In the last century, a new way of looking at the Bible developed. Research into the ancient Near East and its texts recreated for us the civilizations out of which the Bible emerged. In this century, there has been a revival of Jewish biblical scholarship; Israeli and American scholars, in particular, concentrating in the fields of archaeology, biblical history, Semitic languages, and the religion of Israel, have opened exciting new vistas into the world of the Scriptures. For the first time in history, we have at our disposal information and methodological tools that enable us to explore the biblical text in a way that could never have been done before. This new world of knowledge, as seen through the eyes of contemporary Jewish scholars and utilizing at the same time the insights of over twenty centuries of traditional Jewish exegesis, is now available for the first time to a general audience in *The JPS Torah Commentary.*

The Commentary is published in five volumes, each by a single author who has devoted himself to the study of the text. Given the wide range of perspectives that now exist in biblical scholarship, the JPS has recognized the individual expertise of these authors and made no attempt to impose uniformity on the methodology or content of their work.

The Hebrew text is that of the Leningrad Codex B 19A, the oldest dated manuscript of the complete Hebrew Bible. Copied from a text written by the distinguished Masoretic scholar Aaron ben Moses ben Asher, who lived in the first half of the 10th century C.E., the manuscript was completed in 1009 C.E. In this edition it has been arranged according to the weekly synagogue Torah readings. The format has been adjusted to correspond to that adopted by the TANAKH, the new translation of the Hebrew Bible, published by the Jewish Publication Society and utilized in the present *Commentary.*

The Jewish Publication Society has completed this project with a full awareness of the great tradition of Jewish Bible commentary, with a profound sense of the sanctity of the biblical text and an understanding of the awe and love that our people has accorded its Bible. The voice of our new *Commentary* resounds with the spirit and concerns of our times—just as the Jewish spirit has always found its most sincere and heartfelt expression in its appreciation of the Bible; yet it acknowledges the intrinsic value of the tools of modern scholarship in helping to establish the original sense and setting of Scripture.

With all this fixed firmly in mind, the Jewish Publication Society commits its good name and its decades of pioneering in the world of English-language Jewish publishing to this *Torah Commentary* with the hope that it will serve as the contemporary addition to the classic commentaries created by Jews during past epochs in Jewish history.

Nahum M. Sarna, GENERAL EDITOR
Chaim Potok, LITERARY EDITOR

וְהַמַּשְׂכִּלִים יַזְהִרוּ כְּזֹהַר הָרָקִיעַ
וּמַצְדִּיקֵי הָרַבִּים כַּכּוֹכָבִים לְעוֹלָם וָעֶד

Sander H., Alan, and David C. Mendelson

Joseph and Rebecca Meyerhoff

Warren G. and Gay H. Miller

Mr. and Mrs. Hershel Muchnick
In memory of Max and Annie Sherman
and Lt. Louis O. Sherman

Joseph Muchnick
In memory of his wife, Mollie

Nancy and Morris W. Offit

Mr. and Mrs. Mitchell E. Panzer
In memory of their parents

Edith and Charles Pascal
In memory of their parents,
Harry and Lena Chidakel
Harry and Marion Pascal

Mr. and Mrs. Frank J. Pasquerilla

Leon J. Perelman

Mr. and Mrs. Ronald O. Perelman

Harry M. and Esther L. Plotkin

Anne and Henry S. Reich

Arleen and Robert S. Rifkind

Judy and Arthur Robbins
In honor of Sheila F. Segal

Mr. and Mrs. Daniel Rose

Sam Rothberg

Rabbi Stephen A. and Nina Berman Schafer
In memory of Joel Michael Schafer

Drs. Amiel and Chariklia-Tziraki Segal

Bernard G. Segal

Norma L. Shapiro
In memory of her parents,
Jane K. and Bert Levy

Lola and Gerald Sherman
In memory of Jean and Al Sherman
and Ada and Jack Kay

Jerome J. and Marciarose Shestack
In memory of Olga and Isadore Shestack
and Clara Ruth Schleifer

Jonathan and Jennifer Shestack
In memory of their great-grandfathers,
Rabbi Israel Shankman and
Rabbi Judah Shestack

Dr. and Mrs. Edward B. Shils

Charles E. Smith
In honor of Mr. and Mrs. Robert P. Kogod
and Mr. and Mrs. Robert H. Smith

Marian Scheuer Sofaer

William and Radine Spier

The Oscar and Lillian Stempler Foundation
In memory of Rose and Isadore Engel
and Lillian Stempler
In honor of Oscar Stempler

David B. Sykes
In memory of his wife, Shirley

Mr. and Mrs. Sylvan M. Tobin

Sami and Annie Totah
In honor of their parents

Adele and Bert M. Tracy
In memory of their parents

Elizabeth R. and Michael A. Varet

Edna and Charles Weiner

Simon and Trudy Weker
In honor of their children,
Laurie, Jonathan, and Robert

Morton H. Wilner

Mr. and Mrs. Seymour D. Wolf
In memory of their parents,
Abraham and Dora Wolf
Abraham and Sarah Krupsaw

Dr. Allen M. and Eleanor B. Wolpe

Ben Zevin

Benjamin Bernard Zucker
In honor of Lotty Gutwirth Zucker

PATRONS

And the knowledgeable will be radiant like the bright expanse of sky,
And those who lead the many to righteousness will be like the stars forever and ever.

DANIEL 12:3

Mr. and Mrs. Robert P. Abrams
In memory of Peter Abrams

D.F. Antonelli, Jr.

Mr. and Mrs. Marvin Anzel and Sons
In memory of Rose and Samuel Anzel

Stephen and Stephanie Axinn

Mr. and Mrs. Ronald S. Baron

Dr. Muriel M. Berman

Nancy Berman and Alan Bloch

Philip I. Berman

Steven M. Berman

Herbert and Nancy Bernhard

Mr. and Mrs. Arthur H. Bienenstock

Goldene and Herschel Blumberg
In memory and in honor of their parents

Irvin J. Borowsky and Laurie Wagman

Elmer Cerin
In memory of Sylvia S. Cerin

Dr. and Mrs. D. Walter Cohen
In honor of their parents,
Abram and Goldie Cohen
Joseph and Bessie Axelrod

Melvin and Ryna Cohen

Rosalie and Joseph Cohen

Elsie B. and Martin D. Cohn
In honor of their children and grandchildren

Mr. and Mrs. Charles M. Diker

Carole and Richard Eisner

Edward E. Elson

The Endowment Fund of the
Greater Hartford Jewish Federation

Edith Brenner Everett and Henry Everett
In memory of their father, Eli Brenner,
and brother, Fred Brenner

Federation of Jewish Agencies
of Greater Philadelphia

Peter I. Feinberg

Myer and Adrienne Arsht Feldman
In honor of Bella Feldman

Mr. Joseph M. and Dr. Helen G. First

Libby and Alan Fishman

Selma and William Fishman

The Foundation for Conservative Judaism
of Greater Philadelphia

Bernard and Muriel Frank

Aaron and Cecile Goldman

Evelyn and Seymour C. Graham

Dorothy Gitter Harman
In memory of her parents,
Morris and Maria Gitter

Irving B. Harris

Shirley and Stanley Hayman
In memory of their parents

Evelyn and Sol Henkind

Erica and Ludwig Jesselson

Leonard Kapiloff

Sol and Rita Kimerling

Lillian and Sid Klemow

Mr. and Mrs. Ronald A. Krancer

William B. and Elaine Kremens

Mr. and Mrs. Harvey M. Krueger

Simon and Rosa Laupheimer

Fanney N. Litvin
In memory of her husband, Philip Litvin

Ruth Meltzer
In memory of her husband, Leon

Martha H. and Joseph L. Mendelson

Martha H. and Joseph L. Mendelson
In memory of their parents,
Alexander and Celia Holstein
Abraham and Dora Mendelson

THE JPS TORAH COMMENTARY

NUMBERS במדבר

GENERAL EDITOR *Nahum M. Sarna*
LITERARY EDITOR *Chaim Potok*

GENESIS *Nahum M. Sarna*
EXODUS *Nahum M. Sarna*
LEVITICUS *Baruch A. Levine*
NUMBERS *Jacob Milgrom*
DEUTERONOMY *Jeffrey H. Tigay*

THE JPS TORAH COMMENTARY

NUMBERS במדבר

The Traditional Hebrew Text with the New JPS Translation

Commentary by JACOB MILGROM

THE JEWISH PUBLICATION SOCIETY
PHILADELPHIA · NEW YORK
5750 / 1990

First edition
Manufactured in the United States of America
Composed by Polebridge Press in Galliard (English text) and Keter (Hebrew text).
Printed and bound by Arcata Graphics.

Library of Congress Cataloging-in-Publication Data

Milgrom, Jacob, 1923–
Numbers = [Ba-midbar] : the traditional Hebrew text with the new JPS translation / commentary by Jacob Milgrom.
p. cm. — (The JPS Torah commentary)
English and Hebrew; commentary in English
Includes bibliographical references.
ISBN 0-8276-0329-0. — ISBN 9-8276-0331-2 (set)
1. Bible. O.T. Numbers—Commentaries. I. Bible. O.T. Numbers. Hebrew. 1989. II. Bible. O.T. Numbers. English. Jewish Publication Society. 1989. III. Title. IV. Title: Ba-midbar. V. Series.
BS1265.3.M55 1989 89-38431
222'.14077—dc20 CIP
HE

GENESIS *ISBN 0-8276-0326-6*
EXODUS *ISBN 0-8276-0327-4*
LEVITICUS *ISBN 0-8276-0328-2*
DEUTERONOMY *ISBN 0-8276-0330-4*
Five-volume set ISBN 0-8276-0331-2

Designed by ADRIANNE ONDERDONK DUDDEN

The author wishes to thank Rabbi Israel Stein for his careful reading and excellent suggestions.

To Moshe Greenberg

When his companion corrects him and recites Scripture with him, it is said: "Two are better than one, because they have a good reward for their labor."

(Eccl. 4:9; ARN[1]8)

CONTENTS

WEEKLY TORAH READINGS FROM THE BOOK OF NUMBERS

INTRODUCTION

Preliminaries

The Title The fourth book of the Torah is called ***Bemidbar*** (literally, "In the Wilderness") in Hebrew. The English title ***Numbers*** goes back to the Latin ***Numeri*** and the earlier Greek (Septuagint) ***arithmoi***. However, these titles are probably derived from the oldest Hebrew title ***ḥomesh ha-pekudim*** "the fifth (of the Torah) the mustered" (Mish. Yoma 7:1, Mish. Men. 4:3), so named because of the several censuses recorded in the book (chaps. 1–4,26). It was also entitled ***va-yedabber*** after the first word (see Rashi on Exod. 38:26), as is the case with the other Torah books. The present Hebrew title ***Bemidbar*** (the fifth word of the opening verse) seems more apt since it actually encompasses all the events described in the book that took place "in the wilderness."

The Text Except for a few lines of ancient poetry (see the Comments to 21:14,30; 24:22–24), the text of Numbers is in an excellent state of preservation. The variations in Masoretic manuscripts are few and insignificant. Greater deviations from the Hebrew are found in the Septuagint and Samaritan versions. However, these are not evidence of a different Hebrew text but, probably, curtailments or enlargements of the Masoretic version. The Samaritan, for instance, has freely incorporated parallel material from Deuteronomy in order to harmonize the Numbers accounts with that book. Such additions from the Samaritan are pointed out in the Comments to 12:6; 14:41,45; 20:13; and 21:13,22.

The Chronology The tradition that Israel spent forty years in the wilderness following its Exodus from Egypt is demonstrably old (Deut. 1:46; Amos 2:10; 5:25). Yet the chronology within that forty-year period is marred by two major problems. The events of 1:1–10:11 cover nineteen days from the first to the nineteenth of the second month of the second year. Those of the final chapters 21:10–36:13 occur within five months of the fortieth year (see 20:28=33:38; 20:29; Deut. 1:3). The material in between, 10:12–21:9, is undated but must fall in the intervening thirty-eight years. Even then the first part of this middle block, 10:12–14:45, occurs at the very beginning of this period (to judge by 14:34) and the last part, 20:1–21:10, at the end of this period (see the Comment to 20:1). This would leave the events of the Korahite rebellions (chaps. 16–17) and several laws (chaps. 15,18–19) as all that can be attributed to the intervening thirty-eight of the forty years spent in the wilderness. At present there is no satisfactory solution to this puzzle. All that can be said is that the wilderness traditions survived, in the main, without fixed dates, and they were clustered at the beginning and at the end of the wilderness sojourn. It would seem that the intent of the Book of Numbers is to concentrate on the aftermath of the Sinaitic revelation and the preparations for entering the land. The forty years serve as a period of transition, allowing for a new generation to arise (26:65).

Another chronological problem concerns the first block of material, 1:1–10:11, which by its terminal dates (see 1:1 and 10:11) falls between the first and the twentieth day of the second month of the second year. But within this block, chapters 7–9 ostensibly revert to the first month of the second year (see 7:1 and 9:1). This problem, however, is capable of resolution. The word ***be-yom*** (in 7:1 and 9:15) should be rendered "when," and the verbs in 7:1 and 9:1,5 should be taken as pluperfects (see 9:11). Thus the entire block dates to the second month of the second year, except for a few flashbacks to events occurring at the beginning of the first month.

Methodology For more than a century the Torah has been subjected to critical literary analysis and found to comprise four main sources whose composition and final redaction span half a millennium (approximately the 9th to the 5th century B.C.E.). That is, the grouping of similar vocabulary, institutions, and concepts led to the discernment of four distinct scribal schools that were fused into the Hebrew text and preserved to this day. This source criticism, better known as the ***documentary hypothesis,*** still reigns supreme.

An alternative approach, generally termed ***form criticism,*** was developed earlier this century. Focusing instead on the literary forms, structures, and genres embedded in the Hebrew text, it traced their origins to short units in order to discover their original form and the sociohistorical context that produced them. This approach was applied, in the main, to the poetic sections of the Bible, such as the Prophets and the Psalms, but it found its way into pentateuchal studies as well. A third approach, ***tradition criticism,*** chose to isolate motifs and larger themes, such as exodus and wilderness, and to study their reflexes in the rest of Scripture.

These three theories share one basic trait: They are all diachronic, proceeding from early to late. They virtually ignore the present text except as a base from which to probe into its origins. During the past two decades a strong reaction, amounting to open rebellion, has set in. Against the historicism of its predecessors, this new approach assumes that the preserved text is an organic unit and searches for the stylistic and structural devices that bind each literary unit into a cohesive and artistic whole. Only upon the disclosure of irreconcilable elements does it entertain the possibility that more than one hand is discernible in the composition. In any case, this theory assumes that the text, whether the product of an author or a redactor, is a work of art whose artistry can be divulged by a "close reading." To be sure, this theory is not really new; it is influenced by antecedent trends in literary criticism. Indeed, just as the established theories reflect the previous *Zeitgeist* of their time—historicism, evolution, linear development—so does this present trend echo the "new criticism" of today, which concentrates on the text as it is.

This newest approach in biblical research is termed ***redaction criticism*** and treats the text synchronically, not just diachronically. It refuses to dissect the whole into parts and then consider these parts as having meaning apart from the whole. Rather, it studies a literary piece as a whole by demonstrating the interaction of its parts. Actually, this approach is not new at all. For the medieval Jewish exegetes, the unity of the Torah was axiomatic; they were therefore pressed into finding associative terms and themes that linked together the material, much of which—especially in the case of Numbers—was heterogeneous and disjunctive (see below, pp. xiii–xv). Their insights have illumined almost every page of this Commentary. I differ with them only in this respect: The Masoretic text is but the final redaction. However, there are enough places where editorial sutures are clearly visible, thereby exposing a penultimate stage in the development of the text (e.g., Excursus 39).

The truth be told, the medievalists themselves were not unaware of the likelihood that the Torah experienced literary growth. Indeed, in one outstanding case, their hints in this direction led to the resolution of a major theological crux (Excursus 50).

This commentary aims to be critical, unapologetic, and objective. At the same time, it offers reliable support to those who believe that this book and the Torah at large were divinely revealed. The two generations of Israel's founders who walk through its pages alternately obeyed and resisted the covenantal demands of Sinai. Their encounters with God, devoutly interpreted and dutifully recorded by subsequent generations, manifest occasional ambiguities and discrepancies. It could not be otherwise. These uncertainties represent the flawed human perception of the infinite faces of the divine. They were entered into the books of the Torah because they all were regarded as equally authentic and sacred. They were accorded the same verdict as the much later disagreements between the schools of Hillel and Shammai: "Both are the words of the living God" (*b.Er.* 13b).

Being a Jewish commentary, it also dips freely and frequently into the vast reservoir of rabbinic literature for some of its examples of literary insight and moral teaching.

Inner Cohesion and Links with Other Texts in the Hexateuch

Subdivisions and Associative Terms and Themes The generic variety that characterizes Numbers surpasses that of any other book of the Bible. Note these examples: narrative (4:1–3), poetry (21:17–18), prophecy (24:3–9), victory song (21:27–30, pre-Israelite), prayer (12:13), blessing (6:24–26), lampoon (22:22–35), diplomatic letter (21:14–19), civil law (27:1–11), cultic law (15:17–21), oracular decision (15:32–36), census list (26:1–51), temple archive (7:10–88), itinerary (33:1–49).

This literary richness adds to the difficulties of finding the book's inner cohesion. However, topographical and chronological data clearly provide the main organizational criteria. The Book of Numbers describes the journey of the Israelites from Mount Sinai to the borders of Canaan. Their forty-year trek comprises forty stations (see chap. 33) that can be subsumed under three main stages: the wilderness of Sinai (1:1–10:10), where the preparations for the journey are made; the vicinity of Kadesh (10:11–20:13), where the bulk of the forty years is spent; and from Kadesh to the steppes of Moab (20:14–36:13), where they prepare for the conquest and settlement of the promised land.

Numbers also subdivides according to temporal as well as spatial criteria. The forty years embrace two generations, both of whose accounts begin with a census (chaps. 1 and 26).[1] The generation of the Exodus, doomed to die in the wilderness (14:32–34), is finally extinguished by a plague at Baal-peor (25:9,18–29). Thus, the second census, which follows immediately upon the plague (25:19), states unambiguously: "Among these there was not one of those enrolled by Moses and Aaron the priest when they recorded the Israelites in the wilderness of Sinai. For the LORD had said of them, 'They shall die in the wilderness.' Not one of them survived, except Caleb the son of Jephunneh and Joshua son of Nun" (26:64–65). The chapters that follow the second census (27–36) differ sharply from the preceding ones, which are informed by murmuring and rebellion (chaps. 11–14; 16–17; 20:1–13; 21:4–9). These chapters describe the fidelity and stoutheartedness of the new generation (chap. 32), which, as a reward, does not lose a single life, even in battle (31:49). That these chapters constitute an organic literary block is indicated by the accounts concerning the daughters of Zelophehad that flank them at both ends (27:1–11; 36:1–12).[2]

Regardless of how one conceives the overarching organizational structure of the book, it is more important to note the thematic and verbal links that bind the material together. Chapters 1–10 deal with the preparations for the march through the wilderness. Chapters 1 and 2 constitute the census and camp arrangement predicated upon military criteria. Chapters 3–4 and 7–8 deal with the Levites: They undergo a census for guarding and transporting the Tabernacle (chaps. 3–4); they receive carts from the tribal chieftains for the Tabernacle transport (7:1–9); they are purified prior to their entry into Tabernacle service (8:1–22); and they are informed of their retirement regulations (8:23–26).

The laws comprising chapters 5–6 are inserted into these preparations for the march since they have as their common denominator the prevention and elimination of defilement in Israel's camp. Thus 5:1–4 banishes the bearers of severe impurity; 5:5–8 prescribes reparation for the desecration of God's name in a false oath; 5:11–31 ordains a test for the suspected (defiled) adulteress; 6:1–21 highlights the law of the defiled Nazirite. However, the most likely basis for the joining of these pericopes is that in each the priest plays a prominent role: It is he who determines and terminates ritual impurity (5:1–4; see Lev. 13–15), officiates at the reparation sacrifice (5:5–8), is the recipient of all sanctuary donations (5:8–10), executes the ordeal for the suspected adulteress (5:11–31), officiates at the ritual for the Nazirite (6:1–21), and offers the Priestly Blessing (6:22–27). If so, then chapters 5–6—perhaps originally an independent scroll—were inserted here because of their opening law, the impurity of the wilderness camp. Certain words bind the inner chapters: ***maʿal***, "trespass" (5:6, 12); ***'ishah***, "woman" (5:31; 6:2); ***tame'***, "impure" (5:2; 5:13,14,19,20,28,29; 6:9) and, of course, ***kohen***, "priest" (5:8,9,10; 5:15–26; 6:10,11,16,19,20; 6:23 [equivalent]).

Chapters 11–14 and 16–17 detail Israel's rebellions in the wilderness. Ostensibly, chapter 15, a legal miscellany, jarringly interrupts this sequence. However, its thematic and literary links with the previous unit prove otherwise. Chapter 15 begins with two laws that are operative in Canaan (see vv. 2,18). They are a reassurance to the Israelites, condemned to die in the wilderness, that their children will indeed inherit the promised land (see 14:31). A third law (vv. 22–31), bearing no heading, may originally have referred to the two preceding laws. The case of the Sabbath violator follows (vv. 32–36) since his punishment is not certain: Will he be subject to ***karet,*** mentioned in the previous law (vv. 30–31; see Exod. 31:14); or is he to be put to death, as demanded by Exodus 31:15? A fifth and final law, tassels, has no apparent connection with the immediately preceding material but was probably placed here to provide a verbal inclusion (see below, p. xxix) to the episode of the scouts (chaps. 13–14): By wearing the tassels (***tsitsit***), Israel will henceforth be warned about "scouting" and "whoring" in sight and thought (see 14:33–34; 15:39).

Demoralized by the majority report of the scouts and condemned to die in the wilderness, the people are psychologically receptive to demagogic appeals to overthrow their leadership and return to Egypt. Three, possibly four, discrete rebellions have been fused in chapter 16, all attributed to machinations of Korah. The aftermath vindicates Aaron when his fire pan of incense brings not death (16:35–17:5) but life (17:6–15) and when his rod blossoms miraculously (17:16–26). As a result of their hazardous responsibility in guarding the Tabernacle against encroachment, the priests and Levites are granted specified endowments (17:27–18:32).

The position of chapter 19, purification rites for corpse contamination, is an enigma. By dint of its theme, corpse contamination, one would have expected it to have been placed with the other impurity sources described in Leviticus 11–15 (see Excursus 48) or, at least, with Numbers 5:1–4, which presumes a knowledge of the laws of corpse contamination (see 5:2). Why was it placed here? Perhaps the twice-mentioned warning that corpse contami-

nation may pollute the sanctuary (vv. 13,20) made this chapter a natural sequel to the ***parashah*** of Korah (chaps. 16–18), which deals especially with the issue of the desecration of the sanctuary by encroachment. For other possible associative links, see the introductory Comment to chapter 19.

The traditions concerning the final stage of the wilderness march from Kadesh to the steppes of Moab are collected in chapters 20–21. They are grouped in two parallel panels (see below, pp. xxvii–xxviii, and Excursus 55), the first detailing the failure and punishment of Moses and Aaron and the second, the failure and deliverance of the people. The unifying theme is that God provides water (and all of Israel's other needs) even when the leaders fail to do so. The emphasis on God's Providence is perhaps what accounts for the insertion of the episode of the bronze serpent (21:4–9) and a new itinerary list (21:12–20), the latter containing two ancient poems (21:14–15,17–18). A third poem, the Song of Heshbon (21:27–30), has been inserted to justify Israel's conquest of Transjordan (21:21–25,31–35).

The Document of Balaam, as chapters 22–24 are called in rabbinic tradition, is the largest independent section in Numbers. It has absolutely no verbal or thematic link with the contiguous chapters. The only connecting link is its setting: the steppes of Moab. Perhaps it performs the same function as chapter 15: It reassures Israel that despite its defection, it is blessed and will live, through its posterity, in the promised land. With the exception of the ass episode (22:22–35), itself an interpolation (see Excursus 57), these chapters, comprising both prose and poetry, are an integrated, interlocking, artfully structured unity (Excursus 56).

The apostasy at Baal-peor (chap. 25) resembles the apostasy of the golden calf (Exod. 32) in context and placement. Both involve illicit worship, the slaughter of the guilty, and the choice of the line of the Levites/Phinehas. Both describe the fall of Israel after having previously attained the sublime heights of the Lord's promise of future greatness (the Sinaitic covenant, Exod. 19–20,24; Balaam's blessings, Num. 23–24). According to one tradition (31:16), it was Balaam who plotted the Baal-peor apostasy. If so, it would account for its placement here.

The final eleven chapters of Numbers (26–36) are motivated by a single theme, the immediate occupation of the promised land: a (second) census of able-bodied men for war in the land and for the apportionment of the land (chap. 26); inheritance rights of women in the land (27:1–11; 36); the succession to Moses in the land (27:12–13); the cultic calendar of the land (chaps. 28–29) and the fulfillment of vows (chap. 30); the war against Midian (chap. 31); the allotment of Transjordan (chap. 32); a summary of the wilderness stations (33:1–49); evicting the inhabitants of the land and extirpating their cult (33:50–56); the boundaries of the land (34:1–15); supervisors for the division of the land (34:16–29); the Levitical holdings in the land (35:1–8); preventing the pollution of the land by homicide (35:9–34). The final chapter (36), further instructions on women's inheritance rights in the land, is an appendix; however, it forms an inclusion with the earlier material on the daughters of Zelophehad (27:11), thereby locking the chapters on the new generation into a closed unit, beginning with chapter 27 and ending with chapter 36.

Alternation of Law and Narrative A striking feature of Numbers is that law (L) and narrative (N) alternate regularly, as follows: 1–10:10 (L); 10:11–14:45 (N); 15 (L); 16–17 (N); 18–19 (L); 20–25 (N); 26–27:11 (L); 27:12–23 (N); 28–30 (L); 31–33:49 (N); 33:50–56; 34–36 (L).

In the main, the narrative is confined to the wilderness march; the law, to the three main stations of the march: Sinai (1–10:10), Kadesh (chaps. 15, 18–19), and the steppes of

Moab (chaps. 28–30, 34–36). However, there are exceptions. Certain events are associated with stations, for example, the scouts (chaps. 13–14), the Korahite rebellions (chaps. 16–17), the Midianite war and Transjordanian settlement (chaps. 31–32). And some laws arise from test cases composed in narrative style, for example, the *pesaḥ* (9:1–14), the wood gatherer (15:32–36), and Zelophehad's daughters (27:1–11). Thus this alternation is not a function of whether Israel was stationary or in motion.

The admixture of these two genres comes as no surprise to anyone conversant with ancient Near Eastern vassal treaties, which open with a recounting of the suzerain's benefactions to his vassal (narrative) and follow with the stipulations imposed upon the vassal (law). The Book of Deuteronomy is a parade example of this literary type: The law code of chapters 12–26 is preceded by a recital of God's salvific acts for Israel in chapters 1–11. The Book of Numbers also operates in the shadow of Sinai: Israel has accepted the suzerainty of its God and is bound to His law, while the narratives continue to manifest divine Providence (and Israel's backsliding).

Links with Exodus, Deuteronomy, and Joshua In the twelfth century, the commentator Bekhor Shor noted that a number of wilderness narratives in Exodus and Numbers duplicate each other, in particular, the incidents of the water from the rock (20:2–13; Exod. 17:1–7) and the manna and the quail (11:4–9,31–34; Exod. 16:1–15). Evidently, it is the duplication of the quail incident that led Bekhor Shor to this conclusion. For he asks: "If Moses saw that the quail arrived in sufficient quantities the first time, how could he on the second occasion doubt: 'Could enough flocks and herds be slaughtered to suffice them?' (11:22)." He finds additional evidence in Deuteronomy 33:8b: "Whom you tested at Massah/Challenged at the waters of Meribah." Since a poetic line consists of parallel clauses, Massah and Meribah, the sites for the rock incidents in Exodus and Numbers (Exod. 17:7; Num. 20:13) must be identical. Moreover, their names are interchanged in Psalms 78:15–31 and 95:8–9. Further evidence for this duplication is cited in Excursus 50.

Of course, these duplicate accounts differ in some details. But their main difference lies in one fact that holds the key to their duplication: Only Numbers records that God punished Israel (Lev. R. 1:10).[3] Indeed, this distinction holds true for the other wilderness narratives as well. In Exodus, God does not punish Israel for its murmuring; in Numbers, He does so consistently. There can be only one explanation for this state of affairs. The Exodus incidents are pre-Sinai; those of Numbers are post-Sinai. Before Israel accepted the covenant it was not responsible for its violation; indeed, it could claim ignorance of its stipulations. However, all the incidents of Numbers take place after Israel has left Sinai—where it swore allegiance to the covenant and was warned of the divine sanctions for its infringement. Thus it can be postulated that for a number of wilderness narratives two traditions were reported, the one involving punishment, and the other, not. The redactor, then, with Mount Sinai as his great divide, dutifully recorded both, as either pre- or post-Sinai.

This distinction is nowhere better illustrated than in the initial stage of the wilderness march as recorded in each book. Both the Exodus and Numbers phases of the trek begin with a three-day march (Exod. 15:22; Num. 10:33). In Exodus, however, Israel's complaint goes unpunished—indeed, even unreprimanded—whereas in Numbers, Israel is severely dealt with (Exod. 15:22–26; Num. 11:1–3). Sinai, then, is the watershed in Israel's wilderness experience. Indeed, it is the pivot as well as the summit for the Torah books as a whole.

A more significant structural link between Exodus and Numbers lies in the itinerary

formula "departed from X and encamped at Y." Frank Cross[4] has noticed that in Exodus and Numbers there are exactly twelve such formulas that correspond to the itinerary list of Numbers 33. Six take Israel from Egypt to Rephidim, the station before Sinai (Exod. 12:37; 13:20; 14:1–2; 15:22; 16:1; 17:1), and six, from Sinai to the steppes of Moab (Exod. 19:2; Num. 10:12; 20:1; 20:22; 21:10–11; 22:1). Thus Exodus and Numbers, at least in their wilderness narratives, reveal the same redactional hand.

Recensional activity involving Exodus and Numbers is also evident in regard to the census recorded in both books, taken only several months apart and yielding identical results (Exod. 30:12–16; 38:26; Num. 1:46). The likelihood is that the same census is intended. Exodus probably provides the more authentic setting. With the Tabernacle under construction at Sinai, a census was taken to determine the military deployment of the camp and the guarding of the Tabernacle by the Levites. Subsequently, this account would have been moved to Numbers and joined with other material that described Israel's preparations for the march from Sinai (Num. 1:1–10:10); only the prescription to pay the half-shekel ransom remained in its original place in Exodus. For details, see Excursus 2.

Finally, it is also important to see how Numbers fits into the grand design of the Hexateuch, the five books of the Torah plus the Book of Joshua, which cover the entire history of early Israel from the time their forefather Abraham entered the promised land until they returned to it under Joshua.

The accompanying diagram (courtesy of Newing) takes the form of a grand introversion, ABCDEFG X G′F′E′D′C′B′A′, a pattern that, as will be shown, is the dominant structure of the individual pericopes of Numbers. The following points should be noted. As in all introverted structures, the center (X) is crucial. Once again it is Sinai. Not only is it the watershed of the wilderness narratives (Exodus-Numbers); it is the great divide of the Hexateuch. Sinai marks the end of slavery and the beginning of freedom. After Sinai, Israel repeats the failures and promises that had preceded it, repairing the former and fulfilling the latter. Also to be noted are the key concepts, terms, and phrases that mark the symmetrical sections: the "bones of Joseph" (Gen. 49:25; Josh. 24:32; AA′); "put off your shoes . . . holy" (Exod. 3:5; Josh. 5:15; BB′); circumcision (Exod. 4:25; Josh. 5:2–9; BB′); *pesaḥ* (Exod. 12:1–28; Josh. 5:10–12; BB′); crossing the sea/Jordan (Exod. 14:9–15:21; Josh. 3:4; CC′); the three days, manna, quail, rock narratives (Exod. 16–17; Num. 11, 20; DD′); theophany in fire (Exod. 19:18; Lev. 9:24; EE′); encroaching upon Sinai/Tabernacle incurs death (Exod. 19:13; Num. 1:51; EE′); architectural detail of the Tabernacle (Exod. 25–31; Exod. 35–40; FF′); Sabbath law precedes Tabernacle construction (Exod. 31:12–17; Exod. 35:1–3; FF′); broken and renewed covenant (Exod. 32; Exod. 34:10–28; GG′); and the unparalleled theophany to Moses (33:17–34:9; X). Finally, the two large wedges on either side of Sinai (which balance the structure) are subsequent additions to the corpus: the primeval history (Gen. 1–11) and Deuteronomy.

The Sources

Discrete sources have been fused into the literary units that comprise Numbers. They can be shown to be of two types, composites or inserts, some of which are borrowings.

Composites Composite structure is best exemplified in the intertwining of the quail and assistance motifs in the Kibroth-hattaavah episode (11:4–34). The braided effect is

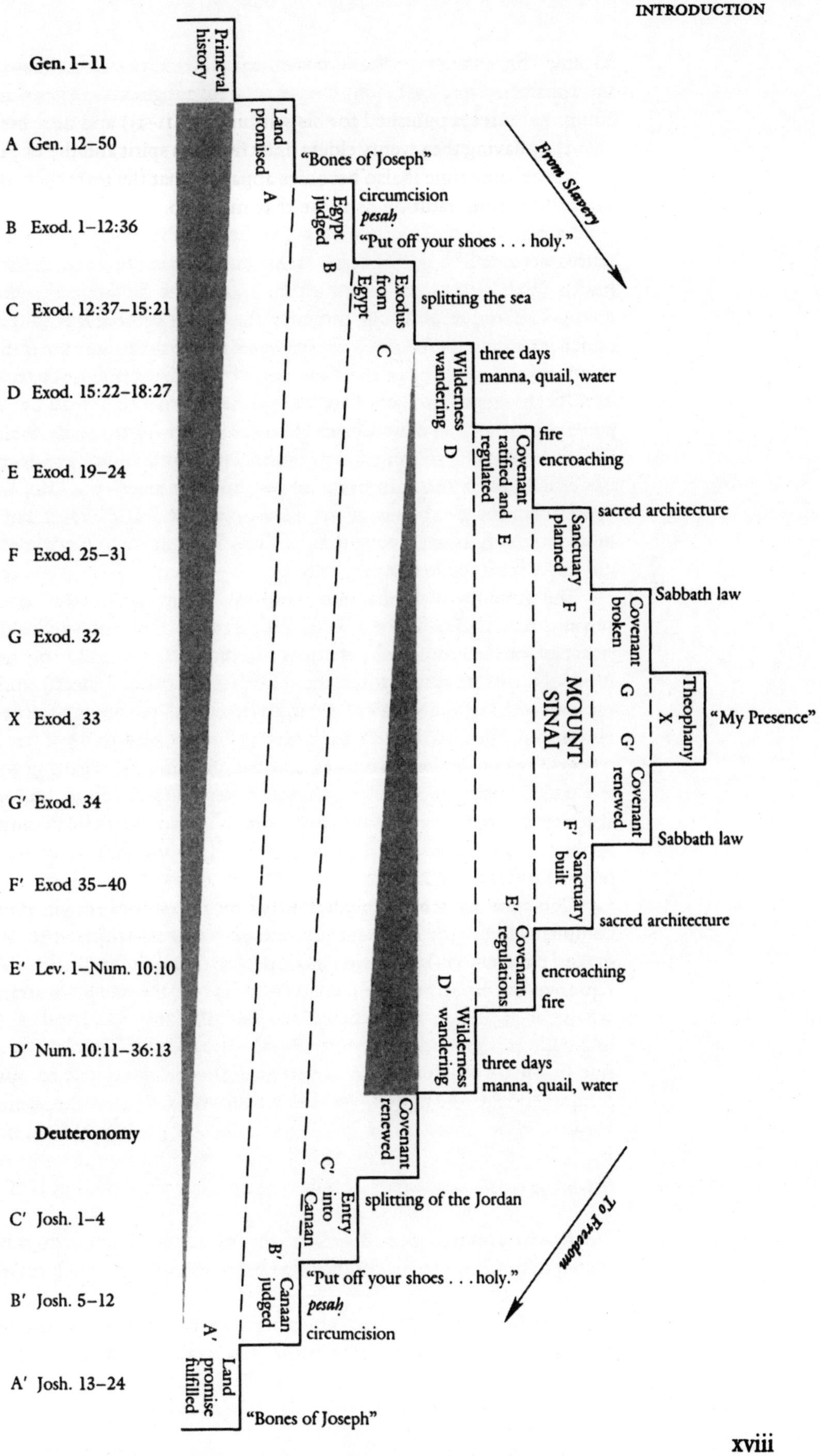

THE THEOLOGICAL-LITERARY STRUCTURE OF THE HEXATEUCH

apparent once the two strands are separated: quail (vv. 4–9,13,19–23,31–34) and assistance (vv. 10–12,14–18,24–30). Why the plaiting? As suggested in Excursus 24, in this manner the author had Moses punished for his self-pity (vv. 11–15) and near heretical faithlessness (vv. 21–22) by having the seventy elders draw from his spirit and thereby diminish him.

At the same time it also becomes apparent that the texts that comprise this episode are not of the same tradition as those that make up the previous chapters. This is so for the reason, among others, that the Tent of Meeting here (11:24–27) is different from the one heretofore mentioned. The latter Tent is situated in the center of the camp, even during the march (2:17; 3:38; 10:21), and the Lord addresses the petitioner from the inner sanctum (7:89). The former Tent is located outside the camp at rest (11:26) and in front during the march (10:33), and the Lord speaks at its entrance to the petitioner stationed inside (12:5; see Exod. 33:9). For other distinctions between the two Tents, see Excursus 28.

The scouts episode of chapters 13–14 must also be judged as being of two strands: At times it speaks of Joshua among the scouts (13:8; 14:6,30,38), yet it also holds that Caleb was the lone dissenting voice (14:24). In addition, it maintains two irreconcilable views concerning the land reconnoitered: only the Hebron area (13:22–24) and the full extent of the promised land (13:21). It seems likely that the author of this artfully constructed scout episode had two discrete traditions of the reconnaissance mission to Canaan and had no choice but to interweave them into his composition (see Excursus 29).

The account of the Korahite rebellion (chap. 16) has also been shown to be a composite—an interlacing of several rebellions: Korah and the chieftains/Levites versus Aaron; Dathan and Abiram versus Moses; and the congregation versus Moses and Aaron. Nowhere is the conflation better exhibited than in verses 24 and 27, where a probable original reading, ***mishkan YHVH***, "Tabernacle of the Lord," has been replaced by "abodes (***mishkan*** [*sic*]) of Korah, Dathan, and Abiram"; and in verse 32, where the conjectured original ***lahem***, "their" (i.e., Dathan and Abiram; see Deut. 11:6), became ***le-koraḥ***, "of Korah." Other signs of the conflation are detailed in Excursus 39, where it is also suggested that the motivation behind this intricate (and not so artful) composite is the attempt to attach to the person of Korah all the traditions of wilderness rebellions against the leadership of Moses and Aaron.

Conventional scholarship holds that the two stories entwined in the Kibroth-hattaavah complaint (11:4–34) represent discrete epic sources (referred to as J and E), whereas the earlier chapters (1–10), which maintain a different tradition of the Tent of Meeting, represent the priestly source (called P). Similarly, the two main strands of the scout episode (chaps. 13–14) and of the Korah episode (chap. 16) are attributed to the epic and priestly sources. Since the existence of a discrete literary source for the priestly writings is highly questionable (see below, pp. xxi, xvi and Excursuses 29 and 39), I shall use the term "source" circumspectly. On the other hand, there is a clear distinction in style and ideology between those texts called priestly and those called epic. Therefore, when focusing on matters of style and ideology, I will not hesitate to use the terms priestly and epic for the reason that they are convenient sigla to designate these two kinds of writing.

Inserts When the smooth flow of narrative is interrupted by the insertion of new material, the existence of more than one strand is indicated. Thus, for example, an analysis of chapter 21 shows that the itinerary formula has been broken (vv. 4a,10) to make room for the incident of the brazen serpent (vv. 4b–9). Also a new itinerary source has been inserted,

verses 12–20—to judge by both its changed style and itinerary overlap (vv. 19–20; cf. vv. 21–31). The reason for both interpolations is shown to be the same: to provide a parallel panel to chapter 20 (see below, p. xxviii), whereby God no longer depends on Moses and Aaron—who had failed Him at Meribah—to provide Israel with water. God Himself will continue to care for His people despite their contentiousness: He heals those whom He has afflicted (vv. 4–9) and provides them with wells in the wilderness (vv. 16–17) and victory over their enemies (vv. 21–35). For details, see Excursus 55.

Another obvious insertion in chapter 21 is the Song of Heshbon (vv. 27–30), whose interpolative nature is revealed by the repetitive resumption of verse 25b in 31 (see p. xxviii, below). The purpose of this insert is not difficult to discern: to justify Israel's conquest of Transjordan (see Excursus 56).

Another patent insertion is the ass episode (22:22–35) into the prose narrative of Balaam. It not only portrays Balaam in a different light, but it is poorly stitched to the main story. It creates a blatant contradiction in the attitude of the Lord to Balaam's request for permission to curse Israel: Having given permission (v. 20), He now is angry at Balaam for proceeding (v. 22). Indeed, a resumptive repetition betrays the seams of the insert (vv. 21b, 35b; see below, p. xxx).

Further evidence of inserted material is exhibited by the account of the war against Midian in chapter 31. Its original purpose, to promulgate the law of spoil distribution (vv. 25–47), was supplemented by two additional laws concerning the purification procedures for organic and inorganic spoil (vv. 13–24). That the latter are two discrete interpolations is shown by the inlaying of verses 21–23 into verses 13–20,24 (see further in Excursus 67).

A final example of an insert can be adduced from the account of the settlement of Transjordan in chapter 32. Two inserts are attested: the summary of the scout episode (vv. 7–15), which is marked by a different (deuteronomic) idiom, and, more strikingly, the belated mention of Manasseh (vv. 39–42, and in v. 33; deuteronomic?), which attempts to justify the separate and, probably, subsequent intrusions of Manassite clans into Transjordan. Details are supplied in Excursuses 69 and 70.

Borrowings The Book of Numbers contains a fair sampling of poetry, ranging from the four poems that comprise Balaam's oracles (chaps. 23–24) to smaller pieces of a few lines. The latter most likely stem from earlier sources. The Priestly Blessing (6:24–26) probably originates in the cult of the First Temple (see Lev. 9:23 and Excursus 13); the outside origin of the Song of the Ark (10:35–36) is probably indicated by the inserted ***nuns*** that frame it (see Excursus 23); the excerpt on God the Warrior (see the Comments to 21:14–15) is expressly borrowed from the "Book of the Wars of the Lord"; the Song of the Well (21:17–18) may plausibly be traced to the time and region in which Israel found itself during its wilderness sojourn, but it required a special prose introduction (21:16) to emphasize that it was the Lord rather than man who provided the water (see also Excursus 53); and the Song of Heshbon (21:27–30) is most likely an Amorite victory song over the Moabites borrowed by Israel to substantiate its claim that it took Transjordan from the Amorites and not from the Moabites, which demonstrates that the Bible contains pre-Israelite poetry (see Excursus 54).

There is also evidence in Numbers of borrowings from epic sources found in the narratives of Exodus. Thus the statement that the Levites were chosen at Mount Sinai (3:1, 5–13) alludes to their consecration at the time of the episode of the golden calf (Exod.

32:26–29), and the comprehensive wilderness itinerary (chap. 33) includes the opening line of a narrative found in Exodus (for 33:14, see Exod. 17:1; see also 33:40 and the beginning of 21:1–3). Also, the calendar of Leviticus 23 presumes a knowledge of chaps. 28–29.

Borrowings from Leviticus are also in evidence, especially from the second half of the book (chaps. 17–26), generally known as the Holiness Code (H). The frequent inclusion of the *ger*, the "resident alien," in the legislation of Numbers (e.g., 9:13–14; 15:26–30; 19:13,20; 35:15) is an indication that these passages are dependent on the doctrine that the Land of Israel is holy, and hence all its inhabitants, Israelites and non-Israelites alike, are under obligation not to pollute it by violating the Lord's prohibitive commandments (Excursus 34). This doctrine, however, is the expressed teaching of Leviticus 17–26 (H), which may imply that all the passages that cite the *ger* are dependent on these chapters—which would then mandate that the final redaction of the Book of Numbers took place later than that of Leviticus. This conclusion would be supported by the observation that the law of corpse contamination (Num. 19; note the *ger*, vv. 13,20) was not inserted in the Book of Leviticus, which deals with human impurities (chaps. 12–15) and presumes the knowledge of corpse impurity (e.g., 5:3; 7:21; 21:1–4; and esp. 22:3–4), because the law in Numbers reflects a time subsequent to that presupposed by the impurity laws of Leviticus. Details are found in Excursus 48.

Further evidence that Numbers is posterior to Leviticus is the large number of clearly demonstrable interpolations evident in Numbers, as presented above. Indeed, the fact that its editorial sutures are, in the main, fully visible, and at times crudely done, renders this material subject to the exegetical principle: "The less integrated the disturbance is into the context, the later it may be assumed to have been combined. . . . The grossest disturbances are thus to be ascribed to the last redactional stage of combination, while lesser disturbances belong to earlier development of the tradition complexes."[5] For glaring examples of interpolation, see the structural schemes charted below, on pages xxiv to xxviii and in their respective Excursuses. Leviticus, on the other hand, contains many fewer interpolations, and even this material, as I demonstrate in my Leviticus commentary,[6] has been smoothly integrated into the text.

There is also evidence of borrowing from Deuteronomy. The victory over Og in Numbers 21:33–35 must be adjudged a copy of Deuteronomy 3:1–2, made for the purpose of conforming the Numbers narrative to the deuteronomic position that all of Transjordan was conquered at once (see the Comments to 21:33–35, and Excursus 55).

Conversely, Numbers itself may be the source for other Torah books. The wilderness itinerary list (chap. 33) may well be the basis for the individual itinerary statements in Exodus and Numbers (Exod. 12:37; 13:20; 14:1–2; 15:22; 17:1; 19:2; Num. 10:12; 20:1,22; 21:10–11; 22:1; see Excursus 71). Deuteronomy has picked up items from Numbers. For example, Deuteronomy 1:39 is clearly a reworking and condensation of Numbers 14:30–33. At the same time, two pericopes characterized by the same subject and vocabulary need not be interdependent; for example, the two laws on the purification offering (15:22 and Lev. 4:13–21) probably reflect discrete traditions.

In sum, the pericopes of Numbers are not, in the main, unitary compositions but are composites of or contain insertions from other sources. Some of these sources are old poems, narratives in Exodus, and cultic material in Leviticus. Conversely, Numbers material can be shown to have influenced the composition of Exodus and Deuteronomy.

The Structure of the Units

Every writer employs the literary conventions of his time. The biblical writer is no exception. In particular, he organized his material according to established structural schemes. Since the recovery of these structural forms has recensional and theological implications, I shall devote a great deal of space to their analysis.

Chiasm and Introversion The main structural device, to judge by its attestation in nearly every chapter of Numbers, is chiasm and introversion. Chiasm is named after the Greek letter X and denotes a pair of items that reverses itself, yielding the structure ABB′A′. When there is a series—more than two members—for example ABXB′A′ or ABCC′B′A′, then the term introversion will be used. These two types must be distinguished, for whereas the chiasm is purely an aesthetic device, the introversion can have didactic implications. In the scheme ABXB′A′, the central member frequently contains the main point of the author, climaxing what precedes and anticipating what follows. This scheme is especially propitious in pericopes telling of God's command and its fulfillment or, to cite a more striking usage, of man's proposal and God's disposal. In this latter instance, as the examples below demonstrate, structure is theology.

SMALLER UNITS

1. ***Simple chiasm***

A. If only we had died
  B. in the land of Egypt
  B′. or in this wilderness
A′. if only we had died (14:2)

2. ***Complex chiasm***

A. If her husband offers no objection from that day to the next,
  B. he has upheld all the vows and obligations she has assumed;
  B′. he has upheld them
A′. by offering no objection on the day he found out (30:15)

3. ***Chiasm in Subsequent Repetition***

A. We will build here sheepfolds for our flocks
  B. and towns for our children (32:16)
  B′. Build towns for your children
A′. and sheepfolds for your flocks (32:24)

4. ***Chiasm in Summation***

A. (Case of a woman under authority of her father, 30:4–6)
  B. (Case of a woman under authority of her husband, 30:7–16)
  B′. These are the laws . . . between a man and his wife
A′. and as between a father and his daughter . . . (30:17)

5. ***Introversion in a Speech*** (11:11–15)

A. dealt ill (11a*α*)
  B. I enjoyed your favor (11a*β*)
    C. burden of all this people (11b)
      D. all this people (12a*β*)

X. Where am I to get meat (13aα)
D′. all this people (13aβ)
C′. carry all this people (14a)
B′. I enjoy your favor (15a)
A′. my wretchedness (15b)

This structure clearly shows that although Moses' complaint seemingly stresses his need for assistance in administration (CDD′C′) his main concern is expressed in the pivot (X), where his whining discloses his lack of faith that God will enable him to provide Israel with meat.

6. *Introversion in Poetry* (12:6–8)

Introduction: Hear these My words
A. When a prophet of the LORD arises among you
B. I make myself known to him in a vision
C. I speak with him in a dream
D. Not so with My servant Moses
D′. He (alone) is trusted throughout My household
C′. With him I speak mouth to mouth
B′. Plainly and not in riddles
A′. And he beholds the likeness of YHVH
Conclusion: How then did you not shrink
from speaking against My servant Moses?

The first half describes God's communication with other prophets (ABC), the second half, His unique communication with Moses (C′B′A′). The pivot sets Moses apart from his prophetic analogues (D) by declaring that God confides in him alone (D′).

7. *Chiasm Within Introversion* (33:52–56)

A. The reward for obedience (vv. 52–53)
X. The division of the land (v. 54)
a. by lot for clan location
x. by population for size
a′. by lot for tribe location
A′. The punishment for disobedience (vv. 55–56)

A′ is the inverse of A. The pivot, X, is itself a chiasm. The pair aa′ speaks of the decisions of the lot; x, the pivot, focuses on the criterion of population. Both are determinants of the land apportionment in 26:54–55; here they are summarized in this doubly introverted but symmetrical scheme. For details see Excursus 72.

LARGER UNITS (UNINTERPOLATED)

8. *The Nazirite* (6:1–21)

A. Introduction (vv. 1–2)
B. Prohibitions (vv. 3–8)
X. Defilement (vv. 9–12)
B′. Completion (vv. 13–20)
A′. Summary (v. 21)

The Nazirite who successfully heeds the prohibitions entailed in his vow undergoes a prescribed ritual ABB′A′). However, if his vow is aborted by his contamination, another ritual is prescribed (X). The latter, holding the pivot position in the text, is the main point. It explains the placement of this pericope here. After the census of the Israelites, the positioning of the laity and Levites, and the detailing of the responsibilities of the latter in the wilderness march (chaps. 1–4), concern is expressed regarding the defilement of the camp both ritually (5:1–3,5–8) and ethically (5:11–31). Thus the possibility of the defilement of the holy Nazirite occupies center stage in this scheme. For details, see Excursus 12.

9. *The Purification Rites of the Levitical Work For* (8:5–22)

A. Introduction (vv. 5–7a)
  B. Prescriptive procedure (vv. 7b–15)
    X. Rationale (vv. 16–19)
  B′. Descriptive procedure (vv. 20–22a)
A′. Conclusion (v. 22b)

The prescriptive and descriptive texts are symmetrically balanced (ABB′A′), with their singular rationale (X) placed at the center. For details see Excursus 18. Though the rationale is traceable to a previous source (3:9,12–13), a new element is added—the Levites as ransom for the Israelites (v. 19), a factor that will play a crucial role in defining the Levitical responsibilities in the sanctuary (18:23; Excursus 40).

10. *The Complaints at Kibroth-hattaavah* (11:4–34)

A. People's complaint: meat (vv. 4–10a)
  B. Moses' complaint: assistance (vv. 10b–15)
    X. God's reply to both complaints (vv. 16–23)
      a. God's reply (vv. 16–20): ostensibly positive
        x. Moses' reaction (vv. 21–22): faithless
      a′. God's reply (v. 23): restrained
  B′. God diminishes Moses by authorizing the elders (vv. 24–30)
A′. God punishes people by supplying meat (vv. 31–34)

The introverted symmetry of this pericope is clear. God punishes the people's complaint (AA′) and that of Moses (BB′). Section X, the divine reply (condemnation) to both complaints, is pivotal, anticipating the punishment. It has a chiastic structure; Moses' panicky outburst, bordering on heresy, is its pivot. That Moses is penalized for his self-pity (v. 15) and his loss of faith (vv. 21–22) is explained in Excursus 24.

LARGER UNITS (INTERPOLATED)

11. *The Suspected Adulteress* (5:11–31)

A. The case (vv. 11–14)
  B. Preparation of the ritual-ordeal (vv. 15–18)
    X. The oath-imprecation (vv. 19–24)
      [interpolation (v. 21)]
  B′. Execution of the ritual-ordeal (vv. 25–28)
A′. The case (vv. 29–30)
  [postscript (v. 31)]

Here too the prescriptive and descriptive passages (BB′) balance each other as well as the facts of the case that frame the text (AA′). It is, however, the oath-imprecation, in both its original and its interpolated form, that powers the ordeal and, hence, occupies the central pivot section in the scheme. The earlier, pre-Israelite form, as hypothesized, ascribed innate powers to the ordeal waters; the interpolated, Israelite form insists that the efficacy of the oath-ordeal owes to the God of Israel. For details see Excursus 10.

12. *The Settlement of Transjordan* (chap. 32)

A. Gad and Reuben request land (vv. 1–6)
    [interpolation (vv. 7–15)]
    B. Gad and Reuben's second proposal and Moses' revisions (vv. 16–24)
        X. Gad and Reuben accept Moses' revisions (vv. 25–27)
    B′. Gad and Reuben repeat acceptance of Moses' revisions (vv. 28–32)
A′. Moses provisionally grants land (vv. 33–38)
    [interpolation (vv. 39–42)]

Section X (vv. 25–27) is the true center of the chapter since it expresses Gad and Reuben's full acceptance of the revisions made by Moses. The balance of request and grant (AA′) is enhanced by the inner chiasm contained in BB′, as follows:

B_1. Gad and Reuben's proposal (vv. 16–19)
    B_2. Moses repeats proposal (vv. 20–24)
    B'_2. Moses repeats proposal before witnesses (vv. 28–30)
B'_1. Gad and Reuben accept before witnesses (vv. 31–32)

This structure underscores the need for the proposal to be stated twice by Moses (vv. 20–24,28–30; $B'_2B'_2$) and twice by Gad and Reuben (vv. 16–19,31–32; $B_1B'_1$) to answer the requirements of the structure and create a symmetric chiasm. To build a chiastic structure, the proposal must be stated twice by Moses and be flanked by statements of Gad and Reuben. Logically, there is no need for Moses' repetition in B_2. The ideal flow might be: Gad and Reuben make the proposal; Moses repeats it before witnesses; Gad and Reuben accept it before witnesses. B_2 is inserted, therefore, for symmetry of structure. Here, then, is a clear example where aesthetics determines the writing, and those who seek other motivations for the duplications—ideological, historical, editorial, and so on—seek in vain (see Excursus 69).

13. *The War Against Midian* (chap. 31)

A. Battlefront. The war (vv. 1–12)
    [B. Purification of spoil—organic (vv. 13–20,24)]
        [Purification of spoil—inorganic (vv. 21–23)]
    B′. Distribution of the animate spoil (vv. 25–47)
A′. Battlefront (flashback) and camp (vv. 48–54)

The dedication of the spoil took place at the battlefront (in A) but was placed in A′ as a flashback out of literary considerations: constructing an introversion. The original structure, I submit (see Excursus 68), was AB′A′, with B′, the distribution of the spoils, occupying the center as the main thrust of the story. Subsequently, however, the purification of the organic and inorganic spoil at the command of Moses and Eleazar, respectively, was interpolated (vv. 13–20,24,21–23; B). Since the matter and style of the inter-

polations are characteristic of the priestly material, this text was reworked by two subsequent priestly hands. For details, see Excursus 68.

14. *The Korahite Rebellions (chap. 16): Penultimate Recension*

Introduction (vv. 1–4), earlier version
A. Dathan and Abiram versus Moses (vv. 12–15)
  B. Korah and chieftains versus Aaron (vv. 16–18)
    C. Korah and *ʿedah* versus Moses and Aaron (vv. 19–22)
    C′. *ʿEdah* spared at the Tabernacle (vv. 23–24,26aα,27a)
  B′. Korah and the chieftains incinerated at the Tabernacle (v. 35)
A′. Dathan and Abiram swallowed by the earth (vv. 25–26,27b–34)

This hypothetical, penultimate recension of the present Masoretic text reveals an introverted structure that is as logical as it is aesthetic. The rebellions proceed in an ever-widening scope. They are led respectively by individuals, 250 chieftains, and finally by the entire *ʿedah*. The rebellions are first against Moses, then against Aaron, and finally against both (ABC). The outcome of the rebellions is presented in inverse order: the *ʿedah* is spared, Korah and the chieftains perish by fire, and Dathan and Abiram by earthquake (C′B′A′). The pivot (CC′) provides both the climax of the rebellions—the entire congregation versus Moses and Aaron—as well as the beginning of the denouement, the intervention of the Deity. The omitted text (vv. 5–11) was inserted in the ultimate recension, as explained in Excursus 39. Since both penultimate and ultimate recensions contain priestly material, and the additions are exclusively priestly, it becomes plain that, at least in this instance, one may no longer speak of priestly sources but of two priestly recensions.

15. *The Reconnaissance of Canaan* (chaps. 13–14)

A. The scouts' expedition (13:1–24)
  [interpolation (v. 21)]
  B. The scouts' report (13:25–33)
    X. The people's response (14:1–10a)
  B′. God's response (14:10b–38)
  [interpolation (vv. 26–38)]
A′. The people's expedition (14:39–45)

AA′, the frame of the structure, shows that the people retrace the steps of the scouts. BB′ reflects God's response to the majority report of the scouts. X, the pivot, describes the nadir of the story: The demoralized people plan to stone Moses and Aaron and return to Egypt. The two interpolations (13:21; 14:26–28) bear witness to a variant tradition concerning the extent of the reconnoitered land and the participation of Joshua (see Excursus 29 for details). Both the main story and the interpolations contain priestly material, indicating, as in the case of chapters 16 and 31 (nos. 13 and 14, above) that they are the products of two priestly recensions.

Parallel Panels Two pericopes can be juxtaposed not only in inverse order (introversion) but also in parallel panels, described by the scheme ABCD . . . A′B′C′D′ . . . Three examples follow:

1. *The Ashes of the Red Cow* (chap. 19). Not only is the septenary principle a binding element (see below, p. xxxi); the chapter as a whole has been structured as two parallel panels:

A. "This is the ritual law" (v. 2a)	A'_1. "This is the law" (v. 14)
B. Preparation of the ashes renders impure (vv. 2b–10)	B′. Touching a corpse or derivatives renders impure (vv. 14–16)
C. Purification procedures (vv. 11–12)	C′. Purification procedure (vv. 17–19)
D. Penalty for nonpurification (v. 13)	D′. Penalty for nonpurification (v. 20)
	A'_2. "Ritual" (v. 21a) [addition (vv. 21b–22)]

A′ has been split into A'_1 and A'_2 to provide the second panel with its beginning and end, thereby forming an inclusion to the entire chapter (vv. 21b–22 were added subsequently). Furthermore, the middle elements in DD′ are reversed to form an inner chiasm. For further details, see Excursus 47.

2. *Two Complaint Narratives*

Complaint 1: Taberah *(11:1–3)*	***Complaint 2: Hazeroth*** (12:1–15)
a. People complain (v. 1a)	a′. Miriam and Aaron complain
b. God hears, fumes, punishes (v. 1b)	b′. God hears, fumes, punishes (vv. 2b,4–5,9–10)
c. People appeal to Moses (v. 2a)	c′. Aaron appeals to Moses (vv. 11–12)
d. Moses intercedes (v. 2bα)	d′. Moses intercedes (v. 13)
e. Appeal answered (v. 2bβ)	e′. Appeal answered (v. 14)
f. March delayed (see v. 3)	f′. March delayed (v. 15)

These two panels frame another narrative complaint (11:4–34; see above, p. xxiv) as an inclusion. The resulting scheme can be diagrammed as follows:

CHAPTERS 11–12

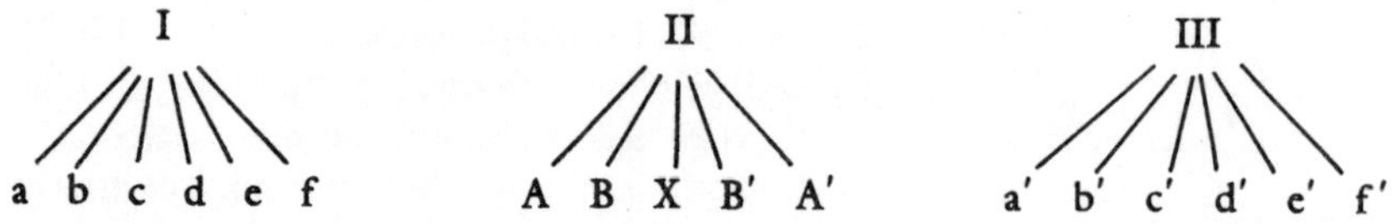

The last item (ff′) requires explanation. The entire people suffer by the forced delay of their journey: seven days in the case of Miriam (12:15), and an unspecified period at Taberah. The latter can be derived from the lack of a travel notice from Taberah to the next station, Kibroth-hattaavah, implying that for the redactor these two sites were identical. For details, see Excursus 24.

3. *From Kadesh to the Jordan* (chaps. 20–21). The many episodes that comprise the final leg of Israel's march in the wilderness have been structured into two parallel panels:

The Failure of the Leaders (32 verses)	***The Failure of the People*** (32 verses)
A. Ominous beginning: Miriam's death (20:1)	A′. Ominous beginning: arduous detour (21:4)
B. People murmur for water (20:2–6) and leaders rebel against God (20:9–11a)	B′. People murmur for water, and *they* rebel against God (21:5)
C. God provides water (20:7–8,11b)	D′. People punished (21:6)
D. Leaders punished (20:12–13)	C′. God heals and provides water (21:7–9,16–18) [interpolation (21:12–20)]
E. Three reverses (20:14–21,22–29; 21:1–3)	E′. Three victories (21:21–31,32,33–35)

The panels consist of five parallel sections with one pair in chiastic relation (CDD′C′), an interlocking feature. AA′ are portents of future tragedy. BB′ reveal a significant difference. In B, the people murmur against the leaders but not against God, whereas in B′, the people murmur against God as well—thereby clarifying why in the first panel, God punishes only the leaders who defy His command (D), whereas in the second panel, God punishes the people because they direct their murmuring expressly against Him (D′). The battle with the Canaanites (21:1–3, E) is interpreted as a reverse, especially for Moses, since Israel's victory led to their retreat rather than to their entry into Canaan. For further details and another possible alignment of the two panels, see Excursus 55.

Inclusions The writer may end the way he begins, thus enclosing his text in a frame that sets it off from contiguous material. Select examples follow, from the simple to the complex:

1. *In inventories*: "These are the duties of the Gershonite clans" (4:24,28). For variations, see 4:4,15b and 4:31,34.

2. *In dialogues*: "you have gone too far" (16:3,7); "we will not come" (16:12,14).

3. *In cultic law*: "Their dedicated gifts . . . of the Israelites I give to you, to your sons, and to your daughters that are with you, as a due for all time. . . . All the sacred gifts that the Israelites set aside for the LORD I give to you, to your sons, and to the daughters that are with you, as a due for all time" (18:11a,19a).

4. *In introversions*:

A. "Then the LORD said to Moses,
  B. The man shall be put to death:
    C. shall pelt him with stones
      D. the whole community outside the camp.
      D′. So took him the whole community outside the camp
    C′. and stoned him
  B′. so that he died
A′. as the LORD had commanded Moses" (15:35–36)

These two verses have been rewritten literally according to the Hebrew sequence in order to demonstrate that they form a perfect introverted inclusion, for not a single word is left outside this scheme.

A. "The LORD spoke to Moses saying . . .
  B. remove from camp . . .
    C. The Israelites did so,

B′. putting them outside the camp;
A′. as the LORD had spoken to Moses,
C′. so the Israelites did" (5:1–2,4)

ABB′A′ form an inclusion in chiastic order. Moreover the subscript (v. 4) is in itself an inclusion, CC′. For another example of this type, see 8:1–4.

5. "This is the ritual for the nazirite" (6:13,21). This inclusion is exegetically important. It indicates that the final verse of the text (v. 21) only applies to the last mentioned case—the Nazirite who completes his/her vow (vv. 13–20). It should be noted that the subscript is an inclusion in itself: "This is the obligation for the nazirite . . . his obligation as a nazirite" (v. 21). The identical inclusion formula is found in the subscript for the text of the suspected adulteress (5:29–30).

6. "The initiation offering for the altar upon its being anointed. . . . This was the initiation offering for the altar upon its being anointed. . . . This was the initiation offering for the altar after its anointing" (7:10,84,88). As above, the subscript (vv. 84–88) is itself framed in an inclusion. Its exegetical significance lies in the equation of ***be-yom*** (vv. 10,84) and ***'aḥarei*** (v. 88), proving that the former should not be rendered as "day" but "upon, after." This insight also clears other alleged difficulties in the text (see the Comment to 7:1).

7. "When Moses finished setting up the Tabernacle. . . . When the Tabernacle was set up" (7:1; 9:15). This inclusion sets off the intervening texts from their contiguous material. In addition, it performs a useful chronological function: informing the reader that these same texts were revealed to Moses not at a fixed date but some time after the Tabernacle was completed (on 1/1) and before Israel began its march (on 2/20). A conflict with the date of the census (2/1) is thereby avoided (see Excursus 16).

8. All introversions are by definition framed by inclusions, if not in language then in subject matter (nos. 5–15, above). As a locking device, the inclusion is at times written in reverse order (chiastically), as in the cited example of a woman's vow (30:17; see above, p. xxii).

9. Entire pericopes can be written or employed as inclusions. Such is the case with the law of tassels (15:37–41), whose vocabulary allows it to act as an inclusion to the episode of the reconnaissance of Canaan of chapters 13–14; that is, by wearing tassels, one will not be seduced by sight and thought as happened with the scouting expedition to Canaan.

Repetitive Subscripts and Resumptions The repetitive subscript is a known archival technique in the ancient Near East (see the Comment to 5:28–29). In inventories it gives totals (7:84–88), and in legal documents it repeats the facts of the case either verbatim (5:29–30) or in summary fashion (30:17; note the chiasm). The subscript itself can be framed by an inclusion, for example, ***zo't torat . . . ha-torah ha-zo't*** (5:29,30; note the chiasm); ***torat ha-nazir . . . torat nizro*** (6:21). Notices that God's command was executed generally take the form of the chiastic subscript: ***va-ya'asu . . . ken 'asu*** (1:54; see 5:4; 8:24; 9:5; 17:25; etc.). In pericopes with introverted structures, subscripts can form the second part of the AA′ inclusion, as in the following examples: the suspected adulteress (5:12–14,29–30); the Nazirite law (6:1–2,13–14aα,21); Moses' speech (11:11,15).

Repetitive resumptions, on the other hand, pick up the thread of an interrupted sequence by repeating the last clause prior to the interruption. Let these few examples suffice:

1. "He anointed and sanctified" (7:1aα,b) is intersected by a string of objects (7:1aβ).
2. The narrative "Moses sent them" (13:3a,17a) is interrupted by the list of the scouts.
3. Moses' challenge to Korah is given twice in nearly identical language (16:6–7a and

16–17a). Since the Levite and Dathan and Abiram passages intervene, the second version may be a repetitive resumption of the challenge. However, it may also be the sign of yet another rebellion against Moses.

4. "Israel settled . . ." (21:25b,31) is interrupted by the Song of Heshbon, an interpolation (see above, p. xx, and Excursus 54).

5. "Balaam . . . departed with the Moabite dignitaries" (22:21a,35b) frames the ass episode, which, as shown, is an interpolation (see above, p. xx, and Excursus 57).

6. "Set out from Rameses" (33:3a*a*,5a) encloses an aside on the exodus that is irrelevant to the itinerary.

Prolepses (Anticipatory Passages) Another distinctive redactional technique evidenced in Numbers is the divulging of information that is patently irrelevant to its context but that prepares the way for what follows. This phenomenon has been noticed in other books of the Torah (see Rashbam on Gen. 1:1).[7] Rather than being dismissed as editorial interpolations and glosses constituting later additions to the text, these proleptic passages should be regarded as integral to the composition. This redactional device is illustrated by the following examples:

1. The description of the Levites' responsibilities (1:48–54) is not germane to the fact that they were not included in the national census (v. 47), but it summarizes and anticipates the Levitical duties as delineated in chapters 3 and 4.

2. The fact that the camp traveled in the same formation as at rest (2:34) anticipates the description of the camp in motion (10:11–28).

3. The naming of Aaron's sons and their fate (3:1–4) is strange in its context. However, it obviates the need to include them in the Levitical census that follows. Contrast the second census, where such information needs to be inserted into the census itself (26:59–61).

4. The subordination of the Levites to the priests (3:9) is irrelevant to their census, but it anticipates the notice that Eleazar was chief of the Levitical guards (3:32) and that the Levites, in general, were made subservient to the priests (8:16,19; 18:3–4).

5. Similarly, the remark that the priests are to "guard their priesthood" (3:10a) remains opaque until clarified and specified in 18:7.

6. The need for the Levites to ransom the Israelites (8:19) is resolved in 18:23.

7. Israel's guidance in the wilderness by God's Presence as condensed in the fire-cloud (9:15–23) has already been anticipated in Exodus 40:36–38. The former also serves as a repetitive resumption (see the Comment to 9:15–23).

8. The advent of the chief villain and the hero of Israel's rebellions in the wilderness, Korah (chap. 16) and Phinehas (chap. 25), has been anticipated by the genealogy of Exodus 6:14–25, which purposefully terminates with these two names.

9. The notice that Israel settled in the Transjordanian territory it conquered from the Amorites (21:25,31) prepares the way for the story of the settlement of the two and a half tribes (chap. 32).

10. The mention of the asylum towns in the account of the Levitical towns (35:6) anticipates the creation of the asylums for cases of homicide (35:9–34).

There can be no doubt that anticipation is a key technique in the redactor's art. It piques the curiosity of the reader, sustains his attentiveness, and prods him to read on so that he can discover the full meaning of each allusive prolepsis. One final note: Since this technique bridges Exodus and Numbers (above, nos. 7 and 8), the conclusion is ineluctable

that the final redaction of Numbers took place when it was already part of a literary corpus containing Exodus and Leviticus (see above, pp. xx–xxi).

Septenary Repetitions A word or phrase repeated seven times, if not an accident, is a device to underscore its significance. Three examples follow in which the number seven predominates:

1. *The Transjordanian Settlement* (chap. 32): Five terms exhibit this septenary pattern: "holding/share," "Gad and Reuben," "cross," "be picked, shock troops," "before the Lord." In effect, these terms summarize the chapter: If Gad and Reuben will cross (the Jordan) as the vanguard before the Lord (i.e., the Ark), they will receive the land holdings (they desire). See further in Excursus 69.

2. *The Ashes of the Red Cow* (chap. 19): Here, not terms but subjects—seven of them—are repeated seven times: (*a*) the cow and its ashes; (*b*) seven items burnt; (*c*) the sprinkling; (*d*) seven persons wash; (*e*) seven persons are contaminated; (*f*) seven are purified; (*g*) seven priests (see Excursus 47).

3. *"At the command of the Lord"* appears seven times in chapters 3–4 (3:16,39,51; 4:37,41, 45,49) to emphasize that the Lord Himself counted the Levites in contrast to the census of the Israelites. It appears seven times again in chapter 9 (vv. 18a,18b,20a,20b,23a,23b,23c) to emphasize that the Lord alone directs Israel's march through the wilderness.

Recapitulation and Conclusions The individual pericopes of Numbers manifest design. Their main structural device is chiasm and introversion. Also evidenced are such artifices as parallel panels, inclusions, subscripts and repetitive resumptions, prolepses, and septenary enumerations. The pericopes are linked to each other by associative terms and themes and to similar narratives in Exodus by the same itinerary formula. The revelation to Moses at Sinai (Exod. 33) is the pivot not only for the Exodus and Numbers narratives but also for the entire Hexateuch, which takes the shape of a grand introversion in which the events after Sinai repeat the failures and fulfill the promises of the pre-Sinaitic period.

Yet, despite this unmistakable evidence of recensional activity, one cannot with confidence speak of the redaction of Numbers. Redaction implies a single mind or, if several persons are involved, a single mind-set or school. To be sure, marks left by two editors from the priestly school have been detected in the account of the scouts (chaps. 13–14; see above, p. xxvi), the Korahite rebellions (chap. 16; see above, p. xxvi), the war against Midian (chap. 31; see above, p. xxv), and in other pericopes (e.g., chap. 36; see Excursus 77). However, there is as yet no way to ascertain whether these strands were deposited by the same person. And even if they betray the same style and ideology, other pericopes reveal that another (deuteronomic) school was at work. There are only two places where a deuteronomic hand can be detected (21:33–35; 32:7–15); and there is a strong possibility that it represents the last editorial activity in Numbers, even after the priestly recension had been completed. This possibility will be augmented by the evidence, presented below, that the priestly material is of high antiquity. Yet, until new evidence is adduced, it would be more prudent to speak of the composition of Numbers rather than its redaction.

One conclusion, however, can be asserted with relative certainty. The interpolations bearing the priestly trademark show that the priestly material does not comprise an independent source but is the product of at least two recensions. In other words, two writers of the priestly school—possibly redactors—added their interpolations to combined priestly and epic material and thereby composed the Book of Numbers.

Special Features

The Antiquity of the Priestly Materials There is general scholarly consensus on the antiquity of the poetry and narratives that comprise the nonpriestly stratum in Numbers. The same verdict must be passed on those texts assigned to the priestly stratum as well: The sheer weight of the demonstrably ancient terms and institutions contained in that material renders such a conclusion ineluctable. The evidence of the technical terms will be marshaled first.

TERMS The sociopolitical divisions of ancient Israel are described by (1) *ʿedah*, (2) *moʿed*, "(national) assembly," (3) *matteh*, "tribe," (4) *ʾelef*, "clan," (5) *nasiʾ*, "chieftain," terms that cease being used after the ninth century (see Excursus 1 and the Comment to 16:2). Even more compelling is the term (6) *ʿavodah*: In the Tetrateuch (Genesis–Numbers) it means only "physical work" and is the occupation not of the priests but of the Levites. In the postexilic literature (e.g., Ezra, Nehemiah, Chronicles), it means "cultic service," the occupation of the priests. However, these two meanings are mutually exclusive: Levites perform cultic service on pain of death. Thus the fact that *ʿavodah* is ascribed only to Levites in Numbers, whereas in the Second Temple period priests alone are permitted *ʿavodah*, necessarily leads to the conclusion that Levitical *ʿavodah* is a preexilic phenomenon. And since this term proliferates throughout Numbers (chaps. 1, 3, 4, 7, 8, 16, 18), the cultic contexts in which this term is found must all be adjudged to be old (see further in Excursus 6). Similarly the term (7) *mishmeret*, meaning "guard duty" in Numbers, changes to "course of duty" in postexilic texts, a meaning it does not have in Numbers and therefore another indication that its cultic contexts in Numbers must be old (see Excursus 4). Evidence of another sort is provided by (8) *ʾasham*, "feel guilt," the priestly forerunner of the prophetic *shav*, "repent." Since the latter word is totally absent from the priestly texts (and in general from the Tetrateuch), it stands to reason that *ʾasham* is a preexilic term. Indeed, it was most likely current before the seventh (and possibly eighth) century, when prophetic *shav* became the prominent term for repentance. Further evidence has been adduced by (9) *mi . . . va-maʿalah*, "from . . . and upwards" (1:3) and (10) *yityalledu*, "registered," which was replaced in postexilic texts by *mi . . . u-le-maʿalah* and *hityaḥes*, respectively.[8] Also (11) *ḥallah*, "loaf" (6:15,19; 15:20), which appears only in the priestly texts and in 2 Samuel 6:19, is changed to the frequently attested *kikkar* when the latter passage is cited in 2 Chronicles 16:3. And (12) *leḥem tamid*, "regular bread" (4:7), called *leḥem panim*, "display bread," in the priestly texts (e.g., Exod. 25:30; 35:13) and in the early narratives (1 Sam. 21:5; 1 Kings 7:48 [= 2 Chron. 4:19]), is always referred to in postexilic books by the term *maʿarekhet* (e.g., Neh. 10:34; 2 Chron. 2:3).[9] Finally (13) *ʾummah*, a rare word for "tribe" (25:15), attested in the Akkadian of ancient Mari (a city on the Euphrates in modern Iraq), is replaced in later literature, except for archaizing poetry, by *leʾom*.[10]

In addition to the above thirteen terms, which can be shown to have fallen out of usage by the time of the Babylonian exile, there remains a host of other technical terms that are attested in literature—especially Mesopotamian—antecedent to the Bible. The term used at ancient Mari for (14) "muster the troops" is the exact cognate of *pakad tsavaʾ* (1:3). (15) None of the twenty-four names found in the list of chieftains (1:5–15) is compounded of the divine element YH (YHVH), a fact that corresponds with the tradition that the Tetra-

grammaton was first revealed to Moses. (16) Old Aramaic *'dn* and Akkadian *adê* correspond to biblical *'edut*, "pact" (1:53). (17) *Karav*, "encroach" (3:10), has an exact cognate in fifteenth-century Nuzi Akkadian (see Excursus 5). (18) *Mille' yad*, "ordain," also has an older Akkadian equivalent (see the Comment to 3:3). (19) *Tsava'*, "service" (4:3), in Akkadian as well as Hebrew, has a military and a nonmilitary meaning. Other old Akkadian terms surfacing in the priestly texts of Numbers are (20) *tsav*, "draught animal" (7:3); (21) *'amud*, "pillar" (14:14), that is, the "standard" of the Deity; (22) *peresh*, "specify (by oracle)" (15:34); (23) *mishḥah*, "perquisite, allotted measure" (18:8); (24) *tsamad*, "couple (sexually)" (25:2); (25) *mekhes*, "tax" (31:27); and (26) *sikkim*, "pointed object" (33:55). To be sure, this latter group of thirteen terms, although attested in antecedent Mesopotamian literature, could have survived even in late biblical Hebrew. But in their aggregate and coupled with the preceding thirteen terms, which demonstrably did not survive in postexilic Hebrew, they make a strong case for the preexilic provenience of their contexts.

INSTITUTIONS The antiquity of the terminology is matched by the antiquity of the institutions represented in the priestly texts:

1. Israel's camp in the wilderness is square-shaped; in later Israel the war camp was round. The wilderness camp most resembles the war camp of Ramses II, the probable pharaoh of the Exodus. Not only is the latter camp square in shape, but its tent-sanctuary is in its center, surrounded by thick walls as protection against defilement, a function filled in Israel's camp by the Levitical cordon (see Excursus 3).

2. The custody of the Tabernacle is shared by the priests who guarded inside the sacred precincts and by the Levites without, a tradition that is found solely in the anterior Hittite cult. In the texts dealing with Solomon's Temple, however, the Levites do not appear at all; they only surface in Ezekiel's visionary Temple and in the postexilic writings that were influenced by the Torah literature. Moreover, the Levite guards of the Tabernacle were armed, ready to strike down any encroacher, a fact that explains the action of Phinehas at Baal-peor who slew the encroaching couple in his capacity as chief of the Levitical guards. Armed Levitical guards are not, however, attested for the two Jerusalem Temples (see Excursuses 4, 5, 40).

3. The first-born originally held a sacred status, possibly as officiants at the worship of the family's ancestors. Their replacement by the nonsacred Levites may reflect an ancient polemic and struggle against ancestral cults in Israel (see the Comments to 3:11–14).

4. The purification offering required of the Nazirite who successfully completed his vow conflicts with the Torah's definition of the *ḥatta't*. Following Ramban, the *ḥatta't* here serves to desanctify the Nazirite, a function that is more characteristic of the reparation offering. Like the boiled shoulder eaten by the Nazirite in the sanctuary court (see below), it probably reflects a more ancient usage of the purification offering prior to the latter's differentiation from the reparation offering (see the Comment to 6:14).

5. The boiled shoulder of the Nazirite ram (6:19) is at odds with the Israelite sacrificial system, which never requires the shoulder. Nor does it require that the lay offerer cook his sacrificial portion inside the sacred precincts. However, both practices are attested in pre-Israelite Lachish and pre-Temple Shiloh (see the Comment to 6:19).

6. The details of the form and manufacture of the Tabernacle menorah do not correspond with those of Solomon's Temple or of later periods. They most closely resemble the design of lampstands of the late Bronze Age (see Excursus 17).

7. That the Midianites constituted an *'ummah* (25:15), an ancient word for tribe, replaced in later texts by *le'om* (see example 10, below, and Excursus 67) indicates the antiquity of this passage.

8. Ecstatic prophecy as a group phenomenon (11:25) is last attested in the time of Saul (1 Sam. 19:20–24).

9. The rebellions that are conflated in the Korah pericope (chap. 16) are redolent of high antiquity: that of the Reubenites Dathan and Abiram against Moses before their tribe lost its first-born leadership status and that of the Levites against Aaron before the struggle over which priestly family would control the Temple had been settled (Excursus 39).

10. The account of the war against the Midianites (chap. 31) bears many hallmarks of antiquity, chief of which is the absence of camels from the spoils: By contrast, they predominate in the inventory of booty taken from the Midianites in Gideon's war (Judg. 6–8). Thus the Mosaic account must have originated before the eleventh century, when the Midianites developed a camel cavalry (Excursus 67).

11. Moses permits his soldiers to marry their Midianite captive women (31:18), a precedent set by Moses himself (Exod. 2:16–21) but that was anathema to the postexilic age (e.g., Ezra 9).

12. The boundaries of the promised land (chap. 34) do not conform to any historical situation in Israel's national existence but are congruent with Egypt's Asian province during the period of the New Empire (15th–13th cents.). Transjordan, notably, lies outside the promised land (and the Egyptian province), although it is occupied by Reuben and Gad during the period of conquest and settlement. The Book of Deuteronomy, on the other hand, adjusts to historical reality by making the conquest of all of Transjordan a divine command (see Excursus 73).

13. Deuteronomy, the product of the eighth and seventh centuries, is familiar with the following priestly materials in Numbers: (*a*) details of the scouting expedition attributed to the priestly strand (for example, 14:31–33; Deut. 1:39); (*b*) the priestly dues (18:20; Deut. 18:2); (*c*) the death of Moses (27:12–14; Deut. 32:48–52); (*d*) the succession of Joshua (27:18; Deut. 34:9); (*e*) the asylum cities (35:13–14; Deut. 19:8–9; see Excursus 75). In addition, Deuteronomy exhibits knowledge of priestly laws from other Torah books, for example, (*f*) priests are in charge of leprosy cases (Deut. 24:8; Lev. 13:2,9, etc.); (*g*) blemished sacrifices (Deut. 17:1; Lev. 22:20); (*h*) the reciprocal covenant (Deut. 29:12; Exod. 6:7; Lev. 26:12). To be sure, it can be (and has been) maintained that a later editor interpolated the priestly elements in all these deuteronomic passages. However, it can be shown in many instances that the so-called additions are too integrated into their contexts to allow for their excision; furthermore, it is more logical to posit that Deuteronomy borrowed from the priestly material than to assume that a later hand reworked so many deuteronomic passages.

14. The big bulge in the story of Gad and Reuben (32:7–15) is replete with deuteronomic phrases. Thus it seems probable that the final redaction of this piece was done by a Deuteronomist. Of course, it can be maintained that this latter-day Deuteronomist lived in the postexilic period. This, however, is unlikely since it presupposes that the deuteronomic school extended over several centuries. In any event, the existence of this deuteronomic bulge proves that the last editorial hand in Numbers is not of the priestly school.

15. As Y. Kaufmann has already argued, the absence of priestly sancta such as the Ark, the Urim and Thummin (27:21; Excursus 64), and the anointing oil (4:16) in the postexilic age speaks eloquently for their antiquity. Similarly, the 12:1 ratio of priests to Levites in

postexilic times (Ezra 2:36–42; 8:15) cannot be reconciled with the 1:10 ratio presupposed by the tithe laws (18:26) unless the latter stem from a much earlier period.

In addition, there are many other institutions reflected in the priestly texts of Numbers that are demonstrably old, as follows: (16) the census (1:2,3,49), whose closest model is that of ancient Mari (Excursus 2); (17) the golden libation bowls inside the Tent (4:7; cf. Exod. 25:29), which may reflect a pre-Mosaic usage; (18) the priestly doctrine of repentance, which precedes the prophetic doctrine (see the introductory Comments to 5:5–8 and Excursus 33); (19) the antiquity of the Temple tithe, in general, and the Levitical tithe (18:25–32), in particular (see Excursus 46); (20) the letter to Edom (20:14–17), which resembles second millennium diplomatic notes; (21) the copper serpent worshiped by Israel in the wilderness (21:4–9) and that was found in a shrine in Timna—at approximately the same place and time as in the Numbers passage (Excursus 52); (22) the possibility that it is the priestly tradition that Balaam seduced Israel to engage in the idolatrous rites at Baal-peor that is reflected in the eighth-century Deir ʿAlla inscription (Excursus 60); (23) the second census (chap. 26) of Israel's clans (and not its tribes) probably belongs to the premonarchic age (see the introductory Comment to chap. 26); (24) the Manassite clans (26:29–34) are shown by the eighth-century Samaria Ostraca to be names of districts, indicating that the Manassites settled there in a much earlier period (see the introductory Comment to 26:29–34); (25) the master itinerary of the wilderness march (chap. 33) most closely resembles, in form, ninth-century Assyrian itineraries (see Excursus 71); (26) the probability that the original plan for the Levitical and asylum towns (Excursuses 74 and 75) is to be found in the priestly (rather than the deuteronomic) texts.

RECAPITULATION Thus, eleven priestly terms and fifteen priestly institutions mentioned in Numbers disappear from usage in the postexilic age. In addition, thirteen priestly terms and ten priestly institutions, although they may have continued in use in later times, originate in the earliest period of (or prior to) Israel's national existence. In sum, we have twenty-six strong reasons and twenty-three supportive ones for affirming the antiquity of the priestly material in the Book of Numbers.

Polemics Israel's ideological war with its pagan surroundings is reflected in Numbers. Its first encounter with the Baal fertility cult in the steppes of Moab is calamitous, resulting in a devastating plague (25:1–9) and an avenging attack against the Midianites (25:16–19; 31:1–54). Balaam, the foreign diviner who instigates the Baal apostasy—according to one tradition (31:16)—must unlearn his heathen arts before he can qualify for direct revelation from God. First, as he consistently insists to Balak, he is a diviner not a sorcerer; that is, he can discern the divine will but not alter it (Excursus 59). Second—and here he enters the realm of Israelite prophecy—he discards the divinatory technique and seeks a direct communication from the Lord (Excursus 58).

The transformation of Balaam is matched by the transformation of two rituals that were clearly pagan in origin. The ritual for the suspected adulteress (5:11–31), minus the interpolated verse 21, originally called for an incantation-ordeal employing magical water, but it did not invoke the name of any deity. The priestly legislators, however, found the formula unacceptable since it ostensibly attributed the effect of the incantation to the water itself. They therefore inserted a statement affirming that the efficacy of the ritual was due to the God of Israel (v. 21b).

An even more striking transformation of a widespread, long-enduring pagan belief is

evident in the purification ritual for those contaminated by contact with a corpse (chap. 19). The preparation of the exorcistic medium, the ashes of the red cow, was totally overhauled so as to incorporate it into Israel's monotheistic sacrificial system. Moreover, the hitherto demonic impurity attributed to corpses was devitalized by denying it the automatic power to contaminate the sanctuary. Considering that the belief in demonic possession and exorcism still prevails in our own time—even in sophisticated circles—the wonder is all the greater that the priestly legislators, nearly three millennia ago, effectively uprooted this belief and practice from the official religion of Israel. For further documentation, see Excursus 48.

A polemic against paganism may also lie behind the replacement of the first-born by the Levites (3:11–14; 8:16–19). That the human first-born originally held a sacred status is indicated by their being "dedicated, sanctified, transferred, to the Lord" (Exod. 13:1,12; 22:28) and by the need to "ransom" them from the Lord (18:15). This terminology may be a reflex of an attested custom in the ancient Near East whereby the first-born was expected to nurture and worship the spirits of his departed parents and grandparents. Thus the substitution of the Levite for the first-born may reflect Israel's ancient struggle against the deeply rooted ancestor worship in its environment. For greater detail, see the Comments to 3:11–14.

In Numbers, priestly concerns play a major role. It is therefore not surprising that a number of issues addressed in this book express priestly points of view and thus are brushed with polemical colorations. For example, 5:9–10 declares the right of each worshiper to choose the priestly recipient of his donations. The inflated language of this passage betrays its polemical character. The controversy within priestly circles over the issue of egalitarian division versus worshiper's choice may be reflected here. (Details are provided in the Comments to 5:9–10.) The law of the temporary Nazirite (6:1–21) may also be a polemic. The priests may have frowned on lifelong Nazirites (e.g., Samuel and Samson) and their asceticism. Instead, they proposed a terminal period that could be brought under priestly control (6:1–21). For details, see Excursus 11. Finally, the possibility should be entertained that the priestly texts deny that Moses could communicate with God "face to face." Rather, he could only hear God's voice while standing in the outer room of the Tent of Meeting where the veil blocked his vision of the Ark and cherubim upon which the divine fire-cloud had descended. Thus the priests may have taught that the privilege Moses received to penetrate the fire-cloud at Sinai's summit in order to receive the Decalogue was unique: Moses was not vouchsafed the experience again (see Excursus 15).

Realism It has been frequently averred that the priestly laws predicate a utopia and do not reflect the existential conditions of Israel's life. However, even those who posit that the priestly laws were written in the Babylonian exile affirm that they are future oriented—preparing the way for Israel's restoration and reoccupation of its land. To be sure, there can be no doubt that idealism permeates the priestly legislation. (Indeed, every code sets forth ideals; otherwise why promulgate it!) Yet it is also true that these laws are permeated by a realism that reflects the social, economic, and political conditions that obtained in ancient Israel. Thus they provide a window to the life of ancient Israel. Evidence will be adduced from several laws in Numbers:

1. The census and organization of Israel's camp (chaps. 1–2) are grounded in military principles that reflect the actual dangers inherent in a trek through the wilderness (see Excursuses 2 and 3).

2. The law of the suspected adulteress (5:11–31) is geared toward curbing the lynch-law mentality that prevailed in society and was thus meant to protect the hapless woman from the uncontrollable rage of her husband and/or community (see Excursuses 8 and 10).

3. As discussed above, the Nazirite law (6:1–21) may be the priestly countermeasure to the prevailing institution of the lifelong Nazirite (see Excursus 11).

4. Though the purification procedure for corpse contamination in chapter 19 uses wilderness terminology, it nonetheless reflects settled conditions. The bearer of impurity, for example, need not leave his community; as is mandated by the older law of Israel's wilderness camp (5:1–4). This change, therefore, reflects the changed conditions of Israel's national existence—again an instance of law as a mirror of society (see Excursus 48).

5. The fact that the Shavuot festival is not called a *ḥag* (28:26), despite its designation as such in the other calendars of the Torah (Exod. 23:16; 34:22; Deut. 16:10,16), implies that realism prevailed over idealism: The middle of the harvest season was no time to make a pilgrimage to the sanctuary. Furthermore, that this festival is not designated as *ḥag* in the one other priestly calendar (Lev. 23:16–21) proves that the omission of the term is deliberate, a clear example of how the priestly legislator accommodated the law to changing socioeconomic conditions (see the Comment to 28:6).

6. The Levitical settlements are a model of town planning. They not only allow for variations in size at the moment of their settlement but also for their future growth. This is realism at its finest (see Excursus 74).

7. The appendix to the case of Zelophehad's daughters in chapter 36 reflects the changeover from clan to tribal dominance. Thus two stages of adjustment to reality are manifested here: first, the fear that daughters who inherit may marry outside their clan and then, outside the tribe (see Excursus 77). Once again, the priestly legislation is shown to have been amended in order to address changing needs.

Theology and Anthropology

The Presence of God The principal actor in the Book of Numbers is, of course, YHVH. Even under extreme provocation, He keeps His covenant with the Israelites, guides them through the wilderness, and provides for their needs.

FIDELITY It is to YHVH's attribute of *ḥesed* that Moses appeals in his plea that God not destroy Israel (14:18–20). *Ḥesed* stands for God's constancy, His fidelity to His covenant with Israel (see Excursus 32). It is this unimpeachable reliability of God's word that Balaam, the heathen prophet, lauds: "God is not man to be capricious/Or mortal to change His mind./Would He speak and not act,/Promise and not fulfill?" (23:19).

UNMEDIATED ACCESSIBILITY The high point in Balaam's praise of Israel is reached when he exclaims: "Lo, there is no augury in Jacob, No divining in Israel:/Jacob is told at once,/Yea Israel, what God has planned" (23:23). Israel, then, is unique among the nations. Having direct access to God, it needs neither diviners nor divination to learn the Deity's will. Indeed, the Balaam story is nothing but the education of a prophet. At the outset, having associated himself with the God of Israel, Balaam rejects Balak's request that he curse Israel, an act that would have made him a sorcerer who could coerce the Deity to accede to his desires. Balaam, however, will only admit to divinatory powers, which, by

virtue of God's grace, enable him to discern His will (see Excursus 59). As Balaam proceeds and blesses Israel he learns something else: Complex techniques are not needed to approach the Lord. Balaam then casts aside his divinatory apparatus and becomes a true prophet "who hears God's speech,/who beholds visions from the Almighty,/Prostrate, but with eyes unveiled" (24:4; see Excursus 58).

To be sure, there is a qualitative difference between Moses and any other prophet. To the latter, "I make myself known to him in a vision, I speak with him in a dream" (12:6). Not so with Moses: "With him I speak mouth to mouth, plainly and not in riddles" (12:8). This distinction is also apparent in the degree of approachability to God: When Moses is in the company of Aaron or the people, God's Presence (***kavod***) is beheld in the Tabernacle courtyard (14:10; 17:8,15; 20:6), to which all of Israel has access. However, when Moses meets with God alone, he is permitted to stand inside the Tent, before the veil (7:89; 17:19; see Excursus 15). However, it must be remembered, this latter distinction is not in kind but in degree. Divination presumes that the Deity leaves traces of his plans imprinted upon natural phenomena, traces that the skilled diviner can discern. Not so, proclaims Israel: God will disclose His will to a prophet only when He so desires; and He does so directly, eschewing mediation.

GUIDANCE The ***kavod*** at Sinai's summit has transferred itself to the Tabernacle, where it is visible as a cloud by day and as fire by night (9:15–16). Its starts and stops determine Israel's stages and stations. Its constant visibility is a sign to Israel and the nations "that you, O LORD, are in the midst of this people; that you, O LORD, appear in plain sight when Your cloud rests over them and when You go before them in a pillar of cloud by day and in a pillar of fire by night" (14:14b). Thus the divine Presence will enter with Israel into the promised land. Just as God's Presence mandates the purity of His camp (5:1–4; 31:19,24), so His Presence in the land mandates that Israel not pollute His land (35:34).

Since God's fire-cloud descends upon the Ark whenever He wishes to address Moses (7:89; see Excursus 15), the Ark too serves as a tangible witness to the divine Presence. The sight of the Ark in battle holds out the promise that Israel will be victorious over its enemies (10:35–36; 31:6), and its absence is a sure sign that Israel will be defeated (14:43–44). That the Ark is flanked by winged cherubim indicates that it represents a flying chariot, a symbol that God is not confined to His Tabernacle-Ark except when He descends upon it to communicate with man. During the march, the Ark, distinguished by its blue cover (4:6), occupies the very center of the camp (10:21), but according to another tradition, it is placed at the head of the camp to lead the march (10:33; see Excursus 22).

PROVIDENCE God supplies Israel with all of its nutritional needs: manna, quail (11:4–34), and water, even when spurned by the people at large or its leadership (20:12–13; 21:5; Excursuses 50 and 55). God also assures Israel's victory over its enemies (21:21–35; 24:8–9, 17–18).

Sacrifice The doctrine of collective responsibility is nowhere better illustrated than in the ***ḥatta't***, the purification offering. This sacrifice, brought for severe physical impurity or inadvertent violations, presumes that these offenses produce a miasma that is attracted magnetlike to the sanctuary and accumulates there until God abandons His sanctuary and His people to their doom. Thus this sacrifice preserves a vivid image of how the individual

can affect the common weal. For the details of the purification effected by the *ḥatta't*, see Excursuses 35 and 49.

The other sacrifice with a total expiatory function is the *'asham*, the reparation offering (see the Comments to 5:5–8). It is brought for the desecration of the sancta, whether cult objects or God's holy name. The latter offense, even if committed deliberately, may be expiated by this offering, provided that remorse and confession have taken place. Thus only unrepented sins are ineligible for sacrificial expiation. Repentance alone, however, cannot absolve sin (in contrast to the later teaching of the prophets). According to the priestly theology, repentance must be augmented by sacrifice; otherwise divine forgiveness is unavailable (see below).

Intercession

PROPHETIC The prophet's job is to defend his people before the divine judge, an intercessory role underscored by the Lord's statement to Moses after the scout heresy: "I will strike them with pestilence and disown them; and I will make of you a nation . . ." (14:12). This is the semantic equivalent of the Lord's request of Moses following the apostasy of the golden calf: "Now, let Me be, that My anger may blaze forth against them and that I may destroy them, and make of you a great nation" (Exod. 32:10). First, by asking Moses not to intercede, God as much as admits that prophetic intercession is effective. Moreover, God seems to be hinting to Moses—perhaps even testing him—that he should intercede if he wants to save Israel. The psalmist, citing a striking image from Ezekiel 22:30, pays this tribute to Moses' intercessory achievement: "He would have destroyed them, had not Moses His chosen one confronted Him in the breach to avert His destructive wrath" (Ps. 106:23). So, indeed, Numbers confirms that Moses interceded for his people at every turn and thereby assuaged the divine wrath (see 11:2; 12:13; 14:13–20; 16:22; 21:7).

PRIESTLY And yet a prophet, even a Moses, can only avert punishment; he cannot expunge the sin. Sin remains suspended over the heads of the sinners, capable of exacting retribution at a future date. Thus Moses' intercession mitigates or postpones the punishment, but it does not abolish it: God's anger will take its toll and the sinners will die, be they Korah and his cohorts (chap. 16) or the entire generation of the Exodus (chap. 14).

On the other hand, not only can a priest intercede, but he can win absolution as well. Aaron stems the plague by offering incense (17:6–14), and his grandson Phinehas does the same by force (25:7–8). More typically, however, the priest obtains forgiveness by means of sacrifice (see 15:22–29). To be sure, sacrifice is not inherently efficacious; it must be accompanied by contrition and confession (for deliberate sins) and, even then, forgiveness is not assured but is dependent on the grace of God. Still, the impact of repentance and sacrifice in tandem is total: The sin is erased from the divine record. This priestly teaching predates the subsequent prophetic doctrine that repentance alone can eradicate sin (Excursus 33), but it demonstrates that the older priestly circles fully appreciated the power of repentance, even if they hitched it to the sacrificial system.

That repentance by itself in Numbers (and in the preceding Torah books) is incapable of shriving sin is evident from the fact that Moses never asks God for forgiveness nor his people for repentance. He takes for granted that punishment is the ineluctable conse-

quence of sin. True, he asks for reconciliation (*salaḥ*, 14:19); however, this means only that God should not abandon Israel but should continue to maintain His covenant with them (see Excursus 32).

Levites The Book of Leviticus is the domain of the priests; the Levites do not appear there at all. But they proliferate in Numbers; indeed, they dominate the book. They are expressly excluded from the national census (1:47–53; 2:33) and are to be mustered separately (chaps. 3–4). They are assigned wagons for their transport duties (7:6–9), undergo purificatory rites when they join the work force (8:5–22), and are assigned guard duty in their retirement years (8:23–28). They march between the tribal units laden with the disassembled Tabernacle (10:17,21). Having joined Korah's rebellion against Aaron (16:7–10) they, henceforth, are represented by Aaron (17:18,23). They are assigned to potentially lethal guard duties in the Tabernacle precincts, for which they are rewarded with the tithe (18:1–6,21–24). In the second census, they once again are counted apart from the rest of the people (26:57–62). They receive two percent of the spoils (31:30,47) as well as forty-eight cities in the settled land, six of which are designated as asylums for those who commit unintentional homicide (35:6,9–15).

The most important function of the Levites, one that invests their entire adult life, is to guard the sanctuary against encroachers. In fact they are identified by this function—"guardians of the Tabernacle of the Lord" (31:30,47). In the ancient world, the entrances to temples were adorned with images of protector gods to ward off supernal demons. In Israel, where the world of the demons has been abolished, the sanctuary remains in danger of defilement by the one creature capable of the demonic: man. His sin can pollute the sacred precincts and his physical encroachment upon the sancta can bring down the wrath of the Deity upon the entire community. The Levitical cordon is therefore empowered to strike down the encroacher (see Excursuses 4 and 5); moreover, it is held fully responsible if any encroachment occurs. Just as in the human sphere the guard pays with his life if anyone manages to slip through his watch (e.g., 2 Kings 10:24), so in the divine sphere the Levitical guards are guilty of a capital crime before God if they fail to prevent encroachment upon the sanctuary. Henceforth, the Israelites need not worry that God will punish the entire community; only the encroacher and the negligent Levitical cordon will pay the penalty. For Israel's sake, God will compromise His doctrine of collective responsibility. The Levites will be the lightning rod to absorb the divine anger so that Israel may worship at the sanctuary without fear (see Excursus 40).

Priests The centrality of the priesthood in assuring divine favor for Israel by means of sacrifice has already been discussed. The story of the Korahite rebellions (chaps. 16–17) vindicates the Aaronides as the sole priestly line and declares that any encroacher on their prerogatives is to be put to death (18:3,7).

In Numbers, the priests are assigned the following roles: (1) to serve as guards at the entrance and in the courtyard of the Tabernacle (3:38; 18:5); (2) to dismantle and cover the Tabernacle sancta before the Kohathite Levites carry them (4:1–20); (3) to officiate at the ordeal of the suspected adulteress (5:11–31), the rite terminating the aborted or successfully completed Nazirite period (6:1–21), the Priestly Blessing (6:22–26), the purification of the Levitical work force (8:5–26), blowing the trumpets (10:8), and preparing the ashes of the red cow (19:1–10).

The High Priest is assigned even loftier responsibilities: (1) to intercede for Israel by

offering incense (17:6–15); (2) to consult the Urim and Thummim oracle (27:21); (3) to serve by his death as vicarious atonement for the unintentional homicide (35:28).

For their service, the priests are granted the following emoluments: assigned sacrificial portions, *ḥerem*, firstlings of pure animals and the redemption price of impure firstlings and human first-born (18:8–20), a tithe of the Levitical tithe (18:25–32), and .02 percent of the spoil (31:30,41–46). The worshiper is permitted to designate his priestly officiant and recipient of his edible donations (5:9–10).

Israelites All Israelites—men and women alike—are to attach tassels, each containing one violet cord, to the edges of their outer garments (15:37–41). The tassels render their garments *sha'atnez*, a mixture otherwise permitted only to priests; and the violet cord is the emblem of royalty. Thus the tassels remind Israel that they belong to a royal priesthood (Exod. 19:6). Though only priests are holy from birth, all of Israel can aspire to a life of holiness (Lev. 19:2). Belonging to royalty, they serve no mortal king; they are servants of God (see Excursus 38).

Israelites who crave the austere life of the priesthood can achieve it by taking the Nazirite vow (6:1–21), although this practice, it seems, is transitory and discouraged (Excursus 11). Indeed, even Levites (see above, p. xl) are not inherently holy. Although they are bound to the sanctuary as much as the priests, in ritual requirements they differ not at all from the laity. The priesthood, then, is the prerogative of the descendants of Aaron. Attempts on the part of the laity to break into this circle led to disaster (chap. 16). Enough that Israel's special relationship to God sets her on a path that leads to a life of holiness!

Another tradition in Numbers, however, puts forward the prophet not the priest as the ideal and Moses as the paragon (12:6–8). Just as one cannot choose to be a priest, so one cannot be a prophet except by divine election (11:16–17,23–25). Still, though Eldad and Medad's prophesying is regarded by Joshua as a threat to Moses' leadership, Moses rises to the summit of altruism when he proclaims: "Would that all the LORD's people were prophets, that the LORD put His spirit upon them" (11:29). This teaching is echoed by a later prophet: "After that, I will pour out My spirit on all flesh; Your sons and daughters shall prophesy; Your old men shall dream dreams, And your young men shall see visions" (Joel 3:1).

Moses One would expect the traditions about the founder of a nation to be embellished with legend and hyperbole. Yet what surprises about Moses, particularly as he appears in Numbers, is that he is all too human, a personage of flesh and blood. Betraying a streak of self-doubt (11:14; see Exod. 4:10–14), he indulges in self-pity (11:11,15) and even begins to question God (11:21–22). He becomes more intemperate (20:10–11) and—in the plain hearing of his assembled people—he allows his anger to overrun his words and commit the ultimate heresy: He attributes the miracle to himself (20:10; see Excursus 50). We know this man Moses; we recognize him in ourselves. He is burnt out, worn down by his grueling task and chapters 11–20 record his steady decline (see Excursuses 24 and 39). Though it has been years since his people have been liberated from Egypt, they reveal that they still are slaves—by their hankering after their past material security (11:5) and their panic that the promised land promises only disaster (14:3). Moses cannot handle them: His leadership falters and he cannot be entrusted to bring them into the land.

Yet despite these lapses, Moses remains a giant. Indeed, it is in this book that he attains unprecedented moral stature. Though he selflessly intercedes with God for his people

whenever the occasion demands it (11:2; 12:13; 14:13–20; 16:22; 21:7), he refuses to utter one word in his own defense when his own family pillories his reputation, producing the editorial comment: "Moses was a very humble man, more so than any other man on earth" (12:3). He bears no grudge against his sister Miriam when she defames him (12:1–2); to the contrary, he prays that her punishment be remitted (12:13). Moses brushes aside Joshua's warning that Eldad and Medad's prophesying is a threat to his leadership: "Are you wrought up on my account? Would that all the LORD's people were prophets" (11:29). The Numbers traditions about Moses thus prove him capable of reaching new spiritual heights. True, he plummets to his nadir, but it is matched by his zenith.

Moses' lapses, though fatal, are few and momentary. Otherwise he is the unfailing leader. He has prepared his people militarily for the conquest. Organizing them into an effective army (chap. 1; Excursuses 2 and 3), he succeeds in establishing a secure bridgehead on the Jordan by conquering much of the east bank (21:12–22:1) and by crushing the Midianites (chap. 31). His administrative acumen is in evidence when he provides for the succession, first to Aaron and then to himself (20:22–29; 27:12–23), and when he successfully negotiates with the tribes of Reuben and Gad to lead their brethren in the campaign of conquest in exchange for the privilege of settling in the conquered Transjordanian territory (chap. 32). To the end of his days he functions as covenantal mediator when he renders oracular decisions: the second Passover for impurity bearers (9:1–14); the punishment for the Sabbath violation (15:32–36); inheritance rights for women (27:1–11; 36:1–10). His continued success as prophet-intercessor has already been discussed (see above, p. xxxix). Having consecrated the Tabernacle and its clergy (Lev. 8), Moses no longer officiates as priest (contrast Exod. 24:8; and see Ps. 99:6). However, he is still credited as the author of Israel's cultic institutions: purificatory rites (5:1–4; 31:19–20,24), sacrificial accompaniments (15:1–16), priestly gifts (15:17–21; 18:25–32), and the cultic calendar (chaps. 28–29). To be sure, the priestly tradition refutes the legendary superhuman status accorded to the figure of Moses: It allows Moses an aural but not a visual audience with God (7:89, and despite Exod. 33:11) by barring him from the Holy of Holies (see Excursus 15); yet it never denies that he was the greatest of men.

The Commentators

Medieval My commentary is selective in citing other interpretations. It grapples with many widely held views that differ from my own and acknowledges all with which I agree. In the latter category, the reader will find that I draw heavily from medieval Jewish exegetes whose insights have largely been neglected. Indeed, some of their very names will draw a blank even from scholars. Having lived in a premodern age, they are a priori written off as precritical. However, in page after page of this commentary, it will be demonstrated that they frequently anticipate the moderns and at times even supersede them. Unfortunately, except for Rashi and Ramban, their commentaries, composed in Hebrew (and Saadia's in Arabic), still await translation into English. At the least they deserve some identification. A thumbnail biography follows in chronological order.

SAADIA ben Joseph Gaon (882–942). Arguably, the greatest leader, philosopher, and halakhist of the gaonic period, he was born and raised in Egypt and settled in Babylonia

where he became the head (*gaon*) of the academy of Sura. His Arabic translation and partial commentary (*Tafsir*) of the Bible has remained standard for Arabic-speaking Jews. His translation is not literal, yet he strives for the plain meaning of the text. For examples of his exegesis see the Comments to 22:41 and 23:2,10,22.

IBN JANAḤ, Jonah (first half of 11th cent.) Spanish physician, grammarian, and lexicographer. He compiled the first complete book on Hebrew philology, which is preserved in its entirety. Its second half, known as *Sefer ha-Shorashim* (The Book of Roots), is a complete dictionary of biblical Hebrew, which also contains exegetical excursuses on difficult biblical passages. His influence on succeeding generations of exegetes is enormous. See his Comments to 10:29,36; 14:4; 23:18; and 25:8.

RASHI Solomon ben Isaac (1040–1105), of Troyes, France. His commentary to the Bible and the Babylonian Talmud remains standard curriculum in all traditional Jewish schools to this day. His Bible commentary is a blend of the literal and midrashic. Its methodology is defined in his Comment to Genesis 3:8: "As for me, I am only concerned with the literal meaning of Scriptures and with such aggadot (i.e., midrashim) as explain the biblical passages in a fitting manner." There exists an annotated English translation (Rosenbaum-Silbermann). For examples of his exegesis, see Comments to 11:4,16, and 13:2,3 in this work.

RASHBAM Samuel ben Meir (ca. 1080–ca. 1174), grandson of Rashi and commentator on the Bible and Babylonian Talmud. Of the former, only his commentaries on the Torah and Ecclesiastes survive. A confirmed literalist, he states his position in his Comment to Exodus 21:1 as follows: "I have not come to explain the halakhot. . . . Derived as they are from textual redundancies, they can partly be found in the commentaries of Rabbi Solomon, my maternal grandfather. My aim is to interpret the literal meaning of Scripture." See his exegesis of 11:1, 12:1,4,7, and 13:2.

IBN EZRA, Abraham (1089–1164), poet, grammarian, exegete, philosopher, astronomer, and physician. Until 1140, he lived in Tudela, Spain. Thereafter, he was an itinerant scholar, mainly in Italy and France. Etymology and grammar are his main concerns. In his introduction to the Torah, he states his intention to determine the literal meaning of the text as well as to adhere to the decisions of the rabbis in interpreting the legal portions. Unfortunately, no English translation of Ibn Ezra exists except for his commentary on Isaiah (Friedlaender) and Genesis (Strickman-Silver). For examples of his exegesis, see Comments to 11:8,20,33, and 12:4,5,6,8.

BEKHOR SHOR Joseph ben Isaac (12th cent.), of Orléans, France. In his Torah commentary, he follows the literal approach of his French predecessors, Rashi and Rashbam, stressing the rational basis of the commandments. See his comments to 12:4,5,6,14, and 13:17,30.

RADAK David Kimḥi (1160?–1235?), of Narbonne, France, grammarian and exegete. Following the methodology of Ibn Ezra, he concentrates on philological analysis. However, relying on rabbinic literature, he also includes homiletical interpretations. He wrote

commentaries to Genesis, all the prophetic books, Psalms, and Chronicles. His collected comments on the rest of the Pentateuch and Proverbs were probably culled from his philological writings. For examples of his exegesis, see the Comments to 13:17,32, 14:32, 17:5, and 25:8.

RAMBAN Moses ben Naḥman (1194–1270), philosopher, kabbalist, exegete, talmudist, poet, and physician. He was born in Gerona, Spain, and spent his final years in Palestine. His Torah commentary always gives the literal interpretation but also makes frequent use of the Talmud, Midrash, and Zohar in order to cite a reason for each commandment. An annotated English translation is available (Chavel). For examples of his exegesis, see the Comments to 11:1,12,29, and 12:4,16.

BAḤYA ben Asher (13th cent.), of Saragossa, Spain, exegete, preacher, and kabbalist. He interprets the Pentateuch (published in 1291) in four ways: literally, homiletically, allegorically, and mystically. The clarity of his style and the moralistic thrust of his exposition made his commentary popular through the ages. See his Comments to 14:9 and 16:25.

ḤAZZEKUNI (also Ḥizkuni) A commentary on the Torah and on Rashi's commentary by the Hezekiah ben Manoah of France (13th century). He largely bases himself on his predecessors: Rashi, Rashbam, and Bekhor Shor; but he also quotes many midrashim that are no longer extant.

SEFER HA-MIVḤAR A Torah commentary by Aaron ben Joseph ha-Rofe (Aaron the Elder) (ca. 1250–1320), a Karaite scholar and physician. He lived in Sokhet, Crimea, and in Constantinople. Though a strict literalist, he occasionally introduces a midrashic interpretation taken as a rule from Rashi. For examples of his exegesis, see the Comments to 11:1, 12:5, 16:4, 17:25, and 18:10.

TIRAT KESEF A supercommentary on *Sefer ha-Mivḥar*, written by the Karaite scholar Joseph Solomon ben Moses Lutzki (d. 1844). He was raised in Poland and settled in the Crimea where he became *ḥazzan* (rabbi) of the Karaites. See his comment to 15:19.

KETER TORAH A Torah commentary authored by Aaron ben Elijah (1328?–1369), a Karaite scholar, philosopher, and jurist. He lived in Nicomedia (near Izmir, Turkey). He was called Aaron the Younger to distinguish him from Aaron the Elder who lived a century earlier. His commitment to the literal interpretation of the text did not prevent him from introducing allegorical and metaphysical interpretations. For examples of his exegesis, see the Comments to 12:6, 13:17, 14:9, 15:11, and 23:18.

ABRAVANEL Isaac ben Judah (1437–1508), statesman, philosopher, and exegete. He served as treasurer to Alfonso V of Portugal and in 1484 entered the service of Ferdinand and Isabella of Castille. Expelled from Spain together with its Jewish population, he made his home in Italy where he wrote his Torah commentary. His exegesis is characterized by lengthy answers to questions, sometimes numbering over forty, which he raises before each unit. Eschewing grammar and philology, he concentrates on the rationale for the commandments, stressing their moral significance. See his Comments to 12:5, 13:32, 14:5,9, and 22:7.

MEYUḤAS ben Elijah (probably 15th cent.), Greek exegete and talmudist. Little else is known. See his Comments to 16:12, 22:3,33, 23:18, and 32:32.

SFORNO Obadiah ben Jacob (ca. 1470–ca. 1550), Italian exegete and physician. His brief Torah commentary focuses on the literal meaning of the text, avoiding philosophy and grammar. See his Comments to 11:28,29,33, 12:8, and 13:30.

SHADAL Samuel David Luzzato (1800–1865), Italian scholar, philosopher, exegete, and translator. In his Torah commentary he favors the views of Rashi and Rashbam but also offers his own novel interpretations. He frequently quotes his students, citing them by name. Though chronologically he belongs to the modern period, his faithful pursuit of the plain meaning of the text qualifies him for the company of the above-cited medievalists. See his comments to 11:4,29, 12:2, 13:30, and 14:5.

Modern I have benefited from the following commentators whose works were written during the past century: Dillmann (1886 [German]), Ehrlich (1899–1901 [Hebrew]; 1908–1914 [German]), Paterson (1900), Baentsch (1903 [German]), Gray (1903), Binns (1927), Greenstone (1939), Snaith (1967), Noth (1968), deVaulx (1972 [French]), Wenham (1982), and Budd (1984). In this list the only verse by verse commentaries are those of Dillmann, Baentsch, and Gray—the latter in English. On a popular level the reader is referred to the recent English works of Wenham and the fuller one of Budd. A comprehensive commentary in Hebrew by Licht is now in progress, of which chapters 1–10 have been published (1985).

My Students and Other Acknowledgments This work has been forged on the anvil of my graduate seminar over a period of five years. The feedback of my students was indispensable in challenging and refining my ideas. Their contributions are incorporated in the commentary and acknowledged in the notes. To distinguish them from authors listed in the bibliography, I cite them with their first initial.

I also welcome the opportunity to thank my colleagues M. Greenberg, E. L. Greenstein, S. Talmon, M. Weinfeld, Y. Zakovitch, and my editor, N. M. Sarna, who gave of their time and wisdom to comment on all or part of my manuscript, as well as Chaim Potok, Sheila Segal, and Amy Gewirtzman, of the editorial staff of JPS, for their stylistic improvements.

Notes to the Introduction

1. D. T. Olson, *The Death of the Old and the Birth of the New* (Chico, Calif.: Scholars Press, 1985).
2. Ibid.
3. Cf. G. E. Mendenhall, "Covenant," *Interpreter's Dictionary of the Bible* (Nashville: Abingdon, 1962), 719b; J. A. Wilcoxen, "Some Anthropocentric Aspects of Israel's Sacred History," JR 48 (1968): 333–350.
4. F. M. Cross, *Canaanite Myth and Hebrew Epic* (Cambridge, MA: Harvard University Press, 1973).

5. M. Greenberg, "The Redaction of the Plague Narratives in Exodus," *Near Eastern Studies in Honor of W. F. Albright*, ed. H. Goedicke (Baltimore: Johns Hopkins Press, 1971), 245.

6. J. Milgrom, *Leviticus*, vol. 1, Anchor Bible 3A (New York: Doubleday, in press).

7. N. M. Sarna, "The Anticipatory Use of Information as a Literary Feature of the Genesis Narratives," in *The Creation of Sacred Literature*, ed. R. E. Friedman (Berkeley: University of California Press, 1981), 76–82.

8. A. Hurvitz, "The Evidence of Language in Dating the Priestly Code," RB 81 (1974): 24–56.

9. M. Paran, "Literary Features of the Priestly Code" (in Hebrew) (Ph.D. diss., Hebrew University, 1983).

10. A. Malamat, "*Ummatum* in Old Babylonian Texts and Its Ugaritic and Biblical Counterparts," UF 11 (1979): 527–536.

GLOSSARY

Abravanel, Isaac ben Judah (1437–1508) Statesman, Bible commentator, and religious philosopher. Portugal and Spain.

Aggadah The nonhalakhic (nonlegal) homiletic side of rabbinic teaching, mostly anchored to the biblical text.

Akkadian An ancient Semitic language spoken in Mesopotamia; its chief dialects were Babylonian and Assyrian.

Aquila A convert to Judaism from Pontus, Anatolia, and a disciple of Rabbi Akiba. He translated the standardized biblical Hebrew text into Greek in the 2nd century C.E.

Aramaic A Semitic language closely related to biblical Hebrew and known in many dialects and phases, including Syriac. Aramaic flourished throughout the biblical period and thereafter, and is the language of the Targums, the Gemaras, and large sections of midrashic literature.

Avot de-Rabbi Nathan An exposition of an early form of Mishnah Avot (Ethics of the Fathers), transmitted in two versions.

Baḥya ben Asher See Introduction, p. xliv.

Bekhor Shor Commentary on the Torah by Joseph ben Isaac, 12th century. Northern France.

Exodus Rabba Aggadic midrash on the Book of Exodus, originally two separate compositions, combined ca. 11th or 12th centuries.

Gemara An exposition of the Mishnah in Aramaic and Hebrew.

Genesis Apocryphon An elaboration of the Genesis narratives in Aramaic from 1st century B.C.E. or C.E., found in cave 1 at Qumran near the Dead Sea.

Genesis Rabba Palestinian aggadic midrash on the Book of Genesis, edited ca. 425 C.E.

Halakhah The individual and collective rabbinic legal rulings that regulate all aspects of Jewish life, both individual and corporate.

Ḥazzekuni Commentary on the Torah by Hezekiah ben Rabbi Manoah, mid-13th century. France.

Ibn Ezra, Abraham (1089–1164) Poet, grammarian, and Bible commentator. Spain.

Ibn Janaḥ, Jonah (first half 11th century) Grammarian and lexicographer. Spain.

Judah ben Samuel he-Ḥasid (the Pious) (ca. 1150–1217) Ethical writer and mystic; authored a commentary on the Torah. Regensburg.

Judah Ḥayyuj (ca. end of 10th century) Hebrew grammarian. Cordova, Spain.

Kere The way the Masorah requires a word to be read, especially when it diverges from the ***kethib***.

Keter Torah See Introduction, p. xliv.

Kethib The way a word, usually unvocalized, is written in the Bible; see ***kere***.

Lekaḥ Tov A midrashic compilation on the Torah and the Five Megillot by Tobias ben Eliezer, 11th century. Balkans.

Leviticus Rabba Palestinian aggadic midrash on the Book of Leviticus, edited in the 5th century C.E.

Likkutim or ***Sefer ha-Likkutim*** A midrashic collection, six volumes, edited by E. H. Gruenhut (Jerusalem, 1898–1902).

Maimonides, Moses ben Maimon, known as Rambam (1135–1204) Halakhic codifier (*Yad Ḥazakah = Mishneh Torah*), philosopher (*Moreh Nevukhim = Guide of the Perplexed*), and commentator on the Mishnah. Spain and Egypt.

Malbim (1809–1879) Acronym for Meir Loeb ben Yehiel Michael. Rabbi, preacher, and Bible commentator. Eastern Europe.

Masorah The traditional, authoritative Hebrew text of the Bible with its consonants, vowels, and cantillation signs, as well as marginal notes that relate to orthographic, grammatical, and lexicographic oddities; developed by the school of Masoretes in Tiberias between the 6th and 9th centuries.

Mekhilta Halakhic midrash on the Book of Exodus in two forms, the Mekhilta de-R. Ishmael and the Mekhilta de-R. Simeon ben Yoḥai, 1st and 2nd centuries C.E.

Menahem ben Jacob ibn Saruq (10th century) Authored *Maḥberet,* a dictionary of biblical Hebrew. Spain.

Meyuḥas See Introduction, p. xlv.

Midrash Legal and homiletical expositions of the biblical text, and anthologies and compilations of such.

Mishnah The written compilation of orally transmitted legal teachings covering all aspects of Jewish law, arranged in six orders that, in turn, are divided into tractates; executed by Judah ha-Nasi, ca. 200 C.E. Palestine.

Natziv (1817–1893) Acronym for Naphtali Zevi Yehuda Berlin. Rabbinic scholar and head of yeshivah at Volozhin, Poland. Authored *Ha'amek Davar,* a commentary on the Torah.

Numbers Rabba Aggadic midrash on the Book of Numbers, originally two separate compositions, combined ca. 13th century.

Peshitta A translation of the Bible into Syriac, parts of which are said to have been made in the first century C.E.

Pirkei de-Rabbi Eliezer Aggadic work on scriptural narratives, 8th century. Palestine.

Pesikta de-Rav Kahana Homilies on the synagogue lectionaries, (?)5th century C.E. Palestine.

Pesikta Rabbati Medieval midrash on the festivals.

Qumran The site of the caves where Bible manuscripts were found in 1949/50. The manuscripts are identified by such symbols as 4QSam[a] (for manuscript *a* of Samuel, found in the fourth cave of Qumran); 1QIS[a] (for manuscript *a* of Isaiah found in the first cave of Qumran).

Radak Acronym for Rabbi David ben Joseph Kimḥi (?1060–?1235) Grammarian, lexicographer, and Bible commentator. Narbonne, Provence.

Ralbag Acronym for Rabbi Levi ben Gershom, known as Gersonides (1248–1344) Mathematician, astronomer, philosopher, and Bible commentator. Southeastern France.

Rambam See Maimonides.

Ramban Acronym for Rabbi Moses ben Naḥman, known as Naḥmanides (1194–1270) Philosopher, halakhist, and Bible commentator. Spain.

Rashbam Acronym for Rabbi Samuel ben Meir (ca. 1080–1174) Grandson of Rashi. Commentator on the Bible and Talmud. Northern France.

Rashi Acronym for Rabbi Solomon ben Isaac (1040–1105) Commentator on the Bible and Talmud. Troyes, France.

Saadia ben Joseph (882–942) Philosopher, halakhist, liturgical poet, grammarian, and Bible commentator and translator. Gaon (head of academy) of Pumbedita, Babylonia.

Seder Olam (Rabba) Midrashic chronological work ascribed to Yose ben Ḥalafta, 2nd century C.E. Palestine.

Sefer ha-Mivḥar See Introduction, p. xliv.

Septuagint The Greek translation of the Torah made for the Jewish community of Alexandria, Egypt, 3rd century B.C.E.

Sforno, Obadiah ben Jacob (ca. 1470–ca. 1550) Bible commentator. Italy.

Shadal See Introduction, p. xlv.

Sifra = Torat Kohanim Tannaitic midrashic commentary to the Book of Leviticus, probably compiled about the end of the 4th century C.E. Palestine.

Sifrei Tannaitic halakhic midrash to the Books of Numbers and Deuteronomy, probably compiled at the end of the 4th century C.E.

Sumerian A non-Semitic language, written in cuneiform, spoken in the southern part of ancient Babylonia.

Symmachus (2nd century C.E.) Translator of the Bible into Greek.

Talmud The body of rabbinic law, dialectic, and lore comprising the Mishnah and Gemara, the latter being a commentary and elaboration on the former in Hebrew and Aramaic. Two separate talmudic compilations exist: the Babylonian Talmud and the Palestinian Talmud (also known as the Jerusalem Talmud).

Tanḥuma (Yelammedenu) Collection of homiletical midrashim on the Torah, arranged according to the triennial lectionary cycle. Attributed to Tanḥum bar Abba, Palestinian preacher, 4th century C.E.

Tanna(im) The Palestinian sages of the 1st and 2nd centuries C.E. whose rulings are cited in the Mishnah and Tosefta.

Targum Literally, "translation"; specifically of the Bible into Aramaic.

Targum Jonathan An unofficial Aramaic free translation of the Torah, erroneously ascribed to Jonathan ben Uzziel through misinterpretation of the initials "T.Y." (= Targum Yerushalmi). That scholar is the reputed author of the Targum to the Prophets.

Targum Onkelos The standard, official Aramaic translation of the Torah, made in the 2nd century C.E. and attributed to Onkelos, reputed nephew of the Roman emperor Hadrian and convert to Judaism. The name is probably a corruption of Aquila.

Theodotian (2nd century C.E.) Reviser of the Septuagint.

Tirat Kesef See Introduction, p. xliv.

Tosefta A compilation of tannaitic rulings either omitted from the Mishnah or containing material parallel or supplementary to it. It is arranged according to the six orders of the Mishnah.

Ugaritic A language of inscriptions found at Ras Shamra, on the Syrian coast, dating from the second millennium B.C.E. Both the language and its literature have shed much light on the Hebrew Bible.

Vulgate The Latin translation of the Bible made by the Church father Jerome about 400 C.E. It became the official Bible of the Roman Catholic Church.

Yalkut Shimoni Midrashic anthology on the Bible attributed to a certain Simeon, 13th century.

ABBREVIATIONS

AASOR	*Annual of the American Schools of Oriental Research*
AB	Anchor Bible
ADAJ	*Annual of the Department of Antiquities of Jordan*
AfO	*Archiv für Orientforschung*
AHW	W. von Soden, *Akkadisches Handwörterbuch*
AJSL	*American Journal of Semitic Languages and Literatures*
Akk.	Akkadian
ANEP	J. B. Pritchard, ed., *Ancient Near East in Pictures*
ANET	J. B. Pritchard, ed., *Ancient Near Eastern Texts*
Ant.	Josephus, *Antiquities*
AOAT	*Alter Orient und Altes Testament*
Aq.	Aquila
Ar.	Arakhin
Arab.	Arabic
Aram.	Aramaic
ARM	*Archives royales de Mari*
$ARN^{1,2}$	Avot de-Rabbi Nathan, versions 1 and 2, ed. S. Schechter (1887, reprinted 1967)
ASTI	*Annual of the Swedish Theological Institute,* Jerusalem
AusBR	*Australian Biblical Review*
Av. Zar.	Avodah Zarah
BA	*Biblical Archaeologist*
BAP	E. C. Kraeling, ed., *The Brooklyn Museum Aramaic Papyri,* or Philo of Byblos
BAR	*Biblical Archaeologist Reader*
BARev	*Biblical Archaeology Review*
BASOR	*Bulletin of the American Schools of Oriental Research*
BB	Bava Batra
BDB	F. Brown, S. R. Driver, and C. A. Briggs, *Hebrew and English Lexicon of the Old Testament*
Bek.	Bekhorot
Ber.	Berakhot
Bets.	Betsah
Bib	*Biblica*
BIES	*Bulletin of the Israel Exploration Society* (= *Yediot*)
Bik.	Bikkurim
BK	Bava Kamma
BM	Bava Metsia
BO	*Bibliotheca orientalis*
BR	*Biblical Research*

BSOAS	*Bulletin of the School of Oriental and African Studies,* University of London
BTS	*Bible et terre sainte*
BZ	*Biblische Zeitschrift*
CAD	*The Assyrian Dictionary of the Oriental Institute of the University of Chicago*
CAP	A. Cowley, *Aramaic Papyri of the Fifth Century B. C.*
CBQ	*Catholic Biblical Quarterly*
CD	Damascus Document from the Cairo Genizah
CRAIBL	*Comptes rendus de l'Académie des inscriptions et belles-lettres*
Dem.	Demai
Deut. R.	Deuteronomy Rabba
DISO	C.-F. Jean and J. Hoftijzer, *Dictionnaire des inscriptions sémitiques de l'ouest*
EB	*Encyclopaedia Biblica* (Hebrew)
Eduy.	Eduyyot
EncJud	*Encyclopaedia Judaica* (1971)
Er.	Eruvin
Exod. R.	Exodus Rabba
Exp Tim	*Expository Times*
Gen. Apoc.	Genesis Apocryphon
Gen. R.	Genesis Rabba
Git.	Gittin
Gk.	Greek
GKC	*Gesenius' Hebrew Grammar,* ed. E. Kautzsch and trans. A. E. Cowley
Ḥag.	Ḥagigah
Ḥal.	Ḥallah
HALAT	W. Baumgartner et al., *Hebräisches und aramäisches Lexicon zum Alten Testament*
Heb.	Hebrew
HKAT	*Handkommentar zum Alten Testament*
Hor.	Horayot
HTR	*Harvard Theological Review*
HUCA	*Hebrew Union College Annual*
Ḥul.	Ḥullin
IEJ	*Israel Exploration Journal*
Int	*Interpretation*
JANES	*Journal of the Ancient Near Eastern Society of Columbia University*
JAOS	*Journal of the American Oriental Society*
JBC	*Jerome Biblical Commentary*
JBL	*Journal of Biblical Literature*
JCS	*Journal of Cuneiform Studies*
JJS	*Journal of Jewish Studies*
JNES	*Journal of Near Eastern Studies*
JPOS	*Journal of the Palestine Oriental Society*
JQR	*Jewish Quarterly Review*
JR	*Journal of Religion*
JSJ	*Journal for the Study of Judaism in the Persian, Hellenistic, and Roman Period*
JSOT	*Journal for the Study of the Old Testament*
JSOTSup	*Journal for the Study of the Old Testament: Supplement Series*
JSS	*Journal of Semitic Studies*

JTS	*Journal of Theological Studies*
KAI	H. Donner and W. Röllig, *Kanaanäische und aramäische Inschriften*
Ker.	Keritot
Ket.	Ketubbot
Kid.	Kiddushin
Kil.	Kilayim
Kin.	Kinnim
Lam. R.	Lamentations Rabba
Lev. R.	Leviticus Rabba
LXX	Septuagint
Maʿas.	Maʿaserot
Maʿas. Sh.	Maʿaser Sheni
Mak.	Makkot
Makhsh.	Makhshirin
Meg.	Megillah
Meʿil.	Meʿilah
MdRY	Mekhilta de-R. Ishmael
MdRSbY	Mekhilta de-R. Simeon bar Yoḥai
Men.	Menaḥot
Mid.	Midrash
Mid. Ag.	Midrash Aggadah
Mik.	Mikva'ot
Mish.	Mishnah
MK	Moʿed Katan
Naz.	Nazir
Ned.	Nedarim
Neg.	Negaʿim
Nid.	Niddah
NJPS	New Jewish Publication Society translation
Num. R.	Numbers Rabba
OB	Old Babylonian
Oho.	Oholot
Or.	Orlah
OrAnt	*Oriens antiquus*
OTS	*Oudtestamentische Studiën*
Par.	Parah
PdRE	Pesikta de-Rav Eliezer
PdRK	Pesikta de-Rav Kahana
PEQ	*Palestine Exploration Quarterly*
Pes.	Pesaḥim
Pesh.	Peshitta
Pesik.	Pesikta
Phoen.	Phoenician
PJ	*Palästina-Jahrbuch*
PRU	*Le Palais royal d'Ugarit*
Q	Qumran
1QapGen	Genesis Apocryphon from Qumran, cave 1

1QM	War between the Children of Light and the Children of Darkness from Qumran, cave 1
1QS	Rule of the Congregation from Qumran, cave 1
1QSa	Appendix A to 1QS
11QTemple	Temple Scroll from Qumran, cave 11
RA	*Revue d'assyriologie et d'archéologie orientale*
RB	*Revue biblique*
RevQ	*Revue de Qumran*
RH	Rosh Ha-Shanah
Sam.	Samaritan
Sanh.	Sanhedrin
SANT	*Studien zum Alten und Neuen Testament*
SBT	*Studies in Biblical Theology*
Sem	*Semitica*
SER	Seder Eliyahu Rabba
Shab.	Shabbat
Shek.	Shekalim
Shev.	Shevi'it
Shevu.	Shevu'ot
Sif.	Sifrei
Sif. Zut.	Sifrei Zuta
Sifra	Sifra
SOR	Seder Olam Rabba
Sot.	Sotah
Suk.	Sukkah
Sum.	Sumerian
Sym.	Symmachus
Syr.	Syriac
SyroP.	Syro-Palestinian
Ta'an.	Ta'anit
Tam.	Tamid
Tanḥ.	Tanḥuma
Targ. Onk.	Targum Onkelos
Targ. Jon.	Targum Jonathan
Targ. Neof.	Targum Neofiti
Targ. Yer.	Targum Yerushalmi
TDOT	G. J. Botterweck and H. Ringgren, eds., *Theological Dictionary of the Old Testament*
Tem.	Temurah
Ter.	Terumot
Theod.	Theodotian
TJ	Jerusalem Talmud
TLZ	*Theologische Literaturzeitung*
Toh.	Tohorot
Tosafot	Tosafot
Tosef.	Tosefta
TY	Tevul Yom
TynBul	*Tyndale Bulletin*
UF	*Ugarit-Forschungen*

Uk.	Uktsin
UM	Tablets in the collection of the University Museum of the University of Pennsylvania
UT	C. H. Gordon, *Ugaritic Textbook* (1965)
VT	*Vetus Testamentum*
VTSup	*Vetus Testamentum: Supplements*
Vulg.	Vulgate
WO	*Die Welt des Orients*
Yad.	Yadayim
Yal.	Yalkut
Yal. Reub.	Yalkut Reubeni
YD	Yoreh De'ah
Yev.	Yevamot
Zav.	Zavim
ZAW	*Zeitschrift für die alttestamentliche Wissenschaft*
ZDPV	*Zeitschrift des deutschen Palästina-Vereins*
Zev.	Zevaḥim

The editors have adopted a popular system for transliteration of Hebrew, except for the following letters, which have no English equivalent:

’= alef
‘= ayin
ḥ= ḥet (pronounced as the guttural "ch" in German)
kh= khaf (pronounced as the guttural "ch" in German)

1. The Route of the Israelites from Goshen to Kadesh

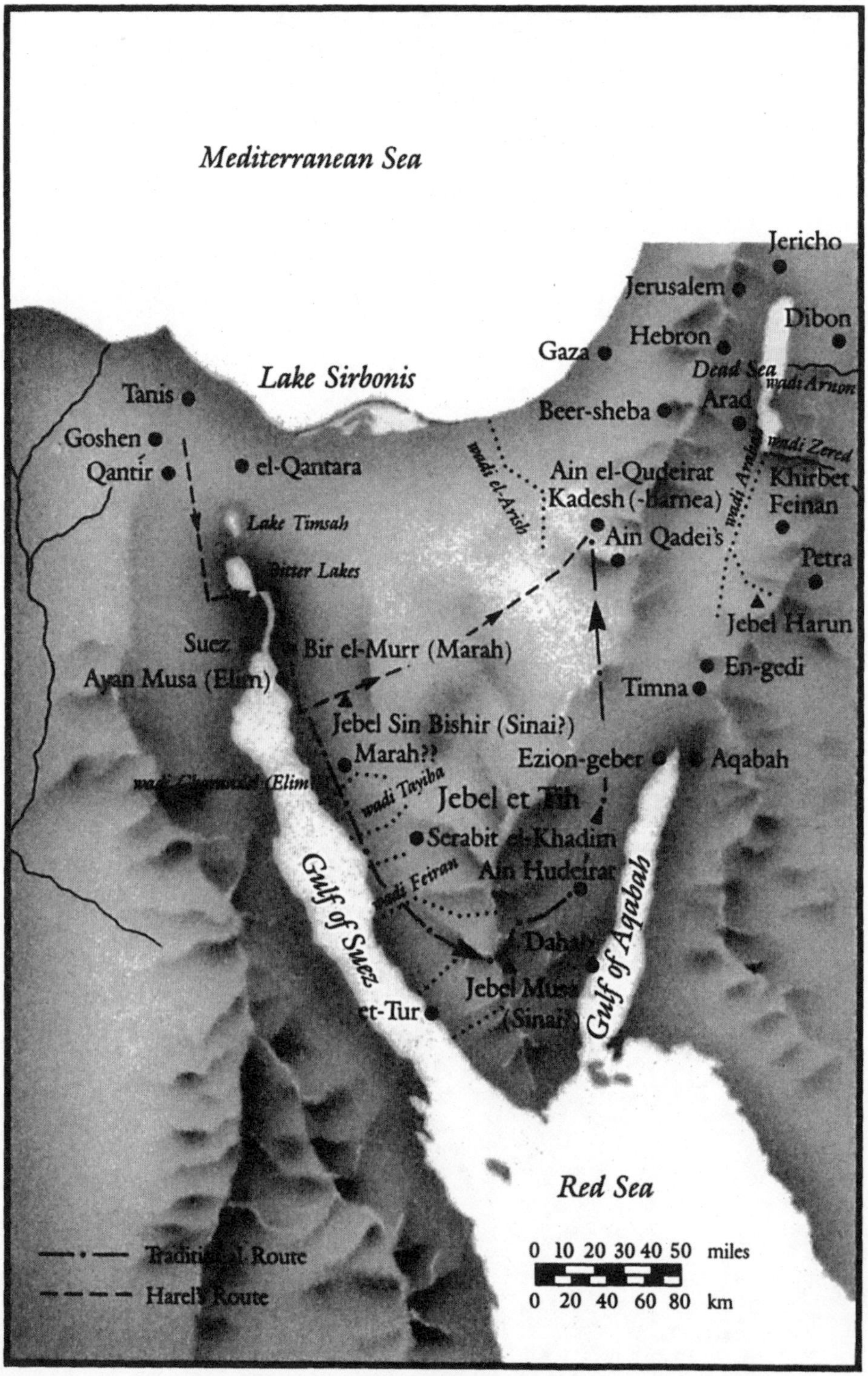

Adapted from G. J. Wenham, *Numbers*, Tyndale Commentaries, 1981.

2. *The Route of the Israelites from Kadesh to the Jordan*

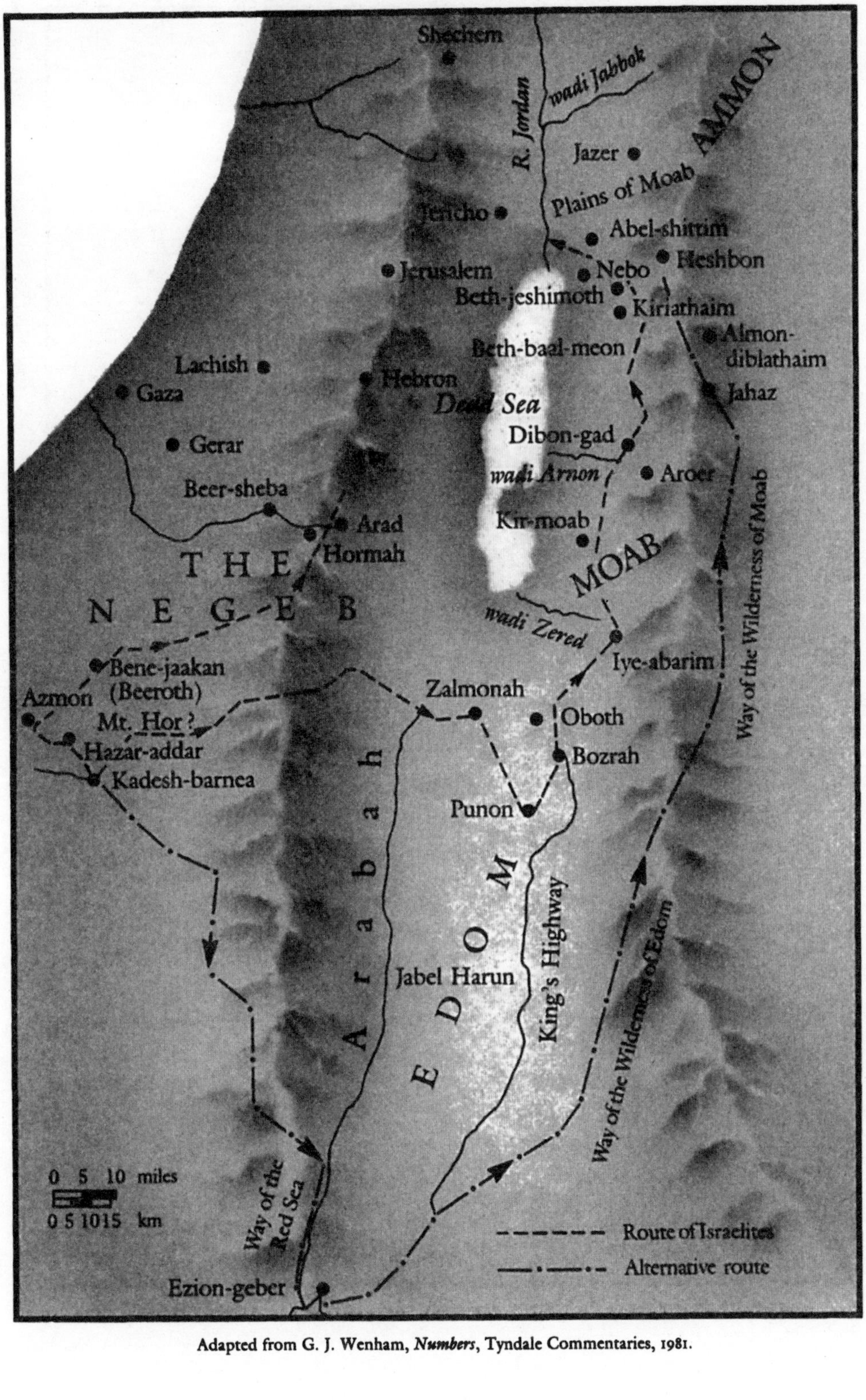

Adapted from G. J. Wenham, *Numbers*, Tyndale Commentaries, 1981.

3. The Borders of Canaan and the Mission of the Scouts

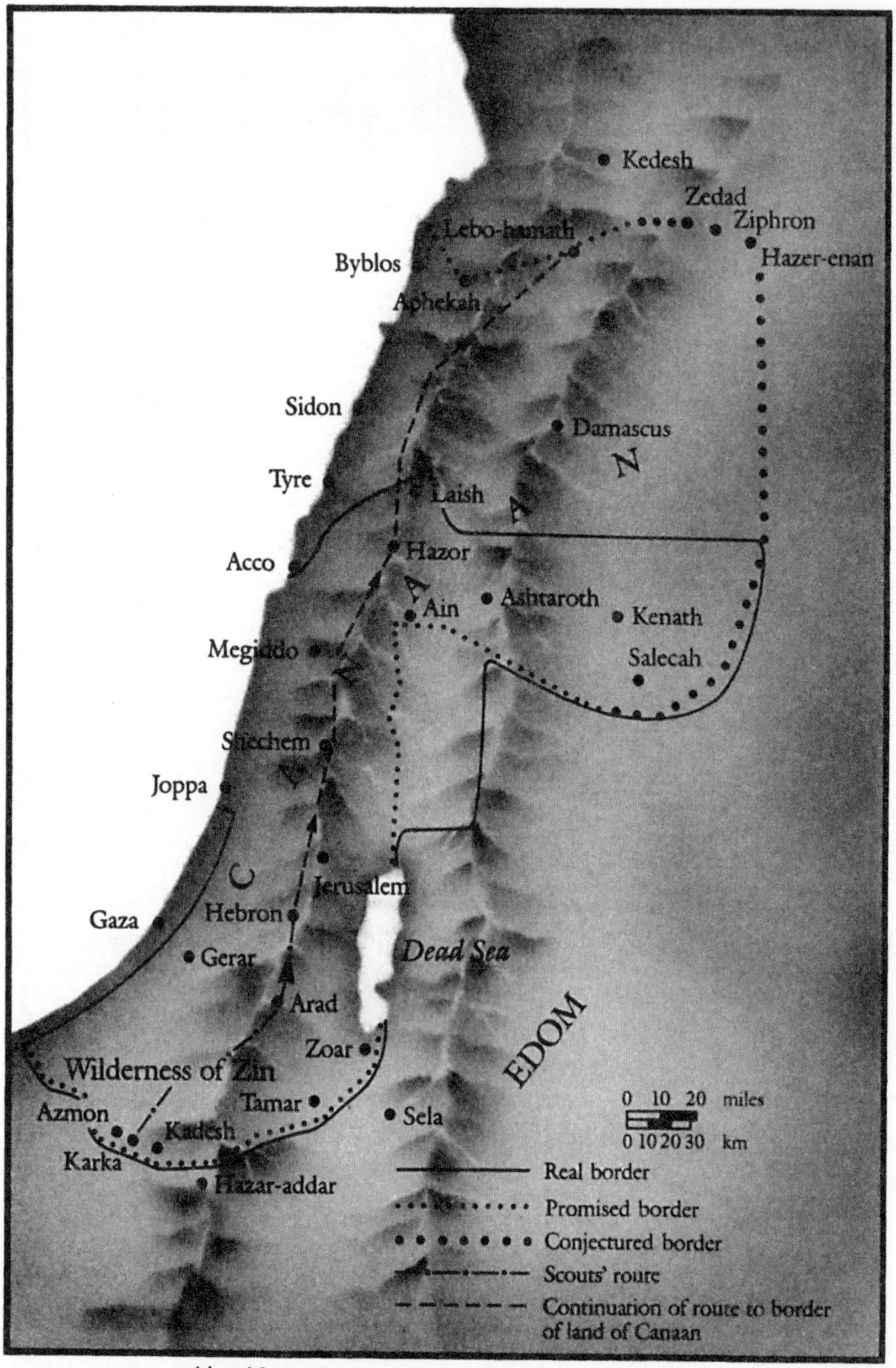

Adapted from G. J. Wenham, *Numbers*, Tyndale Commentaries, 1981.

4. *Mt. Ephraim in the Light of the Samaria Ostraca*

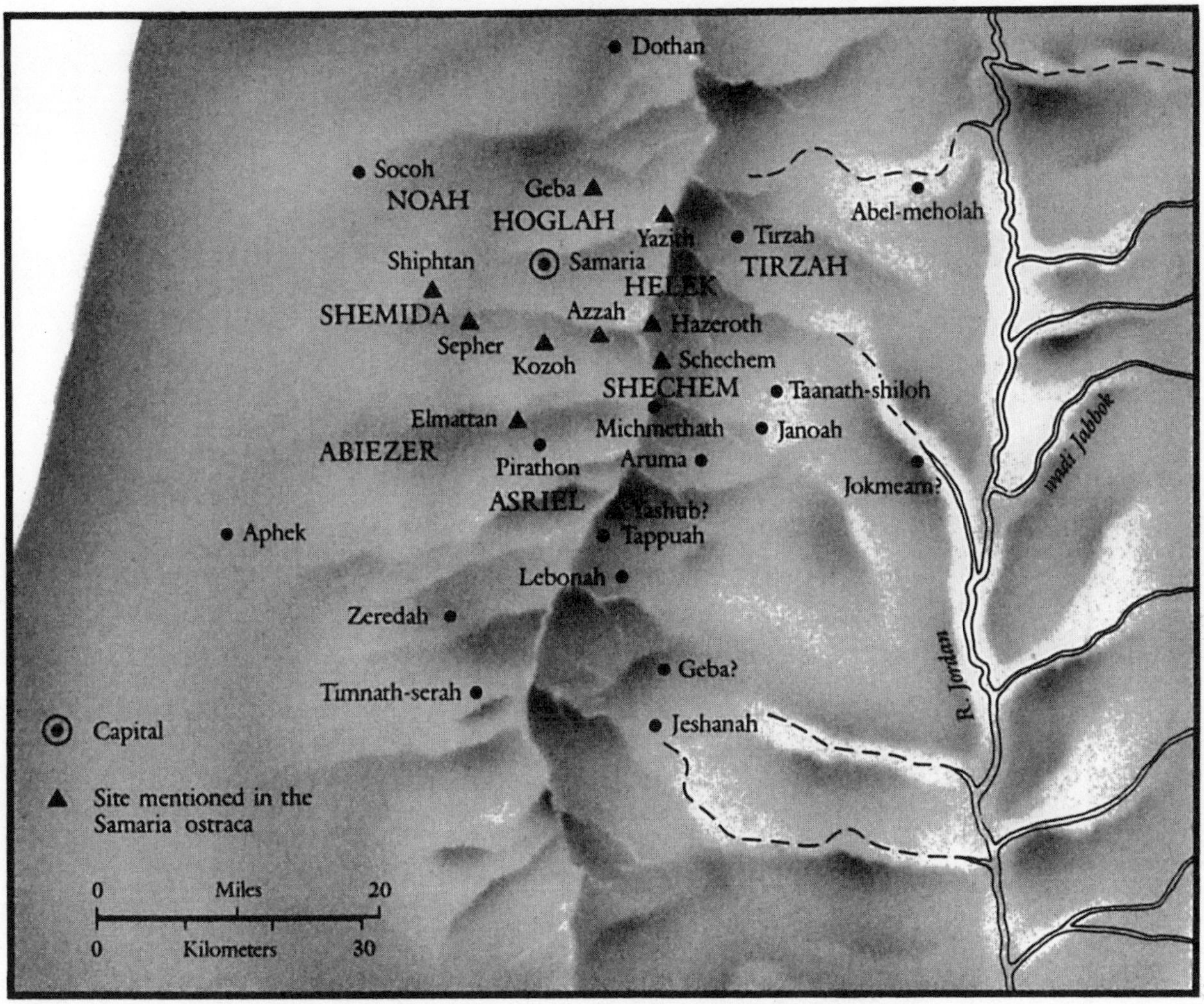

Adapted from Y. Aharoni, *The Land of the Bible,* 1962, 1979.

5. The Cities of Reuben and Gad

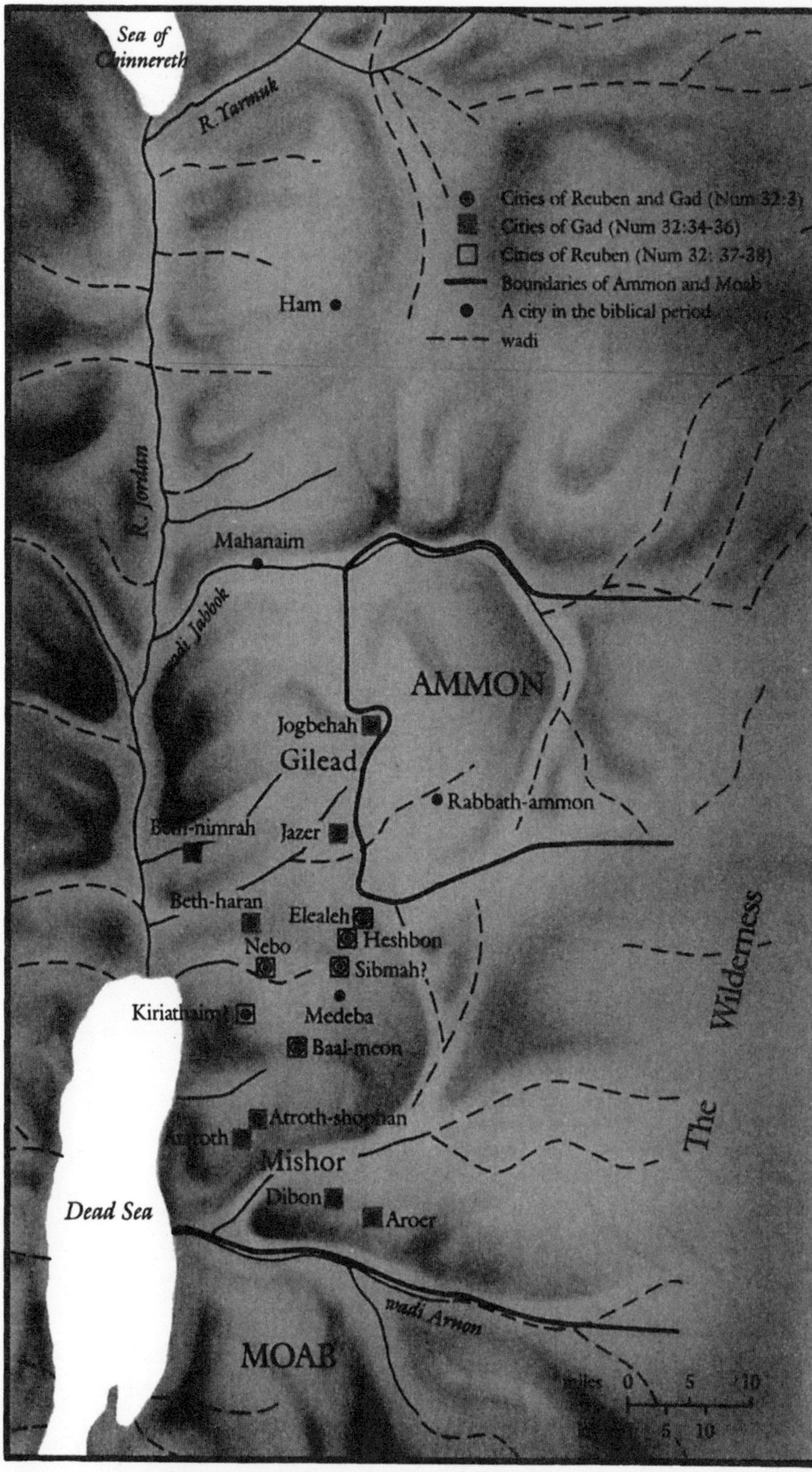

Adapted from *Numbers: The World of the Bible* (Hebrew), J. Milgrom ed., 1985.

THE COMMENTARY TO NUMBERS

THE GENERATION OF THE EXODUS (1:1–25:19)

THE ORGANIZATION OF THE WILDERNESS CAMP (1:1–10:10)

Bemidbar

The Israelites who escaped from Egypt, witnessed the Sinaitic revelation, erected the Tabernacle, and were instructed in the operation of it (as described in Exodus and Leviticus) now prepare themselves militarily and spiritually for their march through the wilderness. They are organized as a war camp centered about the Tabernacle (1.1–10:10), but they become progressively demoralized by complaints, rebellions, and finally by apostasy, leading to their death in the wilderness (10:11–25:19). The first of the three sections of the Book of Numbers takes place in "the wilderness of Sinai" (1:1,19; 3:4,14; 9:1,5; 10:12) over the course of twenty days, from the first day of the second month of the second year (1:1) to the twentieth day of the second month of the second year (10:11), the day that the Israelites leave Sinai to meander through the wilderness for thirty-eight years until they reach the Jordan River (22:1). These twenty days are spent in putting the camp on a war footing to protect it against potential adversaries. First, a census of able-bodied men is taken (chap. 1). Then, the camp is organized for maximum security (chap. 2), while the Levites, who undergo a separate census, are encamped around the Tabernacle and charged with guarding and transporting it (chaps. 3–4). This is followed by a miscellany of legislation concerned with the purity of the camp (5:1–4) and the cultic responsibilities of the priests (5:5–6:27). The tribal chieftains bring gifts of transport (oxen and carts) to the newly dedicated altar for the use of the Levite porters (chap. 7). The Levites are inducted into this service (8:5–22), with work assigned on the basis of age (8:23–26). A month's postponement is permitted for those who are ritually impure (9:1–14), and the divine guidance system for the wilderness trek is explained (9:15–23), as well as the various trumpet calls by which the camp can meet emergencies (10:1–10).

CHAPTER 1

Census in the Wilderness (vv. 1–54)

The march of the Israelites through the wilderness, from Mount Sinai to the promised land, will take them through hostile environments, both natural and human. To meet those dangers, the people must be organized into a military camp, which requires a census. Under the supervision of Moses, Aaron, and the tribal chieftains, all males over twenty, other than Levites, are registered by their respective clans. The Levites, who are assigned special functions, are subject to a special census (3:14–39; 4:21–49).

BEMIDBAR

1 On the first day of the second month, in the second year following the exodus from the land of Egypt, the LORD spoke to Moses in the wilderness of Sinai, in the Tent of Meeting, saying:

²Take a census of the whole Israelite community by the clans of its ancestral houses, listing the names, every male, head by head. ³You and Aaron shall record them by their

א וַיְדַבֵּ֨ר יְהֹוָ֧ה אֶל־מֹשֶׁ֛ה בְּמִדְבַּ֥ר סִינַ֖י בְּאֹ֣הֶל
מוֹעֵ֑ד בְּאֶחָד֩ לַחֹ֨דֶשׁ הַשֵּׁנִ֜י בַּשָּׁנָ֣ה הַשֵּׁנִ֗ית
לְצֵאתָ֛ם מֵאֶ֥רֶץ מִצְרַ֖יִם לֵאמֹֽר: ² שְׂא֗וּ אֶת־רֹ֨אשׁ
כָּל־עֲדַ֣ת בְּנֵֽי־יִשְׂרָאֵ֔ל לְמִשְׁפְּחֹתָ֖ם לְבֵ֣ית אֲבֹתָ֑ם
בְּמִסְפַּ֣ר שֵׁמ֔וֹת כָּל־זָכָ֖ר לְגֻלְגְּלֹתָֽם: ³ מִבֶּ֨ן עֶשְׂרִ֜ים

---

1. The first day In ancient times, the first day of each month was a holiday (Num. 10:10; 28:11) and provided a convenient opportunity to bring the people together for important announcements (Num. 9:1; Deut. 1:3; Ezek. 26:1), as noted by Ehrlich.

of the second month The sanctuary, called the "Tent of Meeting," had been completed one month earlier (Exod. 40:17), which implies that all the instructions of Leviticus (except those in chaps. 25–27) had been given in the intervening month.

in the wilderness of Sinai This locale is cited in Exodus 19:1–2, in Leviticus 7:38, and frequently in the Book of Numbers. Here its mention is intended either to distinguish this chapter from the preceding ones (Lev. 25–27), which took place on Mount Sinai itself, according to Ramban, or to differentiate between the commands of God that were issued on Mount Sinai before the sanctuary was completed (Exod. 40:17), and those, beginning with Leviticus, that were promulgated after its completion.[1] Wilderness, *midbar,* does not mean "desert," for although its scant rainfall cannot support cultivation, it can provide adequate pasturage for flocks.

The LORD spoke ... in the Tent of Meeting The Lord's voice came from within (Lev. 1:1), from between the two cherubim that flanked the Ark (Exod. 25:22; Num. 7:89). The tent was regarded as a portable Sinai: As Moses was permitted to ascend to the presence of God atop the mountain (Exod. 19:20; 34:2) so might he enter the Holy of Holies, a concession also granted the High Priest under special circumstances (Lev. 16:2–17); as Moses was accompanied by priests and elders only until he reached the cloud perimeter of Mount Sinai (Exod. 24:1–2,9,15), so the priests could enter the Tent only up to the veil that sealed off God's beclouded Presence (Exod. 28:43; 30:20; Lev. 10:9; 16:2); as the Israelites gathered on the lower slopes of Mount Sinai (Exod. 19:7) where they witnessed the theophany and worshiped at an altar, so were they given access to the "entrance of the Tent" where they might witness future theophanies (Lev. 9:24) and worship at God's altar (see Excursus 14).[2] On only one occasion was Moses himself not permitted to enter the Tent (Lev. 1:1): during its dedicatory service when the Presence of God overflowed beyond the veil to fill the entire Tent (Exod. 40:35).

2. Take a census That is, for the purpose of military conscription. Such censuses were frequent occurrences during the monarchy (2 Sam. 24:1–9; 2 Chron. 14:7). A head count of the troops was always taken before a campaign (for example, Josh. 8:10) and at its conclusion (Num. 31:48–49; cf. 1 Sam. 14:17). For another example of a military census list based on tribal conscription, see 1 Chronicles 7. This usage of *nasa' ro'sh,* literally "lift the head," is unique to the priestly texts.

This ancient institution was indispensable for any government levy upon persons or property. The census described here follows the same procedures and even uses the same terminology as those found earlier, in Near Eastern cultures that had been intimately associated with Israel's origins. Thus at the ancient Mesopotamian town of Mari (modern Tell el-Hariri in Syria), the Akkadian term for "muster the troops,"[3] is the exact cognate of the Hebrew *pakad tsava'* (see v. 3). Similarly, the men of Mari were inscribed "on a tablet and by name" (see the Comment to v. 18; and see 4:32).

community Hebrew *'edah,* also rendered "assembly" in verse 16. Its basic meaning is the entire nation—men, women, and children. This usage occurs over one hundred times in the early narratives (e.g., Exod. 16:1; Num. 17:11) and laws (e.g., Exod. 12:19,47; Num. 1:53). It can also refer to all adult males (e.g., Num. 14:1–4; 31:26,28,43), especially those bearing arms (e.g., Judg. 20:1). Finally, *'edah* can be used of tribal leaders meeting as an executive body, as in Exodus 12:3,21, Joshua

שָׁנָה וָמַעְלָה כָּל־יֹצֵא צָבָא בְּיִשְׂרָאֵל תִּפְקְדוּ
אֹתָם לְצִבְאֹתָם אַתָּה וְאַהֲרֹן: 4 וְאִתְּכֶם יִהְיוּ אִישׁ
אִישׁ לַמַּטֶּה אִישׁ רֹאשׁ לְבֵית־אֲבֹתָיו הוּא:

groups, from the age of twenty years up, all those in Israel who are able to bear arms. [4]Associated with you shall be a man from each tribe, each one the head of his ancestral house.

22:14–16, and Judges 21:10,13. In these three latter instances, the term really implies the entire nation, not just a segment thereof.

of its ancestral houses Hebrew *le-veit 'avotam,* a synonym for clan *(mishpaḥah),* indicating that the latter comprises a number of closely related households (*beit 'av;* see v. 16).

listing the names From 10:11, it is clear that the census was completed in fewer than twenty days. By contrast, David's census, which likewise encompassed some 600,000 names, took nine months and twenty days to complete (2 Sam.24:8)! The divergence is to be explained by the different procedures adopted. David's census was laboriously conducted, tribe by tribe, district by district. Moses, on the other hand, made each clan responsible for its own count (vv. 2,18,20); he and the tribal chieftains merely supervised. In this way, all clans were mustered simultaneously, and their individual totals had only to be collated. The practice at Mari, where the mustering of the tribal population was delegated to the chieftains, indicates the antiquity of this procedure. It seems that the system continued to be operative in the period of the monarchy, for some Judean kings are on record as having delegated military conscription to each household (2 Chron. 17:14; 25:5).

3. You and Aaron Though God speaks solely to Moses (vv. 1,19,54), the command is addressed to Aaron as well (vv. 17,44; 26:64); hence, it is given in the plural in verses 2–5.

twenty years up This was the age of conscription in Israel. The census taken by King Amaziah early in the eighth century B.C.E. also began with those aged twenty (2 Chron. 25:5). In the classical world the age for entering military service was twenty in Sparta, eighteen in Athens, and seventeen in Rome.

It is to be noted that no upper age is given. This is strange because such a limit is set for the Levites (8:24–26) and because later censuses in Israel are expressly limited to the militarily fit (e.g., 2 Sam. 24:9; 2 Chron. 14:7). One would also have expected, as exists in the Mari texts, a separate census of the aged as well as of those physically incapacitated and unable to bear arms. The unusual nature of this census was probably caused by the fact that it was taken in preparation for achieving the overriding national goal, the conquest of the promised land. In critical wars there was neither exemption nor retirement from military service.[4]

The Legend of King Keret, found at Ugarit, modern Ras Shamra on the Syrian coast, and dated in the centuries immediately preceding the Exodus, contains a legendary account of an expedition to capture a bride. Since the instructions stem from the god El, the expedition is mandatory, and the text expressly denies exemption to the bachelor, the bedridden, the blind, and the newlywed (contrast Deut. 20:7). Early rabbinic law, in fact, restricts the exemptions of Deuteronomy 20 to offensive wars *(reshut),* making them inapplicable in defensive wars *(ḥovah),* when not even the bride and the groom could be released from military service (Mish. Sot. 8:7, Tosef. Sot. 7:24). Finally, the account of the Levite census shows that, while its labor force is indeed given an upper age limit, its sanctuary guards are not because their task was crucial (8:25–26; see the Comment to 3:6–10).

able to bear arms Hebrew *yotsei' tsava',* literally "go out (as an) army" (31:36);[5] contrast the verb used with *tsava'* in 4:3,23; 8:24. This expression is later defined as those "able to bear spear and shield" (2 Chron. 25:5). The previous statement of no age limit is thus qualified—only those "able to bear arms."

4. tribe Hebrew *matteh.* Like *'edah,* this term is absent from any biblical source that can be dated with certainty after the ninth century B.C.E., another indication that Numbers 1 reflects the sociopolitical life of Israel before the rise of the monarchy. Later literature, unless it is copying an earlier source, uses the synonyms *shevet* and *kahal* exclusively (see Excursus 1).

head Hebrew *ro'sh,* elsewhere called "chieftain" *(nasi')* (see the Comment to v. 16 and Excursus 1).

5These are the names of the men who shall assist you:

From Reuben, Elizur son of Shedeur.

6From Simeon, Shelumiel son of Zurishaddai.

7From Judah, Nahshon son of Amminadab.

8From Issachar, Nethanel son of Zuar.

9From Zebulun, Eliab son of Helon.

10From the sons of Joseph:

from Ephraim, Elishama son of Ammihud;

from Manasseh, Gamaliel son of Pedahzur.

11From Benjamin, Abidan son of Gideoni.

12From Dan, Ahiezer son of Ammishaddai.

13From Asher, Pagiel son of Ochran.

14From Gad, Eliasaph son of Deuel.

15From Naphtali, Ahira son of Enan.

16Those are the elected of the assembly, the chieftains of their ancestral tribes: they are the heads of the contingents of Israel.

5 וְאֵ֙לֶּה֙ שְׁמ֣וֹת הָֽאֲנָשִׁ֔ים אֲשֶׁ֥ר יַֽעַמְד֖וּ אִתְּכֶ֑ם
לִרְאוּבֵ֕ן אֱלִיצ֖וּר בֶּן־שְׁדֵיא֑וּר׃
6 לְשִׁמְע֕וֹן שְׁלֻֽמִיאֵ֖ל בֶּן־צוּרִֽישַׁדָּֽי׃
7 לִֽיהוּדָ֕ה נַחְשׁ֖וֹן בֶּן־עַמִּֽינָדָֽב׃
8 לְיִ֨שָּׂשכָ֔ר נְתַנְאֵ֖ל בֶּן־צוּעָֽר׃
9 לִזְבוּלֻ֕ן אֱלִיאָ֖ב בֶּן־חֵלֹֽן׃
10 לִבְנֵ֣י יוֹסֵ֔ף
לְאֶפְרַ֕יִם אֱלִֽישָׁמָ֖ע בֶּן־עַמִּיה֑וּד
לִמְנַשֶּׁ֕ה גַּמְלִיאֵ֖ל בֶּן־פְּדָהצֽוּר׃
11 לְבִ֨נְיָמִ֔ן אֲבִידָ֖ן בֶּן־גִּדְעֹנִֽי׃
12 לְדָ֕ן אֲחִיעֶ֖זֶר בֶּן־עַמִּֽישַׁדָּֽי׃
13 לְאָשֵׁ֕ר פַּגְעִיאֵ֖ל בֶּן־עָכְרָֽן׃
14 לְגָ֕ד אֶלְיָסָ֖ף בֶּן־דְּעוּאֵֽל׃
15 לְנַפְתָּלִ֕י אֲחִירַ֖ע בֶּן־עֵינָֽן׃
16 אֵ֚לֶּה קְרוּאֵ֣י הָֽעֵדָ֔ה נְשִׂיאֵ֖י מַטּ֣וֹת אֲבוֹתָ֑ם
רָאשֵׁ֛י אַלְפֵ֥י יִשְׂרָאֵ֖ל הֵֽם׃ 17 וַיִּקַּ֥ח מֹשֶׁ֖ה וְאַֽהֲרֹ֑ן

קְרוּאֵי ק׳   v. 16.

5. *These are the names* The census supervisors, who are mandatory according to verse 4, are nominated by God. The identical situation exists in 34:18–28: Israel is ordered to appoint divinely selected chieftains who will help apportion the land.

5–15. The list of twenty-four names betrays evidence of great antiquity. Sixteen of them never recur in later biblical literature, and not one is compounded of the divine element YH(YHVH), as is precisely the case with all the names in the Book of Genesis. This corresponds with the tradition of Exodus 6:3 that the Tetragrammaton was first revealed to Moses. Moreover, the list displays features mainly prevalent in early and pre-Israelite lists of names: ten of the twenty-four names are noun sentences (e.g., Elizur, "God is a rock," v. 5); and in four names that are verb sentences, the verb is in the perfect and is the second element (e.g., Amminadab, "the [divine] kinsman is generous," v. 7). Furthermore, the theophoric (divine) elements, Shaddai and Zur, are found in ancient Mari texts, and Shaddai is the earliest attested name of Israel's God (Gen. 17:1; 49:25; Num. 24:4; and especially Exod. 6:3);[6] and the use of 'am, "clan, kindred," is prevalent in Semitic nomadic groups and, hence, in early Israel.[7]

The tribal lists throughout the Bible may vary in the names and order of the tribes, but they share in common the concern for preserving the number twelve. These lists can be divided into two groups: those that include the tribe of Levi and those that omit it. All the tribal lists in Numbers fall into the latter category. The reason for Levi's absence from the first of these lists is decisive for the other lists: It is exempt from military conscription. In the lists where Levi occurs, it invariably occupies the third position and is followed by Judah (e.g., Gen. 29:31–30:24; 49:3–27). In the lists where Levi is absent, the third position is held either by Judah (Num. 1:7) or Gad (Num. 1:24), on which see the Comment to verse 24. Other than the omission of Levi, the list follows the chronological order of the birth of Jacob's sons (Gen. 35:22–26) grouped according to their mothers: Leah, Rachel, and the concubines.

It should be noted that neither this list nor that of the spies in chapter 13 nor that of the chieftains in chapter 34 has a single name with the theophoric element YH. However, many of the names are compounded with El and Shaddai.[8]

16. *elected* Rather, "called" *(keru'ei,* the *Kere),* that is, called (to decide) any important matter, according to Rashi (see 16:2).

assembly See Excursus 1.

[17]So Moses and Aaron took those men, who were designated by name, [18]and on the first day of the second month they convoked the whole community, who were registered by the clans of their ancestral houses—the names of those aged twenty years and over being listed head by head. [19]As the Lord had commanded Moses, so he recorded them in the wilderness of Sinai.

[20]They totaled as follows:

The descendants of Reuben, Israel's first-born, the registration of the clans of their ancestral house, as listed by name, head by head, all males aged twenty years and over, all who were able to bear arms—[21]those enrolled from the tribe of Reuben: 46,500.

אֵ֚ת הָאֲנָשִׁ֣ים הָאֵ֔לֶּה אֲשֶׁ֥ר נִקְּב֖וּ בְּשֵׁמֽוֹת׃ 18 וְאֵ֨ת
כָּל־הָעֵדָ֜ה הִקְהִ֗ילוּ בְּאֶחָד֙ לַחֹ֣דֶשׁ הַשֵּׁנִ֔י וַיִּתְיַֽלְד֥וּ
עַל־מִשְׁפְּחֹתָ֖ם לְבֵ֣ית אֲבֹתָ֑ם בְּמִסְפַּ֣ר שֵׁמ֗וֹת מִבֶּ֨ן
עֶשְׂרִ֥ים שָׁנָ֛ה וָמַ֖עְלָה לְגֻלְגְּלֹתָֽם׃ 19 כַּאֲשֶׁ֛ר צִוָּ֥ה
יְהוָ֖ה אֶת־מֹשֶׁ֑ה וַֽיִּפְקְדֵ֖ם בְּמִדְבַּ֥ר סִינָֽי׃ פ
שני 20 וַיִּהְי֤וּ בְנֵֽי־רְאוּבֵן֙ בְּכֹ֣ר יִשְׂרָאֵ֔ל תּוֹלְדֹתָ֥ם
לְמִשְׁפְּחֹתָ֖ם לְבֵ֣ית אֲבֹתָ֑ם בְּמִסְפַּ֤ר שֵׁמוֹת֙
לְגֻלְגְּלֹתָ֔ם כָּל־זָכָ֗ר מִבֶּ֨ן עֶשְׂרִ֤ים שָׁנָה֙ וָמַ֔עְלָה כֹּ֖ל
יֹצֵ֥א צָבָֽא׃ 21 פְּקֻדֵיהֶ֖ם לְמַטֵּ֣ה רְאוּבֵ֑ן שִׁשָּׁ֧ה
וְאַרְבָּעִ֛ים אֶ֖לֶף וַחֲמֵ֥שׁ מֵאֽוֹת׃ פ

chieftains Hebrew *nasi'*, the established leader of his clan, as is clear from the title "chieftain of the ancestral house," both in connection with the clans that comprise the tribe of Levi (Num. 3:24,30,35) and the Midianites (Num. 25:15,18). The term *nasi'* is frequently equated with the title "head of the ancestral house" (Heb. *ro'sh beit 'avot;* e.g., Num. 7:2; 36:1). Indeed, whenever the phrase "heads of the clans/ancestral houses" (Heb. *ra'shei 'alafim/'avot*) occurs alone it may be safely assumed that the chieftain *(nasi')* is intended (e.g., Josh. 14:1; 22:21).

Since each tribe comprised more than one clan, it follows that there was more than one *nasi'* per tribe. Thus the title of Eleazar is *nasi' nesi'ei ha-levi,* "the head chieftain of the Levites" (3:32). There are three separate lists of the chieftains of the twelve tribes, none of which duplicates the other (Num. 1:5–16; 13:1–15; 34:16–29). Most significantly, 250 chieftains of the *'edah* spearheaded the rebellion of Korah against Moses; and these men are also referred to as those "chosen in the assembly, men of repute" (Num. 16:2), indicating that they represented only a portion of the chieftains (see Excursus 1).

contingents Hebrew *'elef,* the largest tribal subdivision, better rendered "clan." It is sometimes interchangeable with *mishpaḥah* (1 Sam. 10:19,21). Joshua 7:14 (cf. 16–18) shows the following units in order of decreasing size: tribe, clan *(mishpaḥah),* household *(bayit),* individual.

'Elef is the more precise term, for the clan leaders *(nasi', ro'sh)* are never associated with *mishpaḥah,* only with *'elef* and its equivalent, *beit 'avot,* "ancestral house." This is a strong indication that *'elef* is an ancient term harking back to the time when clan structure was fully operative (see Excursus 1). A synonymous term is *'alluf,* "clan leader," from the same root. This is attested not only in the verifiably ancient Song of the Sea (Exod. 15:15) but in the designation for the chieftains of the Edomites during their nomadic, premonarchic period (Gen. 36:15–30).

17. designated by name[9]

18. and on the first day . . . The date of verse 1 is repeated to emphasize that the census was begun on the very day it was commanded.

were registered Hebrew *va-yityalledu,* "declared their lineage," according to their households and clans. The phrase occurs only here and is so understood by Targum Onkelos and Targum Jonathan, which use the verb *hityaḥes.*[10] The Greek, however, renders "they inscribed them on tablets." This terminology is also used in the Mari texts; for example, a census of soldiers (ARM 9.298) consists of numbers of contingents and a final line of totals. It is of interest to note that the War Scroll of the Dead Sea sectarians probably registered all of its members on its banners,[11] and according to other scrolls, these banners may have been used in the sect's peacetime assemblies as well as in war.[12]

20. They totaled as follows Hebrew *va-yihyu.* The same word begins the total sum (v. 46), framing the entire census with an inclusion.

Israel's first-born Reuben's title is given to account for the fact that he heads the list even though Judah is to lead the march (10:14).

22Of the descendants of Simeon, the registration of the clans of their ancestral house, their enrollment as listed by name, head by head, all males aged twenty years and over, all who were able to bear arms—23those enrolled from the tribe of Simeon: 59,300.

24Of the descendants of Gad, the registration of the clans of their ancestral house, as listed by name, aged twenty years and over, all who were able to bear arms—25those enrolled from the tribe of Gad: 45,650.

26Of the descendants of Judah, the registration of the clans of their ancestral house, as listed by name, aged twenty years and over, all who were able to bear arms—27those enrolled from the tribe of Judah: 74,600.

28Of the descendants of Issachar, the registration of the clans of their ancestral house, as listed by name, aged twenty years and over, all who were able to bear arms—29those enrolled from the tribe of Issachar: 54,400.

30Of the descendants of Zebulun, the registration of the clans of their ancestral house, as listed by name, aged twenty years and over, all who were able to bear arms—31those enrolled from the tribe of Zebulun: 57,400.

32Of the descendants of Joseph:

Of the descendants of Ephraim, the registration of the clans of their ancestral house, as listed by name, aged twenty years and over, all who were able to bear arms—33those enrolled from the tribe of Ephraim: 40,500.

34Of the descendants of Manasseh, the registration of the clans of their ancestral house, as listed by name, aged twenty years and over, all who were able to bear arms—35those enrolled from the tribe of Manasseh: 32,200.

22 לִבְנֵי שִׁמְעוֹן תּוֹלְדֹתָם לְמִשְׁפְּחֹתָם לְבֵית
אֲבֹתָם פְּקֻדָיו בְּמִסְפַּר שֵׁמוֹת לְגֻלְגְּלֹתָם כָּל־זָכָר
מִבֶּן עֶשְׂרִים שָׁנָה וָמַעְלָה כֹּל יֹצֵא צָבָא׃
23 פְּקֻדֵיהֶם לְמַטֵּה שִׁמְעוֹן תִּשְׁעָה וַחֲמִשִּׁים אֶלֶף
וּשְׁלֹשׁ מֵאוֹת׃ פ

24 לִבְנֵי גָד תּוֹלְדֹתָם לְמִשְׁפְּחֹתָם לְבֵית
אֲבֹתָם בְּמִסְפַּר שֵׁמוֹת מִבֶּן עֶשְׂרִים שָׁנָה וָמַעְלָה
כֹּל יֹצֵא צָבָא׃ 25 פְּקֻדֵיהֶם לְמַטֵּה גָד חֲמִשָּׁה
וְאַרְבָּעִים אֶלֶף וְשֵׁשׁ מֵאוֹת וַחֲמִשִּׁים׃ פ

26 לִבְנֵי יְהוּדָה תּוֹלְדֹתָם לְמִשְׁפְּחֹתָם לְבֵית
אֲבֹתָם בְּמִסְפַּר שֵׁמֹת מִבֶּן עֶשְׂרִים שָׁנָה וָמַעְלָה
כֹּל יֹצֵא צָבָא׃ 27 פְּקֻדֵיהֶם לְמַטֵּה יְהוּדָה אַרְבָּעָה
וְשִׁבְעִים אֶלֶף וְשֵׁשׁ מֵאוֹת׃ פ

28 לִבְנֵי יִשָּׂשכָר תּוֹלְדֹתָם לְמִשְׁפְּחֹתָם לְבֵית
אֲבֹתָם בְּמִסְפַּר שֵׁמֹת מִבֶּן עֶשְׂרִים שָׁנָה וָמַעְלָה
כֹּל יֹצֵא צָבָא׃ 29 פְּקֻדֵיהֶם לְמַטֵּה יִשָּׂשכָר
אַרְבָּעָה וַחֲמִשִּׁים אֶלֶף וְאַרְבַּע מֵאוֹת׃ פ

30 לִבְנֵי זְבוּלֻן תּוֹלְדֹתָם לְמִשְׁפְּחֹתָם לְבֵית
אֲבֹתָם בְּמִסְפַּר שֵׁמֹת מִבֶּן עֶשְׂרִים שָׁנָה וָמַעְלָה
כֹּל יֹצֵא צָבָא׃ 31 פְּקֻדֵיהֶם לְמַטֵּה זְבוּלֻן שִׁבְעָה
וַחֲמִשִּׁים אֶלֶף וְאַרְבַּע מֵאוֹת׃ פ

32 לִבְנֵי יוֹסֵף

לִבְנֵי אֶפְרַיִם תּוֹלְדֹתָם לְמִשְׁפְּחֹתָם לְבֵית
אֲבֹתָם בְּמִסְפַּר שֵׁמֹת מִבֶּן עֶשְׂרִים שָׁנָה וָמַעְלָה
כֹּל יֹצֵא צָבָא׃ 33 פְּקֻדֵיהֶם לְמַטֵּה אֶפְרָיִם
אַרְבָּעִים אֶלֶף וַחֲמֵשׁ מֵאוֹת׃ פ

34 לִבְנֵי מְנַשֶּׁה תּוֹלְדֹתָם לְמִשְׁפְּחֹתָם לְבֵית
אֲבֹתָם בְּמִסְפַּר שֵׁמוֹת מִבֶּן עֶשְׂרִים שָׁנָה וָמַעְלָה
כֹּל יֹצֵא צָבָא׃ 35 פְּקֻדֵיהֶם לְמַטֵּה מְנַשֶּׁה שְׁנַיִם
וּשְׁלֹשִׁים אֶלֶף וּמָאתָיִם׃ פ

22. *their enrollment*[13]

24. *Gad* Gad replaces Judah in the third position both here and in chapter 2 because these two lists are ordered according to the arrangement of the camp: Gad is assigned to Reuben's division, whereas Judah heads one of its own (2:3,10–16). The Septuagint, however, places Gad after Benjamin, with the sons of the concubines. Why Judah was replaced by Gad—and not by another lesser tribe such as Dan, Asher, or Naphtali who also were descended from Jacob's concubines (Gen. 30:1–13)—may be explained on geographical grounds. According to Kuschke, the territory of the tribe of Gad was located close to that of Judah, Reuben, and Simeon, whereas Dan, Asher, and Naphtali form a contiguous grouping in the Galilee.[14] Also, since the first six in the usual tribal list (Gen. 46:8–27) are the six sons of Leah, the first alternate would naturally be Gad who was the first-born of Leah's concubine (Gen. 30:9–11) and hence considered one of her sons (see Gen. 30:3,6).

³⁶Of the descendants of Benjamin, the registration of the clans of their ancestral house, as listed by name, aged twenty years and over, all who were able to bear arms—²⁷those enrolled from the tribe of Benjamin: 35,400.

³⁸Of the descendants of Dan, the registration of the clans of their ancestral house, as listed by name, aged twenty years and over, all who were able to bear arms—³⁹those enrolled from the tribe of Dan: 62,700.

⁴⁰Of the descendants of Asher, the registration of the clans of their ancestral house, as listed by name, aged twenty years and over, all who were able to bear arms—⁴¹those enrolled from the tribe of Asher: 41,500.

⁴²[Of] the descendants of Naphtali, the registration of the clans of their ancestral house as listed by name, aged twenty years and over, all who were able to bear arms—⁴³those enrolled from the tribe of Naphtali: 53,400.

⁴⁴Those are the enrollments recorded by Moses and Aaron and by the chieftains of Israel, who were twelve in number, one man to each ancestral house. ⁴⁵All the Israelites, aged twenty years and over, enrolled by ancestral houses, all those in Israel who were able to bear arms—⁴⁶all who were enrolled came to 603,550.

⁴⁷The Levites, however, were not recorded among them by their ancestral tribe. ⁴⁸For the LORD had spoken to

36 לִבְנֵ֣י בִנְיָמִ֔ן תּוֹלְדֹתָ֥ם לְמִשְׁפְּחֹתָ֖ם לְבֵ֣ית אֲבֹתָ֑ם בְּמִסְפַּ֣ר שֵׁמֹ֗ת מִבֶּ֨ן עֶשְׂרִ֤ים שָׁנָה֙ וָמַ֔עְלָה כֹּ֖ל יֹצֵ֥א צָבָֽא: 37 פְּקֻדֵיהֶ֖ם לְמַטֵּ֣ה בִנְיָמִ֑ן חֲמִשָּׁ֥ה וּשְׁלֹשִׁ֛ים אֶ֖לֶף וְאַרְבַּ֥ע מֵאֽוֹת: פ

38 לִבְנֵ֣י דָ֔ן תּוֹלְדֹתָ֥ם לְמִשְׁפְּחֹתָ֖ם לְבֵ֣ית אֲבֹתָ֑ם בְּמִסְפַּ֣ר שֵׁמֹ֗ת מִבֶּ֨ן עֶשְׂרִ֤ים שָׁנָה֙ וָמַ֔עְלָה כֹּ֖ל יֹצֵ֥א צָבָֽא: 39 פְּקֻדֵיהֶ֖ם לְמַטֵּ֣ה דָ֑ן שְׁנַ֤יִם וְשִׁשִּׁ֛ים אֶ֖לֶף וּשְׁבַ֥ע מֵאֽוֹת: פ

40 לִבְנֵ֣י אָשֵׁ֔ר תּוֹלְדֹתָ֥ם לְמִשְׁפְּחֹתָ֖ם לְבֵ֣ית אֲבֹתָ֑ם בְּמִסְפַּ֣ר שֵׁמֹ֗ת מִבֶּ֨ן עֶשְׂרִ֤ים שָׁנָה֙ וָמַ֔עְלָה כֹּ֖ל יֹצֵ֥א צָבָֽא: 41 פְּקֻדֵיהֶ֖ם לְמַטֵּ֣ה אָשֵׁ֑ר אֶחָ֤ד וְאַרְבָּעִ֤ים אֶ֖לֶף וַחֲמֵ֥שׁ מֵאֽוֹת: פ

42 בְּנֵ֣י נַפְתָּלִ֔י תּוֹלְדֹתָ֥ם לְמִשְׁפְּחֹתָ֖ם לְבֵ֣ית אֲבֹתָ֑ם בְּמִסְפַּ֣ר שֵׁמֹ֗ת מִבֶּ֨ן עֶשְׂרִ֤ים שָׁנָה֙ וָמַ֔עְלָה כֹּ֖ל יֹצֵ֥א צָבָֽא: 43 פְּקֻדֵיהֶ֖ם לְמַטֵּ֣ה נַפְתָּלִ֑י שְׁלֹשָׁ֤ה וַחֲמִשִּׁים֙ אֶ֖לֶף וְאַרְבַּ֥ע מֵאֽוֹת: פ

44 אֵ֣לֶּה הַפְּקֻדִ֗ים אֲשֶׁ֨ר פָּקַ֤ד מֹשֶׁה֙ וְאַהֲרֹ֔ן וּנְשִׂיאֵ֖י יִשְׂרָאֵ֑ל שְׁנֵ֣ים עָשָׂ֣ר אִ֑ישׁ אִישׁ־אֶחָ֛ד לְבֵית־אֲבֹתָ֖יו הָיֽוּ: 45 וַיִּֽהְי֞וּ כָּל־פְּקוּדֵ֣י בְנֵֽי־יִשְׂרָאֵל֮ לְבֵ֣ית אֲבֹתָ֑ם מִבֶּ֨ן עֶשְׂרִ֤ים שָׁנָה֙ וָמַ֔עְלָה כָּל־יֹצֵ֥א צָבָ֖א בְּיִשְׂרָאֵֽל: 46 וַיִּֽהְיוּ֙ כָּל־הַפְּקֻדִ֔ים שֵׁשׁ־מֵא֥וֹת אֶ֖לֶף וּשְׁלֹ֣שֶׁת אֲלָפִ֑ים וַחֲמֵ֥שׁ מֵא֖וֹת וַחֲמִשִּֽׁים: 47 וְהַלְוִיִּ֖ם לְמַטֵּ֣ה אֲבֹתָ֑ם לֹ֥א הָתְפָּקְד֖וּ בְּתוֹכָֽם: פ 48 וַיְדַבֵּ֥ר יְהוָ֖ה אֶל־מֹשֶׁ֥ה לֵּאמֹֽר: 49 אַ֣ךְ

---

42.   *The descendants*[15]

45.   *by ancestral houses*[16]

46.   *603,550*   This figure is identical with that yielded by an earlier census taken during the first year in the wilderness (Exod. 30:12–16; 38:26). Another census taken in the fortieth year netted a total of 601,730 (Num. 26:51). These figures accord with the other traditions about the numbers of adult males who left Egypt (Exod. 12:37; Num. 11:21). They presuppose a population of over two million supporting itself for forty years in the Sinai Peninsula.

DUTIES OF THE LEVITES   (vv. 47–54)

This is an anticipatory summary of the Levites' encampment and guard duties for the sanctuary, which are detailed in chapters 3–4.

47.   *recorded*[17]

48.   *For the LORD had spoken*   *Va-yedabber YHVH* must be rendered a pluperfect so that Moses would have received the divine order not to count the Levites before he took the census.

Moses, saying: 49Do not on any account enroll the tribe of
Levi or take a census of them with the Israelites. 50You shall
put the Levites in charge of the Tabernacle of the Pact, all
its furnishings, and everything that pertains to it: they shall
carry the Tabernacle and all its furnishings, and they shall
tend it; and they shall camp around the Tabernacle.
51When the Tabernacle is to set out, the Levites shall take it
down, and when the Tabernacle is to be pitched, the Levites
shall set it up; any outsider who encroaches shall be put to
death. 52The Israelites shall encamp troop by troop, each
man with his division and each under his standard. 53The
Levites, however, shall camp around the Tabernacle of the

אֶת־מַטֵּה לֵוִי לֹא תִפְקֹד וְאֶת־רֹאשָׁם לֹא תִשָּׂא
בְּתוֹךְ בְּנֵי יִשְׂרָאֵל׃ 50 וְאַתָּה הַפְקֵד אֶת־הַלְוִיִּם
עַל־מִשְׁכַּן הָעֵדֻת וְעַל כָּל־כֵּלָיו וְעַל כָּל־אֲשֶׁר־לוֹ
הֵמָּה יִשְׂאוּ אֶת־הַמִּשְׁכָּן וְאֶת־כָּל־כֵּלָיו וְהֵם
יְשָׁרְתֻהוּ וְסָבִיב לַמִּשְׁכָּן יַחֲנוּ׃ 51 וּבִנְסֹעַ הַמִּשְׁכָּן
יוֹרִידוּ אֹתוֹ הַלְוִיִּם וּבַחֲנֹת הַמִּשְׁכָּן יָקִימוּ אֹתוֹ
הַלְוִיִּם וְהַזָּר הַקָּרֵב יוּמָת׃ 52 וְחָנוּ בְּנֵי יִשְׂרָאֵל
אִישׁ עַל־מַחֲנֵהוּ וְאִישׁ עַל־דִּגְלוֹ לְצִבְאֹתָם׃
53 וְהַלְוִיִּם יַחֲנוּ סָבִיב לְמִשְׁכַּן הָעֵדֻת וְלֹא־יִהְיֶה

49. ***Do not*** The imperative is used because the prohibition is binding forever, for all subsequent censuses.[18]

on any account Hebrew *'akh,* a particle that frequently begins a law (Exod. 31:13; Lev. 23:27,39).

enroll . . . take a census The difference between the two terms may be that the Hebrew *pakad,* "enroll," refers to the individual count, whereas *nasa' ro'sh,* "take a census," refers to the totals, that is, "take their sum."

The separate mustering of the Levites (chaps. 3–4) is illumined by the Mari documents. One of its censuses is divided into three separate registrations: soldiers, those exempt from military service, and the aged. Since the Levites were exempt from the regular militia, they would have been separately mustered in accord with ancient practice (3:15; 4:2,22,29). It is significant that King David also omitted the tribe of Levi from his national military census (1 Chron. 21:6) at the end of his reign (1 Chron. 23:1) because of his intention to use them exclusively in the administration of his projected temple (1 Chron. 23:24–32).

A midrash explains that the exemption of the Levites and their assignment to guard duty in the sanctuary was their reward for having remained faithful to God during the brief rebellion at the foot of Mount Sinai, when the Israelites worshiped the golden calf (Exod. 32:25–29). They were excluded from the census of the tribes because those that were numbered were fated to die in the desert (Num. R. 1:10).

50. ***You*** Hebrew *ve-'attah,* literally "But you," the *vav* of antithesis[19]; that is, the Levites are not to serve in the regular militia but are assigned to the Tabernacle.

put . . . in charge Hebrew *hafked.* Rather, "make . . . responsible" (Num. 3:32; 4:16; Gen. 39:4; 2 Kings 7:17).

Pact *'Edut,* synonymous with *berit,* "covenant," as in the Ark of *'edut* (4:5)/*berit* (Josh. 3:6).[20]

they shall carry Verses 50–51 summarize and introduce the work load of the Levites to be detailed in chapter 4.

tend it By guarding it, as explained in verse 53. *Shamar,* "guard," is subsumed under *sheret,* "tend" (3:6b,7a; 18:2a,3a).[21]

take it down That is, dismantle, according to Targum Onkelos.

51. ***outsider*** That is, unauthorized person, in this case any Israelite. This prohibition is dealt with in Excursus 5.

52. ***standard*** Rather, "unit" (see the Comment to 2:2).

53. ***wrath*** God's wrath will befall the Israelites if they encroach upon the sancta (see Excursus 5). For the implications of God's wrath, see the Comment to 8:19.

Pact, that wrath may not strike the Israelite community; the Levites shall stand guard around the Tabernacle of the Pact.

54The Israelites did accordingly; just as the LORD had commanded Moses, so they did.

קֶצֶף עַל־עֲדַת בְּנֵי יִשְׂרָאֵל וְשָׁמְרוּ הַלְוִיִּם אֶת־
מִשְׁמֶרֶת מִשְׁכַּן הָעֵדוּת׃ 54 וַיַּעֲשׂוּ בְּנֵי יִשְׂרָאֵל
כְּכֹל אֲשֶׁר צִוָּה יְהוָה אֶת־מֹשֶׁה כֵּן עָשׂוּ׃ פ
שלישי

2 The LORD spoke to Moses and Aaron, saying: 2The Israelites shall camp each with his standard, under the banners of their ancestral house; they shall camp around the Tent of Meeting at a distance.

ב וַיְדַבֵּר יְהוָה אֶל־מֹשֶׁה וְאֶל־אַהֲרֹן לֵאמֹר׃
2 אִישׁ עַל־דִּגְלוֹ בְאֹתֹת לְבֵית אֲבֹתָם יַחֲנוּ בְּנֵי
יִשְׂרָאֵל מִנֶּגֶד סָבִיב לְאֹהֶל־מוֹעֵד יַחֲנוּ׃

shall stand guard around the Tabernacle Hebrew *ve-shamru 'et mishmeret ha-mishkan.*[22] Effective guard duty will prevent the outbreak of God's wrath.

54. ***so they did*** A repetition of the beginning of the verse, that is, an inclusion device indicating the conclusion of the account.[23]

CHAPTER 2

The Arrangement of the Camp (vv. 1–34)

Chapter 1 recorded the census of the militarily able men in Israel. This chapter (vv. 1–31) deals with their deployment to defend the camp when it is at rest (see Excursus 3).

THE ORDERING OF THE TRIBES (vv. 1–31)

The tribes are ordered in military divisions around the Tabernacle, each under its chieftain. The list of chieftains in the previous chapter (1:5–16) reoccurs here in the description of the military camp and again later, when the chieftains present gifts and sacrifices to the sanctuary (7:12–88) and when the militia is organized for the march (10:14–28). The totals for the fighting force of each tribe and of the entire people are also repeated.

1. ***and Aaron*** Missing in the recapitulation of verse 34.[1] Aaron also seems secondary in 1:17,44; and compare 1:1,19,48,54.

2. ***standard*** Hebrew ***degel*** possibly originally meant a military banner. This is supported by the Akkadian ***dagalu,*** "to look," and ***diglu,*** "sight." The meaning "banner" was later extended by association to include the army division, just as ***shevet*** and ***matteh,*** the two terms for "tribe," were probably derived from the "rod" that served as the official tribal insignia (cf. 1:45; 14:17–18). The meaning "unit" better fits the context here, as verse 3 shows, and is supported by the Targums and the Septuagint as well as by Aramaic usage as evidenced from the Persian period by an ostracon from Arad (no. 12) and the papyri from Elephantine. It comprised a garrison of 1,000 men that lived together with their families and, as attested by the Aramaic documents of the Persian period, was an economic and legal unit as well as a military one. This situation corresponds closely to the makeup and function of the Israelite tribes in the wilderness, as depicted in the Book of Numbers.[2] The meaning "military unit" is also present in the War Scroll from Qumran.[3]

banners Hebrew ***'ot*** (cf. Ps. 74:4) is used for a fire signal in the Lachish letters (4:10). Here it means that each household had its distinctive insignia. According to Numbers Rabba 2:7, based on Exodus 39:14, each tribe had a banner bearing the same color as its corresponding stone on the High Priest's breastplate, and according to the War Scroll of the Dead Sea sectarians, each unit of three tribes (cf. also Targ. Jon.), down to the smallest unit—whether a myriad, thousand, hundred, fifty, or ten—had its own standard.[4]

3 Camped on the front, or east side: the standard of the
division of Judah, troop by troop. Chieftain of the Judites:
Nahshon son of Amminadab. 4 His troop, as enrolled:
74,600. 5 Camping next to it: the tribe of Issachar. Chieftain of the Issacharites: Nethanel son of Zuar. 6 His troop,
as enrolled: 54,400. 7 The tribe of Zebulun. Chieftain of the
Zebulunites: Eliab son of Helon. 8 His troop, as enrolled:
57,400. 9 The total enrolled in the division of Judah:
186,400, for all troops. These shall march first.

3 וְהַחֹנִים קֵדְמָה מִזְרָחָה דֶּגֶל מַחֲנֵה יְהוּדָה
לְצִבְאֹתָם וְנָשִׂיא לִבְנֵי יְהוּדָה נַחְשׁוֹן בֶּן־עַמִּינָדָב׃
4 וּצְבָאוֹ וּפְקֻדֵיהֶם אַרְבָּעָה וְשִׁבְעִים אֶלֶף וְשֵׁשׁ
מֵאוֹת׃ 5 וְהַחֹנִים עָלָיו מַטֵּה יִשָּׂשכָר וְנָשִׂיא לִבְנֵי
יִשָּׂשכָר נְתַנְאֵל בֶּן־צוּעָר׃ 6 וּצְבָאוֹ וּפְקֻדָיו
אַרְבָּעָה וַחֲמִשִּׁים אֶלֶף וְאַרְבַּע מֵאוֹת׃ ס
7 מַטֵּה זְבוּלֻן וְנָשִׂיא לִבְנֵי זְבוּלֻן אֱלִיאָב בֶּן־חֵלֹן׃
8 וּצְבָאוֹ וּפְקֻדָיו שִׁבְעָה וַחֲמִשִּׁים אֶלֶף וְאַרְבַּע
מֵאוֹת׃ 9 כָּל־הַפְּקֻדִים לְמַחֲנֵה יְהוּדָה מְאַת אֶלֶף
וּשְׁמֹנִים אֶלֶף וְשֵׁשֶׁת־אֲלָפִים וְאַרְבַּע־מֵאוֹת
לְצִבְאֹתָם רִאשֹׁנָה יִסָּעוּ׃ ס

10 On the south: the standard of the division of Reuben,
troop by troop. Chieftain of the Reubenites: Elizur son of
Shedeur. 11 His troop, as enrolled: 46,500. 12 Camping next
to it: The tribe of Simeon. Chieftain of the Simeonites:
Shelumiel son of Zurishaddai. 13 His troop, as enrolled:
59,300. 14 And the tribe of Gad. Chieftain of the Gadites:
Eliasaph son of Reuel. 15 His troop, as enrolled: 45,650.

10 דֶּגֶל מַחֲנֵה רְאוּבֵן תֵּימָנָה לְצִבְאֹתָם וְנָשִׂיא
לִבְנֵי רְאוּבֵן אֱלִיצוּר בֶּן־שְׁדֵיאוּר׃ 11 וּצְבָאוֹ
וּפְקֻדָיו שִׁשָּׁה וְאַרְבָּעִים אֶלֶף וַחֲמֵשׁ מֵאוֹת׃
12 וְהַחוֹנִם עָלָיו מַטֵּה שִׁמְעוֹן וְנָשִׂיא לִבְנֵי שִׁמְעוֹן
שְׁלֻמִיאֵל בֶּן־צוּרִי־שַׁדָּי׃ 13 וּצְבָאוֹ וּפְקֻדֵיהֶם
תִּשְׁעָה וַחֲמִשִּׁים אֶלֶף וּשְׁלֹשׁ מֵאוֹת׃ 14 וּמַטֵּה גָּד
וְנָשִׂיא לִבְנֵי גָד אֶלְיָסָף בֶּן־רְעוּאֵל׃ 15 וּצְבָאוֹ

at a distance Hebrew *mi-neged* implies distance[5] (see Gen. 21:16; Exod. 19:2; Deut. 32:52; Num. R. 2:9). It was necessary to make room for the Levitical encampment, which was set up between the sanctuary and the Israelite camp and which is detailed in chapters 3 and 4. The rabbis (Num. R. 2:1) surmise that this distance was 2,000 cubits, approximately 900 meters (1,000 yd.); this was the farthest walking distance permitted on the Sabbath, so all of Israel could worship at the sanctuary (this figure is the distance of the Israelites from the Ark when they crossed the Jordan; see Josh. 3:4).

3. ***camped . . . the standard*** Rather, "camped . . . the unit." The verb "camped" renders the translation of *degel* more likely as "unit" than "standard"; see verse 2.

on the front, or east side Occasionally two terms are recorded for the same compass direction, for example, east (here and 34:15); south (Exod. 26:18; 27:9).[6] See further at Numbers 3:38.

division Hebrew *maḥaneh*. Here it is synonymous with *degel,* the "unit" of three tribes.[7]

Judah According to 1 Chronicles 5:1–2, Judah replaced Reuben, the first-born, as the leader of the tribes, and Joseph (i.e., Ephraim) retained the birthright, thus accounting for the fact that Judah (v. 3), Reuben (v. 10), and Ephraim (v. 18) are the heads of their respective divisions. On Dan, see verse 25.

Naḥshon His sister, Elisheba, was the wife of Aaron (Exod. 6:23).[8]

4. ***His troop*** See 10:14–27. The chieftain is always associated with his troop. Literally, the text reads: "As for his troop, its enrollment was . . ."

5. ***Camping next to it*** The plural participle refers to both tribes, Issachar and Zebulun, implying that Judah was in the center. By the same token, the names of the remaining three units also refer to the tribe in the center; see the diagram in Excursus 3. These three tribes occupy the third, fourth, and fifth places in the list of 1:20–46, and they may have been inserted in front of the first unit—Reuben, Simeon, Gad—in order to give Judah primacy.

10. ***On the south . . . troop by troop*** In the Hebrew text these two terms are contiguous; they appear in the same order in verse 25 and in reverse order in verse 18, a chiastic construction.

14. ***Reuel*** Read *Deuel* as in 1:14 and many manuscripts and versions.

16 The total enrolled in the division of Reuben: 151,450, for all troops. These shall march second.

17 Then, midway between the divisions, the Tent of Meeting, the division of the Levites, shall move. As they camp, so they shall march, each in position, by their standards.

18 On the west: the standard of the division of Ephraim, troop by troop. Chieftain of the Ephraimites: Elishama son of Ammihud. 19 His troop, as enrolled: 40,500. 20 Next to it: the tribe of Manasseh. Chieftain of the Manassites: Gamaliel son of Pedahzur. 21 His troop, as enrolled: 32,200. 22 And the tribe of Benjamin. Chieftain of the Benjaminites: Abidan son of Gideoni. 23 His troop, as enrolled: 35,400. 24 The total enrolled in the division of Ephraim: 108,100 for all troops. These shall march third.

25 On the north: the standard of the division of Dan, troop by troop. Chieftain of the Danites: Ahiezer son of Ammishaddai. 26 His troop, as enrolled: 62,700.

וּפְקֻדֵיהֶ֑ם חֲמִשָּׁ֤ה וְאַרְבָּעִים֙ אֶ֔לֶף וְשֵׁ֥שׁ מֵא֖וֹת
וַחֲמִשִּֽׁים׃ 16 כָּֽל־הַפְּקֻדִ֞ים לְמַחֲנֵ֣ה רְאוּבֵ֗ן מְאַ֨ת
אֶ֜לֶף וְאֶחָ֨ד וַחֲמִשִּׁ֥ים אֶ֛לֶף וְאַרְבַּע־מֵא֥וֹת וַחֲמִשִּׁ֖ים
לְצִבְאֹתָ֑ם וּשְׁנִיִּ֖ם יִסָּֽעוּ׃ ס
17 וְנָסַ֧ע אֹֽהֶל־מוֹעֵ֛ד מַחֲנֵ֥ה הַלְוִיִּ֖ם בְּת֣וֹךְ
הַֽמַּחֲנֹ֑ת כַּאֲשֶׁ֤ר יַחֲנוּ֙ כֵּ֣ן יִסָּ֔עוּ אִ֥ישׁ עַל־יָד֖וֹ
לְדִגְלֵיהֶֽם׃ ס
18 דֶּ֣גֶל מַחֲנֵ֥ה אֶפְרַ֛יִם לְצִבְאֹתָ֖ם יָ֑מָּה וְנָשִׂיא֙
לִבְנֵ֣י אֶפְרַ֔יִם אֱלִישָׁמָ֖ע בֶּן־עַמִּיהֽוּד׃ 19 וּצְבָא֖וֹ
וּפְקֻדֵיהֶ֑ם אַרְבָּעִ֣ים אֶ֔לֶף וַחֲמֵ֖שׁ מֵאֽוֹת׃ 20 וְעָלָ֖יו
מַטֵּ֣ה מְנַשֶּׁ֑ה וְנָשִׂיא֙ לִבְנֵ֣י מְנַשֶּׁ֔ה גַּמְלִיאֵ֖ל בֶּן־
פְּדָהצֽוּר׃ 21 וּצְבָא֖וֹ וּפְקֻדֵיהֶ֑ם שְׁנַ֤יִם וּשְׁלֹשִׁים֙
אֶ֖לֶף וּמָאתָֽיִם׃ 22 וּמַטֵּ֖ה בִּנְיָמִ֑ן וְנָשִׂיא֙ לִבְנֵ֣י בִנְיָמִ֔ן
אֲבִידָ֖ן בֶּן־גִּדְעֹנִֽי׃ 23 וּצְבָא֖וֹ וּפְקֻדֵיהֶ֑ם חֲמִשָּׁ֧ה
וּשְׁלֹשִׁ֛ים אֶ֖לֶף וְאַרְבַּ֥ע מֵאֽוֹת׃ 24 כָּֽל־הַפְּקֻדִ֞ים
לְמַחֲנֵ֣ה אֶפְרַ֗יִם מְאַ֥ת אֶ֛לֶף וּשְׁמֹנַֽת־אֲלָפִ֥ים וּמֵאָ֖ה
לְצִבְאֹתָ֑ם וּשְׁלִשִׁ֖ים יִסָּֽעוּ׃ ס
25 דֶּ֣גֶל מַחֲנֵ֥ה דָ֛ן צָפֹ֖נָה לְצִבְאֹתָ֑ם וְנָשִׂיא֙ לִבְנֵ֣י
דָ֔ן אֲחִיעֶ֖זֶר בֶּן־עַמִּישַׁדָּֽי׃ 26 וּצְבָא֖וֹ וּפְקֻדֵיהֶ֑ם

17. ***midway between*** Rather, "in the midst of" (see 10:17). The Tabernacle and its Levitical guards were divided into two groups during the march. The dismantled structure was transported by the Gershonites and Merarites who marched between the first and second divisions, whereas the cult objects were carried by the Kohathites in the very center of the column, between the second and third divisions.

the Tent of Meeting, the division of the Levites These two phrases are either appositional, to be understood as "the Tent of Meeting, which is in the Levitical division," or they should be understood as being connected by the conjunction "and," which is the reading of the Septuagint. Since the other tribal divisions were called after the chief tribe (i.e., Judah, Reuben, Ephraim, and Dan), one would hardly expect the Levite division to be called "the Tent of Meeting." Therefore the second alternative is preferable.[9] It should also be noted that, whereas all the other tribes are described in their stationary position around the encamped Tabernacle, only the Levite division is mentioned as being in transit. This is because the details on the stationary Tabernacle in relation to the Levitical encampment will be given in chapter 3.

in position Hebrew *yad,* literally "hand," can mean "place" (Deut. 23:13; Jer. 6:3). However, it may be equivalent to "banner" (both modifying *degel,* v. 2), indicating a semantic development from signals by hand to signals by banner,[10] hence rendered, "(each) by his banner (according to their units)."

standards Rather, "units"; see verse 2. The plural indicates that "divisions" (of all the tribes) is the antecedent, as shown by the same word in verse 34. The meaning of the second half of this verse would then be that, whereas the Levites are broken into two units during the march, the Israelite troops remain intact at all times.

20. ***Next to it*** That is, camping next to it, referring to the two tribes associated with a leader.

25. ***Dan*** Dan was made head of its division because he was the first-born of all of Jacob's children from his concubines (Gen. 30:1–13).[11] Moreover, Dan stood out among the tribes because it provided the hero judge Samson (Judg. 13–16), its sanctuary was staffed by a priestly line descended

27Camping next to it: The tribe of Asher. Chieftain of the Asherites: Pagiel son of Ochran. 28His troop, as enrolled: 41,500. 29And the tribe of Naphtali. Chieftain of the Naphtalites: Ahira son of Enan. 30His troop, as enrolled: 53,400. 31The total enrolled in the division of Dan: 157,600. These shall march last, by their standards.

32Those are the enrollments of the Israelites by ancestral houses. The total enrolled in the divisions, for all troops: 603,550. 33The Levites, however, were not recorded among the Israelites, as the LORD had commanded Moses.

34The Israelites did accordingly; just as the LORD had commanded Moses, so they camped by their standards, and so they marched, each with his clan according to his ancestral house.

שְׁנַ֥יִם וַחֲמִשִּׁ֛ים אֶ֖לֶף וּשְׁבַ֥ע מֵא֖וֹת: 27 וְהַחֹנִ֥ים עָלָ֖יו מַטֵּ֣ה אָשֵׁ֑ר וְנָשִׂיא֙ לִבְנֵ֣י אָשֵׁ֔ר פַּגְעִיאֵ֖ל בֶּן־עָכְרָֽן: 28 וּצְבָא֖וֹ וּפְקֻדֵיהֶ֑ם אֶחָ֧ד וְאַרְבָּעִ֛ים אֶ֖לֶף וַחֲמֵ֥שׁ מֵאֽוֹת: 29 וּמַטֵּ֖ה נַפְתָּלִ֑י וְנָשִׂיא֙ לִבְנֵ֣י נַפְתָּלִ֔י אֲחִירַ֖ע בֶּן־עֵינָֽן: 30 וּצְבָא֖וֹ וּפְקֻדֵיהֶ֑ם שְׁלֹשָׁ֧ה וַחֲמִשִּׁ֛ים אֶ֖לֶף וְאַרְבַּ֥ע מֵאֽוֹת: 31 כָּל־הַפְּקֻדִים֙ לְמַ֣חֲנֵה דָ֔ן מְאַ֥ת אֶ֖לֶף וְשִׁבְעָ֧ה וַחֲמִשִּׁ֛ים אֶ֖לֶף וְשֵׁ֥שׁ מֵא֖וֹת לָאַחֲרֹנָ֥ה יִסְע֖וּ לְדִגְלֵיהֶֽם: פ

32 אֵ֣לֶּה פְּקוּדֵ֣י בְנֵֽי־יִשְׂרָאֵ֔ל לְבֵ֖ית אֲבֹתָ֑ם כָּל־פְּקוּדֵ֧י הַֽמַּחֲנֹ֛ת לְצִבְאֹתָ֖ם שֵׁשׁ־מֵא֥וֹת אֶ֛לֶף וּשְׁלֹ֥שֶׁת אֲלָפִ֖ים וַחֲמֵ֥שׁ מֵא֖וֹת וַחֲמִשִּֽׁים: 33 וְהַ֨לְוִיִּ֔ם לֹ֣א הָתְפָּקְד֔וּ בְּת֖וֹךְ בְּנֵ֣י יִשְׂרָאֵ֑ל כַּאֲשֶׁ֛ר צִוָּ֥ה יְהֹוָ֖ה אֶת־מֹשֶֽׁה:

34 וַיַּעֲשׂ֖וּ בְּנֵ֣י יִשְׂרָאֵ֑ל כְּ֠כֹל אֲשֶׁר־צִוָּ֤ה יְהֹוָה֙ אֶת־מֹשֶׁ֔ה כֵּ֥ן חָנ֖וּ לְדִגְלֵיהֶ֑ם וְכֵ֣ן נָסָ֗עוּ אִ֚ישׁ לְמִשְׁפְּחֹתָ֖יו עַל־בֵּ֥ית אֲבֹתָֽיו: ס רביעי

from Moses (Judg. 18:30), and it was noted for two of its artisans, who designed the wilderness Tabernacle (Exod. 31:6) and Solomon's Temple (2 Chron. 2:12–13).

   31. by their standards   Not only is the plural here difficult, but the usual "for all troops" after the number is missing from the formula (cf. vv. 9,16,24). Perhaps the intent of the plural is to include all four camps.[12]

A SUMMARY (vv. 32–34)

These verses reproduce 1:46–47 with two relevant additions. The phrase "the total enrolled in the divisions, for all troops" shows the objective to be military deployment. The appended "as the LORD had commanded Moses" refers back to 1:48 to explain the omission of the enrollment and deployment of the Levitical division. Verse 34 relates the execution of the divine command to form divisions. It anticipates (as does also 17b) the marching orders given in full in 10:11–28.

CHAPTER 3

The First Levite Census   (vv. 1–51)

Chapter 3 divides itself into two main sections: Verses 1–13 take place *at Mount Sinai* (v. 1) where the Levites are designated as the guards and porters of the Tabernacle (vv. 5–10) in place of the first-born (vv. 11–13); and verses 14–51 take place in the *wilderness of Sinai* where the Levites are counted and assigned their guarding duties; see Ibn Ezra.

AT MOUNT SINAI (vv. 1–13)

The priestly genealogy properly precedes that of the Levites (vv. 1–4) and also serves to identify Aaron's sons (vv. 9–10) under whom the Levites will serve. Above all, these verses anticipate the Levitical census that follows and therefore obviates the need to count the Aaronides. Contrast the

3 This is the line of Aaron and Moses at the time that the
LORD spoke with Moses on Mount Sinai. [2]These were the
names of Aaron's sons: Nadab, the first-born, and Abihu,
Eleazar and Ithamar; [3]those were the names of Aaron's
sons, the anointed priests who were ordained for priesthood. [4]But Nadab and Abihu died by the will of the LORD,
when they offered alien fire before the LORD in the wilderness of Sinai; and they left no sons. So it was Eleazar and
Ithamar who served as priests in the lifetime of their father
Aaron.

ג וְאֵלֶּה תּוֹלְדֹת אַהֲרֹן וּמֹשֶׁה בְּיוֹם דִּבֶּר יְהוָה
אֶת־מֹשֶׁה בְּהַר סִינָי׃ 2 וְאֵלֶּה שְׁמוֹת בְּנֵי־אַהֲרֹן
הַבְּכוֹר ׀ נָדָב וַאֲבִיהוּא אֶלְעָזָר וְאִיתָמָר׃ 3 אֵלֶּה
שְׁמוֹת בְּנֵי אַהֲרֹן הַכֹּהֲנִים הַמְּשֻׁחִים אֲשֶׁר־מִלֵּא
יָדָם לְכַהֵן׃ 4 וַיָּמָת נָדָב וַאֲבִיהוּא לִפְנֵי יְהוָה
בְּהַקְרִבָם אֵשׁ זָרָה לִפְנֵי יְהוָה בְּמִדְבַּר סִינַי וּבָנִים
לֹא־הָיוּ לָהֶם וַיְכַהֵן אֶלְעָזָר וְאִיתָמָר עַל־פְּנֵי אַהֲרֹן
אֲבִיהֶם׃ פ

second Israelite census where these facts concerning the Aaronides need be repeated (26:59–61). In substance these verses are a repetition of Exodus 6:23 and Leviticus 10:1–2.

THE PRIESTS (vv. 1–4)

*1. **This is the line*** For a similar genealogical heading, see, for example, Genesis 10:1.

Moses That Moses is mentioned at all is due to the notice of his encampment alongside of Aaron (v. 38); he is counted with Aaron and not with the Levites (see also 26:59–61). That he is mentioned after Aaron can be explained by the fact that Aaron is the first-born. Similarly, Aaron's sons and the Levitical clans in this chapter are listed in chronological order (see chap. 4). However, the line of Moses is not given at all. We must infer from the mention of the Amramites (v. 27) that Moses' line was reckoned among the Levites (so Num. 26:59; 1 Chron. 23:13–14). Perhaps the genealogy of Moses was ignored because one branch of his descendants seems to have become the priests of the condemned golden calf of Dan (Judg. 18:30; LXX manuscripts; 1 Kings 12:28–30). In any event, this genealogical notice is a clear attempt to separate the Aaronide line from the rest of the Levites (see the Comment to v. 38). It is not without significance that of the seventy-eight times Moses and Aaron are mentioned together, Aaron precedes Moses only in the genealogical texts (Exod. 6:20; Num. 3:1; 26:59; 1 Chron. 5:29; 23:13).

Mount Sinai As distinct from the wilderness of Sinai (v. 14). Verses 1–13 describe the designation of the Levites at Mount Sinai as the cultic replacements of the first-born, presumably after the episode of the golden calf apostasy, in Exodus 32, according to Ibn Ezra and Sefer ha-Mivḥar.

*2. **These were the names*** That is, when they were at Mount Sinai, for Nadab and Abihu died a while later (cf. Exod. 24:1 with Lev. 10:1–2). The double rubric "This is the line" and "These are (were) the names" is also found in Genesis 25:12–13 and 36:9–10.

*3. **anointed*** The anointment of Aaron's sons by the sprinkling of sanctified oil and blood is described in Exodus 29:21 and Leviticus 8:30 (cf. Exod. 30:30; 40:15).

ordained Hebrew ***mille' yadam,*** literally "fill the hand" (see Exod. 28:41). Their anointing and ordination entitles them to the priesthood and to authority over the Levites (v. 9).[1] This idiom always refers to the installation of persons in priestly functions (e.g., Judg. 17:5; 1 Kings 13:33).

*4. **by the will of*** Rather, "before" the Lord; i.e., within the sanctuary.[2]

in the lifetime On Hebrew ***'al penei,*** compare Genesis 11:28.[3] Ramban transposes this phrase to the beginning of the verse, thereby indicating not that Eleazar and Ithamar served in the lifetime of the father but that Nadab and Abihu *died* in the lifetime of their father. The Chronicler understands this verse similarly (1 Chron. 24:2).

and they left no sons This essential point is new (cf. Lev. 10:1–7). The detailing of the Levitical duties in the Tabernacle is preceded by a general summary (vv. 5–10).

[5]The Lord spoke to Moses, saying: [6]Advance the tribe of
Levi and place them in attendance upon Aaron the priest to
serve him. [7]They shall perform duties for him and for the
whole community before the Tent of Meeting, doing the
work of the Tabernacle. [8]They shall take charge of all the

5 וַיְדַבֵּר יְהוָה אֶל־מֹשֶׁה לֵּאמֹר: 6 הַקְרֵב אֶת־
מַטֵּה לֵוִי וְהַעֲמַדְתָּ אֹתוֹ לִפְנֵי אַהֲרֹן הַכֹּהֵן וְשֵׁרְתוּ
אֹתוֹ: 7 וְשָׁמְרוּ אֶת־מִשְׁמַרְתּוֹ וְאֶת־מִשְׁמֶרֶת כָּל־
הָעֵדָה לִפְנֵי אֹהֶל מוֹעֵד לַעֲבֹד אֶת־עֲבֹדַת
הַמִּשְׁכָּן: 8 וְשָׁמְרוּ אֶת־כָּל־כְּלֵי אֹהֶל מוֹעֵד וְאֶת־

SUBORDINATION OF THE LEVITES (vv. 5–13)

6. ***advance*** Rather, "qualify." *Hakrev* has a cultic connotation (Exod. 28:1; 29:3,8; 40:12; Num. 16:5,9–10). The Levites are "qualified" in a ceremony (described in chap. 8) that will subordinate them as assistants to Aaron and his sons.[4]

place them in attendance upon Hebrew *ʿamad lifnei* is an idiom of subordination (cf. 1 Sam. 16:22; 1 Kings 1:2).

serve Rather, "assist." The verb *sheret* has multiple nuances.[5]

7. ***duties*** Rather, "guard duty" (and so throughout). In connection with the Tabernacle, *mishmeret* means "guard duty" and nothing else.[6] Numbers 1:53 has indicated in advance that the Levitical cordon around the Tabernacle both guards it from incursion by the laity and protects the latter from suffering the consequent wrath of God. This dual role of guarding is fully explained in Excursus 40. The guard duty of the Levites is a lifelong responsibility that, presumably, would begin at adolescence and continue into old age (8:25–26), knowing no retirement. In contrast to this, the hard labor of dismantling, transporting, and reassembling the Tabernacle (called *ʿavodah,* see Excursus 6) terminates at age fifty; it is limited to the age of maximum physical strength (4:3,23,30; 8:24).

Verses 14–39 itemize the Tabernacle furnishings to the last detail as they are distributed among the Levitical clans for their safekeeping during the march. Chapter 4 itemizes these same furnishings and assigns them to the same Levitical clans in regard to their transport duties. The guarding duties of the Levites while the camp is at rest were generalized in the anticipatory statement, 1:53, and will be referred to again when the "occupational hazards" of guarding are mentioned in 18:1–7. In this introductory pericope, the Levitical job profile in regard to the sanctuary can be summarized in just two verses: while the camp is at rest (v. 7) and in transit (v. 8).

for him . . . before the Tent of Meeting Guarding the Tabernacle proper and the courtyard altar is the responsibility of the priests exclusively (18:5); the Levite is forbidden access (18:3). Thus "before the Tent of Meeting," that is, the Tabernacle, must be understood literally: before but not within. The Levites guarded outside the sacred area, whereas the priests were stationed within (3:10; 18:3b,7a). However, since the layman was permitted into the "entrance of the Tent of Meeting" (e.g., 16:19) for ritual purposes (e.g., Lev. 1:3), it was here that presumably the Levitical guard shared the custodial duties with the priests. This is what is meant by "for him" (cf. also Num. 18:3a).[7] The ancient Hittite temple was also guarded by two classes of officials: "keepers" on the outside and priests on the inside.[8] Two occasions in the Hittite "Instructions for Temple Officials" are given when the keeper performed guard duty inside the temple precinct: to escort the layman who enters to perform a sacred rite and to search for or guard against the unauthorized infiltrator.[9] Similarly, Israel's Levite leaves his post to escort the worshiper when he assists him in his sacrificial preparations (Num. 16:9) and to assist the priests in protecting the sancta against encroachment (Num. 3:6b,7a; 18:2–4).

and for the whole community By replacing the first-born; see the Comments to verses 11–14.

doing Rather, "in doing"; that is, guard duty constituted half of their work, whereas their removal labors constituted the other half.[10]

work On *ʿavodah,* see chapter 4.

8. ***take charge . . . duty*** Rather, "guard . . . guard duty." Verse 8 is not a repetition of verse 7 but is its essential complement. Both together spell out the total guard duty encumbent upon the

furnishings of the Tent of Meeting—a duty on behalf of the Israelites—doing the work of the Tabernacle. 9You shall assign the Levites to Aaron and to his sons: they are formally assigned to him from among the Israelites. 10You shall make Aaron and his sons responsible for observing their priestly duties; and any outsider who encroaches shall be put to death.

11The LORD spoke to Moses, saying: 12I hereby take the

מִשְׁמֶרֶת בְּנֵי יִשְׂרָאֵל לַעֲבֹד אֶת־עֲבֹדַת הַמִּשְׁכָּן׃
9 וְנָתַתָּה אֶת־הַלְוִיִּם לְאַהֲרֹן וּלְבָנָיו נְתוּנִם נְתוּנִם
הֵמָּה לוֹ מֵאֵת בְּנֵי יִשְׂרָאֵל׃ 10 וְאֶת־אַהֲרֹן וְאֶת־
בָּנָיו תִּפְקֹד וְשָׁמְרוּ אֶת־כְּהֻנָּתָם וְהַזָּר הַקָּרֵב
יוּמָת׃ פ
11 וַיְדַבֵּר יְהוָה אֶל־מֹשֶׁה לֵּאמֹר׃ 12 וַאֲנִי הִנֵּה

Levites: when the camp was at rest (v. 7) and in transit (v. 8). The latter is ascertained by the reference to the "furnishings of the Tent." The Levites guarded these while transporting them during the march (see the Comments to 3:25,31,36), but had no access to them when they were set up in camp and were under the sole supervision of the priests (18:5).

on behalf of the Israelites By replacing their first-born (vv. 11–13). For another interpretation, see verse 38.

doing Rather, "in doing" (see v. 7) or "in addition to doing" or "while doing." This phrase makes perfect sense here since it speaks of Levitical guard duty in transit at a time when they also had removal duty (specified in chap. 4; see also 18:4). It is thus possible that this phrase in verse 7b, which speaks of Levitical guard duty when the camp was at rest, is a dittography.

9. formally assigned The root ***n-t-n*** implies dedication.[11] By replacing the first-born in their cultic duties (see the Comments to 3:11–13), the Levites are dedicated *(n–t–n)* to the Lord (8:16–18; cf. 3:41) and in a special dedication ritual (8:5–22) are transferred to the jurisdiction of the priests.[12]

The Levites are dedicated ***(n-t-n),*** whereas the priests are sanctified ***(k-d-sh).*** This distinction is consistently maintained in the priestly sources, thereby emphasizing that only the priests—but never the Levites—are authorized to have access to the most sacred sancta. It is also of significance that a later class of Temple servants is called ***netinim*** (e.g., Ezra 8:20).[13]

from among the Israelites The Israelites actually donate the Levites to God (cf. 8:10; and the Comment to 4:2).

10. responsible Compare Rashi. The verb ***tifkod*** usually requires an object; the Septuagint adds "over the Tent of Meeting."

observing their priestly duties Rather, "guarding their priesthood," that is, against encroachment[14] (see v. 10b; 18:1b), a function that is spelled out in the Septuagint on this verse and in 18:7: "in everything pertaining to the altar and to what is behind the curtain." This verse thus clearly stipulates that the priests are the sole custodians of the most sacred objects (see the table in Excursus 40).

encroaches See Excursus 5.

Verses 11–13 The replacement of the first-born by the Levites implies that the former originally held a sacred status. This is supported by the biblical laws regarding the human first-born that utilize the phrase "dedicate [***natan***]/sanctify [***kiddesh***]/transfer [***heʿevir***] to the Lord" (Exod. 13:1,12; 22:28) as well as "redeem [***padah***] from the Lord" (Num. 18:15). This is reflected in an ancient custom whereby the first-born was expected to care for the burial and worship of his deceased parents. Traces of ancestor worship are found in Mesopotamia: the first-born inherits the family gods at Nuzi and cultic objects at Nippur; many Akkadian adoption documents specify that inheritance depends on the fulfillment of the funerary cult; the ***kudurru*** boundary stone curses include the lack of a son who will offer libations after death. The one responsible for the care of the ancestral spirit ***(eṭemmu)*** is called by the title ***pāqidu,*** literally "the one who takes care of," and seems in most cases to have been a relative of the deceased. His duties were to "make funerary offerings," "pour water," and "call the name," meaning to keep the name of the individual alive. The cared-for spirit would then be expected

Levites from among the Israelites in place of all the first-born, the first issue of the womb among the Israelites: the Levites shall be Mine. [13]For every first-born is Mine: at the time that I smote every first-born in the land of Egypt, I consecrated every first-born in Israel, man and beast, to Myself, to be Mine, the LORD's.

[14]The LORD spoke to Moses in the wilderness of Sinai, saying: [15]Record the Levites by ancestral house and by clan;

לָקַחְתִּי אֶת־הַלְוִיִּם מִתּוֹךְ בְּנֵי יִשְׂרָאֵל תַּחַת כָּל־
בְּכוֹר פֶּטֶר רֶחֶם מִבְּנֵי יִשְׂרָאֵל וְהָיוּ לִי הַלְוִיִּם׃
13 כִּי לִי כָּל־בְּכוֹר בְּיוֹם הַכֹּתִי כָל־בְּכוֹר בְּאֶרֶץ
מִצְרַיִם הִקְדַּשְׁתִּי לִי כָל־בְּכוֹר בְּיִשְׂרָאֵל מֵאָדָם
עַד־בְּהֵמָה לִי יִהְיוּ אֲנִי יְהוָה׃ ס חמישי
14 וַיְדַבֵּר יְהוָה אֶל־מֹשֶׁה בְּמִדְבַּר סִינַי לֵאמֹר׃

to exert a beneficial influence, such as interceding on behalf of his family with the gods; otherwise, his influence might be malevolent. Whereas in Mesopotamia, the popular funerary cult was observed for ascendants no further back than grandparents, in the royal funerary cult all previous kings whose names had been recorded for posterity on king lists and monuments were included.[15]

Ancestor worship is also attested in Egypt, among pre-Islamic Arabs, in Ugarit, and in Israelite popular religion (e.g., Isa. 8:19; cf. Deut. 26:14). Thus the Bible may be preserving a memory of the first-born bearing a sacred status; his replacement by the Levites may reflect the establishment of a professional, inherited priestly class. The deliberate avoidance by the priestly texts of the word ***kadosh,*** "holy," in regard to the Levites (v. 9) may also be due to the fear of the priestly legists that the family ancestral worship, heretofore conducted by the first-born, might be continued by the Levites. The tradition of reciting ***kaddish*** for one's departed parents, falling upon the male children, especially the first-born, but recast as a declaration of faith in the establishment of God's kingdom on earth, may be a lineal descendant of an original form of ancestor worship, the reinterpretation of which is reflected in the substitution of the Levites for the first-born. The rabbis also maintained that the first-born originally held a priestly status.[16] There is no support, however, for the theory that the first-born was originally offered for sacrifice. As to why this section was inserted here rather than before verses 40–51, which deal with the first-born, see the Comment to verse 16.

12. ***I hereby take*** That is, by means of a ritual (chap. 8), although the designation of the Levites had already been determined (see the Comments to vv. 41,44; 8:14,18).

in place of The Septuagint renders "as ransom for"; expiation is explicitly stated as the Levites' function in 8:19.

first issue of the womb It was the first-born of the mother who held sacred status, but the rights of inheritance (primogeniture) were claimed by the first-born of the father (see Deut. 21:15–17).

The Levites shall be Mine That is, to serve Me, according to Targum Onkelos, by means of an ordination ritual; see 8:14.[17]

13. ***at the time that I smote . . . I consecrated*** Referring to Exodus 13:1–2,11–16 (see also 8:17). The logic seems to be that by sparing Israel's first-born, God thereby acquired them (Exod. 13:15).

to be Mine Possibly "they shall be Mine," referring to the Levites in verse 12b, according to Ramban.

the LORD's The same phrase is found in verses 41,45 and often in the second half of the Book of Leviticus.

IN THE WILDERNESS OF SINAI (vv. 14–51)

These verses concern the first Levitical census and the assignment of guard duty for the Tabernacle furnishings ***while in transit.*** That this guard duty refers only to the march is shown both by its association with the term ***ʿavodah,*** "removal" (vv. 26,31,36), and by its description in chapter 4 as "the guarding of their porterage" (4:31,32; cf. 4:27).

14. ***wilderness of Sinai*** See the Comment to verse 1.

record every male among them from the age of one month
up. 16So Moses recorded them at the command of the
LORD, as he was bidden. 17These were the sons of Levi by
name: Gershon, Kohath, and Merari. 18These were the
names of the sons of Gershon by clan: Libni and Shimei.
19The sons of Kohath by clan: Amram and Izhar, Hebron
and Uzziel. 20The sons of Merari by clan: Mahli and Mushi.

These were the clans of the Levites within their ancestral houses:

21To Gershon belonged the clan of the Libnites and the
clan of the Shimeites; those were the clans of the Gershonites. 22The recorded entries of all their males from the age
of one month up, as recorded, came to 7,500. 23The clans of
the Gershonites were to camp behind the Tabernacle, to the
west. 24The chieftain of the ancestral house of the Gershonites was Eliasaph son of Lael. 25The duties of the Ger-

15 פְּקֹד אֶת־בְּנֵי לֵוִי לְבֵית אֲבֹתָם לְמִשְׁפְּחֹתָם
כָּל־זָכָר מִבֶּן־חֹדֶשׁ וָמַעְלָה תִּפְקְדֵם׃ 16 וַיִּפְקֹד
אֹתָם מֹשֶׁה עַל־פִּי יְהוָה כַּאֲשֶׁר צֻוָּה׃ 17 וַיִּהְיוּ־
אֵלֶּה בְנֵי־לֵוִי בִּשְׁמֹתָם גֵּרְשׁוֹן וּקְהָת וּמְרָרִי׃
18 וְאֵלֶּה שְׁמוֹת בְּנֵי־גֵרְשׁוֹן לְמִשְׁפְּחֹתָם לִבְנִי
וְשִׁמְעִי׃ 19 וּבְנֵי קְהָת לְמִשְׁפְּחֹתָם עַמְרָם וְיִצְהָר
חֶבְרוֹן וְעֻזִּיאֵל׃ 20 וּבְנֵי מְרָרִי לְמִשְׁפְּחֹתָם מַחְלִי
וּמוּשִׁי

אֵלֶּה הֵם מִשְׁפְּחֹת הַלֵּוִי לְבֵית אֲבֹתָם׃

21 לְגֵרְשׁוֹן מִשְׁפַּחַת הַלִּבְנִי וּמִשְׁפַּחַת הַשִּׁמְעִי
אֵלֶּה הֵם מִשְׁפְּחֹת הַגֵּרְשֻׁנִּי׃ 22 פְּקֻדֵיהֶם בְּמִסְפַּר
כָּל־זָכָר מִבֶּן־חֹדֶשׁ וָמָעְלָה פְּקֻדֵיהֶם שִׁבְעַת
אֲלָפִים וַחֲמֵשׁ מֵאוֹת׃ 23 מִשְׁפְּחֹת הַגֵּרְשֻׁנִּי אַחֲרֵי
הַמִּשְׁכָּן יַחֲנוּ יָמָּה׃ 24 וּנְשִׂיא בֵית־אָב לַגֵּרְשֻׁנִּי
אֶלְיָסָף בֶּן־לָאֵל׃ 25 וּמִשְׁמֶרֶת בְּנֵי־גֵרְשׁוֹן בְּאֹהֶל

*15. **one month up*** The Levite census begins at the age of one month because the first-born must be one month old to be eligible for redemption. See further in the Comments to 3:46–51.

*16. **command*** Hebrew *'al pi* should be rendered "oracle" (cf. 9:18; 27:21; Num. R. 3:9);[18] otherwise *tsuvvah,* "commanded," is a tautology (see also 4:49). Thus the two Levitical censuses (chaps. 3–4), in contrast to the Israelite census (chap. 1), are taken by God. Moses is merely to record the totals (see 3:16) and the work assignments (4:49). Significantly, this reference to the Lord's oracle occurs seven times in chapters 3 and 4.[19] The supposition that the Levitical censuses are conducted with divine assistance is further supported by the absence of any mention of the procedure of writing down names as is indicated for the Israelite census (1:2,18) and that of the Israelite first-born (3:40,43). The reason for this distinction may be rooted in the fear of taking a census: Its dire consequences can be avoided only if each individual pays a half-shekel ransom (Exod. 30:11–16; Num. 31:48–54). But this ransom, presumed in the account of the census of Israel's fighting force (see Excursus 2), is obviated in the census of the Levites because God Himself has taken their count. This indeed may explain why the notice of God's selection of the Levites (3:11–13) precedes the account of their census: God counts them personally, thereby avoiding the dangers of a census. Significantly, the oracle is again resorted to in the account of redemption of the 273 remaining first-born (3:51), for how was Moses to select which of the surplus individuals had to pay five shekels each except by leaving the matter to God? Rabbinic tradition suggests that lots were drawn, a form of oracle.[20] The Urim and Thummim could not have been used for this purpose since they were the exclusive reserve of the High Priest, as noted in Exodus 28:30 and Leviticus 8:8 (and cf. especially Num. 27:21).

*18–20a. **by name . . . the names*** The sons and grandsons of Levi are listed here, though they will be mentioned again in the census of the Levite clans (vv. 21–39) in order to correspond to the list of the priests' names, given earlier (vv. 2–3). This genealogy seems to have been borrowed from Exodus 6:16–19.[21]

*20. **Mushi*** See 26:58.

*21 (27). **Libnites . . . Hebronites*** These are clearly associated with place-names; see 26:58.

*22. **as recorded*** See verse 28.

*23 (29, 35). **camp*** Wherever the three Levitical clans camped (south, west, and north, respectively), they presumably performed their guard duty for the Tabernacle. Concerning the east side, see verse 38.

*24 (30, 35). **ancestral house*** Here ancestral house (Hebrew *beit 'av*) stands for the larger

shonites in the Tent of Meeting comprised: the tabernacle, the tent, its covering, and the screen for the entrance of the Tent of Meeting; 26 the hangings of the enclosure, the screen for the entrance of the enclosure which surrounds the Tabernacle, the cords thereof, and the altar—all the service connected with these.

27 To Kohath belonged the clan of the Amramites, the clan of the Izharites, the clan of the Hebronites, and the clan of the Uzzielites; those were the clans of the Kohathites. 28 All the listed males from the age of one month up

מוֹעֵ֔ד הַמִּשְׁכָּ֖ן וְהָאֹ֑הֶל מִכְסֵ֕הוּ וּמָסַ֕ךְ פֶּ֖תַח אֹ֥הֶל
מוֹעֵֽד׃ 26 וְקַלְעֵ֣י הֶֽחָצֵ֗ר וְאֶת־מָסַךְ֙ פֶּ֣תַח הֶֽחָצֵ֔ר
אֲשֶׁ֧ר עַל־הַמִּשְׁכָּ֛ן וְעַל־הַמִּזְבֵּ֖חַ סָבִ֑יב וְאֵת֙ מֵֽיתָרָ֔יו
לְכֹ֖ל עֲבֹדָתֽוֹ׃
27 וְלִקְהָ֗ת מִשְׁפַּ֤חַת הָֽעַמְרָמִי֙ וּמִשְׁפַּ֣חַת
הַיִּצְהָרִ֔י וּמִשְׁפַּ֙חַת֙ הַֽחֶבְרֹנִ֔י וּמִשְׁפַּ֖חַת הָֽעָזִּיאֵלִ֑י
אֵ֥לֶּה הֵ֖ם מִשְׁפְּחֹ֥ת הַקְּהָתִֽי׃ 28 בְּמִסְפַּר֙ כָּל־זָכָ֔ר
מִבֶּן־חֹ֖דֶשׁ וָמָ֑עְלָה שְׁמֹנַ֤ת אֲלָפִים֙ וְשֵׁ֣שׁ מֵא֔וֹת

unit of the clans comprising the Gershonites, Kohathites, and Merarites. In 17:17, ***beit 'av*** will actually indicate the entire tribe.

25. ***duties*** Rather, "guard duty" (see v. 7). The Tabernacle furnishings placed in the custody of the Gershonites and Merarites are clearly distinguished: The former guard all the fabrics, whereas the latter guard the Tabernacle planks and posts (vv. 25–28,36–37).

the tabernacle Refers here to the innermost tent covering composed of ten finely twisted linen and woolen cloths "with a design of cherubim worked into them" (Exod. 26:1). Since the inner Tabernacle curtains were anointed (Lev. 8:10), they theoretically had the same sacred status as the sancta (Exod. 30:29). Why, then, were they handled by the Gershonites and not by the Kohathites, who transported all the sancta (4:15; 7:9)? Clearly these curtains do not communicate holiness.[22]

the tent A second covering made up of eleven cloths of goat's hair (Exod. 26:7).

its covering The outermost covering made of tanned ram skins and yellow-orange skins (but cf. Exod. 26:14; Num. 4:25).

the screen The entrance to the Tent was of embroidered work (Exod. 26:36) and, hence, of lesser sanctity than the inner curtains, which contained designs of cherubim (Exod. 26:1,31). The reason is clear: The screen could be seen by anyone in the Tabernacle court, whereas the inner curtains could not be seen from the outside.

26. ***the cords thereof, and the altar*** Rather, "and the altar, and the cords thereof," implying that the cords belong to the previously mentioned Tabernacle curtains (v. 25) and enclosure hangings (v. 26)—an interpretation that is verified by 4:26 and Exodus 35:18.[23] Midrash records, instead, that the cords assigned to the Gershonites (3:26; 4:26) had the sole function of tying the sanctuary and enclosure curtains so they could be loaded onto the transport wagons.[24]

26 (31, 36). ***all the service connected with these*** Rather, "including their removal." For Hebrew ***lekhol*** meaning "including," see 4:31. That ***'avodah*** means "removal," see Excursus 6. The removal tasks of the Gershonites and the Merarites (v. 36) consisted of dismantling, loading, unloading, and reassembling, as specified in chapter 4.

27. ***Amramites*** To which the descendants of Moses ostensibly would belong (see v. 1).

28. ***All the listed males*** Rather, "the recorded entries of all their males," as in verses 22, 34; so the Peshitta. The redundant ***pekudeihem,*** "recorded entries," in verse 22b (and omitted by the Sam. and Pesh.) may well belong here.[25]

8,600 If this figure be added to the 7,500 of verse 22 and the 6,200 of verse 34, the total is 22,300 instead of the 22,000 given in verse 39. The Septuagint here reads 8,300, its Hebrew text having had ***shin, lamed, shin*** in place of ***shin, shin.***

attending to the duties of the sanctuary Rather, "performing the guard duty for the sancta." The Kohathites were responsible for transporting and guarding the most sacred objects, as itemized in verse 31.

came to 8,600, attending to the duties of the sanctuary. 29 The clans of the Kohathites were to camp along the south side of the Tabernacle. 30 The chieftain of the ancestral house of the Kohathite clans was Elizaphan son of Uzziel. 31 Their duties comprised: the ark, the table, the lampstand, the altars, and the sacred utensils that were used with them, and the screen—all the service connected with these. 32 The head chieftain of the Levites was Eleazar son of Aaron the priest, in charge of those attending to the duties of the sanctuary.

33 To Merari belonged the clan of the Mahlites and the clan of the Mushites; those were the clans of Merari. 34 The recorded entries of all their males from the age of one month up came to 6,200. 35 The chieftain of the ancestral house of the clans of Merari was Zuriel son of Abihail. They were to camp along the north side of the Tabernacle. 36 The assigned duties of the Merarites comprised: the planks of the Tabernacle, its bars, posts, and sockets, and all its furnishings—all the service connected with these; 37 also the posts around the enclosure and their sockets, pegs, and cords.

שֹׁמְרֵי מִשְׁמֶרֶת הַקֹּדֶשׁ׃ 29 מִשְׁפְּחֹת בְּנֵי־קְהָת
יַחֲנוּ עַל יֶרֶךְ הַמִּשְׁכָּן תֵּימָנָה׃ 30 וּנְשִׂיא בֵית־אָב
לְמִשְׁפְּחֹת הַקְּהָתִי אֱלִיצָפָן בֶּן־עֻזִּיאֵל׃
31 וּמִשְׁמַרְתָּם הָאָרֹן וְהַשֻּׁלְחָן וְהַמְּנֹרָה וְהַמִּזְבְּחֹת
וּכְלֵי הַקֹּדֶשׁ אֲשֶׁר יְשָׁרְתוּ בָּהֶם וְהַמָּסָךְ וְכֹל
עֲבֹדָתוֹ׃ 32 וּנְשִׂיא נְשִׂיאֵי הַלֵּוִי אֶלְעָזָר בֶּן־אַהֲרֹן
הַכֹּהֵן פְּקֻדַּת שֹׁמְרֵי מִשְׁמֶרֶת הַקֹּדֶשׁ׃

33 לִמְרָרִי מִשְׁפַּחַת הַמַּחְלִי וּמִשְׁפַּחַת הַמּוּשִׁי
אֵלֶּה הֵם מִשְׁפְּחֹת מְרָרִי׃ 34 וּפְקֻדֵיהֶם בְּמִסְפַּר
כָּל־זָכָר מִבֶּן־חֹדֶשׁ וָמָעְלָה שֵׁשֶׁת אֲלָפִים
וּמָאתָיִם׃ 35 וּנְשִׂיא בֵית־אָב לְמִשְׁפְּחֹת מְרָרִי
צוּרִיאֵל בֶּן־אֲבִיחָיִל עַל יֶרֶךְ הַמִּשְׁכָּן יַחֲנוּ צָפֹנָה׃
36 וּפְקֻדַּת מִשְׁמֶרֶת בְּנֵי מְרָרִי קַרְשֵׁי הַמִּשְׁכָּן
וּבְרִיחָיו וְעַמֻּדָיו וַאֲדָנָיו וְכָל־כֵּלָיו וְכֹל עֲבֹדָתוֹ׃
37 וְעַמֻּדֵי הֶחָצֵר סָבִיב וְאַדְנֵיהֶם וִיתֵדֹתָם
וּמֵיתְרֵיהֶם׃

29. south side Starting with the east, which is the most prestigious position (see v. 38), the position next in importance, rotating to the right (clockwise), is the south. The Kohathites merited this because it was their honored task to carry the most sacred objects. The term for side, *yerekh,* is used only in connection with the longer dimension of the Tabernacle, the north and south (3:35; see Exod. 40:22,24). Elsewhere *pe'ah* is also used (e.g., Exod. 26:18,20).

31. sacred utensils Itemized in 4:7,9,14.

screen Hebrew *masakh,* also called *parokhet;* see Exodus 26:1–33, Numbers 4:5. The Peshitta adds here "the laver and its base," for these also constituted "most sacred" sancta (Exod. 30:28) and would be expected to be placed in the custody of the Kohathites. The same addition is made in 4:14 by the Septuagint, the Samaritan, and the Peshitta.

all the service connected with these Rather, "including their removal"; see verse 26. *'Avodah* of the Kohathites is limited to porterage.

32. attending to the duties Rather, "performing the guard duty" (cf. v. 7). The Hittite "Instructions for Temple Officials" stipulate: "One of the high priests shall be in charge of the patrols" (III.12; ANET, p. 209). Thus Eleazar was head of all the Levite chieftains not only in respect to guard duty but also for their labors (4:16).

in charge of Hebrew *pekudat,* "responsible for" (see 4:16).

sanctuary Rather, "sancta," *kodesh* (see 4:15–16). Eleazar was in charge of the Levitical guards and was personally responsible for guarding the sacred objects enumerated in verse 31.

36. furnishings Rather, "tools." *Kelim* are called literally "work tools" in 4:26,32 and distinguished from *kelei kodesh/sharet,* literally "holy/service vessels" (e.g., 3:31; 4:12).

all the service connected with these Rather, "including their removal"; see the Comment to verse 26.

³⁸Those who were to camp before the Tabernacle, in front—before the Tent of Meeting, on the east—were Moses and Aaron and his sons, attending to the duties of the sanctuary, as a duty on behalf of the Israelites; and any outsider who encroached was to be put to death. ³⁹All the Levites who were recorded, whom at the LORD's command Moses and Aaron recorded by their clans, all the males from the age of one month up, came to 22,000.

⁴⁰The LORD said to Moses: Record every first-born male of the Israelite people from the age of one month up, and make a list of their names; ⁴¹and take the Levites for Me, the

38 וְהַחֹנִ֣ים לִפְנֵ֣י הַמִּשְׁכָּ֡ן קֵ֣דְמָה לִפְנֵי֩ אֹֽהֶל־
מוֹעֵ֨ד ׀ מִזְרָ֜חָה מֹשֶׁ֣ה ׀ וְאַהֲרֹ֣ן וּבָנָ֗יו שֹֽׁמְרִים֙
מִשְׁמֶ֣רֶת הַמִּקְדָּ֔שׁ לְמִשְׁמֶ֖רֶת בְּנֵ֣י יִשְׂרָאֵ֑ל וְהַזָּ֥ר
הַקָּרֵ֖ב יוּמָֽת׃ 39 כָּל־פְּקוּדֵ֨י הַלְוִיִּ֜ם אֲשֶׁר֩ פָּקַ֨ד
מֹשֶׁ֧ה וְ֯אַהֲרֹ֛ן עַל־פִּ֥י יְהוָ֖ה לְמִשְׁפְּחֹתָ֑ם כָּל־זָכָ֛ר
מִבֶּן־חֹ֥דֶשׁ וָמַ֖עְלָה שְׁנַ֥יִם וְעֶשְׂרִ֖ים אָֽלֶף׃ ס
שׁשׁי

40 וַיֹּ֨אמֶר יְהוָ֜ה אֶל־מֹשֶׁ֗ה פְּקֹ֨ד כָּל־בְּכֹ֤ר זָכָר֙
לִבְנֵ֣י יִשְׂרָאֵ֔ל מִבֶּן־חֹ֖דֶשׁ וָמָ֑עְלָה וְשָׂ֕א אֵ֖ת מִסְפַּ֥ר
שְׁמֹתָֽם׃ 41 וְלָקַחְתָּ֨ אֶת־הַלְוִיִּ֤ם לִי֙ אֲנִ֣י יְהוָ֔ה תַּ֣חַת

v. 39. נקוד על ואהרן

38. to camp Since the priests had no watch posts outside the sacred area, "camp" refers only to their place of residence, located in the east, which was closest to their guarding assignment, the entrance to and interior of the sacred area. The participles *ḥonim* and *shomerim* (contrast *yaḥanu* for the Levitical clans, vv. 23,29,35) indicate that the priestly encampment was also the place of their watch. This is what one would expect, for the entrance to the Tabernacle was in the east, where it was most vulnerable to encroachment.

sanctuary Rather, "sacred area." Hebrew *mikdash* in the priestly writings never means the sanctuary building but refers to the sacred *area* (e.g., Lev. 12:4) or to the sacred *objects,* that is, the sancta (e.g., Lev. 21:23). Thus *mikdash* here is distinguished from *kodesh,* literally "sancta" in verse 32.

on behalf of the Israelites By replacing their first-born. Another interpretation is suggested by Numbers Rabba 3:12 (followed by Ibn Ezra, Abravanel, and *Sefer ha-Mivḥar*): as a guard duty *against* the Israelites since the very purpose of guard duty is to prevent Israelite encroachment upon the sanctuary (see Excursuses 4 and 5). Thus the two halves of this verse would be logically connected; but this rendering is difficult on syntactical grounds.

and any outsider who encroached was Rather, "any outsider who encroaches shall" (see Excursus 5). The singular of this repeated formula stands out in startling relief against its plural context (1:51; 3:10; 18:7). In this verse, in particular, the contrast is even more striking. The first half of the text concludes with "Israelites," but it does not continue with the same subject or its pronoun (or a purpose clause; cf. 18:22) but with a new subject, *ha-zar,* "the stranger," in the singular. Clearly, this is a standard formula that must have had its own independent history (see Excursus 5 for details).

39. at the LORD's command Rather, "by the Lord's oracle" (see v. 16).

Aaron Missing in some Hebrew manuscripts and in the Samaritan and the Peshitta. The superlinear points over the name indicate that the Masoretes regarded it suspiciously. That Aaron's name may have been originally omitted is further supported by the singular verb *pakad* and by Aaron's absence once again in verses 14 and 16. However, Aaron is included in the second census of chapter 4, as Eleazar, the High Priest, is in the second census in 26:1,3,63.

REPLACING THE ISRAELITE FIRST-BORN   (vv. 40–51)

The number of Israelite first-born exceeds that of the Levites by 273. The latter, chosen by lot, are redeemed by the payment of five shekels per person to the priests. This procedure becomes the standard for the redemption of all Israelite first-born (see the Comment to 18:16). The cattle of the Levites are also substituted for the cattle of the first-born, thereby freeing the latter for common use. The number of the first-born, 22,273, cannot be reconciled with the totals of the Israelite fighting force, 603,550 (1:46). Even assuming as many first-born females as males, these figures presume an average Israelite family of fourteen male children.

LORD, in place of every first-born among the Israelite people, and the cattle of the Levites in place of every first-born among the cattle of the Israelites. 42So Moses recorded all the first-born among the Israelites, as the LORD had commanded him. 43All the first-born males as listed by name, recorded from the age of one month up, came to 22,273.

44The LORD spoke to Moses, saying: 45Take the Levites in place of all the first-born among the Israelite people, and the cattle of the Levites in place of their cattle; and the Levites shall be Mine, the LORD's. 46And as the redemption price of the 273 Israelite first-born over and above the number of the Levites, 47take five shekels per head—take this by the sanctuary weight, twenty *gerahs* to the shekel—48and give the money to Aaron and his sons as the redemption price for those who are in excess. 49So Moses took the

כָּל־בְּכֹר בִּבְנֵי יִשְׂרָאֵל וְאֵת בֶּהֱמַת הַלְוִיִּם תַּחַת
כָּל־בְּכוֹר בְּבֶהֱמַת בְּנֵי יִשְׂרָאֵל׃ 42 וַיִּפְקֹד מֹשֶׁה
כַּאֲשֶׁר צִוָּה יְהוָה אֹתוֹ אֶת־כָּל־בְּכֹר בִּבְנֵי
יִשְׂרָאֵל׃ 43 וַיְהִי כָל־בְּכוֹר זָכָר בְּמִסְפַּר שֵׁמֹת
מִבֶּן־חֹדֶשׁ וָמַעְלָה לִפְקֻדֵיהֶם שְׁנַיִם וְעֶשְׂרִים אֶלֶף
שְׁלֹשָׁה וְשִׁבְעִים וּמָאתָיִם׃ פ
44 וַיְדַבֵּר יְהוָה אֶל־מֹשֶׁה לֵּאמֹר׃ 45 קַח אֶת־
הַלְוִיִּם תַּחַת כָּל־בְּכוֹר בִּבְנֵי יִשְׂרָאֵל וְאֶת־בֶּהֱמַת
הַלְוִיִּם תַּחַת בְּהֶמְתָּם וְהָיוּ־לִי הַלְוִיִּם אֲנִי יְהוָה׃
46 וְאֵת פְּדוּיֵי הַשְּׁלֹשָׁה וְהַשִּׁבְעִים וְהַמָּאתָיִם
הָעֹדְפִים עַל־הַלְוִיִּם מִבְּכוֹר בְּנֵי יִשְׂרָאֵל׃
47 וְלָקַחְתָּ חֲמֵשֶׁת חֲמֵשֶׁת שְׁקָלִים לַגֻּלְגֹּלֶת
בְּשֶׁקֶל הַקֹּדֶשׁ תִּקָּח עֶשְׂרִים גֵּרָה הַשָּׁקֶל׃
48 וְנָתַתָּה הַכֶּסֶף לְאַהֲרֹן וּלְבָנָיו פְּדוּיֵי הָעֹדְפִים
בָּהֶם׃ 49 וַיִּקַּח מֹשֶׁה אֵת כֶּסֶף הַפִּדְיוֹם מֵאֵת

40. one month up An infant younger than thirty days old was not considered a person,[26] presumably because of the high rate of infant mortality.[27] This principle is still operative in Jewish practice. Thus, no mourning rites are maintained for an infant under thirty days old.[28]

make Rather, "by making" (cf. 1:2).

a list of their names In distinction to the Levites, who were tallied by oracle (see v. 15).

41. and take In verse 12, God is the subject of this verb. The difference is clear: God's taking implies His choosing; Moses' taking is for performing the ceremony (see the Comment to 8:5).

every first-born among the cattle of the Israelites Since the first-born of pure animals automatically belonged to the Lord (they must anyway be sacrificed on the altar and may not be redeemed, Lev. 27:26; Num. 18:15,17), the rabbis, in Bekhorot 4b, conclude that the redeemed Israelite animals must have been impure, ineligible for the altar, and therefore redeemable.[29]

45. their cattle That is, of the Israelite first-born. Just as the erstwhile sacred first-born Israelites must be redeemed, so must their cattle, which belong to God and would otherwise be destined for the altar if pure and for sanctuary use if impure.[30] The cattle of the Levites release the animals of the first-born from their erstwhile sacred status. However, this does not mean that the Levites' cattle now become sacred any more than do the Levites themselves when they replace the first-born (see the Comment to v. 9).

It would appear that animals given to the priests are intended for the sanctuary and not for their personal possession. The Levites, however, retained their animals. Significantly, only the Levites received cities and pastureland (Num. 35:1–8), not the priests (Josh. 21). Moreover, when the Midianite spoils are apportioned (Num. 31), the priests' share is given to Eleazar alone (not to the other priests). It is called *terumat YHVH,* "a contribution to the LORD" (31:29,41), that is, to the sanctuary. The Levites, on the other hand, receive their share directly as their personal property (31:30,47). Thus their cattle release the animals of the Israelite first-born from their sacred status. The purpose of the exchange, then, is to ensure that the sanctuary not be deprived of its animals when the first-born Israelites are desacralized.[31]

46. redemption price[32] The Hebrew verb *padah* generally denotes a process by which something lost to the original owner can be recovered through the payment of money (e.g., 18:15–16).

47. by the sanctuary weight See Exodus 30:13. The shekel is a silver weight not a coin (coinage was not invented until the 7th cent. B.C.E. and was not minted in Judah until the 4th cent.). It weighed about 11.5 grams.

redemption money from those over and above the ones
redeemed by the Levites; 50he took the money from the
first-born of the Israelites, 1,365 sanctuary shekels. 51And
Moses gave the redemption money to Aaron and his sons at
the LORD's bidding, as the LORD had commanded Moses.

הָעֹדְפִים עַל פְּדוּיֵי הַלְוִיִּם׃ 50 מֵאֵת בְּכוֹר בְּנֵי
יִשְׂרָאֵל לָקַח אֶת־הַכָּסֶף חֲמִשָּׁה וְשִׁשִּׁים וּשְׁלֹשׁ
מֵאוֹת וָאֶלֶף בְּשֶׁקֶל הַקֹּדֶשׁ׃ 51 וַיִּתֵּן מֹשֶׁה אֶת־
כֶּסֶף הַפְּדֻיִם* לְאַהֲרֹן וּלְבָנָיו עַל־פִּי יְהוָה כַּאֲשֶׁר
צִוָּה יְהוָה אֶת־מֹשֶׁה׃ פ שביעי

4 The LORD spoke to Moses and Aaron, saying:
2Take a [separate] census of the Kohathites among the
Levites, by the clans of their ancestral house, 3from the age
of thirty years up to the age of fifty, all who are subject to
service, to perform tasks for the Tent of Meeting. 4This is

ד וַיְדַבֵּר יְהוָה אֶל־מֹשֶׁה וְאֶל־אַהֲרֹן לֵאמֹר׃
2 נָשֹׂא אֶת־רֹאשׁ בְּנֵי קְהָת מִתּוֹךְ בְּנֵי לֵוִי
לְמִשְׁפְּחֹתָם לְבֵית אֲבֹתָם׃ 3 מִבֶּן שְׁלֹשִׁים שָׁנָה
וָמַעְלָה וְעַד בֶּן־חֲמִשִּׁים שָׁנָה כָּל־בָּא לַצָּבָא

v. 51. חסר ו'

49. *redemption* Here the Hebrew word is written *pidyom,* a parallel form of *pidyon* (e.g., Exod. 21:30).[33]

51. *bidding* By an oracle (see v. 15).

CHAPTER 4

The Second Levite Census (vv. 1–49)

This chapter records a second census of the Levites between the ages of thirty and fifty for the purpose of ascertaining the size of the work force necessary for the transport of the sanctuary during the wilderness march.

REMOVAL DUTIES OF THE KOHATHITES (vv. 1–20)

The Kohathites are listed first, even though Kohath is not the first-born. This contrasts with the first Levitical census (3:14–39) where the clan of Gershon, the first-born, is mustered first (cf. v. 17). There are two reasons for the ordering here: The work of the Kohathites involved greater responsibility because they transported the most sacred sancta (Num. R. 4:12; 6:1), and their work was more hazardous since they risked their lives (vv. 15–20; 18:1). Behind the shift in clan preeminence among the Levites is a historic change discussed in Excursus 39.

1. *Aaron* His name is missing from this verse in a few manuscripts; it is also not found in the command to count the Gershonites (v. 21) and Merarites (v. 29). Perhaps Aaron is introduced now because the most sacred sancta were assigned to the Kohathites for transport under the direction of Aaron and his sons specifically (v. 19; Num. R. 6:5). Aaron is, however, mentioned when the census is carried out for each of the Levitical clans (vv. 34,41,45).[1]

2. *among the Levites* This phrase is not used in connection with the Gershonites and Merarites, indicating that the Kohathites were distinguished from their fellow clans by being privileged to carry the sancta. For a different tradition concerning the starting age, see 8:24.

3. *subject to service* Hebrew *ba' la-tsava'* implies nonmilitary service (cf. 4:23; 8:24) as opposed to *yotsei' tsava',* "go to war" (cf. 1:3).[2] *Ba'* bears the technical meaning of "qualify" (cf. 8:22 and especially v. 24).[3]

tasks Hebrew *mela'khah* implies skilled labor[4] as opposed to *'avodah,* the physical labor of the other Levites. The Kohathites had to be more circumspect and skillful in carrying the lethal sancta (cf. vv. 15–20).

לַעֲשׂוֹת מְלָאכָה בְּאֹהֶל מוֹעֵד׃ 4 זֹאת עֲבֹדַת בְּנֵי־
קְהָת בְּאֹהֶל מוֹעֵד קֹדֶשׁ הַקֳּדָשִׁים׃ 5 וּבָא אַהֲרֹן
וּבָנָיו בִּנְסֹעַ הַמַּחֲנֶה וְהוֹרִדוּ אֵת פָּרֹכֶת הַמָּסָךְ
וְכִסּוּ־בָהּ אֵת אֲרֹן הָעֵדֻת׃ 6 וְנָתְנוּ עָלָיו כְּסוּי עוֹר

the responsibility of the Kohathites in the Tent of Meeting: the most sacred objects.

5 At the breaking of camp, Aaron and his sons shall go in and take down the screening curtain and cover the Ark of the Pact with it. 6 They shall lay a covering of dolphin skin

4. *the most sacred objects* The specific job of the Kohathites is the porterage of the most sacred objects (enumerated in vv. 5–15) by shoulder (4:15; 7:9).

Only the priests, who were sacred, were qualified to handle the Ark and the other sancta. The Kohathites, however, had no sacred status (see 3:9) and hence their touching and even seeing the uncovered sancta could be fatal (vv. 15–20). Thus Aaron and his sons had to cover the sancta before the Kohathites could enter the sacred area to attend to their transport (Num. R. 4:19).

The sancta are distinguished from each other in accordance with their degree of sanctity by their number, color, and the quality of their covers. The covers themselves are graded according to their colors. Their established sequence, attested consistently throughout Scripture (e.g., Exod. 25:4), reveals the order of their sanctity: ***tekhelet,*** "violet" (blue-purple); ***'argaman,*** "purple" (red-purple); and ***tola'at shani,*** "crimson." ***Taḥash,*** "yellow-orange," is not one of the sacred colors but is used to dye skins (i.e., leather, not cloth) for the sole purpose of protecting the objects it covers from the elements. Hence, with the exception of the Ark, the Tabernacle in camp and the sancta in transit are always covered with the yellow-orange skins (vv. 8,10,11,14; Exod. 26:14).

The Ark, the holiest of the sancta, was covered first by the screening curtain, which itself was composed of all three sacred colors (Exod. 26:31), followed by a yellow-orange and, last, a violet cover. The table, next in sequence and, hence, in holiness, was covered first by a violet cloth, followed by a crimson and then a yellow-orange cloth. The lampstand and golden altar were covered by violet and yellow-orange cloths. The sacrificial altar and probably the laver (see the Comment to vv. 13–14)—the least holy of the sancta since they stood outside in the court and not in the tent—were provided with purple and yellow-orange cloths.

Thus, the sacred colors of the sancta as well as their sequence indicate their holiness rank. The Ark, covered by all three sacred colors, is the holiest. The table, next in holiness, claimed two sacred colors. The golden altar and the lampstand were provided with one sacred color, violet, denoting that they were equal in holiness. The sacrificial altar and probably the laver were also granted one sacred color, but it was purple not violet. In this manner the sequence of the sancta is marked by the differentiation in the colors of their covers, both signifying a descending order in holiness. These distinctions are matched by the quality and workmanship of the sancta themselves: The inner sancta are made of gold, the outer altar of copper[5] (cf. Exod. 25–27). The order of dismantling the sancta is the same as for reassembling them (Exod. 40:17–33).

5–6. *the Ark* The most sacred of the sancta, the Ark, is covered first. The midrash considers it the earthly counterpart of the heavenly throne (Num. R. 4:13), a reflex of the ancient tradition that the Ark was indeed the divine throne/chariot upon which the Lord is either seated, as in 1 Samuel 4:4 and 2 Samuel 6:2, or riding, as in 2 Samuel 22:11 and Psalms 68:5,34. The Ark was protected by three covers.

It should be noted that the cloths of the other sacred objects are not qualified by the adjective ***kalil,*** "pure." Another distinction for the Ark was that the violet cloth was uppermost, probably to distinguish it from the other sancta, which were covered on top by yellow-orange cloths (Num. R. 14:3). Since the function of the latter was to protect the sancta against dust and rain, perhaps the Ark's violet cover was allowed to be topmost only when weather permitted (cf. Ibn Ezra). For the meaning of the name "Ark of the Pact," see the Comment to 7:89.

the screening curtain It separated the Holy of Holies from the rest of the sanctuary (Exod. 26:31–33). Why was it not given to the Gershonites as were the other Tabernacle curtains made of the same material and workmanship and, hence, possessing the same degree of holiness? The answer lies

תַּחַשׁ וּפָרְשׂוּ בֶגֶד־כְּלִיל תְּכֵלֶת מִלְמַעְלָה וְשָׂמוּ
בַּדָּיו׃ 7 וְעַל ׀ שֻׁלְחַן הַפָּנִים יִפְרְשׂוּ בֶּגֶד תְּכֵלֶת
וְנָתְנוּ עָלָיו אֶת־הַקְּעָרֹת וְאֶת־הַכַּפֹּת וְאֶת־
הַמְּנַקִּיֹּת וְאֵת קְשׂוֹת הַנָּסֶךְ וְלֶחֶם הַתָּמִיד עָלָיו
יִהְיֶה׃ 8 וּפָרְשׂוּ עֲלֵיהֶם בֶּגֶד תּוֹלַעַת שָׁנִי וְכִסּוּ
אֹתוֹ בְּמִכְסֵה עוֹר תָּחַשׁ וְשָׂמוּ אֶת־בַּדָּיו׃
9 וְלָקְחוּ ׀ בֶּגֶד תְּכֵלֶת וְכִסּוּ אֶת־מְנֹרַת הַמָּאוֹר

over it and spread a cloth of pure blue on top; and they shall put its poles in place.
7Over the table of display they shall spread a blue cloth; they shall place upon it the bowls, the ladles, the jars, and the libation jugs; and the regular bread shall rest upon it.
8They shall spread over these a crimson cloth which they shall cover with a covering of dolphin skin; and they shall put the poles in place.
9Then they shall take a blue cloth and cover the lamp-

in the fact that the priests, like everyone else, were forbidden to look at the Ark. That it is the Ark's first cover suggests the possibility that when the priests entered the sanctuary they first removed the screening curtain and, holding it high before them, proceeded forward until they could lay it upon the Ark. In this way, the curtain would function like the cloud of incense that Aaron raised in the shrine on the Day of Atonement (Lev. 16:2,13); even for the High Priest, the sight of the exposed Ark was considered to be fatal.[6]

dolphin Hebrew *taḥash*. Rather, "yellow-orange"[7] (and so in vv. 8,10,11,12).

cloth Rather, "garment" (and so throughout vv. 6–14). In Scripture, *beged* usually covers only human beings; it is no accident that a conspicuous exception is made with all the sancta in that they too are initially covered by a *beged*. They are treated with the same respect as human beings, indeed, like royalty since they are dressed in regal clothing made of violet or purple (see Excursus 38). Since the *beged* must totally enclose the sanctum so that no part is exposed, it must have been a garment into which the entire sanctum could be fitted, with an opening for the protruding poles. The fact that the *beged* acted like a bag is shown by its use for the service vessels where the verbal phrase is *ve-natnu 'el*, "put (them) into" (v. 12).

blue Hebrew *tekhelet*. Rather, "violet" (so throughout); see Excursus 38.

put its poles in place The Ark, the display table, and the altars were fitted with rings into which poles were inserted for carrying, whereas the lampstand (probably the laver, see v. 14) and some utensils were set into carrying frames.[8]

7–8. table of display The fuller term for this object is the table of display bread, so-called because every Sabbath twelve loaves of bread arranged in two rows were displayed on a table before God in the sanctuary (Lev. 24:5–9). The table had three covers. Its colors were violet, crimson, and yellow-orange. It ranked second in importance among the sancta, as is clear from its listing after the Ark and from the fact that it had three covers like the Ark whereas the other sancta were assigned only two.[9]

libation jugs Since they were made of gold (Exod. 25:29; 37:16), they were not originally intended for the wine libations on the outer altar (Num. 15:5,7,10), for the latter's vessels were exclusively bronze (Exod. 27:3; 38:3). Nor could they have served the inner altar upon which libations were strictly forbidden (Exod. 30:9). In pre-Israelite pagan practice food and drink were regularly offered up on the god's table. In Israel this notion—that God needs food—was vigorously denied (cf. Ps. 50:13); and the Israelite cult, in its polemic against paganism, prohibited any food offerings inside the shrine (Exod. 30:9), restricting them to the outer altar.[10] As a result of this prohibition, the bread on the table was eaten in its entirety by the priests (Lev. 24:9), and the libation jugs, also associated with the table, may have been used for the wine libations for the outer altar. This was the practice of the Second Temple, according to the rabbis (e.g., Tosef. Zev. 1:12). According to rabbinic sources, they were also used for water libations (Mish. Sanh. 9:6). Perhaps it is no accident that, in the Second Temple, the vessel containing the libation water was made of gold (Mish. Suk. 4:9).

regular bread Hebrew *leḥem ha-tamid*, that is, the twelve loaves of bread regularly changed every Sabbath (Lev. 24:8); an ellipsis of *leḥem panim lefanai tamid*, literally "bread of display before Me regularly" (Exod. 25:30).

stand for lighting, with its lamps, its tongs, and its fire pans, as well as all the oil vessels that are used in its service. 10They shall put it and all its furnishings into a covering of dolphin skin, which they shall then place on a carrying frame.

11Next they shall spread a blue cloth over the altar of gold and cover it with a covering of dolphin skin; and they shall put its poles in place. 12They shall take all the service vessels with which the service in the sanctuary is performed, put them into a blue cloth and cover them with a covering of dolphin skin, which they shall then place on a carrying frame. 13They shall remove the ashes from the [copper] altar and spread a purple cloth over it. 14Upon it they shall place

וְאֶת־נֵרֹתֶיהָ וְאֶת־מַלְקָחֶיהָ וְאֶת־מַחְתֹּתֶיהָ וְאֵת
כָּל־כְּלֵי שַׁמְנָהּ אֲשֶׁר יְשָׁרְתוּ־לָהּ בָּהֶם׃ 10 וְנָתְנוּ
אֹתָהּ וְאֶת־כָּל־כֵּלֶיהָ אֶל־מִכְסֵה עוֹר תָּחַשׁ וְנָתְנוּ
עַל־הַמּוֹט׃ 11 וְעַל ׀ מִזְבַּח הַזָּהָב יִפְרְשׂוּ בֶּגֶד
תְּכֵלֶת וְכִסּוּ אֹתוֹ בְּמִכְסֵה עוֹר תָּחַשׁ וְשָׂמוּ אֶת־
בַּדָּיו׃ 12 וְלָקְחוּ אֶת־כָּל־כְּלֵי הַשָּׁרֵת אֲשֶׁר
יְשָׁרְתוּ־בָם בַּקֹּדֶשׁ וְנָתְנוּ אֶל־בֶּגֶד תְּכֵלֶת וְכִסּוּ
אוֹתָם בְּמִכְסֵה עוֹר תָּחַשׁ וְנָתְנוּ עַל־הַמּוֹט׃
13 וְדִשְּׁנוּ אֶת־הַמִּזְבֵּחַ וּפָרְשׂוּ עָלָיו בֶּגֶד אַרְגָּמָן׃

9–10. The lampstand For greater details on the composition of the lampstand, the menorah, see Exodus 25:31–40. Here, as in Exodus 35:14, it is given the fuller title, "the lampstand for lighting."

lamps The lamps and the lampstand are separate objects.[11]

fire pans For removing the ashes from the lamps, according to Rashi.

carrying frame The menorah and its utensils could not be suspended on poles like the Ark and table and thus required the construction of a special carrying frame, perhaps a "flat surface on which a variety of objects could be placed and carried."[12]

dolphin See the Comment to verse 6.

11. altar of gold It was also known as the altar of incense (Exod. 31:8; cf. 30:1) and was carried on poles. The utensils of the incense altar are not mentioned, although some, like Rashi, find them intimated in verse 12. The likelihood is that there were none. It must be remembered that the surface of this altar was only one cubit square. Nothing was burnt on it but incense, which left no residue. Thus there was no need for any of the utensils mentioned in connection with the sacrificial altar (v. 14). Supporting evidence is found in the sancta list of Exodus 30:27–28, where again the incense altar is the only sanctum mentioned without utensils (Exod. 40:21–29; cf. Num. R. 4:18).

12. service vessels The *kelei ha-sharet* is a general designation of the utensils associated with the major cult objects (vv. 4,9,14; cf. 2 Chron. 24:14). But here the reference is to whatever additional vessels are used inside the Tent, especially with the incense altar. The verb *sheret* with the priests as its subject means "perform in the service" or "officiate" (see 3:6).

in the sanctuary Hebrew *ba-kodesh* literally means "inside the sanctuary" (see v. 15), excluding the sancta and utensils of the courtyard, proved by the fact that the service vessels are put into a violet garment, the same which covers all the interior sancta.

13–14. the altar All the sancta inside the sanctuary having been covered, the text turns to the last and lowest ranking of the sancta, the copper sacrificial altar of the courtyard.

remove the ashes from[13]

purple cloth[14] Rather, "purple garment" (see the Comment to v. 6). In distinction to the sancta of the sanctuary whose covering was made of violet[15] (Num. R. 4:16), the outer altar was wrapped in a purple garment, an indication of the decreasing degree of holiness in moving from the shrine outward into the courtyard.

The Septuagint and the Samaritan add at the end of verse 14: "and they shall take a purple

all the vessels that are used in its service: the fire pans, the flesh hooks, the scrapers, and the basins—all the vessels of the altar—and over it they shall spread a covering of dolphin skin; and they shall put its poles in place.

15 When Aaron and his sons have finished covering the sacred objects and all the furnishings of the sacred objects at the breaking of camp, only then shall the Kohathites come and lift them, so that they do not come in contact with the sacred objects and die. These things in the Tent of Meeting shall be the porterage of the Kohathites.

16 Responsibility shall rest with Eleazar son of Aaron the priest for the lighting oil, the aromatic incense, the regular meal offering, and the anointing oil—responsibility for the whole Tabernacle and for everything consecrated that is in it or in its vessels.

14 וְנָתְנ֣וּ עָלָ֗יו אֶֽת־כָּל־כֵּלָ֞יו אֲשֶׁ֣ר יְשָׁרְת֣וּ עָלָ֪יו
בָּהֶ֟ם אֶת־הַמַּחְתֹּ֤ת אֶת־הַמִּזְלָגֹת֙ וְאֶת־הַיָּעִ֣ים
וְאֶת־הַמִּזְרָקֹ֔ת כֹּ֖ל כְּלֵ֣י הַמִּזְבֵּ֑חַ וּפָרְשׂ֣וּ עָלָ֗יו כְּס֛וּי
ע֥וֹר תַּ֖חַשׁ וְשָׂמ֥וּ בַדָּֽיו׃ 15 וְכִלָּ֣ה אַהֲרֹן֩ וּבָנָ֨יו
לְכַסֹּ֜ת אֶת־הַקֹּ֣דֶשׁ וְאֶת־כָּל־כְּלֵ֣י הַקֹּדֶשׁ֮ בִּנְסֹ֣עַ
הַֽמַּחֲנֶה֒ וְאַחֲרֵי־כֵ֗ן יָבֹ֤אוּ בְנֵֽי־קְהָת֙ לָשֵׂ֔את וְלֹֽא־
יִגְּע֥וּ אֶל־הַקֹּ֖דֶשׁ וָמֵ֑תוּ אֵ֛לֶּה מַשָּׂ֥א בְנֵֽי־קְהָ֖ת
בְּאֹ֥הֶל מוֹעֵֽד׃ 16 וּפְקֻדַּ֞ת אֶלְעָזָ֣ר ׀ בֶּן־אַהֲרֹ֣ן הַכֹּהֵ֗ן
שֶׁ֤מֶן הַמָּאוֹר֙ וּקְטֹ֣רֶת הַסַּמִּ֔ים וּמִנְחַ֥ת הַתָּמִ֖יד
וְשֶׁ֣מֶן הַמִּשְׁחָ֑ה פְּקֻדַּ֗ת כָּל־הַמִּשְׁכָּן֙ וְכָל־אֲשֶׁר־בּ֔וֹ
בְּקֹ֖דֶשׁ וּבְכֵלָֽיו׃ ס מפטיר 17 וַיְדַבֵּ֣ר יְהוָ֔ה

garment and cover the laver and its base and shall put them within a covering of yellow-orange and place them on a carrying frame." This addition is essential since the laver is elsewhere ranked among the most sacred objects, as in Exodus 30:28–29, hence requiring covering for transport.

14. all the vessels Mentioned in Exodus 27:3 with the exception of "the pails for removing the ashes."[16]

the basins Rather, "the tossing bowls," to dash the sacrificial blood on the altar.

15. Aaron and his sons have finished The conclusion of the priestly assignment that began with "Aaron and his sons shall go in" (v. 5). Both verbs are in the singular.

sacred objects Hebrew *kodesh* can refer either to sacred space (shrine, sanctuary, or sacred area; cf. v. 12) or to sacred cult objects. The latter meaning is intended here (as in v. 16; 3:32).

furnishings of the sacred objects Rather, "sacred utensils" (= "service vessels"; see v. 12; enumerated in vv. 7,9,14).

shall the Kohathites come That is, go in. Hebrew *yavo'u* corresponds to "Aaron and his sons shall go in," *u-va'* (v. 5).

contact Even contact with the covered sancta can be as fatal as seeing them uncovered (v. 20). No wonder the removal labors of the Kohathites are termed *mela'khah,* "skilled labor" (v. 3).

porterage Hebrew *massa',* an inclusion to verse 49. The removal labor, *'avodah,* requires skill, *mela'khah,* since it concerns specifically the lethal sancta that must be carried *(massa')* by shoulder. Since the dismantling and reassembling of the sancta is performed by the priests, the Kohathites are responsible only for their porterage. Thus *massa'* can be used to describe the job profile of the Kohathites (as in 7:9).

16. Responsibility Two areas of responsibility (*pekudah;* cf. 3:32) are delineated for Eleazar the priest. First, as the overseer of the Kohathites, he is personally in charge of the sacred ingredients used with the sancta carried by the Kohathites: the oil for lighting the menorah, the incense for the incense altar, the regular meal offering of the High Priest, Aaron (sacrificed twice daily on behalf of the priesthood, Lev. 6:12–16, and prepared by the priest anointed to succeed Aaron, Lev. 6:15, i.e., Eleazar), and the anointing oil used in consecrating both the sancta and the priests (Exod. 30:22–30). Eleazar is not to carry these ingredients personally[17] but is to supervise scrupulously their porterage by reliable Kohathites.[18] The second responsibility, indicated in the second half of the verse, refers to Eleazar's supervisory role over the Gershonite and Merarite clans in addition to his own. As Eleazar is chief of the Levite guards (3:32), he is also chief of the Levite labor battalions.

17The LORD spoke to Moses and Aaron, saying: 18Do not
let the group of Kohathite clans be cut off from the Levites.
19Do this with them, that they may live and not die when
they approach the most sacred objects: let Aaron and his
sons go in and assign each of them to his duties and to his
porterage. 20But let not [the Kohathites] go inside and
witness the dismantling of the sanctuary, lest they die.

אֶל־מֹשֶׁה וְאֶל־אַהֲרֹן לֵאמֹר: 18 אַל־תַּכְרִיתוּ אֶת־
שֵׁבֶט מִשְׁפְּחֹת הַקְּהָתִי מִתּוֹךְ הַלְוִיִּם: 19 וְזֹאת ׀
עֲשׂוּ לָהֶם וְחָיוּ וְלֹא יָמֻתוּ בְּגִשְׁתָּם אֶת־קֹדֶשׁ
הַקֳּדָשִׁים אַהֲרֹן וּבָנָיו יָבֹאוּ וְשָׂמוּ אוֹתָם אִישׁ
אִישׁ עַל־עֲבֹדָתוֹ וְאֶל־מַשָּׂאוֹ: 20 וְלֹא־יָבֹאוּ
לִרְאוֹת כְּבַלַּע אֶת־הַקֹּדֶשׁ וָמֵתוּ: פ

regular meal offering The exact reference is uncertain. The display bread, which was inseparable from the table (v. 7), may be intended, as might also be the supplement of the daily ***tamid*** sacrifice (Exod. 29:40). If the latter, it is not clear why the accompanying wine is not mentioned. Most probably the private daily offering of the anointed priest is meant. In Aaron's time, this was offered by Eleazar (Lev. 6:15).

everything consecrated that is in it or in its vessels Rather, "everything in it, whether the sacred objects or their utensils" (cf. v. 15).

17–20. An elaboration of verse 15, these verses detail the lethal hazards of the removal job assigned to the Kohathites.

18. ***group*** Hebrew *shevet,* literally "tribe"; but since there is no other term for a group of clans *(mishpaḥot),* it can only be rendered "group." However, the synonymous term ***matteh*** is not so fluid but can only mean "tribe" (see Excursus 1).

be cut off Hebrew ***takhritu.*** The penalty of ***karet,*** "to be cut off," is inflicted only by God; since the Kohathites face divine wrath for any mishap with the sancta, this term is quite appropriate here. For the meaning of ***karet*** see Excursus 36.

from the Levites Only the Kohathites, who carry the sancta, are in mortal danger, not the Gershonites or Merarites.

19. ***approach*** Rather, "make contact with." The Hebrew word ***nagash,*** like its synonym, ***karav,*** does not in these cultic contexts mean "approach" but "have access, handle," implying direct contact. There is no prohibition against approaching sancta (with the exception of the Ark), only against encroaching upon them (see Excursus 5).[19]

most sacred objects Hebrew ***kodesh ha-kodashim.*** Elsewhere in this section the sancta are called ***kodesh*** (vv. 15,20), although technically the cult objects are in the category of "most sacred" by virtue of their consecration with the anointing oil (Exod. 30:29). They are called "most sacred" here to emphasize the reason for the death penalty. Also, it forms an inclusion with the same term in verse 4.[20]

to his duties and to his porterage Rather, "to his porterage work." The Kohathites have no other duties in the sanctuary removal except the porterage of the sancta. Therefore the Hebrew ***'al-'avodato ve-'el-massa'o*** should be regarded as a hendiadys, the equivalent of ***'avodat massa',*** "porterage work" (v. 47). The tandem ***'avad/massa'*** appears seven times in this chapter (vv. 19,24, 27,31,32,47,49), a probable literary device that emphasizes the main theme.[21]

20. ***go inside*** That is, into the Tent. Even the accidental viewing of the exposed sancta inside the sanctuary (but not of the courtyard altar, cf. Exod. 30:30) could prove fatal.[22] Rabbi Judah in the name of Rav, however, restricts the lethal power of the sancta only during the time of their dismantling but not when they are at rest (Yoma 54a). The taboo and the lethal danger in viewing sancta stem from ancient Near Eastern concepts. Thus, in one text, the city of Agade is cursed because "the Akkadians saw the holy vessels of the gods."[23] Another relates that Ur is destroyed because "the holy kettles that no one (was permitted) to look upon the enemy looked upon."[24]

the dismantling of Hebrew ***kevalla'.***[25]

sanctuary See verse 12 above or render "sacred objects" (v. 15, above).

NASO'

[21]The LORD spoke to Moses: [22]Take a census of the Gershonites also, by their ancestral house and by their clans. [23]Record them from the age of thirty years up to the age of fifty, all who are subject to service in the performance of tasks for the Tent of Meeting. [24]These are the duties of the Gershonite clans as to labor and porterage: [25]they shall carry the cloths of the Tabernacle, the Tent of Meeting with its covering, the covering of dolphin skin that is on top of it, and the screen for the entrance of the Tent of Meeting; [26]the hangings of the enclosure, the screen at the entrance of the gate of the enclosure that surrounds the Tabernacle, the cords thereof, and the altar, and all their service equipment and all their accessories; and they shall perform the service. [27]All the duties of the Gershonites, all their porter-

נשא

21 וַיְדַבֵּר יְהוָה אֶל־מֹשֶׁה לֵּאמֹר׃ 22 נָשֹׂא אֶת־
רֹאשׁ בְּנֵי גֵרְשׁוֹן גַּם־הֵם לְבֵית אֲבֹתָם
לְמִשְׁפְּחֹתָם׃ 23 מִבֶּן שְׁלֹשִׁים שָׁנָה וָמַעְלָה עַד
בֶּן־חֲמִשִּׁים שָׁנָה תִּפְקֹד אוֹתָם כָּל־הַבָּא לִצְבֹא
צָבָא לַעֲבֹד עֲבֹדָה בְּאֹהֶל מוֹעֵד׃ 24 זֹאת עֲבֹדַת
מִשְׁפְּחֹת הַגֵּרְשֻׁנִּי לַעֲבֹד וּלְמַשָּׂא׃ 25 וְנָשְׂאוּ אֶת־
יְרִיעֹת הַמִּשְׁכָּן וְאֶת־אֹהֶל מוֹעֵד מִכְסֵהוּ וּמִכְסֵה
הַתַּחַשׁ אֲשֶׁר־עָלָיו מִלְמָעְלָה וְאֶת־מָסַךְ פֶּתַח
אֹהֶל מוֹעֵד׃ 26 וְאֵת קַלְעֵי הֶחָצֵר וְאֶת־מָסַךְ ׀
פֶּתַח ׀ שַׁעַר הֶחָצֵר אֲשֶׁר עַל־הַמִּשְׁכָּן וְעַל־הַמִּזְבֵּחַ
סָבִיב וְאֵת מֵיתְרֵיהֶם וְאֶת־כָּל־כְּלֵי עֲבֹדָתָם וְאֵת
כָּל־אֲשֶׁר יֵעָשֶׂה לָהֶם וְעָבָדוּ׃ 27 עַל־פִּי אַהֲרֹן

REMOVAL DUTIES OF THE GERSHONITES AND MERARITES (vv. 21–33)

Naso' The former are assigned to the Tabernacle curtains and the latter to the Ṭabernacle structure. According to Abravanel, *parashat Naso'* was made to begin here, even though it interrupted the context, in order to restore prestige to the first-born Gershon, who had been displaced by Kohath in chapter 3.

22. *by their ancestral house and by their clans* These terms are in reverse order in verses 2 and 29, thereby forming a chiasm.[26]

23. *subject to service in the performance of tasks* Rather, "all who qualify to serve in the work force." *Ba'*, "qualify," is the opposite of *shav,* "retire" (see the Comment to 8:25 and Excursus 6).

24. *duties* Rather, "labors" (see Excursus 6).

labor Rather, "packing." *'Avodah* for the Gershonites and Merarites is limited to dismantling and assembling the Tabernacle (see Excursus 6).

and porterage Hebrew *u-le-massa'*.[27]

25. *carry* Rather, "transport," by packing and loading the curtains onto the wagons.

with its covering This layer consisted of reddened ram skins, followed by a fourth made of yellow-orange skins (Exod. 26:14). Numbers 3:25, on the other hand, implies that the red and yellow-orange skins comprised a single curtain.[28] This ambiguity may be a reflection of the fact that some sancta were covered by three cloths (the Ark and table) and others by two (the menorah and altars). Since the innermost Tabernacle curtain was anointed (Exod. 30:26; 40:9) and, hence, a sanctum, it was also in need of being covered either by two coverings (Num. 3:25) or, according to the tradition reflected in this verse, by three.

The difference between chapters 3 and 4 is nowhere as clear as in 3:25 and 4:25. The implements are the same, but chapter 3 speaks of their *mishmeret,* "guarding," and chapter 4 speaks of their *'avodah,* "removal."

26. *the cords thereof, and the altar* The cords held up the enclosure curtains (3:26), whereas the curtains of the Tent needed no cords; they were simply draped over the frame. However, the cords mentioned in verse 32 connect the posts to the pegs.

service equipment Rather, "work tools" (cf. Exod. 27:19).

and all their accessories Literally, "and all that is done to/for them," referring either to the Tabernacle curtains or to the work tools (i.e., their repair).[29]

age and all their service, shall be performed on orders from
Aaron and his sons; you shall make them responsible for
attending to all their porterage. 28 Those are the duties of
the Gershonite clans for the Tent of Meeting; they shall
attend to them under the direction of Ithamar son of Aaron
the priest.

29 As for the Merarites, you shall record them by the clans
of their ancestral house; 30 you shall record them from the
age of thirty years up to the age of fifty, all who are subject
to service in the performance of the duties for the Tent of
Meeting. 31 These are their porterage tasks in connection
with their various duties for the Tent of Meeting: the
planks, the bars, the posts, and the sockets of the Tabernacle; 32 the posts around the enclosure and their sockets,
pegs, and cords—all these furnishings and their service:
you shall list by name the objects that are their porterage
tasks. 33 Those are the duties of the Merarite clans, pertaining to their various duties in the Tent of Meeting under
the direction of Ithamar son of Aaron the priest.

וּבָנָיו תִּהְיֶה כָּל־עֲבֹדַת בְּנֵי הַגֵּרְשֻׁנִּי לְכָל־מַשָּׂאָם
וּלְכֹל עֲבֹדָתָם וּפְקַדְתֶּם עֲלֵהֶם בְּמִשְׁמֶרֶת אֵת
כָּל־מַשָּׂאָם׃ 28 זֹאת עֲבֹדַת מִשְׁפְּחֹת בְּנֵי הַגֵּרְשֻׁנִּי
בְּאֹהֶל מוֹעֵד וּמִשְׁמַרְתָּם בְּיַד אִיתָמָר בֶּן־אַהֲרֹן
הַכֹּהֵן׃ פ 29 בְּנֵי מְרָרִי לְמִשְׁפְּחֹתָם לְבֵית־
אֲבֹתָם תִּפְקֹד אֹתָם׃ 30 מִבֶּן שְׁלֹשִׁים שָׁנָה
וָמַעְלָה וְעַד בֶּן־חֲמִשִּׁים שָׁנָה תִּפְקְדֵם כָּל־הַבָּא
לַצָּבָא לַעֲבֹד אֶת־עֲבֹדַת אֹהֶל מוֹעֵד׃ 31 וְזֹאת
מִשְׁמֶרֶת מַשָּׂאָם לְכָל־עֲבֹדָתָם בְּאֹהֶל מוֹעֵד
קַרְשֵׁי הַמִּשְׁכָּן וּבְרִיחָיו וְעַמּוּדָיו וַאֲדָנָיו׃
32 וְעַמּוּדֵי הֶחָצֵר סָבִיב וְאַדְנֵיהֶם וִיתֵדֹתָם
וּמֵיתְרֵיהֶם לְכָל־כְּלֵיהֶם וּלְכֹל עֲבֹדָתָם וּבְשֵׁמֹת
תִּפְקְדוּ אֶת־כְּלֵי מִשְׁמֶרֶת מַשָּׂאָם׃ 33 זֹאת עֲבֹדַת
מִשְׁפְּחֹת בְּנֵי מְרָרִי לְכָל־עֲבֹדָתָם בְּאֹהֶל מוֹעֵד
בְּיַד אִיתָמָר בֶּן־אַהֲרֹן הַכֹּהֵן׃ [שני לספרדים]

27. Aaron and his sons They assign the Gershonites to their tasks. But it is Aaron's son Ithamar who is their supervisor (v. 28).

attending Rather, "guarding" (cf. 3:7). The absence of *'avodah,* "labor," is to be expected here. Since the Tabernacle curtains dismantled by the Gershonites and the Tabernacle structure dismantled by the Merarites (vv. 31,32, below) are to be transported by carts, these Levite clans have no labor as such during the march; their duties are limited to guarding.[30]

28. they shall attend to them Rather, "and their guard duty" (cf. 3:7); the phrase belongs to the preceding clause. In this way, the job profile is parallel to that of the Merarites (v. 33). Both the removal and guard duties of the Gershonites and the Merarites as well as the Tabernacle records kept by the Levites (Exod. 38:21) were under the jurisdiction of Ithamar. (For a Hittite parallel, see the Comment to 3:32.)

29. As for the Merarites The subject precedes the verb in contrast to verses 2 and 22, giving a chiastic effect.[31]

30. subject to service in the performance of the duties Rather, "all who are qualified for the work force" (cf. 4:3 and Excursus 6).

31. These are their porterage tasks . . . for the Tent of Meeting Rather, "The guarding of their porterage, inclusive of their removal labor for the Tent of Meeting, shall comprise . . ."

32. all these furnishings and their service Rather, "including their work tools."[32]

posts . . . pegs, and cords The cords fasten the posts to the pegs. No pegs are mentioned in connection with the Tabernacle curtains (absent in v. 26); nor are they needed since the Tabernacle frame gives the curtains sufficient stability.

by name It was essential to label the numerous objects under Merarite charge, such as sockets, pegs, bars, and cords (vv. 30–31). Four wagons were needed to transport them all.

that are their porterage tasks Rather, "of their porterage watch" (cf. v. 28).

33. duties Rather, "labors."

pertaining to their various duties Rather, "all their work" (see Excursus 6).

[34]So Moses, Aaron, and the chieftains of the community recorded the Kohathites by the clans of their ancestral house, [35]from the age of thirty years up to the age of fifty, all who were subject to service for work relating to the Tent of Meeting. [36]Those recorded by their clans came to 2,750. [37]That was the enrollment of the Kohathite clans, all those who performed duties relating to the Tent of Meeting, whom Moses and Aaron recorded at the command of the LORD through Moses.

[38]The Gershonites who were recorded by the clans of their ancestral house, [39]from the age of thirty years up to the age of fifty, all who were subject to service for work relating to the Tent of Meeting—[40]those recorded by the clans of their ancestral house came to 2,630. [41]That was the enrollment of the Gershonite clans, all those performing duties relating to the Tent of Meeting whom Moses and Aaron recorded at the command of the LORD.

[42]The enrollment of the Merarite clans by the clans of their ancestral house, [43]from the age of thirty years up to the age of fifty, all who were subject to service for work relating to the Tent of Meeting—[44]those recorded by their clans came to 3,200. [45]That was the enrollment of the Merarite clans which Moses and Aaron recorded at the command of the LORD through Moses.

[46]All the Levites whom Moses, Aaron, and the chieftains of Israel recorded by the clans of their ancestral houses, [47]from the age of thirty years up to the age of fifty, all who were subject to duties of service and porterage relating to the Tent of Meeting—[48]those recorded came to 8,580. [49]Each one was given responsibility for his service and porterage at the command of the LORD through Moses, and each was recorded as the LORD had commanded Moses.

34 וַיִּפְקֹד מֹשֶׁה וְאַהֲרֹן וּנְשִׂיאֵי הָעֵדָה אֶת־בְּנֵי
הַקְּהָתִי לְמִשְׁפְּחֹתָם וּלְבֵית אֲבֹתָם׃ 35 מִבֶּן
שְׁלֹשִׁים שָׁנָה וָמַעְלָה וְעַד בֶּן־חֲמִשִּׁים שָׁנָה כָּל־
הַבָּא לַצָּבָא לַעֲבֹדָה בְּאֹהֶל מוֹעֵד׃ 36 וַיִּהְיוּ
פְקֻדֵיהֶם לְמִשְׁפְּחֹתָם אַלְפַּיִם שְׁבַע מֵאוֹת
וַחֲמִשִּׁים׃ 37 אֵלֶּה פְקוּדֵי מִשְׁפְּחֹת הַקְּהָתִי כָּל־
הָעֹבֵד בְּאֹהֶל מוֹעֵד אֲשֶׁר פָּקַד מֹשֶׁה וְאַהֲרֹן עַל־
פִּי יְהוָה בְּיַד־מֹשֶׁה׃ ס שני 38 וּפְקוּדֵי בְּנֵי
גֵּרְשׁוֹן לְמִשְׁפְּחוֹתָם וּלְבֵית אֲבֹתָם׃ 39 מִבֶּן
שְׁלֹשִׁים שָׁנָה וָמַעְלָה וְעַד בֶּן־חֲמִשִּׁים שָׁנָה כָּל־
הַבָּא לַצָּבָא לַעֲבֹדָה בְּאֹהֶל מוֹעֵד׃ 40 וַיִּהְיוּ
פְּקֻדֵיהֶם לְמִשְׁפְּחֹתָם לְבֵית אֲבֹתָם אַלְפַּיִם וְשֵׁשׁ
מֵאוֹת וּשְׁלֹשִׁים׃ 41 אֵלֶּה פְקוּדֵי מִשְׁפְּחֹת בְּנֵי
גֵרְשׁוֹן כָּל־הָעֹבֵד בְּאֹהֶל מוֹעֵד אֲשֶׁר פָּקַד מֹשֶׁה
וְאַהֲרֹן עַל־פִּי יְהוָה׃ 42 וּפְקוּדֵי מִשְׁפְּחֹת בְּנֵי מְרָרִי
לְמִשְׁפְּחֹתָם לְבֵית אֲבֹתָם׃ 43 מִבֶּן שְׁלֹשִׁים שָׁנָה
וָמַעְלָה וְעַד בֶּן־חֲמִשִּׁים שָׁנָה כָּל־הַבָּא לַצָּבָא
לַעֲבֹדָה בְּאֹהֶל מוֹעֵד׃ 44 וַיִּהְיוּ פְקֻדֵיהֶם
לְמִשְׁפְּחֹתָם שְׁלֹשֶׁת אֲלָפִים וּמָאתָיִם׃ 45 אֵלֶּה
פְקוּדֵי מִשְׁפְּחֹת בְּנֵי מְרָרִי אֲשֶׁר פָּקַד מֹשֶׁה
וְאַהֲרֹן עַל־פִּי יְהוָה בְּיַד־מֹשֶׁה׃ 46 כָּל־הַפְּקֻדִים
אֲשֶׁר פָּקַד מֹשֶׁה וְאַהֲרֹן וּנְשִׂיאֵי יִשְׂרָאֵל אֶת־
הַלְוִיִּם לְמִשְׁפְּחֹתָם וּלְבֵית אֲבֹתָם׃ 47 מִבֶּן
שְׁלֹשִׁים שָׁנָה וָמַעְלָה וְעַד בֶּן־חֲמִשִּׁים שָׁנָה כָּל־
הַבָּא לַעֲבֹד עֲבֹדַת עֲבֹדָה וַעֲבֹדַת מַשָּׂא בְּאֹהֶל
מוֹעֵד׃ 48 וַיִּהְיוּ פְּקֻדֵיהֶם שְׁמֹנַת אֲלָפִים וַחֲמֵשׁ
מֵאוֹת וּשְׁמֹנִים׃ 49 עַל־פִּי יְהוָה פָּקַד אוֹתָם בְּיַד־
מֹשֶׁה אִישׁ אִישׁ עַל־עֲבֹדָתוֹ וְעַל־מַשָּׂאוֹ וּפְקֻדָיו
אֲשֶׁר־צִוָּה יְהוָה אֶת־מֹשֶׁה׃ פ שלישי

34–49. These verses describe the carrying out of the second Levitical census with the assistance of the tribal chieftains (see 1:44). The totals for the Levites over the age of twenty (8,580) are in harmony with the totals of all the Levites over the age of one month (22,000). However, the former list appears the more realistic; Merari and not Kohath is the largest clan and the totals for each clan are rounded to the nearest ten not hundred.

35. See the Comment to verses 3,23.

49. Each was given responsibility . . . at the command of the LORD through Moses Rather, "they were counted by the Lord's oracle through Moses, each according to his packing and porterage" (cf. 3:16 and Excursus 6).

and each was recorded Hebrew *u-fekudav*. This rendering is difficult to explain. Perhaps it should be translated "and his assignment/responsibility" (see v. 27 for this usage of the verb). Though the census was by oracle, the work assignment was by God's direct command to Moses.

as Rather, "which" for Hebrew *'asher*. Most versions read *ka'asher*, "as." No change in the text is needed, however, if the previous term *u-fekudav* is rendered "assignment/responsibility" (cf. 3:36; 4:16).

5 The LORD spoke to Moses, saying: [2]Instruct the Israelites to remove from camp anyone with an eruption or a discharge and anyone defiled by a corpse. [3]Remove male and female alike; put them outside the camp so that they do not defile the camp of those in whose midst I dwell.

ה וַיְדַבֵּר יְהוָה אֶל־מֹשֶׁה לֵּאמֹר׃ 2 צַו אֶת־בְּנֵי
יִשְׂרָאֵל וִישַׁלְּחוּ מִן־הַמַּחֲנֶה כָּל־צָרוּעַ וְכָל־זָב
וְכֹל טָמֵא לָנָפֶשׁ׃ 3 מִזָּכָר עַד־נְקֵבָה תְּשַׁלֵּחוּ אֶל־
מִחוּץ לַמַּחֲנֶה תְּשַׁלְּחוּם וְלֹא יְטַמְּאוּ אֶת־מַחֲנֵיהֶם
אֲשֶׁר אֲנִי שֹׁכֵן בְּתוֹכָם׃ 4 וַיַּעֲשׂוּ־כֵן בְּנֵי יִשְׂרָאֵל

Purification of the Camp (5:1–6:27)

Chapters 5 and 6 constitute an insertion of several laws into the account of the preparations for the march through the wilderness. Their common denominator is the prevention and elimination of impurity from the camp of the Israelites lest the Lord abandon His sanctuary and people.

CHAPTER 5 THE REMOVAL OF SEVERELY IMPURE PERSONS (vv. 1–4)

The camp of Israel has been organized for its sojourn through the wilderness in chapters 1–4. The camp is sacred and must retain its purity. This next law (5:1–4) stipulates situations in which Israelite individuals should be removed to areas outside the camp: when they have specific skin diseases (called "leper," ***metsora'*** in Lev. 13f. and ***tsarua'***, "with an eruption," here); when they suffer from chronic discharges from their genitalia, perhaps gonorrheic individuals (***zav;*** cf. Lev. 15); and when they are contaminated by a corpse (***tame' le-nefesh***; cf. Num. 19; Mish. Kel. 1:8). These three categories of affliction were seen as severe impurities, as is obvious from the fact that their purification is of seven-day duration and involves a complex ritual. Furthermore, their impurity is contagious through contact with persons and objects; in the case of leprosy, it is enough to be under the same roof (Lev. 14:46).[1] However, it is not the threat of contagion to man and his objects that causes the banishment. Rather, as the text makes amply clear, it is the threat to the sanctuary, that is, "the camp in whose midst I dwell" (v. 3). In contrast to the religion of its neighbors, Israelite religion has divested impurity of its demonic nature: It is not a threat to the life and health of man. In monotheistic Israel, demons are nonexistent. Therefore, whoever bears or contracts impurity eliminates it by ritual means: lustration and sacrifice (see Excursus 7).

2. *remove* The Piel verb ***shillah*** is found three times in verses 2–3, underscoring the urgency of expelling these carriers of impurity from the camp.

eruption[2]

discharge The omission from the legislation of the parturient (Lev. 12), the menstruating woman (Lev. 15:19–24), and those with impurities that last seven days or more is not accidental. All of these, in contrast to the other conditions, are natural and expected. There is evidence that their bearers were quarantined within the community during their period of impurity (see Isa. 30:22).[3]

corpse Hebrew ***nefesh,*** short for ***nefesh met,*** "dead person" (see 6:6). For the rules concerning this impurity, see chapter 19 and Excursus 48.

3. *male and female alike* Emphasizing that females are also subject to these impurities (see Lev. 15:19–30).

outside the camp The outside of the camp, like the camp itself, is neutral in regard to impurity (***ḥol,*** lit. "nonholy"). Hence it can be either clean, ***tahor*** (e.g., Num. 19:9), or unclean, ***tame'*** (e.g., Lev. 14:40–41). "Outside the camp" differs from "within" in one respect only: It is out of the contamination range of the sanctuary, so that impurities there cannot pollute the sanctuary.

[4]The Israelites did so, putting them outside the camp; as the LORD had spoken to Moses, so the Israelites did.

[5]The LORD spoke to Moses, saying: [6]Speak to the Israelites: When a man or woman commits any wrong toward a fellow man, thus breaking faith with the LORD, and that person realizes his guilt, [7]he shall confess the wrong that he

וַיִּֽשְׁלְחוּ אוֹתָם אֶל־מִחוּץ לַמַּחֲנֶה כַּאֲשֶׁר דִּבֶּר
יְהוָה אֶל־מֹשֶׁה כֵּן עָשׂוּ בְּנֵי יִשְׂרָאֵל׃ פ
5 וַיְדַבֵּר יְהוָה אֶל־מֹשֶׁה לֵּאמֹר׃ 6 דַּבֵּר אֶל־בְּנֵי
יִשְׂרָאֵל אִישׁ אוֹ־אִשָּׁה כִּי יַעֲשׂוּ מִכָּל־חַטֹּאת
הָאָדָם לִמְעֹל מַעַל בַּיהוָה וְאָשְׁמָה הַנֶּפֶשׁ הַהִוא׃

dwell Hebrew *shokhen,* a denominative of *mishkan,* "Tabernacle." The Lord's consent to dwell in the Tabernacle must be matched by Israel's scrupulousness in keeping the camp pure. Implied is that any impurity in the camp threatens the purity of the Tabernacle (see the introductory Comment to vv. 1–4). In Canaan, the demand for purity is extended to all of God's land (35:34).

4. The fulfillment is stated thrice, corresponding to the threefold command "remove" in verse 2. This verse is a self-contained unit enveloped by the chiastic inclusion, "the Israelites did so . . . so the Israelites did."

THE *'ASHAM* FOR A FALSE OATH[4] (vv. 5–8)

The case is that of a person who has defrauded his fellow and then denied it under oath. Instances of such fraud are detailed in Leviticus 5:20–26.[5] The *'asham* law here is a generalization of the one in Leviticus, but it supplements it in two ways: (1) when the defrauded person dies leaving no kin, the reparation belongs to the officiating priest; (2) the reparation must be preceded by confession. This second innovation is momentous. The priestly laws stipulate confession only in those cases in which deliberate sin against God is permitted to be expiated by sacrifice (cf. Lev. 5:1–4; 16:21). It leads to the conclusion that even if one has deliberately offended God, as in the case of a false oath, this deliberate sin is reduced to an inadvertency and qualifies for sacrificial expiation if the sinner shows remorse (*'asham;* cf. v. 6b) and then acknowledges the sin by confessing his crime and accepting blame. The radical nature of this innovation can only be appreciated in view of the fundamental premise that brazen, presumptuous sins cannot be expiated by sacrifice (cf. 15:30–31). Moreover, the Bible presumes that brazen offenses against God, such as a false oath, are punished by Him with death (cf. Jer. 5:2–3; Zech. 5:4; Mal. 3:5).[6] This background projects the true magnitude of the priestly innovation: For the sake of the repentant sinner, God will compromise His justice by reducing the crime from a deliberate act punishable by death to an inadvertency, expiable by sacrifice. For a discussion of the priestly doctrine of repentance, see Excursus 33.

The reason for placing this law here is not clear. Perhaps it is the association of the leper in verse 2 with the reparation offering, his most important sacrifice (Lev. 14:12–14,24–25).[7] Perhaps the association is thematic: The law of the pollution of the sacred (5:1–4) is followed by the law of the desecration of the sacred, the reparation offering (5:5–8). Most likely, the thread that unites all the legal miscellanea of chapters 5–6 is the priest, who plays a prominent role in each case. It is the priest who determines and terminates ritual impurity (5:1–4); who officiates at the *'asham* sacrifice, is awarded its meat, and, in the case of the defrauded person who dies leaving no kin, receives the reparation as well (5:5–8); who is the recipient of all sanctuary donations (5:9–10); and who executes the ordeal for the suspected adulteress (5:11–31) and all the rituals for the Nazirite (6:1–21). Most likely, chapters 5–6 constituted a special scroll that dealt with sacrificial rites relating to various forms of impurity; it was attached here because of the relevance of its opening law (5:1–4) and its concern with the purity of the wilderness camp. For Israel, about to set out on its march through the wilderness, nothing was more vital than the assurance of God's Presence, which depended on the strict maintenance of the purity of the camp.

6. wrong toward a fellow man Hebrew *ḥatt'ot ha-'adam* can mean either "the wrongs of (i.e., committed by) the person" or "the wrongs toward the person." The phrase is a general statement about the cases detailed in Leviticus 5:20–26. The formulation, however, is independent of that passage, for in Leviticus 5 the sacrifice itself is named *'asham.* Here *'asham* is used specifically for

has done. He shall make restitution in the principal
amount and add one-fifth to it, giving it to him whom he
has wronged. 8 If the man has no kinsman to whom restitution can be made, the amount repaid shall go to the LORD
for the priest—in addition to the ram of expiation with
which expiation is made on his behalf. 9 So, too, any gift

7 וְהִתְוַדּוּ אֶת־חַטָּאתָם אֲשֶׁר עָשׂוּ וְהֵשִׁיב אֶת־
אֲשָׁמוֹ בְּרֹאשׁוֹ וַחֲמִישִׁתוֹ יֹסֵף עָלָיו וְנָתַן לַאֲשֶׁר
אָשַׁם לוֹ׃ 8 וְאִם־אֵין לָאִישׁ גֹּאֵל לְהָשִׁיב הָאָשָׁם
אֵלָיו הָאָשָׁם הַמּוּשָׁב לַיהוָה לַכֹּהֵן מִלְּבַד אֵיל
הַכִּפֻּרִים אֲשֶׁר יְכַפֶּר־בּוֹ עָלָיו׃ 9 וְכָל־תְּרוּמָה

the restitution paid to the victim (vv. 7,8), whereas the actual sacrifice is called *'eil ha-kippurim,* "the ram of expiation" (v. 8). The variation in terminology shows that the definite article here in *ha-'adam* (lit. "the man") cannot refer to the same word in Leviticus 5:22 to support a meaning "wrongs of the person"; it must mean "the wrongs toward the person."[8]

thus breaking faith with Hebrew *li-m'ol ma'al be.* Rather, "whereby he commits sacrilege against." There are two prerequisites for this crime: defrauding his fellow and committing sacrilege against God by means of a false oath.[9] For *ma'al* as the sacrilege that can refer to oath violation, see Leviticus 26:40 and Ezekiel 17:18–20.

and that person realizes his guilt Rather, "when that person feels guilt." This is the beginning of the main sentence: the *sine qua non* for the reduced penalty.[10]

7. ***confess*** The Septuagint correctly translates Hebrew *ve-hitvadu* as "declare"; the penitent's remorse must be articulated.[11]

he shall confess . . . he has done[12]

make restitution The *'asham* is the only sacrifice that regularly uses the verb *heshiv* (Num. 5:7,8), meaning "restore" and implying monetary compensation.[13]

in the principal amount In its entirety.[14]

one-fifth The penalty for apprehended theft is double the value of the stolen article (Exod. 22:3) or more (Exod. 21:37). The intent of the sharp reduction of this penalty here to 20 percent is to encourage the voluntary surrender of the theft. It is found in ancient Near Eastern practice[15] and in rabbinic law, where it is called *takkanat ha-shavim,* "a dispensation for the repentant."[16]

has wronged Hebrew *'asham lo* means "has incurred liability"; cf. Leviticus 5:19b.[17]

8. ***kinsman*** Literally, "redeemer." The law of redemption is defined in Leviticus 25:48–49 (cf. Lev. 25:25; Jer. 32:7).

restitution . . . amount Both words are expressed by *'asham* (also in v. 7), which, however, is the term for the required sacrifice in Leviticus 5:14–26.[18]

go to the LORD for the priest In the absence of kinsmen, the sanctuary is the beneficiary, specifically, the officiating priest, chosen by the offerer. The monetary restitution, as it were, is added to the reparation of the sacrificial ram to expiate for the trespass to the Lord. The sacrifice could also be in monetary equivalents.[19]

The significance of this provision rests in what it silently denies: *The restitution does not go to the state.* Under the monarchy, ownerless property fell to the state, even if it entailed a crime against God (e.g., Ahab's confiscation of Naboth's land; 1 Kings 21:10,13,15). Similarly in ancient Assyria, "if the line of the original owner of land which has been sold dies out, the land reverts to the crown, even though the land is actually in the possession of another."[20] This law may be intended as a polemic against royal "eminent domain." More likely, it harks back to an older, premonarchic tradition.

in addition to The restitution to the defrauded man or his kin precedes the sacrificial restitution to God, as Leviticus 5:24b–25 makes clear. This rule is accentuated and expanded by the rabbis, who declare: "The Day of Atonement atones for the sins between man and God. But the Day of Atonement does not atone for the sins between man and his fellow until he has made restitution to his fellow."[21]

the ram of expiation Hebrew *'eil ha-kippurim.* Rather than its proper name, *'asham,* this

among the sacred donations that the Israelites offer shall be
the priest's. 10And each shall retain his sacred donations:
each priest shall keep what is given to him.

לְכָל־קָדְשֵׁי בְנֵי־יִשְׂרָאֵל אֲשֶׁר־יַקְרִיבוּ לַכֹּהֵן לוֹ
יִהְיֶה׃ 10 וְאִישׁ אֶת־קֳדָשָׁיו לוֹ יִהְיוּ אִישׁ אֲשֶׁר־יִתֵּן
לַכֹּהֵן לוֹ יִהְיֶה׃ פ רביעי 11 וַיְדַבֵּר יְהוָה

term is used to designate the sacrifice, since the former was already appropriated by the legislator to denote "restitution" in verse 7.

THE PRIEST OF CHOICE (vv. 9–10)

The *'asham* passage (vv. 5–8) concludes with the remark that the officiating priest receives the meat of the animal victim in return for performing the expiatory rites (cf. Lev. 7:7). The next two verses add that when a person makes a donation to the sanctuary, he has the right to give it to the priest of his choice.[22] The sacred donation in question clearly must be an item of food; nonperishables would be kept by the sanctuary and would not be the property of any single priest.

The inflated nature of this passage (v. 10 is virtually tautologous) indicates its emphasis and betrays a long controversy in early priestly circles concerning the recipient of offerings. At the sanctuary at Shiloh, and probably at other small sanctuaries, the custom prevailed to give the officiating priest a portion of the *shelamim,* the sacrifice eaten by the worshiper. This custom was violated by the sons of Eli, who committed a sacrilege by taking their portion before the Lord received His portion on the altar (1 Sam. 2:13–17).

Later, probably in the Jerusalem Temple, it was mandated that certain sacrificial portions be divided equally among all the priests (e.g., the dry meal offering, Lev. 7:10, and the breast of the *shelamim,* Lev. 7:31) in order to prevent strife within the large priestly staff. However, the older custom of rewarding the officiating priest was still observed when it came to other sacrificial portions (e.g., Lev. 7:7–9,14,32–33). Our text may be focusing on nonsacrificial donations such as first fruits[23] or the first yield of baking (cf. Num. 15:17–21), which are given directly to the priest. However, it is most likely that all sacred donations are intended here.[24] If so, the text underscores the inalienable right of the worshiper to designate the priestly recipient of his food offerings when they are not explicitly assigned to all the priests. Historical corroboration can be found in King Jehoash's demand that the priests underwrite the cost of the Temple repairs with the sacred donations received "each from his benefactor" (2 Kings 12:6; cf. v. 8), implying that each person chose the priestly recipient for his donations.[25]

Finally, one cannot help noticing that the catchword *la-kohen,* literally "to the priest," is twice repeated in verses 9, 10, and again in verse 8, impelling one to ask why this emphatic insistence on the right of the worshiper to designate the priestly recipient of his gifts was inserted here? It is after all somewhat of a surprise that the officiating priest is entitled to the perquisites from the reparation offering as well as the monetary reparation normally due the embezzled person but who, in this case, is no longer alive and has left no heirs. Thus, the fact that the officiating priest gains both the sacrificial meat and the reparation money may have been responsible for the rule that the offerer should at least have the option to choose his officiant.

9. gift Hebrew *terumah,* literally "that which is set aside" for the sanctuary, or "dedication" (cf. 18:8,19).

any gift among the sacred donations[26]

offer[27]

shall be the priest's Hebrew *la-kohen lo yihyeh,* literally "it is the priest's; it belongs to him" (cf. Lev. 7:8,9,14).

10. each That is, each priest. Hebrew *'ish* occurs twice in this verse; the second time it refers to the worshiper. Alternatively, this *'ish* also refers to the worshiper, implying that he has the right to give his donations to the priest of his choice despite the fact that as donations to the sanctuary they are its property.[28]

each priest . . . to him[29]

[11]The LORD spoke to Moses, saying: [12]Speak to the Israelite people and say to them:
If any man's wife has gone astray and broken faith with
him [13]in that a man has had carnal relations with her
unbeknown to her husband, and she keeps secret the fact
that she has defiled herself without being forced, and there
is no witness against her—[14]but a fit of jealousy comes over

אֶל־מֹשֶׁה לֵּאמֹר׃ 12 דַּבֵּר אֶל־בְּנֵי יִשְׂרָאֵל
וְאָמַרְתָּ אֲלֵהֶם אִישׁ אִישׁ כִּֽי־תִשְׂטֶה אִשְׁתּוֹ
וּמָעֲלָה בוֹ מָֽעַל׃ 13 וְשָׁכַב אִישׁ אֹתָהּ שִׁכְבַת־
זֶרַע וְנֶעְלַם מֵעֵינֵי אִישָׁהּ וְנִסְתְּרָה וְהִיא נִטְמָאָה
וְעֵד אֵין בָּהּ וְהִוא לֹא נִתְפָּשָׂה׃ 14 וְעָבַר עָלָיו

THE CASE OF THE SUSPECTED ADULTERESS (vv. 11–31)

An irate husband suspects that his wife has been unfaithful. Having no proof, his only recourse is to bring her to the sanctuary where she undergoes an ordeal. The priest makes her drink a potion consisting of sacred water to which dust from the sanctuary floor and a parchment containing a curse have been added. The curse spells out the consequences. If she is guilty, her genital area will distend and she will no longer be able to conceive. If, however, the water has no effect on her, she is declared innocent and she will be blessed with seed. Alleged duplications and inconsistencies in the text will be discussed in the Commentary and notes. The larger issues of the treatment of adultery and the role of the ordeal in Israel and the ancient Near East are discussed in Excursuses 8 and 9. The analysis of the composition of this text is reserved for Excursus 10.

THE CASE (vv. 12–14)

The husband accuses his wife of conjugal infidelity whether or not she is guilty (vv. 12b–14).

*12. **has gone astray*** Hebrew ***tisteh,*** used elsewhere in the Bible only in connection with harlotry (Prov. 4:15; 7:25). From this verb is derived the noun ***sotah,*** which is the technical name in rabbinic literature for the woman convicted of adultery by the ordeal.

broken faith with him Hebrew ***maʿalah bo maʿal.*** This is the only time that the term ***maʿal*** is used outside the sacred sphere of sancta and oath violations, where the object of ***maʿal*** is invariably the Deity. Here its usage in connection with the betrayal of the husband bears a literary rather than legal character. Just as the term ***berit,*** "covenant," is at times used by the prophets for the marriage relationship (cf. Ezek. 16:8; Mal. 2:14), where no oath of marital fidelity is actually involved, so here ***maʿal*** has a figurative meaning.[30] The unfaithful wife is a recurring prophetic image for Israel's infidelity to God (e.g., Hos. 2:4–22; Jer. 3:8f.; Ezek. 23:37). Moreover, ***maʿal*** is used in priestly texts for idolatry (cf. Lev. 26:40; Num. 31:16). Since ***maʿal*** denotes straying after other gods, its extension to straying after other men is obvious. As the only term used in common in the laws of oath violation (5:6–8) and the laws of adultery (5:11–31), it provides the link between these two otherwise unrelated cases.[31]

*13. **carnal relations*** Hebrew ***shikhvat zeraʿ*** means "semen" (cf. Lev. 15:16).[32]

unbeknown Literally, "hidden from the eyes of." The meaning is not that the husband did not witness the act but was unaware of it. For this usage, see Leviticus 4:12.

she keeps secret[33]

defiled herself[34] The defilement must be understood in an ethical sense (as is its antonym, ***tehorah,*** "pure," in v. 28). Ritual defilement is not intended since it can result from legitimate cohabitation (e.g., Lev. 15:18), whereas here the term has a purely pejorative meaning. For a similar usage in law, see Deuteronomy 24:4.[35]

forced Hebrew ***nitpasah,*** a rendering based on Deuteronomy 22:28.[36] It also can be rendered "apprehended."[37] However, if the latter is accepted, then the next clause, "there is no witness against her," is tautologous.[38] If the former is accepted, then one would expect the clause to

him and he is wrought up about the wife who has defiled
herself; or if a fit of jealousy comes over one and he is
wrought up about his wife although she has not defiled
herself—
15 the man shall bring his wife to the priest. And he
shall bring as an offering for her one-tenth of an *ephah* of
barley flour. No oil shall be poured upon it and no frankincense shall be laid on it, for it is a meal offering of
jealousy, a meal offering of remembrance which recalls
wrongdoing.

רוּחַ־קִנְאָה וְקִנֵּא אֶת־אִשְׁתּוֹ וְהִוא נִטְמָאָה אוֹ־
עָבַר עָלָיו רוּחַ־קִנְאָה וְקִנֵּא אֶת־אִשְׁתּוֹ וְהִיא לֹא
נִטְמָאָה׃ 15 וְהֵבִיא הָאִישׁ אֶת־אִשְׁתּוֹ אֶל־הַכֹּהֵן
וְהֵבִיא אֶת־קָרְבָּנָהּ עָלֶיהָ עֲשִׂירִת הָאֵיפָה קֶמַח
שְׂעֹרִים לֹא־יִצֹק עָלָיו שֶׁמֶן וְלֹא־יִתֵּן עָלָיו לְבֹנָה
כִּי־מִנְחַת קְנָאֹת הוּא מִנְחַת זִכָּרוֹן מַזְכֶּרֶת עָוֺן׃

be included in the curse formula of verse 19;[39] also the terminology presumes that she was not forced but willing, for example, "has gone astray," "breaking faith with him," "she keeps secret." Thus both renderings, although plausible, are flawed. However, the preference must be given to the translation "apprehended," as explained in Excursus 9.

no witness Although capital punishment may not be imposed on the basis of the testimony of a single witness (Num. 35:30), this verse implies that the case of an adulteress is an exception. The rabbis circumvent this possibility by requiring that she be previously warned by her husband in the presence of two witnesses against secluding herself with her suspected paramour.[40] Philo requires that both husband and wife argue their case before the high court in Jerusalem, thus enabling the wife to refute her husband's charges and thereby circumvent the ordeal.[41]

14. ***fit*** For this sense of ***ruaḥ,*** compare Isaiah 19:14 and Hosea 4:12; 5:4.

jealousy Hebrew ***kin'ah*** connotes possessive emotion (see Prov. 6:34). Note the rendering "wrought up" for ***kinne'*** in the next clause or the rendering "impassioned God" for ***'el kanna'*** in Exodus 20:5.[42]

who has defiled herself . . . although she has not defiled herself[43]

THE PROCEDURE: OATH, SACRIFICE, AND ORDEAL (vv. 15–26)

15. ***the man shall bring his wife*** Only the husband can press charges, not the community as in Hammurabi's code (see Excursus 8).

for her Hebrew ***'aleha.***[44] Since she is under suspicion of being a brazen, unrepentant sinner, she is not qualified to bring her own sacrifice (cf. Num. 15:30). Hence, her offering is brought by her husband on her behalf (see v. 18). Ramban renders "instead of her," since the purpose of this offering is to expose her sin and exact revenge. The preposition ***'al*** frequently means "for, on behalf of" in the priestly writings (e.g., Exod. 30:16; Lev. 1:4).

ephah Estimated as equivalent to 22.8 liters.

barley flour The ***minḥah*** meal offering, which was normally composed of ***solet,*** fine wheat flour (see Lev. 2). In the purification offering of the poor (Lev. 5:11), as here, neither oil nor frankincense is added, for these ingredients are associated with joy (e.g., Ps. 104:15). Their absence is a sign that the occasion is one of real or suspected wrongdoing.[45] An expiatory sacrifice such as the burnt, purification, or reparation offering (Lev. 1:4,5) is not required since there is neither proof nor acknowledgment of sin. Accordingly, the term for expiation, ***kipper,*** is missing. The purpose of the ***minḥah*** is explained below.

Barley, being much cheaper than wheat (e.g., 2 Kings 7:1), was a staple of the poor (Ruth 2:17), as well as of animals (1 Kings 5:8; cf. v. 2). Indeed, this fact prompted Rabban Gamaliel to explain this offering as follows: "Because her act was the act of a beast, so her offering is the food of a beast."[46]

jealousy Probably "suspicions"; see verse 14. The plural ***kena'ot*** is used here because there are two cases of suspicion;[47] see the introductory Comment to this chapter and verse 29.

a meal offering of remembrance which recalls wrongdoing This offering of the remembrance (Heb. ***zikkaron***) is inconsistent with prescribed usage, since elsewhere a remembrance offering

16The priest shall bring her forward and have her stand before the LORD. 17The priest shall take sacral water in an earthen vessel and, taking some of the earth that is on the floor of the Tabernacle, the priest shall put it into the water. 18After he has made the woman stand before the LORD, the priest shall bare the woman's head and place upon her hands the meal offering of remembrance, which is a meal offering of jealousy. And in the priest's hands shall be the water of bitterness that induces the spell. 19The priest shall

16 וְהִקְרִיב אֹתָהּ הַכֹּהֵן וְהֶעֱמִדָהּ לִפְנֵי יְהוָה׃
17 וְלָקַח הַכֹּהֵן מַיִם קְדֹשִׁים בִּכְלִי־חָרֶשׂ וּמִן־
הֶעָפָר אֲשֶׁר יִהְיֶה בְּקַרְקַע הַמִּשְׁכָּן יִקַּח הַכֹּהֵן
וְנָתַן אֶל־הַמָּיִם׃ 18 וְהֶעֱמִיד הַכֹּהֵן אֶת־הָאִשָּׁה
לִפְנֵי יְהוָה וּפָרַע אֶת־רֹאשׁ הָאִשָּׁה וְנָתַן עַל־
כַּפֶּיהָ אֵת מִנְחַת הַזִּכָּרוֹן מִנְחַת קְנָאֹת הִוא וּבְיַד
הַכֹּהֵן יִהְיוּ מֵי הַמָּרִים הַמְאָרְרִים׃ 19 וְהִשְׁבִּיעַ

is always for the benefit of the offerer (e.g., Exod. 28:12). Thus the text must add the clause "which recalls wrongdoing" in order to explain this anomaly.

recalls wrongdoing Hebrew ***hizkir ʿavon*** means "exposes" wrongdoing so that punishment is inevitable (cf. 1 Kings 17:18).

16. her The antecedent can also be the meal offering, but then the verb ***heʿemid,*** "have stand," could not apply (cf. v. 18) since the sacrifice is placed on the altar. For the use of ***heʿemid . . . hikriv*** with persons, compare 3:6.

before the LORD She stands before the altar so that the imprecation she takes upon herself will most certainly be effective (cf. 1 Kings 8:31–32).

17. This entire verse stands as a parenthetical explanation in the procedural order; that is, the items enumerated in this verse were prepared earlier, whereas the actual procedure is given in verse 18.[48] Alternatively, the potion was prepared in the presence of the woman to heighten its psychological effect,[49] in which case verse 17 would follow verse 16 chronologically. However, the repetition (known by the term repetitive resumption) of the statement that the priest stands the woman before the Lord (vv. 16,18) implies that the intervening statement—the preparation of the potion—is out of chronological sequence and describes an earlier act.

sacral water Probably taken from the consecrated laver; compare Exodus 30:17–21,29.[50] The water had to be specified as "sacred" since ordinary water was used by the lay worshiper to wash the legs and entrails of his burnt offering (Lev. 1:9). However, in the Solomonic Temple, water used within the sacred precincts, for whatever purpose, had to be taken from the consecrated laver(s) (2 Chron. 4:6).[51]

earthen vessel Also required in the purification ritual of the healed leper and leprous house (Lev. 14:5,50). If earthen vessels became contaminated they could not be reused but had to be broken (cf. Lev. 6:21; 11:33); and in all probability, the earthen vessels specified for use with the leper and suspected adulteress also were broken because of the association of these persons with impurity.

earth . . . on the floor of the Tabernacle Josephus claims that the earth was taken from anywhere within the sacred area.[52] Surprisingly, however, the floor of the Tabernacle was not consecrated with the anointment oil (cf. Exod. 30:26–30) and, theoretically, bore no sacred status and could be traversed by the laity. The rabbinic view, therefore, may be correct: The earth came from the floor of the Temple building, interpreting ***mishkan,*** "Tabernacle," as the sanctuary tent.[53] Dust from the temple gate (i.e., the courtyard) was an ingredient in a prophylactic potion for the horses and troops of the Babylonian kings,[54] and, as noted in Excursus 8, dust from the city gates of Mari was used in a water ordeal. The ground of the sacred area was regarded as having greater potency, whether for warding off evil (Mesopotamia) or causing it (Israel).

is Hebrew ***yihyeh*** should be rendered "will be." Since the Tabernacle is constantly on the move, the earthen floor is never the same.

18. After he has made Literally, "the priest shall make," a repetitive resumption of verse 16, following the parenthetical comment of verse 17.

adjure the woman, saying to her, "If no man has lain with
you, if you have not gone astray in defilement while
married to your husband, be immune to harm from this
water of bitterness that induces the spell. 20But if you have
gone astray while married to your husband and have defiled
yourself, if a man other than your husband has had carnal
relations with you"—21here the priest shall administer the
curse of adjuration to the woman, as the priest goes on to
say to the woman—"may the LORD make you a curse and
an imprecation among your people, as the LORD causes
your thigh to sag and your belly to distend; 22may this water

אֹתָהּ הַכֹּהֵן וְאָמַר אֶל־הָאִשָּׁה אִם־לֹא שָׁכַב אִישׁ
אֹתָךְ וְאִם־לֹא שָׂטִית טֻמְאָה תַּחַת אִישֵׁךְ הִנָּקִי
מִמֵּי הַמָּרִים הַמְאָרְרִים הָאֵלֶּה׃ 20 וְאַתְּ כִּי שָׂטִית
תַּחַת אִישֵׁךְ וְכִי נִטְמֵאת וַיִּתֵּן אִישׁ בָּךְ אֶת־
שְׁכָבְתּוֹ מִבַּלְעֲדֵי אִישֵׁךְ׃ 21 וְהִשְׁבִּיעַ הַכֹּהֵן אֶת־
הָאִשָּׁה בִּשְׁבֻעַת הָאָלָה וְאָמַר הַכֹּהֵן לָאִשָּׁה יִתֵּן
יְהוָה אוֹתָךְ לְאָלָה וְלִשְׁבֻעָה בְּתוֹךְ עַמֵּךְ בְּתֵת
יְהוָה אֶת־יְרֵכֵךְ נֹפֶלֶת וְאֶת־בִּטְנֵךְ צָבָה׃ 22 וּבָאוּ

bare the woman's head A sign of mourning (cf. Lev. 10:6; 21:10) or of a leper (Lev. 13:45), an indication that the woman was in disgrace.[55] What would happen to her if she did indeed confess? The rabbis claim that the only legal consequence she would suffer would be that her husband would be obligated to divorce her immediately.[56] The biblical law, however, is unclear in this regard. One might argue that voluntary confession for unapprehended crime always mitigates the penalty (e.g., Lev. 5:5). But this applies only when the crime is committed against God.[57] In our case, however, it is the husband, not God, who is victimized by the wife's infidelity, and as in all other cases of adultery, capital punishment may have been imposed.

place upon her hands Since it was her sacrifice, even though her husband brought it (v. 15), it was she who had to present it to the priest, just as other offerings must be brought by the worshipers themselves (e.g., Lev. 7:30). The underlying principle is that the sacrifice has an effect only on the one who brings it.

water of bitterness Since the earth of the Tabernacle could not have given the waters a bitter taste, some rabbis attribute this description to the effect of the waters upon the woman (as in v. 24); others conjecture that a bitter ingredient was added.[58] The meaning of this term is yet to be resolved.

induces the spell See Exodus 14:20; compare Numbers 22:6.[59]

19–24. These verses present the prescription for the oath: its adjuration, writing it down, and dissolving it into the waters.

19–20. ***adjure*** To which the woman will respond, "Amen, amen" (v. 22). According to the rabbis, the priest encourages her to confess by adding these words: "Wine can be responsible for much, or frivolity can be responsible for much, or childishness can be responsible for much. Many have been guilty before you and were swept away (when they refused to confess and then drank the water). Do not cause the great Name to be blotted out in the water of bitterness." He then tells her of the affair of Reuben with Bilhah (Gen. 35:22) and of Judah with Tamar (Gen. 38:15ff.). Both of them then confessed and inherited life in the next world.[60]

lain . . . gone astray in defilement The adultery is expressed twice in these two verses by the use of three of the clauses used in the formulation of the case in verses 12b–13, stated in chiastic order.

while married Hebrew *taḥat,* literally "under" the husband's authority (cf. Ezek. 23:5).

be immune to harm Hebrew *hinnaki,* literally "be cleansed."[61] An alternative rendering, "be clear of guilt," is a legal term as in verse 31 and Genesis 24:8 (cf. Exod. 21:19, 23:7).

21. This verse is almost a verbatim repetition of verses 19 and 22, necessitated, according to Ramban, by the lengthy condition of the curse. It also can be explained as an early textual interpolation. See below and Excursus 10.

curse Hebrew *'alah,* the imprecation appended to an oath (cf. Deut. 29:11,18–19). Thus it is possible to explain verse 21a not as a repetition of verse 19a but as a continuation of the priest's adjuration, which began with the accusation (vv. 19–20) and is now followed by the imprecation-punishment (vv. 21–22). An alternative interpretation is discussed below.

that induces the spell enter your body, causing the belly to distend and the thigh to sag." And the woman shall say, "Amen, amen!"

23The priest shall put these curses down in writing and rub it off into the water of bitterness. 24He is to make the woman drink the water of bitterness that induces the spell, so that the spell-inducing water may enter into her to bring on bitterness. 25Then the priest shall take from the woman's hand the meal offering of jealousy, elevate the

הַמַּיִם הַמְאָרְרִים הָאֵלֶּה בְּמֵעַיִךְ לַצְבּוֹת בֶּטֶן
וְלַנְפִּל יָרֵךְ וְאָמְרָה הָאִשָּׁה אָמֵן ׀ אָמֵן׃ 23 וְכָתַב
אֶת־הָאָלֹת הָאֵלֶּה הַכֹּהֵן בַּסֵּפֶר וּמָחָה אֶל־מֵי
הַמָּרִים׃ 24 וְהִשְׁקָה אֶת־הָאִשָּׁה אֶת־מֵי הַמָּרִים
הַמְאָרְרִים וּבָאוּ בָהּ הַמַּיִם הַמְאָרְרִים לְמָרִים׃
25 וְלָקַח הַכֹּהֵן מִיַּד הָאִשָּׁה אֵת מִנְחַת הַקְּנָאֹת
וְהֵנִיף אֶת־הַמִּנְחָה לִפְנֵי יְהוָה וְהִקְרִיב אֹתָהּ אֶל־

among your people This implies: "All the women will use you in their imprecations and when they curse each other they will say: 'If you have done such a thing may your end be like that of so-and-so.'"[62] For a biblical example of this type of curse, see Jeremiah 29:22; compare also Isaiah 65:15.

as the LORD causes . . . In contrast to "may this water that induces the spell . . . causing . . ." in verse 22a. The ostensible redundancy between verses 21b and 22a is thereby explained: The punishment suffered by the guilty woman is not to be attributed to inherent magical powers of the water (v. 22a) but to the sovereign will of God (v. 21b). Thus it seems likely that verse 21, which interrupts the smooth sequence of verses 20 and 22, was added to emphasize the point that the imprecation derives its powers not from the waters but from the Lord. This insertion must be early since the element stating that the guilty woman will be an object of derision (v. 21a) is present in the wording of the final prognosis (v. 27b).[63] See Excursus 10.

thigh to sag and your belly to distend There is disagreement among scholars concerning the import of these symptoms. "Thigh" probably is a euphemism for the procreative organs (e.g., Gen. 24:2,9), thus referring to the physical inability to beget children (cf. v. 27).[64]

distend Hebrew *tsavah*. A unique usage, of unknown etymology. If related to Akkadian *ṣabû,* "flood," then the effect of the curse would be to flood the woman's uterus, thereby making certain that she would be unable to conceive.

22. ***Amen, amen*** Amen confirms the acceptance of the curse;[65] see Deuteronomy 27:15–26 (twelve times) and Nehemiah 5:13. The oath sworn by Hittite soldiers demanded a similar affirmation.[66] Cases are attested of Bedouin ordeals where the victim "fooled" the ordeal by altering his or her intention while taking the oath.[67] The double "amen" is found at the end of doxologies (Pss. 41:14; 72:19; 89:53) and in solemn acknowledgment of guilt (Neh. 8:6).

23. ***curses*** Rather, "curse." Despite the plural *'alot,* there is only one curse.[68] But perhaps the plural is deliberate, referring to the two symptoms of the punishment or to the punishment and its effect, that she will become an object of derision.

in writing and rub it off into the water Jeremiah is commanded to write down his prophecy against Babylonia on a scroll, read it aloud to the Babylonians, and then tie the scroll to a stone and throw it into the river and say, "Thus shall Babylon sink" (Jer. 51:59–64). This example of sympathetic magic is relevant here in illustrating the belief in the power of the curse when it is written down, read aloud, and then carried out—even in symbolic form. In Egypt, a cure for illness calls for passages of the Koran to be written on the inner surface of a bowl, water to be poured in and stirred until the writing is dissolved, and the potion to be drunk by the patient.[69]

24. Since the offering of the sacrifice precedes the drinking of the potion in verses 25–27, this verse is either anticipatory, as rendered (cf. Lev. 16:6,10),[70] or purposive "so that when he makes . . . spell-inducing water . . ." explaining the purpose of dissolving the curse into the water.

25–26. The ritual procedure is a continuation of verse 18, which had been interrupted by the prescription for the oath in verses 19–24.

25. ***elevate*** A special dedicatory rite, *tenufah,* whereby the offering is brought to the special attention of God (cf. Lev. 14:12,24)[71] before it can be brought to the altar.[72]

meal offering before the LORD, and present it on the altar.
26The priest shall scoop out of the meal offering a token part of it and turn it into smoke on the altar. Last, he shall make the woman drink the water.
27Once he has made her drink the water—if she has defiled herself by breaking faith with her husband, the spell-inducing water shall enter into her to bring on bitterness, so that her belly shall distend and her thigh shall sag; and the woman shall become a curse among her people.
28But if the woman has not defiled herself and is pure, she shall be unharmed and able to retain seed.

29This is the ritual in cases of jealousy, when a woman goes astray while married to her husband and defiles her-

הַמִּזְבֵּחַ׃ 26 וְקָמַץ הַכֹּהֵן מִן־הַמִּנְחָה אֶת־אַזְכָּרָתָהּ
וְהִקְטִיר הַמִּזְבֵּחָה וְאַחַר יַשְׁקֶה אֶת־הָאִשָּׁה אֶת־
הַמָּיִם׃ 27 וְהִשְׁקָהּ אֶת־הַמַּיִם וְהָיְתָה אִם־נִטְמְאָה
וַתִּמְעֹל מַעַל בְּאִישָׁהּ וּבָאוּ בָהּ הַמַּיִם הַמְאָרְרִים
לְמָרִים וְצָבְתָה בִטְנָהּ וְנָפְלָה יְרֵכָהּ וְהָיְתָה הָאִשָּׁה
לְאָלָה בְּקֶרֶב עַמָּהּ׃ 28 וְאִם־לֹא נִטְמְאָה הָאִשָּׁה
וּטְהֹרָה הִוא וְנִקְּתָה וְנִזְרְעָה זָרַע׃ 29 זֹאת תּוֹרַת
הַקְּנָאֹת אֲשֶׁר תִּשְׂטֶה אִשָּׁה תַּחַת אִישָׁהּ
וְנִטְמָאָה׃ 30 אוֹ אִישׁ אֲשֶׁר תַּעֲבֹר עָלָיו רוּחַ

jealousy Rather, "jealousies" or better, "suspicions" for plural ***kena'ot*** (cf. vv. 15,30).

26. The sacrificial procedure follows that of a regular meal offering, ***minḥah*** (cf. Lev. 2:2).

AN EDITORIAL SUMMATION[73] (vv. 27–28)

27. ***Once he has made her drink the water*** This clause is omitted in the Septuagint and the Syriac and looks like an accidental repetition (dittography) of verse 26b. However, once verses 27–28 are understood as an editorial summation of the prognosis, it is not superfluous.

28. ***pure*** That is, the waters having had no effect.

unharmed Literally, "shall be cleansed" (cf. v. 19).

able to retain seed Rather, "bear seed," as opposed to the punishment of sterility inflicted on the guilty wife (cf. v. 21).[74]

A RESUMPTIVE SUBSCRIPT[75] (vv. 29–30)

A typical feature of priestly legislation is to conclude a prescriptive ritual with a summation beginning with the words: "This is the ritual *(torah)*." Thus Leviticus 7:37 summarizes the prescriptive text of chapters 6–7, which lists the individual sacrifices (each headed by the same rubric: "this is the ritual"). Leviticus 11:46–47 recapitulates the animal dietary laws of chapter 11. Leviticus 12:7b concludes the laws of the new mother (with a concessionary supplement, v. 8). Leviticus 13:59 repeats the categories of skin diseases previously discussed. Leviticus 14:32 constitutes a midpoint subscript; it concludes the ritual of the healed leper (which also begins with the word *torah,* 14:2), thus separating it from the leprosy laws that obtain only in the land of Canaan. By contrast, Leviticus 14:54–57 is a resumptive subscript for all the leprosy laws in Leviticus 13–14. Leviticus 15:32–33 concludes the laws of polluting discharges (see Num. 6:13,21). Subscripts themselves can be framed by an inclusion, for example, using the word *torah* at the end as well as at the beginning of the inclusion (Lev. 14:54–57; Ezek. 43:12; and occasionally as here in an inverted position, e.g., 6:21; and cf. further 7:84–88, where a different inclusion occurs).[76]

29. ***goes astray*** Rather, "may go astray" (cf. vv. 12,14b). That the imperfect may be conditional, see 6:20. This resumptive postscript uses the language of the oath (vv. 19–20) in order to summarize the case.

jealousy Rather, "jealousies" or "suspicions" (cf. vv. 15,18). The plural ***kena'ot*** is apt since the text cites two cases that lead to the ordeal (vv. 29–30; cf. the introductory Comment to vv. 11–31 for details).

30. ***jealousy*** Rather, "suspicion" (cf. v. 14). This rendering corresponds with ***kinne',*** "wrought up," in this verse.

self, 30or when a fit of jealousy comes over a man and he is wrought up over his wife: the woman shall be made to stand before the LORD and the priest shall carry out all this ritual with her. 31The man shall be clear of guilt; but that woman shall suffer for her guilt.

קִנְאָה וְקִנֵּא אֶת־אִשְׁתּוֹ וְהֶעֱמִיד אֶת־הָאִשָּׁה לִפְנֵי
יְהוָה וְעָשָׂה לָהּ הַכֹּהֵן אֵת כָּל־הַתּוֹרָה הַזֹּאת׃
31 וְנִקָּה הָאִישׁ מֵעָוֺן וְהָאִשָּׁה הַהִוא תִּשָּׂא אֶת־
עֲוֺנָהּ׃ פ

A POSTSCRIPT (v. 31)

The following is added: The husband goes unpunished if his wife is proved innocent,[77] whereas the wife bears her punishment if she is guilty.[78] Presumably, the point of this addendum is to assure a suspicious husband that he has nothing to lose by bringing his wife to the ordeal. Thus his suspicions will either be proved or laid to rest; in the latter case, a harmonious relationship may be restored.

man That is, the husband (cf. v. 12).

clear of guilt Rather, "free from punishment"; *'avon* means crime or punishment but never guilt.[79]

suffer for her guilt Rather, "suffer her punishment" (see the preceding Comment). The punishment, of course, is the consequence of the ordeal-oath. For other examples of this phrase following the specifications of the punishment, see Leviticus 20:17,19.[80] This clause gives a second reason for the postscript: It is a reminder to the husband and the community that if the adulteress is convicted by the ordeal, her punishment rests solely with God (see Excursus 9).

The rabbis[81] read this verse as follows: "If the man is clear of sin then that woman shall suffer her guilt." They quote the prophet Hosea for support: "I will not punish their daughters for fornicating / Nor their daughters-in-law for committing adultery; / For they themselves turn aside with whores / And sacrifice with prostitutes" (Hos. 4:14). Thus the rabbis limited the efficacy of the ordeal to the case of an impure wife of a sexually pure husband.[82] Similar reasoning prompted Rabbi Johanan ben Zakkai to abolish the ordeal even while the Temple still existed.[83]

CHAPTER 6

THE LAW OF THE NAZIRITE (vv. 1–21)

One becomes a Nazirite by means of a vow (cf. 15:3,8). The law first outlines the obligation of the Nazirite (vv. 1–8), then the ritual procedure of renewing the Nazirite period if it is interrupted by corpse contamination (vv. 9–12), and, finally, the ritual procedure at the termination of the vow (vv. 13–21). The law deals only with a temporary Nazirite, one whose vow is for a limited period; it ignores the lifelong Nazirite (e.g., Samson and Samuel; see Excursus 11) most likely because the latter was not involved with sanctuary ritual. The need of the temporary Nazirite for the priest and the sanctuary probably accounts for the juxtaposition of this section to the law of the suspected adulteress (5:11ff.).[1] Possibly the verbal association of "bare [lit. loosen the hair of] the woman's head" (5:18) and "the hair of his head being left to grow untrimmed" (6:5)—note the same verb *para'*—prompted the connection of the sections.[2]

The prohibitions are minutely detailed, resembling the growth of a terse, uncomplicated mishnah into an intricate, complex gemara.[3] The law of the Nazirite is certainly unusual in biblical jurisprudence, which usually contents itself with generalizations: Its paradigm is the prohibition of work on the Sabbath without ever defining what constitutes work. Thus the original Nazirite prohibitions may have read: "He shall abstain from wine and any other intoxicant (v. 3a); no razor shall touch his head (v. 5a); he is consecrated to the LORD (v. 8b)."[4] The remaining text represents expansions necessitated by the establishment of the temporary vow, the resort to the sanctuary, and the need for defining the prohibitions with greater precision (see Excursus 11).

6 The LORD spoke to Moses, saying: [2]Speak to the Israelites and say to them: If anyone, man or woman, explicitly
utters a nazirite's vow, to set himself apart for the LORD, [3]he
shall abstain from wine and any other intoxicant; he shall
not drink vinegar of wine or of any other intoxicant,
neither shall he drink anything in which grapes have been
steeped, nor eat grapes fresh or dried. [4]Throughout his

ו וַיְדַבֵּר יְהוָה אֶל־מֹשֶׁה לֵּאמֹר׃ 2 דַּבֵּר אֶל־בְּנֵי
יִשְׂרָאֵל וְאָמַרְתָּ אֲלֵהֶם אִישׁ אוֹ־אִשָּׁה כִּי יַפְלִא
לִנְדֹּר נֶדֶר נָזִיר לְהַזִּיר לַיהוָה׃ 3 מִיַּיִן וְשֵׁכָר יַזִּיר
חֹמֶץ יַיִן וְחֹמֶץ שֵׁכָר לֹא יִשְׁתֶּה וְכָל־מִשְׁרַת
עֲנָבִים לֹא יִשְׁתֶּה וַעֲנָבִים לַחִים וִיבֵשִׁים לֹא
יֹאכֵל׃ 4 כֹּל יְמֵי נִזְרוֹ מִכֹּל אֲשֶׁר יֵעָשֶׂה מִגֶּפֶן

2. ***or woman*** The inclusion of the woman indicates that the Nazirite vow was widely practiced. The woman, however, needed the consent of her father or husband, as with all her other vows (30:3ff.). At the end of the Second Temple period, many women took the vow, which accounts for the technical term for the female Nazirite, ***nezirah,*** and for the many laws pertaining to her status (e.g., Mish. Naz. 4:1ff.). A celebrated case of a woman Nazirite was Helena, the convert queen of Abiabene, who took a seven-year vow on the condition that her son return safely from war, but her Nazirite period lasted twice or thrice as long (Mish. Naz. 3:6). Berenice, sister of King Agrippa II, also took the vow when she recovered from illness (Josephus, Wars 2.15.1).

explicitly utters The Hebrew root ***p-l-'*** is frequently used in the making of a vow, either in the Piel (e.g., Lev. 15:3,8; 22:21) or Hifil, as here (also Lev. 27:2). The versions render "express, make explicit," implying that the vow cannot be silent but must be articulated.[5] Ibn Ezra (ii) renders "makes a remarkable vow [from Heb. ***pele',*** "marvel, wonder"] since most people would rather indulge their appetites" (cf. Judg. 13:19). Philo, following the Septuagint, calls it "the great vow," explaining: "His own self is the greatest possession which anyone has and this self he forgoes."[6] This verb may also imply an impulsive act.[7]

nazirite's vow to set himself apart for the LORD Hebrew ***nazir . . . le-hazzir.*** The root ***n-z-r*** means "separate oneself," and if the separation is for God then it implies sanctification (cf. Lev. 15:31).[8] The implication is clear: Only by separating oneself, by abstaining from certain acts permitted to all others, can one be sanctified to God. The noun ***nazir*** is probably an abbreviation of ***nezir 'elohim*** (cf. Judg. 13:5,7): one who is separated or consecrated to God. It is applied metaphorically to one who is singled out from his group (e.g., Gen. 49:26; Deut. 33:16). The noun ***nezer*** also refers to the hair of the head (v. 9; cf. Jer. 7:29) and, figuratively, to the consecrated head (Lev. 21:12) or headgear (Exod. 39:30) and to the unpruned vine (Lev. 25:5).

PROHIBITIONS FOR THE TEMPORARY NAZIRITE (vv. 3–8)

The temporary Nazirite was forbidden from (1) imbibing wine or ale or any product of the vine; (2) cutting the hair; (3) coming into contact with a corpse. Although the first and third prohibitions resemble those of the priest, who also may not drink intoxicants or be contaminated by the dead, the Nazirite's prohibitions are more severe. Thus the priest may not partake of strong drink when he enters the sanctuary (Lev. 10:9; Ezek. 44:21), but outside he is under no such restrictions (e.g., Isa. 28:7), not to speak of having to refrain from the unfermented grape. In regard to corpse contamination, the Nazirite more closely resembles the High Priest, who also was forbidden to approach the dead (i.e., attend the funerals) of his own immediate family (Lev. 21:11). However, in regard to his unpolled hair, the Nazirite was *sui generis.* Although the priest was forbidden to shave his hair (deliberately distinguishing him from his Egyptian counterpart)[9] he was also forbidden to let it grow wild and was expected to trim it regularly (Ezek. 44:20). Indeed, it is the uniqueness of his uncut hair that is the mark of the Nazirite and the part of him that is truly holy, to judge by the treatment of the hair when the Nazirite period is accidentally aborted or successfully terminated. For the distinction between the temporary Nazirite and the lifelong Nazirite, as recorded in Scripture, see Excursus 11.

3–4. Wine and ale are forbidden to the Nazirite. A more precise definition of what is meant by wine and ale follows, consisting of three items in increasing order of severity: (1) wine turned sour (vinegar); (2) the grapes themselves, whether fresh or dry; (3) even the nonjuicy part of the grape, the seeds and the skin.

term as nazirite, he may not eat anything that is obtained
from the grapevine, even seeds or skin.
5 Throughout the term of his vow as nazirite, no razor
shall touch his head; it shall remain consecrated until the
completion of his term as nazirite of the LORD, the hair of
his head being left to grow untrimmed. 6 Throughout the
term that he has set apart for the LORD, he shall not go in
where there is a dead person. 7 Even if his father or mother,

הַיַּ֔יִן מֵחַרְצַנִּ֥ים וְעַד־זָ֖ג לֹ֥א יֹאכֵֽל׃ 5 כָּל־יְמֵי֙ נֶ֣דֶר
נִזְר֔וֹ תַּ֖עַר לֹא־יַעֲבֹ֣ר עַל־רֹאשׁ֑וֹ עַד־מְלֹ֨את הַיָּמִ֜ם
אֲשֶׁר־יַזִּ֤יר לַֽיהוָה֙ קָדֹ֣שׁ יִהְיֶ֔ה גַּדֵּ֥ל פֶּ֖רַע שְׂעַ֥ר
רֹאשֽׁוֹ׃ 6 כָּל־יְמֵ֥י הַזִּיר֖וֹ לַֽיהוָ֑ה עַל־נֶ֥פֶשׁ מֵ֖ת לֹ֥א
יָבֹֽא׃ 7 לְאָבִ֣יו וּלְאִמּ֗וֹ לְאָחִיו֙ וּלְאַ֣חֹת֔וֹ לֹֽא־יִטַּמָּ֥א

any other intoxicant Hebrew *shekhar*, alternatively "old wine."[10] The exact cognate in Akkadian *šikru, šikaru,* means "beer." The beer and ale industry is attested in earliest times in the predominantly grain-growing countries of Egypt and Mesopotamia. Canaan, however, was celebrated for its wine, which figured among its chief exports in every age (see also 28:7). Typical of Philistine pottery is a jug "usually provided with a strainer spout . . . in order to strain out the beer without swallowing barley husks. It is not difficult to infer from the ubiquity of these . . . beer jugs that the Philistines were mighty carousers. In this respect, archaeology is in full agreement with biblical tradition, as we see from the story of Samson, where drinking bouts are mentioned several times in connection with the Philistines, though it is said emphatically of Samson that he drank neither wine nor beer."[11]

vinegar Hebrew *ḥomets,* that is, wine turned sour, used as food by the poor (Ruth 2:14).

steeped[12]

dried That is, raisins. Pressed into a cake, it was a common article of food (cf. 2 Sam. 6:19; Hos. 3:1).

4. obtained The Hebrew root *ʿ-s-h* can mean "produce," as in Genesis 1:11 and Job 1:14.

grapevine Literally, "vine of the wine"; compare Judges 13:14, where Samson's mother is explicitly forbidden to partake of "anything that comes from the grapevine."

even seeds or skin Hebrew *ḥartsannim* and *zag* are unique words, and all renderings are conjectures derived from the context.[13]

5. shall touch Literally, "shall press over." The usual verb with the subject razor is *gillaḥ,* "shave." Its avoidance is deliberate: Not only shaving is prohibited but any form of trimming.

it That is, the hair.[14] However, the rendering "he," meaning the Nazirite, is preferable (cf. v. 8). True, the hair remains a permanent sanctum: It cannot undergo desanctification and must be burnt when the Nazirite vow is terminated. But all during the Nazirite period the entire person is holy. He is the lay equivalent of a priest and must observe similar prohibitions (see Excursus 11).

hair That the Nazirite's uncut hair is more significant than his other two characteristics is indicated in verse 7; it is the sole reason cited for abstaining from corpse contamination. Also it is the only characteristic common to both the temporary Nazirite, legislated here, and the lifelong Nazirite, discussed in the biblical narratives. Indeed, of both Samson and Samuel it is expressly specified that they did not cut their hair: "No razor has ever touched my head, for I have been a nazirite to God since I was in my mother's womb" (Judg. 16:17); "no razor shall ever touch his head" (1 Sam. 1:11). In other contexts, the word *nazir* takes on the figurative meaning of an untrimmed vine (Lev. 25:5,11), again indicating that the Nazirite's distinctive trait is his uncut hair (see Excursus 11).

6–7. In respect to the prohibition of coming into contact with the dead, the Nazirite resembles the High Priest, who is also forbidden to contaminate himself by attending the burial rites of the members of his immediate family (Lev. 21:11).

he has set apart Hebrew *hazziro* is perhaps used reflexively, "he has set himself apart."

go in Hebrew *yavo' ʿal.* Defilement results from being under the same roof as the corpse (see 19:14–16).

or his brother or sister should die, he must not defile
himself for them, since hair set apart for his God is upon his
head: 8 throughout his term as nazirite he is consecrated to
the LORD.
9 If a person dies suddenly near him, defiling his consecrated hair, he shall shave his head on the day he becomes
clean; he shall shave it on the seventh day. 10 On the eighth

לָהֶם בְּמֹתָם כִּי נֵזֶר אֱלֹהָיו עַל־רֹאשׁוֹ׃ 8 כֹּל יְמֵי
נִזְרוֹ קָדֹשׁ הוּא לַיהוָה׃ 9 וְכִי־יָמוּת מֵת עָלָיו
בְּפֶתַע פִּתְאֹם וְטִמֵּא רֹאשׁ נִזְרוֹ וְגִלַּח רֹאשׁוֹ בְּיוֹם
טָהֳרָתוֹ בַּיּוֹם הַשְּׁבִיעִי יְגַלְּחֶנּוּ׃ 10 וּבַיּוֹם הַשְּׁמִינִי

7. ***hair set apart*** Hebrew ***nezer;*** compare verse 2.

8. ***consecrated*** The fourth and final use of the introductory phrase "throughout his term as nazirite" (see vv. 4,5,6) sums up his status as one who is "consecrated to the Lord." All the restrictions previously enumerated have but one function, to consecrate him and thus endow him with a status equivalent to the priesthood (see Excursus 11).

CONTAMINATION BY CORPSE (vv. 9–12)

When the Nazirite period ends because of corpse contamination it must start over again after a special rite of purification. In this respect, the Nazirite stands higher than the corpse-contaminated priest who, as in the case of a layman, undergoes only a seven-day ritual of purification and does not have to bring any sacrifices (19:11–12). The prophet Ezekiel, however, requires the priest to supplement the layman's purification by barring him from the sanctuary for an additional week, at the end of which he brings a purification offering (Ezek. 44:26–27). Thus the Nazirite may reflect a more severe code of impurities for the priest, one mitigated by the Torah but preserved by Ezekiel. (For another example of an ancient priestly practice preserved by the Nazirite's ritual, see v. 19.) The corpse-contaminated priest of Ezekiel and the Nazirite bear an impurity of the same severe degree as the parturient, the gonorrheic individual, and the leper, who also had to bring purification sacrifices at the end of their impurity (Lev. 12:6–8; 14:10; 15:14,29). The other sacrifices incumbent on the Nazirite will be explained below.

9. ***near him*** Hebrew ***ʿalav.*** In contrast to the layman, who is contaminated by a corpse only by direct contact or by being under the same roof, the Nazirite (v. 6, and the High Priest, cf. Lev. 21:11, which uses the same word ***ʿal,*** "near") is contaminated merely by being in its proximity.[15] Such is the added power of the Nazirite's holiness that it contracts impurity at a distance. This idea that impurity could be contracted by sight as well as by touch, especially by holy persons, is widely attested in the ancient world.[16] That this view prevailed in the priestly legislation in the Bible is discussed in Excursus 11. It is thus probable that the mere sight of the corpse aborted the Nazirite vow.

What if the Nazirite came into contact with the leper or gonorrheic? *A fortiori* it must be deduced that, since these impurities are as severe (and indeed severer) than corpse contamination, they automatically cancel the Nazirite vow.[17] However, this would not hold for lesser impurities. For example, the Nazirite is not prohibited from sexual relations even though they cause defilement (Lev. 15:18); and clearly the vow of the woman Nazirite is not terminated by her menses, though it causes defilement (Lev. 15:19).[18]

suddenly Hebrew ***be-fetaʿ pitʾom,***[19] indicating that the occurrence was accidental.[20] Indeed, if the contamination were deliberate, sacrificial expiation (v. 12) would be inadmissible (15:27–31).[21]

defiling his consecrated hair Only his hair is permanently sanctified, in contrast to his person, which is desanctified at the termination of his vow (see v. 18).

shave his head According to Mishnah Temurah 7:4, the shaved hair was buried, probably to prevent it from polluting other objects.[22]

he shall shave it on the seventh day An explanatory gloss on the "day he becomes clean," that is, after he has been sprinkled on the third and seventh day with the purificatory waters (19:11–12).[23]

day he shall bring two turtledoves or two pigeons to the
priest, at the entrance of the Tent of Meeting. 11The priest
shall offer one as a sin offering and the other as a burnt
offering, and make expiation on his behalf for the guilt that
he incurred through the corpse. That same day he shall
reconsecrate his head 12and rededicate to the LORD his term
as nazirite; and he shall bring a lamb in its first year as a
penalty offering. The previous period shall be void, since
his consecrated hair was defiled.

יָבִא֙ שְׁתֵּ֣י תֹרִ֔ים א֥וֹ שְׁנֵ֖י בְּנֵ֣י יוֹנָ֑ה אֶל־הַכֹּהֵ֔ן אֶל־
פֶּ֖תַח אֹ֥הֶל מוֹעֵֽד׃ 11 וְעָשָׂ֣ה הַכֹּהֵ֗ן אֶחָ֤ד לְחַטָּאת֙
וְאֶחָ֣ד לְעֹלָ֔ה וְכִפֶּ֣ר עָלָ֔יו מֵאֲשֶׁ֥ר חָטָ֖א עַל־הַנָּ֑פֶשׁ
וְקִדַּ֥שׁ אֶת־רֹאשׁ֖וֹ בַּיּ֥וֹם הַהֽוּא׃ 12 וְהִזִּ֤יר לַֽיהוָה֙
אֶת־יְמֵ֣י נִזְר֔וֹ וְהֵבִ֛יא כֶּ֥בֶשׂ בֶּן־שְׁנָת֖וֹ לְאָשָׁ֑ם
וְהַיָּמִ֤ים הָרִאשֹׁנִים֙ יִפְּל֔וּ כִּ֥י טָמֵ֖א נִזְרֽוֹ׃ 13 וְזֹ֥את

*10. **two turtledoves or two pigeons*** The most inexpensive animal offerings (cf. Lev. 5:7; 12:8). However, he is not given the option of bringing instead the cheaper meal offering allowed the indigent layman who has accidentally prolonged his impurity (Lev. 5:3,11–13), probably because animal blood is required for the purgation of the altar (Lev. 4:27–35; 8:15). R. Shemayah was wont to say: "What reason had the Torah for being lenient to an unclean Nazirite and making him bring only turtledoves or young pigeons? Because, when assuming Naziriteship, he intended the act for the glory of heaven, and when defiled he forfeited all that he accomplished and would have to recommence from the beginning; the Torah consequently showed consideration for him by enabling him to free himself from his obligation through a poor man's offering."[24]

*11. **sin offering*** Hebrew *ḥatta't*. Rather, "purification offering."

burnt offering Hebrew *'olah* is actually superfluous since only the purification offering is needed in order to purge the sanctuary of the impurity caused by the Nazirite's contamination. However, as noted by Ibn Ezra (on Lev. 5:7, and endorsed by Ramban), the burnt offering was added in the case of birds to provide an adequate gift for the altar.

guilt Rather, "wrongdoing" or "error." Hebrew *ḥata'* does not imply sin but failure, as in Judges 20:16: "sling a stone at a hair and not miss."[25]

*12. **rededicate to the LORD*** Presumably by a new vow.

penalty offering Hebrew *'asham*. Rather, "reparation offering." Its purpose is to make expiation for the inadvertent desecration of the consecrated hair and vow. (That a vow is in itself a sanctum capable of desecration is explicitly stated by 30:2.) This is shown not only by the general function of the *'asham* to expiate a desecrated sanctum but by the sacrificial order required for the contaminated Nazirite. The *'asham* is last in the series, following the purification and burnt offering; moreover, it is separated from the latter by a nonsacrificial ritual whereby the Nazirite reconsecrates his hair and renews his vow. This break is unprecedented, for in every other biblical rite the prescribed sacrifices follow each other without interruption. In this case, the act of reconsecration could have taken place before or after the sacrificial service. Why was it put before the reparation offering? The answer is to be found in the unchangeable procedure for all reparation offerings: Before the offender can look for expiation through his sacrifice, he must repay the sanctuary for the desecrated sanctum (cf. Lev. 5:14–16). The purpose of the ritual order is clear: The sanctum must be restored before God's forgiveness may be sought. The same sacrificial principles are invoked for the contaminated Nazirite. Before his reparation offering can be acceptable to God he must replace the desecrated sancta—the consecrated hair that has been shaven and the preceding Nazirite period that has been canceled. Total restitution has been rendered only after he reconsecrates his new hair and renews his vow; then, and only then, can the priest proceed with the reparation offering in the hope of achieving divine forgiveness.

A historic case illustrating this law is recorded in the Mishnah. Queen Helena had taken a seven-year Nazirite vow. At the end of the period she accidentally became contaminated and had to renew her vow for another seven years.[26]

The reparation animal is a lamb, in contrast to the relatively inexpensive purification birds. This is in keeping with the nature of the *'asham,* which always demands a ram and less frequently a lamb (cf. Lev. 14:12,21); it may never be reduced to fit the economic status of the offerer, as is the case with the purification offering (e.g., Lev. 5:1–13). The reason is that the reparation expiation is offered for an

¹³This is the ritual for the nazirite: On the day that his term as nazirite is completed, he shall be brought to the entrance of the Tent of Meeting. ¹⁴As his offering to the LORD he shall present: one male lamb in its first year, without blemish, for a burnt offering; one ewe lamb in its first year, without blemish, for a sin offering; one ram without blemish for an offering of well-being; ¹⁵a basket of unleavened cakes of choice flour with oil mixed in, and unleavened wafers spread with oil; and the proper meal offerings and libations.

¹⁶The priest shall present them before the LORD and offer the sin offering and the burnt offering. ¹⁷He shall offer the

תּוֹרַ֣ת הַנָּזִ֑יר בְּי֗וֹם מְלֹאת֙ יְמֵ֣י נִזְר֔וֹ יָבִ֣יא אֹת֔וֹ
אֶל־פֶּ֖תַח אֹ֥הֶל מוֹעֵֽד׃ ¹⁴ וְהִקְרִ֣יב אֶת־קָרְבָּנ֣וֹ
לַיהוָ֡ה כֶּ֩בֶשׂ בֶּן־שְׁנָת֨וֹ תָמִ֤ים אֶחָד֙ לְעֹלָ֔ה וְכַבְשָׂ֨ה
אַחַ֧ת בַּת־שְׁנָתָ֛הּ תְּמִימָ֖ה לְחַטָּ֑את וְאַֽיִל־אֶחָ֥ד
תָּמִ֖ים לִשְׁלָמִֽים׃ ¹⁵ וְסַ֣ל מַצּ֗וֹת סֹ֤לֶת חַלֹּת֙
בְּלוּלֹ֣ת בַּשֶּׁ֔מֶן וּרְקִיקֵ֥י מַצּ֖וֹת מְשֻׁחִ֣ים בַּשָּׁ֑מֶן
וּמִנְחָתָ֖ם וְנִסְכֵּיהֶֽם׃ ¹⁶ וְהִקְרִ֥יב הַכֹּהֵ֖ן לִפְנֵ֣י יְהוָ֑ה
וְעָשָׂ֥ה אֶת־חַטָּאת֖וֹ וְאֶת־עֹלָתֽוֹ׃ ¹⁷ וְאֶת־הָאַ֜יִל

offense committed against God—by desecrating His property or name in an oath; it is therefore never subject to amelioration because of economic circumstances.

THE COMPLETION RITUAL (vv. 13–21)

The Nazirite, at the completion of the term of his vow, brings the following sacrifices: one female lamb for a purification offering, one male lamb for a burnt offering, one ram for a well-being offering, and a basket of unleavened cakes together with the requisite meal offerings and libations. The priest sacrifices them (except the cakes) in that order. The Nazirite shaves his consecrated hair and has it burnt. The priestly portion of the well-being ram and the basket of unleavened cakes undergo an elevation offering after which the Nazirite may drink wine.

13. _he shall be brought_ Literally, "one shall bring it." Ibn Ezra (ii) suggests that the priests force the Nazirite to bring the sacrifice to prevent him from prolonging his Nazirite period beyond the term of his vow. However, it hardly seems feasible that the sanctuary would keep track of every Nazirite's term and enforce its termination on the expiration date. Furthermore, how could the priests know the exact date when the vow began? It was not taken at the sanctuary![27]

14. The requirement for a purification offering[28] presents an enigma. The Nazirite has successfully completed his vow. Had he contaminated the sanctuary by some major impurity, his Naziriteship would have been aborted, as in the previously mentioned case. Had he incurred some impurity or wrongdoing unknowingly, he could not have brought a purification offering, which requires awareness of the offense. It is Ramban (followed by Abravanel) who points to the most likely answer: his self-removal from the sacred to the profane realm requires sacrificial expiation. This expiation cannot be fulfilled by the reparation offering that is imposed only for illegitimate desanctification—the Nazirite's desanctification is perfectly legitimate. His sacred status more resembles that of property dedicated to the sanctuary (see Excursus 11 for details) and then desanctified, that is, redeemed, by a monetary fine (cf. Lev. 27:14–33). The use of the purification offering for this purpose is nonetheless unique.[29]

The animal offerings for the successfully completed and abortive Nazirite period are the same, with this major difference: The 'asham for desecration has been replaced by the shelamim for joy.[30]

sin offering Rather, "purification offering" (cf. Lev. 4).

15. _cakes_ Hebrew ḥallot in the form of cakes, as distinct from wafers, the other grain offering in the basket. The offering of well-being resembles that of the todah, the thanksgiving offering, in respect to the accompanying grain offerings (Lev. 7:11–12).

the proper meal offerings and libations For the burnt offerings and the offering of well-being but not for the purification offering.[31] This fact had to be expressed in order to distinguish the Nazirite's well-being offering from the thanksgiving offering (Lev. 7:11–15), which does not require meal offerings and libations.[32]

16. _them_ Omitted in the Hebrew but understood. Alternatively, render "him," that is, the Nazirite.

ram as a sacrifice of well-being to the Lord, together with
the basket of unleavened cakes; the priest shall also offer the
meal offerings and the libations. 18 The nazirite shall then
shave his consecrated hair, at the entrance of the Tent of
Meeting, and take the locks of his consecrated hair and put
them on the fire that is under the sacrifice of well-being.

19 The priest shall take the shoulder of the ram when it has
been boiled, one unleavened cake from the basket, and one
unleavened wafer, and place them on the hands of the
nazirite after he has shaved his consecrated hair. 20 The

יַעֲשֶׂה זֶבַח שְׁלָמִים לַיהוָה עַל סַל הַמַּצּוֹת וְעָשָׂה
הַכֹּהֵן אֶת־מִנְחָתוֹ וְאֶת־נִסְכּוֹ׃ 18 וְגִלַּח הַנָּזִיר
פֶּתַח אֹהֶל מוֹעֵד אֶת־רֹאשׁ נִזְרוֹ וְלָקַח אֶת־שְׂעַר
רֹאשׁ נִזְרוֹ וְנָתַן עַל־הָאֵשׁ אֲשֶׁר־תַּחַת זֶבַח
הַשְּׁלָמִים׃ 19 וְלָקַח הַכֹּהֵן אֶת־הַזְּרֹעַ בְּשֵׁלָה מִן־
הָאַיִל וְחַלַּת מַצָּה אַחַת מִן־הַסַּל וּרְקִיק מַצָּה
אֶחָד וְנָתַן עַל־כַּפֵּי הַנָּזִיר אַחַר הִתְגַּלְּחוֹ אֶת־נִזְרוֹ׃

*17. **offer . . . together with the basket of unleavened cakes*** The cakes, however, are only presented. They are not sacrificed but are eaten by the priest and Nazirite (see v. 19). The purpose of their presentation (probably by setting the basket before the altar) is to sanctify them.[33]

the priest shall also offer the meal offerings and libations Rather, "when the priest shall offer its meal offering and libation." The sacrifices accompanying the offering of well-being are singled out (but not those of the burnt offering) in order to emphasize that only after all the sacrifices have been offered up on the altar may the Nazirite shave his consecrated hair (v. 18).

*18. **at the entrance of the Tent of Meeting*** That is, between the entrance and the altar, the area permitted to the lay worshiper when he brought his offerings. The Second Temple provided a special room in the outer court, where the Nazirites had their heads shaved and boiled the meat of their offering of well-being.[34]

the fire that is under the sacrifice of well-being The meat of this sacrifice belonged to the worshiper. This verse preserves the custom, attested in the ancient sources, that the sacrifice was cooked and eaten in the sacred precincts (Lev. 8:31; 1 Sam. 2:13; Ezek. 46:24). The hair was burned not in the altar fire but in the special hearth set up "under the pot"[35] to cook the sacrifice of well-being (cf. v. 19).

Because the hair is holy (vv. 5,7) even after it is shaved, it must be destroyed by fire. Its destruction prevents it from being defiled. In this respect, it resembles the uneaten portion of the well-being offering, which similarly must be burnt (Lev. 7:17; 19:6) because it is holy (Lev. 19:8).

*19. **the shoulder*** Hebrew *zeroʿa,* the upper part of the foreleg, is mentioned only once again as a priestly perquisite, in Deuteronomy 18:3, which assigns it to the priest from every offering of well-being. Elsewhere, the breast and thigh of the right hind leg of this sacrifice are allotted to the priest (see v. 20 and Lev. 7:30–33). The priestly right to the shoulder of the sacrificial animal has hallowed precedent both in the ancient Near East and in Israel. Egyptian rituals depicted on rock tombs and temple murals clearly show that the entire foreleg, including the shoulder, was carried in sacred processions and placed upon the god's table.[36] Early Mesopotamian sources also verify that the shoulder was considered a sacred portion reserved for the gods and priests. For example, the hero Gilgamesh "severed the shoulder from the Bull of Heaven and tossed it in her (Ishtar's) face."[37] The priest "removes the shoulder of the bull together with its skin."[38] The shoulder was a sacred portion also among the Hittites.[39] And the Jewish sect that lived at the Dead Sea awarded the shoulder to the Levites.[40]

boiled The priest received the shoulder after it was boiled,[41] another indication of the antiquity of this sacrifice. Near the altar of the Lachish temple dating from pre-Israelite Canaan, bones from the right foreleg of a number of animals were found. Significantly, these bones were not burned, indicating that these portions were not consumed on the altar but cooked nearby and eaten.[42] Clearer and more striking witness is provided by the Bible itself. During the days of Samuel, before the Jerusalem Temple was built, the following was the practice at Shiloh and other sanctuaries: "This is how the priests used to deal with the people: When anyone brought a sacrifice, the priest's boy would come along with a three-pronged fork while the meat was boiling, and he would thrust it into the cauldron, or the kettle, or the great pot, or the small cooking pot; and what the fork brought

20 וְהֵנִיף אוֹתָם הַכֹּהֵן ׀ תְּנוּפָה לִפְנֵי יְהוָה קֹדֶשׁ
הוּא לַכֹּהֵן עַל חֲזֵה הַתְּנוּפָה וְעַל שׁוֹק הַתְּרוּמָה
וְאַחַר יִשְׁתֶּה הַנָּזִיר יָיִן׃ 21 זֹאת תּוֹרַת הַנָּזִיר
אֲשֶׁר יִדֹּר קָרְבָּנוֹ לַיהוָה עַל־נִזְרוֹ מִלְּבַד אֲשֶׁר־
תַּשִּׂיג יָדוֹ כְּפִי נִדְרוֹ אֲשֶׁר יִדֹּר כֵּן יַעֲשֶׂה עַל
תּוֹרַת נִזְרוֹ׃ פ 22 וַיְדַבֵּר יְהוָה אֶל־מֹשֶׁה

priest shall elevate them as an elevation offering before the LORD; and this shall be a sacred donation for the priest, in addition to the breast of the elevation offering and the thigh of gift offering. After that the nazirite may drink wine.

21 Such is the obligation of a nazirite; except that he who vows an offering to the LORD of what he can afford, beyond his nazirite requirements, must do exactly according to the vow that he has made beyond his obligation as a nazirite.

up, the priest would take away on it" (1 Sam. 2:13–14). Two bits of relevant information can be derived from this pregnant text: The offerer's sacrifice (of well-being) was boiled on the sanctuary premises, and the priests received their due not from the raw but from the boiled meat. Hence, the boiled shoulder, attested at pre-Israelite Lachish and pre-Temple Shiloh (in distinction to the other priestly portions, the raw breast and thigh; cf. v. 20), is based on very ancient precedent. The tradition of cooking the meat of the offering of well-being near the altar is also attested in Ezekiel's blueprint for the Temple (Ezek. 46:24) and in the actual practice in the Second Temple[43] as well as by the rabbinic rule, "the Nazirite cooked (his offering) where he shaved."[44]

one unleavened cake from the basket The basket had been set down "before the LORD" (Lev. 8:26), probably by the altar (Deut. 26:4,10). Its contents, except for the set belonging to the priest, will be eaten by the Nazirite together with the well-being offering, in accordance with the procedure for a thanksgiving offering (Lev. 7:11–15).

hands Hebrew *kappei.* Rather, "palms."

20. elevate . . . elevation offering The *tenufah* is a rite of dedication that transfers the elevated objects from the property of the offerer to God. That is why all the portions given to the priests are first placed on the palms of the donor to indicate that they initially belonged to him, that they are his to donate. Then the elevation movement is performed by the priest (probably by placing his hands under the palms of the donor),[45] graphically transferring the objects to God, after which they may be eaten by the priest.[46]

gift offering Rather, "dedication." Hebrew *terumah* means that which is set aside or dedicated.[47] The *terumah* is not an offering as is the *tenufah.*[48]

21. Such is the obligation of a nazirite . . . beyond his obligation as a nazirite A resumptive subscript, forming an inclusion with verse 13a (cf. also 5:29).[49]

except . . . This clause adds that the sacrifices enumerated above are the minimum due. The Nazirite who vows additional offerings must fulfill his vow (cf. 30:3; Deut. 23:22). The rabbis derive from this verse that if he is too poor to discharge his required offerings, the community could defray the costs.[50] Indeed, there are recorded instances in Roman times when kings and aristocrats undertook to pay for the offerings of Jewish Nazirites.[51]

APPENDIX: THE PRIESTLY BLESSING (vv. 22–27)

Among the chief duties of the priest is to bless Israel in the name of the Lord (Deut. 10:8; 21:5). However, the blessing issues solely from the Lord; the priests' function is to channel it. This point is made emphatically clear by the threefold use of the divine Name in the blessing formula itself (vv. 24–26). And if this were not enough, the authorization for the priests to pronounce the blessing concludes with the admonition (v. 27) that even though the priests utter the divine Name, it is not they but the Lord who alone can activate the blessing.[52] This repeated emphasis on the divine source of the blessing is projected into even bolder relief when it is contrasted with the formula of welcome pronounced upon the worshiper (by the priest?) as he entered the Temple: "We bless you from the

²²The Lord spoke to Moses: ²³Speak to Aaron and his sons: Thus shall you bless the people of Israel. Say to them:

²⁴The Lord bless you and protect you!

²⁵The Lord deal kindly and graciously with you!

לֵאמֹֽר: 23 דַּבֵּ֤ר אֶֽל־אַהֲרֹן֙ וְאֶל־בָּנָ֣יו לֵאמֹ֔ר כֹּ֥ה תְבָרֲכ֖וּ אֶת־בְּנֵ֣י יִשְׂרָאֵ֑ל אָמ֖וֹר לָהֶֽם: ס

24 יְבָרֶכְךָ֥ יְהוָ֖ה וְיִשְׁמְרֶֽךָ: ס

25 יָאֵ֨ר יְהוָ֧ה ׀ פָּנָ֛יו אֵלֶ֖יךָ וִֽיחֻנֶּֽךָּ: ס

House of the Lord" (Ps. 118:26). Clearly our text has taken great pains to underscore that, although the priest is holy (Lev. 8:30; 22:9), indeed, one of God's intimates (Lev. 10:3), he possesses no divine powers of his own. He is the invested technician of the cult, but whether his purpose is blessing or forgiveness (see Lev. 4:20), consent and implementation reside solely with God.

The structure of the formula is simple, and in its simplicity lies its strength. The threefold blessing is a rising crescendo of 3, 5, and 7 words, respectively. The number of consonants are respectively 15, 20, and 25. The increased progression is also evidenced in the number of words (15, 20, 25), of stressed syllables or meter (3, 5, 7) and of total syllables (12, 14, 16). The first and last cola of the poem are exactly the same length (7 syllables), and they form an envelope about the poem that summarizes its essence: "The Lord bless you / and grant you peace," which is also the conclusion of Psalm 29.[53]

The first part of each line invokes the movement of God toward His people, the second, His activity on their behalf.[54] As rendered here, God initiates six actions: bless *and* protect; shine *and* be gracious; bestow *and* grant peace. However, the transitional *and* may indicate consequence: blessing results in protection; God's shining face results in grace; the bestowal of God's favor results in peace. Thus the Priestly Blessing may actually express three actions.[55]

The blessing itself is couched in the singular, whereas the framework (vv. 23,27) is in the plural. There are those (e.g., Karaites, cited by Ibn Ezra) who connect this section with the formula in the last verse of the preceding section (6:21) and claim that the priest recited it at the conclusion of every individual sacrifice. However, the collective of Israel is addressed in the singular elsewhere, for example, in the Decalogue; in Exodus 20:2–17 and Deuteronomy 5:6–18, and in formulas of blessing in Deuteronomy 28:1–14. It is of significance that in the one attestation of a priest blessing an individual, he does so in response to her specific need, not in the generalities of the Priestly Blessing (1 Sam. 2:20). Ibn Ezra, following the rabbis,[56] feels that the Priestly Blessing is a community blessing. He identifies it with the blessing recited by Aaron at the conclusion of the first public service after the consecration of the Tabernacle (Lev. 9:21–22). And he explains its placement here, following the Nazirite, in terms of associative reasoning: Both the Nazirite and priest were holy. However, a satisfactory explanation of the occurrence of the Priestly Benediction in its present setting has yet to be found.

23. Thus That is, when you bless, use this formula, not one of your devising. The rabbis identify this formula with the blessing recited by Aaron at the conclusion of the first public service in the newly consecrated Tabernacle (Lev. 9:22), thereby deducing that it should be recited by the priests while they are standing, with hands raised, in Hebrew.[57]

to them To the assembled worshipers, indicating the communal nature of the blessing despite its wording in the singular.[58]

24. The Lord That is, "May the Lord" (and so in vv. 25,26).

bless Generally in the Bible, God's blessing comprises mainly material bounty, specifically: posterity (Gen. 28:3; Deut. 1:11); possessions and wealth (Gen. 24:35); land (Gen. 35:12; 48:3); fertility, health, victory (Deut. 7:12–16); strength and peace (Ps. 29:11). For a complete catalogue of wholly material blessings, see Deuteronomy 28:3–14.[59]

protect That is, protect you from evil spirits (Ps. 91:11) and from all forms of evil (Ps. 121).[60]

25. deal kindly Hebrew *ya'er panav*, literally "make His face to shine," that is, illumine.[61] The Hebrew anthropomorphic expression likewise indicates God's friendly concern (e.g., Ps. 31:17). This can also be derived from its semantic opposite, the hiding of God's face, indicating His anger

²⁶The LORD bestow His favor upon you and grant you peace!

²⁷Thus they shall link My name with the people of Israel, and I will bless them.

26 יִשָּׂ֨א יְהֹוָ֤ה ׀ פָּנָיו֙ אֵלֶ֔יךָ וְיָשֵׂ֥ם לְךָ֖ שָׁלֽוֹם׃ ס

27 וְשָׂמ֥וּ אֶת־שְׁמִ֖י עַל־בְּנֵ֣י יִשְׂרָאֵ֑ל וַאֲנִ֖י אֲבָרְכֵֽם׃

פ   חמישי [רביעי לספרדים]

(e.g., Deut. 31:18). It is especially noteworthy that the synonym of "the light of the kings" is "his favor" (Prov. 16:15), and its antithesis is "his wrath" (v. 14).

graciously The root ḥ-n-n is used exclusively in connection with God's mercy and grace, meaning that God will temper His justice by His mercy.[62] He will not judge Israel according to its sins but will deal kindly with it as His free gift.[63] That the root ḥ-n-n is not found elsewhere in the priestly texts probably indicates that the formula here adapted as the Priestly Blessing is an ancient one.

26. bestow His favor The idiom nasa' panim, literally "lift the face," can mean either "to look" without qualifying the action (e.g., 2 Sam. 2:22; 2 Kings 9:32) or "to look with favor" (e.g., Gen. 19:21; 32:21; Job 42:8–9), that is, "smile."[64] Targum Jonathan suggests that this phrase means that God will answer the petitioner's prayer.

peace Hebrew shalom means in its negative sense the freedom from all disasters (Lev. 26:6; Job 21:9). But in its broadest scope it encompasses the positive blessings of prosperity (Deut. 23:7; Prov. 3:2); good health (Ps. 38:4); friendship (Jer. 20:10; 38:22); and general well-being (in greeting, 1 Sam. 16:4f.; 2 Sam. 18:28; cf. shelamim, the well-being offering).

Among the ramifications of this term in the midrash we find: "Great is peace, for the divine Name which was inscribed with all holiness was ordered by the Holy One Blessed be He to be blotted out in water (Num. 5:23) for the sake of bringing about peace between a man and his wife. . . . R. Eleazar, son of R. Eleazar ha-Kappar, says that even if Israel serves idols and peace reigns among them, the Holy One Blessed be He, as it were, says: 'Satan shall not touch them.'"[65]

27. In the Septuagint this verse follows verse 23, thus expressing God's command to Moses in a continuous statement. However the Masoretic order is superior since the formula follows directly upon "say to them." Furthermore, the second person address to the priest in verse 23 is altered to the third person in verse 27, a change that makes sense if the formula intervenes.

Thus they shall link My name with Literally, "And they (the priests) shall place My name on." In the light of the Ketef Hinnom silver plaques, which demonstrate that in seventh (or sixth)-century Jerusalem the Priestly Benediction was worn on the body in the form of amulets, the possibility exists that the literal meaning of this phrase is the correct one, that is, that the Priestly Benediction delivered by the priests in the sanctuary was also to be placed on the Israelites as prophylactics (see Excursus 13). The usual interpretation, adopted in the translation, is that God's Name is figuratively "placed" by the priests on the Israelites through the medium of the benediction. Alternatively, God's name is nikra', "called" upon Israel (Deut. 28:10). Both verbs imply ownership (Deut. 12:5; Jer. 7:10).

and I Rather, "and it is I" or "I Myself." Hebrew va-'ani is emphatic, thrusting home the point that not the priests but the Lord is the sole author of the blessing.[66]

Final Preparations for the Tabernacle Cult   (7:1–8:26)

The wilderness camp having been organized (2:1–4:20) and purified (5:1–6:27), attention is now given to last details for making the cult operative. These include supplying the Tabernacle with its initial sacrificial implements and ingredients—gifts of the tribal chieftains (7:1–89), mounting the menorah lights (8:1–4), and inducting the Levites into service (8:5–26).

7 On the day that Moses finished setting up the Tabernacle, he anointed and consecrated it and all its furnishings, as well as the altar and its utensils. When he had anointed and consecrated them, [2]the chieftains of Israel, the heads of ancestral houses, namely, the chieftains of the tribes, those who were in charge of enrollment, drew near [3]and brought their offering before the LORD: six draught carts and twelve oxen, a cart for every two chieftains and an ox for each one.

When they had brought them before the Tabernacle, [4]the

ז וַיְהִי בְּיוֹם כַּלּוֹת מֹשֶׁה לְהָקִים אֶת־הַמִּשְׁכָּן
וַיִּמְשַׁח אֹתוֹ וַיְקַדֵּשׁ אֹתוֹ וְאֶת־כָּל־כֵּלָיו וְאֶת־
הַמִּזְבֵּחַ וְאֶת־כָּל־כֵּלָיו וַיִּמְשָׁחֵם וַיְקַדֵּשׁ אֹתָם׃
2 וַיַּקְרִיבוּ נְשִׂיאֵי יִשְׂרָאֵל רָאשֵׁי בֵּית אֲבֹתָם הֵם
נְשִׂיאֵי הַמַּטֹּת הֵם הָעֹמְדִים עַל־הַפְּקֻדִים׃
3 וַיָּבִיאוּ אֶת־קָרְבָּנָם לִפְנֵי יְהוָה שֵׁשׁ־עֶגְלֹת צָב
וּשְׁנֵי עָשָׂר בָּקָר עֲגָלָה עַל־שְׁנֵי הַנְּשִׂאִים וְשׁוֹר
לְאֶחָד וַיַּקְרִיבוּ אוֹתָם לִפְנֵי הַמִּשְׁכָּן׃ 4 וַיֹּאמֶר

CHAPTER 7 THE CHIEFTAINS' INITIATORY GIFTS (7:1–89)

The twelve tribal chieftains jointly contribute expensive gifts to the completed and consecrated Tabernacle. These gifts consist of six carts and twelve oxen for the use of the Gershonites and Merarites in transporting the dismantled Tabernacle. Then, individually and on successive days, each chieftain contributes to the consecrated altar the identical gift, as follows: one silver bowl and one silver basin, each filled with choice flour and oil for cereal offerings, one gold ladle filled with incense, and the same number and kind of sacrificial animals. The contribution of each chieftain is duly recorded and the totals are summed up (vv. 84–88); the names of the chieftains are identical with those listed in 1:5–15, and they follow the order of the camp in 2:3–31. The conclusion, verse 89, describes how God communicated with Moses.

It is not clear why this document concerning the initiatory gifts of the tribal chieftains was placed here. Ibn Ezra conjectures that the previously mentioned Priestly Blessing is to be identified with Aaron's blessing, recited at the end of the first public service (the eighth day following the seven-day consecration of the Tabernacle, Lev. 9:22–23), and that immediately after the blessing the chieftains brought their gifts. The context, however, offers another, more plausible reason. In chapter 4, the Levites have been assigned their transport duties. The carts required for the Gershonite and Merarite labors are now donated by the chieftains (vv. 1–9). The altar gifts of the chieftains (vv. 10–88) are incidental and are included only because they form part of the same archival document.

1. On the day Rather, "when" for Hebrew *be-yom* in all of its occurrences in this chapter (vv. 10,84). For other instances in the priestly texts, see Leviticus 7:38, 14:2,57, and especially Numbers 3:1. The implications of this rendering are drawn in Excursus 14.[1]

anointed and consecrated According to Ramban, the consecration was by oil, not by sacrificial blood as Ibn Ezra suggests; compare Exodus 40:9–10 and Leviticus 8:10–11.

as well as the altar and its utensils The altar is singled out since it will receive discrete dedicatory gifts from the chieftains (vv. 10–88), according to Ibn Ezra. Alternatively, according to Meyuḥas, the reason may be that "Tabernacle" refers only to the tent, thus excluding the altar that stood in the court.

When he had anointed and consecrated A repetitive resumption. This again supports the rendering of "when" for *be-yom,* since the erection, the anointing, and the chieftains' contributions can hardly all have taken place on the same day.

2. namely Since there were many chieftains (heads) in each tribe, the text had to specify that the clan head was also the chieftain of the entire tribe. They were chosen by God (cf. 1:5,16–17); hence, the choice could not be protested by other chieftains.

in charge of enrollment Compare 1:4–16. Perhaps the purpose of this qualification is to preclude the participation of the tribe of Levi, which was not enrolled in the general census.[2]

3. draught Wagons strong enough to carry heavy loads.[3] Each draught requires two ox power.

LORD said to Moses: 5Accept these from them for use in the
service of the Tent of Meeting, and give them to the Levites
according to their respective services.

6Moses took the carts and the oxen and gave them to the
Levites. 7Two carts and four oxen he gave to the Gershonites, as required for their service, 8and four carts and
eight oxen he gave to the Merarites, as required for their
service—under the direction of Ithamar son of Aaron the
priest. 9But to the Kohathites he did not give any; since
theirs was the service of the [most] sacred objects, their
porterage was by shoulder.

10The chieftains also brought the dedication offering for
the altar upon its being anointed. As the chieftains were
presenting their offerings before the altar, 11the LORD said
to Moses: Let them present their offerings for the dedication of the altar, one chieftain each day.

12The one who presented his offering on the first day was
Nahshon son of Amminadab of the tribe of Judah. 13His

יְהוָה אֶל־מֹשֶׁה לֵּאמֹר: 5 קַח מֵאִתָּם וְהָיוּ לַעֲבֹד
אֶת־עֲבֹדַת אֹהֶל מוֹעֵד וְנָתַתָּה אוֹתָם אֶל־הַלְוִיִּם
אִישׁ כְּפִי עֲבֹדָתוֹ: 6 וַיִּקַּח מֹשֶׁה אֶת־הָעֲגָלֹת
וְאֶת־הַבָּקָר וַיִּתֵּן אוֹתָם אֶל־הַלְוִיִּם: 7 אֵת | שְׁתֵּי
הָעֲגָלוֹת וְאֵת אַרְבַּעַת הַבָּקָר נָתַן לִבְנֵי גֵרְשׁוֹן
כְּפִי עֲבֹדָתָם: 8 וְאֵת | אַרְבַּע הָעֲגָלֹת וְאֵת שְׁמֹנַת
הַבָּקָר נָתַן לִבְנֵי מְרָרִי כְּפִי עֲבֹדָתָם בְּיַד אִיתָמָר
בֶּן־אַהֲרֹן הַכֹּהֵן: 9 וְלִבְנֵי קְהָת לֹא נָתָן כִּי־עֲבֹדַת
הַקֹּדֶשׁ עֲלֵהֶם בַּכָּתֵף יִשָּׂאוּ: 10 וַיַּקְרִיבוּ הַנְּשִׂאִים
אֵת חֲנֻכַּת הַמִּזְבֵּחַ בְּיוֹם הִמָּשַׁח אֹתוֹ וַיַּקְרִיבוּ
הַנְּשִׂיאִם אֶת־קָרְבָּנָם לִפְנֵי הַמִּזְבֵּחַ: 11 וַיֹּאמֶר
יְהוָה אֶל־מֹשֶׁה נָשִׂיא אֶחָד לַיּוֹם נָשִׂיא אֶחָד
לַיּוֹם יַקְרִיבוּ אֶת־קָרְבָּנָם לַחֲנֻכַּת הַמִּזְבֵּחַ:
ס [חמישי לספרדים] 12 וַיְהִי הַמַּקְרִיב
בַּיּוֹם הָרִאשׁוֹן אֶת־קָרְבָּנוֹ נַחְשׁוֹן בֶּן־עַמִּינָדָב
לְמַטֵּה יְהוּדָה: 13 וְקָרְבָּנוֹ קַעֲרַת־כֶּסֶף אַחַת

oxen . . . ox Hebrew *bakar,* "oxen," stands for the collective and *shor,* "ox," for the single member, without indicating sex or age (e.g., Lev. 22:28).[4]

before the Tabernacle Neither the wood of the carts nor their animals were destined for the altar and, hence, were ineligible to enter the sacred area, which was reserved for the people's sacrifice alone.[5] The midrash explains that the haste with which the chieftains made this donation compensated for the way they delayed their donation of materials for the building of the Tabernacle: They had waited until after the people had "oversubscribed" the Tabernacle needs (Exod. 36:5–7), leaving only the jewels for the High Priest's garment for the chieftains to contribute (Exod. 35:27).[6]

5. use in the service Rather, "for the transport" (and so vv. 5,7,8). For *'avodah* in its restricted use as transport labor, see Excursus 6.

service Rather, "jobs"; see Excursus 6.

7–8. service (2) The planks of the Tabernacle borne by the Merarites were bulkier than the Tabernacle curtains carried by the Gershonites; hence, the Merarites were given four carts, and the Gershonites, two carts.[7]

9. by shoulder According to 1 Chronicles 13:7–10, the death of Uzzah (cf. 2 Sam. 6:3–8) was caused by David's negligence in allowing the Ark to be transported by wagon instead of by shoulder.[8]

10. dedication offering Hebrew *ḥanukkah.* Rather, "initiation offering" (also in vv. 84, 88), gifts brought upon initiating the use of a structure.[9] In the same way, the holiday of Hanukkah celebrates the time when the Temple altar, purified and reconsecrated by the Maccabees, was once again initiated into use.[10] The Bible records initiation ceremonies for homes (Deut. 20:5), temples (1 Kings 8:63), altars (Num. 7:10–88; 2 Chron. 7:9), and city walls (Neh. 12:27). Initiation should not be confused with dedication/consecration, the latter being performed by anointing (cf. v. 88).

12. Nahshon He is the only one of the twelve tribal chieftains who is not explicitly called a chieftain, "so if he should ever feel tempted to lord it over the other chieftains by saying 'I am your king, since I was the first to present the offering,' they could retort by saying, 'You are no more than a commoner, for every one of the others is called a chieftain while you are not described as a chieftain.'"[11]

offering: one silver bowl weighing 130 shekels and one silver basin of 70 shekels by the sanctuary weight, both filled with choice flour with oil mixed in, for a meal offering; 14one gold ladle of 10 shekels, filled with incense; 15one bull of the herd, one ram, and one lamb in its first year, for a burnt offering; 16one goat for a sin offering; 17and for his sacrifice of well-being: two oxen, five rams, five he-goats, and five yearling lambs. That was the offering of Nahshon son of Amminadab.

18On the second day, Nethanel son of Zuar, chieftain of Issachar, made his offering. 19He presented as his offering: one silver bowl weighing 130 shekels and one silver basin of 70 shekels by the sanctuary weight, both filled with choice flour with oil mixed in, for a meal offering; 20one gold ladle of 10 shekels, filled with incense; 21one bull of the herd, one ram, and one lamb in its first year, for a burnt offering; 22one goat for a sin offering; 23and for his sacrifice of well-

שְׁלֹשִׁים וּמֵאָה מִשְׁקָלָהּ מִזְרָק אֶחָד כֶּסֶף שִׁבְעִים
שֶׁקֶל בְּשֶׁקֶל הַקֹּדֶשׁ שְׁנֵיהֶם ׀ מְלֵאִים סֹלֶת
בְּלוּלָה בַשֶּׁמֶן לְמִנְחָה׃ 14 כַּף אַחַת עֲשָׂרָה זָהָב
מְלֵאָה קְטֹרֶת׃ 15 פַּר אֶחָד בֶּן־בָּקָר אַיִל אֶחָד
כֶּבֶשׂ־אֶחָד בֶּן־שְׁנָתוֹ לְעֹלָה׃ 16 שְׂעִיר־עִזִּים אֶחָד
לְחַטָּאת׃ 17 וּלְזֶבַח הַשְּׁלָמִים בָּקָר שְׁנַיִם אֵילִם
חֲמִשָּׁה עַתּוּדִים חֲמִשָּׁה כְּבָשִׂים בְּנֵי־שָׁנָה חֲמִשָּׁה
זֶה קָרְבַּן נַחְשׁוֹן בֶּן־עַמִּינָדָב׃ פ 18 בַּיּוֹם
הַשֵּׁנִי הִקְרִיב נְתַנְאֵל בֶּן־צוּעָר נְשִׂיא יִשָּׂשכָר׃
19 הִקְרִב אֶת־קָרְבָּנוֹ קַעֲרַת־כֶּסֶף אַחַת שְׁלֹשִׁים
וּמֵאָה מִשְׁקָלָהּ מִזְרָק אֶחָד כֶּסֶף שִׁבְעִים שֶׁקֶל
בְּשֶׁקֶל הַקֹּדֶשׁ שְׁנֵיהֶם ׀ מְלֵאִים סֹלֶת בְּלוּלָה
בַשֶּׁמֶן לְמִנְחָה׃ 20 כַּף אַחַת עֲשָׂרָה זָהָב מְלֵאָה
קְטֹרֶת׃ 21 פַּר אֶחָד בֶּן־בָּקָר אַיִל אֶחָד כֶּבֶשׂ־
אֶחָד בֶּן־שְׁנָתוֹ לְעֹלָה׃ 22 שְׂעִיר־עִזִּים אֶחָד
לְחַטָּאת׃ 23 וּלְזֶבַח הַשְּׁלָמִים בָּקָר שְׁנַיִם אֵילִם

*13. **His offering*** The term ***korban*** applies to both the vessels and the animals enumerated in the list. Just as the former were not "offered up" on the altar, neither were the latter, at least, not immediately. Compare also 31:50, where ***korban*** refers to golden ornaments taken in spoil and dedicated to the sanctuary (cf. also 16:17; 17:3–4).[12]

shekels This word is always missing in connection with the bowls and ladles (e.g., v. 14 and frequently elsewhere; cf. Gen. 20:16), but it appears in the totals given in verse 85. A shekel weighed about 12 grams (0.42 oz.). Thus each silver bowl weighed about 1.3 kilograms (3 lbs.), each basin about 1 kilogram (2 lbs.), and each ladle about 250 grams (4 oz.).

bowl . . . basin According to the rabbis, these vessels had the same capacities, but they differed in weight because the bowl was thicker.[13] The bowls were probably used for dry ingredients, such as flour, and the basin for liquids, such as libations and blood (cf. Amos 6:6).[14]

*14. **10 shekels*** Although the ladle was made of gold, its weight was computed in silver.[15]

incense Hebrew ***ketoret,*** probably for use on the altar of incense (cf. Exod. 30:7). The incense used with the ***minḥah*** offering on the altar and with the bread of presence was made exclusively of ***levonah,*** frankincense (Lev. 2:2; 24:7).

15–17. The fact that each variety of sacrificial animal is represented in the ***ʿolah*** and ***shelamim*** is further evidence that the animals were contributed to the sacrificial store and not offered at once. Even though the ***shelamim*** is not offered on the festivals (except for Lev. 23:19), it is attested for gala celebrations such as the Temple dedication (1 Kings 8:63), Hezekiah's Feast of Unleavened Bread (2 Chron. 30:21–24), and others (cf. 10:10). That the ***ḥatta't*** is limited to the he-goat proves that the animals were contributed to the sacrificial store, since the he-goat is the ***only*** animal prescribed as a ***ḥatta't*** for the fixed festival offerings (cf. chaps. 28–29). Also note the absence of he-goats from the ***ʿolah*** animals in this list and in chapters 28–29 (and cf. Lev. 1:10). See further Excursus 14.

*15. **bull of the herd*** Rather, "domestic bull."[16] Wild animals are precluded from the altar (see the Comment to v. 16). In the offerings of the individual chieftains, Hebrew ***bakar*** is shorthand for "bulls of the herd" (vv. 17,23, etc.; and cf. v. 88).

*16. **goat*** Rather, "domestic goat."

*17 (23 etc.). **oxen*** Rather, "bulls" (cf. v. 15). Oxen and other castrated animals are forbidden in sacrifice (cf. Lev. 22:20).

being: two oxen, five rams, five he-goats, and five yearling lambs. That was the offering of Nethanel son of Zuar.

24On the third day, it was the chieftain of the Zebulunites, Eliab son of Helon. 25His offering: one silver bowl weighing 130 shekels and one silver basin of 70 shekels by the sanctuary weight, both filled with choice flour with oil mixed in, for a meal offering; 26one gold ladle of 10 shekels, filled with incense; 27one bull of the herd, one ram, and one lamb in its first year, for a burnt offering; 28one goat for a sin offering; 29and for his sacrifice of well-being: two oxen, five rams, five he-goats, and five yearling lambs. That was the offering of Eliab son of Helon.

30On the fourth day, it was the chieftain of the Reubenites, Elizur son of Shedeur. 31His offering: one silver bowl weighing 130 shekels and one silver basin of 70 shekels by the sanctuary weight, both filled with choice flour with oil mixed in, for a meal offering; 32one gold ladle of 10 shekels, filled with incense; 33one bull of the herd, one ram, and one lamb in its first year, for a burnt offering; 34one goat for a sin offering; 35and for his sacrifice of well-being: two oxen, five rams, five he-goats, and five yearling lambs. That was the offering of Elizur son of Shedeur.

36On the fifth day, it was the chieftain of the Simeonites, Shelumiel son of Zurishaddai. 37His offering: one silver bowl weighing 130 shekels and one silver basin of 70 shekels by the sanctuary weight, both filled with choice flour with oil mixed in, for a meal offering; 38one gold ladle of 10 shekels, filled with incense; 39one bull of the herd, one ram, and one lamb in its first year, for a burnt offering; 40one goat for a sin offering; 41and for his sacrifice of well-being: two oxen, five rams, five he-goats, and five yearling lambs. That was the offering of Shelumiel son of Zurishaddai.

42On the sixth day, it was the chieftain of the Gadites, Eliasaph son of Deuel. 43His offering: one silver bowl weighing 130 shekels and one silver basin of 70 shekels by the sanctuary weight, both filled with choice flour with oil mixed in, for a meal offering; 44one gold ladle of 10 shekels, filled with incense; 45one bull of the herd, one ram, and one lamb in its first year, for a burnt offering; 46one goat for a sin offering; 47and for his sacrifice of well-being: two oxen, five rams, five he-goats, and five yearling lambs. That was the offering of Eliasaph son of Deuel.

חֲמִשָּׁה עַתּוּדִים חֲמִשָּׁה כְּבָשִׂים בְּנֵי־שָׁנָה חֲמִשָּׁה
זֶה קָרְבַּן נְתַנְאֵל בֶּן־צוּעָר׃ פ 24 בַּיּוֹם
הַשְּׁלִישִׁי נָשִׂיא לִבְנֵי זְבוּלֻן אֱלִיאָב בֶּן־חֵלֹן׃
25 קָרְבָּנוֹ קַעֲרַת־כֶּסֶף אַחַת שְׁלֹשִׁים וּמֵאָה
מִשְׁקָלָהּ מִזְרָק אֶחָד כֶּסֶף שִׁבְעִים שֶׁקֶל בְּשֶׁקֶל
הַקֹּדֶשׁ שְׁנֵיהֶם׀ מְלֵאִים סֹלֶת בְּלוּלָה בַשֶּׁמֶן
לְמִנְחָה׃ 26 כַּף אַחַת עֲשָׂרָה זָהָב מְלֵאָה קְטֹרֶת׃
27 פַּר אֶחָד בֶּן־בָּקָר אַיִל אֶחָד כֶּבֶשׂ־אֶחָד בֶּן־
שְׁנָתוֹ לְעֹלָה׃ 28 שְׂעִיר־עִזִּים אֶחָד לְחַטָּאת׃
29 וּלְזֶבַח הַשְּׁלָמִים בָּקָר שְׁנַיִם אֵילִם חֲמִשָּׁה
עַתֻּדִים חֲמִשָּׁה כְּבָשִׂים בְּנֵי־שָׁנָה חֲמִשָּׁה זֶה קָרְבַּן
אֱלִיאָב בֶּן־חֵלֹן׃ פ 30 בַּיּוֹם הָרְבִיעִי נָשִׂיא
לִבְנֵי רְאוּבֵן אֱלִיצוּר בֶּן־שְׁדֵיאוּר׃ 31 קָרְבָּנוֹ
קַעֲרַת־כֶּסֶף אַחַת שְׁלֹשִׁים וּמֵאָה מִשְׁקָלָהּ מִזְרָק
אֶחָד כֶּסֶף שִׁבְעִים שֶׁקֶל בְּשֶׁקֶל הַקֹּדֶשׁ שְׁנֵיהֶם׀
מְלֵאִים סֹלֶת בְּלוּלָה בַשֶּׁמֶן לְמִנְחָה׃ 32 כַּף אַחַת
עֲשָׂרָה זָהָב מְלֵאָה קְטֹרֶת׃ 33 פַּר אֶחָד בֶּן־בָּקָר
אַיִל אֶחָד כֶּבֶשׂ־אֶחָד בֶּן־שְׁנָתוֹ לְעֹלָה׃ 34 שְׂעִיר־
עִזִּים אֶחָד לְחַטָּאת׃ 35 וּלְזֶבַח הַשְּׁלָמִים בָּקָר
שְׁנַיִם אֵילִם חֲמִשָּׁה עַתֻּדִים חֲמִשָּׁה כְּבָשִׂים בְּנֵי־
שָׁנָה חֲמִשָּׁה זֶה קָרְבַּן אֱלִיצוּר בֶּן־שְׁדֵיאוּר׃
פ 36 בַּיּוֹם הַחֲמִישִׁי נָשִׂיא לִבְנֵי שִׁמְעוֹן
שְׁלֻמִיאֵל בֶּן־צוּרִישַׁדָּי׃ 37 קָרְבָּנוֹ קַעֲרַת־כֶּסֶף
אַחַת שְׁלֹשִׁים וּמֵאָה מִשְׁקָלָהּ מִזְרָק אֶחָד כֶּסֶף
שִׁבְעִים שֶׁקֶל בְּשֶׁקֶל הַקֹּדֶשׁ שְׁנֵיהֶם׀ מְלֵאִים
סֹלֶת בְּלוּלָה בַשֶּׁמֶן לְמִנְחָה׃ 38 כַּף אַחַת עֲשָׂרָה
זָהָב מְלֵאָה קְטֹרֶת׃ 39 פַּר אֶחָד בֶּן־בָּקָר אַיִל
אֶחָד כֶּבֶשׂ־אֶחָד בֶּן־שְׁנָתוֹ לְעֹלָה׃ 40 שְׂעִיר־עִזִּים
אֶחָד לְחַטָּאת׃ 41 וּלְזֶבַח הַשְּׁלָמִים בָּקָר שְׁנַיִם
אֵילִם חֲמִשָּׁה עַתֻּדִים חֲמִשָּׁה כְּבָשִׂים בְּנֵי־שָׁנָה
חֲמִשָּׁה זֶה קָרְבַּן שְׁלֻמִיאֵל בֶּן־צוּרִישַׁדָּי׃ פ
ששי 42 בַּיּוֹם הַשִּׁשִּׁי נָשִׂיא לִבְנֵי גָד אֶלְיָסָף בֶּן־
דְּעוּאֵל׃ 43 קָרְבָּנוֹ קַעֲרַת־כֶּסֶף אַחַת שְׁלֹשִׁים
וּמֵאָה מִשְׁקָלָהּ מִזְרָק אֶחָד כֶּסֶף שִׁבְעִים שֶׁקֶל
בְּשֶׁקֶל הַקֹּדֶשׁ שְׁנֵיהֶם׀ מְלֵאִים סֹלֶת בְּלוּלָה
בַשֶּׁמֶן לְמִנְחָה׃ 44 כַּף אַחַת עֲשָׂרָה זָהָב מְלֵאָה
קְטֹרֶת׃ 45 פַּר אֶחָד בֶּן־בָּקָר אַיִל אֶחָד כֶּבֶשׂ־
אֶחָד בֶּן־שְׁנָתוֹ לְעֹלָה׃ 46 שְׂעִיר־עִזִּים אֶחָד
לְחַטָּאת׃ 47 וּלְזֶבַח הַשְּׁלָמִים בָּקָר שְׁנַיִם אֵילִם
חֲמִשָּׁה עַתֻּדִים חֲמִשָּׁה כְּבָשִׂים בְּנֵי־שָׁנָה חֲמִשָּׁה
זֶה קָרְבַּן אֶלְיָסָף בֶּן־דְּעוּאֵל׃ פ 48 בַּיּוֹם

48On the seventh day, it was the chieftain of the Ephraimites, Elishama son of Ammihud. 49His offering: one silver bowl weighing 130 shekels and one silver basin of 70 shekels by the sanctuary weight, both filled with choice flour with oil mixed in, for a meal offering; 50one gold ladle of 10 shekels, filled with incense; 51one bull of the herd, one ram, and one lamb in its first year, for a burnt offering; 52one goat for a sin offering; 53and for his sacrifice of well-being: two oxen, five rams, five he-goats, and five yearling lambs. That was the offering of Elishama son of Ammihud.

54On the eighth day, it was the chieftain of the Manassites, Gamaliel son of Pedahzur. 55His offering: one silver bowl weighing 130 shekels and one silver basin of 70 shekels by the sanctuary weight, both filled with choice flour with oil mixed in, for a meal offering; 56one gold ladle of 10 shekels, filled with incense; 57one bull of the herd, one ram, and one lamb in its first year, for a burnt offering; 58one goat for a sin offering; 59and for his sacrifice of well-being: two oxen, five rams, five he-goats, and five yearling lambs. That was the offering of Gamaliel son of Pedahzur.

60On the ninth day, it was the chieftain of the Benjaminites, Abidan son of Gideoni. 61His offering: one silver bowl weighing 130 shekels and one silver basin of 70 shekels by the sanctuary weight, both filled with choice flour with oil mixed in, for a meal offering; 62one gold ladle of 10 shekels, filled with incense; 63one bull of the herd, one ram, and one lamb in its first year, for a burnt offering; 64one goat for a sin offering; 65and for his sacrifice of well-being: two oxen, five rams, five he-goats, and five yearling lambs. That was the offering of Abidan son of Gideoni.

66On the tenth day, it was the chieftain of the Danites, Ahiezer son of Ammishaddai. 67His offering: one silver bowl weighing 130 shekels and one silver basin of 70 shekels by the sanctuary weight, both filled with choice flour with oil mixed in, for a meal offering; 68one gold ladle of 10 shekels, filled with incense; 69one bull of the herd, one ram, and one lamb in its first year, for a burnt offering; 70one goat for a sin offering; 71and for his sacrifice of well-being: two oxen, five rams, five he-goats, and five yearling lambs. That was the offering of Ahiezer son of Ammishaddai.

הַשְּׁבִיעִ֔י נָשִׂ֖יא לִבְנֵ֣י אֶפְרָ֑יִם אֱלִֽישָׁמָ֖ע בֶּן־
עַמִּיהֽוּד׃ 49 קָרְבָּנ֞וֹ קַֽעֲרַת־כֶּ֣סֶף אַחַ֗ת שְׁלֹשִׁ֣ים
וּמֵאָה֮ מִשְׁקָלָהּ֒ מִזְרָ֤ק אֶחָד֙ כֶּ֔סֶף שִׁבְעִ֥ים שֶׁ֖קֶל
בְּשֶׁ֣קֶל הַקֹּ֑דֶשׁ שְׁנֵיהֶ֣ם ׀ מְלֵאִ֗ים סֹ֛לֶת בְּלוּלָ֥ה
בַשֶּׁ֖מֶן לְמִנְחָֽה׃ 50 כַּ֥ף אַחַ֛ת עֲשָׂרָ֥ה זָהָ֖ב מְלֵאָ֥ה
קְטֹֽרֶת׃ 51 פַּ֣ר אֶחָ֞ד בֶּן־בָּקָ֗ר אַ֧יִל אֶחָ֛ד כֶּֽבֶשׂ־
אֶחָ֥ד בֶּן־שְׁנָת֖וֹ לְעֹלָֽה׃ 52 שְׂעִיר־עִזִּ֥ים אֶחָ֖ד
לְחַטָּֽאת׃ 53 וּלְזֶ֣בַח הַשְּׁלָמִים֮ בָּקָ֣ר שְׁנַיִם֒ אֵילִ֤ם
חֲמִשָּׁה֙ עַתֻּדִ֣ים חֲמִשָּׁ֔ה כְּבָשִׂ֥ים בְּנֵי־שָׁנָ֖ה חֲמִשָּׁ֑ה
זֶ֛ה קָרְבַּ֥ן אֱלִֽישָׁמָ֖ע בֶּן־עַמִּיהֽוּד׃ פ 54 בַּיּוֹם֙
הַשְּׁמִינִ֔י נָשִׂ֖יא לִבְנֵ֣י מְנַשֶּׁ֑ה גַּמְלִיאֵ֖ל בֶּן־פְּדָה־צֽוּר׃
55 קָרְבָּנ֞וֹ קַֽעֲרַת־כֶּ֣סֶף אַחַ֗ת שְׁלֹשִׁ֣ים וּמֵאָה֮
מִשְׁקָלָהּ֒ מִזְרָ֤ק אֶחָד֙ כֶּ֔סֶף שִׁבְעִ֥ים שֶׁ֖קֶל בְּשֶׁ֣קֶל
הַקֹּ֑דֶשׁ שְׁנֵיהֶ֣ם ׀ מְלֵאִ֗ים סֹ֛לֶת בְּלוּלָ֥ה בַשֶּׁ֖מֶן
לְמִנְחָֽה׃ 56 כַּ֥ף אַחַ֛ת עֲשָׂרָ֥ה זָהָ֖ב מְלֵאָ֥ה קְטֹֽרֶת׃
57 פַּ֣ר אֶחָ֞ד בֶּן־בָּקָ֗ר אַ֧יִל אֶחָ֛ד כֶּֽבֶשׂ־אֶחָ֥ד בֶּן־
שְׁנָת֖וֹ לְעֹלָֽה׃ 58 שְׂעִיר־עִזִּ֥ים אֶחָ֖ד לְחַטָּֽאת׃
59 וּלְזֶ֣בַח הַשְּׁלָמִים֮ בָּקָ֣ר שְׁנַיִם֒ אֵילִ֤ם חֲמִשָּׁה֙
עַתֻּדִ֣ים חֲמִשָּׁ֔ה כְּבָשִׂ֥ים בְּנֵי־שָׁנָ֖ה חֲמִשָּׁ֑ה זֶ֛ה קָרְבַּ֥ן
גַּמְלִיאֵ֖ל בֶּן־פְּדָה־צֽוּר׃ פ 60 בַּיּוֹם֙ הַתְּשִׁיעִ֔י
נָשִׂ֖יא לִבְנֵ֣י בִנְיָמִ֑ן אֲבִידָ֖ן בֶּן־גִּדְעֹנִֽי׃ 61 קָרְבָּנ֞וֹ
קַֽעֲרַת־כֶּ֣סֶף אַחַ֗ת שְׁלֹשִׁ֣ים וּמֵאָה֮ מִשְׁקָלָהּ֒ מִזְרָ֤ק
אֶחָד֙ כֶּ֔סֶף שִׁבְעִ֥ים שֶׁ֖קֶל בְּשֶׁ֣קֶל הַקֹּ֑דֶשׁ שְׁנֵיהֶ֣ם ׀
מְלֵאִ֗ים סֹ֛לֶת בְּלוּלָ֥ה בַשֶּׁ֖מֶן לְמִנְחָֽה׃ 62 כַּ֥ף אַחַ֛ת
עֲשָׂרָ֥ה זָהָ֖ב מְלֵאָ֥ה קְטֹֽרֶת׃ 63 פַּ֣ר אֶחָ֞ד בֶּן־בָּקָ֗ר
אַ֧יִל אֶחָ֛ד כֶּֽבֶשׂ־אֶחָ֥ד בֶּן־שְׁנָת֖וֹ לְעֹלָֽה׃ 64 שְׂעִיר־
עִזִּ֥ים אֶחָ֖ד לְחַטָּֽאת׃ 65 וּלְזֶ֣בַח הַשְּׁלָמִים֮ בָּקָ֣ר
שְׁנַיִם֒ אֵילִ֤ם חֲמִשָּׁה֙ עַתֻּדִ֣ים חֲמִשָּׁ֔ה כְּבָשִׂ֥ים בְּנֵי־
שָׁנָ֖ה חֲמִשָּׁ֑ה זֶ֛ה קָרְבַּ֥ן אֲבִידָ֖ן בֶּן־גִּדְעֹנִֽי׃ פ
66 בַּיּוֹם֙ הָֽעֲשִׂירִ֔י נָשִׂ֖יא לִבְנֵ֣י דָ֑ן אֲחִיעֶ֖זֶר בֶּן־
עַמִּישַׁדָּֽי׃ 67 קָרְבָּנ֞וֹ קַֽעֲרַת־כֶּ֣סֶף אַחַ֗ת שְׁלֹשִׁ֣ים
וּמֵאָה֮ מִשְׁקָלָהּ֒ מִזְרָ֤ק אֶחָד֙ כֶּ֔סֶף שִׁבְעִ֥ים שֶׁ֖קֶל
בְּשֶׁ֣קֶל הַקֹּ֑דֶשׁ שְׁנֵיהֶ֣ם ׀ מְלֵאִ֗ים סֹ֛לֶת בְּלוּלָ֥ה
בַשֶּׁ֖מֶן לְמִנְחָֽה׃ 68 כַּ֥ף אַחַ֛ת עֲשָׂרָ֥ה זָהָ֖ב מְלֵאָ֥ה
קְטֹֽרֶת׃ 69 פַּ֣ר אֶחָ֞ד בֶּן־בָּקָ֗ר אַ֧יִל אֶחָ֛ד כֶּֽבֶשׂ־
אֶחָ֥ד בֶּן־שְׁנָת֖וֹ לְעֹלָֽה׃ 70 שְׂעִיר־עִזִּ֥ים אֶחָ֖ד
לְחַטָּֽאת׃ 71 וּלְזֶ֣בַח הַשְּׁלָמִים֮ בָּקָ֣ר שְׁנַיִם֒ אֵילִ֤ם
חֲמִשָּׁה֙ עַתֻּדִ֣ים חֲמִשָּׁ֔ה כְּבָשִׂ֥ים בְּנֵי־שָׁנָ֖ה חֲמִשָּׁ֑ה
זֶ֛ה קָרְבַּ֥ן אֲחִיעֶ֖זֶר בֶּן־עַמִּישַׁדָּֽי׃ פ שביעי

48. seventh day According to rabbinic tradition, the seventh day fell on the Sabbath, and despite the prohibition against an individual offering sacrifice on the Sabbath, an exception was made for the chieftain of the tribe of Ephraim.[17]

72 On the eleventh day, it was the chieftain of the Asherites, Pagiel son of Ochran. 73 His offering: one silver bowl weighing 130 shekels and one silver basin of 70 shekels by the sanctuary weight, both filled with choice flour with oil mixed in, for a meal offering; 74 one gold ladle of 10 shekels, filled with incense; 75 one bull of the herd, one ram, and one lamb in its first year, for a burnt offering; 76 one goat for a sin offering; 77 and for his sacrifice of well-being: two oxen, five rams, five he-goats, and five yearling lambs. That was the offering of Pagiel son of Ochran.

78 On the twelfth day, it was the chieftain of the Naphtalites, Ahira son of Enan. 79 His offering: one silver bowl weighing 130 shekels and one silver basin of 70 shekels by the sanctuary weight, both filled with choice flour with oil mixed in, for a meal offering; 80 one gold ladle of 10 shekels, filled with incense; 81 one bull of the herd, one ram, and one lamb in its first year, for a burnt offering; 82 one goat for a sin offering; 83 and for his sacrifice of well-being: two oxen, five rams, five he-goats, and five yearling lambs. That was the offering of Ahira son of Enan.

84 This was the dedication offering for the altar from the chieftains of Israel upon its being anointed: silver bowls, 12; silver basins, 12; gold ladles, 12. 85 Silver per bowl, 130; per basin, 70. Total silver of vessels, 2,400 sanctuary shekels. 86 The 12 gold ladles filled with incense—10 sanctuary shekels per ladle—total gold of the ladles, 120.

87 Total of herd animals for burnt offerings, 12 bulls; of rams, 12; of yearling lambs, 12—with their proper meal offerings; of goats for sin offerings, 12. 88 Total of herd animals for sacrifices of well-being, 24 bulls; of rams, 60; of he-goats, 60; of yearling lambs, 60. That was the dedication offering for the altar after its anointing.

89 When Moses went into the Tent of Meeting to speak

72 בְּיוֹם עַשְׁתֵּי עָשָׂר יוֹם נָשִׂיא לִבְנֵי אָשֵׁר
פַּגְעִיאֵל בֶּן־עָכְרָן׃ 73 קָרְבָּנוֹ קַעֲרַת־כֶּסֶף אַחַת
שְׁלֹשִׁים וּמֵאָה מִשְׁקָלָהּ מִזְרָק אֶחָד כֶּסֶף שִׁבְעִים
שֶׁקֶל בְּשֶׁקֶל הַקֹּדֶשׁ שְׁנֵיהֶם ׀ מְלֵאִים סֹלֶת
בְּלוּלָה בַשֶּׁמֶן לְמִנְחָה׃ 74 כַּף אַחַת עֲשָׂרָה זָהָב
מְלֵאָה קְטֹרֶת׃ 75 פַּר אֶחָד בֶּן־בָּקָר אַיִל אֶחָד
כֶּבֶשׂ־אֶחָד בֶּן־שְׁנָתוֹ לְעֹלָה׃ 76 שְׂעִיר־עִזִּים אֶחָד
לְחַטָּאת׃ 77 וּלְזֶבַח הַשְּׁלָמִים בָּקָר שְׁנַיִם אֵילִם
חֲמִשָּׁה עַתֻּדִים חֲמִשָּׁה כְּבָשִׂים בְּנֵי־שָׁנָה חֲמִשָּׁה
זֶה קָרְבַּן פַּגְעִיאֵל בֶּן־עָכְרָן׃ פ 78 בְּיוֹם
שְׁנֵים עָשָׂר יוֹם נָשִׂיא לִבְנֵי נַפְתָּלִי אֲחִירַע בֶּן־
עֵינָן׃ 79 קָרְבָּנוֹ קַעֲרַת־כֶּסֶף אַחַת שְׁלֹשִׁים וּמֵאָה
מִשְׁקָלָהּ מִזְרָק אֶחָד כֶּסֶף שִׁבְעִים שֶׁקֶל בְּשֶׁקֶל
הַקֹּדֶשׁ שְׁנֵיהֶם ׀ מְלֵאִים סֹלֶת בְּלוּלָה בַשֶּׁמֶן
לְמִנְחָה׃ 80 כַּף אַחַת עֲשָׂרָה זָהָב מְלֵאָה קְטֹרֶת׃
81 פַּר אֶחָד בֶּן־בָּקָר אַיִל אֶחָד כֶּבֶשׂ־אֶחָד בֶּן־
שְׁנָתוֹ לְעֹלָה׃ 82 שְׂעִיר־עִזִּים אֶחָד לְחַטָּאת׃
83 וּלְזֶבַח הַשְּׁלָמִים בָּקָר שְׁנַיִם אֵילִם חֲמִשָּׁה
עַתֻּדִים חֲמִשָּׁה כְּבָשִׂים בְּנֵי־שָׁנָה חֲמִשָּׁה זֶה קָרְבַּן
אֲחִירַע בֶּן־עֵינָן׃ פ 84 זֹאת ׀ חֲנֻכַּת הַמִּזְבֵּחַ
בְּיוֹם הִמָּשַׁח אֹתוֹ מֵאֵת נְשִׂיאֵי יִשְׂרָאֵל קַעֲרֹת
כֶּסֶף שְׁתֵּים עֶשְׂרֵה מִזְרְקֵי־כֶסֶף שְׁנֵים עָשָׂר
כַּפּוֹת זָהָב שְׁתֵּים עֶשְׂרֵה׃ 85 שְׁלֹשִׁים וּמֵאָה
הַקְּעָרָה הָאַחַת כֶּסֶף וְשִׁבְעִים הַמִּזְרָק הָאֶחָד כֹּל
כֶּסֶף הַכֵּלִים אַלְפַּיִם וְאַרְבַּע־מֵאוֹת בְּשֶׁקֶל
הַקֹּדֶשׁ׃ 86 כַּפּוֹת זָהָב שְׁתֵּים־עֶשְׂרֵה מְלֵאֹת
קְטֹרֶת עֲשָׂרָה עֲשָׂרָה הַכַּף בְּשֶׁקֶל הַקֹּדֶשׁ כָּל־
זְהַב הַכַּפּוֹת עֶשְׂרִים וּמֵאָה׃ מפטיר 87 כָּל־הַבָּקָר
לָעֹלָה שְׁנֵים עָשָׂר פָּרִים אֵילִם שְׁנֵים־עָשָׂר
כְּבָשִׂים בְּנֵי־שָׁנָה שְׁנֵים עָשָׂר וּמִנְחָתָם וּשְׂעִירֵי
עִזִּים שְׁנֵים עָשָׂר לְחַטָּאת׃ 88 וְכֹל בְּקַר ׀ זֶבַח
הַשְּׁלָמִים עֶשְׂרִים וְאַרְבָּעָה פָּרִים אֵילִם שִׁשִּׁים
עַתֻּדִים שִׁשִּׁים כְּבָשִׂים בְּנֵי־שָׁנָה שִׁשִּׁים זֹאת
חֲנֻכַּת הַמִּזְבֵּחַ אַחֲרֵי הִמָּשַׁח אֹתוֹ׃ 89 וּבְבֹא מֹשֶׁה

84–88. These verses give the totals, framed by the phrase "when/after (*be-yom/'aḥarei*) its (the Tabernacle's) anointing" (see above to v. 1). Other examples of summaries framed by inclusions are Leviticus 14:54–57 and Ezekiel 43:12. The order that is kept throughout the chapter of an item followed by a numeral is twice broken in the summary: 12 bulls (v. 87) and 24 bulls (v. 88).

84. the dedication offering Rather, "the initiation offering" (cf. v. 10). Verse 84a is a near verbatim repetition of verse 10a, an inclusion that marks off this section as a literary unit.

88. anointing The Septuagint adds *'aḥarei mille' yadav,* "after its inauguration" (cf. Ezek. 43:26, also in regard to the altar), a phrase that is frequently coupled with anointing (3:3; Exod. 28:41; 29:29).

with Him, he would hear the Voice addressing him from above the cover that was on top of the Ark of the Pact between the two cherubim; thus He spoke to him.

אֶל־אֹ֣הֶל מוֹעֵד֮ לְדַבֵּ֣ר אִתּוֹ֒ וַיִּשְׁמַ֨ע אֶת־הַקּ֜וֹל
מִדַּבֵּ֣ר אֵלָ֗יו מֵעַ֤ל הַכַּפֹּ֙רֶת֙ אֲשֶׁר֙ עַל־אֲרֹ֣ן הָעֵדֻ֔ת
מִבֵּ֖ין שְׁנֵ֣י הַכְּרֻבִ֑ים וַיְדַבֵּ֖ר אֵלָֽיו׃ פ

BEHA'ALOTEKHA

8 The LORD spoke to Moses, saying: [2]Speak to Aaron and

בהעלתך

ח וַיְדַבֵּ֥ר יְהוָ֖ה אֶל־מֹשֶׁ֥ה לֵּאמֹֽר׃ 2 דַּבֵּר֙ אֶֽל־

89. Him Both the thought of this verse and the word Him lack any antecedent. It has been noted[18] that the *promise* in Exodus 25:22 that God would communicate with Moses from above the Ark is not fulfilled in any of the passages that speak of the building of the Tabernacle (e.g., Exod. 37,40). Moreover, its absence there is deliberate, since Exodus 40:34–35 explicitly states that Moses was not able to enter the Tent because of the density and power of God's Presence when the sacrificial laws (Lev. 1–7) were revealed to him (Lev. 1:1).[19] Only upon the conclusion of the first public service after the seven-day consecration of the Tabernacle, was Moses (and also Aaron) permitted to enter the Tent (Lev. 9:23). This is perhaps what our text means to convey. Beginning with the Priestly Blessing at the first service (Num. 6:22–27; Lev. 9:22–23), God's commands to Moses, like the instructions concerning the chieftains' gifts (7:4), were delivered to him from the Ark-throne while he stood alone inside the Tent.

went into the Tent That is, into the outer room of the Tent, separated from the Ark by the screening veil.[20] The implications are investigated in Excursus 15.

speak with Him Hebrew *dibber* means "converse, confer" when it is followed by *'et,* "with," rather than by *'el,* "to" (cf. Num. 3:1; Gen. 17:3,22,23; 23:8). This verse implies that Moses entered the Tent not only upon being summoned by God, but also (and perhaps mainly) on his own initiative in order to elicit an oracle from God (see Excursus 15).[21]

the Voice As understood by the Septuagint and Targum Jonathan, *kol* is a surrogate for the name of God, a forerunner of the later rabbinic *bat kol,* a heavenly voice.

addressing him Hebrew *middabber,* the Hitpael participle, is also found in Ezekiel 2:2 and 43:6; there, too, it appears in connection with the voice of God speaking to the prophet from the recesses of the Temple.[22]

cover Hebrew *kapporet* may be of Egyptian origin, as are many of the technical terms regarding the priestly garments (Exod. 28).[23]

Ark of the Pact Hebrew *'aron ha-'edut.* "The Pact," with the definite article, can only mean the two tablets of the Decalogue that were deposited in the Ark (Exod. 25:10–16). In the ancient Near East, important documents were deposited at the feet of the gods to indicate their authority and guarantee. In Israel, too, the Ark was conceived as God's footstool or the pedestal of His throne (see Excursus 15).[24]

thus He spoke to him Hebrew *va-yedabber.* Fulfilling God's promise in Exodus 25:22: "I shall speak *(ve-dibbarti)* to you from above the cover, from between the two cherubim that are on top of the Ark of the Pact."

CHAPTER 8 LIGHTING THE MENORAH (8:1–4)

Beha'alotekha Like the sacrificial altar, the menorah had to be tended by priests twice daily (Exod. 29:38–42; 30:7–8); and on both sacred objects a fire had to be kept burning continually (Lev. 6:2; 24:2–4). In the passages dealing with the construction of the cult objects in the Tabernacle, the menorah is mentioned most often: instructions for its construction (Exod. 25:31–40); instructions for its lighting (Exod. 27:20–21; 30:7–8; 40:4; Lev. 24:1–3); the execution of the construction (Exod. 37:17–24); and

say to him, "When you mount the lamps, let the seven lamps give light at the front of the lampstand." [3]Aaron did so; he mounted the lamps at the front of the lampstand, as the LORD had commanded Moses.—[4]Now this is how the lampstand was made: it was hammered work of gold, hammered from base to petal. According to the pattern that the LORD had shown Moses, so was the lampstand made.

אַהֲרֹן וְאָמַרְתָּ אֵלָיו בְּהַעֲלֹתְךָ אֶת־הַנֵּרֹת אֶל־מוּל
פְּנֵי הַמְּנוֹרָה יָאִירוּ שִׁבְעַת הַנֵּרוֹת׃ 3 וַיַּעַשׂ כֵּן
אַהֲרֹן אֶל־מוּל פְּנֵי הַמְּנוֹרָה הֶעֱלָה נֵרֹתֶיהָ כַּאֲשֶׁר
צִוָּה יְהוָה אֶת־מֹשֶׁה׃ 4 וְזֶה מַעֲשֵׂה הַמְּנֹרָה מִקְשָׁה
זָהָב עַד־יְרֵכָהּ עַד־פִּרְחָהּ מִקְשָׁה הִוא כַּמַּרְאֶה
אֲשֶׁר הֶרְאָה יְהוָה אֶת־מֹשֶׁה כֵּן עָשָׂה אֶת־
הַמְּנֹרָה׃ פ 5 וַיְדַבֵּר יְהוָה אֶל־מֹשֶׁה לֵּאמֹר׃

here, instructions on how to mount the lamps and the execution of these instructions (Num. 8:1–3). It must be remembered that the lamps were detachable pieces (cf. 4:9) that were cleansed in the morning (Exod. 30:7) and lit in the evening (Exod. 30:8). This passage now adds that the lamps must be affixed so that they will cast their light forward. Since the menorah is located against the southern wall of the Tabernacle (Exod. 26:35), the lamps should cast their light northward for the maximum illumination of the altar of incense and the table of the bread of presence, which stand in the center and along the north wall, respectively.[1]

The positioning of the lamps has already been commanded (Exod. 25:37b), but the account of the construction of the menorah omits this detail (Exod. 37:17–24). Thus there is a need for some statement that this command was fulfilled. Our passage serves this purpose (just as Num. 7:89 is the fulfillment of Exod. 25:22). The repetition of the command (v. 2) might be explained as a resumptive prescription, necessitated by the long interval between Exodus 25 and Numbers 8.[2] It would be the fulfillment verse (v. 3) that would account for this text not being included in one of the abovementioned menorah passages in Exodus: The fulfillment can only take place after the services in the Tabernacle had begun—after Leviticus 9.[3] An alternative explanation is that the text of Exodus and Leviticus was already canonized and there was no choice but to place this passage in Numbers (see the Introduction).

The question as to why this text was placed here, at the head of chapter 8, may be resolved by the previous verse (7:89): Only when God began to speak to Moses from the Holy of Holies, after the consecration of the Tabernacle, did Moses receive the final instructions concerning the operation of the menorah.[4]

2. *Aaron* The cultic service inside the tent was performed solely by the High Priest.[5]

mount Rather, "kindle."[6] True, the literal translation of *heʿelah* is "mount." However, since the mounting, positioning (*ʿarakh,* Exod. 27:21; Lev. 24:3–4), and lighting of the lamps were all part of the same operation, the verb *heʿelah* can imply all these acts (see Exod. 25:37; 27:20; 30:8; 40:4). Most decisive is Leviticus 24:2, where the wording can only refer to the lighting of the menorah. The menorah was lit only at night (Exod. 27:21), a practice attested in Shiloh during the days of Samuel (1 Sam. 3:3).

at the front Hebrew *ʾel-mul penei.* If the intent is that the light should be thrown toward the central lampstand (2 Sam. 11:15),[7] then the pinched lips or nozzles of the lamps atop the six branches would face the lampstand. However, one would expect the text to read "six" not "seven" lamps. Perhaps, then, the light is thrown forward (i.e., northward) toward the table,[8] an interpretation supported by Exodus 25:37, where the synonymous expression *ʿal ʿever penei* clearly means "forward."

3. *at the front* The fact that the idiom *ʾel-mul penei* is repeated indicates that the purpose of this passage is to stress the positioning of the lamps.

4. This verse is a repetition of the most important data concerning the construction of the menorah (Exod. 25:31,40). For the antiquity of its design, see Excursus 17.

hammered from base to petal Rather "even to its stem and petals it was of hammered work." *Yarekh* means "side, flank" (e.g., 3:29,35) and refers here to the trunk or stem of the menorah.[9] *Pirḥah* is a collective noun,[10] referring to all of the twenty-two floral projections on the central stem and on the six branches of the menorah (see Exod. 25:31–36). The point here is that the entire menorah was made of hammered gold[11] (cf. Exod. 25:3), with the exception of the lamps, which were

5The Lord spoke to Moses, saying: 6Take the Levites from among the Israelites and cleanse them. 7This is what you shall do to them to cleanse them: sprinkle on them water of purification, and let them go over their whole body with a razor, and wash their clothes; thus they shall be cleansed. 8Let them take a bull of the herd, and with it a

6 קַח אֶת־הַלְוִיִּם מִתּוֹךְ בְּנֵי יִשְׂרָאֵל וְטִהַרְתָּ
אֹתָם׃ 7 וְכֹה־תַעֲשֶׂה לָהֶם לְטַהֲרָם הַזֵּה עֲלֵיהֶם
מֵי חַטָּאת וְהֶעֱבִירוּ תַעַר עַל־כָּל־בְּשָׂרָם וְכִבְּסוּ
בִגְדֵיהֶם וְהִטֶּהָרוּ׃ 8 וְלָקְחוּ פַּר בֶּן־בָּקָר וּמִנְחָתוֹ

removable (cf. Num. 4:9; Lev. 24:4). All other sacred objects inside the Tabernacle were made of gold-plated wood (Exod. 25:10–30; 30:3–5).

THE PURIFICATION OF THE LEVITES' WORK FORCE (vv. 5–22)

The Levites have replaced the Israelite first-born (3:11–13,40–51) and have been assigned to the duties of guarding (3:14–39) and removing (4:1–33) the Tabernacle. But before the Levite work force is permitted to dismantle and handle the sancta, it must be ritually qualified, which requires that it be purified of impurities such as contact with the dead. This purification, however, should not be compared with the consecration service of the priests (Exod. 29; Lev. 8), who are consecrated[12] with the anointment oil (Exod. 29:7,21) in order to gain a holy status so that they may have access to the sacred objects, that is, officiate at the altar and enter the Tent. The Levites, on the other hand, are forbidden to enter the Tent or officiate at the altar (cf. 18:3–4): They may only transport the dismantled Tabernacle and its sacred objects after they are covered by the priests, a task that does not require sanctification but purification.[13]

That the only Levites who had to undergo purification were those belonging to the work force, the males between ages thirty (or twenty-five; cf. v. 24) and fifty (chap. 4), is demonstrable on the following grounds: (1) only the term *'avodah* occurs (vv. 11,15,19,22), but guard duty *(mishmeret)* does not appear at all (contrast vv. 23–26); (2) guard duty would require no purification, since it is performed outside the sacred area where there would be no contact with sancta; (3) one of the purification rites reads: "let them go over their whole body with a razor" (v. 7), implying that only mature males are involved; (4) verses 23–26, which focus on the retirement age of the Levite work force, constitute a logical continuation of this section, which speaks of the induction of the Levite work force. This being the case, then, the text does not posit an induction "service." Rather, it only calls for the cleansing of the Levite work force as a prerequisite to its handling of the Tabernacle and its sancta, which would imply that when the younger Levites reached the age of thirty, they too would undergo similar purification, but individually.

6. *cleanse them* Or, "have them cleansed." The avowed purpose of the ritual is purification.[14] Moses must see to it that the ritual is accomplished, but its execution is mainly carried out by Aaron. Herein is another distinction between the consecration of the priests and the purification of the Levites: The former ritual is conducted by Moses; however, once the priests are consecrated—and this text assumes they are—then Moses no longer has any right to officiate.

7. *sprinkle* This first rite in the purification apparently is carried out by Moses. Purification with the ashes of the red cow need not be done by a priest (19:18). The fact that this sprinkling with these special waters precedes shaving and washing indicates that its function is purely symbolic.[15]

water of purification Hebrew *mei ḥatta't*. The latter word is that of the purification offering (v. 8) and refers to the ashes of the red cow, also called a *ḥatta't* (19:9). Mixed with fresh water they are sprinkled *(hizzah,* 19:18,19,21) on any person or object contaminated by the dead. These waters are also called *mei niddah,* waters of lustration (19:9, 21; 31:23). This passage presumes knowledge of the law of chapter 19, a presumption that also underlies 5:1–4, since the expulsion of the corpse-contaminated individual from the camp also implies the person's eventual restoration.[16]

These waters cannot be drawn from the Tabernacle laver,[17] a sanctum reserved for priestly use only (Exod. 30:17–21) and whose waters are called "holy water" (5:17), an appropriate designation because only those who themselves are holy (priests) are entitled to partake of them. The washing of the priests *prior* to their consecration was also done with ordinary water (Exod. 29:4; Lev. 8:6).

meal offering of choice flour with oil mixed in, and you take a second bull of the herd for a sin offering. ⁹You shall bring the Levites forward before the Tent of Meeting. Assemble the whole Israelite community, ¹⁰and bring the Levites forward before the LORD. Let the Israelites lay their hands upon the Levites, ¹¹and let Aaron designate the Levites before the LORD as an elevation offering from the Israelites, that they may perform the service of the LORD. ¹²The

סֹ֣לֶת בְּלוּלָ֖ה בַשֶּׁ֑מֶן וּפַר־שֵׁנִ֥י בֶן־בָּקָ֖ר תִּקַּ֥ח לְחַטָּֽאת׃ 9 וְהִקְרַבְתָּ֙ אֶת־הַלְוִיִּ֔ם לִפְנֵ֖י אֹ֣הֶל מוֹעֵ֑ד וְהִ֨קְהַלְתָּ֔ אֶֽת־כָּל־עֲדַ֖ת בְּנֵ֥י יִשְׂרָאֵֽל׃ 10 וְהִקְרַבְתָּ֥ אֶת־הַלְוִיִּ֖ם לִפְנֵ֣י יְהֹוָ֑ה וְסָמְכ֧וּ בְנֵֽי־יִשְׂרָאֵ֛ל אֶת־יְדֵיהֶ֖ם עַל־הַלְוִיִּֽם׃ 11 וְהֵנִיף֩ אַהֲרֹ֨ן אֶת־הַלְוִיִּ֤ם תְּנוּפָה֙ לִפְנֵ֣י יְהֹוָ֔ה מֵאֵ֖ת בְּנֵ֣י יִשְׂרָאֵ֑ל וְהָי֕וּ לַעֲבֹ֖ד אֶת־עֲבֹדַ֥ת יְהֹוָֽה׃ 12 וְהַלְוִיִּ֖ם יִסְמְכוּ֙ אֶת־יְדֵיהֶ֔ם

go over Close shaving is hardly intended, as shown by the absence of the verb *gillaḥ*, used for shaving the leper (Lev. 14:8–9) and the Nazirite (6:9).[18]

thus they shall be cleansed Rather, "and cleanse themselves."[19] *Ve-hitteharu* is a Hitpael and always implies bathing (cf. Gen. 35:2; Ezra 6:20). A synonymous term is *hitkaddesh*, "sanctify one-self" (cf. 11:18 and Excursus 27). It is obvious that for purposes of purification, laundering without bathing would be self-defeating (cf. Num. 19:19; Lev. 15:5–13). Finally, the prescribed sequence for the purification of the corpse-contaminated person is sprinkling, laundering, and bathing;[20] bathing is also the final act in the purification of the leper (Lev. 14:8). Priests, on their consecration, also must undergo a bathing ritual (Exod. 29:4; Lev. 8:6). But in addition, and unlike the Levites, priests may not possess certain physical blemishes (Lev. 21:16–21). An Assyrian ritual for the consecration of a priest to the god Enlil provides that the priest be examined for blemishes during his ritual bath and, strikingly, moral as well as physical blemishes are included.[21]

8. *you take* That is, from them (cf. Lev. 16:5), because the purification offering works expiation only for its offerer (Lev. 4:14).

second bull The purification offering requires a bull in the case of the High Priest (cf. Lev. 16:6) or the community (Lev. 4:13–21). Since the bull is on behalf of the Levitical work force, the latter is considered a community, according to Abravanel. The function of this purification bull can be deduced from its place in the total rite. Bathing cleanses them of minor impurities, and the *ḥaṭṭa't* waters and sacrifice cleanse them of severe impurities that have impinged on the sanctuary and polluted its altar (see Excursus 49).

sin offering Rather, "purification offering" (and so throughout; see Excursus 48).

10. *before the LORD* The equivalent to "at the entrance of the Tent of Meeting" (e.g., 16:17–18), whereas prior to that the Levites were standing "in front of the Tent of Meeting" (v. 9), a term that can connote the space outside the entrance (e.g., 3:7,38; cf. 7:3). However, since these two expressions can also be synonymous, this verse may also be rendered, according to Ibn Ezra: "When you bring the Levites forward before the Lord, let the Israelites . . ."

lay Rather, "lean" (and so throughout). The verb *samakh* implies pressure (e.g., Judg. 16:29).

Israelites lay their hands upon the Levites This rite was conducted by representatives, that is, elders.[22] It must be assumed that the elders used one hand just as the Levites did upon their offerings (v. 12). Thus the Levites are designated as Israel's "sacrifice"—their representatives in the sanctuary. Just as the Levites replace the Israelite first-born in performing guard duty at the sanctuary (see 3:11–13), so they now replace all of Israel in the responsibility of transporting the Tabernacle (v. 11).

11. *designate . . . elevation offering* This ritual must be presumed to have been executed only in symbolic form.

from the Israelites The hand leaning performed by the Israelites (v. 10) combined with the elevation offering of the Levites performed by Aaron on behalf of the Israelites together form the ritual whereby the Levites are transferred from the ranks of the Israelites to the property of the Lord.

service Rather, "work," meaning removal labor; see Excursus 6.

Levites shall now lay their hands upon the heads of the bulls; one shall be offered to the LORD as a sin offering and the other as a burnt offering, to make expiation for the Levites.

[13]You shall place the Levites in attendance upon Aaron and his sons, and designate them as an elevation offering to the LORD. [14]Thus you shall set the Levites apart from the Israelites, and the Levites shall be Mine. [15]Thereafter the Levites shall be qualified for the service of the Tent of Meeting, once you have cleansed them and designated them as an elevation offering. [16]For they are formally assigned to Me from among the Israelites: I have taken them for Myself in place of all the first issue of the womb, of all the first-born of the Israelites. [17]For every first-born

עַל רֹאשׁ הַפָּרִים וַעֲשֵׂה אֶת־הָאֶחָד חַטָּאת וְאֶת־
הָאֶחָד עֹלָה לַיהוָה לְכַפֵּר עַל־הַלְוִיִּם׃
13 וְהַעֲמַדְתָּ אֶת־הַלְוִיִּם לִפְנֵי אַהֲרֹן וְלִפְנֵי בָנָיו
וְהֵנַפְתָּ אֹתָם תְּנוּפָה לַיהוָה׃ 14 וְהִבְדַּלְתָּ אֶת־
הַלְוִיִּם מִתּוֹךְ בְּנֵי יִשְׂרָאֵל וְהָיוּ לִי הַלְוִיִּם׃ שני
15 וְאַחֲרֵי־כֵן יָבֹאוּ הַלְוִיִּם לַעֲבֹד אֶת־אֹהֶל מוֹעֵד
וְטִהַרְתָּ אֹתָם וְהֵנַפְתָּ אֹתָם תְּנוּפָה׃ 16 כִּי נְתֻנִים
נְתֻנִים הֵמָּה לִי מִתּוֹךְ בְּנֵי יִשְׂרָאֵל תַּחַת פִּטְרַת
כָּל־רֶחֶם בְּכוֹר כֹּל מִבְּנֵי יִשְׂרָאֵל לָקַחְתִּי אֹתָם
לִי׃ 17 כִּי לִי כָל־בְּכוֹר בִּבְנֵי יִשְׂרָאֵל בָּאָדָם

12. ***one shall be offered*** If Moses had been the officiant, as claimed by some scholars, then the text would read *ve-ʿasita,* "you shall offer."[23] That Aaron was the officiant is expressly declared in verse 21b.[24] The active verb *ʿaseh* can imply a passive, a common phenomenon in cultic texts. It might better be rendered "have one offered."[25]

to make expiation The burnt offering can also be employed for expiatory purposes, as in Leviticus 1:4; 14:20. The physical cleansing of the Levites (v. 7) is followed immediately by their moral cleansing by means of sacrificial expiation. The purification offering is required to purge the sanctuary of the impurities caused by any of the Levites' moral (and physical) lapses.

13. ***You shall place*** Rather, "Thus you shall place." This verse concludes the instructions to Moses (paralleling v. 22a; see Excursus 18).

place . . . in attendance upon Hebrew *heʿemid lifnei* implies subordination (cf. 3:6).

and designate them as an elevation offering And so in verses 15,21.[26] Only the elevation offering is mentioned, but it is shorthand for the entire sacrifice ritual, including the double hand leaning and the offering of the two purification bulls (vv. 9–12). It points to the prime function of the ritual: to dedicate the Levitical work force to the Lord so that it will be eligible to handle the removal of the Tabernacle.

to the LORD Rather, "before the Lord" *(lifnei YHVH)* with many manuscripts and the Septuagint and as in all other cases of the elevation offering *(tenufah);* this is in contrast to the dedication rite *(terumah),* which is always "to the Lord."

14. ***Thus*** This word should be deleted. This verse begins a new section (vv. 14–19), which gives the rationale for the Levitical service in the Tabernacle (vv. 16–19; see Excursus 18).

15. ***be qualified*** The idiomatic meaning of *ba',* as encountered in 4:47 (cf. vv. 22,24).

service Rather, "to perform the work," that is, removal labors, adding *ʿavodat* with some manuscripts and most of the versions, as in verse 19.

once you have cleansed[27]

16–19. These verses provide the rationale for the investiture of the Levites, a repetition of 3:9,11–13; however, they add the new point that the Levites are a "ransom" for lay encroachment upon the sanctuary (see Excursus 19).

16. ***formally assigned*** Hebrew *netunim netunim* (cf. 3:9 and v. 19). The root *n-t-n* is the technical term to designate the nature of the Levites' relationship to the Lord (cf. 18:6).[28] This relationship is accurately described by Targum Onkelos, which renders "dedicated" (to God) here and "transmitted" (to Aaron) in verse 19 and 3:9. By this ritual the Levites are assigned to the Lord, who then reassigns them to the priests. This usage of *natan* is found in other, similar biblical contexts.

among the Israelites, man as well as beast, is Mine; I consecrated them to Myself at the time that I smote every first-
born in the land of Egypt. 18Now I take the Levites instead
of every first-born of the Israelites; 19and from among the
Israelites I formally assign the Levites to Aaron and his
sons, to perform the service for the Israelites in the Tent of
Meeting and to make expiation for the Israelites, so that no
plague may afflict the Israelites for coming too near the
sanctuary.
20Moses, Aaron, and the whole Israelite community did
with the Levites accordingly; just as the LORD had commanded Moses in regard to the Levites, so the Israelites did
with them. 21The Levites purified themselves and washed

וּבַבְּהֵמָה בְּיוֹם הַכֹּתִי כָל־בְּכוֹר בְּאֶרֶץ מִצְרַיִם
הִקְדַּשְׁתִּי אֹתָם לִי׃ 18 וָאֶקַּח אֶת־הַלְוִיִּם תַּחַת
כָּל־בְּכוֹר בִּבְנֵי יִשְׂרָאֵל׃ 19 וָאֶתְּנָה אֶת־הַלְוִיִּם
נְתֻנִים ׀ לְאַהֲרֹן וּלְבָנָיו מִתּוֹךְ בְּנֵי יִשְׂרָאֵל לַעֲבֹד
אֶת־עֲבֹדַת בְּנֵי־יִשְׂרָאֵל בְּאֹהֶל מוֹעֵד וּלְכַפֵּר עַל־
בְּנֵי יִשְׂרָאֵל וְלֹא יִהְיֶה בִּבְנֵי יִשְׂרָאֵל נֶגֶף בְּגֶשֶׁת
בְּנֵי־יִשְׂרָאֵל אֶל־הַקֹּדֶשׁ׃ 20 וַיַּעַשׂ מֹשֶׁה וְאַהֲרֹן
וְכָל־עֲדַת בְּנֵי־יִשְׂרָאֵל לַלְוִיִּם כְּכֹל אֲשֶׁר־צִוָּה
יְהוָה אֶת־מֹשֶׁה לַלְוִיִּם כֵּן־עָשׂוּ לָהֶם בְּנֵי יִשְׂרָאֵל׃
21 וַיִּתְחַטְּאוּ הַלְוִיִּם וַיְכַבְּסוּ בִּגְדֵיהֶם וַיָּנֶף אַהֲרֹן

Hannah vows that she will dedicate ***(titten)*** her son Samuel to the Lord (1 Sam. 1:11). Joshua assigned/dedicated ***(natan)*** the Gibeonites as manual laborers in the Temple (Josh. 9:26). Later we read of a class of Temple servants called ***netinim*** who were assigned ***(netunim)*** to the Levites (Ezra 8:2).

It should be noted that the Levitical status is never designated by the root ***k-d-sh*** for, in contrast to the priests, they are like any other Israelite laymen in terms of status. Hence the Levites, unlike the priests, can never have access to the stationary sancta (cf. 18:3b). This verse amplifies and thereby corrects the misinterpretation to which this idiom in 3:9 is open.

first issue Hebrew ***pitrat*** is unique.[29]

of all the first-born[30]

17. consecrated The first-born, like the priests, were holy (3:13). The Levites, in replacing the first-born, did not, however, assume their sacred status (cf. v. 16; 3:9).

18. Now I take That is, formally, through this ritual, though the intention was declared previously (3:12).

19. make expiation Rather, "ransom"; that is, the Levites will assume the responsibility for any Israelite encroachment upon the sancta. For this meaning of ***kippur*** and its implications, see Excursus 19.

plague ***Negef*** or ***ketsef,*** "wrath" (1:53), is technically not a legal penalty; it is reflex action, God's angry response in the wake of idolatry (25:9,18–19; 31:16), rebellion (17:11–15), an unexpiated census (Exod. 30:12), as well as the inevitable outcome of illicit contact with sancta (1:53; 18:5). However, the priestly tradition effectively restricts the outbreak of divine plague/wrath for encroachment upon sancta to the clergy alone (see Excursus 40).

coming too near Rather, "encroaching on." For Hebrew ***be-geshet,*** from the verb ***nagash,*** a synonym of ***karav,*** see Excursus 5.

the sanctuary Rather, "the sancta," Hebrew ***kodesh,*** as in 3:38 and 4:15,20. Encroachment by the laity is more likely during the time when the Levites are engaged in ***ʿavodah,*** their removal labors, when the Tabernacle is dismantled and transported. But it is also possible when the sancta are installed in the Tabernacle (see 1:53 and Excursus 40).

20. Moses, Aaron . . . community According to Ibn Ezra, Moses commanded, Aaron officiated, and the community performed the leaning of the hands.

in regard to The preposition ***le-*** here corresponds to ***ʿal*** in verse 22.

did with the Levites . . . Israelites did with them An inclusion formula, the completion of an account (cf. 1:54; 5:4). However, verses 21–22 summarize the procedure with emphasis on Aaron's role, the intention being either to offset the impression given by the final words of the inclusion—

their clothes; and Aaron designated them as an elevation offering before the LORD, and Aaron made expiation for them to cleanse them. [22]Thereafter the Levites were qualified to perform their service in the Tent of Meeting, under Aaron and his sons. As the LORD had commanded Moses in regard to the Levites, so they did to them.

אֹתָם תְּנוּפָה לִפְנֵי יְהוָה וַיְכַפֵּר עֲלֵיהֶם אַהֲרֹן
לְטַהֲרָם׃ 22 וְאַחֲרֵי־כֵן בָּאוּ הַלְוִיִּם לַעֲבֹד אֶת־
עֲבֹדָתָם בְּאֹהֶל מוֹעֵד לִפְנֵי אַהֲרֹן וְלִפְנֵי בָנָיו
כַּאֲשֶׁר צִוָּה יְהוָה אֶת־מֹשֶׁה עַל־הַלְוִיִּם כֵּן עָשׂוּ
לָהֶם׃ ס 23 וַיְדַבֵּר יְהוָה אֶל־מֹשֶׁה לֵּאמֹר׃

that the Israelites but not the Levites participated in the rite—or, more probably, to offset the impression of verses 13–15 that Moses rather than Aaron was the officiant for the Levites' induction.

21. purified themselves Hebrew *va-yithatte'u* refers to the use of the waters containing the ashes of the red cow, a *hatta't,* purification offering (e.g., 19:12,13,20; see Excursus 48), though shaving (v. 7) must also be implied.

washed their clothes Bathing is omitted, but it is implied whenever laundering is required. A person who eats from a carcass must bathe and launder (Lev. 17:15–16). Leviticus 11:40 describes a similar case and there, too, bathing is omitted (twice), as in the rest of the same chapter (vv. 11,25,28), because it is taken for granted.

made expiation Hebrew *va-yekhapper,* referring to the *kippur* sacrifices of verse 12.

22. they did Rather, "was done," with Hebrew *'asu* taken passively.

AGE LIMITS FOR LEVITICAL DUTIES (vv. 23–26)

The final section of rules regarding the Levites in the Book of Numbers gives the age limits for the Levitical labors. These figures have already been stated in the Levitical census of chapter 4. However, the present passage is essential not only because it informs us that the Levite must cease from the arduous task of removing the Tabernacle when he reaches the age of fifty but also because it stipulates that he does not withdraw into retirement but continues to perform guard duty, the other main Levitical function (cf. 3:7).[31]

The starting age of twenty-five, given here, conflicts with the starting age of thirty stipulated in the census (4:3,23,30; cf. 1 Chron. 23:3). The problem is compounded by yet a third variant starting age, that of twenty, cited in the postexilic literature (1 Chron. 23:21,27; cf. Ezra 3:8; 2 Chron. 31:17).

The latter problem is usually resolved by resorting to the list of returnees from the Babylonian exile, which shows 74 Levites over against 4,289 priests (Ezra 2:36–40; Neh. 7:39–41). Thus it is conjectured that the paucity of Levites available for the Temple service made necessary the extension of their term of service.[32] However, the Chronicler, by his own admission, attests to an ample supply of Levites (1 Chron. 23:3).

The answer, rather, is to be found in the changed work profile of the Levites. The key to the change is the elimination of the upper age limit. As the Chronicler himself testifies, by the time of David, the Levite no longer had to transport the Tabernacle and its sancta but was responsible for the maintenance of the Temple, the preparation of sacrificial ingredients, the guarding of the Temple (continuing the ancient function), and the musical liturgy (1 Chron. 23:28–31). Thus the additional duties of the Levite, which did not entail excessive physical labor, made necessary the extension of his employ from the age of twenty until death (cf. Ramban on 8:24–26). This is reflected in the rabbinic statement that upon entry into the promised land, the Levite could be disqualified not by age but only by an impaired singing voice (Sif. Num. 63; Sif. Zut. on 8:26).

Nonetheless, the discrepancy of ages thirty (chap. 4) and twenty-five (chap. 8) still remains within the priestly text. The Septuagint simply cuts the Gordian knot: It conveniently reads twenty-five instead of thirty in 4:3,23,30. The rabbis harmonize the discrepancy by conjecturing that at age twenty-five the Levite entered into training and perhaps served as an assistant, but only at age thirty did he assume his full role in the ranks of Levite laborers.[33] The members of the Dead Sea sect at Qumran resolved this discrepancy precisely in the same way except that they applied the Levitical ages

[23]The LORD spoke to Moses, saying: [24]This is the rule for the Levites. From twenty-five years of age up they shall participate in the work force in the service of the Tent of Meeting; [25]but at the age of fifty they shall retire from the work force and shall serve no more. [26]They may assist their brother Levites at the Tent of Meeting by standing guard, but they shall perform no labor. Thus you shall deal with the Levites in regard to their duties.

24 זֹאת אֲשֶׁר לַלְוִיִּם מִבֶּן חָמֵשׁ וְעֶשְׂרִים שָׁנָה
וָמַעְלָה יָבוֹא לִצְבֹא צָבָא בַּעֲבֹדַת אֹהֶל מוֹעֵד׃
25 וּמִבֶּן חֲמִשִּׁים שָׁנָה יָשׁוּב מִצְּבָא הָעֲבֹדָה וְלֹא
יַעֲבֹד עוֹד׃ 26 וְשֵׁרֵת אֶת־אֶחָיו בְּאֹהֶל מוֹעֵד
לִשְׁמֹר מִשְׁמֶרֶת וַעֲבֹדָה לֹא יַעֲבֹד כָּכָה תַּעֲשֶׂה
לַלְוִיִּם בְּמִשְׁמְרֹתָם׃ פ שלישי

for Tabernacle service to their entire community. Rendering the word for the Levitical work force, *tsava'* (e.g., 4:3; 8:24), as "army" (cf. 1:3), they mandated that each male was mobilized to begin his military training at age twenty-five; he then performed menial tasks until age thirty, when he was fully enrolled into the military ranks (1QSa 1:12–19; 1QM 7:3). This interpretation, incidentally, clearly shows that the Qumranites had the Masoretic text and not the Septuagint before them.

At present, this age discrepancy within the Book of Numbers cannot be satisfactorily resolved; perhaps it reflects variant traditions.

24. This is the rule . . . Hebrew *zo't . . .*, literally, "This is for the Levites." The addition of *ha-torah*, "the rule," is implied.[34]

from . . . age up Initially, all the Levites between ages thirty and fifty were mustered for the work force (4:46–47). Henceforth, the mustering will take place at age twenty-five.[35]

participate in the work force in the service of Rather, "qualify to serve in the work force for." (For *ba'* as "qualify" and *tsava'* as "work force," see 4:3.)

25. at the age Hebrew *u-mi-ben*, literally "and from the age," probably influenced by "from . . . age" in the previous verse. Of course the exact age of fifty is intended.

fifty In contrast to the priests, "age not bodily defects disqualifies Levites."[36]

retire Hebrew *yashuv*, literally "he shall return," is the opposite of *ba'*, "qualify, be admitted."

serve Hebrew *ya'avod.* Rather, "labor." See Excursus 6.

26. assists Hebrew *sheret* frequently is defined as *mishmeret*, "guarding" (cf. 1:50b, 53b).

labor This is anticipated by Sifrei Zuta: "This refers to (Levitical) porterage in the wilderness."

duties Rather, "guard duty" (cf. 3:7).

Final Preparations for Departure (9:1–10:10)

Chapters 9–10 tell of final preparation before the departure from Sinai on the twentieth of the second month of the second year (10:11); the observance of the second Passover six days earlier (9:1–14); the divine cloud as guide (9:15–23); the trumpet signals for assembling the people and its leaders and for breaking camp (10:1–10); the order of the march (10:11–28) and a narrative relating a variant marching order (10:29–36).

9 The LORD spoke to Moses in the wilderness of Sinai, on the first new moon of the second year following the exodus from the land of Egypt, saying: [2]Let the Israelite people offer the passover sacrifice at its set time: [3]you shall offer it on the fourteenth day of this month, at twilight, at its set time; you shall offer it in accordance with all its rules and rites.

[4]Moses instructed the Israelites to offer the passover sacrifice; [5]and they offered the passover sacrifice in the first month, on the fourteenth day of the month, at twilight, in the wilderness of Sinai. Just as the LORD had commanded Moses, so the Israelites did.

ט וַיְדַבֵּר יְהוָה אֶל־מֹשֶׁה בְמִדְבַּר־סִינַי בַּשָּׁנָה
הַשֵּׁנִית לְצֵאתָם מֵאֶרֶץ מִצְרַיִם בַּחֹדֶשׁ הָרִאשׁוֹן
לֵאמֹר: 2 וְיַעֲשׂוּ בְנֵי־יִשְׂרָאֵל אֶת־הַפָּסַח בְּמוֹעֲדוֹ:
3 בְּאַרְבָּעָה עָשָׂר־יוֹם בַּחֹדֶשׁ הַזֶּה בֵּין הָעֲרְבַּיִם
תַּעֲשׂוּ אֹתוֹ בְּמוֹעֲדוֹ כְּכָל־חֻקֹּתָיו וּכְכָל־מִשְׁפָּטָיו
תַּעֲשׂוּ אֹתוֹ: 4 וַיְדַבֵּר מֹשֶׁה אֶל־בְּנֵי יִשְׂרָאֵל
לַעֲשֹׂת הַפָּסַח: 5 וַיַּעֲשׂוּ אֶת־הַפֶּסַח בָּרִאשׁוֹן
בְּאַרְבָּעָה עָשָׂר יוֹם לַחֹדֶשׁ בֵּין הָעַרְבַּיִם בְּמִדְבַּר
סִינָי כְּכֹל אֲשֶׁר צִוָּה יְהוָה אֶת־מֹשֶׁה כֵּן עָשׂוּ בְּנֵי
יִשְׂרָאֵל: 6 וַיְהִי אֲנָשִׁים אֲשֶׁר הָיוּ טְמֵאִים לְנֶפֶשׁ

CHAPTER 9 THE SECOND PASSOVER (vv. 1–14)

This passage is divided into three parts: the observance of the first Passover sacrifice in the wilderness during the twilight hours of the fourteenth day of the first month of the second year (vv. 1–5); the account of those who complained to Moses of being barred from participating in the Passover sacrifice *(pesaḥ)* because of corpse contamination and of Moses bringing their complaint to God (vv. 6–8); and the giving of the divine decision that those who cannot observe the Passover because of corpse contamination or who are on a journey may observe the festival one month later, on the fourteenth day of the second month. The chronology is not out of joint. The census of 2/1 (1:1) is followed by the observance of the second Passover on 2/14 (9:11) just before Israel departs from Sinai on 2/20 (10:11). And the prescription of the regular Passover (9:1–5) must be considered a flashback, inserted here to distinguish it and all subsequent Passover observances from the original one in Egypt: Henceforth, according to Rashbam, the sacrifice had to be observed in the sanctuary. Also, it may be no accident that the instructions concerning the Passover immediately precede the march from Sinai. This sequence duplicates the sequence of the events of the Exodus: Then too, instructions (Exod. 12–13) had preceded the march out of Egypt (Exod. 13:17; 15:27).

1–5. It is no accident that Passover, falling on the fourteenth day of the month, follows the erection and dedication (on the first through eighth days) of the Tabernacle, followed by the altar dedication and purification of the Levites (chaps. 7–8). In later times the dedication of the Temple in Jerusalem is climaxed by the observance of one of the great pilgrimage festivals: Solomon on Sukkot (1 Kings 8:65–66), Hezekiah on Passover (2 Chron. 29–30), Josiah on Passover (2 Kings 23:21–23), the exiles on Sukkot (Ezra 3:4), Ezra and Nehemiah on Sukkot (Neh. 8:13–18), and perhaps Jeroboam on Sukkot (one month later, 1 Kings 12:32–33).

1. first new moon Hebrew *ḥodesh ha-ri'shon.* Hebrew *ḥodesh* can mean new moon as well as month, as in Exodus 19:1. This statement is a flashback, as has been noted.

2. Let . . . offer Missing is the usual introductory phrase: "Command (Lev. 5:2), or say (LXX; cf. Num. 17:2), or speak (Exod. 25:2; Lev. 16:2) to the Israelites." However, the ellipsis is not unusual; compare Genesis 27:28.[1] The verb *'asah* in a cultic context means to offer a sacrifice (e.g., 6:11,17) or to celebrate a festival (e.g., Exod. 12:47–48).

at its set time Hebrew *be-mo'ado,* even if it coincides with the Sabbath.[2]

3. you shall offer The change from indirect speech (v. 2) to direct is characteristic of the priestly texts (e.g., Lev. 22:1–3; 24:1–3).[3]

at twilight Hebrew *bein ha-'arbayim,* literally "between the two evenings," meaning between sunset and darkness (Exod. 16:12).

in accordance with all its rules and rites The blood of the first Passover was smeared on the doorposts and lintels of Israel's homes in Egypt. This time, in the wilderness of Sinai, the blood would have had to have been smeared on the entrances to Israel's tents.

⁶But there were some men who were unclean by reason of a corpse and could not offer the passover sacrifice on that day. Appearing that same day before Moses and Aaron, ⁷those men said to them, "Unclean though we are by reason of a corpse, why must we be debarred from presenting the LORD's offering at its set time with the rest of the Israelites?" ⁸Moses said to them, "Stand by, and let me hear what instructions the LORD gives about you."

⁹And the LORD spoke to Moses, saying: ¹⁰Speak to the Israelite people, saying: When any of you or of your posterity who are defiled by a corpse or are on a long journey would offer a passover sacrifice to the LORD, ¹¹they shall offer it in the second month, on the fourteenth day of the

אָדָ֗ם וְלֹא־יָכְל֛וּ לַעֲשֹׂת־הַפֶּ֖סַח בַּיּ֣וֹם הַה֑וּא וַיִּקְרְב֞וּ לִפְנֵ֤י מֹשֶׁה֙ וְלִפְנֵ֣י אַהֲרֹ֔ן בַּיּ֖וֹם הַהֽוּא׃ 7 וַ֠יֹּאמְרוּ הָאֲנָשִׁ֤ים הָהֵ֙מָּה֙ אֵלָ֔יו אֲנַ֥חְנוּ טְמֵאִ֖ים לְנֶ֣פֶשׁ אָדָ֑ם לָ֣מָּה נִגָּרַ֗ע לְבִלְתִּ֞י הַקְרִ֣ב אֶת־קָרְבַּ֤ן יְהוָה֙ בְּמֹ֣עֲד֔וֹ בְּת֖וֹךְ בְּנֵ֥י יִשְׂרָאֵֽל׃ 8 וַיֹּ֥אמֶר אֲלֵהֶ֖ם מֹשֶׁ֑ה עִמְד֣וּ וְאֶשְׁמְעָ֔ה מַה־יְצַוֶּ֥ה יְהוָ֖ה לָכֶֽם׃ פ

9 וַיְדַבֵּ֥ר יְהוָ֖ה אֶל־מֹשֶׁ֥ה לֵּאמֹֽר׃ 10 דַּבֵּ֞ר אֶל־בְּנֵ֤י יִשְׂרָאֵל֙ לֵאמֹ֔ר אִ֣ישׁ אִ֣ישׁ כִּי־יִהְיֶֽה־טָמֵ֣א ׀ לָנֶ֡פֶשׁ אוֹ֩ בְדֶ֨רֶךְ רְחֹקָ֜הׄ לָכֶ֗ם א֚וֹ לְדֹרֹ֣תֵיכֶ֔ם וְעָ֥שָׂה פֶ֖סַח לַיהוָֽה׃ 11 בַּחֹ֨דֶשׁ הַשֵּׁנִ֜י בְּאַרְבָּעָ֨ה עָשָׂ֥ר י֛וֹם בֵּ֥ין הָעַרְבַּ֖יִם יַעֲשֹׂ֣וּ אֹת֑וֹ עַל־מַצּ֥וֹת

v. 10. נקוד על ה׳

6–14. A particular circumstance occasions a query directed to Moses. He, in turn, refers the matter to God and receives appropriate instructions. The procedure recalls the case of the blasphemer in Leviticus (24:10–22) in that, possibly just as there, so here an individual case and its resolution became part of the larger law code. The wilderness incident and the divine decision provide the pretext for the law of the second Passover, which actually applies to conditions in the settled land (v. 10).⁴ However, since the condition of "long journey" appears only in the law (v. 10) but not in the wilderness incident (vv. 6–7), it is more likely that an actual incident became the basis for the generalized law (this pattern is also exemplified in the law of inheritance; see 27:1–11; 36:1–12).

6. But there were⁵

Appearing . . . before The use of *lifnei*, "before," instead of *'el*, "to," with the verb *karav* is deliberate, indicating proximity but not contact. It is used whenever ritual or etiquette requires one to keep one's distance, for example, women before communal leaders (27:2; Josh. 17:4), lay Israelites before God (e.g., Exod. 16:9), or, as here, contaminated persons before Moses.

and Aaron Since only Moses is addressed (v. 7a) and only Moses answers (v. 8a), Aaron's presence seems to be superfluous. This is admitted by Rabbi Eliezer, who suggests that Aaron just happened to be present when Moses was presented with the problem.⁶

7. debarred Hebrew *niggara'*. This verb implies the withdrawal of a part from the whole (e.g., 27:4; 36:3). The fear is that they would be excluded from the national festival as if they were foreigners (cf. Exod. 12:43).

the LORD's offering Compare verse 13. This phrase implies that this second Passover offering and all subsequent ones, in distinction to the first in Egypt (Exod. 12:6–7), was really a formal sacrifice, in which the blood and suet of the animal were offered on the authorized sanctuary altar (see Excursus 20).

8. Stand by Hebrew *'imdu*, at the entrance of the Tent of Meeting (cf. 11:16).⁷

10. Speak to the Israelite people But not to the resident aliens, who are not required to observe the Passover but may do so if they are circumcised (v. 14; Exod. 12:48).

defiled by a corpse Hebrew *tame' le-nefesh* (cf. 5:2). According to the rabbis, this specific impurity includes all other causes of impurity: "The following observe the Second [Passover]: gonorrheics, menstruants, parturients, those who [do not observe the First Passover] forcibly, accidentally, or deliberately, lepers, those who have intercourse with menstruants, and those who are corpse-contaminated or on a long journey."⁸ Such certainly was the understanding of the Chronicler, who attributes Hezekiah's postponement of the Passover to the second month most likely to the two reasons cited by this law: the absence of the people, presumably because of the distance, and the negligence of the officiating priests in purifying themselves (2 Chron. 30:3). The nature of the

month, at twilight. They shall eat it with unleavened bread and bitter herbs, 12and they shall not leave any of it over until morning. They shall not break a bone of it. They shall offer it in strict accord with the law of the passover sacrifice. 13But if a man who is clean and not on a journey refrains from offering the passover sacrifice, that person shall be cut off from his kin, for he did not present the LORD's offering at its set time; that man shall bear his guilt.

14And when a stranger who resides with you would offer

וּמְרֹרִים יֹאכְלֻהוּ׃ 12 לֹא־יַשְׁאִירוּ מִמֶּנּוּ עַד־בֹּקֶר
וְעֶצֶם לֹא יִשְׁבְּרוּ־בוֹ כְּכָל־חֻקַּת הַפֶּסַח יַעֲשׂוּ
אֹתוֹ׃ 13 וְהָאִישׁ אֲשֶׁר־הוּא טָהוֹר וּבְדֶרֶךְ לֹא־הָיָה
וְחָדַל לַעֲשׂוֹת הַפֶּסַח וְנִכְרְתָה הַנֶּפֶשׁ הַהִוא
מֵעַמֶּיהָ כִּי ׀ קָרְבַּן יְהוָה לֹא הִקְרִיב בְּמֹעֲדוֹ חֶטְאוֹ
יִשָּׂא הָאִישׁ הַהוּא׃ 14 וְכִי־יָגוּר אִתְּכֶם גֵּר וְעָשָׂה

impurity is not stated, nor is it specified even for the people who are impure on the second Passover (2 Chron. 17–20). Thus one can infer, following the rabbis, that ***any kind*** of impurity disqualifies the individual from partaking of the Passover sacrifice, which is in keeping with the general law barring those impure for whatever cause from contact with a sacrifice (Lev. 7:20–21).

long journey The rabbis disagree how far away from the Temple an Israelite must dwell in order to be exempt from observing the Passover on its appointed date in the first month. Rabbi Eliezer and Rabbi Yose apply this exemption to anyone who cannot reach the Temple threshold, whereas Rabbi Akiba (more logically according to Ramban) applies it to anyone living beyond the city of Modin (the home of the Maccabees), that is, a radius of 28 km. (17.5 miles).[9]

The superlinear dot over the final ***heh*** of ***reḥokah*** in the Hebrew text perhaps calls attention to this controversy.[10] The question is: a "long journey" from where? Two answers are possible: (1) from the authorized altar at the Tabernacle (later the Temple in Jerusalem) on which the suet and blood of the "Lord's offering" (vv. 6,13) would be burnt; or (2) from the household, implying that the ***pesaḥ*** could be eaten only within the family circle but not elsewhere. This was the law that pertained in Egypt (Exod. 12:3–4, especially v. 14). However, the existence of the Tabernacle from the second Passover and thereafter implies that the "Lord's offering" was sacrificed there. Interestingly, in contrast to other ancient Near Eastern cults that regard being on a journey as inexcusable and subject to divine punishment,[11] the Bible renders it a legitimate excuse by divine decree.

11. unleavened bread and bitter herbs The third requirement of the original paschal sacrifice in Egypt, that it be "roasted over the fire" (Exod. 12:8), is missing. This leads some commentators[12] to conclude that this passage was influenced by the Deuteronomic paschal sacrifice, which was cooked and not roasted (Deut. 16:7). However, this omission is covered by the general law of verse 12b. Similarly, the absence of the circumcision requirement for the resident alien who wishes to observe the Passover (v. 14; cf. Exod. 12:48) does not mean that the requirement was dropped; it is covered by the statement "he must offer it in accordance with the rules and rites of the passover sacrifice" (v. 14).

12. until morning Compare Exodus 12:10. In this respect the paschal sacrifice resembles the ***todah*** and ***millu'im*** offerings, which, of all the sacrifices eaten by the worshiper ***(shelamim),*** are the only ones that must be consumed the same day (Exod. 29:34; Lev. 7:15; 22:30). For this reason the rabbis accord the paschal sacrifice a higher degree of sanctity than the ***shelamim.***[13]

not break a bone of it Compare Exodus 12:46. The antiquity of the paschal sacrifice is attested by this prohibition. Comparative research among the nomadic tribes in the ancient Semitic world and elsewhere indicates that its underlying belief was that the survival of the entire skeleton was essential for resurrection in the afterlife. This belief may be implied by Ezekiel's vision of the dry bones that God must knit together before they can live again (Ezek. 37:1–14; cf. Pss. 34:21; 53:6). Alternatively, this prohibition has been viewed as a prophylactic rite to ensure that no harm befall its consumers during the Exodus from Egypt[14] and, thereafter, from one Passover to the next (Jub. 49:13–15). In either case, the underlying principle is that the treatment of the animal affects the fate of its consumer.

the law of the passover sacrifice Compare Exodus 12:43–49. This clause proves the dependency of our passage on Exodus.

13. cut off . . . bear his guilt Hebrew ***ve-nikhretah . . . het'o yissa'*** are synonymous (cf. the parallel passages Lev. 7:18; 19:8), both implying death by divine agency if the neglect was deliberate

a passover sacrifice to the Lord, he must offer it in accordance with the rules and rites of the passover sacrifice. There shall be one law for you, whether stranger or citizen of the country.

[15]On the day that the Tabernacle was set up, the cloud covered the Tabernacle, the Tent of the Pact; and in the evening it rested over the Tabernacle in the likeness of fire

פֶּסַח לַיהוָה כְּחֻקַּת הַפֶּסַח וּכְמִשְׁפָּטוֹ כֵּן יַעֲשֶׂה
חֻקָּה אַחַת יִהְיֶה לָכֶם וְלַגֵּר וּלְאֶזְרַח הָאָרֶץ׃
פ רביעי 15 וּבְיוֹם הָקִים אֶת־הַמִּשְׁכָּן כִּסָּה
הֶעָנָן אֶת־הַמִּשְׁכָּן לְאֹהֶל הָעֵדֻת וּבָעֶרֶב יִהְיֶה
עַל־הַמִּשְׁכָּן כְּמַרְאֵה־אֵשׁ עַד־בֹּקֶר׃ 16 כֵּן יִהְיֶה

(cf. 15:30–31 and Excursus 36). The fact that the penalty applies only to the nonobservance of the fixed Passover[15] implies that the observance of the second Passover (by those exempted from the first, v. 10) is not required but voluntary.[16]

at its set time *be-mo'ado* (see vv. 2,3,7). The paschal sacrifice is the only holiday observance whose willful neglect is punishable by the divine penalty of ***karet***. The reason for this is that all other occasions of sacred time involve only prohibitive but not performative commandments. For example, on Sabbaths and festivals one may not do any work and on Yom Kippur one may not eat. However, neither on the Sabbath nor on festivals (in the priestly texts) is there a performative commandment, for example, that one has to worship. The paschal sacrifice alone, among all the festival commandments, is performative: Every family in Israel absolutely must participate in the offering "at its set time," except for the mitigating circumstances stated here.

Ostensibly, there are two other performative commandments in connection with the festivals: (1) dwelling in the ***sukkah*** and taking specified vegetation to the sanctuary during Sukkot (Lev. 23:40–42) and (2) appearing at the sanctuary on the three pilgrimage festivals (Exod. 23:14–17; 34:23; Deut. 16:1–17). The latter commandment, however, is not a requirement of the priestly tradition. As for Sukkot, it clearly is not of the same rank as Passover since its nonobservance is not threatened by ***karet***. Put otherwise: Residing in ***sukkot*** or rejoicing "before the Lord" is a privilege, a boon and, hence, a commandment without sanctions. Passover, however, has national significance: As a commemoration of the Exodus, its observance is a reaffirmation of the covenant struck by God with Israel at the beginning of its national existence. As a consequence, failure to participate in the rite—except for the circumstances stipulated here—is tantamount to a breach of the covenant. And by a similar rationale, circumcision is the only other performative commandment whose neglect is subject to ***karet*** (Gen. 17:14). It is the sign of the covenant and its neglect is therefore also equivalent to a violation of the covenant.

14. This law ostensibly adds nothing to Exodus 12:49. Ramban would have the latter verse apply only for the first Passover in Egypt, the observance of which is here made permanent. Another possibility, according to Ibn Ezra, is to extend to the resident alien the privilege of observing the second Passover.

would offer The resident alien may participate in the paschal offering if he is circumcised (Exod. 12:48).

stranger Hebrew ***ger,*** literally "resident alien" (see Excursus 34).

THE FIRE-CLOUD (vv. 15–23)

The lengthy priestly legislation beginning with Leviticus 1 is now concluded by an elaboration of the passage that ends the Book of Exodus (40:36–38), thereby forming an inclusion around the entire section (Lev. 1:1–Num. 9:14). Thus Israel's movement in the wilderness (Exod. 15–18), interrupted by the Sinaitic legislation (Exod. 19–Num. 9), is now resumed.[17] The elevated prose expresses the excitement of the impending march—Israel is headed for its land!

God leads Israel in its wilderness march not by His voiced commands but by His appointed sign, a cloud-encased fire (cf. Exod. 40:38). During the day only the cloud is visible, the fire, presumably, dimmed by the sunlight. But night renders the cloud invisible, and the luminous fire can be clearly seen. The fire is also called ***kavod*** (Exod. 24:17; 2 Chron. 7:3; cf. Ezek. 1:27–28). The Lord's cloud and

until morning. 16It was always so: the cloud covered it, appearing as fire by night. 17And whenever the cloud lifted from the Tent, the Israelites would set out accordingly; and at the spot where the cloud settled, there the Israelites would make camp. 18At a command of the LORD the Israelites broke camp, and at a command of the LORD they made camp: they remained encamped as long as the cloud stayed over the Tabernacle. 19When the cloud lingered over the

תָּמִיד הֶעָנָן יְכַסֶּנּוּ וּמַרְאֵה־אֵשׁ לָיְלָה׃ 17 וּלְפִי
הֵעָלֹת הֶעָנָן מֵעַל הָאֹהֶל וְאַחֲרֵי־כֵן יִסְעוּ בְּנֵי
יִשְׂרָאֵל וּבִמְקוֹם אֲשֶׁר יִשְׁכָּן־שָׁם הֶעָנָן שָׁם יַחֲנוּ
בְּנֵי יִשְׂרָאֵל׃ 18 עַל־פִּי יְהוָה יִסְעוּ בְּנֵי יִשְׂרָאֵל
וְעַל־פִּי יְהוָה יַחֲנוּ כָּל־יְמֵי אֲשֶׁר יִשְׁכֹּן הֶעָנָן עַל־
הַמִּשְׁכָּן יַחֲנוּ׃ 19 וּבְהַאֲרִיךְ הֶעָנָן עַל־הַמִּשְׁכָּן יָמִים

kavod can be compared with Akkadian ***melammu*** and ***puluhtu,*** which describe, respectively, the refulgent aureole and garment of fire surrounding the gods and the sancta. The ***melammu*** can also refer to the mask that hides the natural body of gods, demons, and kings.[18] Thus, the Lord's ***kavod*** is enveloped by a cloud but is visible, especially at night, "in the likeness of fire" (9:15).[19]

When the fire-cloud descends upon the Tabernacle (Exod. 40:34) or leaves it (Ezek. 10:4a), it expands into the courtyard (Ezek. 10:4b) so that the consecrated personnel cannot enter (Exod. 40:35). In effect, the power of the numinous is increased when in motion. Our passage states unequivocally that it is the ascending and descending fire-cloud that determines whether Israel moves or encamps (cf. v. 18). As soon as the Tabernacle is reassembled, it is enveloped by the cloud; and whenever the Lord seeks to speak with Moses or manifests Himself to Israel, the ***kavod***-fire leaves the cloud and descends upon the Ark-throne in the Holy of Holies (see Excursus 22). The cloud-encased fire or ***kavod,*** while suspended above the Tabernacle, initially informs Moses that God wishes to address him. Presumably it does this by becoming so luminous that it can be seen in daylight (20:6). The fire-cloud was seen for the first time by Israel when it descended to the top of Mount Sinai (Exod. 24:15–18). The sevenfold repetition of the two key terms "Tabernacle" and "at a command of/on a sign from the Lord" is the linguistic cement that unifies this passage (see the Comments to vv. 17 and 18).

15. ***On the day*** That is, the first day of the first month of the second year (cf. Exod. 40:17, 34); or render "when" (see the Comment to 7:1). In this verse, the verbs are in the perfect tense, referring to a historical event. In the following verses the verbs are imperfect, referring to continuous occurrences.

the Tabernacle, the Tent of Pact The purpose of the apposition is to emphasize that by the Tabernacle is meant the Tent-shrine and not the entire enclosure. On the other hand, Ramban may be right in understanding these two terms not as an apposition but as a construct: "the Tabernacle of the Tent of Pact," which also implies that the cloud rested solely on the Tabernacle shrine but not in the Tent courtyard. The expression "Tent of Pact" occurs again only in 17:7–8 and 18:2. The usual idiom is "Tent of Meeting" or, less frequently, "Tabernacle of Pact" (1:50,53; 10:11).

17. ***Tent*** Hebrew *'ohel,* here a synonym of ***mishkan,*** "Tabernacle," in contrast to "the Tent of the Pact" (v. 15). "Tabernacle" appears seven times in this section as does the phrase "at a command of/on a sign from the Lord" (see the Comment to v. 18). These two septenary expressions sum up the main idea of this passage: God's Tabernacle, His earthly Presence, moved when He and not Israel so desired.

settled Hebrew *yishkon,* literally "tabernacled" (cf. 10:12). Presumably, the spot under the cloud marked the center of the camp, where the Tabernacle was to be erected. As soon as the latter operation was completed, the cloud would descend to "tabernacle," envelop, the Tent.

18. ***At a command*** Rather "On a sign from," that is, the fire-cloud, according to Ibn Ezra and Bekhor Shor. This interpretation is supported by *u-lefi . . . he-'anan,* literally "by the sign of . . . the cloud" in verse 17.[20] Furthermore, the function of the second half of the verse, with its repetition of the verb *yaḥanu,* is to explain the first half, i.e., the cloud is the Lord's sign.[21] Moreover, since the movement of the cloud directed Israel's march, what purpose would be served by the verbal command of God? For *'al pi YHVH* as indicating the will of God expressed through oracular signs, see the Comment to 3:16.[22] It must be assumed that when the cloud lifted, it proceeded to the head of

Tabernacle many days, the Israelites observed the LORD's mandate and did not journey on. 20 At such times as the cloud rested over the Tabernacle for but a few days, they remained encamped at a command of the LORD, and broke camp at a command of the LORD. 21 And at such times as the cloud stayed from evening until morning, they broke camp as soon as the cloud lifted in the morning. Day or night, whenever the cloud lifted, they would break camp. 22 Whether it was two days or a month or a year—however long the cloud lingered over the Tabernacle—the Israelites remained encamped and did not set out; only when it lifted did they break camp. 23 On a sign from the LORD they made camp and on a sign from the LORD they broke camp; they observed the LORD's mandate at the LORD's bidding through Moses.

רַבִּים וְשָׁמְרוּ בְנֵי־יִשְׂרָאֵל אֶת־מִשְׁמֶרֶת יְהוָה וְלֹא
יִסָּעוּ׃ 20 וְיֵשׁ אֲשֶׁר יִהְיֶה הֶעָנָן יָמִים מִסְפָּר עַל־
הַמִּשְׁכָּן עַל־פִּי יְהוָה יַחֲנוּ וְעַל־פִּי יְהוָה יִסָּעוּ׃
21 וְיֵשׁ אֲשֶׁר־יִהְיֶה הֶעָנָן מֵעֶרֶב עַד־בֹּקֶר וְנַעֲלָה
הֶעָנָן בַּבֹּקֶר וְנָסָעוּ אוֹ יוֹמָם וָלַיְלָה וְנַעֲלָה הֶעָנָן
וְנָסָעוּ׃ 22 אוֹ־יֹמַיִם אוֹ־חֹדֶשׁ אוֹ־יָמִים בְּהַאֲרִיךְ
הֶעָנָן עַל־הַמִּשְׁכָּן לִשְׁכֹּן עָלָיו יַחֲנוּ בְנֵי־יִשְׂרָאֵל
וְלֹא יִסָּעוּ וּבְהֵעָלֹתוֹ יִסָּעוּ׃ 23 עַל־פִּי יְהוָה יַחֲנוּ
וְעַל־פִּי יְהוָה יִסָּעוּ אֶת־מִשְׁמֶרֶת יְהוָה שָׁמָרוּ עַל־
פִּי יְהוָה בְּיַד־מֹשֶׁה׃ פ

the column (in conformity with the nonpriestly tradition, e.g., Exod. 13:21–22) and wherever it stopped the Tabernacle was reassembled beneath it (cf. 10:12). It is quite deliberate that the phrase *'al pi YHVH* occurs seven times in this passage, for it emphasizes that Israel's march to its promised land was conducted only by the direction of God, not by man, not even by a Moses.

*19. **cloud*** The fact that the cloud alone (and not the fire) decided the line of march (vv. 19–22) must mean that Israel marched only by day, a conclusion confirmed by 10:34.

observed the LORD's mandate Hebrew *Ve-shamru . . . 'et mishmeret YHVH.* Although *mishmeret* means guarding or guard duty (cf. 3:7), when it takes the Lord as its object, it refers to His negative commandments, prohibitions whose violation must be scrupulously guarded against (cf. Lev. 18:30 on sexual prohibitions; Lev. 22:9 on the contaminated priest and his food; Num. 18:7a on priestly prohibitions involving the altar and shrine). Here the prohibition is clear: No man, not even Moses, directs the march but only God.[23]

*20. **few days***[24]

*21. **Day*** Hebrew *yomam* means daylight as opposed to *yom,* the twenty-four-hour period.[25]

*22. **or a year*** Hebrew *'o-yamim.* The Septuagint and many manuscripts read "a full month," *ḥodesh yamim,* omitting the intervening *'o.*[26]

*23. **observed the LORD's mandate*** Hebrew *'et mishmeret YHVH shamaru,* repeated from verse 19 (but in reverse order) to complete the inclusion. This is the only verb, outside of those in verse 15a, that is not an imperfect frequentive but the simple past. It registers a fulfillment, that the Israelites faithfully followed the directions of the fire-cloud.

bidding Rather, "sign" (cf. v. 18).

CHAPTER 10 THE TRUMPETS *(ḤATSOTSEROT)* (vv. 1–10)

This section concludes the preparation for the march. At God's command, the trumpets sound and the people assemble in marching formation. Thus, the use of the trumpets is Israel's response to the divine signal given by the fire-cloud.[1] The other usages of the trumpet are also explained.

To judge by the many illustrations of the ancient Egyptian trumpet[2] and the ones portrayed on Judean coins,[3] the trumpet was a short, slender tube with a widened mouth, and, according to Josephus (Ant. 3.291), slightly more than one foot in length. Those depicted on the Arch of Titus would be too long to fit Josephus' measurements. In ancient Egypt, the trumpets were used in war

10 The LORD spoke to Moses, saying: [2]Have two silver
trumpets made; make them of hammered work. They shall
serve you to summon the community and to set the divisions in motion. [3]When both are blown in long blasts, the
whole community shall assemble before you at the entrance
of the Tent of Meeting; [4]and if only one is blown, the
chieftains, heads of Israel's contingents, shall assemble
before you. [5]But when you sound short blasts, the divisions
encamped on the east shall move forward; [6]and when you

י וַיְדַבֵּר יְהוָה אֶל־מֹשֶׁה לֵּאמֹר׃ 2 עֲשֵׂה לְךָ שְׁתֵּי
חֲצוֹצְרֹת כֶּסֶף מִקְשָׁה תַּעֲשֶׂה אֹתָם וְהָיוּ לְךָ
לְמִקְרָא הָעֵדָה וּלְמַסַּע אֶת־הַמַּחֲנוֹת׃ 3 וְתָקְעוּ
בָּהֵן וְנוֹעֲדוּ אֵלֶיךָ כָּל־הָעֵדָה אֶל־פֶּתַח אֹהֶל
מוֹעֵד׃ 4 וְאִם־בְּאַחַת יִתְקָעוּ וְנוֹעֲדוּ אֵלֶיךָ
הַנְּשִׂיאִים רָאשֵׁי אַלְפֵי יִשְׂרָאֵל׃ 5 וּתְקַעְתֶּם
תְּרוּעָה וְנָסְעוּ הַמַּחֲנוֹת הַחֹנִים קֵדְמָה׃

and to summon the people to worship.[4] In Israel, too, according to our passage, the two trumpets were used singly or together for administrative, military (cf. also 2 Chron. 13:12–14), and cultic functions. The latter, as indicated by verse 10, were solely occasions of joy, verified by the ample attestations of the trumpet in the Bible: in coronations (2 Kings 11:14; cf. Ps. 98:6); the installation of the Ark in David's tent (1 Chron. 16:6,42); the dedication of Solomon's Temple (2 Chron. 5:12–13); the rededication of the altar and covenant under Asa (2 Chron. 15:8–15); the purification of Hezekiah's Temple (2 Chron. 29:27); the laying of the foundation of the Second Temple (Ezra 3:10); consecrating the walls of Jerusalem (Neh. 12:35,41). The use of the trumpet in the Dead Sea War Scroll will be adduced in relevant verses below. The difference between the trumpet and the shofar is discussed in Excursus 21.

2. silver Since the trumpets were made of precious metal, they were prized as spoil (cf. the Arch of Titus).

hammered work Hebrew ***mikshah,*** made like the menorah (cf. 8:4). The trumpets were probably molded by rubbing the metallic foil over a model.

summon . . . set . . . in motion[5] The War Scroll of the ancient Jewish sect residing at Qumran, along the Dead Sea, prescribed sets of trumpets for both functions mentioned in this verse: summoning the community and setting the divisions in motion. The warlike purpose of the latter call is made clear by the trumpet's inscription: "God's mighty deeds to scatter the enemy, and to put to flight all opponents of justice, and disgraceful retribution to the opponents of God." This paraphrase of 10:35 was written in similar language upon the standard of the Judahite division.[6] The Qumranites also had trumpets called "triumph of the camps" (not in our passage), which, to judge from their inscription, were used during peacetime: "Peace of God in the encampment of His saints."

community Hebrew ***'edah,*** most likely limited to males over twenty years of age (cf. Excursus 1).

divisions Hebrew ***maḥanot*** refers to the individual tribal camps (cf. vv. 5–6).

*4. **chieftains*** That the community ***('edah),*** represented by grown males, and the chieftains ***(nesi'im)*** were assembled separately has given rise to the suggestion that early Israel was governed by a bicameral legislative body as found in early premonarchic cities of Mesopotamia and Anatolia (see Excursus 1). The Dead Sea War Scroll (3:2–3), basing itself upon this verse, prescribed special sets of trumpets (not just discrete signals) for calling up of the ***'edah***[7] and the commanders ***(sarim);*** the inscription on the latter trumpets read ***nesi'ei 'el,*** "chieftains of God." In addition, the scroll prescribes for two other related trumpets: "trumpets of the formation" and "trumpets of the clans of the congregation."

heads of Israel's contingents The auxiliary title of the chieftains (cf. 1:16). Some versions, however, prefix this title with the conjunction, reading "and the heads . . ." Perhaps this reading explains the War Scroll's prescription for two additional trumpets: "trumpets of the formations" (of the battle units) and "trumpets of the men of renown, chieftains of the contingents of the community."

assemble before you Also at the entrance of the Tent of Meeting.[8]

*5. **short blasts*** Hebrew ***teru'ah,*** verbal form ***heria'***, in contrast to "blow long blasts," ***taka'***. It should be noted that the term "blow long blasts" is expressed simply by the verb ***taka'*** (vv.

sound short blasts a second time, those encamped on the south shall move forward. Thus short blasts shall be blown for setting them in motion, [7]while to convoke the congregation you shall blow long blasts, not short ones. [8]The trumpets shall be blown by Aaron's sons, the priests; they shall be for you an institution for all time throughout the ages.

[9]When you are at war in your land against an aggressor who attacks you, you shall sound short blasts on the trumpets, that you may be remembered before the LORD

6 וּתְקַעְתֶּם תְּרוּעָה שֵׁנִית וְנָסְעוּ הַמַּחֲנוֹת הַחֹנִים
תֵּימָנָה תְּרוּעָה יִתְקְעוּ לְמַסְעֵיהֶם׃ 7 וּבְהַקְהִיל
אֶת־הַקָּהָל תִּתְקְעוּ וְלֹא תָרִיעוּ׃ 8 וּבְנֵי אַהֲרֹן
הַכֹּהֲנִים יִתְקְעוּ בַּחֲצֹצְרוֹת וְהָיוּ לָכֶם לְחֻקַּת עוֹלָם
לְדֹרֹתֵיכֶם׃ 9 וְכִי־תָבֹאוּ מִלְחָמָה בְּאַרְצְכֶם עַל־
הַצַּר הַצֹּרֵר אֶתְכֶם וַהֲרֵעֹתֶם בַּחֲצֹצְרוֹת וְנִזְכַּרְתֶּם
לִפְנֵי יְהוָה אֱלֹהֵיכֶם וְנוֹשַׁעְתֶּם מֵאֹיְבֵיכֶם׃

3–4), but "blow short blasts" requires the compound expression *taka' teru'ah* (vv. 5–6). The reason for these distinct forms is twofold. (1) The term *teru'ah* and its corresponding verb *heria'* refer elsewhere to a loud shout by warriors (e.g., Josh. 6:5,10,16,20), and worshipers (e.g., Pss. 47:2; 95:2), whereas the sole verb signifying the blowing of a horn is *taka'* (e.g., Josh. 6:13). Hence when the text wishes to express the idea of blowing the *teru'ah* signal on the trumpet it must either use the verb *taka'*, signifying blowing on an instrument, and the object *teru'ah* to indicate the appropriate signal or, if it uses the verb *heria'*, it must specify that the sound was produced by a trumpet (v. 9). (2) *Teru'ah* can refer to a battle cry (cf. Amos 1:14; Jer. 14:19); and, hence, its use in breaking camp implies signaling the Israelites to move from an encamped peaceful position to a mobile battle formation. Thus the trumpets taken into the Midianite war are actually called "the trumpets of *teru'ah*" (31:6; cf. 2 Chron. 13:12). The rabbis define the length of the calls by the following equation: a *teki'ah* (verbal noun from *taka'*) is equivalent to three *teru'ah* sounds;[9] hence the translation "long blasts" and "short blasts" respectively.[10] According to Josephus (Wars 3.5.4), the Romans issued three calls upon breaking camp: (1) to dismantle the tents; (2) to load the animals; and (3) to begin the march.

6. *forward* The Septuagint adds: "When you shall sound short blasts a third time, the divisions encamped westward shall move forward, and when you shall sound short blasts a fourth time, the divisions encamped northward shall move forward."[11] Ibn Ezra, however, denies altogether the possibility of these additional third and fourth blasts since the priests, who had to blow the horns (v. 8), moved with the cult objects following the second division (2:17; 10:21). Even so, they could have sounded the trumpets a third time; moreover, the priestly trumpeters could have remained behind. Thus the blasts for the remaining divisions are to be anticipated and these are adumbrated in the second half of the verse. The Vulgate addition, "and according to this manner shall the rest do," captures the sense.

them That is, the remaining divisions.

7. *while* Rather, "however."[12]

congregation Hebrew *kahal,* a synonym of *'edah,* "community" (v. 2; and cf. Excursus 1).

you shall blow . . . That is, blow the trumpet but not with martial notes.[13]

8. *the priests* And henceforth the trumpets are blown only by the priests (e.g., 31:6), whereas the shofar could be blown by anyone (see Excursus 21).

In the ancient Near East, priests were an integral part of a military force, as attested in Ugarit[14] and Alalakh[15] and later in biblical Israel (Deut. 20:2–4; 1 Sam. 23:9; 30:7), the Neo-Babylonian empire (Ezek. 21:26), and classical Greece.[16] Basing themselves on Deuteronomy 20:2, the rabbis speak of a special priest "anointed for war."[17] The War Scroll of the Dead Sea sectarians goes into great detail concerning the part that the "head (= high) priest," the "priest chosen for the day of revenge," and the six priestly trumpeters assume in battle (7:8–11; 15:4ff.).

generations The perpetual use of the trumpets is meant for the assembly (vv. 3–4) and for war but not for the divisions breaking camp, according to Ibn Ezra. However, it is precisely for the latter function that the trumpets are usually employed in the Dead Sea War Scroll.

9. *are at war* Hebrew *tavo'u milḥamah.* Read *be-milḥamah* (1 Kings 22:30) or *le-*

your God and be delivered from your enemies. [10]And on your joyous occasions—your fixed festivals and new moon days—you shall sound the trumpets over your burnt offerings and your sacrifices of well-being. They shall be a reminder of you before your God: I, the LORD, am your God.

10 וּבְי֨וֹם שִׂמְחַתְכֶ֥ם וּֽבְמוֹעֲדֵיכֶם֮ וּבְרָאשֵׁ֣י
חָדְשֵׁיכֶם֒ וּתְקַעְתֶּ֣ם בַּחֲצֹֽצְרֹ֗ת עַ֚ל עֹלֹ֣תֵיכֶ֔ם וְעַ֖ל
זִבְחֵ֣י שַׁלְמֵיכֶ֑ם וְהָי֨וּ לָכֶ֤ם לְזִכָּרוֹן֙ לִפְנֵ֣י אֱלֹהֵיכֶ֔ם
אֲנִ֖י יְהוָ֥ה אֱלֹהֵיכֶֽם׃ פ חמישי 11 וַיְהִ֗י

milhamah. The usual expression is ***ba' le-milhamah*** (e.g., 31:21; 32:6), literally "enter war." Rabbi Akiba extends the notion of war to include all forms of natural disasters.[18]

you may be remembered The trumpet blasts serve also as a prayer whose efficacy is recorded in the war between Abijah and Jeroboam (2 Chron. 13:12–16). The Dead Sea War Scroll prescribed trumpets named "trumpets of remembrance" to be used "when the battle intervals open for the skirmishers to go forth" and bearing the inscription "vengeful remembrance at the appointed time of God" (cf. "the Lord's vengeance on Midian," 31:3; cf. v. 6).[19] Trumpets used as instruments of prayer appear to be unique to Israel. "R. Josiah said: It is written, 'Happy is the people that know the sound of the ***teru'ah.***' But do not the nations of the world know how to sound the ***teru'ah***? What a host of horns they have! What a host of ***bucinae*** (horns) they have! What a host of trumpets they have! Yet you say, 'Happy is the people that know the sound of the ***teru'ah.***' It can only mean that they (Israel) know how to sway their Creator with the ***teru'ah.***"[20]

10. your joyous occasions Many examples of joyous occasions accompanied by trumpet blasts are attested in Scripture, such as those cited in the introductory Comment to 10:1–10. The wording of 2 Kings 11:14 (the coronation of Joash): "rejoicing and blowing trumpets" is precisely the same as here. According to Ibn Ezra, "joyous occasions" refer mainly to victory on the battlefield since this verse follows the description of war (v. 9).

your fixed festivals Enumerated in Leviticus 23:4–38. In late Second Temple times the trumpet was also blown twice daily during the sacrifice of the ***tamid;***[21] this was, perhaps, based on the inclusion of the ***tamid*** among the ***mo'adim,*** "fixed festivals," in 28:1,2–8; 29:39 (see Excursus 65).

sound Hebrew ***u-teka'tem.*** Hence only the long blast, the ***teki'ah,*** is sounded on festive occasions. Ostensibly, this is contradicted by the description of Rosh Hashanah as "commemorated by ***teru'ah***" (Lev. 23:24) and "a day of ***teru'ah***" (Num. 29:1). However, that ***teru'ah*** is sounded by the shofar and not by the trumpet, by the people and not the priests (cf. Ps. 47:6).

burnt offerings Public offerings;[22] see chapters 28–29.

sacrifices of well-being Public offerings[23] (Lev. 23:19).

I, the LORD, am your God The rabbis regard this verse as the basis for the three major sections of the Musaf prayer of the Rosh Hashanah service. This clause stands for God's sovereignty ***(malkhuyot);*** "you shall sound the trumpets" stands for ***shofarot;*** and "they shall be a reminder of you" stands for God's remembrance, ***zikhronot.***[24]

a reminder Hebrew ***zikkaron.*** The function of a ritual reminder is described in Excursus 38.

THE MARCH FROM SINAI TO TRANSJORDAN (10:11–22:1)

The march took about forty years (14:33; 33:38), but the bulk of this section is concerned with the opening months (10:11–14:45) and the closing months (20:1–22:1). Israel's movements are generated solely by the Lord. He leads Israel to the land He has promised (10:29), moves it (9:15–23; 10:11), retards it (12:14–15; 14:26–35; 20:27–28), and causes it to detour (14:25), advises (13:1–2), nourishes (11:31–32), and gives it victory (21:1–3,33). In so doing, the Lord renews the wonders of the Exodus: manna (Num. 11:7–9; Exod. 16:14–36), quail (Num. 11:31; Exod. 16:11–13), water from the rock (20:2–13; 21:16; Exod. 17:1–7). And the victories in the Negeb and Transjordan anticipate those in Canaan

11 In the second year, on the twentieth day of the second
month, the cloud lifted from the Tabernacle of the Pact
12 and the Israelites set out on their journeys from the
wilderness of Sinai. The cloud came to rest in the wilderness of Paran.
13 When the march was to begin, at the LORD's command
through Moses, 14 the first standard to set out, troop by
troop, was the division of Judah. In command of its troops

בַּשָּׁנָה הַשֵּׁנִית בַּחֹדֶשׁ הַשֵּׁנִי בְּעֶשְׂרִים בַּחֹדֶשׁ
נַעֲלָה הֶעָנָן מֵעַל מִשְׁכַּן הָעֵדֻת: 12 וַיִּסְעוּ בְנֵי־
יִשְׂרָאֵל לְמַסְעֵיהֶם מִמִּדְבַּר סִינָי וַיִּשְׁכֹּן הֶעָנָן
בְּמִדְבַּר פָּארָן: 13 וַיִּסְעוּ בָּרִאשֹׁנָה עַל־פִּי יְהוָה
בְּיַד־מֹשֶׁה: 14 וַיִּסַּע דֶּגֶל מַחֲנֵה בְנֵי־יְהוּדָה

(13:1–24; 21:1–3; 10:35; Josh. 2:6; 8:10). However, Israel responds with unbelief and rebellion (11:1,5–6; 14:1–10; 17:6–7; 20:1–6; 21:4–5; 25:1), and so do its leaders: the chieftains (13:30–33; 16; 25:14), Miriam and Aaron (12:1), and Moses himself (20:10–12).[25]

From Sinai to Kadesh (10:11–12:16)

The notice that the desert of Paran is the first major stop, without mention of the minor intermediary ones (cf. 11:3,34–35), is intended to form an inclusion with the notice of the actual arrival at Paran (12:16), thus structurally defining the section 10:11–12:16 as a complete literary unit.[26]

THE ORDER OF THE MARCH (10:11–28)

Guided by the fire-cloud, Israel leaves Sinai on the twentieth day of the second month of the second year and encamps in the wilderness of Paran. The names of the tribal princes and the order of the march coincide with the data of chapters 1 and 2. They march in a single column, the square (the shape of the camp) becoming a beam, but, as Shadal notes, the order of the divisions, tribes, and clans remains unchanged; the only exception is the dismantled Tabernacle, which is transported between the divisions.

11. the cloud The ascending and descending cloud was the divine sign of when to break and make camp (see the Comment to 9:18); its motion indicated the direction of the march (see the introductory Comment to 9:15–23).

12. set out on their journeys The verb ***nasaʿ*** means "pull up stakes" (cf. Judg. 16:3; Isa. 33:20), a term related to nomadic travel, where journeys are begun and ended by pulling up the tent pins and by implanting them in a new site (e.g., Gen. 35:21). Thus, ***nasaʿ*** means "journey in stages" and its noun ***massaʿ*** means "stages"; so henceforth in the book.[27]

came to rest Hebrew ***shakhan*** is the verb used when the subject is God (5:3; 35:34), His Tabernacle (***mishkan***, Josh. 22:19), or His cloud (Exod. 40:35).

Paran Verse 12 summarizes several stations, since the Israelites stop at Kibroth-hattaavah and Hazeroth before they reach the wilderness of Paran (11:35; 12:16).[28] The likelihood, however, is that the wilderness of Paran is not a station but is the general name for the northern half of the Sinai Peninsula, between Midian (in Transjordan) and Egypt (1 Kings 11:18) on the east and west, Sinai on the south (10:11) and Kadesh-barnea (13:26) and Elath (Gen. 14:6) on the north.[29] Paran may be the ancient name for the entire Sinai Peninsula since Feiran (= Paran) is the name of the main oasis in the southern Sinai.[30] (See Map 1.)

13. When the march was to begin Verses 13 and 14 form a single sentence.[31] Alternatively, render "they set out for the first time,"[32] that is, from Sinai, a reflection of the long and seminal sojourn at Sinai.

at the LORD's command Rather, "sign" (see the Comment to 9:18).[33]

was Nahshon son of Amminadab; 15 in command of the
tribal troop of Issachar, Nethanel son of Zuar; 16 and in
command of the tribal troop of Zebulun, Eliab son of
Helon.

17 Then the Tabernacle would be taken apart; and the
Gershonites and the Merarites, who carried the Tabernacle,
would set out.

18 The next standard to set out, troop by troop, was the
division of Reuben. In command of its troop was Elizur
son of Shedeur; 19 in command of the tribal troop of
Simeon, Shelumiel son of Zurishaddai; 20 and in command
of the tribal troop of Gad, Eliasaph son of Deuel.

21 Then the Kohathites, who carried the sacred objects,
would set out; and by the time they arrived, the Tabernacle
would be set up again.

22 The next standard to set out, troop by troop, was the
division of Ephraim. In command of its troop was
Elishama son of Ammihud; 23 in command of the tribal
troop of Manasseh, Gamaliel son of Pedahzur; 24 and in
command of the tribal troop of Benjamin, Abidan son of
Gideoni.

25 Then, as the rear guard of all the divisions, the standard
of the division of Dan would set out, troop by troop. In
command of its troop was Ahiezer son of Ammishaddai;
26 in command of the tribal troop of Asher, Pagiel son of

בָּרִאשֹׁנָה לְצִבְאֹתָם וְעַל־צְבָאוֹ נַחְשׁוֹן בֶּן־
עַמִּינָדָב: 15 וְעַל־צְבָא מַטֵּה בְּנֵי יִשָּׂשכָר נְתַנְאֵל
בֶּן־צוּעָר: 16 וְעַל־צְבָא מַטֵּה בְּנֵי זְבוּלֻן אֱלִיאָב
בֶּן־חֵלֹן: 17 וְהוּרַד הַמִּשְׁכָּן וְנָסְעוּ בְנֵי־גֵרְשׁוֹן וּבְנֵי
מְרָרִי נֹשְׂאֵי הַמִּשְׁכָּן: ס 18 וְנָסַע דֶּגֶל מַחֲנֵה
רְאוּבֵן לְצִבְאֹתָם וְעַל־צְבָאוֹ אֱלִיצוּר בֶּן־שְׁדֵיאוּר:
19 וְעַל־צְבָא מַטֵּה בְּנֵי שִׁמְעוֹן שְׁלֻמִיאֵל בֶּן־
צוּרִישַׁדָּי: 20 וְעַל־צְבָא מַטֵּה בְנֵי־גָד אֶלְיָסָף בֶּן־
דְּעוּאֵל: 21 וְנָסְעוּ הַקְּהָתִים נֹשְׂאֵי הַמִּקְדָּשׁ
וְהֵקִימוּ אֶת־הַמִּשְׁכָּן עַד־בֹּאָם: ס 22 וְנָסַע
דֶּגֶל מַחֲנֵה בְנֵי־אֶפְרַיִם לְצִבְאֹתָם וְעַל־צְבָאוֹ
אֱלִישָׁמָע בֶּן־עַמִּיהוּד: 23 וְעַל־צְבָא מַטֵּה בְּנֵי
מְנַשֶּׁה גַּמְלִיאֵל בֶּן־פְּדָהצוּר: 24 וְעַל־צְבָא מַטֵּה
בְּנֵי בִנְיָמִן אֲבִידָן בֶּן־גִּדְעוֹנִי: ס 25 וְנָסַע
דֶּגֶל מַחֲנֵה בְנֵי־דָן מְאַסֵּף לְכָל־הַמַּחֲנֹת
לְצִבְאֹתָם וְעַל־צְבָאוֹ אֲחִיעֶזֶר בֶּן־עַמִּישַׁדָּי:
26 וְעַל־צְבָא מַטֵּה בְּנֵי אָשֵׁר פַּגְעִיאֵל בֶּן־עָכְרָן:

through Moses Even though the sign, the ascending cloud, is visible to the entire people (9:15–23), Moses alone determined when the march would resume.

14. first[34]

its That is, the tribe (not the division) of Judah; compare 2:3–5, of which this verse is an abbreviation.

Nahshon The names of the chieftains are those enumerated in chapters 1 and 2. They are repeated here to inform us that they led in the march, that is, in war, and in the camp, that is, in peace; so Ramban.

17. Gershonite and Merarite Levites transported the Tabernacle by wagon ahead of the Kohathites. When the latter entered the new encampment bearing the sacred objects on their shoulders, they would find the Tabernacle reassembled, prepared to receive these objects (v. 21).[35]

21. sacred objects Hebrew ***mikdash*** refers here to the sacred cult objects of the Tabernacle.[36] In the priestly texts the term ***mikdash*** never means the sanctuary building. It either refers to "the sacred area" (Num. 19:20; Lev. 12:4) or to all "the sacred objects" (3:38), of which the Tabernacle is one (Exod. 25:8–9). Regarding the latter understanding, especially compelling are Numbers 18:1, where the Kohathites are solely responsible for the sacred objects during their transit, and Leviticus 21:23, where the impaired priest is not prohibited from the sacred area but only from the sacred objects.

the Tabernacle would be set up Hebrew ***hekimu,*** literally "they (the Gershonites and Merarites) would set up the Tabernacle."

Ochran; 27 and in command of the tribal troop of Naphtali, Ahira son of Enan.

28 Such was the order of march of the Israelites, as they marched troop by troop.

29 Moses said to Hobab son of Reuel the Midianite, Moses' father-in-law, "We are setting out for the place of which the LORD has said, 'I will give it to you.' Come with us and we will be generous with you; for the LORD has promised to be generous to Israel."

27 וְעַל־צְבָא מַטֵּה בְּנֵי נַפְתָּלִי אֲחִירַע בֶּן־עֵינָן׃
28 אֵלֶּה מַסְעֵי בְנֵי־יִשְׂרָאֵל לְצִבְאֹתָם וַיִּסָּעוּ׃
ס [ששי לספרדים] 29 וַיֹּאמֶר מֹשֶׁה
לְחֹבָב בֶּן־רְעוּאֵל הַמִּדְיָנִי חֹתֵן מֹשֶׁה נֹסְעִים ׀
אֲנַחְנוּ אֶל־הַמָּקוֹם אֲשֶׁר אָמַר יְהוָה אֹתוֹ אֶתֵּן
לָכֶם לְכָה אִתָּנוּ וְהֵטַבְנוּ לָךְ כִּי־יְהוָה דִּבֶּר־טוֹב
עַל־יִשְׂרָאֵל׃ 30 וַיֹּאמֶר אֵלָיו לֹא אֵלֵךְ כִּי אִם־אֶל־

28. ***as they marched troop by troop***[37] This verse forms an inclusion with verse 12, adding the significant fact that Israel marched in military formation.

GUIDANCE IN THE WILDERNESS: HOBAB (vv. 29–32)

Moses asks Hobab to serve as Israel's guide in the wilderness. The dialogue reveals Moses' diplomatic skills. He does not at first state his real purpose but invites Hobab to share in the Lord's bounty to Israel. Hobab's refusal is taken by Moses as a sign that he is too proud to accept an undeserved boon. Only then does Moses make his proposal.[38] These verses barely conceal the ebullience of Moses and Israel in their certainty that theirs is but a short journey through the wilderness (cf. the Comments to vv. 29,33).

29. ***Hobab son of Reuel the Midianite*** Probably "Hobab of the Midianite clan of Reuel." The identification of Hobab is difficult. He is designated here as Moses' father-in-law (also in Judg. 1:16; 4:11), a role assigned to Reuel in Exodus 2:18 and to Jethro in Exodus 18. Three solutions have been proposed: (1) Hobab and Jethro are the same person and Reuel is their father;[39] (2) the term *ḥoten* means a relation of the bride, hence, brother-in-law as well as father-in-law, by which Reuel becomes the father of Hobab/Jethro and the father-in-law of Moses;[40] (3) Reuel is a clan name,[41] as seen by its association with Midian (Gen. 25:3 LXX) and Edom (Gen. 36:17; 1 Chron. 1:35,37), and therefore *ḥoten* in this verse should be read *ḥatan,* "son-in-law,"[42] thereby making Hobab, the young desert scout of the Midianite clan of Reuel, Moses' son-in-law.[43]

A second difficulty is that Hobab the Midianite is elsewhere called a Kenite (Judg. 1:16 LXX; 4:11). This problem, however, can be satisfactorily explained. Midian, it now appears, is not the name of a people but of a confederation of peoples,[44] one of which is the Kenites. Similarly, Enoch is both a Kenite (i.e., the son of Cain, Gen. 4:17) and a Midianite (the son of Midian, Gen. 25:4). The name Kenites means smiths (cf. Gen. 4:22). Probably they worked the mines in the mountain regions of Sinai or Midian (Num. 24:21).

If Hobab is identical with Jethro, then the Hobabites/Kenites were not only smiths but a clan of priests (Exod. 18:1) who settled among the Judahites at Negeb-Arad (Judg. 1:16 LXX) (and were responsible perhaps for the recently excavated Israelite shrine at Arad) and also at Kedesh in Naphtali at the sacred terebinth of Elon-bazaanannim (Judg. 4:11), at which Sisera the Canaanite general sought refuge.[45]

Biblical tradition asserts that Jethro was a worshiper of the Lord (Exod. 18:10–12), giving rise to the possibility that Moses learned of the Lord from his father-in-law during his sojourn in Midian (Exod. 3:1,13–18). This theory has received recent support from a fourteenth-century Egyptian (Nubian) inscription that speaks of "the land of Shasu YHW'." The Shasu, a group of Bedouin tribes, are located in a contemporary (El-Amarna) inscription in "the land of Shasu *S'rr'*," identified with Seir (24:18), bordering on the Gulf of Elath—also the home of the Midianites (v. 30).[46] That the Lord originally was worshiped in this area is supported by the early statement: "The LORD came from Sinai; He shone upon them from Seir" (Deut. 33:2; see Judg. 5:4; Isa. 63:1; Hab. 3:3).

The tradition that the Midianites were kinsmen by marriage of Moses the Israelite must be

30"I will not go," he replied to him, "but will return to my native land." 31He said, "Please do not leave us, inasmuch as you know where we should camp in the wilderness and can be our guide. So if you come with us, we will extend to you the same bounty that the LORD grants us."

אַרְצִי וְאֶל־מוֹלַדְתִּי אֵלֵךְ׃ 31 וַיֹּאמֶר אַל־נָא תַּעֲזֹב
אֹתָנוּ כִּי ׀ עַל־כֵּן יָדַעְתָּ חֲנֹתֵנוּ בַּמִּדְבָּר וְהָיִיתָ לָּנוּ
לְעֵינָיִם׃ 32 וְהָיָה כִּי־תֵלֵךְ עִמָּנוּ וְהָיָה ׀ הַטּוֹב
הַהוּא אֲשֶׁר יֵיטִיב יְהוָה עִמָּנוּ וְהֵטַבְנוּ לָךְ׃

reckoned with seriously (cf. chaps. 25, 31). The subsequent history of the Kenites/Hobabites, however, indicates that a faction of the Reuelite clan of the Midianites allied itself with Israel in the wilderness and settled among them in the promised land. This tradition is reflected in the excellent relations that prevailed between the Kenites and Israelites during the time of Saul and David (1 Sam. 15:6; 30:29).

We are setting out Immediately, for the promised land (cf. Exod. 33:1).[47] At this point Moses had no premonition of the catastrophic episode of the scouts (chaps. 13–14), which would result in forty years of wandering in the wilderness.

place Hebrew ***makom,*** frequently a synonym for "land" (see Exod. 3:8; 23:20; Jer. 7:3,14).

promised Hebrew ***dibber*** can mean "promise" as well as "speak," especially in the Deuteronomic phrase "as (God) promised" (Deut. 1:11,21).

to be generous Hebrew ***tov,*** literally "a bounty," as in verse 32. The bounty clearly refers to the aforementioned "place"—the promised land. The vagueness of the offer perhaps reflects the anomalous status of the Kenites who resided with Israel (cf. the Comment to v. 32). The root ***t-w-b*** occurs five times in verses 29 and 32, emphasizing the pure goodness that awaits the Israelites if they but follow God's directions. This will contrast with the "goodness" they begin to see in Egypt (11:18; 14:3) and the ***ra'***, "evil," with which they respond (11:1,10,11,15 [even Moses!]; 14:26,35). However, the noun ***tov*** also functions as a synonym of ***berit,*** "covenant,"[48] and, hence, part of the verse may also be rendered, "for the Lord has negotiated a treaty with Israel."[49] This covenantal reference automatically implies that Hobab will be entitled to inherit together with Israel in the promised land.[50] Scripture confirms that the Kenites indeed settled in the Negeb of Judah (Judg. 1:16; see 1 Sam. 15:6).

30. native land Hebrew ***'el-'artsi ve-'el-moladeti*** taken as a hendiadys (cf. Gen. 12:1). However, ***moledet*** generally means "family" (Gen. 24:4), and the phrase may also be rendered "to my land and my family." Midian, Hobab's native land, is located in the vicinity of the Gulf of Elath and thus would be in the direction of Israel's march.

31. inasmuch as Hebrew ***ki 'al-ken,*** literally "for on the basis of the fact that" (see Gen. 38:26), according to Rashi.

know Hebrew ***yada'ta.***[51] The Septuagint, Targum Onkelos, and Targum Jonathan render the perfect as a past, "have known."[52] According to this interpretation, Hobab is rewarded for past services. Thus the theological paradox is avoided whereby Israel seemingly engages a human guide, Hobab, at the same time that a divinely designated guide, the Ark or cloud (v. 33; 9:15–23), is performing the same function! The paradox is resolved once it is recognized that the narrative has conflated two traditions concerning Israel's guidance in the wilderness, the one natural, the other supernatural. The juxtaposition of these two elements is present throughout the wilderness and conquest traditions. A striking example is the capture of Jericho by the crumbling of the city walls at the sound of trumpets (Josh. 6) but also by sending scouts to probe for weaknesses in the city walls—which they find at Rahab's wallhouse (her outside window overlooks the wall); they mark it with a red string to indicate the point of entry to the attacking Israelites (Josh. 2). It should also be noted that sending scouts from the wilderness to reconnoiter the promised land is initiated by God, according to one source (Num. 13:2), and by Israel, according to another (Deut. 1:22), again indicative of the coexistence of two traditions, exclusive divine action and assistance by human agents.

This "double causality" is also present in the Genesis narratives. Jacob's prosperity as a shepherd is attributed to both his cunning (Gen. 30:32ff.) and God's directives (31:10–12), and Joseph's enslavement in Egypt is attributed to his brothers' machinations (37:18ff.) and to divine design (45:5–8; 50:20).

33 They marched from the mountain of the LORD a distance of three days. The Ark of the Covenant of the LORD traveled in front of them on that three days' journey to seek out a resting place for them; 34 and the LORD's cloud kept above them by day, as they moved on from camp.

33 וַיִּסְעוּ֙ מֵהַ֣ר יְהוָ֔ה דֶּ֖רֶךְ שְׁלֹ֣שֶׁת יָמִ֑ים וַאֲר֨וֹן
בְּרִית־יְהוָ֜ה נֹסֵ֣עַ לִפְנֵיהֶ֗ם דֶּ֚רֶךְ שְׁלֹ֣שֶׁת יָמִ֔ים
לָת֥וּר לָהֶ֖ם מְנוּחָֽה׃ 34 וַעֲנַ֧ן יְהוָ֛ה עֲלֵיהֶ֖ם יוֹמָ֑ם
בְּנָסְעָ֖ם מִן־הַֽמַּחֲנֶֽה׃ נ* ס ששי 35 וַיְהִ֛י

guide Literally, "eyes."[53] The exegetical thrust is clear. The Ark is the sole guide; hence, Hobab must serve another function. But once he is equated with Jethro, the function is self-evident: He will continue to advise Moses as he did in the past (Exod. 18) and ***yadaʿta*** will have the connotation of "have known," as noted above.[54]

32. Hobab's reply is not given, but the later presence of his descendants in the Holy Land (Judg. 1:16; 4:11), clearly indicates it must have been in the affirmative. Perhaps his reply was omitted because it would have provided the Kenites and their descendants with a scriptural basis for claiming land rights in the promised land.[55] However, it is more likely due to the conviction that Israel's safe journey through the wilderness was due to the guidance of the Ark, not of Hobab.

GUIDANCE IN THE WILDERNESS: THE ARK (vv. 33–36)

The first stage of the march is a three-day journey to Taberah (11:3) in the wilderness of Paran (10:12). According to the midrash, Israel was so delighted to leave Sinai—for staying there might mean receiving additional laws—that they marched uninterruptedly for three days; in this way they were like the schoolboy who runs out when class is dismissed lest the teacher call him back.[56] Strikingly, when Israel left Egypt after the victory of the sea they also marched without stop for three days (Exod. 15:22–24). Their complaint about the lack of water had not been punished, but here their complaint—probably about this forced march (see the Comment to 11:1)—is severely punished. For this crucial difference between the marchings before and after Sinai, see the Introduction.

mountain of the LORD Here alone this phrase designates Mount Sinai, which everywhere else is called "the mountain of God," as in Exodus 3:1 and 4:27. After the Temple is built the mountain of the Lord is the Temple Mount (Isa. 2:3).

a distance of three days To their first station, presumably Taberah (11:3). Thus, this initial march from Sinai is equivalent to the entire distance from Egypt to Sinai, which is also a three-day march (Exod. 3:18).

the Ark . . . traveled in front The contradiction with verse 21 and 2:17 is self-evident. Probably during this initial stage the Ark did precede the marchers because the people feared the dangers in the wilderness; so Ibn Ezra and Ramban. Some rabbis conjecture that there were two Arks, one in front and one in their midst.[57] Three traditions are recorded concerning the nature of Israel's divinely designated guide: a cloud-encased fire (Num. 9:15–23; 14:14; Deut. 1:33); the Ark (Num. 10:33; Josh. 3:3,6,11); and an angel (Exod. 14:19a; 23:20–23).

on that three days' journey So Ramban and Abravanel; the literal rendering "a distance of three days" cannot be sustained; clearly, the Ark had to be visible in order to serve as a guide.[58] Of course, a respectable distance would separate the sacred Ark from the people; elsewhere this distance is given as 2,000 cubits (approximately 1,000 yards; cf. Josh. 3:4).

resting place Hebrew ***menuḥah***. This word accounts for the following juxtaposition of the song of the Ark (vv. 35–36), which also describes its "resting," ***u-ve-nuḥoh*** (v. 36).

LORD's cloud kept above them Whereas the Ark served as a guide (cf. Josh. 3:3), the cloud was suspended over them as shade and protection (14:14b).[59] However, most commentators claim the reverse: The cloud was the guide, whereas the Ark was transported in the center of the marching columns. The Septuagint places this verse after verse 36, thereby connecting the song of the Ark with the statement about the Ark (v. 33).

35 When the Ark was to set out, Moses would say:
Advance, O LORD!
May Your enemies be scattered,
And may Your foes flee before You!
36 And when it halted, he would say:
Return, O LORD,
You who are Israel's myriads of thousands!

בִּנְסֹעַ הָאָרֹן וַיֹּאמֶר מֹשֶׁה
קוּמָה ׀ יְהוָה
וְיָפֻצוּ אֹיְבֶיךָ
וְיָנֻסוּ מְשַׂנְאֶיךָ מִפָּנֶיךָ׃
36 ובנחה יֹאמַר
שׁוּבָה יְהוָה
רִבְבוֹת אַלְפֵי יִשְׂרָאֵל׃ *[פ

נון הפוכה v. 36. 35.
וּבְנֻחֹה ק' v. 36.

35–36. This couplet, The Song of the Ark, may be a fragment of a larger saga on the life of Moses. It may have been attached here because of the association of the words for travel, ***be-nosʿam*** (v. 34) and ***bi-nsoʿa*** (v. 35), and rest, ***menuḥah*** (v. 33) and ***u-ve-nuḥoh*** (v. 36). That the poem does not belong to its context is indicated by the inverted ***nuns*** that frame it (see Excursus 23).

The first verse of the couplet is repeated almost verbatim in Psalms 68:2; and both verses are condensed in Psalms 132:8: "Advance, O LORD, to Your resting-place, You and Your mighty Ark!" The prayer for the scattering of the enemy is there omitted because once the Lord has consented to advance it is certain that He will "rest" only after victory is assured. In the Psalm, the "resting place" refers to the installation of the Ark in the tent that David erected for it in Jerusalem (cf. v. 14; 2 Sam. 6:17).

35. ***Advance*** Or, "arise," a rendering that better suits the image of the Ark as the chariot-throne of the Lord (see Excursus 22). The verb ***kam*** signifies advancing or rising in order to attack[60] (cf. Judg. 5:12), and the noun ***kam*** means "attacker" (Exod. 15:7).

36. ***Return*** Rather, "rest, sit,"[61] again suiting the image of the Ark as the Lord's throne-chariot (see Excursus 22).[62]

You who are Just as the prophets Elijah and Elisha are called "Israel's chariots and horsemen" (2 Kings 2:12; 13:14), so Israel's God is called "Israel's myriads of thousands."[63] So in Egypt, King Sesostris III is praised: "He alone is a million"; and the victory of Ramses II after the battle of Kadesh reads: "Amun is worth more to me than millions of foot-soldiers, and hundreds of thousands of chariots."[64] In other words, precisely as in this couplet, the god or deified king is declared equivalent to hordes of his armies.

Alternatively, the phrase can be translated (according to Sforno): "O YHVH of Israel's myriads of thousands," as indicated by the parallel but more frequent designation of God as "YHVH of hosts,"[65] especially when this epithet is compounded with other constructs such as "God of Israel" (Isa. 21:10; Zeph. 2:9), "Mighty One of Israel" (Isa. 1:24), and in particular "the God of the ranks of Israel" (1 Sam. 17:45).[66] The word "hosts" (from ***tsava'***) refers to celestial hosts or armies (Josh. 5:14–15), including the sun, moon, and stars (e.g., Deut. 4:19). Indeed, the old war epics in Scripture describe how the heavenly bodies warred on the side of Israel (Josh. 10:12–13; Judg. 5:20). Thus, according to this poem, Israel's myriads of thousands on earth are the counterpart of the Lord's hosts in heaven. One striking rabbinic statement indeed understands it in this way: "This verse states that the divine Presence rules above with thousands of myriads, as it is written: 'God's chariots are myriads upon myriads, thousands upon thousands' (Ps. 68:18). Just as the divine Presence rules above with thousands of myriads so the divine Presence rules below with thousands of myriads."[67]

myriads of thousands That is, an astronomic number, also found in reverse order: "thousands of myriads" (Gen. 24:60). Alternatively, ***rivevot 'alfei*** can be rendered "the countless armed units" (see Excursus 1).[68]

11 The people took to complaining bitterly before the LORD. The LORD heard and was incensed: a fire of the LORD broke out against them, ravaging the outskirts of the camp.

י״א וַיְהִי הָעָם כְּמִתְאֹנְנִים רַע בְּאָזְנֵי יְהוָה
וַיִּשְׁמַע יְהוָה וַיִּחַר אַפּוֹ וַתִּבְעַר־בָּם אֵשׁ יְהוָה
וַתֹּאכַל בִּקְצֵה הַמַּחֲנֶה׃ 2 וַיִּצְעַק הָעָם אֶל־מֹשֶׁה

The wilderness narrative recounts the incidents befalling the Israelites as they moved in stages from their encampment at Sinai to the plains of Moab on the border of Canaan. The incidents are often marked by the people's complaints for which, in contrast to the complaints levied before the Revelation at Sinai, they are severely punished.[1] Chapters 11–14 are nothing more than an itemization of Israel's rebellious acts that progressively slow down the march until it comes to a complete halt at Kadesh (13:26), where Moses and Aaron are also told that they cannot enter the promised land (20:1–13). Chapters 11 and 12 exhibit a structural unity, as is demonstrated in Excursus 24. The narrative is interspersed with legal and cultic material.

CHAPTER 11 THE COMPLAINT AT TABERAH (vv. 1–3)

This short section of three verses contains all of the essential elements of all the subsequent narratives describing Israel's complaints: complaint (11:4–5; 12:1–2; 14:1–4; 17:6–7; 20:3–5; 21:5), divine punishment (11:33; 12:9–10; 14:20–37; 16:32; 17:11; 21:7), and immortalizing the incident by giving a name to the site (11:34; 20:13; 21:3; Exod. 15:23; 17:7).

The same pattern is also evident in the stories of the judges, the intercessor-successors to Moses, for example, Othniel (Judg. 3:7–11). But the intercession changes form: Moses prays, whereas the judge wars.[2] Nonetheless, the result is much the same. Both leaders, in effect, defend Israel *against the Lord.* True, the judge does battle with Israel's enemies, but the latter are the Lord's agents whose role is to test Israel (e.g., Judg. 2:14–16).

Moses' intercession is verbal but nonetheless militant. He defends Israel almost to the point of *lèse-majesté*, accusing God of breaking His promises to the patriarchs (Exod. 32:13)—thereby showing unconcern for His people (Exod. 33:13b) and giving the nations a pretext for asserting His inability to carry out His promises (Num. 14:15–16). In this respect, Moses is the archetypical prophet. Indeed, so is the prophetic role defined in Ezekiel 22:30: "I sought a man among them to repair the wall or to stand in the breach *before Me* [italics mine] in behalf of this land, that I might not destroy it."

1. took to complaining[3] The basis for the complaint is not stated. But if these verses are seen as a continuation of those preceding (10:29–36), then the complaint becomes manifest. According to Rashbam, the people objected to their living conditions in the wilderness (explicitly stated in vv. 4–6; see 21:4–5). Specifically, they complained about the forced marches,[4] according to Ramban. The connection with the preceding passage is even more manifest on linguistic grounds. Israel responds to the *tov,* "the goodness," that the Lord has prepared for them (this root appears five times in 10:29,32) with its opposite—*ra'*, "evil."

A comparison of the wanderings recounted in Exodus and Numbers may shed further light on the complaint. It can be shown that the wilderness narratives in these two books are, in the main, parallel (see Excursus 50). The murmuring over water in Exodus (15:22–26) follows the three-day march from the Sea and precedes the manna/quail episode (chap. 16). Similarly in Numbers, the Taberah incident (11:1–3) follows upon a three-day march from Sinai (10:33) and precedes the manna/quail account (11:4–34). The Taberah complaint—unspecified in the text—may therefore be assumed to be the lack of water.

bitterly Hebrew *ra'* is here understood adverbially rather than as a noun because the prefix *'al,* "of misfortune," would be required in the latter instance,[5] as in 1 Kings 22:8.

before the LORD Literally, "in the ears of the Lord," implying that they voiced their complaints directly, brazenly to God.[6]

fire of the LORD Probably lightning (cf. Exod. 9:23–24; 19:18). Some claim it took the form of a plague[7] or that it was actual fire,[8] an interpretation that would be supported by the verb "died down" and by the description of God's wrath: "You send forth Your fury, it consumes them like

[2]The people cried out to Moses. Moses prayed to the LORD, and the fire died down. [3]That place was named Taberah, because a fire of the LORD had broken out against them.

[4]The riffraff in their midst felt a gluttonous craving; and then the Israelites wept and said, "If only we had meat to eat! [5]We remember the fish that we used to eat free in Egypt, the cucumbers, the melons, the leeks, the onions,

וַיִּתְפַּלֵּל מֹשֶׁה אֶל־יְהוָה וַתִּשְׁקַע הָאֵשׁ׃ 3 וַיִּקְרָא
שֵׁם־הַמָּקוֹם הַהוּא תַּבְעֵרָה כִּי־בָעֲרָה בָם אֵשׁ
יְהוָה׃ 4 וְהָאסַפְסֻף אֲשֶׁר בְּקִרְבּוֹ הִתְאַוּוּ תַּאֲוָה
וַיָּשֻׁבוּ וַיִּבְכּוּ גַּם בְּנֵי יִשְׂרָאֵל וַיֹּאמְרוּ מִי יַאֲכִלֵנוּ
בָּשָׂר׃ 5 זָכַרְנוּ אֶת־הַדָּגָה אֲשֶׁר־נֹאכַל בְּמִצְרַיִם
חִנָּם אֵת הַקִּשֻּׁאִים וְאֵת הָאֲבַטִּחִים וְאֶת־הֶחָצִיר
וְאֶת־הַבְּצָלִים וְאֶת־הַשּׁוּמִים׃ 6 וְעַתָּה נַפְשֵׁנוּ

straw" (Exod. 15:7). For instances of fire as divine punishment, see Numbers 16:35, Leviticus 10:2, and 2 Kings 1:10,12. In any case, the outbreak of the fire is the result of a miracle, an indication that miracles can serve as divine punishment as well as salvation. The miracles of the quail in the next episode must be viewed in the same way (see Excursus 24).

broke out Compare verse 3. Hebrew *b-ʿ-r* usually means "burn," but it can also mean "kindle, ignite" (Exod. 22:5; 35:3).

outskirts This shows that the destructive fire did not come from the Tabernacle as in cases cited in other (priestly) texts (e.g., Num. 16:35; cf. Lev. 10:2). Hebrew ***bi-ketseh*** can also be interpreted to refer to people, either the alien element who live at the edges of society or the important people of Israel.[9] (Cf. ***katseh,*** "officer," Gen. 47:2,[10] 1 Kings 12:31.)

2. ***prayed*** An example of Moses, the archetype of the prophetic intercessor (cf. Exod. 32:11–14,31–32; and see the Introduction).[11]

3. ***Taberah*** This place is cited again in Deuteronomy 9:22 but ignored in the itinerary of Numbers 33:16 where it is apparently subsumed under Kibroth-hattaavah, a plausible omission since there is no record of a journey between these two stations. Perhaps there was none. Israel might have been detained at Taberah/Kibroth-hattaavah as punishment for its complaining.

THE COMPLAINT AT KIBROTH-HATTAAVAH (vv. 4–35)

The craving for meat was previously voiced after the crossing of the Red Sea (Exod. 16:3), and the divine answer came in the form of manna and quail, which arrived together (Exod. 16:14,31; cf. Ps. 78:21–31). In this narrative it is clear that the quail constitute the new element, whereas the manna (whose appearance and taste is described differently; cf. vv. 7–9 with Exod. 16:14,31) is regarded as a familiar phenomenon (v. 6).

4. ***riffraff*** The rendering excellently conveys the assonance of Hebrew ***ʾasafsuf.*** This term refers to the non-Israelites who joined them in their break for freedom, also called ***ʿerev rav,*** "mixed multitude" (Exod. 12:38). One rabbinic interpretation locates this riffraff at the edges of the camp,[12] thereby connecting it with the preceding incident: The alien element, having been scorched by God's wrath for its complaint about the forced marches (v. 1), now incites the rest of Israel to complain about the forced food.

felt a gluttonous craving Compare verse 34 and Psalms 78:29–35 and 106:14.[13]

moreover For this usage of ***va-yashuvu,*** see Deuteronomy 23:14.[14]

meat This verse seems to stem from a tradition that did not credit the Israelites with possessing livestock. The rabbis explain the implied discrepancy with Exodus 10:24,26; 12:38 and Numbers 32:1 as an example of gratuitous complaining.[15] However, the contradiction is resolved by the next verse, which indicates that the "meat" requested by the Israelites meant fish (cf. also v. 22)—a plentiful and cheap commodity in Egypt.

5. For Egypt as a "vegetable garden," compare Deuteronomy 11:10. Around the year 1900, an authority on Egypt wrote that its poor subsist on "bread (made of millet or maize), milk, new cheese, eggs, small salted fish, cucumbers and melons and gourds of a great variety of kinds, onions and leeks, beans, chick peas, the fruit of the black egg-plant, lentils, etc."[16]

and the garlic. [6]Now our gullets are shriveled. There is
nothing at all! Nothing but this manna to look to!"
[7]Now the manna was like coriander seed, and in color it
was like bdellium. [8]The people would go about and gather
it, grind it between millstones or pound it in a mortar, boil
it in a pot, and make it into cakes. It tasted like rich cream.

יָבֵשָׁה אֵין כֹּל בִּלְתִּי אֶל־הַמָּן עֵינֵינוּ׃ 7 וְהַמָּן
כִּזְרַע־גַּד הוּא וְעֵינוֹ כְּעֵין הַבְּדֹלַח׃ 8 שָׁטוּ הָעָם
וְלָֽקְטוּ וְטָחֲנוּ בָרֵחַיִם אוֹ דָכוּ בַּמְּדֹכָה וּבִשְּׁלוּ
בַּפָּרוּר וְעָשׂוּ אֹתוֹ עֻגוֹת וְהָיָה טַעְמוֹ כְּטַעַם לְשַׁד
הַשָּׁמֶן׃ 9 וּבְרֶדֶת הַטַּל עַל־הַמַּחֲנֶה לָיְלָה יֵרֵד

The regret at leaving Egypt is a constant motif of the wilderness rebellion. Here, however, a deeper level of meaning is struck. Egypt symbolizes materialism, the craving for food produced of the earth in contrast to the manna, the "heavenly grain/bread," food produced of faith (Pss. 78:24; 105:40).

fish Fish was reckoned as meat (cf. v. 22). Alternatively, render "produce" in general, preceding specifications (*Da'at Zekenim*, and cf. Gen. 48:16).

leeks Hebrew *ḥatsir* is attested with this meaning only in rabbinic Hebrew.[17] Elsewhere in the Bible it refers to grass. Perhaps one should read *ḥeṣin,* Egyptian for "leeks."[18]

garlic Panammu of Yaudi, who ruled over a northern Syrian state during the ninth century B.C.E., boasted of his "land of garlic."[19]

used to eat Hebrew ***no'khal*** is an imperfect, indicating that the food supply was unceasing.

free According to the midrash, this implies they did not want to slaughter their own cattle but they wanted their meat free, like the manna, at no cost to themselves.[20]

*6. **gullets*** Hebrew ***nefesh,*** as in Akkadian ***napishtu*** (cf. Isa. 5:14).

shriveled Literally, "dry," contrasting with the actual taste of the manna (v. 8).

MANNA (vv. 7–9)

This botanical and culinary description of the manna was deliberately inserted here to refute each point in the people's complaint.[21] The manna was (1) a seed, hence easy to pick; (2) white (Exod. 16:31), hence easy to spot; (3) clean, since it fell on a layer of dew; (4) eaten raw or cooked, hence not monotonous fare, and (5) like cream in taste and hence would not shrivel the gullet.

The manna has been identified with a natural substance formed in the wilderness of northern Arabia. "There forms from the sap of the tamarisk tree a species of yellowish-white flake or ball, which results from the activity of a type of plant lice ***(Trabutina mannipara*** and ***Najococcus serpentinus).*** The insect punctures the fruit of the tree and excretes a substance from this juice. During the warmth of the day it (the substance) melts, but it congeals when cold. It has a sweet taste. These pellets or cakes are gathered by the natives in the early morning and, when cooked, provide a sort of bread. The food decays quickly and attracts ants. The annual crop in the Sinai Peninsula is exceedingly small and some years fails completely."[22] If the identification is correct, its ephemeral nature and its undependableness—appearing irregularly and only for several hours each day—would have stamped it as supernatural, originating in heaven. In Scripture, however, the food itself, as well as its appearance, is a miracle.

The narrative assumes that the Israelites were familiar with the manna, thus presuming a knowledge of the Exodus version of the manna story (Exod. 16:4–36).

*7. **coriander*** Hebrew ***gad,*** a plant, the seeds of which are used in flavoring (cf. Exod. 16:31).

color That is, appearance (Lev. 13:55).

bdellium Hebrew ***bedolaḥ.*** An aromatic resin that is pale yellow or white (Exod. 16:31).[23]

*8. **millstones*** A common household utensil, still in use today among the Arab Bedouin.[24]

rich cream Hebrew ***lashad,*** like Akkadian ***lishdu,*** means cream (cf. Ps. 32:4) and refers to the upper layer of the first pressing of olive oil.[25] Midrashic lore tells that it possessed "the virtue of every pleasant savor and was agreeable to every taste."[26]

9 When the dew fell on the camp at night, the manna would fall upon it.

10 Moses heard the people weeping, every clan apart, each person at the entrance of his tent. The LORD was very angry, and Moses was distressed. 11 And Moses said to the LORD, "Why have You dealt ill with Your servant, and why have I not enjoyed Your favor, that You have laid the burden of all this people upon me? 12 Did I conceive all this people, did I bear them, that You should say to me, 'Carry them in your bosom as a nurse carries an infant,' to the land that You have promised on oath to their fathers? 13 Where am I to get

הַמָּן עָלָיו׃ 10 וַיִּשְׁמַע מֹשֶׁה אֶת־הָעָם בֹּכֶה
לְמִשְׁפְּחֹתָיו אִישׁ לְפֶתַח אָהֳלוֹ וַיִּחַר־אַף יְהוָה
מְאֹד וּבְעֵינֵי מֹשֶׁה רָע׃ 11 וַיֹּאמֶר מֹשֶׁה אֶל־יְהוָה
לָמָה הֲרֵעֹתָ לְעַבְדֶּךָ וְלָמָּה לֹא־מָצָתִי חֵן בְּעֵינֶיךָ
לָשׂוּם אֶת־מַשָּׂא כָּל־הָעָם הַזֶּה עָלָי׃ 12 הֶאָנֹכִי
הָרִיתִי אֵת כָּל־הָעָם הַזֶּה אִם־אָנֹכִי יְלִדְתִּיהוּ כִּי־
תֹאמַר אֵלַי שָׂאֵהוּ בְחֵיקֶךָ כַּאֲשֶׁר יִשָּׂא הָאֹמֵן
אֶת־הַיֹּנֵק עַל הָאֲדָמָה אֲשֶׁר נִשְׁבַּעְתָּ לַאֲבֹתָיו׃

v. 11. חסר א׳

*9. **upon it*** Hebrew *'alav* has also been rendered "with it"[27] to harmonize with Exodus 16:14, which relates that the manna fell on the dew. According to the rabbis, the dew encased the manna, the bottom layer protecting it from the sand while the upper prevented it from being eaten by insects and flies.[28]

MOSES COMPLAINS TO GOD (vv. 10–15)

Moses can neither supply Israel with sufficient food nor shoulder the burden of leadership. Exhausted physically and psychologically, he requests that his life be terminated.

*10. **Moses heard*** When "the Lord heard" (v. 1), it led to His anger (vv. 1,10) and punishment (11:33; 12:9–10). In Moses' case Israel's complaint leads to his demoralization and self-pity (vv. 11–15).

every clan apart Hebrew *le-mishpeḥotav,* literally "by families," an expression that connotes the universality of the weeping (cf. Zech. 12:12–14) but not that the people congregated in groups, since they did not move from their tents.[29]

entrance That is, openly, defiantly. Their weeping constituted a public demonstration.

and Moses was distressed Literally, "in the eyes of Moses it was evil *(ra')*." Is the referent of "it" the people's complaint or the Lord's actions? That is, with whom did Moses side—with God, that the people's complaint was evil, or with the people in their complaint against God? Moses' own discomfiture with God in the following verse (note especially ***hare 'ota,*** "dealt ill," lit. "evil") indicates that he concurred with Israel that the Lord had dealt ill with it (contrast 10:29,32).

*11. **Why have You dealt ill with Your servant*** Hebrew ***lamah hare'ota le-'avedekha*** contrasts with ***lamah hare'ota la-'am ha-zeh,*** "Why have You dealt ill with this people" (Exod. 5:22). Moses' selfless concern for his people has apparently evaporated.

this people Rather than "my people" (cf. vv. 12,14). The use of this derisive term by Moses contrasts tellingly with the golden calf episode where it is God who employs this term (Exod. 32:9; 33:12) and Moses who argues with Him that "this people" is "Your people" (Exod. 33:13).

*12. **Did I*** Hebrew ***he'anokhi*** emphasizes the "I," that is, I am not the parent of this people—but you, God.

conceive . . . bear Maternal metaphors are used because "it is the mother who suffers the pains of rearing children," according to Ramban.

nurse Rather, "guardian." According to Ramban, ***'omen*** is a male caretaker of children, found frequently among wealthy families in ancient Israel (cf. 2 Kings 10:1,5; Isa. 49:23).

to the land Reading ***'el*** for ***'al*** (with the versions).

You have promised Hebrew ***nishba'ta.*** In the Samaritan version that reads ***nishba'ti,*** "I have promised," the direct speech continues to the end of the verse.[30]

meat to give to all this people, when they whine before me and say, 'Give us meat to eat!' [14]I cannot carry all this people by myself, for it is too much for me. [15]If You would deal thus with me, kill me rather, I beg You, and let me see no more of my wretchedness!"

[16]Then the LORD said to Moses, "Gather for Me seventy of Israel's elders of whom you have experience as elders and officers of the people, and bring them to the Tent of Meeting and let them take their place there with you. [17]I will

13 מֵאַ֣יִן לִ֔י בָּשָׂ֕ר לָתֵ֖ת לְכָל־הָעָ֣ם הַזֶּ֑ה כִּֽי־יִבְכּ֤וּ עָלַי֙ לֵאמֹ֔ר תְּנָה־לָּ֥נוּ בָשָׂ֖ר וְנֹאכֵֽלָה׃ 14 לֹֽא־אוּכַ֤ל אָנֹכִי֙ לְבַדִּ֔י לָשֵׂ֖את אֶת־כָּל־הָעָ֣ם הַזֶּ֑ה כִּ֥י כָבֵ֖ד מִמֶּֽנִּי׃ 15 וְאִם־כָּ֣כָה ׀ אַתְּ־עֹ֣שֶׂה לִּ֗י הָרְגֵ֤נִי נָא֙ הָרֹ֔ג אִם־מָצָ֥אתִי חֵ֖ן בְּעֵינֶ֑יךָ וְאַל־אֶרְאֶ֖ה בְּרָעָתִֽי׃ פ 16 וַיֹּ֨אמֶר יְהֹוָ֜ה אֶל־מֹשֶׁ֗ה אֶסְפָה־לִּ֞י שִׁבְעִ֣ים אִישׁ֮ מִזִּקְנֵ֣י יִשְׂרָאֵל֒ אֲשֶׁ֣ר יָדַ֔עְתָּ כִּי־הֵ֛ם זִקְנֵ֥י הָעָ֖ם וְשֹׁטְרָ֑יו וְלָקַחְתָּ֤ אֹתָם֙ אֶל־אֹ֣הֶל מוֹעֵ֔ד וְהִֽתְיַצְּב֥וּ שָׁ֖ם עִמָּֽךְ׃ 17 וְיָרַדְתִּ֗י וְדִבַּרְתִּ֣י עִמְּךָ֮ שָׁם֒

13. whine before me That is, nag, the particular meaning of *bakhah 'al* (cf. Judg. 14:16–17).

14. carry . . . by myself The addition of *'anokhi*, emphatic I, can be interpreted as meaning that Moses is all too willing to share his leadership, a point graphically confirmed by the story of Eldad and Medad (vv. 26–29) and that effectively refutes the charges leveled against him by Miriam and Aaron (12:2). Alternatively, emphatic I, now occurring for the third time (cf. v. 2) may be a confession of Moses' helplessness in supplying the people's sustenance, a need that only God can fill. Thus Moses may be asking for divine rather than human assistance, an interpretation supported by the context (cf. v. 13). If so, then God's answer is not what Moses expected: He must henceforth share his leadership with seventy elders. In the Deuteronomic version (Deut. 1:12–13), however, Moses requests human assistance.

much Literally, "heavy"; the weight of the people is too much.

15. You Hebrew *'at*, normally the feminine form for "you" (found again in Deut. 5:24; Ezek. 28:14).[31]

kill me For a similar death wish, see the case of Elijah (1 Kings 19:4), whose visit to Horeb is clearly modeled after that of Moses (cf. also Jer. 20:14–18).

I beg you Literally, "if I have found favor in your eyes," that is, do me a favor.[32]

see *Ra'ah be-* means "witness" (e.g., Gen. 21:16; 44:34; Exod. 2:11).

of my wretchedness Hebrew *be-ra'ati*. This is one of the eighteen places in the Bible where, according to some rabbis, the scribes made changes *(tikkun soferim)* to avoid disrespect to God, the original reading being either *be-ra'atekha*, "your punishment,"[33] or *be-ra'atam*, "their punishment."[34] However, if the text can allow for *hare'ota*, "(why have) You (i.e., God) dealt ill" (v. 11), there would have been no need to make substitutions for this word. The text here, therefore, must be considered correct and should not be understood as a euphemism. In fact it is essential, for it makes the entire passage an outpouring of Moses' self-pity, climaxed by this remark: Since God is the author of his wretchedness, He might as well finish the job—and take his life.

GOD'S SOLUTION FOR MOSES: SEVENTY LEADERS (vv. 16–17)

The number seventy is not accidental. There are seventy nations (cf. Gen. 10), each having its guardian angel.[35] The number seventy is also found in the following instances, among others: the descendants of Jacob (Exod. 1:5; Deut. 10:22), the elders of Israel (Exod. 24:1; Ezek. 8:11), the submissive kings (Judg. 1:7), those struck by the Lord (1 Sam. 6:19), the sons or brothers of a judge or king (Judg. 8:30; 12:14; 2 Kings 10:1–7).[36] As a symbolic number, like seven, it is not intended as an exact number but only as an approximation of a large group of people.

16. seventy of Israel's elders As Israel numbered many elders (e.g., Exod. 4:29; 12:21) these need not be the same seventy that accompanied Moses at Sinai (Exod. 24:9). The rabbis are sensitive to the fact that Moses already had an advisory council of seventy elders at Sinai but claim

come down and speak with you there, and I will draw upon
the spirit that is on you and put it upon them; they shall
share the burden of the people with you, and you shall not
bear it alone. 18And say to the people: Purify yourselves for

וְאָצַלְתִּ֗י מִן־הָר֛וּחַ אֲשֶׁ֥ר עָלֶ֖יךָ וְשַׂמְתִּ֣י עֲלֵיהֶ֑ם
וְנָשְׂא֤וּ אִתְּךָ֙ בְּמַשָּׂ֣א הָעָ֔ם וְלֹא־תִשָּׂ֥א אַתָּ֖ה
לְבַדֶּֽךָ׃ 18 וְאֶל־הָעָ֨ם תֹּאמַ֜ר הִתְקַדְּשׁ֣וּ לְמָחָ֗ר

that they were guilty of unseemly conduct at Taberah (vv. 1–3) and were destroyed by the divine fire.[37]

The institution of a council of seventy attached to a ruler is well attested in the ancient Near East. The eighth-century B.C.E. inscription of Barrakab king of Yaudi (located in northern Syria) speaks of the murder of an earlier king together with seventy of his "brothers."[38] The same occurrence is recorded twice in the Bible: Abimelech puts to death his seventy "brothers, the sons of Jerubbaal" (Judg. 9:5); and Jehu puts to death "the princes, seventy in number" (2 Kings 10:6). The likelihood is strong that the terms "brothers" and "princes/sons" refer to the members of the royal council.[39] This institution survived in the seventy-member Sanhedrin, the supreme political, religious, and judicial body in Palestine during the Roman period.[40]

officers Rather, "assistants," such as the foremen who assisted the taskmasters in Egypt.[41]

take their place Hebrew *ve-hityatstsevu* is the technical term for readiness[42] required before a theophany (cf. Exod. 14:13; 19:17; Deut. 31:14); the priestly texts employ instead the root *ʿ-m-d* (cf. 9:8).

with you According to Rashi, the powers given to the elders will derive from God not from Moses.

17. ***I will come down*** Compare Exodus 33:9–11 for a fuller description of God's descent. The Bible records ten occurrences when God descended from on high.[43]

speak with you But not with the elders.[44] The purpose or content of God's speech is not stated here nor in its execution (v. 25). Perhaps the content *per se* was not significant; the purpose was for God to speak to Moses in order to assure him that he would continue to serve as God's intermediary, despite the diminution of his spirit.

draw upon Hebrew *ve-ʾatsalti min.* The root *ʾ-ts-l* actually means "withdraw, reserve" (Gen. 27:36; Eccles. 2:10). The divine spirit will either be drawn from Moses,[45] thereby diminishing him (as his authority was diminished when it was transferred to Joshua, 27:2, and as Elijah's spirit was transferred to Elisha, 2 Kings 2:10)[46] or the divine spirit that has been bestowed on Moses will now also rest on the elders.[47] According to the latter explanation, the divine spirit, like wisdom[48] or candlelight,[49] can be given to others without any diminution of its source.[50] Note the example of Samuel who, as the head of a band of ecstatics, was able to transmit "the spirit of God"—not his own—to the messengers of Saul (1 Sam. 19:20). However, from the fact that Joshua attempts to stifle Eldad and Medad (v. 28), it is clear that the elders derive their spirit from Moses.[51] See further in Excursus 24.

the spirit Hebrew *ruaḥ;* see Excursus 25.

share the burden of the people . . . not bear it alone God's answer incorporates the very wording of Moses' plea in verse 14. It should be noted that the transplanting of Moses' spirit onto the elders must take place at the Tent of Meeting (cf. also vv. 24–25)—not that God is incapable of endowing His spirit at any other place. Indeed, this is precisely what will happen to Eldad and Medad (v. 26). But the situations are not alike. The latter receive their spirit directly from God, whereas the elders receive theirs from Moses. At any other site but the Tent, observers might attribute the miracle not to the invisible God but to the visible Moses! Only at the Tent upon which the divine cloud descends (v. 25) can God's visible Presence leave no doubts concerning the source of the spirit.

GOD'S SOLUTION FOR THE PEOPLE: MEAT (vv. 18–23)

In Exodus 16:11–13, the quail (as well as the manna) were God's gracious gift to Israel in response to its hankering after meat (Exod. 16:3) in order that they may behold the Lord's power and, henceforth,

וַאֲכַלְתֶּם בָּשָׂר כִּי בְּכִיתֶם בְּאָזְנֵי יְהוָה לֵאמֹר מִי
יַאֲכִלֵנוּ בָּשָׂר כִּי־טוֹב לָנוּ בְּמִצְרָיִם וְנָתַן יְהוָה
לָכֶם בָּשָׂר וַאֲכַלְתֶּם׃ 19 לֹא יוֹם אֶחָד תֹּאכְלוּן
וְלֹא יוֹמָיִם וְלֹא ׀ חֲמִשָּׁה יָמִים וְלֹא עֲשָׂרָה יָמִים
וְלֹא עֶשְׂרִים יוֹם׃ 20 עַד ׀ חֹדֶשׁ יָמִים עַד אֲשֶׁר־
יֵצֵא מֵאַפְּכֶם וְהָיָה לָכֶם לְזָרָא יַעַן כִּי־מְאַסְתֶּם
אֶת־יְהוָה אֲשֶׁר בְּקִרְבְּכֶם וַתִּבְכּוּ לְפָנָיו לֵאמֹר
לָמָּה זֶּה יָצָאנוּ מִמִּצְרָיִם׃ 21 וַיֹּאמֶר מֹשֶׁה שֵׁשׁ־
מֵאוֹת אֶלֶף רַגְלִי הָעָם אֲשֶׁר אָנֹכִי בְּקִרְבּוֹ וְאַתָּה
אָמַרְתָּ בָּשָׂר אֶתֵּן לָהֶם וְאָכְלוּ חֹדֶשׁ יָמִים׃

tomorrow and you shall eat meat, for you have kept
whining before the LORD and saying, 'If only we had meat
to eat! Indeed, we were better off in Egypt!' The LORD will
give you meat and you shall eat. 19 You shall eat not one
day, not two, not even five days or ten or twenty, 20 but a
whole month, until it comes out of your nostrils and becomes loathsome to you. For you have rejected the LORD who is among you, by whining before Him and saying, 'Oh, why did we ever leave Egypt!'"

21 But Moses said, "The people who are with me number six hundred thousand men; yet You say, 'I will give them enough meat to eat for a whole month.'
22 Could enough

trust in Him (Exod. 16:4,6,12). By contrast, the gift of quail in verse 20 of this passage is given in anger and will result in many fatalities (vv. 33–34).[52] God's words expose the real reason behind the complaint: The craving for meat expresses a disguised desire to return to Egypt and is tantamount to a rejection of God (v. 20). Indeed, from God's response (v. 23) to Moses' faltering faith (vv. 21–22), it would almost seem that the quail are brought to Israel in order to prove God's powers to Moses!

It should be noted that the motif of "return to Egypt" is present in the wilderness complaints and constitute the essence of the rebellions (Exod. 16:3; 20:5; 21:5). It is missing in two episodes, Marah (Exod. 15:22–26) and Taberah (Num. 11:1–3). But it is hardly accidental that both places are the very first stations in Israel's journey from the Red Sea and Sinai, respectively, when the people were buoyed up with confidence and hope.

18. Purify yourselves Hebrew *hitkaddeshu.* That is, "sanctify yourselves" by a rite of laundering and bathing that precedes a sacrifice (cf. Excursus 27). However, this notion may be double-edged: It also intimates that the coming sacrifice will be Israel (vv. 33–34).[53]

before the LORD Literally, "in the ears of the Lord," as in verse 1, intended to provoke the Lord.[54]

If only . . . in Egypt The first part of the quotation is cited verbatim from verse 4; the second part is a synopsis of verse 5.

20. whole month Hebrew *ḥodesh yamim,* literally "a month of days," used for stylistic reasons, completing the series of numbers of days in verse 19.

nostrils Rather, "nose." (Nostrils would have been expressed by the dual *'appeikhem.*) Ibn Ezra understands this to mean: You will not be able to stand the stench. For causing God's anger (lit. "his nose to flare"), the stench from the meat will fill the people's noses—a fitting punishment.

loathsome Hebrew *le-zara'*. The Septuagint renders it as cholera, a disease characterized by nausea and vomiting.[55]

21. who are with me *'Asher 'anokhi be-kirbo,* literally "in whose midst I am," which counterbalances "the Lord who is among you" *(YHVH 'asher be-kirbekhem)* in the previous verse. In effect, Moses is saying: I too am in the midst of this people and their large number leads me to doubt that you can feed them. Moses' words border on disbelief—for which he is summarily punished by having his powers diminished (v. 25; see Excursus 24). His subsequent disbelief at Meribah, however, is punished even more severely. For the qualitative difference between these two situations, see the Comment to 20:12.

men Hebrew *ragli,* literally "footmen, infantry" (cf. Exod. 12:37). The reference to 600,000 in this latter verse clearly excludes the riffraff. This also may be the intention here,[56] that is, to dissociate the riffraff who instigate the rebellion (v. 4) from Israel, an intimation of their coming destruction (v. 34).

flocks and herds be slaughtered to suffice them? Or could all the fish of the sea be gathered for them to suffice them?"
23 And the LORD answered Moses, "Is there a limit to the LORD's power? You shall soon see whether what I have said happens to you or not!"

24 Moses went out and reported the words of the LORD to the people. He gathered seventy of the people's elders and stationed them around the Tent.
25 Then the LORD came down in a cloud and spoke to him; He drew upon the spirit that was on him and put it upon the seventy elders. And when the spirit rested upon them, they spoke in ecstasy, but did not continue.

22 הֲצֹאן וּבָקָר יִשָּׁחֵט לָהֶם וּמָצָא לָהֶם אִם אֶת־
כָּל־דְּגֵי הַיָּם יֵאָסֵף לָהֶם וּמָצָא לָהֶם׃ פ
23 וַיֹּאמֶר יְהוָה אֶל־מֹשֶׁה הֲיַד יְהוָה תִּקְצָר עַתָּה
תִרְאֶה הֲיִקְרְךָ דְבָרִי אִם־לֹא׃ 24 וַיֵּצֵא מֹשֶׁה
וַיְדַבֵּר אֶל־הָעָם אֵת דִּבְרֵי יְהוָה וַיֶּאֱסֹף שִׁבְעִים
אִישׁ מִזִּקְנֵי הָעָם וַיַּעֲמֵד אֹתָם סְבִיבֹת הָאֹהֶל׃
25 וַיֵּרֶד יְהוָה׀ בֶּעָנָן וַיְדַבֵּר אֵלָיו וַיָּאצֶל מִן־
הָרוּחַ אֲשֶׁר עָלָיו וַיִּתֵּן עַל־שִׁבְעִים אִישׁ הַזְּקֵנִים
וַיְהִי כְּנוֹחַ עֲלֵיהֶם הָרוּחַ וַיִּתְנַבְּאוּ וְלֹא יָסָפוּ׃

yet You *Ve-'attah,* adversative *vav.*[57]

22. ***flocks and herds*** They had enough meat at hand (Exod. 12:38; cf. Num. 32:1), but they were looking for a pretext to complain.[58]

suffice So Targum Onkelos; see also Zechariah 10:10.

sea "The Great Sea," that is, the Mediterranean, according to Targum Jonathan.

23. ***"Is there a limit to the LORD's power?"*** Literally, "Is the Lord's hand too short" (e.g., Isa. 50:2; 59:1).[59]

what I have said Hebrew ***devari,*** literally "my word." God's ***davar,*** once uttered, must be fulfilled: "So is the word that issues from My mouth: It does not come back to Me unfulfilled" (Isa. 55:11).

THE SPIRIT IS GIVEN TO THE ELDERS, ELDAD, AND MEDAD (vv. 24–30)

The elders, gathered around Moses' tent, are possessed by God's spirit, a sign that their selection by Moses is ratified by God. At the same time, Eldad and Medad, two of the elders designated as Moses' administrative assistants for reasons that are unknown, remain behind in the camp. Nevertheless, they too begin to prophesy. Joshua, who is with Moses inside the tent (cf. Exod. 33:11), becomes alarmed over this possible threat to Moses' authority and urges that they be restrained. Moses replies that ideally all of Israel should qualify as prophets, and that this endowment stems directly from God. Nonetheless, the prophecy characterizing the selected elders is temporary and not permanent, ecstatic and not direct, and thus differs markedly from the prophetic gifts of Moses (cf. Excursuses 25 and 26).

24. ***went out*** From the Tabernacle, according to Targum Jonathan, where God would speak with him (v. 17; Exod. 33:9).

words of the LORD Concerning meat. (Hence v. 24a belongs with the previous passage, vv. 18–23.)

around In contrast to Moses, who entered the Tent (Exod. 33:9).

25. This is the fulfillment of the promise given in verse 17.

spoke to him To distinguish Moses from the elders; compare verse 17.

spoke in ecstasy The function of their ecstasy is not to render them prophets—their ecstatic state is never again repeated—but to provide divine validation for their selection as leaders (cf. Excursus 25).

not continue Hebrew ***lo' yasafu.***[60] Others read ***yasufu,*** "not cease,"[61] that is, their prophetic gift was lifelong, or ***yissafu;*** "not die" (cf. 16:26),[62] that is, from the theophany (cf. Exod. 24:11).

26 Two men, one named Eldad and the other Medad, had
remained in camp; yet the spirit rested upon them—they
were among those recorded, but they had not gone out to
the Tent—and they spoke in ecstasy in the camp. 27 A youth
ran out and told Moses, saying, "Eldad and Medad are
acting the prophet in the camp!" 28 And Joshua son of Nun,
Moses' attendant from his youth, spoke up and said, "My
lord Moses, restrain them!" 29 But Moses said to him, "Are
you wrought up on my account? Would that all the LORD's
people were prophets, that the LORD put His spirit upon

26 וַיִּשָּׁאֲר֣וּ שְׁנֵֽי־אֲנָשִׁ֣ים ׀ בַּֽמַּחֲנֶ֗ה שֵׁ֣ם הָאֶחָ֣ד ׀
אֶלְדָּ֡ד וְשֵׁם֩ הַשֵּׁנִ֨י מֵידָ֜ד וַתָּ֧נַח עֲלֵהֶ֣ם הָר֗וּחַ
וְהֵ֙מָּה֙ בַּכְּתֻבִ֔ים וְלֹ֥א יָצְא֖וּ הָאֹ֑הֱלָה וַיִּֽתְנַבְּא֖וּ
בַּֽמַּחֲנֶֽה׃ 27 וַיָּ֣רָץ הַנַּ֔עַר וַיַּגֵּ֥ד לְמֹשֶׁ֖ה וַיֹּאמַ֑ר
אֶלְדָּ֣ד וּמֵידָ֔ד מִֽתְנַבְּאִ֖ים בַּֽמַּחֲנֶֽה׃ 28 וַיַּ֜עַן יְהוֹשֻׁ֣עַ
בִּן־נ֗וּן מְשָׁרֵ֥ת מֹשֶׁ֛ה מִבְּחֻרָ֖יו וַיֹּאמַ֑ר אֲדֹנִ֥י מֹשֶׁ֖ה
כְּלָאֵֽם׃ 29 וַיֹּ֤אמֶר לוֹ֙ מֹשֶׁ֔ה הַֽמְקַנֵּ֥א אַתָּ֖ה לִ֑י וּמִ֨י
יִתֵּ֜ן כָּל־עַ֤ם יְהוָה֙ נְבִיאִ֔ים כִּֽי־יִתֵּ֧ן יְהוָ֛ה אֶת־רוּח֖וֹ

26. Eldad The name means "God loves."[63]

Medad[64]

the spirit That is, of God not of Moses (cf. v. 29).

recorded Hebrew *ba-ketuvim* is equivalent to ***mispar shemot,*** "list of names" (1:2). This means either that they were recorded as elders but were not among the seventy whom Moses gathered about the tent (v. 24) or that, though selected by Moses among the seventy elders, they declined to come out (v. 26) because of feelings of inadequacy.[65] The rabbinic view that holds the first opinion provides this embellishment (Sanh. 17a): "Some say: they (e.g., their names) remained in the urn. For when the Holy One Blessed Be He said to Moses: 'Gather for Me seventy of Israel's elders,' Moses said (to himself): 'How shall I do it? (v. 16); if I select five (from each tribe) ten will be wanting. If, on the other hand, I choose six out of one and five out of another, I shall cause jealousy among the tribes.' What did he do? He selected six men (out of each tribe), and brought seventy-two slips, on seventy of which he wrote the word 'elder,' leaving the other two blank. He then mixed them all up, deposited them in an urn, and said to them, 'Come and draw your slips.' To each who drew a slip bearing the word 'elder,' he said, 'Heaven has already consecrated you.' To him who drew a blank, he said, 'Heaven has rejected you, what can I do?'" As the rabbis recognize there, a similar type of lottery was used to redeem the extras among the first-born (cf. the Comment to 3:44–51).

gone out to the Tent . . . in the camp According to this tradition, the Tent was stationed outside the camp (cf. Num. 12:4; Exod. 33:7–11).

27. A youth Hebrew ***ha-na'ar,*** one of Moses' attendants, according to Ibn Ezra. The term is synonymous with ***mesharet,*** "attendant" (v. 28; cf. 2 Kings 4:38,43; 6:15).

28. Joshua The presence of Joshua with Moses in the Tent is presumed (cf. Exod. 33:11) and requires no explanation.

attendant Hebrew ***mesharet*** (cf. Exod. 33:11). The stories about the prophets Elijah and Elisha also speak of their attendants (e.g., 1 Kings 19:21; 2 Kings 4:43; 6:15).

from his youth Hebrew ***mi-beḥurav.*** So Targum Onkelos.[66] Ibn Ezra objects that Joshua's service only began in the wilderness with the construction of the Tent and therefore renders the word "of his chosen ones" (as though reading ***mi-beḥirav***).[67]

restrain them So Targum Jonathan (cf. Ps. 40:10,12). Others render "imprison them."[68] Joshua's alarm was motivated by his loyalty to Moses. He feared that since Eldad and Medad received their spirit directly from God,[69] not from Moses, they might now contend with him for the leadership.[70] The fact that they had to be restrained means that they did not cease prophesying as did the elders but continued on.[71] Also the fact that their spirit stemmed directly from God implies that the quality of their prophecy was of a higher order than that of the elders.

29. wrought up For this meaning of ***kinna',*** see 25:11,13.

prophets It is significant that Moses uses the term ***nevi'im,*** "prophets," rather than ***mitnabbe'im,*** "ecstatics," implying a qualitative as well as quantitative distribution of the Lord's

them!" 30 Moses then reentered the camp together with the
elders of Israel.

31 A wind from the Lord started up, swept quail from the
sea and strewed them over the camp, about a day's journey
on this side and about a day's journey on that side, all

עֲלֵיהֶם׃ שביעי 30 וַיֵּאָסֵף מֹשֶׁה אֶל־הַמַּחֲנֶה הוּא
וְזִקְנֵי יִשְׂרָאֵל׃ 31 וְרוּחַ נָסַע ׀ מֵאֵת יְהוָה וַיָּגָז
שַׂלְוִים מִן־הַיָּם וַיִּטֹּשׁ עַל־הַמַּחֲנֶה כְּדֶרֶךְ יוֹם כֹּה
וּכְדֶרֶךְ יוֹם כֹּה סְבִיבוֹת הַמַּחֲנֶה וּכְאַמָּתַיִם עַל־

spirit. In effect, Moses proclaims that not only is it a desideratum that all of Israel qualify (through ecstasy) to become elders but that they may even attain a higher level—to be prophets like Moses himself.

Would that . . . the Lord But not I, that is, Moses.[72]

Would that . . . them The Lord does not restrict His gifts to particular individuals or classes. This lesson inspired a later prophet to predict: "After that, I will pour out My spirit on all flesh; Your sons and daughters shall prophesy . . ." (Joel 3:1).[73]

His spirit But not Moses', again emphasizing that it was not the spirit of Moses that was transmitted to Eldad and Medad but the Lord's (cf. v. 17).

30. reentered ***Ba'*** and ***ne'esaf*** both mean "enter," but the latter is used when one returns to where one belongs, whether to one's home, family, ancestors, or community (cf. 12:14).

Moses' selflessness reaches its apogee in this passage and thereby merits the accolade awarded him: "Now Moses was a very humble man, more so than any other man on earth" (12:3).

THE QUAIL (vv. 31–35)

This is the fulfillment of the promise of verses 18–23, a point emphasized by the brief reference to the incident in Psalms 105:40: "They asked and He brought them quail." Psalms 78:26–31 gives a fuller poetic summary: "He set the east wind moving in heaven, and drove the south wind by His might. He rained meat on them like dust, winged birds like the sands of the sea, making them come down inside His camp, around His dwelling-place. They ate till they were sated; He gave them what they craved. They had not yet wearied of what they craved, the food was still in their mouths when God's anger flared up at them. He slew their sturdiest, struck down the youth of Israel." According to Exodus 16:13, the quail had already made an appearance. This led Bekhor Shor (followed by many moderns) to speculate that the Exodus passage refers to the same incident described here. That the quail were intended, to begin with, as punishment, see Excursus 24.

Quail migrate in great numbers across the Sinai Peninsula, northward in the spring and southward in the fall, propelled by winds from the Red Sea or the Mediterranean. Once they fall, exhausted, upon the Sinai sands,[74] they are easy prey for the hunter. (Since the quail land near the shore, it must be assumed that Israel was still near the Gulf of Suez and had not yet penetrated into the interior of Sinai.)[75] The fourteenth-century Arab writer Al-Qazwini relates that the natives of El-ʿArish, near Gaza, caught and slaughtered quail in wholesale fashion during the seasonal flights from Europe.[76] The phenomenon of the quail would not in itself be a miracle but, as the text emphasizes, it is Moses' prayer for flesh and the immediate answer in the form of these birds—caused by "a wind from the Lord"—that constitutes the divine intervention.

31. A wind from the Lord God answers both Moses and the people through His ***ruaḥ,*** a term that means either spirit or wind. God's spirit on Moses has been shared by the elders. Now it is God's wind that brings meat to the people. Wind and spirit are two aspects of the same divine agency (cf. 1 Kings 22:19–23). God employs a wind to drive back the waters of Creation (Gen. 1:2; Ps. 104:4), the Flood (Gen. 8:1), and the Red Sea (Exod. 14:21), to endanger Jonah's ship (Jon. 1:4), and to remove the plague of the locusts (Exod. 10:13,19). That quail follow the prevailing winds was already noted by Aristotle.[77] Psalms 78:26 speaks of an east wind.

started up Hebrew ***nasaʿ***. The Hifil ***yassaʿ*** is used in Psalms 78:26—"He set the east wind moving"—emphasizing the wind's divine origins.

swept[78]

around the camp, and some two cubits deep on the ground. 32The people set to gathering quail all that day and night and all the next day—even he who gathered least had ten *homers*—and they spread them out all around the camp. 33The meat was still between their teeth, nor yet chewed, when the anger of the LORD blazed forth against the people and the LORD struck the people with a very severe plague.

פְּנֵ֥י הָאָֽרֶץ׃ 32 וַיָּ֣קָם הָעָ֡ם כָּל־הַיּוֹם֩ הַה֨וּא וְכָל־
הַלַּ֜יְלָה וְכֹ֣ל ׀ י֣וֹם הַֽמָּחֳרָ֗ת וַיַּֽאַסְפוּ֙ אֶת־הַשְּׂלָ֔ו
הַמַּמְעִ֕יט אָסַ֖ף עֲשָׂרָ֣ה חֳמָרִ֑ים וַיִּשְׁטְח֤וּ לָהֶם֙
שָׁט֔וֹחַ סְבִיב֖וֹת הַֽמַּחֲנֶֽה׃ 33 הַבָּשָׂ֗ר עוֹדֶ֙נּוּ֙ בֵּ֣ין
שִׁנֵּיהֶ֔ם טֶ֖רֶם יִכָּרֵ֑ת וְאַ֤ף יְהוָה֙ חָרָ֣ה בָעָ֔ם וַיַּ֤ךְ יְהוָה֙
בָּעָ֔ם מַכָּ֖ה רַבָּ֥ה מְאֹֽד׃ 34 וַיִּקְרָ֛א אֶת־שֵֽׁם־הַמָּק֥וֹם

quail Hebrew *selav*[79] has been identified with quail,[80] and *salva* is the word for quail in modern Egyptian Arabic.

sea This would be the Gulf of Elath according to Psalms 78:20, which speaks of a south and east wind, thereby placing the coming of the quail in the spring, a date which accords with the chronology of 10:11,33.

strewed For this meaning of the root *n-t-sh,* compare 1 Samuel 30:16. The poetical account of the descent of the quail (Ps. 78:27) places all the quail within the camp, an understanding that accords with the tradition of Exodus 16:13, which confines the quail to the camp and the manna to its outskirts. Also, the fact that in the Psalm the sanctuary is in the middle of the camp conforms to the narrative of Exodus 16 (cf. vv. 33–34).

over Rather, "around," according to Ibn Ezra. The point is that the quail fell outside the camp, whereas God's food, the manna, fell within the camp (v. 9). This topographic distinction between the camp, which contains the Lord's presence, and the non-Godly, impure environs indicates that the quail are a curse not a blessing.[81]

32. ***set to gathering*** Hebrew *va-yakom* is perhaps an ironic comment on its antonym, the proposed *va-yeshvu* (v. 4); that is, Israel sat down to complain but rose quickly to glut its lust.

homers So Targum Jonathan, a dry measure that equals 5.16 bushels or 220 liters. Hebrew *ḥomarim* can also mean "heaps."[82]

spread them out In the sun,[83] to cure them by drying.[84] For this meaning of *shataḥ,* see Ezekiel 26:5 and Psalms 88:10. Most Septuagint manuscripts render "refreshed themselves," that is, spread them out for a feast. The Samaritan and the Vatican manuscripts of the Septuagint render "slaughtered them," reading the root as *sh-ḥ-t* rather than *sh-t-ḥ*.[85] This reading has the advantage of answering Moses' challenge to God in verse 22 to provide enough meat for the people to "gather" *('asaf)* and "slaughter" *(shaḥat)* "for them" *(lahem)*. Also implied is that they ate the meat raw: They were so lustful for meat that as soon as they slaughtered the birds they gorged themselves on the raw flesh.

33. ***chewed*** An alternative rendering would be "failed," i.e., there were ample quail still left.[86] For this meaning of *karet,* see Josh. 3:16; 2 Sam. 3:29.

the people Rather, "a portion of the people." Hebrew *ba-'am* literally means "among the people," implying that only some of the people were smitten, presumably the riffraff (v. 4; see the Comment to v. 34). This rendering would also resolve the theological difficulty that the Lord, on the one hand, promised meat for thirty days (v. 19) but, on the other hand, struck down the Israelites on the very first day they ate of the quail. What then actually transpired was that only the instigators of Israel's discontent, the riffraff, were summarily punished, whereas, presumably, the Israelites continued to eat quail for a whole month or until it became loathsome.[87]

plague Resulting from overeating, according to Ibn Ezra, or they choked on the meat (v. 33a). Others, however, regard the punishment as a supernatural affliction stemming from God for their unjustified complaint against the manna, since, according to the text, the only anticipated result of stuffing themselves with quail was revulsion (v. 20).[88]

34 That place was named Kibroth-hattaavah, because the people who had the craving were buried there.

35 Then the people set out from Kibroth-hattaavah for Hazeroth.

הַהוּא קִבְרוֹת הַתַּאֲוָה כִּי־שָׁם קָבְרוּ אֶת־הָעָם
הַמִּתְאַוִּים׃ 35 מִקִּבְרוֹת הַתַּאֲוָה נָסְעוּ הָעָם
חֲצֵרוֹת וַיִּהְיוּ בַּחֲצֵרוֹת׃ פ

12 When they were in Hazeroth, 1 Miriam and Aaron spoke against Moses because of the Cushite woman he had married: "He married a Cushite woman!"

י״ב וַתְּדַבֵּר מִרְיָם וְאַהֲרֹן בְּמֹשֶׁה עַל־אֹדוֹת
הָאִשָּׁה הַכֻּשִׁית אֲשֶׁר לָקָח כִּי־אִשָּׁה כֻשִׁית לָקָח׃

34. Kibroth-hattaavah . . . the people who had the craving Hebrew *ha-ta'avah . . . ha-mit'avvim* is a verbal reference to the riffraff who "felt a gluttonous craving" *(hit'avvu ta'avah),* implying that the main body of Israelites escaped punishment (see the Comment to "the people," v. 33).

CHAPTER 12 THE UNIQUENESS OF MOSES (vv. 1–16)

The uniqueness of Moses is the sole theme of this chapter. It is reflected in the challenge to his authority (v. 2); his humility (v. 3); God's affirmation of his uniqueness (vv. 6–8); the punishment of Miriam (vv. 9–10); and Moses' successful intercession on her behalf (vv. 11–15). The previous chapter (11:14–17,24–31) has contrasted Moses with the ecstatics. This chapter contrasts him with prophets, in particular, with Miriam and Aaron who, on the basis of their own prophetic gifts, contest Moses' leadership. This theme serves as the link that connects the two chapters. Miriam and Aaron summon the courage to challenge Moses from the example of Eldad and Medad (11:26–29), who also have received their prophetic gift directly from God, prophesying independently of Moses and with the latter's encouragement. As God's intimate confidant, Moses is now proclaimed the prophet *par excellence.*

1. Miriam and Aaron spoke against The verb *va-tedabber* is in the feminine singular, indicating that Miriam was the principal instigator of the gossip (also note that Miriam is mentioned ahead of Aaron, the reverse of the normal order; cf. vv. 4,5). This would therefore account for the fact that she and not Aaron was punished.[1] Singular verbs are also used with Moses and Deborah, the authors of their songs, even though their names are followed by "the Israelites" and "Barak," respectively (Exod. 15:1; Judg. 5:1). And similarly with Esther: Although she is coupled with Mordecai, it is she who is the principal author of the decree to observe Purim (Esther 9:29; cf. v. 32).

For *dibber be,* denoting "speak against," see 21:5,7.

because of the Cushite woman Those who claim that Cush is Ethiopia[2] clearly cannot identify the woman with his wife Zipporah.[3] They cite an elaborate legend of how Moses had married an Ethiopian. Others, however, place Cush in Midianite territory (Hab. 3:7) or understand Cushite as an adjective meaning beautiful,[4] thus allowing for the identification with Zipporah. That the marriage with Zipporah, consummated so much earlier (Exod. 2:21), would cause such a belated shock can be explained by the fact that her husband had left her behind when he went to Egypt to redeem his people, and she only rejoined him at Sinai, to be seen for the first time by the Israelites (Exod. 18:5–6).[5]

Regardless of whether Moses' wife was Ethiopian or Midianite, the objection to her, it is implied, was ethnic (cf. Lev. 24:10). Strikingly, the rabbis raise no objection to her Cushite origin but, to the contrary, defend her, claiming that Moses refused to have sexual intercourse after his descent from Sinai.[6]

"He married a Cushite woman!" So Ibn Ezra. The particle *ki* can introduce direct speech (cf. Gen. 21:30; 29:33; Exod. 3:12).

2 They said, "Has the LORD spoken only through Moses? Has He not spoken through us as well?" The LORD heard it. 3 Now Moses was a very humble man, more so than any other man on earth. 4 Suddenly the LORD called to Moses, Aaron, and Miriam, "Come out, you three, to the Tent of Meeting." So the three of them went out. 5 The LORD came down in a pillar of cloud, stopped at the entrance of the Tent, and called out, "Aaron and Miriam!" The two of them came forward; 6 and He said, "Hear these My words:

2 וַיֹּאמְרוּ הֲרַק אַךְ־בְּמֹשֶׁה דִּבֶּר יְהוָה הֲלֹא גַּם־
בָּנוּ דִבֵּר וַיִּשְׁמַע יְהוָה׃ 3 וְהָאִישׁ מֹשֶׁה ענו מְאֹד
מִכֹּל הָאָדָם אֲשֶׁר עַל־פְּנֵי הָאֲדָמָה׃ ס
4 וַיֹּאמֶר יְהוָה פִּתְאֹם אֶל־מֹשֶׁה וְאֶל־אַהֲרֹן וְאֶל־
מִרְיָם צְאוּ שְׁלָשְׁתְּכֶם אֶל־אֹהֶל מוֹעֵד וַיֵּצְאוּ
שְׁלָשְׁתָּם׃ 5 וַיֵּרֶד יְהוָה בְּעַמּוּד עָנָן וַיַּעֲמֹד פֶּתַח
הָאֹהֶל וַיִּקְרָא אַהֲרֹן וּמִרְיָם וַיֵּצְאוּ שְׁנֵיהֶם׃

v. 3. עָנָיו ק'

2. Herein lies the true reason for Miriam and Aaron's complaint; the previous one was only a pretext. What they were really after was a share in Moses' leadership.

only Hebrew *ha-rak 'akh,* literally "only and solely," is a doubling for the sake of emphasis (cf. Gen. 14:24; Exod. 14:11).

spoken (only) through So Rashbam. Examples of this usage of *dibber be* are 2 Samuel 23:2, 1 Kings 22:28, Hosea 1:2, and Habakkuk 2:1, all of which are divine commands to Israel communicated through a prophet.[7] However, this rendering is impossible in verse 8, where God's speech is directed to Moses alone. Hence the rendering "speak to" or "speak with" would be preferable.[8]

us The tradition does exist that Miriam and Aaron were prophets, as is clear from Exodus 4:16 and 15:20 and Micah 6:4. That Miriam and Aaron are Moses' siblings also may have spurred their claim to prophetic equality with their brother. The divinatory profession is known to have been handed down within families, especially among the early Arabs.[9] That this familial prerogative is herewith denied may also be part of the prophetic revolution within Israel. Beginning with Moses, prophecy is an individual not a group phenomenon.[10]

The LORD heard it But not Moses, according to Shadal. The consequence of the Lord's hearing is self-understood and is more powerful by the text's deliberate silence on the matter than if it had put it in words (similarly, cf. Gen. 35:22). The expected result, God's anger, is withheld until verse 9 (cf. 11:1); the punishment then follows.

3. *Now Moses . . .* An editorial reply to the charge that Moses did not deign to answer.[11] The literal rendering of the text is "the man Moses," worded in this manner, perhaps, to emphasize that he was only a man. The use of this same expression in Exodus 11:3 is instructive: To the Egyptians, Moses appears great but not in his own eyes.

humble Hebrew *'anav* (cf. Zeph. 2:3). This is the only instance of the singular in the Bible. Its meaning is clarified by its synonymous parallel "who seek the Lord" (Ps. 22:27), hence, "devout, trusting." It also applies to the weak and exploited (Amos 2:7; Isa. 11:4).[12] However, it never means "meek."

4. *Suddenly* That is, at once, to prevent Miriam and Aaron from saying that Moses had complained to God;[13] or while they were speaking about Moses;[14] or unexpectedly.[15]

Come out . . . went out Again, indicating that the Tent of Meeting, according to this tradition, was located outside the camp (cf. Excursus 28).

you three Moses was summoned together with Miriam and Aaron because all litigants must appear before the bar of (divine) justice, according to Bekhor Shor. The same legal principle will be enforced in Korah's rebellion (16:16–18).

5. *The LORD came down . . . entrance of the Tent* Each Tent tradition transmitted a different mode for the Lord's revelation (cf. Excursus 28).

"Aaron and Miriam!" Direct discourse,[16] which provides an ironic twist. The Lord declares that He speaks directly only to Moses (v. 8) but here He avoids Moses and speaks directly to Aaron and Miriam.

When a prophet of the LORD arises among you, I make
Myself known to him in a vision, I speak with him in a
dream. 7 Not so with My servant Moses; he is trusted
throughout My household. 8 With him I speak mouth to

6 וַיֹּאמֶר שִׁמְעוּ־נָא דְבָרָי אִם־יִהְיֶה נְבִיאֲכֶם יְהוָה
בַּמַּרְאָה אֵלָיו אֶתְוַדָּע בַּחֲלוֹם אֲדַבֶּר־בּוֹ׃ 7 לֹא־כֵן
עַבְדִּי מֹשֶׁה בְּכָל־בֵּיתִי נֶאֱמָן הוּא׃ 8 פֶּה אֶל־פֶּה

came forward Rather, "came out," either (1) from the position they had taken with Moses outside the sacred enclosure, according to the principle that "persons summoned to or seeking God await His appearance, not He theirs"[17] (cf. Exod. 33:7–11; Num. 11:16–17,24–25) or (2) from the Tent[18] that the seeker of the divine word would enter (Excursus 28), in order to prevent it from being contaminated by Miriam's leprosy.[19] A similar procedure to the first interpretation obtained during the induction service of the Levites. First the Levites and the community gathered before the sacred enclosure (8:9). Then the Levites and representatives of the community advanced before the altar (8:10). A midrash adds an ethical motivation: so that Moses should not hear his praise, in keeping with the rule that one should never praise a man fully to his face.[20]

6–8. These verses are poetry (and probably originate in an ancient epic concerning Moses). This is apparent when they are typographically reset.[21] They reveal an introverted structure.[22] The number of syllables per line is indicated in parentheses. Alterations of the translation are explained in the Commentary and notes.

Introduction: Hear these My words (7)
A. If either of you is YHVH's prophet (9)
B. I make Myself known to him in a vision (8)
C. I speak with him in a dream (7)
D. Not so with My servant Moses (6)
D′. He (alone) is trusted in all My household (7)
C′. With him I speak mouth to mouth (7)
B′. Plainly and not in riddles (8)
A′. And he beholds the likeness of the Lord (7)
Conclusion: How then did you not shrink (7)
from speaking against My servant Moses. (9)

This introverted structure clarifies the point of the poem. The first half describes God's communication with other prophets (ABC), the second half, His unique transmission to Moses (C′B′A′). The pivot sets Moses apart from his prophetic counterparts (D) by declaring that God confides in him alone (D′).

6. Hear these My words A fitting opening for a poem (cf. Gen 4:23).

When a prophet of the LORD arises among you[23]

vision[24] The usual term for vision is ***maḥazeh*** (24:4,16; Gen. 15:1) or ***ḥazon, ḥizayon*** (2 Sam. 7:17; Isa. 1:1) from the root ***ḥ-z-h,*** a synonym of ***ra'ah.*** The specialist in visions, that is, the clairvoyant, is called by the derived nouns, ***ḥozeh*** and ***ro'eh*** (e.g., Isa. 30:10; 1 Chron. 29:29), and a seminal verse informs us that the prophet ***(navi')*** was previously called a ***ro'eh*** (1 Sam. 9:9; see Excursus 26).

dream Dreams are mentioned alongside of prophecy as authentic vehicles of God's revelation (Deut. 13:2,4,6), and there are several attestations to this effect: Abimelech (Gen. 20:7), Jacob (Gen. 31:10–13), Solomon (1 Kings 3:5–14), and Job (Job 33:14–18). However, when Deuteronomy describes a true prophet (18:14–20), it speaks of direct divine communication and does not mention the dream.[25] And some of the higher prophets—perhaps under Deuteronomic influence—clearly held the dream to be inferior to prophecy: "Let the prophet who has a dream tell the dream; and let him who has received My word report My word faithfully! How can straw be compared to grain?—says the LORD" (Jer. 23:28). Moreover, dreams are a form of divination. In essence, there is no difference between trying to interpret the number and position of stars (Joseph's dream; Gen. 37:9) and the number and position of clouds in the sky or spots on a liver (divination). Also, according to Bekhor Shor, since dreams and visions require interpretation they cannot be ranked with prophecy. Dreams and visions are distinguished from each other at ancient Mari.[26] And when Saul complains that God will not answer him through the legitimate means of dreams and prophets (1 Sam. 28:15), he

mouth, plainly and not in riddles, and he beholds the likeness of the LORD. How then did you not shrink from speaking against My servant Moses!" 9 Still incensed with them, the LORD departed.

אֲדַבֶּר־בּוֹ וּמַרְאֶה וְלֹא בְחִידֹת וּתְמֻנַת יְהוָה יַבִּיט
וּמַדּוּעַ לֹא יְרֵאתֶם לְדַבֵּר בְּעַבְדִּי בְמֹשֶׁה: 9 וַיִּחַר
אַף יְהוָה בָּם וַיֵּלַךְ: 10 וְהֶעָנָן סָר מֵעַל הָאֹהֶל

probably means by the latter term clairvoyants, for indeed, as an editorial note informs us, the prophet Samuel was heretofore known as a *ro'eh,* a clairvoyant (1 Sam. 9:9).

7. ***Not so*** In 11:7,25, Moses was distinguished from the ecstatic prophets *(mitnabbe'im).* Here he is set apart from and above prophets *(nevi'im)* like Aaron and Miriam (cf. Exod. 4:16; 15:20; Mic. 6:4), although all share the same title (Deut. 18:15; 34:10).[27]

My servant Elsewhere, this epithet is bestowed on Moses (cf. Exod. 14:31; Deut. 34:5), Abraham (Gen. 26:24), and Caleb (14:24), as well as on the prophets (2 Kings 9:7) and all Israel (Isa. 41:8).

trusted Hebrew *ne'eman.* Compare 1 Samuel 22:14, implying reliability (Rashbam), or that he can enter without permission (Ibn Ezra), or that he can speak harshly to his Master without arousing his ire (Ehrlich).

My household Hebrew *beiti;* that is, Moses is entrusted with the administration of the house of Israel as were Eliezer (Gen. 24:2) and Joseph (Gen. 39:4–5) in the households of Abraham and Pharaoh, respectively. For Israel as God's *bayit,* "house," compare Jeremiah 12:7 and Hosea 8:1. Alternatively, the verse may intend the divine council in God's celestial "house," to whose deliberations the prophets are privy (cf. Isa. 6) and who, like Moses, are called "the Lord's servants" (2 Kings 9:7).[28] In this latter interpretation, *be-khol* would not be rendered "throughout" but "of": Of all of God's household, Moses is the most trusted; he alone has direct access to the Deity and obtains an audience with Him at will.

8. ***mouth to mouth*** By direct revelation (Ibn Ezra) and while fully conscious (Sforno). This expression is synonymous with "face to face" in Exodus 33:11 and Deuteronomy 34:10. Both expressions imply a dialogue: The prophet is the intercessor for his people as well as the conveyor of God's word. The image is that of a royal house in which only the most trusted servant has regular access to the monarch. Such ones are called literally "those who see the face of the king" (2 Kings 25:19).

plainly Hebrew *u-mar'eh.* The reading *be-mar'eh*[29] seems preferable, unless the *bet* in *be-ḥidot,* "riddles," is doing double duty and the *vav* is explicative[30] (e.g., Exod. 6:3; Deut. 33:4). In any case, it should be taken adverbially from the noun *mar'eh,* "appearance" (e.g., Lev. 13:3).[31] The midrash speaks of Moses seeing through a clear mirror, whereas other prophets see through a murky mirror.[32] In other words, Moses' visions do not require any interpretation, but the visions (or dreams, riddles) of other prophets do. Some attribute Moses' distinction to his vision of the burning bush,[33] or to his theophany at Sinai[34] (cf. Exod. 33:23), or to his being shown the blueprint of the Tabernacle (e.g., Exod. 25:40).[35]

riddles Hebrew *ḥidot,* enigmatic, perplexing statements (1 Kings 10:1). Dreams, the parallel term in verse 6, also fall into this category. The difficulty of dream interpretation accounts for Joseph's rise to power (Gen. 41).

likeness Hebrew *temunah* is less distinct than *mar'eh,* "appearance" (Job 4:16). "The intangible, yet quasi-sensual manifestation of the Godhead vouchsafed to Moses, as contrasted with the less distinct manifestation by the vision, or the dream (v. 6) which might need interpretation (v. 8), granted to other prophets."[36] According to Deuteronomy, at Horeb/Sinai, the people saw no likeness but only heard a voice (Deut. 4:12,15). The prophet Elijah, who in many respects is patterned after Moses, especially in being granted a theophany at Sinai/Horeb, is graphically instructed that God reveals Himself only in a voice (1 Kings 19:12–13).[37]

How then . . . servant Moses The conclusion of this poetic fragment. Containing sixteen syllables, it balances perfectly the sixteen syllables of the opening two lines in verse 6.[38] God's speech ends using the same vocabulary *(dibber be)* as Miriam and Aaron did in their charge (v. 2) but with boomerang effect: God speaks to Moses (2) but Miriam and Aaron speak against Moses (8, cf. v. 1).

10 As the cloud withdrew from the Tent, there was
Miriam stricken with snow-white scales! When Aaron
turned toward Miriam, he saw that she was stricken with
scales. 11 And Aaron said to Moses, "O my lord, account
not to us the sin which we committed in our folly. 12 Let her
not be as one dead, who emerges from his mother's womb

וְהִנֵּה מִרְיָם מְצֹרַעַת כַּשָּׁלֶג וַיִּפֶן אַהֲרֹן אֶל־מִרְיָם
וְהִנֵּה מְצֹרָעַת׃ 11 וַיֹּאמֶר אַהֲרֹן אֶל־מֹשֶׁה בִּי
אֲדֹנִי אַל־נָא תָשֵׁת עָלֵינוּ חַטָּאת אֲשֶׁר נוֹאַלְנוּ
וַאֲשֶׁר חָטָאנוּ׃ 12 אַל־נָא תְהִי כַּמֵּת אֲשֶׁר
בְּצֵאתוֹ מֵרֶחֶם אִמּוֹ וַיֵּאָכֵל חֲצִי בְשָׂרוֹ׃ 13 וַיִּצְעַק

9. Still incensed with them Literally, "The Lord was incensed with them," referring back to verse 2, when God heard Miriam and Aaron murmuring against Moses (cf. 11:1 and Excursus 24). The displacement of the anger to verse 9 means that God's anger did not abate but only mounted during the confrontation. The literal rendering also makes sense if it is understood as an expression of divine punishment. Thus, "The Lord heard it" (v. 2) implies His anger, and "The Lord was incensed with them" (v. 9) implies His punishment.

the LORD departed God's departure brings punishment in its wake. Also, God's departure from Miriam and Aaron suggests the cancellation of their prophetic gifts,[39] a fact underscored by Aaron's plea to Moses to intercede—a basic prophetic function—implying that he, Aaron, no longer could.

10. As the cloud withdrew The use of the perfect preceded by the subject breaks the narrative sequence, thus equating the Lord (v. 9) with the cloud. A midrash informs us that God's withdrawal was a sign of his love and compassion. It is like a king who tells the teacher: Discipline my son, but only after I leave.[40]

from Rather, "from beside" (cf. 16:26–27).

snow-white scales Rather, "scaly as snow" (cf. Exod. 4:6; Lev. 13:3). Leprosy was considered a punishment for offenses against the Deity in Israel (and elsewhere in the ancient Near East).[41] According to the rabbis, the chief cause for leprosy is defamation, interpreting *metsora'* as *motsi' shem ra'*, "slander."[42] If Cushite means Ethiopian then the whiteness of Miriam would be a fit punishment for objecting to Moses' dark-skinned wife.[43] However, the simile of snow indicates the flakiness associated with the disease, not whiteness (cf. Pss. 68:15; 147:16).[44]

he saw Since Aaron was a priest, *his* seeing her condition confirmed the diagnosis (cf. Lev. 13:2–17).

11. Moses' intercession has ironic implications: Only he whom Miriam and Aaron have wronged can help them. This motif occurs elsewhere: Abimelech is told that only Abraham whose wife he has taken can remove the plague (Gen. 20:7), and the friends who wronged Job must turn to him for their expiation (Job 42:7–8).

O Hebrew *bi* always precedes "my lord/God." It designates a petition to speak (e.g., Gen. 43:20; 44:11).

my lord Aaron acknowledges Moses' superiority by using this title that one bestows upon a superior, whether man (e.g., Gen. 43:20; 44:18) or God (Exod. 4:10,13). It constitutes Moses' final vindication: Aaron who had denied Moses' supremacy (vv. 1–2) is now forced to acknowledge it.

committed in our folly He attempts to reduce the gravity of the wrong: It was not done with malice and, hence, was expiable by intercession. The Septuagint reads: "for we were ignorant wherein we sinned."

12. Let her not be as one dead In antiquity, the leper was regarded as a dead person.[45] The Septuagint adds "like an abortion."[46] Rashbam takes Aaron's statement as a rebuke of Moses[47] and renders the verse: "Let *you* be not like one dead, inasmuch as all who come from the same mother's womb partly die (when any brother or sister dies)";[48] that is, Moses himself would be as one dead since his own flesh—his sister Miriam—would be consumed.

half his flesh eaten away When a fetus that has died in the womb is delivered, its skin flakes off, giving it the appearance of a "leper."[49]

with half his flesh eaten away." 13So Moses cried out to the
LORD, saying, "O God, pray heal her!"
14But the LORD said to Moses, "If her father spat in her
face, would she not bear her shame for seven days? Let her

מֹשֶׁ֔ה אֶל־יְהוָ֖ה לֵאמֹ֑ר אֵ֕ל נָ֛א רְפָ֥א נָ֖א לָֽהּ׃
פ מפטיר 14 וַיֹּ֨אמֶר יְהוָ֜ה אֶל־מֹשֶׁ֗ה וְאָבִ֙יהָ֙
יָרֹ֤ק יָרַק֙ בְּפָנֶ֔יהָ הֲלֹ֥א תִכָּלֵ֖ם שִׁבְעַ֣ת יָמִ֑ים תִּסָּגֵ֞ר
שִׁבְעַ֤ת יָמִים֙ מִח֣וּץ לַֽמַּחֲנֶ֔ה וְאַחַ֖ר תֵּאָסֵֽף׃

13. Moses is caught in a dilemma. On the one hand, Miriam had openly spoken against him and deserved to be punished. On the other hand, as his sister, she evoked his compassion. Moses' terse prayer—bereft of emotion and substantiation—is the result. It is a model of brevity, perhaps lest he be accused of showing favoritism to his sister.[50] It is more likely, however, that the prayer's brevity indicates Moses' lack of enthusiasm and minimal compliance with Aaron's plea, an attitude supported by the fact that Miriam is not referred to by name but by the impersonal third person.[51] The prayer's structure is a near perfect introversion: *'el na' refa' na' lah,* ABXB′A′. The key word *refa',* "heal," is the pivotal center X, BB′ contain the identical word, and AA′ are monosyllables consisting of the same voiced consonant, *lamed.*

cried out Hebrew *va-yits'ak,* a term used for Moses' intercession in crisis situations (e.g., Exod. 15:25; 17:4).

O God Hebrew *'el,* although found in compound expressions, never exists by itself in prose. But Moses' prayer may be a poetic fragment, as are verses 6–8, from a larger epic; and in poetry, *'el* by itself is frequently attested (e.g., 23:8,19,22,23). The assonance *'al . . . 'al . . . 'el* creates the impression that Moses begins his intercession with Aaron's plea.[52] Moreover, the use of *'el* allows the entire prayer to consist of monosyllables—an index of Moses' unenthusiasm—and forms an inclusion with the final word *lah.*

14. ***spat in her face*** In the ancient Near East, magical powers are attributed to spittle, for example, "fill your eyes with spit" is juxtaposed with "tear out your tongue" as part of the treatment performed by the Mesopotamian exorcist.[53] In the Bible, however, this magical background has been uprooted: All spitting, whether part of a ritual or not, is simply a matter of humiliation (cf. Deut. 25:9; Isa. 50:6).

bear her shame for seven days The nature of the shame and the length of its duration are taken for granted, but thus far they have received no illumination from literature of the ancient Near East. The purpose of this analogy may have been as follows: If a human father's rebuke by spitting entails seven days of banishment, should not the leprosy rebuke of the Heavenly Father at least require the same banishment?

seven days Miriam's penalty is sharply reduced from lifelong leprosy to a seven-day exclusion from camp. Here too an additional concession is made, for an ordinary case of leprosy lasts a minimum of fourteen days (Lev. 13:5).[54] It may be implied that Miriam was healed at once; if so the seven-day quarantine (Lev. 13:5) was not required but only the seven-day ritual of purification (Lev. 14:1–20). Indeed, God's response that Miriam's exclusion is due to shame and not her illness implies that Moses' prayer for a complete healing has been answered: Miriam is totally cured. Why then was she excluded?

The fact that her leprosy was white (v. 10) may point to the solution.[55] According to the leprosy laws of Leviticus, whiteness is a sign that the affected person is clean (Lev. 13:13,17), that the disease is noncontagious and is probably a form of leukoderma (vitiligo) or psoriasis.[56] Thus, from the outset Miriam's "leprosy" did not imply banishment from the camp. Rather, her punishment was that she was marked for life! By the same token, the white leprosy of the Aramean general Naaman (2 Kings 5:1,27) assuredly did not prevent him from performing the duties of his office. It also can be assumed that the leprosy that temporarily afflicted Moses (Exod. 4:6–7) was of the same type. Thus the stigma (and discomfort) of Miriam's punishment is removed by the intercession of the true prophet, Moses. And her exclusion from camp has nothing to do with the laws of leprosy but, as the text itself states, with the norms of shame. Furthermore the analogy of Miriam's condition to that of the daughter is now clarified. Miriam's white (and hence, pure) leprosy is equivalent to the daughter who is spat upon. Both are ostracized because they are humiliated not because they are impure.

be shut out of camp for seven days, and then let her be readmitted." [15]So Miriam was shut out of camp seven days; and the people did not march on until Miriam was readmitted. [16]After that the people set out from Hazeroth and encamped in the wilderness of Paran.

15 וַתִּסָּגֵ֥ר מִרְיָ֛ם מִח֥וּץ לַֽמַּחֲנֶ֖ה שִׁבְעַ֣ת יָמִ֑ים
וְהָעָם֙ לֹ֣א נָסַ֔ע עַד־הֵאָסֵ֖ף מִרְיָֽם׃ 16 וְאַחַ֛ר נָסְע֥וּ
הָעָ֖ם מֵחֲצֵר֑וֹת וַֽיַּחֲנ֖וּ בְּמִדְבַּ֥ר פָּארָֽן׃ פ

*15. **people did not march*** Out of respect for Miriam, because Miriam had watched over Moses at the river bank for a short while.[57] A more cogent reason, however, is that all of Israel pays a penalty for Miriam's sin: Their march to the promised land must be delayed a full week.

readmitted Or "cleansed," according to the Septuagint, referring to the purification ritual of the healed leper (cf. Lev. 14:9). In regard to leprosy, *'asaf* can mean either readmit (v. 14) or heal (cf. 2 Kings 5:6,11).

*16. **Paran*** That is, at Kadesh (cf. Num. 13:26; Deut. 1:19), according to Ramban.

Because of the faithlessness of most members of the reconnaissance expedition to Canaan, Israel is condemned to spend forty years in the wilderness, mostly in the area of Kadesh-barnea (see Map 1), where they receive new laws (chaps. 15, 18–19) and where the authority of Aaron and Moses (chaps. 16–17) and even God (20:1–13) is flouted.

The Reconnaissance of Canaan (13:1–14:45)

According to the Torah, the wilderness period was marked by two egregious sins: the apostasy of the golden calf (Exod. 32–34) and the faithlessness of the scouts (Num. 13–14). Only these two sins are singled out for special mention in the survey of the wilderness trek given by Deuteronomy (1:22–45; 9:12–25), and only in connection with these two sins does God threaten the annihilation of Israel and the fulfillment of the patriarchal promise through Moses (Exod. 32:10; Num. 14:12). Echoes of the scout episode resonate throughout Scripture. The story of Israel's rebellion is artfully constructed. The scouts' factual but negative report (13:28–29) sets off a wave of murmuring (13:30a): The exaggerated description of the dangers (13:32–33) leads to organized vocal opposition (14:1–3) and a threat to return to Egypt under new leadership (14:4–10).

The juxtaposition of chapters 13–14 with chapter 12 derives from the tradition that Israel's rebellion following the reconnaissance of Canaan took place in the wilderness of Paran (12:16; 13:26). There also is a psychological connection: Miriam and Aaron's public outburst against Moses (12:1–2,8b) may have encouraged the malcontents among the Israelites to do the same.

CHAPTER 13 SCOUTS ARE CHOSEN (vv. 1–20)

Shelah-lekha

Moses, bidden by God to send scouts to reconnoiter the land, chooses twelve chieftains, one from each tribe, and gives them specific questions to investigate concerning the land and its inhabitants. Their names differ from the tribal chieftains previously listed in chapters 1,2,7; whereas the census and altar initiation had called for the most senior leaders, a mission of arduous and dangerous reconnaissance requires younger leaders.[1]

SHELAḤ-LEKHA

13 The LORD spoke to Moses, saying, 2"Send men to
scout the land of Canaan, which I am giving to the Israelite
people; send one man from each of their ancestral tribes,
each one a chieftain among them." 3So Moses, by the

שלח לך

י״ג וַיְדַבֵּר יְהוָה אֶל־מֹשֶׁה לֵּאמֹר: 2 שְׁלַח־לְךָ
אֲנָשִׁים וְיָתֻרוּ אֶת־אֶרֶץ כְּנַעַן אֲשֶׁר־אֲנִי נֹתֵן לִבְנֵי
יִשְׂרָאֵל אִישׁ אֶחָד אִישׁ אֶחָד לְמַטֵּה אֲבֹתָיו
תִּשְׁלָחוּ כֹּל נָשִׂיא בָהֶם: 3 וַיִּשְׁלַח אֹתָם מֹשֶׁה

1. The LORD spoke According to the tradition recorded in Deuteronomy (1:22,23,37), the initiative to scout the land stemmed from the people, not from God—constituting a breach of faith because God had already scouted the land. Hence, since Moses approved the expedition, he was condemned with the people to die in the desert. The Samaritan Pentateuch conflates the two traditions by inserting Deuteronomy 1:20–23a at the head of Numbers 13. Others would suggest that Deuteronomy transferred the initiative to the people because it did not want to attribute the failure of the scouts to God.[2] Most likely, the Torah reflects two independent traditions (see Excursus 29).

2. send Hebrew ***shelaḥ-lekha,*** literally "send for yourself" (cf. Gen. 12:1; Num. 14:25), an idiom that forms the basis for the following midrash. "A rich man possessed a vineyard. Whenever he saw that the wine was good he would say to his men: 'Bring the wine into *my* house,' but when he saw that the wine had turned to vinegar, he would say: 'Bring the wine into *your* houses.' It was the same with the Holy One, Blessed Be He. When he saw the elders and how worthy their deeds were, He called them His own; as it says, 'Gather for *Me* seventy of Israel's elders' (Num. 11:16). But when He saw the scouts and how they would later sin, He ascribed them to Moses, saying, ***shelaḥ-lekha,*** 'Send men for *yourself.*'"[3]

This idiom, as described by the midrash, reveals an important insight. In contrast to the chieftains who were chosen by God (e.g., to conduct the census, 1:4–17, and to parcel the land, 34:16–29), the chieftains sent to scout the land were to be chosen by Moses—an indication that the Lord disapproved of the project from the start. Ramban also notes that no lot was used to select the scouts (cf. 1:5–15; 34:19–28), a further indication of the Lord's displeasure with the idea of sending scouts. Therefore, God, as it were, told Moses: If you want them, you must pick them.

to scout Hebrew root ***t-w-r,*** "scout, seek out" (10:33; 15:39; Ezek. 20:6); compare Akkadian ***târu,*** "turn around," that is, gather information but not necessarily of a military nature (cf. Excursus 30). This verb contrasts with ***r-g-l,*** "spy out" (cf. Num. 21:32; Josh. 7:2; Judg. 18:2). The Deuteronomic account (Deut. 1:24) uses the verb "spy out" (cf. Josh. 14:7), but this is not surprising since in its view, the reconnaissance was initiated by the people, not God (v. 22). Military intelligence would therefore have been essential.

However, it is hardly conceivable that Moses would have sent twelve clan heads on a spying mission. Were such the case, he would neither have risked sending the chieftains nor have resorted to such a large number. It is noteworthy that for a true case of espionage—at Jericho—Joshua sent two (probably trained) spies (Josh. 2:1). Therefore, Moses' intention could only have been to send a cross-section of the tribal leaders so that their (hopefully positive) report would dispute the people's self-doubts concerning their ability to conquer the land.

men Hebrew ***'anashim*** can refer to important and brave men,[4] such as the members of the city council (Gen. 34:20; Judg. 8:15–17). Thus the men were not ordinary military scouts (Heb. ***meraggelim;*** cf. Josh. 6:23) but distinguished leaders of each tribe who were chosen to witness God's truth by verifying the virtues of His land. According to this tradition, then, the venture was more a test of faith than a military expedition.

land of Canaan The promised land, according to this tradition (v. 21), extended as far north as Antioch[5] or the Amanus Mountains.[6] Thus the purpose of the expedition was to claim possession symbolically and not just to reconnoiter the land (cf. Gen. 13:17).

a chieftain Hebrew ***nasi'***. For the meaning of this term, see Excursus 1. The root ***n-s-'*** used with the subject ***lev*** means "volunteer" (lit. "whom the heart lifts," e.g., Exod. 35:21), giving Rashbam the opportunity to suggest that Moses called for volunteers.

LORD's command, sent them out from the wilderness of Paran, all the men being leaders of the Israelites. 4And these were their names:

From the tribe of Reuben, Shammua son of Zaccur.

5From the tribe of Simeon, Shaphat son of Hori.

6From the tribe of Judah, Caleb son of Jephunneh.

7From the tribe of Issachar, Igal son of Joseph.

8From the tribe of Ephraim, Hosea son of Nun.

9From the tribe of Benjamin, Palti son of Rafu.

10From the tribe of Zebulun, Gaddiel son of Sodi.

11From the tribe of Joseph, namely, the tribe of Manasseh, Gaddi son of Susi.

12From the tribe of Dan, Ammiel son of Gemalli.

13From the tribe of Asher, Sethur son of Michael.

14From the tribe of Naphtali, Nahbi son of Vophsi.

15From the tribe of Gad, Geuel son of Machi.

16Those were the names of the men whom Moses sent to scout the land; but Moses changed the name of Hosea son of Nun to Joshua.

17When Moses sent them to scout the land of Canaan, he said to them, "Go up there into the Negeb and on into the hill country, 18and see what kind of country it is. Are the

מִמִּדְבַּר פָּארָן עַל־פִּי יְהוָה כֻּלָּם אֲנָשִׁים רָאשֵׁי
בְנֵי־יִשְׂרָאֵל הֵמָּה׃ 4 וְאֵלֶּה שְׁמוֹתָם
לְמַטֵּה רְאוּבֵן שַׁמּוּעַ בֶּן־זַכּוּר׃
5 לְמַטֵּה שִׁמְעוֹן שָׁפָט בֶּן־חוֹרִי׃
6 לְמַטֵּה יְהוּדָה כָּלֵב בֶּן־יְפֻנֶּה׃
7 לְמַטֵּה יִשָּׂשכָר יִגְאָל בֶּן־יוֹסֵף׃
8 לְמַטֵּה אֶפְרָיִם הוֹשֵׁעַ בִּן־נוּן׃
9 לְמַטֵּה בִנְיָמִן פַּלְטִי בֶּן־רָפוּא׃
10 לְמַטֵּה זְבוּלֻן גַּדִּיאֵל בֶּן־סוֹדִי׃
11 לְמַטֵּה יוֹסֵף לְמַטֵּה מְנַשֶּׁה גַּדִּי בֶּן־סוּסִי׃
12 לְמַטֵּה דָן עַמִּיאֵל בֶּן־גְּמַלִּי׃
13 לְמַטֵּה אָשֵׁר סְתוּר בֶּן־מִיכָאֵל׃
14 לְמַטֵּה נַפְתָּלִי נַחְבִּי בֶּן־וָפְסִי׃
15 לְמַטֵּה גָד גְּאוּאֵל בֶּן־מָכִי׃
16 אֵלֶּה שְׁמוֹת הָאֲנָשִׁים אֲשֶׁר־שָׁלַח מֹשֶׁה לָתוּר
אֶת־הָאָרֶץ וַיִּקְרָא מֹשֶׁה לְהוֹשֵׁעַ בִּן־נוּן יְהוֹשֻׁעַ׃
17 וַיִּשְׁלַח אֹתָם מֹשֶׁה לָתוּר אֶת־אֶרֶץ כְּנָעַן
וַיֹּאמֶר אֲלֵהֶם עֲלוּ זֶה בַּנֶּגֶב וַעֲלִיתֶם אֶת־הָהָר׃

3. ***by the LORD's command*** According to Rashi, the scouting mission stemmed from God's will.

all the men Hebrew *kullam 'anashim.* Rather, "all of them dignitaries"[7] (cf. the Comment to v. 2).

Paran Where they have camped (12:16).

4. ***Shammua*** Compare 2 Samuel 5:14.

Zaccur Compare Nehemiah 3:2.

5. ***Shaphat*** Also the name of the father of the prophet Elisha, in 1 Kings 19:16.

Hori Compare Genesis 36:22.

6. ***Caleb*** The name Caleb, from *kelev,* "dog," is probably part of a longer theophoric name like the Akkadian kalbi-Sin/Marduk, "the obedient servant of the god so-and-so." Dog as a metaphor for an obsequious servant is amply attested in the literature of the ancient Near East.[8]

7. ***Igal*** Also the name of one of David's heroes (2 Sam. 23:36).

9. ***Palti*** Short for Paltiel (2 Sam. 3:15).

10. ***Gaddiel*** The full name of Gad (v. 15; cf. Dan and Daniel) and Gaddi (v. 11).

12. ***Ammiel*** Compare 2 Samuel 9:4 and 1 Chronicles 3:5.

16. ***Joshua*** Hebrew *yehoshua',* originally *hoshea'* (v. 8; Deut. 32:44). Since the priestly tradition maintains that the theophoric element *yeho* (standing for the Tetragrammaton YHVH) was unknown before the Exodus (cf. Exod. 6:2), Joshua, who was born in Egypt, could not have carried this name from birth.[9]

17. ***When ... Canaan*** A resumption of verse 3a, necessitated by the long list of names,[10] a stylistic device called *Wiederaufnahme,* "repetitive resumption."

18 וּרְאִיתֶ֥ם אֶת־הָאָ֖רֶץ מַה־הִ֑וא וְאֶת־הָעָם֙ הַיֹּשֵׁ֣ב
עָלֶ֔יהָ הֶחָזָ֥ק הוּא֙ הֲרָפֶ֔ה הַמְעַ֥ט ה֖וּא אִם־רָֽב׃
19 וּמָ֣ה הָאָ֗רֶץ אֲשֶׁר־הוּא֙ יֹשֵׁ֣ב בָּ֔הּ הֲטוֹבָ֥ה הִ֖וא
אִם־רָעָ֑ה וּמָ֣ה הֶֽעָרִ֗ים אֲשֶׁר־הוּא֙ יוֹשֵׁ֣ב בָּהֵ֔נָּה
הַבְּמַֽחֲנִ֖ים אִ֥ם בְּמִבְצָרִֽים׃ 20 וּמָ֣ה הָ֠אָרֶץ הַשְּׁמֵנָ֨ה
הִ֜וא אִם־רָזָ֗ה הֲיֵֽשׁ־בָּ֥הּ עֵץ֙ אִם־אַ֔יִן וְהִ֨תְחַזַּקְתֶּ֔ם
וּלְקַחְתֶּ֖ם מִפְּרִ֣י הָאָ֑רֶץ וְהַ֨יָּמִ֔ים יְמֵ֖י בִּכּוּרֵ֥י עֲנָבִֽים׃
שני 21 וַֽיַּעֲל֖וּ וַיָּתֻ֣רוּ אֶת־הָאָ֑רֶץ מִמִּדְבַּר־צִ֥ן עַד־
רְחֹ֖ב לְבֹ֥א חֲמָֽת׃ 22 וַיַּעֲל֣וּ בַנֶּגֶב֮ וַיָּבֹ֣א עַד־חֶבְרוֹן֒

people who dwell in it strong or weak, few or many? 19 Is the country in which they dwell good or bad? Are the towns they live in open or fortified? 20 Is the soil rich or poor? Is it wooded or not? And take pains to bring back some of the fruit of the land."—Now it happened to be the season of the first ripe grapes.

21 They went up and scouted the land, from the wilderness of Zin to Rehob, at Lebo-hamath. 22 They went up into the Negeb and came to Hebron, where lived Ahiman,

there into Hebrew *zeh* is either an enclitic (e.g., 1 Kings 19:5) or, preferably, should be rendered "this way through," the equivalent of *ba-zeh*.[11] For *'alah be*, meaning "ascend by means of," see Genesis 28:12, Ezekiel 40:22,49; and compare verse 22. The goal is the hill country; the Negeb is the means of getting there.

Negeb Literally, "arid land," referring to the southern part of Judah below the central mountain range (between Beer-sheba and the Sinai Peninsula). The midrash compares Moses with a shrewd merchant who shows his poorest wares first (the Negeb) then the better kind (the hill country).[12]

and on into Hebrew *va-'alitem,* literally "and ascend." The ascent begins in the Negeb, and the altitude reaches 900 meters (3,000 ft.) at Hebron (v. 22).

hill country Of Judah (cf. Josh. 15:48; Judg. 1:19).

18. That is, God will give you the land but not without an effort of your own; so Rashbam.

19. country . . . good or bad According to Ibn Ezra, the reference is to climate; and according to Ramban it is to fertility. But fertility is the subject of the following verse (v. 20) and to judge by the scouts' report (vv. 26–28,32–33), climate was never a subject of their inquiry. Rather, "good or bad" is a general question concerning the land, as shown by the summary statement: "the land is exceedingly good" (14:7).

open So Targum Onkelos and Targum Jonathan. The Septuagint reads "unwalled."

20. rich Hebrew *shemenah,* literally "fat," that is, fertile. Targum Neofiti reads "whether its fruits are fat" (for this meaning cf. Gen. 27:28).

take pains The root *ḥ-z-k* in the Hitpael means "exert oneself" (cf. Gen. 48:2; Deut. 12:23).

season of the first ripe grapes Hence, July/August. According to the ritual calendar of the Dead Sea sect at Qumran, this was celebrated as a festival of first fruits on the third day of the month of Ab, seven weeks after Shavuot.[13]

THE EXPEDITION (vv. 21–24)

Two traditions have been conflated (see Excursus 29): that the scouts covered the entire land (v. 21) and that they journeyed only as far as Hebron (vv. 22–24). Note the double mention of "They went up" in verses 21 and 22. They meet up with Anakites at Hebron and return with samples of the fruit of the land.

21. Zin The wilderness of Zin above the wilderness of Paran, the point of origin of the scouts (v. 3). Like the scouts, Israel will also traverse it after leaving Paran (20:1). The exact bounds of either wilderness are not precisely known, but elsewhere Zin is cited as the southern border of the promised land (34:3–4; Josh. 15:1,3). The oasis of Kadesh-barnea possibly lies on the border between Paran and Zin (cf. v. 26 and see Map 3).

Sheshai, and Talmai, the Anakites.—Now Hebron was founded seven years before Zoan of Egypt.—23 They reached the wadi Eshcol, and there they cut down a branch with a single cluster of grapes—it had to be borne on a carrying frame by two of them—and some pomegranates and figs. 24 That place was named the wadi Eshcol because of the cluster that the Israelites cut down there.

וְשָׁם אֲחִימַן שֵׁשַׁי וְתַלְמַי יְלִידֵי הָעֲנָק וְחֶבְרוֹן
שֶׁבַע שָׁנִים נִבְנְתָה לִפְנֵי צֹעַן מִצְרָיִם׃ 23 וַיָּבֹאוּ
עַד־נַחַל אֶשְׁכֹּל וַיִּכְרְתוּ מִשָּׁם זְמוֹרָה וְאֶשְׁכּוֹל
עֲנָבִים אֶחָד וַיִּשָּׂאֻהוּ בַמּוֹט בִּשְׁנָיִם וּמִן־הָרִמֹּנִים
וּמִן־הַתְּאֵנִים׃ 24 לַמָּקוֹם הַהוּא קָרָא נַחַל אֶשְׁכּוֹל
עַל אֹדוֹת הָאֶשְׁכּוֹל אֲשֶׁר־כָּרְתוּ מִשָּׁם בְּנֵי

Rehob This site is unknown but must be distinguished from sites with the same name in the tribal territory of Asher (Josh. 19:28; Judg. 1:31). The text itself wishes to avoid this confusion by placing it at Lebo-hamath.

Lebo-hamath Lebo, identified with Libweh, was an important city on the southern border of the kingdom of Hamath on one of the sources of the Orontes River, which flows northward from there and turns westward to reach the Mediterranean about 50 kilometers (30 mi.) north of Ugarit. Lebo coincides with the northern boundary of Israel under David and Solomon (1 Kings 8:65) and Jeroboam II (2 Kings 14:25; Amos 6:14) and is specified as forming the northern boundary of the promised land (cf. Num. 34:7–9; Ezek. 48:1).

22. into Perhaps "by means of"; for this use of *ʿalah be,* compare verse 17.

Hebron The most sacred site in the southern part of the land, comparable in sanctity to Shechem in the north (see Map 3). Here all the forefathers and their wives (except for Rachel) were buried. Here Abraham was first promised the land, thereby making the scouts' rejection of it even more heinous.[14]

Hebron was the capital of the tribe of Judah, and David reigned there for seven years. Its earlier name was Kiriath-arba (Gen. 23:2; Josh. 14:15). Caleb had a special interest in Hebron, as explained in this story (see Excursus 31) and in the story of the conquest (cf. Josh. 14:6–15).

the Anakites Hebrew ***yelidei ha-ʿanak,*** also ***benei ha-ʿanak*** (v. 33), of the autochthonous population of Canaan before Israel's conquest; although, possibly, they were a family of Hittite noblemen (Gen. 23).[15] They were known and feared for their size (v. 33, LXX). Assuming the equivalence of ***ʿanakim*** and ***refaʾim*** (Deut. 2:11), descendants of these giants were still found along the Philistine coast (Josh. 11:21–22). Four of them were slain by David's warriors (2 Sam. 21:18–22), and their most famous representative, Goliath, was slain by David himself (1 Sam. 17). However, the possibility exists that the tradition of aboriginal giants stemmed from the dolmens and the great size and strength of the Canaanite fortresses. "We find this same idea among the Greeks, who reported that the huge walls of their ancient cities had been built by the Cyclops, giant artisans from Asia Minor. This tradition led to the expression 'Cyclopean' masonry, to describe the huge blocks used in constructing some ancient cities."[16]

The etymology of the name is uncertain. The rabbis associate it with the word for necklace (cf. Song 4:9; Gen. R. 26:7). Others claim it either refers to the ***Iy-ʿanaq*** mentioned in the Egyptian execration texts[17] or is of Hurrian or Philistine origin, the former related to the Khanaqqa of the Mezi texts,[18] the latter to the Greek ***anax,*** "lord," referring to the Philistine aristocracy.[19]

Zoan Also known as Tanis in Hellenistic sources.[20] Its identification with Avaris, the capital of the Hyksos pharaohs (1720–1570 B.C.E.) and the royal residence of Ramses II (1290–1233), generally thought to be the pharaoh of the Exodus, has now been proved to be wrong.[21] Zoan/Tanis was rebuilt as the capital of Egypt at the same time that Jerusalem became the capital of Israel under David. Thus it may not be an accident that the seven years David reigned in Hebron before moving his capital to Jerusalem (2 Sam. 2:11; 5:4–5) are identical with the seven years by which Hebron antedates the city of Zoan/Tanis,[22] in which case the verse is unrelated to the time of the Exodus. Rather, as the rabbis suggest, it enhances the status of Hebron; that is, it is even older than Egypt's capital Zoan/Tanis.[23]

23. wadi Eshcol Probably a proper name like the nearby grove called the terebinths of Mamre (cf. Gen. 14:13, where Eshkol is the brother of Mamre). *Eshkol* means "cluster"; thus the story may have arisen from the name of the wadi rather than the reverse (v. 24).

25At the end of forty days they returned from scouting
the land. 26They went straight to Moses and Aaron and the
whole Israelite community at Kadesh in the wilderness of
Paran, and they made their report to them and to the whole
community, as they showed them the fruit of the land.
27This is what they told him: "We came to the land you sent
us to; it does indeed flow with milk and honey, and this is
its fruit. 28However, the people who inhabit the country are

יִשְׂרָאֵל׃ 25 וַיָּשֻׁבוּ מִתּוּר הָאָרֶץ מִקֵּץ אַרְבָּעִים
יוֹם׃ 26 וַיֵּלְכוּ וַיָּבֹאוּ אֶל־מֹשֶׁה וְאֶל־אַהֲרֹן וְאֶל־
כָּל־עֲדַת בְּנֵי־יִשְׂרָאֵל אֶל־מִדְבַּר פָּארָן קָדֵשָׁה
וַיָּשִׁיבוּ אוֹתָם דָּבָר וְאֶת־כָּל־הָעֵדָה וַיַּרְאוּם אֶת־
פְּרִי הָאָרֶץ׃ 27 וַיְסַפְּרוּ־לוֹ וַיֹּאמְרוּ בָּאנוּ אֶל־
הָאָרֶץ אֲשֶׁר שְׁלַחְתָּנוּ וְגַם זָבַת חָלָב וּדְבַשׁ הִוא
וְזֶה־פִּרְיָהּ׃ 28 אֶפֶס כִּי־עַז הָעָם הַיֹּשֵׁב בָּאָרֶץ

single . . . two Emphasizing that a single cluster could only be borne by two men.[24] The Testament of Jacob (Gen. 49:11) uses the metaphor of tethering an ass to a vine to indicate the fertility of the same territory (of Judah).

carrying frame Hebrew *mot* (cf. 4:10). The unlikelihood that the scouts carried the grape cluster with them to the north has led critics to assign the northern expedition (v. 21) to a separate source (see Excursus 29).

THE REPORT (vv. 25–33)

The scouts give a balanced report of their findings, beginning with the positive side. However, the following detailed description of the obstacles clearly implies that they favor abandoning the idea of conquering the land. When Caleb, a minority of one, registers his opinion that the land can be taken, his colleagues make their opposition explicit: The inhabitants were so powerful and of such size that the scouts felt like grasshoppers.

26. Kadesh Also known as Kadesh-barnea (32:8), En-mishpat (Gen. 14:7), Meribah (Num. 20:13), or Meribath-kadesh (27:14). It forms part of the southern boundary of the promised land (34:4) and, hence, of the territory of Judah (Josh. 15:3). It is located either in the wilderness of Paran (Num. 13:26) or Zin (20:1). Perhaps it is to be located on the border of these two adjoining wildernesses (cf. the Comment to 10:12). The site is identified with a group of oases 80 kilometers (50 mi.) south of Beer-sheba, one of which still bears the name ʿAin Qadesh (see Map 1). Excavations have uncovered a large Iron Age fortress dating to the tenth century B.C.E., the time of King Solomon; but as yet there are no remains that date back to the time of Moses. Kadesh means "sanctuary" and its synonym, En-mishpat, means "the well of jurisprudence" or "judgment," names that are appropriate for a site in which Israel was settled for most of its wilderness sojourn (Deut. 2:14) and where it probably developed the fundamental rules of the cultic and legal system that molded it into a unified people.

27–28. him That is, Moses. According to the previous verse a report was made to Moses ***and*** to the entire community—indicating the possibility of different traditions.

the land you sent us to A hint of the attitude of the scouts: It is not the land "which the Lord promised" (see 13:2; 14:16,23,30,40).[25]

indeed Hebrew *ve-gam* means indeed it is true.[26] For the idiom "we came . . . (literally) indeed," compare Genesis 32:7.

flow with milk and honey The traditional phrase for the fruitfulness of the promised land (e.g., Exod. 3:8,17).[27] Hebrew *devash,* "honey," stems from wild bees or dates, most likely the latter; compare Joel 4:18, where milk and fruit juice (must) are parallel (cf. also Gen. 43:11; Deut. 8:8). The figure may be metaphoric: "fruits pure as milk and sweet as honey."[28]

The scouts answer Moses' questions factually: "flowing with milk and honey" in response to "Is the soil rich or poor" (v. 20); "this is its fruit" to "Is it wooded or not" (v. 20); "the cities are fortified" to "open or fortified" (v. 19). But the last answer is qualified by "however" (v. 28), indicating their wickedness. The rabbis sum it up: "Slander which does not have some truth in the beginning will not be accepted in the end."[29] Hence, "the scouts began with the truth, a favorable report, so as not to arouse suspicion."[30]

powerful, and the cities are fortified and very large; moreover, we saw the Anakites there. [29]Amalekites dwell in the Negeb region; Hittites, Jebusites, and Amorites inhabit the hill country; and Canaanites dwell by the Sea and along the Jordan."

[30]Caleb hushed the people before Moses and said, "Let us

וְהֶעָרִים בְּצֻרוֹת גְּדֹלֹת מְאֹד וְגַם־יְלִדֵי הָעֲנָק
רָאִינוּ שָׁם׃ 29 עֲמָלֵק יוֹשֵׁב בְּאֶרֶץ הַנֶּגֶב וְהַחִתִּי
וְהַיְבוּסִי וְהָאֱמֹרִי יוֹשֵׁב בָּהָר וְהַכְּנַעֲנִי יֹשֵׁב עַל־
הַיָּם וְעַל יַד הַיַּרְדֵּן׃ 30 וַיַּהַס* כָּלֵב אֶת־הָעָם

ס׳ רבתי לדעת קצת סופרים v. 30.

*28. **fortified*** The walls of ancient Canaanite cities were 9 to 15 meters high (30–50 ft.) and sometimes 4.5 meters (15 ft.) thick.

*29. **Amalekites*** A nomadic tribe whose domain extended from the Negeb of Judah into the Sinai Peninsula, virtually the same extent of Israel's wilderness trek. It was probably the dominant people in this region at this time (24:20). Thus the few oases and pasturages were probably points of contention between these two peoples, and their mutual hostility is readily understandable (Exod. 17:8–16; Deut. 25:19). The Amalekites also engaged in cattle breeding (1 Sam. 15), indicating that their sedentation had already begun. Wars against Amalek were waged during the reign of Saul to prevent their incursion across the southern border, and David won a decisive victory over them (1 Sam. 30:17–19). Their remnants are last recorded at Mount Seir in Transjordan (1 Chron. 4:41–43).

Negeb region Compare Numbers 14:43–45 and also Genesis 14:7, where the Amalekites are located near Kadesh.

Hittites The non-Semitic Hittite empire of Anatolia was destroyed around 1200 B.C.E., but the Hittite language and culture, carried by Hittite enclaves, persisted in northern Syria for another 500 years. Thus the Assyrians called northern Syria Hatti (Hittite land), which name they applied also to Canaan when they extended their conquests there. Hittite, therefore, like the older name Amorite (Amurru), is another designation for the population of Canaan (Ezek. 16:3,45). There is no evidence for discrete Hittite enclaves in Canaan. However, Hittite refugees may have entered Canaan from the north.[31]

Jebusites This is the name for the inhabitants of Jerusalem from at least as early as the conquest until it was captured by King David (2 Sam. 5:5–9). David allowed the Jebusite survivors to remain in the city (1 Chron. 21:7) and even purchased from the Jebusite Araunah the rocky hilltop to the north of Jebusite Jerusalem (renamed the City of David, 2 Sam. 5:9) for the building of the Temple.

Amorites *Amurru* in Akkadian means "west," and the term was used in the Mesopotamian cuneiform sources as early as the second half of the third millennium to designate the Semitic herdsmen and their territory in the Syrian steppe west of the Euphrates. In the eighteenth-century Mari texts, Amurru is a territory and kingdom in central Syria. As such it continues in Egyptian and Mesopotamian sources of the fourteenth and thirteenth centuries when its boundaries are most clearly defined: from the Mediterranean to the Orontes and to Canaan on the south. In the Bible "Amorite" occurs only as an ethnic label and does not refer to the Amurru kingdom, which disappeared around 1200 B.C.E. The Amorites are listed among the peoples that occupied Canaan (e.g., Gen. 15:21) but also as its total population (e.g., Gen. 15:16; Deut. 1:7,27), analogous to its usage in the Mesopotamian sources. Most specifically, Amorites are located in Transjordan, in the kingdoms of Sihon and Og (Num. 21:21,33), who are expressly labeled "the two Kings of the Amorites" (e.g., Deut. 3:8). Solomon is said to have pressed the remaining Cisjordanian Amorites into his labor gang (1 Kings 9:20–21).

Canaanites According to the El-Amarna letters of the fourteenth century B.C.E., Canaan was an Egyptian province ruled by Egyptian governors and local princes. Canaan was thus a geographical and political unit—Egypt's Asian province—that extended from the fortress of Sile (present El-Qantara on the Suez Canal) until its border with the Hittite empire near the source of the Orontes, that is, Lebo-hamath. In effect, the Egyptian province of Canaan is congruent with the borders of the promised land (34:1–12). The biblical term "land of Canaan" is an accurate historical reflex of this Egyptian province (e.g., 13:2,17). Thus it is natural that the name Canaanite could refer to all the inhabitants of this territory (e.g., Gen. 12:6; 50:11). But in this verse and in other passages

by all means go up, and we shall gain possession of it, for we shall surely overcome it."

31 But the men who had gone up with him said, "We cannot attack that people, for it is stronger than we." 32 Thus they spread calumnies among the Israelites about the land they had scouted, saying, "The country that we traversed and scouted is one that devours its settlers. All the people that we saw in it are men of great size; 33 we saw the

אֶל־מֹשֶׁה וַיֹּאמֶר עָלֹה נַעֲלֶה וְיָרַשְׁנוּ אֹתָהּ כִּי־
יָכוֹל נוּכַל לָהּ׃ 31 וְהָאֲנָשִׁים אֲשֶׁר־עָלוּ עִמּוֹ
אָמְרוּ לֹא נוּכַל לַעֲלוֹת אֶל־הָעָם כִּי־חָזָק הוּא
מִמֶּנּוּ׃ 32 וַיֹּצִיאוּ דִּבַּת הָאָרֶץ אֲשֶׁר תָּרוּ אֹתָהּ
אֶל־בְּנֵי יִשְׂרָאֵל לֵאמֹר הָאָרֶץ אֲשֶׁר עָבַרְנוּ בָהּ
לָתוּר אֹתָהּ אֶרֶץ אֹכֶלֶת יוֹשְׁבֶיהָ הִוא וְכָל־הָעָם
אֲשֶׁר־רָאִינוּ בְתוֹכָהּ אַנְשֵׁי מִדּוֹת׃ 33 וְשָׁם רָאִינוּ

(e.g., 14:25; Josh. 11:3), Canaanites are only one of the various autochthonous peoples residing there. The name "Amorite," as discussed previously, possesses the same dual connotation. In other passages, Canaanite designates a merchant class (cf. Isa. 23:8; Ezek. 17:4; Prov. 31:8). Its Akkadian equivalent, ***kinaḫḫu,*** also means "red purple"; since the eastern Mediterranean littoral was the source for this dye, it was handled exclusively by the Canaanite merchants, who in turn came to be identified with their product.

Negeb . . . hill country . . . Sea . . . Jordan Corresponding to the four major geographical divisions of the promised land: the southern wilderness, the central mountain chain above it from Beer-sheba northward and the plains on either side, the sea coast, and the Jordan rift.

30. Caleb Joshua took no part because his close affiliation with Moses would have discredited his opinion, according to Shadal. Alternatively, this verse reflects the tradition that Joshua was not one of the scouts (see Excursus 29).

hushed Hebrew *va-yahas,* a verb formed from the interjection *has,* "hush" (Judg. 3:19; Zech. 2:17).

before Hebrew *'el,* literally "to," according to the Septuagint, Targum Neofiti, and Peshitta.

before Moses So that they might listen to him, according to Targum Jonathan, Sforno, and Bekhor Shor. Deuteronomy 1:29 records Moses' reply. Some commentators feel that the verse is out of place since the people do not record their opposition until 14:1–3.[32] However, the negative report of verses 28–29 probably set off an audible murmuring, which Caleb and, presumably, Moses tried to quell. Moreover, the very structure of this story requires an opposing argument at this point (see Excursus 29).

all means . . . surely Expressed by adding the infinitive to the verb: *'aloh na'aleh, yakhol nukhal.* Caleb does not contradict the content of the scouts' report but only their conclusions.

31. gone up . . . attack Hebrew *'alu . . . la-'alot.* The same verb is used for the sake of irony: The few scouts who were able to "go up" now claim that a whole people cannot "go up."

attack So Targum Neofti; Hebrew *'el.*

32. spread calumnies Hebrew *hotsi' dibbah,* a false report, must be distinguished from *mevi' dibbah* (Gen. 37:2), a true report; so Ibn Ezra, Ramban, Radak. *Dibbah* from the root *d-b-b,* "to utter," is a neutral term and originally had to be qualified by the adjective *ra'ah,* "evil," to indicate calumny (cf. Num. 14:37; Gen. 37:2). However, it eventually developed this negative connotation even when used without qualification (e.g., 14:36).

among the Israelites Implied is that the scouts bypassed Moses and Aaron (v. 26) and spread the following calumnies (vv. 32–33) directly among the people.[33]

devours its settlers Israel hesitated up to this point. This statement is what tipped the scales to the negative side, according to Abravanel. The metaphor is usually explained as a reference to the land's infertility.[34] If so, the scouts would have been guilty of self-contradiction since they unequivocally affirmed the land's fertility and abundant population (vv. 27–28). Moreover, the people's only complaint is that they will die by the sword, but they say nothing about the natural condition of the land (14:3). The same metaphor occurs in Ezekiel 36:13–14, where the destruction of the land is clearly

Nephilim there—the Anakites are part of the Nephilim—and we looked like grasshoppers to ourselves, and so we must have looked to them."

אֶת־הַנְּפִילִים בְּנֵי עֲנָק מִן־הַנְּפִלִים וַנְּהִי בְעֵינֵינוּ
כַּחֲגָבִים וְכֵן הָיִינוּ בְּעֵינֵיהֶם׃

14 The whole community broke into loud cries, and the people wept that night. 2 All the Israelites railed against Moses and Aaron. "If only we had died in the land of Egypt," the whole community shouted at them, "or if only we might die in this wilderness! 3 Why is the LORD taking us

י״ד וַתִּשָּׂא כָּל־הָעֵדָה וַיִּתְּנוּ אֶת־קוֹלָם וַיִּבְכּוּ
הָעָם בַּלַּיְלָה הַהוּא׃ 2 וַיִּלֹּנוּ עַל־מֹשֶׁה וְעַל־אַהֲרֹן
כֹּל בְּנֵי יִשְׂרָאֵל וַיֹּאמְרוּ אֲלֵהֶם כָּל־הָעֵדָה לוּ־
מַתְנוּ בְּאֶרֶץ מִצְרַיִם אוֹ בַּמִּדְבָּר הַזֶּה לוּ־מָתְנוּ׃

the result of the wars waged upon it (cf. also Lev. 26:38).[35] An Assyrian king proclaims: "I destroyed (and) razed the city. I set it on fire. (Thus) I ravaged it."[36] The Arabic cognate "to eat" also means to conquer. An Islamic tradition states: "I was given orders concerning a town which eats other towns, i.e., its inhabitants conquer all other towns and take spoil."[37] Thus this idiom can only mean that the nature of the land is such that it will perpetually keep its inhabitants at war, perhaps a reflection of the geopolitical position of Canaan as a land bridge whose city-states were either fighting each other or stemming invasion from Asia or Africa.

A more fanciful rendering, given by Targum Jonathan, is "a land that slays its inhabitants with diseases," which the midrash explains in this way: As soon as the scouts entered the city, plagues struck. The inhabitants were so busy burying the dead that their attention was diverted from the scouts. The latter, instead of acknowledging God's miraculous salvation, reported that the land "devours its settlers."[38]

great size Hebrew *'anshei middot. Middah* means "measure" or "large measure" (1 Sam. 21:20 Ketiv; Isa. 45:14); compare *beit middot,* "large house, mansion."

33. ***Nephilim*** Literally, "fallen ones" (LXX reads "giants"); a reference to them appears in Genesis 6:4 as being the products of marriages between divine beings and mortal women. In the scouts' first report they are called Anakites (v. 28). Now their identification as the Nephilim could have only one purpose—to instill greater fear in the hearts of the people, for the gigantic stature and strength of these Anakites are now measured against a primordial and divine dimension.

grasshoppers The choice of this metaphor may have stemmed from dietary considerations. The grasshopper was the smallest edible creature (Lev. 11:22), a hint that this land that "devours its settlers" would easily devour them. Alternatively, the term grasshopper in biblical terms may be equivalent to the usage of "shrimp" in ours, that is, a designation of lilliputian dimensions. In either case, the effect of this vivid contrast was shattering. The scouts clearly have panicked and their panic infects the people. God's reaction is conjectured by the midrash: "I take no objection to your saying: 'we looked like grasshoppers to ourselves' but I take offense when you say 'so we must have looked to them.' How do you know how I made you look to them? Perhaps you appeared to them as angels?"[39]

CHAPTER 14 THE PEOPLE'S RESPONSE (vv. 1–5)

Demoralized by the scouts' report, the people panic and rail against Moses and even suggest finding another leader to take them back to Egypt.

1. ***broke into loud cries*** Hebrew *va-tisa' . . . va-yittnu 'et kolam va-yivku.* The idiom usually contains only one verb, *natan* (e.g., Gen. 45:2); here it is expanded into three verbs to heighten the effect.

that night "It was confirmed that they should weep on that night throughout their generations,"[1] reflecting the tradition that it fell on Tisha b'Av.

2. ***If only we had died . . . if only we might die*** Both clauses are expressed by the same

3 וְלָמָה יְהוָה מֵבִיא אֹתָנוּ אֶל־הָאָרֶץ הַזֹּאת
לִנְפֹּל בַּחֶרֶב נָשֵׁינוּ וְטַפֵּנוּ יִהְיוּ לָבַז הֲלוֹא טוֹב
לָנוּ שׁוּב מִצְרָיְמָה׃ 4 וַיֹּאמְרוּ אִישׁ אֶל־אָחִיו
נִתְּנָה רֹאשׁ וְנָשׁוּבָה מִצְרָיְמָה׃ 5 וַיִּפֹּל מֹשֶׁה
וְאַהֲרֹן עַל־פְּנֵיהֶם לִפְנֵי כָּל־קְהַל עֲדַת בְּנֵי
יִשְׂרָאֵל׃ 6 וִיהוֹשֻׁעַ בִּן־נוּן וְכָלֵב בֶּן־יְפֻנֶּה מִן־
הַתָּרִים אֶת־הָאָרֶץ קָרְעוּ בִּגְדֵיהֶם׃ 7 וַיֹּאמְרוּ אֶל־
כָּל־עֲדַת בְּנֵי־יִשְׂרָאֵל לֵאמֹר הָאָרֶץ אֲשֶׁר עָבַרְנוּ
בָהּ לָתוּר אֹתָהּ טוֹבָה הָאָרֶץ מְאֹד מְאֹד׃ שלישי

to that land to fall by the sword? Our wives and children will be carried off! It would be better for us to go back to
Egypt!" 4And they said to one another, "Let us head back for Egypt."

5Then Moses and Aaron fell on their faces before all the assembled congregation of the Israelites. 6And Joshua son of Nun and Caleb son of Jephunneh, of those who had scouted the land, rent their clothes 7and exhorted the whole Israelite community: "The land that we traversed and scouted is an exceedingly good land. 8If the LORD is pleased

Hebrew phrase, ***lu matnu,*** in reverse order: literally "If only we had died in the land of Egypt . . . if only in this wilderness we might die."

*3. **Why is the LORD*** The Deuteronomic version turns the question into a charge: "It is because [He] hates us" (Deut. 1:27).

better for us In contrast to the purported evil of the Lord (cf. the Comment to 11:1).

to go back to Egypt Forbidden forever (Deut. 17:16; 28:68; Hos. 11:15). In Egypt they were forced into slavery; now they return to it willingly. The yearning for Egypt is a symbol of Israel's apostasy (Isa. 30:1–7).

*4. **head back for*** Hebrew ***natan ro'sh,*** literally "set the head," may be equivalent to ***natan lev,*** "set the heart" or "set the mind, decide" (cf. Eccles. 1:13,17; cf. Neh. 9:29).[2] Alternatively, ***natan*** in the sense of "appoint" (e.g., Gen. 41:41) would mean "appoint a leader,"[3] implying insurrection, a complete break with Moses—and with God (cf. v. 9). For the defecting militia to succeed, new leadership would be required.[4]

*5. **fell on their faces*** If this act took place in the Tent of Meeting (support for which may be drawn from vv. 10–11: God speaks to Moses from there), then its purpose would be to propitiate God on behalf of Israel (e.g., 20:6). However, a propitiatory act would be premature before the announcement of the punishment. Besides, this act takes place before the people and not in the Shrine. Rather, comparison with 16:4–5 indicates that its purpose is to propitiate not God but the people.[5] Indeed, it is because of the leaders' self-humiliation that Joshua and Caleb now intervene.[6] Alternatively, the act may reflect the leaders' helplessness and despair before their distempered people (cf. 16:4).

THE COUNTERRESPONSE OF JOSHUA AND CALEB (vv. 6–10)

The land is good, the enemy impotent, and God is with us. Their words anger the people, who threaten to stone them.

*6. **of those who had scouted the land*** This explanation is needed either because Joshua has not yet been introduced into the dialogue, or because it stems from the tradition in which no dialogue has yet taken place (see Excursus 29), or simply to indicate that the other spies did not rend their clothes.

rent their clothes Out of grief and distress (cf. Gen. 37:29) because of the humiliation heaped on Moses and particularly because of the implied rebellion against God. To this day clothes or a symbolic substitute, such as a ribbon, are rent *(keri'ah)* by Jews upon learning of the death of a close member of the family.

*7. **good*** In answer to Moses' query concerning the land (13:19) and in contrast to the "good" of returning to Egypt (v. 3).

with us, He will bring us into that land, a land that flows with milk and honey, and give it to us; 9only you must not rebel against the LORD. Have no fear then of the people of the country, for they are our prey: their protection has departed from them, but the LORD is with us. Have no fear of them!" 10As the whole community threatened to pelt them with stones, the Presence of the LORD appeared in the Tent of Meeting to all the Israelites.

11And the LORD said to Moses, "How long will this people spurn Me, and how long will they have no faith in Me despite all the signs that I have performed in their midst? 12I will strike them with pestilence and disown them, and I will make of you a nation far more numerous than they!" 13But Moses said to the LORD, "When the

8 אִם־חָפֵץ בָּנוּ יְהוָה וְהֵבִיא אֹתָנוּ אֶל־הָאָרֶץ
הַזֹּאת וּנְתָנָהּ לָנוּ אֶרֶץ אֲשֶׁר־הִוא זָבַת חָלָב
וּדְבָשׁ׃ 9 אַךְ בַּיהוָה אַל־תִּמְרֹדוּ וְאַתֶּם אַל־
תִּירְאוּ אֶת־עַם הָאָרֶץ כִּי לַחְמֵנוּ הֵם סָר צִלָּם
מֵעֲלֵיהֶם וַיהוָה אִתָּנוּ אַל־תִּירָאֻם׃ 10 וַיֹּאמְרוּ כָּל־
הָעֵדָה לִרְגּוֹם אֹתָם בָּאֲבָנִים וּכְבוֹד יְהוָה נִרְאָה
בְּאֹהֶל מוֹעֵד אֶל־כָּל־בְּנֵי יִשְׂרָאֵל׃ פ
11 וַיֹּאמֶר יְהוָה אֶל־מֹשֶׁה עַד־אָנָה יְנַאֲצֻנִי הָעָם
הַזֶּה וְעַד־אָנָה לֹא־יַאֲמִינוּ בִי בְּכֹל הָאֹתוֹת אֲשֶׁר
עָשִׂיתִי בְּקִרְבּוֹ׃ 12 אַכֶּנּוּ בַדֶּבֶר וְאוֹרִשֶׁנּוּ וְאֶעֱשֶׂה
אֹתְךָ לְגוֹי־גָּדוֹל וְעָצוּם מִמֶּנּוּ׃ 13 וַיֹּאמֶר מֹשֶׁה

*9. **Have no fear*** Literally, "And you have no fear." The addition of ***ve-'attem*** implies that others may have cause to fear these nations but not Israel, for "the Lord is with us."

prey The Targums paraphrase: "for they are delivered into our hands." To eat means to conquer (e.g., Jer. 2:3; Pss. 14:4; 79:7).

protection Hebrew *tsel,* literally "shade," an appropriate term for those who live under a tropical sun (cf. Isa. 32:2). Others say it refers to the shade cast by the shield;[7] some render "strength."[8] However, the mention of "the Lord" indicates that "shade" is a metaphor for divine protection, attested elsewhere (e.g., Pss. 91:1; 121:5)[9] and supported by the verb ***sur me'al,*** "depart," used of divine withdrawal (e.g., 1 Sam. 28:15; Judg. 16:20). Some of the rabbis believe that this term is an allusion to the guardian angel appointed over each nation,[10] a belief that has firm support in Scripture (e.g., Deut. 32:30–31).

*10. **threatened*** Hebrew ***'amar*** can mean "think, desire" (e.g., Gen. 20:11).

to pelt them with stones "Them" refers to Moses and Aaron (v. 5) or to Joshua and Caleb (vv. 6–9). Cf. Exod. 17:4 for a similar threat.

Presence of the LORD Hebrew ***kavod*** stands for the cloud-encased fire that descended over the Tabernacle (cf. 9:15–23). Some of the versions actually insert "appeared in [the cloud over] the Tent."[11] The purpose of God's descent is to speak to Moses (v. 11) and to deter Israel from attacking Moses (and Aaron). While God appears to Israel in the Tabernacle courtyard, Moses enters the Tent to hear His command (cf. 7:89; Excursus 28).

GOD'S RESPONSE (vv. 11–38)

God wishes to destroy Israel at once, sparing only Moses. But Moses argues that the nations will regard Israel's destruction not as the result of its sin but of God's inability to bring them to the land. His intercession tempers God's judgment: The present generation will die in the wilderness, save Joshua and Caleb; their children who are now under the age of twenty will inherit the land.

*12. **I will . . . I will*** Rather, "Let me . . . let me." The verbs should be taken as cohortatives, equivalent to "Now let Me be, that My anger may blaze forth against them and that I may destroy them and make of you a great nation" (Exod. 32:10); that is, in the two major demonstrations of apostasy, the incidents of the golden calf and the scouts, God asks Moses to intercede on behalf of Israel. Here, then, is a recognition that prophetic intercession can block divine retribution. This and more: God is actually cuing Moses in his role as intercessor and intermediary—perhaps even testing him—that by his intercession he may save his people (cf. Exod. 32:10).[12] The contrast between God's

Egyptians, from whose midst You brought up this people
in Your might, hear the news, 14they will tell it to the
inhabitants of that land. Now they have heard that You, O
Lord, are in the midst of this people; that You, O Lord,
appear in plain sight when Your cloud rests over them and
when You go before them in a pillar of cloud by day and in
a pillar of fire by night. 15If then You slay this people to a
man, the nations who have heard Your fame will say, 16'It

אֶל־יְהוָה וְשָׁמְעוּ מִצְרַיִם כִּי־הֶעֱלִיתָ בְכֹחֲךָ אֶת־
הָעָם הַזֶּה מִקִּרְבּוֹ: 14 וְאָמְרוּ אֶל־יוֹשֵׁב הָאָרֶץ
הַזֹּאת שָׁמְעוּ כִּי־אַתָּה יְהוָה בְּקֶרֶב הָעָם הַזֶּה
אֲשֶׁר־עַיִן בְּעַיִן נִרְאָה | אַתָּה יְהוָה וַעֲנָנְךָ עֹמֵד
עֲלֵהֶם וּבְעַמֻּד עָנָן אַתָּה הֹלֵךְ לִפְנֵיהֶם יוֹמָם
וּבְעַמּוּד אֵשׁ לָיְלָה: 15 וְהֵמַתָּה אֶת־הָעָם הַזֶּה
כְּאִישׁ אֶחָד וְאָמְרוּ הַגּוֹיִם אֲשֶׁר־שָׁמְעוּ אֶת־
שִׁמְעֲךָ לֵאמֹר: 16 מִבִּלְתִּי יְכֹלֶת יְהוָה לְהָבִיא

offer to Moses and his subsequent "offer" to Israel is striking. The former is stated as a question; the latter, however, is a decision made irrevocable by an oath (vv. 21,28),[13] another indication that God was trying Moses and that by His question, He sought to evoke an intercessional response (cf. Amos 7:1–9; Jer. 7:16; 11:14).

disown Hebrew ***horish*** (Hifil) reverses the meaning of ***yarash*** (Kal), "inherit." Israel will no longer be God's inheritance (cf. Exod. 34:9; Deut. 32:9).

I will make of you *Ve-'et beit 'avikha,* "and your father's house," is added by the Septuagint and the Samaritan, thereby including Aaron and the priesthood among the survivors. God's initial reaction is identical to the one He expressed at the apostasy of the golden calf (Exod. 32:10), except that here the comparative is used: not a great nation but a greater one.

far more numerous Hebrew ***gadol ve-'atsum min,*** literally "greater and mightier than," in a physical not a spiritual sense (cf. Gen. 18:18; Deut. 26:5).

13–19. Moses intercedes. In his first argument (vv. 13–16) he poses the following theological problem: How is God to punish Israel and yet maintain the reputation of His power in the world? Ezekiel saw the same problem in Israel's exile and, hence, predicted Israel's restoration, even though undeserved (Ezek. 36:16–36; 39:21–29).[14]

13. from whose . . . might Hebrew ***ki . . . mi-kirbo*** is parenthetic.[15]

the news Not in the text but implied by the verb ***ve-sham'u,*** "hear."

14. they will tell it to Hebrew ***ve-'amru 'el.*** The word "it" is omitted and is understood. The Septuagint reads ***ve-'ulam kol,*** "However all (the inhabitants of this land have heard . . .)," providing a clearer text. In any case, the passage reflects two potential comments on God's proposed destruction of Israel, one made by Egypt, the other by Canaan; both are fused in verses 15b–16.

Now they Must be inferred or supplied, reading ***'asher.***[16] However, these words need not be inserted if the Septuagint reading is original.

appear Hebrew ***nir'ah,*** literally "appeared" (past tense), referring to the Sinaitic theophany beheld by the elders (Exod. 24:10).[17]

in plain sight Hebrew ***'ayin be-'ayin,*** literally "eye for eye" (cf. Isa. 52:8).

Your cloud rests over them Cf. 10:34.

pillar Hebrew ***'amud.*** The Assyrians carried the emblems of their gods on a standard called ***imittu,*** which is cognate with Hebrew ***'amud.*** Placed on a chariot the divine emblems went before the Assyrian armies as ***ālikāt maḫri,*** "forerunners." Since graven images were forbidden in Israelite religion, the presence of the divine guide was indicated by the pillar of the cloud.

15. If then Not in the text but implied. Targum Yerushalmi elaborates: "And after all these miracles, will you . . ."

the nations That is, Egypt and Canaan.

your fame Hebrew ***shim'akha.*** The Septuagint reads ***shimkha,*** "your name," a rendering it follows elsewhere (e.g., Gen. 29:13; Deut. 2:25).

must be because the LORD was powerless to bring that people into the land He had promised them on oath that He slaughtered them in the wilderness.' 17Therefore, I pray, let my LORD's forbearance be great, as You have declared, saying, 18'The LORD! slow to anger and abounding in kindness; forgiving iniquity and transgression; yet not remitting all punishment, but visiting the iniquity of fathers upon children, upon the third and fourth generations.'

אֶת־הָעָם הַזֶּה אֶל־הָאָרֶץ אֲשֶׁר־נִשְׁבַּע לָהֶם
וַיִּשְׁחָטֵם בַּמִּדְבָּר׃ 17 וְעַתָּה יִגְדַּל־נָא כֹּחַ אֲדֹנָי
כַּאֲשֶׁר דִּבַּרְתָּ לֵאמֹר׃ 18 יְהוָה אֶרֶךְ אַפַּיִם וְרַב־
חֶסֶד נֹשֵׂא עָוֺן וָפָשַׁע וְנַקֵּה לֹא יְנַקֶּה פֹּקֵד עֲוֺן
אָבוֹת עַל־בָּנִים עַל־שִׁלֵּשִׁים וְעַל־רִבֵּעִים׃

v. 17. י׳ רבתי

16. It must be Not in the text, but understood.

powerless Not because of hate (Exod. 32:12; Deut. 1:27) but impotence.[18]

promised them on oath Such an oath is explicitly recorded only as given to Abraham (e.g., Gen. 15:18; 22:16; 26:3) but not to the generation of the Exodus. In the Exodus narratives only the oath to the fathers is mentioned (Exod. 6:8, the basis for v. 30; see below). However, the oath must be alluded to in God's promises of fulfillment (Exod. 3:8,17), and God's promise is equivalent to an oath (cf. Deut. 19:8, where *nishba'* "swear," and *dibber* "promise," are equivalent).[19] One other verse ostensibly mentions the oath to the Exodus generation: "as He swore to you and to your fathers, and has given it to you" (Exod. 13:11). However, its meaning probably is "swore to your fathers to give to you" (Exod. 13:5; cf. Ramban on Exod. 13:11).

17–18. A second argument: God's nature is merciful (cf. Exod. 34:6–7).

forbearance Hebrew *koaḥ,* literally "strength," that is, "the strength to hold back from destroying Israel."[20] *Koaḥ* meaning "forbearance" is found in Job 6:12 and especially Nahum 1:3, a passage clearly based on this verse, where *gedal koaḥ* follows "slow to anger" and hence also emphasizes divine forbearance. "Who is mighty? He who conquers his passion" (Mish. Avot 4:1).

be great As opposed to the Lord's wish to make Moses great (v. 12), Moses asks God to make His forbearance great.

18. The LORD! slow to anger . . . A comparison with the full formula of God's attributes in Exodus 34:6–7 reveals the following omissions: (1) "A God compassionate and gracious . . ., (2) and faithfulness . . ., (3) extending kindness to the thousandth generation . . ., (4) and sin . . ., (5) children's children." Since the formula is curtailed even more drastically elsewhere (cf. Exod. 20:6, Deut. 5:10, etc.), it stands to reason that only those portions are quoted that are applicable to the situation. The major omissions (1) and (3) are due to the particular nature of Moses' plea. He did not ask for the cancellation of punishment but only for its postponement[21] or for its execution as long as God would maintain His covenant with Israel (see Excursus 32). *'Emet,* "faithfulness" (2) is actually supplied in a few manuscripts as well as by most of the versions;[22] others justify its omission on the grounds that *'emet,* literally "truth," focusing on God's justice, is inappropriate in a plea for mercy.[23] "And sin" (4) is also supplied in the above manuscripts and versions, but its omission can be rationalized on the grounds that *ḥatta'ah* generally refers to inadvertent sin (e.g., Lev. 4:2), an inappropriate designation for Israel's open rebellion.[24] The omission of (5) has no meaningful consequence.

not remitting all punishment Hebrew *ve-nakkeh lo' yenakkeh,* literally "acquitting not acquitting," that is, not completely acquitting, an idiom that allows for the midrashic interpretation: "acquitting those who return to His law but not acquitting those who will not return."[25] This is an early echo of the rabbis' interpretation, which allowed them to cut off the quotation at *ve-nakkeh* (see Excursus 32).

visiting the iniquity Ostensibly it exacerbates God's retribution, but it is actually an aspect of God's mercy,[26] for if He cannot forgive, at least He can attenuate the punishment by distributing it over a number of generations.[27] Deuteronomy, however, reinterprets this attribute to mean that God will punish (or bless) succeeding generations only if they follow in the ways of their fathers (e.g., Deut. 5:9–10; 7:9). However, the probability is that God's right to punish children for their father's sins is indeed invoked; for details, see Excursus 32.

¹⁹Pardon, I pray, the iniquity of this people according to Your great kindness, as You have forgiven this people ever since Egypt."

²⁰And the LORD said, "I pardon, as you have asked. ²¹Nevertheless, as I live and as the LORD's Presence fills the whole world, ²²none of the men who have seen My Presence and the signs that I have performed in Egypt and in the wilderness, and who have tried Me these many times and have disobeyed Me, ²³shall see the land that I promised

סְלַח־נָ֗א לַעֲוֺ֤ן הָעָ֣ם הַזֶּה֙ כְּגֹ֣דֶל חַסְדֶּ֔ךָ וְכַאֲשֶׁ֤ר נָשָׂ֙אתָה֙ לָעָ֣ם הַזֶּ֔ה מִמִּצְרַ֖יִם וְעַד־הֵֽנָּה: 20 וַיֹּ֣אמֶר יְהֹוָ֔ה סָלַ֖חְתִּי כִּדְבָרֶֽךָ: 21 וְאוּלָ֖ם חַי־אָ֑נִי וְיִמָּלֵ֥א כְבוֹד־יְהֹוָ֖ה אֶת־כׇּל־הָאָֽרֶץ: 22 כִּ֣י כׇל־הָאֲנָשִׁ֗ים הָרֹאִ֤ים אֶת־כְּבֹדִי֙ וְאֶת־אֹ֣תֹתַ֔י אֲשֶׁר־עָשִׂ֥יתִי בְמִצְרַ֖יִם וּבַמִּדְבָּ֑ר וַיְנַסּ֣וּ אֹתִ֗י זֶ֚ה עֶ֣שֶׂר פְּעָמִ֔ים וְלֹ֥א שָׁמְע֖וּ בְּקוֹלִֽי: 23 אִם־יִרְאוּ֙ אֶת־הָאָ֔רֶץ אֲשֶׁ֥ר

children All the Targums render "rebellious children," implying the Deuteronomic and rabbinic interpretation, above.

19. *Pardon* Hebrew *salaḥ*, implying not the absolution of sin but the suspension of anger;[28] that they not die immediately and their children may survive;[29] that they live out their lives and their children inherit;[30] that they not be destroyed and the covenant maintained (e.g., Jer. 5:1,7).[31] See further, Excursus 32.

as You have forgiven The objection is raised that no previous forgiveness is recorded in the wilderness murmuring tradition, just a stay of punishment. Thus God can offer neither forgiveness nor reconciliation.[32] However, neither does the revelation of God's attributes in the original passage (Exod. 34:6–7) result in pardon, and yet the covenant is renewed (Exod. 34:10). The problem can be resolved if the verb *salaḥ* is understood as denoting reconciliation, not pardon (see Excursus 32).

kindness Rather, "constancy." For this connotation of *ḥesed*, see Excursus 32.

forgiven Hebrew *nasa'* has three meanings: (1) carry a burden, that is, bear with Israel; (2) be gracious (with the object *panim*, "face"; cf. 6:26); and (3) forgive (with the object *'avon/ḥet'*, "sin"). Only the first meaning (and possibly the second) applies. Moses does not ask God to forgive Israel but to bear with (lit. "carry") His people and, despite their failings, continue to maintain His covenant with them (see Excursus 32). That the notion of covenant is paramount here is evidenced by the use of the terms *'avon, ḥesed,* and *nasa'* in this verse, which corresponds with the consecutive sequence of *ḥesed, nose' 'avon* in the last of the Lord's attributes (v. 18), implying that it is the Lord's *ḥesed,* His fidelity, that motivates Him to preserve His covenantal relationship with Israel.

ever since Hebrew *'ad hennah*, a temporal designation (e.g., Gen. 44:28). But it could also be rendered spatially, "(from Egypt) till this place" (cf. Job 2:2).[33]

21. *as I live* Man swears by God but the Lord God swears by His own life, essence, or being since there is no superior entity (e.g., Gen. 22:16).

and . . . fills Hebrew *ve-yimmale'*; that is, as God's power is worldwide, He has the power to fulfill his oath.[34] Or interpreting the *vav* as purposive: God will fulfill His oath so that the whole world will acknowledge His justice.[35] Or so that the whole world (especially Egypt and Canaan) will see that God is not powerless.[36] Or reading *va-yimmale'* the clause bears a parenthetical sense: "while the whole world was filled by His Presence" (during the oath).

This parenthesis is integral to the literary structure of God's reply (vv. 20–24): The words (written consonantally) *vyml'* and *'rts* are repeated chiastically, that is, in reverse order (vv. 20,24). The repetition of *kavod* (vv. 21,22) also binds this unit together, and the "measure for measure" principle of divine retribution can be fully appreciated—the land full of God's Presence will not be seen by those who have seen God's Presence.[37]

22. *men* Generic for persons but does not include children, who could not be the subjects of the following verbs: "seen . . . tried . . . disobeyed." In the Deuteronomic version the phrase "this evil generation" (Deut. 1:35) is added, but it is already implied here.

Presence Hebrew *kavod*, as in the previous verse, implies the manifestation of God's power (e.g., Ps. 96:3).

on oath to their fathers; none of those who spurn Me shall see it. 24 But My servant Caleb, because he was imbued with a different spirit and remained loyal to Me—him will I bring into the land that he entered, and his offspring shall hold it as a possession. 25 Now the Amalekites and the Canaanites occupy the valleys. Start out, then, tomorrow and march into the wilderness by way of the Sea of Reeds."

26 The LORD spoke further to Moses and Aaron, 27 "How

נִשְׁבַּעְתִּי לַאֲבֹתָם וְכָל־מְנַאֲצַי לֹא יִרְאוּהָ׃
24 וְעַבְדִּי כָלֵב עֵקֶב הָיְתָה רוּחַ אַחֶרֶת עִמּוֹ
וַיְמַלֵּא אַחֲרָי וַהֲבִיאֹתִיו אֶל־הָאָרֶץ אֲשֶׁר־בָּא
שָׁמָּה וְזַרְעוֹ יוֹרִשֶׁנָּה׃ 25 וְהָעֲמָלֵקִי וְהַכְּנַעֲנִי יוֹשֵׁב
בָּעֵמֶק מָחָר פְּנוּ וּסְעוּ לָכֶם הַמִּדְבָּר דֶּרֶךְ יַם־סוּף׃
פ רביעי 26 וַיְדַבֵּר יְהוָה אֶל־מֹשֶׁה וְאֶל־
אַהֲרֹן לֵאמֹר׃ 27 עַד־מָתַי לָעֵדָה הָרָעָה הַזֹּאת

many The Septuagint renders "the tenth time," the earliest allusion to the later rabbinic tradition that Israel was subjected to ten trials in the wilderness.[38]

23. shall see "None . . . who have seen (v. 22) . . . shall see"; measure for measure.

spurn Me shall see it An addition to the oath in order to form an inclusion with God's opening words (cf. "spurn Me" in v. 11).[39]

24. Caleb See Excursus 31.

spirit Here *ruaḥ* bears a psychological connotation (e.g., Gen. 26:35).

remained loyal to Me Hebrew *mille' 'aḥar*, literally "follow fully,"[40] is used almost exclusively in describing Caleb (32:11–12). Caleb's loyalty consists of confirming God's word (cf. 1 Kings 1:14), bearing witness to His truth (so 1 Macc. 2:56).

shall hold it as a possession For this meaning of *yorishennah,* see the Comment to 33:54; others vocalize it *yirashennah.*[41] Caleb will be granted the right to enter the land he traversed (13:22) and bequeath it to his children as their inheritance. This does not mean that the rest of Canaan, which was not scouted according to the Calebite tradition, will not be possessed by the rest of the Israelites (see Excursus 29).

25. the Amalekites and the Canaanites Compare 13:29. Again measure for measure: The scouts frightened Israel by mentioning these nations, although they posed no threat; now that Israel has spurned God, they indeed become a threat.[42]

occupy the valleys In 13:29 the Canaanites are located along the sea (also Josh. 5:1; 11:3) and the Amalekites in the Negeb (cf. v. 45). The point here is that all entrances are blocked.

by way of the Sea of Reeds Although the reference here probably is to the Gulf of Elath, the fact that the same name is used for the sea that Israel crossed in leaving Egypt illustrates the measure for measure principle again. If Israel desires to return to Egypt (v. 4), then it should turn back—but only to die in the wilderness (vv. 28–29). Implied is that Israel must leave Kadesh at once but the later reference to Kadesh in 20:1 may signify that they remained in the vicinity of Kadesh until the fortieth year (see 33:38).

26–38. These verses interrupt the sequence of verses 25, 39–45, as is confirmed by Deuteronomy 1:40–41; that is, as soon as God orders Israel to retreat, they attempt an incursion into Canaan on their own. That this passage contains an alternative response of the Lord to the people's rebellion is clear from the similarity in content and wording: the question, "how long" (v. 11), "How much longer" (v. 20); the oath, "as I live" (vv. 21,28); the punishment, death in the wilderness for the adults (vv. 23,29). In the second passage, Joshua and Caleb are exempted from this punishment, and the entrance to the land is postponed for forty years. These new stipulations account for the inclusion of the second version. Verses 36–38 are an editorial note anticipating the execution of the punishment.

26. Aaron Aaron and the Levites are also exempt from God's oath of retribution since the tribe of Levi was not represented among the scouts.[43] Furthermore, the oath implicitly exempts Levi in specifying the census of those over twenty (v. 29; cf. 1:3), which did not include Levi (1:47–48): Levi was counted from the age of one month (3:15) in a separate census.[44] Finally, Eleazar, Aaron's son and successor, is assuredly over twenty at the time of the census (cf. 3:32; 4:16) and yet is vouchsafed entrance into the land (e.g., Josh. 24:33).

much longer shall that wicked community keep muttering
against Me? Very well, I have heeded the incessant muttering of the Israelites against Me. 28Say to them: 'As I live,'
says the LORD, 'I will do to you just as you have urged Me.
29In this very wilderness shall your carcasses drop. Of all of
you who were recorded in your various lists from the age of
twenty years up, you who have muttered against Me, 30not
one shall enter the land in which I swore to settle you—
save Caleb son of Jephunneh and Joshua son of Nun.
31Your children who, you said, would be carried off—these

אֲשֶׁר הֵמָּה מַלִּינִים עָלַי אֶת־תְּלֻנּוֹת בְּנֵי יִשְׂרָאֵל
אֲשֶׁר הֵמָּה מַלִּינִים עָלַי שָׁמָעְתִּי׃ 28 אֱמֹר אֲלֵהֶם
חַי־אָנִי נְאֻם־יְהוָה אִם־לֹא כַּאֲשֶׁר דִּבַּרְתֶּם בְּאָזְנָי
כֵּן אֶעֱשֶׂה לָכֶם׃ 29 בַּמִּדְבָּר הַזֶּה יִפְּלוּ פִגְרֵיכֶם
וְכָל־פְּקֻדֵיכֶם לְכָל־מִסְפַּרְכֶם מִבֶּן עֶשְׂרִים שָׁנָה
וָמָעְלָה אֲשֶׁר הֲלִינֹתֶם עָלָי׃ 30 אִם־אַתֶּם תָּבֹאוּ
אֶל־הָאָרֶץ אֲשֶׁר נָשָׂאתִי אֶת־יָדִי לְשַׁכֵּן אֶתְכֶם
בָּהּ כִּי אִם־כָּלֵב בֶּן־יְפֻנֶּה וִיהוֹשֻׁעַ בִּן־נוּן׃
31 וְטַפְּכֶם אֲשֶׁר אֲמַרְתֶּם לָבַז יִהְיֶה וְהֵבֵיאתִי
אֹתָם וְיָדְעוּ אֶת־הָאָרֶץ אֲשֶׁר מְאַסְתֶּם בָּהּ׃

27. wicked community That is, the scouts, the subject of the first mention of muttering in this verse.[45] However, this very phrase, "wicked community," reoccurs in verse 35 where it clearly refers to Israel.[46]

heeded Hebrew *shama'ti.* Rather, "heard." The second half of this verse is not a mechanical repetition of the first half (cf. Lev. 21:21 for a similar structure). It is modeled, together with the beginning of the next verse, on Exodus 16:11–12: God speaks to Moses, acknowledges *(shama')* the muttering *(telunnot)* and concludes with the words "say to them."[47] The pre-Sinai muttering was answered by God's gracious gift; here, in the post-Sinai wanderings, their mutterings are met with punishment (see the Introduction).

28. As I live Compare verse 21.

says the LORD Hebrew *ne'um YHVH,* a favored expression in the prophetic books, is found in only one other place in the Torah, Genesis 22:16, where it also introduces an oath.

I will do just as you Israel is about to achieve its wish, "if only we might die in this wilderness!" (v. 2).

urged Me Literally, "spoken into my ear." This idiom conveys a tone of belligerency and presumptuousness, just as in 11:1,18, that is, "pestered me."

29. this very wilderness That is, Paran.

drop As you were afraid "to drop" *(nafal)* by the sword (v. 3) in the land, so you will drop *(nafal)* in the wilderness. "Drop" may also imply without burial (cf. *yittammu,* vv. 33,35). However, the full measure for measure principle is realized in verse 43. Here it is anticipated.[48]

twenty years up Because they were of fighting age (cf. 1:3) and they refused to fight.[49]

30–33. Judging by the vocabulary and structure, these verses are a literary unit.[50]

30. swore Hebrew *nasa' yad,* "raise the hand," that is, heavenward,[51] calling God to witness. It is the same gesticulation as raising the hand(s) in prayer (e.g., Pss. 25:2; 63:5), but it also symbolizes the direct address to God.[52] (For biblical examples of raising the hand in oath, cf. Gen. 14:22; Exod. 6:8.) Exodus 6:8 provides the backdrop against which to see the ironic turn that this oath has taken. There God swears that He will bring the generation of the Exodus to the land; here He swears He will bring not the parents but the children to the land (cf. Ps. 106:26).

31. Your children Hebrew *ve-tappkhem,* referring to all up to the age of twenty (v. 29).[53]

carried off Compare verse 3.[54]

they shall know the land In contrast to their fathers, who shall know God's punishment (v. 34).

you have rejected Compare Psalms 106:24.

will I allow to enter; they shall know the land that you have
rejected. 32 But your carcasses shall drop in this wilderness,
33 while your children roam the wilderness for forty years,
suffering for your faithlessness, until the last of your carcasses is down in the wilderness. 34 You shall bear your
punishment for forty years, corresponding to the number
of days—forty days—that you scouted the land: a year for
each day. Thus you shall know what it means to thwart Me.
35 I the LORD have spoken: Thus will I do to all that wicked
band that has banded together against Me: in this very
wilderness they shall die to the last man.'"

32 וּפִגְרֵיכֶם אַתֶּם יִפְּלוּ בַּמִּדְבָּר הַזֶּה׃ 33 וּבְנֵיכֶם
יִהְיוּ רֹעִים בַּמִּדְבָּר אַרְבָּעִים שָׁנָה וְנָשְׂאוּ אֶת־
זְנוּתֵיכֶם עַד־תֹּם פִּגְרֵיכֶם בַּמִּדְבָּר׃ 34 בְּמִסְפַּר
הַיָּמִים אֲשֶׁר־תַּרְתֶּם אֶת־הָאָרֶץ אַרְבָּעִים יוֹם יוֹם
לַשָּׁנָה יוֹם לַשָּׁנָה תִּשְׂאוּ אֶת־עֲוֺנֹתֵיכֶם אַרְבָּעִים
שָׁנָה וִידַעְתֶּם אֶת־תְּנוּאָתִי׃ 35 אֲנִי יְהוָה דִּבַּרְתִּי
אִם־לֹא זֹאת אֶעֱשֶׂה לְכָל־הָעֵדָה הָרָעָה הַזֹּאת
הַנּוֹעָדִים עָלָי בַּמִּדְבָּר הַזֶּה יִתַּמּוּ וְשָׁם יָמֻתוּ׃

32. ***your carcasses*** Hebrew *u-figreikhem 'attem,* literally "As for you, your carcasses"[55]; that is, "your own carcasses." *'Attem* contrasts with *'otam,* "these," that is, the children (v. 31; cf. children, v. 33).[56] Thus verse 32 is no mere repetition of verse 29, but as verse 30 contrasts with verse 31, "you . . . your children," so verse 32 contrasts with verse 33, "you . . . your children."

33. ***roam*** Hebrew *ro'im,* literally "will be shepherds/nomads" (cf. 27:17). Of interest is the implied denigration of the nomadic existence.[57]

suffering for your faithlessness Literally, "bearing your harlotry." The verb *zanah,* "to whore," is frequently a metaphor for idolatry (e.g., Exod. 34:16–17) and for any defection from God's commandments (e.g., 15:39). The children suffering for the fathers' sins is the precise application of God's attribute: "visiting the iniquity of fathers upon children" (v. 18; Sefer ha-Mivḥar). It is possibly an aspect of God's mercy; that is, He delays the punishment to a future generation (see Excursus 32). A later age interpreted the children's punishment not as referring to the next generation's wilderness wandering but to a future generation's exile from the land (Ezek. 20:23; Ps. 106:27).

last of your carcasses is down Hebrew *tom pigreikhem,* literally "your carcasses are finished, consumed." (For this use of the root *t-m-m,* cf. v. 35; 17:28.) The implication is that burial is denied.

34. ***bear your punishment*** Hebrew *nasa' 'avon (ḥet'),* like its Akkadian equivalent *zabālu arna (ḫiṭu),* means literally "carry (the consequences of) sin," that is, suffer punishment. The idiom *nasa' 'avon* also bears the antithetical meaning "forgive iniquity" (v. 18). Thus, this verse provides an ironic contrast to God's attributes: He will fulfill his attribute of *nasa' 'avon* not as Israel expects it, as forgiveness, but as punishment.[58]

forty days . . . a year for each day Another instance of measure for measure. The same scale is adopted by Ezekiel whose forty days lying on his side represent forty years of Judah's sin (Ezek. 4:6). Forty years will allow a fourth generation to be born in the wilderness, thereby fulfilling God's attribute of punishing to the fourth generation.[59] Thus God punishes the succeeding generation only as long as the evildoers live.

you shall know Your knowing shall be the reverse of your children's knowing. They shall "know" the land (v. 31), but you will know the price for frustrating the Lord.

what it means to thwart Me Hebrew *tenu'ati,* literally "my frustration" or "the annulment of My intention."[60] The versions recoil from such a bold statement and adopt euphemisms,[61] "you murmured against Me."[62] The verb *heni'* means "frustrate" (e.g., 32:9).

35. ***band that has banded together against Me*** When the Israelites banded together to stone Moses and Aaron (v. 5), what they really intended was to rebel against God.[63]

shall die to the last man Literally, "they will be finished . . . die," that is, "they will completely die" (cf. 17:28).

³⁶As for the men whom Moses sent to scout the land, those who came back and caused the whole community to mutter against him by spreading calumnies about the land—³⁷those who spread such calumnies about the land died of plague, by the will of the LORD. ³⁸Of those men who had gone to scout the land, only Joshua son of Nun and Caleb son of Jephunneh survived.

³⁹When Moses repeated these words to all the Israelites, the people were overcome by grief. ⁴⁰Early next morning they set out toward the crest of the hill country, saying, "We are prepared to go up to the place that the LORD has spoken of, for we were wrong." ⁴¹But Moses said, "Why do you transgress the LORD's command? This will not succeed. ⁴²Do not go up, lest you be routed by your enemies, for the LORD is not in your midst. ⁴³For the Amalekites and the

³⁶ וְהָ֣אֲנָשִׁ֔ים אֲשֶׁר־שָׁלַ֥ח מֹשֶׁ֖ה לָת֣וּר אֶת־הָאָ֑רֶץ
וַיָּשֻׁ֗בוּ וַיַּלִּ֤ונוּ עָלָיו֙ אֶת־כָּל־הָ֣עֵדָ֔ה לְהוֹצִ֥יא דִבָּ֖ה
עַל־הָאָֽרֶץ: ³⁷ וַיָּמֻ֙תוּ֙ הָֽאֲנָשִׁ֔ים מוֹצִאֵ֥י דִבַּת־
הָאָ֖רֶץ רָעָ֑ה בַּמַּגֵּפָ֖ה לִפְנֵ֥י יְהוָֽה: ³⁸ וִיהוֹשֻׁ֣עַ בִּן־נ֔וּן
וְכָלֵ֖ב בֶּן־יְפֻנֶּ֑ה חָיוּ֙ מִן־הָֽאֲנָשִׁ֣ים הָהֵ֔ם הַהֹלְכִ֖ים
לָת֥וּר אֶת־הָאָֽרֶץ: ³⁹ וַיְדַבֵּ֤ר מֹשֶׁה֙ אֶת־הַדְּבָרִ֣ים
הָאֵ֔לֶּה אֶל־כָּל־בְּנֵ֖י יִשְׂרָאֵ֑ל וַיִּֽתְאַבְּל֥וּ הָעָ֖ם מְאֹֽד:
⁴⁰ וַיַּשְׁכִּ֣מוּ בַבֹּ֔קֶר וַיַּֽעֲל֥וּ אֶל־רֹאשׁ־הָהָ֖ר לֵאמֹ֑ר
הִנֶּ֗נּוּ וְעָלִ֛ינוּ אֶל־הַמָּק֛וֹם אֲשֶׁר־אָמַ֥ר יְהוָ֖ה כִּ֥י
חָטָֽאנוּ: ⁴¹ וַיֹּ֣אמֶר מֹשֶׁ֔ה לָ֥מָּה זֶּ֛ה אַתֶּ֥ם עֹבְרִ֖ים
אֶת־פִּ֣י יְהוָ֑ה וְהִ֖וא לֹ֥א תִצְלָֽח: ⁴² אַֽל־תַּעֲל֔וּ כִּ֣י
אֵ֤ין יְהוָה֙ בְּקִרְבְּכֶ֔ם וְלֹא֙ תִּנָּ֣גְפ֔וּ לִפְנֵ֖י אֹיְבֵיכֶֽם:

וַיַּלִּ֥ינוּ ק' v. 36.

36-38. These verses are an editorial interpolation explaining that, except for Joshua and Caleb, the rebellious scouts did not die a natural death in the wilderness but were struck down by plague.⁶⁴

36. *against him* Following the *Kere* reading *va-yalinu*, "caused (the community) to mutter,"⁶⁵ whereas the Septuagint, following the *Ketiv* spelling *va-yilonu*, renders "muttered against it (i.e., the land) to the community."

37. *by the will of the LORD* Hebrew *lifnei YHVH*; compare 3:4 and Genesis 10:9; 27:7.

THE PEOPLE'S EXPEDITION (vv. 39-45)

Stricken by guilt and grief the people attempt to invade Canaan, but the end is disastrous. It is too late. The Lord's oath—that the generation of the Exodus must die in the desert (vv. 21-23,28-32)—is irrevocable. The account assumes that after the spies' report, God commanded Israel to attack from the south.⁶⁶ This is implied by verse 40 and made explicit in the Deuteronomic account: "just as the LORD our God commanded us" (Deut. 1:41; cf. v. 21), a formula peculiar to Deuteronomy whereby it refers back to an earlier source.⁶⁷

39. *these words* That is, verses 21-25 and/or verses 28-35 (see the Comment to v. 25).

40. *Early next morning they set out* As they were commanded (v. 25). But instead of retreating they defied the Lord and invaded Canaan.

crest of the hill country That is, toward Hebron, one of the highest points in the Judean mountains.

wrong Compare 21:7 for a similar confession. Since it follows God's decree, the remorse here is too late. It contrasts with the golden calf apostasy, where the expression of remorse preceded the final decree (Exod. 33:4,14), which perhaps is why God consents to renew the covenant with the sinners in Exodus (34:10) but only with their children in Numbers.

41. *But Moses said* In the Deuteronomic account, Moses' warning is issued first by God: "The LORD said to me, 'Warn them: Do not go up and do not fight, since I am not in your midst; else you will be routed by your enemies'" (Deut. 1:42).⁶⁸

42. *The LORD is not in your midst* Because the Lord so told Moses (cf. Deut. 1:42; cf. v. 40, above) or because the Ark did not accompany them in battle (v. 44; cf. v. 14 and 10:35-36; see Excursus 22), whereas, heretofore, the Lord had been in Israel's midst (vv. 11,14).

Canaanites will be there to face you, and you will fall by the sword, inasmuch as you have turned from following the LORD and the LORD will not be with you."

44Yet defiantly they marched toward the crest of the hill country, though neither the LORD's Ark of the Covenant nor Moses stirred from the camp. 45And the Amalekites and the Canaanites who dwelt in that hill country came down and dealt them a shattering blow at Hormah.

43 כִּי֩ הָעֲמָלֵקִ֨י וְהַכְּנַעֲנִ֥י שָׁם֙ לִפְנֵיכֶ֔ם וּנְפַלְתֶּ֖ם
בֶּחָ֑רֶב כִּֽי־עַל־כֵּ֤ן שַׁבְתֶּם֙ מֵאַחֲרֵ֣י יְהוָ֔ה וְלֹא־יִהְיֶ֥ה
יְהוָ֖ה עִמָּכֶֽם׃ 44 וַיַּעְפִּ֕לוּ לַעֲל֖וֹת אֶל־רֹ֣אשׁ הָהָ֑ר
וַאֲר֤וֹן בְּרִית־יְהוָה֙ וּמֹשֶׁ֔ה לֹא־מָ֖שׁוּ מִקֶּ֥רֶב הַֽמַּחֲנֶֽה׃
45 וַיֵּ֤רֶד הָעֲמָלֵקִי֙ וְהַכְּנַעֲנִ֔י הַיֹּשֵׁ֖ב בָּהָ֣ר הַה֑וּא
וַיַּכּ֥וּם וַֽיַּכְּת֖וּם עַד־הַֽחָרְמָֽה׃ פ

43. the Amalekites and the Canaanites The same nations appear in verse 45. But Deuteronomy 1:44 reads Amorites. Amorites and Canaanites can stand for the entire population of Canaan (cf. 13:29).[69]

fall by the sword Measure for measure, for so they feared (14:3).[70]

44. Yet defiantly The meaning of Hebrew *va-ya'pilu* is uncertain. Others render: "committed the wickedness";[71] "armed themselves/went up in the dark before morning";[72] "they went up to the *'ofel*, the top of the mountain."[73] The parallel account in Deuteronomy uses the verb ***va-tazidu***, "you acted willfully" (Deut. 1:43).

LORD's Ark of the Covenant Outside of Deuteronomy, this name for the Ark is found only here and in 10:33.

45. dealt them a shattering blow Hebrew ***va-yakkum va-yaktum*** are a hendiadys, two words denoting one idea.[74]

at Rather, "until, as far as" (cf. Deut. 1:44), but see below.

Hormah The Hebrew contains the definite article, which is unusual for proper names, leading Targum Jonathan to render "to destruction" (cf. root *ḥ-r-m* in 21:2–3).[75]

CHAPTER 15

A Miscellany of Laws (15:1–41)

Chapter 15 is a miscellany of diverse laws: the tariff of the meal and oil offering and wine libation accompanying the sacrifices (vv. 1–16); the bread dough offering (vv. 17–21); sacrificial expiation for individual and communal inadvertencies (vv. 22–31); the case of the wood gatherer on the Sabbath (vv. 32–36); and the command to wear *tsitsit* (vv. 37–41). The chapter clearly interrupts the narrative sequence of the spy story (chaps. 13–14) and the rebellion of Korah, Dathan, and Abiram (chaps. 16–17).

Why was this chapter placed here? The reason suggested by the medieval commentators is most plausible: After the generation of the Exodus is told that it must die in the wilderness (14:32), it is given some laws that will take effect in the promised land, "when you enter the land . . ." (v. 2; cf. v. 18). Thus the members of that generation are assured that their children will inherit the land. It is also possible that during the long sojourn at Kadesh the people began to engage in agriculture and in other phases of settled life, thus requiring new legal and cultic provisions. Another reason may be the emphasis on the equality of the ***ger*** with the native born (vv. 14–16,26,29), which would explain why the celebrated ***ger*** Caleb (see Excursus 31) was awarded choice territory in the promised land (see the Comment to 14:24).

15 The LORD spoke to Moses, saying: 2Speak to the
Israelite people and say to them:
When you enter the land that I am giving you to settle in,
3and would present an offering by fire to the LORD from the
herd or from the flock, be it burnt offering or sacrifice, in
fulfillment of a vow explicitly uttered, or as a freewill
offering, or at your fixed occasions, producing an odor
pleasing to the LORD:
4The person who presents the offering to the LORD shall

ט״ו וַיְדַבֵּר יְהוָה אֶל־מֹשֶׁה לֵּאמֹר: 2 דַּבֵּר אֶל־
בְּנֵי יִשְׂרָאֵל וְאָמַרְתָּ אֲלֵהֶם כִּי תָבֹאוּ אֶל־אֶרֶץ
מוֹשְׁבֹתֵיכֶם אֲשֶׁר אֲנִי נֹתֵן לָכֶם: 3 וַעֲשִׂיתֶם אִשֶּׁה
לַיהוָה עֹלָה אוֹ־זֶבַח לְפַלֵּא־נֶדֶר אוֹ בִנְדָבָה אוֹ
בְּמֹעֲדֵיכֶם לַעֲשׂוֹת רֵיחַ נִיחֹחַ לַיהוָה מִן־הַבָּקָר אוֹ
מִן־הַצֹּאן: 4 וְהִקְרִיב הַמַּקְרִיב קָרְבָּנוֹ לַיהוָה מִנְחָה

ACCOMPANIMENTS TO THE SACRIFICE (vv. 1–16)

The offering on the "table of the Lord" corresponded to the human meal. Since meat was eaten together with bread and wine, these last two items accompanied an animal sacrifice. The meal offering and the wine libation were not required in the wilderness because they are products of an agricultural society. Their antiquity in Israel is attested by 1 Samuel 1:24 and 10:3 (cf. Judg. 9:9,13). Indeed, the entire sacrificial system reflected in this passage represents a merger between two ways of life, that of the shepherd and that of the farmer.

The wine libation as an ancillary offering is of great antiquity. It was practiced in Mesopotamia,[1] among the Hittites,[2] and in Ugarit.[3] The ancient Greeks too accompanied the well-being sacrifice *(thusia)* with a wine libation. In the Second Temple, the wine libation marked the climax of the service (Ecclus. 50:14–21).[4]

2. *When you enter the land* This introductory phrase is often found in connection with laws that presume a settled agricultural life (e.g., Lev. 23:10; 25:2).

to settle in That is, in permanent settlements not tents. This phrase led Rabbi Ishmael to maintain that the meal and wine accompaniments to the sacrifices were not brought until after the Israelite conquest was completed.[5]

3. *would present* The continuation of the condition implied in the previous verse, and not a command.

an offering by fire Rather, "a gift" (cf. v. 25).[6]

herd . . . flock But birds do not require accompanying meal and libation offerings.

sacrifice *Zevaḥ,* short for *zevaḥ shelamim,* "offering of well-being" as in the parallel verse, Leviticus 22:21.

explicitly uttered Hebrew *le-falle';* compare 6:2.

vow . . . freewill offering *Neder . . . nedavah*—two motivations for the "offering of well-being" (e.g., Lev. 7:16; 22:21) and the burnt offering (Lev. 22:18; Num. 29:39). The third kind of well-being offering, the *todah,* "thanksgiving offering," is missing, implying that it is not accompanied by meal and wine. The rabbis deduced from these two motivations that the purification and reparation offerings are also exempt from meal and wine accompaniments because they are mandatory and not voluntary sacrifices.[7] The Dead Sea sectaries, however, prescribed them.[8]

at your fixed occasions The burnt offerings required for the fixed, public cult (cf. 28:2, 29–39; Lev. 23:4–37).

an odor pleasing to the LORD Hebrew *reaḥ niḥoaḥ* is a term found in connection with the burnt offering, the offering of well-being, the meal offering, and the libation. It is absent from the contexts dealing with the reparation offering, and it is found only once in connection with the purification offering.[9] This distribution clearly shows that, like its companion term *'isheh,* discussed below in verse 25, it must connote something pleasing to God. Conversely, a rendering like "appeasing, placating, soothing" that is favored by many commentators and translators should be

bring as a meal offering: a tenth of a measure of choice flour with a quarter of a *hin* of oil mixed in. [5]You shall also offer, with the burnt offering or the sacrifice, a quarter of a *hin* of wine as a libation for each sheep.

[6]In the case of a ram, you shall present as a meal offering: two-tenths of a measure of choice flour with a third of a *hin* of oil mixed in; [7]and a third of a *hin* of wine as a libation—as an offering of pleasing odor to the LORD.

[8]And if it is an animal from the herd that you offer to the LORD as a burnt offering or as a sacrifice, in fulfillment of a

סֹלֶת עִשָּׂרוֹן בָּלוּל בִּרְבִעִית הַהִין שָׁמֶן׃ 5 וְיַיִן
לַנֶּסֶךְ רְבִיעִית הַהִין תַּעֲשֶׂה עַל־הָעֹלָה אוֹ לַזָּבַח
לַכֶּבֶשׂ הָאֶחָד׃ 6 אוֹ לָאַיִל תַּעֲשֶׂה מִנְחָה סֹלֶת
שְׁנֵי עֶשְׂרֹנִים בְּלוּלָה בַשֶּׁמֶן שְׁלִשִׁית הַהִין׃ 7 וְיַיִן
לַנֶּסֶךְ שְׁלִשִׁית הַהִין תַּקְרִיב רֵיחַ־נִיחֹחַ לַיהוָה׃
חמישי 8 וְכִי־תַעֲשֶׂה בֶן־בָּקָר עֹלָה אוֹ־זָבַח
לְפַלֵּא־נֶדֶר אוֹ־שְׁלָמִים לַיהוָה׃ 9 וְהִקְרִיב עַל־בֶּן־

avoided. To be sure, such a meaning might be present in passages like Genesis 8:21 and Leviticus 26:31. A case for it can be based on the root ***n-w-ḥ,*** which in the Hifil can mean "appease," as in Ezekiel 5:13. Further, its Akkadian cognate ***nuḫḫu*** similarly denotes "appease," especially in connection with the gods. Support might also be sought from the Greek world, where Apollo may be willing to ward off a plague if he receives the aroma of lambs or perfect goats. Nevertheless, the rarity of the phrase ***reaḥ niḥoaḥ*** in connection with Israel's expiatory sacrifices can only signify that even if the Hebrew had this meaning originally, it lost it in the cultic terminology of the priestly texts. Hence, the Septuagint rendering "sweet savor" and the rabbinic explanation "pleasure" are accurate.

4. ***The person*** Either a man or a woman.[10]

meal offering The private meal offering became a priestly revenue after a token portion was offered on the altar, but one that accompanied a meat offering was burnt completely on the altar as prescribed in Leviticus 14:20 and 23:13. According to Megillat Taʿanit 7, the Sadducees, however, held that the meal offering accompanying the offering of well-being was eaten by the priests.

tenth of a measure The measure is an ephah, implied but not stated in the text, approximately equal to a bushel. A tenth of an ephah is also called omer in Exodus 16:36.

choice flour That is, semolina, the finest grade of flour.

hin Approximately 5.7 liters (12 pts. or 1.5 gal.).[11]

5. ***You*** Hebrew ***taʿaseh*** is singular. The frequent change of person in the direct address to Israel is characteristic of the priestly style.

sacrifice Compare verse 4.

libation According to rabbinic tradition, the wine was placed in perforated bowls atop the altar from which the wine drained into the ground underneath.[12] Most likely the wine originally was poured upon the base of the altar and not burnt upon its hearth, the flames of which might be extinguished, in violation of Leviticus 6:6.

sheep This rule applies to goats as well, as verse 11 shows.

6. ***In the case*** Hebrew ***'o*** in contradiction to ***ki,*** as in verses 2a, 8, and 14, indicates a subcase. Therefore all details such as the sacrifices and their motivation need not be repeated.

ram The rabbis in Mishnah Parah 1:3 differ on the age of the ram; some hold it to be thirteen months, others two years.

two-tenths Twice the amount of flour required for a sheep, which approximates their respective weights. A yearling ***(keves)*** yields about 16 kilograms of meat, whereas a mature ram ***('ayil),*** about 34 kilograms.

7. ***of pleasing odor to the LORD*** This phrase applies to the case of the sheep as well, mentioned in verses 4–5. It marks the end of the subsections, as in verses 1–3,4–7,8–10,11–13.

8. ***offering of well-being*** This corresponds to "freewill offering" in verse 3. The assumption is that the ***nedavah,*** "freewill offering," is the most usual kind of ***shelamim,*** "offering of well-

vow explicitly uttered or as an offering of well-being, [9]there shall be offered a meal offering along with the animal: three-tenths of a measure of choice flour with half a *hin* of oil mixed in; [10]and as libation you shall offer half a *hin* of wine—these being offerings by fire of pleasing odor to the LORD.

[11]Thus shall be done with each ox, with each ram, and with any sheep or goat, [12]as many as you offer; you shall do thus with each one, as many as there are. [13]Every citizen, when presenting an offering by fire of pleasing odor to the LORD, shall do so with them.

[14]And when, throughout the ages, a stranger who has taken up residence with you, or one who lives among you,

הַבָּקָר מִנְחָה סֹלֶת שְׁלֹשָׁה עֶשְׂרֹנִים בָּלוּל בַּשֶּׁמֶן
חֲצִי הַהִין׃ 10 וְיַיִן תַּקְרִיב לַנֶּסֶךְ חֲצִי הַהִין אִשֵּׁה
רֵיחַ־נִיחֹחַ לַיהוָה׃ 11 כָּכָה יֵעָשֶׂה לַשּׁוֹר הָאֶחָד אוֹ
לָאַיִל הָאֶחָד אוֹ־לַשֶּׂה בַכְּבָשִׂים אוֹ בָעִזִּים׃
12 כַּמִּסְפָּר אֲשֶׁר תַּעֲשׂוּ כָּכָה תַּעֲשׂוּ לָאֶחָד
כְּמִסְפָּרָם׃ 13 כָּל־הָאֶזְרָח יַעֲשֶׂה־כָּכָה אֶת־אֵלֶּה
לְהַקְרִיב אִשֵּׁה רֵיחַ־נִיחֹחַ לַיהוָה׃ 14 וְכִי־יָגוּר
אִתְּכֶם גֵּר אוֹ אֲשֶׁר־בְּתוֹכְכֶם לְדֹרֹתֵיכֶם וְעָשָׂה
אִשֵּׁה רֵיחַ־נִיחֹחַ לַיהוָה כַּאֲשֶׁר תַּעֲשׂוּ כֵּן יַעֲשֶׂה׃

being." The thanksgiving offering is also subsumed under the title *shelamim* (Lev. 7:11–12), but it was originally a discrete sacrifice known as *zevaḥ todah* (Lev. 7:12; 22:29). It was eaten in one day in distinction to the *zevaḥ shelamim* (i.e., the votive or freewill offering), which may be eaten over the course of two days (Lev. 19:5–6). Its expanded name *zevaḥ todat shelamav* (Lev. 7:13–15) also indicates that its incorporation into the *shelamim* was a later development.

9. mixed in[13]

10. these being offerings by fire Rather, "these being offerings." For *'isheh* as "offering, gift," see the Comment to verse 25. The term would then apply to the wine as well as to the animal and meal offerings. Rashi, however, who follows the traditional rendering "fire offering," must therefore disqualify the wine as an *'isheh* since it was not burned on the altar hearth.[14]

of pleasing odor to the LORD Though the wine was poured at the base of the altar and not on its hearth, it still exuded a pleasing aroma.[15] So indeed proclaims Ben Sira: "Pouring it [the wine] at the foot of the altar, an appeasing fragrance to the Most High, the King of all" (Ecclus. 50:15).

11. Thus shall be done A summary, enumerating the animals in inverse order: ox, ram, lamb.[16]

ox *Shor,* here, is equivalent to *ben bakar,* "animal from the herd," in verse 8, and can be either masculine or feminine as in Leviticus 22:28. That a female bovine is acceptable for the well-being offering is clear from Leviticus 3:1.

any sheep or goat Literally, "with any kid, whether sheep or goat." Hebrew *seh* is the young of either sheep or goats, as Exodus 12:5 shows. Again, both genders are encompassed.

12. as many as you offer . . . as many as there are The first "many" refers to the animals, the second (pl.) refers to the sacrificial accompaniment—the meal, oil, and wine, as Ibn Ezra noted. However, according to the present rendering, both incidents of "many" refer to the animals, the first being attached to the previous verse.

14. And when, throughout the ages Although Hebrew *be-doroteikhem* is found at the end of the second clause, it belongs here at the beginning of the verse.[17]

stranger Hebrew *ger* specifies: "A man of another tribe or district who, coming to sojourn in a place where he was not strengthened by the presence of his own kin, put himself under the protection of a clan or of a powerful chief."[18] For a discussion of the *ger,* see Excursus 34.

or one who lives among you Literally, "or one who is among you." This phrase may refer to the *nokhri,* the foreigner who does not actually reside among the Israelites, as does the *ger,* but who sojourns or visits. He too may offer sacrifices provided they follow these regulations (Lev. 22:25).

15. the rest of the congregation This rendering follows the Septuagint and Samaritan texts in attaching *ha-kahal* to the previous verse. But this is open to the objections that the Hebrew

would present an offering by fire of pleasing odor to the LORD—as you do, so shall it be done by [15]the rest of the congregation. There shall be one law for you and for the resident stranger; it shall be a law for all time throughout the ages. You and the stranger shall be alike before the LORD; [16]the same ritual and the same rule shall apply to you and to the stranger who resides among you.

[17]The LORD spoke to Moses, saying: [18]Speak to the Israelite people and say to them:

When you enter the land to which I am taking you [19]and you eat of the bread of the land, you shall set some aside as a

15 הַקָּהָל חֻקָּה אַחַת לָכֶם וְלַגֵּר הַגָּר חֻקַּת עוֹלָם
לְדֹרֹתֵיכֶם כָּכֶם כַּגֵּר יִהְיֶה לִפְנֵי יְהוָה׃ 16 תּוֹרָה
אַחַת וּמִשְׁפָּט אֶחָד יִהְיֶה לָכֶם וְלַגֵּר הַגָּר אִתְּכֶם׃
פ ששי 17 וַיְדַבֵּר יְהוָה אֶל־מֹשֶׁה לֵּאמֹר׃
18 דַּבֵּר אֶל־בְּנֵי יִשְׂרָאֵל וְאָמַרְתָּ אֲלֵהֶם בְּבֹאֲכֶם
אֶל־הָאָרֶץ אֲשֶׁר אֲנִי מֵבִיא אֶתְכֶם שָׁמָּה׃ 19 וְהָיָה
בַּאֲכָלְכֶם מִלֶּחֶם הָאָרֶץ תָּרִימוּ תְרוּמָה לַיהוָה׃

cannot yield "the rest of" and that *ger* cannot be included in the *kahal* (cf. Josh. 8:35). An acceptable solution is possible once verse 29a is brought in for comparison. Its similar construction to verse 15a allows for the equation of *ha-kahal* with *ha-'ezraḥ,* "citizen," and the passage should therefore be rendered: "As for the congregation (i.e., Israelites), there shall be one law for you and for the resident stranger."[19]

16. the same ritual Applies in this case. Although the stranger is placed on an equal footing with the citizen in civil law, there are a few significant differences between them in religious law, on which see Excursus 34.

THE FIRST OF THE DOUGH: A PRIESTLY EMOLUMENT (vv. 17–21)

This passage prescribes that the *re'shit,* the first of the *'arisah,* dough or kneading trough (called by the rabbis *ḥallah*), be given to the priest. Its purpose, according to the prophet Ezekiel in 44:30, is that a "blessing may rest upon your home." This verse is instructive. It specifies "home" not "crop." Verses 17–21 are therefore directed to the nonfarmer, who, like the farmer, is also made to feel that his provender should be subjected to a "first fruits" offering. In the case of the farmer the first fruits offering brings a blessing on the remainder of the crop (Lev. 19:24–25; 23:10–11). In the case of the nonfarmer the *ḥallah* brings a blessing on his labors, as is made explicit by the rabbis: "R. Josiah said: For the sin of (neglecting) *ḥallah* the fruits are not blessed and man's labors do not yield enough."[20]

The gift of the first fruits *(bikkurim)* is due not only from the first ripe crops of the soil but also from the first processed *(re'shit),* that is, threshed grain, new wine, new (olive) oil, fruit syrup, leavened food, and, as discussed here, bread dough (Num. 18:12). The identification of this gift with bread dough is virtually certain because it is called *ḥallah,* "loaf," in verse 20, where it is compared with the "gift of the threshing floor," a term that cannot refer to the standing grain but only to the processed product. Further, in verses 20–21 it is called *re'shit* rather than *bikkurim,* the latter being the first of the freshly harvested produce, whereas the former is the first of the produce after it has been processed (cf. 18:12–13; Excursus 43).

In Mishnah Ḥallah 1:1, the rabbis applied this law to five kinds of grain indigenous to the land of Israel: wheat, barley, spelt, oats, and rye, but not to rice, millet, or pulse.[21] Since this law is operative only when Israel enters its land, it is therefore juxtaposed to the law of sacrificial accompaniments, which is also qualified by this provision (v. 2).

18. When you enter the land Hebrew *be-vo'akhem* instead of the usual *ki tavo'u* is used to avoid the impression that this law is independent of the preceding one; both take effect simultaneously upon entering the land.

19. bread of the land From this phrase, the rabbis derived the rule that the bread made from grain grown outside the land of Israel is not subject to *ḥallah.*[22] In the Diaspora, however, as well as in the land itself after the destruction of the Second Temple, the law is observed symbolically by reciting a blessing and throwing a small portion of the dough into the fire.[23] The reason cited by the rabbis is that "the Torah should not be forgotten."[24]

gift to the Lord: 20as the first yield of your baking, you shall set aside a loaf as a gift; you shall set it aside as a gift like the gift from the threshing floor. 21You shall make a gift to the Lord from the first yield of your baking, throughout the ages.

22If you unwittingly fail to observe any one of the commandments that the Lord has declared to Moses 23—any-

20 רֵאשִׁית֙ עֲרִסֹ֣תֵכֶ֔ם חַלָּ֖ה תָּרִ֣ימוּ תְרוּמָ֑ה
כִּתְרוּמַ֣ת גֹּ֔רֶן כֵּ֖ן תָּרִ֥ימוּ אֹתָֽהּ׃ 21 מֵרֵאשִׁית֙
עֲרִסֹ֣תֵיכֶ֔ם תִּתְּנ֥וּ לַֽיהוָ֖ה תְּרוּמָ֑ה לְדֹרֹתֵיכֶֽם׃
ס 22 וְכִ֣י תִשְׁגּ֔וּ וְלֹ֣א תַעֲשׂ֔וּ אֵ֥ת כָּל־
הַמִּצְוֺ֖ת הָאֵ֑לֶּה אֲשֶׁר־דִּבֶּ֥ר יְהוָ֖ה אֶל־מֹשֶֽׁה׃

to the Lord From this expression, one would not know if the gift is assigned to the altar or to the priest. But we have Ezekiel's explicit instructions in 44:30: "You are to give the first of your *'arisah* to the priest."[25]

set some aside as a gift Hebrew *tarimu terumah.* The function of the *terumah* is to transfer an object from its owner to the Deity. In this respect it is similar to the *tenufah,* but with this crucial distinction: The *tenufah* is performed "before the Lord," whereas the *terumah* is never "before" but always "to the Lord." Thus *tenufah* and *terumah* comprise two means of dedication to the Lord, the former by a ritual in the sanctuary and the latter by a dedication without ritual outside the sanctuary, effected either by an oral declaration, such as that found in Judges 17:3, or by a physical act, such as setting it apart as in Leviticus 27:32. The verb *herim* in this context means "to set apart, dedicate," as indicated by its synonym *nivdal* in 16:21 and 17:10 and by *hesir,* as for example in Leviticus 4:8–10,31,35. Thus the noun *terumah* must refer to that which is set apart or dedicated to the sanctuary and should be rendered "dedication, gift."[26]

20. of your baking The term *'arisah* seems clearly to refer to the bread that is in the process of baking, but its precise meaning is still debated. While the Septuagint renders "dough," the Targums and Syriac Peshitta render "kneading trough." The latter, perhaps, is preferable because *'arisah* also means "cradle" in rabbinic Hebrew.[27]

gift from the threshing floor The priest was entitled to the *re'shit,* the first yield of the threshing floor (wheat) and the vat (wine, oil), as prescribed in 18:12. This text, then, presumes a knowledge of the priestly emoluments listed in 18:8–32. The amount of the *re'shit* is never specified. It would seem to refer to the first loaf. The rabbis, however, stipulate that *ḥallah* is minimally one omer, enough to fill a vessel 10x10x3.25 inches,[28] of which 1/24 goes to the priest in the case of a private householder and 1/48 in the case of a bakery.[29]

21. from the first yield That is, not all of it.[30]

INADVERTENT AND BRAZEN WRONGDOING (vv. 22–31)

This passage deals with sacrifices required for the inadvertent violation of any of the laws either by the community (vv. 24–26) or by an individual (vv. 27–28). This rule applies equally to the native and to the stranger (v. 29). A brazen, high-handed wrong, however, cannot be expiated by sacrifice; the offender bears the punishment of *karet* for his sin (vv. 30–31). On this term, see Excursus 36. A more elaborate statement regarding sacrifices required for inadvertent wrongs is found in Leviticus 4, but there are significant differences in the details, on which see Excursus 35. The lack of an introductory phrase, as in verses 1 and 17, indicates that this section was intended to be a continuation of the previous one.

22. unwittingly Hebrew *tishgu* is, rather, "inadvertently," and so throughout.[31]

any one The emphasis here is that the prescribed sacrifice is brought for any inadvertent sin not just for the violation of prohibitive commandments (see Excursus 36).[32]

of the commandments Rather, "of these commandments." There is, however, no clear antecedent for "these." There are two possibilities. The first is that "these" refers to a body of laws found elsewhere. The other possibility is that since no heading separates this section from the preceding, "these" refers to the two previous laws in the chapter, the sacrificial supplements (vv. 1–10)

thing that the LORD has enjoined upon you through Moses —from the day that the LORD gave the commandment and on through the ages:

[24]If this was done unwittingly, through the inadvertence of the community, the whole community shall present one bull of the herd as a burnt offering of pleasing odor to the LORD, with its proper meal offering and libation, and one he-goat as a sin offering. [25]The priest shall make expiation for the whole Israelite community and they shall be forgiven; for it was an error, and for their error they have brought their offering, an offering by fire to the LORD and their sin offering before the LORD. [26]The whole Israelite

23 אֵת֩ כׇּל־אֲשֶׁ֨ר צִוָּ֧ה יְהֹוָ֛ה אֲלֵיכֶ֖ם בְּיַד־מֹשֶׁ֑ה
מִן־הַיּ֞וֹם אֲשֶׁ֨ר צִוָּ֧ה יְהֹוָ֛ה וָהָ֖לְאָה לְדֹרֹתֵיכֶֽם׃
24 וְהָיָ֗ה אִ֣ם מֵעֵינֵ֣י הָעֵדָה֮ נֶעֶשְׂתָ֣ה לִשְׁגָגָה֒ וְעָשׂ֣וּ
כׇל־הָעֵדָ֡ה פַּ֣ר בֶּן־בָּקָ֩ר אֶחָ֨ד לְעֹלָ֜ה לְרֵ֣יחַ נִיחֹ֗חַ
לַֽיהֹוָ֔ה וּמִנְחָת֥וֹ וְנִסְכּ֖וֹ כַּמִּשְׁפָּ֑ט וּשְׂעִיר־עִזִּ֥ים אֶחָ֖ד
לְחַטָּֽת*׃ 25 וְכִפֶּ֣ר הַכֹּהֵ֗ן עַֽל־כׇּל־עֲדַ֛ת בְּנֵ֥י יִשְׂרָאֵ֖ל
וְנִסְלַ֣ח לָהֶ֑ם כִּֽי־שְׁגָגָ֣ה הִ֔וא וְהֵם֩ הֵבִ֨יאוּ אֶת־
קׇרְבָּנָ֜ם אִשֶּׁ֣ה לַֽיהֹוָ֗ה וְחַטָּאתָ֛ם לִפְנֵ֥י יְהֹוָ֖ה עַל־
שִׁגְגָתָֽם׃ 26 וְנִסְלַ֗ח לְכׇל־עֲדַת֙ בְּנֵ֣י יִשְׂרָאֵ֔ל וְלַגֵּ֖ר

v. 24. חסר א׳

and the *ḥallah* (vv. 17–21). If this latter view is adopted, then the following verse would be an attempt to broaden the applicability of this law to all the commandments (cf. Excursus 35).

23. ***anything*** The first half of this verse restates the previous verse, that is, that this law applies to any of the commandments spoken by God to Moses. And the second half adds a temporal dimension, that is, that the laws commanded by God are operative not only for the time of Moses but for all future time. Again, the emphasis is upon the application of the principle of inadvertency or presumptuousness to all commandments, regardless of whether they refer to prohibited acts (as in Lev. 4:2) or to prescribed ones (see Excursus 35).

from the day that the LORD gave the commandment That is, at Mount Sinai, as Rashbam and Sforno explain. However, *min ha-yom 'asher tsivvah* may also be rendered "from that day which the Lord commanded," that is, from the day "when you enter the land" (v. 2). This would imply that only the laws operative in the land are meant, such as the Omer and Shavuot festivals (Lev. 23:10–22), the leprous houses (Lev. 14:34), the fourth year for fruit trees (Lev. 19:23), Sabbatical and Jubilee years (Lev. 35:2), and so forth. However, as shown by Shadal, the phrase probably refers to all the laws given "from whatever day," that is, given at any time.

and on through the ages According to the rabbis,[33] it includes even laws revealed by the prophets, thus pointing to continuous revelation. However, this phrase more likely refers to the eternal validity of the laws given to Moses.[34]

THE INADVERTENT WRONGS OF THE COMMUNITY (vv. 24–26)
(Based on Lev. 4:13–21)

24. ***If*** Hebrew *ve-hayah 'im,* the beginning of the subcase, in contrast to *ve-khi,* "if," in the previous verse, which sets forth the general case.

through the inadvertence of the community Hebrew *me-ʿeinei ha-ʿedah.* Rather, "unnoticed by the community," literally "from the notice ["eyes"] of the community." It is analogous to *ve-neʿelem . . . me-ʿeinei ha-kahal,* "escape the notice [lit. "eyes"] of the congregation," in Leviticus 4:13.

the whole community That is, through its national representatives. (See Excursus 1 and the Comment to 8:10.)

present Rather, "sacrifice." The root *ʿ-s-h* embraces the entire sacrificial ritual, as in 6:11, 8:5, and 8:12.[35]

with its proper meal offering and libation The proper amounts have been given in verses 9–10 and constitute another link between this section and the preceding one.

sin offering Rather, "purification offering," and so throughout.

25. ***and they shall be forgiven*** Rather, "that they may be forgiven," as in verse 28b. Forgiveness is not automatic. It does not inhere in the ritual but is entirely dependent on the will of

הַגֵּ֤ר בְּתוֹכְכֶ֔ם כִּ֥י לְכָל־הָעָ֖ם בִּשְׁגָגָֽה: ס

27 וְאִם־נֶ֥פֶשׁ אַחַ֖ת תֶּחֱטָ֣א בִשְׁגָגָ֑ה וְהִקְרִ֛יבָה עֵ֥ז בַּת־שְׁנָתָ֖הּ לְחַטָּֽאת: 28 וְכִפֶּ֣ר הַכֹּהֵ֗ן עַל־הַנֶּ֧פֶשׁ הַשֹּׁגֶ֛גֶת בְּחֶטְאָ֥ה בִשְׁגָגָ֖ה לִפְנֵ֣י יְהוָ֑ה לְכַפֵּ֥ר עָלָ֖יו וְנִסְלַ֥ח לֽוֹ: 29 הָֽאֶזְרָח֙ בִּבְנֵ֣י יִשְׂרָאֵ֔ל וְלַגֵּ֖ר הַגָּ֣ר בְּתוֹכָ֑ם תּוֹרָ֤ה אַחַת֙ יִהְיֶ֣ה לָכֶ֔ם לָעֹשֶׂ֖ה בִּשְׁגָגָֽה: 30 וְהַנֶּ֜פֶשׁ אֲשֶֽׁר־תַּעֲשֶׂ֣ה ׀ בְּיָ֣ד רָמָ֗ה מִן־

community and the stranger residing among them shall be forgiven, for it happened to the entire people through error.

27In case it is an individual who has sinned unwittingly, he shall offer a she-goat in its first year as a sin offering. 28The priest shall make expiation before the LORD on behalf of the person who erred, for he sinned unwittingly, making such expiation for him that he may be forgiven. 29For the citizen among the Israelites and for the stranger who resides among them—you shall have one ritual for anyone who acts in error.

God. These words actually end the law as in most other cases of expiatory offering, such as in Leviticus 4:20,26,31,35 and 5:10,13. Verses 25b–26 were added in order to emphasize the condition of inadvertency and to include the stranger (see Excursus 34).

their offering   That is, the burnt offering.[36]

an offering by fire   Rather, "gift" (of food). Hebrew 'isheh cannot mean "fire offering,"[37] for then there would be no reason to exclude the purification offering, listed separately in the next phrase, which was also burned, in part, on the altar. If, however, 'isheh is understood as "gift," then the discrete purification offering makes sense since a sacrifice that purges the pollution caused by the collective accumulation of sin can hardly be termed a gift.[38] Indeed, the term 'isheh is conspicuously missing in all texts dealing with the purification offering ritual. Two ostensible exceptions (Lev. 4:35; 5:12) only prove the rule. The purification offering is not called an 'isheh but is burned on the altar 'al 'ishe YHVH, "together with the Lord's gifts." Furthermore, the term 'isheh is applied to oblations that are never burned on the altar, such as wine (v. 10), the priestly allowance from the well-being offering (Lev. 7:30,31–36), and the bread of display (Lev. 24:9). Finally, the fact that all the most holy sacrifices, including the purification offering, are called min ha-'esh, "from the fire," in 18:9 can only mean that the term 'isheh was deliberately avoided because it does not mean "an offering by fire."[39]

26. stranger   See Excursus 34. The ger, "stranger," is mentioned three times in this section: the community's inadvertency (v. 20), the individual's inadvertency (v. 29), and the individual's presumptuousness (v. 30). It constitutes another link between this section and the previous one dealing with supplementary offerings (vv. 1–6), which is also directed to the stranger (vv. 14–16).

people   The stranger is included in the 'am, "people," but not in the 'edah, the covenantal community. See Excursus 1.

THE INADVERTENT WRONGS OF THE INDIVIDUAL (vv. 27–29)
(Based on Lev. 4:27–31)

27. In case it is   This is the second subcase of the individual, introduced by ve-'im; 27a is a verbatim citation from Leviticus 4:27.

offer   The Hebrew verb hikriv usually means "present," but it can also connote the performance of the entire ritual, as in Leviticus 10:19 and 16:11.

in its first year   A stipulation not found in Leviticus 4:28.

28. The priest shall make expiation . . . for him that he may be forgiven   Hebrew ve-khipper ha-kohen . . . 'alav ve-nislah lo. This is an exact citation of Leviticus 4:31b, except for one change in the word order. The additional, medial words thereby convey the specific intent of the law; that is, they emphasize the element of inadvertency.

29. stranger   Another innovation of this law: The ger who commits an inadvertent wrong is equally liable as the citizen to bring the required expiatory sacrifice (see Excursuses 34 and 35). The

30 But the person, be he citizen or stranger, who acts defiantly reviles the LORD; that person shall be cut off from among his people. 31 Because he has spurned the word of the LORD and violated His commandment, that person shall be cut off—he bears his guilt.

32 Once, when the Israelites were in the wilderness, they came upon a man gathering wood on the sabbath day.

הָאֶזְרָח֙ וּמִן־הַגֵּ֔ר אֶת־יְהוָ֖ה ה֣וּא מְגַדֵּ֑ף וְנִכְרְתָ֛ה
הַנֶּ֥פֶשׁ הַהִ֖וא מִקֶּ֥רֶב עַמָּֽהּ׃ 31 כִּ֤י דְבַר־יְהוָה֙ בָּזָ֔ה
וְאֶת־מִצְוָת֖וֹ הֵפַ֑ר הִכָּרֵ֧ת ׀ תִּכָּרֵ֛ת הַנֶּ֥פֶשׁ הַהִ֖וא
עֲוֺנָ֥ה בָֽהּ׃ פ 32 וַיִּהְי֥וּ בְנֵֽי־יִשְׂרָאֵ֖ל בַּמִּדְבָּ֑ר
וַֽיִּמְצְא֗וּ אִ֛ישׁ מְקֹשֵׁ֥שׁ עֵצִ֖ים בְּי֥וֹם הַשַּׁבָּֽת׃

implicit reason is that the Holy Land will become polluted by sins committed upon it, be they ritual or ethical, whether by citizen or stranger (Lev. 18:24–30).

30–31. The main innovation of this section is the ***karet*** penalty for those who brazenly violate God's commandments. The nature of ***karet*** is discussed in Excursus 36. The verbal form in the Nifal is attested seventy-one times in the Bible and always with regard to a crime committed against God but not against man. In other words, ***karet*** is imposed for ritual and not ethical sins. This fact alone mandates that these same sins, when committed inadvertently, require sacrificial expiation. That the ***karet*** injunction is the main point and climax of this section (vv. 22–31) is also indicated by its being preceded by nine mentions of the root for inadvertency *sh-g-h/sh-g-g,* leaving ***karet*** in the tenth and climactic position.[40]

30. ***But the person*** Hebrew *ve-ha-nefesh.* The conjunctive *vav* indicates that no new subsection is being introduced. What follows is a continuation: The individual sins either inadvertently or brazenly.

acts defiantly Literally, "with upraised hand." The original setting of this metaphor is seen in the statues of ancient Near Eastern deities who were sculpted with an uplifted or outstretched right hand, bearing a spear, war ax, or lightning bolt.[41] Similarly, the mighty acts of the God of Israel are described as being performed "by a mighty hand and an outstretched arm" (Deut. 4:34; 5:15; 26:8) or by this very expression, "with an upraised hand" (33:3; Exod. 14:8). The upraised hand is therefore poised to strike; it is a threatening gesture of the Deity against His enemies or of man against God Himself.[42] Thus, this literary image is most apposite for the brazen sinner who commits his acts in open defiance of the Lord (cf. Job 38:15). The essence of this sin is that it is committed flauntingly.[43] However, sins performed in secret, even deliberately, can be commuted to the status of inadvertencies by means of repentance.[44]

reviles the LORD Hebrew *'et YHVH hu' megaddef,* an expression that appears once again in the Bible in Ezekiel 20:27, in connection with illicit worship. Here, however, it connotes the brazen violation of any of God's commandments.[45]

shall be cut off The penalty of ***karet*** is discussed in Excursus 36.

31. ***violated His commandment*** Hebrew *ve-'et mitsvato hefer* occurs only once more, in Ezra 9:14. It stands in synonymous parallelism with the previous phrase and is more akin to poetic and prophetic style, thus giving a crescendo effect to this section.[46]

shall be cut off Hebrew ***hikkaret tikkaret.*** There are three mentions of ***karet*** in verses 30–31, thereby indicating that it is the main point of the section.

he bears his guilt Rather, "he bears his punishment." Hebrew *'avon* can mean sin or its consequent punishment but not guilt.[47]

THE CASE OF THE WOOD GATHERER (vv. 32–36)

Although brazen defiance of the Lord is punished with ***karet,*** willful desecration of the Sabbath is met with even severer punishment: In addition to ***karet,*** the offender is put to death. This double penalty for Sabbath violation is cited as a law in Exodus 31:14, which, however, may be based on this case of

33Those who found him as he was gathering wood brought him before Moses, Aaron, and the whole community. 34He was placed in custody, for it had not been specified what should be done to him. 35Then the LORD said to Moses, "The man shall be put to death: the whole community shall pelt him with stones outside the camp." 36So the whole community took him outside the camp and stoned him to death—as the LORD had commanded Moses.

33 וַיַּקְרִ֨יבוּ אֹת֜וֹ הַמֹּצְאִ֥ים אֹת֛וֹ מְקֹשֵׁ֥שׁ עֵצִ֖ים
אֶל־מֹשֶׁה֙ וְאֶֽל־אַהֲרֹ֔ן וְאֶ֖ל כָּל־הָעֵדָֽה׃ 34 וַיַּנִּ֥יחוּ
אֹת֖וֹ בַּמִּשְׁמָ֑ר כִּ֛י לֹ֥א פֹרַ֖שׁ מַה־יֵּעָשֶׂ֥ה לֽוֹ׃ ס
35 וַיֹּ֤אמֶר יְהוָה֙ אֶל־מֹשֶׁ֔ה מ֥וֹת יוּמַ֖ת
הָאִ֑ישׁ רָג֨וֹם אֹת֤וֹ בָֽאֲבָנִים֙ כָּל־הָ֣עֵדָ֔ה מִח֖וּץ
לַֽמַּחֲנֶֽה׃ 36 וַיֹּצִ֨יאוּ אֹת֜וֹ כָּל־הָעֵדָ֗ה אֶל־מִחוּץ֙
לַֽמַּחֲנֶ֔ה וַיִּרְגְּמ֥וּ אֹת֛וֹ בָּאֲבָנִ֖ים וַיָּמֹ֑ת כַּאֲשֶׁ֛ר צִוָּ֥ה
יְהוָ֖ה אֶת־מֹשֶֽׁה׃ פ 37 מפטיר וַיֹּ֥אמֶר יְהוָ֖ה

the person who was apprehended gathering wood on the Sabbath and whose penalty is decreed by oracle. For details, see Excursus 37. This is one of four oracular legal decisions attributed to Moses (see v. 34).

32. Once, when the Israelites were in the wilderness Ramban claims that this incident was placed here for chronological reasons: It took place on the first Sabbath after the fiasco of the reconnaissance mission (chaps. 13–14).

gathering Hebrew *mekoshesh* is a verb formed from the noun *kash*, "stubble."[48] The verb is used for gathering of stubble (Exod. 5:12) or pieces of wood (1 Kings 17:10,12).

33. found[49]

34. in custody[50]

specified[51]

what should be done to him Targum Jonathan explains: "The decree of the Sabbath was known to them but not the punishment for its violation." The Targum Neofiti comments as follows:

> This is one of the four legal cases that came up before Moses our master. In two of them Moses was quick (to act) and in two of them Moses was tardy. And in each case Moses said: I have not heard (the like). (He was quick to act) in the case of the unclean persons who could not keep the passover at its appointed time (Num. 9:6–13) and in the case of the daughters of Zelophehad (27:1–11; 36:1–12) because civil cases were involved. But in the case of the wood gatherer who profaned the Sabbath willfully and in the case of the blasphemer who pronounced the holy Name blasphemously (Lev. 24:10–23), Moses was tardy because these were capital cases. This was in order to teach the judges who would succeed Moses that they should be quick in civil cases and tardy in capital cases, so that they would not be in a hurry to put to death even one condemned to death; so that they would not be ashamed to say: We have not heard (a similar case), since Moses our master has also said: I have not heard.

Moses hesitated either in regard to the problem of whether the act of the Sabbath violator constituted work (and hence was a crime whether the violation was intended or not—a specific instance of verses 22–31) or in regard to the particular mode of the death penalty. These alternatives are discussed in Excursus 37.

35. This verse and the next exhibit a chiastic (inverse) structure. Command and fulfillment are related to each other chiastically and are therefore a single unit.[52]

shall pelt Hebrew *ragom* is an infinitive with the force of an imperative.

outside the camp Executions took place only outside the camp (Lev. 24:14,23) or the city (1 Kings 21:10,13). They took the form of stoning either (1) to avoid corpse ritual contamination, which would be transmitted by direct contact or by being under the same roof as the dead body (Num. 19:11,14; cf. Exod. 19:13) or (2) to avoid the shedding of blood and subsequent blood guilt (Gen. 9:5–6; Num. 35:33).[53]

36. the whole community The whole community participates in the execution[54] in order to indicate that they share the responsibility (see Lev. 24:14,16,23).

37 The LORD said to Moses as follows: 38 Speak to the
Israelite people and instruct them to make for themselves
fringes on the corners of their garments throughout the
ages; let them attach a cord of blue to the fringe at each
corner. 39 That shall be your fringe; look at it and recall all
the commandments of the LORD and observe them, so that
you do not follow your heart and eyes in your lustful urge.

אֶל־מֹשֶׁה לֵּאמֹר׃ 38 דַּבֵּר אֶל־בְּנֵי יִשְׂרָאֵל
וְאָמַרְתָּ אֲלֵהֶם וְעָשׂוּ לָהֶם צִיצִת עַל־כַּנְפֵי
בִגְדֵיהֶם לְדֹרֹתָם וְנָתְנוּ עַל־צִיצִת הַכָּנָף פְּתִיל
תְּכֵלֶת׃ 39 וְהָיָה לָכֶם לְצִיצִת וּרְאִיתֶם אֹתוֹ
וּזְכַרְתֶּם אֶת־כָּל־מִצְוֺת יְהוָה וַעֲשִׂיתֶם אֹתָם וְלֹא־
תָתֻרוּ אַחֲרֵי לְבַבְכֶם וְאַחֲרֵי עֵינֵיכֶם אֲשֶׁר־אַתֶּם
זֹנִים אַחֲרֵיהֶם׃ 40 לְמַעַן תִּזְכְּרוּ וַעֲשִׂיתֶם אֶת־כָּל־

TSITSIT ("TASSELS") (vv. 37–41)

These are also called *gedilim* in Deuteronomy 22:12. The origin, nature, and history of the *tsitsit* are discussed in Excursus 38. Most probably, the *tsitsit* section was placed here to form a verbal inclusion with the episode of the spies recounted in chapters 13–14. In "scouting" (*tur,* 13:2,25; 14:34), the spies whored (*zanah,* 14:33) after their eyes and brought a false report. So by wearing the *tsitsit,* Israel would be prevented from ever again "scouting" (*tur,* 15:39) and "whoring" (*zanah,* 15:39) "after their heart and eyes." Moreover, wearing the *tsitsit* would convert their dress into uniforms of the royal priests of God (see Excursus 38).

38. fringes The *tsitsit* resemble a lock of hair (cf. "and took me by the *tsitsit* of my head" in Ezek. 8:3). Hence, one should perhaps render it "tassels." The Targums and the Septuagint render "edges, hems"; the relation of the hem to the tassels is discussed in Excursus 38.

Presently, the *tsitsit* are attached to the four corners of a prayer shawl *(tallit).* Each *tsitsit* consists of four white threads, one of which is longer than the others. Holes are made in each of the four corners of the *tallit,* and the threads are inserted into them and folded over. The two collections of threads are then tied with a double knot. The long thread is wound round the others seven, eight, eleven, and thirteen times, each joint being separated from the other by a double knot. The Hebrew numerical value of the consonants of the word *tsitsit* is 600. If five (for the sets of double knots) and eight (for the number of thread ends) be added, they yield a total of 613, which, according to rabbinic tradition, represents the number of biblical commandments of which the *tsitsit* are to remind the wearer.

corners Hebrew *kanfei,* literally "wings." The rendering "corners" is really inappropriate here since, in ancient days, men wore closed robes or skirts just as did women. The term may, however, refer to the scalloped hems resembling wings or to the embroidered threads that hung from the hem at quarter points.

blue Rather, "violet" or "blue-purple," the sign of royalty. The violet, or blue-purple, dye was extracted from the gland of the *Murex trunculus* snail found in shallow waters off the coast of northern Israel and Lebanon. Since it has been shown that 12,000 snails yield only 1.4 grams of dye, it can be readily understood why only royalty could afford it; and hence the term "royal blue or purple."

39. That shall be your fringe Literally, "that shall be a *tsitsit* for you." Possibly *tsitsit* in this phrase should be rendered "ornament, something to look at"—from the verb *hetsits,* "peek, glimpse,"[55] or from *tsits,* "ornament, frontlet," mentioned in Exodus 28:36. The Septuagint renders "and it (the blue-purple cord) shall be on your fringe."[56] Its function is clearly symbolic, like that of an *'ot,* "sign." For other signs and their respective functions, compare the rainbow in Genesis 9:8–17; the blood of the paschal sacrifice in Exodus 12:7,12–14; the Sabbath in Exodus 31:12–17; the altar covering in Numbers 17:1–5; and Aaron's rod in Numbers 17:25–26.

look . . . recall . . . observe Hebrew *ra'ah . . . zakhar . . . 'asah.* Most *zikhronot*—reminders in the priestly texts of the Torah—remind God to remember Israel: the breastplate (Exod. 28:12), the silver ransom (Exod. 30:16), the gold booty (Num. 31:54), the jealousy offering (Num. 5:18), and the blowing of the trumpets (Num. 10:9). However, four reminders are not directed to God but to Israel: the altar plating (Num. 17:5), the Passover day (Exod. 12:14), the *tefillin* (Exod. 13:7), and the cairn

40 Thus you shall be reminded to observe all My commandments and to be holy to your God. 41 I the LORD am your God, who brought you out of the land of Egypt to be your God: I, the LORD your God.

מִצְוֺתָ֑י וִהְיִיתֶ֥ם קְדֹשִׁ֖ים לֵֽאלֹהֵיכֶֽם׃ 41 אֲנִ֞י יְהוָ֣ה
אֱלֹֽהֵיכֶ֗ם אֲשֶׁ֨ר הוֹצֵ֤אתִי אֶתְכֶם֙ מֵאֶ֣רֶץ מִצְרַ֔יִם
לִהְי֥וֹת לָכֶ֖ם לֵאלֹהִ֑ים אֲנִ֖י יְהוָ֥ה אֱלֹהֵיכֶֽם׃ פ

erected after crossing the Jordan (Josh. 4:6–7,21–24). The fringes are in the latter category; they are mnemotechnical devices to remind Israel of God's commandments. Indeed, the purpose of all ritual is, by means of sensual experience, to lead to conviction and finally to action. The rabbis formulated it thus: "Sight leads to memory and memory to action."[57]

it Hebrew *'oto,* masculine, cannot refer to the tassel, which is a feminine noun, but must refer to the entire combination of tassel and thread.[58]

lustful urge The root *z-n-h* means "fornicate" and is used figuratively in connection with intercourse with other gods (e.g., Exod. 34:15–16; especially Ezek. 6:9) and of moral defection (e.g., Isa. 1:21). Both usages are echoed in the rabbinic comment: "'Your heart' implies heresy; 'eyes' implies harlotry."[59] The sectaries of Qumran applied these images to all wrongdoing, as for instance: "Stubbornly follow a sinful ***heart*** and ***lustful eyes*** committing all manner of evil" (1QS 1:7).

40. reminded to observe The roots *z-kh-r* and *'-s-h* are repeated because they lead to the highest spiritual attainment—holiness (see Excursus 38).

holy to your God The *tsitsit* are a reminder of the priestly robes. In other words, the Israelites, although not priests, can still attain a life of holiness! "The *tsitsit* add holiness to Israel."[60]

41. to be your God The redemption of Israel from Egypt was the act by which the Lord claimed Israel's allegiance (Exod. 6:7; 20:2–5).[61] Israel is thereby enjoined to follow His commandments (Exod. 20:2ff.) and achieve holiness (Lev. 11:45; Deut. 26:17–19).

> Why at every performance of a commandment must we have the Exodus in our thoughts? Here is a parable: It can be likened to a king whose friend's son was taken prisoner. The king redeemed him but expressly upon the understanding that he should become a slave, so that at any time, if he should disobey the king, the latter would say: "You are my slave!" As soon as they entered the country, the king said to him: "Put on my sandals! Take my clothes to the bathhouse!" When the son began to protest the king pulled out the bill of sale and said to him: "You are my slave!" So when the Holy One redeemed the descendants of Abraham, His friend, He did not redeem them so that they should be His sons but His slaves, so that when He commands and they do not obey He could say to them: "You are My slaves." And as soon as they went out into the wilderness, He began to issue some light commandments and some weighty ones, for instance: the laws concerning Sabbath and incest (weighty ones) and *tsitsit* and *tefillin* (light ones). When Israel began to protest, He said to them: "You are My slaves! For this reason have I redeemed you, that I might issue decrees and you should keep them."[62]

This rabbinic parable neatly captures the nexus between the Exodus and Sinai: The Exodus entitled God to impose His covenant upon Israel. By rescuing Israel from the Egyptian bondage, the Lord acquired Israel as His slave. Israel, then, exchanged masters—the Lord replaced Pharaoh—and was subsequently obligated to fulfill the Lord's commandments.

KORAḤ

16 Now Korah, son of Izhar son of Kohath son of Levi, betook himself, along with Dathan and Abiram sons of Eliab, and On son of Peleth—descendants of Reuben—[2]to

קרח

ט״ז וַיִּקַּח קֹרַח בֶּן־יִצְהָר בֶּן־קְהָת בֶּן־לֵוִי וְדָתָן
וַאֲבִירָם בְּנֵי אֱלִיאָב וְאוֹן בֶּן־פֶּלֶת בְּנֵי רְאוּבֵן׃

Encroachment on the Tabernacle (16:1–18:32)

Koraḥ

The theme of this entire ***parashah*** (chaps. 16–18) is encroachment on the Tabernacle. Korah, vying with Aaron for the priesthood, leads a rebellion of tribal chieftains. They are incinerated by a divine fire when their incense offering—a test devised by Moses—is rejected. (The story of Dathan and Abiram's uprising against Moses is also woven into the narrative; see Excursus 39.) The fire pans of the slain aspirants are then hammered into plating for the altar—a warning to future encroachers. When the people complain about the death of their chieftains, they, in turn, are afflicted with a deadly plague. And a new test involving chieftains' staffs again proves Aaron's rights to the priesthood.

At this point the people panic. Having witnessed the massacre of their leaders at the Tabernacle and the massacre of fellow Israelites in the subsequent plague, they are in mortal fear of entering the Tabernacle lest they too be guilty of encroachment. Divine assurance is then given that, henceforth, the priests and Levites, whose job it is to guard the Tabernacle, will assume responsibility for any encroachment: The Israelites can now worship at the Tabernacle without fear. The ***parashah*** concludes with a list of emoluments granted the priests and Levites as recompense for the risks they assume in guarding and transporting the Tabernacle.

The thematic unity of this ***parashah*** can best be seen by the following outline of its contents:

The Korahite encroachment: vindication of Aaron (and Moses) (16:1–35)
The encroachers' fire pans as a sign (17:1–5)
The plague: further vindication of Aaron (17:6–15)
The staffs: final vindication of Aaron (17:16–26)
Priestly and Levitical responsibility for encroachment (17:27–18:7)
Priestly and Levitical emoluments for assuming the risks in guarding the Tabernacle against encroachment (18:8–32)

CHAPTER 16 THE KORAHITE REBELLIONS (vv. 1–35)

Israel's fortunes have reached a low ebb. Demoralized by the majority report of the scouts and condemned by their God to die in the wilderness, the people are psychologically receptive to demagogic appeals to overthrow their leadership and return to Egypt. Four separate rebellions are herewith recorded and fused: the Levites against Aaron; Dathan and Abiram against Moses; the tribal chieftains against Aaron; and the entire community against Moses and Aaron. The archconspirator, however, is the Levite Korah, who instigates or is associated with all four rebellious groups. The punishment is swift and dreadful: Dathan and Abiram are swallowed by the earth; the encroaching chieftains are incinerated by a divine fire (the fate of the rebellious Levites is not recorded); the community, however, is saved from destruction by the intercession of Moses and Aaron. As for Korah, the nature of his punishment is not clear. He probably perished with the chieftains, but a variant tradition records that he perished with Dathan and Abiram in the earthquake (26:10). For details, see Excursus 39.

DRAMATIS PERSONAE: THE LEADERS OF THE REBELLION (vv. 1–2)

1. ***Korah, son of Izhar son of Kohath*** According to the rabbis, Korah maintains that since the sons of Amram, the eldest of Kohath, assumed the leadership of the people (Moses) and the priesthood (Aaron), the position of the head of the family should have gone to himself, the eldest of the second son of Kohath. Instead, it was given to Elizaphan son of Uzziel, the youngest son of Kohath,[1] as demonstrated by the following genealogical chart (cf. Exod. 6:16–22):

rise up against Moses, together with two hundred and fifty Israelites, chieftains of the community, chosen in the assembly, men of repute. [3]They combined against Moses and Aaron and said to them, "You have gone too far! For all the community are holy, all of them, and the LORD is in their midst. Why then do you raise yourselves above the LORD's congregation?"

² וַיָּקֻ֙מוּ֙ לִפְנֵ֣י מֹשֶׁ֔ה וַאֲנָשִׁ֥ים מִבְּנֵֽי־יִשְׂרָאֵ֖ל חֲמִשִּׁ֣ים וּמָאתָ֑יִם נְשִׂיאֵ֥י עֵדָ֛ה קְרִאֵ֥י מוֹעֵ֖ד אַנְשֵׁי־שֵֽׁם: 3 וַיִּקָּהֲל֞וּ עַל־מֹשֶׁ֣ה וְעַֽל־אַהֲרֹ֗ן וַיֹּאמְר֣וּ אֲלֵהֶם֮ רַב־לָכֶם֒ כִּ֤י כָל־הָֽעֵדָה֙ כֻּלָּ֣ם קְדֹשִׁ֔ים וּבְתוֹכָ֖ם יְהוָ֑ה וּמַדּ֥וּעַ תִּֽתְנַשְּׂא֖וּ עַל־קְהַ֥ל יְהוָֽה:

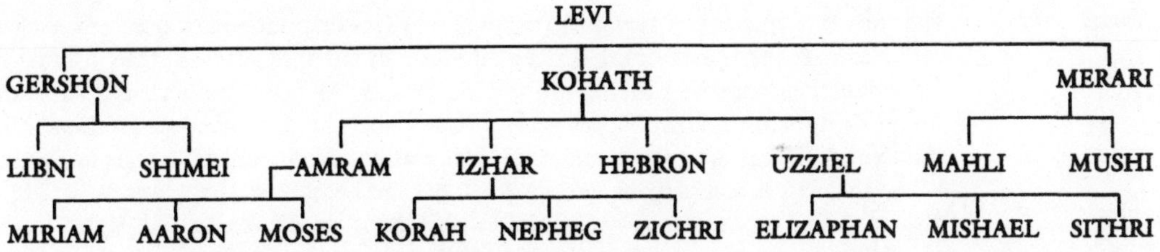

betook himself So Ibn Janaḥ (cited by Ibn Ezra). Hebrew *va-yikkaḥ*, literally "he took," has no object here. Many solutions have been proposed.[2]

Dathan and Abiram . . . Reuben The mention of the entire tribal line fulfills two purposes: (1) Being descended from Reuben, the first-born of Jacob and, hence, the original leader of the tribes, they resented Moses' leadership; and (2) being encamped to the south alongside the Kohathites (see diagram in Excursus 3), they were neighbors of Korah, from which "one can learn: Woe unto the wicked, woe unto his neighbor."[3]

On son of Peleth He is never mentioned again.[4]

2. rise up against Hebrew *va-yakumu lifnei*. The preposition '*al* would normally be expected with this verb, but the analogies of 26:37 and Joshua 7:12,13 suggest that the meaning seems to be "confront, stand up to."

Israelites Rather, "Israelite dignitaries." '*Anashim* means not only "men" but "dignitaries" (see 13:2–3).[5]

chieftains of Hebrew *nesi'ei*. See the Comment to 1:16 and Excursus 1. These 250 chieftains were not only Levites, but represented a cross section of the tribes, as is indirectly implied by 27:3, where Zelophehad, the Manassite chieftain, is exonerated from the suspicion that he had joined Korah's rebellion (cf. also 20:3).

community Hebrew '*edah*. See Excursus 1.

chosen in Hebrew *keri'ei* (cf. 1:16; 26:9). Rather, "called to" (as the Greek). Chieftains were heads of clans and were called to the national assembly by virtue of this office, as noted in Excursus 1.

assembly Hebrew *mo'ed*. The same term occurs in the account of the eleventh-century B.C.E. journey of the Egyptian official Wen-Amon[6] in regard to the assembly called by the king of Byblos on the Phoenician coast. From the documents of Ugarit, a city just north of Byblos, a few centuries earlier, we learn of the *phr m'd*, "the gathering of the assembly" (137. 14, 31). The name of Israel's national assembly is '*edah* (cf. 1:16; 26:9).

repute Hebrew *shem*, literally "name." Hence ignoble persons are "nameless" as in Job 30:8, "scoundrels, nobodies," literally "sons without a name."

THE INCENSE TEST FOR HOLINESS (vv. 3–7)

3. They combined[7]

You have gone too far Hebrew *rav lakhem*, literally "you have too much," that is, power and prestige.[8]

4 וַיִּשְׁמַע מֹשֶׁה וַיִּפֹּל עַל־פָּנָיו׃ 5 וַיְדַבֵּר אֶל־קֹרַח
וְאֶל־כָּל־עֲדָתוֹ לֵאמֹר בֹּקֶר וְיֹדַע יְהוָה אֶת־
אֲשֶׁר־לוֹ וְאֶת־הַקָּדוֹשׁ וְהִקְרִיב אֵלָיו וְאֵת אֲשֶׁר
יִבְחַר־בּוֹ יַקְרִיב אֵלָיו׃ 6 זֹאת עֲשׂוּ קְחוּ־לָכֶם
מַחְתּוֹת קֹרַח וְכָל־עֲדָתוֹ׃ 7 וּתְנוּ בָהֵן ׀ אֵשׁ

4When Moses heard this, he fell on his face. 5Then he
spoke to Korah and all his company, saying, "Come morning, the LORD will make known who is His and who is holy,
and will grant him access to Himself; He will grant access
to the one He has chosen. 6Do this: You, Korah and all your
band, take fire pans, 7and tomorrow put fire in them and lay

all the community are holy This claim is anathema to the priestly teaching that only priests are holy (see Excursus 11).[9] It is a clever application of the command to "be holy" at the end of the previous section (15:40), and it may account for the juxtaposition of the story of Korah's rebellion to the commandment on fringes. In effect, Korah argues that if all of Israel aspires to holiness by wearing a priestly mixture in their garments (see Excursus 38), why should they not be eligible for the priesthood itself? Buber suggests that Moses' own words were used against him: If all of Israel were worthy of being prophets (11:29), then there was no need for Moses' mediation. However, prophets are not "holy." Therefore, either Aaron is the intended target of the attack (and Moses is bracketed with him because it was he who appointed and consecrated Aaron), or Moses too is accused of presuming to be holy because he, on occasion, assumed priestly powers, such as when he officiated at Aaron's consecration, as recounted in Exodus 29 and Leviticus 8 (see also Exod. 24:6–8).

raise yourself Hebrew *titnasse'u,* a play on the word *nasi'* "chieftain," that is, play the chieftain.

community . . . congregation Hebrew *'edah* and *kahal* are synonymous terms, but whereas the former is the technical term for the national "assembly" (see Excursus 1), the latter is a verbal noun meaning "assemblage, gathering."

4. ***fell on his face*** So that God would provide him an answer.[10] This view assumes that Moses (but not Aaron) had entered the Tabernacle enclosure to consult God. The midrash, however, claims that Moses fell on his face in despair; he was afraid that his many intercessions on his people's behalf may have exhausted his influence with God,[11] in which case Moses did not enter the Tabernacle but prostrated himself before Korah.

5. ***morning*** Presumably, a day is needed for the required purification rituals before appearing at the Tabernacle (cf. Lev. 15:16–18 and Excursus 27).

who is His and who is holy To lead Israel and the priesthood, respectively.[12] These two clauses may reflect a fusion of two phases of the rebellion, one against Moses, the other against Aaron.[13]

will grant him access to Himself Hebrew *ve-hikriv 'elav.* The verb *karav* in cultic contexts frequently means "be qualified," and with the preposition *'el* it means "have access to,"[14] as is correctly rendered in the Targum's additional "to serve Him."

grant access . . . has chosen Hebrew *yivḥar . . . yakriv.*[15] "Grant access" also occurs earlier in the verse, but this time it appears in the imperfect to indicate that God intends to designate His priest for all time.[16]

chosen Because the Hebrew verb *baḥar* is found in the priestly texts only in connection with the priesthood itself, as, for instance, in 16:7 and 17:20, Aaron must be the referent of both "holy" and "chosen." In Deuteronomy, however, all of Israel, not just the priesthood, is holy; and therefore Israel too is "chosen" (Deut. 7:6; 14:2).

6. ***Do this*** The offering of incense is an exclusive priestly prerogative and nonpriests offer it only at the peril of their lives, be they Levites (17:5) or kings (2 Chron. 26:16–20). Even priests incur death if they offer it incorrectly (Lev. 10:1–2).

Korah and all your band Literally, "Korah and all his band."[17] Strangely, Aaron is not asked to submit to the same test (but see below, vv. 16–17).

fire pans Hebrew *maḥtot,* a flat pan used for removing ashes or live coals from the altar[18] and upon which incense is placed (16:18; 17:11).

incense on them before the LORD. Then the man whom the LORD chooses, he shall be the holy one. You have gone too far, sons of Levi!"

[8]Moses said further to Korah, "Hear me, sons of Levi. [9]Is it not enough for you that the God of Israel has set you apart from the community of Israel and given you access to Him, to perform the duties of the LORD's Tabernacle and to minister to the community and serve them? [10]Now that He has advanced you and all your fellow Levites with you, do you seek the priesthood too? [11]Truly, it is against the LORD

וְשִׂימוּ עֲלֵיהֶן קְטֹרֶת לִפְנֵי יְהֹוָה מָחָר וְהָיָה הָאִישׁ
אֲשֶׁר־יִבְחַר יְהֹוָה הוּא הַקָּדוֹשׁ רַב־לָכֶם בְּנֵי לֵוִי׃
8 וַיֹּאמֶר מֹשֶׁה אֶל־קֹרַח שִׁמְעוּ־נָא בְּנֵי לֵוִי׃
9 הַמְעַט מִכֶּם כִּי־הִבְדִּיל אֱלֹהֵי יִשְׂרָאֵל אֶתְכֶם
מֵעֲדַת יִשְׂרָאֵל לְהַקְרִיב אֶתְכֶם אֵלָיו לַעֲבֹד אֶת־
עֲבֹדַת מִשְׁכַּן יְהֹוָה וְלַעֲמֹד לִפְנֵי הָעֵדָה לְשָׁרְתָם׃
10 וַיַּקְרֵב אֹתְךָ וְאֶת־כָּל־אַחֶיךָ בְנֵי־לֵוִי אִתָּךְ
וּבִקַּשְׁתֶּם גַּם־כְּהֻנָּה׃ 11 לָכֵן אַתָּה וְכָל־עֲדָתְךָ

7. fire in them Hebrew *bahen,* probably in the sense of *'alehem,* "on them" (16:18; 17:11; see the Comment to v. 6), in which case *'esh,* "fire," should be rendered "coals" (17:2; Gen. 22:6).

before the LORD That is, at the entrance to the Tabernacle court (v. 18).

chooses . . . holy one Two clauses of verse 5 are herein telescoped, indicating their synonymity.

You have gone too far The same words begin Korah's address (v. 3), thus forming an inclusion to the dialogue (vv. 3–7). Similarly, the phrase "we will not come" frames Dathan and Abiram's address (vv. 12–14). The midrash explains this repetition as a sign that Moses became impatient with Korah and refused to hear him any further and then God said, "With what you have struck you will be struck. You have said *rav lakhem,* later I will tell you *rav lakh* (Deut. 3:26)," thereby cutting off Moses' plea to enter the promised land.[19]

sons of Levi Not all the followers of Korah (vv. 5–7), or even the major part, were Levites.[20] On this, see Excursus 39.

MOSES REBUKES THE LEVITES (vv. 8–11)

When Moses' own leadership is contested, he does not defend himself but leaves his defense to God (12:2–3; 16:4–5). When Aaron is the target, however, Moses springs to his defense.

8. Hear me[21]

sons of Levi Earlier, in verse 2, we are told that Korah's allies are the tribal chieftains, but here they seem to be Levites.

9. not enough Literally, "too little."

has set you apart See 8:14.

given you access to Him See Comment to verse 5.

the duties Rather, "the labors," referring to the Levitical responsibility and privilege of dismantling, transporting, and reassembling the Tabernacle and its sancta. For the meaning of Levitical *'avodah,* see Excursus 6.

minister Hebrew *'amad lifnei* is language of subordination (3:6; 1 Sam. 16:22; 1 Kings 1:2).

serve them That is, by assisting the Israelites in the preparation of their sacrifices.[22] The lay worshiper must pass through a Levitical watch post at the entrance of the Tabernacle. It then becomes the responsibility of the Levites to keep him under guard lest he encroach upon the sancta (3:7). It is only natural that this Levite guard also assist him with the noncultic preliminary acts of preparing the sacrifice: slaughtering, flaying, and washing the animal, tasks that normally are performed by the offerer himself (cf. Lev. 1:5,6,9). The combination of *'amad lifnei* and *sheret,* "minister" and "serve," also delineates the assistance rendered to the priests by the Levites (3:6), which, however, takes a different form—sharing with them the custody of the Tabernacle (see 3:7).

10. Now that[23]

that you and all your company have banded together. For who is Aaron that you should rail against him?"

12Moses sent for Dathan and Abiram, sons of Eliab; but they said, "We will not come! 13Is it not enough that you brought us from a land flowing with milk and honey to have us die in the wilderness, that you would also lord it over us? 14Even if you had brought us to a land flowing with milk and honey, and given us possession of fields and vineyards, should you gouge out those men's eyes? We will not come!" 15Moses was much aggrieved and he said to the

הַנֹּעָדִים עַל־יְהוָה וְאַהֲרֹן מַה־הוּא כִּי תלונו עָלָיו׃
12 וַיִּשְׁלַח מֹשֶׁה לִקְרֹא לְדָתָן וְלַאֲבִירָם בְּנֵי
אֱלִיאָב וַיֹּאמְרוּ לֹא נַעֲלֶה׃ 13 הַמְעַט כִּי הֶעֱלִיתָנוּ
מֵאֶרֶץ זָבַת חָלָב וּדְבַשׁ לַהֲמִיתֵנוּ בַּמִּדְבָּר כִּי־
תִשְׂתָּרֵר עָלֵינוּ גַּם־הִשְׂתָּרֵר׃ שני 14 אַף לֹא אֶל־
אֶרֶץ זָבַת חָלָב וּדְבַשׁ הֲבִיאֹתָנוּ וַתִּתֶּן־לָנוּ נַחֲלַת
שָׂדֶה וָכָרֶם הַעֵינֵי הָאֲנָשִׁים הָהֵם תְּנַקֵּר לֹא
נַעֲלֶה׃ 15 וַיִּחַר לְמֹשֶׁה מְאֹד וַיֹּאמֶר אֶל־יְהוָה

v. 11. תַּלִּינוּ ק'

advanced you Hebrew *va-yakrev,* "qualified"; see verse 5. "You" (sing.) contrasts with "you" (pl.) in verse 9, referring to Korah's loftier position as a Kohathite (over his fellow Levites), one who has the privilege of carrying the sacred vessels.[24]

priesthood The Targums render "High Priesthood," intimating that Korah desired to usurp Aaron's role.

11. ***Truly*** Targum Neofiti renders "on oath" or "I swear (in an oath)."

against Hebrew *ʿal.* For this usage, see 26:9 and Psalms 2:2.

the LORD The real thrust of the rebellion is against the Lord, who has chosen Moses and Aaron.[25]

who Hebrew *mah,* literally "what." Perhaps the meaning is "what is Aaron's part" (cf. *naḥnu mah,* "what is our part," Exod. 16:8); that is, Aaron did not assume the priesthood by his own initiative but was so chosen by God. This verse makes it clear that the rebellion was really directed against Aaron and not Moses.

MOSES DEFIED (vv. 12–15)

Although Dathan and Abiram's motive is not explicitly stated, it is hinted at by their accusation that Moses wants to "lord it over us" (v. 13). Thus, "We will not come" (vv. 12,14) clearly implies "We will no longer obey your orders"—an open break with Moses' authority. That Dathan and Abiram stem from Reuben, Jacob's first-born, may point to the underlying cause for their rebellion (see Excursus 39).

12. ***We will not come!*** Hebrew *lo' naʿaleh.* The verb *ʿalah,* literally "go up," is used in connection with appearing before a court (Deut. 25:7; Judg. 4:5; Ruth 4:1).[26] A word play is also evident here: Since Moses has not brought up *(heʿelah)* Israel to the land (v. 13), they too will not *naʿaleh* to the land but return to Egypt.[27]

13. ***Is it not enough*** Hebrew *ha-meʿat,* literally "is it too little." The same word that Moses used in verse 9 is now turned against him. Similarly, Dathan and Abiram contradict Moses' major claim: Egypt and not Canaan is the true land of milk and honey (14:8; cf. Exod. 3:17). Furthermore, Israel will not reach the promised land but will die in the wilderness (14:29).

also lord it over us Hebrew *tistarer ʿalenu gam histarer.*[28] The Hitpael of *s-r-r* has the connotation of "playing or pretending to be the lord" (cf. *titnaseʾu,* v. 3). This root *s-r-r* was also flung at Moses by his fellow Hebrew in Egypt: "Who made you chief *(sar)* and ruler over us?" (Exod. 2:14), an association that leads the midrash to identify this Hebrew with Dathan.[29]

14. ***Even if you had*** This rendering follows Ibn Ezra who understands *'af lu* for *'af lo',* which literally means "you have not even."

brought us to a land flowing with milk and honey That is, as you promised (Exod. 3:8,17; 4:3).

Lord, "Pay no regard to their oblation. I have not taken the ass of any one of them, nor have I wronged any one of them."

16And Moses said to Korah, "Tomorrow, you and all your company appear before the Lord, you and they and Aaron. 17Each of you take his fire pan and lay incense on it, and each of you bring his fire pan before the Lord, two hundred and fifty fire pans; you and Aaron also [bring] your fire pans." 18Each of them took his fire pan, put fire in it, laid incense on it, and took his place at the entrance of the Tent of Meeting, as did Moses and Aaron. 19Korah gath-

אַל־תֵּ֖פֶן אֶל־מִנְחָתָ֑ם לֹ֠א חֲמ֨וֹר אֶחָ֤ד מֵהֶם֙
נָשָׂ֔אתִי וְלֹ֥א הֲרֵעֹ֖תִי אֶת־אַחַ֥ד מֵהֶֽם׃ 16 וַיֹּ֤אמֶר
מֹשֶׁה֙ אֶל־קֹ֔רַח אַתָּה֙ וְכָל־עֲדָ֣תְךָ֔ הֱי֖וּ לִפְנֵ֣י יְהוָ֑ה
אַתָּ֥ה וָהֵ֛ם וְאַהֲרֹ֖ן מָחָֽר׃ 17 וּקְח֣וּ ׀ אִ֣ישׁ מַחְתָּת֗וֹ
וּנְתַתֶּ֤ם עֲלֵיהֶם֙ קְטֹ֔רֶת וְהִקְרַבְתֶּ֞ם לִפְנֵ֤י יְהוָה֙ אִ֣ישׁ
מַחְתָּת֔וֹ חֲמִשִּׁ֥ים וּמָאתַ֖יִם מַחְתֹּ֑ת וְאַתָּ֥ה וְאַהֲרֹ֖ן
אִ֥ישׁ מַחְתָּתֽוֹ׃ 18 וַיִּקְח֞וּ אִ֣ישׁ מַחְתָּת֗וֹ וַיִּתְּנ֤וּ
עֲלֵיהֶם֙ אֵ֔שׁ וַיָּשִׂ֥ימוּ עֲלֵיהֶ֖ם קְטֹ֑רֶת וַיַּֽעַמְד֗וּ פֶּ֛תַח
אֹ֥הֶל מוֹעֵ֖ד וּמֹשֶׁ֥ה וְאַהֲרֹֽן׃ 19 וַיַּקְהֵ֨ל עֲלֵיהֶ֥ם קֹ֙רַח֙

gouge out those men's eyes This idiom also means "hoodwink"[30] and corresponds to the modern idioms "throw dust in the eyes"[31] or "pull the wool over the eyes."[32] "Those men" refers either to the elders who accompanied Moses (v. 25)[33] or, more likely, to themselves.[34]

We will not come! These words frame the speech of defiance in an inclusion (see v. 12).

15. ***aggrieved*** The verb ***ḥarah*** alone means "be upset, distressed" (e.g., Gen. 4:5), whereas with ***'af*** it means "be angry" (as in 11:1,10).

oblation Hebrew ***minḥatam,*** referring to their incense offering,[35] to their prior but unmentioned offering,[36] or to any sacrifice they might wish to offer prior to the test.[37] The possibility must also be considered that this verse belongs with the next section (vv. 16–22), in which case ***minḥatam*** refers to the incense offering of Korah and the 250 chieftains. (Whereas ***minḥah*** can mean only "cereal offering" in the priestly texts, it can connote any sacrifice in the narrative material.)

taken Hebrew ***nasa'ti. Nasa'*** followed by the preposition ***min*** means "take," literally "lift from" (as in Josh. 21:23; 1 Sam. 17:34).[38]

ass[39]

THE INCENSE TEST AT THE TENT OF MEETING (vv. 16–24)

Korah instigates the entire community to join him and the 250 chieftains in the rebellion against Moses and Aaron. God intervenes, threatening to destroy them all. Moses and Aaron intercede on behalf of the community.

16. ***And Moses said to Korah . . .*** Verses 16–17 are a repetition of verses 6–7, except that Aaron, missing there, is explicitly mentioned here. And the Levites, who are addressed in verses 6–7, are missing here. Possibly Korah stands for all the rebellious Levites.

you and all[40]

before the Lord That is, at the entrance to the Tent of Meeting (v. 19).

18. ***Each . . .*** The execution of the test, presumably on the next day.

put fire But Moses did not command this here (v. 17) although he did so in the earlier command (v. 7). Is this omission a hint that Korah and the chieftains were guilty of offering ***'esh zarah,*** "unauthorized fire," that is, not from the altar—the sin of Nadab and Abihu (Lev. 10:2)?[41] It is hardly accidental that when Moses asks Aaron to offer incense on a fire pan he specifies that the fire be taken from the altar (17:11).[42]

in it Hebrew ***'aleihem.*** Rather, "on it" (see 17:11 and the Comment to v. 6).

as did Moses and Aaron[43]

19. ***whole community*** Hebrew ***kol ha-'edah*** presupposes that Korah rallied all of Israel behind him;[44] hence, God intended to destroy them (v. 21).[45]

ered the whole community against them at the entrance of the Tent of Meeting.

Then the Presence of the Lord appeared to the whole community, [20]and the Lord spoke to Moses and Aaron, saying, [21]"Stand back from this community that I may annihilate them in an instant!" [22]But they fell on their faces and said, "O God, Source of the breath of all flesh! When one man sins, will You be wrathful with the whole community?"

[23]The Lord spoke to Moses, saying, [24]"Speak to the community and say: Withdraw from about the abodes of Korah, Dathan, and Abiram." [25]Moses rose and went to

אֶת־כָּל־הָעֵדָה אֶל־פֶּתַח אֹהֶל מוֹעֵד וַיֵּרָא כְבוֹד־
יְהוָה אֶל־כָּל־הָעֵדָה׃ פ שלישי 20 וַיְדַבֵּר
יְהוָה אֶל־מֹשֶׁה וְאֶל־אַהֲרֹן לֵאמֹר׃ 21 הִבָּדְלוּ
מִתּוֹךְ הָעֵדָה הַזֹּאת וַאֲכַלֶּה אֹתָם כְּרָגַע׃ 22 וַיִּפְּלוּ
עַל־פְּנֵיהֶם וַיֹּאמְרוּ אֵל אֱלֹהֵי הָרוּחֹת לְכָל־בָּשָׂר
הָאִישׁ אֶחָד יֶחֱטָא וְעַל כָּל־הָעֵדָה תִּקְצֹף׃
פ 23 וַיְדַבֵּר יְהוָה אֶל־מֹשֶׁה לֵּאמֹר׃ 24 דַּבֵּר
אֶל־הָעֵדָה לֵאמֹר הֵעָלוּ מִסָּבִיב לְמִשְׁכַּן־קֹרַח
דָּתָן וַאֲבִירָם׃ 25 וַיָּקָם מֹשֶׁה וַיֵּלֶךְ אֶל־דָּתָן

21. Stand back Hebrew *hibbadelu,* literally "separate yourselves" (17:10). This separation from the community is reminiscent of the "separation" (same root) by the Levites from the community (v. 9). The former case is a separation from the fate of the Israelites; the latter, for the service of God.

this community This refers to the community of Israel (v. 19) who are not among the conspirators but who are the innocent sheep (v. 22); compare 17:10 for the same usage but not the same innocence.

22. they fell on their faces That is, in prayer[46] (see v. 4).

Source of Hebrew *'elohei,* literally "God of."

the breath Hebrew *ha-ruḥot* (see 27:16). God gives man His breath at birth and withdraws it at death. This idea is found in Isaiah 42:5, Zechariah 12:1, and elsewhere. The implication of this divine epithet is that since God is the creator of life, He alone determines who is to live and who is to die; hence, His anger need not engulf the wicked. In the midrash we read:

> They said to Him: "Sovereign of the Universe! In the case of a mortal king, if a province rebels against him and rises and curses the king or his deputies, even if only ten or twenty of them have done so, he sends his legions there and carries out a massacre, slaying the good with the bad, because he cannot tell which of them has rebelled and which has not, or who has honored the king and who has cursed him. You, however, know the thoughts of man and what the hearts and reins counsel. You discern the inclinations of your creatures and know which man has sinned and which has not, who has rebelled and who has not. You know the spirit *(ruaḥ)* of each and every one."[47]

When one man[48] Since more than Korah were implicated in the rebellion, the entire statement may originally have been a popular saying.[49] The reference, however, may be to Korah, since he alone instigated the community.

wrathful with the whole community The divine right to punish collectively is herewith both assumed and questioned (see Lev. 10:6).[50]

24. community But the community was gathered at the Tent of Meeting! This is one of the indications that originally the rebellion of Dathan and Abiram and the rebellion of Korah may have been separate events.

Withdraw[51] The verb *'alah,* "go up," was chosen as a contrast to *yarad,* "go down," the punishment meted out to Dathan and Abiram (cf. the Comment to v. 30). For an explanation of why the people must separate themselves from the sinners in order to escape divine punishment, see the Comment to 17:10.

Dathan and Abiram, the elders of Israel following him.
26 He addressed the community, saying, "Move away from
the tents of these wicked men and touch nothing that
belongs to them, lest you be wiped out for all their sins."

וַאֲבִירָם וַיֵּלְכוּ אַחֲרָיו זִקְנֵי יִשְׂרָאֵל׃ 26 וַיְדַבֵּר אֶל־
הָעֵדָה לֵאמֹר סוּרוּ נָא מֵעַל אָהֳלֵי הָאֲנָשִׁים
הָרְשָׁעִים הָאֵלֶּה וְאַל־תִּגְּעוּ בְּכָל־אֲשֶׁר לָהֶם פֶּן־
תִּסָּפוּ בְּכָל־חַטֹּאתָם׃ 27 וַיֵּעָלוּ מֵעַל מִשְׁכַּן־קֹרַח

abodes The singular *mishkan* is reserved for the Tabernacle; for human abodes only the plural *mishkenot* is used and, then, only in poetry, where it is usually in parallel with *'ohalim,* "tents" (e.g., 24:5; Isa. 54:2). In this chapter, too, plural "tents" occurs in verse 26, which makes the oddity of singular *mishkan* here and in verse 27 even more striking. One view is that it is used deliberately for the sake of irony: Since the rebels really directed their attack against God (v. 11), in effect their abode replaced the Tabernacle.[52] However, if this chapter fuses several rebellions, as is shown in Excursus 39, then *mishkan* should be rendered "Tabernacle," reading *ha-mishkan,* "the Tabernacle," or adding the Tetragrammaton, "of the Lord," as in 17:28. The proper names that follow would thus have been inserted in order to substantiate the tradition that Korah died with Dathan and Abiram in the earthquake (v. 35; 26:10).[53] According to this reconstruction, only the community gathered at the Tent of Meeting (v. 19) was told to withdraw so that God could destroy the incense offerers with His fire (v. 35).

THE PUNISHMENT OF THE REBELS (vv. 25–35)

The punishment of the 250 at the Tabernacle was by divine fire, presumably God's *kavod,* the pendulous cloud-encased fire over the Tabernacle (v. 35). Dathan and Abiram, however, having refused to leave their tents, had to suffer a divine punishment of a different order. Moses requests that the punishment be unprecedented: to be swallowed alive by the earth. Thus, they perish with their families and possessions (v. 32), in accordance with the divine principle of collective retribution (17:6–15,27–28; see Excursus 40).

25. elders of Israel Perhaps the seventy elders of 11:16.[54] Thus, Dathan and Abiram had no support from the other tribes. Also implied is that the elders, or at least a goodly number, were also chieftains, thus providing another support for the theory that the rebellion of Dathan and Abiram, which had no support from the elders/chieftains, must have occurred separately from the rebellion of the chieftains.

26. the community Hebrew *ha-'edah* without a pronominal suffix refers, in this chapter, to the Israelites who did not participate in the rebellion (see the Comment to v. 19). Also the use of *ha-'edah,* a term typical of the stratum that deals with the rebellion of the 250 chieftains, indicates that what originally followed was Moses' command to the Israelites to withdraw from the Tabernacle (see Excursus 39).

Move away Hebrew *suru na' me-'al* contrasts with the synonymous *he'alu mi-saviv,* "withdraw from about" (v. 24; cf. v. 27), indicating the possibility that they reflect different rebellion traditions.

tents The term *'ohel* refers not only to the tent's curtains but also to its contents (see Gen. 13:5).

touch nothing Since it will be subject to the ban *(ḥerem)* and will be destroyed.[55] The same prohibition occurs at the convocation at Sinai in Exodus 19:12–13. The implication is that contact with sancta can be fatal. Even more relevant is the banned spoil of Jericho, which is fatally contagious to Achan and his entire household, including his animals (Josh. 7:24), a contagion that can be imparted by touch (Num. 4:15) and even by sight (Num. 4:20; cf. Gen. 19:17).[56]

wiped out[57]

for all their sins[58]

27. withdrew[59]

27So they withdrew from about the abodes of Korah, Dathan, and Abiram.

Now Dathan and Abiram had come out and they stood at the entrance of their tents, with their wives, their children, and their little ones. 28And Moses said, "By this you shall know that it was the LORD who sent me to do all these things; that they are not of my own devising: 29if these men die as all men do, if their lot be the common fate of all mankind, it was not the LORD who sent me. 30But if the LORD brings about something unheard-of, so that the ground opens its mouth and swallows them up with all that belongs to them, and they go down alive into Sheol, you shall know that these men have spurned the LORD."

דָּתָ֣ן וַאֲבִירָ֗ם מִסָּבִ֔יב וְדָתָ֤ן וַאֲבִירָם֙ יָצְא֣וּ נִצָּבִ֔ים פֶּ֚תַח אָֽהֳלֵיהֶ֔ם וּנְשֵׁיהֶ֥ם וּבְנֵיהֶ֖ם וְטַפָּֽם׃ 28 וַיֹּ֣אמֶר מֹשֶׁ֔ה בְּזֹאת֙ תֵּֽדְע֔וּן כִּֽי־יְהוָ֣ה שְׁלָחַ֔נִי לַעֲשׂ֕וֹת אֵ֥ת כָּל־הַֽמַּעֲשִׂ֖ים הָאֵ֑לֶּה כִּי־לֹ֖א מִלִּבִּֽי׃ 29 אִם־כְּמ֤וֹת כָּל־הָֽאָדָם֙ יְמֻת֣וּן אֵ֔לֶּה וּפְקֻדַּת֙ כָּל־הָ֣אָדָ֔ם יִפָּקֵ֖ד עֲלֵיהֶ֑ם לֹ֥א יְהוָ֖ה שְׁלָחָֽנִי׃ 30 וְאִם־בְּרִיאָ֞ה יִבְרָ֣א יְהוָ֗ה וּפָצְתָ֨ה הָאֲדָמָ֤ה אֶת־פִּ֙יהָ֙ וּבָלְעָ֤ה אֹתָם֙ וְאֶת־כָּל־אֲשֶׁ֣ר לָהֶ֔ם וְיָרְד֥וּ חַיִּ֖ים שְׁאֹ֑לָה וִֽידַעְתֶּ֕ם כִּ֧י נִֽאֲצ֛וּ הָאֲנָשִׁ֥ים הָאֵ֖לֶּה אֶת־יְהוָֽה׃ 31 וַיְהִי֙ כְּכַלֹּת֔וֹ לְדַבֵּ֕ר אֵ֥ת כָּל־הַדְּבָרִ֖ים הָאֵ֑לֶּה וַתִּבָּקַ֥ע

had come out Hebrew *yatse'u,* with pluperfect force. This detail is crucial to the narrative. It presumes that for a curse to be effective, the object of the curse must be in view. Dathan, Abiram, and their families had to be seen by Moses. So, too, Balaam must see Israel, the object of his intended curse (22:41; 23:13).[60] There is also an ironic literary touch here: Dathan and Abiram have accused Moses of blinding the people's eyes (v. 14); now with Dathan, Abiram, and their families in full view, all of Israel will behold their punishment. The midrash finds yet another motive for their standing in front of their tents: a sign of their open defiance of Moses.[61]

28. all these things This refers to Moses' leadership, declared a failure by Dathan and Abiram (vv. 13–14),[62] or to Moses' appointment either of the Levites in place of the first-born[63] or of Aaron and his sons to the priesthood.[64]

my own devising Literally, "my own heart," the heart being the seat of thought. Moses wishes to demonstrate that he is not "lording" over Israel (v. 13) but merely executing the will of God (cf. 24:13).

29. if their lot be the common fate of all mankind Rather, "if these men are cared for as are all men." This rendering is based on Akkadian *pāqidu* "caretaker." Moses denies post-mortem burial rites to the accursed Korahites (Bloch-Smith, *Journal of Biblical Literature* 110 [1991], 329). That is, their corpses will somehow disappear.

30. brings about something unheard-of Literally, "will create a creation," that is, something unprecedented that did not exist before (e.g., Jer. 31:21). However, a preferable rendering is "makes a great chasm,"[65] corroborated by the fulfillment passage (vv. 31–33), as follows:

VERSE 30	VERSES 31b–33a
1. But if the LORD makes a great chasm	1. the ground under them burst asunder
2. So that the ground opens its mouth	2. and the earth opened its mouth
3. and swallows them up with all that belongs to them,	3. and swallowed them up with their households . . .
4. and they go down alive into Sheol.	4. They went down alive into Sheol.

go down alive Because Dathan and Abiram refused to "go up" (*'alah,* vv. 12,14) they will "go down" (*yarad,* vv. 30,33).[66] For complaining that God had "brought us up" (*he'elitanu,* v. 12) from Egypt to "have us die *(le-hamitenu)* in the wilderness" (v. 12), they will not "die *(yamutu)* as all men do" (v. 29) but will "go down alive *(ve-yardu hayyim,* vv. 30,33) in Sheol."[67]

Sheol The term for the underworld, the abode of the dead, as in Isaiah 14:9–11. Later it was believed that only the wicked descend to Sheol (see Pss. 9:18; 31:18) and that the egregious wicked "go

31Scarcely had he finished speaking all these words when the
ground under them burst asunder, 32and the earth opened
its mouth and swallowed them up with their households,
all Korah's people and all their possessions. 33They went
down alive into Sheol, with all that belonged to them; the
earth closed over them and they vanished from the midst of
the congregation. 34All Israel around them fled at their
shrieks, for they said, "The earth might swallow us!"
35And a fire went forth from the LORD and consumed the
two hundred and fifty men offering the incense.

הָֽאֲדָמָ֖ה אֲשֶׁ֥ר תַּחְתֵּיהֶֽם׃ 32 וַתִּפְתַּ֤ח הָאָ֙רֶץ֙ אֶת־
פִּ֔יהָ וַתִּבְלַ֥ע אֹתָ֖ם וְאֶת־בָּתֵּיהֶ֑ם וְאֵ֤ת כָּל־הָֽאָדָם֙
אֲשֶׁ֣ר לְקֹ֔רַח וְאֵ֖ת כָּל־הָרְכֽוּשׁ׃ 33 וַיֵּ֨רְד֜וּ הֵ֣ם וְכָל־
אֲשֶׁ֥ר לָהֶ֛ם חַיִּ֖ים שְׁאֹ֑לָה וַתְּכַ֤ס עֲלֵיהֶם֙ הָאָ֔רֶץ
וַיֹּאבְד֖וּ מִתּ֥וֹךְ הַקָּהָֽל׃ 34 וְכָל־יִשְׂרָאֵ֗ל אֲשֶׁ֛ר
סְבִיבֹתֵיהֶ֖ם נָ֣סוּ לְקֹלָ֑ם כִּ֣י אָֽמְר֔וּ פֶּן־תִּבְלָעֵ֖נוּ
הָאָֽרֶץ׃ 35 וְאֵ֥שׁ יָצְאָ֖ה מֵאֵ֣ת יְהוָ֑ה וַתֹּ֗אכַל אֵ֣ת
הַחֲמִשִּׁ֤ים וּמָאתַ֙יִם֙ אִ֔ישׁ מַקְרִיבֵ֖י הַקְּטֹֽרֶת׃
פ

down alive to Sheol" (see Ps. 55:16), whereas the righteous ascend heavenward (Prov. 15:24; Eccles. 3:20–23). In rabbinic times Sheol is replaced by the term Gehinnom (Gehenna).

The metaphoric language in this verse is a heritage of the pre-Israelite myth that death *(mavet;* Ugar. *mot)* was one of the gods (see Jer. 9:20), as can be seen from the linguistic fossil "the ground/ Sheol opens wide its mouth" to receive the dead (Isa. 5:14; Hab. 2:5; Prov. 1:12).[68] Perhaps it is the pagan background of the imagery that this verse tries to counter by emphasizing that it is solely the creative act of the Lord that is responsible for the activity of the earth.

you shall know The "unheard-of thing" was not that the earth swallowed the culprits, since earthquakes were well known;[69] rather, like the plagues in Egypt, the earthquake occurred precisely at the command of Moses.[70] According to Josephus, had Moses failed, he would have suffered the fate he proposed for them.[71]

spurned[72]

the LORD But not me.

32. ***earth*** Hebrew *'erets* here, and in verses 33,34, as in Ugaritic *arṣ* and Akkadian *erṣetu,* can only mean "netherworld" and is equivalent to Sheol in verse 33.[73]

households This may originally have referred only to the families of Dathan and Abiram (see Ps. 106:17 and Excursus 39).

all Korah's people The fate of Korah himself is not mentioned here, although 26:10 relates that he too was swallowed by the earth. The implication here is that Korah met his fate elsewhere, that is, at the entrance of the Tent of Meeting together with the 250 chieftains (vv. 17,35; 17:5). On the other hand, the version of this story in Deuteronomy 11:6, which ascribes only the death of Dathan and Abiram to the earthquake, reads as follows: "when the earth opened her mouth and swallowed them, along with their households, their tents, and every living thing *(yekum)* in their train." Thus, the possibility should be entertained that originally the Numbers text read *ve-khol ha'adam,* "and all the people," and that *'asher le-koraḥ,* "belonging to Korah," was interpolated in order to include Korah in the fate of Dathan and Abiram (see Excursus 39). Whether Korah was swallowed by the earth or burned by fire (or both, or neither!) is discussed in detail by the rabbis.[74]

33. ***the earth closed over them*** This, and not the earth's opening, is what constitutes the "unheard-of" creation.[75]

vanished from the midst of the congregation This expression implies the penalty of *karet,* extirpation (cf. Excursus 36), and indeed all traces of the line of Dathan and Abiram were eliminated.[76]

35. ***A fire went forth from the LORD*** That is, from the *mishkan,* the Tabernacle.[77] Nadab and Abihu, who died a similar death, also offered incense (Lev. 10:1–2), but their sins were different. They were legitimate priests who offered illegitimate incense (strange fire), whereas the 250 chieftains were illegitimate aspirants for the priesthood whose offering was legitimate.

Korah is not mentioned here, but it must be presumed that he too died by the divine fire in the original story (see 17:5). In our Hebrew text, Dathan, Abiram, and Korah are swallowed up together

17 The LORD spoke to Moses, saying: ²Order Eleazar son of Aaron the priest to remove the fire pans—for they have become sacred—from among the charred remains; and scatter the coals abroad. ³[Remove] the fire pans of those who have sinned at the cost of their lives, and let them be made into hammered sheets as plating for the altar—for once they have been used for offering to the LORD, they have become sacred—and let them serve as a warning to the people of Israel. ⁴Eleazar the priest took the copper fire

יז וַיְדַבֵּ֥ר יְהֹוָ֖ה אֶל־מֹשֶׁ֥ה לֵּאמֹֽר: 2 אֱמֹ֣ר אֶל־אֶלְעָזָ֞ר בֶּן־אַהֲרֹ֣ן הַכֹּהֵ֗ן וְיָרֵ֤ם אֶת־הַמַּחְתֹּת֙ מִבֵּ֣ין הַשְּׂרֵפָ֔ה וְאֶת־הָאֵ֖שׁ זְרֵה־הָ֑לְאָה כִּ֖י קָדֵֽשׁוּ: 3 אֵ֡ת מַחְתּוֹת֩ הַֽחַטָּאִ֨ים הָאֵ֜לֶּה בְּנַפְשֹׁתָ֗ם וְעָשׂ֨וּ אֹתָ֜ם רִקֻּעֵ֤י פַחִים֙ צִפּ֣וּי לַמִּזְבֵּ֔חַ כִּֽי־הִקְרִיבֻ֥ם לִפְנֵֽי־יְהֹוָ֖ה וַיִּקְדָּ֑שׁוּ וְיִהְי֥וּ לְא֖וֹת לִבְנֵ֥י יִשְׂרָאֵֽל: 4 וַיִּקַּ֞ח אֶלְעָזָ֤ר

(vv. 24–33)—a version that is verified by 26:10—thus necessitating the absence of Korah's name from this verse (see Excursus 39).

CHAPTER 17   THE AFTERMATH OF KORAH'S REBELLION   (17:1–18:32)

THE FIRE PANS AS REMINDERS (vv. 1–5)

This passage is a continuation of 16:35. The fire pans of the slain priestly pretenders, sanctified by their contact with divine fire (or by their use in the Tabernacle), are made into (another) plating for the bronze sacrificial altar as a warning to future would-be encroachers upon the sanctuary.

2. Eleazar   Not Aaron but Eleazar was ordered to remove the fire pans, presumably because Aaron, as High Priest, had to be more scrupulous in avoiding contact with the dead and their possessions[1] or, perhaps, because he figured in the controversy.[2] It is more likely, however, that this was simply a job delegated to Eleazar, in keeping with the contention of the entire book that Aaron's days were numbered and Eleazar was gradually assuming more and more of his father's duties.

remove   Hebrew *va-yarem.* Rather, "set aside, dedicate" (see 15:19). As a priest, Eleazar would not have been allowed to touch the fire pans before they were purified from having been in the hands of the slain chieftains. Presumably, they were handled initially by some nonpriestly persons, perhaps Levites.[3]

sacred   The fire pans became sacred by their use in the sacred precincts[4] or because they were touched by the divine fire. Fire from the altar, if it had been used to burn the incense, would also have sanctified the fire pans, but this possibility is unlikely.

charred remains   That is, of Korah and his cohorts (see v. 4).[5]

scatter the coals abroad   That Hebrew *'esh* can refer to the fuel as well as the flame is shown by Numbers 16:7 and Genesis 22:7. Two questions need to be answered: If the coals came from the altar why were they not returned there? And since only authorized priests had access to the altar, how could Korah and the chieftains have acquired the coals? The Greek here has "the unauthorized coals," which would make the present case similar to that of Nadab and Abihu in Leviticus 10:1. But this interpretation implies that Korah and his band were condemned for not taking coals from the altar, a right they did not have in the first place! Rather than predicate a "loaded" test, better assume that the coals mentioned here did not come from the altar. This would explain why Eleazar was commanded to have the coals scattered, an act that would be inexplicable if the coals had derived from the sacred altar. Thus both questions evaporate when their premise is removed: There was no need for the altar because the coals came from some other source. To be sure, when a priest offers incense, the coals must be taken from the altar (17:11; see Lev. 10:1), but the circumstances of this test are unique.

3. [Remove]   The verb is missing and must be supplied. The ancient versions do so from *kadeshu,* the last Hebrew word of the previous verse, either by (1) simply connecting it with this verse[6] and rendering: "For the fire pans of those who have sinned at the cost of their lives have become sacred";[7] or (2) reading with the Greek: "For they have sanctified *(kiddeshu)* the fire pans."

pans which had been used for offering by those who died in
the fire; and they were hammered into plating for the altar,
5as the LORD had ordered him through Moses. It was to be a
reminder to the Israelites, so that no outsider—one not of
Aaron's offspring—should presume to offer incense before
the LORD and suffer the fate of Korah and his band.

6Next day the whole Israelite community railed against
Moses and Aaron, saying, "You two have brought death
upon the LORD's people!" 7But as the community gathered

הַכֹּהֵן אֵת מַחְתּוֹת הַנְּחֹשֶׁת אֲשֶׁר הִקְרִיבוּ
הַשְּׂרֻפִים וַיְרַקְּעוּם צִפּוּי לַמִּזְבֵּחַ: 5 זִכָּרוֹן לִבְנֵי
יִשְׂרָאֵל לְמַעַן אֲשֶׁר לֹא־יִקְרַב אִישׁ זָר אֲשֶׁר לֹא
מִזֶּרַע אַהֲרֹן הוּא לְהַקְטִיר קְטֹרֶת לִפְנֵי יְהוָה
וְלֹא־יִהְיֶה כְקֹרַח וְכַעֲדָתוֹ כַּאֲשֶׁר דִּבֶּר יְהוָה בְּיַד־
מֹשֶׁה לוֹ: 6 וַיִּלֹּנוּ כָּל־עֲדַת בְּנֵי־יִשְׂרָאֵל מִמָּחֳרָת
עַל־מֹשֶׁה וְעַל־אַהֲרֹן לֵאמֹר אַתֶּם הֲמִתֶּם אֶת־עַם
יְהוָה: 7 וַיְהִי בְּהִקָּהֵל הָעֵדָה עַל־מֹשֶׁה וְעַל־אַהֲרֹן

at the cost of their lives[8]

let them be made[9]

hammered sheets Hebrew *paḥ* occurs again only in Exodus 39:3. The bronze fire pans were hammered into thin layers.[10]

plating for the altar But according to Exodus 27:2 and 38:2, the altar was already plated with bronze. This ostensible contradiction is eliminated by the Greek, which adds the following to Exodus 38:2 (38:22 LXX): "He made the bronze altar out of the bronze censers that belonged to the men who had revolted with the company of Korah." Consequently, some moderns regard the present passage as the story accounting for the installation of the bronze plating of the altar. However, the text can be accepted at face value; it merely indicates that the altar was bronze plated a second time in order to serve as a warning sign to unauthorized encroachers.

once they have been used[11]

warning[12]

5. *him* That is, Eleazar.[13]

outsider Hebrew *zar,* that is, an unauthorized person, either a nonpriest or non-Levite (cf. 1:51; 3:10,38) or even a disqualified priest (18:7). Hence the text must add "one not of Aaron's offspring," an obvious reference to Korah the Levite.

presume[14]

Korah Here it is explicitly stated that Korah died with his company in the incense trial.

THE OUTBREAK OF THE PLAGUE (vv. 6–15)

The *'edah* rebels a second time (see 16:19–24) as a result of the death of their leaders. Moses and Aaron again intercede, but this time they fail because the excuse that "one man has sinned" is not now applicable (v. 22). But where prayer fails, ritual succeeds. It is performed by Aaron, and its implication is significant: The same fire pan that brought death to the unauthorized 250 averts death in the hands of the authorized.[15]

6. *Next day* This phrase connects the plague with the previous story of the fire pans.

You two Hebrew *'attem* is emphatic. It was you two who devised the incense test by which they lost their lives.[16] Actually, the text attributes the test solely to Moses' initiative (16:6–7,16–17), but Moses and Aaron are accused of collusion.

the LORD's people Hebrew *'am YHVH* (as in 11:29) is equivalent to "the LORD's congregation" (16:3). The phrase implies that the people are not convinced by the incense test but continue to believe that, as the Lord's people, all are equally holy. Thus, in effect, they pick up Korah's refrain: Moses and Aaron are lording it over the people. Now they have a new charge against them: They conspired to slay "the LORD's people." This phrase, of course, refers to the slain chieftains and is more than hyperbole. Because the latter represented Israel in the national assembly (*'edah;* 16:2), their decision may have been considered as having divine sanction.

against them, Moses and Aaron turned toward the Tent of Meeting; the cloud had covered it and the Presence of the LORD appeared.

[8]When Moses and Aaron reached the Tent of Meeting, [9]the LORD spoke to Moses, saying, [10]"Remove yourselves from this community, that I may annihilate them in an instant." They fell on their faces. [11]Then Moses said to Aaron, "Take the fire pan, and put on it fire from the altar. Add incense and take it quickly to the community and make expiation for them. For wrath has gone forth from the LORD: the plague has begun!" [12]Aaron took it, as Moses

וַיִּפְנוּ֙ אֶל־אֹ֣הֶל מוֹעֵ֔ד וְהִנֵּ֥ה כִסָּ֖הוּ הֶעָנָ֑ן וַיֵּרָ֖א
כְּב֥וֹד יְהוָֽה׃ 8 וַיָּבֹ֤א מֹשֶׁה֙ וְאַהֲרֹ֔ן אֶל־פְּנֵ֖י אֹ֥הֶל
מוֹעֵֽד׃ פ רביעי 9 וַיְדַבֵּ֥ר יְהוָ֖ה אֶל־מֹשֶׁ֥ה
לֵּאמֹֽר׃ 10 הֵרֹ֗מּוּ מִתּוֹךְ֙ הָעֵדָ֣ה הַזֹּ֔את וַאֲכַלֶּ֥ה
אֹתָ֖ם כְּרָ֑גַע וַֽיִּפְּל֖וּ עַל־פְּנֵיהֶֽם׃ 11 וַיֹּ֨אמֶר מֹשֶׁ֜ה
אֶֽל־אַהֲרֹ֗ן קַ֣ח אֶת־הַ֠מַּחְתָּה וְתֶן־עָלֶ֨יהָ אֵ֜שׁ מֵעַ֤ל
הַמִּזְבֵּ֙חַ֙ וְשִׂ֣ים קְטֹ֔רֶת וְהוֹלֵ֧ךְ מְהֵרָ֛ה אֶל־הָעֵדָ֖ה
וְכַפֵּ֣ר עֲלֵיהֶ֑ם כִּֽי־יָצָ֥א הַקֶּ֛צֶף מִלִּפְנֵ֥י יְהוָ֖ה הֵחֵ֥ל
הַנָּֽגֶף׃ 12 וַיִּקַּ֨ח אַהֲרֹ֜ן כַּאֲשֶׁ֣ר ׀ דִּבֶּ֣ר מֹשֶׁ֗ה וַיָּ֙רָץ֙

7. ***the cloud had covered it*** When the Tent of Meeting/Tabernacle was stationary it was always covered by the divine cloud (see the introductory Comment to 9:15–23).

the Presence of the LORD appeared The pillar of fire within the cloud, usually visible only at night, probably increased its brightness so that it could be seen by day, thereby signaling to Moses that God desired an audience with him (introductory Comment to 9:15–23).

8. ***reached***[17] Moses' audiences with God took place inside the Shrine, but when he was accompanied by Aaron or the people (as in Lev. 9:5) they took place in the courtyard that served as the entrance to the Shrine (cf. Excursus 15).

9. ***Moses*** Although Aaron was with him, God's voice was heard only by Moses.[18]

10. ***Remove yourselves***[19] Why must Moses and Aaron withdraw from the people in order to escape the plague? Will God sweep away the innocent with the wicked? Genesis 18:23 informs us that this was the very question that Abraham had put to God. The answer given there and throughout the Bible is—yes! When God punishes a community by natural disasters—earthquake, flood, plague—the righteous perish together with the wicked unless they leave the arena of punishment. Thus Lot and his family must flee the plains of Sodom; Noah must be given the means of riding out the flood; Israelites in Egypt require blood on their doorposts to ward off the destroyer (Exod. 12:23). Here, the people must distance themselves from Dathan and Abiram lest the earth swallow them up too (16:26), and Moses and Aaron must remove themselves if they are to escape the plague. Indeed, as the story unfolds, only ritual intercession, Aaron's incense (vv. 12–13),[20] can stop the plague.

Of course, God can spare the innocent but only—as in the case of Abraham in Genesis 18:20–32—if He also spares the guilty. However, as the midrash tells us: "Once leave has been given to the 'destroyer' to do injury, it no longer discriminates between the innocent and the guilty."[21]

that I may annihilate them in an instant The same expression is used in 16:21. As it had already been decreed that they would die in the wilderness, the only additional punishment left was their instantaneous death.[22]

fell on their faces That is, in prayer, as in 16:22, although here the prayer is not recorded.

11. ***Then Moses said to Aaron*** Is it to be assumed that Moses' directive to Aaron was not of his own initiative but was God's response to his prayer? Or, conversely, was it the lack of divine response that impelled Moses to attempt his own solution? That God does not explicitly answer and that His wrath continues unabated indicates the probability of the latter. Moreover, that the incense is offered outside the sacred precincts—an unprecedented act—indicates that it was a special emergency measure, improvised on the spot.

the fire pan The definite article indicates a familiar fire pan, the one that Aaron always used[23] of the several fire pans attached to the altar (4:14).

incense The same incense that causes destruction when used by unauthorized persons averts destruction when used by authorized persons.[24]

take it[25]

had ordered, and ran to the midst of the congregation, where the plague had begun among the people. He put on the incense and made expiation for the people; 13he stood between the dead and the living until the plague was checked. 14Those who died of the plague came to fourteen thousand and seven hundred, aside from those who died on account of Korah. 15Aaron then returned to Moses at the entrance of the Tent of Meeting, since the plague was checked.

אֶל־תּ֣וֹךְ הַקָּהָ֔ל וְהִנֵּ֛ה הֵחֵ֥ל הַנֶּ֖גֶף בָּעָ֑ם וַיִּתֵּן֙ אֶת־
הַקְּטֹ֔רֶת וַיְכַפֵּ֖ר עַל־הָעָֽם׃ 13 וַיַּעֲמֹ֥ד בֵּין־הַמֵּתִ֖ים
וּבֵ֣ין הַחַיִּ֑ים וַתֵּעָצַ֖ר הַמַּגֵּפָֽה׃ 14 וַיִּהְי֗וּ הַמֵּתִים֙
בַּמַּגֵּפָ֔ה אַרְבָּעָ֥ה עָשָׂ֛ר אֶ֖לֶף וּשְׁבַ֣ע מֵא֑וֹת מִלְּבַ֥ד
הַמֵּתִ֖ים עַל־דְּבַר־קֹֽרַח׃ 15 וַיָּ֤שָׁב אַהֲרֹן֙ אֶל־מֹשֶׁ֔ה
אֶל־פֶּ֖תַח אֹ֣הֶל מוֹעֵ֑ד וְהַמַּגֵּפָ֖ה נֶעֱצָֽרָה׃ פ
חמישי 16 וַיְדַבֵּ֥ר יְהוָ֖ה אֶל־מֹשֶׁ֥ה לֵּאמֹֽר׃

make expiation for them The verb *kipper* in this context carries the connotation of "make appeasement." In the cults of the ancient Near East, incense served to appease and soothe divine wrath. This is strikingly illustrated by the Egyptian reliefs depicting Canaanite ruler-priests standing on the parapets and offering incense to the Pharaoh, who towers over the city slaughtering its inhabitants.[26] The offering of incense serves both to acknowledge Pharaoh as god and to implore his mercy.[27]

wrath . . . from the Lord Wrath is conceived as an independent entity (see 1:53; 18:5), equivalent to the destroyer (Hebrew *ha-mashḥit;* Exod. 12:23) who acts as God's agent of destruction (2 Chron. 19:2). According to Rashi, the rabbis believed that this function was assumed by the angel of death,[28] who is also called "the Anger before the Lord with the authority to kill."[29] God's destroyer, according to the rabbis, did not distinguish between the innocent and the wicked.[30] Thus the divine wrath/plague/destroyer is regarded as an amoral force, which can be overcome only by blood, incense, or some other ritual (cf. the Comments to vv. 10,13).

12. ***it***[31]

put on That is, on the fire pan.

made expiation Rather, "propitiate" (see v. 11).

13. ***he stood between the dead and the living*** Although Aaron, as High Priest, is forbidden to come into contact with the dead (see Lev. 21:11), he does so in this case in order to save the living. Rashbam explains: "The destroyer could not pass beyond the place of the incense offering." Targum Neofiti paraphrases: "He stood among the dead, begging mercy for the living." Aaron is herewith praised because he risked his life by confronting the destroyer.[32] A similar kind of intercession is attributed to David: He stops a plague at its most advanced point by building an altar there and sacrificing upon it (2 Sam. 24:18–25). Strikingly, it is the prophet, at *the command of God* (v. 19) who suggests this solution, implying that God Himself could stop the "destroyer Angel" (v. 16) only by sacrificial means (see the Comment to v. 11).

14. ***died on account of Korah*** This refers to the death of the 250 chieftains (16:35) and probably also to the death of Dathan, Abiram, and their families; see Excursus 39.

15. ***since the plague was checked*** According to Ibn Ezra, Hebrew *neʿetsarah* is a redundancy (see v. 13), unless the entire verse is connected with the next one, as follows: "When Aaron returned to Moses at the Tent of Meeting—the plague being checked—the Lord spoke to Moses." Moses' presence at the Tent is repeated in order to emphasize Aaron's achievement: Not Moses' prayer but Aaron's ritual assuaged God's wrath.

THE TEST OF THE STAFFS (vv. 16–26)

The principal instigators have died by earthquake and fire. Great numbers of the contentious people have been cut down by the plague. However, more persuasion is necessary if all are to be convinced that Aaron has been chosen above "the Lord's people" (17:6), that is, the chieftains. The test of the staffs is devised to settle this doubt once and for all. The double meaning of *matteh* is significant: The dead *matteh* (staff) springs to life and represents the living *matteh* (tribe) that God blesses.[33] Furthermore, only the *matteh* (staff/tribe) of Levi is qualified to be in the Presence of God.[34]

[16]The LORD spoke to Moses, saying: [17]Speak to the Israelite people and take from them—from the chieftains of their ancestral houses—one staff for each chieftain of an ancestral house: twelve staffs in all. Inscribe each man's name on his staff, [18]there being one staff for each head of an ancestral house; also inscribe Aaron's name on the staff of Levi. [19]Deposit them in the Tent of Meeting before the Pact, where I meet with you. [20]The staff of the man whom I choose shall sprout, and I will rid Myself of the incessant mutterings of the Israelites against you.

17 דַּבֵּר ׀ אֶל־בְּנֵי יִשְׂרָאֵל וְקַח מֵאִתָּם מַטֶּה מַטֶּה
לְבֵית אָב מֵאֵת כָּל־נְשִׂיאֵהֶם לְבֵית אֲבֹתָם שְׁנֵים
עָשָׂר מַטּוֹת אִישׁ אֶת־שְׁמוֹ תִּכְתֹּב עַל־מַטֵּהוּ׃
18 וְאֵת שֵׁם אַהֲרֹן תִּכְתֹּב עַל־מַטֵּה לֵוִי כִּי מַטֶּה
אֶחָד לְרֹאשׁ בֵּית אֲבוֹתָם׃ 19 וְהִנַּחְתָּם בְּאֹהֶל
מוֹעֵד לִפְנֵי הָעֵדוּת אֲשֶׁר אִוָּעֵד לָכֶם שָׁמָּה׃
20 *וְהָיָה הָאִישׁ אֲשֶׁר אֶבְחַר־בּוֹ מַטֵּהוּ יִפְרָח
וַהֲשִׁכֹּתִי מֵעָלַי אֶת־תְּלֻנּוֹת בְּנֵי יִשְׂרָאֵל אֲשֶׁר הֵם
מַלִּינִם עֲלֵיכֶם׃ 21 וַיְדַבֵּר מֹשֶׁה אֶל־בְּנֵי יִשְׂרָאֵל

v. 20. חצי הספר בפסוקים

17. staff Hebrew ***matteh*** also means "tribe," as in 1:16. The staff was the official insignia of a tribal chieftain (see Gen. 49:10). But it also designated the ordinary walking stick (Gen. 38:18,25), which in ancient Babylonia bore a distinctive design to designate its owner.[35]

an ancestral house Hebrew ***beit 'av*** ordinarily refers to the family household or clan (as in 1:2), but in this passage it designates the entire tribe. This special usage is mandated because the technical term for tribe, ***matteh,*** is preempted for "staff." To avoid the confusion arising from using ***matteh*** for both staff and tribe in the same passage, a near synonym for tribe, ***beit 'av,*** is employed.[36]

each man's name But not the name of the tribe. As the test was designed to choose God's priest from among the tribal chieftains, the individual mattered, not his tribe.

18. head Hebrew ***ro'sh,*** synonym for ***nasi',*** "chieftain" (see 1:16).

Aaron's name on the staff of Levi It is presumed that the priestly and Levitical orders are subservient to Aaron.[37] This relationship was determined when all the Levitical guards—according to 3:32—were assigned to Eleazar and the entire Levitical work force—according to 3:9 and 8:19,22—was placed under Aaron. The contest, therefore, is between Aaron and the other chieftains (v. 20a), who, like their 250 fallen colleagues (16:2–3), are still reluctant to see Aaron as the head of the priesthood (for the meaning of this struggle, see Excursus 39).

The objection is raised by Rabbi Judah ben Samuel he-Ḥasid that the Levites would not have been convinced by this demonstration. They could have argued that if any of their names had been written on Levi's staff it would still have blossomed. Judah therefore suggests that (1) the rod test was intended to prove the superiority of Levi over the other tribes and that (2) the test *preceded* and, indeed, motivated the rebellion of Korah, which then developed into an internal struggle among the Levites concerning the leadership of their tribe. Supporting this view is the tradition, recorded in Josephus,[38] that Aaron wrote the name of Levi on the Levitical staff and that the other contending chieftains inscribed the names of their tribes on their staffs.

19. the Pact Hebrew ***ha-'edut*** (cf. Exod. 16:34; 30:36), short for ***'aron ha'edut,*** "the Ark of the Pact" (4:5; 7:84), refers to the chief function of the Ark as the receptacle for the Decalogue, the symbol of the Pact or Covenant between God and Israel (see Exod. 25:16; 40:20). Thus the staffs were placed in the Holy of Holies in front of the Ark (v. 25).

where I meet[39]

with you Hebrew ***lakhem,*** plural, referring to the Israelites (see Exod. 28:42,43), even though the Israelites actually stand in the courtyard, not inside the Tent, for a divine audience (see Excursus 15). However, the Septuagint, the Samaritan, and the Vulgate read ***lekha,*** singular, referring to God's meetings with Moses, which take place inside the Shrine (Exod. 25:22; 30:6,36).[40]

20. the man whom I choose That is, either Aaron or one of the other tribal chieftains. The verb ***baḥar*** is used in the priestly texts only in connection with the priesthood (see the Comment to 16:7).

21Moses spoke thus to the Israelites. Their chieftains gave him a staff for each chieftain of an ancestral house, twelve staffs in all; among these staffs was that of Aaron. 22Moses deposited the staffs before the LORD, in the Tent of the Pact. 23The next day Moses entered the Tent of the Pact, and there the staff of Aaron of the house of Levi had sprouted: it had brought forth sprouts, produced blossoms, and borne almonds. 24Moses then brought out all the staffs from before the LORD to all the Israelites; each identified and recovered his staff.

25The LORD said to Moses, "Put Aaron's staff back before the Pact, to be kept as a lesson to rebels, so that their mutterings against Me may cease, lest they die." 26This

וַיִּתְּנ֨וּ אֵלָ֜יו ׀ כָּל־נְשִׂיאֵיהֶ֗ם מַטֶּה֩ לְנָשִׂ֨יא אֶחָ֜ד
מַטֶּ֨ה לְנָשִׂ֥יא אֶחָ֛ד לְבֵ֥ית אֲבֹתָ֖ם שְׁנֵ֣ים עָשָׂ֑ר
מַטּ֑וֹת וּמַטֵּ֥ה אַהֲרֹ֖ן בְּת֥וֹךְ מַטּוֹתָֽם׃ 22 וַיַּנַּ֥ח מֹשֶׁ֛ה
אֶת־הַמַּטֹּ֖ת לִפְנֵ֣י יְהוָ֑ה בְּאֹ֖הֶל הָעֵדֻֽת׃ 23 וַיְהִ֣י
מִֽמָּחֳרָ֗ת וַיָּבֹ֤א מֹשֶׁה֙ אֶל־אֹ֣הֶל הָעֵד֔וּת וְהִנֵּ֛ה פָּרַ֥ח
מַטֵּֽה־אַהֲרֹ֖ן לְבֵ֣ית לֵוִ֑י וַיֹּ֤צֵא פֶ֙רַח֙ וַיָּ֣צֵֽץ צִ֔יץ וַיִּגְמֹ֖ל
שְׁקֵדִֽים׃ 24 וַיֹּצֵ֨א מֹשֶׁ֤ה אֶת־כָּל־הַמַּטֹּת֙ מִלִּפְנֵ֣י
יְהוָ֔ה אֶל־כָּל־בְּנֵ֖י יִשְׂרָאֵ֑ל וַיִּרְא֥וּ וַיִּקְח֖וּ אִ֥ישׁ
מַטֵּֽהוּ׃ ס ששי 25 וַיֹּ֩אמֶר֩ יְהוָ֨ה אֶל־מֹשֶׁ֜ה
הָשֵׁ֞ב אֶת־מַטֵּ֤ה אַהֲרֹן֙ לִפְנֵ֣י הָעֵד֔וּת לְמִשְׁמֶ֥רֶת
לְא֖וֹת לִבְנֵי־מֶ֑רִי וּתְכַ֧ל תְּלוּנֹּתָ֛ם מֵעָלַ֖י וְלֹ֥א יָמֻֽתוּ׃

rid myself The Kal stem ***sh-kh-kh*** is used to indicate the subsiding of Noah's flood (Gen. 8:1). So perhaps here, where it is a Hifil causative, it means that God will settle the matter once and for all.[41]

against you Hebrew *'aleikhem* is puzzling given that the purpose of the test is to vindicate Aaron alone. The antecedent, therefore, must also include the previous plague incident in which the people direct their complaint against Moses as well as Aaron (vv. 6–7). Indeed, Moses has been blamed from the beginning for appointing his brother Aaron to the High Priesthood (16:3,11). The opening and concluding verses of this section (vv. 15–16,25–26) also show that the plague and staff incidents have been soldered by connectives and allusions.

21. ***among these staffs*** Were there twelve or thirteen staffs? The former number would require that Manasseh and Ephraim be subsumed under the tribe of Joseph. But in all the tribal lists in the priestly texts, neither Joseph nor Levi appears. Furthermore, there is not a single attestation of a chieftain for Joseph, but one each for Manasseh and Ephraim. If then Levi now appears among the tribes it must be the thirteenth. This conclusion finds support in ***betokh mattotam,*** which should be rendered "among their staffs," that is, the chieftains'.[42]

22. ***before the LORD, in the Tent of the Pact*** That is, in the Holy of Holies before the Ark, as indicated in verse 25.[43]

23. ***house of Levi*** Hebrew ***beit levi. Bayit,*** "house," frequently occurs with the meaning "tribe," as in Exodus 2:1 and Judges 10:9. Here its use is mandated because ***matteh,*** the usual term for tribe, has been preempted for "staff" (see v. 17, where "ancestral house" also stands for "tribe" for the same reason).

sprouts . . . blossoms . . . almonds If almonds, the final product of the miraculous growth, had been achieved, then the two earlier stages had to be conjectured. Rashbam and Bekhor Shor suggest that when Moses entered the Tent, the staff had only sprouted but that while he held it in his hand it blossomed and bore fruit. Shadal, citing one of his pupils, suggests that some of the sprouts were still in bud and in flower. The sequence, however, may simply mean that the cycle of growth had been completed.

borne Hebrew ***va-yigmol,*** "ripened" (see Isa. 18:5).

24. ***each*** That is, chieftain.

identified So Targum Onkelos for ***va-yir'u,*** the subject being the chieftains. However, the subject may as well be the Israelites, in which case this verb means "looked, inspected"; that is, the Israelites had a chance to verify for themselves that it was Aaron's staff that had sprouted.

25. ***Pact*** Short for "Ark of the Pact" (see the Comment to v. 19).

as a lesson Rather, "for safekeeping, as a warning." Hebrew ***mishmeret*** is used in the sense of "safekeeping" in connection with the manna (Exod. 16:23,32–34) and the ashes of the red cow

Moses did; just as the LORD had commanded him, so he did.

[27]But the Israelites said to Moses, "Lo, we perish! We are lost, all of us lost! [28]Everyone who so much as ventures near the LORD's Tabernacle must die. Alas, we are doomed to perish!"

26 וַיַּ֖עַשׂ מֹשֶׁ֑ה כַּאֲשֶׁ֨ר צִוָּ֧ה יְהוָ֛ה אֹת֖וֹ כֵּ֥ן עָשָֽׂה׃
ס 27 וַיֹּֽאמְרוּ֙ בְּנֵ֣י יִשְׂרָאֵ֔ל אֶל־מֹשֶׁ֖ה לֵאמֹ֑ר
הֵ֥ן גָּוַ֛עְנוּ אָבַ֖דְנוּ כֻּלָּ֥נוּ אָבָֽדְנוּ׃ 28 כֹּ֣ל הַקָּרֵ֧ב ׀
הַקָּרֵ֛ב אֶל־מִשְׁכַּ֥ן יְהוָ֖ה יָמ֑וּת הַאִ֥ם תַּ֖מְנוּ לִגְוֹֽעַ׃
ס

(19:9). The staff as an admonitory sign puts it in the same class as the altar plating made of the illicit fire pans (v. 3). Since divine staffs were kept in the sanctuaries of Egypt and Phoenicia,[44] it is possible that the purpose of assigning a mnemonic role to Aaron's staff (like Moses' staff it may also have been regarded as "God's staff"; Exod. 4:20; 17:9)[45] was to deprive it of any magical or mythical significance.[46] However, it is not possible to conceive of Aaron's staff having divine properties, for then he would have had an unfair advantage over the other contestants. His staff, then, must have been an ordinary one.[47]

rebels Hebrew ***benei meri,*** literally "rebellious children." The prophet Ezekiel, basing himself on this term, frequently refers to Israel as ***beit meri,*** "rebellious household/line." It is one of Ezekiel's fundamental theses that each generation, beginning with the wilderness and down to his own, has rebelled against the Lord and His commandments (see Ezekiel 20:5–29).

their mutterings Hebrew ***telunnotam*** connects with ***va-yillonu*** (v. 6), tying together the plague and staff incidents.

may cease[48]

26. so he did Hebrew ***ken 'asah*** forms an inclusion with the first two words of this verse, ***va-ya'as mosheh,*** reversing their order. This is a clear literary sign that the passage, verses 16–26, is completed[49] and that the final two verses of this chapter belong to the next chapter.

THE PANIC AND THE REMEDY (17:27–18:7)

As a consequence of the death of their chieftains at the Tabernacle (16:35–17:5) and the toll taken by the plague, the Israelites begin to dread the Tabernacle and will not come near it. To allay their fright, they are given the assurance that henceforth priests and Levites alone will bear the responsibility for encroachment. This responsibility is divided into three groupings: priests and Kohathites are liable for Israelites (18:1a); priests and Levites for Levites (18:3); and priests for priests (18:1b). A fourth grouping, Levites for Israelites, is postponed to 18:22–23. This assignment of responsibility guarantees that "wrath may not again strike the Israelites" (18:5b; see Excursus 40, for the table of responsibility). This section contains many technical terms and code words that describe the Levitical tasks in the sanctuary; they are discussed in chapters 3–4.

27. perish . . . lost . . . lost The threefold cry of despair is rendered by Targum Onkelos as follows: "Behold some of us were killed by the sword (14:45), some were swallowed up by the earth (16:32), while others died in the plague (17:14)."

28. so much as ventures near The Hebrew verb ***karev*** has the meaning of "encroach" (see Excursus 5). Here, however, the doubling of the term tells us that the Israelite now fears to enter the Tabernacle even in order to offer his sacrifices lest he, like the chieftains who offered incense, be guilty of encroachment and struck down. The consoling answer is forthcoming (18:1–7): Responsibility for angering God by encroaching upon His sancta will henceforth reside with the priestly and Levitical guards who failed to prevent its occurrence.

must die That is, at the hands of God. The people fear that even inadvertent encroachment upon the sanctuary will be fatal.

Alas Hebrew ***ha-'im*** (usually "is it not?") otherwise implies "no" as an answer (as in 11:22; Gen. 17:17; 37:8). Hence, it is here something like "alas."[50]

we are doomed to perish Hebrew ***tamnu li-gvo'a***[51] here means "we are being wiped out."

18 The LORD said to Aaron: You and your sons and the ancestral house under your charge shall bear any guilt connected with the sanctuary; you and your sons alone shall bear any guilt connected with your priesthood. 2You shall also associate with yourself your kinsmen the tribe of Levi, your ancestral tribe, to be attached to you and to minister to you, while you and your sons under your charge are before the Tent of the Pact. 3They shall discharge their

י״ח וַיֹּאמֶר יְהוָה אֶל־אַהֲרֹן אַתָּה וּבָנֶיךָ וּבֵית־
אָבִיךָ אִתָּךְ תִּשְׂאוּ אֶת־עֲוֹן הַמִּקְדָּשׁ וְאַתָּה וּבָנֶיךָ
אִתָּךְ תִּשְׂאוּ אֶת־עֲוֹן כְּהֻנַּתְכֶם׃ 2 וְגַם אֶת־אַחֶיךָ
מַטֵּה לֵוִי שֵׁבֶט אָבִיךָ הַקְרֵב אִתָּךְ וְיִלָּווּ עָלֶיךָ
וִישָׁרְתוּךָ וְאַתָּה וּבָנֶיךָ אִתָּךְ לִפְנֵי אֹהֶל הָעֵדֻת׃
3 וְשָׁמְרוּ מִשְׁמַרְתְּךָ וּמִשְׁמֶרֶת כָּל־הָאֹהֶל אַךְ

CHAPTER 18

1. to Aaron Only in this chapter (see vv. 1, 8, 20) and in Leviticus 10:8–11 are instructions given by God directly to Aaron. Otherwise they are transmitted to him via Moses (e.g., 6:23; 8:2). This extraordinary fact only underscores the hazards and rewards for performing the priestly and Levitical duties of guarding the sanctuary: The Lord personally wishes to communicate this information to the chief of the Levitical tribe. Furthermore, the direct address to Aaron is a fitting climax to the rebellious contention for the priesthood: God further vindicates Aaron by granting him a personal revelation.[1]

the ancestral house That is, the clan of Kohath,[2] which bore the responsibility of transporting the sacred objects by shoulder during the wilderness march (4:1–20; 7:9).

under your charge Hebrew *'ittekha,* here and in verses 2,7,19, should be rendered "after you" (see the Comment to v. 19).

guilt Rather, "penalty." Hebrew *'avon,* as with most behavioral nouns, can mean either the act (sin) or its consequence (penalty).[3]

connected with Hebrew *'avon ha-mikdash*, that is, they shall bear the consequences for encroachment upon the sancta.

sanctuary Rather, "sancta." *Mikdash* means either "sacred area" (as in Lev. 12:4) or, as here, "sacred objects, sancta" (3:38; 10:21). The first half of this verse thus proclaims that both priests and Kohathites bear the responsibility for encroachment upon the sancta: the priests, when the Tabernacle is at rest and the sancta are in their charge, and the Kohathites, when they carry the sancta during the march.

alone Rather, "after you." For this rendering of Hebrew *'ittekha,* see the Comment to "that are with you," v. 19.

your priesthood But only priests can be responsible for encroachment committed by fellow priests; that is, if disqualified priests—those who are blemished (Lev. 21:23), inebriated (Lev. 10:9), unwashed (Exod. 30:20), or improperly dressed (Exod. 28:43)—attempt to officiate at the altar or enter the Shrine. Further, if priests dare enter the Holy of Holies (cf. v. 7) or if the High Priest does so without proper safeguards (Lev. 16:2)—this, too, is encroachment. The principle that priests are responsible for priestly encroachment can be deduced from the following mishnah: "A priest who has officiated in a state of impurity is not brought by his fellow priest to the court, but the apprentices to the priesthood remove him from the Temple courtyard and smash his brain with clubs."[4]

2. also The priests in no way reduce their own guarding responsibilities by sharing the custody of the Tabernacle with the Levites. To the contrary, the Levites are now an added source for encroachment and priestly blame (see v. 3).

associate[5]

your kinsmen The entire tribe of Levi is to share the custody of the Tabernacle with the priests. Rashi suggests that this term refers to the Merarites and Gershonites but not to the Kohathites, the remaining Levitical clan (v. 1). But the Levites' responsibility must include that of the Kohathites *(ve-gam);* hence, the entire Levitical tribe is meant.

duties to you and to the Tent as a whole, but they must not
have any contact with the furnishings of the Shrine or with
the altar, lest both they and you die. 4They shall be attached
to you and discharge the duties of the Tent of Meeting, all
the service of the Tent; but no outsider shall intrude upon
you 5as you discharge the duties connected with the Shrine

אֶל־כְּלֵי הַקֹּדֶשׁ וְאֶל־הַמִּזְבֵּחַ לֹא יִקְרָבוּ וְלֹא־יָמֻתוּ
גַם־הֵם גַּם־אַתֶּם׃ 4 וְנִלְווּ עָלֶיךָ וְשָׁמְרוּ אֶת־
מִשְׁמֶרֶת אֹהֶל מוֹעֵד לְכֹל עֲבֹדַת הָאֹהֶל וְזָר לֹא־
יִקְרַב אֲלֵיכֶם׃ 5 וּשְׁמַרְתֶּם אֵת מִשְׁמֶרֶת הַקֹּדֶשׁ

tribe . . . tribe Hebrew synonyms ***matteh*** . . . ***shevet.*** Synonyms are used to avoid monotonous repetition. In the cultic texts, however, tribe is designated by ***matteh*** (as in 1:49; 3:6) and not by its imprecise synonym ***shevet.***[6]

your ancestral Hebrew ***'avikha,*** literally "your father," a reminder that the Levites are ***'aḥekha,*** literally "your brothers," and hence, by reason of blood, deserve to be your associates.

attached Hebrew ***ve-yillavu 'al,*** a play on the word ***levi,*** "Levi." With the preposition ***'im*** the attachment is between equals (Ps. 83:9), but with ***'el*** or ***'al*** (v. 4; Isa. 14:1; 56:3) the attachment implies subordination.[7]

minister to you Rather, "assist you," that is, in your guarding duties (v. 3).[8]

and your sons Literally, "namely you and your sons."

before the Tent of the Pact That is, outside the sacred area, where the Levites perform their guard duty.

3. *discharge their duties to you and to* Rather, "perform your guard duty and the guarding of." The Hebrew verb ***shamar*** means "guard" only in the priestly texts of the Torah (see the Comment to 3:7).

The guarding of the Tabernacle tent and the courtyard altar is the exclusive responsibility of the priests (v. 5). However, since the lay worshiper was admitted with his offering to the entrance of the Tabernacle courtyard and, presumably, the Levite guard also had access to it, it is there that the latter assisted the priests on duty (as well as the lay worshiper; 16:9). Thus the custody of the Tabernacle was neatly divided between the two sacral orders: priests on the inside, Levites on the outside, and both at the entrance. Rabbinic traditions concerning the Second Temple confirm this division: Of the twenty-four watches at the entrance to the sacred precincts, three were occupied by priests and the rest by Levites who, it should be noted, guarded only from the outside.[9]

Although the priests are encamped at the entrance (3:38a) and hence might be expected to guard it, their guarding duties at the entrance are assigned to the Levites. As a result, the Levite cordon rings the entire Sanctuary.

have any contact with Rather, "encroach on" (see Excursus 5). Levites, forbidden to handle the sancta, may carry them during the march only after the priests have covered them (4:1–20).

the furnishings of the Shrine Rather, "sacred utensils" (3:31; 4:15), probably referring to the altar utensils (4:12,14) which were placed in the courtyard and, like the altar itself, would be vulnerable to encroachment by the Levite guards and the lay worshiper. Alternatively, this term can refer to the sancta within the Tent but not to the Ark (1 Kings 8:4 = 2 Chron. 5:5).

both they and you die If a Levite encroaches upon a sanctum then the negligent guards, both priestly and Levitical, are held responsible and suffer death by divine agency in contrast to the encroaching layman, who is slain by the guards. Encroachment by the clergy is punishable by God because only He can carry out the death sentence: Since the clerical encroacher himself is an armed guard, what mortal can punish him? Thus, this prescription is most realistic. The entire Tabernacle cordon, including all priests and Levites on guard duty, is responsible for Levitical encroachment: They will guard very carefully.

4. *discharge the duties* Rather, "perform the guard duty" (see the Comment to 3:7).

all the service Rather, "including all the labor."[10] For ***'avodah*** as physical work or "labor," see Excursus 6. The first half of this verse states that the Levites share with the priests the custody of the Tabernacle in addition to their transport labors (8:11, etc.).

and the altar, that wrath may not again strike the Israelites.
6 I hereby take your fellow Levites from among the Israelites; they are assigned to you in dedication to the LORD, to do the work of the Tent of Meeting; 7 while you and your sons shall be careful to perform your priestly duties in everything pertaining to the altar and to what is behind the curtain. I make your priesthood a service of dedication; any outsider who encroaches shall be put to death.

וְאֵת מִשְׁמֶרֶת הַמִּזְבֵּחַ וְלֹא־יִהְיֶה עוֹד קֶצֶף עַל־
בְּנֵי יִשְׂרָאֵל׃ 6 וַאֲנִי הִנֵּה לָקַחְתִּי אֶת־אֲחֵיכֶם
הַלְוִיִּם מִתּוֹךְ בְּנֵי יִשְׂרָאֵל לָכֶם מַתָּנָה נְתֻנִים
לַיהוָה לַעֲבֹד אֶת־עֲבֹדַת אֹהֶל מוֹעֵד׃ 7 וְאַתָּה
וּבָנֶיךָ אִתְּךָ תִּשְׁמְרוּ אֶת־כְּהֻנַּתְכֶם לְכָל־דְּבַר
הַמִּזְבֵּחַ וּלְמִבֵּית לַפָּרֹכֶת וַעֲבַדְתֶּם עֲבֹדַת מַתָּנָה
אֶתֵּן אֶת־כְּהֻנַּתְכֶם וְהַזָּר הַקָּרֵב יוּמָת׃ ס

outsider That is, a nonpriest (as in 17:5).

no . . . intrude upon you Rather, "(the outsider shall) not be associated with you."[11]

5. ***as you discharge the duties connected with*** Rather, "you shall perform the guard duty of" (see the Comment to 3:7).

the Shrine and the altar These must be protected against encroachment by the unauthorized.

wrath For Hebrew *ketsef* as an autonomous destructive force, see the Comment to 17:11.

6. ***assigned to you in dedication to the LORD***[12] The Levites' exclusive tasks in regard to the Tabernacle transport[13] are contrasted with the priests' exclusive responsibility for guarding the altar and inner sancta against encroachment (v. 7).

work That is, the removal of the Tabernacle (as in 8:11,15,19,22).

7. ***while you*** Hebrew *ve-'attah* contrasts with *va-'ani*, "I" (v. 6); that is, for the boon of Levitical assistance, see to it that no encroachment occurs.

be careful to perform your priestly duties Literally, "guard your priesthood," explicates and forms an inclusion with verse 1b: Priests will be penalized for failing to guard the sancta against encroaching nonpriests and disqualified priests.[14]

everything pertaining to[15]

the altar . . . behind the curtain Nonpriests and disqualified priests are prohibited from officiating on the altar, and all priests are prohibited from entering the Holy of Holies, the inner Shrine (see the Comment to v. 1b).

behind[16]

I make your priesthood a service of dedication This is a problematic translation. There are alternatives.[17]

any outsider who encroaches[18] This is the last of four occurrences of the formula (1:51; 3:10,38), and its application differs slightly from the others in that it is directed against the priest himself: the one who dares enter the Holy of Holies or who is unqualified to officiate on the altar (see the Comment to v. 1b).

THE PRIESTLY EMOLUMENTS (vv. 8–19)

After an introductory verse (v. 8), the priestly gifts are enumerated according to the accepted division: *kodesh kodashim*, "most sacred" (vv. 9–10), and *kodesh*, "sacred" (vv. 11–19). Three gifts are specified in the first group and eight in the second, for a total of eleven. The rabbis, however, list twenty-four priestly perquisites, enumerating them under two headings: twelve gifts given the priests in the Temple and twelve outside the Temple. Those in the Temple are: (1) purification offerings (Lev. 6:19,22); (2) reparation offerings (Lev. 7:6); (3) the communal well-being offering brought on Shavuot (Lev. 23:20); (4) the skin of the burnt offering (Lev. 7:8); (5) the remainder of the oil brought

[8]The LORD spoke further to Aaron: I hereby give you
charge of My gifts, all the sacred donations of the Israelites;
I grant them to you and to your sons as a perquisite, a due
for all time. [9]This shall be yours from the most holy sacri-

8 וַיְדַבֵּר יְהוָה אֶל־אַהֲרֹן וַאֲנִי הִנֵּה נָתַתִּי לְךָ אֶת־
מִשְׁמֶרֶת תְּרוּמֹתָי לְכָל־קָדְשֵׁי בְנֵי־יִשְׂרָאֵל לְךָ
נְתַתִּים לְמָשְׁחָה וּלְבָנֶיךָ לְחָק־עוֹלָם׃ 9 זֶה־יִּהְיֶה

by the healed leper (cf. Lev. 14:18,29); (6) the remainder of the omer of the first fruit barley offering (cf. Lev. 23:12–13); (7) the two first fruit wheat loaves (Lev. 23:17,20); (8) the display bread (Lev. 24:5–9); (9) the remainder of the meal offerings (Lev. 6:9; 10:12); (10) the breads that accompany the thanksgiving offering (Lev. 7:12–14); (11) the breast and right thigh of the individual well-being offering (Lev. 7:34; 10:35); (12) the shoulder of the well-being offering brought by the Nazirite and its accompanying loaves (Num. 6:19–20). The gifts outside the Temple are: (1) the ***terumah*** (about one-fifteenth of the produce; cf. Num. 18:12); (2) a tenth of the Levite tithe (Num. 18:25–32); (3) the first of the dough (Num. 15:17–21); (4) the first fruits (Num. 18:13); (5) the first of the shorn wool (Deut. 18:4); (6) the shoulder, cheeks, and stomach (Deut. 18:3); (7) the male first-born of women (Num. 18:15); (8) the first-born of clean animals (Num. 18:15); (9) the first-born of the ass (cf. Exod. 12:13; 34:20); (10) ***ḥerem*** (Num. 18:16); (11) a field that was dedicated to the sanctuary but not redeemed before the Jubilee (Lev. 27:21); (12) property stolen from a ***ger*** and returned by the repentant robber (cf. Num. 5:8).[19]

The midrash explains by the following parable why this list was appended to the story of Korah. A king gave a field to his favorite but without a deed. Someone contested the gift. The king then wrote a deed and recorded it. Thus after Korah contested Aaron's right to the priesthood, God wrote down the deed and recorded it. That is why the list of priestly perquisites is appended to the story of Korah.[20]

8. The general introduction to the list of priestly perquisites.

I Whereas you, Aaron, will be held responsible in the event of the desecration of the sanctuary (vv. 1,7), I, in turn, will provide you Levitical assistance (v. 6) and ample perquisites as a reward (vv. 8–19).[21]

give Hebrew ***natatti.*** Rather, "assign" (as in v. 6; 8:19).

charge of My gifts Hebrew ***mishmeret terumotai.*** Because the noun ***mishmeret*** can mean "guarding" (see the Comment to 3:7) or "safekeeping, reserved" (17:25), the phrase can mean either "the guarding of the gifts due Me" (i.e., that they may not be profaned or used improperly)[22] or "the reserved of My gifts" (i.e., those gifts kept back from the altar as perquisites for the priests).[23] A third possibility is, "My gifts for guarding": Just as the Levites are expressly assigned tithes as a reward for their guard duties (vv. 23,31), the priestly perquisites may fulfill a similar function. "If you guard the sancta as you are commanded, I shall assign you the priestly revenues listed in this section:"[24] Targum Jonathan specifies that the dough (see 15:17–21) and first fruits are among "My gifts"; the former is missing in the list of priestly perquisites, below.

all Rather, "including all." Thus the Hebrew phrase ***terumotai le-khol kodshei*** is rendered "My donations including the sacred gifts." The same combination of terms is found in 5:9, ***ve-khol terumah le-khol kodshei,*** "every donation including all the sacred gifts." This would imply that there are two categories of gifts to the priests: those they received from the sacrifices and those they received directly, bypassing the altar. This section lists the required gifts of both types.

to your sons Although this verse is the general heading of the priestly perquisites, including those from which the entire priestly household may benefit (v. 11), the common denominator of all the perquisites is that they may be eaten by male priests.

perquisite On the basis of cognate languages,[25] Hebrew ***moshḥah*** probably means the allotted measure or perquisite. The Levites, however, receive ***sakhar,*** "wages" (v. 31); the tithe is considered their proper compensation for their sanctuary labors.

due for all time[26]

fices, the offerings by fire: every such offering that they render to Me as most holy sacrifices, namely, every meal offering, sin offering, and guilt offering of theirs, shall belong to you and your sons. 10 You shall partake of them as most sacred donations: only males may eat them; you shall treat them as consecrated.

לְךָ מִקֹּדֶשׁ הַקֳּדָשִׁים מִן־הָאֵשׁ כָּל־קָרְבָּנָם לְכָל־
מִנְחָתָם וּלְכָל־חַטָּאתָם וּלְכָל־אֲשָׁמָם אֲשֶׁר יָשִׁיבוּ
לִי קֹדֶשׁ קֳדָשִׁים לְךָ הוּא וּלְבָנֶיךָ׃ 10 בְּקֹדֶשׁ
הַקֳּדָשִׁים תֹּאכְלֶנּוּ כָּל־זָכָר יֹאכַל אֹתוֹ קֹדֶשׁ

The Perquisites from the "Most Holy" Sacrifices (vv. 9–10)

from the most holy sacrifices Hebrew ***mi-kodesh kodashim,*** distinguished from ***kodashim,*** "holy sacrifice" (see v. 19), known in rabbinic Hebrew as ***kodashim kallim,*** "less holy sacrifices." "From" implies that there are most holy sacrifices from which the priests do not receive an altar gift of flesh. This would be the *ʿolah,* "burnt offering," from which the priest receives the skin (Lev. 7:8) but whose flesh is entirely burned on the altar.

The offerings by fire Hebrew ***min ha-ʾesh,*** literally "from the fire," referring to the portions of the sacrifices not burned on the altar but reserved for the priests. The implication is that the entire sacrifice is intended for the altar but that God has assigned parts of it to the priesthood. These priestly perquisites are the cereal offering (after a handful is burned on the altar; Lev. 2:3; 5:13; 6:9), the purification and reparation offerings (after the suet, some internal organs, and the blood are offered on the altar; Lev. 4:25,26; 7:2–5), and the skin of the burnt offering (Lev. 7:8).[27] The rabbis take the Hebrew literally: The priestly perquisites stem "from the fire"; that is, what is left after the Lord receives His portion on the altar.[28] Thus, excluded is the burnt offering, whose meat is entirely burned on the altar.[29]

every such offering Add "of theirs," transferred from the end of the verse.

render Rather, "restore," a phrase that is associated exclusively with the *ʾasham,* "reparation offering" (see 5:7–8). It should be transposed after "reparation offering."

as most holy sacrifices Transfer to the end of the verse, which now should read "and reparation offerings they restore to Me shall be most holy for you and your sons"; that is, these enumerated sacrifices shall be treated by you as most holy. In this way, verse 9b connects with verse 10a.

meal offering Or "cereal offering," which, but for a token burned on the altar, is eaten by the priests, according to Leviticus 6:7–9. The bread of display in Leviticus 24:5–9 falls into the same category.

sin offering Rather, "purification offering," the meat of which, like that of the reparation offering (cf. 5:5–8), belongs to the officiating priest (Lev. 6:19; 7:7).

10. as most sacred donation Rather, "in a most sacred state";[30] that is, eaten in the Tabernacle courtyard on the same day by male priests, in accordance with Leviticus 6:9,19 and 7:6.[31]

The Perquisites from the "Holy" Sacrifices (vv. 11–19)

Specifically enumerated are (1) the first fruits of the soil (v. 13); (2) certain foods processed from them, including grain, wine, and (olive) oil (omitted are fruit syrup, the fourth year produce of fruit trees, and bread dough, presumably because they have already been mentioned in Lev. 2:12; 19:24; Num. 15:17–20, respectively); (3) the meat of the first-born male of sacrificial animals; (4) the redemption price for the first-born male of nonsacrificial animals and of women; (5) everything proscribed, that is, placed under ban, *ḥerem.* The right thigh and breast of the well-being offerings, referred to incidentally in verse 18, have already been stipulated in Exodus 29:27–28 and Leviticus 10:14–15. The tenth of the Levitical tithe is listed separately with the latter in verses 25–32. These cited gifts are encased by an inclusion (vv. 11,19) that states that all gifts to the sanctuary, be they dedicated in advance (*terumah;* vv. 11,19) or at the sanctuary (*tenufah;* v. 11) also belong to the priests (see Excursuses 41 and 42). All these perquisites bear the lesser grade of sanctity, ***kodashim,*** which entitle

[11]This, too, shall be yours: the gift offerings of their
contributions, all the elevation offerings of the Israelites, I
give to you, to your sons, and to the daughters that are with
you, as a due for all time; everyone of your household who
is clean may eat it.
[12]All the best of the new oil, wine, and grain—the choice
parts that they present to the LORD—I give to you. [13]The
first fruits of everything in their land, that they bring to the
LORD, shall be yours; everyone of your household who is
clean may eat them. [14]Everything that has been proscribed

יִֽהְיֶה־לָּֽךְ׃ 11 וְזֶה־לְּךָ֞ תְּרוּמַ֣ת מַתָּנָ֗ם לְכָל־תְּנוּפֹת֮
בְּנֵ֣י יִשְׂרָאֵל֒ לְךָ֣ נְתַתִּ֗ים וּלְבָנֶ֧יךָ וְלִבְנֹתֶ֛יךָ אִתְּךָ֖
לְחָק־עוֹלָ֑ם כָּל־טָה֥וֹר בְּבֵיתְךָ֖ יֹאכַ֥ל אֹתֽוֹ׃ 12 כֹּ֚ל
חֵ֣לֶב יִצְהָ֔ר וְכָל־חֵ֖לֶב תִּיר֣וֹשׁ וְדָגָ֑ן רֵאשִׁיתָ֛ם
אֲשֶׁר־יִתְּנ֥וּ לַֽיהוָ֖ה לְךָ֥ נְתַתִּֽים׃ 13 בִּכּוּרֵ֞י כָּל־אֲשֶׁ֧ר
בְּאַרְצָ֛ם אֲשֶׁר־יָבִ֥יאוּ לַֽיהוָ֖ה לְךָ֣ יִהְיֶ֑ה כָּל־טָה֥וֹר
בְּבֵיתְךָ֖ יֹאכֲלֶֽנּוּ׃ 14 כָּל־חֵ֥רֶם בְּיִשְׂרָאֵ֖ל לְךָ֥ יִהְיֶֽה׃

them to be eaten not just by the priests but also by members of their household who are in a state of ritual purity (vv. 11,13).

11. The gift offerings . . . the elevation offerings Rather, "their dedication gifts, including their elevation offerings" (see 5:9; 8:11; 15:19). The *terumah* refers to the nonsacrificial "gifts," that is, those dedicated to the Lord outside the sanctuary (e.g., *ḥallah;* 15:17–21). But the *tenufah* refers to those gifts brought to the sanctuary and dedicated by an elevation ritual (e.g., the breast of the well-being offering; Lev. 7:30). However, not all elevation offerings are meant, as some are wholly consigned to the altar (e.g., the bread of the priestly consecration offering; Exod. 29:22–26) and others are by nature most sacred offerings, which are reserved solely for male priests (e.g., the grain offering of the suspected adulteress in Num. 5:25; the leper's reparation offering in Lev. 14:12–13).

give That is, "assign" (see the Comments to 8:19; 18:6).

daughters that are with you The implication is that married daughters who have joined their lay husbands' households are not eligible to partake of sacred food (see Lev. 22:12–13). All other members of the priest's household, including his slaves (Lev. 22:11)—but not his hired laborers since they maintain their own households (Lev. 22:10)—may also share his sacred food.[32]

clean Rather, "pure." Those who knowingly eat sacred food in a state of ritual impurity are liable to *karet* (Lev. 7:20–21; see Excursus 36); if they do so by accident, they must bring a purification offering (Lev. 4:27–35; Excursus 35).

12. best Literally, "fat," as in the expression "the fat of the wheat," that is, the germ, kernel of the wheat (e.g., Deut. 32:14).

the choice parts Rather, "the first processed." Grain, wine, and oil, as well as fruit syrup, leaven, dough, and wool (Lev. 2:12; Num. 15:20–21; Deut. 18:4) are clearly processed and not products in their natural state; priestly terminology distinguishes them from *bikkurim,* "first ripe" (see Excursus 43). The rabbis, however, take *re'shit* to mean "the first," implying that the priest is entitled to the first portion,[33] which they fix between one-sixtieth and one-fortieth of the crop.[34]

13. the first fruits Literally, "the first ripe" of the crops in the field and orchard (see Excursus 43).

of everything in their land In contrast to the *re'shit,* the priestly perquisites from a limited group of crops (v. 12), the *bikkurim* fall due on all the crops. The rabbis, however, limit them to the seven crops enumerated in Deuteronomy 8:8: wheat, barley, grape, fig, pomegranate, olive oil, and (date) honey.[35]

they bring Hebrew *yavi'u* in contrast to the *re'shit,* which "they present" *(yittenu)* to the priest, that is, even outside the sanctuary.[36] Implied is that the *bikkurim* are brought to the sanctuary (see Exod. 23:19; 34:26). During Second Temple times this was celebrated by lavish pilgrimages featuring music, song, and ornate decoration.[37] Indeed, a first fruit pilgrimage is predicated by the ceremony described in Deuteronomy 26:1–11: Although the text speaks of *re'shit,* it clearly has *bikkurim,* first fruits, in mind.

14. that has been proscribed Leviticus 27:28 reads: "But of all that anyone owns, be it man or beast or land of his holding, nothing that he has proscribed *(ḥerem 'asher yaḥarim)* for the LORD may be sold or redeemed; every proscribed thing *(ḥerem)* is totally consecrated to the LORD."

in Israel shall be yours. [15]The first issue of the womb of every being, man or beast, that is offered to the LORD, shall be yours; but you shall have the first-born of man redeemed, and you shall also have the firstling of unclean animals redeemed. [16]Take as their redemption price, from the age of one month up, the money equivalent of five shekels by the sanctuary weight, which is twenty *gerahs*.

15 כָּל־פֶּטֶר רֶחֶם לְכָל־בָּשָׂר אֲשֶׁר־יַקְרִיבוּ לַיהוָה
בָּאָדָם וּבַבְּהֵמָה יִהְיֶה־לָּךְ אַךְ ׀ פָּדֹה תִפְדֶּה אֵת
בְּכוֹר הָאָדָם וְאֵת בְּכוֹר־הַבְּהֵמָה הַטְּמֵאָה תִּפְדֶּה׃
16 וּפְדוּיָו מִבֶּן־חֹדֶשׁ תִּפְדֶּה בְּעֶרְכְּךָ כֶּסֶף חֲמֵשֶׁת
שְׁקָלִים בְּשֶׁקֶל הַקֹּדֶשׁ עֶשְׂרִים גֵּרָה הוּא׃ 17 אַךְ

Ḥerem is the ultimate case of dedication. Not only does it belong to the sanctuary, but it may never be redeemed: It remains in the sanctuary permanently. That which is of no value to the sanctuary must be destroyed. Thus, when the Israelites under Joshua imposed the ***ḥerem*** upon Jericho, all life and property were put to fire, except for the precious metals and metallic wares, which were "deposited in the treasury of the House of the LORD" (Josh. 6:24). The verb ***heḥerim,*** a denominative from ***ḥerem,*** translated here "proscribe," actually means "dedicate" (Mic. 4:13), a meaning it has in Moabite, Aramaic, and Nabatean as well. It implies that the sanctuary alone may benefit from the dedicated object. Thus, if the object is land or an impure (nonsacrificial) animal, it can be put to work for the sanctuary. For example, the ***ḥerem*** land can be cultivated by ***ḥerem*** animals. Pure ***ḥerem*** animals must be sacrificed on the altar, and the grain harvested from ***ḥerem*** lands comprises the grain offerings ***(minḥah)*** on the altar. However, this verse informs us that the meat of the ***ḥerem*** offerings belongs to the priests, meaning that they are sacrificed as ***shelamim,*** well-being offerings. And they are similar to the two well-being lambs sacrificed on the Shavuot festival; this meat also belongs entirely to the priests (Lev. 23:20). It goes without saying that the ***minḥah,*** the grain offering, is a priestly revenue: Only a token handful is offered up on the altar; the rest is eaten by the priests (Lev. 2:2–3; 6:7–11). Thus, this verse states in effect that any food that is ***ḥerem*** or is produced from ***ḥerem*** property is a perquisite of the priests. (For the various kinds of ***ḥerem*** and its role in Israelite history, see Excursus 44.)

15. first issue of the womb That is, the first-born of the mother, provided—it is assumed—that it is a male (see Exod. 13:12b; 34:19b).

that is offered to the LORD All first-born of the mother, whether of man or beast, are the innate property of the Lord (Exod. 13:1–2,12a; 22:28b–29). Hence they can only be "offered," not "given" (v. 12; see Lev. 27:26). Support for this is that the verb for "redeem" is ***padah*** (buy what was not his originally) rather than ***ga'al*** (buy back what was his originally).[38]

shall be yours That is, the priests'. However, the text goes on to divide the first-born into three categories: pure (sacrificial) animals whose flesh is eaten by the priests; impure (unofferable) animals, which may be redeemed by their owners; and humans who must be redeemed by their parents, the redemption price belonging to the priests. This threefold division is found in all the laws of the first-born (e.g., Exod. 13:12b–13; 34:19b–20), but the law codes differ in regard to the impure animal (cf. Excursus 45).

you shall have . . . redeemed Hebrew ***tifdeh,*** the active verb understood passively: You, the priest, shall conduct the redemption proceedings, but the redeemers are, obviously, the owners or parents. Since the subject of the entire section (vv. 8–20) is Aaron (see vv. 8,20), it is only natural that the priest should be addressed in the matter of the redemption of the first-born.

Notice should be taken of the difference between the verbs used in the redemption of the first-born human and the first-born impure animal. The former is ***padoh tifdeh,*** an emphatic, whereas the latter is the simple imperfect ***tifdeh,*** which should be rendered "you may have redeemed." The distinction is important: The redemption of the first-born human is mandatory; the redemption of the first-born animal is optional. Its owner may decline to redeem it, in which case the sanctuary may keep it as a work animal or sell it (Lev. 27:27).

The rabbis limit the requirement to redeem the first-born animal to the ass, basing themselves on Exodus 13:13.[39] In that verse, however, the redemption is optional (for further discussion, see Excursus 45).

16. their redemption price Hebrew ***u-feduyav,*** plural (Sam. reads ***u-feduyo,*** sing.). However, as this noun has already been attested as an abstract plural (***peduyim*** in 3:51; ***peduyei*** in 3:46,49), it

17But the firstlings of cattle, sheep, or goats may not be redeemed; they are consecrated. You shall dash their blood against the altar, and turn their fat into smoke as an offering by fire for a pleasing odor to the LORD. 18But their meat shall be yours: it shall be yours like the breast of elevation offering and like the right thigh.

19All the sacred gifts that the Israelites set aside for the LORD I give to you, to your sons, and to the daughters that are with you, as a due for all time. It shall be an everlasting covenant of salt before the LORD for you and for your offspring as well. 20And the LORD said to Aaron: You shall,

בְּכוֹר־שׁוֹר אוֹ־בְכוֹר כֶּשֶׂב אוֹ־בְכוֹר עֵז לֹא תִפְדֶּה
קֹדֶשׁ הֵם אֶת־דָּמָם תִּזְרֹק עַל־הַמִּזְבֵּחַ וְאֶת־חֶלְבָּם
תַּקְטִיר אִשֶּׁה לְרֵיחַ נִיחֹחַ לַיהוָה׃ 18 וּבְשָׂרָם
יִהְיֶה־לָּךְ כַּחֲזֵה הַתְּנוּפָה וּכְשׁוֹק הַיָּמִין לְךָ יִהְיֶה׃
19 כֹּל ׀ תְּרוּמֹת הַקֳּדָשִׁים אֲשֶׁר יָרִימוּ בְנֵי־יִשְׂרָאֵל
לַיהוָה נָתַתִּי לְךָ וּלְבָנֶיךָ וְלִבְנֹתֶיךָ אִתְּךָ לְחָק־
עוֹלָם בְּרִית מֶלַח עוֹלָם הִוא לִפְנֵי יְהוָה לְךָ
וּלְזַרְעֲךָ אִתָּךְ׃ 20 וַיֹּאמֶר יְהוָה אֶל־אַהֲרֹן בְּאַרְצָם

should be rendered here "its redemption price," referring exclusively to the human first-born who is redeemed by the fixed sum of five shekels (see Num. 3:47; Lev. 27:6). On the other hand, the animal first-born is redeemed at market value, as determined by the priest. The redemption price of the human first-born is stated explicitly; the redemption procedure for the impure animal, having already been cited in Leviticus 27:27, can be omitted here.

one month The child must be at least one month old to be eligible for redemption (see the Comment to 3:15; and see Lev. 27:6). In Jewish law the child is not considered fully viable until that age.[40] Therefore, neither funeral nor mourning rites are observed for the child who has not reached one month.[41] As there seems to be no minimum age for redemption of impure animals, it may take place at birth.[42]

up The first time all the first-born were redeemed (3:40). Henceforth, this redemption of the first-born must take place at age one month.

Jewish tradition has developed a set rite, ***pidyon ha-ben,*** for the redemption of the mother's first-born son. On the thirty-first day (postponed until evening if it falls on a Sabbath or holy day), the father presents his son symbolically to a ***kohen,*** a descendant of a priestly family, and then receives the child back in exchange for the redemption price of five silver dollars. "The idea that the child belongs to God first and foremost is at the heart of the ***pidyon ha-ben,*** and this realization can be a sobering and important experience for the parents who set out to raise their first child."[43]

the money equivalent Literally, "in accordance with the evaluation," referring to earlier notices that fixed the redemption price at five shekels (Lev. 27:6; Num. 3:47).[44] The democratic, egalitarian nature of the fixed, low redemption price of five shekels is emphasized by Philo.[45]

by the sanctuary weight See the Comment to 3:47.

17–18. cattle Hebrew ***shor*** stands for an individual member of the bovine species without specifying its sex. Here, of course, it stands for the female, as in Leviticus 22:28.

may not be redeemed Hebrew ***lo' tifdeh,*** an active verb with passive meaning (see v. 16); that is, you shall not accept their redemptive price.[46]

blood . . . fat . . . meat The first-born sacrificial animal is to be treated as a well-being offering whose blood, suet, and certain internal organs (Lev. 3:9; 7:3) are offered up on the altar but whose meat is eaten by its owner (Lev. 7:11–16). Since the priest is the ***de jure*** owner of the animal as soon as it is born (Lev. 27:26), he sacrifices it as a ***shelamim*** whose meat belongs to the owner. (For Deuteronomy's divergence from the provision, see Excursus 45.) The identification with the ***shelamim,*** the well-being offering, is further underscored by the analogy with the right thigh and breast, which are the established priestly perquisites from the well-being offering (Lev. 7:31–34; 10:14–15). The knowledge of Exodus 29:27–28 and Leviticus 7:34 is clearly presumed by this text.

19. A summary of the priestly perquisites from the sacred gifts, ***kodesh,*** forming a framing inclusion with verse 11: "There are pericopes which begin with a generalization followed by itemization, begin with itemization and end with generalization, but this pericope begins and ends with a generalization and the itemization comes in the middle."[47]

however, have no territorial share among them or own any portion in their midst; I am your portion and your share among the Israelites.

לֹ֤א תִנְחָל֙ וְחֵ֔לֶק לֹא־יִהְיֶ֥ה לְךָ֖ בְּתוֹכָ֑ם אֲנִ֤י חֶלְקְךָ֙
וְנַחֲלָ֣תְךָ֔ בְּת֖וֹךְ בְּנֵ֥י יִשְׂרָאֵֽל׃ ס שביעי

sacred gifts Hebrew ***terumot ha-kodashim,*** the equivalent of ***terumat mattanam,*** "their dedicated gifts" (v. 11), referring to the intervening list of fixed perquisites from sacred (but not most sacred) offerings that the priest and his household may eat. The term ***kodashim*** has the technical meaning of sacred food allowable to the priestly household as opposed to the most sacred food, ***kodesh ha-kodashim*** (v. 9), which may be eaten only by the male priests (Lev. 21:22).

that are with you Rather, "that are after you." (Heb. *'ittekha* can denote "after you," as shown by the alternation of *'et* and *'aḥarei* in the patriarchal promises.[48] Besides, the given rendering cannot be correct since Aaron had no daughters [see also Lev. 10:14]).

covenant of salt Hebrew ***berit melaḥ*** (see Lev. 2:13; 2 Chron. 13:15). Salt was the food preservative ***par excellence*** in antiquity. Its use was required for all sacrifices (Lev. 2:13; Ezek. 43:24), and it stands in contrast to leaven and other fermentatives, whose use is forbidden on the altar (Lev. 2:11). Thus salt is a symbol of permanence, and a "salt covenant," therefore, means an unbreakable covenant.[49] Most likely salt played a central role at the solemn meal that sealed a covenant, as in Genesis 26:13 and 31:54 and Exodus 24:11. A Neo-Babylonian letter speaks of "all who have tasted the salt of the Jakin tribe,"[50] referring to the tribe's covenanted allies. Loyalty to the Persian monarch is claimed by having tasted the "salt of the palace" in Ezra 4:14. And Arabic ***milḥat,*** a derivative of ***malaḥa,*** "to salt," means "a treaty."[51]

REWARD FOR THE LEVITES (vv. 20–24)

The introductory phrase indicates a new section. God speaks to Aaron for the third time: the first (vv. 1–7), to have the priests and Levites share the responsibility for the custody of the Tabernacle; the second (vv. 8–19), designating the priestly perquisites; and the third (vv. 20–24), denying priests and Levites any share in the promised land and assigning the tithes to the Levites as a reward for their potentially lethal guard duties.

20. And the LORD said to Aaron But not to or concerning his sons (contrast vv. 1,8). Aaron, then, is addressed not as the head of the priests but as the head of the Levites (see 17:18,23); the land prohibition, therefore, applies to the Levites as well as the priests.[52] This statement is the antecedent of "therefore I have said" in verse 24.

however This does not translate a specific word, but beginning the sentence with the ***be-'artsam,*** "in their land," gives this effect.

your portion . . . your share Hebrew ***ḥelkekha ve-naḥalatekha*** are synonymous terms that refer to the land allotted each family within its tribal territory in the promised land. Because land was denied to the families of priests and Levites (v. 24), they received, as compensation, the perquisites enumerated here.[53]

Since the tribal inheritance involved agricultural land only, the assignment of forty-eight cities and their surrounding pasture to the Levites (35:1–8) and to the priests (Josh. 21:13–19) does not contradict the prohibition against clergy owning land. Indeed, Ezekiel also forbids any landed inheritance to priests (Ezek. 44:28)—although he ostensibly assigns them land (Ezek. 45:4; 48:10–11). But in this case it is for residences only ("for houses"; 45:4). It is true that dedicated lands produce food for the priests (e.g., Lev. 27:21,28), but they belong to the sanctuary not to the individual priests. In practice, however, this rule seems to have been breached (see 1 Kings 2:26).

The implication of this verse is clear: Because the priests and Levites are "My portion" and receive "My gifts" (v. 8), they need no landed inheritance.

[21]And to the Levites I hereby give all the tithes in Israel as their share in return for the services that they perform, the services of the Tent of Meeting. [22]Henceforth, Israelites shall not trespass on the Tent of Meeting, and thus incur guilt and die: [23]only Levites shall perform the services of the Tent of Meeting; others would incur guilt. It is the law for all time throughout the ages. But they shall have no territorial share among the Israelites; [24]for it is the tithes set aside by the Israelites as a gift to the LORD that I give to the Levites as their share. Therefore I have said concerning them: They shall have no territorial share among the Israelites.

21 וְלִבְנֵי לֵוִי הִנֵּה נָתַתִּי כָּל־מַעֲשֵׂר בְּיִשְׂרָאֵל
לְנַחֲלָה חֵלֶף עֲבֹדָתָם אֲשֶׁר־הֵם עֹבְדִים אֶת־
עֲבֹדַת אֹהֶל מוֹעֵד׃ 22 וְלֹא־יִקְרְבוּ עוֹד בְּנֵי
יִשְׂרָאֵל אֶל־אֹהֶל מוֹעֵד לָשֵׂאת חֵטְא לָמוּת׃
23 וְעָבַד הַלֵּוִי הוּא אֶת־עֲבֹדַת אֹהֶל מוֹעֵד וְהֵם
יִשְׂאוּ עֲוֺנָם חֻקַּת עוֹלָם לְדֹרֹתֵיכֶם וּבְתוֹךְ בְּנֵי
יִשְׂרָאֵל לֹא יִנְחֲלוּ נַחֲלָה׃ 24 כִּי אֶת־מַעְשַׂר בְּנֵי־
יִשְׂרָאֵל אֲשֶׁר יָרִימוּ לַיהוָה תְּרוּמָה נָתַתִּי לַלְוִיִּם
לְנַחֲלָה עַל־כֵּן אָמַרְתִּי לָהֶם בְּתוֹךְ בְּנֵי יִשְׂרָאֵל
לֹא יִנְחֲלוּ נַחֲלָה׃ פ 25 וַיְדַבֵּר יְהוָה אֶל־

21. and to the Levites This is a continuation of the address to Aaron, implying that Aaron, as head of the tribe of Levi (vv. 17–18), is responsible for seeing to it that the Levites receive their tithes.

give Rather, "assign." The tithe is a compulsory, permanent grant to the Levites. It falls due on every crop in the promised land (Lev. 27:30) as annual wages (v. 31) for the Levitical labors in the sanctuary. Deuteronomy imposes the tithe obligation only on the grain, wine, and (olive) oil crops (Deut. 14:23; cf. Excursus 46).

all the tithes Hebrew *kol maʿaser* may be a reference to the same phrase in Leviticus 27:30, in which case this passage also holds that the tithe falls due on all crops.

in return[54]

services (2) Rather, "labor," referring to all the tasks assigned the Levites in the Tabernacle, embracing both their guarding and removal responsibilities (see Excursus 6).

22. trespass Or, "encroach" (cf. Excursus 5).

guilt Hebrew *ḥet'*, like its synonym *ʿavon,* means either sin or its consequence, but in the expression *nasa' ḥet'/ʿavon* it means the latter, "incur punishment."[55]

23. only This expresses the pronoun *hu',* that is, the Levite alone.[56]

others would incur guilt Rather, "they (the Levites) would incur their (the Israelites') punishment." Henceforth, the Levites will bear the full responsibility for Israelite encroachment (see the Comment to 8:19). In effect, the Levitical guards who failed in their duties to prevent encroachment by Israelites will be punished with death by God (see Excursus 40). By this measure, the people's fears—that they will continue to suffer God's wrath as a result of their sanctuary encroachment—are to be allayed (17:27–28).

law for all time That the Levites will perform the removal and guarding duties of the Tabernacle.

no territorial share Hebrew *naḥalah.* For the full meaning of this term, see the Comment to 27:7. The territory referred to here is farmland. Since the Levites will receive a tithe of the grain, wine, and oil of their brothers' crops, they need not produce these crops on their own. However, they will need permanent residences (see 35:1–8).

24. a gift to the LORD The tithe properly belongs to the Lord, which He, in turn, assigns to the Levites as payment for their sanctuary labors. Thus, both Levitical and priestly perquisites are grants from the divine domain. This may explain why the tithes are still called "the Lord's" in Leviticus 27:30: It may reflect an earlier period, when the tithes were the property of the sanctuary, before they were transferred to the exclusive possession of the Levites.

give Rather, "assign" (see the Comment to v. 21).

25The Lord spoke to Moses, saying: 26Speak to the Levites and say to them: When you receive from the Israelites their tithes, which I have assigned to you as your share, you shall set aside from them one-tenth of the tithe as a gift to the Lord. 27This shall be accounted to you as your gift. As with the new grain from the threshing floor or the flow from the vat, 28so shall you on your part set aside a gift for the Lord from all the tithes that you receive from the Israelites; and from them you shall bring the gift for the Lord to Aaron the priest. 29You shall set aside all gifts due to the Lord from everything that is donated to you, from each thing its best portion, the part thereof that is to be consecrated.

מֹשֶׁה לֵּאמֹר׃ 26 וְאֶל־הַלְוִיִּם תְּדַבֵּר וְאָמַרְתָּ
אֲלֵהֶם כִּי־תִקְחוּ מֵאֵת בְּנֵי־יִשְׂרָאֵל אֶת־הַמַּעֲשֵׂר
אֲשֶׁר נָתַתִּי לָכֶם מֵאִתָּם בְּנַחֲלַתְכֶם וַהֲרֵמֹתֶם
מִמֶּנּוּ תְּרוּמַת יְהוָה מַעֲשֵׂר מִן־הַמַּעֲשֵׂר׃
27 וְנֶחְשַׁב לָכֶם תְּרוּמַתְכֶם כַּדָּגָן מִן־הַגֹּרֶן
וְכַמְלֵאָה מִן־הַיָּקֶב׃ 28 כֵּן תָּרִימוּ גַם־אַתֶּם
תְּרוּמַת יְהוָה מִכֹּל מַעְשְׂרֹתֵיכֶם אֲשֶׁר תִּקְחוּ
מֵאֵת בְּנֵי יִשְׂרָאֵל וּנְתַתֶּם מִמֶּנּוּ אֶת־תְּרוּמַת יְהוָה
לְאַהֲרֹן הַכֹּהֵן׃ 29 מִכֹּל מַתְּנֹתֵיכֶם תָּרִימוּ אֵת כָּל־
תְּרוּמַת יְהוָה מִכָּל־חֶלְבּוֹ אֶת־מִקְדְּשׁוֹ מִמֶּנּוּ׃

A TENTH OF THE TITHE: A PRIESTLY PERQUISITE (vv. 25–32)

The Levites are not exempt from the tithe, but their tithe goes to the priests; who are exempt. In sixth- and fifth-century Babylonia, by contrast, temple officials also are obligated to pay annual tithes to the sanctuary. Tithes are collected at the source from the owner (v. 26).

25. *The Lord spoke to Moses* But not to Aaron, as He did previously (vv. 1,8), in order to avoid the conflict of interest that would result if Aaron were told to collect the tenth of the Levitical tithe assigned to him (v. 28).[57]

26. *receive* Rather, "take." The Levites are not dependent upon the philanthropic whims of the landowner; they may seize the tithe that has been assigned them (vv. 21,24,26). The verb ***lakaḥ*** can mean "take possession" (8:16; 31:29,30; see Excursus 46).

as your share[58]

set aside As in verse 28. Hebrew ***herim*** is the technical term for dedication outside of the sanctuary (see Excursus 42).

27. *This shall be accounted to you as your gift*[59]

As with the new grain From which the Israelites set aside a gift to the priests (v. 12), so shall you Levites also set aside a tithe for the priests.[60] Does this verse imply that the tithe is collected only from grain, wine, and oil? Or is it collected from all produce?

flow Literally, "fullness," that is, full crop (see Deut. 22:9). Here, however, this term is associated solely with the vat and, hence, refers to its liquid contents, that is, wine or oil. Alternatively, it may refer to ***re'shit*** (v. 12), the priestly perquisite from the vat (so rendered in the Greek), a meaning it apparently has in Exodus 22:28.

28. *receive* Rather, "take" (see the Comment to v. 26).

gift for the Lord[61]

29. *donated to you* God has commanded that the Israelites donate a tithe to the Levites (***natatti;*** vv. 21,24); likewise the Levites are to donate (***u-netattem;*** v. 28) a tithe to the priests.

its best portion Literally, "its fat"; that is, the priestly perquisite from the Levitical tithe should come from its best portion, just as the priestly perquisite from the laity's first processed is also from its ***ḥelev***—"best" (v. 12).

the part . . . that is to be consecrated Hebrew ***mikdesho.*** The vocalization has been deliberately altered by the Masoretes to distinguish this noun from ***mikdasho,*** "His sanctuary."[62] The tithe of the tithe set aside for the priests automatically assumes a sacred status, as do all priestly perquisites (vv. 8–10,19), whereas the Levitical tithe—as the Levites themselves—is never called sacred in these priestly texts (contrast Lev. 27:30; Deut. 26:13).

30Say to them further: When you have removed the best part from it, you Levites may consider it the same as the yield of threshing floor or vat. 31You and your households may eat it anywhere, for it is your recompense for your services in the Tent of Meeting. 32You will incur no guilt through it, once you have removed the best part from it; but you must not profane the sacred donations of the Israelites, lest you die.

מפטיר 30 וְאָמַרְתָּ אֲלֵהֶם בַּהֲרִימְכֶם אֶת־חֶלְבּוֹ
מִמֶּנּוּ וְנֶחְשַׁב לַלְוִיִּם כִּתְבוּאַת גֹּרֶן וְכִתְבוּאַת
יָקֶב׃ 31 וַאֲכַלְתֶּם אֹתוֹ בְּכָל־מָקוֹם אַתֶּם וּבֵיתְכֶם
כִּי־שָׂכָר הוּא לָכֶם חֵלֶף עֲבֹדַתְכֶם בְּאֹהֶל מוֹעֵד׃
32 וְלֹא־תִשְׂאוּ עָלָיו חֵטְא בַּהֲרִימְכֶם אֶת־חֶלְבּוֹ
מִמֶּנּוּ וְאֶת־קָדְשֵׁי בְנֵי־יִשְׂרָאֵל לֹא תְחַלְּלוּ וְלֹא
תָמוּתוּ׃ פ

*30. **you Levites may consider it*** Rather, "it will be reckoned (by God, not the Levites) to you Levites" ("you" is not in the text but is understood).

as the yield of threshing floor or vat After it is tithed and permitted to its owner.

*31. **eat it anywhere*** After the priestly portion is removed, the tithe's status becomes profane and it may be eaten anywhere without concern for ritual purity.[63] Deuteronomy 26:14 ostensibly disagrees. But the Book of Deuteronomy does not posit the removal of a "sacred" part of the tithe for the priest; hence, the tithe retains its sanctity.

recompense The Levites are entitled to the exorbitant wage of the tithe in compensation for having to expose themselves to lethal dangers in performing their Tabernacle duties (see Excursus 40).

for[64]

your services Rather, "your labors" (see the Comment to v. 21).

*32. **incur no guilt*** See v. 22. As long as the sacred tenth of the tithe has not been set aside for the priests, it is lethal to eat it or touch it if one is in a state of impurity[65]—even to tamper with it in a state of purity. That the punishment is death by God is expressly stated at the end of the verse.

through it Hebrew *'alav*, as in Leviticus 19:17; 22:9.

profane Hebrew *teḥallelu.* The verb *ḥillel,* "profane," must be distinguished from *timme'*, "pollute, render impure." Unauthorized contact with sancta is penalized with a monetary reparation, for example, if sacred food is accidentally eaten (Lev. 22:14–16), or with capital punishment, if the act was performed deliberately. The latter case is not explicitly expressed in scriptural law, but it may be deduced from the examples of sancta trespass by Nadab and Abihu (Lev. 10:1–2) and by Korah and the chieftains (Num. 16).[66]

sacred donations of Hebrew *kodeshei,* a general designation for all the sacred gifts donated by Israelites to the sanctuary. This serves as a warning to the Levites lest they tamper with them and thereby incur death.

Purification from Contamination by a Corpse (vv. 1–22)

Ḥukkat

Contamination through contact with a corpse has been mentioned earlier in the Torah,[1] but only here is the mode of purification prescribed.[2] The connection with the adjoining chapters seems tenuous.[3] Perhaps the twice-mentioned warning that corpse contamination may defile the sanctuary (vv. 13,20) made this chapter a natural sequel to the *parashah* of Korah (chaps. 16–18), in which the main problem is the desecration of the sanctuary by encroachment. The most attractive explanation may be that Eleazar and not Aaron officiates—as is also the case in the previous Korah episode (17:2–4). As both instances involve corpse contamination, Aaron is barred from officiating and Eleazar takes his place. Hence this unit was placed here, between the Korah narrative and the account of Aaron's sin and death (20:1–13,20–29). The structure of this chapter is discussed in Excursus 47.

HUKKAT

19 The LORD spoke to Moses and Aaron, saying: 2 This is the ritual law that the LORD has commanded:

Instruct the Israelite people to bring you a red cow without blemish, in which there is no defect and on which no yoke has been laid. 3 You shall give it to Eleazar the priest. It shall be taken outside the camp and slaughtered in his presence. 4 Eleazar the priest shall take some of its blood with his finger and sprinkle it seven times toward the front of the Tent of Meeting. 5 The cow shall be burned in his

חקת

י״ט וַיְדַבֵּר יְהוָה אֶל־מֹשֶׁה וְאֶל־אַהֲרֹן לֵאמֹר:
2 זֹאת חֻקַּת הַתּוֹרָה אֲשֶׁר־צִוָּה יְהוָה לֵאמֹר
דַּבֵּר ׀ אֶל־בְּנֵי יִשְׂרָאֵל וְיִקְחוּ אֵלֶיךָ פָרָה אֲדֻמָּה
תְּמִימָה אֲשֶׁר אֵין־בָּהּ מוּם אֲשֶׁר לֹא־עָלָה עָלֶיהָ
עֹל: 3 וּנְתַתֶּם אֹתָהּ אֶל־אֶלְעָזָר הַכֹּהֵן וְהוֹצִיא
אֹתָהּ אֶל־מִחוּץ לַמַּחֲנֶה וְשָׁחַט אֹתָהּ לְפָנָיו:
4 וְלָקַח אֶלְעָזָר הַכֹּהֵן מִדָּמָהּ בְּאֶצְבָּעוֹ וְהִזָּה אֶל־
נֹכַח פְּנֵי אֹהֶל־מוֹעֵד מִדָּמָהּ שֶׁבַע פְּעָמִים:

CHAPTER 19 THE RED COW (vv. 1–13)

1. Aaron Because Hebrew ***dabber,*** "instruct," and *'elekha,* "you," are in the singular, the instruction may have been given to Moses alone:[4] Only he, the prophet, relays God's message to Israel. But when the instruction changes from words to action, it is addressed to Aaron as well: "You (pl.) shall give it" (v. 3).

2. ritual law Hebrew *ḥukkat ha-torah* occurs again only in 31:21, which also begins a section on purification from corpse contamination. A similar construct, *ḥukkat ha-mishpat,* "law of procedure," is found in 27:11 and 35:29.

red cow The idea is to increase, if symbolically, the amount of blood in the ashes (see Excursus 48).

without blemish, in which there is no defect This apparent redundancy is for the sake of emphasis; see Leviticus 22:21 for the identical construction. The rabbis, however, interpret "without blemish" as referring to the color: "unblemished red."[5] Hebrew *'adom,* usually rendered "red," probably means "brown" (for which there is no Hebrew word). Brown cows, of course, are plentiful, but one that is completely uniform in color, without specks of white or black or without even two black or white hairs, is extremely rare.[6] Thus the rabbinic interpretation is preferred.

no yoke has been laid That is, it must not be used for profane purposes. This stipulation is made in Deuteronomy 21:2 and 1 Samuel 6:7, where the animals were not intended for sacrifice. Indeed, the rabbis teach that worked animals are not disqualified as sacrifices.[7] However, the firstling, a sacrificial animal, may not be worked.[8] Thus work animals probably could be sacrificed but no sooner were they consecrated as sacrificial animals than no benefit could be derived from them. The Hittites also (see the Comment to 13:29) regarded the working of sacrificial animals as a capital crime.[9]

3. Eleazar According to the majority of the rabbis, henceforth only the High Priest officiated in the ritual of the red cow.[10] This would accord with the ritual of a burnt purification offering (vv. 9,17), whose sacrifice was also performed by the High Priest (cf. Lev. 4:1–23; 16:3–28). It may be that Eleazar officiates instead of Aaron because the latter is close to death (20:22–29). Eleazar, already put in charge of the Tabernacle during the wilderness march (3:32; 4:16), was, in effect, the acting High Priest (17:2–4). However, the most likely explanation is, as in the previous case of the Korahite rebellion (17:2–4), that Aaron was barred from officiating lest he become contaminated.

outside the camp The Greek adds "in a clean place," an essential criterion for the burnt purification offering (Lev. 4:12).

in his presence The cow will also be burned in his presence (v. 5), an indication that it is imperative for the officiating priest to supervise the entire ritual (see Excursus 48).

4. sprinkle it seven times This act consecrates the red cow as a purification offering.

sight—its hide, flesh, and blood shall be burned, its dung
included—6and the priest shall take cedar wood, hyssop,
and crimson stuff, and throw them into the fire consuming
the cow. 7The priest shall wash his garments and bathe his
body in water; after that the priest may reenter the camp,
but he shall be unclean until evening. 8He who performed
the burning shall also wash his garments in water, bathe his
body in water, and be unclean until evening. 9A man who is

5 וְשָׂרַף אֶת־הַפָּרָה לְעֵינָיו אֶת־עֹרָהּ וְאֶת־בְּשָׂרָהּ
וְאֶת־דָּמָהּ עַל־פִּרְשָׁהּ יִשְׂרֹף׃ 6 וְלָקַח הַכֹּהֵן עֵץ
אֶרֶז וְאֵזוֹב וּשְׁנִי תוֹלָעַת וְהִשְׁלִיךְ אֶל־תּוֹךְ שְׂרֵפַת
הַפָּרָה׃ 7 וְכִבֶּס בְּגָדָיו הַכֹּהֵן וְרָחַץ בְּשָׂרוֹ בַּמַּיִם
וְאַחַר יָבוֹא אֶל־הַמַּחֲנֶה וְטָמֵא הַכֹּהֵן עַד־הָעָרֶב׃
8 וְהַשֹּׂרֵף אֹתָהּ יְכַבֵּס בְּגָדָיו בַּמַּיִם וְרָחַץ בְּשָׂרוֹ
בַּמָּיִם וְטָמֵא עַד־הָעָרֶב׃ 9 וְאָסַף ׀ אִישׁ טָהוֹר אֵת

toward the front According to the rabbis, the front, that is, the entrance of the Tent, must be seen. Hence if the wind blows the Tent flap shut, the sprinkling is invalid.[11] During Second Temple times, the High Priest performed the ceremony atop the Mount of Olives, which afforded a view of the entrance to the Temple building.[12]

5. ***and blood*** The blood is the essential ingredient in the ashes of the red cow. It is the blood of a *ḥatta't,* a purification offering, which is the ritual detergent *par excellence* and which will remove the impurity from those contaminated by contact with corpses. Thus all of the blood from the red cow, except for the few drops sprinkled by the priest, is burned in the fire. Indeed, according to the rabbis, after the sevenfold sprinkling, the High Priest wiped his hands on the carcass to assure that not a single drop of blood was wasted.[13]

shall be burned Not necessarily by a priest (see Lev. 4:12,21; 9:11; 16:27).

its dung[14]

6. ***priest*** Any priest, not just Eleazar.[15]

cedar wood, hyssop, and crimson stuff The same materials were used in the purification of the leper (Lev. 14:4,6,49,51–52) and in other purification rituals throughout the ancient Near East. For example, in the Mesopotamian "Ritual . . . When Covering the Temple Kettle-Drum," the bull (whose hide would become the drumskin) was sprinkled with cedar balsam, burned with cedar wood, and buried in a red cloth.[16] Since cedar, *'erez,* was uncommon outside of Lebanon, some tannaim and modern scholars believe that the cyprus tree is meant.[17] The hyssop, *'ezov,* is identified with *Majorana syriaca,* an aromatic plant widespread throughout the Land of Israel. Its hairy surface retains liquid and, hence, is ideal for sprinkling (v. 18; Exod. 12:22). Crimson yarn called *tola'at shani,* literally "red dyed wool,"[18] refers to the dye extracted from a "crimson worm," the *Kermes bilicus,* and used in the weaving of the sacred garments of the High Priest and the inner curtains of the Tabernacle (Exod. 36:8,35,37; 39:1–2). *Shani,* "crimson," seems to be an Egyptian loanword. In postexilic texts (e.g., 2 Chron. 3:14), the term is replaced by *karmil.*[19]

fire According to the rabbis, the cedar and hyssop are added in great quantities to provide ample ashes.[20]

7. ***wash his garments and bathe his body*** This is a logical sequence: If he bathed first, his unwashed garments would recontaminate him.

be unclean So all handlers of the burnt *ḥatta't* (purification) offering; see Excursus 48.

until evening Whoever handles a burnt *ḥatta't* may enter the camp as soon as he has laundered and bathed (see Lev. 16:26,28), provided he does not partake of sacred food until the evening.[21] This rule applies to all other bearers of one-day impurity,[22] who, however, are not required to leave the camp.

8. ***He who performed the burning*** And also he who gathers up the ashes (v. 10) is presumed to remain outside the camp until after he has laundered and bathed precisely as the contaminated priest has done (v. 7).

in water[23]

clean shall gather up the ashes of the cow and deposit them
outside the camp in a clean place, to be kept for water of
lustration for the Israelite community. It is for cleansing.
10He who gathers up the ashes of the cow shall also wash his
clothes and be unclean until evening.

This shall be a permanent law for the Israelites and for
the strangers who reside among you.

11He who touches the corpse of any human being shall be
unclean for seven days. 12He shall cleanse himself with it on
the third day and on the seventh day, and then be clean; if
he fails to cleanse himself on the third and seventh days, he
shall not be clean. 13Whoever touches a corpse, the body of

אֵפֶר הַפָּרָה וְהִנִּיחַ מִחוּץ לַמַּחֲנֶה בְּמָקוֹם טָהוֹר
וְהָיְתָה לַעֲדַת בְּנֵי־יִשְׂרָאֵל לְמִשְׁמֶרֶת לְמֵי נִדָּה
חַטָּאת הִוא׃ 10 וְכִבֶּס הָאֹסֵף אֶת־אֵפֶר הַפָּרָה
אֶת־בְּגָדָיו וְטָמֵא עַד־הָעָרֶב וְהָיְתָה לִבְנֵי יִשְׂרָאֵל
וְלַגֵּר הַגָּר בְּתוֹכָם לְחֻקַּת עוֹלָם׃ 11 הַנֹּגֵעַ בְּמֵת
לְכָל־נֶפֶשׁ אָדָם וְטָמֵא שִׁבְעַת יָמִים׃ 12 הוּא
יִתְחַטָּא־בוֹ בַּיּוֹם הַשְּׁלִישִׁי וּבַיּוֹם הַשְּׁבִיעִי יִטְהָר
וְאִם־לֹא יִתְחַטָּא בַּיּוֹם הַשְּׁלִישִׁי וּבַיּוֹם הַשְּׁבִיעִי
לֹא יִטְהָר׃ 13 כָּל־הַנֹּגֵעַ בְּמֵת בְּנֶפֶשׁ הָאָדָם

9. A man Not necessarily a priest.[24]

to be kept Rather, "to be safeguarded" (see the Comment to 3:7). The ashes of the red cow must be guarded scrupulously lest they become invalidated through contamination. During Second Temple times the ashes were divided into three parts: one-third for sprinkling, one-third for sanctifying new lustral water, and one-third for safekeeping.[25]

water of lustration Hebrew ***mei niddah,*** derived from a privative Piel, "remove impurity" (e.g., ***niddah,*** "menstrual impurity," in Lev. 18:19) and analogous to *ḥitte',* "remove sin" *(ḥet').* Thus the prophet declares: "In that day a fountain shall be open to the House of David and the inhabitants of Jerusalem for purging *(le-ḥatta't)* and for cleansing *(le-niddah)*" (Zech. 13:1).[26]

It is for cleansing Hebrew ***ḥatta't hi'.*** Rather, "It is a purification offering."[27] The antecedent of "it" (read as feminine) is technically "the cow," but clearly "it" (written as masculine) refers to ***'efer,*** the "ashes" containing the ritual detergent, the ***ḥatta't*** blood (see Excursus 48). As explained below, it is these ashes mixed with water that will be sprinkled on the corpse-contaminated individual to remove the impurity.

10. wash his clothes It is understood that he will also bathe his body (v. 21; 31:24).

strangers Hebrew ***ger,*** that is, the "resident alien." All those who dwell in the Holy Land, Israelites and non-Israelites alike, must purify themselves of corpse contamination lest they defile the sanctuary by bearing their impurity within the community (vv. 13,20; cf. 31:19).

11. any human being Literally, "a body of a person" (v. 13). According to Yevamot 61a, this includes non-Israelites but excludes animal carcasses, which only transmit one-day impurity (Lev. 11:24–40).

seven days A week of purification is required for the severe impurity bearers: the new mother (Lev. 12:2), the leper (Lev. 14:9), and the gonorrheic (Lev. 15:13,28). However, they require a ***ḥatta't*** offering on the eighth day (Lev. 14:10,21–23; 15:14–15,28–29), or even later for the new mother (Lev. 12:6–8), whereas the corpse-contaminated individual is aspersed with the ***ḥatta't*** ashes during the week of purification, on the third and seventh days (v. 12). The severity of corpse contamination is unique in another respect: Whereas the other severe impurities (e.g., leprosy, gonorrhea) stem from the contaminated person, corpse contamination stems not from his own person but from his contact with a corpse. The week-long purification for corpse contamination is attested in ancient Babylonia—whoever contacts dust from a place of mourning offers sacrifices to the god Shamash, bathes, changes clothing, and does not leave his house for seven days.[28]

12. cleanse himself Hebrew ***yitḥatte',*** Hitpael from ***ḥitte',*** a term deliberately chosen because it implies the use of a ***ḥatta't*** offering (cf. 8:7,21).

with it Hebrew *bo.* The masculine suffix refers back to ***'efer,*** "ashes" (v. 10).

a person who has died, and does not cleanse himself, defiles
the LORD's Tabernacle; that person shall be cut off from
Israel. Since the water of lustration was not dashed on him,
he remains unclean; his uncleanness is still upon him.
14This is the ritual: When a person dies in a tent, whoever
enters the tent and whoever is in the tent shall be unclean
seven days; 15and every open vessel, with no lid fastened
down, shall be unclean. 16And in the open, anyone who

אֲשֶׁר־יָמוּת וְלֹא יִתְחַטָּא אֶת־מִשְׁכַּן יְהוָה טִמֵּא
וְנִכְרְתָה הַנֶּפֶשׁ הַהִוא מִיִּשְׂרָאֵל כִּי מֵי נִדָּה לֹא־
זֹרַק עָלָיו טָמֵא יִהְיֶה עוֹד טֻמְאָתוֹ בוֹ׃ 14 זֹאת
הַתּוֹרָה אָדָם כִּי־יָמוּת בְּאֹהֶל כָּל־הַבָּא אֶל־הָאֹהֶל
וְכָל־אֲשֶׁר בָּאֹהֶל יִטְמָא שִׁבְעַת יָמִים׃ 15 וְכֹל כְּלִי
פָתוּחַ אֲשֶׁר אֵין־צָמִיד פָּתִיל עָלָיו טָמֵא הוּא׃

third day That the severity of the impurity is diminished by the initial sprinkling on the third day is still reflected in the mourning customs of Judaism: On the third day of the week of mourning *(shivah),* the prohibitions are reduced.[29] In Moʿed Katan 27b we find: "Three days for weeping and seven for lamenting and thirty (to refrain) from cutting the hair and (donning) pressed clothes; hereafter, the Holy One Blessed Be He says, 'You are not more compassionate toward him (the departed) than I.'"

and then be clean Hebrew ***yithar,*** literally "he shall be clean," implying that he is aspersed with the purificatory waters on the third day only. Hence, it is preferable to read ***ve-taher.***[30]

13. ***defiles the LORD's Tabernacle*** The corpse-contaminated individual, by prolonging his impurity, has defiled the sanctuary from afar, even without entering it. This concept that severe impurity is dynamic, attacking the sanctuary through the air, is discussed in Excursus 49.

The demand for purification from corpse contamination was so great during Second Temple times that the purificatory waters were made available in twenty-four districts of the country. Even after the destruction of the Temple these waters were still available in Judea, Galilee, Transjordan, and Ezion-geber (Assia) in the south.[31]

cut off Hebrew ***nikhretah,*** implying the penalty of ***karet,*** the excision of his line (see Excursus 36). The neglect must be deliberate (15:30–31);[32] if accidental, he brings a purification offering (15:27–29).

dashed Hebrew ***zorak***[33] is a singular verb used collectively with a plural subject, ***mayim,*** "waters." This exceptional use is attested elsewhere (e.g., 24:7).

PURIFICATION BY SPRINKLING (vv. 14–22)

14. ***This***[34]

tent Or house.[35]

enters the tent The principle of ***maʾahil,*** "overhang," applies.[36] The impurity exuded by the body, so to speak, is trapped by the roof and cannot rise. Hence, every person and object under the roof is contaminated, another example of the original notion that impurity was a dynamic, physical substance exuded by the contaminated body (Excursus 49).

15. ***every open vessel*** However, a tightly closed vessel will not admit the "vapors" of impurity given off by the corpse; its contents remain pure. The vessels referred to here are limited to those made entirely of earthenware.[37]

lid Hebrew ***tsamid,*** a nominal formation from the verb ***ts-m-d,*** "bind together," as in Ugaritic and Akkadian.

fastened down Hebrew ***patil,*** passive participle from the root ***p-t-l,*** "twist" (cf. Gen. 30:8), from which the noun ***petil,*** "twisted cord," is formed.[38] Archaeological evidence suggests that what may be meant is a lid attached to the vessel by cords passing through holes in the lid and through the handles of the vessel. Such a lid would keep the vessel tightly closed and preserve it from defilement.

touches a person who was killed or who died naturally, or
human bone, or a grave, shall be unclean seven days.
17 Some of the ashes from the fire of cleansing shall be taken
for the unclean person, and fresh water shall be added to
them in a vessel. 18 A person who is clean shall take hyssop,
dip it in the water, and sprinkle on the tent and on all the
vessels and people who were there, or on him who touched
the bones or the person who was killed or died naturally or
the grave. 19 The clean person shall sprinkle it upon the
unclean person on the third day and on the seventh day,
thus cleansing him by the seventh day. He shall then wash
his clothes and bathe in water, and at nightfall he shall be
clean. 20 If anyone who has become unclean fails to cleanse
himself, that person shall be cut off from the congregation,
for he has defiled the LORD's sanctuary. The water of lustration was not dashed on him: he is unclean.

16 וְכֹל אֲשֶׁר־יִגַּע עַל־פְּנֵי הַשָּׂדֶה בַּחֲלַל־חֶרֶב אוֹ
בְמֵת אוֹ־בְעֶצֶם אָדָם אוֹ בְקָבֶר יִטְמָא שִׁבְעַת
יָמִים׃ 17 וְלָקְחוּ לַטָּמֵא מֵעֲפַר שְׂרֵפַת הַחַטָּאת
וְנָתַן עָלָיו מַיִם חַיִּים אֶל־כֶּלִי׃ שני 18 וְלָקַח
אֵזוֹב וְטָבַל בַּמַּיִם אִישׁ טָהוֹר וְהִזָּה עַל־הָאֹהֶל
וְעַל־כָּל־הַכֵּלִים וְעַל־הַנְּפָשׁוֹת אֲשֶׁר הָיוּ־שָׁם וְעַל־
הַנֹּגֵעַ בַּעֶצֶם אוֹ בֶחָלָל אוֹ בַמֵּת אוֹ בַקָּבֶר׃
19 וְהִזָּה הַטָּהֹר עַל־הַטָּמֵא בַּיּוֹם הַשְּׁלִישִׁי וּבַיּוֹם
הַשְּׁבִיעִי וְחִטְּאוֹ בַּיּוֹם הַשְּׁבִיעִי וְכִבֶּס בְּגָדָיו וְרָחַץ
בַּמַּיִם וְטָהֵר בָּעָרֶב׃ 20 וְאִישׁ אֲשֶׁר־יִטְמָא וְלֹא
יִתְחַטָּא וְנִכְרְתָה הַנֶּפֶשׁ הַהִוא מִתּוֹךְ הַקָּהָל כִּי
אֶת־מִקְדַּשׁ יְהוָה טִמֵּא מֵי נִדָּה לֹא־זֹרַק עָלָיו

shall be unclean "Forever,"[39] in contrast to all persons and objects in the tent and everyone who touches a corpse or related item. These "shall be unclean seven days" (vv. 14,16)—another indication that the vessels spoken of here are made exclusively of earthenware. Unless they have fastened covers, they must be broken.[40] The Dead Sea Scrolls say so expressly.[41]

16. ***in the open*** Literally, "on the field" (see Lev. 14:7,53; 17:5).

grave The ancient Mesopotamians regarded the dust around the grave as dangerously defiling (see the Comment to v. 11).

17. ***fire of cleansing*** Hebrew *sereifat ha-ḥatta't*. Rather, "fire of the purification offering" or "burnt purification offering" (see v. 9 and Excursus 48).

added to them Hebrew *ve-natan,* reading *ve-natenu* (pl.),[42] to conform with "shall be taken," also in the plural. The text implies that the water was added to the ashes. The rabbis, however,[43] hold that the ashes were added to the water. Perhaps the ashes were held in a porous cloth through which the water was filtered.[44]

18. ***A person who is clean*** This obvious condition is made explicit in order to bar those who had already handled the ashes (v. 17) and were thereby contaminated.[45]

hyssop See verse 6.

on all the vessels These thereafter must undergo burning or washing (31:23); persons require washing (v. 19).[46]

19. ***thus cleansing*** Rather, "thus purifying him" with the purification offering ashes. He is not fully cleansed until he launders and bathes.

20. This verse is not a pointless repetition of verse 13. The latter verse belongs to the section (vv. 11–13) that speaks of the purification of a person who is contaminated by a corpse, whereas this verse belongs to a new section (vv. 14–21), which itemizes a series of objects and persons contaminated by corpses and parts of corpses.[47]

congregation Hebrew *kahal,* a synonym of *'edah* (v. 13). This latter word, the technical term for the Israelite community before the establishment of the monarchy, was replaced by *kahal.*[48]

sanctuary Hebrew *mikdash.* Rather, "sacred precincts" (3:38), a synonym for *mishkan,* "Tabernacle" (v. 13). Does this change also reflect a later period when the Tabernacle was no longer functioning?

21 That shall be for them a law for all time. Further, he
who sprinkled the water of lustration shall wash his clothes;
and whoever touches the water of lustration shall be unclean until evening. 22 Whatever that unclean person
touches shall be unclean; and the person who touches him
shall be unclean until evening.

טָמֵא הוּא׃ 21 וְהָיְתָה לָהֶם לְחֻקַּת עוֹלָם וּמַזֵּה
מֵי־הַנִּדָּה יְכַבֵּס בְּגָדָיו וְהַנֹּגֵעַ בְּמֵי הַנִּדָּה יִטְמָא
עַד־הָעָרֶב׃ 22 וְכֹל אֲשֶׁר־יִגַּע־בּוֹ הַטָּמֵא יִטְמָא
וְהַנֶּפֶשׁ הַנֹּגַעַת תִּטְמָא עַד־הָעָרֶב׃

20 The Israelites arrived in a body at the wilderness of
Zin on the first new moon, and the people stayed at
Kadesh. Miriam died there and was buried there.

כ וַיָּבֹאוּ בְנֵי־יִשְׂרָאֵל כָּל־הָעֵדָה מִדְבַּר־צִן
בַּחֹדֶשׁ הָרִאשׁוֹן וַיֵּשֶׁב הָעָם בְּקָדֵשׁ וַתָּמָת שָׁם

21. ***wash his clothes*** His bathing is taken for granted (v. 10).

be unclean It may be more than a matter of style that the prescription to launder is omitted. Perhaps if only his fingers touched the waters, he would bathe but not launder (cf. Lev. 15:10–11).

22. ***Whatever*** That is, anything or anyone (e.g., Lev. 15:10).

him Not in the text, but understood.[49]

From Kadesh to the Steppes of Moab (20:1–22:1)

The narrative of the wilderness march is resumed. The following incidents are recorded: Miriam's death (20:1), the murmuring for food and water (20:2–7; 21:4–9), the leaders' sin at the rock (20:7–13), fruitless negotiations with Edom (20:14–21), Aaron's death (20:22–29), victory at Hormah (21:1–3), the plague of snakes (21:4–9), the well and its song (21:16–18), and the conquest of Transjordan (21:21–35). Despite the failings of the people and its leaders (20:1–13,24; 21:4–9) and despite the refusal of nations to give Israel rights of passage (20:18,21; 21:1; 23:33), God provides Israel with all its needs: water (20:7–11; 21:16–18), healing (21:8–9), and victory (21:3,21–35). In contrast to the march from Sinai to Kadesh (10:11–14:45), which began in high spirits and ended in disaster, this final phase of the wilderness trek begins in gloom and ends in jubilation.[1] (See Map 2.)

CHAPTER 20 THE SIN OF MOSES AND AARON (vv. 1–13)

After Miriam's death, the people complain about the lack of water. Moses and Aaron are commanded to bring forth water from the rock. They produce the water but in so doing they are condemned by God to die in the wilderness. Their sin is akin to heresy (see Excursus 50). It constitutes the climax of a series of rebellions: first, by the people (chap. 14); then, by the Levites and chieftains (chap. 16); and, finally, by the leaders, Moses and Aaron. The punishment for all of them is the same: They will not inherit the land but, instead, will die in the wilderness.

1. ***in a body*** Hebrew *kol ha-ʿedah* is repeated in verse 22. Its precise nuance is not clear. The midrash claims that the reference is to the new generation that would be privileged to enter the promised land.[2] The redundancy, it would seem, emphasizes the unanimity of action (v. 29) or that Israel arrived at its destination intact (v. 22).

Zin See the Comment to 13:21.

2The community was without water, and they joined against Moses and Aaron. 3The people quarreled with Moses, saying, "If only we had perished when our brothers perished at the instance of the LORD! 4Why have you brought the LORD's congregation into this wilderness for us and our beasts to die there? 5Why did you make us leave Egypt to bring us to this wretched place, a place with no grain or figs or vines or pomegranates? There is not even water to drink!"

מִרְיָם וַתִּקָּבֵר שָׁם׃ 2 וְלֹא־הָיָה מַיִם לָעֵדָה וַיִּקָּהֲלוּ
עַל־מֹשֶׁה וְעַל־אַהֲרֹן׃ 3 וַיָּרֶב הָעָם עִם־מֹשֶׁה
וַיֹּאמְרוּ לֵאמֹר וְלוּ גָוַעְנוּ בִּגְוַע אַחֵינוּ לִפְנֵי יְהוָה׃
4 וְלָמָה הֲבֵאתֶם אֶת־קְהַל יְהוָה אֶל־הַמִּדְבָּר הַזֶּה
לָמוּת שָׁם אֲנַחְנוּ וּבְעִירֵנוּ׃ 5 וְלָמָה הֶעֱלִיתֻנוּ
מִמִּצְרַיִם לְהָבִיא אֹתָנוּ אֶל־הַמָּקוֹם הָרָע הַזֶּה לֹא
מְקוֹם זֶרַע וּתְאֵנָה וְגֶפֶן וְרִמּוֹן וּמַיִם אַיִן לִשְׁתּוֹת׃

The first new moon Hebrew *ba-ḥodesh ha-ri'shon.*[3] The usual rendering "first month" would not specify the day. But *ḥodesh* also means "new moon" (e.g., 28:14), and the dating is comparable to that of Exodus 19:1. The year, not stated, is uncertain. Most likely it is the fortieth year,[4] since the detailed itinerary of the wilderness march in chapter 33 places Kadesh before the stop where Aaron died in the fifth month of the fortieth year (33:38). Supporting this is the reference to his contemporaries as those eligible to enter the land (see the Comment to v. 12). Hence, the generation of the Exodus must have died out and the date must be the fortieth year. However, according to 13:26, Israel had already arrived at Kadesh at the beginning of the sojourn in the wilderness. Accordingly, some commentators[5] suggest that after having left Kadesh they returned to it in the fortieth year.[6]

On the other hand, Deuteronomy harbors a different tradition: Israel reached Kadesh at once but stayed there "many days" (Deut. 1:46) and then spent thirty-eight years in the wilderness (Deut. 2:14). According to this tradition, then, the date in this verse (v. 1) would refer to the first day of the third year (cf. 10:11). Supporting this interpretation is the clause "our brothers perished" (v. 3) which can only have been said by the survivors of the Korahite plague concerning the death of their peers (17:6–15) and not by the sons concerning the death of their fathers (14:34). Also the murmurers refer to themselves as the generation of the Exodus (vv. 4a,5a). If so, then the events leading to the punishment of Moses and Aaron (vv. 1–13) must be separated from the events of 20:14–21:35. The latter clearly refer to the fortieth year and also proceed from Kadesh (20:14,16,22)—referring either to a second Kadesh or to a return to the previous Kadesh. Thus the question of whether the sojourn at Kadesh took place at the beginning or at the end of the wilderness trek or at both termini cannot be resolved. The chronological uncertainty is compounded by a topographical one: Kadesh, a fertile oasis (see the Comment to 13:26), hardly fits the description of verse 5. However, according to one geographer, Israel probably encamped at Ein Kadesh, which offers insufficient water and actually goes dry in drought years; nearby Ein el-Qudeirat (= Kadesh-barnea), which has ample water, may have been in the hands of the more powerful Amalekites.[7] These obscurities may not be accidental but may reflect the deliberate intent of the redaction; see Excursus 55.

Miriam died there On the tenth day of the first month, according to an ancient tradition.[8]

3. ***Moses*** The quarrel was chiefly with Moses, not Aaron, according to Ibn Ezra.

brothers The reference cannot be to the previous generation, as claimed by Ibn Ezra; the text in that case would have read "fathers" (see the Comment to v. 1).

perished[9] During the Korahite rebellion (16:35; 17:14).

at the instance of the LORD Hebrew *lifnei YHVH.* Rather, "before the Lord," i.e., at the sanctuary (16:35). Although the people identify with the Korahite rebels, God does not punish them because their complaint is legitimate: They are dying of thirst.

4. ***to die***[10]

5. ***make us leave*** Hebrew *he'elitunu,* vocalized as a plural (21:5), refers to Moses and Aaron (see Exod. 16:3).

grain Hebrew *zera',* literally "seed" but also "grain" (Job 39:12).

figs or vines or pomegranates Precisely the items brought back from the promised land by the scouts (13:23).[11]

6 Moses and Aaron came away from the congregation to the entrance of the Tent of Meeting, and fell on their faces. The Presence of the LORD appeared to them, 7 and the LORD spoke to Moses, saying, 8 "You and your brother Aaron take the rod and assemble the community, and before their very eyes order the rock to yield its water. Thus you shall produce water for them from the rock and provide drink for the congregation and their beasts."

9 Moses took the rod from before the LORD, as He had commanded him. 10 Moses and Aaron assembled the congregation in front of the rock; and he said to them, "Listen, you rebels, shall we get water for you out of this rock?" 11 And Moses raised his hand and struck the rock twice with his rod. Out came copious water, and the community and their beasts drank.

6 וַיָּבֹא מֹשֶׁה וְאַהֲרֹן מִפְּנֵי הַקָּהָל אֶל־פֶּתַח אֹהֶל
מוֹעֵד וַיִּפְּלוּ עַל־פְּנֵיהֶם וַיֵּרָא כְבוֹד־יְהוָה אֲלֵיהֶם׃
פ שלישי [שני כשהן מחוברות]
7 וַיְדַבֵּר יְהוָה אֶל־מֹשֶׁה לֵּאמֹר׃ 8 קַח אֶת־הַמַּטֶּה
וְהַקְהֵל אֶת־הָעֵדָה אַתָּה וְאַהֲרֹן אָחִיךָ וְדִבַּרְתֶּם
אֶל־הַסֶּלַע לְעֵינֵיהֶם וְנָתַן מֵימָיו וְהוֹצֵאתָ לָהֶם
מַיִם מִן־הַסֶּלַע וְהִשְׁקִיתָ אֶת־הָעֵדָה וְאֶת־בְּעִירָם׃
9 וַיִּקַּח מֹשֶׁה אֶת־הַמַּטֶּה מִלִּפְנֵי יְהוָה כַּאֲשֶׁר
צִוָּהוּ׃ 10 וַיַּקְהִלוּ מֹשֶׁה וְאַהֲרֹן אֶת־הַקָּהָל אֶל־פְּנֵי
הַסָּלַע וַיֹּאמֶר לָהֶם שִׁמְעוּ־נָא הַמֹּרִים הֲמִן־הַסֶּלַע
הַזֶּה נוֹצִיא לָכֶם מָיִם׃ 11 וַיָּרֶם מֹשֶׁה אֶת־יָדוֹ וַיַּךְ
אֶת־הַסֶּלַע בְּמַטֵּהוּ פַּעֲמָיִם וַיֵּצְאוּ מַיִם רַבִּים
וַתֵּשְׁתְּ הָעֵדָה וּבְעִירָם׃ ס 12 וַיֹּאמֶר יְהוָה

6. *came away from* That is, as refugees.[12]

fell on their faces In prayer[13] or more likely out of fear,[14] since prayer does not require prostration. Perhaps the silence of Moses here, in contrast to his past angry rebuttals to the people's complaints,[15] is meant to underscore the gravity of his sin in his subsequent outburst (v. 10b).[16]

The Presence That is, the fire-encased cloud (9:15).

8. *rod* It could well have been Aaron's since it was kept "before the Lord" (v. 10), in which case it was not for striking but to remind Israel of their contentiousness (17:25).[17] Or it could have been for striking since, according to the priestly texts, Aaron's rod was so used during the plagues (Exod. 7:9,20; 8:1,13). However, it was more likely the rod of Moses, which had been employed in the performance of God's miracles in the wilderness (Exod. 14:16; 17:9). And, more relevantly, it was used in a previous instance of drawing water from a rock (Exod. 17:1–7), in which it was identified as the one used to strike the Nile (e.g., Exod. 7:19–20). Note also "his (Moses') rod" in verse 11. Ibn Ezra assumes that if this is so, then Moses' rod was kept in the sanctuary, a most plausible conjecture since it (as well as Aaron's) was called "the rod of God" (Exod. 4:20).

order the rock See Excursus 50.

to yield its water. Thus you shall produce water Literally, "so that it may yield its water and you shall produce water." The apparent redundancy is made worse by the contrast between the first verb *ve-natan,* in the third person, and the other verbs in this verse, which are in the second person. Its purpose can only be to clarify that the rock would yield its water because of the will of God, not the rod of Moses. Alternatively, the second half of the verse may be rendered: "When you produce for them water from the rock, you shall provide drink."[18]

9. *from before the LORD* That is, from the Tabernacle (see v. 8).

as He had commanded him This statement would have been expected before or after the account of the fulfillment of the command but not in the middle. Its "misplacement" is deliberate; up to this point Moses executes God's command; thereafter he deviates from it.[19]

10. *you rebels* Hebrew *ha-morim,* from *marah,* "rebel," a reminder that Israel had already been labeled *benei meri,* "rebels" (17:25); but see verse 24.

we The fatal pronoun by which Moses ascribes the miracle to himself and to Aaron; see Excursus 50.

11. *twice* This is an indication of Moses' anger, but it is not the cause of his sin.

12But the LORD said to Moses and Aaron, "Because you did not trust Me enough to affirm My sanctity in the sight of the Israelite people, therefore you shall not lead this congregation into the land that I have given them."
13Those are the Waters of Meribah—meaning that the Israelites quarrelled with the LORD—through which He affirmed His sanctity.

אֶל־מֹשֶׁה וְאֶל־אַהֲרֹן יַעַן לֹא־הֶאֱמַנְתֶּם בִּי
לְהַקְדִּישֵׁנִי לְעֵינֵי בְּנֵי יִשְׂרָאֵל לָכֵן לֹא תָבִיאוּ
אֶת־הַקָּהָל הַזֶּה אֶל־הָאָרֶץ אֲשֶׁר־נָתַתִּי לָהֶם׃
13 הֵמָּה מֵי מְרִיבָה אֲשֶׁר־רָבוּ בְנֵי־יִשְׂרָאֵל אֶת־
יְהוָה וַיִּקָּדֵשׁ בָּם׃ ס רביעי 14 וַיִּשְׁלַח

12. trust Me Hebrew *he'emantem bi.* A fitting and fair punishment: Just as Israel who did not *ya'aminu bi,* "trust Me" (14:11), must die in the wilderness (14:23), so must Moses and Aaron.[20]

in the sight of the Israelite people Their sin was aggravated because it was witnessed by all of Israel, as recognized by the following midrash:

> But had not Moses previously said something that was worse than this? For he said: "Could enough flocks and herds be slaughtered to suffice for them? Or could all the fish in the sea be gathered for them to suffice for them?" (Num. 11:22). Faith surely was wanting there too, and to a greater degree than in the present instance. Why then did He not make the decree against him on that occasion? Let me illustrate. To what may this be compared? To the case of a king who had a friend. Now this friend displayed arrogance toward the king privately, using harsh words. The king, however, did not lose his temper with him. After a time he rose, and displayed his arrogance in the presence of his legions, and the king passed sentence of death upon him. So also the Holy one, blessed be He, said to Moses: "The first offense that you committed was a private matter between you and Me. Now, however, that it is done in the presence of the public it is impossible to overlook it," as it says "to affirm My sanctity in the sight of the Israelite people" (20:12).[21]

This midrash encapsulates a great truth. Moses' previous doubts and even his disbelief (11:22) had been uttered in private, but here they were expressed in public, before the assembled throngs of Israel.

therefore Hebrew *lakhen,* which introduces an oath made by God.[22] This is because a declaration by God is equivalent to an oath.[23] Deuteronomy (4:21) actually makes the oath explicit.

you shall not lead this congregation Implied is that "this congregation" refers to the new generation, which is eligible to enter the land, an indication that this event takes place in the fortieth year.

13. Waters of Meribah See Exodus 17:7. The full name Waters of *Meribath-kadesh* (Num. 27:14; Deut. 32:51) is based either on the site Kadesh (v. 1) or on the tradition God "sanctified Himself" (*va-yikadesh*) there (v. 13).

This is not the formula of naming that would have required the verb *kara',* "call." To the contrary, the use of the pronoun *hemmah,* "those," indicates that the place-name that follows is already well known to the reader.[24] This formula is found again in a later passage, "Those are the Waters of Meribath-kadesh" (27:14), which is not a naming but a clear reference to this verse. Thus the Waters of Meribah here are presumed to have been previously named, and indeed they have been, in Exodus 17:7. For the significance, see Excursus 50.

Israelites quarreled with the LORD But they had quarreled only with Moses (v. 3). Elsewhere Israel's quarrel with Moses implies that their real object is God (14:2–4,11,27, esp. v. 9).[25] Indeed, the next quarrel (21:5) makes this explicit. Moreover, Deuteronomy bears the tradition that the people are responsible for Moses' punishment (Deut. 1:37; 3:26; 4:21) as does Psalms 106:32–33, "They provoked wrath at the waters of Meribah and Moses suffered on their account, because they rebelled against Him [or "embittered his spirit"] and he spoke rashly."[26] Psalms 95:7–11 bears yet another variant tradition: Israel's forty years in the wilderness was due to its sin at Massah-Meribah (see Exod. 17:7 and Excursus 50) and not to the scout episode (14:26–35; Deut. 1:34–35). Hence, Moses and Aaron must die with them in the wilderness.[27]

[14]From Kadesh, Moses sent messengers to the king of Edom: "Thus says your brother Israel: You know all the hardships that have befallen us; [15]that our ancestors went

מֹשֶׁה מַלְאָכִים מִקָּדֵשׁ אֶל־מֶלֶךְ אֱדוֹם כֹּה אָמַר
אָחִיךָ יִשְׂרָאֵל אַתָּה יָדַעְתָּ אֵת כָּל־הַתְּלָאָה אֲשֶׁר
מְצָאָתְנוּ׃ 15 וַיֵּרְדוּ אֲבֹתֵינוּ מִצְרַיְמָה וַנֵּשֶׁב

through which He affirmed His sanctity Hebrew *va-yikadesh bam.*[28] What is the antecedent of *bam*? Does it mean "through which" or "through whom"? Three possibilities have been proposed.[29] The first, Moses and Aaron, has the advantage of the nearest parallel, Nadab and Abihu, by whose death the Lord sanctified Himself (Lev. 10:3). However, Moses and Aaron are mentioned only in the previous verse—a distant antecedent. The second, the waters, implies that although Moses and Aaron defied God, God continued to supply Israel with water and thereby caused His name to be sanctified in Israel. The third, Israel, avers that by means of God's deliverance of Israel, He sanctified, that is, exalted, His name in the world (e.g., see Ezek. 20:41). A fourth interpretation is even possible: By God's punishment of Israel (the forty years of wandering attributed to this sin; Ps. 95:7–11), the Lord sanctified His name (e.g., Ezek. 28:22).[30]

THE ENCOUNTER WITH EDOM (vv. 14–21)

After the abortive attempt to enter Canaan from the south (14:40–45; cf. v. 25), Israel attempts to enter from the east, across the Jordan river. But from their base at Kadesh the direct route to the Jordan of necessity takes them through Edomite territory—to the east of the Arabah, bordering the Zered River (Wadi el-Hasa) to the north and near the Red Sea to the south and the desert to the east. During this period (at the end of the twelfth century), the Edomites have no cities and, in fact, are attested in Egyptian sources as Shasu, a nomadic tribe. They are nevertheless able to mount a sizable force to block Israel's entry. Israel's request for passage is turned down, a tradition corroborated by Judges 11:17. Deuteronomy 2:29, however, records the opposite tradition, that Edom did indeed permit Israel passage. But this may reflect the later situation that by the eighth century the Edomites had settled in Elath (2 Kings 16:6), overrunning the territory crossed by Israel.[31]

The parallel story in the lives of the ancestors of Israel and Edom—Jacob's encounter with Esau (Gen. 32:4–5)—has been noted.[32] Jacob sends messengers to his brother Esau. They are repulsed and report back Esau's evil intent. In the end, Esau does consent to greet his brother, as does Edom, according to the Deuteronomic tradition (Deut. 2:6,29). A closer source (Num. 14:39–45) offers another parallel.[33] Moses takes the initiative to conquer Canaan even though he has been rejected by God, resulting in his being thwarted by Edom. Rejected Israel is likewise foiled by the resident nations in its attempt to conquer Canaan. This association carries with it the added advantage of being able to explain why the encounter with Edom (20:14–21) was juxtaposed with the sin of Moses (20:1–13). Deuteronomy 23:4–5 and Judges 11:15 attest additional encounters with Moab and Ammon, which, however, are absent in Numbers.[34]

14. king See Genesis 36:31–39. At this time, the Edomites were probably ruled by chieftains (*'allufim;* Exod. 15:15; Gen. 36:15–19, 40–43). Other nomadic groups are also reported to be led by "kings" (e.g., the Midianites; 31:8; Judg. 8:12).[35] As noted by Ramban, the king is not named.

Edom The Greek adds "saying," *le'mor* (see 21:21; Judg. 11:17). However, the Hebrew text closely resembles the formal epistolary address common throughout the ancient Near East: beginning with the addressee ("to the king of Edom"), followed by the addresser ("thus speaks your brother Israel"), and then the message ("You know . . .").[36] The same style is found in 21:21–22, in abbreviated form (see Ezra 5:7).

your brother The personification of a people in the singular is frequently found in direct address (e.g., Exod. 14:26). Here the personification is that of a brother, a twin brother to be exact (Gen. 25:24), a kinship that is attested elsewhere in Scripture (e.g., Deut. 2:4; 23:8).

hardships Hebrew *tela'ah* (e.g., Exod. 18:3), from the root *l-'-h,* "be weary."[37] The emphasis on Israel's misfortunes is solely to elicit sympathy. Canaan is omitted as the goal (contrast Deut. 2:29, Israel's address to Sihon) so that the Edomites would not envy them.[38]

בְּמִצְרַיִם יָמִים רַבִּים וַיָּרֵעוּ לָנוּ מִצְרַיִם וְלַאֲבֹתֵינוּ׃
16 וַנִּצְעַק אֶל־יְהוָה וַיִּשְׁמַע קֹלֵנוּ וַיִּשְׁלַח מַלְאָךְ
וַיֹּצִאֵנוּ מִמִּצְרָיִם וְהִנֵּה אֲנַחְנוּ בְקָדֵשׁ עִיר קְצֵה
גְבוּלֶךָ׃ 17 נַעְבְּרָה־נָּא בְאַרְצֶךָ לֹא נַעֲבֹר בְּשָׂדֶה
וּבְכֶרֶם וְלֹא נִשְׁתֶּה מֵי בְאֵר דֶּרֶךְ הַמֶּלֶךְ נֵלֵךְ לֹא
נִטֶּה יָמִין וּשְׂמֹאול עַד אֲשֶׁר־נַעֲבֹר גְּבוּלֶךָ׃
18 וַיֹּאמֶר אֵלָיו אֱדוֹם לֹא תַעֲבֹר בִּי פֶּן־בַּחֶרֶב
אֵצֵא לִקְרָאתֶךָ׃ 19 וַיֹּאמְרוּ אֵלָיו בְּנֵי־יִשְׂרָאֵל
בַּמְסִלָּה נַעֲלֶה וְאִם־מֵימֶיךָ נִשְׁתֶּה אֲנִי וּמִקְנַי
וְנָתַתִּי מִכְרָם רַק אֵין־דָּבָר בְּרַגְלַי אֶעֱבֹרָה׃

down to Egypt, that we dwelt in Egypt a long time, and
that the Egyptians dealt harshly with us and our ancestors.
16 We cried to the LORD and He heard our plea, and He sent
a messenger who freed us from Egypt. Now we are in
Kadesh, the town on the border of your territory. 17 Allow
us, then, to cross your country. We will not pass through
fields or vineyards, and we will not drink water from wells.
We will follow the king's highway, turning off neither to
the right nor to the left until we have crossed your territory."

18 But Edom answered him, "You shall not pass through
us, else we will go out against you with the sword." 19 "We
will keep to the beaten track," the Israelites said to them,
"and if we or our cattle drink your water, we will pay for it.

*15. **our ancestors . . .*** The text from here through verse 16a is a capsule of Israel's faith. It resembles the declaration that each Israelite makes when he brings his first fruits to the sanctuary (Deut. 26:5–10).

we dwelt Hebrew ***va-neshev***. The verb *y-sh-v* implies dependence, particularly in regard to the Egyptian bondage (Exod. 12:40; 16:3).[39]

the Egyptians Hebrew ***mitsrayim,*** literally "Egypt." Perhaps with the Samaritan the definite article should be added to read ***ha-mitsrim,*** "the Egyptians."

with us As if it is not the generation of the Exodus speaking. The point is to elicit the sympathy of the Edomites by pointing to the suffering in Egypt.

*16. **messenger*** Hebrew ***mal'akh,*** literally "angel."[40]

the town on the border Kadesh is not a town; nor is it on Edom's border, unless another Kadesh is meant.[41]

*17. **king's highway*** Cf. 21:22. It is the main route through the length of Transjordan. Its function is clarified by the exact Akkadian equivalent, *ḫarrān šarri,* which connects the royal residence with the outlying districts.[42] So too the Hebrew expression means literally "the road to the king" since ***derekh,*** "road," is always followed by its destination (e.g., 14:25; 21:4).

turning off neither Literally, "we will not stray." Targum Jonathan understands it metaphorically: "We will not seduce virgins, nor carry off betrothed, nor commit adultery with men's wives."[43]

territory Hebrew ***gevul;*** see the Comment to 21:13.

*18. **You shall not pass through*** Edom takes vengeance on Israel for what Jacob did to Esau.[44]

us . . . we Literally, "me . . . I."

*19. **beaten track*** Hebrew ***mesillah.*** Rather, "byroad," probably equivalent to Akkadian *ḫarrān zukinim,* "infantry road" (***zūku*** = infantry), a meaning supported by the further comment that Israel will pass through "on foot." In other words, Israel volunteers to leave behind its wagons, that is, its water provisions (hence necessitating the purchase of water from the Edomites), and to march as "backpacking" infantry.[45]

your water Hebrew ***meimekha.*** Most versions read ***mi-memekha,*** "from your water."

we will pay Literally, "I will pay" (see the Comment to v. 18). Ramban points out that this offer does not contradict verse 17 but must be understood as an additional condition: Not only will we not drink your well water—but even water from your rivers and springs—which cost you

We ask only for passage on foot—it is but a small matter."
20But they replied, "You shall not pass through!" And
Edom went out against them in heavy force, strongly
armed. 21So Edom would not let Israel cross their territory,
and Israel turned away from them.

22Setting out from Kadesh, the Israelites arrived in a
body at Mount Hor. 23At Mount Hor, on the boundary of
the land of Edom, the LORD said to Moses and Aaron,
24"Let Aaron be gathered to his kin: he is not to enter the
land that I have assigned to the Israelite people, because
you disobeyed my command about the waters of Meribah.

20 וַיֹּאמֶר לֹא תַעֲבֹר וַיֵּצֵא אֱדוֹם לִקְרָאתוֹ בְּעַם
כָּבֵד וּבְיָד חֲזָקָה: 21 וַיְמָאֵן ׀ אֱדוֹם נְתֹן אֶת־
יִשְׂרָאֵל עֲבֹר בִּגְבֻלוֹ וַיֵּט יִשְׂרָאֵל מֵעָלָיו: פ
חמישי [שלישי כשהן מחוברות] 22 וַיִּסְעוּ
מִקָּדֵשׁ וַיָּבֹאוּ בְנֵי־יִשְׂרָאֵל כָּל־הָעֵדָה הֹר הָהָר:
23 וַיֹּאמֶר יְהוָה אֶל־מֹשֶׁה וְאֶל־אַהֲרֹן בְּהֹר הָהָר
עַל־גְּבוּל אֶרֶץ־אֱדוֹם לֵאמֹר: 24 יֵאָסֵף אַהֲרֹן אֶל־
עַמָּיו כִּי לֹא יָבֹא אֶל־הָאָרֶץ אֲשֶׁר נָתַתִּי לִבְנֵי
יִשְׂרָאֵל עַל אֲשֶׁר־מְרִיתֶם אֶת־פִּי לְמֵי מְרִיבָה:

nothing—we will pay for. However, there is no natural water supply in Edom until the perennial Zered River is reached—Edom's northern border. Thus the purpose of this second proposal is to offer the Edomites a financial boon: Israel will not take along water but will purchase it.[46]

only for passage on foot Hebrew ***rak . . . beraglai.*** These two words, frequently separated syntactically (e.g., Deut. 2:28), go together in meaning.[47]

it is but a small matter Hebrew ***'ein davar,*** literally "it is nothing," where ***davar*** points to dire consequences (e.g., Josh. 22:24).[48]

20. ***strongly armed*** Literally, "mighty hand" (e.g., Exod. 13:9).

21. ***Israel turned away from them***[49] Israel must now turn south toward the Red Sea to skirt the land of Edom (21:4). In the Deuteronomic version it is not Edom's strength but God's injunction that makes Israel retreat. The reason given there is that God has allowed Edom to conquer its territory as He is now doing for Israel.[50]

THE DEATH OF AARON (vv. 22–29)

All Israel observes as Moses, Aaron, and Eleazar ascend Mount Hor and as Moses descends with Eleazar, who is wearing Aaron's priestly garments. Thus all know that Aaron has died on the mountain and that Eleazar has taken his place. They mourn for thirty days. The mystery and grandeur of Aaron's death, so anticipatory of Moses' own death (Num. 27:12–14; Deut. 34:1–8), is befitting the founder of Israel's priesthood and its first High Priest. Subsequently, the death of the successors to his office will have expiatory effect (35:25), thus continuing to be of great moment to all of Israel.

22. ***arrived*** On the first of Av, according to 33:38.

in a body See the Comment to verse 1.

Mount Hor Literally, "Hor, the mountain," always presented in this inverted order. It is the death site for Aaron according to Numbers 33:38 and Deuteronomy 32:50. However, Deuteronomy 10:6 records a variant tradition, that Aaron died at Moseroth, which, according to 33:30, Israel reached six stations before Mount Hor. The location of Mount Hor is disputed. The traditional site, Jebel Nabi Harun near Petra,[51] has to be rejected since it is in the heart of Edom, far from its border. Some have conjectured 'Imaret el-Khurisheh, 13 kilometers (8 mi.) north of Kadesh, in order to be on "the way to Atharim" (21:1) leading from Kadesh to Arad,[52] but this site is far to the east of the border of Edom. Others have suggested Jebel Madrah due west of Kadesh near the Arabah (the Jordan rift), which has the advantage of being close to the Edomite border (and possibly being the same name as Moseroth) but which has inadequate water sources in its vicinity.

24. ***gathered to his kin*** Hebrew *ye'asef 'el 'ammav.* This idiom is found only in the Pentateuch, in connection with the deaths of Abraham (Gen. 25:8), Ishmael (Gen. 25:17), Isaac (Gen. 35:29), Jacob (Gen. 49:29,33), Moses (Num. 27:13; 31:2; Deut. 32:50), and Aaron (Num. 20:24; Deut.

[25]Take Aaron and his son Eleazar and bring them up on Mount Hor. [26]Strip Aaron of his vestments and put them on his son Eleazar. There Aaron shall be gathered unto the dead."

[27]Moses did as the LORD had commanded. They ascended Mount Hor in the sight of the whole community.

25 קַח אֶת־אַהֲרֹן וְאֶת־אֶלְעָזָר בְּנוֹ וְהַעַל אֹתָם
הֹר הָהָר׃ 26 וְהַפְשֵׁט אֶת־אַהֲרֹן אֶת־בְּגָדָיו
וְהִלְבַּשְׁתָּם אֶת־אֶלְעָזָר בְּנוֹ וְאַהֲרֹן יֵאָסֵף וּמֵת
שָׁם׃ 27 וַיַּעַשׂ מֹשֶׁה כַּאֲשֶׁר צִוָּה יְהוָה וַיַּעֲלוּ אֶל־
הֹר הָהָר לְעֵינֵי כָּל־הָעֵדָה׃ 28 וַיַּפְשֵׁט מֹשֶׁה אֶת־

32:50). Thus it is reserved for Israel's forefathers—never for women and never for non-Israelites.[53] Its meaning becomes clear in the stories of the patriarchs: It is the act that takes place ***after dying but before burial.*** Thus it can neither mean to die nor to be buried in the family tomb. Rather, it means "be reunited with one's ancestors" and refers to the afterlife in Sheol.[54] Hence, the opposite term ***ve-nikhrat me-ʿammav,*** "be cut off from one's ancestors," means to be denied any afterlife (see Excursus 36).

disobeyed My command Literally, "rebelled against (the words of) My mouth" (see Deut. 1:26,43). According to the received text, the disobedience occurred when Moses struck the rock instead of speaking to it. Alternatively, it was God's command to sanctify His name that Moses and Aaron violated when they attributed the miracle to their own powers (see Excursus 50). Here, this idiom provides an ironic twist to Moses' words (the source of his disbelief) in referring to Israel as ***morim,*** "rebels." God informs Moses and Aaron that they are the rebels, not Israel.

about[55]

25. ***Take Aaron*** The midrash is sensitive to the fact that in contrast to Aaron, the sons of Moses did not succeed him. It interprets "Take" as meaning "persuade": "The Holy One, Blessed Be He, said to him, 'You can comfort him (Aaron) with the assurance that he is bequeathing his crown as an inheritance to his children, whereas you will not do so to yours.'"[56]

Eleazar He had already succeeded his father ***de facto*** in the priestly responsibilities outside the Tabernacle service: supervising the transport, guarding the Tabernacle (3:32; 4:16), and preparing the purificatory ashes of the red cow (19:3). He now succeeds him ***de jure*** by the command of God as executed by Moses.

26. ***Strip Aaron of his vestments*** Perhaps this was not done at the Tabernacle so that Aaron would remain High Priest up to his last moment.[57] But then how could Eleazar enter the High Priesthood without having first been consecrated with the sacred oil of anointment (see Exod. 29:4–7; Lev. 8:6,12)? It is not necessary to assume from this that the passages requiring anointing for the High Priest are late.[58] Rather, it might simply be the case that Eleazar had already been anointed as his father's successor so that he could take his place whenever his father became incapacitated or ritually impure (see Lev. 6:15).

put them on his son The difference between the investiture of the priest and the prophet should be noted. The High Priest holds office by birth: He inherits his father's garments. The prophet holds office by virtue of divine selection: Moses lays his hands on Joshua to transfer his authority (27:20), or the Lord confers His spirit directly (11:25–26). There seems to be a fusion of the two types of ordination in the transfer of Elijah's prophetic powers to Elisha: Elisha both receives his master's cloak (1 Kings 19:19; 2 Kings 2:13) and performs miracles with it (2 Kings 2:14–15).

unto the dead Hebrew ***u-met,*** literally "and he will die," preceded by ***ye'asef,*** "to be gathered." However, everywhere else the order is reversed, death first, followed by being gathered to one's kin (e.g., Gen. 25:8,17; Deut. 32:50). Since ***'asaf,*** "be gathered," appears by itself in the command without the verb ***met*** (v. 24; see 27:13), it may also have been the case in this fulfillment verse so that ***u-met*** may be an explicative gloss. If so, it was added at an early stage since in the later books of the Bible ***ne'esaf*** becomes a poetic synonym for "die" (e.g., Isa. 57:1).[59]

27. ***they ascended*** Hebrew ***va-yaʿalu.*** The Samaritan reads ***va-yʿalehu,*** "and he (Moses) brought him (Aaron) up." Perhaps the original reading was ***va-yʿalem,*** "and he (Moses) brought them (Aaron and Eleazar) up," corresponding to the command of verse 25.

28 Moses stripped Aaron of his vestments and put them on his son Eleazar, and Aaron died there on the summit of the mountain. When Moses and Eleazar came down from the mountain, 29 the whole community knew that Aaron had breathed his last. All the house of Israel bewailed Aaron thirty days.

אַהֲרֹן אֶת־בְּגָדָיו וַיַּלְבֵּשׁ אֹתָם אֶת־אֶלְעָזָר בְּנוֹ
וַיָּמָת אַהֲרֹן שָׁם בְּרֹאשׁ הָהָר וַיֵּרֶד מֹשֶׁה וְאֶלְעָזָר
מִן־הָהָר: 29 וַיִּרְאוּ כָּל־הָעֵדָה כִּי גָוַע אַהֲרֹן וַיִּבְכּוּ
אֶת־אַהֲרֹן שְׁלֹשִׁים יוֹם כֹּל בֵּית יִשְׂרָאֵל: ס

29. The whole community knew Not because Aaron was missing but because Eleazar was wearing Aaron's garments.[60] According to the midrash, even then the people refused to believe that Aaron was dead: "They objected: 'How could the angel of death strike him? He was a man who had withstood the angel of death and had restrained him, as it is written: "He stood between the dead and the living until the plague was checked" (17:13)! If you bring him back, well and good; if not, we shall stone you!' Thereupon Moses resorted to prayer, and said, 'Sovereign of the Universe! Deliver us from suspicion!' Straightway the Holy One Blessed Be He opened the cave and showed Aaron to them."[61]

breathed his last Hebrew *gava'*, literally "die" (Gen. 25:8,17). But it also connotes "perish," especially as a punishment, for example, in the flood (Gen. 6:17), the Korahite rebels (17:27, 28), and Achan (Josh. 22:20).

All the house of Israel Emphasizing that the loss of Aaron was felt by everyone: "And when Aaron's soul rested, the clouds of Glory moved away, on the first day of the month Av. And the entire congregation saw Moses descend from the mountain with rent garments. And he was weeping and saying, 'Woe is me for you, my brother Aaron, the pillar of Israel's prayer.' And they too wept for Aaron thirty days, the men and women of Israel."[62]

thirty days Moses was also mourned for thirty days (Deut. 34:8), an indication of Aaron's importance since mourning ordinarily lasts for seven days (Gen. 50:10; 1 Sam. 31:13). To be sure, Joseph was mourned for seventy days (Gen. 50:3), but this was in accordance with Egyptian practice. Abravanel asks: Since Moses and Aaron sinned together why did they not die together? Five of his answers are noteworthy: (1) The deaths of the siblings followed the order of their births: Miriam, Aaron, Moses; (2) each deserved to be mourned separately for thirty days; (3) Moses was needed to complete the wilderness march; (4) to bring them safely to the Jordan; and (5) at least to see the promised land.

According to the midrash, the people loved Aaron because he strove to establish peace between the learned and the ignorant, among the learned and among the ignorant, and between man and wife. If he discovered that two men had fallen out, he hastened first to the one, then to the other, saying to each: "My son, do you not know what the one you quarreled with is doing? He beats his heart, rends his garments and says, 'Woe is me? How can I ever again face my friend against whom I have acted so?'" Aaron would then speak to each separately until the former enemies mutually forgave each other and, as soon as they were again face to face, greeted each other as friends. If Aaron heard that husband and wife were living in discord, he would hasten to the husband, saying: "I come to you because I heard that you and your wife live in discord, wherefore you must divorce her. Keep in mind, however, if you should marry another, it is questionable if your second wife will be as good as this one. At your first quarrel she will throw up to you that you are a quarrelsome man, as proved by your divorce from your first wife." Many thousands of unions were saved from impending rupture by the efforts and urgings of Aaron, and the sons born to the couples brought together anew usually received Aaron's name, owing, as they did, their existence to his intercession.[63]

21 When the Canaanite, king of Arad, who dwelt in the Negeb, learned that Israel was coming by the way of Atharim, he engaged Israel in battle and took some of them captive. [2]Then Israel made a vow to the LORD and said, "If You deliver this people into our hand, we will proscribe their towns." [3]The LORD heeded Israel's plea and delivered up the Canaanites; and they and their cities were proscribed. So that place was named Hormah.

כ״א וַיִּשְׁמַע הַכְּנַעֲנִי מֶלֶךְ־עֲרָד יֹשֵׁב הַנֶּגֶב כִּי
בָּא יִשְׂרָאֵל דֶּרֶךְ הָאֲתָרִים וַיִּלָּחֶם בְּיִשְׂרָאֵל
וַיִּשְׁבְּ ׀ מִמֶּנּוּ שֶׁבִי׃ 2 וַיִּדַּר יִשְׂרָאֵל נֶדֶר לַיהוָה
וַיֹּאמַר אִם־נָתֹן תִּתֵּן אֶת־הָעָם הַזֶּה בְּיָדִי
וְהַחֲרַמְתִּי אֶת־עָרֵיהֶם׃ 3 וַיִּשְׁמַע יְהוָה בְּקוֹל
יִשְׂרָאֵל וַיִּתֵּן אֶת־הַכְּנַעֲנִי וַיַּחֲרֵם אֶתְהֶם וְאֶת־
עָרֵיהֶם וַיִּקְרָא שֵׁם־הַמָּקוֹם חָרְמָה׃ פ

CHAPTER 21 ENCOUNTER WITH THE CANAANITES (vv. 1–3)

Israel "turns away" from the Edomites (20:21), first by going northward either to invade Canaan directly or to enter Transjordan via Edom's northern border, the Zered River. However, on the way it must cross the Canaanites of the Negeb, who are identified as the subjects of the king of Arad. The latter succeed in defeating the Israelites, who thereupon vow to place those Canaanites under the ban *(ḥerem),* thereby destroying them and their cities and dedicating the spoil to the sanctuary. God heeds their vow; Israel is victorious and the ban is imposed. The destroyed area is called *ḥormah,* "destruction," from *ḥerem.* Many problems attend the identification of the place-names and the very location of this section here. These are discussed in the Commentary and in detail in Excursuses 51 and 55, respectively. This victory marks a turning point in Israel's military fortunes. They will henceforth be victorious in all their battles (see Excursus 55, second scheme).

1. ***The Canaanite, king of Arad, who dwelt in the Negeb*** Rather, "the Canaanite, king of Arad, who ruled in the Negeb." Hebrew *yoshev* can be rendered "ruler,"[1] in which case, Numbers 21 would imply that the king of Arad ruled over the entire Negeb. The version of Numbers 33 states that he was a ruler *ba-negev,* "*in* the Negeb"; that is, there were other rulers there, a usage attested in Zechariah 9:6.[2]

learned Literally, "heard," which gives Targum Neofiti an opportunity to speculate: "When the Canaanite king of Arad . . . heard that Aaron, the pious man for whose merits the clouds of glory surrounded Israel, had been removed (i.e., had died) and that Miriam the prophetess, for whose merits the well used to come up for them (see the Comments to vv. 16–18), had been removed (i.e., had died) . . . he waged war."[3]

the way of Atharim Unknown. The Targums as well as the Greek renderings of Aquila and Symmachus presuppose a reading of *ha-tarim,* "the scouts" (from *tur;* see the Comment to 13:2), giving rise to the midrash that Israel tried to penetrate into Canaan via the same route employed by the scouts.

2. ***Israel*** For the vow to be effective it had to be taken by every soldier.

this people The antecedent can only be *ha-kena'ani* (v. 1), which provides another support for rendering the latter as "the Canaanites" (see Note 2).

proscribe Hebrew *ve-haḥaramti,* literally "put under ban *(ḥerem).*" *Ḥerem* represents an extreme form of self-denial. Troops were not salaried in ancient times. They were recompensed only by receiving a share of the booty (see chap. 31). To dedicate *all* the booty to God is an act of selflessness intended to win the support of the Deity. It is not unique to Israel, for it appears in the Moabite inscription of King Mesha (1.16). (For the meaning of *ḥerem,* see Excursus 44. For a tragic example of the vow of *ḥerem* taken before a battle, see Judg. 11:30–32,34–40).

3. ***Canaanites***[4] Hebrew *ha-kena'ani* here clearly refers to the people as it probably also does in verse 1 (see Note 2).

place Hebrew *makom,* which must refer to the entire region (cf. 20:5). But no such region called Hormah is attested elsewhere. Thus, it cannot be identical with the *city* of Hormah, previously called Zephath, which was also proscribed (Judg. 1:17; see Excursus 51).

Hormah Rather, "Destruction" (see Excursus 51).

4They set out from Mount Hor by way of the Sea of
Reeds to skirt the land of Edom. But the people grew
restive on the journey, 5and the people spoke against God
and against Moses, "Why did you make us leave Egypt to
die in the wilderness? There is no bread and no water, and
we have come to loathe this miserable food." 6The Lord

4 וַיִּסְעוּ מֵהֹר הָהָר דֶּרֶךְ יַם־סוּף לִסְבֹב אֶת־אֶרֶץ
אֱדוֹם וַתִּקְצַר נֶפֶשׁ־הָעָם בַּדָּרֶךְ׃ 5 וַיְדַבֵּר הָעָם
בֵּאלֹהִים וּבְמֹשֶׁה לָמָה הֶעֱלִיתֻנוּ מִמִּצְרַיִם לָמוּת
בַּמִּדְבָּר כִּי אֵין לֶחֶם וְאֵין מַיִם וְנַפְשֵׁנוּ קָצָה
בַּלֶּחֶם הַקְּלֹקֵל׃ 6 וַיְשַׁלַּח יְהוָה בָּעָם אֵת הַנְּחָשִׁים

THE COPPER SNAKE (vv. 4–9)

While rounding the land of Edom near the Red Sea, the Israelites fall to complaining once again about the lack of food and water. This is the last and most grievous of Israel's wilderness complaints since this time it is in open defiance of the Lord Himself. The Lord punishes them with a plague of seraph snakes. After they acknowledge their wrongdoing, Moses intercedes on their behalf. The Lord bids Moses make a seraph and mount it on a standard. Those who looked at the snake recovered. The form of this episode follows the typological structure of Israel's wilderness complaints already noted in 11:1–3 and 12:1–5 (see Excursus 24). The possibility that the itinerary was broken in order to insert this episode is discussed in the Comment to verse 10, and its significance is considered in Excursus 55.

4. ***Sea of Reeds*** Hebrew *yam suf.* Here, it should be rendered "Red Sea" (cf. 14:25). Israel marched toward Elath at the head of the Red Sea (i.e., its northern end), whereas the Sea of Reeds was traversed upon leaving Egypt (Exod. 13:18; 15:4,22). The Edomites had not yet reached the Red Sea—the first buildings at Ezion-geber (Elath) date from the time of Solomon—and the Israelites could have passed through without difficulty, traversing the land that later became the kingdom of Edom (see Deut. 2:1–9).

to skirt the land of Edom Via the stations of Zalmonah and Punon, according to 33:41–42. The latter, a center for the mining and smelting of copper in antiquity, was thus an appropriate site for the manufacture of the copper snake (see Excursus 52).

on the journey Hebrew *ba-derekh,* alternatively "because of the journey," following Rashi, who comments (probably citing an unknown midrash): "Because of the difficulties of the journey. They said: Now that we are close enough to enter the land yet we have to turn back. Just so had our fathers to turn back and detoured (in the wilderness) thirty-eight years until this day. Consequently they became dismayed because of the hardships of their journey. . . . It would be incorrect to render the phrase '(they were restive) on the journey' because the text does not explain why they were restive. In every passage where Scripture uses *katsar nefesh* it explains the cause. (The preposition *be* prefixed to the word expresses the cause of discouragement.) Thus *va-tiktsar nafshi,* 'I became impatient *[bahem]* of them' (Zech. 11:8), and for example: *va-tiktsar nafsho,* 'He [the Lord] became impatient *[ba-ʿamal]* on account of the misery of Israel' (Judg. 10:16)."

5. ***and the people spoke against God and against Moses*** This is the polar opposite of Israel's attitude when they crossed the Red Sea: "They had faith in the Lord and His servant Moses" (Exod. 14:31). Their murmuring here contrasts with the previous such case where their murmuring was directed solely to the leaders (20:3–4; see Excursus 50). The use of "God" instead of "Lord," the designation of the Deity in the rest of the passage, emphasizes the severity of the offense. Israel has rebelled not only against its personal Deity but against the very principle of divine authority, as conveyed by such idioms as "the fear of God" (Gen. 20:11; 42:18; Deut. 25:18) and "revile God" (Exod. 22:27; Lev. 24:15).

make us leave Hebrew *heʿelitunu* (pl.). But according to the consonantal text it could be vocalized *heʿelitanu* (sing.), where the subject would be Moses, as in previous complaints (16:13; Exod. 17:3).[5]

miserable Hebrew *kelokel*, from *kalal,* "treat lightly."[6]

food Hebrew *leḥem,* literally "bread." The complainants contradict themselves, just as the Song of the Well (vv. 17–18) will disprove their other contention that God does not provide them water (see Excursus 53).

sent *seraph* serpents against the people. They bit the people
and many of the Israelites died. 7The people came to Moses
and said, "We sinned by speaking against the LORD and
against you. Intercede with the LORD to take away the
serpents from us!" And Moses interceded for the people.
8Then the LORD said to Moses, "Make a *seraph* figure and
mount it on a standard. And if anyone who is bitten looks
at it, he shall recover." 9Moses made a copper serpent and
mounted it on a standard; and when anyone was bitten by a
serpent, he would look at the copper serpent and recover.

הַשְּׂרָפִים וַיְנַשְּׁכוּ אֶת־הָעָם וַיָּמָת עַם־רָב
מִיִּשְׂרָאֵל׃ 7 וַיָּבֹא הָעָם אֶל־מֹשֶׁה וַיֹּאמְרוּ חָטָאנוּ
כִּי־דִבַּרְנוּ בַיהוָה וָבָךְ הִתְפַּלֵּל אֶל־יְהוָה וְיָסֵר
מֵעָלֵינוּ אֶת־הַנָּחָשׁ וַיִּתְפַּלֵּל מֹשֶׁה בְּעַד הָעָם׃
8 וַיֹּאמֶר יְהוָה אֶל־מֹשֶׁה עֲשֵׂה לְךָ שָׂרָף וְשִׂים
אֹתוֹ עַל־נֵס וְהָיָה כָּל־הַנָּשׁוּךְ וְרָאָה אֹתוֹ וָחָי׃
9 וַיַּעַשׂ מֹשֶׁה נְחַשׁ נְחֹשֶׁת וַיְשִׂמֵהוּ עַל־הַנֵּס וְהָיָה
אִם־נָשַׁךְ הַנָּחָשׁ אֶת־אִישׁ וְהִבִּיט אֶל־נְחַשׁ
הַנְּחֹשֶׁת וָחָי׃ ששי 10 וַיִּסְעוּ בְּנֵי יִשְׂרָאֵל וַיַּחֲנוּ

6. ***seraph*** Untranslated. It can be synonymous with *naḥash,* "serpent" (Isa. 14:29). The verb *saraf* means "burn." Thus the Greek renders "deadly" and Targum Onkelos, "burning," referring to the serpent's poisonous bite. Targum Neofiti offers this explanation: "The divine voice came forth from the earth and its voice was heard on high: Come see, all you creatures, and come give ear, all you sons of the flesh; the serpent was cursed from the beginning and I said to it: Dust shall be your food (see Gen. 3:14). . . . Let the serpent which does not murmur concerning its food come and rule over the people which has murmured concerning their food."[7]

against As in Deuteronomy 7:20 and 28:20.

bit Hebrew *va-yenashekhu,* the Piel form used iteratively: "many biters and many bitten."[8] The danger of poisonous snakes in the Sinai desert had been noted by the ancients.[9] T. E. Lawrence gives this account of a remarkable experience in the Wadi Sirhan to the east of Jordan: "The plague of snakes which had been with us since our first entry into Sirhan, to-day rose to memorable height, and became a terror. . . . This year the valley seemed creeping with horned vipers and puff-adders, cobras and black snakes. By night movement was dangerous; and at last we found it necessary to walk with sticks, beating the bushes each side."[10]

7. ***We sinned*** Aaron and Miriam made a similar confession (12:11; see vv. 1,8b).

Intercede The standard function of the prophet, as his people's defense attorney before the Supreme Judge (see 11:2; Gen. 20:7,17).

the serpents Hebrew *ha-naḥash,* literally "the serpent," the singular used as a collective, for example, *va-ta'al ha-tsefarde'a* (Exod. 8:2), literally "the frog came up."[11]

8. ***seraph figure*** A winged snake similar to the winged Egyptian uraeus (cobra). Its image, engraved on a bronze bowl inscribed with a Hebrew name, was found in the excavation of the royal palace of Nineveh, dating to the end of the eighth century. It was believed that looking at it would generate its homeopathic healing (see Excursus 52). Yet the question needs to be asked: Why did not God simply remove the plague as He removed all the plagues of Egypt? The answer given by tradition is that He resorted to this means in order to test Israel's obedience; only those who heeded His command to look at the snake would recover. This is precisely how Targum Jonathan understands it: "If he [the victim] directed his heart to the Name of the Memra' of the Lord, he would live";[12] or as expressed in the Wisdom of Solomon (first half of the first century C.E.): "Only for a while were they thrown into disarray as a warning, possessing as they did a symbol of Your salvation to remind them of the commandment of Your law. For whoever turned towards it was saved not by the sight beheld, but through You, the savior of all" (Wisdom of Sol. 16:6–7).

9. ***copper serpent*** How did Moses know that the *seraph* figure should be made of copper? Abravanel says that only copper could imitate the color of the poisonous snakes that are characterized by red spots or stripes. More likely, Moses wished to imitate not the color of the snake but its name, ***neḥash neḥoshet:*** "Moses reasoned thus: If I make it of gold *[zahav]* or silver *[kesef]* these Hebrew words do not resemble each other. Hence I will make it out of copper *(neḥoshet)* since this word resembles the other, namely, ***neḥash neḥoshet***—a copper serpent."[13] Thus the paronomasia, or word play, adds to its homeopathic powers. Note that, according to later biblical tradition, the serpent was called ***neḥushtan*** (2 Kings 18:4), thus perpetuating the paronomasia (see Excursus 52).

10The Israelites marched on and encamped at Oboth.
11They set out from Oboth and encamped at Iye-abarim, in
the wilderness bordering on Moab to the east. 12From there

בְּאֹבֹת׃ 11 וַיִּסְעוּ מֵאֹבֹת וַיַּחֲנוּ בְּעִיֵּי הָעֲבָרִים
בַּמִּדְבָּר אֲשֶׁר עַל־פְּנֵי מוֹאָב מִמִּזְרַח הַשָּׁמֶשׁ׃

copper serpent Rather, "copper snake." It has been suggested that the snake was made out of bronze. By the end of the second millennium the knowledge of how to harden copper by adding tin to make the alloy bronze was widespread through the Near East and bronze objects have been found in Middle Bronze Jericho, Megiddo, and Lachish, that is, in the Canaanite period. Of greater relevance, however, is the copper snake, five inches long, found at Timna, the copper mining and smelting region in the Arabah near the Red Sea, which dates from between 1200 and 900 B.C.E.—approximately the same time and place that Moses fashioned a similar snake. This fact makes it highly probable that the snake story was inserted into the itinerary precisely when Israel was in the vicinity of the Timna copper mines. This thesis is further supported by textual evidence of a break in the next stage of the itinerary (see the Comment to v. 10). The snake was found in the holy place of a tent shrine erected by a nomadic tribe (Midianites?). The place had been the site of a temple to the Egyptian god Hathor that had been abandoned by the Egyptians about 1150 B.C.E.[14]

THE ROUTE THROUGH TRANSJORDAN (vv. 10–20)

This section offers a summary of the stations of Israel's march through Transjordan, given in fuller form in 33:41–49. Since the battle with the Amorites clearly took place prior to Israel's arrival at the Jordan valley, then chronologically 21:21–35 precedes 21:10–20. A few stations are cited from a poetic work, the Book of the Wars of the LORD and a second poem, a well song, is inserted into the narrative when the station Beer, literally "well," is reached. These problems are analyzed in Excursus 55. The unit bristles with textual difficulties.

10. marched on Hebrew *va-yisse'u,* literally "pull up stakes, set out," the first word of the itinerary formula (see v. 11). However, the point of origin, Mount Hor, is missing. Since verse 4 has already related that "they set out from Mount Hor," it is possible that verse 4a originally continued with "and encamped at Oboth" (v. 10b), the itinerary formula being broken in order to insert the story of the copper serpent (vv. 4b–9). In that case, verse 10a would have been added in order to complete the broken sentence.

encamped at Oboth It has been suggested[15] that the text originally read: "The Israelites set out from Mount Hor and encamped in the wilderness bordering on Moab to the east" (v. 11bβ) and that the intervening text (*Oboth . . . Iye-abarim*; vv. 10b–11bα) was copied from the detailed itinerary of 33:43–44.[16]

11. Oboth This site cannot be identified.

Iye-abarim Rather, "*Iyyei-ha-'abarim,*" which means "Iyyim of the Abarim" (mountains) (see 27:12; 33:45); that is, Iyyim on the mountain range that traverses the length of Moab. The name Abarim is related to *'ever,* "across" (see v. 13), probably indicating the viewpoint of a Cisjordanian dweller who to this day cannot but be impressed by the grandeur of the mountain range on his eastern horizon, on the other side *('ever)* of the Jordan. The site Iyyim has not been identified.[17]

Moab to the east See 33:44b. Some hold that this designation contradicts the next stop, the wadi Zered, which forms the southern border of Moab.[18] However, as in Deuteronomy 2:9,13, where Israel ostensibly reaches the wilderness of Moab before it crosses the wadi Zered, the reference is to the ***road*** that leads to Moab's eastern wilderness border.[19]

Also to be noted is that the style of the itinerary changes in verses 12–20 (resembling that of Deut. 10:6–7) and that these verses are an intrusion in the narrative (see the Comment to v. 21). This new list may have been inserted to complete the itinerary before recounting the details of the conquest; but, more likely, it was to furnish evidence showing that God continued to provide His rebellious people with water (see Excursus 55). The intrusion is further amplified by the logistics of the itinerary: Israel would have negotiated with Sihon before crossing the Arnon into his territory.

they set out and encamped at the wadi Zered. [13]From there they set out and encamped beyond the Arnon, that is, in the wilderness that extends from the territory of the Amorites. For the Arnon is the boundary of Moab, between Moab and the Amorites. [14]Therefore the Book of the Wars of the LORD speaks of ". . . Waheb in Suphah, and the wadis: the Arnon [15]with its tributary wadis, stretched along the settled country of Ar, hugging the territory of Moab . . ."

12 מִשָּׁם נָסָעוּ וַיַּחֲנוּ בְּנַחַל זָרֶד׃ 13 מִשָּׁם נָסָעוּ
וַיַּחֲנוּ מֵעֵבֶר אַרְנוֹן אֲשֶׁר בַּמִּדְבָּר הַיֹּצֵא מִגְּבוּל
הָאֱמֹרִי כִּי אַרְנוֹן גְּבוּל מוֹאָב בֵּין מוֹאָב וּבֵין
הָאֱמֹרִי׃ 14 עַל־כֵּן יֵאָמַר בְּסֵפֶר מִלְחֲמֹת יְהוָה
אֶת־וָהֵב בְּסוּפָה וְאֶת־הַנְּחָלִים אַרְנוֹן׃ 15 וְאֶשֶׁד
הַנְּחָלִים אֲשֶׁר נָטָה לְשֶׁבֶת עָר וְנִשְׁעַן לִגְבוּל
מוֹאָב׃ 16 וּמִשָּׁם בְּאֵרָה הִוא הַבְּאֵר אֲשֶׁר אָמַר

12. wadi Zered A wadi *(naḥal)* is a ravine through which a stream flows. In present-day Israel most wadis are dry except during the rainy season. The wadi Zered, however, contains a perennial stream. It is identified with the wadi el-Hesa, 35 miles long, whose waters flow into the southeastern end of the Dead Sea, falling about 1,200 meters (3,900 ft.). It is the northern boundary of Edom and the southern boundary of Moab.

13. From there they set out The Samaritan reads: "They set out from the wadi Zered," an attempt to conform to the general itinerary style (chap. 33 and v. 11).

Arnon A perennial stream flowing midway into the eastern end of the Dead Sea through the Wadi el-Mujib, a tremendous ravine that at one point, south of Dibon (v. 30), is 4 kilometers (2.5 mi.) wide and 500 meters (1,650 ft.) below the tops of the adjoining cliffs. As indicated by this verse (and v. 26), it formed the boundary between Moab and Sihon's kingdom and later the southern boundary of the tribe of Reuben (Deut. 3:8,16; Josh. 13:16).

in the wilderness Hebrew *ba-midbar*. The Samaritan reads *ʿal ha-midbar,* "by the wilderness." But the present text is preferable, since it specifies that Israel crossed the Arnon in the wilderness, that is, to the east and outside of Moabite territory, a statement corroborated by the rest of the text (vv. 11b,15b,23).

territory *Gevul*—in Hebrew, Phoenician, and Punic, and its semantic equivalents in Egyptian, Akkadian, and Hittite—means both "boundary" and "territory," depending on the context.[20] Thus, it is "territory" here (also vv. 21,22) but "boundary" elsewhere in the chapter (vv. 13b,15). In certain expressions, it will have a fixed meaning, for example, *be-khol gevul yisraʾel/bi-gevul yisraʾel* always means "in the whole territory of Israel" (Judg. 19:29) and "in the territory of Israel" (1 Sam. 7:13). Thus the Israelites marched in the wilderness that lies to the east of the territories of the Moabites and Amorites.

Arnon is the boundary of Moab Originally, before it was conquered by Sihon, Moab occupied the territory to the north of the Arnon (v. 26). The territory between the Arnon and the Jabbok, 80 kilometers (50 mi.) north, remained in dispute. The Ammonites of Jephthah's time claimed it (Judg. 11:13) and later occupied it (Jer. 49:1–2). The Moabites under King Mesha conquered it from King Ahab of Israel (2 Kings 3:4–5) and held it for some time. It was settled by the tribes of Reuben and Gad (Num. 32).

the Amorites See the Comment to 13:29.

14. the Book of the Wars of the LORD According to Ibn Ezra, it was a separate book which, together with the Book of Jashar (Josh. 10:13; 2 Sam. 1:18), were anthologies of early songs describing the saga of Israel's battles at the beginning of its national existence. But only these three small fragments survive. According to Ramban (v. 13), a fourth fragment, the victory poem of Sihon (vv. 27–30)—a pagan—was included.

Waheb in Suphah According to Ibn Janaḥ, these are place-names.[21]

and the wadis: the Arnon Hebrew *ve-ʾet ha-neḥalim ʾarnon*. Alternatively, "and the branch wadis of the Arnon," reading *naḥalei-m.*[22] The Arnon consists of a complex of wadis uniting in a deep, long trench that carries their waters to the Dead Sea.[23]

15. with its tributary wadis Hebrew *ve-ʾeshed ha-neḥalim*. The root *ʾšd* in Ugaritic and

16 And from there to Beer, which is the well where the
LORD said to Moses, "Assemble the people that I may give
them water." 17 Then Israel sang this song:
Spring up, O well—sing to it—

יְהֹוָה לְמֹשֶׁה אֱסֹף אֶת־הָעָם וְאֶתְּנָה לָהֶם מָיִם: ס
17 אָז יָשִׁיר יִשְׂרָאֵל אֶת־הַשִּׁירָה הַזֹּאת
עֲלִי בְאֵר עֱנוּ־לָהּ:

išdu in Akkadian means "leg, base." Elsewhere in Scripture it is found only in the plural, either in construct with *pisgah* (Deut. 3:17; 4:49; Josh. 12:3), a mountainous region (v. 20), or in the absolute *'ashedot,* one of the four principal geographical divisions of southern Canaan (Josh. 10:40). Thus etymology and geography point to the rendering "slopes," and the reference here would be to a mountainous area intersected by many ravines. The Targums render "spill," giving rise to the meaning "waterfall." The Samaritan, however, reads *va-'asher hinḥilam,* "[the Lord] who led them." The crux remains.

Ar Either (1) a city on the Arnon (Sam. reads *'ir,* "city"), (2) a district bordering the Arnon (v. 28; Deut. 2:18), or (3) the equivalent of Kir, the capital of Moab (Isa. 15:1), a metonymy for the entire country (Deut. 2:9). The second interpretation seems preferable here.

hugging the territory of Moab According to Ibn Ezra, this description of Israel's position accords with Balak's location of Israel's encampment: "It is settled next to me" (22:5). Thus, it supplies another confirmation that Israel circuited the territory of the Moabites. Here *gevul* should be rendered "boundary" not "territory" (see v. 13).

A recent rendering of this quotation from the Book of the Wars of the Lord[24] is worthy of being cited: YHWH came in a whirlwind, / Came to the Wadis of Arnon; / He marched through the wadis, / Turning aside to the seat of Ar, / Leaning toward the border of Moab.

This construction commends itself chiefly because it is poetry, precisely the form one would expect in a quotation from an ancient paean to God the Warrior. It makes YHVH the subject of the poem, as one would expect in the Book of the Wars of the Lord. The construction utilizes a few plausible emendations.[25]

16. ***Beer*** Literally, "well."[26] However this place-name is well attested: Beer (Judg. 9:21), Beeroth (pl., 2 Sam. 4:2), Beer-elim (Isa. 15:8, situated in Moab).

where . . . said Hebrew *'asher 'amar,* a pluperfect construction (see Num. 10:29; 2 Kings 21:4,7). The purpose of this explanation, followed by the well song, is to indicate that the people's cry for water was not only punished (by the plague of snakes, vv. 4–9) but requited, as God had done in all previous murmuring incidents (11:4–34; 20:1–13).

Assemble . . . that I may give Hebrew *'esof . . . ve-'ettenah.* The Samaritan reads *'esefah li . . . ve-'etten* (the form found in 11:16–17). A comparison with 20:7–8 is revealing. There God commanded Moses "assemble the community . . . you shall produce water." However, Moses failed God's trust and, henceforth, God Himself must furnish the water. Also, the introduction to the following poem is needed to affirm that the digging of the well was at the command of God.

17. ***Then Israel sang*** Rather, "This was when Israel sang," that is, when they were assembled.[27] The same words introduce the Song of the Sea (Exod. 15:1). The midrash puzzles over the absence of the names of God and Moses in this song in contrast to the Song of the Sea: "Why is Moses not mentioned in this context? Because he owed his punishment to water (20:8–13), and no man praises his executioner. Why is not the Holy One Blessed Be He mentioned? This may be illustrated by the case of a governor who made a feast for the king. The king asked : 'Will my friend be there?' 'No,' he was told. Said he: 'Then I also am not going to be there.' In the same way the Holy One Blessed Be He said: 'Since Moses is not mentioned there, I also will not be mentioned there.' "[28] According to the Talmud, this song was sung in the Temple every third Sabbath afternoon and the Song of the Sea on the other two Sabbath afternoons.[29]

Spring up[30]

sing Hebrew *'anu.* For this meaning see Exodus 15:21 and 1 Samuel 18:7.

18The well which the chieftains dug,
Which the nobles of the people started
With maces, with their own staffs.
And from Midbar to Mattanah, 19and from Mattanah to
Nahaliel, and from Nahaliel to Bamoth, 20and from
Bamoth to the valley that is in the country of Moab, at the
peak of Pisgah, overlooking the wasteland.

18 בְּאֵר חֲפָרוּהָ שָׂרִים
כָּרוּהָ נְדִיבֵי הָעָם
בִּמְחֹקֵק בְּמִשְׁעֲנֹתָם
וּמִמִּדְבָּר מַתָּנָה׃ 19 וּמִמַּתָּנָה נַחֲלִיאֵל וּמִנַּחֲלִיאֵל
בָּמוֹת׃ 20 וּמִבָּמוֹת הַגַּיְא אֲשֶׁר בִּשְׂדֵה מוֹאָב
רֹאשׁ הַפִּסְגָּה וְנִשְׁקָפָה עַל־פְּנֵי הַיְשִׁימֹן׃ פ
שביעי [רביעי כשהן מחוברות] 21 וַיִּשְׁלַח

18. the chieftains dug This is not to be taken literally. "Although the (Bedouin) chiefs seldom work themselves with their own hands, yet it is always said: 'Sheikh N dug (the Arab. verb is the same as Heb. *ḥafar*) this well.'"[31] In Wadi el-Thamad, the upper stretch of Wadi Waleh, itself a northern tributary of the Arnon, the Arabs dig out with their hands pits in the gravel of the dry torrent bed in which water gathers. These water pits are called *bir, biyar,* the exact equivalent of Hebrew *be'er,* "well," and this wadi "is the only place north of the Arnon where water comes to the surface in the manner described in Numbers 21:16–18,"[32] the very neighborhood where Israel was encamped.

nobles For *nadiv* meaning "noble," see 1 Samuel 2:8 and Song of Songs 7:2.

started The verb *k-r-h* means "begin to dig" (Gen. 26:25; Exod. 21:23).

With maces Rather, "with their maces" or "with their scepters," the suffix of the following word doing double duty.[33] The word itself is perhaps derived from *ḥ-k-k,* "inscribe," hence, "inscribed staff, scepter." This meaning is most probable in Genesis 49:10, since "*meḥokek* (from between his feet)" is parallel to *shevet,* "scepter"/"staff" and since kings are pictured holding maces or scepters before them.[34] The bas-relief of King Darius of Persia is particularly significant; he is seated on his throne with his scepter literally between his feet.[35]

staffs Hebrew *mish'enet* parallels *shevet,* "staff" (Ps. 23:4). Alternatively, it has been suggested that since *mish'enet* also means "economic support" (Isa. 3:1), and *nadiv* also means "magnanimous person" (Exod. 35:5,22), and *meḥokek* may be related to *ḥok,* "allotment" (Gen. 47:22), the song may be extolling the noble ones whose financial support was responsible for digging the well.[36] However, since the water could easily be reached by probing the loose gravel with an ordinary stick and since such procedures are actually attested in Bedouin well songs (see Excursus 53), there is no reason not to take the poem literally.

And from Midbar to Mattanah Rather, "And from the wilderness a gift,"[37] whereby this clause is the conclusion of the song. The Greek reads *be'er* instead of *midbar* in order to connect with the previous station, Beer (v. 16), and because *midbar,* meaning "wilderness," could hardly be the name of a station. However, this change is superfluous once it is recognized that there are no place-names whatsoever in this clause.

19. and from Mattanah Possibly, it was the misreading of *mattanah* in the previous verse as a place-name that may have caused an original *be'er* (Beer, connecting with v. 16) to be changed to Mattanah.[38] In any event, this site can be neither attested nor identified.

Nahaliel Targum Neofiti renders "swelling torrents," taking the second element *'el* not as "God" but as the adjective "mighty (wadis)" (see *harerei 'el,* "mighty mountains"; Ps. 36:7), an apt description of the terrain north of the Arnon where Israel was encamped (see the Comment to v. 14).

Bamoth This name is frequently attested (Mesha 3; Isa. 15:2; 16:12; Jer. 48:35), also in compound names: Bamoth-arnon (v. 28), Beth Bamoth (Mesha 27), Bamoth-baal (22:41; Josh. 13:17)—all in Moab. Bamoth as a topographical name never appears outside of Moabite territory.[39]

20. the valley Hebrew *ha-gai'*. As distinct from *naḥal* or wadi, where water flows (see the Comment to v. 12), *gai'* refers to a valley between mountains.

country of Moab Hebrew *sedeh moab* (Gen. 36:35; Ruth 1:1,2); see *sedeh* Edom (Gen. 32:4; Judg. 5:4); *sedeh* Aram (Hos. 12:13); *sedeh* Samaria, Ephraim (Obad. 1:19). The name indicates that the country, though now Amorite, once belonged to Moab; similarly "the steppes of Moab" (22:1).

21Israel now sent messengers to Sihon king of the
Amorites, saying, 22"Let me pass through your country. We
will not turn off into fields or vineyards, and we will not
drink water from wells. We will follow the king's highway
until we have crossed your territory." 23But Sihon would

יִשְׂרָאֵל֙ מַלְאָכִ֔ים אֶל־סִיחֹ֥ן מֶֽלֶךְ־הָאֱמֹרִ֖י לֵאמֹֽר׃
22 אֶעְבְּרָ֣ה בְאַרְצֶ֗ךָ לֹ֤א נִטֶּה֙ בְּשָׂדֶ֣ה וּבְכֶ֔רֶם לֹ֥א
נִשְׁתֶּ֖ה מֵ֣י בְאֵ֑ר בְּדֶ֤רֶךְ הַמֶּ֙לֶךְ֙ נֵלֵ֔ךְ עַ֥ד אֲשֶֽׁר־
נַעֲבֹ֖ר גְּבֻלֶֽךָ׃ 23 וְלֹֽא־נָתַ֨ן סִיחֹ֣ן אֶת־יִשְׂרָאֵל֮ עֲבֹ֣ר

Pisgah It is not clear whether it is a mountain, mountain range, or district. The construct *ro'sh,* "peak" (Num. 21:20; 23:14; Deut. 3:27; 34:1), militates against "district" (preferred by Eusebius) and the plural construct *'ashdot,* "slopes" (Deut. 3:17; 4:40; see the Comment to v. 15), militates against the singular "mountain," leaving a "mountain range" as the most likely meaning. Perhaps it refers to part of the larger chain of mountains, Abarim (see the Comment to v. 11), that traverses the length of Moab. This latter interpretation is supported by the fact that Balak, king of Moab, took Balaam to the summit of the Pisgah (23:14). This means that Pisgah had to be in territory under Moabite control, that is, south of the Arnon.

overlooking[40]

the wasteland Hebrew *yeshimon,* from the root *y-sh-m,* "be desolate." Here it refers to a specific wasteland, north of the Dead Sea on both sides of the Jordan, both on the eastern bank where Beth-jeshimoth is located (33:49) and on its western bank (1 Sam. 23:19,24; 26:1,3). Thus the rendering "Jeshimon," a proper name, is preferred.

THE VICTORY OVER SIHON (vv. 21–32)

Moving northward along the eastern (wilderness) edge of Moab, Israel now seeks peaceful passage through the Amorite kingdom of Sihon as it did with Edom. Sihon confronts Israel with an armed force, and the battle, joined in the wilderness at Jahaz, results in a total Israelite victory and the acquisition of Sihon's territory.

Moses actually had no intention of possessing Transjordan—the promised land lay across the Jordan River. Indeed, had not the tribes Reuben and Gad desired to settle there (chap. 32), he would have left it barren.[41] The acquisition of Transjordan, being Israel's first conquest, made a lasting impact upon subsequent generations (Deut. 2:24–37; Judg. 11:19–27) and was ranked with the Exodus as a paradigm of God's miraculous intervention on behalf of his people. A victory song of the Amorites over Moab is inserted (vv. 27–30); its purpose is explained in Excursus 54.

21. Israel now sent messengers Either from Iye-Abarim at Moab's boundary (v. 11) or from the ford of the Arnon, which separates the Moabites and the Amorites (v. 13). Either station conforms to the itinerary of 33:44–45.[42]

the Amorites The Amorite conquest of Transjordan must be associated with the invasion by the Hittites and their Amorite allies of Upi, of the region of Damascus and northern Transjordan following the Hittite defeat of Ramses II at Kadesh, about 1290, not many years before Israel entered this area.[43] For more on the Amorites, see the Comment to 13:29.

The Septuagint and Samaritan add "with an offer of peace," as in Deuteronomy 2:26. The midrash elaborates: "The Holy One Blessed Be He said to him (Moses): Make war with Sihon. Even though he does not seek to interfere with you, you must open hostilities against him (Deut. 2:24). Moses, however, did not do so, but, in accordance with what is written afterward, 'sent messengers' (Deut. 2:26). The Holy One Blessed Be He said to him: By your life, I shall cancel My own words and confirm yours; as it says 'when you approach a town to attack it, you shall offer it terms of peace' (Deut. 20:10)."[44]

22. The text of the message resembles that sent to the Edomites (20:17) but is shorter. Even shorter is its form in Judges 11:19. A much expanded version is found in the Samaritan and in Deuteronomy 2:27–29.

territory For this meaning of *gevul,* see the Comment to verse 13.

not let Israel pass through his territory. Sihon gathered all his people and went out against Israel in the wilderness. He came to Jahaz and engaged Israel in battle.
24But Israel put them to the sword, and took possession of their land, from the Arnon to the Jabbok, as far as [Az] of the Ammonites, for Az marked the boundary of the Ammonites.
25Israel took all those towns. And Israel settled in all the towns of the Amorites, in Heshbon and all its dependencies.

בִּגְבֻלוֹ וַיֶּאֱסֹף סִיחֹן אֶת־כָּל־עַמּוֹ וַיֵּצֵא לִקְרַאת
יִשְׂרָאֵל הַמִּדְבָּרָה וַיָּבֹא יָהְצָה וַיִּלָּחֶם בְּיִשְׂרָאֵל׃
24 וַיַּכֵּהוּ יִשְׂרָאֵל לְפִי־חָרֶב וַיִּירַשׁ אֶת־אַרְצוֹ
מֵאַרְנֹן עַד־יַבֹּק עַד־בְּנֵי עַמּוֹן כִּי עַז גְּבוּל בְּנֵי
עַמּוֹן׃ 25 וַיִּקַּח יִשְׂרָאֵל אֵת כָּל־הֶעָרִים הָאֵלֶּה
וַיֵּשֶׁב יִשְׂרָאֵל בְּכָל־עָרֵי הָאֱמֹרִי בְּחֶשְׁבּוֹן וּבְכָל־

23. *in the wilderness* This is defined in Deuteronomy as "the wilderness of Kedemoth" (Deut. 2:26), further evidence that Israel had skirted the land of Moab.

Jahaz According to Eusebius,[45] it lies between Madaba and Dibon (see Map 5). The Mesha inscription confirms its proximity to Dibon.[46] This battle is firmly anchored in later biblical sources (Deut. 2:33; Judg. 11:20).

24. *put them to the sword* That is, Sihon's army, but nothing is said concerning the Amorite population that Deuteronomy 2:33 claims was placed under the ban *(ḥerem)* and totally destroyed (see vv. 33–35).

Jabbok One of the main eastern tributaries of the Jordan. Its source is near Amman (biblical Rabbah; Deut. 3:11). From there, it flows northward, then turns ninety degrees and flows westward through ever-deepening canyons until it empties into the Jordan, 24 kilometers (15 mi.) north of the Dead Sea. Its upper south-north stretch served as the western boundary of the Ammonites and its lower east-west course formed the boundary between the two Amorite kingdoms of Sihon and Og (see Map 5).

The Jabbok may have been the idealized northern border (Josh. 12:2–3) since Sihon's rule apparently extended only as far north as Jazer (see the Comment to v. 32). The purpose of this claim is explicated in Excursus 54.

[Az][47]

Ammonites Recent archaeological excavations, including the discovery of a Late Bronze Age temple at Amman, point to a settled occupation by 1600 B.C.E., possibly by Ammonites. Thus, in contrast to Edom, which was still seminomadic (see the Comment to 20:14–21), and to Moab, which had just been organized into a kingdom (see the Comment to v. 26), Ammon may have been an established state for several centuries when Israel entered this area. No wonder, then, that confrontation with the Ammonites was avoided.

Az There is no such place-name in the Bible. It also means "strong," referring perhaps to the precipitous Arnon canyon, which formed Ammon's western boundary. According to this reading, Israel refrained from attacking the Ammonites—not because they were a kindred people, the rationale of Deuteronomy 2:19—but on more pragmatic grounds: Ammon was too strong. However, the Septuagint reading, Jazer, implying that the first and last consonants of *(y)ʿz(r)* were accidentally lost—the first by haplography with the preceding word *ki*—should be seriously considered since Jazer and its environs bordered on Ammon (see v. 32 and Map 5).

25. *Israel took all those towns* A list of the towns may originally have preceded.

Israel settled in all the towns of the Amorites Anticipating the settlement of the tribes of Reuben and Gad in this area (chap. 32). Perhaps the emphasis here is that Israel took these towns from the Amorites, not from the Moabites (see Excursus 54).

Heshbon Questionably identified with Tell Hesban whose remains do not antedate the Iron Age. Jalul, the only important Late Bronze site in the vicinity, may have been the Amorite city of Sihon, which was transferred to another site and given the name Heshbon after it was destroyed by Israel. (For a similar conjecture concerning Canaanite Arad, see the Comment to 21:1.)

26Now Heshbon was the city of Sihon king of the Amorites, who had fought against a former king of Moab and taken all his land from him as far as the Arnon. 27Therefore the bards would recite:

"Come to Heshbon; firmly built
And well founded is Sihon's city.

בְּנֹתֶֽיהָ׃ 26 כִּֽי חֶשְׁבּוֹן עִיר סִיחֹן מֶלֶךְ הָאֱמֹרִי הִוא וְהוּא נִלְחַם בְּמֶלֶךְ מוֹאָב הָרִאשׁוֹן וַיִּקַּח אֶת־כָּל־אַרְצוֹ מִיָּדוֹ עַד־אַרְנֹֽן׃ 27 עַל־כֵּן יֹאמְרוּ הַמֹּשְׁלִים בֹּאוּ חֶשְׁבּוֹן תִּבָּנֶה וְתִכּוֹנֵן עִיר סִיחֽוֹן׃

its dependencies   Literally, "its daughters," also called "its towns" in Joshua 13:17, where they are itemized. This suggests that all the cities of the *mishor,* "tableland"—the area from Heshbon (on the wadi Hesban) south to the Arnon River—comprised the kingdom of Sihon (which also included control over certain Midianite clans; Josh. 13:21). However, territory north of Heshbon (around Jazer) had to be conquered in a separate campaign (v. 32). The distinction between "mother" and "daughter" is that of walled city and open village. The latter, for the first time, has been excavated 1.2 kilometers (.75 mi.) southeast of Beth Shemesh, which revealed a Middle Bronze Age village, consisting of a dozen or more simple house-courtyard complexes containing domestic pottery and stone implements such as sickle flints and saddle querns, suggesting agricultural activity.

26. *had fought*   Hebrew *nilḥam,* a pluperfect.

a former   Rather, "the former" or, preferably, "the first." The latter rendering commends itself because, except for nomads, all of Moab (the area south of the Jabbok) was unsettled between the nineteenth and thirteenth centuries. Thus the Moabite state had just been formed when Israel came upon the scene. And as the Israelites later changed their government to a monarchy better to combat the Philistine menace, so perhaps did the Moabites before the advancing Amorites (see the Comment to v. 13). According to this verse, then, their efforts failed and only under later monarchs such as Eglon (Judg. 3) and Mesha (2 Kings 1:1; Mesha stone) did Moab regain suzerainty over this area. Saul, Israel's first king, also failed to overthrow the foreign, Philistine dominion and the task fell to a king of a new line: David.

from him   Hebrew *mi-yado,* literally "from his hand." The Septuagint reads "from Aroer," which commends itself because with it the verse would contain the two termini of Sihon's conquest. This Aroer cannot be the one located at the Arnon (Josh. 13:16) but the one defined as "Aroer, which is close to Rabbah," the Ammonite capital (Josh. 13:25). Some scholars would read *mi-yabbok,* "from the Jabbok," in conformity with verse 24. The present text, however, makes excellent sense since it underscores the main point of the section, that Israel conquered this territory from Sihon himself—and not from the Moabites (see Excursus 54).

27. *bards*   Hebrew *ha-moshelim,* that is, the reciters of *meshalim* (sing. *mashal*), derives from the stem "to be like" and stands for such literary forms as the proverb, parable, riddle (the Septuagint renders "those who speak in enigmas"), and allegory. They could vary from pithy folk maxims (1 Sam. 24:14; 1 Kings 20:11) to longer artistic compositions such as the Balaam poems (Num. 23–24), Ezekiel's allegories (Ezek. 17:2–12), Job's discourses, and the contents of the Book of Proverbs *(mishlei).* They also include mocking taunt songs directed against a foe (Isa. 14:4; Mic. 2:4), such as the following poem, which describes the gloating over the defeated Moabites.[48]

firmly built   Or "may it be built firm/rebuilt" (see Josh. 6:26). According to Ramban, this is a call to the Amorites to settle in conquered Heshbon to rebuild and expand it.

well founded   Hebrew *tikkonen,* an attested synonym of *banah,* "build," in biblical poetry (Hab. 2:12).[49]

Sihon's city   An alternative name for Heshbon in honor of its conqueror, just as Jerusalem was called David's city after he conquered it (2 Sam. 5:7; 1 Kings 2:10). Just as Jerusalem literally became David's personal possession—since he took it by his private army and not by the tribal militia—so too Heshbon may perhaps have become the private fief of Sihon.

28 For fire went forth from Heshbon,
Flame from Sihon's city,
Consuming Ar of Moab,
The lords of Bamoth by the Arnon.
29 Woe to you, O Moab!
You are undone, O people of Chemosh!
His sons are rendered fugitive
And his daughters captive
By an Amorite king, Sihon."
30 Yet we have cast them down utterly,
Heshbon along with Dibon;
We have wrought desolation at Nophah,
Which is hard by Medeba.

28 כִּֽי־אֵשׁ֙ יָֽצְאָ֣ה מֵֽחֶשְׁבּ֔וֹן
לֶהָבָ֖ה מִקִּרְיַ֣ת סִיחֹ֑ן
אָֽכְלָה֙ עָ֣ר מוֹאָ֔ב
בַּעֲלֵ֖י בָּמ֥וֹת אַרְנֹֽן׃
29 אוֹי־לְךָ֣ מוֹאָ֔ב
אָבַ֖דְתָּ עַם־כְּמ֑וֹשׁ
נָתַ֨ן בָּנָ֤יו פְּלֵיטִם֙
וּבְנֹתָ֣יו בַּשְּׁבִ֔ית
לְמֶ֥לֶךְ אֱמֹרִ֖י סִיחֽוֹן׃
30 וַנִּירָ֛ם אָבַ֥ד
חֶשְׁבּ֖וֹן עַד־דִּיבֹ֑ן
וַנַּשִּׁ֣ים עַד־נֹ֔פַח
אֲשֶׁר֖* עַד־מֵֽידְבָֽא׃

v. 30. נקוד על ר׳

28. fire went forth A frequently used image for a ravaging army (Judg. 8:20).

Ar Hebrew *'ar* refers either to a city (see the Comment to 23:26) or to a district near the Arnon (see the Comment to v. 15). It indicates the full extent of Sihon's conquest, from Heshbon southward to the Arnon, and provides a fitting parallel to Bamoth by the Arnon in the next colon.[50]

the lords of Hebrew *ba'alei.* The Septuagint reads *bal'ah,* "devouring," a perfect parallel to "consuming" in the previous colon.

Bamoth by the Arnon So-called to distinguish it from other sites in Moab called Bamoth (v. 19; 22:41). Since *bamah* refers to a cultic place, the plural form Bamoth probably indicates the site of a sanctuary.

29. Woe Hebrew *'oi* also occurs as *hoi,* an exclamation used in facing death (1 Kings 13:30; Jer. 22:18) but also, especially in the prophets, it appears in predictions of catastrophe (e.g., Isa. 3:9,11).

people of Chemosh That is, the Moabites—just as the Israelites are called "the people of YHVH" (Exod. 15:16; Judg. 5:11). Chemosh was the national deity of Moab (Judg. 11:24; 1 Kings 11:7).

are rendered Hebrew *natan,* an active verb understood passively by Rashi. However, Ramban's literal translation "he rendered" is preferable, heightening the irony in the poem whereby the god Chemosh willingly surrenders his subjects. In the ancient Near East it was not unknown for a nationwide disaster to be attributed to the decision of the national deity. Once again, according to Mesha inscription 4–5, Chemosh is said to have made such a decision: "Omri . . . afflicted Moab for many days because Chemosh was angry with his land." So, too, the Assyrians claimed that their invasion of Judah was willed by Israel's God (2 Kings 18:25).

In the citation of this verse in Jeremiah 48:46, *natan* is changed to *lukḥu,* "are carried off," in order to avoid the possible attribution of divinity to Chemosh.[51]

By an Amorite king, Sihon A correct explanatory gloss, although it overloads the verse.

30. This verse is an insoluble crux. It may not even belong to the song but may be part of the itinerary.

Yet we have cast them down utterly Reading *ve-niram* instead of *va-niram* with Targum Onkelos and Targum Yerushalmi. Alternatively, the Hebrew consonants *vnyrm 'bd* can be read *vnyr m'b ['b]d,* "the dominion of Moab has perished," with the bracketed letters accounted for by haplography.[52] *Nir* means yoke or dominion in the cognate languages of Akkadian, Aramaic, and Syriac as well as elsewhere in the Bible (1 Kings 11:36; 15:4).[53]

Heshbon along with Dibon Alternatively, from Heshbon to Dibon.

31So Israel occupied the land of the Amorites. 32Then Moses sent to spy out Jazer, and they captured its dependencies and dispossessed the Amorites who were there.

33They marched on and went up the road to Bashan, and King Og of Bashan, with all his people, came out to Edrei to engage them in battle. 34But the LORD said to Moses,

31 וַיֵּשֶׁב יִשְׂרָאֵל בְּאֶרֶץ הָאֱמֹרִי׃ 32 וַיִּשְׁלַח מֹשֶׁה
לְרַגֵּל אֶת־יַעְזֵר וַיִּלְכְּדוּ בְּנֹתֶיהָ ויירש אֶת־הָאֱמֹרִי
אֲשֶׁר־שָׁם׃ 33 וַיִּפְנוּ וַיַּעֲלוּ דֶּרֶךְ הַבָּשָׁן וַיֵּצֵא עוֹג
מֶלֶךְ־הַבָּשָׁן לִקְרָאתָם הוּא וְכָל־עַמּוֹ לַמִּלְחָמָה
אֶדְרֶעִי׃ מפטיר 34 וַיֹּאמֶר יְהוָה אֶל־מֹשֶׁה אַל־

v. 32. וַיּוֹרֶשׁ ק׳

Dibon Identified with modern Dhiban, 5 kilometers (3 mi.) north of the Arnon River. It was rebuilt by the tribe of Gad (32:34) and thereafter called Dibon-gad (33:45). But according to another tradition it was assigned to the tribe of Reuben (Josh. 13:17). Mesha, king of Moab, was a Dibonite (Mesha 1–2). Excavations at this site have revealed an Early Bronze Age occupation.

We have wrought desolation at Nophah Rather, "and from Nashim to Nophah." Neither place-name occurs elsewhere.[54]

Which is Hebrew *'asher.* The dot over the *r* in the Hebrew text indicates that the Masoretes were doubtful of this letter. Its elimination yields *'esh,* "fire," the reading of the Septuagint and the Samaritan.[55]

hard by Hebrew *'ad,* although the Septuagint, the Samaritan, and some manuscripts read *'al,* "against."

Medeba Identified with modern Madaba on the ancient king's highway (20:17; 21:22), 24 kilometers (15 mi.) southeast of the mouth of the Jordan (see Map 5). It was allocated to the tribe of Reuben (Josh. 13:9,16) and later retaken by Mesha of Moab (Mesha 8,30).

31. This repetitive resumption of verse 25b probably indicates that the intervening verses (the explanation in prose [v. 26] and poetry [vv. 27–30] that Israel conquered the territory not from the Moabites [forbidden to them in Deut. 2:10] but from the Amorites [see Excursus 54]) interrupt the sequence.

32. Jazer Eusebius and Jerome speak of a place called Azer or Jazer about 16 kilometers (10 mi.) west of Rabbah of the Ammonites. It was the main city of a discrete region, being listed separately from the Gilead, and fits the Greek reading of verse 24b. It lay between Heshbon and the Jabbok (see Map 5), another indication that Sihon's dominion did not extend much north of his city Heshbon (see the Comment to v. 25). It was assigned to and rebuilt by the Gadites (Num. 32:35; Josh. 13:25). Excursus 55 discusses the purpose of mentioning this brief campaign while omitting the others that took place in the conquest of the Gilead, between the Jabbok and Yarmuk (32:39–42).[56]

THE VICTORY OVER OG (vv. 33–35)

Verses 33–34 are duplicated in Deuteronomy 3:1–2, except for the change from first to third person. They conform to the Deuteronomic position that all of Transjordan was taken at one stroke. The campaign against Og differs considerably from that against Sihon. No messengers are sent requesting passage since the way across the Jordan has already been secured with the victory over Sihon. Also, whereas the battle against Sihon is undertaken at Israel's initiative (the name of God does not appear in vv. 21–32), here the campaign against Og is expressly commissioned by the Lord (v. 34). The reason for this disparity is that, in contrast to Sihon's land, the land of Og is part of the promised land, which includes the Bashan (34:10–11). Thus the Lord commands the conquest of the Bashan as much as He commands the conquest of Canaan.[57] The Deuteronomic account is more consistent in having both campaigns commissioned by God (Deut. 2:24). This difference probably stems from two different traditions concerning the eastern boundary of the promised land. The priestly tradition, expressed here, holds that it was the Jordan River (34:12); hence, Transjordan was excluded (Josh. 22:19). But Deuteronomy maintains that Israel entered its promised land when it crossed the Arnon—thereafter

"Do not fear him, for I give him and all his people and his
land into your hand. You shall do to him as you did to
Sihon king of the Amorites who dwelt in Heshbon." [35]They
defeated him and his sons and all his people, until no
remnant was left him; and they took possession of his
22 country. [1]The Israelites then marched on and encamped in the steppes of Moab, across the Jordan from
Jericho.

תִּירָא אֹתוֹ כִּי בְיָדְךָ נָתַתִּי אֹתוֹ וְאֶת־כָּל־עַמּוֹ
וְאֶת־אַרְצוֹ וְעָשִׂיתָ לּוֹ כַּאֲשֶׁר עָשִׂיתָ לְסִיחֹן מֶלֶךְ
הָאֱמֹרִי אֲשֶׁר יוֹשֵׁב בְּחֶשְׁבּוֹן׃ 35 וַיַּכּוּ אֹתוֹ וְאֶת־
בָּנָיו וְאֶת־כָּל־עַמּוֹ עַד־בִּלְתִּי הִשְׁאִיר־לוֹ שָׂרִיד
וַיִּירְשׁוּ אֶת־אַרְצוֹ׃

כ״ב וַיִּסְעוּ בְּנֵי יִשְׂרָאֵל וַיַּחֲנוּ בְּעַרְבוֹת מוֹאָב
מֵעֵבֶר לְיַרְדֵּן יְרֵחוֹ׃ ס

it could conquer for possession (Deut. 2:24). In the later literature, both victories were coupled.[58] Excursus 55 addresses the issue of the omission of the conquest of the intervening territory of Gilead (see 32:39–42).

33. Bashan This includes the area bounded by Mount Hermon to the north, Jebel Druze to the east, the hills east of the Sea of Galilee to the west, and extending to about 9.6 kilometers (6 mi.) south of the Yarmuk River (see Map 5).

Og An Amorite. According to the prophet Amos, they were a people "Whose stature was like a cedar's / And who was stout as the oak" (Amos 2:9). Og himself was remembered as the last of the giant Rephaim (Deut. 3:11; see 2 Sam. 21:16–22).

Edrei Identified with modern Derʿa, it was located near the Yarmuk and the desert, probably at the southeast border of Og's kingdom. The site was occupied during the Late Bronze Age. The fact that the battle took place here suggests that Israel marched unopposed from the Jabbok to the Yarmuk.[59]

34. as you did to Sihon According to verse 35, this means that the *ḥerem* or total destruction of the population was imposed on Sihon's kingdom. But this is only claimed in the Deuteronomic version (Deut. 2:34), not in the present account (see the Comment to v. 24). This is further ground for suspecting that originally the text only contained the account of the victory over Sihon and that the Deuteronomic account of Moses' conquest of the Bashan was later appended here.

35. and his sons This phrase is missing in the Samaritan and in Deuteronomy 3:3, but it is found in Deuteronomy 2:33, which describes the defeat of Sihon. It may have been omitted in the Deuteronomic account of Og because it would have clashed with the claim that Og was the last of the giants (Deut. 3:11).[60]

22:1 marched on The point of origin of this last stage of the march is not given. The full itinerary (33:48) identifies it as the mountains of Abarim. The previous occurrence of the standard itinerary formula, "set out . . . encamped," is in verse 11, which mentions the station of Iyyim of the Abarim mountains in "the wilderness bordering on Moab to the east" (v. 11). In the full itinerary it appears four stations back (33:44–45). Perhaps, then, in order to avoid listing all the previous stations, the point of origin is omitted.

This verse is an editorial transition to the last third of the Book of Numbers, which deals with events that occurred and laws that were given at the banks of the Jordan prior to entry into the promised land. It forms an inclusion with the last verse of the book (36:13) as a time bracket (cf. also the Comment to 35:1).

steppes of Moab The eastern portion of the lower Jordan plain before it empties into the Dead Sea, also called the "country of Moab" (Gen. 36:35; 1 Chron. 1:46) and the "land of Moab" (e.g., Deut. 1:5). The name is another indication that the area belonged to Moab before it was conquered by Sihon. The exact site where Israel ended its wilderness trek is given as Shittim (Num. 25:1) or Abel-shittim (33:49).

opposite Jericho Literally, "the Jordan of Jericho," that is, at the point of the Jordan River located at Jericho. This expression is found mainly in the remainder of the Book of Numbers (e.g., 26:3,63).

BALAK

2Balak son of Zippor saw all that Israel had done to the Amorites.

3Moab was alarmed because that people was so numerous. Moab dreaded the Israelites, 4and Moab said to the elders of Midian, "Now this horde will lick clean all that is about us as an ox licks up the grass of the field."

Balak son of Zippor, who was king of Moab at that time,

בלק

2 וַיַּרְא בָּלָק בֶּן־צִפּוֹר אֵת כָּל־אֲשֶׁר־עָשָׂה
יִשְׂרָאֵל לָאֱמֹרִי׃ 3 וַיָּגָר מוֹאָב מִפְּנֵי הָעָם מְאֹד כִּי
רַב־הוּא וַיָּקָץ מוֹאָב מִפְּנֵי בְּנֵי יִשְׂרָאֵל׃ 4 וַיֹּאמֶר
מוֹאָב אֶל־זִקְנֵי מִדְיָן עַתָּה יְלַחֲכוּ הַקָּהָל אֶת־כָּל־
סְבִיבֹתֵינוּ כִּלְחֹךְ הַשּׁוֹר אֵת יֶרֶק הַשָּׂדֶה וּבָלָק
בֶּן־צִפּוֹר מֶלֶךְ לְמוֹאָב בָּעֵת הַהִוא׃ 5 וַיִּשְׁלַח

Balaam (22:2–24:25)

Balak Rabbinic tradition calls these chapters the "Section of Balaam,"[1] a designation that accords with the view that the Torah was compiled from disparate scrolls.[2] Clearly the rabbis believed that the Balaam story was composed independently and only later inserted into the Pentateuchal corpus. Indeed, these chapters are totally distinct from the larger context: Neither the personalities nor the events in them appear in the adjoining chapters. There is only one connecting link: As in chapters 21 and 25, the Israelites are encamped on the borders of Moab. In fact, the juxtaposition of these chapters to chapter 25 reflects the tradition found in 31:16 that it was Balaam who advised the Midianites to seduce Israel at Shittim.

The action moves swiftly. Balak, king of Moab, hires the renowned seer Balaam to curse Israel. Balaam consents only when he receives the Lord's permission and, further, warns Balak that he will speak only as the Lord directs him. On these occasions, involving a sacrificial ritual and change of site, Balaam blesses the Israelites instead of cursing them. And in a fourth oracle he predicts the eventual doom of Moab at the hands of Israel: Balak's curse, intended for Israel, will instead be inflicted by Israel on Moab. The unity of these chapters is discussed in Excursus 56, the episode of the ass in Excursus 57, the character of Balaam in Excursus 58, the profession of Balaam in Excursus 59, and the Balaam inscription in Excursus 60.

CHAPTER 22 THE HIRING OF BALAAM (vv. 2–21)

Israel is encamped at the borders of Moab. Balak, the king of Moab, sends emissaries to the renowned seer Balaam to engage his services to curse the Israelites and thereby weaken them so that Moab can defeat them in battle. Balaam seeks the permission of the Lord in a dream, but it is denied. Balak then sends a more prominent delegation, and this time the Lord grants permission.

2. As Abravanel has noted, there is an abrupt change of subject from Balak to Moab in verses 2 and 3, with the identification of the connection between the two postponed to verse 4b. The problem can be resolved by regarding verse 2 as an editorial link that ties the following Balaam story with the preceding narrative on the conquest of the Amorites.[3] That a personified Moab speaks in verse 4a rather than Balak indicates that the latter has not yet been introduced.

Amorites The kingdom of Sihon, who is mentioned in 21:21,25–26,31–32.[4]

3. This is the true beginning of the Balaam story. The repetition of the subject and the use of synonymous verbs and objects, a characteristic of Hebrew poetry, may actually be due to a poetic substratum underlying the text. See the next verse.

dreaded Hebrew *va-yakots . . . mi-penei*. For the idiom, see Exodus 1:12 and Isaiah 7:16.[5]

4. ***elders of Midian*** Midian was a confederation of peoples (see the Comment to 10:29), and part of its people may have been ruled by the Moabite king.[6] The fact that Midianites lived on Moabite soil is attested by Genesis 36:35. That the Midianite rulers are called "elders" rather than "royal officials" indicates that Midian was not a monarchy at this time as was Moab (see the Comments to v. 8 and 25:15).

5 sent messengers to Balaam son of Beor in Pethor, which is
by the Euphrates, in the land of his kinsfolk, to invite him,
saying, "There is a people that came out of Egypt; it hides
the earth from view, and it is settled next to me. 6 Come
then, put a curse upon this people for me, since they are too
numerous for me; perhaps I can thus defeat them and drive
them out of the land. For I know that he whom you bless is
blessed indeed, and he whom you curse is cursed."

מַלְאָכִים אֶל־בִּלְעָם בֶּן־בְּעֹר פְּתוֹרָה אֲשֶׁר עַל־
הַנָּהָר אֶרֶץ בְּנֵי־עַמּוֹ לִקְרֹא־לוֹ לֵאמֹר הִנֵּה עַם
יָצָא מִמִּצְרַיִם הִנֵּה כִסָּה אֶת־עֵין הָאָרֶץ וְהוּא יֹשֵׁב
מִמֻּלִי׃ 6 וְעַתָּה לְכָה־נָּא אָרָה־לִּי אֶת־הָעָם הַזֶּה
כִּי־עָצוּם הוּא מִמֶּנִּי אוּלַי אוּכַל נַכֶּה־בּוֹ וַאֲגָרְשֶׁנּוּ
מִן־הָאָרֶץ כִּי יָדַעְתִּי אֵת אֲשֶׁר־תְּבָרֵךְ מְבֹרָךְ
וַאֲשֶׁר תָּאֹר יוּאָר׃ 7 וַיֵּלְכוּ זִקְנֵי מוֹאָב וְזִקְנֵי מִדְיָן

According to tradition, the two nations formed an alliance against the Israelite menace: "It is like the case of two dogs that were fighting with one another. A wolf attacked one of them. The other thought: If I do not come to his aid the wolf will kill him today and tomorrow he will attack me. For a similar reason Moab joined with Midian."[7] Another interpretation maintains that Balak himself was a Midianite and that Moab and Midian formed a united kingdom.[8]

"(Now) this (horde)" The ancient versions (LXX, Sam., Pesh.) add "this" (Heb. *ha-zeh*), which is essential since the speaker is a non-Israelite and has to distinguish Israel from his own people. The speech, composed of metaphor and simile befitting a pastoral scene, may again be a vestige of an original poetic substratum.

lick . . . licks up[9]

Balak[10]

5. ***sent*** The absence of a subject makes it necessary to begin the sentence with the previous clause, "Balak . . ." (v. 4).

Balaam son of Beor[11] The animosity of the tradition toward Balaam is revealed by the many explanations proposed for his name: (1) a mad people;[12] (2) he went out of his mind because of the immensity of his knowledge;[13] (3) he who swallows up the people;[14] (4) corrupter of the people;[15] (5) his son is a beast.[16] The Deir ʿAlla inscription features a seer by the same name, Bilʿam the son of Beor (see Excursus 60).[17]

Pethor Identified with Pitru on the Sajur River, a tributary of the Euphrates, some 20 kilometers (12 mi.) south of Carchemish. Targum Onkelos identifies the region as Aram, and this is confirmed by an Egyptian text that designates the area up to the Euphrates as Aram.[18] Furthermore, the annals of Shalmaneser III indicate that in the tenth or the first half of the ninth century B.C.E. Pitru was in Aramean hands.[19] If the identification is correct, then the journey from Pethor to Moab, a distance of about 640 kilometers (400 mi.) would have taken at least twenty days. And since the text records four such journeys, three months would have been occupied in traveling.

Early midrash understands Pethor as "dream interpreter," from the root *p-t-r*.[20]

Euphrates Literally, the River, as in Genesis 31:21, Exodus 23:31, and Joshua 24:2.

his kinsfolk Hebrew *benei ʿammo* (see 24:14); so Ramban. Alternatively, the following interpretations have been offered: (1) Balak's kinsfolk;[21] (2) Ammon, reading *ʿammon* for *ʿammo*.[22] Ammon is located in Transjordan, close to Moab, which would explain how Balaam could travel by ass, an animal that could only negotiate short distances; (3) rendering "(land of) ʿAmau," a proper name possibly mentioned in Egyptian and Akkadian inscriptions,[23] but the reading is disputed.[24]

it hides the earth from view Literally, "it hides the eye of the earth"; by extension, "eye" can mean "appearance, view," as in Numbers 11:7 and Leviticus 13:55. Israel is clearly compared with a locust plague, a common simile for an invading army (cf. Judg. 6:5; 7:12).[25]

6. ***Come then*** Hebrew *ve-ʿattah*, literally "and now," used when the main point of the discourse is reached.[26]

I can thus defeat them[27] Balaam's curse is expected to weaken the Israelites so that Moab can defeat them in battle and expel them from its land. This is made explicit in Joshua 24:9–10 (see Excursus 58).

7The elders of Moab and the elders of Midian, versed in divination, set out. They came to Balaam and gave him Balak's message. 8He said to them, "Spend the night here, and I shall reply to you as the LORD may instruct me." So the Moabite dignitaries stayed with Balaam.

9God came to Balaam and said, "What do these people want of you?" 10Balaam said to God, "Balak son of Zippor, king of Moab, sent me this message: 11Here is a people that came out from Egypt and hides the earth from view. Come now and curse them for me; perhaps I can engage them in battle and drive them off." 12But God said to Balaam, "Do not go with them. You must not curse that people, for they are blessed."

וּקְסָמִים בְּיָדָם וַיָּבֹאוּ אֶל־בִּלְעָם וַיְדַבְּרוּ אֵלָיו
דִּבְרֵי בָלָק׃ 8 וַיֹּאמֶר אֲלֵיהֶם לִינוּ פֹה הַלַּיְלָה
וַהֲשִׁבֹתִי אֶתְכֶם דָּבָר כַּאֲשֶׁר יְדַבֵּר יְהוָה אֵלָי
וַיֵּשְׁבוּ שָׂרֵי־מוֹאָב עִם־בִּלְעָם׃ 9 וַיָּבֹא אֱלֹהִים אֶל־
בִּלְעָם וַיֹּאמֶר מִי הָאֲנָשִׁים הָאֵלֶּה עִמָּךְ׃ 10 וַיֹּאמֶר
בִּלְעָם אֶל־הָאֱלֹהִים בָּלָק בֶּן־צִפֹּר מֶלֶךְ מוֹאָב
שָׁלַח אֵלָי׃ 11 הִנֵּה הָעָם הַיֹּצֵא מִמִּצְרַיִם וַיְכַס
אֶת־עֵין הָאָרֶץ עַתָּה לְכָה קָבָה־לִּי אֹתוֹ אוּלַי
אוּכַל לְהִלָּחֶם בּוֹ וְגֵרַשְׁתִּיו׃ 12 וַיֹּאמֶר אֱלֹהִים
אֶל־בִּלְעָם לֹא תֵלֵךְ עִמָּהֶם לֹא תָאֹר אֶת־הָעָם
כִּי בָרוּךְ הוּא׃ שני [חמישי כשהן
מחוברות] 13 וַיָּקָם בִּלְעָם בַּבֹּקֶר וַיֹּאמֶר אֶל־

7. versed in divination Hebrew ***u-kesamim be-yadam***, literally "with divination in their hands"; that is, they themselves were diviners (see Ezra 7:25) and might, therefore, prevent him from backing out on the pretext that the time was unpropitious.[28] More likely, his colleagues were present for the purpose of honoring him.[29] Alternatively, the phrase has been translated (1) "possessing [the means of] divination" (see Ezek. 21:27)[30] (but that Balaam would have need of his colleagues' divinatory methods is hardly likely)[31] and (2) "possessing [the fees for] divination."[32] However, Balaam is to be rewarded only after the job is done (22:18,37; 24:11).

The mention of divination is not to be taken as a reproof of Balaam. Although divination is elsewhere condemned in Scripture, as in Deuteronomy 17:10,14 (also 1 Sam. 15:23; 28:8; 2 Kings 17:17), in certain quarters its practice was considered both efficacious and legitimate.[33] Balaam's oracles serve to clarify that Israel has no need of it in order to determine God's will. This text is the first of many to emphasize that Balaam is a diviner, one who predicts the future, not a sorcerer, one who can alter the future (through cursing and blessing), as Balak makes him out to be. (For details, see Excursus 59.)

8. Spend the night So that Balaam might receive a divine message in a dream (see v. 20), as dreams are a legitimate means in Israel for divine communication (see the Comment to 12:6). The prophets, however, regarded them as an inferior medium, as noted in Numbers 12:6 and Jeremiah 23:28. Dreams should not be confused with incubation, the ancient custom of sleeping in the temple of a god or goddess in order to obtain a message from him or her.[34]

the Moabite dignitaries Hebrew ***sarei mo'av***, called "Moabite elders," ***ziknei mo'av***, in the previous verse. The terminological change may reflect Moab's transition from a tribal to a monarchic government, the clan elders being replaced by royal bureaucrats. For this phenomenon in Israel, see Judges 8:6,14,16.[35]

9. What do (these people) want God uses this rhetorical question (of course He knows) to open a conversation (as in Gen. 3:9; 4:9).[36] From Balaam's answer in verses 10–11, it becomes clear that God questions the emissaries' business not their names.[37]

10. sent me this message Hebrew ***shalaḥ 'elai***. The Septuagint adds "saying." However, ***shalaḥ*** frequently occurs followed directly by the quote, as, for example, in 20:14 (also Gen. 27:45; 2 Kings 11:4).

11. a people that came out[38]

12. On verse 9 Ibn Ezra asks why God did not allow Balaam to curse Israel and thereby provide a greater miracle by turning the curse into blessing. He answers that if Balaam had been allowed to curse Israel, then the entire world would have attributed the plague of Baal-peor (25:9) to the power of Balaam's curse.

Do not go Three times in the Bible God appears to non-Israelites in order to warn them not to carry out their intentions; the other occasions are Genesis 31:24 (Laban) and Genesis 20:3 (Abimelech).

13 Balaam arose in the morning and said to Balak's dignitaries, "Go back to your own country, for the LORD will not let me go with you." 14 The Moabite dignitaries left, and they came to Balak and said, "Balaam refused to come with us."

15 Then Balak sent other dignitaries, more numerous and distinguished than the first. 16 They came to Balaam and said to him, "Thus says Balak son of Zippor: Please do not refuse to come to me. 17 I will reward you richly and I will do anything you ask of me. Only come and damn this people for me." 18 Balaam replied to Balak's officials, "Though Balak were to give me his house full of silver and gold, I could not do anything, big or little, contrary to the

שָׂרֵי בָלָק לְכוּ אֶל־אַרְצְכֶם כִּי מֵאֵן יְהוָה לְתִתִּי
לַהֲלֹךְ עִמָּכֶם׃ 14 וַיָּקוּמוּ שָׂרֵי מוֹאָב וַיָּבֹאוּ אֶל־
בָּלָק וַיֹּאמְרוּ מֵאֵן בִּלְעָם הֲלֹךְ עִמָּנוּ׃ 15 וַיֹּסֶף עוֹד
בָּלָק שְׁלֹחַ שָׂרִים רַבִּים וְנִכְבָּדִים מֵאֵלֶּה׃
16 וַיָּבֹאוּ אֶל־בִּלְעָם וַיֹּאמְרוּ לוֹ כֹּה אָמַר בָּלָק
בֶּן־צִפּוֹר אַל־נָא תִמָּנַע מֵהֲלֹךְ אֵלָי׃ 17 כִּי־כַבֵּד
אֲכַבֶּדְךָ מְאֹד וְכֹל אֲשֶׁר־תֹּאמַר אֵלַי אֶעֱשֶׂה
וּלְכָה־נָּא קָבָה־לִּי אֵת הָעָם הַזֶּה׃ 18 וַיַּעַן בִּלְעָם
וַיֹּאמֶר אֶל־עַבְדֵי בָלָק אִם־יִתֶּן־לִי בָלָק מְלֹא
בֵיתוֹ כֶּסֶף וְזָהָב לֹא אוּכַל לַעֲבֹר אֶת־פִּי יְהוָה

they are blessed That is, they are already blessed from the time of the patriarchs, and the blessing cannot be reversed by a curse.[39] This is based on Genesis 27:33.

13. *Balaam arose in the morning* Proof that God appeared to him in the night. The identical sentence appears in the Balaam inscription of Deir ʿAlla (1:3; see Excursus 60).

the LORD will not let me go Balaam omits the full reason—that cursing Israel is an exercise in futility—not because he hoped later to change God's mind but because it would have brought the story to an end had the emissaries reported this reason to Balak.

the LORD The fact that a heathen invokes the name of Israel's God is not unprecedented (Abimelech the Philistine does this in Gen. 26:28).

with you The midrash seizes upon these words to denigrate Balaam's intentions: "Shall I go with you? I will only go with greater men than you."[40]

14. *Balaam refused to come with us* Again, an incomplete quotation. The emissaries omit mentioning that the Lord is the author of Balaam's refusal. It may be the narrator's way of indicating that the Moabites were so sure of Balaam's inherent power to curse Israel that they regarded Balaam's reliance upon the Lord as an excuse to back out.

15. *More numerous* Hebrew *rabbim*. Rather, "more powerful," as in Psalms 48:3 and Esther 1:8.[41]

16. *refuse*[42]

17. *I will reward you richly* Literally, "I will honor you greatly," a euphemism for monetary rewards, as the next verse makes explicit.[43]

18. *officials* Hebrew *ʿavdei*, literally "servants." Perhaps the narrator's switch from *sarim*, "dignitaries," in verses 8,14,15 to "servants" here can be explained by Balaam's comment: He is not Balak's servant but the Lord's, and he will hearken solely to His command.[44]

I could not do anything Hebrew *lo' 'ukhal*, denoting a moral impossibility (cf. 22:38; 23:12,26; 24:13).

big or little A literary merism for "anything" (see 1 Sam. 20:2; 22:15; 25:36).

contrary to Hebrew *la-ʿavor*, literally "to transgress, step across the boundary," as in the idiom *laʿavor berit*, "violate the covenant," in Joshua 7:11.

The LORD my God This affirmation perhaps underscores the reason Moab sought Balaam even though he lived so far away (see the Comment to v. 5). Since he professed allegiance to and intimacy with Israel's God he would have had a better chance of convincing Him to curse His people Israel.[45]

command of the LORD my God. 19 So you, too, stay here overnight, and let me find out what else the LORD may say to me." 20 That night God came to Balaam and said to him, "If these men have come to invite you, you may go with them. But whatever I command you, that you shall do."

21 When he arose in the morning, Balaam saddled his ass and departed with the Moabite dignitaries. 22 But God was incensed at his going; so an angel of the LORD placed himself in his way as an adversary.

He was riding on his she-ass, with his two servants alongside, 23 when the ass caught sight of the angel of the LORD

אֱלֹהָי לַעֲשׂוֹת קְטַנָּה אוֹ גְדוֹלָה׃ 19 וְעַתָּה שְׁבוּ
נָא בָזֶה גַּם־אַתֶּם הַלָּיְלָה וְאֵדְעָה מַה־יֹּסֵף יְהוָה
דַּבֵּר עִמִּי׃ 20 וַיָּבֹא אֱלֹהִים ׀ אֶל־בִּלְעָם לַיְלָה
וַיֹּאמֶר לוֹ אִם־לִקְרֹא לְךָ בָּאוּ הָאֲנָשִׁים קוּם לֵךְ
אִתָּם וְאַךְ אֶת־הַדָּבָר אֲשֶׁר־אֲדַבֵּר אֵלֶיךָ אֹתוֹ
תַעֲשֶׂה׃ שלישי 21 וַיָּקָם בִּלְעָם בַּבֹּקֶר וַיַּחֲבֹשׁ
אֶת־אֲתֹנוֹ וַיֵּלֶךְ עִם־שָׂרֵי מוֹאָב׃ 22 וַיִּחַר־אַף
אֱלֹהִים כִּי־הוֹלֵךְ הוּא וַיִּתְיַצֵּב מַלְאַךְ יְהוָה בַּדֶּרֶךְ
לְשָׂטָן לוֹ וְהוּא רֹכֵב עַל־אֲתֹנוֹ וּשְׁנֵי נְעָרָיו עִמּוֹ׃

19. here[46]

what else Perhaps the Lord will change His mind. Such indeed is the unspoken premise behind all forms of divination. The same ritual procedures are repeated until a favorable omen is received. Repeated omen taking is best attested among the ancient Greeks. Xenophon, for example, sacrifices three times on each of two or three consecutive days, based on this hope: "It may be that the victims will turn out favorable to us."[47] Also the Hittite "Ritual against Impotence" is performed for three consecutive days, three times daily,[48] probably for the same reason (see Excursus 59). There exists a pre-Islamic Arabian tale of a female soothsayer who enabled her client to avoid fulfilling his vow to sacrifice his son by continuing to throw the arrow-oracle before the god until the god pointed (via the arrows) at a surrogate (ten camels) instead of at the son.[49] So Balaam will have the king repeat the same sacrificial ritual, albeit in different places, in order to effect the desired result.

Even in dream interpretation, a single dream is not decisive, as in the case of Pharaoh in Genesis 41:5. Similarly, in Mesopotamia, Gilgamesh and Gudea must dream the same dream twice. Thus Balaam can sincerely hope that in his second dream he will learn that the Lord has changed His mind. This basically pagan view is reflected in the midrash that Balaam was privy to the split second when God waxes angry against Israel each day.[50] The difference between Balaam and Israel's prophets contrasts sharply on this matter. Both hope that God will change His mind. But the prophets assume His constancy even while attempting to change His mind, whereas Balaam assumes that God is fickle, and he attempts to exploit that by divination. This premise will be categorically denied in this story. The universe is neither mechanical nor predictable; God's will is neither capricious nor determinable (see the Comment to 23:19).

20. That night God came to Balaam That is, in a dream (see the Comment to v. 8). The same language is used for divine manifestations to non-Israelites, as in the case of Abimelech in Genesis 20:3 and of Laban in Genesis 31:24. It is never used with Israel's prophets, an indication that Balaam is the recipient of an inferior theophany. Strikingly, the identical language is used of Balaam's vision in the Deir ʿAlla inscription: "the gods came to him at night" (1.1); see Excursus 60.

Why indeed did God change His mind and allow Balaam to go? A realistic answer might be that without the change we would have neither the tale nor the oracle.[51] The rabbis, however, see in this tale the source of the doctrine of human responsibility and free will: "From this you learn that a man is led in the way he desires to go";[52] "If one comes to defile himself, he is given an opening," that is, he is given the opportunity.[53]

BALAAM AND THE ASS (vv. 22–35)

God is angered that Balaam is going to Balak. He interposes a sword-bearing angel on the road. Balaam's ass sees the angel and veers aside. Balaam, who does not see the angel, beats his ass. This happens three times until the ass speaks and rebukes its master. The angel, now visible to Balaam,

standing in the way, with his drawn sword in his hand. The ass swerved from the road and went into the fields; and Balaam beat the ass to turn her back onto the road. [24]The angel of the LORD then stationed himself in a lane between the vineyards, with a fence on either side. [25]The ass, seeing

23 וַתֵּרֶא הָאָתוֹן אֶת־מַלְאַךְ יְהוָה נִצָּב בַּדֶּרֶךְ
וְחַרְבּוֹ שְׁלוּפָה בְּיָדוֹ וַתֵּט הָאָתוֹן מִן־הַדֶּרֶךְ וַתֵּלֶךְ
בַּשָּׂדֶה וַיַּךְ בִּלְעָם אֶת־הָאָתוֹן לְהַטֹּתָהּ הַדָּרֶךְ׃
24 וַיַּעֲמֹד מַלְאַךְ יְהוָה בְּמִשְׁעוֹל הַכְּרָמִים גָּדֵר
מִזֶּה וְגָדֵר מִזֶּה׃ 25 וַתֵּרֶא הָאָתוֹן אֶת־מַלְאַךְ יְהוָה

rebukes him for beating his ass, which saved his life. Balaam, recognizing that his mission is displeasing to God, volunteers to return home. But the angel permits him to continue on condition that he speak only as directed by God.

The inner cohesion of this episode is revealed by its carefully constructed plot, which is built around three scenes in which the same actions reoccur: The angel stands in the way three times and is seen three times by the ass, which turns aside three times and is beaten three times by Balaam. The ass speaks only twice; in the third and climactic instance it is replaced by the angel, who reproves Balaam in its stead.[54] The three scenes are interlocked by the following stylistic and thematic links: (1) The sword of the angel (v. 23) is wishfully in Balaam's hand (v. 24). (2) God's anger at Balaam (v. 22) corresponds with Balaam's anger at his ass (v. 27). (3) As the path continues to narrow, the ass veers first to the field, then to the roadside fence, and finally it comes to a halt. All the while Balaam's anger mounts, and he strikes the ass, first to get it back on the road (v. 23), then because it squeezed Balaam's foot against the wall (v. 25), and finally, when it lay down under Balaam, he beat it with a stick (v. 27), which is a surrogate for a sword (v. 29).[55]

The angel acts as the Lord's agent and never initiates any action on his own (for the seeming exception, see the Comment to v. 35). The Lord Himself intrudes upon the scene twice but in each case only when a miracle is called for: to give the ass speech (v. 28) and Balaam sight (v. 31).[56]

22. ***But God was incensed*** According to tradition, Balaam's acquiescence indicates his eagerness to curse Israel, thereby arousing the anger of God.[57]

God[58]

at his going[59]

as an adversary Later the term *satan* is personified as Satan (see 1 Chron. 21:1). Here it is used attributively, as in 1 Samuel 29:4.

two servants Balak's officials (v. 21) have disappeared. Abraham is accompanied by two servants on a three-day journey (Gen. 22:3), as is Saul on his day trip to En-dor (1 Sam. 28:8). This mode of travel, the master riding and the servant walking, suggests that Balaam was close by (see Excursus 57). The theme of two servants is a literary stereotype: "This is the proper way; that is, that when a man [of eminence] goes out on a journey, two people should attend on him."[60]

23. ***sword*** For the motif of an angel with a sword, see Genesis 3:24, Joshua 5:15, and 1 Chronicles 21:16.

into the fields Implying that the fields had no fences along the road.

Balaam beat the ass "This villain went to curse an entire nation which had not sinned against him, yet he had to strike his ass to prevent it from going into a field";[61] that is, his word is ineffectual even with his ass. Furthermore, as a Mesopotamian diviner, Balaam should have recognized that his animal's bizarre actions may have held a divine portent.[62] For other ironies picked up by the midrash, see Excursus 57.

onto the road Hebrew *ha-derekh*. The definite article can have the force of a preposition.[63]

24. ***a lane*** Hebrew *mishʿol*, the only occurrence of this word in Scripture.[64] Since *shaʿal* means "hollow hand, handful," *mishʿal* may be a hollowed-out furrow serving as a path.[65]

vineyards The scenery is not of the Syrian desert (see Excursus 57).

fence Hebrew *gader*, that is, of heaped stones.

the angel of the LORD, pressed herself against the wall and
squeezed Balaam's foot against the wall; so he beat her
again. 26Once more the angel of the LORD moved forward
and stationed himself on a spot so narrow that there was no
room to swerve right or left. 27When the ass now saw the
angel of the LORD, she lay down under Balaam; and Balaam
was furious and beat the ass with his stick.

28Then the LORD opened the ass's mouth, and she said to
Balaam, "What have I done to you that you have beaten me
these three times?" 29Balaam said to the ass, "You have
made a mockery of me! If I had a sword with me, I'd kill
you." 30The ass said to Balaam, "Look, I am the ass that you
have been riding all along until this day! Have I been in the
habit of doing thus to you?" And he answered, "No."

וַתִּלָּחֵץ אֶל־הַקִּיר וַתִּלְחַץ אֶת־רֶגֶל בִּלְעָם אֶל־
הַקִּיר וַיֹּסֶף לְהַכֹּתָהּ׃ 26 וַיּוֹסֶף מַלְאַךְ־יְהֹוָה עֲבוֹר
וַיַּעֲמֹד בְּמָקוֹם צָר אֲשֶׁר אֵין־דֶּרֶךְ לִנְטוֹת יָמִין
וּשְׂמֹאול׃ 27 וַתֵּרֶא הָאָתוֹן אֶת־מַלְאַךְ יְהֹוָה
וַתִּרְבַּץ תַּחַת בִּלְעָם וַיִּחַר־אַף בִּלְעָם וַיַּךְ אֶת־
הָאָתוֹן בַּמַּקֵּל׃ 28 וַיִּפְתַּח יְהֹוָה אֶת־פִּי הָאָתוֹן
וַתֹּאמֶר לְבִלְעָם מֶה־עָשִׂיתִי לְךָ כִּי הִכִּיתַנִי זֶה
שָׁלֹשׁ רְגָלִים׃ 29 וַיֹּאמֶר בִּלְעָם לָאָתוֹן כִּי
הִתְעַלַּלְתְּ בִּי לוּ יֶשׁ־חֶרֶב בְּיָדִי כִּי עַתָּה הֲרַגְתִּיךְ׃
30 וַתֹּאמֶר הָאָתוֹן אֶל־בִּלְעָם הֲלוֹא אָנֹכִי אֲתֹנְךָ
אֲשֶׁר־רָכַבְתָּ עָלַי מֵעוֹדְךָ עַד־הַיּוֹם הַזֶּה הַהַסְכֵּן
הִסְכַּנְתִּי לַעֲשׂוֹת לְךָ כֹּה וַיֹּאמֶר לֹא׃ 31 וַיְגַל

25. pressed herself[66]

wall Hebrew ***kir***, that is, the surface of the stony fence; see ***kir ḥomah***, "the outer side of the wall" (Josh. 2:15; cf. the Comment to Num. 35:4).

beat her again The first time was for a purpose—to get the ass back on the road. The lack of purpose here serves to indicate that Balaam struck his ass in sheer anger (see v. 27).

26. moved forward Hebrew *ʿavor*. For this usage, see Genesis 33:3.

27. When the ass now saw For the third time, in contrast to Balaam's persistent blindness (see Excursus 57).

with his stick An index of his mounting anger; perhaps previously he struck with his hand or a strap.[67] Again, a lampoon: Balaam is more of a brute than his ass (see Excursus 57).

28. The LORD opened the ass's mouth That is, He gave the ass the power of speech (see Ezekiel 3:27 and 33:22). These words are a satiric play on Balaam's reputed prophetic gifts, for the Lord also uses Balaam's mouth as the vehicle for His message (22:38; 23:5,12,16).

Maimonides, the rationalist, understood the entire scene to be a prophetic vision. Earlier, the rabbis tried to reduce the miraculous element by declaring that the speaking ass was ordained by God on the eve of the first Sabbath[68]—that is, as part of Creation—and therefore did not constitute an interruption of the natural order.

these[69]

times Hebrew ***regalim***. The term occurs only once again outside this section (Exod. 23:14), also with the number three. Possibly, it was only used with three.[70] It is a synonym of ***peʿamim*** (Exod. 34:23); both words originally meant "foot" (Pss. 58:11; 85:14; and Ugar.).

29. made a mockery[71]

If I had a sword "[The Moabite officials] said: This fool [boasts] that he can destroy nations with his words; how can he not destroy his ass except with a sword?"[72] The irony rests in the fact that the sword Balaam seeks is close at hand with the angel, whom he, the seer, cannot see.

30. all along[73]

Have I been in the habit[74] The burlesque continues. Balaam's impetuous rage is answered by the measured and justifiable argument of the ass: "Here was this ass, the most stupid of all beasts, and there was the wisest of all wise men, yet as soon as she opened her mouth he could not stand his ground against her."[75]

³¹Then the LORD uncovered Balaam's eyes, and he saw the angel of the LORD standing in the way, his drawn sword in his hand; thereupon he bowed right down to the ground. ³²The angel of the LORD said to him, "Why have you beaten your ass these three times? It is I who came out as an adversary, for the errand is obnoxious to me. ³³And when the ass saw me, she shied away because of me those three times. If she had not shied away from me, you are the one I should have killed, while sparing her." ³⁴Balaam said to the angel of the LORD, "I erred because I did not know that you were standing in my way. If you still disapprove, I will turn back." ³⁵But the angel of the LORD said to Balaam, "Go with the men. But you must say nothing except what I tell you." So Balaam went on with Balak's dignitaries.

³⁶When Balak heard that Balaam was coming, he went out to meet him at Ir-moab, which is on the Arnon border, at its farthest point. ³⁷Balak said to Balaam, "When I first

יְהוָה֙ אֶת־עֵינֵ֣י בִלְעָ֔ם וַיַּ֞רְא אֶת־מַלְאַ֤ךְ יְהוָה֙ נִצָּ֣ב בַּדֶּ֔רֶךְ וְחַרְבֹּ֥ו שְׁלֻפָ֖ה בְּיָדֹ֑ו וַיִּקֹּ֥ד וַיִּשְׁתַּ֖חוּ לְאַפָּֽיו׃ ³² וַיֹּ֤אמֶר אֵלָיו֙ מַלְאַ֣ךְ יְהוָ֔ה עַל־מָ֗ה הִכִּ֙יתָ֙ אֶת־אֲתֹ֣נְךָ֔ זֶ֖ה שָׁלֹ֣ושׁ רְגָלִ֑ים הִנֵּ֤ה אָנֹכִי֙ יָצָ֣אתִי לְשָׂטָ֔ן כִּֽי־יָרַ֥ט הַדֶּ֖רֶךְ לְנֶגְדִּֽי׃ ³³ וַתִּרְאַ֙נִי֙ הָֽאָתֹ֔ון וַתֵּ֣ט לְפָנַ֔י זֶ֖ה שָׁלֹ֣שׁ רְגָלִ֑ים אוּלַי֙ נָטְתָ֣ה מִפָּנַ֔י כִּ֥י עַתָּ֛ה גַּם־אֹתְכָ֥ה הָרַ֖גְתִּי וְאֹותָ֥הּ הֶחֱיֵֽיתִי׃ ³⁴ וַיֹּ֨אמֶר בִּלְעָ֜ם אֶל־מַלְאַ֤ךְ יְהוָה֙ חָטָ֔אתִי כִּ֚י לֹ֣א יָדַ֔עְתִּי כִּ֥י אַתָּ֛ה נִצָּ֥ב לִקְרָאתִ֖י בַּדָּ֑רֶךְ וְעַתָּ֛ה אִם־רַ֥ע בְּעֵינֶ֖יךָ אָשׁ֥וּבָה לִּֽי׃ ³⁵ וַיֹּ֩אמֶר֩ מַלְאַ֨ךְ יְהוָ֜ה אֶל־בִּלְעָ֗ם לֵ֚ךְ עִם־הָ֣אֲנָשִׁ֔ים וְאֶ֗פֶס אֶת־הַדָּבָ֛ר אֲשֶׁר־אֲדַבֵּ֥ר אֵלֶ֖יךָ אֹתֹ֣ו תְדַבֵּ֑ר וַיֵּ֥לֶךְ בִּלְעָ֖ם עִם־שָׂרֵ֥י בָלָֽק׃ ³⁶ וַיִּשְׁמַ֥ע בָּלָ֖ק כִּ֣י בָ֣א בִלְעָ֑ם וַיֵּצֵ֨א לִקְרָאתֹ֜ו אֶל־עִ֣יר מֹואָ֗ב אֲשֶׁר֙ עַל־גְּב֣וּל אַרְנֹ֔ן אֲשֶׁ֖ר בִּקְצֵ֥ה הַגְּבֽוּל׃ ³⁷ וַיֹּ֨אמֶר בָּלָ֜ק אֶל־בִּלְעָ֗ם הֲלֹא֩ שָׁלֹ֨חַ

---

31. the LORD uncovered Balaam's eyes   The wording is deliberate, a sardonic contradiction of Balaam's claim that his "eyes are opened" to God's revelation (24:4,16). In both the ass episode here and the poetry, Balaam's eyes are opened in the third scene, an indication that the poetry and the prose belong together (see Excursus 56).

The Lord intervenes directly only twice in this story, both times to effect a miracle: to give the ass speech (v. 28) and to give Balaam revelatory sight (v. 31); the rest of the action is delegated to the angel.[76]

32. for the errand is obnoxious to me[77]

33. because of me[78]

those three times   This expression is repeated by the angel (see v. 32) in order to mock Balaam: The dumb ass shied away from me three times but you, the all-wise seer, did not shy away from me even once.[79]

If . . . not[80]

you are the one   Hebrew *gam* can be taken as an adversative particle, to be rendered as "rather"; that is, in contrast to the ass, which would have lived, you would have died—the opposite of what Balaam intended (v. 29). For examples of this usage, see Job 2:10 and 18:5.[81] Alternatively, *gam* can be an emphatic particle, hence, untranslatable (e.g., Gen. 44:10; 1 Kings 14:14).[82]

I should have killed   Rather, "I would have killed."

34. I did not know   In contradiction to Balaam's claim that he "obtains knowledge from the Most High" (24:16).

I will turn back[83]

35.   Balaam's two servants (v. 32) have disappeared, replaced by Balak's dignitaries.[84]

nothing except[85]

what I tell you   The angel, here identified with the "I" of the Lord, thus speaks or acts as the Lord's surrogate. This identification is made clear at the end of a narrative.[86]

sent to invite you, why didn't you come to me? Am I really unable to reward you?" [38]But Balaam said to Balak, "And now that I have come to you, have I the power to speak freely? I can utter only the word that God puts into my mouth."

[39]Balaam went with Balak and they came to Kiriath-huzoth. [40]Balak sacrificed oxen and sheep, and had them served to Balaam and the dignitaries with him. [41]In the morning Balak took Balaam up to Bamoth-baal. From there he could see a portion of the people.

שְׁלַחְתִּי אֵלֶיךָ לִקְרֹא־לָךְ לָמָּה לֹא־הָלַכְתָּ אֵלָי
הַאֻמְנָם לֹא אוּכַל כַּבְּדֶךָ׃ 38 וַיֹּאמֶר בִּלְעָם אֶל־
בָּלָק הִנֵּה־בָאתִי אֵלֶיךָ עַתָּה הֲיָכוֹל אוּכַל דַּבֵּר
מְאוּמָה הַדָּבָר אֲשֶׁר יָשִׂים אֱלֹהִים בְּפִי אֹתוֹ
אֲדַבֵּר׃ רביעי [ששי כשהן מחוברות]
39 וַיֵּלֶךְ בִּלְעָם עִם־בָּלָק וַיָּבֹאוּ קִרְיַת חֻצוֹת׃
40 וַיִּזְבַּח בָּלָק בָּקָר וָצֹאן וַיְשַׁלַּח לְבִלְעָם
וְלַשָּׂרִים אֲשֶׁר אִתּוֹ׃ 41 וַיְהִי בַבֹּקֶר וַיִּקַּח בָּלָק
אֶת־בִּלְעָם וַיַּעֲלֵהוּ בָּמוֹת בָּעַל וַיַּרְא מִשָּׁם קְצֵה
הָעָם׃

THE MEETING OF BALAK AND BALAAM (22:36–23:6)

Here, in the continuation of verse 21, Balak greets Balaam at the border of his territory and upbraids him for not returning with the first delegation. Balaam responds, as he did to the delegation, that he will only do the Lord's bidding. Balak arranges a grand feast for Balaam and his company and on the morrow takes Balaam to a height where he might see a portion of Israel's encampment. Balaam first instructs Balak to try to dispose the Lord to their favor through a specified sacrificial ritual; he thereupon sets out in search of omens to interpret for Balak. Instead, the Lord dictates to Balaam a specific message of blessing.

36. Ir-moab Probably identical with Ar of Moab (21:15,28) on the southern shore of the upper Arnon. Alternatively, it is identified with El Medeiyim on the Wadi es Sfei, a tributary of the Arnon in the northeast.

Arnon border That is, the northern border of Moab as noted in 21:26, which presumes that Balaam came from the north, a fact that fits an Aramean provenience for Balaam. It also agrees with chapter 21 that the Arnon was Moab's northern border at the time of the Israelite incursion.

at its farthest point Balak paid Balaam the maximum respect by meeting him at the point at which Balaam crossed into Moabite territory (see Gen. 29:13; 46:29; Exod. 18:7).

37. When I first sent Hebrew *shaloaḥ shalaḥti*. The root *sh-l-ḥ* is repeated for the sake of emphasis: Balak stresses his extraordinary exertions to send a proper delegation to Balaam.

38. Balaam dismisses Balak's question, his answer implying: Never mind your question; I am here. For *ʿattah* introducing the main point, see the Comment to verse 6.

freely Literally, "anything."

God Hebrew *ʾelohim*. An exception to the rule that Balaam refers to God only by the Tetragrammaton.

39. Kiriath-huzoth Unidentified; the site is probably close to Bamoth-baal in verse 41.

40. Sacrificed Hebrew *va-yizbaḥ*; that is, Balak sacrificed a ***zevaḥ shelamim***, a well-being offering, the meat of which is eaten by the worshiper and his guests, as is clear from Exodus 18:12 and 1 Samuel 9:23–24.

41. In the morning Sacrificial ritual implies entering into a state of sanctification, a preliminary requirement for a divine encounter.

Bamoth-baal The Septuagint reads the singular ***bamat baʿal***, "the cultic platform of Baal," probably a shrine[87] (see the Comment to 21:20)

he could see a portion of the people The object must be within sight for a curse against it to be effective. The power of the "evil eye" is captured by Democritus: "From the eyes issue images which are neither without sensation nor without volition, and are filled with the wickedness and malice of those from whom they proceed: imprinting themselves firmly upon the person to be

23 Balaam said to Balak, "Build me seven altars here and have seven bulls and seven rams ready here for me." [2]Balak did as Balaam directed; and Balak and Balaam offered up a bull and a ram on each altar. [3]Then Balaam said to Balak, "Stay here beside your offerings while I am gone. Perhaps the LORD will grant me a manifestation, and whatever He reveals to me I will tell you." And he went off alone.

כ״ג וַיֹּאמֶר בִּלְעָם אֶל־בָּלָק בְּנֵה־לִי בָזֶה
שִׁבְעָה מִזְבְּחֹת וְהָכֵן לִי בָּזֶה שִׁבְעָה פָרִים
וְשִׁבְעָה אֵילִים׃ 2 וַיַּעַשׂ בָּלָק כַּאֲשֶׁר דִּבֶּר בִּלְעָם
וַיַּעַל בָּלָק וּבִלְעָם פָּר וָאַיִל בַּמִּזְבֵּחַ׃ 3 וַיֹּאמֶר
בִּלְעָם לְבָלָק הִתְיַצֵּב עַל־עֹלָתֶךָ וְאֵלְכָה אוּלַי
יִקָּרֵה יְהוָה לִקְרָאתִי וּדְבַר מַה־יַּרְאֵנִי וְהִגַּדְתִּי לָךְ
וַיֵּלֶךְ שֶׁפִי׃ 4 וַיִּקָּר אֱלֹהִים אֶל־בִּלְעָם וַיֹּאמֶר אֵלָיו

enchanted, they become part of him, and disturb and injure both his body and mind."[88] Balak, however, fears that the sight of too many Israelites may nullify and even reverse the curse (see the Comment to 23:13); hence, he allows Balaam to see only a portion of the Israelites.[89]

CHAPTER 23

1. ***seven altars . . . seven bulls and seven rams*** Ibn Ezra points to the frequency of the number seven in the cultic calendar: the seventh day (Sabbath), the seventh week (Shavuot), the seventh month (Tishrei), the seventh year (the Sabbatical for land and remission of debts), seven burnt offering lambs (on festivals, twice seven on Sukkot), seven sprinklings (in the Temple on Yom Kippur and for the purification of the leper). He also points to the sacrificial requirement of seven bulls and seven rams for Job's friends (Job 42:8) and the astrological significance of seven. The magical use of seven is attested in the Bible: leprous Naaman bathes seven times in the Jordan (2 Kings 5:10,14); Elijah orders his servant to scan the skies seven times for signs of rain (1 Kings 18:43); Joshua's army circuits Jericho seven times on the seventh day (Josh. 6:4,10). In the Talmud, a medical prescription requires seven twigs from seven trees, seven nails from seven bridges, and so on.[1]

The use of multiple altars for a single ritual is unattested anywhere else in Scripture. Hence it must derive from a pagan practice, each altar most likely being dedicated to a different deity, for example: "At dawn, in the presence of Ea, Shamash, and Marduk, you shall erect seven altars, you shall set seven censers of cypress, you shall pour the blood of seven sheep."[2]

Midrashic tradition attributes the seven altars to the need to recall the altars erected previously by seven righteous men: Adam, Abel, Noah, Abraham, Isaac, Jacob, and Moses.[3] *Sefer ha-Mivḥar*, in seeking an astrological explanation (i.e., seven altars for the seven planets), is close to the mark—it was part of Balaam's divinatory technique.

have . . . ready Hebrew *hakhen*, that is, prepare for sacrifice (see Zeph. 1:7).

2. ***a bull and a ram*** These are the most expensive (hence, efficacious) animals in the sacrificial system (cf. Job 42:7; 1 Chron. 15:26; 2 Chron. 29:21).

on each altar Hebrew *ba-mizbeaḥ*. The definite article can be distributive.[4]

3. ***Stay*** They worked in tandem: Balak had to stand at his sacrifice while the diviner sought his omens (see also vv. 6,15,17). Its equivalent in Mesopotamia is the *āpilu* offering his prophecy "while (the king's representative) was standing at the sacrificial (omen) entrails."[5] In the Greek world, Xenophon claims that he was able to check on Silanus, the diviner, because "he was always present at the sacrifices."[6]

In Judaism too, the people were present at all the public sacrifices by means of their proxy, known as the *ma'amad* (from *'amad*, "stand"), which the Qumran sect refers to by the verb used here, *hityatstsev*.[7] And the Mishnah asks: "How can a man's sacrifice be offered while he does not stand by it?"[8]

here Not in the text, but see the Comment to verse 15.

your offerings Hebrew *'olatekha*, literally "your burnt offering," the specific sacrifice required. In ancient Mesopotamia, the offerer prayed by his offerings while the diviner did his work.[9] However, Mesopotamia did not know the *'olah*, the burnt offering.[10] In that culture, food was laid out for the god on a sacrificial table, but it was not consumed by fire.[11] Thus, Balaam was not a Mesopotamian or he adapted his practice to that of the cult of Moab (see Excursus 58).

4God manifested Himself to Balaam, who said to Him, "I have set up the seven altars and offered up a bull and a ram on each altar." 5And the LORD put a word in Balaam's mouth and said, "Return to Balak and speak thus."

6So he returned to him and found him standing beside his offerings, and all the Moabite dignitaries with him. 7He took up his theme, and said:

From Aram has Balak brought me,
Moab's king from the hills of the East:
Come, curse me Jacob,
Come, tell Israel's doom!

אֶת־שִׁבְעַת הַמִּזְבְּחֹת עָרַכְתִּי וָאַעַל פָּר וָאַיִל
בַּמִּזְבֵּחַ׃ 5 וַיָּשֶׂם יְהוָה דָּבָר בְּפִי בִלְעָם וַיֹּאמֶר
שׁוּב אֶל־בָּלָק וְכֹה תְדַבֵּר׃ 6 וַיָּשָׁב אֵלָיו וְהִנֵּה
נִצָּב עַל־עֹלָתוֹ הוּא וְכָל־שָׂרֵי מוֹאָב׃ 7 וַיִּשָּׂא
מְשָׁלוֹ וַיֹּאמַר

מִן־אֲרָם יַנְחֵנִי בָלָק
מֶלֶךְ־מוֹאָב מֵהַרְרֵי־קֶדֶם
לְכָה אָרָה־לִּי יַעֲקֹב
וּלְכָה זֹעֲמָה יִשְׂרָאֵל׃

while I am gone Hebrew *ve-'elekha*, which perhaps should be translated "while I go there," adding *koh* (see v. 15), which may have accidentally fallen out because the consonants *kh* appear twice in succession (haplography).

grant me a manifestation Literally, "may chance to appear [to me]."[12]

reveals to me Literally, "shows me," that is, via omens.

I will tell you That is, interpret for you.

alone If this rendering of Hebrew *shefi* (occurring only once again, perhaps, in Job 33:21) is correct,[13] then either Balaam withdraws to practice his divination in private or the God of Israel does not wish to reveal Himself in the presence of heathens, as we find in Exodus 9:29,33, regarding Pharaoh's court.[14] This word has also been rendered "bare height," taken as the singular of *shefayim*, used in Isaiah 41:18 and Jeremiah 3:2,21.[15] But if that were correct, then the verb *va-ya'al*, "ascend," would be expected, not *va-yelekh*, "go."

4. *manifested Himself* Literally, "chanced to appear"[16] (v. 3). According to the midrash, this characterizes the difference between Balaam and Moses: "Two men once knocked on a magistrate's door requesting alms, the one a friend, the other a leprous beggar. The magistrate said, 'Let my friend enter, but I shall bring the beggar's alms to the door that he may not enter and pollute my palace.' God called Moses to Him in His Tabernacle, whereas He betook Himself to Balaam."[17]

offered up The subject must be Balak, not Balaam. Hence, the possibility must be considered that verse 4b belongs to the speech of Balak and should follow verse 2. Balaam is informed that his instructions have been followed.[18] In this case, verse 4a would continue with 5a, just as in verse 16. Two other factors also support this. Balaam implies that God has required the altars,[19] but no such request is recorded; and Balaam addresses God first and not, as one would expect, in response.

5. *the LORD put a word in Balaam's mouth* That is, the Lord told him the exact words.[20] This expression indicates a divine manifestation to a prophet, as occurs with Aaron in Exodus 4:15; with Israel, a prophet-nation, in Isaiah 49:2, 58:16, and 59:21; and with Jeremiah in Jeremiah 1:9 (and so with every prophet, as stated in Deut. 18:18). However, Balaam's revelation here and a second time in verse 16 stand in contrast to the third occasion: Then, he is overwhelmed by the divine spirit (24:2).

LORD If verse 5a follows immediately after verse 4a, as proposed above, then the subject here is self-understood, and "Lord" becomes unnecessary. This would, then, eliminate an obstacle to the theory that Lord, YHVH, was used only in Balaam's speech.[21]

6. *offerings* Hebrew *'olato*, literally "burnt offering," the specific sacrifice required by the ritual (v. 3). The singular stands for the collective as in verse 17.

8 How can I damn whom God has not damned,
How doom when the LORD has not doomed?
9 As I see them from the mountain tops,
Gaze on them from the heights,
There is a people that dwells apart,
Not reckoned among the nations,

8 מָה אֶקֹּב לֹא קַבֹּה אֵל
וּמָה אֶזְעֹם לֹא זָעַם יְהוָה׃
9 כִּי־מֵרֹאשׁ צֻרִים אֶרְאֶנּוּ
וּמִגְּבָעוֹת אֲשׁוּרֶנּוּ
הֶן־עָם לְבָדָד יִשְׁכֹּן
וּבַגּוֹיִם לֹא יִתְחַשָּׁב׃

BALAAM'S FIRST ORACLE (vv. 7–10)

The oracle recounts the events: Balak brought Balaam from Aram to curse Israel, but when Balaam spied Israel from the heights he realized from their strength and numbers that God had no intention of cursing them. Consequently he, Balaam, would be happy to share their fate. The blessing, as Balak formulates it in verse 11, is subdued. Israel's present state is described. Their potential is obvious (v. 10), and the theme is expanded upon in the following oracles. The poetry is inextricably linked to the preceding narrative by the common themes: Balak and Aram (22:5); curse (22:6,17); view of Israel from heights (22:41); Israel's teeming numbers (22:5). (See Excursus 56.)

7. took up[22]

his theme Hebrew ***meshalo*** (see the Comment to 21:27). There is no precise rendering for this term, which applies to many kinds of discourses: apothegms (1 Sam. 10:12; 24:14); proverbs (Ezek. 12:22; 18:23; cf. Deut. 28:37); lamentations (Isa. 14:4; Mic. 2:4; see the Comment to 21:27). It is, however, never used for the discourses of Israel's prophets, a clear indication that the "Book of Balaam" never intended Balaam's oracle to be reckoned as prophecy.

Aram This may possibly fit the Mesopotamian provenience of Balaam (see the Comment to 22:5; Hos. 12:13). Aram occurs as a place-name as early as the twenty-third century B.C.E. in an inscription of Naram-Sin of Akkad, referring to a region on the upper Euphrates. The people called Arameans are not attested until the end of the twelfth century.[23]

hills of the East Hebrew ***harerei kedem***. Rather, "hills of Qedem." From the Egyptian story of Sinuhe,[24] Qedem seems to designate a specific territory in the Syrian desert (east of the Phoenician coast). This accords with its designation here as being synonymous with Aram. Furthermore, an Egyptian geographical list contains the name ***qdm*** along with other place-names in the area of Syro-Palestine.[25] Genesis 29:1 actually identifies Qedem as the region from which the patriarchs stemmed. Elsewhere in Scripture, Qedem applies to the entire desert fringe, beginning in the north at the middle Euphrates and running south to the eastern border of present-day Syria and Jordan (cf. Gen. 25:5–6; 29:1; Judg. 6:3,33). However, the second term "hills" is hardly appropriate since the specific territory of northern Aram/Qedem is not conspicuously mountainous.[26]

Jacob The poet chooses the name ***Ya'akov*** deliberately: The syllable ***kov*** appears three times in verses 7b, 8a to balance the thrice-repeated verb ***za'am***.[27] The word pair "Jacob/Israel" appears more than fifty times in the Bible and six times in the Balaam poems; it even appears once in a verbal form (Hos. 12:4).[28]

tell Israel's doom The Hebrew verb ***za'am*** means "be indignant" (as in Ps. 7:12; Zech. 1:12; Dan. 11:30) and by extension "curse" (as in Prov. 24:24).

8. God Hebrew ***'el***, used again in 23:19 and 24:4,8,16,23—the name of the God of the patriarchs (e.g., Gen. 46:1–2)—was worshiped by Canaanite workers in the mines of Serabit el Khadem in the Sinai Peninsula in the fifteenth century B.C.E. Inscriptions there contain the name "the Eternal El" (see Gen. 21:33).

mountain tops[29]

9. heights Literally, "hills." The pair "mountains/hills" includes all heights, just as the pair "day/night" (e.g., Job 3:3) embraces all time and "silver/gold" (e.g., Job 3:15) includes everything of value.[30]

10Who can count the dust of Jacob,
Number the dust-cloud of Israel?
May I die the death of the upright,
May my fate be like theirs!

11Then Balak said to Balaam, "What have you done to
me? Here I brought you to damn my enemies, and instead
you have blessed them!" 12He replied, "I can only repeat

10 מִי מָנָה עֲפַר יַעֲקֹב
וּמִסְפָּר אֶת־רֹבַע יִשְׂרָאֵל
תָּמֹת נַפְשִׁי מוֹת יְשָׁרִים
וּתְהִי אַחֲרִיתִי כָּמֹהוּ׃
11 וַיֹּאמֶר בָּלָק אֶל־בִּלְעָם מֶה עָשִׂיתָ לִי לָקֹב
אֹיְבַי לְקַחְתִּיךָ וְהִנֵּה בֵּרַכְתָּ בָרֵךְ׃ 12 וַיַּעַן וַיֹּאמַר
הֲלֹא אֵת אֲשֶׁר יָשִׂים יְהוָה בְּפִי אֹתוֹ אֶשְׁמֹר

apart That is, apart in strength and security. This figure of speech is used of God in Deuteronomy 32:12 and of Israel in Deuteronomy 33:28, Jeremiah 49:31, and Psalms 4:9. All are synonyms of *betaḥ*, "security."

reckoned Israel will not share the fate of other nations.[31] Other ancient versions suggest that the laws of Israel differ from those of other nations.[32]

nations Hebrew *goyim*, a political designation, in distinction to *ʿam*, "people," an ethnic designation. However, the usually attested word pair "people/nations" (see Deut. 33:21; 2 Sam. 22:44; Isa. 11:10) is here altered in meaning so that "nations" refers to non-Israelites and "people," the more intimate term, refers to Israel.[33]

10. ***count the dust*** A reflection of the patriarchal promise of Genesis 13:16; the latter contains the same expression, "count the dust," which it relates to "seed." It has also been suggested that this expression bears magical significance. Mesopotamian sorcerers would hex the dust collected from the victim's feet,[34] leaving the sense here as "who can bewitch Israel?"[35] However, the synonymous "dust-cloud" indicates that Israel's military strength is being lauded.

Number[36]

the dust-cloud Hebrew *ʾet rovaʿ*. Since *ʾet* does not occur in ancient poetry, read *turbaʿat*[37] or preferably, *turbaʿ*,[38] meaning "dust-cloud."[39] The image here is of the dust raised by Israel's marching hosts, an image found in the Bible in Ezekiel 26:10 and Nahum 1:4 and also in Akkadian literature.[40] Hebrew *rovaʿ* is otherwise rendered as "one-fourth";[41] that is, who can number even a small fraction of the Israelites (see Gen. 13:16). Saadia and Rashi render "seed," from the root *r-b-ʿ*, "copulate" (see Lev. 18:23), and Ramban suggests "encampment" from the root *r-b-ts*.[42]

my fate Hebrew *ʾaḥariti*, paralleled by "death." Balaam's wish illustrates the blessing that every nation and person will desire to receive from God—to share the fate of Israel. This is expressed in Genesis 12:3, 22:18, and 28:14.

BALAK'S REACTION AND SECOND ATTEMPT (vv. 11–17)

Balak is shocked and hurt by Balaam's praise of Israel, but Balaam disclaims any responsibility for his words since he was only the mouthpiece of the Lord. Balak then takes him to another site on the assumption (1) that it will provoke a change of God's mind, and (2) as a further precaution, that it will allow Balaam to work his curse on an even smaller portion of Israel. The same sacrificial and omen-taking procedure is followed.

11. ***I brought you*** Rather, "I summoned you," as in 23:20, 24:10, and Judges 11:5.

you have blessed them Hebrew *berakhta barekh*. Rather, "you have done nothing but bless," the force of the infinitive absolute.[43] Ostensibly there is no blessing in Balaam's first oracle, only praise. But the blessing resides in Israel's potential, and it will be articulated in the following oracles (see Excursus 56).

12. ***repeat faithfully*** Literally, "be punctilious to speak."

faithfully what the LORD puts in my mouth." [13]Then Balak said to him, "Come with me to another place from which you can see them—you will see only a portion of them; you will not see all of them—and damn them for me from there." [14]With that, he took him to Sedehzophim, on the summit of Pisgah. He built seven altars and offered a bull and a ram on each altar. [15]And [Balaam] said to Balak, "Stay here beside your offerings, while I seek a manifestation yonder."

[16]The LORD manifested Himself to Balaam and put a word in his mouth, saying, "Return to Balak and speak thus." [17]He went to him and found him standing beside his offerings, and the Moabite dignitaries with him. Balak asked him, "What did the LORD say?" [18]And he took up his theme, and said:

לְדַבֵּר: חמישי 13 וַיֹּאמֶר אֵלָיו בָּלָק לְךָ־נָּא
אִתִּי אֶל־מָקוֹם אַחֵר אֲשֶׁר תִּרְאֶנּוּ מִשָּׁם אֶפֶס
קָצֵהוּ תִרְאֶה וְכֻלּוֹ לֹא תִרְאֶה וְקָבְנוֹ־לִי מִשָּׁם:
14 וַיִּקָּחֵהוּ שְׂדֵה צֹפִים אֶל־רֹאשׁ הַפִּסְגָּה וַיִּבֶן
שִׁבְעָה מִזְבְּחֹת וַיַּעַל פָּר וָאַיִל בַּמִּזְבֵּחַ: 15 וַיֹּאמֶר
אֶל־בָּלָק הִתְיַצֵּב כֹּה עַל־עֹלָתֶךָ וְאָנֹכִי אִקָּרֶה כֹּה:
16 וַיִּקָּר יְהוָה אֶל־בִּלְעָם וַיָּשֶׂם דָּבָר בְּפִיו וַיֹּאמֶר
שׁוּב אֶל־בָּלָק וְכֹה תְדַבֵּר: 17 וַיָּבֹא אֵלָיו וְהִנּוֹ
נִצָּב עַל־עֹלָתוֹ וְשָׂרֵי מוֹאָב אִתּוֹ וַיֹּאמֶר לוֹ בָּלָק
מַה־דִּבֶּר יְהוָה: 18 וַיִּשָּׂא מְשָׁלוֹ וַיֹּאמַר

v. 13. חסר ה׳

13. another place Balaam will continue to try the same oracular procedure to effect a favorable omen (see the Comment to 22:19). This time, however, it will be at another place, on the principle "change of place means change of luck."[44]

only a portion Hebrew *'efes katsehu*, literally "the end of its edge." For *'efes* meaning "end," see the Comment to 22:35. The sense then is that Balak was showing Balaam an even smaller segment of the Israelite camp than before[45] out of fear that the sight of too many Israelites would once again turn his curse into a blessing.

14. Sedeh-zophim Literally, "mountain of the watchmen," that is,[46] "lookout post" for astronomical observation or for observing the flight of birds (see Excursus 59). The Phoenicans called the astrologer by the same root, *tsofe shamem*, "watcher of the skies."[47]

Pisgah See the Comment to 21:20.

He That is, Balak (see the Comment to vv. 3,15).

15. here . . . yonder Hebrew *koh . . . koh*. For this idiom, see 11:31, Exodus 2:12, and Genesis 22:5 (*poh . . . koh*).

while I seek a manifestation Literally, "that I may be encountered" by God (see the Comment to v. 3).[48] The technique of manifestation was well understood by the Jewish Hellenist Philo: "(Balak) sent him (Balaam) away to seek good omens through birds or voices."[49]

16. LORD Perhaps "God" (*'elohim*) should be read (with nine manuscripts and the Septuagint) in accordance with the principle that the narrative uses the name "God" exclusively (see the introductory Comment to 22:22–35).

manifested Himself Hebrew *va-yikkar*, a Nifal reflexive. Alternatively, the Nifal is used to stress the element of chance; that is, Balaam could not coerce the Lord to appear, but the Lord "allowed Himself to be encountered" (see the Comment to v. 3).

put a word in his mouth That this phrase is stressed in connection with the first two oracles (22:38; 23:5,12,16) contrasts conspicuously with its total absence in connection with the last two oracles (23:25–24:25), when Balaam is visited by God's spirit (24:2).

17. "What did the LORD say?" This is the first time Balak recognizes that Israel's God and He alone determines Israel's fate (see the Comments to 23:27; 24:11).

Up, Balak, attend,
Give ear unto me, son of Zippor!
19 God is not man to be capricious,
Or mortal to change His mind.
Would He speak and not act,
Promise and not fulfill?
20 My message was to bless:
When He blesses, I cannot reverse it.
21 No harm is in sight for Jacob,
No woe in view for Israel.
The LORD their God is with them,
And their King's acclaim in their midst.

קוּם בָּלָק וּשְׁמָע
הַאֲזִינָה עָדַי בְּנוֹ צִפֹּר׃
19 לֹא אִישׁ אֵל וִיכַזֵּב
וּבֶן־אָדָם וְיִתְנֶחָם
הַהוּא אָמַר וְלֹא יַעֲשֶׂה
וְדִבֶּר וְלֹא יְקִימֶנָּה׃
20 הִנֵּה בָרֵךְ לָקָחְתִּי
וּבֵרֵךְ וְלֹא אֲשִׁיבֶנָּה׃
21 לֹא־הִבִּיט אָוֶן בְּיַעֲקֹב
וְלֹא־רָאָה עָמָל בְּיִשְׂרָאֵל
יְהוָה אֱלֹהָיו עִמּוֹ
וּתְרוּעַת מֶלֶךְ בּוֹ׃

THE SECOND ORACLE (vv. 18–24)

By changing the venue of the sacrificial ritual, Balak had hoped to change God's disposition. In answer, God—through Balaam—instructs Balak that He is not capricious: He does not alter His purpose. God not only intends to bless Israel but reveals His intentions through prophecy, thus dispensing with the need to pry loose divine secrets by divination. With the Lord as King, Israel is invincible.

18. Up Hebrew ***kum***, that is, listen, attention! (see 22:20).[50]

Balak The fact that Balak's name appears in the poetry is further evidence that the prose and poetry are thoroughly integrated.

unto me Hebrew ***'adai***.[51]

son of[52]

19. man Hebrew ***ben 'adam***, literally "son of man." ***Ben***, "son of," also denotes a member of a class, as in ***benei yisra'el***, "Israelites," or ***ben navi'***, "prophet's disciple" (Amos 7:14).[53]

be capricious Hebrew ***vi-yekhazzev***. The usual meaning of this verb is "lie, deceive" (Ps. 78:36), but it also describes a failing spring, in Isaiah 58:11, and an unfulfilled oracle, in Habakkuk 2:3.

change His mind[54] The constancy of God's intention and action contrasts with the gods' caprice, which can be appealed to by man. This is illustrated by a Mesopotamian incantation: "the evil of the ***induḫallatu***-lizard which fell upon me, the portent of the evil which I saw—Ea, Shamash and Marduk turn it to a portent of good, an oracle of good for me."[55] In 1 Samuel 15:29,35, one finds the notion that God's standards are not capricious as are those of man—but not that He is not capable of changing His mind. For example, He may change His mind to punish man as a result of prophetic intercession (Exod. 32:9–14) or man's repentance (Jon. 3:10).[56]

speak . . . Promise God's blessing is implied; see verse 20.

fulfill[57]

20. My message was[58]

When He blesses[59]

reverse it Hebrew ***'ashivennah***. For this meaning, see Isaiah 43:13 and Amos 1:3,6.

21. harm . . . woe Hebrew ***'aven . . . 'amal***. For this connotation of both nouns, see Habakkuk 1:3 and Psalms 90:10. And although inapplicable here, they can also connote moral evil, iniquity, and are so explained in the tradition.[60]

22God who freed them from Egypt
Is for them like the horns of the wild ox.
23Lo, there is no augury in Jacob,
No divining in Israel:
Jacob is told at once,
Yea Israel, what God has planned.
24Lo, a people that rises like a lion,
Leaps up like the king of beasts,
Rests not till it has feasted on prey
And drunk the blood of the slain.

22 אֵל מוֹצִיאָם מִמִּצְרָיִם
כְּתוֹעֲפֹת רְאֵם לוֹ׃
23 כִּי לֹא־נַחַשׁ בְּיַעֲקֹב
וְלֹא־קֶסֶם בְּיִשְׂרָאֵל
כָּעֵת יֵאָמֵר לְיַעֲקֹב
וּלְיִשְׂרָאֵל מַה־פָּעַל אֵל׃
24 הֶן־עָם כְּלָבִיא יָקוּם
וְכַאֲרִי יִתְנַשָּׂא
לֹא יִשְׁכַּב עַד־יֹאכַל טֶרֶף
וְדַם־חֲלָלִים יִשְׁתֶּה׃

is in sight . . . in view[61]

their King's[62]

acclaim Hebrew *teru'ah* is the military alarm sounded by the trumpet (10:5–6) and the shofar (Amos 2:2). But it is also used as a shout of joy in 1 Samuel 4:5–6 and, with particular relevance to this passage, for the acclamation of God as king of Israel by voice, song, and shofar in Psalms 47 and 98:6. It should be understood as an objective genitive, that is, "(Israel's) acclaim of their king." Saadia and Rashi, however, would derive it from the root *r-'-h*, "be friendly" (Judg. 15:6; 2 Sam. 15:37), leading to the rendering "they have their King's friendship."[63]

22. freed them[64] The Hebrew word ***motsi'am*** represents the Exodus as still in progress,[65] in contrast to Balak's claim that "a people *came* out of Egypt" (22:5);[66] it emphasizes that the Lord is the true source of their freedom. Here Balaam subtly corrects Balak's assertion that Israel was "a people come out of Egypt" (22:5), as if it came out without divine help.[67]

horns Hebrew *to'afot*. The meaning of this word is obscure. In Psalms 95:4 it refers to the tops of the mountains. Are the horns of the wild ox its peaks? Elsewhere—Deuteronomy 33:17, Psalms 22:22 and 92:11—the wild ox is celebrated for its horns.[68]

wild ox Hebrew *re'em*; Akkadian *rimu*. The metaphor can refer either to God[69] or to Israel. However, since the subject of the entire oracle is the blessedness of Israel, it probably refers to Israel's divinely endowed power (see Ps. 92:11), in which case the line should be rendered: "They are like the horns of the wild ox" (so too 24:8).[70] King Hammurabi of Babylon proclaims himself as "the fiery wild ox who gores the foe." In the ancient Near East, gods were depicted with horns or wearing horned crowns. On a bas-relief from Ugarit, Baal is pictured wearing the horns of a wild ox.[71]

23. augury Hebrew *naḥash*. This refers to observing omens, for example, the flight of birds (so the Septuagint) or the play of light in water as in Genesis 44:5,15 (see Excursus 59).

in Jacob . . . in Israel[72]

divining Hebrew *kesem*. A synonym of *naḥash*, "augury"; but in Scripture it is attested mainly as the casting of lots—for example, with arrows, as in Ezekiel 21:2b. Here is a tacit admission that magic works but that Israel has no need for it.

planned Hebrew *pa'al*. For this meaning, see Isaiah 5:12. This is the central point of the entire "Book of Balaam": Because God has provided Israel with prophets, it has no need to resort to magical arts to determine His will. This point is expanded in Deuteronomy 18:8–15. The identical idiom occurs in the Deir 'Alla Balaam inscription 1.5 (Excursus 60).

24. like a lion This simile referring to Israel occurs frequently, as in Genesis 49:9, Deuteronomy 33:20, and Micah 5:7.

25Thereupon Balak said to Balaam, "Don't curse them
and don't bless them!" 26In reply, Balaam said to Balak,
"But I told you: Whatever the LORD says, that I must do."
27Then Balak said to Balaam, "Come now, I will take you to
another place. Perhaps God will deem it right that you
damn them for me there." 28Balak took Balaam to the peak
of Peor, which overlooks the wasteland. 29Balaam said to

25 וַיֹּאמֶר בָּלָק אֶל־בִּלְעָם גַּם־קֹב לֹא תִקֳּבֶנּוּ גַּם־
בָּרֵךְ לֹא תְבָרְכֶנּוּ׃ 26 וַיַּעַן בִּלְעָם וַיֹּאמֶר אֶל־
בָּלָק הֲלֹא דִּבַּרְתִּי אֵלֶיךָ לֵאמֹר כֹּל אֲשֶׁר־יְדַבֵּר
יְהוָה אֹתוֹ אֶעֱשֶׂה׃ ששי [שביעי כשהן
מחוברות] 27 וַיֹּאמֶר בָּלָק אֶל־בִּלְעָם לְכָה־נָּא
אֶקָּחֲךָ אֶל־מָקוֹם אַחֵר אוּלַי יִישַׁר בְּעֵינֵי הָאֱלֹהִים
וְקַבֹּתוֹ לִי מִשָּׁם׃ 28 וַיִּקַּח בָּלָק אֶת־בִּלְעָם רֹאשׁ
הַפְּעוֹר הַנִּשְׁקָף עַל־פְּנֵי הַיְשִׁימֹן׃ 29 וַיֹּאמֶר בִּלְעָם

THE THIRD ORACLE (23:25–24:9)

Balak is very upset by Balaam's second oracle, and he blurts out that Balaam—if he cannot curse—should refrain from blessing. Balaam again responds that he is only doing God's bidding. Again at a new height, Balak prepares for a third trial of the ritual and divination. But this time Balaam does not even look for omens. Realizing that the Lord wants him to bless Israel, he moves forward without fear so that he can view the entire Israelite encampment.

*25. **Don't curse . . . don't bless*** This is not a dismissal of Balaam. The negative *lo'* can have the force of *'al*; that is, better don't curse them and (thereby) don't bless them.[73]

*27. **Perhaps God will deem it right that you damn them*** A submissive, almost plaintive tone, acknowledging the power of God. Compare it with Balak's earlier order in verse 13: "Damn them." The brusque imperative has changed to an uncertain imploration. The transformation in Balak is now clear: He must reckon with the power of Israel's God (see the Comment to v. 17).

will deem it right Literally, "be straight in the eyes of," that is, be to his liking (Judg. 14:17; 1 Sam. 18:20,26).

*28. **Peor*** In 21:20, Pisgah replaces Peor. It is probably the name of one of the peaks in the Abarim range (21:11) that overlooks Israel's encampment. The site is as yet unidentified. It contains a sanctuary dedicated to the god Baal (Num. 25:3; Hos. 9:10) and is the subject of chapter 25. Targum Neofiti reads here "idols of Peor" with this juxtaposition in mind.

wasteland Hebrew *yeshimon* (see the Comment to 21:20), equivalent to *ha-midbar*, "the wilderness" (24:1).

CHAPTER 24

*1. **pleased***[1]

the LORD As in the remainder of the narrative (24:11,13), although previously in the narrative *Elohim*, "God," had predominated (see chap. 22, n. 56). Perhaps the change reflects a subtle indication by the author that henceforth Balaam will receive direct revelation from Israel's personal God, the Lord.

to bless Israel As he had learned from God in his previous oracle (23:20), again confirming the tight links between the prose and poetry.

as on previous occasions[2]

in search of omens Balaam has learned from God in the previous oracle (23:23) that His will can be ascertained directly without resort to omens—again, a linkage between the prose and the poetry. Here the purpose of having separated himself from Balak on the previous two occasions is clarified: While Balak attended to the sacrifices, Balaam went off by himself to search for portents of the future. Perhaps, for example, he would render in poetic form his observation of the flight of birds or of clouds, while fixing his gaze on a portion of the Israelite camp (see Excursus 59).

turned his face Rather, "he set out," in consonance with the preceding Hebrew verb *halakh*, "go" (see Gen. 31:21; 2 Kings 12:18).[3]

Balak, "Build me here seven altars, and have seven bulls and seven rams ready for me here." 30Balak did as Balaam said: he offered up a bull and a ram on each altar.

אֶל־בָּלָק בְּנֵה־לִי בָזֶה שִׁבְעָה מִזְבְּחֹת וְהָכֵן לִי
בָּזֶה שִׁבְעָה פָרִים וְשִׁבְעָה אֵילִים׃ 30 וַיַּעַשׂ בָּלָק
כַּאֲשֶׁר אָמַר בִּלְעָם וַיַּעַל פַּר וָאַיִל בַּמִּזְבֵּחַ׃

24 Now Balaam, seeing that it pleased the LORD to bless Israel, did not, as on previous occasions, go in search of omens, but turned his face toward the wilderness. 2As Balaam looked up and saw Israel encamped tribe by tribe, the spirit of God came upon him. 3Taking up his theme, he said:

כ״ד וַיַּרְא בִּלְעָם כִּי טוֹב בְּעֵינֵי יְהוָה לְבָרֵךְ
אֶת־יִשְׂרָאֵל וְלֹא־הָלַךְ כְּפַעַם־בְּפַעַם לִקְרַאת
נְחָשִׁים וַיָּשֶׁת אֶל־הַמִּדְבָּר פָּנָיו׃ 2 וַיִּשָּׂא בִלְעָם
אֶת־עֵינָיו וַיַּרְא אֶת־יִשְׂרָאֵל שֹׁכֵן לִשְׁבָטָיו וַתְּהִי
עָלָיו רוּחַ אֱלֹהִים׃ 3 וַיִּשָּׂא מְשָׁלוֹ וַיֹּאמַר

toward the wilderness Hebrew *'el ha-midbar*, synonymous with *yeshimon* (23:28) and the steppes of Moab (22:1), where Israel was encamped (v. 2). Note also that Beth-jeshimoth (33:49) is in the Jordan plain. The meaning here is clear: Rather than timorously catching a glimpse of the edge of the Israelite camp, Balaam now boldly steps forward so that he can see all of Israel.

The midrash associates *midbar*, "wilderness," with Sinai, meaning that evil Balaam perniciously recalled Israel's apostasy of the golden calf (see the Targums and Excursus 56).

2. encamped tribe by tribe Once Balaam is convinced that God intends only blessing for Israel (23:20), he no longer needs to follow Balak's precaution that he see only a portion of Israel (v. 1) lest the curse be ineffectual (see the Comment to 22:40). He can now view the entire Israelite encampment with impunity. Tradition interprets the fact that Balak's sacrifices are repeated to mean that they are not magical in purpose but are for predisposing the deity to the wishes of the petitioner.[4]

the spirit of God came upon him The assumption here is that instead of seeking God in a dream (22:9,20) or having God's words "put into his mouth" (23:5,16), Balaam is now invested with the divine spirit and falls into an ecstatic state (vv. 3–4),[5] the mark of a prophet (11:25–29). "Spirit of God" should be understood as "divine spirit," as in Exodus 31:3 and 35:31, since in the narrative of this chapter only the Tetragrammaton is used for the name of God.

3–9. Balaam introduces himself—now that he is invested with the divine spirit—as one who is privy to God's direct revelation. He compares Israel with well-watered trees and gardens, whose king is mightier than Amalek's Agag and whose divinely endowed leonine strength will crush all its enemies and deter future aggressors. Indeed, not only is Israel blessed and not cursed but the blessing and curse of others will be empowered to redound to those who utter them.[6] In the opening and closing phrases of this third oracle, Balaam addresses Israel directly for the first time (vv. 3a*a*,b), a fitting frame for the oracle. The mention of the Amalekite king (v. 7; see 1 Sam. 15:8; 2 Sam. 8:12) and the crushing of Israel's enemies (v. 8; see 2 Sam. 12:31; 1 Chron. 20:13; Ps. 18:38–43) apparently refer to the time of Kings Saul and David. This oracle is the climactic one: In the first, only God determines blessing and curse (23:8); in the second, God's blessing cannot be revoked (23:20); in this, the third, those who bless or curse Israel will themselves be blessed or cursed.

3. Word of Balaam Hebrew *ne'um bil'am*. A self-introduction would have been expected at the beginning of a poem, not in its third stanza (e.g., 2 Sam. 23:1). However, in contrast to the prior oracles, God does not this time "put words in his mouth" (see 23:5,16). Thus, Balaam can say that these are truly his words; God has inspired the message, but it is he, Balaam, who has put it into words.[7] The divine origin of his message is made explicit in the next verse. Similarly, King David, after opening his poem with the same formula of self-introduction (*ne'um*), also immediately identifies its divine origin: "The word of David son of Jesse, the word of the man whom God raised up[8] . . . the Spirit of the LORD has spoken through me, His message is on my tongue" (2 Sam. 23:1–2). Indeed, the choice of *ne'um* for "word" is probably deliberate; it nearly always indicates a divine utterance.

son of Hebrew *beno*; see the Comment to 23:18.

Word of Balaam son of Beor,
Word of the man whose eye is true,
4 Word of him who hears God's speech,
Who beholds visions from the Almighty,
Prostrate, but with eyes unveiled:
5 How fair are your tents, O Jacob,
Your dwellings, O Israel!
6 Like palm-groves that stretch out,
Like gardens beside a river,
Like aloes planted by the LORD,
Like cedars beside the water;

נְאֻם בִּלְעָם בְּנוֹ בְעֹר
וּנְאֻם הַגֶּבֶר שְׁתֻם הָעָיִן׃
4 נְאֻם שֹׁמֵעַ אִמְרֵי־אֵל
אֲשֶׁר מַחֲזֵה שַׁדַּי יֶחֱזֶה
נֹפֵל וּגְלוּי עֵינָיִם׃
5 מַה־טֹּבוּ אֹהָלֶיךָ יַעֲקֹב
מִשְׁכְּנֹתֶיךָ יִשְׂרָאֵל׃
6 כִּנְחָלִים נִטָּיוּ
כְּגַנֹּת עֲלֵי נָהָר
כַּאֲהָלִים נָטַע יְהוָה
כַּאֲרָזִים עֲלֵי־מָיִם׃

whose eye is true Hebrew *shetum ha-ʿayin.*[9] Two other renderings have been suggested: (1) "Whose eye is open," the root *sh-t-m* in rabbinic Hebrew meaning "be open,"[10] supported by the parallelism with "eyes unveiled" (v. 4) and by a medical text from Nimrud: "If someone falls to the ground with his eyes wide open, he has been possessed by a *gallu*-demon." (2) "Whose eye is closed" (see Lam. 3:8), where *shatam* is equivalent to *satam,* "close"[11]; that is, Balaam was heretofore blind to God's revelation or he was actually physically blind, which would account for God's having to open his eyes to see the angel.[12] However, this latter interpretation faces the objection that in 22:41 and 23:13, Balaam had to see the Israelites in order to curse them, a fact that he confirms in his oracles in 23:9.

4. *speech* Perhaps the Hebrew words *ve-yodeaʿ daʿat ʿelyon*, "who obtains knowledge from the Most High" (see v. 16aβ), should be inserted here (as in one manuscript) in order to balance the verse.

beholds visions Hebrew *maḥazeh . . . yeḥezeh*. The visions are really auditions, judging by the frequent association of the root *ḥ-z-h* with *davar*, "word," as in Isaiah 2:1 and Amos 1:1 (also Mic. 1:1; cf. Hab. 1:1).

Almighty Hebrew *shaddai* (so rendered in the Septuagint), an ancient name for Israel's God. In Genesis 49:25 it is in parallelism with *ʾel*; and according to a biblical tradition in Exodus 6:4, the patriarchs knew Him only by this name. Its etymology is unknown. It may derive from Akkadian *šadû*, which has two meanings: (1) "mountain" (the gods Asshur and Bel are called *šadû rabû*, "great mountain," i.e., almighty)[13] and, most likely, (2) "steppe" (analogous to Heb. *sadeh*, "field," which in 14-cent. Ugarit was pronounced *šd*). The god of the Amurru in upper Mesopotamia (the homeland of the patriarchs) was called *bēl šadê*, "the Lord of the (Syrian) Steppe."[14] However, like the parallel form *ʾel*, "God," it may not even be a proper name but a generic name for deity, god. Elsewhere too *shaddai* is parallel with *ʾel/ ʾeloah*, "deity" (Job 5:17; 6:4; 8:3,5; 9:7, etc.). In the Deir ʿAlla inscription (1.6; see Excursus 60), *shaddai*, indeed, occurs in the plural, meaning "gods" (so also Job 19:29).

Prostrate An act of acknowledgment of and homage to the presence of God, as in Genesis 17:3 and Joshua 5:14.[15] Balaam remains in full possession of his faculties and testifies that he has seen and heard; there is therefore no need to posit that he fell into a trance.[16]

but with eyes unveiled His eyes were either literally "opened" or, more likely, he was figuratively "enlightened"; that is, he saw with his inner eye.[17]

5. *fair* Hebrew *tovu*, that is, "pleasing" as in Genesis 3:6, 24:16, and Song of Songs 4:10.[18]

dwellings Hebrew *mishkenotekha*, plural of *mishkan*, "Tabernacle." The term designates a temporary structure, as indicated by its parallel, "tents." Tradition refers "dwellings" to the Tabernacle and "tents" to the tent of the patriarch Jacob (Gen. 25:27)—the tent in which he prayed.[19] The midrash sees in this verse the ideal of the Jew in his home and synagogue, and for this reason it was placed at the opening of the daily morning service.

7Their boughs drip with moisture,
Their roots have abundant water.
Their king shall rise above Agag,
Their kingdom shall be exalted.
8God who freed them from Egypt

7 יִזַּל־מַ֙יִם֙ מִדָּ֣לְיָ֔ו
וְזַרְע֖וֹ בְּמַ֣יִם רַבִּ֑ים
וְיָרֹ֤ם מֵֽאֲגַג֙ מַלְכּ֔וֹ
וְתִנַּשֵּׂ֖א מַלְכֻתֽוֹ׃
8 אֵ֚ל מוֹצִיא֣וֹ מִמִּצְרַ֔יִם

6. Like palm-groves Its meaning in Arabic. Others render "canyons, wadis," but then the lush greenery intended by this verse would be missing.

that stretch out Hebrew *nittayu*. So Israel's tents appeared from the heights from which Balaam beheld them. It has also been suggested that this word should be read *natah y(h)w*, "that the Lord stretched out," which would complement the next line in structure and rhythm.[20] The name *yhw* for the Tetragrammaton appears on an eighth-century B.C.E. stone bowl found at Kuntilet 'Ajrud, 50 kilometers (30 mi.) south of Kadesh-barnea.

gardens beside a river A reminder of the Garden of Eden as described in Genesis 2:10.

aloes Hebrew *'ahalim*. A word play with *'oholim*, "tents" (v. 5). A sweet-smelling tree whose sap is used as a perfume.[21] It is an exotic plant not found in Israel and, hence, imported.

cedars beside the waters Since cedars grow on mountains and not by waters, the suggestion has been made to transpose aloes and cedars, yielding: "Like cedars planted by the Lord," exactly as in Psalms 104:16. But it is possible that *'erez* is generic for a variety of evergreens that do not bear fruit. Such appears to be the case in Psalms 148:9. In rabbinic Hebrew a number of coniferous trees are subsumed under this term.[22]

7. Their boughs Hebrew *dalyav*. The usual form of the plural is *daliyotav*, as in Jeremiah 19:13 and Ezekiel 17:7. Ibn Ezra and Shadal explain the image as that of trees (mentioned in the previous verse) so drenched that their boughs drip water; that is, the vegetation will be watered from above and below (see Gen. 49:25). Rashi says that the form of the word is dual and can mean "buckets." The image would be of "Israel's prosperity under the figure of a man returning from his abundant springs with water dripping over the two full buckets carried over his shoulders."[23] In support, Akkadian *dalû* means "irrigate with water drawn from a well."

drip Hebrew *yizzal*. The singular is used, although "water" is a plural, as in 19:13. Water is a common metaphor for prosperity.[24]

Their roots Hebrew *ve-zar'o*. This word can be interpreted in two ways. It may be a reference to posterity (see the translation) or taken literally as "roots." The image tells us that "it was beautiful in its . . . branches [*daliyotav*], because its stock stood by abundant waters" (Ezek. 31:7). Since the antecedent is the coniferous tree of verse 6, the possibility also exists that "seed" could refer to the cones borne by the branches, which, like its boughs, will also be drenched with water.[25]

Their king Thrice promised by God to the patriarchs (Gen. 17:6,16; 35:11).

Agag The king of Amalek in the time of Saul (see 1 Sam. 15:8).[26] Amalek was Israel's most dreaded enemy during the time of Moses (e.g., Exod. 17:8–16; Deut. 25:17–18). Agag may remind the poet of *gag*, "roof," hence his wording "rise above Agag."[27] The Septuagint and Samaritan read "Gog," the legendary future antagonist of Israel mentioned in Ezekiel 38–39, thereby giving the oracle an eschatological thrust.

Their kingdom shall be exalted Rashi says that this description applies to David rather than to Saul, as the latter's kingdom was under incessant Philistine harassment and domination. Indeed, Targum Onkelos and Targum Jonathan render "taken away," referring to the transfer of the kingdom from Saul to David. Other versions give this line a messianic interpretation.[28]

8. freed them[29]

Is for them That is, Israel; see the Comment to 23:22.

Is for them like the horns of the wild ox.
They shall devour enemy nations,
Crush their bones,
And smash their arrows.
9They crouch, they lie down like a lion,
Like the king of beasts; who dare rouse them?
Blessed are they who bless you,
Accursed they who curse you!

כְּתוֹעֲפֹת רְאֵם לוֹ
יֹאכַל גּוֹיִם צָרָיו
וְעַצְמֹתֵיהֶם יְגָרֵם
וְחִצָּיו יִמְחָץ׃
9 כָּרַע שָׁכַב כַּאֲרִי
וּכְלָבִיא מִי יְקִימֶנּוּ
מְבָרֲכֶיךָ בָרוּךְ
וְאֹרְרֶיךָ אָרוּר׃

10Enraged at Balaam, Balak struck his hands together. "I
called you," Balak said to Balaam, "to damn my enemies,
and instead you have blessed them these three times! 11Back
with you at once to your own place! I was going to reward

10 וַיִּחַר־אַף בָּלָק אֶל־בִּלְעָם וַיִּסְפֹּק אֶת־כַּפָּיו
וַיֹּאמֶר בָּלָק אֶל־בִּלְעָם לָקֹב אֹיְבַי קְרָאתִיךָ וְהִנֵּה
בֵּרַכְתָּ בָרֵךְ זֶה שָׁלֹשׁ פְּעָמִים׃ 11 וְעַתָּה בְּרַח־לְךָ
אֶל־מְקוֹמֶךָ אָמַרְתִּי כַּבֵּד אֲכַבֶּדְךָ וְהִנֵּה מְנָעֲךָ

devour Hebrew *yo'khal*, an image of military conquest, as in Numbers 13:32, Isaiah 9:11, and Jeremiah 10:25.

smash their arrows[30]

9. The images in verse 9b are taken from Isaac's blessing to Jacob in Genesis 27:29 and in verse 9a, from Jacob's blessing for Judah in Genesis 49:9.

crouch Hebrew *shakhav*. Rather, "couch, rest." In the previous oracle, the lion rises and does not rest (*shakhav*) until it eats its prey (23:24). Here the sated lion now lies down to rest: Even when it is in a state of repose, who would dare rouse it?[31]

Blessed . . . bless . . . Accursed . . . curse The active participles are in the plural, and the passive participles are in the singular (also in Gen. 27:29), a construction known as the distributive singular,[32] meaning, "Those who bless you, blessed be every one of them." Also implied is that everyone will bless you in order to be blessed and will desist from cursing you for fear of being cursed.[33] Perhaps there is a hint that Balak's very intention to curse Israel will now boomerang on his own kingdom (see v. 17). Also implied is that Balaam, who has blessed Israel, will himself be blessed,[34] supporting the thesis that the "Book of Balaam," with the exception of the ass episode (22:22–34), depicts Balaam as a saint and not as a sinner (see Excursus 58). In any event, a climax is reached by the final words of this oracle: The promise to Abraham (Gen. 12:3; 22:18), to Jacob (Gen. 27:29), and to the Israelites (Exod. 23:22) is now fulfilled by Balaam.

THE FOURTH ORACLE (vv. 10–19)

Balak fires Balaam in a fit of anger. Balaam again spurns Balak's material temptations and persists in his initial claim that he is but the spokesman of the Lord. Still imbued with prophetic inspiration, he now turns his attention to the future of Balak's country, Moab.

10. Enraged at Balaam Note the progression: (1) Balak mildly rebukes Balaam (23:11); (2) his anger surfaces (23:25); (3) his anger bursts forth in words and gestures.

struck his hands together A sign of derision, as in Job 27:23 and Lamentations 2:15.

called you Rather, "summoned you" (see the Comment to 23:11).

blessed them Hebrew *berakhta barekh*. The doubling of the verb implies "you have done nothing but bless" (see 23:11).

11. Back with you Literally, "flee at once," as in Genesis 27:43 and Amos 7:12.

you richly, but the LORD has denied you the reward."
12 Balaam replied to Balak, "But I even told the messengers
you sent to me, 13 'Though Balak were to give me his house
full of silver and gold, I could not of my own accord do
anything good or bad contrary to the LORD's command.
What the LORD says, that I must say.' 14 And now, as I go
back to my people, let me inform you of what this people
will do to your people in days to come." 15 He took up his
theme, and said:

Word of Balaam son of Beor,
Word of the man whose eye is true,

יְהוָה מִכָּבוֹד׃ 12 וַיֹּאמֶר בִּלְעָם אֶל־בָּלָק הֲלֹא גַּם
אֶל־מַלְאָכֶיךָ אֲשֶׁר־שָׁלַחְתָּ אֵלַי דִּבַּרְתִּי לֵאמֹר׃
13 אִם־יִתֶּן־לִי בָלָק מְלֹא בֵיתוֹ כֶּסֶף וְזָהָב לֹא
אוּכַל לַעֲבֹר אֶת־פִּי יְהוָה לַעֲשׂוֹת טוֹבָה אוֹ רָעָה
מִלִּבִּי אֲשֶׁר־יְדַבֵּר יְהוָה אֹתוֹ אֲדַבֵּר׃ שביעי
14 וְעַתָּה הִנְנִי הוֹלֵךְ לְעַמִּי לְכָה אִיעָצְךָ אֲשֶׁר
יַעֲשֶׂה הָעָם הַזֶּה לְעַמְּךָ בְּאַחֲרִית הַיָּמִים׃
15 וַיִּשָּׂא מְשָׁלוֹ וַיֹּאמַר
נְאֻם בִּלְעָם בְּנוֹ בְעֹר
וּנְאֻם הַגֶּבֶר שְׁתֻם הָעָיִן׃

your own place Hebrew ***mekomekha***. The choice of this word is motivated by an ironic purpose: Previously, Balaam had been taken to Balak's "place" (23:13,27).[35]

the LORD This term is used here and in verse 13 instead of *Elohim*, "God." For the significance, see the Comment to verse 1. In addition, this verse should be juxtaposed to 23:12; that is, since Balaam has consistently used the name of the Lord, Balak now utters it with ironic intent: The same Lord—Balaam's God—has now denied Balaam any reward.

12. The messengers[36]

13. of my own accord Balaam, like Moses (see 16:28), acts only on God's instructions.[37]

good or bad A merism for any kind of behavior (e.g., Gen. 24:50; 31:24,29). In 22:18 we find "big or little." Perhaps the change in merism is intentional, to intimate the "bad" tidings in store for Moab (v. 17)[38] or to refer to the oracles, which blessed Israel instead of cursing her.[39]

14. my people Hebrew ***ʿammi***, a reference to 22:5, both verses framing an inclusion to the narrative portion of the "Book of Balaam."

inform you Hebrew ***ʾiyʿatsekha***, that is, of God's plan (see Isa. 14:24,26). The same root *(y-ʿ-ts)* is used in Arabic ***waʿiṣ***, the "augurer," consulted by sheikhs before embarking on a military campaign.[40] Thus Balaam's "information" was prophetic.

The Masoretic accentuation is disjunctive, indicating that the information itself was omitted.[41] Rabbinic tradition, in the light of 31:16, supplied Balaam's information: "Prepare inns and employ seductive women to sell food and drink at lowered prices. And these people [Israel] will come eat, drink, and have sexual intercourse with them; and they will reject their God. And they will be delivered into your hand shortly, and many of them will fall."[42] Other midrashim develop this theme into a total abandonment of Jewish life.[43]

what this people will do to your people Implying that the oracle will deal only with Moab.[44]

in days to come Hebrew ***be-ʾaḥarit ha-yamim*** is not the "end of days" but a reference to the near future from the point of view of the speaker. Thus in Genesis 49:1 the settlement in Canaan is referred to, and Deuteronomy 4:30 and 31:29 refer to adversity following Israel's defection.

15–19. The last and climactic oracle predicts the destruction of Moab and other enemies. It completes the 3 + 1 pattern whereby the last of a triad is enhanced by the addition of a fourth member. For other biblical examples, see Amos 1:3–2:6 and Proverbs 30:18–19,29–31. The mention of Edom and the Sethites is unanticipated, but the function of these oracles is the confirmation and fulfillment of the patriarchal blessings of Genesis 25:23 and 27:29, in which the overthrow of Edom is a prominent theme. In Genesis 27:29—if the Sethites refer to all the nomadic groups descended from Abraham (Gen. 25:1–18)—Jacob/Israel is promised dominion over all his kinsmen. According to Ibn Ezra and many moderns, this prophecy refers to King David, who conquered Moab and Edom, as mentioned in 2 Samuel 8:2,13–14, 1 Kings 11:15–16, and Psalms 60:2,10.[45]

16 Word of him who hears God's speech,	16 נְאֻם שֹׁמֵעַ אִמְרֵי־אֵל
Who obtains knowledge from the Most High,	וְיֹדֵעַ דַּעַת עֶלְיוֹן
And beholds visions from the Almighty,	מַחֲזֵה שַׁדַּי יֶחֱזֶה
Prostrate, but with eyes unveiled:	נֹפֵל וּגְלוּי עֵינָיִם׃
17 What I see for them is not yet,	17 אֶרְאֶנּוּ וְלֹא עַתָּה
What I behold will not be soon:	אֲשׁוּרֶנּוּ וְלֹא קָרוֹב
A star rises from Jacob,	דָּרַךְ כּוֹכָב מִיַּעֲקֹב
A scepter comes forth from Israel;	וְקָם שֵׁבֶט מִיִּשְׂרָאֵל
It smashes the brow of Moab,	וּמָחַץ פַּאֲתֵי מוֹאָב
The foundation of all children of Seth.	וְקַרְקַר כָּל־בְּנֵי־שֵׁת׃

15. Verses 15–16 are almost identical with verses 3–4. The significance of the repetition of Balaam's self-introduction is that he continues to prophesy under the influence of the divine spirit without resort to divination (see the Comment to v. 3).

16. ***Who obtains knowledge from the Most High***[46] Literally, "who knows the knowledge of the Most High." This refers to one who is privy to God's designs, even "the hour of the wrath of the Most High God,"[47] in order to time his curses against Israel.[48] However, the construct may be treated not as a subjective genitive, "the Lord's knowledge," but as an objective genitive, "knowledge from the Lord"; and the verb ***yodea'*** can also connote "apprehend, experience."[49]

Most High Hebrew ***'elyon***, a title for God in Genesis 14:18–22 and Deuteronomy 32:8.[50]

17. ***What I see for them . . . What I behold*** Hebrew ***'er'ennu . . . 'ashurennu***. These two verbs occur in the first oracle, in 23:9a. Their scope is graduated, indicating a heightening of Balaam's visionary powers. In the first oracle, he is endowed with normal physical sight. In the second, he attains the spiritual power to see Israel's invulnerable state in the present. Now his vision soars from the plane of the present to behold the distant future. The verb ***ra'ah*** also means "to divine" (e.g., 1 Kings 22:19), as does its synonym ***ḥazah*** (e.g., Ezek. 13:6), leading to the technical terms for diviner: ***ro'eh*** (e.g., 1 Sam. 9:6) and ***ḥozeh*** (e.g., Mic. 3:7). In the Deir 'Alla inscription (1.1), Balaam is called the ***ḥzh 'lhn***, "the seer of the gods" (see Excursus 60).

is not yet . . . will not be soon Clearly, a prophecy for the distant future. Rashi and Ibn Ezra interpret this oracle as referring to King David, the "star" who will conquer Moab (2 Sam. 8:2) and Edom (2 Sam. 8:14).

A star Hebrew ***kokhav*** has been interpreted in four ways: (1) It is understood as an image of a king, as in Isaiah 14:12, where the Babylonian king is called the morning star (see Ezek. 32:7). This would refer to the rise of King David.[51] (2) Some understand it as the messianic king,[52] identified by Rabbi Akiba as Bar Kokhba: "R. Simeon bar Yoḥai taught: R. Akiba interpreted 'A star rises from Jacob' as Kokhba ('star') came forth out of Jacob. When R. Akiba saw Ben Kosba, he said: This is the king Messiah (Kosba = Kokhba). R. Johanan ben Torta replied: Akiba, grass will grow out of your cheekbones before the son of David comes."[53] Alexander Yannai, 150 years earlier (103–76 B.C.E.), imprinted a star on some of his coins to symbolize that ***he*** was the conquering star that rose from Jacob.[54] (3) In ancient Near Eastern mythology, the gods Resheph, Nergal, and Apollo direct shooting stars or comets to destroy their enemies.[55] (4) ***Kokhab*** (not meaning "star") can mean "host" (Arab. ***kaukabun*** can mean "multitude of an army"): Thus, "a host shall march forth from Jacob."[56]

rises Hebrew ***darakh***.[57] For its military connotation, see Deuteronomy 33:29 and Isaiah 63:3. The rendering here is doubtful, since it regularly means "march, trample" in Scripture. The meaning "prevail" has been suggested, from Ugaritic ***darkatu***, "dominion," and as hinted by Targum Onkelos. And if the ***mem*** of ***mi-ya'akov*** is transferred to the previous word, without changing its

[18]Edom becomes a possession,	18 וְהָיָה אֱדוֹם יְרֵשָׁה
Yea, Seir a possession of its enemies;	וְהָיָה יְרֵשָׁה שֵׂעִיר אֹיְבָיו
But Israel is triumphant.	וְיִשְׂרָאֵל עֹשֶׂה חָיִל׃
[19]A victor issues from Jacob	19 וְיֵרְדְּ מִיַּעֲקֹב
To wipe out what is left of Ir.	וְהֶאֱבִיד שָׂרִיד מֵעִיר׃

meaning (an enclitic), the line will read: "when the stars of Jacob prevail."[58] The meaning "is aimed" (Pss. 58:8; 64:4) has also been suggested,[59] the star/comet imaged as an arrow. If, however, the above interpretation (4) for *kokhav* is adopted, *darakh* can have its attested meaning of "march."

A scepter Hebrew *shevet* also means comet or meteor, based on Akkadian *šibṭu* and on rabbinic *shavit*.[60] It describes both gods and kings. For example, the god Nergal is called *ša šibṭi* "of the comet,"[61] and on the poetical stela of Thutmose III, the god Amen-Re proclaims: "I let them see your majesty as a shooting star, that scatters fire as it sheds its flame."[62] *Shevet* has three usual meanings. (1) "Scepter" refers to the king's insignia, as in Genesis 49:10 and Isaiah 14:5. Ancient Egyptian iconography represents the victorious Pharaoh striking the enemy with his scepter.[63] (2) "Ruler" refers to the one who wields the scepter, as in Genesis 49:10,16 and Deuteronomy 29:9. (3) "Tribe" refers to its military units, as in Judges 20:12 and 1 Samuel 9:21. If *kokhav* can mean "host," then this last rendering for *shevet* is best.

comes forth For *kam* with hostile intent, see the Comment to 10:35.

smashes[64]

the brow of[65]

Moab A fitting and ironic conclusion to the Balaam story: Balak of Moab wished to curse Israel; instead, his hired seer, Balaam, curses Moab—a measure for measure principle (see Excursus 56).

the foundation of[66]

children of Seth Hebrew *benei shet*, or Sethites. Probably identified with the tribal Shutu mentioned in the Egyptian execration texts of the early second millennium B.C.E. as a nomadic people somewhere in Canaan.[67] Hence, this is a general designation for all the nomadic groups descended from Abraham (see Gen. 25) and considered his kinsmen, over whom Israel was promised dominance in the patriarchal blessings, as in Genesis 27:29.[68]

18.[69]

a possession[70]

of its enemies[71]

19. A victor issues from Jacob Hebrew *ve-yerd mi-ya'akov*, from the verb *radah*, "rule, control," as in Genesis 1:28 and Leviticus 25:43.[72] However, this interpretation is forced. A preferable solution is to read *ve-yerd(m) ya'akov 'oyevav* (transposing the last word from v. 18) and reversing the sequence of 19a, 18c, yielding: "Jacob shall rule over his enemies and Israel shall be triumphant."[73] Thus without any consonantal changes, the meter of verses 18–19 is restored; and Jacob and Israel are again a word pair with Jacob the "A" word, as in seven other verses in the Balaam oracles (23:7, 10,21,23[2]; 24:5,17).

of Ir If the reference is to Ir-moab (22:36) or the city of Ar (21:28), then this line belongs in verse 17 with the oracle against Moab. Alternatively, render "of cities" (*'ir*, a collective), a reference to David, who put to death all the Edomite males (1 Kings 11:15–16) and spared one-third of the Moabite fighting force, echoed in the wording of verse 17b.[74] This verse was clearly incorporated into Obadiah's prophecy (1:17–18) against Edom: "The house of Jacob shall dispossess . . . and no savior shall be left of the House of Esau" (see Amos 9:12).[75]

20He saw Amalek and, taking up his theme, he said:
A leading nation is Amalek;
But its fate is to perish forever.

21He saw the Kenites and, taking up his theme, he said:
Though your abode be secure,
And your nest be set among cliffs,
22Yet shall Kain be consumed,
When Asshur takes you captive.

20 וַיַּרְא אֶת־עֲמָלֵק וַיִּשָּׂא מְשָׁלוֹ וַיֹּאמַר
רֵאשִׁית גּוֹיִם עֲמָלֵק
וְאַחֲרִיתוֹ עֲדֵי אֹבֵד׃
21 וַיַּרְא אֶת־הַקֵּינִי וַיִּשָּׂא מְשָׁלוֹ וַיֹּאמַר
אֵיתָן מוֹשָׁבֶךָ
וְשִׂים בַּסֶּלַע קִנֶּךָ׃
22 כִּי אִם־יִהְיֶה לְבָעֵר קָיִן
עַד־מָה אַשּׁוּר תִּשְׁבֶּךָּ׃

ORACLES AGAINST NATIONS (vv. 20–25)

This is the first example of a genre that is fully developed by the classical prophets: Isaiah 13–23, Jeremiah 46–51, Amos 1:3–2:3. It consists of three more oracles introduced by the words "taking up his theme," yielding a total of seven oracles for the "Book of Balaam." They differ from the previous oracle against Moab and Edom (vv. 17–19) in that they do not mention Israel. The scene depicts Balaam, still on the height, as a series of nations come into view. Indeed, from the Moabite plateau one can actually see into the Negeb, the home of the Amalekites, Asshurim, and Kenites. These verses are among the most difficult in all Scripture because of the obscurity of most of the words and references.

20. He saw As he "saw Israel" (v. 2). So it must be assumed that from the peak of Peor he saw the Amalekite and Kenite territories.

leading Hebrew ***re'shit***, as in Amos 6:1. This term was chosen because it is the antonym (lit. "beginning") of ***'aḥarit***, "fate" (lit. "end") in the next line.

its fate Hebrew ***'aḥarito*** (see the Comment to 23:10), or "its remnant," as in Amos 4:2, 9:1, and Ezekiel 23:25, a fitting antonym to Amalek's "beginnings."

to perish forever So Targum Onkelos for Hebrew ***'adei 'oved***, literally "as far as one who perishes." For this meaning, see Proverbs 31:6 and Job 29:13, 31:19.[76]

21. The Kenites A nomadic group that attached itself to Midian, Amalek, and Israel and ranged from the Sinai Peninsula to the Galilee, as far as "Elon-bezaanannim, which is near Kadesh" (Judg. 4:11). The name means "smith,"[77] implying that they were itinerant craftsmen, a guild of metalworkers who plied their metallurgical skills over a wide area. They also raised livestock (Exod. 2:16–22). They are represented as a subgroup of the Midianites (see the Comment to 10:29) through Moses' wife (Judg. 1:16; 4:11; Num. 10:29). In Judges 1:16, 4:11 and 1 Samuel 15:6–7, the Kenites who settled in Canaan are represented as allies of the Israelites, suggesting that the Kenites of the following oracle are of an earlier period.

secure[78]

your nest Hebrew ***kinnekha***, a word play on ***keni***, "Kenites."

be set[79]

22. Kain Hebrew ***kayin***, literally "smith." Tubal-cain (***kayin***) (Gen. 4:22) is the eponymous ancestor of all the smiths and, presumably, of all the Kenites.[80]

be consumed Hebrew ***le-va'er***, that is, "become fuel," a play on the original meaning of ***kayin*** as "smith."[81]

When Asshur takes you captive The likelihood that Assyria (Asshur) is the referent is slight, as it did not enter the horizon of the Israelites until the eighth century B.C.E.. It may, however, refer to the nomadic group Asshurim (see v. 24), of whom nothing is presently known.[82]

23He took up his theme and said:
Alas, who can survive except God has willed it!
24Ships come from the quarter of Kittim;
They subject Asshur, subject Eber.
They, too, shall perish forever.

23 וַיִּשָּׂא מְשָׁלוֹ וַיֹּאמַר
אוֹי מִי יִחְיֶה מִשֻּׂמוֹ אֵל׃
24 וְצִים מִיַּד כִּתִּים
וְעִנּוּ אַשּׁוּר וְעִנּוּ־עֵבֶר
וְגַם־הוּא עֲדֵי אֹבֵד׃

23. He took up No nation is the target of this final oracle. The Septuagint prefaces it by "He saw Og" (see 21:33), but a national grouping not a personal name is needed. Some feel that "Og" in the Septuagint is a mistake for "Agag" (see the Comment to v. 7), a clan name here[83] on the basis of "Agagite" (Esther 3:1). It probably means "a descendant of Agag." Others read "Gog" (as the Septuagint does in v. 7), referring to the northern barbarians (the *gagāya* of the El-Amarna letters). The problem has not even begun to be solved.

Alas, who can survive except God has willed it Hebrew *'oy mi yiḥyeh mi-sumo 'el*. A literal rendering is incomprehensible. Albright reads *'iyyim yoḥyu mi-semo'l*, "the (inhabitants of the) isles shall be gathered from the north," combining *'oy mi* into *'iyyim*, "isles"; detecting the verb *ḥayah*, "gather together" (Zech. 10:9; Neh. 3:34), a denominative from *ḥai*, "clan" (1 Sam. 18:18), *ḥavvot*, "tent village" (32:41); and combining *mi-sumo 'el* into *mi-semo'l*, "from the north" (lit. "left," as one faces east; Gen. 14:15; Josh. 19:27). According to this attractive rendering, the reference would be to the sea peoples, called in Egyptian inscriptions "foreigners from the north . . . from the isles . . of the sea" who invaded the entire eastern Mediterranean littoral during the thirteenth and twelfth centuries. Another proposal suggests that *mi-sumo* derives from the root *som*, akin to Arabic *sham*, "to inflict ill fortune."[84] Thus, this verse would translate: "Alas, who can survive whom God has condemned."

24. Ships Hebrew *tsim*, an Egyptian loan word found also in Isaiah 33:21 and Daniel 11:30. Perhaps this is the source for the anchor imprinted, together with the star, by Alexander Yannai on his coins (see the Comment to v. 17). (Today *tsim*, written Zim, is the name of the commercial fleet of the State of Israel.) Alternatively, some render "demonic beasts," connecting it with *tsiyim* of Isaiah 13:21, 23:13, and 34:14.

come from the quarter of Kittim Kittim is Cyprus (Gen. 10:4). According to Josephus,[85] the name derives from the city of Kition (Phoen. Kiti), present-day Larnaca. It is clear from biblical references (Jer. 2:10; Ezek. 27:6) that it must be an island. Hence, its identification with Macedonia (in 1 Maccabees 1:1 and 8:5) or Italy[86] cannot be correct. The Kittiyim of the Arad inscriptions were probably "Greek or Cypriot mercenaries serving in the Judean army, perhaps especially in garrisons of the more remote fortresses."[87] These ships from Kittim are interpreted in Daniel 11:30 as referring to Roman galleys.[88] The Qumran texts frequently use Kittim as a generic term for a hostile foreign power, such as the Seleucids of Syria, the Ptolemies of Egypt, and the Romans.[89] Here, however, the reference may be to the invasions of the sea peoples in the thirteenth and twelfth centuries.[90]

Asshur Perhaps the Asshurim of Genesis 25:3,18 and Psalms 83:9.

Eber Hebrew *'ever*. The Septuagint reads *'ivrim*, "Hebrews." According to Genesis 11:14–17, Eber is the eponymous ancestor of the Hebrews. Targum Onkelos reads "across [*'ever*] the Euphrates," that is, Assyria (see Josh. 24:2). According to the recently discovered Ebla tablets, in the mid-third millennium, the king of a great empire—stretching from northern Mesopotamia to the Mediterranean—was called Ibrim. However, the identification of Eber is still obscure. Another suggestion is to read *ḥever* instead of *'ever*,[91] possibly referring to the non-Israelite Kenite clan of Heber, which settled in the Galilee around the time of the conquest (Judg. 4:11) and made peace with the Canaanites (Judg. 4:17) before it was absorbed into the tribe of Asher (Num. 26:45; Gen. 46:17). The letters *ḥet* and *ayin* can interchange, for example, *ḥefer* (26:32) and *'efer* (1 Chron. 5:24). This verse, then, would relate to the subjection of the tribe of Asher and the neighboring (non-Israelite) clan of Heber to the invading sea peoples.[92]

25 Then Balaam set out on his journey back home; and Balak also went his way.

25 וַיָּקׇם בִּלְעָם וַיֵּלֶךְ וַיָּשׇׁב לִמְקֹמוֹ וְגַם־בָּלָק הָלַךְ
לְדַרְכּוֹ׃ פ

25 While Israel was staying at Shittim, the people profaned themselves by whoring with the Moabite women,

כ״ה וַיֵּשֶׁב יִשְׂרָאֵל בַּשִּׁטִּים וַיָּחֶל הָעָם לִזְנוֹת
אֶל־בְּנוֹת מוֹאָב׃ 2 וַתִּקְרֶאןָ לָעָם לְזִבְחֵי אֱלֹהֵיהֶן

25. This is the usual literary formula for ending a narrative, as in Genesis 18:33 and 32:1–2a. According to the tradition represented by Numbers 31:8 and Joshua 13:22, Balaam now proceeds to advise the Midianites in their war against Israel.

set out[93]

Idolatry and Expiation at Baal-Peor (vv. 1–19)

This chapter stands in sharp contrast to the preceding one. Balaam's prediction of Israel's glorious promise is immediately dashed by the sickening reality of Israel at Baal-peor. The nation that dwells alone with its God (23:9,21) pollutes itself with idolatry. Moabite women entice the Israelites to participate in the cult of Baal-peor. In punishment, pestilence breaks out, and God commands Moses to impale the ringleaders. Before the order is carried out, an Israelite and a Midianite princess enter an improvised alcove near the sanctuary, where Moses and the assembled Israelites are importuning God to end the plague. Phinehas—priest, grandson of Aaron, chief of the Levitical guards (see Num. 3:32; 1 Chron. 9:20) stationed at the entrance to the sanctuary—enters the alcove, spears the couple during their sexual intercourse, and the plague is halted (see Excursus 61).

CHAPTER 25 THE APOSTASY (vv. 1–9)

The apostasy of Baal-peor and that of the golden calf resemble one another in their inner detail. Both involve worship of other gods (Num. 25:2; Exod. 32:8), the assuaging of God's wrath by the slaughter of the guilty parties (Num. 25:7–8; Exod. 32:26–28), and the designation of the line of the Phinehas/Levites for sacred service in the sanctuary (Num. 25:11–13; Exod. 32:39).[1] Moreover, Baal-peor is the punishment for the sin and the fulfillment of the sentence for the golden calf. The editor who added the notice "Then the Lord sent a plague, for what they did with the calf that Aaron made" (Exod. 32:35) to the divine pronouncement "A day will come when I will punish them for their sin" (v. 34b, NEB), clearly had Baal-peor in mind. Ironically, yet justifiably, the ***coup de grâce*** to the generation of the Exodus is executed when they commit apostasy for the second time. In a real sense, Baal-peor is but an extension of the golden calf.

The story of the reconnaissance of Canaan (chaps. 13–14) provides another illuminating parallel. "In both cases, the people stand on the brink of entering the land of Canaan, a setting filled with hope. The immediate response in the two stories, however, is open rebellion against God. A plague kills the people involved (14:37; 25:9). One or two faithful people separate themselves from the majority and act on behalf of God (Caleb and Joshua—Num. 14:6–10; Phinehas—Num. 25:6–7)."[2]

According to one tradition (31:16), the apostasy at Baal-peor was plotted by Balaam in his attempt to destroy Israel (see the Comment to 24:14). This interpretation is in keeping with Rabbi Akiba's principle: "Every section in Scripture is explained by the one that stands next to it."[3]

1. ***was staying*** Israel did not merely encamp at this site but settled for a while, as it did at Kadesh (20:1). Why? The Baal-peor apostasy is a setback; they cannot enter the land until they are purged.

2 who invited the people to the sacrifices for their god. The
people partook of them and worshiped that god. 3 Thus
Israel attached itself to Baal-peor, and the LORD was incensed with Israel. 4 The LORD said to Moses, "Take all the

וַיֹּאכַל הָעָם וַיִּשְׁתַּחֲווּ לֵאלֹהֵיהֶן׃ 3 וַיִּצָּמֶד יִשְׂרָאֵל
לְבַעַל פְּעוֹר וַיִּחַר־אַף יְהוָה בְּיִשְׂרָאֵל׃ 4 וַיֹּאמֶר
יְהוָה אֶל־מֹשֶׁה קַח אֶת־כָּל־רָאשֵׁי הָעָם וְהוֹקַע

at Shittim Literally, "in the acacias." Its full name was Abel-shittim (33:49). As Israel's last stop in its wilderness trek, it was from there that Joshua sent out spies (Josh. 2:1) and led Israel across the Jordan (Josh. 3:1). It must also have been the site of Israel's new (Deuteronomic) covenant (Deut. 28:69). According to Josephus, it was located 60 stadia (about 7 mi.) from the Jordan[4] and was known for its palms.[5] The site, as yet unidentified, must be located within the territory wrested from Sihon, who had originally conquered it from the Moabites (see the Comment to 21:26). It is otherwise known as "the steppes of Moab" (33:49; see 22:1).

profaned themselves[6]

whoring Hebrew *li-znot*. This is the only place in the Bible where this verb in its literal sense takes a masculine subject. This unusual usage probably connotes Israel's religious defection as a result of cohabitation and intermarriage with Moabite women (see v. 6).

with[7]

Moabite women It is assumed that Moabites continued to dwell in the territory after Sihon and the Israelites conquered it (see the Comment to 21:26).

2\. ***invited*** Literally, "called," also denotes "invite," especially to sacrificial feasts (see Gen. 31:54).

to the sacrifices The sequence, sacrificing following whoring, makes sense. Sexual attraction led to participation in the sacrificial feasts at the shrine of Baal-peor and, ultimately, to intermarriage (see v. 6). This conforms precisely with the prediction in the Book of Exodus: "for they will lust after their gods and sacrifice to their gods and invite you, and you will eat of their sacrifices. And when you take wives from among their daughters for your sons, their daughters will lust after their gods and will cause your sons to lust after their gods" (Exod. 34:15b–16).

Later tradition, however, avers that the whoring was an act of sacred prostitution that constituted an integral part of the ritual that took place during the sacrificial feast. Thus, Targum Jonathan renders *be-marzeḥeihon*, "at their cultic meals."[8] In the Madaba map (6th cent. C.E.), the area of Baal-peor is labeled "Betomarsea" (Beth-Marzeaḥ), also Maiumas. Maiumas was a popular licentious feast connected with water festivals.[9] Thus, tradition associates Baal-peor with a cultic site for ritual prostitution; but see the discussion in Excursus 61.

their god Hebrew *'eloheihem*, plural, which could also be rendered "gods." However, the context indicates that only the deity Baal-peor is intended (vv. 3,5).

3\. ***attached itself to*** Hebrew *va-yitsamed le*, perhaps by covenant; that is, transferring allegiance from YHVH to Baal, since the root *ṣmd*, "attach," was used at Ugarit for the permanent transfer of property.[10] The usual term ***karat berit***, "strike a covenant" (as in the similar context of Exod. 34:12–16), is avoided here, perhaps deliberately. Those who opt for the sexual interpretation of Israel's attachment to Baal-peor render this term "coupled itself for"; that is, Israel engaged in acts of ritual intercourse required in Baal worship.[11] A funerary explanation has also been suggested (see Excursus 61).

This term is found twice again (v. 5; Ps. 106:28) but only in regard to this incident. The prophet Hosea uses another term in referring to this incident: "When they came to Baal-peor, they [literally] dedicated themselves [*va-yinazeru*] to shamefulness [*boshet*, a derogatory name for Baal], and they became as disgusting as their lovemaking" (Hos. 9:10).

Baal-peor Baal is the name of the god, and Peor is the name of the site (also called Beth-peor [Deut. 3:29]). Other examples of the Baal associated with a particular site are Baal-meon (32:38) and Baal-zephon (33:7). The mountain of Peor was Balaam's last recorded station (23:28) and accounts for the linkage of these two episodes: Israel—being encamped at the foot of Mount Peor opposite Beth-peor—began to worship the local deity. Baal means "owner" and refers to the divine

ringleaders and have them publicly impaled before the LORD, so that the LORD's wrath may turn away from Israel."

אוֹתָם לַיהוָה נֶגֶד הַשָּׁמֶשׁ וְיָשֹׁב חֲרוֹן אַף־יְהוָה
מִיִּשְׂרָאֵל׃ 5 וַיֹּאמֶר מֹשֶׁה אֶל־שֹׁפְטֵי יִשְׂרָאֵל

owner of the fields. One woos him by ploughing: if he is not served as he desires there is no luck. "This is what 'the daughters of Moab' taught 'the sons of Israel.'"[12]

For the first time Israel encounters the Baal. The erstwhile pastoral nomads now come into contact with the fringe of agricultural, settled communities. The latter are chiefly concerned with propitiating the gods lest they withhold the needed rain. The worship of the Baal was relatively new to Canaan. The name Baal does not appear in Genesis: The patriarchs did not know him. Ancient Near Eastern records from Mari, Ugarit, and Egypt confirm that Baal was not an important deity in Canaan until the second half of the second millennium.[13] Thus, Israel is unprepared when it first confronts him at the borders of the promised land, and the confrontation is disastrous.

the LORD was incensed God's anger frequently takes the form of a devastating plague (see 17:11);[14] and so it is assumed by two other references to this incident, Numbers 31:16 and Psalm 106:29.

4. ***ringleaders*** Implying that only the guilty leaders were to be punished. However, Hebrew ***ra'shei ha-'am***, literally "heads of the people," simply means "leaders" (see 10:4; 13:3), suggesting that innocent and guilty leaders alike were to be executed.[15] Rabbi Judah concurs that all the leaders fell under the decree; they were guilty since they had allowed the travesty to take place without protest.[16] This also seems to be the view of Rabbi Eleazar ben Shammua: "As it is impossible for a doornail to be taken out from the door without extracting some of the wood, so it is impossible for Israel to separate itself from (the worship) of Peor without (losing) souls";[17] that is, innocent souls must also die.[18]

publicly Hebrew ***neged ha-shemesh***. For this meaning, see 2 Samuel 12:12.[19]

impaled Hebrew ***hoka'***. This verb occurs again only in 1 Samuel 21:6,9,13, in reference to the execution of the sons of Saul (see Excursus 61). Some render "cast down," that is, from a cliff, on the basis of Arabic ***waka'a*** and the fact that Saul's sons "fell" (2 Sam. 21:9).[20] However, in the only instance where such an execution (i.e., tossing off a cliff) is attested (2 Chron. 25:12), this verb is not used; and the verb "fall" is used figuratively for any kind of violent death (e.g., 1 Sam. 4:10). Others claim that dismemberment is implied.[21] However, in such cases other verbs are used (Judg. 19:29; 1 Sam. 11:7).[22] The rabbis maintain that the punishment for idolatry was death by stoning, with the body then hanged for public display[23]—and that this is what is meant here.[24] Similarly, the Septuagint and Symmachus render "expose" and Aquila, "impale," implying that execution could have been by other means and that the hanging or impalement of the corpse followed, a practice clearly envisioned in the law of Deuteronomy: "If a man is guilty of a capital offense and is put to death, and you impale [lit. "hang"] him on a stake, you must not let his corpse remain on the stake overnight, but must bury him the same day. For an impaled body is an affront to God" (Deut. 21:22–23; see Josh. 10:26). The corpses of Saul's sons, contrary to this law, were exposed to the birds of prey and the beasts of the field for many months, as told in 2 Samuel 21:9–10. Similarly, Mesopotamian law (contrary to the Torah) prescribed impalement and no burial for certain crimes.[25] But in the main, both in Israel and in Mesopotamia, impalement was used as a punishment and a deterrent as well as an expiation to the deity for violating his oath (see Excursus 61).

before the LORD Hebrew ***le-YHVH***. Rather, "to the Lord," although in the similar case of the impalement of Saul's sons (see Excursus 61), the expression "for the Lord" also occurs (2 Sam. 21:9) together with "to the Lord" (v. 6). The difference is this: "Before" implies a ritual at the sanctuary; "to" connotes a nonritualistic dedication to the Lord outside the sanctuary.[26] Either explanation is possible here. The fact that the impaled corpses would have brought ritual defilement to the sanctuary (e.g., see Lev. 16:1) is not a consideration because an emergency situation prevailed. Moreover, the impalement of Saul's sons probably took place before the famed altar of Gibeon (cf. 2 Sam. 21:6; LXX; 1 Kings 3:4; see also 1 Sam. 15:33).

In this case the public impalement was not to be regarded as a deterrent to others but as expiation for Israel's apostasy—in the hope that it might terminate the plague (see Excursus 61). Perhaps this is

[5]So Moses said to Israel's officials, "Each of you slay those of his men who attached themselves to Baal-peor."

[6]Just then one of the Israelites came and brought a Midianite woman over to his companions, in the sight of Moses and of the whole Israelite community who were weeping at the entrance of the Tent of Meeting. [7]When Phinehas, son of Eleazar son of Aaron the priest, saw this, he left the assembly and, taking a spear in his hand, [8]he

הִרְגוּ אִישׁ אֲנָשָׁיו הַנִּצְמָדִים לְבַעַל פְּעוֹר׃ 6 וְהִנֵּה
אִישׁ מִבְּנֵי יִשְׂרָאֵל בָּא וַיַּקְרֵב אֶל־אֶחָיו אֶת־
הַמִּדְיָנִית לְעֵינֵי מֹשֶׁה וּלְעֵינֵי כָּל־עֲדַת בְּנֵי־
יִשְׂרָאֵל וְהֵמָּה בֹכִים פֶּתַח אֹהֶל מוֹעֵד׃ מפטיר
7 וַיַּרְא פִּינְחָס בֶּן־אֶלְעָזָר בֶּן־אַהֲרֹן הַכֹּהֵן וַיָּקָם
מִתּוֹךְ הָעֵדָה וַיִּקַּח רֹמַח בְּיָדוֹ׃ 8 וַיָּבֹא אַחַר

what Baḥya had in mind: "As they desecrated (the name of God) in public (by their idolatrous worship) so they must now sanctify His name in public."

the LORD's wrath That is, the plague (see the Comment to v. 3). It is not unusual for the Lord to refer to Himself in the third person (e.g., Exod. 12:11,14).

5. *Israel's officials* The *shofet*, "judge," is also the *sar*, one of the military officers appointed by Moses, on Jethro's advice, as commanders and judges over companies of tens, fifties, hundreds, and thousands (Exod. 18:21). The two functions overlap, the commander frequently acting in judicial capacity, as in Isaiah 32:1 and Jeremiah 26:10–16.[27] Among the Hittites, the *bēl madgalti*, "commander of the guard," had a judicial function, as was true in Mesopotamia.[28]

his men That is, those under his command.[29] The execution is assumed by some to have been carried out.[30] More likely, God's wrath was assuaged by Phinehas's act before Moses' order could be fulfilled.[31]

6. *Just then . . . came*[32]

brought . . . over to his companions For what purpose? The simplest and most probable answer is that, following Ibn Ezra, *'eḥav* should be rendered as "kinsmen," thereby implying that he introduced his Midianite bride to his family. Others, like Rashbam, point to the sexual connotation of the word *va-yakrev*, as in Leviticus 18:6 and Genesis 20:4. The Septuagint interchanges *'el* and *'et* and reads *'eḥav* as the singular *'aḥiv* for the rendering "brought his brother to the Midianite woman"—thereby getting others to join him and aggravating the sexual offense. Another explanation holds that the Israelite was convinced (by his Midianite partner?) that ritual intercourse was the best way to appease God and thereby terminate the plague. All interpretations thus agree that this act constituted a brazen escalation of Israel's sin, committed before the sanctuary in the sight of Moses and the people while they were bewailing the plague in supplication to God. In any case, the result was the same: war with Midian. There can hardly be a more heinous crime than the open and deliberate murder of a princess by one of the highest officials of another nation (see Excursus 61).

in the sight of Moses Tradition explains Moses' lack of response to this brazen outrage by positing that (1) he did not want to attract further attention to it by starting a debate,[33] or that (2) "the Israelite sinner said to Moses: Can this one (the Midianite) be taken? Should you say that it is forbidden, didn't you yourself take a Midianitess, the daughter of Jethro? When Moses heard this, he became agitated and fainted."[34] Tradition recognized that Moses' passivity created a leadership vacuum.

who were weeping That is, while Moses and the community were weeping, the couple passed them by. Alternatively, "while they (Moses and the community) were weeping, Phinehas . . ." (v. 7). The weeping is a rite of penitence,[35] a subtle condemnation of Moses. He was there and witnessed the sacrilegious act; he should have done what Phinehas did. For other examples of Moses' inertia when action was needed, see Exodus 14:15 and Numbers 14:5; 16:4.

7. *Phinehas* An Egyptian name. This is the first mention of Phinehas, aside from the genealogical reference in Exodus 6:25.[36] In some respects, Phinehas's act corresponds to the Levitical role in the apostasy of the golden calf, as told in Exodus 32:25–29. Both had to slay "each his brother," for which both received ordination to the priesthood (see the Comment to v. 13).

followed the Israelite into the chamber and stabbed both of them, the Israelite and the woman, through the belly. Then the plague against the Israelites was checked. ⁹Those who died of the plague numbered twenty-four thousand.

אִישׁ־יִשְׂרָאֵל֙ אֶל־הַקֻּבָּ֔ה וַיִּדְקֹר֙ אֶת־שְׁנֵיהֶ֔ם אֵ֖ת אִ֣ישׁ יִשְׂרָאֵ֑ל וְאֶת־הָאִשָּׁ֖ה אֶל־קֳבָתָ֑הּ וַתֵּעָצַר֙ הַמַּגֵּפָ֔ה מֵעַ֖ל בְּנֵ֥י יִשְׂרָאֵֽל׃ 9 וַיִּהְי֕וּ הַמֵּתִ֖ים בַּמַּגֵּפָ֑ה אַרְבָּעָ֥ה וְעֶשְׂרִ֖ים אָֽלֶף׃ פ

Whence did Phinehas appear? According to the tradition of 1 Chronicles 9:20, he was already there, at the entrance of the Tent of Meeting, in his capacity as chief of the sanctuary guards (an office held by his father before him; Num. 3:32; and see Excursus 4). Eleazar did not act in this instance: As the High Priest, he was forbidden to come into contact with the dead under any circumstances (Lev. 21:10–12). Under similar circumstances, when Aaron had held this office, he, Eleazar, acted in his father's stead (17:2; 19:2–7). Phinehas again acts as protector of Israel's cult in chapter 31 (see also Josh. 22:13–31).

spear Not a long-shafted javelin but a short-shafted pike, which could be held in both hands and, like the modern bayonet, thrust downward upon a recumbent body. Since Phinehas was probably on duty as chief of the sanctuary guards, he was armed.

8. *the chamber* Hebrew *ha-kubbah*.[37] The *qubbah* among pre-Islamic Bedouin tribes was a miniature red leather tent with a domed top, on occasion small enough to be mounted on camelback. It contained tribal idols or betyls and was set up close to the chieftain's tent. It was used for divination; it guided the tribe during its wanderings; and it was occasionally attended by a female priest and occupied, in times of crisis, by women from the noblest tribal families.[38] But the *kubbah* mentioned here was probably not the ancient name for Israel's Tabernacle;[39] it was more likely a marriage canopy[40] (see Excursus 61). The egregious, aggravated crime of this couple was not only their intermarriage but that they flaunted it before Moses and the leaders of Israel.

through the belly Hebrew *'el kovatah*. A play on words with *kubbah*. The rendering "belly" relates it to *kevah* (Deut. 18:3), the maw of the animal assigned to the priest as his perquisite from the sacrifice.[41] Indeed, the midrash explains homiletically that the priestly right to the animal's maw stemmed from Phinehas's deed in the sinners' maw.[42] Alternatively, render "womb,"[43] relating the term to *nekevah*, "female, female genitals,"[44] a "measure for measure" punishment.[45] The word may, however, derive from an original *kovet*,[46] on the model of *boshet* "shame" (Hos. 9:10, cited in the Comment to v. 3), a derogatory term for her genitals. The phrase should accordingly be rendered "through the genitals."[47]

The rabbis were uncomfortable with Phinehas's act. He set a dangerous precedent by taking the law into his own hands and slaying a man impulsively, in disregard of the law. Some argued that Moses and the other leaders would have excommunicated him[48] were it not for the divine decree declaring that Phinehas had acted on God's behalf (vv. 12–13). Regarding this, a recent commentator remarks: "Who can tell whether the perpetrator is not really prompted by some selfish motive, maintaining that he is doing it for the sake of God, when he has actually committed murder? That is why the sages wished to excommunicate Phinehas, had not the Holy Spirit testified that his zeal for God was genuine."[49]

It is also possible that this negative judgment of Phinehas is already reflected in the Bible: "Phinehas stepped forth, *va-yepallel*, . . . and the plague ceased" (Ps. 106:30). The psalmist, who obviously is familiar with the passage in Numbers, avoids the attribution of zeal (*kin'ah*) to Phinehas and, instead, utilizes the verb *pillel*, which, as its occurrences elsewhere attest (e.g., 1 Sam. 2:25), can only signify mediation by prayer.[50] This meaning is clearly reflected in the rabbinic comment: "When Phinehas saw that the angel was causing too much devastation among the people he threw to the ground [the two sinners pierced with Phinehas's spear], stepped forth, and prayed [*va-yepallel*], as it is stated 'Phinehas stepped forth, *va-yepallel*, and the plague ceased'" (Sif. Num. 131).

9. *twenty-four thousand* Presumably, this number included the rest of the older generation who were doomed to die in the wilderness (14:29), since the census that follows this incident expressly certifies this (26:64–65).[51]

PINḤAS

10 The LORD spoke to Moses, saying, 11 "Phinehas, son of Eleazar son of Aaron the priest, has turned back My wrath from the Israelites by displaying among them his passion for Me, so that I did not wipe out the Israelite people in My passion. 12 Say, therefore, 'I grant him My pact of friendship. 13 It shall be for him and his descendants after him a pact of priesthood for all time, because he took impassioned action for his God, thus making expiation for the Israelites.'"

פינחס

10 וַיְדַבֵּר יְהוָה אֶל־מֹשֶׁה לֵּאמֹר: 11 פִּינְחָס בֶּן־
אֶלְעָזָר בֶּן־אַהֲרֹן הַכֹּהֵן הֵשִׁיב אֶת־חֲמָתִי מֵעַל
בְּנֵי־יִשְׂרָאֵל בְּקַנְאוֹ אֶת־קִנְאָתִי בְּתוֹכָם וְלֹא־
כִלִּיתִי אֶת־בְּנֵי־יִשְׂרָאֵל בְּקִנְאָתִי: 12 לָכֵן אֱמֹר
הִנְנִי נֹתֵן לוֹ אֶת־בְּרִיתִי שָׁלוֹם: 13 וְהָיְתָה לּוֹ
וּלְזַרְעוֹ אַחֲרָיו בְּרִית כְּהֻנַּת עוֹלָם תַּחַת אֲשֶׁר
קִנֵּא לֵאלֹהָיו וַיְכַפֵּר עַל־בְּנֵי יִשְׂרָאֵל: 14 וְשֵׁם

THE PACT WITH PHINEHAS (vv. 10–18)

Pinḥas

God rewards Phinehas's zeal by granting him and his offspring (the Zadokites) the priesthood (see Excursus 61). Thus, the covenant with Phinehas matches the later covenant with David: Their lines will control, respectively, the spiritual and civil lives of their people. Phinehas's victims turn out to be from the leading families of their respective nations. Thus, the Midianites who are blamed at the outset for instigating the apostasy of Baal-peor now have yet another reason to perpetuate their enmity toward Israel: to avenge the murder of their princess.

*11. **turned back my wrath***[52]

by displaying among them his passion for Me Literally, "in his becoming impassioned with My passion among them."[53] Phinehas was upset as much as the Lord Himself over the affront to the Lord caused by the people's sin.[54] The verb ***qana'a*** in Arabic and Syriac means "become intensely red" and refers here to the visible effects of anger on the face.[55] God becomes "impassioned," that is, aroused, when Israel flirts with other gods, as in Exodus 20:5 and 34:14. However, this phrase most likely means that Phinehas's passion matched that of God's because he alone, in distinction to Moses and the tribal heads, obeyed God's command to kill Israel's leaders (see Excursus 61).

wipe out the Israelite people Once released, God's anger destroys everything in its path and makes no moral distinctions. This empirical truth concerning natural disasters—in modern actuarial parlance called "acts of God"—is neither glossed over nor treated apologetically by the Torah. It is reckoned with as a cornerstone of its theology (see Excursus 61; also Excursuses 4, 19, 32, and 40).

*12. **Say*** That is, to the people[56] in the form of an oath.[57]

My pact of friendship Hebrew ***beriti shalom***. The idiom is found again in Isaiah 54:10, Ezekiel 34:25, and other texts. The unusual form here (a broken construct) is elliptical for ***beriti berit shalom***, literally "My pact, a pact of friendship,"[58] or ***beriti 'im shalom***, literally "My pact with/of friendship."[59] This latter meaning is confirmed by the equivalent construction ***beriti ya'akov . . . beriti yitsḥak . . . beriti 'avraham***, "My pact with Jacob . . . my pact with Isaac . . . my pact with Abraham," in Leviticus 26:42.[60]

God's covenant meant that Phinehas received divine protection against the revenge that would be sought by Zimri's clan.[61] Targum Jonathan adds: "And I will make him an eternal angel. And he will live forever, to announce the redemption at the end of the days."[62]

*13. **a pact of priesthood for all time*** The biblical notion of an eternal covenant, ***berit 'olam***,[63] is also attested in extrabiblical sources, for example, Akkadian ***adi dāriti, ūmē ṣâti***, "an everlasting covenant, for all time."

The text here mentions "the priesthood," not the High Priesthood, which gives rise to the rabbinic suggestion that Phinehas did not become a priest together with Aaron and his sons (Lev. 8) but only when he killed Zimri.[64] It may be the High Priesthood that is intended here.[65] Phinehas is awarded the High Priesthood just as the Levites have been awarded the priesthood (Exod. 32:29; see Mal. 2:4–8)—for suppressing apostasy. However, the likelihood is that Phinehas is here promised

14The name of the Israelite who was killed, the one who
was killed with the Midianite woman, was Zimri son of
Salu, chieftain of a Simeonite ancestral house. 15The name
of the Midianite woman who was killed was Cozbi daughter of Zur; he was the tribal head of an ancestral house in
Midian.

אִישׁ יִשְׂרָאֵל הַמֻּכֶּה אֲשֶׁר הֻכָּה אֶת־הַמִּדְיָנִית
זִמְרִי בֶּן־סָלוּא נְשִׂיא בֵית־אָב לַשִּׁמְעֹנִי׃ 15 וְשֵׁם
הָאִשָּׁה הַמֻּכָּה הַמִּדְיָנִית כָּזְבִּי בַת־צוּר רֹאשׁ
אֻמּוֹת בֵּית־אָב בְּמִדְיָן הוּא׃ פ 16 וַיְדַבֵּר
יְהוָה אֶל־מֹשֶׁה לֵּאמֹר׃ 17 צָרוֹר אֶת־הַמִּדְיָנִים

that his line, later called the Zadokites (see Ezek. 44:15–16), will be the exclusive officiants in the Temple (see Excursus 61 for details).

This covenant is one of five issued by God: the promise to Noah that humanity will not be destroyed, the promise of seed and soil to Abraham, the Torah to Moses (and Israel), and dynasties to Phinehas and David (cf. Jer. 33:19–22; Ps. 89:29–38). It constitutes another royal gift bestowed upon the High Priest, who, like the king, wears special robes and a crown and is anointed (Lev. 8:12; 2 Kings 11:12). Now, by virtue of this covenant, he is granted a ruling dynasty.

This dynastic promise to Phinehas, however, encounters the historic difficulty that certain High Priests, the Elids, trace their descent to Phinehas's uncle, Ithamar (1 Chron. 24:3,6).[66] This passage, then, may reflect the victory of Zadok (the descendant of Phinehas) over Abiathar (the descendant of Ithamar). The two served jointly as High Priests during the reign of David, but Solomon banished Abiathar from his office, as told in 1 Kings 2:26–27 (see 1 Sam. 2:27–36), leaving the High Priesthood exclusively to the line of Phinehas. However, the text mentions "priesthood" not "High Priesthood." The exact phrase, moreover, is "everlasting (*'olam*) priesthood," which occurs in two other places (Exod. 29:9; 40:15), where Aaron's dynasty is granted the priesthood. Hence, the reference here is not to the office of High Priest but to all those who are authorized to function as priests in the sanctuary. Therefore, it is more likely that the Baal-peor incident served to justify the banishment of Abiathar's entire family from the Jerusalem Temple, leaving the Zadokites alone as the officiating priests. Other priestly families continued to serve on the staff of the First Temple but not as officiants (Ezek. 40:45–46; 43:19; see Excursus 61 for details).

making expiation Rather, "ransoming" (see 8:19 and Excursus 19). By means of his passion (*kin'ah*), Phinehas provided a ransom for Israel, and God's wrath was assuaged. So too, when the Levitical guard cuts down the encroacher on God's sancta, he also provides a ransom that stays God's wrath from venting itself upon Israel (see the Comments to 8:19; 18:22–23).[67] Phinehas, as chief of the Levitical guards, now fulfills this Levitical function.

Later tradition, interpreting "plague" as slaughter,[68] claims that Phinehas's example was followed by his loyal supporters,[69] and it was they who slew the twenty-four thousand Israelites (v. 9).

14–15. A postscript giving the names and pedigrees of the culprits. Ramban explains that this constitutes implicit praise of Phinehas, who, for the sake of his God, killed an Israelite chieftain and a Midianite princess. Abravanel adds that despite their high rank, Phinehas was not afraid of Simeonite and Midianite revenge. Also, it might indicate that Phinehas began to carry out God's command to impale the leaders (see Excursus 61).

14. ***chieftain*** See the Comment to 1:16 and Excursus 1.

ancestral house That is, a household, the basic unit of the clan. Hence, writes Ibn Ezra, the chieftain of a clan (1:4) would be a higher official.

15. ***tribal head*** Hebrew *ro'sh 'ummot*, reading the singular, *'ummat*.[70] Alternatively, the Midianite is called a king (31:8) and a chieftain (Josh. 13:21), indicating in either case that he held a high office. The rare term *'ummah* is found in only one other place in the Bible, in the genealogy of Ishmael (Gen. 25:16). Thus, two tribally based and related peoples, the Midianites and Ishmaelites (see Judg. 8:24–26), utilize the same term to designate the tribal unit. The term also occurs in Akkadian *ummatum* in eighteenth-century documents at Mari and Tell al-Rimah in Upper Mesopotamia, as well as in letters of Hammurabi of Babylon, where the term also applies to a tribal unit.[71]

of an ancestral house Possibly a gloss, explaining the rare term *'ummah* by equating the Midianites' position with that of Zimri. However, *'ummah* is clearly the larger unit.

16The Lord spoke to Moses, saying, 17"Assail the Midianites and defeat them—18for they assailed you by the trickery they practiced against you—because of the affair of Peor and because of the affair of their kinswoman Cozbi, daughter of the Midianite chieftain, who was killed at the time of the plague on account of Peor."

וְהִכִּיתֶם אוֹתָם׃ 18 כִּי צֹרְרִים הֵם לָכֶם בְּנִכְלֵיהֶם
אֲשֶׁר־נִכְּלוּ לָכֶם עַל־דְּבַר־פְּעוֹר וְעַל־דְּבַר כָּזְבִּי
בַת־נְשִׂיא מִדְיָן אֲחֹתָם הַמֻּכָּה בְיוֹם־הַמַּגֵּפָה עַל־
דְּבַר־פְּעוֹר׃ 19 וַיְהִי אַחֲרֵי הַמַּגֵּפָה׃* פ

v. 19. פסקא באמצע פסוק

17. Assail[72]

the Midianites Since it was Moabite women who seduced the Israelites, why are the Midianites assailed? This episode may reflect the period when Moab was part of a Midianite confederation (see the Comments to Num. 10:29; 22:4) that embraced all of Transjordan as its protectorate (e.g., Josh. 13:21). When Israel conquered Sihon's territory, it severed the king's highway (21:22) and thereby threatened the Midianites' hold on the vital spice trade.[73] Thus Midian, Israel's erstwhile ally (10:29–32), now became its implacable foe.

18. ***they assailed you*** Hebrew *tsorerim*, a participle, may also be rendered "they are hostile," indicating both past and continuing hostility.

by the trickery they practiced[74]

because of the affair . . . because of the affair Both Israel's apostasy at Baal-peor and the egregious case of Zimri are attributed to the machinations of the Midianites (see the Comment to 22:4). If the participle *tsorerim* implies ongoing hostility, then the first "because" indicates the Midianites' *past* hostility as evidenced by their role in the Baal-peor incident and their *future* hostility because of their desire to avenge the murder of their princess.[75]

chieftain *Nasi'* of Midian, also called *ro'sh*, "head" (v. 19), "king" (31:8), and *netsiv*, "sheikh" (Josh. 13:21).[76]

their kinswoman Hebrew *'aḥotam* (see Gen. 24:59), implying that the Midianites now felt obligated to avenge her death.

19. ***When the plague was over*** The Masoretic note *piska' be-'emtsa' pasuk* indicates a break in the text at this point, which may mean that originally the account of the war against Midian followed (chap. 31). And since war requires draft registration, the account of the census (chap. 26) was interposed.[77] Philo, in fact, follows his account of chapter 25 with chapter 31.[78] The juxtaposition of the second census (chap. 26) to this clause implies, however, that the plague wiped out the entire generation that had left Egypt (see 26:64–65).[79]

THE GENERATION OF THE CONQUEST (26:1–36:13)

The central theme of the final eleven chapters of the Book of Numbers is the occupation of the promised land. We read of a (second) census of able-bodied men, this time of the new generation, in preparation for war (with Midian) and for the division of the land (chap. 26); the rights of women, under certain conditions, to share in the division and to inherit (27:1–11; 36); the succession to Moses (27:12–23); the cultic calendar (chaps. 28–29) and fulfillment of vows (chap. 30); the war against Midian (chap. 31); the allotment of Transjordan (chap. 32); the various wilderness stations (33:1–49); the attitude toward the Canaanites and their cult (33:50–56); the boundaries of the land (34:1–15); the supervisors for the division of the land (34:16–29); the Levitical holdings in the land (35:1–8); the need to prevent the pollution of the land by homicide (35:9–34). In contrast to the faithlessness of the generation of the Exodus, the following generation is characterized by fidelity and courage; it is successful in battle and deemed worthy to conquer the promised land.

CHAPTER 26

The Second Census (vv. 1–65)

All able-bodied men above the age of twenty are registered for the ultimate purpose of dividing the land among them (also to provide a militia for the forthcoming war against Midian; chap. 31). This census and the earlier census in Numbers (1:20–43) serve to bracket the wilderness trek, the main difference (besides the slight variation in the count) being that this list enumerates the tribal clans—a difference explained by context. The first census is followed, in chapter 2, by the description of Israel's wilderness camp, a tribal arrangement, whereas this chapter prepares the way for the allotment of land in Canaan (vv. 52–56), a clan arrangement.[1] This clan register is clearly old, dating from the premonarchical period, when Israelite society was based solely on a clan structure. The identity of certain clans with towns and districts in the mountains further supports the list's antiquity (see the Comments to vv. 29–34). The existence of two types of census, for war (chap. 1) and for land (chap. 26), is duplicated in the Mari archive, dating to the turn of the nineteenth century B.C.E. There too we find a military census (ARM 1.42) and a land census (ARM 1.7.31–45).[2] Clearly, these two biblical censuses are based on hoary precedent.

The names are closely related to those in Genesis 46:8–24, with the difference that there they are persons, whereas here they are clans. If one includes the daughters of Zelophehad (v. 33) and the Levites in the following census (vv. 57–62), the people of Israel comprises seventy clans. Thus, Israel—having entered Egypt numbering seventy individuals (Gen. 46:27; Exod. 1:5)—has become a nation of seventy clans.[3] Also the order of the tribes is different, following that of the first census (1:20–43) except that here Manasseh precedes Ephraim (for the possible reason, see the Comment to vv. 29–34). Other registers of the Israelite clans are found in Exodus 6 and 1 Chronicles 2, 4, 5, 7, and 8. The variations in the names are slight and need not be discussed.

The list is composed of two formulas. The first gives the clan names—"The X-ites by their clans: Of A, the clan of A; of B, the clan of B . . ."; and the second gives the totals—"Those are the clans of the X-ites; persons enrolled: N," where X stands for the tribe, A for the clan and N for the tribal count. Expansions are found in verses 8–11,29–33. The results of the two wilderness censuses are as follows:

26 [19]When the plague was over, [1]the LORD said to Moses
and to Eleazar son of Aaron the priest, [2]"Take a census of
the whole Israelite community from the age of twenty years
up, by their ancestral houses, all Israelites able to bear
arms." [3]So Moses and Eleazar the priest, on the steppes of
Moab, at the Jordan near Jericho, gave instructions about
them, namely, [4]those from twenty years up, as the LORD
had commanded Moses.

כ״ו וַיֹּאמֶר יְהוָה אֶל־מֹשֶׁה וְאֶל אֶלְעָזָר בֶּן־
אַהֲרֹן הַכֹּהֵן לֵאמֹר: 2 שְׂאוּ אֶת־רֹאשׁ | כָּל־עֲדַת
בְּנֵי־יִשְׂרָאֵל מִבֶּן עֶשְׂרִים שָׁנָה וָמַעְלָה לְבֵית
אֲבֹתָם כָּל־יֹצֵא צָבָא בְּיִשְׂרָאֵל: 3 וַיְדַבֵּר מֹשֶׁה
וְאֶלְעָזָר הַכֹּהֵן אֹתָם בְּעַרְבֹת מוֹאָב עַל־יַרְדֵּן יְרֵחוֹ
לֵאמֹר: 4 מִבֶּן עֶשְׂרִים שָׁנָה וָמָעְלָה כַּאֲשֶׁר° צִוָּה

Tribes	*Census (year 2)*	*Census (year 40)*	*Increase*	*Decrease*
1. Reuben	46,500	43,730		2,770
2. Simeon	59,300	22,200		37,100
3. Gad	45,650	40,500		5,150
4. Judah	74,600	76,500	1,900	
5. Issachar	54,400	64,300	9,900	
6. Zebulun	57,400	60,500	3,100	
7. Ephraim	40,500	32,500		8,000
8. Manasseh	32,200	52,700	20,500	
9. Benjamin	35,400	45,600	10,200	
10. Dan	62,700	64,400	1,700	
11. Asher	41,500	53,600	11,900	
12. Naphtali	53,400	45,400		8,000
TOTAL	603,550	601,730	59,200	61,020

The major changes are the precipitous decline in Simeon and the sizable increase in Manasseh, perhaps reflecting the historical situation of the settlement: Simeon was soon absorbed by Judah (see Judg. 1:3; Josh. 19:1), whereas Manasseh expanded beyond its settled territory (Josh. 17:11,16) and dominated political events during the judgeships of two of its sons, Gideon and Abimelech (Judg. 6–9; see 12:1–6). Alternative proposals for interpreting these tribal totals drastically reduce the numbers so that they are in consonance with the size of armies attested in many documents from the ancient Near East. Thus, if *'elef* is not rendered as "thousand" but as "military unit," then the totals mustered from the tribes in each census are 5,550 and 5,730 men, respectively. For details see Excursus 2.

DIRECTIONS FOR TAKING A CENSUS (vv. 1–4)

The purpose, in part as preparation for war against Midian,[4] is mainly for parceling out the promised land, as is clear from verses 52–56.[5]

*1. **Eleazar*** God's command for the first census was given to Moses and Aaron. Now, following Aaron's death, his successor takes his place. This is the only place that God addresses Eleazar directly. Why he is needed for the census is not clear. It is possible that the tribe of Levi, as in the first census, was counted by oracle (see the Comments to 3:16,39), which, presumably, would have been operated by Eleazar (27:21).

2. The instructions are identical to, but briefer than, the corresponding ones of the first census (1:1–2).

by their ancestral houses Hebrew *le-veit 'avotam*, called *mishpeḥotam* in the tribal list that follows, proving the equivalence of these two terms (see the Comments to 1:2,16).

*3. **gave instruction about them***[6]

The descendants of the Israelites who came out of the land of Egypt were:

[5]Reuben, Israel's first-born. Descendants of Reuben: [Of] Enoch, the clan of the Enochites; of Pallu, the clan of the Palluites; [6]of Hezron, the clan of the Hezronites; of Carmi, the clan of the Carmites. [7]Those are the clans of the Reubenites. The persons enrolled came to 43,730.

[8]Born to Pallu: Eliab. [9]The sons of Eliab were Nemuel,

יְהוָ֤ה אֶת־מֹשֶׁה֙ וּבְנֵ֣י יִשְׂרָאֵ֔ל הַיֹּצְאִ֖ים מֵאֶ֥רֶץ
מִצְרָֽיִם׃ שני 5 רְאוּבֵ֖ן בְּכ֣וֹר יִשְׂרָאֵ֑ל בְּנֵ֣י רְאוּבֵ֗ן
חֲנוֹךְ֙ מִשְׁפַּ֣חַת הַחֲנֹכִ֔י לְפַלּ֕וּא מִשְׁפַּ֖חַת הַפַּלֻּאִֽי׃
6 לְחֶצְרֹ֕ן מִשְׁפַּ֖חַת הַֽחֶצְרוֹנִ֑י לְכַרְמִ֕י מִשְׁפַּ֖חַת
הַכַּרְמִֽי׃ 7 אֵ֖לֶּה מִשְׁפְּחֹ֣ת הָרֻאוּבֵנִ֑י וַיִּהְי֣וּ פְקֻדֵיהֶ֗ם
שְׁלֹשָׁ֤ה וְאַרְבָּעִים֙ אֶ֔לֶף וּשְׁבַ֥ע מֵא֖וֹת וּשְׁלֹשִֽׁים׃
8 וּבְנֵ֥י פַלּ֖וּא אֱלִיאָֽב׃ 9 וּבְנֵ֣י אֱלִיאָ֗ב נְמוּאֵ֛ל וְדָתָ֖ן

at[7]

namely Hebrew *le'mor*, literally "saying," is followed by a direct quotation (v. 4), which is truncated.

4. ***As the Lord had commanded Moses*** This is the customary formula signifying the fulfillment of a command (e.g., 1:19; 2:33), which leads the Peshitta to delete "namely" from the previous verse and to begin this verse with "And Moses numbered." However, most versions and commentators begin the fulfillment passage with verse 3 and supply the missing subject and verb. An alternative rendering of this phrase is cited below.

The descendants of the Israelites Hebrew *u-venei yisra'el* is the common Hebrew expression for "the Israelites." Such a rendering would imply that this second census was also taken of the generation of the Exodus; but according to the explicit statement of the text (vv. 64–65), it had already perished! For the possible resolution of this contradiction, see the next Comment.

who came out Hebrew *ha-yotse'im*. This participle, disconnected from the previous sentence, can only be rendered "who are coming out," referring unmistakably to the generation of the Exodus. If so then this second census was originally a variant of the first (1:20–43). Some commentators attempt to resolve this dilemma by rendering all of verse 4 as a continuous sentence: ". . . as the Lord commanded Moses and the Israelites *when* they came out of the land of Egypt."[8] Thus the phrase "as the Lord commanded . . ." is not a fulfillment formula (see above) but a reference to the first census, meaning that this new census should be carried out in exactly the same way—a most plausible interpretation.

THE RESULTS OF THE CENSUS (vv. 5–51)

This section enumerates the clans, the number of able-bodied men in each tribe, and their total sum; additional information is inserted for Reuben (vv. 8–11), Judah (v. 19), and Manasseh (v. 33).

THE REUBENITES (vv. 5–7)

5. ***Descendants of Reuben*** Rather, "the Reubenites," and so for the other tribes. The four Reubenite clans are identical with those listed in Genesis 46:9, Exodus 6:14, and 1 Chronicles 5:3.

6. ***Hezron . . . Carmi*** Also clan names in Judah (v. 21; 1 Chron. 4:1). Other evidence shows that Reubenite families did indeed live in Judah (Josh. 15:6).

7. ***The persons enrolled came to***[9]

AN ADDENDUM TO THE KORAHITE REBELLION (vv. 8–11)

This section indicates that neither the Reubenites nor the Korahites died out, despite the deaths of Korah and of Dathan and Abiram and their families. This passage follows the tradition that Korah also perished in the quake (see Excursus 39).

8. ***Born to***[10]

and Dathan and Abiram. These are the same Dathan and Abiram, chosen in the assembly, who agitated against Moses and Aaron as part of Korah's band when they agitated against the LORD. 10 Whereupon the earth opened its mouth and swallowed them up with Korah—when that band died, when the fire consumed the two hundred and fifty men—and they became an example. 11 The sons of Korah, however, did not die.

12 Descendants of Simeon by their clans: Of Nemuel, the clan of the Nemuelites; of Jamin, the clan of the Jaminites; of Jachin, the clan of the Jachinites; 13 of Zerah, the clan of the Zerahites; of Saul, the clan of the Saulites. 14 Those are the clans of the Simeonites; [persons enrolled:] 22,200.

15 Descendants of Gad by their clans: Of Zephon, the clan of the Zephonites; of Haggi, the clan of the Haggites; of Shuni, the clan of the Shunites; 16 of Ozni, the clan of the

וַאֲבִירָם הוּא־דָתָן וַאֲבִירָם קרואי הָעֵדָה אֲשֶׁר
הִצּוּ עַל־מֹשֶׁה וְעַל־אַהֲרֹן בַּעֲדַת־קֹרַח בְּהַצֹּתָם
עַל־יְהוָה׃ 10 וַתִּפְתַּח הָאָרֶץ אֶת־פִּיהָ וַתִּבְלַע
אֹתָם וְאֶת־קֹרַח בְּמוֹת הָעֵדָה בַּאֲכֹל הָאֵשׁ אֵת
חֲמִשִּׁים וּמָאתַיִם אִישׁ וַיִּהְיוּ לְנֵס׃ 11 וּבְנֵי־קֹרַח
לֹא־מֵתוּ׃ ס 12 בְּנֵי שִׁמְעוֹן לְמִשְׁפְּחֹתָם
לִנְמוּאֵל מִשְׁפַּחַת הַנְּמוּאֵלִי לְיָמִין מִשְׁפַּחַת
הַיָּמִינִי לְיָכִין מִשְׁפַּחַת הַיָּכִינִי׃ 13 לְזֶרַח מִשְׁפַּחַת
הַזַּרְחִי לְשָׁאוּל מִשְׁפַּחַת הַשָּׁאוּלִי׃ 14 אֵלֶּה
מִשְׁפְּחֹת הַשִּׁמְעֹנִי שְׁנַיִם וְעֶשְׂרִים אֶלֶף וּמָאתָיִם׃
ס 15 בְּנֵי גָד לְמִשְׁפְּחֹתָם לִצְפוֹן מִשְׁפַּחַת
הַצְּפוֹנִי לְחַגִּי מִשְׁפַּחַת הַחַגִּי לְשׁוּנִי מִשְׁפַּחַת
הַשּׁוּנִי׃ 16 לְאָזְנִי מִשְׁפַּחַת הָאָזְנִי לְעֵרִי מִשְׁפַּחַת

v. 9. קְרִיאֵי ק׳

Nemeul Otherwise unknown. It may have been moved up from the next list (the first of the Simeonite clans; v. 12) to suggest that the line of Pallu did not become extinct because of the death of Dathan and Abiram (16:32).[11]

chosen in (the assembly)[12]

9. agitated[13]

10. with Korah Hebrew *ve-'et korah*. The Samaritan reads instead *ha-'arets*; that is, the earth swallowed them (Dathan and Abiram); and after "consume," the Samaritan adds *koraḥ ve-'et*, "Korah and," thereby making this text conform to the tradition that Korah died by the divine fire and not by the quake (see Excursus 39).

an example Hebrew *nes*, literally "standard," equivalent to *'ot*, which can also mean "standard" (see 2:2) or "example, warning" (17:2).[14]

11. The sons of Korah, however, did not die. The Korahite clan survived (v. 58) to become an important Levitical clan of Temple singers. Their name appears in the titles of Psalms 42, 44–49, 84, 85, and 87, and as Temple guards in 1 Chronicles 9:19. The expression "sons of Korah" appears on an ostracon from Arad.[15]

THE SIMEONITES (vv. 12–14)

A sixth clan, Ohad (also missing in 1 Chron. 4:24), occurs in Genesis 46:10 and Exodus 6:15, possibly, as Rashi points out, because it later disappeared. The loss of two-thirds of Simeon's soldiery, as shown in the comparative table featured above, parallels its history of near disappearance and absorption into the tribe of Judah. On this, see Judges 1:3 and Joshua 19:1.

13. Zerah Also one of the chief clans of Judah (Gen. 46:12), but since Simeon was absorbed into Judah, it is plausible to conjecture that representatives of this Simeonite clan became linked to both tribes.

THE GADITES (vv. 15–18)

In the Septuagint Gad follows Zebulun, as in Genesis 46:16.

persons enrolled Hebrew *li-fekudeihem*. As indicated by the formulas for Reuben (v. 7), Manasseh (v. 34), Benjamin (v. 41), and Naphtali (v. 50), this word has to be taken with the number that follows (see the Comment to v. 7).

Oznites; of Eri, the clan of the Erites; [17]of Arod, the clan of the Arodites; of Areli, the clan of the Arelites. [18]Those are the clans of Gad's descendants; persons enrolled: 40,500.

[19]Born to Judah: Er and Onan. Er and Onan died in the land of Canaan.

[20]Descendants of Judah by their clans: Of Shelah, the clan of the Shelanites; of Perez, the clan of the Perezites; of Zerah, the clan of the Zerahites. [21]Descendants of Perez: of Hezron, the clan of the Hezronites; of Hamul, the clan of the Hamulites. [22]Those are the clans of Judah; persons enrolled: 76,500.

[23]Descendants of Issachar by their clans: [Of] Tola, the clan of the Tolaites; of Puvah, the clan of the Punites; [24]of Jashub, the clan of the Jashubites; of Shimron, the clan of the Shimronites. [25]Those are the clans of Issachar; persons enrolled: 64,300.

[26]Descendants of Zebulun by their clans: Of Sered, the clan of the Seredites; of Elon, the clan of the Elonites; of Jahleel, the clan of the Jahleelites. [27]Those are the clans of the Zebulunites; persons enrolled: 60,500.

[28]The sons of Joseph were Manasseh and Ephraim—by their clans.

17 הָעֵרִ֑י לַֽאֲר֕וֹד מִשְׁפַּ֖חַת הָֽאֲרוֹדִ֑י לְאַ֨רְאֵלִ֔י מִשְׁפַּ֖חַת הָֽאַרְאֵלִֽי: 18 אֵ֥לֶּה מִשְׁפְּחֹ֖ת בְּנֵי־גָ֑ד לִפְקֻדֵיהֶ֕ם אַרְבָּעִ֥ים אֶ֖לֶף וַֽחֲמֵ֥שׁ מֵאֽוֹת: ס 19 בְּנֵ֥י יְהוּדָ֖ה עֵ֣ר וְאוֹנָ֑ן וַיָּ֥מָת עֵ֛ר וְאוֹנָ֖ן בְּאֶ֥רֶץ כְּנָֽעַן: 20 וַיִּֽהְי֥וּ בְנֵֽי־יְהוּדָ֖ה לְמִשְׁפְּחֹתָ֑ם לְשֵׁלָ֗ה מִשְׁפַּ֣חַת הַשֵּֽׁלָנִ֔י לְפֶ֨רֶץ֙ מִשְׁפַּ֣חַת הַפַּרְצִ֔י לְזֶ֕רַח מִשְׁפַּ֖חַת הַזַּרְחִֽי: 21 וַיִּֽהְי֣וּ בְנֵי־פֶ֔רֶץ לְחֶצְרֹ֕ן מִשְׁפַּ֖חַת הַֽחֶצְרֹנִ֑י לְחָמ֕וּל מִשְׁפַּ֖חַת הֶֽחָמוּלִֽי: 22 אֵ֥לֶּה מִשְׁפְּחֹ֖ת יְהוּדָ֑ה לִפְקֻֽדֵיהֶ֕ם שִׁשָּׁ֧ה וְשִׁבְעִ֛ים אֶ֖לֶף וַֽחֲמֵ֥שׁ מֵאֽוֹת: ס 23 בְּנֵ֤י יִשָּׂשכָר֙ לְמִשְׁפְּחֹתָ֔ם תּוֹלָ֕ע מִשְׁפַּ֖חַת הַתּֽוֹלָעִ֑י לְפֻוָּ֕ה מִשְׁפַּ֖חַת הַפּוּנִֽי: 24 לְיָשׁ֕וּב מִשְׁפַּ֖חַת הַיָּֽשֻׁבִ֑י לְשִׁמְרֹ֕ן מִשְׁפַּ֖חַת הַשִּׁמְרֹנִֽי: 25 אֵ֥לֶּה מִשְׁפְּחֹ֖ת יִשָּׂשכָ֑ר לִפְקֻֽדֵיהֶ֕ם אַרְבָּעָ֧ה וְשִׁשִּׁ֛ים אֶ֖לֶף וּשְׁלֹ֥שׁ מֵאֽוֹת: ס 26 בְּנֵ֤י זְבוּלֻן֙ לְמִשְׁפְּחֹתָ֔ם לְסֶ֕רֶד מִשְׁפַּ֖חַת הַסַּרְדִּ֑י לְאֵל֕וֹן מִשְׁפַּ֖חַת הָֽאֵֽלֹנִ֑י לְיַחְלְאֵ֕ל מִשְׁפַּ֖חַת הַיַּחְלְאֵלִֽי: 27 אֵ֥לֶּה מִשְׁפְּחֹ֖ת הַזְּבֽוּלֹנִ֑י לִפְקֻֽדֵיהֶ֕ם שִׁשִּׁ֥ים אֶ֖לֶף וַֽחֲמֵ֥שׁ מֵאֽוֹת: ס 28 בְּנֵ֥י יוֹסֵ֖ף לְמִשְׁפְּחֹתָ֑ם מְנַשֶּׁ֖ה וְאֶפְרָֽיִם:

---

19. This verse explains the absence of Er and Onan from the list of clans, since they are referred to in Genesis 46:12.

THE JUDITES (vv. 20–22)

Their clans are described as sons and grandsons.

Descendants Preceded by *va-yihyu*, "and there were," a phrase that is unique in this list. It was inserted to bridge the preceding notice about Er and Onan and for this reason was probably also inserted at the beginning of verse 21.[16]

THE ISSACHARITES (vv. 23–26)

23. *Puvah*[17] It is the clan of the judge Tola (Judg. 10:1–2), who lived in the hill country of Ephraim.

24. *Jashub . . . Shimron* Both clans are place-names in the hill country of Ephraim. They are mentioned in 1 Kings 16:24 and in the Samaria ostraca (no. 48). This points to the family linkages between the contiguous tribes of Issachar and Manasseh.[18] Shimron was a Canaanite stronghold (Josh. 11:1); in another record, however (Josh. 19:15), it was assigned to Zebulun.

THE ZEBULUNITES (vv. 26–27)

26. *Elon* The name of a Zebulunite judge as well as of a Zebulunite town, Aijalon (Judg. 12:11–12).[19]

28. Manasseh and Ephraim are listed according to their order of birth, just as in Genesis 46:20, rather than according to the promise of Genesis 48:19. This is probably because of the former's growth and the latter's diminution during the time between the two censuses (see the comparative table, above).

29 Descendants of Manasseh: Of Machir, the clan of the Machirites.—Machir begot Gilead.—Of Gilead, the clan of the Gileadites. 30 These were the descendants of Gilead: [Of] Iezer, the clan of the Iezerites; of Helek, the clan of the

29 בְּנֵ֣י מְנַשֶּׁ֗ה לְמָכִיר֙ מִשְׁפַּ֣חַת הַמָּכִירִ֔י וּמָכִ֖יר
הוֹלִ֣יד אֶת־גִּלְעָ֑ד לְגִלְעָ֕ד מִשְׁפַּ֖חַת הַגִּלְעָדִֽי׃
30 אֵ֚לֶּה בְּנֵ֣י גִלְעָ֔ד אִיעֶ֕זֶר מִשְׁפַּ֖חַת הָאִיעֶזְרִ֑י

THE MANASSITES (vv. 29–34)

They are described as four generations: Machir (son) possessed Gilead (grandson; see 32:29) whose sons Shechem, Iezer/Abiezer, Hepher, Helek, Shmida, and Asriel settled in Cisjordan.[20] However, Joshua 17:1–3, 1 Chronicles 2:21–23, and 7:14–19 offer different schemes. Also, Manasseh now occupies the important seventh place in the order of the tribes (contrast 1:34) as do the daughters of Zelophehad in the Manassite genealogy (v. 33) in anticipation of the anomalous significance of the latter in the inheritance laws (27:1–11).[21]

The sixty-three Samaria ostraca record the delivery of wine and oil from certain districts near Samaria to the royal palace. Among the districts are Abiezer, Asriel (?), Helek, Shechem, and Shmida, which accord with five of the six Manassite clans in verses 30–32, as well as Noah and Hoglah who are two of the five daughters of Zelophehad in verse 33. Tirzah, another daughter (v. 33), also a place-name, is a former Canaanite city-state (Josh. 12:24) and the ancient capital of northern Israel (1 Kings 14:17; 15:21). Since these ostraca date about 800 B.C.E.,[22] this means that the Manassite clan divisions maintained themselves well into the monarchy. Moreover, since Shechem and Tirzah are former Canaanite city-states mentioned in Joshua 12:24; 24:25 and Judges 9, as are probably the other names as well, and since they are all located in the hill country of northern and northeastern Manasseh while none of them is in the plain, it is clear that this list must date from when Israel controlled only the mountainous territory but not the plain[23]—that is, before the time of King David. Furthermore, since these place-names do not occur among the list of cities Israel had failed to conquer (Judg. 1:27–35), a list that is also pre-Davidic, they must have been in Manasseh's possession and incorporated into its clan system at an early age.

The Samaria ostraca can lead to the same conclusion but on different grounds. The fact that five of Manasseh's six clans and two of Zelophehad's daughters are names of erstwhile Canaanite districts, coupled with the fact that Tirzah, another daughter, as well as Shechem are erstwhile Canaanite city-states, points to a sizable Canaanite element in Manasseh's population. This theory is reinforced by the genealogical datum that the line of Hepher terminates in daughters; that is, it is of lowly status and receives rights of inheritance only through divine decree (27:6–7). A striking parallel is afforded by the case of Caleb who is also of Canaanite (Kenizzite) stock (32:12) and also receives inheritance in Canaan by divine decree (14:24)—a matter all the more surprising since Joshua is not granted such a privilege. Moreover, the fact that the Book of Joshua records that both Caleb and Zelophehad's daughters are forced to remind Joshua of the divine promise (Josh. 14:6–14; 17:4) further supports the hypothesis that the Hepherites and the Calebites were originally Canaanite clans that assimilated into Israel. This would explain why they were not automatically accorded inheritance rights together with their Israelite brethren but had to bring their case before the Lord.[24] This theory also necessitates the premise that this list dates to premonarchic times when the tribe of Manasseh began to settle in the land.

29. Machir Who originally settled in Cisjordan (Judg. 5:14) as did the six "grandsons" (vv. 30–32). This is also shown by Joshua 17:14–18, which states explicitly that the entire house of Joseph, that is, Ephraim and Manasseh, was originally contained in Cisjordan. The Song of Deborah mentions Machir among the Cisjordanian tribes (Judg. 5:14–15). Apparently, only later did families of Machir settle in Gilead, that is, Transjordan (33:39). In this way, Machir was finally identified in the genealogies with Gilead as Gilead's father.[25] See the Comments to 32:39–42.

These were the descendants of Gilead Joshua 17:2 has a variant, probably more accurate tradition that they were "sons" of Manasseh, that is, contemporaneous clans with Machir in Cisjordan before the latter moved into Gilead.

30. Iezer Synonymous with Abiezer (Josh. 17:2), the clan of the judge Gideon (Judg. 6:11,24,34). In the Samaria ostraca this name is a district containing the towns of Elmatan and Tavil. If the latter are modern Ammatin and Till, the clan's territory was just west of Shechem.[26]

Helekites; [31][of] Asriel, the clan of the Asrielites; [of] Shechem, the clan of the Shechemites; [32][of] Shemida, the clan of the Shemidaites; [of] Hepher, the clan of the Hepherites. [33]—Now Zelophehad son of Hepher had no sons, only daughters. The names of Zelophehad's daughters were Mahlah, Noah, Hoglah, Milcah, and Tirzah.—[34]Those are the clans of Manasseh; persons enrolled: 52,700.

[35]These are the descendants of Ephraim by their clans: Of Shuthelah, the clan of the Shuthelahites; of Becher, the clan of the Becherites; of Tahan, the clan of the Tahanites.

לְחֵלֶק מִשְׁפַּחַת הַחֶלְקִי: 31 וְאַשְׂרִיאֵל מִשְׁפַּחַת
הָאַשְׂרְאֵלִי וְשֶׁכֶם מִשְׁפַּחַת הַשִּׁכְמִי: 32 וּשְׁמִידָע
מִשְׁפַּחַת הַשְּׁמִידָעִי וְחֵפֶר מִשְׁפַּחַת הַחֶפְרִי:
33 וּצְלָפְחָד בֶּן־חֵפֶר לֹא־הָיוּ לוֹ בָּנִים כִּי אִם־
בָּנוֹת וְשֵׁם בְּנוֹת צְלָפְחָד מַחְלָה וְנֹעָה חָגְלָה
מִלְכָּה וְתִרְצָה: 34 אֵלֶּה מִשְׁפְּחֹת מְנַשֶּׁה וּפְקֻדֵיהֶם
שְׁנַיִם וַחֲמִשִּׁים אֶלֶף וּשְׁבַע מֵאוֹת: ס
35 אֵלֶּה בְנֵי־אֶפְרַיִם לְמִשְׁפְּחֹתָם לְשׁוּתֶלַח
מִשְׁפַּחַת הַשֻּׁתַלְחִי לְבֶכֶר מִשְׁפַּחַת הַבַּכְרִי לְתַחַן
מִשְׁפַּחַת הַתַּחֲנִי: 36 וְאֵלֶּה בְּנֵי שׁוּתָלַח לְעֵרָן

Helek Containing the village of Ḥatserit in the Samaria ostraca. If identified with modern ʿAṣiret Esh-shamaliyeh,[27] the clan's territory was northeast of Abiezer, northwest of Shechem, and east of Samaria.

31. ***Asriel*** Associated with two villages in the Samaria ostraca, Yashoub and ʿAsheret. If the former is identified with modern Yossouf,[28] Asriel is to be located in the southern portion of Manasseh.

32. ***Shemida*** Embraces Saffarin and Kur in the Samaria ostraca, located north of Abiezer.

33. ***Zelophehad*** He and his daughters bring the Manassites to the sixth and seventh generation and are added here in anticipation of 27:1–11 to indicate that all problems regarding the inheritance of the tribal and clan apportionments of the promised land were ultimately resolved. Implied, then, is that Zelophehad's daughters inherited on an equal basis with their uncles, that is, in accordance with the second census in which they would have been reckoned as five persons.

Hepher The name of a region[29] comprising five "daughters" or districts situated in northeast Manasseh, north of Shechem and east of the central mountain range (see Map 4). These five Hepher districts/clans plus those of his five brothers mentioned in verses 30–32 comprise the ten district/clans of Manasseh in Cisjordan, a fact confirmed by Joshua 17:5 (see the Comment to 27:1).

Noah, Hoglah The only ones of the daughters' names mentioned in the Samaria ostraca. Yaṣid in the district of Hoglah is located east of Samaria (see Map 4).

Tirzah Identified with modern Tell El-Farah, at the head of Wadi Farʿah, northeast of Shechem.

THE EPHRAIMITES (vv. 35–37)

35. ***Becher*** Deleted in the Septuagint, probably because according to Genesis 46:21 it is a Benjaminite clan. However, since Ephraim and Benjamin were neighbors, it is possible that the same family lived on both sides of their common border[30] (see the Comments to vv. 6,13,44).

THE BENJAMINITES (vv. 38–41)

Genesis 46:21 lists three clans that are omitted here: Becher (see v. 35), Gera (the clan of Ehud [Judg. 3:15] and Shimei [2 Sam. 16:5]), and Rosh as well as two more clans, Ard and Naaman, who are Benjamin's grandsons according to verse 40.

THE DANITES (vv. 42–43)

These consist of only one clan, which indicates that the tribe must have been small, despite its large totals. This is indicated by Judges 18:2 and verified by its historical background: Canaanite and Philistine pressures forced it to migrate north where its territory bordered on the city of Laish-Dan (Judg. 18:27–29).

36 These are the descendants of Shuthelah: Of Eran, the clan
of the Eranites. 37 Those are the clans of Ephraim's descendants; persons enrolled: 32,500.

Those are the descendants of Joseph by their clans.

38 The descendants of Benjamin by their clans: Of Bela,
the clan of the Belaites; of Ashbel, the clan of the Ash-
belites; of Ahiram, the clan of the Ahiramites; 39 of Shephu-
pham, the clan of the Shuphamites; of Hupham, the clan of
the Huphamites. 40 The sons of Bela were Ard and Naaman:
[Of Ard,] the clan of the Ardites; of Naaman, the clan of the
Naamanites. 41 Those are the descendants of Benjamin by
their clans; persons enrolled: 45,600.

42 These are the descendants of Dan by their clans: Of
Shuham, the clan of the Shuhamites. Those are the clans of
Dan, by their clans. 43 All the clans of the Shuhamites;
persons enrolled: 64,400.

44 Descendants of Asher by their clans: Of Imnah, the
clan of the Imnites; of Ishvi, the clan of the Ishvites; of
Beriah, the clan of the Beriites. 45 Of the descendants of
Beriah: Of Heber, the clan of the Heberites; of Malchiel,
the clan of the Malchielites. 46—The name of Asher's
daughter was Serah.—47 These are the clans of Asher's
descendants; persons enrolled: 53,400.

48 Descendants of Naphtali by their clans: Of Jahzeel, the
clan of the Jahzeelites; of Guni, the clan of the Gunites; 49 of
Jezer, the clan of the Jezerites; of Shillem, the clan of the
Shillemites. 50 Those are the clans of the Naphtalites, clan
by clan; persons enrolled: 45,400.

51 This is the enrollment of the Israelites: 601,730.

מִשְׁפַּחַת הָעֵרָנִי׃ 37 אֵלֶּה מִשְׁפְּחֹת בְּנֵי־אֶפְרַיִם
לִפְקֻדֵיהֶם שְׁנַיִם וּשְׁלֹשִׁים אֶלֶף וַחֲמֵשׁ מֵאוֹת
אֵלֶּה בְנֵי־יוֹסֵף לְמִשְׁפְּחֹתָם׃ ס 38 בְּנֵי
בִנְיָמִן לְמִשְׁפְּחֹתָם לְבֶלַע מִשְׁפַּחַת הַבַּלְעִי
לְאַשְׁבֵּל מִשְׁפַּחַת הָאַשְׁבֵּלִי לַאֲחִירָם מִשְׁפַּחַת
הָאֲחִירָמִי׃ 39 לִשְׁפוּפָם מִשְׁפַּחַת הַשּׁוּפָמִי לְחוּפָם
מִשְׁפַּחַת הַחוּפָמִי׃ 40 וַיִּהְיוּ בְנֵי־בֶלַע אַרְדְּ וְנַעֲמָן
מִשְׁפַּחַת הָאַרְדִּי לְנַעֲמָן מִשְׁפַּחַת הַנַּעֲמִי׃
41 אֵלֶּה בְנֵי־בִנְיָמִן לְמִשְׁפְּחֹתָם וּפְקֻדֵיהֶם חֲמִשָּׁה
וְאַרְבָּעִים אֶלֶף וְשֵׁשׁ מֵאוֹת׃ ס 42 אֵלֶּה
בְנֵי־דָן לְמִשְׁפְּחֹתָם לְשׁוּחָם מִשְׁפַּחַת הַשּׁוּחָמִי
אֵלֶּה מִשְׁפְּחֹת דָּן לְמִשְׁפְּחֹתָם׃ 43 כָּל־מִשְׁפְּחֹת
הַשּׁוּחָמִי לִפְקֻדֵיהֶם אַרְבָּעָה וְשִׁשִּׁים אֶלֶף וְאַרְבַּע
מֵאוֹת׃ ס 44 בְּנֵי אָשֵׁר לְמִשְׁפְּחֹתָם לְיִמְנָה
מִשְׁפַּחַת הַיִּמְנָה לְיִשְׁוִי מִשְׁפַּחַת הַיִּשְׁוִי לִבְרִיעָה
מִשְׁפַּחַת הַבְּרִיעִי׃ 45 לִבְנֵי בְרִיעָה לְחֶבֶר
מִשְׁפַּחַת הַחֶבְרִי לְמַלְכִּיאֵל מִשְׁפַּחַת הַמַּלְכִּיאֵלִי׃
46 וְשֵׁם בַּת־אָשֵׁר שָׂרַח׃ 47 אֵלֶּה מִשְׁפְּחֹת בְּנֵי־
אָשֵׁר לִפְקֻדֵיהֶם שְׁלֹשָׁה וַחֲמִשִּׁים אֶלֶף וְאַרְבַּע
מֵאוֹת׃ ס 48 בְּנֵי נַפְתָּלִי לְמִשְׁפְּחֹתָם
לְיַחְצְאֵל מִשְׁפַּחַת הַיַּחְצְאֵלִי לְגוּנִי מִשְׁפַּחַת
הַגּוּנִי׃ 49 לְיֵצֶר מִשְׁפַּחַת הַיִּצְרִי לְשִׁלֵּם מִשְׁפַּחַת
הַשִּׁלֵּמִי׃ 50 אֵלֶּה מִשְׁפְּחֹת נַפְתָּלִי לְמִשְׁפְּחֹתָם
וּפְקֻדֵיהֶם חֲמִשָּׁה וְאַרְבָּעִים אֶלֶף וְאַרְבַּע מֵאוֹת׃
51 אֵלֶּה פְּקוּדֵי בְּנֵי יִשְׂרָאֵל שֵׁשׁ־מֵאוֹת אֶלֶף
וָאָלֶף שְׁבַע מֵאוֹת וּשְׁלֹשִׁים׃ פ שלישי

THE ASHERITES (vv. 44–47)

44. *Beriah* Also a clan of Ephraim (1 Chron. 7:21–24) and Benjamin (1 Chron. 8:13) and possibly the same family that migrated.

46. *Serah* The only female in the genealogical lists, she is also mentioned in Genesis 46:17 and 1 Chronicles 7:30. Ramban cites the Targum on this verse: "the name of the daughter of the wife of Asher" (this is not in our Targum texts). This suggests that her father died without male issue. She is therefore in the same category as the daughters of Zelophehad, which explains her being mentioned here. Otherwise, her presence remains a mystery.

THE NAPHTALITES (vv. 48–50)

THE TOTALS (v. 51)

See the comparative table, above.

⁵²The LORD spoke to Moses, saying, ⁵³"Among these shall the land be apportioned as shares, according to the listed names: ⁵⁴with larger groups increase the share, with smaller groups reduce the share. Each is to be assigned its share according to its enrollment. ⁵⁵The land, moreover, is to be apportioned by lot; and the allotment shall be made according to the listings of their ancestral tribes. ⁵⁶Each portion shall be assigned by lot, whether for larger or smaller groups."

וַיְדַבֵּ֥ר יְהוָ֖ה אֶל־מֹשֶׁ֥ה לֵּאמֹֽר׃ 53 לָאֵ֗לֶּה תֵּחָלֵ֥ק הָאָ֛רֶץ בְּנַחֲלָ֖ה בְּמִסְפַּ֥ר שֵׁמֽוֹת׃ 54 לָרַ֗ב תַּרְבֶּה֙ נַחֲלָת֔וֹ וְלַמְעַ֖ט תַּמְעִ֣יט נַחֲלָת֑וֹ אִ֚ישׁ לְפִ֣י פְקֻדָ֔יו יֻתַּ֖ן נַחֲלָתֽוֹ׃ 55 אַךְ־בְּגוֹרָ֕ל יֵחָלֵ֖ק אֶת־הָאָ֑רֶץ לִשְׁמ֥וֹת מַטּוֹת־אֲבֹתָ֖ם יִנְחָֽלוּ׃ 56 עַל־פִּי֙ הַגּוֹרָ֔ל תֵּחָלֵ֖ק נַחֲלָת֑וֹ בֵּ֥ין רַ֖ב לִמְעָֽט׃ ס

THE METHOD OF APPORTIONING THE LAND   (vv. 52–56)

This procedure is based on two seemingly irreconcilable methods: by lot (vv. 55–56) and by the size of each tribe (vv. 53–54). The best solution is a comprehensive one: The location of the tribal territory is determined by lot,[31] but the size of the territory is a function of the tribe's census count.[32] Details are discussed in Excursus 62. These prescriptions will apply only to the nine and a half tribes that settle in Cisjordan (34:13). The two and a half Transjordanian tribes arrange to have the territory they have conquered (34:14–15) awarded to them by Moses (32:33).

53. *Among these* But not, says Rashi, among those who reach the age of twenty before the land is conquered.

as shares See the Comment to 27:7.

according to the listed names See the Comment to 1:2. This implies that only those names entered in this second census were allotted land—not those who were counted in the first census and who died in the wilderness (vv. 64–65). Yet it is possible to argue that since Zelophehad could only have been counted in the first census and since his daughters inherited his share, the land must have been awarded to those in the earlier list.[33] However, Joshua 17:5–6 states unequivocally that each daughter received a share on a par with the share received by each of the five uncles (for a total of ten shares; see the Comment to v. 33), thus indicating that it was the second census that determined the apportionment of the land.

54. *with larger groups* This refers to the more populous tribes (see 35:8), as indicated by the tribal totals in this second census.

Each . . . its . . . its For this use of Hebrew *'ish* referring to the tribe, see 36:9. Alternatively, render "Each person . . . his . . . his"; that is, each person receives his allotment within his clan, not elsewhere.

55. *moreover* Rather, "however." An amendment to the previous statement will now follow—the employment of the lot (see Excursus 62).

apportioned Referring to location (see Excursus 62).

lot In Scripture the lot is used for a variety of purposes.[34] The casting of the lot was preceded by prayer (1 Sam. 10:22; 14:41) and performed at the sanctuary (1 Sam. 10:17) because the result was determined by God (Exod. 28:30; Josh. 19:50). The assignment of fiefs by lot was also practiced elsewhere in the ancient Near East during the second millennium.[35] Indeed, according to the Septuagint and the Qumran texts of Deuteronomy 32:8, even the nations of the world—not only Israel—received their territory by lot, said to have been assigned by God to each nation's protector angel.

according to the listings Literally, "according to the names"; that is, each person will take his share within the territory assigned to his tribe by lot.

56. *Each portion* Literally, "its portion," that is, each tribe's portion.

whether That is, irrespective of its size, each tribe will be assigned its territory by lot (see Excursus 62).

57 This is the enrollment of the Levites by their clans: Of
Gershon, the clan of the Gershonites; of Kohath, the clan of
the Kohathites; of Merari, the clan of the Merarites. 58 These
are the clans of Levi: The clan of the Libnites, the clan of
the Hebronites, the clan of the Mahlites, the clan of the
Mushites, the clan of the Korahites.—Kohath begot
Amram. 59 The name of Amram's wife was Jochebed daugh-

57 וְאֵלֶּה פְקוּדֵי הַלֵּוִי לְמִשְׁפְּחֹתָם לְגֵרְשׁוֹן
מִשְׁפַּחַת הַגֵּרְשֻׁנִּי לִקְהָת מִשְׁפַּחַת הַקְּהָתִי לִמְרָרִי
מִשְׁפַּחַת הַמְּרָרִי׃ 58 אֵלֶּה ׀ מִשְׁפְּחֹת לֵוִי מִשְׁפַּחַת
הַלִּבְנִי מִשְׁפַּחַת הַחֶבְרֹנִי מִשְׁפַּחַת הַמַּחְלִי
מִשְׁפַּחַת הַמּוּשִׁי מִשְׁפַּחַת הַקָּרְחִי וּקְהָת הוֹלִד
אֶת־עַמְרָם׃ 59 וְשֵׁם ׀ אֵשֶׁת עַמְרָם יוֹכֶבֶד בַּת־לֵוִי

THE LEVITICAL CLANS (vv. 57–62)

These are listed separately because they are not entitled to any share of the land (v. 62; see 18:23–24). And as they do not serve in the army, there is no need to limit their census to those males above twenty. The purpose of their census is not stated and must be inferred. Most likely it is for the assignment of their Tabernacle duties, as was the case with their first census, in chapters 3–4 (see the Comment to 3:7 and Excursuses 4, 5, and 6). An additional reason may be related to the subsequent allocation of forty-eight towns to the Levites (35:1–8): An accurate count would be necessary for distributing them among the assigned cities. Where is the Aaronide clan? Some say it is subsumed under the Hebronites (v. 58), since Hebron is a Levitical town assigned to Aaron (Josh. 21:10; 1 Chron. 6:42).[36] However, the text should be taken at face value. There are only two living Aaronides, Eleazar and Ithamar; and they need only be enumerated in the brief account of Aaron's family given in verses 59–62 in precisely the same fashion that the Aaronides were counted in the first census of 3:1–4.

57. The Gershonites, Kohathites, and Merarites comprise the three traditional clans of Levi who are assigned to their respective guarding and transport duties in the Tabernacle, following their initial census (chaps. 3–4). Their order here is determined by birth (Gen. 46:11) not importance (chap. 4).

58a. The problem: According to 3:18–20 (see Exod. 6:17–19), the three main Levitical clans of Gershon, Kohath, and Merari subdivide themselves into eight clans: two for Gershon (Libni and Shimei), four for Kohath (Amram, Izhar, Hebron, Uzziel), and two for Merari (Mahli and Mushi). Yet here five Levite clans are listed without any family connection to the traditional three: Libni, Hebron, Mahli, Mushi, Korah (the last, Korah, is a great-grandson of Levi, according to Exod. 6:21). Most scholars believe that this is an independent, early[37] tradition concerning the clan makeup of the Levites, one that antedates the organization of the three-clan grouping of the Levites into their courses in the Jerusalem Temple (1 Chron. 23).[38] It is, however, also possible that it is only a fragment of a once fuller list of Levitical subclans that derived from the three main ones.[39]

Libnites Libnah, a town in the tribe of Judah, was assigned to the Aaronides, who belong to the Kohathite Levites (Josh. 21:13).

Hebronites Hebron, a major city of Judah, was assigned to the Aaronides, who belong to the Levitical clan of Kohath (Josh. 21:10–11).

Mahlites This name survives on a cosmetic burner found in Lachish, thus attesting to the possible survival of this clan in the postexilic period.[40]

Mushites Many scholars maintain that this name is the gentilic of Moses, that is, the Levitical clan that traced its ancestry to Moses (e.g., Judg. 13:30) rather than to Kohath (via Amram; v. 59). But this conjecture is without warrant because this alleged Mosaic line would hardly have later been attached to the Merarites (3:20), who were in charge of the most menial labors—guarding and carting the sanctuary planks (3:36–37; 4:29–33)—rather than to the Kohathites, who were assigned the privileged duty of guarding and carrying the sancta (3:27–31; 4:1–14) or, at least, to the clan of Gershon who was Levi's first-born.

Korahites They comprised a prominent Levite family of singers in the Temple.[41] They also served as Temple guards (1 Chron. 26:1–3) at the most prestigious location—the entrance (1 Chron.

ter of Levi, who was born to Levi in Egypt; she bore to Amram Aaron and Moses and their sister Miriam. [60]To Aaron were born Nadab and Abihu, Eleazar and Ithamar. [61]Nadab and Abihu died when they offered alien fire before the LORD.—[62]Their enrollment of 23,000 comprised all males from a month up. They were not part of the regular enrollment of the Israelites, since no share was assigned to them among the Israelites.

[63]These are the persons enrolled by Moses and Eleazar the priest who registered the Israelites on the steppes of Moab, at the Jordan near Jericho. [64]Among these there was not one of those enrolled by Moses and Aaron the priest when they recorded the Israelites in the wilderness of Sinai.

אֲשֶׁר יָלְדָה אֹתָהּ לְלֵוִי בְּמִצְרָיִם וַתֵּלֶד לְעַמְרָם
אֶת־אַהֲרֹן וְאֶת־מֹשֶׁה וְאֵת מִרְיָם אֲחֹתָם׃
60 וַיִּוָּלֵד לְאַהֲרֹן אֶת־נָדָב וְאֶת־אֲבִיהוּא אֶת־
אֶלְעָזָר וְאֶת־אִיתָמָר׃ 61 וַיָּמָת נָדָב וַאֲבִיהוּא
בְּהַקְרִיבָם אֵשׁ־זָרָה לִפְנֵי יְהוָה׃ 62 וַיִּהְיוּ פְקֻדֵיהֶם
שְׁלֹשָׁה וְעֶשְׂרִים אֶלֶף כָּל־זָכָר מִבֶּן־חֹדֶשׁ וָמָעְלָה
כִּי ׀ לֹא הָתְפָּקְדוּ בְּתוֹךְ בְּנֵי יִשְׂרָאֵל כִּי לֹא־נִתַּן
לָהֶם נַחֲלָה בְּתוֹךְ בְּנֵי יִשְׂרָאֵל׃ 63 אֵלֶּה פְּקוּדֵי
מֹשֶׁה וְאֶלְעָזָר הַכֹּהֵן אֲשֶׁר פָּקְדוּ אֶת־בְּנֵי יִשְׂרָאֵל
בְּעַרְבֹת מוֹאָב עַל יַרְדֵּן יְרֵחוֹ׃ 64 וּבְאֵלֶּה לֹא־הָיָה
אִישׁ מִפְּקוּדֵי מֹשֶׁה וְאַהֲרֹן הַכֹּהֵן אֲשֶׁר פָּקְדוּ אֶת־
בְּנֵי יִשְׂרָאֵל בְּמִדְבַּר סִינָי׃ 65 כִּי־אָמַר יְהוָה לָהֶם

9:19; see Num. 3:38). In the Septuagint, they are not listed last but follow the Hebronites, a more logical placement, since both are descended from Kohath (Exod. 6:18,21). The term *benei korah*, "Korahites," was found on an eighth-century B.C.E. ostracon in the city of Arad (see the Comment to 21:1), probably indicating a Levitical family that served the sanctuary there.

Kohath begot Amram Thus Moses and Aaron (Amram's sons; v. 59), although Kohathites, are totally separated from them. For example, Moses and Aaron encamp to the east of the Tabernacle, the Kohathites to the south (3:29,38). The brothers are not included in the Kohathite census; nor do they participate in its Tabernacle duties (3:27–30; 4:1–14). Some scholars deny that Amram was a Kohathite.[42] But the more plausible deduction is that Moses and Aaron were singled out from the Kohathites (3:27) because of their respective leadership responsibilities.

59. Jochebed daughter of Levi She is the aunt of Amram, Levi's grandson, and, therefore, by the law of Leviticus 18:12; 20:19, forbidden to him in marriage. However, this law was not operative before Sinai. For other examples of pre-Sinaitic incest, see Genesis 20:12 and 38:24–26.

who was born to Levi Literally, "who bore her to Levi," a difficult construction since the subject, the mother, is unnamed. For a similar construction, see 1 Kings 1:6.[43]

in Egypt According to this tradition, only two generations were slaves in Egypt: Levi-Jochebed-Moses.

60–61. See 3:4.

62. See 1:47 and 2:33.

A POSTSCRIPT (vv. 63–65)

The postscript explains that this census did not include those counted in the previous census who (with the exception of Caleb and Joshua) had perished in the wilderness at God's command (14:29–32). The question remains: Did the Levites also fall under God's decree? A tradition recorded in the Babylonian Talmud tractate Bava Batra 121a claims that the Levites were exempted and offers Eleazar as proof, since he too survived.[44] However, there is no evidence in the given chronology that he had been over the age of twenty at that time; therefore, he would not have been subject to the decree. Further proof for the exemption of the Levites is adduced from the fact that the scouts (13:4–16) did not include a representative of Levi—therefore, goes the argument, the tribe of Levi was exempted from the decree. However, it is hard to conceive that any Pentateuchal source would have excluded the Levites from the fate of the rest of their people without explicitly mentioning it.

65 For the LORD had said of them, "They shall die in the wilderness." Not one of them survived, except Caleb son of Jephunneh and Joshua son of Nun.

מוֹת יָמֻתוּ בַּמִּדְבָּר וְלֹא־נוֹתַר מֵהֶם אִישׁ כִּי אִם־
כָּלֵב בֶּן־יְפֻנֶּה וִיהוֹשֻׁעַ בִּן־נוּן׃ ס

27 The daughters of Zelophehad, of Manassite family—son of Hepher son of Gilead son of Machir son of Manasseh son of Joseph—came forward. The names of the daughters were Mahlah, Noah, Hoglah, Milcah, and Tirzah.
2 They stood before Moses, Eleazar the priest, the chieftains, and the whole assembly, at the entrance of the Tent of Meeting, and they said,
3 "Our father died in the wilder-

כ״ז וַתִּקְרַבְנָה בְּנוֹת צְלָפְחָד בֶּן־חֵפֶר בֶּן־גִּלְעָד
בֶּן־מָכִיר בֶּן־מְנַשֶּׁה לְמִשְׁפְּחֹת מְנַשֶּׁה בֶן־יוֹסֵף
וְאֵלֶּה שְׁמוֹת בְּנֹתָיו מַחְלָה נֹעָה וְחָגְלָה וּמִלְכָּה
וְתִרְצָה׃ 2 וַתַּעֲמֹדְנָה לִפְנֵי מֹשֶׁה וְלִפְנֵי אֶלְעָזָר
הַכֹּהֵן וְלִפְנֵי הַנְּשִׂיאִם וְכָל־הָעֵדָה פֶּתַח אֹהֶל־
מוֹעֵד לֵאמֹר׃ 3 אָבִינוּ מֵת בַּמִּדְבָּר וְהוּא לֹא־הָיָה

The Law of Succession in Inheritance (vv. 1–11)

The census taken in chapter 26 for apportioning the promised land to the tribal clans is followed by a problematic case: What if the deceased leaves daughters but no sons? The resolution of this case leads to the law of succession in inheritance. The laws of inheritance are discussed in Excursus 63.

CHAPTER 27 THE CASE OF THE DAUGHTERS OF ZELOPHEHAD (vv. 1–7)

The basic assumption here is that of Leviticus 25:23: The land belongs to God, who assigned it to the Israelite clans for their use; whoever alienates it from them is subject to divine punishment. This is exemplified in 1 Kings 21:16–19 and Micah 2:1–5. The Jubilee year was instituted to serve this end: At that time (see the Comment to 36:4) all ancestral land that has been sold reverts to its original owner; and even before the Jubilee the nearest relative (*go'el*) is morally obligated to redeem it (see Jer. 32:6–15). Also assumed is that only males can inherit, since the clan is perpetuated through the male line. This being so, the daughters of sonless Zelophehad plead that unless they are permitted to inherit their father's name will be wiped out. Moses brings their case before God, who grants them the right to inherit.

This is the last of four cases not provided for in the original legislation and which, therefore, had to be decided by oracle, the others being: the blasphemer (Lev. 24:10–22), those impure for the paschal sacrifice (Num. 9:6–14), and the Sabbath violator (Num. 15:32–36). These cases are structured according to a common literary pattern: (1) identification and/or genealogy of the individual(s), (2) who "comes forward" and (3) "stands before" Moses and the assembly or priest and (4) states the case, after which (5) the case is brought before the Lord, who (6) gives a decision that is then (7) generalized through the formula, "speak to the Israelite people" (v. 8) and (8) casts it in casuistic form, "if a man (*'ish*) . . . if (*'im*)." The execution of the oracle is recorded either immediately, as in Leviticus 24:23 and Numbers 15:36, or subsequently, as in Numbers 36:10–12 and Joshua 17:4. Chapter 36, an appendix that makes this case more precise, also follows this pattern.

1. ***of Manassite family***[1]

The names They are probably original to this chapter, although they had been cited in 26:33. They were added there secondarily to indicate that the daughters ultimately inherited and became clans of their own. The midrash accounts this repetition to the merit of Israel's women: In contradistinction to their men who feared to invade Canaan and wished to return to Egypt (14:1–4), they boldly stepped forward and demanded an inheritance in the promised land.[2]

2. ***stood . . . at the entrance of the Tent of Meeting*** To present their case. In the cities of Canaan, the judicial court convened by the gate at the entrance to the city (see Gen. 34:20; Deut.

ness. He was not one of the faction, Korah's faction, which banded together against the LORD, but died for his own sin; and he has left no sons. 4 Let not our father's name be lost to his clan just because he had no son! Give us a holding among our father's kinsmen!"

בְּתוֹךְ הָעֵדָה הַנּוֹעָדִים עַל־יְהֹוָה בַּעֲדַת־קֹרַח כִּי־
בְחֶטְאוֹ מֵת וּבָנִים לֹא־הָיוּ לוֹ׃ 4 לָמָּה יִגָּרַע שֵׁם־
אָבִינוּ מִתּוֹךְ מִשְׁפַּחְתּוֹ כִּי אֵין לוֹ בֵּן תְּנָה־לָּנוּ
אֲחֻזָּה בְּתוֹךְ אֲחֵי אָבִינוּ׃ 5 וַיַּקְרֵב מֹשֶׁה אֶת־

21:19; Jer. 26:10; Ruth 4:1) and could comprise the entire male adult population (as in 1 Kings 21:12–13 and Jeremiah 26:7–18).

and they said[3]

3. ***Korah's faction*** See chapter 16 and Excursus 39. The assumption here is that the participants in the Korahite rebellion were denied the right to inherit the land. A similar rule underlies the case of Naboth in 1 Kings 21:10–13. He was (falsely) convicted of blasphemy "against God and the king," and his land was confiscated by the state. Korah and his faction were guilty of a similar charge: They had rebelled against Aaron and Moses who, respectively, represented God and the state.

but[4]

died for his own sin That is, in the punishment meted out to the entire nation following the scout episode recorded in 14:29. However, the meaning of this clause is unclear, for even if Zelophehad had been a member of Korah's faction, he still would have "died for his own sin." This objection leads some commentators to connect this phrase with the following (see the next Comment). The rabbis—surely aware of this objection—claim that this clause only means that Zelophehad did not incite others to sin, that is, he was not one of the leaders in the rebellion.[5]

and he has left no sons As noted in Sifrei Numbers 133, had he left sons, the girls would have no claim. Alternatively, the daughters may be basing their claim on ancient Near Eastern legal practice whereby daughters, on occasion, did inherit (see Excursus 62). A reflex of this is found in Scripture itself: "Have we still a share in the inheritance of our father's house?" (Gen. 31:14). Rachel and Leah may be implying that before their father had sons (who are first mentioned in Gen. 31:1) they would have been entitled to inherit him.

Another suggestion for interpreting this clause has been put forth by Judah Halevi (quoted favorably by Ibn Ezra and Ramban). Connecting causally with the preceding phrase, it yields: "He died for his own sins and *therefore* left no sons." Evidence for such a belief may be found in 2 Samuel 12:13–14 and 1 Kings 17:18.

4. ***Let not*** *Lammah*.[6]

father's name be lost to his clan There are two assumptions inherent in this statement. One is that a name exists as long as it is attached to land. Another is that Zelophehad's name would be perpetuated through his grandsons. Two scriptural examples confirm this: A certain Attai continues the line of Sheshan via the latter's daughter in 1 Chronicles 2:34–35; and Nehemiah 7:63 and Ezra 2:61 record the case of priests who traced their lineage to Barzillai through the marriage of their unnamed father to one of the daughters of Barzillai "and had taken his name." Here the son-in-law, in effect, adopted his father-in-law's name.

be lost Hebrew ***yiggara'***. Rather, "cut off," which is the basic meaning of the Hebrew stem *g-r-'*.[7]

because he had no son The text assumes that the mother was either dead or infertile. In this case, the levirate solution detailed in Deuteronomy 25:5–6 could not be applied. Also assumed is that the daughters were unmarried; otherwise the land would ultimately pass to the clans of their husbands (see the Comment to 36:3).

holding Hebrew *'aḥuzzah*. In distinction to ***naḥalah*** (inalienable property transmitted by inheritance, i.e., patrimony), ***'aḥuzzah*** is inalienable property derived from a sovereign.[8] The terms, however, are nearly synonymous: The daughters request a "holding" that, being inalienable, becomes inherited property (see the Comments to v. 7 and 35:2).

5 Moses brought their case before the LORD.

6 And the LORD said to Moses, 7 "The plea of Zelophehad's daughters is just: you should give them a hereditary holding among their father's kinsmen; transfer their father's share to them.

8 "Further, speak to the Israelite people as follows: 'If a man dies without leaving a son, you shall transfer his property to his daughter. 9 If he has no daughter, you shall

מִשְׁפָּטָ֖ן* לִפְנֵ֥י יְהוָֽה׃ ס רביעי 6 וַיֹּ֥אמֶר
יְהוָ֖ה אֶל־מֹשֶׁ֥ה לֵּאמֹֽר׃ 7 כֵּ֗ן בְּנ֣וֹת צְלָפְחָד֮ דֹּבְרֹת֒
נָתֹ֨ן תִּתֵּ֤ן לָהֶם֙ אֲחֻזַּ֣ת נַחֲלָ֔ה בְּת֖וֹךְ אֲחֵ֣י אֲבִיהֶ֑ם
וְהַעֲבַרְתָּ֛ אֶת־נַחֲלַ֥ת אֲבִיהֶ֖ן לָהֶֽן׃ 8 וְאֶל־בְּנֵ֥י
יִשְׂרָאֵ֖ל תְּדַבֵּ֣ר לֵאמֹ֑ר אִ֣ישׁ כִּֽי־יָמ֗וּת וּבֵן֙ אֵ֣ין ל֔וֹ
וְהַעֲבַרְתֶּ֥ם אֶת־נַחֲלָת֖וֹ לְבִתּֽוֹ׃ 9 וְאִם־אֵ֥ין ל֖וֹ בַּ֑ת

ן׳ רבתי v. 5.

our father's kinsmen That is, of the clan of Hepher (v. 1). The land is parceled out to the tribes according to their clans (26:32).

5. ***Moses*** Moses alone could bring the case before the Lord, as implied in Exodus 18:19, exemplified in Leviticus 24:13 and Numbers 9:8–9 and 15:35–36, and confirmed, in this case, in Joshua 17:4.

before the LORD That is, for an oracle. One midrashic tradition praises Moses since he thereby taught "the heads of the Sanhedrin of Israel that were destined to arise after him, that . . . they should not be embarrassed to ask for assistance in cases too difficult for them. For even Moses, who was Master of Israel, had to say, 'I have not understood.' Therefore Moses brought their cases before the Lord."[9] But another midrash finds his ignorance a source of punitive humiliation: "The Holy One Blessed Be He said to him: Did you not say, 'The case that is too difficult for you, you shall bring to me' (Deut. 1:17). [For this hubris] the law with which you are unacquainted will be decided by these women!"[10]

7. ***the plea*** Literally, "pleading." The verb *dover/dibber* has this legal connotation in Numbers 36:5, Isaiah 32:7, and elsewhere. Similarly the noun *davar* can mean "case, plea, charge" (see Exod. 18:16; 24:14).

just[11]

hereditary holding Hebrew *'aḥuzzat naḥalah*, used again in 32:35 and in the reverse construction, *naḥalat 'aḥuzzatam*, "holdings apportioned to them," in 35:2. However, the two terms are not interchangeable. *'Aḥuzzah* is a technical term denoting inalienable property received from a sovereign; *naḥalah* refers to inalienable property transmitted by inheritance.[12] The land seized by the Israelites (*'aḥuzzah*) will become their inheritance (*naḥalah*). Thus, this conflated expression makes sense, although some books prefer one term over the other; Deuteronomy, for example, uses *naḥalah* exclusively,[13] whereas Leviticus uses *'aḥuzzah* exclusively.[14]

father's kinsmen See the Comment to verse 4.

transfer The verb *he'evir* is used exclusively for the daughter, whereas the verb *natan* is used for the inheriting male.[15] The "transfer" is from the qualified to the unqualified,[16] or it can connote the transfer of the property from the daughter to her husband or son.[17] The basic idea seems to be the transfer from one domain to another. Thus, the first-born male is "transferred" to God's domain (Exod. 13:12), from which the human and impure animal are redeemed (Exod. 13:13; Num. 18:15–18). A pagan rite requires that children be "transferred" to the domain of Molech (Lev. 18:21). The inheriting of sons, however, is not a transfer, as such. Sons are the extension of their fathers and are technically part of the same domain. This also holds true for the other persons in the chain of succession.

A striking example of the transferring function of the daughter is found in 1 Chronicles 2:34–35: Sheshan, who had no sons, gave his daughter to Jarha, his Egyptian slave. The son of that union, Attai, inherited the ancestral land. Thus the daughter acted as a vehicle for the transfer of her father's property to his grandchild—born to a foreign slave!

share[18]

assign his property to his brothers. 10If he has no brothers,
you shall assign his property to his father's brothers. 11If his
father had no brothers, you shall assign his property to his
nearest relative in his own clan, and he shall inherit it.' This
shall be the law of procedure for the Israelites, in accordance with the LORD's command to Moses."

12The LORD said to Moses, "Ascend these heights of
Abarim and view the land that I have given to the Israelite
people. 13When you have seen it, you too shall be gathered

וּנְתַתֶּם אֶת־נַחֲלָתוֹ לְאֶחָיו׃ 10 וְאִם־אֵין לוֹ אַחִים
וּנְתַתֶּם אֶת־נַחֲלָתוֹ לַאֲחֵי אָבִיו׃ 11 וְאִם־אֵין
אַחִים לְאָבִיו וּנְתַתֶּם אֶת־נַחֲלָתוֹ לִשְׁאֵרוֹ הַקָּרֹב
אֵלָיו מִמִּשְׁפַּחְתּוֹ וְיָרַשׁ אֹתָהּ וְהָיְתָה לִבְנֵי יִשְׂרָאֵל
לְחֻקַּת מִשְׁפָּט כַּאֲשֶׁר צִוָּה יְהוָה אֶת־מֹשֶׁה׃
ס 12 וַיֹּאמֶר יְהוָה אֶל־מֹשֶׁה עֲלֵה אֶל־הַר
הָעֲבָרִים הַזֶּה וּרְאֵה אֶת־הָאָרֶץ אֲשֶׁר נָתַתִּי לִבְנֵי
יִשְׂרָאֵל׃ 13 וְרָאִיתָה אֹתָהּ וְנֶאֱסַפְתָּ אֶל־עַמֶּיךָ גַּם־

THE LAW OF SUCCESSION (vv. 8–11)

A man's natural heirs are his sons; but if he has no sons his daughters become his heirs. If he has no children his brothers inherit him; and in the absence of brothers his father's brothers inherit him. If the father had no brothers, the inheritance passes on to the next of kin. Thus the agnatic, or patrilineal, principle of succession through the father's male line is preserved. The daughter does not really inherit; she transfers the inheritance from father to grandson and thereby keeps the ancestral land in the father's line. The possibility of a man's wife surviving him and, where there are no children, marrying his brother (the levir: Deut. 25:5–10) is not considered here, but it must be assumed. Other lacunae in this law are filled in by the rabbis and discussed in Excursus 62.

*8. **his property*** That is, inherited, landed property. The Karaites, in keeping with their strict adherence to biblical law, interpret this literally. They apply it solely to the ancestral inheritance in the Holy Land but not to real estate elsewhere or to movable property, in which case daughters inherit equally with sons (see Excursus 62).

*9. **brothers*** Also of his mother.[19] This, however, is denied by the rabbis, who consistently apply the agnatic principle[20] (see Excursus 62).

*11. **his . . . relative***[21]

in his own clan That is, his male relatives (see the Comment to v. 9), which assumes that the land remains in the clan.

the law of procedure Hebrew *le-ḥukkat mishpat*. The term occurs only once again (35:39). As opposed to *ḥukkat ha-torah*, "the ritual law" followed in the sanctuary (see 19:1), this law relates to the procedure followed by the judiciary.

The Succession of Moses by Joshua (vv. 12–23)

Moses is commanded to ascend the mountain. From there he will see the promised land and then die. The fulfillment of this command is postponed to Deuteronomy 34, for Moses has yet many laws (chaps. 28–36) and a lengthy testament (Deut.) to give to his people. Because of this postponement, the command itself, using many similar words, is repeated in Deuteronomy 32:48–52—a repetitive resumption found elsewhere in the Torah (e.g., Exod. 6:12,30). Why then was the command issued here? Perhaps there was a tradition that Moses was to have died at this point. But the midrash answers differently: "When Moses heard the command 'give them [the daughters] a hereditary holding' (v. 7), he was under the impression that the Holy One Blessed Be He had been reconciled to him and thought: Behold I am the one who will allot to Israel their inheritance. So the Holy One Blessed Be He said to him: 'My decree retains its force. Ascend these heights. . . . You too shall be gathered to your kin, just as your brother Aaron was (vv. 12–13). You are not better than your brother.'"[22]

to your kin, just as your brother Aaron was. 14For, in the wilderness of Zin, when the community was contentious, you disobeyed My command to uphold My sanctity in their sight by means of the water." Those are the Waters of Meribath-kadesh, in the wilderness of Zin.

15Moses spoke to the LORD, saying, 16"Let the LORD, Source of the breath of all flesh, appoint someone over the community 17who shall go out before them and come in before them, and who shall take them out and bring them in, so that the LORD's community may not be like sheep that have no shepherd." 18And the LORD answered Moses,

אַתָּה כַּאֲשֶׁר נֶאֱסַף אַהֲרֹן אָחִיךָ׃ 14 כַּאֲשֶׁר
מְרִיתֶם פִּי בְּמִדְבַּר־צִן בִּמְרִיבַת הָעֵדָה לְהַקְדִּישֵׁנִי
בַמַּיִם לְעֵינֵיהֶם הֵם מֵי־מְרִיבַת קָדֵשׁ מִדְבַּר־צִן׃
פ 15 וַיְדַבֵּר מֹשֶׁה אֶל־יְהוָה לֵאמֹר׃
16 יִפְקֹד יְהוָה אֱלֹהֵי הָרוּחֹת לְכָל־בָּשָׂר אִישׁ עַל־
הָעֵדָה׃ 17 אֲשֶׁר־יֵצֵא לִפְנֵיהֶם וַאֲשֶׁר יָבֹא לִפְנֵיהֶם
וַאֲשֶׁר יוֹצִיאֵם וַאֲשֶׁר יְבִיאֵם וְלֹא תִהְיֶה עֲדַת
יְהוָה כַּצֹּאן אֲשֶׁר אֵין־לָהֶם רֹעֶה׃ 18 וַיֹּאמֶר יְהוָה
אֶל־מֹשֶׁה קַח־לְךָ אֶת־יְהוֹשֻׁעַ בִּן־נוּן אִישׁ אֲשֶׁר־

12. ***these heights of Abarim*** See the Comment to 21:11. The specific peak of this mountain chain is identified as Mount Nebo in Deuteronomy 32:49 (cf. Num. 33:47). At 843 meters (2,740 ft.) high, it offers a view of wide stretches of Cisjordan.

13. ***shall be gathered to your kin*** See the Comment to 20:24.

as your brother Aaron See 20:22–29. The comparison with Aaron suggests that just as Aaron ascended the mountain to die, such was also the purpose of Moses' ascent. But his death is postponed until all his work is done and then is duly recorded in Deuteronomy 34:9. Aaron's successor was chosen at the time he was commanded to die atop the mountain (20:22–29). The difference in this case is striking. Whereas Aaron is given a successor by God, Moses requests one. It is thus another distinctive mark of Moses' leadership that he plans for his own succession. Moreover, his humility and unselfishness are evidenced by his request that his successor be endowed with all his powers, a request, however, that God denies (see the Comments to vv. 17,21).

14. ***For***[23]

disobeyed My command[24]

Those[25]

Meribath-kadesh[26]

16. ***Source of the breath of all flesh*** The same divine epithet occurs in 16:22, but not for the same reason. In the case of Korah's rebellion, Moses calls upon God to distinguish between the guilty and innocent; here, it is to distinguish one who is worthy from "all flesh": "You are acquainted with the spirit of every individual and should appoint a man who will know how to deal with each one of them in accordance with his own temperament."[27]

There is another, more striking distinction between the two prayers. In the Korah episode, Moses addresses God in the second person (16:22); here, he uses the third person. Moses—just rebuked by God (v. 14), who reminded him of his sin at Meribah (20:8–13)—feels that he is no longer the intimate of God. Indeed, he never speaks to Him again directly but only through mediation. Hence, he adopts the third person address characteristic of the sinful petitioner who has fallen out of grace.[28]

appoint "There (Moses) exemplified the merit of the righteous who at the time of their death do not concern themselves with their personal deeds but with the needs of the community."[29] However, the midrash regards Moses' initiative differently: "The Holy One Blessed Be He said to him: . . . 'Instead of charging Me to attend to My sons, command My sons about Me.' Hence it is written: 'Command the Israelite people' (28:2)."[30] In this way the midrash accounts for the fact that Moses did not immediately ascend Mount Nebo to his death: He first completed his task to transmit all of God's commands to Israel—an event recorded at the end of Deuteronomy.

17. ***who shall go before them and come in before them*** An idiom that refers to military leadership.[31] "Not like others do who send out their troops [first] and they come last."[32] So the officers of modern Israel's defense forces are noted for their battle cry *'aḥarai*, "follow me!"[33]

"Single out Joshua son of Nun, an inspired man, and lay
your hand upon him. 19Have him stand before Eleazar the
priest and before the whole community, and commission
him in their sight. 20Invest him with some of your authority, so that the whole Israelite community may obey. 21But

רוּחַ בּוֹ וְסָמַכְתָּ אֶת־יָדְךָ עָלָיו׃ 19 וְהַעֲמַדְתָּ אֹתוֹ
לִפְנֵי אֶלְעָזָר הַכֹּהֵן וְלִפְנֵי כָּל־הָעֵדָה וְצִוִּיתָה אֹתוֹ
לְעֵינֵיהֶם׃ 20 וְנָתַתָּה מֵהוֹדְךָ עָלָיו לְמַעַן יִשְׁמְעוּ
כָּל־עֲדַת בְּנֵי יִשְׂרָאֵל׃ 21 וְלִפְנֵי אֶלְעָזָר הַכֹּהֵן

who shall take them out and bring them in The verbs are the same as those in the previous clause, but these are written in the causative (Hifil) pattern, thereby denoting the military officer who not only leads his troops into battle but who plans its strategy, that is, who initiates military policy. The example of David, which records the only other attestation of this idiom in the Bible, is striking (2 Sam. 5:2): Since he conducted Israel's wars independently of the ailing King Saul, he deserves to be Israel's ruler. This idiom also reveals Moses' selflessness: He does not care if he is equaled or eclipsed and requests a leader just like himself. But this request is not granted by God (see v. 21).

sheep that have no shepherd For this phrase, see 1 Kings 22:17 and Ezekiel 34:5. Both this image and the preceding one are reworked in a description of David: "When Saul was king over us, it was you who led Israel in war [lit. led Israel out and in]; and the LORD said to you: 'You shall shepherd My people Israel'" (2 Sam. 5:2 [= 1 Chron. 11:2]). Thus the image of David is forged along the Mosaic model. The image of Moses as Israel's shepherd also occurs in later biblical texts, such as Isaiah 63:11 and Psalms 77:21.

18. an inspired man Literally, "a man in whom there is spirit," referring to Joshua. A number of interpretations have been suggested: (1) "spirit of wisdom," mentioned in Deuteronomy 34:9.[34] However, wisdom, according to that passage, comes to Joshua as a result of his investiture; here it is clear that he qualifies as Moses' successor because he already possesses the spirit; (2) "spirit of prophecy,"[35] supported by the example of the elders who begin to prophesy upon receiving Moses' spirit (11:17,25). However, Joshua never becomes a prophet and before his investiture is just a military officer (Exod. 17:9–13) and Moses' aide-de-camp (Exod. 24:13; 32:17); (3) "spirit of skill,"[36] supported by the examples of Bezalel whom God "endowed with a divine spirit of skill, ability, and knowledge in every kind of craft" (Exod. 35:31; cf. 31:2) and of Joseph, endowed with the skill of dream interpretation (Gen. 41:38). This "spirit," then, would refer to Joshua's endowed talent (not acquired skill), attested by his military success; (4) "spirit" as a synonym for "courage," as in Joshua 2:11 and 5:1. This courage manifests itself in his victory over the Amalekites (Exod. 17:9–13), and it is exemplified by his willingness to stand up for God and Moses in the scout episode—for which he is nearly stoned (14:6–10), as alluded to in 26:65. Either of the latter two explanations is acceptable.

lay Rather, "lean."[37] Hebrew *samakh* implies pressure. The rabbis state explicitly that the act of *samakh* must be "with all one's strength."[38]

your hand Hebrew *yadkha*. Rather, *yadeikha* (pl.), "hands."[39] Transfer of authority and power can only be performed by the laying of both hands. This is clear from Numbers 8:10 and Leviticus 16:21. The leaning of only one hand is limited to the ritual whereby the offerer of a sacrificial animal identifies himself as its owner and declares its purpose.[40] In Jewish tradition the laying of both hands, called *semikhah*, became the rite for rabbinic ordination.

19. Have him stand Rather, "After you have him stand,"[41] since the hand-leaning procedure follows in verses 22–23.

commission him[42]

20. Invest him Literally, "place upon him." Use of *'alav*, "on him," corresponds to the *'alav* of the hand leaning (v. 18). Moses thus establishes a physical conduit for the transfer of his *hod*, as discussed in the next Comment. Alternatively, render: "You shall have him invested" by the hand leaning, with the actual transfer performed by God. Thus, 1 Chronicles 29:25 states: *va-yitten 'alav hod malkhut*, "[The Lord] invested him [Solomon] with the *hod* of kingship." See the next Comment.

he shall present himself to Eleazar the priest, who shall on his behalf seek the decision of the Urim before the LORD. By such instruction they shall go out and by such instruction they shall come in, he and all the Israelites, the whole community."

22Moses did as the LORD commanded him. He took Joshua and had him stand before Eleazar the priest and before the whole community. 23He laid his hands upon him and commissioned him—as the LORD had spoken through Moses.

יַעֲמֹד וְשָׁאַל לוֹ בְּמִשְׁפַּט הָאוּרִים לִפְנֵי יְהוָה עַל־
פִּיו יֵצְאוּ וְעַל־פִּיו יָבֹאוּ הוּא וְכָל־בְּנֵי־יִשְׂרָאֵל
אִתּוֹ וְכָל־הָעֵדָה׃ 22 וַיַּעַשׂ מֹשֶׁה כַּאֲשֶׁר צִוָּה יְהוָה
אֹתוֹ וַיִּקַּח אֶת־יְהוֹשֻׁעַ וַיַּעֲמִדֵהוּ לִפְנֵי אֶלְעָזָר
הַכֹּהֵן וְלִפְנֵי כָּל־הָעֵדָה׃ 23 וַיִּסְמֹךְ אֶת־יָדָיו עָלָיו
וַיְצַוֵּהוּ כַּאֲשֶׁר דִּבֶּר יְהוָה בְּיַד־מֹשֶׁה׃ פ
חמישי

with some of your authority Hebrew *me-hodekha*. The exact meaning of *hod* in this context is difficult to determine, since it is Moses who is doing the investing. He is empowered to transfer to Joshua only his authority. But if *hod* refers to Moses' spiritual powers, then only God who has endowed them can transfer them—as He did when He allowed the elders to share Moses' prophetic gifts (11:17,25). Alternatively, render "majesty, power, charisma" ("ray of your glory"),[43] since it is possible that the actual transfer was performed by God (via Moses' hand leaning), just as the *hod* of Solomon's kingship (1 Chron. 29:25) was granted by God. Furthermore, the text states that only part of Moses' *hod* was transferred, implying that Joshua, like the elders who received some of Moses' spirit, was not his equal: "but not all of your *hod*, from which we learn that Moses' face was like the appearance of the sun and Joshua's like the moon."[44]

obey[45]

21. who shall . . . seek[46]

the decision[47]

the Urim Short for Urim and Thummim, so abbreviated also in 1 Samuel 28:6. For its significance, see Excursus 64.

go out . . . come in That is, for war (see the Comment to v. 17). Thus Joshua is commanded to consult the Urim and Thummim through the agency of the High Priest only in military matters. The Dead Sea sectaries adopt a similar stance but logically deduce a further step: The king must consult the High Priest only when waging an offensive war but not a war of defense, in which case he may mobilize the nation at once.[48]

By such instruction That is, of the Urim's decision. Alternatively, it may be by Eleazar's instruction, since it is he who consults the Urim. The Bible never states explicitly that Joshua consults the Urim; and whenever he is mentioned with Eleazar, the latter's name appears first (Josh. 14:1; 19:51; 21:1), implying a dependency upon him.[49] In any event, as this verse makes clear, Joshua will never be the equal of Moses, who received divine guidance directly and never required any mediation (see 12:8).

and all the Israelites Rather, "and all the Israelites with him," referring to the troops that Joshua will lead in battle, as noted in the Comment to verse 17.[50]

the whole community Rather, "and the whole community," that is, not only the army but all the Israelites. This public ceremonial of the transfer of authority from Moses to Joshua is subsequently confirmed by God Himself, who appears in the pillar of cloud and speaks to Joshua in the Tabernacle court (Deut. 31:14–15,23).[51]

22. This is the fulfillment passage, but only of Joshua's succession; Moses' death is postponed to Deuteronomy 34.

23. hands Hebrew *yadav*, that is, both hands. See the Comment to verse 18.

commissioned him See the Comment to verse 19.

As the LORD had spoken through Moses[52]

The Calendar of Public Sacrifices (vv. 28:1–30:1)

Having decided the questions of the apportionment of the land among the Israelites and the succession to Moses, the Torah's next step is to establish the cultic calendar that will prevail in the land. Such a nexus between the acquisition of the land and the calendar has already been attested. The agricultural calendar of Leviticus 23, as soon as it deals with the harvest festivals, begins with the words "when you enter the land" (v. 9). The graduated series of sacrificial adjuncts (15:1–12) also begins with "when you enter the land" (v. 2); indeed, these very meal and wine supplements are incorporated into the sacrificial offerings of this calendar. Ezekiel's vision of the restored sacrificial cult (Ezek. 45:13–25) also begins with "when you allot the land as an inheritance" (45:1). The first task of the first "Zionists" returning from the Babylonian exile—indeed, their very goal—is to rebuild the Temple (Ezra 1). Thus, Israel's first duty upon settling in its land is to establish the proper lines of communion with the Lord through the medium of His cult. This priority was already prefigured at Sinai: Israel's first task after witnessing the revelation was to build the Tabernacle (Exod. 25). Hence, whether in the wilderness or in its land, Israel can be assured by God's Presence only through His sanctioned cult and sanctuary. The indispensability of the regular, public cult is presumed in Scripture and made explicit by the following passage: "Sanctify yourselves and sanctify the House of the LORD God of your fathers, and take the abhorrent things out of the holy place. For our fathers trespassed and did what displeased the LORD our God; they forsook Him, and turned their faces away from the dwelling-place of the LORD, turning their backs on it. They also shut the doors of the porch and put out the lights; they did not offer incense and did not make burnt offerings in the holy place to the God of Israel. The wrath of the LORD was upon Judah and Jerusalem" (2 Chron. 29:5–8).

Thirty days of each year, in addition to the daily and Sabbath cultic requirements, are marked for special public offerings. They exhibit the following distinctive features: (1) The offerings are cumulative; that is, the offerings for the Sabbaths and festivals are in addition to the daily offerings, and the offerings for the New Year are in addition to the daily and the New Moon offerings. Hence, should the New Year fall on a Sabbath, there would be offered: (a) the daily offering, (b) the Sabbath offering, (c) the New Moon offering, and (d) the New Year offering. (2) The organizing principle of the calendar is according to descending order of frequency: daily, Sabbath, New Moon. Then the sacrifices for the festivals follow in calendrical order, beginning with Passover.[1] (3) All the sacrificial animals are males: bulls, rams, and lambs as burnt offerings and goats as purification offerings. (4) The sacrificial order is prescriptive not descriptive. In practice, the purification offering would be sacrificed before the additional burnt offering. (5) The number seven and its multiples are very prominent in the number of animals offered, as can be seen in the following table:

Occasion	*Lambs*	*Rams*	*Bulls*	*Goats*
Each day (28:3–8)	2	—	—	—
Each Sabbath (28:9–10)	2	—	—	—
Each New Moon (28:11–15)	7	1	2	1
Each day of Unleavened Bread (28:16–25)	7	1	2	1
Feast of Weeks (28:26–31)	7	1	2	1
New Year (29:1–6)	7	1	1	1
Yom Kippur (29:7–11)	7	1	1	1
1st of Sukkot (29:12–16)	14	2	13	1
2nd of Sukkot (29:17–19)	14	2	12	1
3rd of Sukkot (29:20–22)	14	2	11	1
4th of Sukkot (29:23–25)	14	2	10	1
5th of Sukkot (29:26–28)	14	2	9	1
6th of Sukkot (29:29–31)	14	2	8	1
7th of Sukkot (29:32–34)	14	2	7	1
8th day, *'atseret* (29:35–38)	7	1	1	1

28 The LORD spoke to Moses, saying: 2Command the Israelite people and say to them: Be punctilious in presenting to Me at stated times the offerings of food due Me, as offerings by fire of pleasing odor to Me.

כ״ח וַיְדַבֵּר יְהוָה אֶל־מֹשֶׁה לֵּאמֹר: 2 צַו אֶת־
בְּנֵי יִשְׂרָאֵל וְאָמַרְתָּ אֲלֵהֶם אֶת־קָרְבָּנִי לַחְמִי
לְאִשַּׁי רֵיחַ נִיחֹחִי תִּשְׁמְרוּ לְהַקְרִיב לִי בְּמוֹעֲדוֹ:

In addition to the frequency of the number seven (and its multiple fourteen) in the above table, there are[2] other occurrences of seven: the seven festivals (including the paschal observance, 28:16, and excluding Sabbaths and New Moons); the seven-day Unleavened Bread and Sukkot festivals; the preponderance of festivals in the seventh month (New Year, Yom Kippur, Sukkot, *ʿatseret*); the seven festival days, in addition to the Sabbath, on which work is prohibited, listed in 28:18,25,26; 29:1,7,12, 35; the bulls required for Sukkot add up to seventy; the total number of animals offered on this seven-day festival is 7 × 7 × 2 lambs, 7 × 2 rams, 7 × 10 bulls, and 7 goats.

This catalogue of public offerings concludes with a reminder in 29:39 that the individual Israelite could also bring his private offerings. Omitted, but surely to be assumed, is that a liturgy of music and prayer accompanied the sacrificial offerings. The titles of Psalm 92, of Psalms 24,48, and 94 according to the Septuagint, and also of Psalms 81 and 82 according to Mishnah Tamid 7:4 indicate that a specific psalm was sung each day of the week in the Temple service.

The text parallels much of Leviticus 23. The corresponding parts are: Leviticus 23:5–8 = Numbers 28:16–19a,25; Leviticus 23:21 = Numbers 28:26b; Leviticus 23:24–25 = Numbers 29:1; Leviticus 23:27–28 = Numbers 29:7–8; Leviticus 23:34–36 = Numbers 29:12,35–36. The prescription for the daily offering (28:3–8) draws on Exodus 29:38–41. The other cultic calendars in the Bible should be compared: Exodus 23:14–17; 34:18–26; Deuteronomy 16:1–13; Ezekiel 45:18–25. Ezekiel's schedule of public offerings differs radically and will be noted in the Commentary.

CHAPTER 28

1–2. The LORD spoke ... Moses ... Command Hebrew *va-yedabber YHVH ... mosheh ... tsav*, a rearrangement of the final words of the preceding chapter: *va-yetsavvehu ... dibber YHVH ... mosheh*, which may account for the sequence of chapters 28–29 here.[3]

2. Be punctilious[4]

at stated times Hebrew *be-moʿado* (see 15:3). The sacrifices are invalid if offered at the wrong time.[5] *Moʿed* is merely any "stated time" or "season,"[6] and so can be used collectively for *ḥag* (see the Comment to v. 17), New Moon, and Sabbath (Ezek. 45:17) and for the first and tenth day of the seventh month (Lev. 23:2,24,27). It can also refer specifically to those holy days to which the name *ḥag* does not apply (Ezek. 46:11), although in later usage *moʿed* can replace *ḥag* (2 Chron. 8:13).

the offerings of food due Me Literally, "My offering, My food."[7] The probable original meaning of Hebrew *leḥem* is "food," as in Judges 13:16, 1 Samuel 14:24, and 1 Kings 5:2. In Arabic it became "flesh" and in Hebrew "bread."

These terms are linguistic fossils deriving from a time when it was believed that gods ate and drank (Deut. 32:38; Judg. 9:13), a belief ridiculed in the Bible (Ps. 50:7–15).[8] Accordingly, Targum Jonathan is careful to add: "the priests may eat of My arranged table" (but God does not).

as offerings by fire Rather, "as My gifts" (see the Comment to 15:25).

of pleasing odor to Me Hebrew *reaḥ niḥoḥi* (15:3). In the only other two instances of a suffix occurring with this phrase (Lev. 26:31 and Ezek. 20:28), it refers to the makers of the odor but, as noted above, when it refers to God, it becomes an objective genitive—the odor made to please Him. This divine pleasure is interpreted in the midrash as follows: "There is a pleasurable disposition (*naḥat ruaḥ*) before Him because He has given a command and His will has been done. So the expression is used when an (expensive) bull is offered, and also when a head of small cattle or a bird is offered, in order to teach the lesson that he who offers much and he who offers little is alike before God, for God neither eats nor drinks (i.e., is not placated by receiving more rather than less). Why then does He say, 'Sacrifice to me so that He will do your will?'[9] The Holy One Blessed Be He said: 'My children! It is not because I eat or drink that I told you to offer sacrifices, but on account of the aroma which should remind you that you must be sweet and pleasing (*noḥim*) to Me like a pleasing aroma (*niḥoaḥ*).'"[10]

[3]Say to them: These are the offerings by fire that you are to present to the LORD:

As a regular burnt offering every day, two yearling lambs without blemish. [4]You shall offer one lamb in the morning, and the other lamb you shall offer at twilight. [5]And as a meal offering, there shall be a tenth of an *ephah* of choice flour with a quarter of a *hin* of beaten oil mixed in [6]—the regular burnt offering instituted at Mount Sinai—an offering by fire of pleasing odor to the LORD.

3 וְאָמַרְתָּ֣ לָהֶ֔ם זֶ֚ה הָֽאִשֶּׁ֔ה אֲשֶׁ֥ר תַּקְרִ֖יבוּ לַֽיהוָ֑ה
כְּבָשִׂ֨ים בְּנֵֽי־שָׁנָ֧ה תְמִימִ֛ם שְׁנַ֥יִם לַיּ֖וֹם עֹלָ֥ה תָמִֽיד׃
4 אֶת־הַכֶּ֥בֶשׂ אֶחָ֖ד תַּעֲשֶׂ֣ה בַבֹּ֑קֶר וְאֵת֙ הַכֶּ֣בֶשׂ
הַשֵּׁנִ֔י תַּעֲשֶׂ֖ה בֵּ֥ין הָעַרְבָּֽיִם׃ 5 וַעֲשִׂירִ֧ית הָאֵיפָ֛ה
סֹ֖לֶת לְמִנְחָ֑ה בְּלוּלָ֛ה בְּשֶׁ֥מֶן כָּתִ֖ית רְבִיעִ֥ת הַהִֽין׃
6 עֹלַ֖ת תָּמִ֑יד הָעֲשֻׂיָה֙ בְּהַ֣ר סִינַ֔י לְרֵ֣יחַ נִיחֹ֔חַ

THE DAILY OFFERING (vv. 3–8)

Called the *tamid* from biblical times on, it consisted of a burnt offering of a lamb together with its meal and wine adjuncts. It was offered in the morning and again in the evening. For the background and history of the *tamid*, see Excursus 65.

3. *Say to them* This verse begins the *tamid* section (vv. 3–8), which proves that the previous verse is the superscription for the entire catalogue of public offerings.

offerings by fire Rather, "sacrificial gifts." See the Comment to 15:25.

that you are to present The *tamid* is to be financed by all the people, not merely by the leaders or the rich (Neh. 10:34).[11] It is striking that Ezekiel (45:13–16) insists that the ingredients for the *tamid* be furnished by the people even though in 45:17 he contradicts Nehemiah 10:34 by prescribing that the king, called *nasi'*, is responsible for supplying the sacrifices for the Sabbaths and festivals.

regular burnt offering Hebrew *'olah tamid*.[12] *Tamid* means "regular," not "perpetual, eternal."[13] The term for this daily offering became abbreviated to *tamid* (e.g., Dan. 8:11) and, indeed, is already adumbrated here in verses 6 and 15.

4. *one*[14]

at twilight Hebrew *bein ha-'arbayim* (see the Comment to 9:3), a term that clearly means the time between sunset and dark. This would imply that the *tamid* was the very last sacrifice of the day before the Temple doors were closed. The rabbis, however, interpret the term to mean the waning day or afternoon, which they specify as the ninth hour or about 3:00 P.M.[15] For the Near Eastern background of the twice-daily offering, see Excursus 65.

5. The ingredients for the meal offering of the *tamid* are also given in 15:4.

beaten Hebrew *katit* means "pressed in a mortar," hence, pure oil.[16] Only the menorah (Exod. 27:20; Lev. 24:2) and the *tamid* require such oil. Implied, therefore, is that the oil used in other meal offerings need not be of the same quality.

a tenth of an ephah In the rest of the sacrificial catalogue, *'issaron*, "a tenth," is used alone, but here, in its first occurrence, the name of the measure must be given as well.

6. This verse is a parenthetical insertion that interrupts the sequence of verses 5 and 7 in order to identify the *tamid* with its prescription at Mount Sinai (cited in Exod. 29:38–42).

the regular burnt offering Hebrew *'olat tamid*. The construct form of this expression mandates that *tamid*, though interpreted adjectivally, be treated as a noun, that is, "the burnt offering of the *tamid*." Thus *tamid* is the name of the entire daily sacrifice.

instituted[17] Rather, "performed" (see the Comment to v. 23). The tannaim differ on whether the *tamid* was actually sacrificed in the wilderness. Rabbi Eliezer denies it, citing "Did you offer sacrifice and oblation to Me those forty years in the wilderness, O House of Israel?" (Amos 5:25). Thus the *tamid* was prescribed but not performed at Mount Sinai. Rashi and Ibn Ezra, who follow

7The libation with it shall be a quarter of a *hin* for each lamb, to be poured in the sacred precinct as an offering of fermented drink to the LORD. 8The other lamb you shall offer at twilight, preparing the same meal offering and libation as in the morning—an offering by fire of pleasing odor to the LORD.

אִשֶּׁה לַיהוָה׃ 7 וְנִסְכּוֹ רְבִיעִת הַהִין לַכֶּבֶשׂ הָאֶחָד
בַּקֹּדֶשׁ הַסֵּךְ נֶסֶךְ שֵׁכָר לַיהוָה׃ 8 וְאֵת הַכֶּבֶשׂ
הַשֵּׁנִי תַּעֲשֶׂה בֵּין הָעַרְבָּיִם כְּמִנְחַת הַבֹּקֶר וּכְנִסְכּוֹ
תַּעֲשֶׂה אִשֵּׁה רֵיחַ נִיחֹחַ לַיהוָה׃ פ 9 וּבְיוֹם

this view, render "performed" but suggest that the *tamid* was performed only during the priestly consecration (Exod. 29; Lev. 8) but not again in the wilderness. Rabbi Akiba, on the other hand, insists that the *tamid* was not only performed at Mount Sinai but was never discontinued thereafter.[18] Abravanel remarks that the initial prescription ordaining the *tamid* "throughout the generations at the Tent of Meeting" (Exod. 29:42) means that it never ceased. In support, one should note that the text of the first public sacrifices in the Tabernacle explicitly states that it was offered "in addition to the burnt offering of the morning" (Lev. 9:17), meaning the *tamid*. Moreover, Moses is said to have offered up the burnt offering and meal offering (presumably the *tamid*) as soon as he had erected the Tabernacle (Exod. 40:29). Besides, can one imagine a Tabernacle or, for that matter, any sanctuary in ancient times without a sacrificial service! This verse merely states that the *tamid* alone (and perhaps the Sabbath sacrifices too) was offered in the wilderness but that the festival offerings were ordained only for the promised land. As for the quotation from Amos and other similar sentiments, such as Jeremiah 7:22—these refer to the individual Israelite's private offerings not the regular, public cult.[19]

7. ***with it*** This refers back to the lamb (v. 4, as in v. 8).

hin The Samaritan and the Septuagint (some manuscripts) add "of wine" (as in Exod. 29:40), which is needed here, as it is the first mention of the libation (see the Comment to v. 14).

in the sacred precinct[20] Alternatively, "in a holy vessel"[21] or "in a state of holiness."[22] In the Second Temple, the wine libation was poured at the base of the altar.[23]

Possibly *ba-kodesh* should be rendered "in the sanctuary," that is, inside the Tent of Meeting (see 4:12), where the golden libation cups on the table of display were stored (see the Comment to 4:7). It is clear that these cups were used for libation (Exod. 25:29; 37:16) and, being of gold, they could be used only *inside* the Tent. Only there—and nowhere else—was gold used on the cult objects (menorah, table, altar of incense) and structure (inner curtains, planks, pillars, bars, hooks, and rings). Where this libation was made is not clear. The obvious place, the inner altar—to correspond with the libation on the outer altar—is strictly forbidden by Exodus 30:9. Perhaps this half verse and the cited verses dealing with the golden libation bowls are vestiges of an original libation on the inner altar, one that was later forbidden as a gross anthropomorphism, lest one think that the Deity—in his private chambers—actually imbibed the liquid. The libation, then, would have been set on the table of display together with its loaves of bread. And just as the bread on the table was assigned to the priests (Lev. 24:9), so was the libation contained in the golden cups. This interpretation is supported by the use of the unique term *shekhar* for the libation (see the next Comment). If correct, then the first half of this verse refers to the wine libation on the outer altar (see Exod. 29:40) and the second half to a *shekhar* libation inside the sanctuary, originally on the inner altar (see the Comment to 4:7).

an offering Rather, "a libation."

fermented drink Hebrew *shekhar*, from the root *sh-k-r*, "inebriated," hence, old wine or[24] undiluted wine,[25] not wine from the press.[26] Since Akkadian *šikaru*, *šikru*, the standard temple libation, is of beer, the rendering "ale" (as in 6:3) is also possible. In either case, the liquid must be distinguished from ordinary wine (see the Comment to 6:3).

8. This verse repeats verse 4b and should be rendered: "When you offer the second lamb at twilight, offer [it with] the same morning meal offering and its libation."[27]

same libation Literally, "as its libation," referring to the *tamid* of verse 4b (as in v. 7).

an offering by fire Rather, "sacrificial gift" (see the Comment to 15:25).

9 On the sabbath day: two yearling lambs without blemish, together with two-tenths of a measure of choice flour with oil mixed in as a meal offering, and with the proper libation— 10 a burnt offering for every sabbath, in addition to the regular burnt offering and its libation.

11 On your new moons you shall present a burnt offering to the LORD: two bulls of the herd, one ram, and seven yearling lambs, without blemish. 12 As meal offering for

הַשַּׁבָּת שְׁנֵי־כְבָשִׂים בְּנֵי־שָׁנָה תְּמִימִם וּשְׁנֵי
עֶשְׂרֹנִים סֹלֶת מִנְחָה בְּלוּלָה בַשֶּׁמֶן וְנִסְכּוֹ׃
10 עֹלַת שַׁבַּת בְּשַׁבַּתּוֹ עַל־עֹלַת הַתָּמִיד וְנִסְכָּהּ׃
ס 11 וּבְרָאשֵׁי חָדְשֵׁיכֶם תַּקְרִיבוּ עֹלָה
לַיהוָה פָּרִים בְּנֵי־בָקָר שְׁנַיִם וְאַיִל אֶחָד כְּבָשִׂים
בְּנֵי־שָׁנָה שִׁבְעָה תְּמִימִם׃ 12 וּשְׁלֹשָׁה עֶשְׂרֹנִים

THE SABBATH OFFERING (vv. 9–10)

The offerings for special days, called ***musaf*** in rabbinic Hebrew, are in addition to the ***tamid*** and offered immediately following it[28] (see the Comment to v. 23). The absence of the term ***musaf*** from the Bible may be fortuitous since the ancient Sumerians clearly distinguished between the daily (***tamid***) offerings and the additional offerings for festivals by two discrete terms.[29] Since the Sabbath offering is the same as the ***tamid***, the seventh day thus has double the number of offerings of the other days. The prophet Ezekiel prescribes a much larger Sabbath offering. In his system, however, the ***nasi'*** (i.e., the king) is responsible for all the offerings for special days (Ezek. 45:17; 46:4–5)—as was probably the custom in Temple times (1 Chron. 31:3); a sumptuous contribution could therefore be expected. But, according to the Torah, the Sabbath offering—if not all the others—expressly comes from communal funds.[30]

Obviously there can be no calendrical dating of the Sabbath: It is independent of the calendar (as is also the Feast of Weeks; vv. 26–31). It bespeaks a different and probably older method of demarcating time, that based on a sabbatical cycle—the seventh day, month, year, and week of years—which is not subject to any calendrical restrictions. This is markedly different from the Mesopotamian calendar, which is entirely linked to the phases of the moon. The difference is not just in the method of counting time. Israel's sabbatical system is grounded in socioeconomic postulates: rest each seventh day for both man and earth as a reminder of God's rest and Israel's release from Egyptian bondage (Exod. 20:11; Deut. 5:15), an injunction that achieves its ultimate fulfillment in the return of sold land and persons to their families in the Sabbatical and Jubilee years.[31]

9. On the sabbath day No verb follows as on the other festival days (see vv. 11,19,26). It is added in the Septuagint, the Vulgate, and the Temple Scroll.[32]

10. every sabbath Hebrew ***shabbat be-shabbatto***, literally "sabbath on its sabbath," the same construction as in "every new moon" (v. 14) and "every day" (Exod. 5:13). The problem with this rendering is that the masculine suffix ***o*** refers to ***shabbat***, a feminine noun. Perhaps the idiom is "the weekly offering on the Sabbath," and so "the monthly offering on the new moon"[33] which would explain the masculine suffix (referring to "week" and "month"). However, the word "Sabbath" can also be masculine, as in Isaiah 56:5. The rabbis interpret the phrase literally "on its Sabbath," that is, not to be postponed to another Sabbath.[34] At Qumran, this phrase was interpreted to mean that each Sabbath had its discrete liturgy.[35]

in addition[36]

regular burnt offering The morning ***tamid*** is clearly intended since there could be no offering after the ***tamid*** of the evening (see the Comment to v. 8). The meal offering supplement to the ***tamid*** is not mentioned here (nor in the New Moon offering of v. 15) and is probably included in the name "burnt offering." It should also be noted that there is no purification offering on the sabbath as on the rest of the special days: All is peace on account of the "Sabbath bride."[37] Indeed, no intimation of human wrongdoing is permitted on this joyous day, a principle embodied in the synagogue liturgy, which eschews prayers of petition on the Sabbath.

each bull: three-tenths of a measure of choice flour with oil mixed in. As meal offering for each ram: two-tenths of a measure of choice flour with oil mixed in. ¹³As meal offering for each lamb: a tenth of a measure of fine flour with oil mixed in. Such shall be the burnt offering of pleasing odor, an offering by fire to the LORD. ¹⁴Their libations shall be: half a *hin* of wine for a bull, a third of a *hin* for a ram, and a quarter of a *hin* for a lamb. That shall be the monthly burnt offering for each new moon of the year. ¹⁵And there shall be one goat as a sin offering to the LORD, to be offered in addition to the regular burnt offering and its libation.

סֹ֣לֶת מִנְחָה֩ בְּלוּלָ֨ה בַשֶּׁ֜מֶן לַפָּ֣ר הָֽאֶחָ֗ד וּשְׁנֵ֣י עֶשְׂרֹנִ֗ים סֹ֤לֶת מִנְחָה֙ בְּלוּלָ֣ה בַשֶּׁ֔מֶן לָאַ֖יִל הָֽאֶחָֽד׃ ¹³ וְעִשָּׂרֹ֣ן עִשָּׂר֗וֹן סֹ֤לֶת מִנְחָה֙ בְּלוּלָ֣ה בַשֶּׁ֔מֶן לַכֶּ֖בֶשׂ הָֽאֶחָ֑ד עֹלָה֙ רֵ֣יחַ נִיחֹ֔חַ אִשֶּׁ֖ה לַֽיהֹוָֽה׃ ¹⁴ וְנִסְכֵּיהֶ֗ם חֲצִ֣י הַהִין֩ יִֽהְיֶ֨ה לַפָּ֜ר וּשְׁלִישִׁ֧ת הַהִ֣ין לָאַ֗יִל וּרְבִיעִ֥ת הַהִ֛ין לַכֶּ֖בֶשׂ יָ֑יִן זֹ֣את עֹלַ֥ת חֹ֙דֶשׁ֙ בְּחָדְשׁ֔וֹ לְחָדְשֵׁ֖י הַשָּׁנָֽה׃ ¹⁵ וּשְׂעִ֨יר עִזִּ֥ים אֶחָ֛ד לְחַטָּ֖את לַֽיהֹוָ֑ה עַל־עֹלַ֧ת הַתָּמִ֛יד יֵעָשֶׂ֖ה וְנִסְכּֽוֹ׃ ס ¹⁶ ששי וּבַחֹ֣דֶשׁ הָֽרִאשׁ֔וֹן בְּאַרְבָּעָ֥ה

ROSH ḤODESH, THE NEW MOON (vv. 11–15)

In early Israel, it was an important festival (Isa. 1:12–13; Hos. 2:13) celebrated by families and clans in a state of ritual purity at the local sanctuary (1 Sam. 20:5–6,26). It was a rest day (Amos 8:5) on which one visited a man of God (2 Kings 4:23). References to the fixed Temple offerings of the day are postexilic (e.g., Ezra 3:4–5); however, at least one passage indicates that the New Moons were celebrated in the First Temple (Isa. 1:12–13). The importance of the New Moon is reflected in its sacrificial inventory: it equals the number of offerings on other important festivals (see the table in the introductory Comment to this chap.) and is greater than Ezekiel's prescription for this day (Ezek. 46:6–7).

11. *your new moons* Hebrew *ra'shei ḥodsheikhem.* The Sumerian name for the New Moon festival is "the head of the crescent/month."[38] Like Akkadian *arḫu,* Hebrew *ḥodesh* can mean "new moon" (as in Ugaritic and Phoenician and in several biblical verses) as well as "month." It is also possible to render this phrase "on every first new moon" (see v. 14b and Exod. 12:2), that is, every first of Nisan,[39] which would then explain verse 14b, referring to the other new moons of the year. However, the plural *ra'shei* would then be incongruous with the rest of the calendrical inventory, which never speaks of more than a single day (*yom,* not *yemei;* see vv. 9,26).

12–14. These quantities for the sacrificial supplements have already been given in 15:2–12.

14. *wine*[40] The libation quantities are given here only; since they are always the same, they need not be repeated. But the amounts of the meal offering are subject to change—for Shavuot (Lev. 23:17), for the omer (Lev. 23:13), and for the thanksgiving offering (Lev. 7:12–13; see Men. 77a)—and are therefore repeated.[41]

burnt offering The absence of the auxiliary meal offering and libation is explained by their incorporation into the term "burnt offering."

new moon Hebrew *ḥodesh* here means "new moon," as in 29:6.

15. *sin offering* Rather, "purification offering," and so throughout these two chapters. It is prescribed for all special days but the Sabbath, and it is absent in Ezekiel's system. It is also missing in the subscription to the festival calendar in Leviticus (Lev. 23:37; indicating that its mention in 23:19 is not original). But its omission is not surprising because that calendar is concerned with the sacrificial obligations of the individual Israelite rather than with the official public cult. Its function, as declared in Mishah Shevu'ot 1:4–5, is "to purify the sanctuary and its sancta" of the pollution inflicted upon it by Israel through its ritual and moral impurity (for details, see Excursus 49). As it was offered on the outer altar, its meat was eaten by the priests (Lev. 6:19,23).[42]

to the LORD Maimonides notes that never again do we find the expression "a purification offering to the Lord." He offers the following reason for its presence here: "As it was apprehended that the he-goat offered on the New Moon could be imagined to be a sacrifice to the moon . . . it was explicitly stated that this goat was consecrated to God and not to the moon" (Guide 3.46). Since the New Moon festival was of paramount importance in the lunar calendar of ancient Mesopotamia,[43] there may be grounds for thinking that Maimonides was right (see the Comment to 15:25).

16In the first month, on the fourteenth day of the month,
there shall be a passover sacrifice to the LORD, 17and on the
fifteenth day of that month a festival. Unleavened bread
shall be eaten for seven days. 18The first day shall be a sacred
occasion: you shall not work at your occupations. 19You
shall present an offering by fire, a burnt offering, to the
LORD: two bulls of the herd, one ram, and seven yearling
lambs—see that they are without blemish. 20The meal

עָשָׂר יוֹם לַחֹדֶשׁ פֶּסַח לַיהוָה׃ 17 וּבַחֲמִשָּׁה עָשָׂר
יוֹם לַחֹדֶשׁ הַזֶּה חָג שִׁבְעַת יָמִים מַצּוֹת יֵאָכֵל׃
18 בַּיּוֹם הָרִאשׁוֹן מִקְרָא־קֹדֶשׁ כָּל־מְלֶאכֶת עֲבֹדָה
לֹא תַעֲשׂוּ׃ 19 וְהִקְרַבְתֶּם אִשֶּׁה עֹלָה לַיהוָה פָּרִים
בְּנֵי־בָקָר שְׁנַיִם וְאַיִל אֶחָד וְשִׁבְעָה כְבָשִׂים בְּנֵי
שָׁנָה תְּמִימִם יִהְיוּ לָכֶם׃ 20 וּמִנְחָתָם סֹלֶת בְּלוּלָה

in addition to the regular burnt offering This clause is added here as well as in the prescriptions of the festivals to follow (28:23,31,etc.), lest one of the lambs prescribed for the festival be used for the *tamid*.[44]

its libation Hebrew *nisko*. The masculine suffix refers to the *tamid* (as in v. 24; see v. 31). It also indicates that the offering was called by the abbreviation *tamid* already in biblical times. The Samaritan, however, reads *niskah* (fem., as in 28:10), referring to the burnt offering, *'olah*. The sectaries of the Dead Sea surely had the Masoretic text, since they chose the goat (masc.) as the antecedent and, thereby, legislated that the purification offering also is accompanied by a meal offering and a libation,[45] a doctrine rigorously opposed by the rabbis.[46]

THE PASCHAL SACRIFICE AND UNLEAVENED BREAD (vv. 16–25)

The day of the paschal offering and the seven-day Festival of Unleavened Bread are discrete holidays (see Excursus 20). Yet the fact that the paschal offering is mentioned even though it is a private sacrifice (see Exod. 12:1–11)—and hence no description is given—indicates that the two festivals are already fused.

17. a festival The Festival of Unleavened Bread is called a *ḥag* in all the early sources, such as Exodus 23:15. Otherwise it is the paschal offering that receives this title (Exod. 34:25; Deut. 16:2,6 [implied]), although the distinction in name is sometimes retained, as in Ezra 6:20,22 and 2 Chronicles 35:17. Here the term *ḥag*, although attached to the fifteenth day, is not called by its full name *ḥag ha-matsot* but simply *ḥag*, implying that it includes the paschal observance; that is, both the paschal sacrifice and the first day of the Festival of Unleavened Bread are observed at the sanctuary, precisely as instituted by Deuteronomy 16:1–6. The sources differ about which day of the festival the *ḥag* refers to: Here and in Exodus 12:14 and Leviticus 23:6 it is the first day; in Exodus 13:6 it is the last, that is, the seventh day; in Ezra 6:22 it encompasses the entire week.

18. occasion Hebrew *mikra'*. See Leviticus 23:2,4,7, where it is the object of the verb *kara'*, "proclaim," and apposite to the subject *mo'ed*, "fixed time"; similarly, in Isaiah 1:13–14, it is linked with New Moon and Sabbath and is also the object of *kara'*, "proclaim." Thus it can only refer to a festival day.[47] Other renderings are: (1) "convocation,"[48] which is not attested in any other Semitic language, and (2) "proclamation,"[49] the verbal noun from *kara'*, as in 10:2. This term is found in the list of calendar festivals in association with the prohibition of work, which may account for its omission in the prescriptions for the Sabbath and New Moon where the work prohibition is also missing (contrast Lev. 23:3).

occupations Hebrew *mele'khet 'avodah*. Rather, "laborious work" that is forbidden on the festivals, in contrast to *kol mela'khah*, "any work," forbidden on the Sabbath and Yom Kippur in Numbers 29:7 and Leviticus 23:3,28. The same distinction obtains in regard to the word *shabbat*. The Sabbath and Yom Kippur alone are described as *shabbat shabbaton* (e.g., Exod. 16:23), which can only mean "absolute rest." The nonlaborious work permitted on the festivals is not defined, except for the explicit permission to prepare food on the first and last days of the Passover (Exod. 12:16).[50]

19–24. The offering on each day of the Festival of Unleavened Bread is the same as for the New Moon (vv. 11–15; see the table in the introductory Comment to this chap.). Ezekiel 45:21–24 prescribes a different matrix.

offering with them shall be of choice flour with oil mixed in: prepare three-tenths of a measure for a bull, two-tenths for a ram; 21and for each of the seven lambs prepare one-tenth of a measure. 22And there shall be one goat for a sin offering, to make expiation in your behalf. 23You shall present these in addition to the morning portion of the regular burnt offering. 24You shall offer the like daily for seven days as food, an offering by fire of pleasing odor to the LORD; they shall be offered, with their libations, in addition to the regular burnt offering. 25And the seventh day shall be a sacred occasion for you: you shall not work at your occupations.

26On the day of the first fruits, your Feast of Weeks, when you bring an offering of new grain to the LORD, you shall observe a sacred occasion: you shall not work at your

בַּשָּׁמֶן שְׁלֹשָׁה עֶשְׂרֹנִים לַפָּר וּשְׁנֵי עֶשְׂרֹנִים לָאַיִל
תַּעֲשׂוּ׃ 21 עִשָּׂרוֹן עִשָּׂרוֹן תַּעֲשֶׂה לַכֶּבֶשׂ הָאֶחָד
לְשִׁבְעַת הַכְּבָשִׂים׃ 22 וּשְׂעִיר חַטָּאת אֶחָד לְכַפֵּר
עֲלֵיכֶם׃ 23 מִלְּבַד עֹלַת הַבֹּקֶר אֲשֶׁר לְעֹלַת
הַתָּמִיד תַּעֲשׂוּ אֶת־אֵלֶּה׃ 24 כָּאֵלֶּה תַּעֲשׂוּ לַיּוֹם
שִׁבְעַת יָמִים לֶחֶם אִשֵּׁה רֵיחַ־נִיחֹחַ לַיהוָה עַל־
עוֹלַת הַתָּמִיד יֵעָשֶׂה וְנִסְכּוֹ׃ 25 וּבַיּוֹם הַשְּׁבִיעִי
מִקְרָא־קֹדֶשׁ יִהְיֶה לָכֶם כָּל־מְלֶאכֶת עֲבֹדָה לֹא
תַעֲשׂוּ׃ ס 26 וּבְיוֹם הַבִּכּוּרִים בְּהַקְרִיבְכֶם
מִנְחָה חֲדָשָׁה לַיהוָה בְּשָׁבֻעֹתֵיכֶם מִקְרָא־קֹדֶשׁ
יִהְיֶה לָכֶם כָּל־מְלֶאכֶת עֲבֹדָה לֹא תַעֲשׂוּ׃

22. ***to make expiation*** Rather, "to make purgation" (see the Comment to v. 15 and Excursuses 19 and 49).

23. This verse seems superfluous in view of verse 24b. Its interpolative nature may be detected by its use of ***milvad*** rather than *ʿal* to denote "in addition to" (see note 36).[51] Its purpose is to specify the order for sacrificing the ***musaf***.

present Rather, "sacrifice." The verb *ʿasah* is used for the entire sacrificial procedure (e.g., see Lev. 9:7,16).

the morning portion Literally, "the morning burnt offering," proof that the ***musaf*** offering follows the morning ***tamid***, from which the tannaim derive the principle: "What is offered more often than another precedes that other. The daily burnt offerings precede the ***musaf*** offerings; the Sabbath offerings precede the New Moon offerings; the New Moon offerings precede the New Year offerings."[52]

of the regular burnt offering Sacrificed twice daily (vv. 3–8).

24. ***the like daily for seven days*** In contradistinction to the Sukkot festival, when the number of bulls varies each day (Sif. Num. 147 and see the table in the introductory Comment to this chap.), but not in Ezekiel's system (Ezek. 45:23).

an offering by fire of pleasing odor Rather, "a gift" (see the Comment to 15:25). The reference is to the burnt offerings not to the purification offerings, which are neither "gifts" nor of "pleasing odor."

with their libations Hebrew ***ve-nisko***, reading ***ve-niskeihem***,[53] to include the libations of both the ***tamid*** and the festival.

25. A repetition of Leviticus 23:8. For the terms, see the Comment to verse 18.

THE FEAST OF WEEKS (vv. 26–31)

Like the Sabbath, the Feast of Weeks is independent of the lunar calendar. It marks the beginning of the wheat harvest, which occurs seven weeks after the beginning of the barley harvest (Lev. 23:15–16). The offerings listed here are also given in Leviticus 23:18–19, except that the quantities for the bulls and the rams are reversed. The rabbis hold that the list here is a ***musaf***, a supplement to those listed in Leviticus 23.[54]

26. ***day of the first fruits*** Hebrew ***yom ha-bikkurim***. This day is also called ***ḥag ha-katsir***, "the Feast of the Harvest," in Exodus 23:16, and ***ḥag ha-shavuʿot***, "the Feast of Weeks," in Exodus

occupations. ²⁷You shall present a burnt offering of pleasing odor to the LORD: two bulls of the herd, one ram, seven yearling lambs. ²⁸The meal offering with them shall be of choice flour with oil mixed in, three-tenths of a measure for a bull, two-tenths for a ram, ²⁹and one-tenth for each of the seven lambs. ³⁰And there shall be one goat for expiation in your behalf. ³¹You shall present them—see that they are without blemish—with their libations, in addition to the regular burnt offering and its meal offering.

27 וְהִקְרַבְתֶּ֨ם עוֹלָ֜ה לְרֵ֣יחַ נִיחֹ֘חַ֮ לַֽיהֹוָה֒ פָּרִ֨ים בְּנֵֽי־
בָקָ֤ר שְׁנַ֙יִם֙ אַ֣יִל אֶחָ֔ד שִׁבְעָ֥ה כְבָשִׂ֖ים בְּנֵ֥י שָׁנָֽה׃ 28 וּמִנְחָתָ֗ם סֹ֤לֶת בְּלוּלָ֣ה בַשֶּׁ֔מֶן שְׁלֹשָׁ֣ה עֶשְׂרֹנִ֗ים
לַפָּ֣ר הָֽאֶחָ֔ד שְׁנֵ֣י עֶשְׂרֹנִ֔ים לָאַ֖יִל הָֽאֶחָֽד׃ 29 עִשָּׂר֣וֹן
עִשָּׂר֔וֹן לַכֶּ֖בֶשׂ הָֽאֶחָ֑ד לְשִׁבְעַ֖ת הַכְּבָשִֽׂים׃ 30 שְׂעִ֥יר
עִזִּ֖ים אֶחָ֑ד לְכַפֵּ֖ר עֲלֵיכֶֽם׃ 31 מִלְּבַ֞ד עֹלַ֧ת הַתָּמִ֛יד
וּמִנְחָת֖וֹ תַּֽעֲשׂ֑וּ תְּמִימִ֥ם יִֽהְיוּ־לָכֶ֖ם וְנִסְכֵּיהֶֽם׃ פ

29 In the seventh month, on the first day of the month, you shall observe a sacred occasion: you shall not work at your occupations. You shall observe it as a day when the horn is sounded. ²You shall present a burnt offering of

כ״ט וּבַחֹ֨דֶשׁ הַשְּׁבִיעִ֜י בְּאֶחָ֣ד לַחֹ֗דֶשׁ מִקְרָא־
קֹ֙דֶשׁ֙ יִֽהְיֶ֣ה לָכֶ֔ם כׇּל־מְלֶ֥אכֶת עֲבֹדָ֖ה לֹ֣א תַֽעֲשׂ֑וּ
י֥וֹם תְּרוּעָ֖ה יִֽהְיֶ֥ה לָכֶֽם׃ 2 וַֽעֲשִׂיתֶ֨ם עֹלָ֜ה לְרֵ֣יחַ

34:22, Deuteronomy 16:10,16, and 2 Chronicles 8:13. The last term is abbreviated in this verse to *shavuʿot*, "weeks." However, it is significant that the festival is not called *ḥag* in the priestly texts (see Lev. 23:16–21), implying that pilgrimage to the sanctuary was not necessary (nor could it be expected in the midst of the grain harvest). This may account for its absence from the festival list in Ezekiel 45:21–25, which is concerned solely with Temple celebrations.⁵⁵ In any case, the omission of the sanctuary requirement indicates the realistic, rather than the allegedly utopian, character of the priestly texts (see the Comments to 35:1–9 and Excursus 74). In rabbinic times, this festival was also called ʿatseret.⁵⁶

The first fruits are those of wheat in the form of two loaves of bread (Lev. 23:17). A measure, called "omer," of the barley harvest is brought as a first fruits offering seven weeks earlier (Lev. 23:10). First fruits of wine and oil are also required from the grape and olive yield (Num. 18:12) but not at any fixed time. The Dead Sea sectarians, however, prescribe fixed festivals for the latter, that of the New Wine (fifty days after the New Wheat) and that of the New Oil (fifty days after the New Wine),⁵⁷ the dates of which correspond uncannily with their respective harvests.

offering of new grain Literally, "new meal offering"; so called also in Leviticus 23:16, to distinguish it from the previous meal offering made from the first fruits of the barley (Lev. 23:10).

27.⁵⁸

two bulls of the herd, one ram These numbers are reversed in Leviticus 23:18.

30. Perhaps *le-ḥattaʾt*, "as a purification offering," should be inserted after the word "goat."⁵⁹

31. **its meal offering** That is, of the *tamid* (see the Comment to v. 15).

CHAPTER 29   THE FIRST DAY OF THE SEVENTH MONTH   (vv. 1–6)

The offering for this day almost duplicates and is in addition to the offering for the New Moon (see the table in the introductory Comment to chap. 28). Thus the seventh New Moon is to the ordinary New Moon as the seventh day is to the ordinary day, thereby indicating how the sabbatical cycle was preserved in the lunar calendar (see the introductory Comment to chap. 28). The seventh month is actually the beginning of the agricultural year, as is apparent from the oldest calendars of the Bible (see Exod. 23:16; 34:22). Furthermore, the Jubilee year, when land reverts to its original owner, commences at the beginning of the agricultural year.¹ And the Jewish religious calendar still preserves the first day of the seventh month as the beginning of the year: Rosh Hashanah, "The Head of the Year," or New Year's Day.² Except that one bull is required instead of two, the offerings are the same as on previous festivals. This reduction is also attested for Yom Kippur and the eighth day of Sukkot.

pleasing odor to the LORD: one bull of the herd, one ram, and seven yearling lambs, without blemish. 3The meal offering with them—choice flour with oil mixed in—shall be: three-tenths of a measure for a bull, two-tenths for a ram, 4and one-tenth for each of the seven lambs. 5And there shall be one goat for a sin offering, to make expiation in your behalf—6in addition to the burnt offering of the new moon with its meal offering and the regular burnt offering with its meal offering, each with its libation as prescribed, offerings by fire of pleasing odor to the LORD.

7On the tenth day of the same seventh month you shall observe a sacred occasion when you shall practice self-denial. You shall do no work. 8You shall present to the

נִיחֹחַ לַיהוָה פַּר בֶּן־בָּקָר אֶחָד אַיִל אֶחָד כְּבָשִׂים
בְּנֵי־שָׁנָה שִׁבְעָה תְּמִימִם׃ 3 וּמִנְחָתָם סֹלֶת
בְּלוּלָה בַשָּׁמֶן שְׁלֹשָׁה עֶשְׂרֹנִים לַפָּר שְׁנֵי עֶשְׂרֹנִים
לָאָיִל׃ 4 וְעִשָּׂרוֹן אֶחָד לַכֶּבֶשׂ הָאֶחָד לְשִׁבְעַת
הַכְּבָשִׂים׃ 5 וּשְׂעִיר־עִזִּים אֶחָד חַטָּאת לְכַפֵּר
עֲלֵיכֶם׃ 6 מִלְּבַד עֹלַת הַחֹדֶשׁ וּמִנְחָתָהּ וְעֹלַת
הַתָּמִיד וּמִנְחָתָהּ וְנִסְכֵּיהֶם כְּמִשְׁפָּטָם לְרֵיחַ נִיחֹחַ
אִשֶּׁה לַיהוָה׃ ס 7 וּבֶעָשׂוֹר לַחֹדֶשׁ הַשְּׁבִיעִי
הַזֶּה מִקְרָא־קֹדֶשׁ יִהְיֶה לָכֶם וְעִנִּיתֶם אֶת־
נַפְשֹׁתֵיכֶם כָּל־מְלָאכָה לֹא תַעֲשׂוּ׃ 8 וְהִקְרַבְתֶּם

The explanation has been put forth that one bull suffices since additional sacrifices are required for Rosh Hashanah (those of the New Moon; v. 6) and Yom Kippur (v. 11; see Lev. 16) and since only one bull is needed on the eighth day of Sukkot to represent Israel.[3] However, the problem remains unresolved.

1. *a day when the horn is sounded* Hebrew *yom teru'ah*. In Leviticus 23:24 the day is called *zikhron teru'ah*, "commemorated with loud blasts." The horn blowing on this day should not be confused with the prescription that horns should be blown on all festivals (10:10). These latter horns are trumpets, to be blown only by priests, and their signal is called *teki'ah*, not *teru'ah* (for the distinction, see Excursus 21). Hence, the tradition that the horn used on this festival is the shofar and that it need not be blown by priests is correct. Perhaps Psalms 47 and 95–100, in which shofar blowing is prominent, were sung; and their theme of cosmic judgment—"he is coming to rule the earth" (Pss. 96:13; 98:9)—was incorporated as a permanent theme in the liturgy of this day.

2. *one bull . . . seven yearling lambs . . . one goat* The identical combination of sacrificial animals appears in verses 8 and 11. It also shows up in Hittite cultic texts.[4]

6. *as prescribed* See 23:3–8,11–15. The reason for the omission of the purification offering for the New Moon from the prescribed sacrifices for the first day (New Moon) of the seventh month is unclear.

THE TENTH DAY OF THE SEVENTH MONTH (vv. 7–11)

The day is known as *yom ha-kippurim*, "The Day of Purgation" (v. 11; Lev. 23:27), which refers to the purgation of the sanctuary following its yearlong defilement by man. Thus the purgation rituals are entirely within the confines of the sanctuary and performed exclusively by the High Priest (Lev. 16). This explains the absence of this day from the calendars of Deuteronomy 16 and Ezekiel 45 and from Nehemiah 8: The people did not go to the Temple. They abstained from work, fasted, and prayed that their yearlong sinning against God and His sanctuary might be forgiven. It was a sober but not somber day, and great was the rejoicing when it ushered in the Jubilee year with a shofar blast (Lev. 25:9–10).

7. *you shall practice self-denial* Hebrew *ve-'innitem 'et naf-shoteikhem*, literally "you shall afflict yourselves," chiefly by fasting, as testified by Isaiah 58:3,5,10. But other acts of self-denial are also implied and are understood by the rabbis as follows: "Afflict yourselves from food and drink, bathing, anointing, [wearing] sandals, and sexual intercourse."[5] Indeed that the psalmist must specify *'inniti ba-tsom nafshi*, literally "I afflicted myself with a fast" (Ps. 35:13), means that there are other forms of self-affliction, some of which were mandatory for this day. Finally, Daniel's attempt *le-hit'annot* consisted of three weeks of mourning during which, he says, "I ate no tasty food, nor did any meat or wine enter my mouth. I did not anoint myself" (Dan. 10:3,12). Thus his "self-denial" consisted of a partial fast; otherwise it resembled the rabbinic definition. The resort to the Hitpael, the

LORD a burnt offering of pleasing odor: one bull of the herd, one ram, seven yearling lambs; see that they are without blemish. 9The meal offering with them—of choice flour with oil mixed in—shall be: three-tenths of a measure for a bull, two-tenths for the one ram, 10one-tenth for each of the seven lambs. 11And there shall be one goat for a sin offering, in addition to the sin offering of expiation and the regular burnt offering with its meal offering, each with its libation.

12On the fifteenth day of the seventh month, you shall observe a sacred occasion: you shall not work at your occupations.—Seven days you shall observe a festival of the LORD.—13You shall present a burnt offering, an offering by fire of pleasing odor to the LORD: Thirteen bulls of the herd, two rams, fourteen yearling lambs; they shall be without blemish. 14The meal offerings with them—of choice flour with oil mixed in—shall be: three-tenths of a measure for each of the thirteen bulls, two-tenths for each of the two rams, 15and one-tenth for each of the fourteen lambs.

עֹלָה לַיהוָה רֵיחַ נִיחֹחַ פַּר בֶּן־בָּקָר אֶחָד אַיִל
אֶחָד כְּבָשִׂים בְּנֵי־שָׁנָה שִׁבְעָה תְּמִימִם יִהְיוּ לָכֶם׃
9 וּמִנְחָתָם סֹלֶת בְּלוּלָה בַשָּׁמֶן שְׁלֹשָׁה עֶשְׂרֹנִים
לַפָּר שְׁנֵי עֶשְׂרֹנִים לָאַיִל הָאֶחָד׃ 10 עִשָּׂרוֹן
עִשָּׂרוֹן לַכֶּבֶשׂ הָאֶחָד לְשִׁבְעַת הַכְּבָשִׂים׃
11 שְׂעִיר־עִזִּים אֶחָד חַטָּאת מִלְּבַד חַטַּאת
הַכִּפֻּרִים וְעֹלַת הַתָּמִיד וּמִנְחָתָהּ וְנִסְכֵּיהֶם׃
פ שביעי 12 וּבַחֲמִשָּׁה עָשָׂר יוֹם לַחֹדֶשׁ
הַשְּׁבִיעִי מִקְרָא־קֹדֶשׁ יִהְיֶה לָכֶם כָּל־מְלֶאכֶת
עֲבֹדָה לֹא תַעֲשׂוּ וְחַגֹּתֶם חַג לַיהוָה שִׁבְעַת יָמִים׃
13 וְהִקְרַבְתֶּם עֹלָה אִשֵּׁה רֵיחַ נִיחֹחַ לַיהוָה פָּרִים
בְּנֵי־בָקָר שְׁלֹשָׁה עָשָׂר אֵילִם שְׁנָיִם כְּבָשִׂים בְּנֵי־
שָׁנָה אַרְבָּעָה עָשָׂר תְּמִימִם יִהְיוּ׃ 14 וּמִנְחָתָם
סֹלֶת בְּלוּלָה בַשָּׁמֶן שְׁלֹשָׁה עֶשְׂרֹנִים לַפָּר הָאֶחָד
לִשְׁלֹשָׁה עָשָׂר פָּרִים שְׁנֵי עֶשְׂרֹנִים לָאַיִל הָאֶחָד
לִשְׁנֵי הָאֵילִם׃ 15 וְעִשָּׂרוֹן* עִשָּׂרוֹן לַכֶּבֶשׂ הָאֶחָד
לְאַרְבָּעָה עָשָׂר כְּבָשִׂים׃ 16 וּשְׂעִיר־עִזִּים אֶחָד

v. 15. נקוד על ו׳ בתרא

reflexive pattern, without *nefesh*, as also in Psalms 107:17 and Ezra 8:21, implies that the latter term should be rendered "self."[6]

work Literally, "any work," is the same phrase used for the Sabbath (Lev. 23:3), which indicates a severer prohibition of work on these days than on the other festivals (see the Comment to v. 18).

11. ***sin offering of expiation*** Hebrew *ḥatta't ha-kippurim*. Rather, "purification offering of purgation," referring to the purgation ritual of the sanctuary, described in Leviticus 16. It is mentioned to avoid confusing the *ḥatta't* of the *musaf* with the *ḥatta't* of purgation.[7]

THE FIFTEENTH TO THE TWENTY-FIRST OF THE SEVENTH MONTH (vv. 12–34)

Elsewhere it is called *ḥag ha-sukkot*, "the Feast of Booths" (Lev. 23:34; Deut. 16:13); *ḥag ha-'asif*, "the Feast of Ingathering" (Exod. 23:16; 34:22); and *he-ḥag*, "the Feast" (e.g., 1 Kings 8:22; 12:32)—that is, the outstanding festival. When the harvest was in at the end of the agricultural year the Israelite farmer could pilgrimage to Jerusalem for this seven-day festival. The sacrifices ordained for this festival are a measure of its popularity. Five times as many bulls and twice as many rams and lambs are offered on this festival than on the equivalent days of the Festival of Unleavened Bread (see the table in the introductory Comment to chap. 28). Rabbinic tradition may be correct in stating that the total of seventy bulls represents all the nations of the world, assumed to number seventy. This festival, focusing on man's need and desire to give thanks to God for the year's harvest, is of universal appeal. It is small wonder that Zechariah prophesied that Sukkot would become a universally observed festival (Zech. 14:16) and that the Pilgrims at Plymouth modeled the thanksgiving celebration for their first harvest on the biblical paradigm.

12. ***sacred occasion*** For this term, see the Comment to 28:18.

Seven days . . . a festival This *ḥag* differs from the Festival of Unleavened Bread. The latter is also of seven days' duration, but only the first day is a *ḥag* (28:17).

15. The Samaritan adds to the verse.[8]

[16]And there shall be one goat for a sin offering—in addition to the regular burnt offering, its meal offering and libation.

[17]Second day: Twelve bulls of the herd, two rams, fourteen yearling lambs, without blemish; [18]the meal offerings and libations for the bulls, rams, and lambs, in the quantities prescribed; [19]and one goat for a sin offering—in addition to the regular burnt offering, its meal offering and libations.

[20]Third day: Eleven bulls, two rams, fourteen yearling lambs, without blemish; [21]the meal offerings and libations for the bulls, rams, and lambs, in the quantities prescribed; [22]and one goat for a sin offering—in addition to the regular burnt offering, its meal offering and libation.

[23]Fourth day: Ten bulls, two rams, fourteen yearling lambs, without blemish; [24]the meal offerings and libations for the bulls, rams, and lambs, in the quantities prescribed; [25]and one goat for a sin offering—in addition to the regular burnt offering, its meal offering and libation.

[26]Fifth day: Nine bulls, two rams, fourteen yearling lambs, without blemish; [27]the meal offerings and libations for the bulls, rams, and lambs, in the quantities prescribed; [28]and one goat for a sin offering—in addition to the regular burnt offering, its meal offering and libation.

[29]Sixth day: Eight bulls, two rams, fourteen yearling lambs, without blemish; [30]the meal offerings and libations for the bulls, rams, and lambs, in the quantities prescribed; [31]and one goat for a sin offering—in addition to the regular burnt offering, its meal offering and libations.

[32]Seventh day: Seven bulls, two rams, fourteen yearling lambs, without blemish; [33]the meal offerings and libations for the bulls, rams, and lambs, in the quantities prescribed; [34]and one goat for a sin offering—in addition to the regular burnt offering, its meal offering and libation.

חַטָּ֑את מִלְּבַד֙ עֹלַ֣ת הַתָּמִ֔יד מִנְחָתָ֖הּ וְנִסְכָּֽהּ׃
ס 17 וּבַיּ֣וֹם הַשֵּׁנִ֗י פָּרִ֧ים בְּנֵי־בָקָ֛ר שְׁנֵ֥ים
עָשָׂ֖ר אֵילִ֣ם שְׁנָ֑יִם כְּבָשִׂ֧ים בְּנֵי־שָׁנָ֛ה אַרְבָּעָ֥ה
עָשָׂ֖ר תְּמִימִֽם׃ 18 וּמִנְחָתָ֣ם וְנִסְכֵּיהֶ֡ם לַ֠פָּרִים
לָאֵילִ֧ם וְלַכְּבָשִׂ֛ים בְּמִסְפָּרָ֖ם כַּמִּשְׁפָּֽט׃ 19 וּשְׂעִיר־
עִזִּ֥ים אֶחָ֖ד חַטָּ֑את מִלְּבַד֙ עֹלַ֣ת הַתָּמִ֔יד וּמִנְחָתָ֖הּ
וְנִסְכֵּיהֶֽם׃ ס 20 וּבַיּ֧וֹם הַשְּׁלִישִׁ֛י פָּרִ֥ים
עַשְׁתֵּי־עָשָׂ֖ר אֵילִ֣ם שְׁנָ֑יִם כְּבָשִׂ֧ים בְּנֵי־שָׁנָ֛ה
אַרְבָּעָ֥ה עָשָׂ֖ר תְּמִימִֽם׃ 21 וּמִנְחָתָ֣ם וְנִסְכֵּיהֶ֡ם
לַ֠פָּרִים לָאֵילִ֧ם וְלַכְּבָשִׂ֛ים בְּמִסְפָּרָ֖ם כַּמִּשְׁפָּֽט׃
22 וּשְׂעִ֥יר חַטָּ֖את אֶחָ֑ד מִלְּבַד֙ עֹלַ֣ת הַתָּמִ֔יד
וּמִנְחָתָ֖הּ וְנִסְכָּֽהּ׃ ס 23 וּבַיּ֧וֹם הָרְבִיעִ֛י פָּרִ֥ים
עֲשָׂרָ֖ה אֵילִ֣ם שְׁנָ֑יִם כְּבָשִׂ֧ים בְּנֵי־שָׁנָ֛ה אַרְבָּעָ֥ה
עָשָׂ֖ר תְּמִימִֽם׃ 24 מִנְחָתָ֣ם וְנִסְכֵּיהֶ֡ם לַ֠פָּרִים
לָאֵילִ֧ם וְלַכְּבָשִׂ֛ים בְּמִסְפָּרָ֖ם כַּמִּשְׁפָּֽט׃ 25 וּשְׂעִיר־
עִזִּ֥ים אֶחָ֖ד חַטָּ֑את מִלְּבַד֙ עֹלַ֣ת הַתָּמִ֔יד מִנְחָתָ֖הּ
וְנִסְכָּֽהּ׃ ס 26 וּבַיּ֧וֹם הַחֲמִישִׁ֛י פָּרִ֥ים תִּשְׁעָ֖ה
אֵילִ֣ם שְׁנָ֑יִם כְּבָשִׂ֧ים בְּנֵי־שָׁנָ֛ה אַרְבָּעָ֥ה עָשָׂ֖ר
תְּמִימִֽם׃ 27 וּמִנְחָתָ֣ם וְנִסְכֵּיהֶ֡ם לַ֠פָּרִים לָאֵילִ֧ם
וְלַכְּבָשִׂ֛ים בְּמִסְפָּרָ֖ם כַּמִּשְׁפָּֽט׃ 28 וּשְׂעִ֥יר חַטָּ֖את
אֶחָ֑ד מִלְּבַד֙ עֹלַ֣ת הַתָּמִ֔יד וּמִנְחָתָ֖הּ וְנִסְכָּֽהּ׃
ס 29 וּבַיּ֧וֹם הַשִּׁשִּׁ֛י פָּרִ֥ים שְׁמֹנָ֖ה אֵילִ֣ם
שְׁנָ֑יִם כְּבָשִׂ֧ים בְּנֵי־שָׁנָ֛ה אַרְבָּעָ֥ה עָשָׂ֖ר תְּמִימִֽם׃
30 וּמִנְחָתָ֣ם וְנִסְכֵּיהֶ֡ם לַ֠פָּרִים לָאֵילִ֧ם וְלַכְּבָשִׂ֛ים
בְּמִסְפָּרָ֖ם כַּמִּשְׁפָּֽט׃ 31 וּשְׂעִ֥יר חַטָּ֖את אֶחָ֑ד מִלְּבַד֙
עֹלַ֣ת הַתָּמִ֔יד מִנְחָתָ֖הּ וּנְסָכֶֽיהָ׃ פ 32 וּבַיּ֧וֹם
הַשְּׁבִיעִ֛י פָּרִ֥ים שִׁבְעָ֖ה אֵילִ֣ם שְׁנָ֑יִם כְּבָשִׂ֧ים בְּנֵי־
שָׁנָ֛ה אַרְבָּעָ֥ה עָשָׂ֖ר תְּמִימִֽם׃ 33 וּמִנְחָתָ֣ם
וְנִסְכֵּהֶ֡ם* לַ֠פָּרִים לָאֵילִ֧ם וְלַכְּבָשִׂ֛ים בְּמִסְפָּרָ֖ם
כְּמִשְׁפָּטָֽם׃ 34 וּשְׂעִ֥יר חַטָּ֖את אֶחָ֑ד מִלְּבַד֙ עֹלַ֣ת
הַתָּמִ֔יד מִנְחָתָ֖הּ וְנִסְכָּֽהּ׃ פ מפטיר 35 בַּיּוֹם

v. 33. חסר יו״ד

19. libations[9]

31. libations[10] Rabbi Akiba interprets the plural as including a water libation,[11] which he explains as follows: "An omer [of barley] is brought on the *pesaḥ,* that the grain of the fields be blessed; first fruits are brought on *'atseret* (Shavuot), that fruits of the trees will be blessed; so there is a water libation on the Festival (Sukkot), that the year's rains will be blessed."[12]

32. Seven bulls In this manner, the decreasing number of bulls offered each day ends with the key number seven on the seventh day, a number that insinuates itself into the entirety of this cultic calendar (see the introductory Comment to chap. 28). The midrash understands the total of ninety-eight lambs offered during the seven days to be an atonement for the ninety-eight curses in Deuteronomy 28.[13]

³⁵On the eighth day you shall hold a solemn gathering; you shall not work at your occupations. ³⁶You shall present a burnt offering, an offering by fire of pleasing odor to the LORD; one bull, one ram, seven yearling lambs, without blemish; ³⁷the meal offerings and libations for the bull, the ram, and the lambs, in the quantities prescribed; ³⁸and one goat for a sin offering—in addition to the regular burnt offering, its meal offering and libation.

³⁹All these you shall offer to the LORD at the stated times, in addition to your votive and freewill offerings, be they

הַשְּׁמִינִ֕י עֲצֶ֖רֶת תִּהְיֶ֣ה לָכֶ֑ם כָּל־מְלֶ֥אכֶת עֲבֹדָ֖ה
לֹ֥א תַעֲשֽׂוּ׃ 36 וְהִקְרַבְתֶּ֨ם עֹלָ֜ה אִשֵּׁ֨ה רֵ֤יחַ נִיחֹ֙חַ֙
לַֽיהֹוָ֔ה פַּ֥ר אֶחָ֖ד אַ֣יִל אֶחָ֑ד כְּבָשִׂ֥ים בְּנֵֽי־שָׁנָ֖ה
שִׁבְעָ֥ה תְּמִימִֽם׃ 37 מִנְחָתָ֣ם וְנִסְכֵּיהֶ֗ם לַפָּ֨ר לָאַ֜יִל
וְלַכְּבָשִׂ֛ים בְּמִסְפָּרָ֖ם כַּמִּשְׁפָּֽט׃ 38 וּשְׂעִ֥יר חַטָּ֖את
אֶחָ֑ד מִלְּבַד֙ עֹלַ֣ת הַתָּמִ֔יד וּמִנְחָתָ֖הּ וְנִסְכָּֽהּ׃
39 אֵ֛לֶּה תַּעֲשׂ֥וּ לַֽיהֹוָ֖ה בְּמוֹעֲדֵיכֶ֑ם לְבַ֣ד מִנִּדְרֵיכֶ֗ם
וְנִדְבֹֽתֵיכֶם֙ לְעֹלֹ֣תֵיכֶ֔ם וּלְמִנְחֹֽתֵיכֶ֖ם וּלְנִסְכֵּיכֶ֑ם
וּֽלְשַׁלְמֵיכֶֽם׃

THE EIGHTH DAY   (vv. 35–38)

Although Sukkot is a seven-day festival (v. 12), an eighth festival day is added. But its offerings are not the same as those of the preceding festival; rather, they are the same as those of the first and tenth of this month. The origin of this day is obscure. Whereas King Solomon sends the celebrants of the Temple dedication home on this eighth day (1 Kings 8:66), the Book of Chronicles lets it be known that the king observed the eighth day as a festival and only released the people on the following day (2 Chron. 7:9–10).

The sharp contrast in the number of sacrificed bulls, seventy during the seven days and only one on the eighth day, gave rise to the following midrash:

> You find that on Sukkot, Israel offers to Him seventy bulls as an atonement for the seventy nations. Israel says: "Sovereign of the worlds! Behold, we offer for them seventy bulls and they ought to love us, yet they hate us! As it says, 'In return for my love they are my adversaries'" (Ps. 109:4). The Holy One Blessed Be He, in consequence, said to them: "Now, therefore, offer a sacrifice on your own behalf: 'On the eighth day . . . one bull'" (29:35–36). This may be compared to the case of a king who made a banquet for seven days and invited all the people in the province during the seven days of the feast. When the seven days of the feast were over he said to his friend: "We have already done our duty to all the people of the province, let us now make shift, you and I, with whatever you can find—a pound of meat, or of fish, or vegetables." In like manner the Holy One Blessed Be He said to Israel: "'On the eighth day, you shall hold a solemn gathering'; make shift with whatever you can find; with 'one bull . . .'" (29:35–36).[14]

35. On the (eighth) day Hebrew *ba-yom*. In distinction to the previous days, which read *u-va-yom*, there is no conjunctive *vav* here, indicating that this, the eighth day, is an independent celebration that is unconnected with the preceding festival.

a solemn gathering Hebrew *'atseret*.[15] For this meaning, see 2 Kings 10:20, Isaiah 1:13, Amos 5:21, and Joel 1:14. Alternatively, render "a concluding solemnity,"[16] with the Septuagint. In rabbinic Hebrew, Shavuot is called the "*'atseret* of Passover," that is, its concluding solemnity.[17] From the fact that work is prohibited on this day, it must also be a "sacred occasion" as the first day of Sukkot (v. 12); and it is so termed in Leviticus 23:36.

A SUBSCRIPT   (v. 39)

Private offerings may be presented in addition to the public offerings stipulated above.

be they . . . That is, the meal offerings and libations here are not meant as discrete offerings.

30 burnt offerings, meal offerings, libations, or offerings of well-being. [1]So Moses spoke to the Israelites just as the LORD had commanded Moses.

ל וַיֹּאמֶר מֹשֶׁה אֶל־בְּנֵי יִשְׂרָאֵל כְּכֹל אֲשֶׁר־צִוָּה
יְהוָה אֶת־מֹשֶׁה׃ פ

MATTOT

[2]Moses spoke to the heads of the Israelite tribes, saying: This is what the LORD has commanded:

[3]If a man makes a vow to the LORD or takes an oath imposing an obligation on himself, he shall not break his pledge; he must carry out all that has crossed his lips.

מטות

2 וַיְדַבֵּר מֹשֶׁה אֶל־רָאשֵׁי הַמַּטּוֹת לִבְנֵי יִשְׂרָאֵל
לֵאמֹר זֶה הַדָּבָר אֲשֶׁר צִוָּה יְהוָה׃ 3 אִישׁ כִּי־יִדֹּר
נֶדֶר לַיהוָה אוֹ־הִשָּׁבַע שְׁבֻעָה לֶאְסֹר אִסָּר עַל־
נַפְשׁוֹ לֹא יַחֵל דְּבָרוֹ כְּכָל־הַיֹּצֵא מִפִּיו יַעֲשֶׂה׃

The sense is that votive and free-will offerings can be either burnt offerings or offerings of well-being together with their meal and libation supplements (15:1–12). The thanksgiving offering (Lev. 7:11–14) is not listed since it is not accompanied by the above-prescribed meal offering and libation.[18] Purification and reparation offerings (Lev. 4–5), although brought by individuals, are mandatory; they are expiations for certain wrongdoing and, hence, are not of the same nature as votive or free-will offerings.

CHAPTER 30

30:1. A fulfillment subscript (see 5:4, etc.), essential here lest one think that Moses went on to address the Israelites (30:2) without informing them of the cultic calendar.[19]

The Annulment of Vows and Oaths Made by Women (vv. 2–17)

Mattot

This section was probably placed here because vows ("votive offerings") were mentioned in the last verse of the previous chapter (29:39),[1] a connection that is further strengthened by the fact that the payment of vows generally took the form of a sacrifice. On similar associative grounds, the Scripture of the Dead Sea sectaries attaches this section to the deuteronomic law of sacrificial vows (Deut. 12:26).[2] The present section informs us that any pledge made by a man in the name of God must be fulfilled. A woman's vow or oath, however, can be countermanded and annulled by her father or husband (depending on whose authority she is under) on the day he learns of it. Thereafter, if he has not objected, the vow or oath is valid, and if he forces her to break it, he must suffer the consequences. By contrast, the vows and oaths of widows and divorcées cannot be annulled, as those individuals are considered to be autonomous. This law reflects the sociological reality that women in biblical days were subservient to their fathers or husbands: As a minor she was under her father's control, and it was presumed that all adult women were married. The case of a spinster is not discussed, presumably because it was rare. The text is constructed according to classical casuistic legal style; that is, the primary case is introduced by *ki*, "when" (vv. 3,4), and the subsections begin with *'im*, "if" (vv. 5,6). The distinction between a vow and an oath is discussed in Excursus 66.

*2. **heads of the Israelite tribes*** Hebrew *ra'shei ha-mattot li-vnei yisra'el* is perhaps an ellipsis of ***ra'shei 'avot ha-mattot***, "the heads of the [Israelite] tribal clans,"[3] which is also a more accurate designation since the tribal leadership consisted of the clan heads. In either case, it is rare to find a law addressed to Israel's leaders rather than to the people themselves. Some conjecture that it was deliberately restricted so that women would not, with impunity, make vows or oaths they did not intend to keep—knowing that their fathers or husbands could always nullify them.[4]

This is what the LORD has commanded This refers to the section that follows, as confirmed by the concluding verse (v. 17).[5]

*3. **man*** Hebrew *'ish*, but not a minor or woman,[6] unless he or she is aware of the significance of the vow: "A child came before Rabbi Akiba and said: 'Rabbi, I dedicated my shovel.'

4 If a woman makes a vow to the LORD or assumes an obligation while still in her father's household by reason of her youth, 5 and her father learns of her vow or her self-

4 וְאִשָּׁה כִּי־תִדֹּר נֶדֶר לַיהוָה וְאָסְרָה אִסָּר בְּבֵית
אָבִיהָ בִּנְעֻרֶיהָ׃ 5 וְשָׁמַע אָבִיהָ אֶת־נִדְרָהּ וֶאֱסָרָהּ

He asked: 'Perhaps you dedicated it to the sun or moon.' He answered: 'Rabbi, do not worry. I dedicated it to the One who created them.' He said 'Go, my son, your vow is valid.'"[7] (See Excursus 66 on dedications.)

vow to the LORD A conditional dedication to the sanctuary (see Excursus 66) either of a person's value or of an animal (Lev. 27:1–13).[8] The vow of a Nazirite fits this definition since it too constitutes a dedication of a person to the Lord for a stipulated period.[9] The beneficiary of the vow, in contradistinction to the oath, is always the Lord (see Excursus 66).[10]

takes an oath[11]

imposing an obligation Hebrew *le'sor 'issar*, literally "binding a binding," that is, an oral/verbal agreement.[12] Thus, since *'issar* as "obligation" can be either positive or negative (i.e., either performing or abstaining from a specified act[s]), it needs to be qualified by another term as, for instance, in verse 14. The same result is obtained by rendering *'issar* as "prohibition," a meaning it has in biblical Aramaic (Dan. 6:8,13,16) or in rabbinic Hebrew. Both renderings, "obligation" or "prohibition," are possible.

break Literally, "desecrate."[13] In Mesopotamian ritual, a sick person confesses: "I promised then reneged; I gave my word but then did not pay."[14] This confession presumes that an oath was taken; its nonfulfillment meant the desecration of the oath and, in its wake, divine retribution.

A vow was generally taken in a moment of crisis (e.g., Gen. 28:20–22; Num. 21:2). But once the crisis had passed and the vow had been answered, there remained the ever-present temptation to forget the vow—even unconsciously (Lev. 5:4). Hence, the frequent scriptural admonition not to desecrate one's vows (see Deut. 23:21–23; Eccles. 5:4).

The Dead Sea sectaries held that any act that was intrinsically a violation of the Torah was automatically annulled: "Everything that a man has imposed upon himself by oath so as to depart from the Torah let him not carry it out even at the price of death."[15] The rabbis, however, allowed for the annulment even of legitimate vows under some circumstances (see Excursus 66). Despite this, however, they were opposed to the very principle of making vows because of the many possibilities (and probable instances) of nonfulfillment: "If one vows it is as if one has built a *bamah* (a forbidden altar), and if one fulfills the vow it is as if one had sacrificed upon it."[16]

has crossed his lips Literally, "has come out of his mouth." Since vows and oaths are made in the name of God, they are endowed with self-fulfilling powers regardless of the consequences. The exchange between Jephthah and his daughter is most instructive: "'I have uttered a vow [lit. opened my mouth] to the LORD and I cannot retract.' 'Father,' said she, 'you have uttered a vow [lit. opened your mouth] to the LORD; do to me as you have vowed [*yatsa' mi-pikha*, lit. what came forth from your mouth]'" (Judg. 11:35–36). Once expressed, then, words are binding, even when the expression does not correspond with the intention (see Isaac's blessing of Jacob; Gen. 27:33–35). The rabbis correct this situation: "A statement is not binding unless intention and expression agree,"[17] thereby paving the way for the annulment of vows (see Excursus 66).

CASE ONE (vv. 4–6)

The vows and oaths of an unmarried girl, still under the authority of her father, can be annulled by her father if he expresses his disapproval on the very day he learns of them.

4. If a woman . . . but not a man;[18] but see the Comment to v. 3.

and assumes Rather, "or assumes."[19]

imposed obligation and offers no objection, all her vows shall stand and every self-imposed obligation shall stand. [6]But if her father restrains her on the day he finds out, none of her vows or self-imposed obligations shall stand; and the LORD will forgive her, since her father restrained her.

[7]If she should marry while her vow or the commitment to which she bound herself is still in force, [8]and her hus-

אֲשֶׁר אָסְרָה עַל־נַפְשָׁהּ וְהֶחֱרִישׁ לָהּ אָבִיהָ וְקָמוּ
כָּל־נְדָרֶיהָ וְכָל־אִסָּר אֲשֶׁר־אָסְרָה עַל־נַפְשָׁהּ
יָקוּם׃ 6 וְאִם־הֵנִיא אָבִיהָ אֹתָהּ בְּיוֹם שָׁמְעוֹ כָּל־
נְדָרֶיהָ וֶאֱסָרֶיהָ אֲשֶׁר־אָסְרָה עַל־נַפְשָׁהּ לֹא יָקוּם
וַיהוָה יִסְלַח־לָהּ כִּי־הֵנִיא אָבִיהָ אֹתָהּ׃ 7 וְאִם־הָיוֹ
תִהְיֶה לְאִישׁ וּנְדָרֶיהָ עָלֶיהָ אוֹ מִבְטָא שְׂפָתֶיהָ

an obligation Or "prohibition" (see v. 3).

in her father's household The Temple Scroll adds *bi-shevu'ah*, "in an oath," correctly clarifying the point (see v. 11).

by reason of her youth Hebrew *bi-ne'ureiha*, literally "in her youth"; that is, when she is young and even marriageable but still in her father's house. For this meaning, note the same expression in "the priest's daughter . . . is back in her father's house as in her youth [*ki-ne'ureiha*]" (Lev. 22:13). Hence, the term means a period embracing childhood up to the point she is married. The rabbis, however, limit this period to the brief span when the first signs of puberty become visible. This is defined as a girl between eleven years and one day and twelve years and one day who, on examination, is found to be aware of the significance of a vow;[20] however, "when a woman has attained puberty, her father no longer has authority over her."[21]

5. *learns* Literally, "hears," but clearly the notion here is when he is apprised of it.[22]

offers no objection Literally, "made himself deaf to her"; that is, he keeps silent, giving rise to the rabbinic dictum, "silence gives consent."[23]

shall stand . . . shall stand Hebrew *yakumu . . . yakum*, a legal term, denoting validity.[24]

6. *restrains* Rather, "opposes, frustrates."[25]

on the day he finds out But if he waits until the next day to express his disapproval, it is too late (see the Comment to v. 15).

forgive Hebrew *yislaḥ*. This active (Kal) form of the verb, also found in verses 9 and 13, contrasts with its passive (Nifal) form as found in sacrificial texts; for example, Leviticus 4:20,26,31,35. The purpose of the latter is to show that, even though the sin is unintentional, the sacrifice is not inherently efficacious but dependent on the divine will. Here, however, the purpose of the verbal form is to show that if the woman is thwarted from fulfilling her vow by her father or husband (vv. 9,13), God will automatically forgive her.

CASE TWO (vv. 7–9)

The woman made her vow or oath when still under her father's control; even though it was approved by the father, her husband may annul it on the day he learns of it.[26] Most of the rabbis, however, posit different circumstances: She is still living with her father but has become betrothed, in which case, both her father and her fiancé must concur in the annulment. They reject what seems the above, more obvious explanation on the grounds that if the husband could annul the vow/oath she made while under her father's authority, then, *a fortiori*, he would certainly have the right to annul a vow/oath made while under his authority—and thus rendering superfluous the exposition of the latter case in verses 11–13.[27] However, their argument can be countered: This case is needed lest one think that since her vow/oath was made while still under her father's authority and with his consent, her husband has no power to annul it.[28]

7. *commitment* Hebrew *mivta' sefateiha*, literally "utterance of her lips," implying an oath.[29] The same expression (in verbal form) in Leviticus 5:4 and Psalms 106:33 connotes rashness, impulsiveness. Perhaps this is what distinguishes the expression from *motsa' sefateiha* (vv. 3,13).

אֲשֶׁר אָסְרָה עַל־נַפְשָׁהּ׃ 8 וְשָׁמַע אִישָׁהּ בְּיוֹם
שָׁמְעוֹ וְהֶחֱרִישׁ לָהּ וְקָמוּ נְדָרֶיהָ וֶאֱסָרֶהָ אֲשֶׁר־
אָסְרָה עַל־נַפְשָׁהּ יָקֻמוּ׃ 9 וְאִם בְּיוֹם שְׁמֹעַ אִישָׁהּ
יָנִיא אוֹתָהּ וְהֵפֵר אֶת־נִדְרָהּ אֲשֶׁר עָלֶיהָ וְאֵת
מִבְטָא שְׂפָתֶיהָ אֲשֶׁר אָסְרָה עַל־נַפְשָׁהּ וַיהוָה
יִסְלַח־לָהּ׃ 10 וְנֵדֶר אַלְמָנָה וּגְרוּשָׁה כֹּל אֲשֶׁר־
אָסְרָה עַל־נַפְשָׁהּ יָקוּם עָלֶיהָ׃ 11 וְאִם־בֵּית אִישָׁהּ
נָדָרָה אוֹ־אָסְרָה אִסָּר עַל־נַפְשָׁהּ בִּשְׁבֻעָה׃

band learns of it and offers no objection on the day he finds out, her vows shall stand and her self-imposed obligations shall stand.
9But if her husband restrains her on the day that he learns of it, he thereby annuls her vow which was in force or the commitment to which she bound herself; and the LORD will forgive her.
10—The vow of a widow or of a divorced woman, however, whatever she has imposed on herself, shall be binding upon her.—
11So, too, if, while in her husband's household, she makes a vow or imposes an obligation on herself by oath,
12and her husband learns of

still in force Hebrew *'aleiha*, literally "upon her"; that is, she made the vow/oath while she was still in her father's house, and her father did not nullify it.[30]

8. ***on the day he finds out***[31]

9. ***he thereby annuls***[32]

or[33]

CASE THREE (v. 10)

An editorial parenthesis, since it is not included in the summation, verse 17.[34] Interestingly, the Dead Sea sectaries transfer this verse to the very end in their section on vows,[35] which is a more logical place. Some exegetes associate this verse with the following case.[36] The principle here differs from the case of the priest's daughter who returns childless to her father's house after being divorced or widowed. In that case, she may still share her father's sacred food as she had done when she was a member of his house (Lev. 22:13) because she needs his food in order to live. No such concession is made for her vows, however. She does not return to her premarital status whereby her father could annul vows.[37] Only for her sustenance does she rejoin her father's household; otherwise she is independent.

CASE FOUR (vv. 11–13)

A wife's vow or oath can be annulled by her husband on the day he learns of it. Thereafter his objections are of no avail: Her vow or oath must be fulfilled. Ibn Ezra, followed by Abravanel, claims that this case is a continuation of the previous one (v. 10) and that it concerns a widow or divorcée who had made a vow or oath while still married and whose husband nullified it but died before it fell due. The law in this case states that the vow remains nullified. The aforementioned exegetes are constrained to adopt this forced interpretation because they agree with the rabbis' objection to the simpler explanation given above: Since the husband can annul a vow/oath made while still under her father's charge, is it not obvious that he can annul it when it was made under his charge (see the Comment to vv. 7–9)? However, the objection may be countered as follows: The former case (vv. 7–9) allows for the vow/oath made by a minor ("in her youth"; see the Comment to v. 4), but in this case (vv. 11–13), she makes her vow/oath as a married woman and, hence, is no longer a minor. Lest one think in this latter case that her husband may not have the right of annulment, the law must explicitly state that he has this right. The Dead Sea sectaries, however, try to restrict the husband's (and father's) powers of annulment: "Concerning a woman's oath, forasmuch as He said: It is for the husband to annul her oath, let no man annul an oath of which he does not know whether it ought to be carried out or annulled. If it is such as to lead to transgression of the covenant, let him annul it and not carry it out. Likewise is the rule for her father."[38] Thus the right of the husband and father to annul is limited to the women's vows and oaths which violate the Torah. Otherwise, she must carry out her verbal commitment.

it, yet offers no objection—thus failing to restrain her—all her vows shall stand and all her self-imposed obligations shall stand. 13But if her husband does annul them on the day he finds out, then nothing that has crossed her lips shall stand, whether vows or self-imposed obligations. Her husband has annulled them, and the LORD will forgive her. 14Every vow and every sworn obligation of self-denial may be upheld by her husband or annulled by her husband. 15If her husband offers no objection from that day to the next, he has upheld all the vows or obligations she has assumed: he has upheld them by offering no objection on the day he found out. 16But if he annuls them after [the day] he finds out, he shall bear her guilt.

12 וְשָׁמַע אִישָׁהּ וְהֶחֱרִשׁ לָהּ לֹא הֵנִיא אֹתָהּ וְקָמוּ
כָּל־נְדָרֶיהָ וְכָל־אִסָּר אֲשֶׁר־אָסְרָה עַל־נַפְשָׁהּ
יָקוּם׃ 13 וְאִם־הָפֵר יָפֵר אֹתָם ׀ אִישָׁהּ בְּיוֹם שָׁמְעוֹ
כָּל־מוֹצָא שְׂפָתֶיהָ לִנְדָרֶיהָ וּלְאִסַּר נַפְשָׁהּ לֹא
יָקוּם אִישָׁהּ הֲפֵרָם וַיהוָה יִסְלַח־לָהּ׃ 14 כָּל־נֵדֶר
וְכָל־שְׁבֻעַת אִסָּר לְעַנֹּת נָפֶשׁ אִישָׁהּ יְקִימֶנּוּ
וְאִישָׁהּ יְפֵרֶנּוּ׃ 15 וְאִם־הַחֲרֵשׁ יַחֲרִישׁ לָהּ אִישָׁהּ
מִיּוֹם אֶל־יוֹם וְהֵקִים אֶת־כָּל־נְדָרֶיהָ אוֹ אֶת־כָּל־
אֱסָרֶיהָ אֲשֶׁר עָלֶיהָ הֵקִים אֹתָם כִּי־הֶחֱרִשׁ לָהּ
בְּיוֹם שָׁמְעוֹ׃ 16 וְאִם־הָפֵר יָפֵר אֹתָם אַחֲרֵי שָׁמְעוֹ

11. by oath Thereby confirming the assertion in verse 3 that the "binding obligation" takes the form of an oath.

12. her husband learns of it, yet offers no objection Hannah's vow is called her husband's (1 Sam. 1:11,21). Is it because, having not objected to it, he is obligated to fulfill it?

A GENERALIZATION (vv. 14–16)

If the husband (and, presumably, the father) annuls her vow/oath after the day he learns of it, he bears the responsibility for its nonfulfillment. This section also defines her oath as one of self-denial. The Temple Scroll of the Dead Sea sectaries prefers to finish its section on a woman's vow/oath with verse 14 since it can be understood not only as a generalization but as a summation.[39]

14. and every[40]

sworn obligation of self-denial For the meaning of "self-denial," see 29:7 and Excursus 66. Regardless of whether Hebrew *'issar* means "prohibition" or "obligation" (see the Comment to v. 3), the qualifying phrase "of self-denial" limits it to oaths of abstention.

15. This verse reveals a chiastic structure, AB || B'A'.

from that day to the next Hebrew ***mi-yom 'el yom***. Rabbi Simeon bar Yoḥai[41] interprets this phrase as meaning the twenty-four-hour period following the utterance. However, there is an attested biblical idiom that denotes this period, *me-ʿet ʿad ʿet* (Ezek. 4:10–11), and that in rabbinic Hebrew becomes ***meʿet le-ʿet***. Hence, it is preferable to take this phrase as meaning that the vow/oath must be annulled on the same day that the father or husband learns of it. Thus, "on the day he finds out" (v. 6) must mean on that day only but not thereafter.[42]

he has upheld Hebrew ***ve-hekim*** is really pluperfect: not now but on the day he had learned of it and was silent.[43]

16. after [the day] he finds out The bracketed word is added for the sake of clarity (see "on the day he found out" in vv. 6,8,9,13,15).

he shall bear her guilt Rather, "he shall bear her punishment" (see the Comment to 5:31) from God, punishment that otherwise would have befallen her for not fulfilling her vow/oath. Either the husband has forced her to break her vow/oath or he has deceived her into believing that he had annulled her vow/oath as soon as he was informed of it.[44] In such a case it is as if he has taken over her vow and has violated it.[45] Indeed, the reading of the Septuagint and the Samaritan, *ʿavono*, "his punishment," supports the latter interpretation, but the Temple Scroll follows the Masoretic text.[46] The same rule applies to the father who delays the annulment of his daughter's vow/oath,[47] as is implied in the summation.

17 Those are the laws that the LORD enjoined upon Moses between a man and his wife, and as between a father and his daughter while in her father's household by reason of her youth.

וְנָשָׂא אֶת־עֲוֺנָהּ׃ 17 אֵלֶּה הַחֻקִּים אֲשֶׁר צִוָּה יְהוָה
אֶת־מֹשֶׁה בֵּין אִישׁ לְאִשְׁתּוֹ בֵּין־אָב לְבִתּוֹ
בִּנְעֻרֶיהָ בֵּית אָבִיהָ׃ פ שני

31 The LORD spoke to Moses, saying, 2 "Avenge the Israelite people on the Midianites; then you shall be gathered to your kin."

3 Moses spoke to the people, saying, "Let men be picked out from among you for a campaign, and let them fall upon Midian to wreak the LORD's vengeance on Midian. 4 You

ל״א וַיְדַבֵּר יְהוָה אֶל־מֹשֶׁה לֵּאמֹר׃ 2 נְקֹם
נִקְמַת בְּנֵי יִשְׂרָאֵל מֵאֵת הַמִּדְיָנִים אַחַר תֵּאָסֵף
אֶל־עַמֶּיךָ׃ 3 וַיְדַבֵּר מֹשֶׁה אֶל־הָעָם לֵאמֹר הֵחָלְצוּ
מֵאִתְּכֶם אֲנָשִׁים לַצָּבָא וְיִהְיוּ עַל־מִדְיָן לָתֵת
נִקְמַת־יְהוָה בְּמִדְיָן׃ 4 אֶלֶף לַמַּטֶּה אֶלֶף לַמַּטֶּה

A SUMMATION (v. 17)

This verse forms an inclusion with verse 2. It adverts in reverse order to the three main cases: The woman is under the authority of the father and husband. It omits the case of a divorcée and widow (see the Comment to v. 10).

The War Against Midian (31:1–54)

Moses' final commission is to execute retribution upon the Midianites for having, on the advice of Balaam, incited their women to seduce the Israelites in the licentious rites of Baal-peor, as recorded in 25:17–19. Moses musters a small army of twelve thousand men (or twelve divisions), one thousand men (or one division) from each tribe. The army annihilates the Midianites without suffering a single casualty. The literary structure of this chapter is discussed in Excursus 67.

CHAPTER 31 THE WAR (vv. 1–12)

2. ***Avenge*** Rather, "Seek the vindication or redress of." The rendering "avenge" has hardly any basis in Scripture and none at all when the subject is God.[1] The verb ***nakam*** bears two closely associated meanings: to redress past wrongs and to exact retribution. The former takes the preposition ***min***, "from," the latter the preposition ***be***, "on."[2] They are found in this and the following verse, respectively (see the Comment to v. 3). This verse is a resumptive repetition of 25:17. There, however, the verb is ***tsaror***, "assail."

on the Midianites Rather, "from."

then Hebrew ***'aḥar***. For this usage, see Genesis 18:5, 24:55 and Judges 19:5.

then you shall be gathered See the Comment to 27:13 for the same command and idiom. Logically, 27:12–14 follows chapter 31, since one would expect the tradition to tell of Moses' death atop the mountain after the victory over the Midianites. In the final form of the canon of the Torah, however, Moses' death is postponed until he delivers his valedictory, the Book of Deuteronomy (see the introductory Comment to 27:12–14).

3. ***let [men] be picked out*** Hebrew ***heḥaletsu***. The rendering, although conjectural, is preferable to "arm [men]" found in many of the versions.[3] It may be related to ***ḥalats***, "remove, withdraw," found in Deuteronomy 25:9–10, Isaiah 20:2, and Hosea 5:6. In the Nifal pattern, it occurs

shall dispatch on the campaign a thousand from every one of the tribes of Israel."

5 So a thousand from each tribe were furnished from the divisions of Israel, twelve thousand picked for the campaign. 6 Moses dispatched them on the campaign, a thousand from each tribe, with Phinehas son of Eleazar serving as a priest on the campaign, equipped with the sacred utensils and the trumpets for sounding the blasts. 7 They

לְכֹל֙ מַטּ֣וֹת יִשְׂרָאֵ֔ל תִּשְׁלְח֖וּ לַצָּבָֽא׃ 5 וַיִּמָּֽסְרוּ֙
מֵאַלְפֵ֣י יִשְׂרָאֵ֔ל אֶ֖לֶף לַמַּטֶּ֑ה שְׁנֵים־עָשָׂ֥ר אֶ֖לֶף
חֲלוּצֵ֥י צָבָֽא׃ 6 וַיִּשְׁלַ֨ח אֹתָ֥ם מֹשֶׁ֛ה אֶ֥לֶף לַמַּטֶּ֖ה
לַצָּבָ֑א אֹתָ֡ם וְאֶת־פִּינְחָ֨ס בֶּן־אֶלְעָזָ֤ר הַכֹּהֵן֙ לַצָּבָ֔א
וּכְלֵ֥י הַקֹּ֛דֶשׁ וַחֲצֹצְר֥וֹת הַתְּרוּעָ֖ה בְּיָדֽוֹ׃ 7 וַיִּצְבְּאוּ֙
עַל־מִדְיָ֔ן כַּאֲשֶׁ֛ר צִוָּ֥ה יְהוָ֖ה אֶת־מֹשֶׁ֑ה וַיַּֽהַרְגוּ֖ כָּל־

again only in 32:17,20, where its meaning is reflexive. Some Samaritan manuscripts[4] read *haḥalitsu*, giving it an active sense, but the Hifil is only attested in Isaiah 58:1, where it has a different meaning. In the War Scroll of the Dead Sea sectaries it occurs twice in the Kal form *yaḥalotsu*,[5] probably based on this verse and with the same meaning. The passive participle *ḥaluts* denotes "vanguard, shock troops" (v. 5, 32:21); as the most exposed of the troops, they must comprise the bravest and most skilled and, hence, are "picked out."[6]

campaign Hebrew *tsava'*, the sole meaning of the word in this chapter (vv. 4,5,6,14, etc.). It connotes more than a battle. It embraces the total operation of a military campaign or any other group service (see the Comment to 4:3).

let them fall upon Hebrew *ve-yihyu 'al*. For this usage, see 2 Samuel 11:23.

to wreak the LORD's vengeance on Rather, "to exact the Lord's retribution on." For the exact idiom, see Ezekiel 25:14,17. Whereas the Israelites seek redress or compensation from the Midianites for causing the devastating plague of Baal-peor, the Lord desires to exact retribution from them for the sacrilege they committed (v. 16) by seducing the Israelites into worshiping Baal-peor.[7]

4. ***thousand*** Given the differences in their size, it is highly unrealistic that the same number was mustered for each tribe. This word is, alternatively, rendered "division" (as in vv. 5,48), a much smaller, elite unit that every tribe could provide. The twelve tribes are those listed in the censuses of chapters 1 and 26. They exclude the Levites since they did not serve in the armed forces (see Excursuses 2, 4, 5, and 6).

5. ***were furnished*** Rather, "were mustered, counted."[8] The verb ***masar*** is unattested in biblical Hebrew outside of this chapter, but it is common in postbiblical Hebrew and Aramaic, meaning "deliver, furnish." The Septuagint correctly renders "counted" but not for the reason, assumed by most critics, that its Hebrew text read ***va-yissaferu***. Rather, it so interpreted ***masar*** of the Masoretic text. Targum Onkelos, Targum Yerushalmi, the Samaritan Targum, and the Peshitta also give this correct rendering. The Samaritan Targum frequently translates ***pakad***, "count," by the verb ***masar***, as in Numbers 4:16,27,34; and ***mesurot*** in the Dead Sea Scrolls[9] means "counted ones, formation," based on this verse. Such also is probably the meaning of ***mesorah***, the work of the Masoretes, those whose job it was to "count" the verses, words, and letters of the Bible in order to preserve the correct biblical text.[10]

divisions of For this meaning see 1 Samuel 10:19,21, where it parallels *mishpaḥah*, "clan." The use of this old meaning of *'elef*, which fell out of use during the monarchy, points to the antiquity of this material (see Excursuses 1 and 67).

twelve thousand Solomon had a cavalry of twelve thousand men (1 Kings 10:26). More relevantly, Ahithophel advised Absalom to allow him to handpick twelve thousand soldiers to pursue David (2 Sam. 17:1). According to the Dead Sea sectaries, the king should handpick twelve thousand men, one thousand from each tribe (based on this verse), as his permanent bodyguard (11QTemple 57:9–11). Alternatively, render "twelve divisions" (see the Comment to v. 4).

picked Rather, "shock troops," as in 32:17. See the Comment to verse 3.

6. ***Phinehas*** And not Eleazar who was the High Priest and therefore forbidden to expose himself to corpse contamination (Lev. 21:10–12; Ramban). Eleazar himself had once replaced his father, Aaron, in a similar situation (see the Comment to 17:2). Here we see Phinehas once again

took the field against Midian, as the LORD had commanded
Moses, and slew every male. 8 Along with their other victims, they slew the kings of Midian: Evi, Rekem, Zur, Hur,
and Reba, the five kings of Midian. They also put Balaam
son of Beor to the sword.

זָכָר׃ 8 וְאֶת־מַלְכֵי מִדְיָן הָרְגוּ עַל־חַלְלֵיהֶם אֶת־
אֱוִי וְאֶת־רֶקֶם וְאֶת־צוּר וְאֶת־חוּר וְאֶת־רֶבַע
חֲמֵשֶׁת מַלְכֵי מִדְיָן וְאֵת בִּלְעָם בֶּן־בְּעוֹר הָרְגוּ
בֶּחָרֶב׃ 9 וַיִּשְׁבּוּ בְנֵי־יִשְׂרָאֵל אֶת־נְשֵׁי מִדְיָן וְאֶת־

acting as the antidote to Balaam. Just as he countered Balaam's plan to seduce the Israelites at Baal-peor (25:7–13), so he now serves as the spiritual leader of Israel's forces as they seek retribution from the Midianites, in whose midst Balaam is also active (v. 8). This leads the midrash to conclude that it must have been Phinehas himself who slew Balaam.[11]

serving as priest on the campaign[12] The *bārû*, "diviner," always accompanied the Mesopotamian armies in order to determine the will of the deity. The Israelite forces also included a priest (Deut. 20:2–4). Rabbinic texts give this priest the title ***meshuaḥ milḥamah***, "anointed for war," and declare him second only to the High Priest.[13] The role of the priesthood in the military is vastly enlarged in the Dead Sea War Scroll (see Excursus 21).

Thus, Phinehas's function is not to lead the army,[14] but to act as chaplain, that is, to render priestly services, especially in consulting the Urim and Thummim. Proof of Phinehas's nonmilitary role is afforded by the fact that Moses does not scold him but only the officers (v. 14).[15] The midrash, however, suggests that Phinehas was chosen over Moses as the campaign general because since Moses "had grown up in the land of Midian, he thought: It is not right that I should assail one who has done good to me. The proverb says: 'Do not cast a stone into the cistern from which you have drunk.' Some say this was not the Midian where Moses grew up [near Egypt], for the one mentioned here is next to Moab and is desolate to the present day. Why did he send Phinehas? He said: 'The one who began the performance of the precept shall finish it. It was he who turned away His wrath and smote the Midianite woman; let him finish the sacred task!'"[16]

equipped with Literally, "in his hand"; that is, in his charge.[17]

the sacred utensils What they comprised can only be conjectured: the Ark,[18] the Ark and the High Priest's gold frontlet (Exod. 28:36),[19] the High Priest's clothing,[20] or the Urim and Thummim.[21] The term's plural formation, "utensils, vessels," and the fact that the High Priest could not approach the battlefront seem to eliminate all the above explanations. However, since the Urim and Thummim were consulted in war, as attested in 1 Samuel 14:41 and 28:6 (see Excursus 64) and since the Ark was brought into battle until the Temple was built (Num. 14:44; 2 Sam. 11:11; 1 Kings 8:8), it is likely that the priest accompanied the troops with all the sacred paraphernalia, including the Ark and Urim and Thummim. He could thereby consult the Lord when necessary, but from a position behind the battle lines in order to protect the sacred vessels both from capture and from contamination (contrast 1 Sam. 4).

the trumpets for sounding the blasts The expression is found again in 2 Chronicles 13:2. The ***teruʿah*** is the specific signal used in war; see the discussion of the trumpets and their signals in Excursus 21.

7. ***They took the field*** Hebrew ***va-yitsbeʾu***. For this usage, see Isaiah 29:7–18 and 31:4.[22]

slew every male That is, every adult male of that Midianite tribe in the Transjordan (see v. 17 and Excursus 67). But other Midianite tribes survived elsewhere, as is clear from Judges 6–8, 1 Kings 11:18, and Isaiah 60:8. The verb ***harag*** implies that they were slain after they were taken captive, not in battle, for which ***hikkah*** is used.[23] The same holds for Balaam and the Midianite chieftains, below.

8. ***kings of Midian*** In Joshua 13:21 these Midianite rulers are listed in the same order but are called ***nesiʾei***, "chieftains of Midian," and ***nesikhei***, "princes of Sihon." Zur (and, presumably, the four others) was called ***roʾsh ʾummah***, "tribal head," in 25:12. The Midianite leaders captured by Gideon are called "kings" in Judges 8:12. Other nomadic groups also have "kings" (e.g., Gen. 36:31–39; Num. 20:14, etc.). The Assyrian King List begins with "twenty-seven kings who lived in tents." At Mari, semi-nomadic Haneans and Benjaminites have kings,[24] although the leaders of the former are alternately called chieftains and kings.[25]

9 The Israelites took the women and children of the Midianites captive, and seized as booty all their beasts, all their herds, and all their wealth. 10 And they destroyed by fire all the towns in which they were settled, and their encampments. 11 They gathered all the spoil and all the booty, man and beast, 12 and they brought the captives, the booty, and the spoil to Moses, Eleazar the priest, and the whole Israelite community, at the camp in the steppes of Moab, at the Jordan near Jericho.

13 Moses, Eleazar the priest, and all the chieftains of the community came out to meet them outside the camp.

טַפָּם וְאֵת כׇּל־בְּהֶמְתָּם וְאֶת־כׇּל־מִקְנֵהֶם וְאֶת־כׇּל־
חֵילָם בָּזָזוּ׃ 10 וְאֵת כׇּל־עָרֵיהֶם בְּמוֹשְׁבֹתָם וְאֵת
כׇּל־טִירֹתָם שָׂרְפוּ בָּאֵשׁ׃ 11 וַיִּקְחוּ אֶת־כׇּל־
הַשָּׁלָל וְאֵת כׇּל־הַמַּלְקוֹחַ בָּאָדָם וּבַבְּהֵמָה׃
12 וַיָּבִאוּ אֶל־מֹשֶׁה וְאֶל־אֶלְעָזָר הַכֹּהֵן וְאֶל־עֲדַת
בְּנֵי־יִשְׂרָאֵל אֶת־הַשְּׁבִי וְאֶת־הַמַּלְקוֹחַ וְאֶת־
הַשָּׁלָל אֶל־הַמַּחֲנֶה אֶל־עַרְבֹת מוֹאָב אֲשֶׁר עַל־
יַרְדֵּן יְרֵחוֹ׃ ס שלישי [שני כשהן
מחוברות] 13 וַיֵּצְאוּ מֹשֶׁה וְאֶלְעָזָר הַכֹּהֵן וְכׇל־
נְשִׂיאֵי הָעֵדָה לִקְרָאתָם אֶל־מִחוּץ לַמַּחֲנֶה׃

Rekem The Semitic name for Petra, an important Edomite city (see Excursus 67).

Zur He is the father of Cozbi (25:15), another link between the Midianite war and the Baal-peor affair.

Hur This is the eponym of the Horites whom the Edomites evicted (Deut. 2:12; Gen. 36:26–30; see Excursus 67).

Balaam In this tradition he is associated with the Midianites (see the Comments to 22:4,7 and Excursus 58).

9. The enumerated booty and captives are consonant with the law of Deuteronomy 20:14 and the case of Genesis 34:28–29. Thus, it is unclear why Moses disapproves of the captured women (vv. 14–16).

beasts That is, the asses (see vv. 34,39). Hebrew ***behemah*** is generic for land animals (e.g., Lev. 11:2). In this verse it stands for the Midianite animals that do not belong to the herd, as in Genesis 36:6; 2 Kings 3:17, leaving only the asses.

10. the towns in which they were settled Perhaps implying that the seminomadic Midianites had just recently become sedentary.

their encampments Probably a tent community[26] protected by a low stone wall (Ezek. 46:23).

11. the booty Hebrew ***ha-malkoaḥ***, that is, animate booty, as opposed to ***shalal*** and ***baz*** (v. 32), "spoil," or inanimate booty (see vv. 26,27,32; Isa. 49:24–25). However, the term can also be restricted to animals, as in the next verse.

12. the booty Here ***ha-malkoaḥ*** is used in conjunction with ***shevi***, "captives," that is, human beings. It is, hence, limited to animals.

THE RETURN (vv. 13–18)

The triumphant army returns with much booty and captive women and children. Moses rebukes the officers for sparing the women since they were responsible for Israel's apostasy at Baal-peor and its resultant plague. He orders the officers to slay all the women and male children but permits them to keep the virgins alive. The execution of Moses' instruction is not recorded.

13. outside the camp The returning army, requiring purification from corpse contamination (v. 19), could not enter the camp. This requirement follows the law of 5:1–4 (and Deut. 23:10–15) and not that of chapter 19, which allows the corpse-contaminated individual to remain inside the camp. In contrast to a settlement, the war camp must always be in a state of purity to allow for God's holy Presence to rest there.

14 Moses became angry with the commanders of the army,
the officers of thousands and the officers of hundreds, who
had come back from the military campaign. 15 Moses said to
them, "You have spared every female! 16 Yet they are the
very ones who, at the bidding of Balaam, induced the
Israelites to trespass against the LORD in the matter of Peor,
so that the LORD's community was struck by the plague.
17 Now, therefore, slay every male among the children, and
slay also every woman who has known a man carnally; 18 but
spare every young woman who has not had carnal relations
with a man.

14 וַיִּקְצֹף מֹשֶׁה עַל פְּקוּדֵי הֶחָיִל שָׂרֵי הָאֲלָפִים
וְשָׂרֵי הַמֵּאוֹת הַבָּאִים מִצְּבָא הַמִּלְחָמָה׃ 15 וַיֹּאמֶר
אֲלֵיהֶם מֹשֶׁה הַחִיִּיתֶם כָּל־נְקֵבָה׃ 16 הֵן הֵנָּה הָיוּ
לִבְנֵי יִשְׂרָאֵל בִּדְבַר בִּלְעָם לִמְסָר־מַעַל בַּיהוָה
עַל־דְּבַר־פְּעוֹר וַתְּהִי הַמַּגֵּפָה בַּעֲדַת יְהוָה׃
17 וְעַתָּה הִרְגוּ כָל־זָכָר בַּטָּף וְכָל־אִשָּׁה יֹדַעַת
אִישׁ לְמִשְׁכַּב זָכָר הֲרֹגוּ׃ 18 וְכֹל הַטַּף בַּנָּשִׁים
אֲשֶׁר לֹא־יָדְעוּ מִשְׁכַּב זָכָר הַחֲיוּ לָכֶם׃ 19 וְאַתֶּם

14. commanders of the army Hebrew *pekudei he-ḥayil* (see v. 48; 2 Kings 11:15).[27] The army apparently has no overall commander, for Moses does not turn to a single leader but to the divisional officers. In this respect it resembles the internecine war of Judges 20–21. The commander's name was most probably lost in the initial, oral transmission of each story.

military campaign Hebrew *tseva' milḥamah* means "army" elsewhere (e.g., Isa. 13:4). In this chapter, however, *tsava'* bears the specific meaning "campaign" (see the Comment to v. 4).

15. The taking of women captives is permitted in any war with non-Canaanites (Deut. 20:14; see Gen. 34:28–29), but in this instance the sight of the Midianite women arouses Moses' wrath: The nonvirgins among them were responsible for the apostasy and plague of Baal-peor (chap. 25)! Moses' anger may be compared with that of Samuel (1 Sam. 15:17–19); both leaders became enraged because the ban against taking spoil had been violated. However, the two bans were not identical: Samuel's required the total destruction of the spoil, human and nonhuman alike; Moses' allowed the goods of the Midianites and their virgin women to be spared.

16. at the bidding of Balaam Reflecting the tradition that after Balaam failed to curse the Israelites he persuaded the Midianites to seduce the Israelites at Baal-peor (see Excursus 61).

induced Hebrew *hayu le*. Rather, "were the cause for, functioned for." For this usage, see Genesis 1:15 and 9:13.

trespass against Hebrew *li-msor ma'al be*. Neither the biblical meaning of *masar*, "count" (see the Comment to v. 5), nor its postbiblical meaning, "deliver," is suitable here. The Targums suggest reading *li-m'ol*, which, with the following word, its cognate accusative *ma'al*, means "transgress, commit sacrilege" (see the Comment to 5:6). Alternatively, read *la-sur me'al*, "turn away from."[28]

17. and slay This verb needs to be repeated lest the second half of this verse be conjoined with the next verse, thereby leaving the impression that these women should be spared.[29]

carnally Literally, lying with a male. These women, because they seduced the Israelites, are to be slain. The idiomatic use of *yada'*, "know sexually," is attested both in the Bible[30] and in Akkadian.[31] The term must refer to married women,[32] the only possible criterion.[33]

18. spare Rather, "spare for yourselves"; that is, the virgins are to be kept alive as slaves or wives.[34] Postexilic Judaism was violently opposed to intermarriage.[35]

young woman Hebrew *taf* usually means "children" but, as used here, also includes girls past puberty. See especially 14:31, where it refers to everyone up to twenty years of age (14:29).

How were the virgins and nonvirgins to be distinguished from one another? The midrash proposes a lie detector test: "Every female child you shall stand before the holy crown (the gold frontlet of the High Priest) and cross-examine her. And whoever has slept with a man, her face will pale; and whoever has not slept with a man, her face will blush like a fire, and you shall spare."[36]

[19]"You shall then stay outside the camp seven days; every one among you or among your captives who has slain a person or touched a corpse shall cleanse himself on the third and seventh days. [20]You shall also cleanse every cloth, every article of skin, everything made of goats' hair, and every object of wood."

[21]Eleazar the priest said to the troops who had taken part in the fighting, "This is the ritual law that the LORD has

חֲנוּ מִחוּץ לַמַּחֲנֶה שִׁבְעַת יָמִים כֹּל הֹרֵג נֶפֶשׁ
וְכֹל ׀ נֹגֵעַ בֶּחָלָל תִּתְחַטְּאוּ בַּיּוֹם הַשְּׁלִישִׁי וּבַיּוֹם
הַשְּׁבִיעִי אַתֶּם וּשְׁבִיכֶם׃ 20 וְכָל־בֶּגֶד וְכָל־כְּלִי־
עוֹר וְכָל־מַעֲשֵׂה עִזִּים וְכָל־כְּלִי־עֵץ תִּתְחַטָּאוּ׃
ס 21 וַיֹּאמֶר אֶלְעָזָר הַכֹּהֵן אֶל־אַנְשֵׁי
הַצָּבָא הַבָּאִים לַמִּלְחָמָה זֹאת חֻקַּת הַתּוֹרָה

THE PURIFICATION OF WARRIORS AND CAPTIVES (vv. 19–24)

All persons and organic materials must be purified with the ashes of the red cow on the third and seventh day (chap. 19). High Priest Eleazar adds another purificatory requirement: Metallic objects must be passed through fire, and all other objects, which cannot withstand fire, must be passed through water. On the seventh day after the bathing and laundering, the warriors and their captives may enter the camp. The purification is from corpse contamination, which can pollute the sanctuary. The execution of these instructions is not recorded (see Excursus 68).

These rules apply solely to the Israelite camp in the wilderness, which is conceived as a war camp from which all impurity is to be excluded as prescribed in Numbers 5:1–4; compare Deuteronomy 23:10–15. In the settlements of Canaan the practice is different. Only the leper is excluded whereas all other impurity bearers, even the corpse-contaminated, undergo their purificatory rites within the settlement (see Excursus 48).

*19. **You shall then . . .*** Moses now turns from the officers and addresses all the troops, as Eleazar will do explicitly in verse 21.

or among your captives The wording implies that all persons, Israelites and non-Israelites alike, are capable of contaminating the sanctuary. Therefore, the captives also must be purified before entering the camp (see Excursuses 47, 48). The rabbis, however, maintain that non-Israelites do not require ritual purification.[37] Hence, they claim that the procedures given here refer not to the captives but to their clothes and utensils, which could contaminate Israelites coming into contact with them.[38]

20. This prescription is not found explicitly in chapter 19. It can be derived, however, from the rules given there in verses 14–18 and in Leviticus 11:32: All exposed objects in a room containing a human corpse must undergo a seven-day purification; articles of wood, cloth, or skin coming into contact with an animal corpse must undergo a one-day purification. Earthenware vessels are absent from this list because they cannot be purified.[39]

cleanse[40]

*21. **ritual law*** Hebrew *ḥukkat ha-torah*. The same expression is found only once more, in 19:2. Indeed, the law here purports to be a continuation of the purification procedures of chapter 19, and it does provide new prescriptions. However, the fact that it is Eleazar who cites them and not Moses affirms that they are not really innovations but had already been revealed by God to Moses. Stemming from Eleazar they serve as supplementary reminders, whereas if Moses had pronounced them they could be understood to constitute a new revelation. Interestingly, the Samaritan text senses that Moses has been slighted and inserts a passage to show that he had initially informed Eleazar of these rules.

A midrash understands Eleazar's intervention differently. God punished Moses for his anger (v. 14) by causing him to forget to communicate the laws of purification to the soldiers; it was Eleazar who made up for Moses' lapse. Others, however, regard the incident as revealing Moses' virtue: Already, while still alive, Moses wished the right of making ritual decisions to be conferred upon Eleazar—so that it could not be challenged after his death.[41]

has enjoined Rather, "had enjoined."

enjoined upon Moses: 22Gold and silver, copper, iron, tin,
and lead23—any article that can withstand fire—these you
shall pass through fire and they shall be clean, except that
they must be cleansed with water of lustration; and anything that cannot withstand fire you must pass through
water. 24On the seventh day you shall wash your clothes
and be clean, and after that you may enter the camp."

אֲשֶׁר־צִוָּה יְהוָה אֶת־מֹשֶׁה׃ 22 אַךְ אֶת־הַזָּהָב
וְאֶת־הַכֶּסֶף אֶת־הַנְּחֹשֶׁת אֶת־הַבַּרְזֶל אֶת־הַבְּדִיל
וְאֶת־הָעֹפָרֶת׃ 23 כָּל־דָּבָר אֲשֶׁר־יָבֹא בָאֵשׁ
תַּעֲבִירוּ בָאֵשׁ וְטָהֵר אַךְ בְּמֵי נִדָּה יִתְחַטָּא וְכֹל
אֲשֶׁר לֹא־יָבֹא בָּאֵשׁ תַּעֲבִירוּ בַמָּיִם׃ 24 וְכִבַּסְתֶּם
בִּגְדֵיכֶם בַּיּוֹם הַשְּׁבִיעִי וּטְהַרְתֶּם וְאַחַר תָּבֹאוּ
אֶל־הַמַּחֲנֶה׃ פ רביעי 25 וַיֹּאמֶר יְהוָה אֶל־

22. The metals are arranged in their descending order of value.[42] Articles made of earthenware or stone, although also able to withstand fire, are not mentioned. Pottery, being porous, can never be purified and must be destroyed if impure (Lev. 6:21); stone, apparently, is not subject to impurity.[43] The sectaries of the Dead Sea, however, did not exempt stone vessels from defilement and the need for purification.[44]

Gold The word is preceded by *'akh*, "however," the particle indicating qualification or amendment (see the Comment to 26:55). The qualification is directed to chapter 19, which does not mention this additional purification by fire or water. This means that in addition to aspersion with the lustral waters (see v. 23aβ), purification by fire or water is mandatory. The discrepancy between what is mandated here and chapter 19 may point to the possibility that the fire/water purification for metals reflects an older tradition that considered corpse contamination to be a more dangerous impurity (see Excursus 48). Indeed, in ancient Hittite birth rituals brand new equipment is required with the exception of metal utensils, which can be purified by burning.[45]

23. ***fire . . . water*** Hebrew *ba-'esh . . . ba-mayim*. The article is generic.[46]

that cannot withstand fire For example, glassware. Fire, however, is the preferred medium of purification. One-day purification, being minor, requires immersion (see Lev. 11:32). But severe impurities, which convey their impurity to others, undergo seven-day purification and, as indicated here, need the stronger purgative of fire.[47]

water of lustration Hebrew *mei niddah* (see the Comment to 19:9), which, when sprinkled on the corpse-contaminated person on the third and seventh day, constitutes its purification (19:18–19). Thus, this passage supplements the rules of purification of corpse-contaminated objects in chapter 19 by insisting that not only must they be sprinkled with the water of lustration, but, in addition, they must be passed through fire or water.[48] However, the rabbis held that the passing of objects through fire or water is not part of the ritual of purification from corpse contamination but that it is a preliminary cleansing of these objects from food they may have absorbed. Thus cooking vessels are heated until they become white hot; silverware is placed in boiling water; and nonporous dishware that is used with cold food only, such as glasses, need only be soaked in cold water—a procedure familiar to every observant Jewish household in preparing for Passover.

must pass through water Presumably this is done on the seventh day (see v. 24) after the objects have been sprinkled with the water of lustration.[49]

24. This verse completes the purification procedure of persons and their clothing. Since this was Moses' and not Eleazar's concern, as can be derived from verses 19–20, the likelihood is that this verse originally was part of Moses' instructions and became severed from them when Eleazar's instructions (vv. 21–23) were interpolated[50] (see Excursus 68). Its content is nearly identical with that of 19:19b, which describes the settled conditions in the Holy Land where the corpse-contaminated person need not leave his community (Excursus 48). Reflected here is the older law of the wilderness that the corpse-contaminated person must leave the camp (see also 5:1–3).

wash your clothes And bathing is assumed (see 19:19b) in purification rules (Lev. 11:25, 28,40). The War Scroll of the Dead Sea documents makes this rule explicit: "In the morning they [the soldiers] shall launder their garments and wash themselves of the blood of the guilty cadavers."[51] Also assumed is that contact with sacred food must wait until evening (see Lev. 22:6–7).[52]

[25]The LORD said to Moses: [26]"You and Eleazar the priest
and the family heads of the community take an inventory of
the booty that was captured, man and beast, [27]and divide
the booty equally between the combatants who engaged in
the campaign and the rest of the community. [28]You shall
exact a levy for the LORD: in the case of the warriors who
engaged in the campaign, one item in five hundred, of
persons, oxen, asses, and sheep, [29]shall be taken from their

מֹשֶׁה לֵּאמֹר: 26 שָׂא אֵת רֹאשׁ מַלְקוֹחַ הַשְּׁבִי
בָּאָדָם וּבַבְּהֵמָה אַתָּה וְאֶלְעָזָר הַכֹּהֵן וְרָאשֵׁי
אֲבוֹת הָעֵדָה: 27 וְחָצִיתָ אֶת־הַמַּלְקוֹחַ בֵּין תֹּפְשֵׂי
הַמִּלְחָמָה הַיֹּצְאִים לַצָּבָא וּבֵין כָּל־הָעֵדָה:
28 וַהֲרֵמֹתָ מֶכֶס לַיהוָה מֵאֵת אַנְשֵׁי הַמִּלְחָמָה
הַיֹּצְאִים לַצָּבָא אֶחָד נֶפֶשׁ מֵחֲמֵשׁ הַמֵּאוֹת מִן־
הָאָדָם וּמִן־הַבָּקָר וּמִן־הַחֲמֹרִים וּמִן־הַצֹּאן:

THE DISTRIBUTION OF SPOILS (vv. 25–47)

Divine decree ordains the division of the persons and animals taken as spoil. The soldiers and civilians each get one-half, from which a levy is exacted for the clergy, the soldiers paying one-tenth as much as the civilians. Specifically, one-five-hundredth of the army's share goes to Eleazar (i.e., the sanctuary) and one-fiftieth of the civilians' share goes to the Levites. The older tradition in the Bible and the ancient Near East is that the temple (and its personnel) receives a tithe (see Gen. 14:20; 28:22).[53] The Koran prescribes that "to God belongs a fifth" of the spoil (8:42). Here the clergy receives a much smaller proportion, but, considering the huge quantities involved, the amount is substantial.

David also decrees that the battlefront and home front should divide the spoil equally, and since the text records that "from that day on it was made a fixed rule for Israel, continuing to the present day" (1 Sam. 30:25), it has been suggested that David's rule was retrojected into this account of the war against the Midianites in the wilderness. Yet the Mosaic ruling does not divide the spoils equitably since the clergy receives unequal shares (the Levites ten times as much as the priests). The mathematics is as follows:

SOLDIERS	CIVILIANS
$\frac{X}{2} - \frac{1}{500}\left(\frac{X}{2}\right) = \frac{499X}{1000}$	$\frac{X}{2} - \frac{1}{50}\left(\frac{X}{2}\right) = \frac{490X}{1000}$

Thus for every thousand persons or animals taken captive the soldiers receive nine more than the civilians. The difference, though paltry, is yet significant enough for the Temple Scroll of the Dead Sea sectaries to ordain that the clergy should receive its share *first*, that is, one-thousandth for the sanctuary and one-hundredth for the Levite to be taken from the *total* spoil; the remainder is then to be divided equally between the soldiers and the civilians.[54] In that way, the prescriptions of Moses and David harmonize perfectly.

26. Moses is assisted in the task of dividing the spoils by Eleazar and the clan heads, the former supervising the distribution to the clergy, and the latter, to the people.

the booty that was captured That is, the living booty (so vv. 27,32; and see the Comment to v. 11).[55]

the family heads of the community[56]

27. ***the combatants*** Hebrew ***tofesei ha-milḥamah*** is synonymous with ***'anshei ha-milḥamah***, "the warriors" (v. 20), literally "those skilled in war."

28. The absence of camels in this inventory of the animal spoils is significant in dating the war (see Excursus 67).

a levy Hebrew ***mekhes***, a term found only in this chapter of the Bible. In postbiblical Hebrew and Aramaic it means "tax." This, however, does not mean that this term (and hence this text) is late, since the word also occurs in Akkadian as ***miksu***. And, furthermore, its usage is attested as early as Old Babylonian and Mari as well as in nearby Ugarit,[57] also as a public tax.[58]

half-share and given to Eleazar the priest as a contribution to the LORD; [30]and from the half-share of the other Israelites you shall withhold one in every fifty human beings as well as cattle, asses, and sheep—all the animals—and give them to the Levites, who attend to the duties of the LORD's Tabernacle."

[31]Moses and Eleazar the priest did as the LORD commanded Moses. [32]The amount of booty, other than the spoil that the troops had plundered, came to 675,000 sheep, [33]72,000 head of cattle, [34]61,000 asses, [35]and a total of 32,000 human beings, namely, the women who had not had carnal relations.

[36]Thus, the half-share of those who had engaged in the campaign [was as follows]: The number of sheep was 337,500, [37]and the LORD's levy from the sheep was 675; [38]the cattle came to 36,000, from which the LORD's levy was 72; [39]the asses came to 30,500, from which the LORD's levy was 61. [40]And the number of human beings was 16,000, from which the LORD's levy was 32. [41]Moses gave the contributions levied for the LORD to Eleazar the priest, as the LORD had commanded Moses.

[42]As for the half-share of the other Israelites, which Moses withdrew from the men who had taken the field, [43]that half-share of the community consisted of 337,500 sheep, [44]36,000 head of cattle, [45]30,500 asses, [46]and 16,000

29 מִמַּחֲצִיתָם תִּקָּחוּ וְנָתַתָּה לְאֶלְעָזָר הַכֹּהֵן
תְּרוּמַת יְהוָה׃ 30 וּמִמַּחֲצִת בְּנֵי־יִשְׂרָאֵל תִּקַּח ׀
אֶחָד ׀ אָחֻז מִן־הַחֲמִשִּׁים מִן־הָאָדָם מִן־הַבָּקָר מִן־
הַחֲמֹרִים וּמִן־הַצֹּאן מִכָּל־הַבְּהֵמָה וְנָתַתָּה אֹתָם
לַלְוִיִּם שֹׁמְרֵי מִשְׁמֶרֶת מִשְׁכַּן יְהוָה׃ 31 וַיַּעַשׂ
מֹשֶׁה וְאֶלְעָזָר הַכֹּהֵן כַּאֲשֶׁר צִוָּה יְהוָה אֶת־מֹשֶׁה׃
32 וַיְהִי הַמַּלְקוֹחַ יֶתֶר הַבָּז אֲשֶׁר בָּזְזוּ עַם הַצָּבָא
צֹאן שֵׁשׁ־מֵאוֹת אֶלֶף וְשִׁבְעִים אֶלֶף וַחֲמֵשֶׁת־
אֲלָפִים׃ 33 וּבָקָר שְׁנַיִם וְשִׁבְעִים אָלֶף׃ 34 וַחֲמֹרִים
אֶחָד וְשִׁשִּׁים אָלֶף׃ 35 וְנֶפֶשׁ אָדָם מִן־הַנָּשִׁים
אֲשֶׁר לֹא־יָדְעוּ מִשְׁכַּב זָכָר כָּל־נֶפֶשׁ שְׁנַיִם
וּשְׁלֹשִׁים אָלֶף׃ 36 וַתְּהִי הַמֶּחֱצָה חֵלֶק הַיֹּצְאִים
בַּצָּבָא מִסְפַּר הַצֹּאן שְׁלֹשׁ־מֵאוֹת אֶלֶף וּשְׁלֹשִׁים
אֶלֶף וְשִׁבְעַת אֲלָפִים וַחֲמֵשׁ מֵאוֹת׃ 37 וַיְהִי
הַמֶּכֶס לַיהוָה מִן־הַצֹּאן שֵׁשׁ מֵאוֹת חָמֵשׁ
וְשִׁבְעִים׃ 38 וְהַבָּקָר שִׁשָּׁה וּשְׁלֹשִׁים אֶלֶף וּמִכְסָם
לַיהוָה שְׁנַיִם וְשִׁבְעִים׃ 39 וַחֲמֹרִים שְׁלֹשִׁים אֶלֶף
וַחֲמֵשׁ מֵאוֹת וּמִכְסָם לַיהוָה אֶחָד וְשִׁשִּׁים׃
40 וְנֶפֶשׁ אָדָם שִׁשָּׁה עָשָׂר אָלֶף וּמִכְסָם לַיהוָה
שְׁנַיִם וּשְׁלֹשִׁים נָפֶשׁ׃ 41 וַיִּתֵּן מֹשֶׁה אֶת־מֶכֶס
תְּרוּמַת יְהוָה לְאֶלְעָזָר הַכֹּהֵן כַּאֲשֶׁר צִוָּה יְהוָה
אֶת־מֹשֶׁה׃ חמישי 42 וּמִמַּחֲצִית בְּנֵי יִשְׂרָאֵל
אֲשֶׁר חָצָה מֹשֶׁה מִן־הָאֲנָשִׁים הַצֹּבְאִים׃ 43 וַתְּהִי
מֶחֱצַת הָעֵדָה מִן־הַצֹּאן שְׁלֹשׁ־מֵאוֹת אֶלֶף
וּשְׁלֹשִׁים אֶלֶף שִׁבְעַת אֲלָפִים וַחֲמֵשׁ מֵאוֹת׃

one item[59]

29. *a contribution to the LORD* For Hebrew *terumah*, see the Comment to 5:9.[60]

30. *you shall withhold one* Literally, "you shall take one seized from." The same usage, withdrawing from a number, is found in 1 Chronicles 24:6. The Levitical share is neither a *mekhes* nor a *terumah*. Those terms are used in construct with "the Lord" (vv. 28,29,37,41) and, therefore, represent contributions to the sanctuary. *'Aḥuz*, by contrast, is a nonsacral term for withholding and is the semantic equivalent of Akkadian *ṣubtu*, a tax imposed on domestic animals.[61] It could be levied by the palace as well as the temple.

one in every fifth Thus, the Levites receive ten times as much as the priests. The ratio is similar to their respective shares in the tithe, the Levites receiving nine times as much (18:25–32).

to the Levites They are not included in the community, having undergone a separate census.[62]

who attend to the duties Rather, "who perform the guard duty" (see the Comment to 3:7 and Excursus 4).

32. *the spoil* Referring to objects that the soldiers plundered for themselves and that were not subject to the levy.

40. *human beings . . . the LORD's levy* These individuals were most likely assigned to menial tasks in the sanctuary, as in Joshua 9:27.

42. *As for the half-share of*[63]

human beings. 47From this half-share of the Israelites, Moses withheld one in every fifty humans and animals; and he gave them to the Levites, who attended to the duties of the LORD's Tabernacle, as the LORD had commanded Moses.

48The commanders of the troop divisions, the officers of thousands and the officers of hundreds, approached Moses. 49They said to Moses, "Your servants have made a check of the warriors in our charge, and not one of us is missing. 50So we have brought as an offering to the LORD such articles of gold as each of us came upon: armlets, bracelets, signet rings, earrings, and pendants, that expiation may be made for our persons before the LORD." 51Moses and

44 וּבָקָר שִׁשָּׁה וּשְׁלֹשִׁים אָלֶף: 45 וַחֲמֹרִים
שְׁלֹשִׁים אֶלֶף וַחֲמֵשׁ מֵאוֹת: 46 וְנֶפֶשׁ אָדָם שִׁשָּׁה
עָשָׂר אָלֶף: 47 וַיִּקַּח מֹשֶׁה מִמַּחֲצִת בְּנֵי־יִשְׂרָאֵל
אֶת־הָאָחֻז אֶחָד מִן־הַחֲמִשִּׁים מִן־הָאָדָם וּמִן־
הַבְּהֵמָה וַיִּתֵּן אֹתָם לַלְוִיִּם שֹׁמְרֵי מִשְׁמֶרֶת מִשְׁכַּן
יְהוָה כַּאֲשֶׁר צִוָּה יְהוָה אֶת־מֹשֶׁה: 48 וַיִּקְרְבוּ אֶל־
מֹשֶׁה הַפְּקֻדִים אֲשֶׁר לְאַלְפֵי הַצָּבָא שָׂרֵי הָאֲלָפִים
וְשָׂרֵי הַמֵּאוֹת: 49 וַיֹּאמְרוּ אֶל־מֹשֶׁה עֲבָדֶיךָ נָשְׂאוּ
אֶת־רֹאשׁ אַנְשֵׁי הַמִּלְחָמָה אֲשֶׁר בְּיָדֵנוּ וְלֹא־נִפְקַד
מִמֶּנּוּ אִישׁ: 50 וַנַּקְרֵב אֶת־קָרְבַּן יְהוָה אִישׁ אֲשֶׁר
מָצָא כְלִי־זָהָב אֶצְעָדָה וְצָמִיד טַבַּעַת עָגִיל וְכוּמָז
לְכַפֵּר עַל־נַפְשֹׁתֵינוּ לִפְנֵי יְהוָה: 51 וַיִּקַּח מֹשֶׁה

THE RANSOM (vv. 48–54)

The officers polled the army after the victory and discovered that Israel had not suffered a single casualty. To ward off any mishap for taking a count of their men, in consonance with Exodus 30:12, the officers voluntarily contribute to the sanctuary all the gold ornaments they had personally rifled from the bodies of the slain. The assumption here is that the officers dedicated their spoil to God before they took count of their men, again in consonance with Exodus 30:12, and are now presenting their dedicated gold to Moses (see Excursus 68). Moses and Eleazar convert the gold into vessels for the sanctuary as a permanent reminder to the Lord on behalf of Israel.

48. commanders See the Comment to verse 14.

49. have made a check Hebrew *nase'u ro'sh* (see v. 26). Rather, "had made a check," since it took place after the battle and before the week of purification and distribution of the spoils. The idiom likely means "took a head count," that is, a census (see the Comment to 1:2).

missing Hebrew *nifkad*, from *pakad*, "count," literally "(not one of us) has not been numbered"; that is, all are accounted for. For this usage, see 1 Samuel 20:25.

50. So we have brought . . . offering Hebrew *va-nakrev . . . korban*. The verb and noun of *k-r-v* are not restricted to an altar sacrifice but can refer to any kind of an offering to the sanctuary.[64] The variety of gold ornaments is not surprising. To this day, nomads wear more ornaments on their persons than do sedentary peoples.

offering to the LORD Implied is that this offering had been set aside and dedicated to the Lord prior to the census, in accordance with Exodus 30:12–16, and is now being turned over to Moses.

armlets[65]

bracelets[66]

earrings[67]

pendants[68]

that expiation may be made for our persons Rather, "to ransom our lives" (see Excursus 19 and 8:19; Exod. 30:15–16; Lev. 17:11). As correctly observed by Rashbam (quoting his father, R. Meir), the ransom to God was a necessary prophylactic against the onslaught of a plague that could be expected for conducting a census (see Exod. 30:12 and Excursus 2). The outbreak of a plague during the reign of King David is attributed to his census of Israel (2 Sam. 24), perhaps for the reason that it was conducted without the prior collection of ransom money. The basis for the taboo against a census is not known, although one plausible suggestion has been offered: As the shepherd counts his sheep, so the counter of persons must be their owner, a title belonging solely to God and not to man.[69] Other explanations for the ransom are: as thanksgiving for not losing a single life in the

Eleazar the priest accepted the gold from them, all kinds of wrought articles. [52]All the gold that was offered by the officers of thousands and the officers of hundreds as a contribution to the LORD came to 16,750 shekels. [53]—But in the ranks, everyone kept his booty for himself.—[54]So Moses and Eleazar the priest accepted the gold from the officers of thousands and the officers of hundreds and brought it to the Tent of Meeting, as a reminder in behalf of the Israelites before the LORD.

וְאֶלְעָזָר הַכֹּהֵן אֶת־הַזָּהָב מֵאִתָּם כֹּל כְּלִי מַעֲשֶׂה׃
52 וַיְהִי ׀ כָּל־זְהַב הַתְּרוּמָה אֲשֶׁר הֵרִימוּ לַיהוָה
שִׁשָּׁה עָשָׂר אֶלֶף שְׁבַע־מֵאוֹת וַחֲמִשִּׁים שָׁקֶל
מֵאֵת שָׂרֵי הָאֲלָפִים וּמֵאֵת שָׂרֵי הַמֵּאוֹת׃
53 אַנְשֵׁי הַצָּבָא בָּזְזוּ אִישׁ לוֹ׃ 54 וַיִּקַּח מֹשֶׁה
וְאֶלְעָזָר הַכֹּהֵן אֶת־הַזָּהָב מֵאֵת שָׂרֵי הָאֲלָפִים
וְהַמֵּאוֹת וַיָּבִאוּ אֹתוֹ אֶל־אֹהֶל מוֹעֵד זִכָּרוֹן לִבְנֵי־
יִשְׂרָאֵל לִפְנֵי יְהוָה׃ פ ששי [שלישי
כשהן מחוברות]

campaign[70] and as a ransom for taking life, even with justification.[71] However, the verb ***kipper*** implies atonement and not thanksgiving. Also ransom for life is correct only in regard to the slaughter of animals for their meat (Lev. 17:11)[72] but not for justified homicide.

*52. **16,750 shekels*** Just over 600 pounds avoirdupois.[73] By contrast, the gold despoiled by Gideon's army from ***all*** Midianites weighed 1,700 (shekels) (Judg. 8:26). Hence, this figure, like the other numbers in this chapter, is not to be taken literally.[74]

53. This parenthetical comment underscores the magnanimity of the officers' contribution. Although a census requires a monetary ransom from each person (Exod. 30:12), the officers donated more than twice the amount needed to ransom the entire army—one-half shekel of silver per soldier (not to speak of gold), totaling 6,000 shekels. Thus, each infantryman could keep his booty (see v. 32).

*54. **So Moses . . . hundreds*** A repetitive resumption of verse 51, necessitated by the explanatory comment of verse 52 and the interpolation of verse 53.

a reminder Hebrew ***zikkaron***. For the significance of this term, see the Comment to 10:10 and Excursus 38. The gold was used to make sanctuary vessels[75] or to repair old ones,[76] in contrast to the silver ransom required in Exodus 30, which was used for the construction (***'avodah***) of the sanctuary (Exod. 30:16; see Exod. 38:25–28). The use of the gold in the sanctuary service was to function as a perpetual reminder to the Lord to prevent the punishment of Israel for taking a census.

A midrash taking an opposite point of view holds that the gold donation to the sanctuary was to remind the Lord of Israel's virtue, for when they stripped the Midianite women of their ornaments they did not violate their persons:

> Each of us had gone into the houses of the Midianites, into the bedchambers of their kings. And we (desired) saw their daughters, pretty and beautiful, delicate and tender; and we unfastened the garlands, the gold crowns from their heads; rings from their ears, necklaces from their necks, chainlets from their arms, chains from their hands, signet rings from their fingers, clasps from the breasts. Nevertheless, not one of us was joined with one of them in this world, so as not to be with her in Gehenna in the world to come. May this stand up in our favor on the day of Great Judgment, to make atonement for us before the Lord.[77]

CHAPTER 32

The Settlement of Transjordan (vv. 1–42)

Whereas 21:21–35 dealt with the conquest of Transjordan, and the subsequent narrative—Balaam (chaps. 22–24), Baal-peor (chap. 25), and the Midianite war (chap. 31)—concerned itself with the threats to Israel's existence, chapter 32 begins a new phase: the settlement period, the record of how the tribes of Israel began to find themselves permanent homes. Gad and Reuben wish to settle in the conquered Transjordanian territory. Their request is emphatically rejected by Moses, who accuses them of betraying the national goal of occupying and settling the promised land. Gad and Reuben

32 The Reubenites and the Gadites owned cattle in very
great numbers. Noting that the lands of Jazer and Gilead
were a region suitable for cattle, 2the Gadites and the

ל״ב וּמִקְנֶה ׀ רַב הָיָה לִבְנֵי רְאוּבֵן וְלִבְנֵי־גָד
עָצוּם מְאֹד וַיִּרְאוּ אֶת־אֶרֶץ יַעְזֵר וְאֶת־אֶרֶץ גִּלְעָד
וְהִנֵּה הַמָּקוֹם מְקוֹם מִקְנֶה׃ 2 וַיָּבֹאוּ בְנֵי־גָד וּבְנֵי

offer a compromise formula: In return for the privilege of settling in Transjordan, they will serve as shock-troops for the forthcoming conquest. Their pledge, in the form of an oath, is repeated before Israel's leaders. They are permitted to rebuild destroyed Transjordanian cities, in which their dependents will remain while they fight alongside the rest of the Israelite tribes. Three Manassite clans, referred to as the half-tribe of Manasseh, conquer and settle territory in northern Transjordan.

THE PROPOSAL (vv. 1–5)

The tribes of Gad and Reuben, seeing that the conquered land in Transjordan affords excellent pasture-land, petition Moses, Eleazar, and the people's leaders to be allowed to settle there instead of crossing the Jordan.

*1. **The Reubenites and the Gadites*** This order prevails in most allusions to this incident (e.g., Deut. 3; Josh. 22). But within the present chapter, as well as in Joshua 18:7 and 2 Kings 10:33, the order is reversed, probably reflecting the original preeminence of Gad.[1] Indeed, in monarchic times Reuben is conspicuously absent from the historical records of Samuel, Kings, and the Moabite stories. For example, Gad but not Reuben is identified during the reign of Saul (1 Sam. 13:7); David's census only mentions Gad (2 Sam. 24:5); Solomon's twelfth district is known as Gad (1 Kings 4:19 LXX), and Mesha of Moab only mentions Gad in his inscription. For the controversy over the fate of the tribe of Reuben, see Excursus 70. Although it may be claimed that this verse was altered to bring it into conformity with the genealogical scheme of Reuben as the first-born, there may be another reason: The order Gad-Reuben (and also other key terms) appears seven times in this chapter (vv. 2,6,25,29,31,33,34/37; see Excursus 70). In order not to break this pattern, the sequence of the tribes in this first verse was reversed. The Septuagint (except for vv. 6 and 33) and the Samaritan, however, put Reuben ahead of Gad. But the fact that the towns of Gad precede those of Reuben (vv. 3,34–38) clearly signifies that the order Gad-Reuben is original; the versions, then, reflect the hand of a harmonizing redactor.

cattle Rather, "livestock," since there were other domesticated animals, such as donkeys, in addition to cattle (see the Comment to v. 26). That this term comprises all domestic hoofed animals, see Exodus 9:3 and 10:26. Reuben, in particular, was later characterized by its investment in grazing animals, as is clear from Judges 5:16 and 1 Chronicles 5:9. The animal spoils from the Midianite war mentioned in the preceding chapter increased the livestock of Gad and Reuben to the point of unmanageability.[2]

The juxtaposition of chapters 31 and 32 is explained in this way by the midrash: "For when He wanted the Reubenites and Gadites to become rich, He cast the Midianites down before Israel in order that the Gadites and Reubenites might grow rich thereby."[3]

in very great numbers Hebrew *rav . . . ʿatsum meʾod*. For this idiom, see Exodus 1:9 and 9:14.

lands of Jazer and Gilead For Jazer, see the Comment to 21:32 where the region of Jazer is distinguished from the Heshbon region. In this chapter, only here is Jazer distinguished from Gilead, but elsewhere (vv. 26,29) it is incorporated into Gilead. Gilead itself is used in three senses. (1) In the broadest sense, it refers to the region from Wadi Heshbon or the Arnon on the south to the Yarmuk on the north, intersected by the Jabbok (e.g., Deut. 3:12–13; Josh. 12:2,5; 13:31). In its narrower sense, it refers to one of the halves, either (2) north of the Jabbok (e.g., Josh. 17:1,5–6), called today ʿAjlun, traces of which are evident in the names Jabesh-gilead and Ramoth-gilead, or (3) south of the Jabbok (e.g., Josh. 13:25), called today the Belqaʿ, traces of which are found in the topographical names Jebel Jelʿad, Khirbet Jelʿad, Khirbet Jalʿud. This chapter features Gilead in its narrow sense, both south of the Jabbok (vv. 1,26,29) and north of the Jabbok (vv. 39,40). The southern Gilead, in particular, is

Reubenites came to Moses, Eleazar the priest, and the
chieftains of the community, and said,
3 "Ataroth, Dibon,
Jazer, Nimrah, Heshbon, Elealeh, Sebam, Nebo, and Beon
—4 the land that the LORD has conquered for the commu-

רְאוּבֵ֔ן וַיֹּאמְר֣וּ אֶל־מֹשֶׁה֙ וְאֶל־אֶלְעָזָ֣ר הַכֹּהֵ֔ן וְאֶל־
נְשִׂיאֵ֥י הָעֵדָ֖ה לֵאמֹֽר׃
3 עֲטָר֤וֹת וְדִיבֹן֙ וְיַעְזֵ֣ר
וְנִמְרָ֔ה וְחֶשְׁבּ֖וֹן וְאֶלְעָלֵ֑ה וּשְׂבָ֥ם וּנְב֖וֹ וּבְעֹֽן׃

famous for its cattle (Mic. 7:14; Song 4:1; 1 Chron. 5:9). A modern Arab saying runs "You cannot find a country like the Belqaʿ" (i.e., between the Arnon and Jabbok) for cattle. More than a century ago, the geographer G. A. Smith described the territory desired by Gad and Reuben as follows:

> Gilead, between the Yarmuk and the Jabbok, has its ridges covered by forests. . . . The valleys hold orchards of pomegranates, apricot, and olive; there are many vineyards; on the open plain are fields of wheat and maize, and the few moors are rich in fragrant herbs. . . . South of the Jabbok, the forests gradually cease and Ammon and Moab are mostly high, bare moors. . . . More famous than the tilth of Eastern Palestine is her pasture. We passed through at the height of the shepherd's year. From the Arabian deserts the Bedouin were swarming to the fresh herbage of these uplands. We should never have believed the amount of their flocks had we not seen and attempted to count them. . . . The Bedouin had also many sheep and goats. The herds of the settled inhabitants were still more numerous. In Moab the dust of the roads bears almost no marks but those of the feet of sheep. The scenes which throng most our memory of Eastern Palestine are . . . the streams of Gilead in the heat of the day with the cattle standing in them, or the evenings when we sat at the door of our tent near the village well, and would hear the shepherd's pipe far away, and the sheep and goats, and cows with heavy bells, would break over the edge of the hill, and come down the slope to wait their turn at the troughs. Over Jordan we were never long out of the sound of the lowing of cattle or of the shepherd's pipe.[4]

region For this usage of Hebrew ***makom***, see 10:29, 14:40, and Exodus 23:20.

2. ***Eleazar*** In the Midianite war, Eleazar appeared in a leadership role (31:12–13) because the sacred vessels accompanied the army into battle (31:6), the sanctuary and its personnel shared in the booty (31:28–30), and the returning army required purification (31:19–24). Eleazar's role here is not as obvious. But it must be remembered that the division of the land is decided by lot, that is, by the Urim and Thummim operated by Eleazar (27:21). Surely, then, the request of Gad and Reuben to withdraw from the forthcoming apportionment of the land (33:50–54; 34:13–15) required the consent of the High Priest Eleazar.

3. These nine towns are mentioned in verses 34–38, where the first four are assigned to Gad and the remainder to Reuben. (They also occur in Isa. 15,16; Jer. 48, where they belong to Moab.) The four assigned to Gad seem to surround Reuben's territory, Ataroth-Dibon to the south and Jazer-Nimrah to the north. Reuben, however, seems restricted to the Heshbon area, which would explain why it was probably eventually absorbed into Gad (but see Excursus 70). These towns are again mentioned in verses 34–38, thereby framing this chapter in an inclusion (see Excursus 69). However, the latter list contains additional names (see Map 5).

Ataroth Identified with *ʿAtarus*, between Libb and Machaerus, 17.5 kilometers (10.5 mi) northwest of Dibon and mentioned in the Mesha stone as a Gadite site.

Dibon Present ***Diban***, located about 5 kilometers (3 mi.) north of the Arnon. Gad's settlement there is confirmed by its alternate name Dibon-gad (33:45,46) and its attribution to Gadite hegemony in the Mesha stone (lines 10, 11). It may have become a Reubenite town (Josh. 13:17) at a later date (see Excursus 70).

Jazer See the Comment to 21:32.

Nimrah Equivalent to Beth-nimrah (v. 36), probably located at Tell Beleibil on Wadi Shaʿib. The name is still preserved in Tell Nimrim, south-southwest of Tell Beleibil. "Waters of Nimrim" (Isa. 15:6; Jer. 48:34) may refer to the lower bend of Wadi Shaʿib.

Heshbon See the Comment to 21:25.

Elealeh Identified with El-ʿal, northwest of Heshbon.

nity of Israel is cattle country, and your servants have
cattle. 5 It would be a favor to us," they continued, "if this
land were given to your servants as a holding; do not move
us across the Jordan."
6 Moses replied to the Gadites and the Reubenites, "Are

4 הָאָ֗רֶץ אֲשֶׁר֩ הִכָּ֨ה יְהוָ֜ה לִפְנֵי֙ עֲדַ֣ת יִשְׂרָאֵ֔ל
אֶ֥רֶץ מִקְנֶ֖ה הִ֑וא וְלַעֲבָדֶ֖יךָ מִקְנֶֽה׃ ס
5 וַיֹּאמְר֗וּ אִם־מָצָ֤אנוּ חֵן֙ בְּעֵינֶ֔יךָ יֻתַּ֞ן אֶת־הָאָ֧רֶץ
הַזֹּ֛את לַעֲבָדֶ֖יךָ לַאֲחֻזָּ֑ה אַל־תַּעֲבִרֵ֖נוּ אֶת־הַיַּרְדֵּֽן׃
6 וַיֹּ֣אמֶר מֹשֶׁ֔ה לִבְנֵי־גָ֖ד וְלִבְנֵ֣י רְאוּבֵ֑ן הַאַחֵיכֶ֗ם

Sebam Or Sibmah (v. 38), identified with Khirbet Carn el-Kibsh between Heshbon and Nebo.

Nebo Identified with Khirbet el-Mukhayyit just south of Mount Nebo. The inscription of King Mesha of Moab (lines 14–18) shows that it was a YHVH cult center in the period before 850 B.C.E.

Beon A conflation of Baal-meon (v. 38; Ezek. 25:9; 1 Chron. 5:8), Beth-baal-meon (Josh. 13:17), or Beth-meon (Jer. 48:23). These variants probably refer to the same place, Maʿin, located 7 kilometers (4 mi.) southwest of Madaba.

4. ***has conquered*** Hebrew ***hikkah***, a term nowhere else used for the conquests of God, is a subtle variation of 21:24, in which Israel is the subject of the same verb. This is precisely the point that Gad and Reuben are making: Since the Lord has conquered Transjordan, it is as much His land as is Cisjordan. This argument, however, is a distortion. Israel had approached Sihon as it had the affine peoples (Edom, Moab, Ammon) whose land was off limits—only to cross it and not to occupy it (cf. 20:14–21 with 21:21–23). In fact, Sihon's land was formerly Moabite, a point stressed by the text (21:26) and, hence, forbidden territory from the beginning (see Excursus 54). Indeed, for Israel this land is not only forbidden but impure (Josh. 22:19). That Israel settled this land without divine permission is reflected in the justification of the rabbinic halakhah that Transjordan is exempt from the law of first fruits (Deut. 26:2) because Israel "took it on its own volition" (Sif. Deut. 299). In nonpriestly, folk narratives, however, there exists the opposing tradition that Transjordan was part of the promised land (e.g., Gen. 15:16–21; Exod. 23:31; see Excursus 73).

5. ***they continued*** Hebrew ***va-yo'meru***. This verb needs to be repeated because of the lengthy remark beginning in verse 2.[5]

if this land were given[6]

do not move us across the Jordan That is, for settlement in Cisjordan. But they had every intention of participating in the conquest, as is made clear by their subsequent clarification (vv. 16–19). Moses, assuming that their intent was not to participate in the forthcoming campaign, interrupts their speech to charge them with disloyalty. The key word *ʿavar*, "cross," occurs seven times (vv. 5,7, 21,27,29,30,32); for the significance, see Excursus 69.

MOSES' REJECTION (vv. 6–15)

He compares them with the scouts of chapters 13–14 who had undermined the unity of Israel and triggered divine wrath and punishment. Moses suspects that Gad and Reuben, like the scouts, are really afraid of the Canaanites;[7] and if ten individuals could demoralize the people, all the more so two entire tribes.[8] The relationship with the scout episode (chap. 14) is actually reversed: There, two (scouts) were positive and ten were negative; here, two (tribes) are negative and ten are positive.[9] The summary of the scout episode of chapters 13–14 is a creative adaptation and not a slavish borrowing.[10]

6. Moses upbraids Gad and Reuben for their selfish disregard of Israel's unity; this is similar to the accusation against the Transjordanian tribes in the time of Joshua (Josh. 22:16–20) and Deborah (Judg. 5:17). Rabbinic tradition also condemns the economic basis of their petition: "You find that they were rich, possessing large numbers of cattle, but they loved their money and settled outside the Land of Israel. Consequently they were the first of the tribes to go into exile (1 Chron. 5:26). What brought it on them? The fact that they separated themselves from their brethren because of their possessions."[11]

your brothers to go to war while you stay here? 7 Why will you turn the minds of the Israelites from crossing into the land that the LORD has given them? 8 That is what your fathers did when I sent them from Kadesh-barnea to survey the land. 9 After going up to the wadi Eshcol and surveying the land, they turned the minds of the Israelites from invading the land that the LORD had given them. 10 Thereupon the LORD was incensed and He swore, 11 'None of the men from twenty years up who came out of Egypt shall see the land that I promised on oath to Abraham, Isaac, and Jacob, for they did not remain loyal to Me— 12 none except Caleb son of Jephunneh the Kenizzite and Joshua son of Nun, for they remained loyal to the LORD.' 13 The LORD was incensed at Israel, and for forty years He made them wander in the wilderness, until the whole generation that had provoked the LORD's displeasure was gone. 14 And now you, a breed of sinful men, have replaced your fathers, to add still further to the LORD's wrath against Israel. 15 If you turn away from Him and He abandons them once more in the wilderness, you will bring calamity upon all this people."

יָבֹאוּ לַמִּלְחָמָה וְאַתֶּם תֵּשְׁבוּ פֹה׃ 7 וְלָמָּה תנואון
אֶת־לֵב בְּנֵי יִשְׂרָאֵל מֵעֲבֹר אֶל־הָאָרֶץ אֲשֶׁר־נָתַן
לָהֶם יְהוָה׃ 8 כֹּה עָשׂוּ אֲבֹתֵיכֶם בְּשָׁלְחִי אֹתָם
מִקָּדֵשׁ בַּרְנֵעַ לִרְאוֹת אֶת־הָאָרֶץ׃ 9 וַיַּעֲלוּ עַד־
נַחַל אֶשְׁכּוֹל וַיִּרְאוּ אֶת־הָאָרֶץ וַיָּנִיאוּ אֶת־לֵב
בְּנֵי יִשְׂרָאֵל לְבִלְתִּי־בֹא אֶל־הָאָרֶץ אֲשֶׁר־נָתַן
לָהֶם יְהוָה׃ 10 וַיִּחַר־אַף יְהוָה בַּיּוֹם הַהוּא וַיִּשָּׁבַע
לֵאמֹר׃ 11 אִם־יִרְאוּ הָאֲנָשִׁים הָעֹלִים מִמִּצְרַיִם
מִבֶּן עֶשְׂרִים שָׁנָה וָמַעְלָה אֵת הָאֲדָמָה אֲשֶׁר
נִשְׁבַּעְתִּי לְאַבְרָהָם לְיִצְחָק וּלְיַעֲקֹב כִּי לֹא־מִלְאוּ
אַחֲרָי׃ 12 בִּלְתִּי כָּלֵב בֶּן־יְפֻנֶּה הַקְּנִזִּי וִיהוֹשֻׁעַ בִּן־
נוּן כִּי מִלְאוּ אַחֲרֵי יְהוָה׃ 13 וַיִּחַר־אַף יְהוָה
בְּיִשְׂרָאֵל וַיְנִעֵם בַּמִּדְבָּר אַרְבָּעִים שָׁנָה עַד־תֹּם
כָּל־הַדּוֹר הָעֹשֶׂה הָרַע בְּעֵינֵי יְהוָה׃ 14 וְהִנֵּה
קַמְתֶּם תַּחַת אֲבֹתֵיכֶם תַּרְבּוּת אֲנָשִׁים חַטָּאִים
לִסְפּוֹת עוֹד עַל חֲרוֹן אַף־יְהוָה אֶל־יִשְׂרָאֵל׃
15 כִּי תְשׁוּבֻן מֵאַחֲרָיו וְיָסַף עוֹד לְהַנִּיחוֹ בַּמִּדְבָּר
וְשִׁחַתֶּם לְכָל־הָעָם הַזֶּה׃ ס 16 וַיִּגְּשׁוּ אֵלָיו

v. 7. תְּנִיאוּן ק׳

7. turn the minds Hebrew *teni'un 'et lev*. Alternatively, "oppose the intention" (see the Comment to 30:6). The idiom also occurs in verse 9.

8. Kadesh-barnea The full name of Kadesh (Num. 34:4; Deut. 1:19; 2:14; 9:23).

10. He swore For the oath, see 14:21–30.

11. from twenty years up In the Bible, twenty is the legal age for majority and, hence, for liability to punishment.[12] The Septuagint adds "who know good and evil," a euphemism for sexual maturity, as in Genesis 2:9, Deuteronomy 1:39, and especially 2 Samuel 19:36. This pairing of twenty years and sex is explicitly made by the Dead Sea sectaries.[13]

not remain loyal to Me For the meaning of the idiom *lo' mile'u 'aḥarai*, see 1 Kings 11:4,6;[14] and see the Comment to 14:24. This contrast of positive and negative action is featured throughout this chapter, in verses 11–12, 19a–19b, 20–23, 29–30, and is a literary characteristic of priestly writings (e.g., Num. 33:52,55; Lev. 26).

12. The Kenizzite In 13:6 and 34:19, Caleb is a Judite; in Joshua 14:6,14, he is a Kenizzite. The latter is implied in Joshua 15:17 and Judges 1:13 and 3:9. Surprisingly, the Septuagint renders, but here only, "who was set apart," echoed in the rabbinic tradition that "he separated himself from the advice of the other scouts."[15] Perhaps the Alexandrian translators did not want to admit to their non-Jewish audience that the brave and faithful Caleb could originally have come from a non-Israelite clan.[16] On Caleb the Kenizzite/Judite see Excursus 31.

13. The Lord was incensed For the second time. The first time He punished the generation of the Exodus (vv. 10–12); the second time He punished their children.[17]

He made them wander Hebrew *va-yeni'em*. For this usage, see 2 Samuel 15:20.

14. a breed[18]

to add[19]

15. abandons them[20]

¹⁶Then they stepped up to him and said, "We will build here sheepfolds for our flocks and towns for our children.

וַיִּגְּשׁ֣וּ אֵלָיו֘ וַיֹּֽאמְרוּ֒ גִּדְרֹ֥ת צֹ֛אן נִבְנֶ֥ה לְמִקְנֵ֖נוּ פֹּ֣ה וְעָרִ֑ים לְטַפֵּֽנוּ׃ ¹⁷ וַאֲנַ֜חְנוּ נֵחָלֵ֣ץ חֻשִׁ֗ים לִפְנֵי֙ בְּנֵ֣י יִשְׂרָאֵ֔ל

you will bring calamity upon If the other tribes tolerate your rebellion.[21] In Joshua 22:18, the building of an altar in Transjordan by these same tribes is also prone to bring calamity upon the entire people (for this idiomatic usage of *shiḥet le*, see 1 Sam. 23:10).

A COMPROMISE FORMULA (vv. 16–19)

Gad and Reuben reveal their true intention.

16. ***Then they stepped up*** Hebrew *va-yiggeshu*. Moses, having interrupted their petition (vv. 5,6–15), is now beseeched in a personal, intimate way. This is the meaning of the verb *va-yiggeshu* when it occurs in the middle of a conversation as in Genesis 44:18 and 45:4; compare Joshua 14:6.

here *Poh*. Thus the tribes respond to Moses' charge that they intend to remain *poh*, "here" (v. 6).[22]

sheepfolds Hebrew *giderot tso'n* (see 1 Sam. 24:3; Zeph. 2:6), the technical term for which is *mishpetayim* (Gen. 49:14; Judg. 5:16). The dual formation may refer to two stone walls in the shape of a V leading to an enclosure in which sheep were penned in time of danger. Such constructions were found in the Arabah and Transjordan but nowhere else.[23] The term *tso'n* means "flock," a more correct rendering since sheep and goats pasture together in the Near East to this day. Moreover, these folds also were built for cattle, to judge by the horned animals that predominate in an ancient Safaitic drawing of such an enclosure.[24]

The towns and sheepfolds would have required adequate manpower to protect them against attack from neighboring tribes. Since the shock-troops comprised a select, elite force, the remainder of the troops could be left behind to construct and protect the home front. That such was the case is demonstrated by the population figures. The two and a half tribes that crossed the Jordan numbered "about forty thousand shock troops" (Josh. 4:13). However, their combined military force numbered 110,580 (26:7,18,34). Thus approximately one-third of the available manpower was utilized for the shock-troops and two-thirds remained behind to protect their tribes' dependents and livestock. Possible confirmation for such a home front is provided by Joshua's order to the Transjordanian shock-troops at the successful completion of the campaign: "Share the spoil of your enemies with your kinsmen" (Josh. 22:8), that is, with the soldiers of the home front.[25]

for our children Rather, "for our dependents." The term *taf* can include women (as in vv. 17,24; see the Comment to 31:18; Exod. 12:37). "Sheepfolds" precedes "children" in this verse but the order is reversed in Moses' response (v. 24), another indication of the chiastic scheme that pervades this chapter.[26] However, a midrash understands it differently: "The Reubenites and Gadites . . . cherished their property more than human life, saying to Moses: 'We will build here sheepfolds for our flocks and towns for our children' (v. 16). Moses said to them: That is not right! Rather do the more important things first. 'Build towns for your children' (v. 24) and afterward 'sheepfolds for your flocks' (v. 24) . . . the Holy One Blessed Be He said to them: 'Seeing that you have shown greater love for your cattle than for human souls, by your life, there will be no blessing in it.'"[27]

And we Literally, "as for us, we"; the pronoun, otherwise superfluous, is for emphasis.

hasten Particularly significant is Joshua 4:12, which records the fulfillment of this pledge: "The Reubenites, the Gadites and the half-tribe of Manasseh went across armed [*ḥamushim*] in the van of the Israelites, as Moses had charged them."[28]

as shock-troops Hebrew *neḥalets*, literally "we shall be picked out" (see the Comment to 31:3), that is, to go first as the vanguard.[29] Without their families and possessions, they have greater mobility than the other tribes and can therefore undertake commando assignments.[30] The root *ḥ-l-ts* occurs seven times in this chapter (vv. 17,20,21,27,29,30,32), the significance of which is explicated in Excursus 69.

[17]And we will hasten as shock-troops in the van of the Israelites until we have established them in their home, while our children stay in the fortified towns because of the inhabitants of the land. [18]We will not return to our homes until every one of the Israelites is in possession of his portion. [19]But we will not have a share with them in the territory beyond the Jordan, for we have received our share on the east side of the Jordan."

[20]Moses said to them, "If you do this, if you go to battle as shock-troops, at the instance of the LORD, [21]and every shock-fighter among you crosses the Jordan, at the instance

עַד אֲשֶׁר אִם־הֲבִיאֹנֻם אֶל־מְקוֹמָם וְיָשַׁב טַפֵּנוּ
בְּעָרֵי הַמִּבְצָר מִפְּנֵי יֹשְׁבֵי הָאָרֶץ׃ 18 לֹא נָשׁוּב
אֶל־בָּתֵּינוּ עַד הִתְנַחֵל בְּנֵי יִשְׂרָאֵל אִישׁ נַחֲלָתוֹ׃
19 כִּי לֹא נִנְחַל אִתָּם מֵעֵבֶר לַיַּרְדֵּן וָהָלְאָה כִּי
בָאָה נַחֲלָתֵנוּ אֵלֵינוּ מֵעֵבֶר הַיַּרְדֵּן מִזְרָחָה׃
פ שביעי [רביעי כשהן מחוברות]
20 וַיֹּאמֶר אֲלֵיהֶם מֹשֶׁה אִם־תַּעֲשׂוּן אֶת־הַדָּבָר
הַזֶּה אִם־תֵּחָלְצוּ לִפְנֵי יְהוָה לַמִּלְחָמָה׃ 21 וְעָבַר
לָכֶם כָּל־חָלוּץ אֶת־הַיַּרְדֵּן לִפְנֵי יְהוָה עַד הוֹרִישׁוֹ

in the van of the Israelites[31]

until[32]

while . . . stay Hebrew *ve-yashav*, an answer to Moses' accusation "while you stay" (v. 6), another indication that verses 16–19 originally followed upon verse 6 (see the Comment to v. 16).

18. ***is in possession*** Literally "possesses for himself." For the usage see 33:54; 34:13.

19. ***have received***[33] Literally, "is coming (to us)," that is, appropriated for us. Gad and Reuben are willing to be the last to settle on their land[34] if they receive it first. Alternatively, render as a future perfect, "when our inheritance has come to us."[35]

east side of the Jordan Literally, "on the other side of the Jordan eastward." Thus, the speaker in this verse places himself on both sides of the Jordan.

MOSES' ACCEPTANCE (vv. 20–24)

Moses repeats the formula offered by Gad and Reuben—rather than merely recording his acceptance—for the purpose of restructuring it in two significant ways. (1) He introduces the name of the Lord, thereby imposing an oath on the tribes. And (2) he reformulates the pledge into a negative as well as positive condition to invoke divine retribution for their noncompliance.

20. ***at the instance of the LORD*** Hebrew *lifnei YHVH*, which occurs seven times in this chapter (vv. 20,21,22 [2], 27,29,32), a number that signifies the importance of the phrase (see Excursus 69). As rendered, it affirms that Israel can only succeed by the grace of the Lord.[36] Alternatively, and preferably, this idiom should be rendered (with the exception of v. 22b) "before the Lord," that is, before the Ark, as in Exodus 16:33,34.[37] Implied is that Gad and Reuben as the *ḥaluts*-vanguard preceded the Ark in battle. According to this tradition, the Ark marched in front of the Israelites (see the Comment to 10:33), but in battle it followed the vanguard, a formation that is strikingly confirmed in the battle of Jericho (Josh. 6:7–13). There, it consisted of (1) the *ḥaluts*-vanguard (identified as Gad and Reuben);[38] (2) seven priests bearing seven trumpets (unique to this battle; see Excursus 21); (3) the Ark; and (4) the rear guard (the rest of the Israelites). Significant here is that ***lifnei 'aron YHVH***, "[the vanguard marching] in front of the Ark of the Lord," is equated in the next verse with ***lifnei YHVH***, "before the Lord" (see Josh. 6:7,8). Further confirmation of this rendering is that ***lifnei YHVH*** uttered by Moses intentionally counters ***lifnei benei yisra'el*** uttered by Gad and Reuben in their proposal (v. 17; and see v. 29). Just as the latter means "in the van of the Israelites" so the former must mean "in front of the Lord," that is, before His Ark. That the two phrases are actually equivalent in meaning is confirmed by the account that records the fulfillment of the pledge taken by Gad and Reuben. It uses both phrases: "The Reubenites, the Gadites . . . went across armed ***in the van of the Israelites***, as Moses had charged them. About forty thousand shock troops went across (literally) ***before the Lord***, to the steppes of Jericho for battle (Josh 4:12–13). Indeed, Targum Onkelos and Targum Jonathan agree to the same equation, rendering ***lifnei YHVH*** as "before the people of the Lord."

of the LORD, until He has dispossessed His enemies before Him, 22 and the land has been subdued, at the instance of the LORD, and then you return—you shall be clear before the LORD and before Israel; and this land shall be your holding under the LORD. 23 But if you do not do so, you will have sinned against the LORD; and know that your sin will overtake you. 24 Build towns for your children and sheepfolds for your flocks, but do what you have promised."

25 The Gadites and the Reubenites answered Moses, "Your servants will do as my lord commands. 26 Our children, our wives, our flocks, and all our other livestock will stay behind in the towns of Gilead; 27 while your servants, all those recruited for war, cross over, at the instance of the LORD, to engage in battle—as my lord orders."

אֶת־אֹיְבָיו מִפָּנָיו׃ 22 וְנִכְבְּשָׁה הָאָרֶץ לִפְנֵי יְהוָה
וְאַחַר תָּשֻׁבוּ וִהְיִיתֶם נְקִיִּם מֵיְהוָה וּמִיִּשְׂרָאֵל
וְהָיְתָה הָאָרֶץ הַזֹּאת לָכֶם לַאֲחֻזָּה לִפְנֵי יְהוָה׃
23 וְאִם־לֹא תַעֲשׂוּן כֵּן הִנֵּה חֲטָאתֶם לַיהוָה וּדְעוּ
חַטַּאתְכֶם אֲשֶׁר תִּמְצָא אֶתְכֶם׃ 24 בְּנוּ־לָכֶם
עָרִים לְטַפְּכֶם וּגְדֵרֹת לְצֹנַאֲכֶם וְהַיֹּצֵא מִפִּיכֶם
תַּעֲשׂוּ׃ 25 וַיֹּאמֶר בְּנֵי־גָד וּבְנֵי רְאוּבֵן אֶל־מֹשֶׁה
לֵאמֹר עֲבָדֶיךָ יַעֲשׂוּ כַּאֲשֶׁר אֲדֹנִי מְצַוֶּה׃ 26 טַפֵּנוּ
נָשֵׁינוּ מִקְנֵנוּ וְכָל־בְּהֶמְתֵּנוּ יִהְיוּ־שָׁם בְּעָרֵי
הַגִּלְעָד׃ 27 וַעֲבָדֶיךָ יַעַבְרוּ כָּל־חֲלוּץ צָבָא לִפְנֵי
יְהוָה לַמִּלְחָמָה כַּאֲשֶׁר אֲדֹנִי דֹּבֵר׃ 28 וַיְצַו לָהֶם

22. ***you shall be clear before*** Hebrew *vi-heyitem nekiyyim min*, that is, free of obligation (see Deut. 24:5), implying that they took an oath (see the Comment to v. 24). The root *n-k-h*, "be clear," is a legal term found in oath contexts.[39] The preposition *min* can mean "before," as in Job 4:17. That the apodosis begins with these words is shown by the negative condition in the next verse.

before the LORD and before Israel From which the rabbis deduce that "a man must satisfy mankind even as he satisfies God."[40]

under the LORD Hebrew *lifnei YHVH*, that is, by the Lord's will, equivalent to Hebrew *'im yirtseh ha-shem* and Arabic *insh'alla*.[41]

23. ***sinned against the LORD*** Implying that they had taken an oath (see the Comment to v. 24).

that your sin Rather, "your punishment";[42] a behavioral term can also imply its consequence.[43]

will overtake[44]

24. A chiastic response to verse 16.

what you have promised In an oath, as indicated by the use of the same phrase in the oath context of 30:3.

GAD AND REUBEN AGREE (vv. 25–27)

25. ***answered*** Hebrew *va-yo'mer*. The plural *va-yo'meru* would be expected and is in fact the reading in many manuscripts, the Septuagint, the Samaritan, and the Peshitta. Midrash, however, sees the singular as a collective implying "as if with one voice."[45]

26. ***our other livestock*** Hebrew *behemtenu*, that is, our donkeys (see the Comment to 31:9). This word had not appeared earlier in this chapter. Similarly the term for "women" appears for the first time. This detailed inventory is deliberate since it is the final comprehensive summary concerning those to be left behind. Heretofore *mikneh* included the livestock (see the Comment to v. 1) and *taf* included the women (see the Comment to v. 16).

behind[46]

27. ***recruited for war*** Hebrew *ḥaluts tsava'*, literally "picked (as shock troops) for the campaign" (see the Comment to 31:5).

at the instance of the LORD Rather, "before the Lord" (see the Comment to v. 20).

[28]Then Moses gave instructions concerning them to Eleazar the priest, Joshua son of Nun, and the family heads of the Israelite tribes. [29]Moses said to them, "If every shock-fighter among the Gadites and the Reubenites crosses the Jordan with you to do battle, at the instance of the LORD, and the land is subdued before you, you shall give them the land of Gilead as a holding. [30]But if they do not cross over with you as shock-troops, they shall receive holdings among you in the land of Canaan."

מֹשֶׁה אֵת אֶלְעָזָר הַכֹּהֵן וְאֵת יְהוֹשֻׁעַ בִּן־נוּן וְאֶת־
רָאשֵׁי אֲבוֹת הַמַּטּוֹת לִבְנֵי יִשְׂרָאֵל׃ 29 וַיֹּאמֶר
מֹשֶׁה אֲלֵהֶם אִם־יַעַבְרוּ בְנֵי־גָד וּבְנֵי־רְאוּבֵן ׀
אִתְּכֶם אֶת־הַיַּרְדֵּן כָּל־חָלוּץ לַמִּלְחָמָה לִפְנֵי
יְהוָה וְנִכְבְּשָׁה הָאָרֶץ לִפְנֵיכֶם וּנְתַתֶּם לָהֶם אֶת־
אֶרֶץ הַגִּלְעָד לַאֲחֻזָּה׃ 30 וְאִם־לֹא יַעַבְרוּ חֲלוּצִים
אִתְּכֶם וְנֹאחֲזוּ בְתֹכְכֶם בְּאֶרֶץ כְּנָעַן׃ 31 וַיַּעֲנוּ

THE ESSENCE OF THE COMPROMISE FORMULA (vv. 28–30)

It is repeated in slightly revised form to those responsible for its execution: Eleazar, Joshua, and the clan leaders.[47] Moses includes the consequences if Gad and Reuben reject the imposed conditions by refusing to take the oath.

28. concerning them[48]

Eleazar He takes precedence over Joshua, also in apportioning the land (34:17) and in war (27:21), where the Urim and Thummim must be employed (see the Comment to 26:55 and Excursus 64).

the family heads[49]

THE VALID CONDITION (vv. 29–30)

From this double statement, positive and negative, Rabbi Meir deduces that "every condition that is not like that imposed on Gad and Reuben is not a valid condition."[50] According to the rabbis, every condition must contain these four elements: (1) It is stated twice, as a positive and negative; (2) the positive precedes the negative; (3) the condition precedes the consequence; (4) the condition is capable of being fulfilled.[51]

at the instance of the LORD See the Comment to verse 20.

30. But if they do not . . . shock troops That is, but if they do not take the oath (see the next Comment). The Septuagint adds: "to war before the Lord, then you shall move across their possessions and their wives and their cattle before you into the land of Canaan, and" explicating the following clause.

they shall receive holdings Hebrew *ve-no'ḥazu*. For this usage, see Genesis 34:10; 47:27; Josh. 22:9,19). The absence of divine punishment as in Moses' original formulation (v. 29) would be disturbing unless Moses again altered his formulation to include a new consequence: If Gad and Reuben reject these conditions, that is, if they refuse to risk their lives as shock troops, and therefore refuse to take the oath, then they will be treated no differently from any other tribe. They will be assigned land to conquer in Cisjordan.[52] This solution is again proposed by Israel when the Transjordanian tribes allegedly commit the heresy of erecting a separate altar (Josh. 22:15).

GAD AND REUBEN REPEAT THEIR ACCEPTANCE (vv. 31–32)

What Gad and Reuben have promised Moses privately (vv. 16–19, especially v. 19) they now repeat publicly before Eleazar, Joshua, and the clan heads, presumably under oath (see the Comment to v. 22) and stipulating the consequences for nonfulfillment (see the Comment to v. 23).

Whatever the LORD has spoken That is, whatever Moses has spoken. Hence, Moses need not fear that we will disobey.[53]

concerning[54]

31 The Gadites and the Reubenites said in reply, "Whatever the LORD has spoken concerning your servants, that we
will do. 32 We ourselves will cross over as shock-troops, at
the instance of the LORD, into the land of Canaan; and we
shall keep our hereditary holding across the Jordan."

33 So Moses assigned to them—to the Gadites, the Reubenites, and the half-tribe of Manasseh son of Joseph—the
kingdom of Sihon king of the Amorites and the kingdom of
King Og of Bashan, the land with its various cities and the
territories of their surrounding towns. 34 The Gadites rebuilt Dibon, Ataroth, Aroer, 35 Atroth-shophan, Jazer, Jog-

בְּנֵי־גָד וּבְנֵי רְאוּבֵן לֵאמֹר אֵת אֲשֶׁר דִּבֶּר יְהוָה
אֶל־עֲבָדֶיךָ כֵּן נַעֲשֶׂה׃ 32 נַחְנוּ נַעֲבֹר חֲלוּצִים
לִפְנֵי יְהוָה אֶרֶץ כְּנָעַן וְאִתָּנוּ אֲחֻזַּת נַחֲלָתֵנוּ
מֵעֵבֶר לַיַּרְדֵּן׃ 33 וַיִּתֵּן לָהֶם ׀ מֹשֶׁה לִבְנֵי־גָד
וְלִבְנֵי רְאוּבֵן וְלַחֲצִי ׀ שֵׁבֶט ׀ מְנַשֶּׁה בֶן־יוֹסֵף אֶת־
מַמְלֶכֶת סִיחֹן מֶלֶךְ הָאֱמֹרִי וְאֶת־מַמְלֶכֶת עוֹג
מֶלֶךְ הַבָּשָׁן הָאָרֶץ לְעָרֶיהָ בִּגְבֻלֹת עָרֵי הָאָרֶץ
סָבִיב׃ 34 וַיִּבְנוּ בְנֵי־גָד אֶת־דִּיבֹן וְאֶת־עֲטָרֹת
וְאֵת עֲרֹעֵר׃ 35 וְאֶת־עַטְרֹת שׁוֹפָן וְאֶת־יַעְזֵר

32. *at the instance of the LORD* See the Comment to verse 20.

and we shall keep Hebrew *ve-'ittanu*, literally "and with us"; that is, it is in our power.[55] Alternatively, "if we can keep."[56] The Septuagint reads *u-tenu*, "and grant" (see v. 33).

THE GRANT OF TRANSJORDAN (vv. 33–38)

Moses grants the conquered areas of Transjordan to Gad and Reuben and the half-tribe of Manasseh. The former two tribes rebuild not only the two of the nine towns they had requested (v. 3) but also five more, perhaps as a reward for their loyalty. But even this larger list is further amplified in Joshua 13, which shows that it is selective.[57] For a discussion of the problems in this section, see Excursus 70.

33. *assigned* Hebrew *va-yitten*, fulfilling Gad and Reuben's request (*yuttan*) of verse 5. This seems to contradict verse 29, which stipulates that their land would be given them by Israel's leaders only upon the subsequent fulfillment of their pledge. However, the difference in the wording should be carefully noted. The tribes request that land as their permanent *'ahuzzah*, "holding," or *nahalah*, "share" (vv. 5,19,32 [2]). And Moses promises that if they carry out their pledge, the land will, indeed, be granted them as their "holding" (vv. 22,29). (The terms *'ahuzzah/nahalah* occur seven times [vv. 5,18,19,22,29,32(2)]—an indication of their importance; see Excursus 69.) Indeed, when Moses accepted their terms, he expressly permitted them to rebuild the destroyed towns (v. 24) but it was not to be for a "holding" (v. 22) until they fulfilled their promise. Here too the term "holding" is conspicuously absent. Moses thus gives Gad and Reuben the land *provisionally*—to rebuild its destroyed towns and settle their dependents and livestock therein but not to possess it until the leaders certify that they have fulfilled their conditions.

The verb *natan*, "assign," is significant in another respect. The nine and one-half remaining tribes will receive their land by lot (33:54), whereas the Transjordanian tribes have their land "assigned," that is, by Moses, not by God. God, as it were, will have nothing to do with the settling of Transjordan (see Excursus 70).

the half-tribe of Manasseh[58]

the kingdom of Sihon Which lies between the Arnon and the Jabbok.[59]

the kingdom of King Og of Bashan Occupied by the half-tribe of Manasseh (see 21:33–35). This phrase is probably a later addition.

the land with its various cities[60]

34. *rebuilt* Hebrew *va-yivnu*. For this usage, see Isaiah 58:12 and 61:4 (also Ezek. 36:36; Amos 9:14; Mesha 9,27).

Dibon, Ataroth See verse 3.

Aroer The name survives in modern 'Ara'ir just north of the Arnon and thus belongs to the southern group of Gadite towns (see the Comment to v. 3). But it may have been absorbed by

behah, 36Beth-nimrah, and Beth-haran as fortified towns or
as enclosures for flocks. 37The Reubenites rebuilt Heshbon,
Elealeh, Kiriathaim, 38Nebo, Baal-meon—some names
being changed—and Sibmah; they gave [their own] names
to towns that they rebuilt. 39The descendants of Machir son
of Manasseh went to Gilead and captured it, dispossessing
the Amorites who were there; 40so Moses gave Gilead to

וְיָגְבְּהָֽה׃ 36 וְאֶת־בֵּ֥ית נִמְרָ֖ה וְאֶת־בֵּ֣ית הָרָ֑ן עָרֵ֥י
מִבְצָ֖ר וְגִדְרֹ֥ת צֹֽאן׃ 37 וּבְנֵ֤י רְאוּבֵן֙ בָּנ֔וּ אֶת־
חֶשְׁבּ֖וֹן וְאֶת־אֶלְעָלֵ֑א וְאֵ֖ת קִרְיָתָֽיִם׃ 38 וְאֶת־נְב֞וֹ
וְאֶת־בַּ֧עַל מְע֛וֹן מֽוּסַבֹּ֥ת שֵׁ֖ם וְאֶת־שִׂבְמָ֑ה וַיִּקְרְא֣וּ
בְשֵׁמֹ֔ת אֶת־שְׁמ֥וֹת הֶעָרִ֖ים אֲשֶׁ֥ר בָּנֽוּ׃ מפטיר
39 וַיֵּ֨לְכ֜וּ בְּנֵ֥י מָכִ֛יר בֶּן־מְנַשֶּׁ֖ה גִּלְעָ֣דָה וַיִּלְכְּדֻ֑הָ
וַיּ֖וֹרֶשׁ אֶת־הָאֱמֹרִ֥י אֲשֶׁר־בָּֽהּ׃ 40 וַיִּתֵּ֤ן מֹשֶׁה֙ אֶת־

Reuben (Josh. 13:16) at a later date (see Excursus 70). It was of strategic importance because the king's highway ran past it (see the Comment to 20:17).

35. Atroth-shophan Mentioned only here, it is probably associated with Ataroth (see the Comment to v. 3).

Jazer See the Comment to 21:32.

Jogbehah Mentioned only once more, together with Nobah (v. 42) in Judges 8:11. It is generally identified with Gubeihat or Khirbet el-Ajbeihat, 11.2 kilometers (7 mi.) northwest of Amman, making it the northernmost Gadite site in this chapter.

36. Beth-nimrah Equivalent to Nimrah (see v. 3).

Beth-haran Written as Beth-haram in Joshua 13:27, generally identified with Tell 'Iktanu, just west of Heshbon.

37. Heshbon See the Comment to 21:25.

Elealeh See verse 3.

Kiriathaim See below on Baal-meon.

38. Nebo See the Comment to verse 3.

Baal-meon So Ezekiel 25:9 and 1 Chronicles 5:8. It is a variant of Beth-meon (Jer. 48:23), conflated as Beth-baal-meon (Josh. 13:17) and as Beon (v. 3). According to Mesha 7–10, Baal-meon and Kiriathaim are located in "Madaba's land" (see Map 5). Both towns are also associated with and, hence, in the proximity of Nebo (Jer. 48:1; Ezek. 25:9). Their exact location is unknown, although Ma'in, 7 kilometers (4 mi.) southwest of Madaba, is probably to be identified with Baal-meon.

some names being changed Hebrew ***musabbot shem*** (as in 2 Kings 23:34) is probably an editorial gloss directing the reader to substitute for the last two names, which are or contain foreign deities.[61] Similarly, the later scribes' dislike of the pagan name Baal led to the change of Eshbaal and Meribbaal to Ish-bosheth and Mephibosheth, respectively (cf. 1 Chron. 8:33 with 2 Sam. 2:8 and 1 Chron. 9:40 with 2 Sam. 4:4). Unfortunately, the new names are not given here. Later sources, such as Isaiah 15:2, Jeremiah 48:22, and Ezekiel 28:9, still use these older pagan names, but by this time the places were under the control of the Moabites who may have restored their use.[62]

Sibmah[63]

[their own] names[64]

MANASSITE INCURSIONS INTO UPPER TRANSJORDAN (vv. 39–42)

This refers to the territory of Og (21:33–35). There are difficulties in the placing of this section after the preceding: (1) Manasseh had previously played no role; (2) the point of origin of the Manassite clans is not mentioned; (3) it defies the basic postulate of the chapter: the unified action of all Israel; (4) its language also differs; resembling that of Judges 1, it looks like an account of conquest following Moses' death. For a fuller discussion see Excursus 70.

Machir son of Manasseh, and he settled there. 41 Jair son of Manasseh went and captured their villages, which he renamed Havvoth-jair. 42 And Nobah went and captured Kenath and its dependencies, renaming it Nobah after himself.

הַגִּלְעָד לְמָכִיר בֶּן־מְנַשֶּׁה וַיֵּשֶׁב בָּהּ: 41 וְיָאִיר בֶּן־
מְנַשֶּׁה הָלַךְ וַיִּלְכֹּד אֶת־חַוֺּתֵיהֶם וַיִּקְרָא אֶתְהֶן
חַוֺּת יָאִיר: 42 וְנֹבַח הָלַךְ וַיִּלְכֹּד אֶת־קְנָת וְאֶת־
בְּנֹתֶיהָ וַיִּקְרָא לָה נֹבַח בִּשְׁמוֹ: פ

39. The descendants of Machir Rather, "the Machirites," that is, members of the clan of Machir (26:29; and see the Comment to v. 40). In the genealogies, Machir is the son of Manasseh (v. 40) and the father of Gilead (26:29; 27:1). That the sons of Machir were adopted by Joseph (Gen. 50:23) probably implies that Machir was considered part of the "house of Joseph." Many scholars theorize that originally Machir was located in Cisjordan (Judg. 5:14) but that after Deborah's time, it migrated east and conquered large tracts of Transjordan. Hence the designation: the father of Gilead. Manasseh then replaced and superseded Machir in the west. Hence Manasseh's designation: the father of Machir.[65]

son of Rather, "descendant of."

Gilead That is, upper Gilead, north of the Jabbok (see the Comment to v. 1).

went . . . captured it[66]

dispossessing[67]

40. This verse is integral to its context: Moses confirms Machir's conquest as he has confirmed the claims of the two and a half tribes in Transjordan (v. 33; Deut. 3:13,16). The verse also complements 21:35—just as Israel "settled" in Sihon's territory, below the Jabbok (21:24), so Machir "settles" in (northern) Gilead, above the Jabbok. That the Manassites first conquered the upper Gilead without receiving Moses' permission is explicable by the fact that this territory (unlike the territory of Reuben and Gad) was part of the promised land but not assigned to any particular tribe (see Excursus 73).

son of Rather, "descendant of."

41. Jair Perhaps Jair, the individual, was made judge of Israel (Judg. 10:3–5) after his victory, as Jephthah was made judge and Saul was made king after their victories over the Ammonites (Judg. 11:8–11; 12:7; 1 Sam. 1:1–15).

son of Rather, "descendant of."

their villages Hebrew *ḥavvoteihem* (with the Targums). Rather, "their fortified villages."[68] To avoid the problem of the absence of an antecedent for "their," it is possible to read *ḥavvoth ham*, "their fortified villages of Ham."[69] Ham (see Gen. 14:5) is located 8 kilometers (5 mi.) south of modern Irbid in the Bashan. Alternatively, *ḥavvah*, "village," is related to the *ḥyy* (2 Sam. 23:11,13) and to the cognates *ḥawâ* (Arabic for a circle of tents) and *wḥyt* (Egyptian for designating a nomadic tribe). However, the rendering "fortified villages" is preferable.

Havvoth-jair This region[70] is identified with the Argob district (Deut. 3:13), probably situated just below the Yarmuk.

42. Nobah Probably a Manassite clan.[71] If identified with Kenath, then it is located in the eastern Bashan and is the only settlement recorded in this chapter north of the Yarmuk. This conquest does not represent a "Transjordanian problem" (see Excursus 69) since the Bashan was part of the promised land (see the Comment to v. 40).

Kenath Probably identified with modern Qanawat, at the foot of Mount Hauran (Jebel Druze), 11 kilometers (7 mi.) northwest of Es-suweida. The reference to its dependencies indicates that it was an important city-state. It is mentioned in Egyptian sources as early as the execration texts (19–18th cent. B.C.E.) and in the conquest lists of Thutmose III and Amenhotep III as well as in the El-Amarna letters (204:4). Its change of name to Nobah is accounted for in this verse. It was conquered

MASE'EI

33 These were the marches of the Israelites who started out from the land of Egypt, troop by troop, in the charge of Moses and Aaron. 2Moses recorded the starting points of

מסעי

ל״ג אֵלֶּה מַסְעֵי בְנֵי־יִשְׂרָאֵל אֲשֶׁר יָצְאוּ מֵאֶרֶץ
מִצְרַיִם לְצִבְאֹתָם בְּיַד־מֹשֶׁה וְאַהֲרֹן: 2 וַיִּכְתֹּב

by Geshur and Aram-Damascus (1 Chron. 2:23) probably during the reign of Baasha, when the name Kenath was restored.[72] In the Hellenistic period it was a member of a federation of Greek cities in Palestine, originally ten in number (Decapolis). Rabbinic tradition cites Kenath as the most north-easterly point of the land of Israel, possessed by the returnees from the Babylonian exile.[73] The identification of Kenath with Nobah is complicated by Judges 8:11, which associates Nobah with Jogbehah (see v. 35). That would place it south of the Jabbok. However, this Nobah, if correctly transmitted, may refer to another site by the same name.

Nobah after himself As the Danites did when they conquered Laish and renamed it Dan (Judg. 18:29).

CHAPTER 33

The Wilderness Itinerary (vv. 1–49)

Mase'ei There are forty-two stations, or forty-one legs, between the starting point, Rameses, and the final encampment at the Jordan. The itinerary divides into three sections: Rameses to the Sinai wilderness (vv. 5–15), the Sinai wilderness to Kadesh (vv. 16–36), and Kadesh to the steppes of Moab (vv. 37–49). (The route is marked on Map 2.) The actual direction of the first two sections is in doubt since the site of Sinai is unknown. Section three assumes (with 21:4; Deut. 2:1–8) that the route from Kadesh cut across the southern border of Edom. The stations in verses 19–30 are attested nowhere else (see Excursus 71).

The placement of the itinerary here is logical. The wilderness has been traversed (chaps. 1–21), and all the incidents that occurred in Transjordan are accounted for (chaps. 22–32). This chapter (vv. 1–49) now sums up the trek through the wilderness. Henceforth, the account concerns itself solely with what transpires in the promised land (33:50–36:13). Also of significance is that the station Dibon-gad (v. 45) presupposes its occupation by the tribe of Gad, an event first recorded in the previous chapter (32:38).

Why the need for this summary? Maimonides explains: "People would think that [the Israelites] sojourned in a desert that was near to cultivated land and in which man can live, like the deserts inhabited at present by the Arabs, or that it consisted of places in which it was possible to till and to reap or to feed on plants that were to be found there, or that there were wells of water in those places. Therefore all these fancies are rebutted and the traditional relation of all these miracles is confirmed through the enumeration of those stations."[1] The midrash testifies to a similar motivation: "The Holy One Blessed Be He said to Moses: 'Write down the stages by which Israel journeyed in the wilderness, in order that they shall know what miracles I wrought for them.'"[2] The midrash also records the following view: "The Holy One Blessed Be He said to Moses: 'Recount to them all the places where they provoked Me.'"[3] The ambivalence of the midrash is justified: Scripture attests to both motivations for remembering the wilderness sojourn (e.g., Deut. 8:14–16; 9:7).

*1. **These*** Hebrew *'elleh*, a sign of an archival document.[4]

the marches of Alternatively, "the stages of" with the Septuagint. See the Comment to 10:12, and see Genesis 13:3.

troop by troop Another reminder that Israel marched in military formation. See the Comments to 1:3 and 10:14–28.

in the charge of Hebrew *be-yad*. For this usage, see 31:49 and 2 Samuel 18:2.

their various marches as directed by the LORD. Their
marches, by starting points, were as follows:
3 They set out from Rameses in the first month, on the
fifteenth day of the first month. It was on the morrow of the
passover offering that the Israelites started out defiantly, in
plain view of all the Egyptians.
4 The Egyptians meanwhile
were burying those among them whom the LORD had
struck down, every first-born—whereby the LORD executed
judgment on their gods.
5 The Israelites set out from Rameses and encamped at
Succoth.
6 They set out from Succoth and encamped at
Etham, which is on the edge of the wilderness.
7 They set
out from Etham and turned about toward Pi-hahiroth,
which faces Baal-zephon, and they encamped before
Migdol.
8 They set out from Pene-hahiroth and passed
through the sea into the wilderness; and they made a three-
days' journey in the wilderness of Etham and encamped at

מֹשֶׁה אֶת־מוֹצָאֵיהֶם לְמַסְעֵיהֶם עַל־פִּי יְהוָה וְאֵלֶּה
מַסְעֵיהֶם לְמוֹצָאֵיהֶם׃
3 וַיִּסְעוּ מֵרַעְמְסֵס בַּחֹדֶשׁ
הָרִאשׁוֹן בַּחֲמִשָּׁה עָשָׂר יוֹם לַחֹדֶשׁ הָרִאשׁוֹן
מִמָּחֳרַת הַפֶּסַח יָצְאוּ בְנֵי־יִשְׂרָאֵל בְּיָד רָמָה לְעֵינֵי
כָּל־מִצְרָיִם׃
4 וּמִצְרַיִם מְקַבְּרִים אֵת אֲשֶׁר הִכָּה
יְהוָה בָּהֶם כָּל־בְּכוֹר וּבֵאלֹהֵיהֶם עָשָׂה יְהוָה
שְׁפָטִים׃
5 וַיִּסְעוּ בְנֵי־יִשְׂרָאֵל מֵרַעְמְסֵס וַיַּחֲנוּ
בְּסֻכֹּת׃
6 וַיִּסְעוּ מִסֻּכֹּת וַיַּחֲנוּ בְאֵתָם אֲשֶׁר בִּקְצֵה
הַמִּדְבָּר׃
7 וַיִּסְעוּ מֵאֵתָם וַיָּשָׁב עַל־פִּי הַחִירֹת
אֲשֶׁר עַל־פְּנֵי בַּעַל צְפוֹן וַיַּחֲנוּ לִפְנֵי מִגְדֹּל׃
8 וַיִּסְעוּ מִפְּנֵי הַחִירֹת וַיַּעַבְרוּ בְתוֹךְ־הַיָּם
הַמִּדְבָּרָה וַיֵּלְכוּ דֶּרֶךְ שְׁלֹשֶׁת יָמִים בְּמִדְבַּר אֵתָם
וַיַּחֲנוּ בְּמָרָה׃
9 וַיִּסְעוּ מִמָּרָה וַיָּבֹאוּ אֵילִמָה

2. ***Moses recorded*** This notice must be taken seriously; see Excursus 71.[5]

the starting points But Moses did not record other data such as the date and distance covered for each stage in the journey. For the genre of itinerary reflected here and its significance, see Excursus 71.

as directed by the LORD Refers to Israel's marches, as Ibn Ezra noted (see 9:20,23). However, Ramban believes that this phrase refers to Moses' recording of the itinerary. According to the former view, Moses wrote down the itinerary on his own initiative.

Their marches, by starting points The notice of Mosaic authorship (v. 2a) necessitates this repetitive resumption of verse 1a, but in chiastic order.

3. ***morrow of the passover offering*** It was sacrificed at twilight on the previous day, as noted in 9:3 and Exodus 12:2,6.

defiantly Literally, "with upraised hand." The rendering, as also in 15:30, is supported by the next clause, "in plain view of all the Egyptians."

in plain view That is, in broad daylight, the same tradition as in Numbers 25:6 and Exodus 12:10,22. Deuteronomy 16:1 declares that the Exodus took place at night.

4. ***meanwhile***[6]

whereby Implied is that the means of punishing Egypt's gods, otherwise undescribed, was by striking down the first-born. Alternatively, the *vav* should be rendered "and," the judgment on Egypt's gods being a discrete punishment. This view presupposes an older story that told of the Lord's battles against the gods of Egypt, hinted at in Exodus 12:12.

5. ***Rameses*** See Exodus 12:37. It is identified with Qantir or Tanis in the eastern delta of the Nile. The journey from Rameses is repeated (from v. 3a) because of the long intervening parenthetical note on the date and event of the Exodus.

6. ***Succoth . . . Etham*** See Exodus 13:20. They are generally taken to be situated in Wadi Tumilat between Lake Timsah and the Bitter Lakes (see Map 1).

7. ***turned about***[7] Instead of marching east into the desert, Israel turned southward along the Bitter Lakes where the pursuing Egyptians caught up with them.

8. ***passed through the sea*** Before the Suez Canal was dug, there had been a shallow fordable stretch of water about 3.2 kilometers (2 mi.) wide below the Bitter Lakes. In ancient times the

Marah. 9They set out from Marah and came to Elim. There
were twelve springs in Elim and seventy palm trees, so they
encamped there. 10They set out from Elim and encamped
by the Sea of Reeds. 11They set out from the Sea of Reeds
and encamped in the wilderness of Sin. 12They set out from
the wilderness of Sin and encamped at Dophkah. 13They set
out from Dophkah and encamped at Alush. 14They set out
from Alush and encamped at Rephidim; it was there that
the people had no water to drink. 15They set out from

וּבְאֵילִ֗ם שְׁתֵּ֥ים עֶשְׂרֵ֛ה עֵינֹ֥ת מַ֖יִם וְשִׁבְעִ֣ים
תְּמָרִ֑ים וַיַּחֲנוּ־שָֽׁם׃ 10 וַיִּסְע֖וּ מֵאֵילִ֑ם וַֽיַּחֲנ֖וּ עַל־
יַם־סֽוּף׃ שני 11 וַיִּסְע֖וּ מִיַּם־ס֑וּף וַֽיַּחֲנ֖וּ בְּמִדְבַּר־
סִֽין׃ 12 וַיִּסְע֖וּ מִמִּדְבַּר־סִ֑ין וַֽיַּחֲנ֖וּ בְּדָפְקָֽה׃
13 וַיִּסְע֖וּ מִדָּפְקָ֑ה וַֽיַּחֲנ֖וּ בְּאָלֽוּשׁ׃ 14 וַיִּסְע֖וּ
מֵאָל֑וּשׁ וַֽיַּחֲנוּ֙ בִּרְפִידִ֔ם וְלֹא־הָ֨יָה שָׁ֥ם מַ֛יִם לָעָ֖ם
לִשְׁתּֽוֹת׃ 15 וַיִּסְע֖וּ מֵרְפִידִ֑ם וַֽיַּחֲנ֖וּ בְּמִדְבַּ֥ר סִינָֽי׃

Bitter Lakes, at present only 1.8 meters (6 ft.) above the level of the Gulf of Suez, were probably connected with it.[8]

they made a three-days' journey This is the only reference in this chapter to the time it took to cover one of the stages. It may be an allusion to the three-day journey into the wilderness that Israel pledged to Pharaoh, as recorded in Exodus 3:18, and implies that they kept their word (Exod. 15:22). This gloss is not the work of an editor but is integral to the itinerary (see Excursus 71).

wilderness of Etham Although identified as Shur in Exodus 15:22, this need not imply two versions. Etham is simply Egyptian for Hebrew Shur, both meaning "wall, fortification." The location probably refers to the defense line built by the Egyptians along the present Suez Canal.

Marah See Exodus 15:23. Bir el-Muwrah, 14.4 kilometers (9 mi.) east of Suez has been suggested.[9] There are no springs between the Bitter Lakes, the possible site of Israel's crossing, and Bir el-Muwrah.

9. Elim See Exodus 15:27. The comment is typical of ancient Near Eastern military itineraries: an account of the sources of water and food (see Excursus 71). Midrash would seek a loftier significance: "In Elim there were twelve fountains of water for the twelve tribes, and seventy palm trees corresponding to the seventy sages"[10] (mentioned in 11:16). Uyun-Musa ("Springs of Moses"), a large oasis just south of Suez along the eastern coast, has been suggested.[11] Today it has twelve wells and palm and tamarisk groves, the latter the natural source for the manna (see the Comment to 11:6).

10. Sea of Reeds Rather, "Red Sea"[12] (see the Comment to 21:4). This station is not mentioned elsewhere. The same holds true for the Gulf of Akaba (see the Comment to 21:4). In the open waters of either gulf there are no reeds. This station clearly indicates that the line of march, at this point in the itinerary, was southward.

11. wilderness of Sin See Exodus 16:1. It is in this wilderness that there appeared the manna covered by a layer of dew, as described in Exodus 16:14–15. The phenomenon can be explained on natural grounds by positing an oasis of tamarisk groves and a relatively high humidity. The only area in the Sinai Peninsula that meets these two requirements is near Suez.[13] The miracle of the quail may also have occurred here since these birds do not fly too far inland (on which see the Comment to 11:31).

12–13. Dophkah ... Alush Unidentified. The term *le-mas'eihem*, "by stages," used in the description of the journey between the wilderness of Sin and Rephidim (Exod. 17:1), alludes to these intermediate stations.[14] This would suggest the conclusion that the itinerary of Numbers 33 was the source of the individual itinerary notes in Exodus and elsewhere in Numbers (see Excursus 71).

14. Rephidim If Israel traveled along the eastern shore of the Gulf of Suez, it would reach the modern Wadi Refayid, 48 kilometers (30 mi.) from the southern tip of the Sinai Peninsula, which is the usually accepted location. However, the absence of water there indicates that Israel left the Suez coast with its many springs and approached the hills of at-Tiya, east of Uyum-Musa, near the entrance of Wadi Suder.[15]

no water to drink See Exodus 17:1. The narrative omits the war with Amalek at Rephidim as well as the manna at Sin, the revelation at Sinai, and other notable events of the wilderness trek for

Rephidim and encamped in the wilderness of Sinai. 16They
set out from the wilderness of Sinai and encamped at
Kibroth-hattaavah. 17They set out from Kibroth-hattaavah
and encamped at Hazeroth. 18They set out from Hazeroth
and encamped at Rithmah. 19They set out from Rithmah
and encamped at Rimmon-perez. 20They set out from
Rimmon-perez and encamped at Libnah. 21They set out
from Libnah and encamped at Rissah. 22They set out from
Rissah and encamped at Kehelath. 23They set out from
Kehelath and encamped at Mount Shepher. 24They set out
from Mount Shepher and encamped at Haradah. 25They set
out from Haradah and encamped at Makheloth. 26They set
out from Makheloth and encamped at Tahath. 27They set
out from Tahath and encamped at Terah. 28They set out
from Terah and encamped at Mithkah. 29They set out from
Mithkah and encamped at Hashmonah. 30They set out
from Hashmonah and encamped at Moseroth. 31They set
out from Moseroth and encamped at Bene-jaakan. 32They
set out from Bene-jaakan and encamped at Hor-haggidgad.

16 וַיִּסְעוּ מִמִּדְבַּר סִינָי וַיַּחֲנוּ בְּקִבְרֹת הַתַּאֲוָה׃
17 וַיִּסְעוּ מִקִּבְרֹת הַתַּאֲוָה וַיַּחֲנוּ בַּחֲצֵרֹת׃
18 וַיִּסְעוּ מֵחֲצֵרֹת וַיַּחֲנוּ בְּרִתְמָה׃ 19 וַיִּסְעוּ
מֵרִתְמָה וַיַּחֲנוּ בְּרִמֹּן פָּרֶץ׃ 20 וַיִּסְעוּ מֵרִמֹּן פָּרֶץ
וַיַּחֲנוּ בְּלִבְנָה׃ 21 וַיִּסְעוּ מִלִּבְנָה וַיַּחֲנוּ בְּרִסָּה׃
22 וַיִּסְעוּ מֵרִסָּה וַיַּחֲנוּ בִּקְהֵלָתָה׃ 23 וַיִּסְעוּ
מִקְּהֵלָתָה וַיַּחֲנוּ בְּהַר־שָׁפֶר׃ 24 וַיִּסְעוּ מֵהַר־שָׁפֶר
וַיַּחֲנוּ בַּחֲרָדָה׃ 25 וַיִּסְעוּ מֵחֲרָדָה וַיַּחֲנוּ בְּמַקְהֵלֹת׃
26 וַיִּסְעוּ מִמַּקְהֵלֹת וַיַּחֲנוּ בְּתָחַת׃ 27 וַיִּסְעוּ
מִתָּחַת וַיַּחֲנוּ בְּתָרַח׃ 28 וַיִּסְעוּ מִתָּרַח וַיַּחֲנוּ
בְּמִתְקָה׃ 29 וַיִּסְעוּ מִמִּתְקָה וַיַּחֲנוּ בְּחַשְׁמֹנָה׃
30 וַיִּסְעוּ מֵחַשְׁמֹנָה וַיַּחֲנוּ בְּמֹסֵרוֹת׃ 31 וַיִּסְעוּ
מִמֹּסֵרוֹת וַיַּחֲנוּ בִּבְנֵי יַעֲקָן׃ 32 וַיִּסְעוּ מִבְּנֵי יַעֲקָן
וַיַּחֲנוּ בְּחֹר הַגִּדְגָּד׃ 33 וַיִּסְעוּ מֵחֹר הַגִּדְגָּד וַיַּחֲנוּ

the reason that these are so well known that they need no repetition.[16] In the present case, however, only the beginning of the account is cited. The rest of it, found in Exodus 17:1–16, presumably not only lay before the writer of the itinerary but was also known to his readers (see further at v. 40).

15. the wilderness of Sinai See Exodus 19:1–2. The region has not been identified with certainty. The identification of Sinai with Jebel Sin Bisher,[17] about 48 kilometers (30 mi.) southeast of Suez, has much to commend it. At 579 meters (1,900 ft.) high and 305 meters (1,000 ft.) above the plain, it alone fits the two distances specified in Scripture: a three-day journey from Egypt (Exod. 3:18) and eleven days from Kadesh-barnea (Deut. 1:2). The widely accepted identification of Mount Sinai with Jebel Musa in southern Sinai has been effectively refuted by Harel on the following grounds: (1) The area cannot support many people; (2) fishing is good here (whereas 11:5 bewails the lack of fish); (3) the many Egyptian-owned mines that were in the area at the time were guarded by Egyptian troops; (4) Jebel Musa is more than a three-day trip from Egypt (Exod. 5:3) and an eleven-day trip to Kadesh (350 km.; 210 mi.). A location in Edom or Midian (northwestern Arabia) is equally improbable since it would place Mount Sinai too far from Egypt and would also render absurd Hobab's wish to return to his homeland (10:29). He would already have been there!

16. See 11:34–35. The site is unidentified. On the absence of Taberah from the itinerary see the Comment to 11:3. Also missing are Mattanah, Nahaliel and Bamoth, mentioned in 21:19.[18]

17. See 11:35 and 12:16. Hazeroth has been equated with the philologically equivalent Ain/Wadi Hudeirat, about 64 kilometers (40 mi.) northeast of Jebel Musa. However, doubts about the latter identification are automatically transferred to the former.

18–29. None of these stations is mentioned elsewhere.[19] The area occupied by these stations, identified with the desert of Paran,[20] is covered with gravel and contains little vegetation and scant sources of water, fitting the description: "We set out from Horeb [Sinai] and traveled the great and terrible wilderness" (Deut. 1:19).

30–34. These sites are unidentified. In spite of differences in order and form, the four stations are identical with those in the itinerary fragment of Deuteronomy 10:6–7. The latter also differs in placing Aaron's death at Moserah instead of at Mount Hor in verse 38 here (see the Comment to 20:23). Jotbath (written in the text as *yotbatah*) has given its name to Kibbutz Yotbatah, 40 kilometers (25 mi.) north of Elath.

[33]They set out from Hor-haggidgad and encamped at Jotbath. [34]They set out from Jotbath and encamped at Abronah. [35]They set out from Abronah and encamped at Ezion-geber. [36]They set out from Ezion-geber and encamped in the wilderness of Zin, that is, Kadesh. [37]They set out from Kadesh and encamped at Mount Hor, on the edge of the land of Edom.

[38]Aaron the priest ascended Mount Hor at the command of the LORD and died there, in the fortieth year after the Israelites had left the land of Egypt, on the first day of the fifth month. [39]Aaron was a hundred and twenty-three years old when he died on Mount Hor. [40]And the Canaanite, king of Arad, who dwelt in the Negeb, in the land of Canaan, learned of the coming of the Israelites.

[41]They set out from Mount Hor and encamped at Zalmonah. [42]They set out from Zalmonah and encamped at Punon. [43]They set out from Punon and encamped at Oboth. [44]They set out from Oboth and encamped at Iye-abarim, in the territory of Moab. [45]They set out from Iyim

בְּיָטְבָתָה: 34 וַיִּסְעוּ מִיָּטְבָתָה וַיַּחֲנוּ בְּעַבְרֹנָה:
35 וַיִּסְעוּ מֵעַבְרֹנָה וַיַּחֲנוּ בְּעֶצְיֹן גָּבֶר: 36 וַיִּסְעוּ
מֵעֶצְיֹן גָּבֶר וַיַּחֲנוּ בְמִדְבַּר־צִן הִוא קָדֵשׁ:
37 וַיִּסְעוּ מִקָּדֵשׁ וַיַּחֲנוּ בְּהֹר הָהָר בִּקְצֵה אֶרֶץ
אֱדוֹם: 38 וַיַּעַל אַהֲרֹן הַכֹּהֵן אֶל־הֹר הָהָר עַל־פִּי
יְהוָה וַיָּמָת שָׁם בִּשְׁנַת הָאַרְבָּעִים לְצֵאת בְּנֵי־
יִשְׂרָאֵל מֵאֶרֶץ מִצְרַיִם בַּחֹדֶשׁ הַחֲמִישִׁי בְּאֶחָד
לַחֹדֶשׁ: 39 וְאַהֲרֹן בֶּן־שָׁלֹשׁ וְעֶשְׂרִים וּמְאַת שָׁנָה
בְּמֹתוֹ בְּהֹר הָהָר: ס 40 וַיִּשְׁמַע הַכְּנַעֲנִי
מֶלֶךְ עֲרָד וְהוּא־יֹשֵׁב בַּנֶּגֶב בְּאֶרֶץ כְּנָעַן בְּבֹא בְּנֵי
יִשְׂרָאֵל: 41 וַיִּסְעוּ מֵהֹר הָהָר וַיַּחֲנוּ בְּצַלְמֹנָה:
42 וַיִּסְעוּ מִצַּלְמֹנָה וַיַּחֲנוּ בְּפוּנֹן: 43 וַיִּסְעוּ מִפּוּנֹן
וַיַּחֲנוּ בְּאֹבֹת: 44 וַיִּסְעוּ מֵאֹבֹת וַיַּחֲנוּ בְּעִיֵּי
הָעֲבָרִים בִּגְבוּל מוֹאָב: 45 וַיִּסְעוּ מֵעִיִּים וַיַּחֲנוּ

35. Ezion-geber Usually identified with Tell el-Kheleifeh at modern Elath.[21] Ezion-geber has recently been identified with nearby Akaba, whereas Abronah (v. 34) has been identified with Tell el-Kheleifeh.[22]

36. Kadesh The general location of the site seems certain (see the Comment to 13:26), which raises a problem: As it is more than 80 kilometers (50 mi.) from Ezion-geber, it could not have been reached in one day. The following solutions have been proposed: (1) The route was well known and used by the Israelites in the time of the monarchy, as demonstrated by recent excavations at Kuntilet ʿAjrud, a point along the way. A route that was familiar would have been only cursorily described, omitting intermediate stages. (2) Two routes have been incorporated in this chapter: Egypt–Ezion-geber via southern Sinai and a northern route, Kadesh-Transjordan.[23] (3) Verses 36b–41a should be transposed to follow verse 30a[24] or verse 18a.[25] Or (4) this may be a different Kadesh on the border of Edom (see the Comment to 20:16). Proposals 2, 3, and 4 are highly conjectural. Proposal 1 is more satisfactory, especially if one assumes that not every place where Israel encamped for the night was named and recorded.

A more difficult problem is that Kadesh is one of the last stations on this itinerary. This would mean, presumably, that Israel reached it at the end of its wilderness sojourn, since they arrive at their next stop in the fortieth year (v. 38). However, this itinerary, which does not record the length of stay at each station, may presuppose a long stay at Kadesh. Furthermore, a late arrival would clash with Deuteronomy 2:14, which holds that Israel spent thirty-eight years at Kadesh. This problem has not been satisfactorily resolved (for details see the Comment to 20:2).

38. See 20:22–29.

40. This verse recounts almost verbatim the beginning of the brief story of the victorious battle against the Canaanites of 21:1–3. Clearly, then, the account of 21:1–3 was before the writer and known to his readers; he had merely to quote the opening line to allude to the complete version.

the coming[26]

41–42. Zalmonah . . . Punon See the Comment to 21:4.

43–44. Oboth . . . Iye-abarim See the Comment to 21:10–11. Verses 41–49 give the impression that Israel cut through the territory of Edom and Moab, a view also held by Deuteronomy 2:2–13,29 (see the Comment to 20:19–21).

and encamped at Dibon-gad. 46They set out from Dibon-gad and encamped at Almon-diblathaim. 47They set out from Almon-diblathaim and encamped in the hills of Abarim, before Nebo. 48They set out from the hills of Abarim and encamped in the steppes of Moab, at the Jordan near Jericho; 49they encamped by the Jordan from Beth-jeshimoth as far as Abel-shittim, in the steppes of Moab.

50In the steppes of Moab, at the Jordan near Jericho, the LORD spoke to Moses, saying: 51Speak to the Israelite

בְּדִיבֹן גָּד׃ 46 וַיִּסְעוּ מִדִּיבֹן גָּד וַיַּחֲנוּ בְּעַלְמֹן
דִּבְלָתָיְמָה׃ 47 וַיִּסְעוּ מֵעַלְמֹן דִּבְלָתָיְמָה וַיַּחֲנוּ
בְּהָרֵי הָעֲבָרִים לִפְנֵי נְבוֹ׃ 48 וַיִּסְעוּ מֵהָרֵי הָעֲבָרִים
וַיַּחֲנוּ בְּעַרְבֹת מוֹאָב עַל יַרְדֵּן יְרֵחוֹ׃ 49 וַיַּחֲנוּ עַל־
הַיַּרְדֵּן מִבֵּית הַיְשִׁמֹת עַד אָבֵל הַשִּׁטִּים בְּעַרְבֹת
מוֹאָב׃ ס שלישי [חמישי כשהן
מחוברות] 50 וַיְדַבֵּר יְהוָה אֶל־מֹשֶׁה בְּעַרְבֹת
מוֹאָב עַל־יַרְדֵּן יְרֵחוֹ לֵאמֹר׃ 51 דַּבֵּר אֶל־בְּנֵי

45. *Dibon-gad* Presupposes the occupation of Dibon by the tribe of Gad (32:34), which may account for placing the itinerary here.

46. *Almon-diblathaim* Perhaps it is identical with Beth-diblathaim mentioned in Jeremiah 48:22 (and see the Mesha inscription, line 30). It may be a conflation of two names: Baal-meon and Beth-diblathaim.[27]

47. *hills of Abarim* See 27:12.

49. *Beth-jeshimoth* See Joshua 12:3 and 13:20 and Ezekiel 25:9. It is identified with Tell el-ʿAzeimah, 19 kilometers (12 mi.) southeast of Jericho. According to Eusebius's *Onomasticon*, it is by the Dead Sea, 16 kilometers (10 mi.) south of Jericho.

as far as Abel-shittim Identified with Tell Kefrein in the highlands, about 8 kilometers (5 mi.) from the Jordan, and 11 kilometers (7 mi.) from the Dead Sea, according to Josephus.[28] If correct, these figures give an idea of the dimensions of the encampment. Rabba bar Bar Ḥana estimates that it measured 3-by-3 parsangs (a parsang is a Persian mile, about 1,219 meters [4000 yds.]).[29] The next stage is the crossing of the Jordan into the promised land (see Josh. 3:1).

The Division of Canaan (vv. 33:50–35:44)

Having completed its wilderness trek (chaps. 1–21, 33:1–49), secured its base at the Jordan against all enemies (chaps. 22–25,31), allowed two and a half tribes to settle in Transjordan (chap. 32), and resolved the problem of who will be its leader (27:12–23), Israel can turn its undivided attention to the conquest and apportionment of Canaan. Each pericope begins in an identical manner: God commands Moses to transmit instructions to Israel (33:50; 34:1,16; 35:1,9). The instructions begin, nearly always, the same way: "When you cross the Jordan to the land of Canaan" (33:51; 34:2; 35:10). The topics of the divine command are sequentially logical: the conquest and apportionment of the land (33:50–56), defined by precise boundaries (34:1–15), under the supervision of designated chieftains (34:16–29), who will also appropriate forty-eight towns for the Levites (35:1–8) and six Levitical towns as asylums for the involuntary homicide (35:9–34).

This entire section serves as a consolation to Moses: Barred from the promised land, he at least merits the privilege of drawing the blueprint for its apportionment.[30]

THE COMMAND (vv. 50–56)

The command to apportion the land was given in 26:52–56. Why is it repeated here in verse 54? In chapter 26, the land was apportioned to the clans of all twelve tribes. In chapter 32, two tribes chose instead to settle in Transjordan, and subsequently some Manassite clans settled there (see the

people and say to them: When you cross the Jordan into the
land of Canaan, 52 you shall dispossess all the inhabitants of
the land; you shall destroy all their figured objects; you
shall destroy all their molten images, and you shall demolish all their cult places. 53 And you shall take possession of
the land and settle in it, for I have assigned the land to you
to possess. 54 You shall apportion the land among yourselves by lot, clan by clan: with larger groups increase the
share, with smaller groups reduce the share. Wherever the

יִשְׂרָאֵל וְאָמַרְתָּ אֲלֵהֶם כִּי אַתֶּם עֹבְרִים אֶת־
הַיַּרְדֵּן אֶל־אֶרֶץ כְּנָעַן׃ 52 וְהוֹרַשְׁתֶּם אֶת־כָּל־
יֹשְׁבֵי הָאָרֶץ מִפְּנֵיכֶם וְאִבַּדְתֶּם אֵת כָּל־מַשְׂכִּיֹּתָם
וְאֵת כָּל־צַלְמֵי מַסֵּכֹתָם תְּאַבֵּדוּ וְאֵת כָּל־בָּמוֹתָם
תַּשְׁמִידוּ׃ 53 וְהוֹרַשְׁתֶּם אֶת־הָאָרֶץ וִישַׁבְתֶּם־בָּהּ
כִּי לָכֶם נָתַתִּי אֶת־הָאָרֶץ לָרֶשֶׁת אֹתָהּ׃
54 וְהִתְנַחַלְתֶּם אֶת־הָאָרֶץ בְּגוֹרָל לְמִשְׁפְּחֹתֵיכֶם
לָרַב תַּרְבּוּ אֶת־נַחֲלָתוֹ וְלַמְעַט תַּמְעִיט אֶת־

introductory Comment to 32:39–42). Thus, the land needs to be divided among the remaining nine tribes, and it is to them that the command is now addressed.

50. *In the steppes of Moab* Having encamped there at the end of its wilderness trek (v. 48), Israel still has not reached its goal: the conquest of Canaan. The divine command is now issued.

near Hebrew *ʿal*, but on the other side of the Jordan (see the Comment to 22:1).

51. *When you cross* Hebrew *ki ʾatem ʿoverim*. The participle is used because the crossing is imminent (also in 34:2; 35:10).[31]

52. *you shall dispossess* Hebrew *ve-horashtem*. God is usually the subject of this verb, as in Joshua 23:5. Divine aid is presumed here, even though Israel is commanded to drive out the Canaanites (see the Comment to v. 56).

You shall destroy[32]

their figured objects Hebrew *maskiyotam*. This translation is an educated guess, as the etymology is unknown (see Lev. 26:1; Ezek. 8:12; Prov. 25:11). Perhaps the reference is to inlaid work.

their molten[33]

images Perhaps *tselem* was chosen to balance the alliterative series of *ts* words in verse 55 (see Excursus 72).

their cult places Leviticus 26:30 is the only other passage in the Torah (and in Joshua) where ***bamah*** is used in this sense. It occurs frequently in the early historical narratives dealing with Israel in Canaan. There is no description of a ***bamah*** in the Bible nor is there, as yet, any archaeological find that can with certainty be identified as the ***bamah***. Most likely it is an open-air altar.[34]

53. *And* Rather, "Then," the beginning of the apodosis, which states the reward for clearing the land of its inhabitants and their cult objects (see Excursus 72).

take possession Hebrew *ve-horashtem*[35] usually means "dispossess" (as in v. 52). In this case, however, that would make sense only if followed by "the inhabitants of" (as in v. 52)—a reading given by the Septuagint and the Targums and supported by the symmetry of verse 55b (see Excursus 72). Nevertheless, the rendering "take possession" also has scriptural warrant. It is so used in 14:24 and especially in Joshua 8:7 and 17:12. Indeed, it makes more sense in this context since the insertion of "the inhabitants of" would equate both protasis and apodosis (see v. 52a), creating an unintelligible redundancy.

for I have assigned the land to you Literally, "[for it is] to you [that I have given the land]"; ***lakhem***, "to you," is expressed first for emphasis.

54. *You shall apportion . . . among yourselves*[36]

clan by clan The tribal boundaries are to be decided by lot (end of verse; 26:55), but the actual division of the land is by clan (see Excursus 62).

the share . . . the share Literally, "its share . . . its share," the antecedent of which is the clan.

lot falls for anyone, that shall be his. You shall have your portions according to your ancestral tribes. 55 But if you do not dispossess the inhabitants of the land, those whom you allow to remain shall be stings in your eyes and thorns in your sides, and they shall harass you in the land in which you live; 56 so that I will do to you what I planned to do to them.

נַחֲלָתוֹ אֶל֩ אֲשֶׁר־יֵ֨צֵא לוֹ שָׁמָּה הַגּוֹרָל לוֹ יִהְיֶה
לְמַטּוֹת אֲבֹתֵיכֶם תִּתְנֶחָלוּ׃ 55 וְאִם־לֹא תוֹרִישׁוּ
אֶת־יֹשְׁבֵי הָאָרֶץ֮ מִפְּנֵיכֶם֒ וְהָיָה אֲשֶׁר תּוֹתִירוּ
מֵהֶם לְשִׂכִּים בְּעֵינֵיכֶם וְלִצְנִינִם בְּצִדֵּיכֶם וְצָרְרוּ
אֶתְכֶם עַל־הָאָרֶץ אֲשֶׁר אַתֶּם יֹשְׁבִים בָּהּ׃
56 וְהָיָה כַּאֲשֶׁר דִּמִּיתִי לַעֲשׂוֹת לָהֶם אֶעֱשֶׂה
לָכֶם׃ פ

anyone . . . his Hebrew *lo . . . lo*, again referring to the individual clan. The implication is that the location of the clan, as well as of the tribe, will be determined by lot.

according to your ancestral tribes The clan can be assigned land only within its tribe's boundaries.

55. ***stings*** Hebrew *sikkim*, found only here, is related to Akkadian *šikkatu*, "nail, point," *šakāku*, "be pointed." In the parallel passage, Joshua 23:13, the word *shotet*, "scourge," is used. *Sikkim* may have been chosen to match ***maskiyotam*** in verse 52 (see Excursus 72).

The "stings" and "thorns" imply acts of physical violence committed against the Israelites by the remaining Canaanite enclaves, as indicated by the following clause: "they shall harass you." However, the two clauses may also convey discrete meanings: In the parallel passages, stings and thorns are either bracketed with or replaced by "snares" and "traps" (see Exod. 23:33; 34:12; Deut. 7:16; Josh. 23:13), implying that the remaining inhabitants will entice the Israelites to embrace their religion.[37] This danger is stated explicitly in Exodus 23:33: "They shall not remain in your land, lest they cause you to sin against Me; for you will serve their gods—and it will prove a snare to you." This interpretation is supported by the literary structure of this pericope (see Excursus 72).

thorns Hebrew *tseninim*. Used elsewhere only in Joshua 23:13, where it replaces and is equivalent to "stings."

thorns in your sides, and they shall harass Hebrew *tseninim be-tsiddeikhem ve-tsareru*, a succession of three alliterative *ts* sounds, perhaps accounting for the choice of these words and balancing the alliteration of verse 52.[38]

harass Hebrew *tsareru*. For the usage, see the Comment to 25:16.

56. ***I planned*** Hebrew *dimiti*.[39] For this usage, see Judges 20:5, Isaiah 14:24, and Psalms 50:21. The means used by God to destroy the Canaanites is made explicit in Exodus 23:27–28.

to do to them Although Israel is commanded to evict the Canaanites, it is the divine will that guarantees their success. Regarding the fate of the Canaanites—only the older sources state that they will be evicted, either by divine agency, as in Exodus 23:20–31, or by Israel's efforts, as maintained here in verses 52–56. Deuteronomy, however, imposes the *ḥerem* on the Canaanites (see Excursus 44), specifying that none of them shall be spared (Deut. 7:2,16; 20:16). That neither option was adopted and that Canaanites coexisted with Israel is explicitly stated by Scripture, as in 1 Kings 9:21.[40]

CHAPTER 34 THE BOUNDARIES OF THE PROMISED LAND (vv. 1–15)

Its area includes the mountains of Lebanon and Sirion (Anti-Lebanon), extending as far north as Lebo, thereby including the Damascus region and the Bashan, reaching the Galilee along the Yarmuk valley (but excluding the Gilead and southern Transjordan), and extending as far south as Kadesh before entering the Mediterranean at El-ʿArish (see Map 3). The boundaries are described by a series of border points just as are the boundaries of the individual tribes in Joshua 15–19. These borders do not correspond to Israel's territory at any time in its history; they do, however, coincide with the Egyptian province of Canaan during the fifteenth through thirteenth centuries (see Excursus 73 for the significance of this fact). This map was reflected in the account of the scouts' reconnaissance of

34 The LORD spoke to Moses, saying: 2 Instruct the Israelite people and say to them: When you enter the land of Canaan, this is the land that shall fall to you as your portion, the land of Canaan with its various boundaries:

3 Your southern sector shall extend from the wilderness of Zin alongside Edom. Your southern boundary shall start on the east from the tip of the Dead Sea. 4 Your boundary shall then turn to pass south of the ascent of Akrabbim and continue to Zin, and its limits shall be south of Kadesh-barnea, reaching Hazar-addar and continuing to Azmon.

ל״ד וַיְדַבֵּר יְהוָה אֶל־מֹשֶׁה לֵּאמֹר׃ 2 צַו אֶת־
בְּנֵי יִשְׂרָאֵל וְאָמַרְתָּ אֲלֵהֶם כִּי־אַתֶּם בָּאִים אֶל־
הָאָרֶץ כְּנָעַן זֹאת הָאָרֶץ אֲשֶׁר תִּפֹּל לָכֶם בְּנַחֲלָה
אֶרֶץ כְּנַעַן לִגְבֻלֹתֶיהָ׃ 3 וְהָיָה לָכֶם פְּאַת־נֶגֶב
מִמִּדְבַּר־צִן עַל־יְדֵי אֱדוֹם וְהָיָה לָכֶם גְּבוּל נֶגֶב
מִקְצֵה יָם־הַמֶּלַח קֵדְמָה׃ 4 וְנָסַב לָכֶם הַגְּבוּל
מִנֶּגֶב לְמַעֲלֵה עַקְרַבִּים וְעָבַר צִנָה והיה תּוֹצְאֹתָיו
מִנֶּגֶב לְקָדֵשׁ בַּרְנֵעַ וְיָצָא חֲצַר־אַדָּר וְעָבַר
עַצְמֹנָה׃ 5 וְנָסַב הַגְּבוּל מֵעַצְמוֹן נַחְלָה מִצְרָיִם

v. 4 וְהָיוּ ק׳

Canaan in 13:21 (see also Josh. 13:2–5). However, its chief influence is upon the prophet Ezekiel who, in 47:15–48:29, rearranged the tribal territories in his futuristic map of Israel to accord with the borders of ancient (Egyptian) Canaan. The present map, although ascribed to Moses, reflects the period after the conquest when the chieftains actually apportioned the land (see Josh. 15–19) to the tribes in the exact geographical order from south to north as the tribal chieftains are listed (vv. 16–29). This chapter follows logically upon 33:50–56. Having been commanded to displace and replace the present occupants of the land, it becomes imperative to know its boundaries.[1]

2. ***When*** See the Comment to 33:51.

the land of Canaan Hebrew *ha-'arets kena'an*, literally "the land, Canaan."[2] It can also be an ellipsis for "the land [the land of], Canaan."[3]

fall That is, by lot (see v. 13). For this usage of Hebrew *tipol*, see Judges 18:9 and Ezekiel 47:14. The command to apportion the land, already given, as in 26:52–56 and 33:54, needs to be repeated since Canaan will now be divided among nine and a half tribes, not twelve, as originally planned.[4]

as your portion Rather, "as your perpetual patrimony" (see the Comment to 27:7).

the land of Canaan Its borders are congruent with those of the Egyptian province of Canaan during the second half of the second millennium (see Excursus 73).

with its various boundaries Rather, "as defined by its borders."

3. ***sector*** Hebrew *pe'ah*. Rather, "limit, side" (Num. 35:5; Josh. 18:12; Ezek. 47:19; 48:23–29).

alongside Edom[5] Since the southern border begins on the eastern side of the Dead Sea, it abuts the northern and western edges of Edom (see Map 3). Alternatively, the territory of Edom may have extended west of the Arabah (see the Comments to 20:16,23; see also Josh. 15:1), in which case a longer stretch of Israel's southern border would have adjoined Edom's northern border.

on the east Hebrew *kedmah*, in place of which Joshua 15:2 reads "from the tongue that projects southward," that is, from the southernmost tip of the Dead Sea. This implies that "on the east" does not refer to the Dead Sea but to the boundary, the description of which will begin on the east (see v. 15).

Dead Sea Hebrew *yam ha-melaḥ*, literally "Salt Sea," also called "Eastern Sea" in Ezekiel 47:18 and "Arabah Sea" in Deuteronomy 3:17 and 4:49.

4. ***turn*** At this point the boundary changes its course.[6]

ascent of Akrabbim Literally, "ascent of Scorpions," a site at present unknown.

Zin Perhaps a point along the boundary rather than the wilderness of the same name (20:1).

limits The terminus of the southwestern line (see Map 3).

5From Azmon the boundary shall turn toward the Wadi of Egypt and terminate at the Sea.

6For the western boundary you shall have the coast of the Great Sea; that shall serve as your western boundary.

7This shall be your northern boundary: Draw a line from the Great Sea to Mount Hor; 8from Mount Hor draw a line to Lebo-hamath, and let the boundary reach Zedad. 9The

וְהָי֥וּ תוֹצְאֹתָ֖יו הַיָּֽמָּה׃ 6 וּגְב֣וּל יָ֔ם וְהָיָ֥ה לָכֶ֛ם הַיָּ֥ם
הַגָּד֖וֹל וּגְב֑וּל זֶה־יִהְיֶ֥ה לָכֶ֖ם גְּב֥וּל יָֽם׃ 7 וְזֶה־יִהְיֶ֥ה
לָכֶ֖ם גְּב֣וּל צָפ֑וֹן מִן־הַיָּם֙ הַגָּדֹ֔ל תְּתָא֥וּ לָכֶ֖ם הֹ֥ר
הָהָֽר׃ 8 מֵהֹ֣ר הָהָ֔ר תְּתָא֖וּ לְבֹ֣א חֲמָ֑ת וְהָי֛וּ תּוֹצְאֹ֥ת
הַגְּבֻ֖ל צְדָֽדָה׃ 9 וְיָצָ֤א הַגְּבֻל֙ זִפְרֹ֔נָה וְהָי֥וּ תוֹצְאֹתָ֖יו

south of Kadesh-barnea It is thus within Israel's territory (see Josh. 10:41). Its location is not certain. Kadesh has been identified with ʿAin Qadesh (see the Comment to 13:26) and Kadesh-barnea, with the area around Kadesh that boasts additional oases, including Ein el-Qudeirat. ʿAin Qadesh suffers from insufficient water—perhaps accounting for Israel's murmuring there (20:1–12)—but Ein el-Qudeirat has an ample supply because it lies west of the watershed and is exposed to the prevailing westerlies from the sea. It may have been controlled then by the stronger Amalekites (14:45).[7] Kadesh-barnea, located on the natural border between the Negev and Sinai, was settled and fortified at the beginning of the Davidic monarchy.[8]

Hazar-addar The southern boundary of Canaan is identical with the southern boundary of Judah, as described in Joshua 15:3. This place-name is there broken into two, Hezron and Addar, and another boundary point, Karka, is added. These three place-names may refer to three known additional oases in the Kadesh area.[9]

Azmon Unknown.

5. ***turn*** To the northwest (see Map 3).

toward the Wadi of Egypt Hebrew ***naḥlah mitsrayim***, modern Wadi El-ʿArish, a long and deep watercourse that is full only after a substantial rain. It constitutes a natural barrier between the Negev and the Sinai Peninsula.

the Sea The Mediterranean. One would expect the concluding phrase: "That shall be your southern boundary" (see vv. 6,9,12).

6. ***western*** Hebrew ***yam***, literally "sea." The Mediterranean is the western border of Canaan.

the coast Hebrew ***u-gevul***,[10] literally "and the boundary." For the usage, see Deuteronomy 3:16–17 and Joshua 13:23,27 and 15:12,47. All these citations refer to bodies of water. Thus the expression signifies the shore or land's edge. Alternatively, read ***u-gevulo***, "its coast."[11]

7. ***Draw a line***[12]

from the Great Sea That is, the Mediterranean. But where? The probable point lies just north of Byblos, in present-day Lebanon, which marked the northern boundary of the Egyptian province of Canaan according to the peace treaty between Ramses II and the Hittites at the beginning of the thirteenth century B.C.E. (see Map 3 and Excursus 73).

Mount Hor Not the Mount Hor that lies near the border of Edom where Aaron died (20:22–29; 33:38). It is probably one of the northwestern summits of the Lebanese range north of Byblos (perhaps Ras Shaqqah or Jebel Akkar). Ezekiel 47:15 gives Hethlon as a northern boundary point; it is identified with modern Heitela, northwest of Tripoli at the foot of Jebel Akkar and south of the Eleuthera River, which separates Syria and Lebanon.[13] The rabbis identify it with Mount Amana (Song 4:8), modern Zebedani, the source of the Amanah River (2 Kings 5:12), modern Barada, which flows through Damascus.[14]

8. ***Lebo-hamath*** See the Comment to 13:21. The description of the northern border in Joshua 13:4 adds Aphek, modern Afqa, 24 kilometers (15 mi.) east of Byblos (see Map 3).

reach Rather, "terminate." The boundary line from Lebo-hamath terminates at Zedad and from there takes a different direction (see Map 3).

boundary shall then run to Ziphron and terminate at
Hazar-enan. That shall be your northern boundary.
10 For your eastern boundary you shall draw a line from
Hazar-enan to Shepham. 11 From Shepham the boundary
shall descend to Riblah on the east side of Ain; from there
the boundary shall continue downward and abut on the
eastern slopes of the Sea of Chinnereth. 12 The boundary
shall then descend along the Jordan and terminate at the
Dead Sea.
That shall be your land as defined by its boundaries on all
sides.

13 Moses instructed the Israelites, saying: This is the land
you are to receive by lot as your hereditary portion, which
the LORD has commanded to be given to the nine and a half
tribes. 14 For the Reubenite tribe by its ancestral houses, the
Gadite tribe by its ancestral houses, and the half-tribe of
Manasseh have already received their portions: 15 those two
and a half tribes have received their portions across the
Jordan, opposite Jericho, on the east, the orient side.
16 The LORD spoke to Moses, saying: 17 These are the

חֲצַר עֵינָן זֶה־יִהְיֶה לָכֶם גְּבוּל צָפוֹן׃
10 וְהִתְאַוִּיתֶם לָכֶם לִגְבוּל קֵדְמָה מֵחֲצַר עֵינָן
שְׁפָמָה׃ 11 וְיָרַד הַגְּבֻל מִשְּׁפָם הָרִבְלָה מִקֶּדֶם
לָעָיִן וְיָרַד הַגְּבוּל וּמָחָה עַל־כֶּתֶף יָם־כִּנֶּרֶת
קֵדְמָה׃ 12 וְיָרַד הַגְּבוּל הַיַּרְדֵּנָה וְהָיוּ תוֹצְאֹתָיו יָם
הַמֶּלַח זֹאת תִּהְיֶה לָכֶם הָאָרֶץ לִגְבֻלֹתֶיהָ סָבִיב׃
13 וַיְצַו מֹשֶׁה אֶת־בְּנֵי יִשְׂרָאֵל לֵאמֹר זֹאת הָאָרֶץ
אֲשֶׁר תִּתְנַחֲלוּ אֹתָהּ בְּגוֹרָל אֲשֶׁר צִוָּה יְהֹוָה לָתֵת
לְתִשְׁעַת הַמַּטּוֹת וַחֲצִי הַמַּטֶּה׃ 14 כִּי לָקְחוּ מַטֵּה
בְנֵי הָראוּבֵנִי לְבֵית אֲבֹתָם וּמַטֵּה בְנֵי־הַגָּדִי לְבֵית
אֲבֹתָם וַחֲצִי מַטֵּה מְנַשֶּׁה לָקְחוּ נַחֲלָתָם׃ 15 שְׁנֵי
הַמַּטּוֹת וַחֲצִי הַמַּטֶּה לָקְחוּ נַחֲלָתָם מֵעֵבֶר לְיַרְדֵּן
יְרֵחוֹ קֵדְמָה מִזְרָחָה׃ פ רביעי [ששי
כשהן מחוברות] 16 וַיְדַבֵּר יְהֹוָה אֶל־מֹשֶׁה
לֵּאמֹר׃ 17 אֵלֶּה שְׁמוֹת הָאֲנָשִׁים אֲשֶׁר־יִנְחֲלוּ
לָכֶם אֶת־הָאָרֶץ אֶלְעָזָר הַכֹּהֵן וִיהוֹשֻׁעַ בִּן־נוּן׃

Zedad Present-day Tsada, east of the Sirion (Anti-Lebanon range) near the Damascus-Homs highway, 56 kilometers (35 mi.) northeast of Lebweh (Lebo).

*9. **Ziphron . . . Hazar-enan*** Unknown. They may be the two known oases east of Zedad, Hawwarin and Qaryatein.

*10. **draw a line*** See the Comment to verse 7.

*11. **Shepham . . . Riblah . . . Ain*** Unknown. Riblah is not to be confused with the Riblah in the Lebanese Bika north of Lebo.[15] The uncertain identification of any of the sites mentioned in verses 9–11a renders the northeast boundary conjectural (see Map 3).

abut Hebrew ***maḥah***, "strike" (Ps. 98:8),[16] which, like ***naga'***[17] and ***paga'*** (35:21), can mean both "touch" and "strike."

slopes Hebrew ***ketef***, literally "shoulder." In Joshua (15:8,10–11; 18:12–13) and Isaiah (11:14), it means "side, flank."

Sea of Chinnereth Probably named after the town on its shores (Deut. 3:17; Josh. 19:35). In Second Temple days it was called Gennesar (1 Macc. 11:67) or Gennesaret (Matt. 14:34) and, in talmudic times, the Sea of Tiberias.[18]

13–15. These verses repeat the opening statement of verse 2b, thereby framing verses 1–15 in an inclusion while adding the explanation that the land has to be reallotted in order to be divided among nine and a half tribes and not twelve as originally planned (see the Comment to 33:50–56).

*13. **you are to receive by lot*** Hebrew *titnaḥalu . . . be-goral*. For the usage, see 33:54.

*14. **and the half-tribe of Manasseh***[19]

THE APPORTIONMENT (vv. 16–29)

The chieftains listed here appear for the first time—with the exception of Caleb and Joshua, the lone survivors of the generation of the Exodus to enter the promised land (see 14:30,38). The order of the

names of the men through whom the land shall be apportioned for you: Eleazar the priest and Joshua son of Nun. [18]And you shall also take a chieftain from each tribe through whom the land shall be apportioned. [19]These are the names of the men: from the tribe of Judah: Caleb son of Jephunneh. [20]From the Simeonite tribe: Samuel son of Ammihud. [21]From the tribe of Benjamin: Elidad son of Chislon. [22]From the Danite tribe: a chieftain, Bukki son of Jogli. [23]For the descendants of Joseph: from the Manassite tribe: a chieftain, Hanniel son of Ephod; [24]and from the Ephraimite tribe: a chieftain, Kemuel son of Shiphtan. [25]From the Zebulunite tribe: a chieftain, Elizaphan son of Parnach. [26]From the Issacharite tribe: a chieftain, Paltiel son of Azzan. [27]From the Asherite tribe: a chieftain, Ahihud son of Shelomi. [28]From the Naphtalite tribe: a chieftain, Pedahel son of Ammihud.

[29]It was these whom the LORD designated to allot portions to the Israelites in the land of Canaan.

18 וְנָשִׂיא אֶחָד נָשִׂיא אֶחָד מִמַּטֶּה תִּקְחוּ לִנְחֹל
אֶת־הָאָרֶץ׃ 19 וְאֵלֶּה שְׁמוֹת הָאֲנָשִׁים לְמַטֵּה
יְהוּדָה כָּלֵב בֶּן־יְפֻנֶּה׃ 20 וּלְמַטֵּה בְּנֵי שִׁמְעוֹן
שְׁמוּאֵל בֶּן־עַמִּיהוּד׃ 21 לְמַטֵּה בִנְיָמִן אֱלִידָד בֶּן־
כִּסְלוֹן׃ 22 וּלְמַטֵּה בְנֵי־דָן נָשִׂיא בֻּקִּי בֶּן־יָגְלִי׃
23 לִבְנֵי יוֹסֵף לְמַטֵּה בְנֵי־מְנַשֶּׁה נָשִׂיא חַנִּיאֵל בֶּן־
אֵפֹד׃ 24 וּלְמַטֵּה בְנֵי־אֶפְרַיִם נָשִׂיא קְמוּאֵל בֶּן־
שִׁפְטָן׃ 25 וּלְמַטֵּה בְנֵי־זְבוּלֻן נָשִׂיא אֱלִיצָפָן בֶּן־
פַּרְנָךְ׃ 26 וּלְמַטֵּה בְנֵי־יִשָּׂשכָר נָשִׂיא פַּלְטִיאֵל בֶּן־
עַזָּן׃ 27 וּלְמַטֵּה בְנֵי־אָשֵׁר נָשִׂיא אֲחִיהוּד בֶּן־
שְׁלֹמִי׃ 28 וּלְמַטֵּה בְנֵי־נַפְתָּלִי נָשִׂיא פְּדַהְאֵל בֶּן־
עַמִּיהוּד׃ 29 אֵלֶּה אֲשֶׁר צִוָּה יְהוָה לְנַחֵל אֶת־בְּנֵי־
יִשְׂרָאֵל בְּאֶרֶץ כְּנָעַן׃ פ חמישי

35 The LORD spoke to Moses in the steppes of Moab at the Jordan near Jericho, saying: [2]Instruct the Israelite

ל״ה וַיְדַבֵּר יְהוָה אֶל־מֹשֶׁה בְּעַרְבֹת מוֹאָב עַל־
יַרְדֵּן יְרֵחוֹ לֵאמֹר׃ 2 צַו אֶת־בְּנֵי יִשְׂרָאֵל וְנָתְנוּ

tribes follows their geographical relationship in Canaan, from south to north, except that Judah precedes Simeon (so that Judah, the chief tribe, may head the list) and Manasseh (the first-born) precedes Ephraim (see also the Comment to 26:28). There is, as yet, no satisfactory explanation of why the leaders of the first three tribes enumerated—Judah, Simeon, and Benjamin—are not given the title "chieftain."

17. through whom . . . shall be apportioned for you Rather, "who shall apportion . . . to you."[20]

Eleazar . . . Joshua They take the place of Moses and Aaron in the generation of the conquest. Eleazar is named first since Joshua will have to consult him (27:21).[21]

18. you shall also take The plural verb *tikḥu* probably refers to Eleazar and Joshua, who will supervise the apportionment of the land.

through whom . . . shall be apportioned Rather, "who shall apportion." (See the Comment to v. 17.)

19. These are the names of the men Repeated from verse 17a because of the intervening parenthetical comment.[22]

21. tribe of Benjamin[23]

25. Parnach A Persian name.[24] The original Hebrew form, which is probably close to the received form, cannot be restored.

CHAPTER 35 THE LEVITICAL TOWNS (vv. 1–8)

Instructions to the Levites always follow those given to the other tribes.[1] Hence, here too, the Levites only receive their apportionment after the other tribes have received theirs. Although the Levites are

people to assign, out of the holdings apportioned to them,
towns for the Levites to dwell in; you shall also assign to
the Levites pasture land around their towns. [3]The towns
shall be theirs to dwell in, and the pasture shall be for the
cattle they own and all their other beasts. [4]The town
pasture that you are to assign to the Levites shall extend a
thousand cubits outside the town wall all around. [5]You

לַלְוִיִּם מִנַּחֲלַת אֲחֻזָּתָם עָרִים לָשָׁבֶת וּמִגְרָשׁ
לֶעָרִים סְבִיבֹתֵיהֶם תִּתְּנוּ לַלְוִיִּם׃ 3 וְהָיוּ הֶעָרִים
לָהֶם לָשָׁבֶת וּמִגְרְשֵׁיהֶם יִהְיוּ לִבְהֶמְתָּם וְלִרְכֻשָׁם
וּלְכֹל חַיָּתָם׃ 4 וּמִגְרְשֵׁי הֶעָרִים אֲשֶׁר תִּתְּנוּ
לַלְוִיִּם מִקִּיר הָעִיר וָחוּצָה אֶלֶף אַמָּה סָבִיב׃

to receive no permanent property in the promised land (18:23), this restriction applies solely to farmland. They are, however, provided permanent residences for themselves and pasturage for their livestock in the form of forty-eight towns and their surrounding fields (the measurements of which take into account variations in the size of the towns and the possibility of their growth; see Excursus 74). The execution of these prescriptions is recorded in Joshua 21.[2] The realistic and utilitarian aspects of the town planning is explained in Excursuses 74 and 75.[3]

1. at the Jordan near Jericho Literally, "at the Jordan of Jericho," that is, at the Jordan, which flows by Jericho. This is more precisely designated as *me-ʿever*, "opposite," the Jordan near Jericho in 22:1. This entire verse is identical to 33:50.

2. assign For the verb *natan*, "assign," see the Comments to 3:9 and 8:16,19. The assignment of the Levitical towns will be done by lot, as reported in Joshua 21:4,10,20.

out of the holdings apportioned to them Hebrew *mi-naḥalat ʾaḥuzzatam*, literally "from the inherited land of their holdings," a combination found only here. The reverse order is also attested, *ʾaḥuzzat naḥalah*, literally "holding of inherited land" or "hereditary holding" (27:7). For the meaning of the two terms that comprise this idiom, see the Comments to 27:4,7.

to dwell in The Levites require dwellings[4] although they are to receive no apportioned land (18:23). The prohibition, however, is on owning *naḥalah*, fields for farming.[5]

pasture land Hebrew *migrash*, a word that is possibly derived from *garash*, "drive, chase," referring to land in which flocks can be driven from one pasture to another.[6]

Here *migrash* is the technical term for the outskirts of a settled area that is not designated for agriculture[7] or human habitation[8] but for livestock.[9] The ancient Mesopotamian towns were also surrounded by pastureland, called *tamertu*. Another characteristic of pastureland is that it is common property, such as obtained in ancient Ugarit; farmland, by contrast, is owned by individuals (see Excursus 74). It is clear that the *migrash* was legally a part of the city (see Josh. 21). Hence the city limits (v. 26), within which the manslayer was safe from the blood redeemer, were not the city walls but the extent of its *migrash*.

3. the cattle they own Literally, "their cattle and their possessions," a hendiadys.[10]

beasts Hebrew *ḥayatam*,[11] referring to impure domesticated animals like donkeys.[12]

4. a thousand cubits About 450 meters (500 yds.). On the basis of this verse, the sectaries of Qumran ordained that one may not walk a distance greater than 1,000 cubits on the Sabbath; but, based on verse 5, they ordained that one may pasture livestock a distance of 2,000 cubits. The rabbis, however, take 2,000 cubits as the Sabbath walking limit for any purpose.

outside the town wall Literally, "from the town wall outward." The measurement is taken perpendicular to the town wall, not from the wall itself but from the rectangle that circumscribes it. This enables the pasturage to grow in proportion to the size of the town (see Excursus 74, fig. 3).

wall Hebrew *kir*, a rare word for a town wall. (The term elsewhere is *ḥomah*.) It probably refers to the outside surface of the town wall (see *kir ha-ḥomah* in Josh. 2:15). Since large cities had walls up to several meters thick, it had to be specified that the measurement was to be taken from the walls' exterior face. Thus *mi-kir ha-ʿir* should be taken as an ellipsis of *mi-kir ḥomat ha-ʿir*, "from the outer surface of the town wall."[13]

5 וּמַדֹּתֶם מִחוּץ לָעִיר אֶת־פְּאַת־קֵדְמָה אַלְפַּיִם
בָּאַמָּה וְאֶת־פְּאַת־נֶגֶב אַלְפַּיִם בָּאַמָּה וְאֶת־פְּאַת־
יָם ׀ אַלְפַּיִם בָּאַמָּה וְאֵת פְּאַת צָפוֹן אַלְפַּיִם בָּאַמָּה
וְהָעִיר בַּתָּוֶךְ זֶה יִהְיֶה לָהֶם מִגְרְשֵׁי הֶעָרִים׃
6 וְאֵת הֶעָרִים אֲשֶׁר תִּתְּנוּ לַלְוִיִּם אֵת שֵׁשׁ־עָרֵי
הַמִּקְלָט אֲשֶׁר תִּתְּנוּ לָנֻס שָׁמָּה הָרֹצֵחַ וַעֲלֵיהֶם
תִּתְּנוּ אַרְבָּעִים וּשְׁתַּיִם עִיר׃ 7 כָּל־הֶעָרִים אֲשֶׁר
תִּתְּנוּ לַלְוִיִּם אַרְבָּעִים וּשְׁמֹנֶה עִיר אֶתְהֶן וְאֶת־
מִגְרְשֵׁיהֶן׃ 8 וְהֶעָרִים אֲשֶׁר תִּתְּנוּ מֵאֲחֻזַּת בְּנֵי־
יִשְׂרָאֵל מֵאֵת הָרַב תַּרְבּוּ וּמֵאֵת הַמְעַט תַּמְעִיטוּ
אִישׁ כְּפִי נַחֲלָתוֹ אֲשֶׁר יִנְחָלוּ יִתֵּן מֵעָרָיו לַלְוִיִּם׃
פ ששי [שביעי כשהן מחוברות]

shall measure off two thousand cubits outside the town on the east side, two thousand on the south side, two thousand on the west side, and two thousand on the north side, with the town in the center. That shall be the pasture for their towns.

6The towns that you assign to the Levites shall comprise the six cities of refuge that you are to designate for a manslayer to flee to, to which you shall add forty-two towns. 7Thus the total of the towns that you assign to the Levites shall be forty-eight towns, with their pasture. 8In assigning towns from the holdings of the Israelites, take more from the larger groups and less from the smaller, so that each assigns towns to the Levites in proportion to the share it receives.

5. two thousand cubits About 900 meters (1,000 yds.) These are the dimensions of the pastureland assuming the town is a point (Excursus 74, fig. 1). This measurement became the basis of the rabbinic law of *teḥum shabbat*, the limit one may walk outside of a city on the Sabbath.

outside Hebrew *mi-ḥuts*.[14] This term is the antonym of *mi-bayit*, "inside," and it must be distinguished from the 1,000-cubit measurement prescribed in the previous verse, which is taken as *ḥutsah*, "outward," from the town wall. Thus the 1,000 cubits in each direction from the town (assumed to be a point) form a square of 2,000 cubits per side (Excursus 74, fig. 1), which increases in area in proportion to the growth of the town (Excursus 74, figs. 2 and 3).

in the center The measures given here presume that the center (and town) is a point.

their Hebrew *lahem*. Many versions[15] read *lakhem*, "your." But the Levites are referred to in the third person throughout this pericope; hence, the received Hebrew text is preferable.

6. cities of refuge Hebrew *ʿarei miklat*. This verse anticipates the section on the cities of refuge for those who commit involuntary homicide, beginning with verse 9 (see also Excursus 75). The manslayer is put in the custody of the Levites, who could be relied upon to adminster justice impartially and not be influenced by the clan/tribe of the slain/slayer.

manslayer The term *rotseaḥ* embraces both the deliberate and involuntary homicide (see the Comment to v. 30).

7. forty-eight towns Named and located in Joshua 21.

8. the larger groups Literally, "the greater." Although there is no Hebrew word here for "groups," clearly the Israelite tribes are meant.[16] However, the referent for "larger" is ambiguous. It cannot be the tribal territory since in the Book of Joshua the forty-eight towns were subsequently distributed (nearly) equally among the tribes, four cities per tribe regardless of their size.[17] Neither can "larger" refer to the tribal population because it would leave unexplained why Issachar and Dan and also Ephraim (which was half as populous) were all assigned the same number of cities, or why Naphtali, more populous than either Gad or Ephraim, was assigned one city fewer (the tribal populations are listed in the introduction to chap. 26). Ramban suggests that the importance of the towns was also a criterion in their distribution, but this is not intimated by the text.

This discrepancy between Numbers and Joshua on the Levitical towns is significant. The Numbers passage cannot be later than the one in Joshua because no writer having Joshua 21 before him would have blatantly contradicted it by concocting this verse. It is more logical to posit that the prescription of Numbers was adapted by the compiler of Joshua to accord with changed historical circumstances (see Excursus 75).

it receives[18]

9The LORD spoke further to Moses: 10Speak to the Israelite people and say to them: When you cross the Jordan into
the land of Canaan, 11you shall provide yourselves with
places to serve you as cities of refuge to which a manslayer
who has killed a person unintentionally may flee. 12The
cities shall serve you as a refuge from the avenger, so that
the manslayer may not die unless he has stood trial before
the assembly.

9 וַיְדַבֵּר יְהוָה אֶל־מֹשֶׁה לֵּאמֹר׃ 10 דַּבֵּר אֶל־בְּנֵי
יִשְׂרָאֵל וְאָמַרְתָּ אֲלֵהֶם כִּי אַתֶּם עֹבְרִים אֶת־
הַיַּרְדֵּן אַרְצָה כְּנָעַן׃ 11 וְהִקְרִיתֶם לָכֶם עָרִים עָרֵי
מִקְלָט תִּהְיֶינָה לָכֶם וְנָס שָׁמָּה רֹצֵחַ מַכֵּה־נֶפֶשׁ
בִּשְׁגָגָה׃ 12 וְהָיוּ לָכֶם הֶעָרִים לְמִקְלָט מִגֹּאֵל וְלֹא
יָמוּת הָרֹצֵחַ עַד־עָמְדוֹ לִפְנֵי הָעֵדָה לַמִּשְׁפָּט׃

THE CITIES OF REFUGE (vv. 9–15)

It is a basic theological postulate that the divine Presence cannot abide in a land polluted by murder; the offense leads to the pollution of earth and the abandonment by God of His sanctuary and people. For this reason the laws of homicide are given special treatment here. The establishment of asylums for homicides was further necessitated because of the prevalence of the institution of blood vengeance in the ancient Near East. Accordingly, the blood of the slain was avenged by his nearest kinsman, called *go'el*, either by taking the blood of the slayer or of a member of the latter's family or by accepting monetary compensation. Israel's laws of homicide and its system of asylum cities presuppose the following basic modifications in the prevailing practice: (1) Only the guilty party is involved; thus, no other member of his family may be slain. (2) Guilt is determined by the slayer's intention: The involuntary homicide is not put to death. (3) No ransom is acceptable in place of the death of the murderer. (4) The verdict of deliberate or involuntary homicide is made by the state and not by the bereaved kinsman, and to this end asylum cities for the homicide are established. (5) His trial is by a national tribunal and not by the kinsmen of either party. (6) The deliberate homicide is executed by the *go'el*, and the involuntary homicide is banished to the asylum until the death of the High Priest. The institution of asylum is attested elsewhere, but the form adopted by Israel is characterized by a revolutionary principle: The right of asylum is limited solely to the unpremeditated manslayer. Details are discussed in Excursus 76.

10. See the Comment to 33:51.

11. you shall provide[19]

refuge Hebrew ***miklat***. *Kalat* in rabbinic Hebrew means "receive" or "contain."[20] In modern Hebrew ***miklat*** means "(air raid) shelter."

manslayer Hebrew ***rotseaḥ*** is used indiscriminately for manslaughter, irrespective of intention and authorization (see v. 30). The underlying postulate is clear: The blood of one slain even accidentally must be redeemed. See the Comment to verse 25 and Excursus 76.

unintentionally Hebrew ***bi-shegagah***. Here this term implies awareness of the law but not of the act. In cases of sacrificial expiation it has the reverse implication (see the Comment to 15:22).

12. avenger Hebrew ***go'el***. Rather, "redeemer," the restorer of the status quo, a responsibility that rests on the next of kin. Thus the ***go'el*** is variously (1) the levir or widow's brother-in-law who, as in Ruth 3:13, provides his deceased kinsman with a survivor by marrying the childless widow; (2) the receiver of reparations due the deceased (5:8); (3) the one obligated to bring the debtor out of slavery, as in Leviticus 25:47–54, and buy back his inherited field, as in Leviticus 25:25–28, 48, and Jeremiah 32:7–12. The redeemer in cases of homicide is called the ***go'el ha-dam***, "the blood redeemer" (vv. 19,21,24,27), and the Septuagint so reads in this verse. The obligation of redemption falls on the brother, the father's brother, and the latter's son—in that order and on through the father's line (Lev. 25:48–49; see the Comment to Num. 27:9–11). The cities of refuge do not abrogate the rights of the blood redeemer but make him an agent of the state; that is, he becomes the state's executioner (see Excursus 75). Thus, the ***go'el***, as exemplified in the above cases, restores the equilibrium—by delivering a descendant to the deceased, the slave to freedom, the land to its rightful owner. The same holds true for murder. Bloodshed pollutes the land (v. 33), and the land becomes barren. With the

13The towns that you thus assign shall be six cities of refuge in all. 14Three cities shall be designated beyond the Jordan, and the other three shall be designated in the land of Canaan: they shall serve as cities of refuge. 15These six cities shall serve the Israelites and the resident aliens among them for refuge, so that anyone who kills a person unintentionally may flee there.

16Anyone, however, who strikes another with an iron object so that death results is a murderer; the murderer must be put to death. 17If he struck him with a stone tool

13 וְהֶעָרִים֙ אֲשֶׁ֣ר תִּתֵּ֔נוּ שֵׁשׁ־עָרֵ֥י מִקְלָ֖ט תִּהְיֶ֥ינָה
לָכֶֽם׃ 14 אֵ֣ת ׀ שְׁלֹ֣שׁ הֶעָרִ֗ים תִּתְּנוּ֙ מֵעֵ֣בֶר לַיַּרְדֵּ֔ן
וְאֵת֙ שְׁלֹ֣שׁ הֶֽעָרִ֔ים תִּתְּנ֖וּ בְּאֶ֣רֶץ כְּנָ֑עַן עָרֵ֥י מִקְלָ֖ט
תִּהְיֶֽינָה׃ 15 לִבְנֵ֣י יִשְׂרָאֵ֗ל וְלַגֵּ֤ר וְלַתּוֹשָׁב֙ בְּתוֹכָ֔ם
תִּהְיֶ֛ינָה שֵׁשׁ־הֶעָרִ֥ים הָאֵ֖לֶּה לְמִקְלָ֑ט לָנ֣וּס שָׁ֔מָּה
כָּל־מַכֵּה־נֶ֖פֶשׁ בִּשְׁגָגָֽה׃ 16 וְאִם־בִּכְלִ֨י בַרְזֶ֧ל ׀
הִכָּ֛הוּ וַיָּמֹ֖ת רֹצֵ֣חַ ה֑וּא מ֥וֹת יוּמַ֖ת הָרֹצֵֽחַ׃ 17 וְאִם

blood of the slayer, the *go'el* neutralizes the deleterious effect of the blood of the slain, restoring the ecological balance. The earth again yields its fruit.

die[21]

be has stood trial[22]

the assembly Deuteronomy 19:11–12 implies that state-appointed judges (see Deut. 16:18; 17:8) conduct the trial in the city of refuge. This text, however, presumes that the trial takes place somewhere else (see the Comment to v. 25), conducted by national representatives of the *'edah* (see Excursus 1). Thus, according to this legislation, all homicides must be tried in a national court.

14. The two and a half tribes in Transjordan are to have the same number of asylums as the more numerous—and more populous—tribes in Cisjordan, a geographic criterion for their distribution. The murderer should not have to flee too far lest the blood redeemer overtake him (see Deut. 19:3).[23] Indeed, Deuteronomy 19:9 provides for an additional three cities in Cisjordan, bringing the total to nine once the conquest is complete. The six cities are named in Joshua 20:7–8.

beyond the Jordan According to Deuteronomy 4:41, Moses himself designated the Transjordanian cities. The rabbis, however, in Mishnah Makkot 2:4, claim that they did not become operative until the three cities in Cisjordan were also ready to function. Because the perspective is that of the postconquest period, Transjordan is called "beyond the Jordan" even though Israel is still in the plains of Moab (v. 1).

15. ***resident aliens*** Hebrew *ve-la-ger ve-la-toshav*, a hendiadys, equivalent to the single word *ger* and used in the equivalent law of Joshua 20:9. It is amply clear from this law that the alien is entitled to the same protection of his basic rights as the Israelite.

DELIBERATE AND INVOLUNTARY HOMICIDE (vv. 16–23)

The distinction is one of intention, evidence for which is the nature of the instrument and the manslayer's state of mind. The distinction is made not by abstract definition but by concrete examples, six for deliberate homicide (vv. 16–18,20–21) and three for involuntary homicide (vv. 22–23). Their arrangement is chiastic, ABB′A′, as follows: Intentional—Implements (vv. 16–18), Intentional (vv. 20–22); Unintentional (v. 22), Unintentional—Implements (v. 23). The words that recur in AA′ are "stone that could cause death" and in BB′, "hate, hurled, on purpose, pushed."[24] The burden of proof is always on the slayer. If, for example, he uses a murderous instrument, he must prove his lack of intention (see the Comment to v. 23). The instrument is categorized by its material: iron, stone, or wood. The latter two must be capable of producing death. In addition to intention, Deuteronomy 19:4–5 adds two other criteria: prior enmity between the slayer and slain and the circumstances of the murder.

16. ***iron object*** Iron of any size can cause death,[25] perhaps reflecting the very beginnings of the Iron Age, when it was used exclusively for weapons. Because they were instruments of death,

that could cause death, and death resulted, he is a murderer; the murderer must be put to death. [18]Similarly, if the object with which he struck him was a wooden tool that could cause death, and death resulted, he is a murderer; the murderer must be put to death. [19]The blood-avenger himself shall put the murderer to death; it is he who shall put him to death upon encounter. [20]So, too, if he pushed him in hate or hurled something at him on purpose and death resulted, [21]or if he struck him with his hand in enmity and death resulted, the assailant shall be put to death; he is a murderer. The blood-avenger shall put the murderer to death upon encounter. [22]But if he pushed him without malice aforethought or hurled any object at him unintentionally, [23]or inadvertently dropped upon him any deadly object of stone, and death resulted—though he was not an enemy of his and did not seek his harm—[24]in such cases the assembly shall decide between the slayer and the blood-avenger. [25]The assembly shall protect the manslayer from

בְּאֶבֶן יָד אֲשֶׁר־יָמוּת בָּהּ הִכָּהוּ וַיָּמֹת רֹצֵחַ הוּא
מוֹת יוּמַת הָרֹצֵחַ׃ 18 אוֹ בִּכְלִי עֵץ־יָד אֲשֶׁר־
יָמוּת בּוֹ הִכָּהוּ וַיָּמֹת רֹצֵחַ הוּא מוֹת יוּמַת הָרֹצֵחַ׃
19 גֹּאֵל הַדָּם הוּא יָמִית אֶת־הָרֹצֵחַ בְּפִגְעוֹ־בוֹ
הוּא יְמִתֶנּוּ׃ 20 וְאִם־בְּשִׂנְאָה יֶהְדֳּפֶנּוּ אוֹ־הִשְׁלִיךְ
עָלָיו בִּצְדִיָּה וַיָּמֹת׃ 21 אוֹ בְאֵיבָה הִכָּהוּ בְיָדוֹ
וַיָּמֹת מוֹת־יוּמַת הַמַּכֶּה רֹצֵחַ הוּא גֹּאֵל הַדָּם
יָמִית אֶת־הָרֹצֵחַ בְּפִגְעוֹ־בוֹ׃ 22 וְאִם־בְּפֶתַע בְּלֹא־
אֵיבָה הֲדָפוֹ אוֹ־הִשְׁלִיךְ עָלָיו כָּל־כְּלִי בְּלֹא צְדִיָּה׃
23 אוֹ בְכָל־אֶבֶן אֲשֶׁר־יָמוּת בָּהּ בְּלֹא רְאוֹת וַיַּפֵּל
עָלָיו וַיָּמֹת וְהוּא לֹא־אוֹיֵב לוֹ וְלֹא מְבַקֵּשׁ רָעָתוֹ׃
24 וְשָׁפְטוּ הָעֵדָה בֵּין הַמַּכֶּה וּבֵין גֹּאֵל הַדָּם עַל
הַמִּשְׁפָּטִים הָאֵלֶּה׃ 25 וְהִצִּילוּ הָעֵדָה אֶת־הָרֹצֵחַ

iron tools were forbidden in the building of the altar and Temple (Exod. 20:25; 1 Kings 6:7). (And to this day, the knife is covered during the recitation of grace in the observant Jewish home.) That the iron object is in a class by itself is shown grammatically by the use of *ve- 'im*, here rendered "anyone, however, who . . ." in this and the following verse describing the stone tool, whereas the wooden tool that follows (v. 18) is introduced by *'o*.

17. ***stone tool*** Hebrew *'even yad*, literally "stone of the hand": (1) It can be gripped by the hand;[26] (2) it is large enough to fill the hand;[27] or (3) it is directed by the hand, that is, thrown.[28] In any case, the stone and wooden (v. 18) implements must be large enough to kill—"that could cause death."

18. ***Similarly***[29]

wooden tool Literally, "a wooden tool of the hand," that is, a cane (Ezek. 33:9).

19. ***the blood-avenger*** Rather, "the blood redeemer" (see the Comment to v. 12).

upon encounter Hebrew *be-fig'o bo*. For this usage, see Genesis 32:2 and Joshua 2:16. The verb *paga'*, like other verbs of contact (e.g., *matsa'*, "find," *naga'*, "touch," *mahah*, "abut"; 34:11), can also mean "strike," as in Exodus 5:3, 1 Samuel 22:17, 2 Samuel 1:15, and 1 Kings 2:25,29,31.

20. ***he pushed him*** Hebrew *yehdafenu*. For this meaning of *hadaf*, see 2 Kings 4:27 and Ezekiel 34:21.

something Not in our Hebrew text. It is either understood or supplied, as by the Septuagint's *kol keli*, "any object" (as in v. 22).

on purpose Hebrew *bi-tsediyah*.[30] The verbal form is found in Exodus 21:13 and 1 Samuel 24:12. Alternatively, "from ambush."[31]

21. A man may kill with his hands, in which case malice must be proved.

22. ***without . . . aforethought*** Literally, "suddenly," that is, unawares.[32]

23. Even if death resulted from the use of a murderous implement, the slaying is adjudged involuntary if the manslayer did not see his victim and bore no grudge against him.

the blood-avenger, and the assembly shall restore him to the city of refuge to which he fled, and there he shall remain until the death of the high priest who was anointed with the sacred oil. 26 But if the manslayer ever goes outside the limits of the city of refuge to which he has fled, 27 and the blood-avenger comes upon him outside the limits of his city of refuge, and the blood-avenger kills the manslayer, there is no bloodguilt on his account. 28 For he must remain inside his city of refuge until the death of the high priest; after the death of the high priest, the manslayer may return to his land holding.

29 Such shall be your law of procedure throughout the ages in all your settlements.

מִיַּד גֹּאֵל הַדָּם וְהֵשִׁיבוּ אֹתוֹ הָעֵדָה אֶל־עִיר
מִקְלָטוֹ אֲשֶׁר־נָס שָׁמָּה וְיָשַׁב בָּהּ עַד־מוֹת הַכֹּהֵן
הַגָּדֹל אֲשֶׁר־מָשַׁח אֹתוֹ בְּשֶׁמֶן הַקֹּדֶשׁ׃ 26 וְאִם־
יָצֹא יֵצֵא הָרֹצֵחַ אֶת־גְּבוּל עִיר מִקְלָטוֹ אֲשֶׁר יָנוּס
שָׁמָּה׃ 27 וּמָצָא אֹתוֹ גֹּאֵל הַדָּם מִחוּץ לִגְבוּל עִיר
מִקְלָטוֹ וְרָצַח גֹּאֵל הַדָּם אֶת־הָרֹצֵחַ אֵין לוֹ דָּם׃
28 כִּי בְעִיר מִקְלָטוֹ יֵשֵׁב עַד־מוֹת הַכֹּהֵן הַגָּדֹל
וְאַחֲרֵי מוֹת הַכֹּהֵן הַגָּדֹל יָשׁוּב הָרֹצֵחַ אֶל־אֶרֶץ
אֲחֻזָּתוֹ׃ 29 וְהָיוּ אֵלֶּה לָכֶם לְחֻקַּת מִשְׁפָּט
לְדֹרֹתֵיכֶם בְּכֹל מוֹשְׁבֹתֵיכֶם׃ 30 כָּל־מַכֵּה־נֶפֶשׁ

INVOLUNTARY HOMICIDE: THE PROCEDURE (vv. 24–29)

The trial is conducted by national judges; if the manslayer is found guilty of second-degree murder (involuntary homicide), he is returned to his city of refuge where he remains until the death of the High Priest. This pericope is framed by the term ***mishpat***, "procedure."

24. ***in such cases*** Alternatively, "according to these rules" (vv. 16–23).

the assembly shall decide The sectaries of the Dead Sea ordained that a court should comprise ten judges (CD 10:4), basing themselves on 14:27, where *ʿ**edah*** refers to the ten scouts who rendered the majority opinion.[33]

25. ***restore him*** Proof that the trial is held outside the city of refuge.[34]

death of the high priest The term ***kohen gadol***, "High Priest," is found in Leviticus 21:10 and Joshua 20:6 (also 2 Kings 2:11; 22:4; Hag. 1:1,12; Zech. 3:1; Neh. 3:1). As the High Priest atones for Israel's sins through his cultic service in his lifetime (Exod. 28:36; Lev. 16:16,21), so he atones for homicide through his death. Since the blood of the slain, although spilled accidentally, cannot be avenged through the death of the slayer, it is ransomed through the death of the High Priest, which releases all homicides from their cities of refuge. That it is not the exile of the manslayer but the death of the High Priest that expiates his crime is confirmed by the Mishnah: "If, after the slayer has been sentenced as an accidental homicide, the High Priest dies, he need not go into exile."[35] The Talmud, in turn, comments thereon: "But is it not the exile that expiates? It is not the exile that expiates, but the death of the High Priest."[36] For details see Excursus 76.

anointed with sacred oil The High Priest is similarly defined in Leviticus 21:10. However, this is no redundancy;[37] it makes certain that "High" should not be defined on any other grounds.

26. ***the limits*** Hebrew ***gevul***. Whether these limits include the pastureland is not clear.

27. ***there is no bloodguilt on his account*** Hebrew ***ʾein lo dam***. The term "bloodguilt" is usually expressed by the plural ***damim*** as in Exodus 22:1 and Leviticus 20:9, but the singular is also attested (Lev. 17:4; 19:16; Deut. 21:8). The blood redeemer cannot be an official of the community,[38] for who but the nearest kinsman would defy the *ʿ**edah***'s verdict that the homicide was accidental?

28. ***his land holding***[39]

29. ***Such***[40]

law of procedure Hebrew ***le-ḥukat mishpat***, also found in 27:11. This expression refers to civil law, as opposed to ***ḥukat torah***, "ritual law," as in 19:2 and 31:21.

30If anyone kills a person, the manslayer may be executed
only on the evidence of witnesses; the testimony of a single
witness against a person shall not suffice for a sentence of
death. 31You may not accept a ransom for the life of a
murderer who is guilty of a capital crime; he must be put to
death. 32Nor may you accept ransom in lieu of flight to a
city of refuge, enabling one to return to live on his land
before the death of the priest. 33You shall not pollute the
land in which you live; for blood pollutes the land, and the
land can have no expiation for blood that is shed on it,
except by the blood of him who shed it. 34You shall not

לְפִי עֵדִים יִרְצַח אֶת־הָרֹצֵחַ וְעֵד אֶחָד לֹא־יַעֲנֶה
בְנֶפֶשׁ לָמוּת׃ 31 וְלֹא־תִקְחוּ כֹפֶר לְנֶפֶשׁ רֹצֵחַ
אֲשֶׁר־הוּא רָשָׁע לָמוּת כִּי־מוֹת יוּמָת׃ 32 וְלֹא־
תִקְחוּ כֹפֶר לָנוּס אֶל־עִיר מִקְלָטוֹ לָשׁוּב לָשֶׁבֶת
בָּאָרֶץ עַד־מוֹת הַכֹּהֵן׃ 33 וְלֹא־תַחֲנִיפוּ אֶת־הָאָרֶץ
אֲשֶׁר אַתֶּם בָּהּ כִּי הַדָּם הוּא יַחֲנִיף אֶת־הָאָרֶץ
וְלָאָרֶץ לֹא־יְכֻפַּר לַדָּם אֲשֶׁר שֻׁפַּךְ־בָּהּ כִּי־אִם
בְּדַם שֹׁפְכוֹ׃ 34 וְלֹא תְטַמֵּא אֶת־הָאָרֶץ אֲשֶׁר

SUPPLEMENT AND PERORATION (vv. 30–34)

Whereas compensation for murder is provided for in all law codes of the ancient Near East, Israel alone maintains that the homicide must pay with his life. Otherwise, the land becomes polluted with the consequence that neither God nor Israel can abide there, a concept expressed in Leviticus 18:25–28. Perhaps, because the law of talion ("life for life . . .") had come to mean monetary compensation for all bodily injuries and even for the life of an animal, as in Leviticus 24:18,21, it is not quoted here. Instead, it is asserted explicitly and emphatically that talion for the life of a person is to be taken literally (see Excursus 76).

30. the manslayer may be executed Literally, "[one] shall murder the murderer." That person must be the *go'el* (vv. 19,21). The verb *ratsaḥ* is also used for unpremeditated killing (v. 25) and for nonculpable killing (v. 27).

31. who is guilty of a capital crime[41] This prohibition clearly has in mind the blood redeemer who might accept monetary compensation for the life of his slain kinsman (see 2 Sam. 21:4). If he does, the nation (*'edah*) cannot acquiesce but must bring the murderer to his death (see Excursus 76). There may be a more theoretical reason for explicitly prohibiting ransom for homicide. The talion law implies compensation in all torts except for loss of life (see Exod. 21:23–24; Lev. 24:17–21; Deut. 19:21). Lest taking of life also be regarded as a tort and, hence, subject to monetary compensation, the talion law is not quoted here, and murder is explicitly excluded from monetary compensation.

32. in lieu of flight[42] The principle enunciated in verse 31 applies to involuntary as well as deliberate homicide (see Excursus 76).

on his land[43]

the priest Many ancient versions read "the High Priest."[44] However, the definite article suffices to specify him.

33. pollute Hebrew *taḥanifu*. The Hebrew verb *ḥ-n-f* means "be corrupt, polluted," especially when it refers to the land, as in Isaiah 24:9, Jeremiah 3:1,2,9, and Psalms 106:38. The Holy Land (like the Israelites) must observe its Sabbaths (Lev. 25:2,5; 26:34–35) and is polluted by bloodshed, idolatry, and incest (Ezek. 36:17–18) until it vomits out its inhabitants (Lev. 18:28). The notion that illicit bloodshed pollutes the land so that it does not yield its fruit is attested in the oldest sources (Gen. 4:10–12; 2 Sam. 21:1).

live[45]

have no expiation Rather, "have no ransom" (see the Comment to 8:1 and Excursus 19). Jubilees 21:19 expressly warns Israel not to allow compensation for murder lest the (unredeemed) blood of the slain pollute the earth.

by the blood[46]

defile the land in which you live, in which I Myself abide, for I the LORD abide among the Israelite people.

אַתֶּם֙ יֹשְׁבִ֣ים בָּ֔הּ אֲשֶׁ֥ר אֲנִ֖י שֹׁכֵ֣ן בְּתוֹכָ֑הּ כִּ֚י אֲנִ֣י
יְהוָ֔ה שֹׁכֵ֖ן בְּת֥וֹךְ בְּנֵ֥י יִשְׂרָאֵֽל׃ פ שביעי

36 The family heads in the clan of the descendants of Gilead son of Machir son of Manasseh, one of the Josephite clans, came forward and appealed to Moses and the chieftains, family heads of the Israelites. 2They said, "The LORD

ל״ו וַֽיִּקְרְב֞וּ רָאשֵׁ֣י הָֽאָב֗וֹת לְמִשְׁפַּ֣חַת בְּנֵי־
גִלְעָד֙ בֶּן־מָכִ֣יר בֶּן־מְנַשֶּׁ֔ה מִֽמִּשְׁפְּחֹ֖ת בְּנֵ֣י יוֹסֵ֑ף
וַֽיְדַבְּר֞וּ לִפְנֵ֤י מֹשֶׁה֙ וְלִפְנֵ֣י הַנְּשִׂאִ֔ים רָאשֵׁ֥י אָב֖וֹת
לִבְנֵ֥י יִשְׂרָאֵֽל׃ 2 וַיֹּאמְר֗וּ אֶת־אֲדֹנִי֙ צִוָּ֣ה יְהוָ֔ה

34. abide Hebrew *shokhen* refers to the indwelling of God in his earthly Tabernacle, *mishkan*, from which derives the rabbinic term Shekhinah to represent the earthly Presence of the Deity. The rabbis state the underlying postulate succinctly: "Because of the crime of bloodshed the Shekhinah departs and the sanctuary is polluted"[47] (see Excursus 49). The double metaphor of land and sanctuary are but two sides of the same coin: The land of Israel is also God's residence and is therefore equivalent in holiness to His sanctuary. The Lord's demand in the wilderness that the camp be kept pure (see 5:3) is, in Canaan, extended to all of God's land.

for I the LORD abide among the Israelite people A reminder that the Lord had consented to transfer His Presence from the summit of Sinai to the portable Sinai of the Tabernacle so that He will forever abide within Israel.

CHAPTER 36

Marriage Requirements for Heiresses (vv. 1–13)

Moses has ruled that daughters may inherit where there are no sons (27:1–11). The leaders of Zelophehad's clan respond with the following objection: If they marry outside their tribe then their land will pass to their husbands' tribes. Moses informs them that God finds their complaint justified and, as a result, He has decreed that all heiresses must marry within their tribe. Zelophehad's daughters marry their first cousins on their father's side. The possibility that this ruling originally directed heiresses to marry within their own clan is discussed in Excursus 77.

Why was this chapter placed at the end of the book and not where it belongs contextually, after 27:1–11? Most critics would answer that this chapter was composed after the Book of Numbers was completed (see Excursus 77). Another possibility is that this chapter "may reflect the Torah's pervasive genealogical interest: there are ten generations from Adam to Noah; ten generations from Noah to Terah (Abraham's father); and ten generations from Abraham to the daughters of Zelophehad. The end of the wanderings is thus related to creation, and Genesis and Numbers are placed in a unified structure."[1] A literary explanation also bears merit: "The accounts of the daughters of Zelophehad in Numbers 27 and 36 . . . form an *inclusio* for the events and organization of the new generation whose emergence is marked by the second census list in chapter 26."[2]

1. family heads Hebrew *ra'shei ha-'avot*. Rather, "clan heads," an ellipsis for *ra'shei beit ha-'avot* (see the Comment to 31:26). *Beit 'avot*, literally a collection of households, is the more technical term for *mishpaḥah*, "clan" (see Excursus 1).

in the clan Hebrew *le-mishpaḥat*. Rather, "in a clan," referring to the clan of Hepher (26:30–33; 27:1), which was one of the Gileadite clans. However, vocalizing *le-mishpeḥot*, "in the clans,"[3] might be preferable since each clan (*mishpaḥah* or *beit 'avot*) had only one head (*ro'sh* or *nasi'*). The plural form *ra'shei*, "heads," therefore implies that all the Gileadite clans protested, not just the clan of Hepher.

Moses After which the Septuagint adds, "and before Eleazar the priest," perhaps in order to harmonize this text with 27:2.

commanded my lord to assign the land to the Israelites as shares by lot, and my lord was further commanded by the LORD to assign the share of our kinsman Zelophehad to his daughters. [3]Now, if they marry persons from another Israelite tribe, their share will be cut off from our ancestral portion and be added to the portion of the tribe into which they marry; thus our allotted portion will be diminished. [4]And even when the Israelites observe the jubilee, their share will be added to that of the tribe into which they marry, and their share will be cut off from the ancestral portion of our tribe."

[5]So Moses, at the LORD's bidding, instructed the Israelites, saying: "The plea of the Josephite tribe is just. [6]This is what the LORD has commanded concerning the daughters

לָתֵת אֶת־הָאָרֶץ בְּנַחֲלָה בְּגוֹרָל לִבְנֵי יִשְׂרָאֵל
וַאדֹנִי צֻוָּה בַיהוָֹה לָתֵת אֶת־נַחֲלַת צְלָפְחָד
אָחִינוּ לִבְנֹתָיו׃ 3 וְהָיוּ לְאֶחָד מִבְּנֵי שִׁבְטֵי בְנֵי־
יִשְׂרָאֵל לְנָשִׁים וְנִגְרְעָה נַחֲלָתָן מִנַּחֲלַת אֲבֹתֵינוּ
וְנוֹסַף עַל נַחֲלַת הַמַּטֶּה אֲשֶׁר תִּהְיֶינָה לָהֶם
וּמִגֹּרַל נַחֲלָתֵנוּ יִגָּרֵעַ׃ 4 וְאִם־יִהְיֶה הַיֹּבֵל לִבְנֵי
יִשְׂרָאֵל וְנוֹסְפָה נַחֲלָתָן עַל נַחֲלַת הַמַּטֶּה אֲשֶׁר
תִּהְיֶינָה לָהֶם וּמִנַּחֲלַת מַטֵּה אֲבֹתֵינוּ יִגָּרַע
נַחֲלָתָן׃ 5 וַיְצַו מֹשֶׁה אֶת־בְּנֵי יִשְׂרָאֵל עַל־פִּי יְהוָֹה
לֵאמֹר כֵּן מַטֵּה בְנֵי־יוֹסֵף דֹּבְרִים׃ 6 זֶה הַדָּבָר
אֲשֶׁר־צִוָּה יְהוָֹה לִבְנוֹת צְלָפְחָד לֵאמֹר לַטּוֹב

the chieftains, family heads One term explains the other and they are synonymous;[4] see Excursus 1.

2. ***my lord*** Hebrew *'adoni*. Moses is addressed in this deferential manner by Joshua (11:25), Aaron (12:11; Exod. 32:22), the chieftains of Reuben and Gad (32:25,27), and now by the chieftains of Gileadite clans.

by lot The location of each tribe's territory was determined by lot (26:55; see Excursus 62).

commanded[5]

by the LORD[6]

3. ***persons from another . . . tribe*** Literally, "to one of the sons of the tribes of." It is assumed that the daughters are presently unmarried: If they were married they would have no claim, since their patrimony would have been automatically transferred to their husbands' tribes.

our ancestral portion Hebrew *'avoteinu*, literally "[the portion] of our fathers." Since the land has been apportioned to the present generation, that is, to the speakers themselves, this term "our fathers" indicates that this chapter was written at a later age (see vv. 4,6,7,8; Lev. 25:41). Peshitta reads *'avihen*, "their father," that is, Zelophehad (also in vv. 4,8), which shows that it was aware of the problem (see further in Excursus 77).

will be cut off[7]

which they marry Literally, "which they will be [wives] to them," that is, to the "persons from another tribe."

4. ***And even when***[8]

the jubilee Hebrew *ha-yovel*. Sold ancestral land, but not inherited land, reverts to its original owner in the Jubilee year (Lev. 25:10).[9]

5. ***at the LORD's bidding*** Implied is that once again Moses consulted the oracle on the Zelophehad case (27:5); that is, he was incapable of rendering a decision on his own. However, because no mention is made of Moses taking the matter before the Lord (as in 27:5) but only that he orders "what the Lord has commanded" (v. 6), it is also possible that God had already anticipated the problem: When He assigned the daughters their father's portion, He enjoined them to marry within their clan, a fact that Moses reports only now.[10]

the Josephite tribe Actually the Gileadites or the clan of Hepher is meant (see the Comment to 27:7).

just Hebrew *ken*. See the Comment to 27:7.

of Zelophehad: They may marry anyone they wish, provided they marry into a clan of their father's tribe. [7]No inheritance of the Israelites may pass over from one tribe to another, but the Israelites must remain bound each to the ancestral portion of his tribe. [8]Every daughter among the Israelite tribes who inherits a share must marry someone from a clan of her father's tribe, in order that every Israelite may keep his ancestral share. [9]Thus no inheritance shall pass over from one tribe to another, but the Israelite tribes shall remain bound each to its portion."

[10]The daughters of Zelophehad did as the LORD had commanded Moses: [11]Mahlah, Tirzah, Hoglah, Milcah, and Noah, Zelophehad's daughters, were married to sons of their uncles, [12]marrying into clans of descendants of Manasseh son of Joseph; and so their share remained in the tribe of their father's clan.

בְּעֵינֵיהֶם תִּהְיֶינָה לְנָשִׁים אַךְ לְמִשְׁפַּחַת מַטֵּה
אֲבִיהֶם תִּהְיֶינָה לְנָשִׁים׃ 7 וְלֹא־תִסֹּב נַחֲלָה לִבְנֵי
יִשְׂרָאֵל מִמַּטֶּה אֶל־מַטֶּה כִּי אִישׁ בְּנַחֲלַת מַטֵּה
אֲבֹתָיו יִדְבְּקוּ בְּנֵי יִשְׂרָאֵל׃ 8 וְכָל־בַּת יֹרֶשֶׁת
נַחֲלָה מִמַּטּוֹת בְּנֵי יִשְׂרָאֵל לְאֶחָד מִמִּשְׁפַּחַת
מַטֵּה אָבִיהָ תִּהְיֶה לְאִשָּׁה לְמַעַן יִירְשׁוּ בְּנֵי
יִשְׂרָאֵל אִישׁ נַחֲלַת אֲבֹתָיו׃ 9 וְלֹא־תִסֹּב נַחֲלָה
מִמַּטֶּה לְמַטֶּה אַחֵר כִּי־אִישׁ בְּנַחֲלָתוֹ יִדְבְּקוּ
מַטּוֹת בְּנֵי יִשְׂרָאֵל׃ מפטיר 10 כַּאֲשֶׁר צִוָּה יְהֹוָה
אֶת־מֹשֶׁה כֵּן עָשׂוּ בְּנוֹת צְלָפְחָד׃ [מפטיר
לספרדים] 11 וַתִּהְיֶינָה מַחְלָה תִרְצָה וְחָגְלָה
וּמִלְכָּה וְנֹעָה בְּנוֹת צְלָפְחָד לִבְנֵי דֹדֵיהֶן לְנָשִׁים׃
12 מִמִּשְׁפְּחֹת בְּנֵי־מְנַשֶּׁה בֶן־יוֹסֵף הָיוּ לְנָשִׁים
וַתְּהִי נַחֲלָתָן עַל־מַטֵּה מִשְׁפַּחַת אֲבִיהֶן׃ 13 אֵלֶּה

6. concerning the daughters of Zelophehad But not future generations, according to the rabbis,[11] a reflection of rabbinic times when the Jewish people had long been alienated from their ancestral portions in the promised land. However, the Book of Tobit follows this law literally and even imposes two additional stipulations: (1) The father who has no sons is responsible for marrying off his daughter to one of his kinsmen, and (2) violation of this law is punishable by death "according to the law of the Book of Moses" (Tob. 6:13).

a clan[12]

8–9. A general law is formulated. Hence, some of the facts and the rationale of the case are repeated.[13] It follows the literary format of such legal innovations (see the introductory Comment to 27:1–11). The rabbis, however, limit the application of this law to the wilderness generation, before the land was actually possessed and divided.[14]

8. inherits Hebrew *yoreshet*, literally "possesses." The noun *yerushah* means "land, holding," and the verb *yarash* means "possess" (see Deut. 3:20). Only in a few instances, as here, does it refer to the possession of the patrimonial estates, that is, in the sense "inherit" (see Gen. 15:3–4; 21:10).[15]

from a clan of her father's tribe[16]

his ancestral share Literally, "his father's share." But this can only occur if the land remains within the clan, not the tribe (see Excursus 77).

9. each Hebrew *'ish*, literally "man," can refer to a single tribe (see 26:54).

11. sons of their uncles Although the daughters could have married anyone from their tribe, they selected husbands from their clan, a fact that also coincides with the law of succession: Where there are no children, the brothers of the deceased inherit the property (27:9). Thus, in effect, the daughters did not inherit. They merely transferred the property to those who, in any event, stood next in the line of succession—another indication that the original formulation of this law directed heiresses to marry within their clan, not the tribe (see the comments to vv. 6,8 and Excursus 77).

The husbands are not named. Neither are the husband of the daughter of Barzillai (Neh. 7:63)[17] and the husbands of the daughters of Kish (1 Chron. 23:22). Their function is to transmit the inheritance to the male offspring of the deceased via his daughters.

12. clans Hebrew *mishpeḥot*. Since they married cousins they remained in their own clan. Therefore vocalize *mishpaḥat*, "clan" (with one manuscript and LXX).

13 These are the commandments and regulations that the LORD enjoined upon the Israelites, through Moses, on the steppes of Moab, at the Jordan near Jericho.

הַמִּצְוֺת וְהַמִּשְׁפָּטִים אֲשֶׁר צִוָּה יְהוָה בְּיַד־מֹשֶׁה
אֶל־בְּנֵי יִשְׂרָאֵל בְּעַרְבֹת מוֹאָב עַל יַרְדֵּן יְרֵחוֹ׃

the tribe of their father's clan See Note 12 and Excursus 77.

13. ***on the steppes of Moab*** This phrase occurs in 22:1, 26:3,63, 31:2, and 35:1 (see Deut. 34:1,8). The final note then clearly refers to all the laws given to Israel once they encamped at the steppes of Moab (22:1). These include the regular public sacrifices (chaps. 28–29), the division of the land (26:52–56), the law of succession in inheritance (27:1–11; 36), the leadership succession both religious (chap. 25) and civil (27:12–23), a woman's vows and oaths (chap. 30), the division of the spoils (chap. 31), and the laws of homicide (35:9–34).[18] Alternatively, since large portions within chapters 22–36 are not laws but narratives, this note may refer only to chapters 35–36, which are headed by a verse (35:1) specifying the identical locale.[19]

חזק
סכום הפסוקים של ספר
אלף ומאתים שמונים
ושמונה
אפרח
וחציו והיה האיש
וסדרים ל״ג

תם ונשלם תהלה לאל בורא עולם
חזק חזק ונתחזק

NOTES TO THE COMMENTARY

Chapter 1

1. Tanḥ. Num. 3.
2. Ramban, introduction to Num.; J. Milgrom, ***Studies in Levitical Terminology*** (Berkeley: University of California Press, 1970), 44–46.
3. ARM 3.19.
4. Contra Philo, Moses 147, Josephus, Ant. 2.37, and Ramban on 1:3.
5. Cf. Krt 85–89, 176–178.
6. Most recently, F. M. Cross, ***Canaanite Myth and Hebrew Epic*** (Cambridge: Harvard University Press, 1973), 52–60.
7. W. F. Albright, "The Names Shaddai and Abram," JBL 54 (1935): 180–187.
8. But, since all these lists stem from the priestly source, it is not surprising since "I appeared to Abraham, Isaac, and Jacob as El Shaddai, but I did not make Myself known to them by My name YHVH" (Exod. 6:2).
9. The leaders of Kaniš were called ***nibum,*** "the named ones." For the use of the verb ***nakav,*** "designate," cf. Gen. 30:28; and for the expression, see 2 Chron. 28:15; 31:19.
10. A. Hurvitz, "The Evidence of Language in Dating the Priestly Code," RB 81 (1974): 24–56.
11. 1QM 4:11.
12. CD 12:22–23, 13:1–2, 14:3ff., and especially 1QS 2:19ff.
13. *Pekudav.* Missing in some manuscripts, LXX, Pesh., Targ. Jon., and in the census accounts of the other tribes.
14. A. Kuschke, "Die Lagervorstellung der priesterlichen Erzählung," ZAW 63 (1951): 74–105.
15. Some manuscripts, LXX, and Pesh. prefix the preposition ***le,*** "for," in keeping with the listings of the other tribes.
16. ***Le-veit 'avotam.*** LXX and Sam. read ***le-tsiv'otam,*** "by their troops."
17. Heb. ***hotpakedu,*** a rare passive form of the Hitpael (2:33; 26:62; 1 Kings 20:27).
18. J. Bright, "The Apodictic Prohibition: Some Observations," JBL 92 (1973): 185–204.
19. G. B. Gray, ***Numbers,*** ICC (New York: Scribners, 1903).
20. Most scholars admit this is an archaic term (e.g., W. F. Albright, ***Yahweh and the Gods of Canaan*** [Garden City, N.Y.: Doubleday, 1968], 92 n. 135, but some would call it an archaism (e.g., Cross, ***Canaanite Myth,*** pp. 267, 300). It may be related to Akk. ***adû*** (pl. ***adê***), Aram. ***'dn,*** and Egyptian ***'dwt'i;*** see J. M. Grintz, "Early Terms in the Priestly Torah," ***Leshonenu*** 39 (1974/1975): 170–172 (Hebrew). See also M. Weinfeld, TDOT, s.v. ***bĕrîth;*** M. Parnas, "***'ĒDŪT, 'ĒDŌT, 'ĒDWŌT in the Bible,***" ***Shnaton*** 1 (1975): 235–246 (Hebrew).
21. Milgrom, ***Studies in Levitical Terminology,*** n. 245.
22. Equivalent to Akk. ***maškanan inaṣṣar;*** Malamat, EB (Hebrew), s.v. ***gedud.***
23. For other examples of this literary technique, see Num. 5:4; 8:4, 20; Exod. 7:6; 12:28; 25:8–9; 39:32, 43. V. 54 follows logically upon v. 47 and refers to the execution of the census. Thus, vv. 48–53 are an editorial insertion.

Chapter 2

1. Num. R. 2:20 is aware of the problem.
2. A. Temerev, "Social Organizations in Egyptian Military Settlements of the Sixth-Fourth Centuries B.C.E.: ***Dgl*** and ***M't,***" in ***The Word of the Lord Shall Go Forth: Essays in Honor of D. N. Freedman,*** ed. C. L. Meyers and M. O'Connor (Winona Lake, Ind.: Eisenbrauns, 1983), 523–525.
3. Cf. also Exod. R. 15:6, Num. R. 2:3; Targ. Jon. on Ps. 20:6.
4. For a pictorial representation of an Ancient Near Eastern standard, see Y. Yadin, ***The Art of Warfare in Biblical Lands*** (New York: McGraw-Hill, 1963), 122, 139.
5. Rashi, Ibn Ezra, Bekhor Shor.
6. According to M. Harel, the need for the gloss "east side" contrasts with Egypt, where the "front," or main, direction was toward the south.
7. That ***maḥaneh*** means an army as well as a camp, see the Zakir and Ahiram steles; and in the Bible, see Judg. 7:21; 1 Sam. 17:1, 46; 1 Kings 22:34. It is synonymous with, but older than, the term ***degel.*** The latter was entered as a gloss here and in vv. 10, 18, 25 and in 1:51 but not in vv. 9, 16, 17, 24, 31, 32.
8. Since marriage ties in biblical genealogies may reflect a covenantal link between two kinship groups, the marriage between Aaron and Elisheba may symbolize the link between the Aaronide priests and the tribe of Judah. Thus the priestly house of Jerusalem's Temple would be regarded as relatives of the Davidic royal line (G. Galil, "The Sons of Judah and the Sons of Aaron in Biblical Historiography," VT 35 [1985]: 488–495).
9. Priests were excluded from the Elephantine ***degel*** (B. Porten, ***Archives from Elephantine*** [Berkeley: University of California Press, 1968]).
10. Y. Yadin, ***The Scroll of the War of the Sons of Light against the Sons of Darkness*** (London: Oxford University Press, 1962), 100 n. 3.
11. Sefer ha-Mivḥar.
12. A. Dillmann, ***Die Bücher Numeri, Deuteronomium, und Josua*** (Leipzig: S. Hirzel, 1886).

Chapter 3

1. For the Akk. equivalent ***mullû qāta,*** see AHW, s.v. ***malû*** 4d,e and CAD, s.v. ***malû*** 9C, p. 187, which allude to the possibility that originally some symbol of authority was placed in the person's hands.
2. For "by the will of," see 14:37; Shadal on Gen. 10:9; Rashi on Gen. 27:7.
3. R. Isaac in PdRK 26:10, Rashi, and Ibn Ezra.
4. J. Milgrom, ***Studies in Levitical Terminology*** (Berkeley: University of California Press, 1970), 33–34.
5. With priests it connotes "officiate," in which case it does not take a direct object (e.g., Exod. 28:35); but with the Levites, it connotes either "guard" (the Tabernacle, 1:50) or "assist" (the priests, 18:2, or laity, 16:9).
6. Abravanel on 3:5, Num. R. 3:8, 6:3.
7. Significantly, the guarding of the tent-shrine at Mari is also performed by a member of a nonpriestly class—the ***āpilum***-prophet (ARM 1.91.26–27).
8. Milgrom, ***Studies in Levitical Terminology,*** pp. 50–52.
9. III.23–90; ANET, p. 209.
10. Sefer ha-Mivḥar; and see chap. 4.
11. The passive participle ***natun/natin*** is the semantic equivalent of Akk. ***širku,*** "presented, devoted, devotee," A. E. Speiser, "Unrecognized Dedication," *IEJ* 13 (1963), 69–73. The ***netinim*** were a special class of servants in the Second Temple who performed "the labor of the Levites" (Ezra 8:20). See also vv. 12,41; 8:18–19; 18:6; Exod. 30:16; Josh. 9:27; 1 Sam. 1:11.

12. In view of this process, LXX and Sam. read *li,* i.e., "Me" (the Lord), instead of "him." It may be significant that in South Arabic inscriptions, the root *lwh* (the same as Levi) refers to a person donated to the sanctuary as the result of a debt or vow.

13. Perhaps, then, the double occurrence of ***netunim netunim*** (also in 8:16) should be read as ***netinim netunim,*** "assigned servants" (J. Licht, *A Commentary on the Book of Numbers 1–10* [Hebrew] [Jerusalem: Magnes Press, 1985]).

14. Meyuḥas.

15. M. Bayliss, "The Cult of Dead Kin in Assyria and Babylonia," *Iraq* 35 (1973): 115–125.

16. Mish. Zev. 14:4, Mekh. SbY on Exod. 24:5, Targ. Jon. on Exod. 24:5, Num. R. 4:8.

17. LXX and Sam. precede this statement with "They shall be their (the first-borns') redemption," referring to vv. 40–51.

18. Sefer ha-Mivḥar on 3:46.

19. C. J. Labuschagne, "The Pattern of the Divine Speech Formulas in the Pentateuch: The Key to Its Literary Structure," VT 32 (1982): 268–296.

20. E.g., Num. R. 4:10, Tanḥ. Num. 25, Sanh. 17a.

21. Licht, *A Commentary.*

22. J. Milgrom, "Sancta Contagion and Altar/City Asylum," VTSup 32 (1981): 278–310.

23. The particle *'et* before "the cords" (and before previously mentioned "the screen") indicates apposition (cf. 1 Sam. 17:34; Ezek. 14:22b; Hag. 2:17). However, it is also possible that this verse was borrowed from 4:26, indicating that the entire list here may have been copied from that in chap. 4 (Licht, *A Commentary*).

24. Num. R. 6:3, 4.

25. G. B. Gray.

26. Cf. Lev. 27:6 and Tosef. Shab. 15[16]:7.

27. Cf. Tanḥ. Num. 21.

28. Cf. MK 24b.

29. Alternatively, the words "first-born among the" *(bekhor be)* may be an incorrect gloss (see the following note).

30. G. B. Gray arrives at this same conclusion by emending, in v. 41, ***kol bekhor bi-vehemat,*** "every first-born among the cattle (of the Israelites)," to ***kol behemat bekhor,*** "all the cattle of the first-born." The emendation, however, is unnecessary. V. 41 seems to be a doublet of v. 45 since a repetition of the command "Take the Levites . . ." is superfluous. V. 41 may be an incorrect gloss to explain the possessive of ***behemtam,*** "their cattle," in v. 45. Thus without v. 41, the structure of vv. 40–51 is flawless: Vv. 40, 42–43 relate the counting of the first-born, and vv. 44–51 describe this substitution together with their animals by the Levites and their animals.

Chapter 4

1. It may be of redactional significance that God's address to Moses ***and*** Aaron occurs precisely seven times (Lev. 11:1; 13:1; 14:33; 15:1; Num. 2:1; 4:1, 17; C. J. Labuschagne, "The Pattern of the Divine Speech Formulas in the Pentateuch: The Key to Its Literary Structure," VT 32 (1982): 268–296.

2. ***Ṣābu,*** the exact Akk. cognate of Heb. ***tsava',*** also exhibits the same semantic range. The multivalent range of ***tsava'*** was recognized by the midrash (Gen. R. 10:5): "R. Eleazar said: There are three periods of service *(tseva'im):* for the heaven and earth (Gen. 2:1), for disciples (Job 14:14), and for suffering (Job 7:1)."

3. Sam. reads ***ha-ba'*** (cf. vv. 23, 30).

4. J. Milgrom, ***Studies in Levitical Terminology*** (Berkeley: University of California Press, 1970), 77–82.

5. Cf. also M. Haran, "The Priestly Image of the Tabernacle," HUCA 36 (1965): 191–226.

6. The possibility must also be entertained that ***parokhet hamasakh*** should be rendered as "the covering canopy" (see the use of ***sukkah*** in Tabernacle contexts, Ps. 27:5; Lam. 2:6; and especially Exod. 40:3), implying that the ***parokhet*** was a smaller, inner tent that housed the Ark (the verb ***ve-horidu,*** "take down" or dismantle, is especially appropriate for a tent [see 1:51; 10:17]). See R. E. Friedman, "The Tabernacle in the Temple," BA 43 (1980): 241–247.

7. The color of the ***dušu*** stone, as proposed by H. Tadmor, EB (Hebrew), s.v. ***taḥash;*** cf. CAD, s.v. ***dušû*** 3D, Sum. DU_8.ŠI.A, a loanword from Hurrian (Nuzi) ***tuḫsiwe,*** used in dying leather for luxury sandals (Ezek. 16:10) and for the uppermost curtains of the Tabernacle (Exod. 25:4; 26:14). Heb. ***taḥash*** represents the original Hurrian pronunciation.

8. Regarding the Ark, however, another tradition states that the poles of the Ark, once inserted, were never removed (Exod. 25:15). Some harmonize this discrepancy by rendering ***ve-samu*** as "adjust" instead of "put" (Yoma 72a; also Ramban and Ehrlich on Exod. 25:15). But the use of this verb in vv. 11 and 14 argues against this interpretation.

9. The reason may be that the display bread itself was never removed from the table during the march (notice its absence from the list of sacred ingredients assigned to Eleazar, v. 16), whereas the lampstand and gold altar were covered only with their respective utensils but not with the ingredients for their cultic use, the oil and incense that were transported separately by Eleazar (v. 16). Ramban conjectures that the additional cover for the table (the violet cloth) was for separating the bread from the other utensils placed on the table, interpreting the second "upon it" (v. 7) as on the table. Others surmise that the third cloth was necessary for packing the larger number of utensils associated with the table.

10. Haran, "The Priestly Image of the Tabernacle."

11. See ANEP, fig. 657, for a picture of a Babylonian lampstand and lamp.

12. G. B. Gray; and cf. 13:23.

13. LXX renders "put the ***kalupter*** on," corresponding to the rabbinic view that the altar was covered with a vessel called ***pesukter*** (Sifra Tsav 2:10) so that the altar fire would never be extinguished (Lev. 6:6).

14. Actually red-purple, Akk. ***argamannu.***

15. Actually blue-purple, Akk. ***takiltu.***

16. Possibly because the removal of the ashes has already been prescribed (v. 13; J. Licht, *A Commentary on the Book of Numbers* [Hebrew] [Jerusalem: Magnes Press, 1985]).

17. So Rashi; see TJ Shab. 10:3.

18. Ibn Ezra, Ramban.

19. The NJPS rendering can also be justified. See the next note.

20. The possibility also exists that this term might be rendered "the shrine," i.e., the inner room of the sanctuary containing the Ark (e.g., Exod. 26:33–34) as opposed to the sanctuary as a whole (***kodesh,*** vv. 15, 20), in which case the rendering "approach" should be retained. The meaning of this verse would then be that the Kohathites are in maximum peril if they dare approach the uncovered Ark (see v. 20).

21. Y. Avishur, in ***Numbers*** (Hebrew), by J. Milgrom et al., ***Encyclopedia of the Biblical World*** (Ramat Gan: Revivim, 1985), ad loc.

22. See 1 Sam. 6:19, Num. R. 5:9; cf. Ibn Ezra, Ramban.

23. ANET, p. 649, lines 128–129.

24. ANET, p. 618, lines 449–450.

25. So Num. R. 5:9, Ibn Ezra (i), Rashbam, and Ramban (see 2 Sam. 20:19–20; Isa. 3:12; 25:7–8; Job 8:18). The LXX renders "suddenly," presumably on the basis of ***billa',*** "swallow" (e.g., Job 7:19). The Dead Sea sect also understood this verse in this way: "and they shall not enter suddenly *(bela')* into My sanctuary" (11QTemple 46:9).

26. My student, G. Marcus.

27. An infinitive form (Ibn Ezra) like ***u-le-massa',*** "set in motion" (10:2; GKC, secs. 45e, 115).

28. See the rabbinic controversy (Shab. 28a).

29. Shadal, A. Ehrlich, Hamiqra Kifshuto (Heb.), 3 vols. (Berlin: Poppelauer, 1899–90). The reading ***bahem***, "with them," i.e., with the work tools, for ***lahem*** (so LXX) would refer to such tasks as undoing the beams and bolts of the Tabernacle and the enclosure curtains (cf. Ezek. 44:14).

30. The LXX reads ***be-shemot***, "by name," as in v. 32, but it is meaningless here. Labeling would be essential for the numerous objects under Merarite charge, e.g., sockets, pegs, bars, and cords (vv. 30–31). The Gershonites, however, had only the Tabernacle curtains as their removal duty, few in number and large in size; their loss or misplacement would be inconceivable. It should also be noted that the Merarites need four wagons to transport their load in comparison with the Gershonites' two wagons (7:7–8). Moreover, the Merarites are twice reminded of their guarding duties (vv. 31, 32). It should be mentioned, therefore, in connection with the Gershonites at least once!

31. My student, G. Marcus.

32. Taking ***le-khol keleihem u-le-khol ʿavodatam*** as a hendiadys. The ***lamed*** of ***le-khol*** is found at the end of a list (cf. 3:26).

Chapter 5

1. Cf. Sif. Num. 1, Mish. Kelim 1:8.

2. Heb. ***tsaruʿa***. The passive participle can be used adjectivally (Lev. 13:44) or as a noun, as here (also in Lev. 14:3; 22:4). The Pual participle ***metsoraʿ*** is more usual (e.g., Lev. 14:2; 2 Sam. 3:29; 2 Kings 5:1, 11).

3. Mish. Nid. 7:4, Josephus, Ant. 3.11.3.

4. So called in Ket. 42a.

5. That this law assumes and supplements the law of Lev. 5:20–26 bears momentous weight in determining the redaction of the Book of Numbers. The fact that the redactor could not merely attach this supplement to the main body of the law in Leviticus can only mean that, for him at least, the text of Leviticus was already fixed. Thus, if this supplement was incorporated into the Book of Numbers, the only possible conclusion is that it was assembled after the Book of Leviticus had achieved its final form. This same conclusion will be drawn from the discussion of 9:14; 19; 27:1–11; 36 (see Excursuses 20, 48, and 77).

6. Rabbinic halakhah prescribes flagellation for such a crime. However, it also bears witness to an ancient tradition that the penalty was death by God (Targ. Jon. on Lev. 5:1; Mish. Sanh. 4:5; Tosef. Shevu. 3:4; Tosef. Sot. 7:2f.; Philo, 2 L.A. 26; CD 15:4).

7. J. Milgrom, ***Cult and Conscience*** (Leiden: E. J. Brill, 1976), 80–82; U. Cassuto, ***Biblical and Oriental Studies***, vol. 1 (Jerusalem: Magnes Press, 1973), 3–4.

8. Contra Ramban.

9. Cf. Targums Onk. and Jon., "tells a lie."

10. Interestingly, the Dead Sea sectarians also interpreted this clause as the beginning of the apodosis, for their law of the false oath reads: "If he transgresses (his oath), he becomes guilty and confesses and makes restitution . . . (CD 15:4). When the root ***ʾ-sh-m*** has no object it means "feel guilt"; see Lev. 4–5 (Milgrom, ***Cult and Conscience***, pp. 1–12).

11. Cf. Philo, 1 Laws 235–238.

12. ***Ve-hitvadu . . . ʿasu***. The plural endings on these verbs are surprising in view of this law, which, otherwise, is couched in the singular. However, since both verbs are III-***he***, which stem from original III-***waw*** forms (GKC, sec. 75a, b), the possibility must be entertained that the ***waw*** at the end of these verbs represents the third radical and should be read as ***aw*** (not ***u***)—singular in form.

13. Cf. Sif. Num. 3.

14. Heb. ***be-roʾsho*** as the Akk. semantic equivalent ***ana qaqqadam*** (lit. "in its head"); cf. English "capital," which always means "the principal" (Sif. Num. 3).

15. E.g., the Hittite "Instructions for Palace Personnel to Insure the King's Purity" (ANET, p. 207).

16. E.g., Tosef. BK 10:5, Mish. Git. 5:5, Mish. Eduy. 7:9.

17. J. Milgrom, "The Cultic ʾAsham," in ***Proceedings of the Sixth World Congress of Jewish Studies, 1973*** (Jerusalem: World Union of Jewish Studies, 1978), 299–308.

18. Cf. BK 109a.

19. Cf. Lev. 5:15, 18, 25 and ***kesef ʾasham***, "ʾasham silver," 2 Kings 12:17. The LXX reads ***yihyeh*** for ***la-YHVH***, yielding "go to the priest."

20. J. N. Postgate, "Land Tenure in the Middle Assyrian Period: A Reconstruction," BSOAS 34 (1971): 496–520.

21. Mish. Yoma 8:9; cf. Mish. BK 9:5.

22. Rashi, Ibn Ezra; cf. Sif. Num. 6.

23. Num. 18:12, R. Ishmael in Sif. Num. 5.

24. Sif. Num. 6.

25. This interpretation is further supported by the active verbs occurring in each verse of our text. ***Yakrivu*** (v. 9) refers to donations to the sanctuary (but not necessarily to the altar, e.g., Exod. 40:12; Lev. 7:14; Num. 5:16; 8:9–10; 17:3). And ***yitten*** (v. 10), a noncultic term, then refers to dedicated foods that bypass the sanctuary and are given directly to the priest, e.g., a tithe of the tithe (Num. 18:28) and, indeed, all the priestly prebends listed in Num. 18:11–19 (note ***mattanam*** at the head of the list, v. 1).

26. ***Ve-khol . . . le-khol*** has the force of a hendiadys (e.g., 4:32a) and is the equivalent of ***terumot ha-kadashim***, "the sacred gifts" (18:19; cf. Lev. 22:12).

27. LXX adds "to the Lord," the only fitting object for ***hikriv***, "offer." The latter, however, need not take an object, in which case it should have a disjunctive accent, as in Lev. 7:8.

28. Sif. Naso' 6. For the possible historical background of this law, see J. Milgrom, ***Studies in Cultic Theology and Terminology*** (Leiden: E. J. Brill, 1983), 168–170.

29. Here the Masoretic cantillation is correct; "priest" is a fitting object of the verb ***natan***, "give" (cf. Lev. 5:16; 22:14; Deut. 18:3; 1 Sam. 2:15; Ezek. 44:30).

30. Milgrom, ***Cult and Conscience***, pp. 133– 136.

31. Ibn Ezra; Targums Onk. and Jon. render "lied to him" (cf. v. 6), an excellent rendering, considering that a false oath is the most notorious form of ***maʿal*** (see Lev. 5:20ff.; Milgrom, ***Cult and Conscience***, pp. 19–22).

32. Therefore ***ve-shakhav . . . ʾotah shikhvat zeraʿ*** must mean "he had semen-producing sexual intercourse" (cf. Lev. 15:18; 18:20), implying that only completed coitus would make him "impure" and liable to the charge of adultery (cf. Rabbi Judah in Sifra Metsoraʿ 6:8). This expression is abbreviated in the adjuration (vv. 19, 20).

33. Heb. ***ve-nisterah***. The Nifal is taken as a reflexive, literally "she keeps herself secret" (Ehrlich).

34. The force of the pronoun ***ve-hiʾ*** (she) is to render the verb a pluperfect (cf. Lev. 5:2–4).

35. In the priestly writings, it is the land that is capable of an unexpiable, nonritual defilement (Lev. 18:25, 27f.; Num. 35:33–34).

36. Sif. Num. 7, Num. R. 9:29, Ket. 51b; cf. Rashi, Rashbam, Bekhor Shor.

37. Cf. Targums, Ibn Ezra, Karaites, Shadal. The concept is also attested in Hammurabi, par. 132, e.g., "apprehend PN's [proper noun] wife there . . . and the witnesses should make their deposition" (Babylonian Inscriptions in the Collection of J. B. Nies 6.69.21 [Old Assyrian], CAD, s.v. *ṣabātu* 2b). It would be supported by Ezek. 21:28–29, where its coupling with the idiom ***mazkir ʿavon*** is clearly borrowed from this passage (cf. v. 15).

38. A. Ehrlich, ***Randglossen zur hebräischen Bibel***, 7 vols. (Leipzig: J. Hinrichs, 1908–14).

39. Karaites.

40. Cf. Mish. Sot. 1:1, Sif. Num. 7, Num. R. 9:29.

41. 3 Laws 53–54.

42. The root *qn'* means "become intensely red" in Arab. and Syr., referring to the effects of anger on the facial complexion (Shadal on Exod. 20:5; see 25:11).

43. *Ve-hi' nitma'ah . . . ve-hi' lo' nitma'ah.* The balanced ends of the two protases-cases: The husband suspects her regardless of whether she is or is not guilty. The need to effect this stylistic balance would account for the double use of "has defiled herself" in the first case.

44. A rendering adopted by the LXX, followed by Philo, 3 L.A. 55.

45. Cf. Sot. 15a, Men. 6a, Num. R. 9:13.

46. Mish. Sot. 2:1; cf. Philo, 3 L.A. 55ff.

47. Sefer ha-Mivḥar.

48. Philo, 3 L.A. 59–60.

49. T. Frymer-Kensky, "The Strange Case of the Suspected Sotah," VT 34 (1984): 11–26.

50. Cf. also Targums, Mish. Sot. 2:2. The LXX reads "pure living water," followed by Philo, 3 L.A. 58, on the analogy of the gonorrheic (Lev. 14:5) and the corpse-contaminated (Num. 19:17). However, the latter persons are purified outside the sanctuary and camp; thus, the water from the sanctuary laver could not be used.

51. The concept of sacred waters seems also to have been present among the Hittites (KUB XVII.1.i.15–18).

52. Ant. 3.272.

53. See Mish. Sot. 2:2 for the procedure.

54. Tablets in the Collections of the British Museum 36. Sm. 340, tablet 2.11.46ff.; see R. I. Caplice, "Namburbi Texts in the British Museum," *Orientalia* 39 (1970): 119f.; 40 (1971): 135f.

55. This rendering is confirmed by the cognate idiom in Akk., *pè-ra-sà wašarat,* "her hair is unloosed" (W. von Soden, "Eine Altassyrische Beschwoerung gegen die Damonim Lamuštum," *Orientalia* 25 [1956]: 143). Strikingly, the Akk. text continues: *daduša šaḫtu,* "her breast (genitalia?) is bared." The Bible also records that part of the punishment of an adulteress (Ezek. 16:38) was to strip off her clothes (cf. Ezek. 16:39; Hos. 2:5). Thus the rabbinic claim that the breast of the suspected (not just the convicted) adulteress was bared as part of her humiliation (Mish. Sot. 1:5f., Sif. Num. 13, Num. R. 9:33), though not explicit in Scripture, may be based on ancient precedent. Two probable reasons account for the rabbinic addition to her humiliation: to motivate her voluntary confession if she was guilty and to discourage her from resorting to the ordeal.

56. Cf. Mish. Sot. 1:5.

57. Milgrom, *Cult and Conscience,* pp. 108–119.

58. Cf. Sif. Num. 11, Sot. 20a. However, since *marim* is an adjective, one would expect the phrase *mayim marim* (without the article), as in *mayim kedoshim,* "sacral water," in v. 17 (H. C. Brichto, "The Case of the Sota and a Reconsideration of Biblical 'Law,'" HUCA 46 [1975]: 55–70). *Ha-marim,* however, as part of a construct formation, can only be a noun. The LXX reads "waters of proof," or "waters of testing" (so interpreted by Philo, 4 L.A. 61), i.e., oracle, perhaps reading *morim;* cf. Gen. 12:6, from the root *y-r-h,* "to instruct (by oracle," Brichto, "The Case of the Sota"; cf. *torah*). Others relate it to the root *m-r-h,* "rebel," rendering "waters of contention" (G. R. Driver, "Two Problems in the Old Testament Examined in the Light of Assyriology," *Syria* 33 [1956]: 73–77), or *mrr,* "bless," in Ugar., hence, part of a merism, "waters that bless and curse," i.e., waters of judgment (J. M. Sasson, "Reflections on an Unusual Practise Reported in ARM X:4," *Orientalia* 43 [1974]: 404–410).

59. A. E. Speiser, "An Angelic 'Curse': Exodus 14:20," JAOS 80 (1960): 198–200.

60. Num. R. 9:17; cf. Sif. Num. 9.

61. So in the Mesopotamian ordeal, the river "cleansed" *(ebēbu)* the innocent (Hammurabi, par. 2, line 48); so also in v. 28.

62. Num. R. 9:18; cf. 9:35.

63. Mish. Sot. 2:3 acknowledges the confusion concerning the exact wording of the oath (cf. also Philo, 3 L.A. 61).

64. It is also possible to interpret Heb. *nofelet* not as "sag" or "shrivel" (LXX) but as "miscarry" (cf. Ps. 58:9; Job 3:16; Eccles. 6:3; G. R. Driver, "Three Technical Terms," JSS 1 [1956]: 97–105). However, since the effect of the ordeal need be immediate, the latter interpretation is hardly likely. The distended belly is understood either as a sign of false pregnancy, a hysterical condition (Brichto, "The Case of the Sota"), or as a sign of sterility, rendering "be parched" instead of "distend" (Driver, "Three Technical Terms"); or both symptoms can be understood as pointing to a prolapsed uterus caused by dropsy (Josephus, Ant. 3.11.6). This latter interpretation is supported by Akk. texts in which Ea inflicts this disease upon perjurers (CAD, s.v. *agannutilû* A1; Sasson, "Reflections on an Unusual Practise"). The midrash evokes the measure for measure principle: She is punished in the exact place and according to the manner in which she sinned (Num. R. 9:18; cf. Tosef. Sot. 3:1–19, Mish. Sot. 1:7, Philo, 3 L.A. 62). Abimelech's wives became sterile as a result of his intention to commit adultery (Gen. 20:17); and sterility is indeed one of the prescribed divine penalties for incestuous marriages (Lev. 20:20–21). The rabbis clearly posited that the effects of the waters were immediate: "Hardly had she finished drinking before her face turns yellow and her eyes bulge and her veins swell and they (the priests) say: 'Take her away! Take her away! That the Temple court not be defiled'" (Mish. Sot. 3:4).

65. Num. R. 9:35.

66. ANET, 353.

67. J. Morganstern, "Trial by Ordeal Among the Semites and in Ancient Israel," *Hebrew Union College Jubilee Volume* (Cincinnati, 1925), 113–143.

68. Cf. Deut. 29:19f. where the singular and plural of this word occur together (Brichto, "The Case of the Sota").

69. G. B. Gray.

70. Rashi, Bekhor Shor.

71. Milgrom, *Studies in Cultic Theology and Terminology,* pp. 133–158.

72. Mish. Men. 5:6.

73. The vocabulary of v. 27 is borrowed from vv. 24, 13, 12, 24, 22, 21 in that order but with slight changes (cf. Sefer ha-Mivḥar).

74. Tosef. Sot. 2:3; Num. R. 9:25; Josephus, Ant. 3.271, Philo, 3 L.A. 62. The Nifal *nizra'* means to "bear seed, conceive," whereas the Hifil *hizri'a* means to "bring forth the seed, deliver" (Lev. 12:2).

75. Cf. Sif. Num. 20.

76. Resumptive subscripts are part of archival techniques not just in Israel but elsewhere in the ancient Near East, i.e., in Mesopotamia (M. Fishbane, "Biblical Colophons: Textual Criticism and Legal Analogies," CBQ 42 [1980]: 438–439), Ugarit (B. A. Levine, "Comments on Some Technical Terms of the Biblical Cult" [Hebrew], *Leshonenu* 30 [1965]: 3–11), Elephantine and other Aramaic papyri (L. R. Fisher, "A New Ritual Calendar for Ugarit," HTR 63 [1970]: 485–501; Yochanan Muffs, *Studies in the Aramaic Legal Papyri from Elephantine* [Leiden: E. J. Brill, 1969]). This ancient archival practice probably is responsible for the phenomenon of encasing a tablet in a clay envelope on which was inscribed a summary of the contents (cf. Jer. 32:6–15; also Isa. 29:11f.; Neh. 6:5; H. Gevaryahu, "Various Observations on Scribes and Books in the Biblical Period" [Hebrew], *Beth Mikra* 43 [1970]: 368–374), and the rabbinic divorce writ *(get mekushar),* whose earliest exemplars were found at Nahal Hever (Y. Yadin, "Camp IV: The Cave of Letters" [Hebrew], BIES 26 [1962]: 214 n. 10).

77. Sif. Num. 21.

78. Sforno.

79. Brichto, "The Case of the Sota."

80. The term *nasa' ʿavon* always implies punishment through divine agency (e.g., Lev. 5:1, 17; 7:18; 17:6; 19:8; 20:17, 19; Num. 9:13 [with the synonym *ḥet'*]; 14:34; 30:16).

81. Sif. Num. 21.

82. Cf. Sot. 47b.

83. Mish. Sot. 9:9; cf. Excursus 9.

Chapter 6

1. The midrash suggests that the association is temperance: Two kinds of women are contrasted, the virtuous Nazirite who abstains from wine and the adulterous wife who strayed, probably under the influence of wine (Num. R. 10:1–4; cf. Ibn Ezra).

2. U. Cassuto, *Biblical and Oriental Studies,* vol. 1 (Jerusalem: Magnes Press, 1973), 3–4.

3. M. Jastrow, "The 'Nazir' Legislation," JBL 32 (1913): 266–285.

4. Cf. E. Zuckerschwerdt, "Zur literarischen Vorgeschichte des priesterlichen Nazir-Gesetzes," ZAW 88 (1976): 191–204.

5. Sif. Zut. on 6:2.

6. 1 L.A. 248.

7. Cf. Num. R. 10:7.

8. Sif. Num. 23, Sifra Metsoraʿ 9:6.

9. Herodotus, Histories 2.37.

10. Targums Onk., Jon., and Yer., followed by Rashi, Ibn Ezra, and Sefer ha-Mivḥar. R. Eleazar ha-Kappar renders "undiluted wine" (Sif. Num. 23). However, this rendering is contradicted by the following phrase: "vinegar of wine or vinegar of *shekhar*" (J. Licht, *A Commentary on the Book of Numbers 1–10* [Jerusalem: Magnes Press, 1985]). The LXX followed by Philo renders "strong drink." Abravanel and Baḥya claim it refers to other intoxicants.

11. W. F. Albright, *The Archaeology of Palestine* (Middlesex: Penguin Books, 1949), 115.

12. The unique Heb. *mishrat* is so understood in Sif. Num. 23, followed by Ibn Ezra. In rabbinic Heb. the verbal form means "soak" (e.g., Mish. Shab. 1:5, Mish. Naz. 6:1; cf. Naz. 37a).

13. The first word, being in the plural, lends itself to the interpretation "seeds." However, the reverse tradition is recorded in Mish. Naz. 6:2 and in Targ. Jon. The fact that these two are products of the vine and not the ripe grape (v. 3) may indicate that they refer to other parts of the plant. Possibly, the *ḥartsannim* are related to Arab. *ḥuṣrum,* the unripe grape used by housewives as a souring agent like lemon or sumac, or to Arabic *ḥariṣ,* the vine twig whose leaves are stuffed with meat or rice and cooked (H. R. Cohen, *Biblical Hapax Legomena in the Light of Akkadian and Ugaritic* [Missoula, Mont.: Scholars Press, 1978], 37–39).

14. So Sif. Num. 25, followed by Rashi.

15. It is so interpreted by the Samaritans; cf. Abravanel.

16. Lucian (2nd cent. C.E.) reports that in Syria the pagan priests (galli) who looked upon a corpse had to undergo purification and could only enter the sanctuary the following day (De Dea Syria 53). In Rome, the high priest, called the Flamen Dialis, was prohibited from viewing a corpse (S. Lieberman, *Hellenism in Jewish Palestine* [New York: Jewish Theological Seminary of America, 1950], 165 n. 12). In ancient Greece, seeing the dead barred one from entering a temple (T. Wachter, *Reinheitsvorschriften im Griechischen Kult* [Giessen, 1910]). Ritual texts from Mesopotamia, earlier by two millennia, also indicate that impurity could be contracted—and not only by priests—simply by looking upon a corpse (G. Meier, "Die assyrische Beschwörungssamlung Maqlu," AfO 2 [1937]: iv.1.29, 30; H. Zimmern, *Ritualtafeln* [Leipzig, 1901], 164).

17. Though the rabbis deny that this is the case (Sif. Num. 26, Naz. 48a).

18. The question remains why then is the impurity of corpse contamination singled out. The question is reinforced by other laws where the corpse-contaminated individual is mentioned to the exclusion of other impurities, e.g., the Passover (9:10). The answer may reside in the prevalence of ancestor worship in ancient times (see Excursus 48).

19. Cf. Akk. *ina pitti.*

20. Beraita, Ker. 9a.

21. This phrase gives Philo a springboard to discuss the difference between voluntary and involuntary sin (On Husbandry 175–177).

22. Cf. also W. R. Smith, *Lectures on the Religion of the Semites,* 3rd ed. (London: A. and C. Black, 1927), 369ff.

23. Cf. Naz. 18a, Num. R. 10:13.

24. Num. R. 10:25.

25. Bekhor Shor.

26. Mish. Naz. 3:6; cf. v. 2.

27. Targ. Jon. and R. Ishmael (Sif. Num. 32, based on Lev. 22:1–6 and Deut. 34:6, followed by Rashi and Ibn Ezra (i), interpret, "he shall bring himself" (e.g., Exod. 5:19); Rashbam believes the Nazirite's sacrifice and Shadal, his hair to be the object of the verb, but neither has grammatical warrant.

28. This is the prescriptive, administrative order in which the burnt offering is always listed first in contrast to the descriptive, procedural order, which begins in v. 16, where the purification offering always precedes the burnt offering (cf. Mish. Zev. 10:2, Tosef. Zev. 14:4).

29. It may indicate that at an earlier period the purification offering was also used for purposes of desanctification.

30. It is also noteworthy that pigeons, ordinarily permitted for the individual's whole and purification offering (Lev. 1:14–17; 5:7–10), are here not allowed, indicating the severity and sanctity of the Nazirite's vow (G. J. Wenham).

31. Sif. Num. 34.

32. Sefer ha-Mivḥar. However since these latter ancillary offerings are required only after Israel is settled in its land (15:2), the law of the Nazirite, in its present form, is also intended for this future time and not for the wilderness.

33. Men. 46b.

34. Mish. Mid. 2:5.

35. Targums Onk. and Jon.; contrast Philo, 1 L.A. 254.

36. See B. Mazar, *Views of the Biblical World,* vol. 1 (Chicago: Jordan Publications, 1959), 185.

37. Gilgamesh 6.161, 167 (ANET, p. 85); corrected by von Brandenstein and Gueterbock.

38. F. Thureau-Dangin, *Rituels accadiens* (Paris: E. Leroux, 1921), 68f., 118ff.

39. E.g., ANET, p. 348.

40. Cf. J. Milgrom, "A Shoulder for the Levites," in *The Temple Scroll,* vol. 1, ed. Y. Yadin (Jerusalem: Israel Exploration Society, 1983), 169–176.

41. Sif. Num. 36.

42. O. Tufnell et al., *Lachish,* vol. 2, *The Fosse Temple* (London: Oxford University Press, 1940), Appendix B, "The Animal Bones," 93f.

43. Mish. Mid. 2:5.

44. Num. R. 10:21.

45. According to Sifra Tsav 11:3.

46. An elevation is attested in the Egyptian cult, revealing many similar characteristics to the *tenufah:* (1) the Egyptian formula "elevate . . . before the face of the god" is the exact equivalent of the wording in this verse, "elevate . . . before (the face of) the Lord"; (2) the Egyptian offering as depicted in the reliefs (H. H. Nelson, "Certain Reliefs at Karnak and Medinat Habu," JNES 8 [1949]: 329–333) is an aggregate, containing a sampling of all the food placed on the god's table. Correspondingly, all the objects subject to the *tenufah* must undergo the act together, never separately; (3) like its Egyptian counterpart, the *tenufah* offering is placed on the palms of the hands (J. Milgrom, "The Tenufah" [Hebrew], in *Zer le-gevurot: The*

Zalman Shazar Jubilee Volume, ed. B. Z. Lurie [Jerusalem: Kiriat Sefer, 1973], 38–55). The Babylonians also "elevated" a person to a high office (CAD, s.v. *našû* A1), a metaphoric use of the term that originally, however, may have involved some physical movement. Thus, the elevation of the Levites may also have been only symbolic.

47. Correctly rendered by the Targums and the LXX and confirmed by the exact Akk. cognate *tarimtu*.

48. For this and other distinctions between them, see J. Milgrom, "The Alleged Wave Offering in Israel and the Ancient Near East," IEJ 22 (1972): 33–38; and idem, "The Tenufah."

49. The phrase *torat ha-nazir (nizro)* frames this concluding verse as an inclusion (similarly 5:29, 30; 7:84–88).

50. Tem. 10a.

51. Cf. Mish. Naz. 2:5; Sif. Zut. on 6:13; TJ Naz. 5:3; Josephus, Ant. 19.6.1; Acts 21:24.

52. Sif. Num. 43, Num. R. 11:8; cf. Rashbam.

53. D. N. Freedman, "The Aaronic Benedictions," in *No Famine in the Land*, ed. J. W. Flanagan (Missoula, Mont.: Scholars Press, 1975), 411–442.

54. P. D. Miller, Jr., "The Blessing of God," Int 29 (1975): 240–251.

55. M. Fishbane, "Forms and Reformulation of the Biblical Priestly Blessing," JAOS 103 (1983): 115–121.

56. Sif. Num. 39; and see v. 23.

57. Sif. Num. 39.

58. Sif. Num. 39; and see Excursus 13.

59. Cf. Sif. Num. 40, Num. R. 11:13.

60. Cf. Targ. Jon., Sif. Num. 40, Num. R. 11:5, PdRK 1:5.

61. Akk. possesses the exact cognate *nuwwur pānam;* also note Sum. GIRÌ.ZAL, "face-shine," translated in Akk. as *tašîltu*, "joy, pleasure."

62. So Targums.

63. Exod. 33:19; Ps. 123:2–3; cf. Sif. Num. 41.

64. Its semantic equivalent in Akk., *pānam wabālum/nadānum/šakānum*, is used with this same meaning in describing the favor shown by Mesopotamian deities; cf. M. I. Gruber, "The Many Faces of Hebrew *nasa' panim* 'Lift Up the Face,'" *ZAW* 95 (1983): 252–260.

65. Num. R. 11:7.

66. Sif. Num. 43.

Chapter 7

1. See also Gen. 2:4, 17; 3:5; Exod. 10:28; 32:34. Akk. *ūm ša*, literally "on the day that," also can mean "when." The word *be-yom* in the priestly writings can also denote "from the time" (e.g., Lev. 6:13; 7:36; Ezek. 38:18; 43:18). It is equivalent to *mi-yom:* the letters *mem* and *bet*, when serving as prepositions, are often interchangeable, especially in priestly texts (e.g., Exod. 12:19; Lev. 8:32; 14:18; 17:15; 22:4; cf. Saadia, Ibn Janaḥ 84; see N. M. Sarna, "The Interchange of the Prepositions *Beth* and *Min* in Biblical Hebrew," JBL 78 [1959]: 310–316).

2. Sefer ha-Mivḥar.

3. Heb. *tsav;* Akk. *ṣubbu/ṣumbu* means "drays" (cf. Isa. 66:20). Targ. Onk. and most versions and the Sif. render "covered wagons"; Pesh. and Targ. Jon., "equipped"; Targ. Yer. and Targ. Neof., "harnessed"; and Sym., "for military services," perhaps reading *tsava'*, "army." Bekhor Shor renders "plodding" like the *tsav*, "turtle."

4. R. Péter, "*Par* et *shor*," VT 25 (1975): 486–496.

5. J. Milgrom, *Studies in Levitical Terminology* (Berkeley: University of California Press, 1970), 17–18.

6. Cf. Sif. Num. 45, Num. R. 12:16.

7. Num. R. 12:19.

8. Sif. Num. 46, Sot. 35a, Num. R. 12:20.

9. Rashi on Gen. 14:14; Deut. 20:5; S. C. Reif, "Dedicated to *ḥnk*," VT 22 (1972): 495–501.

10. O. S. Rankin, *The Origins of the Festival of Hanukkah* (Edinburgh: T. and T. Clark, 1930), 27–45.

11. Num. R. 13:17.

12. Similarly the denominative verb *hikriv* not only means "sacrifice" but "dedicate," e.g., persons (3:6; 18:2) and other nonsacrificial offerings (28:26; cf. Lev. 23:16).

13. Num. R. 13:13.

14. Cf. Mish. Yoma 4:3, 11QTemple 23:12, 26:6.

15. Sif. Num. 54, Num. R. 13:13, 14:15.

16. My student, S. Rattray. Akk. *parrû* and Syr. *pa'ra'* designate the lamb (Péter, "*Par* et *shor*").

17. Sif. Num. 51, Num. R. 14:1, 2.

18. A. W. Knobel, *Die Bücher Exodus und Leviticus* (Leipzig: S. Hirzel, 1857); G. B. Gray.

19. Contra Ibn Ezra.

20. Sifra Nedavah 2:12, Sif. Num. 58; cf. Rashbam.

21. Cf. Num. R. 14:9, Abravanel.

22. The word could also be vocalized as a normal Piel participle *(medabber)*. Why the Masoretes pointed it as a Hitpael participle is not clear.

23. Friedrich, meaning either "sole of the foot," a contraction of *kp(n) rdwj* (cf. *kappot raglai*, Ezek. 43:7, cited by M. Görg, "Eine neue Deutung für *Kapporet*," ZAW 89 [1977]: 115–118; and idem, "Die Function der Sarafen bei Jesaja," *Biblische Notizen* 5 [1978]: 28–39), or "seat," *k3pt (3>r* plus metathesis) (J. M. Grintz, "Early Terms in the Priestly Torah" [Hebrew], *Leshonenu* 40 [1975/1976]: 5–32).

24. In Egypt the pedestal of Pharaoh's throne was represented by the hieroglyph *maat*, the symbol of the cosmic, divine order (M. Görg, "Nachtrag zu *Kapporet*," *Biblische Notizen* 5 [1978]: 28–39).

Chapter 8

1. Rashbam, Sefer ha-Mivḥar.

2. Perhaps D. Kellermann (*Die Priesterschrift von Numeri 1:1 bis 10:10* [Berlin: de Gruyer, 1970]) is correct in contending that the instructions for the lamp positioning in Exod. 25:37b are secondary, a redactional gloss whose purpose is to claim that Moses received this instruction on Mount Sinai along with the blueprint vision of the menorah (Exod. 25:40). The following support his contention: (1) The positioning of the lamps is part of the day-to-day functions of the High Priest and does not belong with construction directions; (2) Exod. 25:37b switches from second to third person and interrupts the flow of vv. 37a, 38 (note the absence of the verb in v. 38, supplied in v. 37a); and (3) our passage, 8:1–3, is a complete unit—command and fulfillment—requiring no anticipatory statement.

3. Vv. 1–3, in the Heb. order, are an inclusion in chiastic relationship, ABCC'B'A': "(A) the Lord spoke to Moses . . .; (B) when you mount the lamps . . .; (C) toward the front of the lampstand . . .; (C') toward the front of the lampstand; (B') he mounted the lamps; (A') as the Lord commanded Moses." V. 4 forms its own inclusion: "This is how the lampstand was made . . . so was the lampstand made."

4. Abravanel discerns a descending hierarchy: Moses (7:89), Aaron (8:1–4), Levites (8:5–22). The Karaites (cf. Sefer ha-Mivḥar) note that though the command concerned Aaron alone, it was given to Moses, and this was the reason why the previous verse (7:89) was inserted here.

5. Sefer ha-Mivḥar.

6. Targ. Onk., Targ. Jon.; cf. Rashi.

7. Cf. LXX, Sif. Num. 59.

8. Cf. Rabbi in Men. 98b.

9. With LXX and Targ. Onk.

10. With LXX and Sam.

11. Rashi.

12. *K-d-sh;* cf. Exod. 29:1, 21, 33.

13. *T-h-r,* vv. 7, 21.

14. *T-h-r,* a root repeated at the end of the ritual, v. 21b, forms an inclusion with this opening verse.

15. Ibn Ezra reverses the order and has the sprinkling following the shaving. However, in addition to disturbing the order of the text, his interpretation is contradicted by the procedure for the corpse-contaminated Nazirite (6:9), who is cleansed (i.e., sprinkled) before he is shaved.

16. According to Shadal, chaps. 1–19 were given in the second month of the second year of the wilderness period, whereas chaps. 20ff. are to be dated in the fortieth year.

17. So K. F. Keil, *The Pentateuch,* vol. 3 (Edinburgh: T. and T. Clark, 1865); J. H. Greenstone, *Numbers with Commentary* (Philadelphia: Jewish Publication Society of America, 1939).

18. A shaving accompanied by washing and laundering (or changing clothes) is a frequent requirement in Mesopotamian purification rites (R. I. Caplice, *The Akkadian Namburbi Texts: An Introduction* (Los Angeles: Undena Publications, 1974).

19. Cf. Targ. Jon.

20. *R-ḥ-ts,* 19:19.

21. R. Borger, "Die Weihe eines Ehlil-Priesters," BO 30 (1973): 163–176.

22. Sefer ha-Mivḥar. In ancient Ugarit, the village elders took an oath in the sanctuary on behalf of the entire population (PRU V.29 [= UT 2029], 21–30).

23. Ehrlich.

24. Ibn Ezra, Sefer ha-Mivḥar. The LXX reads *ve-ʿasah,* "he (Aaron) shall offer."

25. Another example with the same verb is Exod. 28:42: "You shall also have made (Heb. *ʿaseh*) for them linen breeches."

26. As in the previous verse, the active verb *ve-henafta* can be understood as a passive. A striking example with the same verb is Lev. 23:12: "On the day you have the sheaf elevated" (by the priest, v. 11).

27. Heb. *ve-tiharta* ("once you have cleansed") looks like a perfect attached to a sequential *waw.* But the sequence is the reverse: The ritual is the prerequisite for the job. Hence the verb can only be taken as a past introduced by a *waw* that has the force of a relative conjunction.

28. A. E. Speiser, "Unrecognized Dedication," *IEJ* 13 (1969): 69–73. A parade example of *n-t-n* as "dedicate" is Josh. 20:7–8, where *natenu* stands parallel to *va-yakdishu,* "sanctified."

29. But since v. 16b is clearly based on 3:12, this word may be considered as the feminine form of *peter* used there (cf. *tsedek, tsedakah;* Ibn Ezra, Radak).

30. The Hebrew word order should be reversed (Meyuḥas) as in v. 18 (cf. 3:13).

31. There is good reason to believe that this section and the previous one, the purification of the Levitical work force (vv. 5–22), were originally attached to chaps. 1–4, thereby bringing all the material on the Levites together. A literary criterion also points in this direction: Chap. 4 contains the tandem *tsava'/ʿavad* five times (4:23, 30, 35, 39, 43). The present section has two more occurrences (8:24, 25), giving a total of seven. Since sevenfold repetition is clearly a stylistic device in chap. 4 (see the Comment to 4:19), there is a strong probability that 8:23–26 was originally attached to chap. 4 (Y. Avishur, in *Numbers* [Hebrew], by J. Milgrom et al., *Encyclopedia of the Biblical World* [Ramat Gan: Revivim, 1985]).

32. M. Noth, *Numbers: A Commentary,* trans. J. D. Martin (London: S. C. M. Press, 1968); Kellermann, *Die Priesterschrift von Numeri.*

33. Tosef. Shek. 3:26, Sif. Num. 62, Num. R. 11; cf. Rashi, Rashbam, Ramban.

34. Alternatively, read *taʿaseh* instead of *'asher* (cf. v. 26).

35. G. Brin, "The Formulae 'From . . . and Onward/Upward,'" JBL 99 (1980): 161–171.

36. Sif. Num. 62, Sif. Zut. on 8:23.

Chapter 9

1. Ehrlich.

2. Sif. Num. 65.

3. Thus the emendation of the LXX (*yaʿasu* instead of *taʿasu*) is to be rejected.

4. D. Kellermann, *Die Priesterschrift von Numeri 1:1 bis 10:10* (Berlin: de Gruyter, 1970).

5. According to LXX, Targums, Sam. and some manuscripts, Heb. *va-yehi* should be read as a plural *va-yihyu.*

6. Sif. Num. 68.

7. Ibn Ezra. In this meaning, this verb is usually followed by *poh,* "here" (e.g., Deut. 5:28; 2 Sam. 20:4), though its synonym *hityatstsevu* can stand by itself (e.g., Exod. 14:13).

8. Tosef. Pes. 8:1; cf. Targ. Jon., Sif. Num. 69, Sif. Zut. on 9:10.

9. Mish. Pes. 9:2.

10. Mish. Pes. 9:2; cf. S. Lieberman, *Hellenism in Jewish Palestine* (New York: Jewish Theological Seminary of America, 1950), 43–46.

11. E.g., "Instructions for Temple Officials" (ANET, pp. 207–209).

12. E.g., Kellermann, *Die Priesterschrift von Numeri.*

13. Cf. Mish. Zev. 5:8, 10:2.

14. Mekh. Bo' 12.

15. Cf. Mish. Pes. 9:1, Tosef. Pes. 3:7.

16. So Mish. Ḥul. 4:11.

17. R. E. Friedman, in an oral communication.

18. A. L. Oppenheim, *Ancient Mesopotamia* (Chicago: University of Chicago Press, 1964).

19. The winged sun disk of Egypt is also associated with fire and clouds (G. E. Mendenhall, *The Tenth Generation* [Baltimore: Johns Hopkins University Press, 1973]).

20. Keter Torah.

21. M. Paran, "Literary Features of the Priestly Code" (Hebrew) (Ph.D. diss., Hebrew University, 1983), 54.

22. Abravanel, however, maintains that it means "at the command of the Lord."

23. The Akk. cognate *naṣārum maṣṣartam* (Heb. *natsar* is a synonym of *shamar*) exhibits a similar semantic range.

24. Ehrlich. The additional *mem* is accounted for as a dittography of the first letter of the following word. The construct form is the rule everywhere else (cf. Gen. 34:30; Deut. 4:27; Job 16:22). The form *yamim* seems to have been influenced by its occurrence with the adjective *rabbim,* "many," in the previous verse.

25. Keter Torah.

26. Targ. Onk. takes *yamim* for an indefinite period (as in Gen. 40:4), whereas Targ. Jon. renders it "a full year" (cf. Lev. 25:29).

Chapter 10

1. P. J. Budd, *Numbers* (Waco, Tex.: Word Books, 1984).

2. H. Hickman, *La trompette dans l'Égypte Ancienne* (Cairo: Institut français d'archéologie orientale, 1946), pl. 1, figs. 1–24; B. Mazar et al., *Views of the Biblical World,* vol. 1 (Chicago: Jordan Publications, 1959), 206.

3. E.g., the pair on the Bar Kokhba coin, EB, s.v. *neginah ve-zimrah,* p. 762.

4. Hickman, *La trompette.*

5. Heb. *mikra' . . . massaʿ.* These are verbal nouns used as

infinitives (Ibn Ezra); cf. *massa'*, "porterage" (4:24). The root *n-s-'* means "pull up stakes" hence, "to break camp."

6. According to Targ. Jon. on 2:3.

7. Alternatively, called *kahal,* CD 11:21–23, based on v. 7.

8. Sif. Num. 73.

9. Mish. RH 4:9.

10. The Qumranites seem to have held a similar interpretation for they divide their multiple trumpet calls into two main categories (1QM 8:7, 12): low-pitched legato *(noaḥ ve-samukh)* and high-pitched staccato *(ḥad ve-tarud).*

11. Also Beraita Demelekhet Hamishkan, chap. 13, Ramban.

12. Since the verb in v. 6b is in third person plural and the verb in v. 7 is in the second person plural, the two clauses should not be connected. Besides, v. 6b is needed to indicate the signaling of the remaining two divisions.

13. G. B. Gray.

14. *Khnm,* UT 400.VI.25.

15. *Bārû,* UT 180.20.

16. Thucydides 7.50.

17. Cf. Mish. Sot. 8:1.

18. Sif. Num. 76, Sif. Zut.; cf. Mish. RH 3:4.

19. Tanḥ. Mattot 2.

20. Lev. R. 29:4.

21. Cf. Ecclus. 50:16, Mish. Tam. 7:3.

22. Sif. Num. 76.

23. Ibid.

24. Ibid.

25. J. de Vaulx, *Les Nombres* (Paris: J. Gabalda, 1972).

26. Ibid.

27. M. Delcor, "Quelques cas de survivances du vocabulaire nomade en hébreu biblique," VT 25 (1935): 312f.

28. G. J. Wenham.

29. For this reason it is not part of the list of stations in chap. 33 (Ibn Ezra), but it comprises all the stations mentioned there between Sinai and the wilderness of Zin (33:16–36; note that the last station is Ezion-geber/Elath)—except for one citation (12:16) where Paran is probably a station (Keter Torah). According to F. M. Cross (*Canaanite Myth and Hebrew Epic* [Cambridge: Harvard University Press, 1973]), the Paran stations are located in 33:18b–30a, 34b. Paran is the place of refuge for Ishmael (Gen. 21:21), Hadad, king of Edom (1 Kings 11:18), and David (1 Sam. 25:1, where the LXX, however, reads Maon).

30. Y. Aharoni, *The Land of the Bible* (Philadelphia: Westminster Press, 1967), 181–187.

31. Keter Torah.

32. T. W. Mann, *Divine Presence and Guidance in Israelite Tradition* (Baltimore: Johns Hopkins University Press, 1977).

33. Similarly when the Assyrian monarch begins a campaign or resumes his march, he does so "at the command of my lord Anu/Adad/Ashur" (e.g., ANET, p. 275).

34. Heb. *ba-ri'shonah*. Perhaps the *bet* should be deleted (cf. 2:9, Ehrlich) as a dittography from v. 13.

35. This verse does not contradict 2:17.

36. Beraita Demelekhet ha-Mishkan, chap. 13, Mid. Ag.

37. This is the reading in the LXX, which inverts the Masoretic *le-tsiv'otam va-yissa'u,* which would translate, "troop by troop. Thus they marched."

38. Ehrlich.

39. Father and daughter in Exod. 2:16, 18 are taken to mean grandfather and granddaughter; cf. Gen. 32:10; 29:5; Rashi; Ramban.

40. Ibn Janaḥ, Ibn Ezra.

41. G. B. Gray.

42. W. F. Albright, "Jethro, Hobab, and Reuel in Early Hebrew Tradition," CBQ 25 (1963): 1–11.

43. This last hypothesis harmonizes all the names. However, aside from the emendation it rests on two unproved assumptions: that Moses had a daughter and that Exod. 2:18 must be restored to read "their father [Jethro son of] Reuel."

44. W. J. Dumbrell, "Midian: A Land or a League?" VT 25 (1975): 323–337.

45. B. Mazar, "The Sanctuary of Arad and the Family of Hobab the Kenite," JNES 24 (1965): 297–303.

46. R. Giveon, *Les bedouins Shosu des documents égyptiens* (Leiden: E. J. Brill, 1971), documents 6a, 16a; S. Hermann, *A History of Israel in Old Testament Times,* 2nd ed. (Philadelphia: Fortress Press, 1981), 76–77.

47. Sif. Num. 78; cf. Sif. Deut. 2.

48. For *tov/tovah,* "covenant," cf. Gen. 26:28–29; 2 Sam. 2:6; 7:28. This identical meaning is attested by its Aram. cognate *tovta'* and its semantic equivalent in Akk., *damqu* (M. Weinfeld, "The King-People Relationship in the Light of 1 Kings 12:7" [Hebrew], *Leshonenu* 36 [1971]: 3–13).

49. For *dibber tov/tovah,* "negotiate a treaty," see 1 Sam. 25:30; 2 Sam. 7:28; 2 Kings 25:28 (M. Weinfeld, "The Counsel of the 'Elders' to Rehoboam and Its Implications," *Maarav* 3/1 [1982]: 27–53).

50. See Sif. Num. 81, Rashi, Ramban, Abravanel.

51. Meyuḥas.

52. Also Rashi, Ibn Ezra, Rashbam, Shadal.

53. Which the LXX renders *presbútēs,* "elder," and Targ. Jon., "instructor" (cf. also Rashi, "the light of our eyes"; Rashbam, Shadal).

54. Arab. *'ayn* has the meaning of "military scout" (A. Musil, *Arabia Petraea,* vol. 3 [Vienna: A. Hölder, 1908], 259), but it is not attested as such in the Bible. However, a metaphoric usage is possible once the poetic origins of this passage are recognized; it is part of a bicolon of ten syllables each: *yada'tah ḥanotenu ba-midbar/ve-hayita lanu le-'einayim* (Albright, "Jethro, Hobab, and Reuel").

55. J. Licht, *A Commentary on the Book of Numbers 1–10* (Hebrew) (Jerusalem: Magnes Press, 1985); cf. Sif. Naso' 78, 81.

56. Likkutim 2.17.

57. Sif. Num. 82, Sif. Zut.

58. Hence, Pesh. reads "one day."

59. Targums, LXX; cf. Sforno.

60. Ibn Ezra, Maimonides, Guide 1.12.

61. Heb. *sh-w-b* is a by-form of *y-sh-b,* "sit," as *t-w-b/y-t-b,* "be good," *g-w-r/y-g-r,* "fear," etc. The rendering "rest" or "sit" is particularly apt in Amos 1:3; Ps. 7:7–8 (cf. *kumah*); 23:6; 78:38; Prov. 1:32 (11 *shalvah,* Moses Kimḥi) (A. Ahuvya, "*Yšb* and *šwb* is like *ytb* and *twb*" [Hebrew], *Leshonenu* 39 [1974/1975]: 21–36), Ugar. *Aṯbn wanḫn* (UT 49.III.18f.) *šwb/yšb,* "sit, rest" is frequently attested in combination with *nwḥ,* "halt," in cognate Semitic tongues: Akk. *šubat neḫtim* (AHW, s.v. *neḫtu*), Phoen. *lšbtbtnm bnḥt* (Asitawak I.17–18), and biblical Heb. (Deut. 12:9; Isa. 30:15; Ps. 132:14; Lam. 1:3), all meaning "rest in peace" (J. C. Greenfield, "Notes on the Asitawada [Karatepe] Inscription," *Eretz Israel* 14 [1978]: 75–77).

62. Menahem ibn Saruq, quoted by Rashi, and Judah Ḥayyuj, quoted by Ibn Ezra (citing Isa. 30:15), followed by Ibn Janaḥ, Radak, Shadal.

63. Ehrlich.

64. A. Erman, *The Ancient Egyptians* (New York: Harper and Row, 1966), 135, 264.

65. T. N. D. Mettinger, "YHWH SABAOTH: The Heavenly King on the Cherubim Throne," in *Studies in the Period of David and Solomon,* ed. T. Ishida (Winona Lake, Ind.: Eisenbrauns, 1982), 109–138.

66. That two proper names can be in construct; see, e.g., Baal-peor (25:3), Zoan of Egypt (13:22), Dibon-gad (33:45; cf. 32:34). There is also one indisputable attestation of two personal names in construct, "Gog of the land of Magog" (Ezek. 38:2; G. R. Driver, "Reflections on Recent Articles," JBL 73 [1954]: 125–128). Support for the linguistic phenomenon now stems from the recently published inscriptions from Kuntillet 'Ajrud, which twice feature the Tetragrammaton in construct: "YHVH of Samaria" and "YHVH of Teman" (J. A. Emerton,

"New Light on Israelite Religion: The Implications of the Inscriptions from Kuntillet 'Ajrud," ZAW 94 [1982]: 2–20).

67. Sif. Num. 84.

68. N. K. Gottwald, *The Tribes of Yahweh* (New York: Orbis Books, 1979), 281; M. Margaliot ("The Hobab Pericope: Numbers 10:29–36" [Hebrew], *Shnaton* 7–8 [1984]: 91–108) renders the entire phrase as "Return, O Lord, Israel's countless armed units," treating *shuvah* as a transitive verb (as in Deut. 30:3; Ps. 126:1; Nah. 2:3).

Chapter 11

1. See Lev. R. 1:10 and the Introduction.

2. J. de Vaulx, *Les Nombres* (Paris: J. Gabalda, 1972).

3. The present rendering is based on the root *'-n-n,* which in Arab., Syr., and Aram. means "complain" (cf. Lam. 3:3) and in Akk. *(unninu)* means "sigh" (cf. Ramban). Other roots that have been suggested are: *'-n-h,* implying a plot or provocation (Sif. Num. 85; cf. Judg. 14:4; 2 Kings 5:7) and *'-w-n,* a denominative from *'aven,* "evil," yielding "they schemed evil" (Ibn Ezra; cf. Targ. Onk., Targ. Jon.) or (from this root, cf. Ugar. *'n*), "they acted like mourners" (Bekhor Shor, Radak; cf. Gen. 35:18; Deut. 26:14). The initial *kaf* has also been explained as a device to compare an object with its class or ideal form (BDB 454a), i.e., "veritable" (cf. Isa. 13:6; 29:2) or as a relative, e.g., "*as soon* as they complained . . . the anger of the Lord" (Shadal; cf. Gen. 38:29; 40:10).

4. Mid. Ag. on 11:1.

5. G. B. Gray.

6. Sif. Num. 85. Many manuscripts read "eyes" instead of "ears" (cf. v. 10), but the expression is repeated: "whining before (lit. in the ears of) the LORD" (v. 18), and "ears" makes better sense following a verb of utterance, *'-n-n.*

7. G. E. Mendenhall, *The Tenth Generation* (Baltimore: Johns Hopkins University Press, 1973), 109.

8. Sefer ha-Mivḥar.

9. Sif. Num. 85.

10. Ehrlich.

11. The verb *hitpallel* has conative force, "to seek a judgment" either for oneself or, as in this case, for others (also 21:7).

12. Sif. Num. 85, Rashi.

13. The Hitpael term *hit'avvah* must be distinguished in meaning from the Piel *'ivvah.* The two refer to illegitimate and legitimate desire, respectively. The former, in particular, is largely employed in connection with illicit bodily appetites, e.g., Deut. 5:18 (neighbor's possessions || *ḥamad,* "covet"); Prov. 13:4; 23:3, 6; 2 Sam. 23:15 (food).

14. Shadal. However, LXX and Vulg. read *va-yeshvu,* which goes well with the following *va-yivku,* "wept"; cf. Judg. 20:26; 21:2; Ps. 137:1; Job 2:12–13; Lam. 2:10; Neh. 1:4 (and cf. also Deut. 1:45, LXX, and UT 67.VI.11–15).

15. Sif. Num. 86.

16. Lane, quoted by G. B. Gray.

17. E.g., Mish. Kelim 17:5.

18. J. Feliks, *Plant World of the Bible* (Hebrew) (Ramat Gan: Masada Press, 1968), 174.

19. KAI 214.6.

20. Mekh. SbY.

21. Sif. Num. 88, Sif. Zut. 195; cf. LXX, Targ. Jon.

22. B. S. Childs, *The Book of Exodus* (Philadelphia: Westminster Press, 1974), 282.

23. Cf. Josephus, Ant. 3.1.6. Aram. *bedolḥa,* Akk. *budulḫu,* and Gk. *bdellion,* whence English bdellium.

24. G. Dalman, *Arbeit und Sitte in Palästina,* vol. 3 (1928; reprint, Hildesheim: Alms, 1964). Heb. *reḥayim* is a dual formation since it consisted of an upper and lower stone (cf. Jer. 25:10).

25. Ibn Ezra. The LXX renders it *egkris,* a cake made of oil and honey, an attempt to conflate the description here with that of Exod. 16:31 (as do Targ. Yer. and Targ. Neof.; cf. Josephus, Ant. 3.1.28).

26. Wisd. of Sol. 16:20.

27. Ehrlich.

28. Sif. Num. 89.

29. Ehrlich.

30. Ehrlich.

31. This is the original form of the masculine pronoun (Ehrlich).

32. Ehrlich.

33. Two manuscripts; cf. Rashi on Job 32:3.

34. Targ. Yer., Mekh. Beshallaḥ 6, Sif. Num. 91.

35. Sanh. 17a. The divine council also consists of seventy (PRE 24, Ramban), as alluded to in Targ. Jon. and in the LXX and Qumran texts of Deut. 32:8 (cf. also Test. Naph. 8:3–5).

36. Cf. the Aram. inscription of Pahammua II of Sam'al; UT 51.VI.46.

37. Tanḥ. B. Num. 60–61.

38. KAI 215.2–3.

39. M. Weinfeld, "The Counsel of the 'Elders' to Rehoboam and Its Implications," *Maarav* 3/1 (1982): 27–53.

40. Mish. Sanh. 4:3–4, Josephus, Ant. 14.168–170, 15.173, 176, 365ff.; Mark 14:53ff.; John 18:13; Acts 4:3–6, 22–50.

41. Targ. Jon.; cf. Exod. 5:6. The LXX renders "scribes" (the basic meaning of this root in Akk.), but here it clearly refers to executive duties.

42. Correctly understood by Song R. 2:21.

43. As noted by ARN[1] 34: Gen. 3:8; 11:5; 18:21; Exod. 3:8; 19:20; Num. 11:25; 2 Sam. 22:10; Ezek. 44:2; Zech. 14:4.

44. Sif. Num. 93.

45. So LXX, Pesh.; cf. Tanḥ. B. Num. 61, Num. R. 15:25.

46. The same verb *naḥah,* "rest," describes the final stage of the transfer of the spirit of Moses and Elijah (Num. 11:25; 2 Kings 2:15), and, except for Isa. 11:2, this verb does not appear in any other description of the manifestation of the spirit in the Bible (Z. Weisman, "The Personal Spirit as Imparting Authority," ZAW 93 [1981]: 225–234).

47. Ramban.

48. Ibn Ezra.

49. Sif. Num. 43.

50. Targ. Jon.

51. The Targums read "make them chiefs," taking this verb as a denominative of *'atsil,* "leader" (Exod. 24:11).

52. Apparently Ps. 105:40; Wisd. of Sol. 16:2–3; 19:11–12 follow the Exodus tradition, whereas Ps. 78:26–31 echoes that of Numbers.

53. P. J. Budd, *Numbers* (Waco, Tex.: Word Books, 1984). For this negative usage, see Jer. 12:3; Zeph. 1:7; Isa. 34:6; Jer. 46:10; Ezek. 39:17, 19; and cf. Excursus 24.

54. Sif. Zut.

55. Found only in a marginal gloss to Eccles. 37:3. There may be a reference to this word in Ps. 78:30, *lo'* zaru, "they did not weary (from their craving)" (from the root *z-w-r*), referring to a jaded palate.

56. D. Jobling, "The Sense of Biblical Narrative," JSOTSup 7 (1978): 26–62.

57. G. B. Gray.

58. Sif. Num. 95.

59. *Katsrah yad* is the opposite of *hissigah yad,* literally "the hand attains," i.e., the person can afford (cf. 6:21), or *ha-yad ha-gedolah,* literally "the great hand," i.e., wondrous power (cf. Exod. 14:31).

60. So LXX, Sif. Zuta, ad. loc.; cf. Deut. 5:19; Gen. 38:26.

61. Targ. Onk., Targ. Jon.

62. Cf. *he'asfu* (Sam.).

63. Perhaps it is the same name as Elidad (34:21; cf. Num. R. 15:19), equivalent to Jedidiah, "the beloved of the Lord," Solomon's name at birth (2 Sam. 12:25).

64. Written Modad in the LXX and Sam., perhaps short for Almodad, "beloved of God" (cf. Gen. 10:26). Medad is a dialectic variant of Modad; so ***mo'av*** (Gen. 19:37) = ***me'av*** and ***mesha'*** (2 Kings 3:4) = ***mosha'*** (LXX) = ***moshi'a***, "savior" (e.g., 2 Kings 13:5); cf. Ruth 2:1; ***Kere-Ketiv*** (Sarna).

65. Targ. Jon., Sif. Num. 95, Sanh. 17a.

66. ***Mi-beḥurav*** is an abstract plural as in Eccles. 11:9; 12:1, where, however, the feminine form is used.

67. Cf. LXX, Sam.

68. Targ. Onk., Sif. Num. 95 (cf. 1 Kings 22:27).

69. Num. R. 15:19.

70. Cf. Sforno.

71. Sif. Num. 95.

72. Ramban, Sforno.

73. Cf. Num. R. 25.

74. Cf. Josephus, Ant. 3.1.5.

75. If so, then the incident occurred between Elim and the wilderness of Sin (Exod. 16:1); and Taberah and Kibroth-hattaavah would also have to be located there (M. Harel, *The Sinai Journeys* [Hebrew] [Tel Aviv: Am Oved, 1968]).

76. J. Gray, "The Desert Sojourn of the Hebrews and the Sinai-Horeb Tradition," VT 4 (1954): 148–154.

77. History of Animals 8.597b.

78. Heb. ***va-yagaz,*** which perhaps should be read as a Hifil, ***va-yagez*** (A. Dillmann, *Die Bücher Numeri, Deuteronomium, und Josua* [Leipzig: S. Hirzel, 1886]). However, Kal verbs can be both transitive and intransitive (e.g., ***natah***; J. Blau, in *Numbers* [Hebrew], by J. Milgrom et al., *Encyclopedia of the Biblical World* [Ramat Gan: Revivim, 1985]). For the meaning of this root, cf. Nah. 1:12; Ps. 90:10.

79. Syr. and Arab. ***salvay;*** cf. Sam.

80. Cf. Josephus, Ant. 3.1.5; 3.13.1.

81. Jobling, "The Sense of Biblical Narrative."

82. Targ. Onk., Shadal; cf. Exod. 8:10.

83. Pesh.

84. Cf. Herodotus, *Histories* 2.77.

85. Cf. R. Judah in Sif. Num. 98, Yoma 75b.

86. Targ. Onk., Targ. Jon., LXX.

87. Sforno; J. Licht, *A Commentary on the Book of Numbers 1–10* (Hebrew) (Jerusalem: Magnes Press, 1985).

88. G. B. Gray.

Chapter 12

1. Sif. Num. 99, ARN[1] 9, 39.

2. Cf. LXX, Josephus, Ant. 2.10.

3. So Targ. Jon.; cf. Rashbam.

4. Targ. Onk., Targ. Yer., Sif. Num. 99.

5. H. M. Wiener, *Essays in Pentateuchal Criticism* (Oberlin: Bibliotheca Sacra Co., 1909).

6. Sif. Num. 99.

7. It would be equivalent to the idiom ***dibber be-yad*** (e.g., 17:5; 27:23).

8. Yet G. B. Gray may be correct in stating that ***dibber be*** implies "a closer and more intimate conversation than ***dibber 'el***" on the analogy of ***ra'ah be,*** which signifies either an intense look of pleasure (Ps. 54:9) or an intense look of distress (Num. 11:15; cf. Gen. 21:16). Similarly, ***dibber be*** would imply an intensity of speech, either of hostility (vv. 1, 8) or intimacy (vv. 2, 6, 8).

9. A. Musil, *Arabia Petraea,* vol. 3 (Vienna: A. Hölder, 1908), 400.

10. Y. Kaufmann, *The History of Israelite Religion* (Hebrew), vol. 2 (Tel Aviv: Dvir, 1947).

11. Targ. Jon., Sif. Num. 100; cf. Ramban.

12. G. Coats, "The Way of Obedience," *Semeia* 24 (1982): 53–79; G. J. Wenham.

13. Bekhor Shor.

14. Targums, Rashbam.

15. Ibn Ezra, Ramban.

16. Ehrlich.

17. G. B. Gray.

18. Ibn Ezra.

19. Bekhor Shor, Sefer ha-Mivḥar, R. Nissim cited by Abravanel.

20. Sif. Num. 102.

21. F. M. Cross, *Canaanite Myth and Hebrew Epic* (Cambridge: Harvard University Press, 1973), 203–224; D. N. Freedman, "The Broken Construct Chain," Bib 53 (1972): 534–536; and idem, "The Aaronic Benedictions," in *No Famine in the Land,* ed. J. W. Flanagan and A. W. Robinson (Missoula, Mont.: Scholars Press, 1975), 411–442.

22. J. S. Kselman, "A Note on Num. XII 6–8," VT 26 (1976): 500–505; M. Margaliot, "Num. 12: The Nature of Moses' Prophecy" (Hebrew), *Beth Mikra* 81 (1980): 132–149.

23. Heb. ***'im yihyeh nevi'akhem YHVH,*** literally "If your prophet is the Lord," which makes no sense. Some interpret it to mean: "If your prophet is (a prophet) of the Lord," citing Ps. 45:7; 2 Chron. 15:8 (Ibn Ezra, Keter Torah). The LXX reads: "If a prophet among you is of the Lord" (***navi' mi-kem le***), a reading that motivates Gray, among others, to render "If there is a prophet among you" (***navi' bakhem),*** while transferring the name of the Lord to the beginning of the verse: "And the Lord said" (cf. Pesh., LXX, Lucian). However, it is possible that the LXX simply read ***mYHVH*** (A. Ben-Ezra, "The Criterion of '*oleh veyored,*' in the Bible" [Hebrew], in *I. 'Z. Frishberg Memorial Volume* [New York: Twersky, 1958]), 74–85, presuming that the ***mem*** accidentally fell out because of the ***mem*** that ends the preceding word (called haplography), thereby yielding: "If your prophet is from the Lord." (It should be noted that Ps. 45:7, cited by Ibn Ezra, exhibits the same phenomenon: a ***mem*** missing by haplography.) Targ. Onk. reaches the same conclusion without emendation, regarding ***nevi'akhem*** to be equivalent to ***navi' lakhem,*** "a prophet among you" and begins a new line with the name of the Lord. This is supported by the cantillation: ***Nevi'akhem*** bears a disjunctive accent. Shadal understands it similarly, citing Ps. 115:7, where ***yedeihem*** and ***ragleihem,*** literally "their hands" and "their legs" mean "they have hands" and "they have legs"; Ehrlich agrees (citing Lev. 26:42; Song 1:15; 4:1). Freedman offers a new reason for rejecting any emendations: The construction ***nevi'akhem YHVH*** is a broken construct chain (e.g., Lev. 26:42; Hab. 3:8), which gives the line this meaning: "If either of you (Aaron or Miriam) is (or claims to be) YHVH's prophet."

24. So rendered by Sif. Num. 103, Targ. Onk., Targ. Jon. Heb. ***mar'ah*** is deliberately vocalized in this way (cf. 1 Sam. 3:15; Dan. 10:16; Gen. 46:2; Ezek. 1:1; 8:3; 40:2; Job 4:16) to distinguish it from ***mar'eh*** in v. 8, though both words are from the same root, ***ra'ah,*** "see." They are rendered the same in Targ. Jon. and Pesh. but differently in the LXX.

25. A. Rofé, *Introduction to Deuteronomy,* vol. 1 (Hebrew) (Jerusalem: Akadamon, 1975).

26. W. L. Moran, "New Evidence from Mari on the History of Prophecy," Bib 50 (1969): 15–59.

27. It is also possible to prefix a ***vav*** to Heb. ***lo' khen*** (lost by haplography from the previous word ***bo***) and render the line: "But my servant Moses is surely loyal" (Kselman, "A Note on Num. XII 6–8"). The meaning of ***lo'*** here would not be negative but emphatic, i.e., "surely" (e.g., 1 Sam. 20:9; 2 Kings 5:26; Isa. 38:20; Ps. 89:19; Eccles. 9:4), a usage attested in other cognate languages: Akk., Ugar., Phoen., Nabatean, Arab., and Ethiopic (F. Nötscher, "Zum emphatischen Lamed," VT 3 [1953]: 372–380; C. F. Whitley, "Some Remarks on *lû* and *lō',*" ZAW 87 [1975]: 202–204). Also this rendering would create a parallelism between "loyal" ***(ken)*** and "trusted" ***(ne'eman),*** attested elsewhere (e.g., 2 Sam. 7:16; Pss. 78:8, 37; 89:38). However, the

contrast between Moses and the other prophets is thereby blurred.

28. Cf. Targ. Yer., Targ. Neof., Ramban.

29. Few manuscripts, LXX, Pesh., most Targums.

30. Margaliot, "Num. 12."

31. This word is vocalized differently from *be-mar'ah,* "in visions" (v. 8; cf. LXX). The Pesh. and Targ. Jon., however, render both words by the same root. Others, claiming that this word is identical to that of v. 6 and means "vision," are forced to add the negative particle *lo'* before it, rendering the line "not in a vision or in riddles" (W. F. Albright, *Yahweh and the Gods of Canaan* [Garden City, N.Y.: Doubleday, 1968], 42–43) or to have the negative *ve-lo'* applied to both nouns (Freedman, "The Broken Construct Chain"; and idem, "The Aaronic Benedictions").

32. Lev. R. 1:14; cf. Yev. 49b.

33. Targ. Jon.

34. Sif. Num. 103.

35. Ibn Ezra.

36. S. R. Driver on Deut. 4:12.

37. Indeed, the very point of the vision to Elijah may be to counter the tradition that Moses actually saw a likeness (Exod. 33:23). Albright (*Yahweh and the Gods of Canaan,* p. 42 n. 86) vocalizes the term *tamnit* equating it with *tabnit,* "structure, form, image," claiming that it refers to the enveloping brilliance of the deity like Akk. *melammu* (cf. Introduction to 9:15–23) and pointing to this term's poetic parallel "face" in the Bible (Ps. 17:15) and in Ugar. literature.

38. Freedman, "The Aaronic Benedictions."

39. D. Jobling, "A Structural Analysis of Numbers 11 and 12."

40. Sif. Num. 105.

41. J. Milgrom, *Cult and Conscience* (Leiden: E. J. Brill, 1976), 80–82.

42. ARN[1] 9, 39, Shab. 97a, Lev. R. 16:1–6.

43. Cross, *Canaanite Myth,* pp. 203–204.

44. E. V. Hulse, "The Nature of Biblical 'Leprosy' and the Use of Alternative Medical Terms in Modern Translations of the Bible," PEQ 107 (1975): 115–128.

45. Sanh. 47a, Av. Zar. 5a; cf. Josephus, Ant. 3.11.3, Mish. Kelim 1:4, Sif. Num. 105.

46. Cf. Ibn Ezra.

47. *Tehi* being understood as a second person masculine.

48. Probably reading "our mother's womb" and "our flesh" (*tikkun soferim;* cf. Mekh. 135, Tanḥ. Beshallaḥ 16). Rabbi Akiba presumes that this "original" reading implied that Aaron too was stricken by leprosy but that the Torah tried to cover up this fact by this emendation (Shab. 97a; A. Cooper, "The 'Euphemism' in Numbers 12:12," JJS 22 [1981]: 56–64).

49. The Gk. term for *tsara't, lepra,* refers to scaliness; Hulse, "The Nature of Biblical 'Leprosy,'" p. 93.

50. Sif. Num. 105.

51. M. Greenberg, *Biblical Prose Prayer* (Berkeley: University of California Press, 1983), 9–12.

52. Margaliot, "Num. 12."

53. G. Meier, "Die assyrische Beschwörungssamlung Maqlu," AfO 2 (1937): VII.102; cf. AHW, s.v. *ru'tu.*

54. Bekhor Shor.

55. Jobling, "A Structural Analysis of Numbers 11 and 12."

56. R. K. Harrison, IDB, s.v. "Leprosy."

57. Targ. Jon., Targ. Yer., Sif. Num. 106.

Chapter 13

1. G. J. Wenham.

2. Ehrlich; cf. Ramban.

3. Num. R. 16:4.

4. Rashi, Ibn Ezra, Rashbam.

5. Present Antakya; Targ. Jon. and Targ. Neof. on 13:21.

6. 1 QapGen 21:15–18.

7. Cf. Rashi; *'anashim* like Akk. *awilum* can mean either "men" or "important men," i.e., dignitaries.

8. E.g., El-Amarna 61.2, 71.6; 2 Kings 8:13; Lachish 2.2–3, 5.3.

9. G. B. Gray.

10. Keter Torah.

11. Targ. Neof., Pesh.; and cf. Ibn Ezra, Radak, Bekhor Shor.

12. Num. R. 16:12.

13. 11QTemple 19:11–20:10.

14. G. J. Wenham.

15. B. Mazar, "The Early Israelite Settlement in the Hill Country," BASOR 241 (1981): 75–86.

16. JBC.

17. ANET, p. 328; R. Dussaud, "Nouveaux renseignements sur la Palestine et la Syrie vers 2000 avant notre ère," *Syria* 8 (1927): 220.

18. R. de Vaux, *Early History of Israel* (Philadelphia: Westminster, 1978), 135; idem, "Les patriarches hébreux et les decouvertes modernes," RB 55 (1948): 326 n. 1.

19. E. C. B. MacLaurin, "Anak/Anaks," VT 15 (1965): 468–474.

20. LXX; cf. Targ. Jon.

21. E. P. Uphill, "Pithom Ramses: Their Location and Significance," JNES 27 and 28 (1968 and 1969): 291–316 and 15–39; M. Bietak, "Tanis," AfO 22 and 23 (1968/1969 and 1970): 182 and 199.

22. N. Na'aman, "Hebron Was Build Seven Years before Zoan in Egypt (Numbers 13:22)," VT 31 (1981): 488–492.

23. Tanḥ. Shelaḥ 1:8.

24. Ehrlich.

25. G. J. Wenham.

26. Ehrlich.

27. Cf. the description of the land of Yaa in the Egyptian Story of Sinuhe (ANET, p. 19b).

28. Targ. Neof.

29. Sot. 35a.

30. Num. R. 16:17.

31. Mazar, "The Early Israelite Settlement"; LXX and Sam. read Hivites (see Gen. 34:2).

32. G. B. Gray.

33. J. Licht, *A Commentary on Numbers 11–20* [Hebrew] (Jerusalem: Magnes Press, forthcoming).

34. E.g., G. B. Gray.

35. M. H. Segal, *Introduction to the Bible,* vol. 1 (Hebrew) (Jerusalem: Kiriat Sefer, 1950–1951).

36. *A-kul-šu,* literally "I ate it"; CAD, s.v. *akālu* 5d.

37. Cited by M. S. Seale, "Numbers xiii, 32," ExpTim 68 (1986): 25.

38. Sot. 35a, Num. R. 16:13, Tanḥ. B. Num. 67.

39. Num. R. 16:11, Tanḥ. B. Num. 66.

Chapter 14

1. Targ. Jon.

2. Ibn Janaḥ.

3. Cf. LXX, Targums.

4. Cf. Xenophon, Anabasis 3.1.

5. Ramban, Abravanel.

6. Shadal.

7. Ibn Ezra.

8. Targ. Onk., Targ. Jon.

9. Baḥya.

10. Exod. R. 21:5; cf. Ramban, Abravanel, Keter Torah, and Sefer ha-Mivḥar, citing Isa. 24:21; Dan. 10:13.

11. LXX, Targ. Jon., Pesh.

12. Ted Newing, orally.

13. D. T. Olson, *The Death of the Old and the Birth of the New* (Chico, Calif.: Scholars Press, 1985), 227 n. 43.

14. A repetition of key words spans the intercession and locks it together: "might" (vv. 13, 17), "Egypt" (vv. 13, 19), "this people" (vv. 13, 14, 15, 16, 19, 19), "YHVH" (vv. 14, 14, 16, 18). "Egypt" is an inclusion and with "might" forms a chiasm. "This people" and "YHVH" form an alternating sequence, ABABABAA (Newing, orally).

15. Targ. Onk., Syr.; cf. Ibn Ezra.

16. Cf. *desham'u*, Targ. Onk., Targ. Jon.; cf. Pesh.

17. Ibn Ezra.

18. Bekhor Shor. The negation of an infinitive construct requires *bilti* (e.g., 3:11; 4:15). The unusual form of the infinitive construct *yekholet* is attested with *yevoshet* (Gen. 8:7) and *ḥaroshet* (Ezek. 31:5).

19. J. Milgrom, "Profane Slaughter and a Formulaic Key to the Composition of Deuteronomy," HUCA 47 (1976): 1–17.

20. PdRK 26:1.

21. Ramban.

22. LXX, Sam., Targ. Onk., Targ. Yer., Targ. Neof. (in the margin).

23. Bekhor Shor.

24. Ibid.

25. Targ. Onk.; cf. LXX, Targ. Jon.

26. Ramban, Bekhor Shor.

27. Ramban.

28. Ibn Ezra, Sefer ha-Mivḥar, Abravanel.

29. Ramban.

30. Shadal.

31. K. D. Sakenfeld, "The Problem of Divine Forgiveness in Numbers 14," CBQ 37 (1975): 317–330.

32. G. W. Coats, *Rebellion in the Wilderness* (Nashville: Abingdon Press, 1968).

33. Ibn Ezra.

34. Ehrlich.

35. Ibn Ezra.

36. Bekhor Shor.

37. Newing, orally.

38. Cf. Ar. 15a.

39. The LXX adds Deut. 1:39, as the Sam. does in v. 29, below.

40. Targ. Neof.

41. The *vav* and *yod* can be confused, and in some ancient texts (e.g., the Dead Sea Scrolls) they are virtually indistinguishable.

42. Bekhor Shor.

43. Ibn Ezra. Sefer ha-Mivḥar.

44. Ibn Ezra on v. 24.

45. Rashi.

46. Shadal.

47. The LXX avoids the repetition by reading the second "against Me" as "against you," i.e., Moses.

48. My son, A. M. Milgrom.

49. BB 121b, Bekhor Shor.

50. The words *'attem . . . ve-tappekhem . . . 'attem . . . u-figreikhem* are echoed in Deut. 1:39; and note the repeated vocabulary: *b-w-'* and *'erets 'asher* (vv. 30, 31) and *pigreikhem* and *ha-midbar* (vv. 32, 33); S. E. McEvenue, "A Source-Critical Problem in Nm 14, 26–38," Bib 50 (1969): 453–465.

51. Ibn Ezra.

52. The exact semantic equivalent in Akk., *našû qāta* (and *niš qāti*), also bears a dual meaning of oath and prayer.

53. Contrast Deut. 1:39 "your little ones *(ve-tappekhem)* who you said would be carried off, your children *(u-veneikhem)* who do not yet know good from bad (i.e., sex)," which emends this text so that *taf* has its normal meaning of "your children."

54. The Sam. text conflates Deut. 1:39: "and your sons who today do not know good and evil, they shall enter [the land]" (as the LXX has done in v. 23).

55. Targ. Neof.

56. Radak.

57. Some, however, would read *na'im*, "wander," on the basis of 32:13; others *to'im*, "wander aimlessly" (Targ. Jon., Targ. Neof.).

58. Sarna, oral communication.

59. My son, A. M. Milgrom.

60. Sforno.

61. R. Loewe, "Divine Frustration Exegetically Frustrated: Numbers 14:34 *tenu*'ati," in *Words and Meanings*, ed. P. R. Ackroyd and B. Lindars (London: Cambridge University Press, 1968), 137–158.

62. Targ. Onk., Targ. Jon.

63. Ibn Ezra.

64. A self-contained unit cemented by repeated words and phrases. Each verse contains "men" and twice repeated are "spread calumnies about the land" and "scout the land," the latter forming an inclusion (McEvenue, "A Source-Critical Problem").

65. So Targ. Neof., Syr.

66. Coats, *Rebellion in the Wilderness.*

67. Milgrom, "Profane Slaughter."

68. The Sam. and Hexapla Syr. have conflated this quotation into their texts.

69. Cf. Ibn Ezra on 14:25.

70. Bekhor Shor.

71. Targ. Onk.

72. Targ. Jon., Targ. Neof.

73. Ibn Ezra, citing Isa. 32:14.

74. The latter word (root *k-t-t*) should be punctuated *va-yekhattum* (Ibn Ezra, Radak).

75. Targ. Neof. omits the definite article. The LXX and Sam. conclude the chapter with: "They returned to the camp" (based on Deut. 1:45a).

Chapter 15

1. ANET, p. 343.

2. Ibid., p. 358.

3. Krt 156–171.

4. Mish. Tam. 7:3.

The prophet Ezekiel proposes a different scale for the meal and wine accompaniments in his visionary temple. The following table projects the variations in clear relief:

	Ezekiel		Numbers		
Animal	Meal	Oil	Meal	Oil	Wine
lamb					
(regular)	optional	1 hin	1/10 ephah	1/4 hin	1/4 hin
(tamid)	1/6 ephah	1/3 hin			
ram	1 ephah	1 hin	2/10 ephah	1/3 hin	1/3 hin
ox	1 ephah	1 hin	3/10 ephah	1/2 hin	1/2 hin

The biblical measures transposed to ours would approximate the following:

1/10 ephah = 7 1/2 pints	1/4 hin = 3 pints
2/10 ephah = 15 pints	1/3 hin = 4 pints
3/10 ephah = 22 1/2 pints	1/2 hin = 6 pints

5. Sif. Num. 107.

6. The association of *'isheh* and *neder*, "vow," is paralleled in the Ugar. text Krt 199.

7. Sif. Num. 107.

8. 11QTemple 17:13–15, 18:4–6, 23:4–5, etc.

9. Cf. Exod. 29:18, 41; Lev. 1:9, 13, 17; 8:21, 28; 23:18; Num. 28:6, 8, 27; 29:2, 8, 13, 26, the burnt offering; cf. Exod. 29:25; Lev. 3:5, 16; 17:6; Num. 18:17, the offering of well-being; cf. Lev.

2:2, 9, 12; 6:8, 14; 23:13, the cereal offering; Lev. 4:31, the purification offering; and Num. 15:3, 7, 10, 13, 14; 28:13, 24; 29:6, the libation. For the Gk. analogy, cf. Iliad 1.66–67, 9:497–500. For the rabbinic explanation, see Sif. Num. 143; cf. Targums. See also Maimonides, Guide 3.46.67–68.

10. Sif. Num. 107.

11. Perhaps it derives from the Egyptian wet measure *hnw* (Ibn Ezra on Exod. 30:24, short version; J. M. Grintz, "Early Terms in the Priestly Torah" (Hebrew), *Leshonenu* 39 (1974/1975): 15–17, 181.

12. Cf. Targ. Jon. on v. 7, Mish. Suk. 4:9, Ecclus. 50:15, Josephus, Ant. 2.234, Sif. Num. 107.

13. Since *balul* is masculine, it cannot modify either "meal offering" or "flour," which are feminine. Therefore, the text should read *belulah* as in v. 6, or *balol,* infinitive absolute; so Ehrlich.

14. Sifra Tsav, Millu'im 18.

15. J. H. Greenstone, *Numbers with Commentary* (Philadelphia: Jewish Publication Society of America, 1939).

16. Keter Torah.

17. Bekhor Shor.

18. W. R. Smith, *Lectures on the Religion of the Semites,* 3rd ed. (London: A. and C. Black, 1927), 75ff.

19. For *kahal* excluding the *ger,* cf. Josh. 8:35; 2 Chron. 30:25. For another example of the unusual syntax, cf. Gen. 41:40: *ha-kisse',* "With respect to the throne." Cf. also Gen. 34:8; Lev. 7:18; 1 Sam. 9:20; 2 Kings 2:4; and especially Eccles. 2:14; M. Fruchtman, "Notes on the Study of Biblical Narrative" (Hebrew), *Ha-Sifrut* 22 (1976): 63–66.

20. ARN[1] 38; cf. Shab. 32b.

21. Sif. Num. 110.

22. TJ Ḥal. 2:1.

23. Ibid., 4:8–11.

24. Bek. 27a.

25. Tirat Kesef.

26. This rendering is confirmed by the Targums (cf. Meyuḥas) and the Septuagint and by the exact Akk. cognate *tarimtu* (J. Milgrom, IDBSup, s.v. "First Fruits; First Processed"; idem, "Akkadian Confirmation for the Meaning of Terumah," *Tarbiz* 44 [1974]: 189).

27. E.g., Gen. R. 53:10. That *'arisah* can mean "kneading trough," cf. R. Patai, "'Arisah," JQR 35 (1944–1945): 165–172.

28. Mish. Ḥal. 2:5.

29. Mish. Eduy. 1:7.

30. TJ Ḥal. 1:6; cf. Mish. Ḥal. 1:9.

31. The roots *sh-g-h/sh-g-g* in expiatory sacrifices imply awareness of the act but not of the law (J. Milgrom, "The Cultic *Šegaga* and Its Influence in Psalms and Job," JQR 58 [1967]: 73–79). The fact that this verse uses the stem *sh-g-h,* whereas only *sh-g-g* occurs elsewhere in this section (eight times) may indicate that this verse is based on *yishgu* of Lev. 4:13, which is the only other attestation of the stem *sh-g-h* in the Torah; cf. *q-l-h* (Deut. 27:16) and *q-l-l* (Exod. 21:17; M. Weinfeld, *Deuteronomy and the Deuteronomic School* [Oxford: Clarendon Press, 1972], 277). That the third person plural of Lev. 4:13 has been replaced by the second person plural may be due to the inclusion effect, whereby the beginning and ending of this pericope are deliberately changed from the third person impersonal style of Lev. 4:13–21 (A. Toeg, "A Halakhic Midrash in Num. 15:22–31" [Hebrew], *Tarbiz* 43 [1973/1974]: 1–20).

32. Heb. *kol;* so Targ. Jon., Ramban. "Hebrew idiom in certain cases affirms, or denies, of an *entire* class, where English idiom affirms, or denies, of an *individual* of the class" (BDB, p. 482). Cf. Lev. 4:2; 19:23; Num. 21:8; 35:22.

33. Sif. Num. 111.

34. Ramban.

35. The use of this term is surprising in this context since it implies that the burnt offering was sacrificed before the purification offering (cf. Hor. 13a), whereas elsewhere the reverse is the case (J. Milgrom, *Cult and Conscience* [Leiden: E. J. Brill, 1976], n. 251). This anomaly supports the possibility that originally the text read: "the whole community shall sacrifice one bull of the herd as a purification offering," and that the intervening words were interpolated so that this law would conform to the usual pattern for expiatory sacrifices (Toeg, "A Halakhic Midrash"; but cf. Excursus 35).

36. Sif. Num. 111.

37. Ibid.

38. Maimonides, Guide 3.46.

39. Most likely, *'isheh* is derived from Ugar. *'iṯt,* "gift" (J. Hoftijzer, "Das sogennante Feueropfer," VTSup 16 [1967]: 114–134), or Arab. *'aṯaṯu,* "possessions of every kind" (G. R. Driver, "Ugaritic and Hebrew Words," in *Ugaritica,* vol. 6 [Paris: Paul Geuthner, 1969], 181–184; and idem, "The New English Bible: The Old Testament," JSS 24 [1973]: 5).

40. Toeg, "A Halakhic Midrash."

41. *ANEP,* nos. 466, 480–484, 490–497; cf. C. J. Labuschagne, "The Meaning of *b^eyād rāmā* in the Old Testament," in *Von Kanaan bis Kerala,* ed. W. C. Delsman et al. (Neukirchen-Vluyn: Neukirchener Verlag, 1982), 143–148.

42. D. Kellermann, "Bemerkungen zum Sündopfergesetz in Num. 15,22ff.," in *Wort und Geschichte,* ed. H. Gese and H. P. Rüger (Kevelaer: Butzon and Bercker, 1973), 107–113.

43. Targ. Onk. and Targ. Neof. aptly render *beresh galei,* "publicly."

44. J. Milgrom, "The Priestly Doctrine of Repentance," RB 82 (1975): 186–205.

45. R. Akiba, Sif. Num. 70, Mekh. Bo', par. 8.

46. Toeg, "A Halakhic Midrash."

47. Heb. *'avonah bah* is a hybrid term comprised of *'avono yissa'* (Lev. 7:18; 19:8) and *damav bo,* "bloodguilt is upon him" (Lev. 20:9; Ramban).

48. Cf. Akk. *kissatu.*

49. Rather, "caught." *Motsi'* can also mean "strike" (e.g., 32:23; Deut. 19:5; 1 Sam. 31:3) or "apprehend" (e.g., Gen. 44:16; Deut. 22:28b).

50. Heb. *mishmar* from *sh-m-r,* "to guard," occurs again in Lev. 24:12; cf. Gen. 40:3, 4, 7; cf. *mattarah* (Jer. 32:2, 8, 12) from the synonym *n-t-r* with the same meaning.

51. Akk. *parāsu, purrusu* is used in this sense; cf. AHW, s.v. *parāsu(m)* G9, N6; I. Heinemann, "The Development of Technical Terms for the Interpretation of Scripture" (Hebrew), *Leshonenu* 15 (1947): 108–115; cf. Lev. 24:12, where this stem *p-r-sh* is found again in an oracular decision.

52. N. M. Lund, "The Presence of Chiasmus in the Old Testament," AJSL 46 (1930): 104–126.

53. N. H. Snaith, *Leviticus and Numbers* (London: Nelson, 1967).

54. Sif. Num. 114.

55. Sif. Num. 115, Num. R. 17:5.

56. Reading *ba-tsitsit* for *le-tsitsit.*

57. Men. 43b.

58. Unless the LXX reading of Note 56 is adopted.

59. Sif. Num. 115; cf. M. Weinfeld, "All Who Declare Their Willingness to Serve His Trust Must Bring All of Their Mind, Strength, and Wealth into the Community of God (1QS 1:12)" (Hebrew), in *Studies in Bible (Grintz Volume),* ed. B. Uffenheimer (Tel Aviv: Tel Aviv University, 1982), 37–39.

60. Ibid.

61. Ibid.

62. Ibid.; cf. Sifra Shemini 12:4.

Chapter 16

1. Tanḥ. Korah 3, Num. R. 18:2.

2. The following solutions have been proposed: (1) No translation is required since the verb need not imply any specific action but only the preparation for it (Ramban, citing 2 Sam.

18:18); (2) "took men," "men" being understood (Ibn Ezra, Shadal); (3) LXX renders "spoke," indicating the reading *va-yo'mer;* (4) some versions render "separate himself, started a faction, made a division" (Pesh., Targ. Onk., Targ. Neof.; cf. Tanḥ., reading *va-yeḥallek,* i.e., from the root *ḥ-l-k* instead of *l-k-ḥ*); (5) Korah "took" 250 men, rose up against Moses, and combined against Moses and Aaron (Ramban, thus transposing 2aα to the end of 2.

The following emendations have also been proposed: (6) *va-yakom,* "arose" (A. Kuenen, *A Historico-Critical Enquiry into the Origin and Composition of the Hexateuch,* trans. P. H. Wickstead [London: Macmillan, 1886]); (7) *va-yakhel,* "gathered" (Baentsch); (8) *va-yekanne'u,* "envied" (G. Richter, "Die Einheitlichkeit der Geschichte von der Rotte Korah," ZAW 39 (1921), 123–137; (9) *va-yekaḥ,* "was bold, insolent," from Arab. *wqḥ;* cf. Job 15:12 (G. R. Driver, "Misreadings in the Old Testament," WO 1 [1949–1950]: 235–236); (10) connect "took" with "250 Israelites" (Ibn Ezra, cf. Rashbam, Ramban), deleting "to rise up against Moses, together with" (Ehrlich).

Targ. Jon. reads: "And he took his robe which was all of blue," echoing the following midrash: "What is written in the preceding passage? 'Instruct them to make for themselves fringes . . . attach a cord of blue to the fringe at each corner' (15:38). Korah jumped up and asked Moses: 'If a cloak is entirely of blue, what is the law as regards its being exempted from the obligation of fringes?' Moses answered him: 'It is subject to the obligation of fringes,' Korah retorted: 'A cloak that is entirely composed of blue cannot free itself from the obligation, yet four blue threads do free it! These are things,' he continued, 'which you have not been commanded, but you are inventing them out of your mind!' Hence it is written *va-yikkaḥ,* which cannot but signify discord, his heart having carried him away; as it is born out by the text 'why does your heart carry you away, *yikkaḥakha* (Job 15:12)'" (Num. R. 18:3).

A possible solution is that "men" indeed is the object of *va-yikkaḥ,* "took" (Ramban), but it is not understood by the context (Ibn Ezra) but supplied by the text (v. 2). Thus this verb would be followed by the verb *kahal* (v. 3), "gather," just as in 1:16–17. It need not take the particle *'et* as a sign of the direct object (cf. vv. 6, 17, 18, etc.). Then transfer v. 2aα before v. 1b to read "Dathan and Abiram rose against Moses," thus indicating that originally this text spoke of two discrete rebellions, one led by Korah and the chieftains, the other by Dathan and Abiram (see Excursus 39 for details).

3. Tanḥ. Korah 8; cf. v. 25.

4. It has been suggested that the text should read: "Dathan and Abiram sons of Eliab, son of Pallu, son of Reuben," precisely as is found in Num. 26:5, 8. Peleth would then be a scribal confusion for Pallu, and On for Eliab, while *ben* would replace *benei,* as is found in a manuscript and in LXX, Sam. Alternatively, one might justify the retention of the name On the son of Peleth on the basis of the fact that both names occur in the genealogical lists of the tribe of Judah (1 Chron. 2:26, 33). There is evidence that the tribes of Reuben and Judah shared the same clans, e.g., Hezron and Carmi (Num. 26:5–6; 1 Chron. 2:2–7; G. Galil in *Numbers* [Hebrew], by J. Milgrom et al., *Encyclopedia of the Biblical World* [Ramat Gan: Revivim, 1985], *ad loc.*).

5. Cf. 2 Sam. 10:6, 8; similarly Akk. *amēlu.*

6. ANET, p. 29.

7. *Va-yikkahalu.* The verbs *nikhal* and *no'ad* (Nifal) with the preposition *'al,* "against," predominate in the wilderness rebellion stories (Num. 14:35; 16:3, 11, 19; 17:7; 20:2; 27:3; Exod. 32:1).

8. Rashi, Ibn Ezra; cf. Targ. Jon., Ezek. 44:6.

9. M. Fishbane, *Biblical Interpretation in Ancient Israel* (Oxford: Clarendon Press, 1985), 122 n. 86.

10. Ibn Ezra, Sefer ha-Mivḥar.

11. Num. R. 18:6.

12. Keter Torah.

13. Or they are vestiges of an epic substratum characterized by poetic parallelism, a hypothesis supported by the appearance of a third redundancy, "the one He has chosen"; cf. v. 5.

14. J. Milgrom, *Studies in Levitical Terminology* (Berkeley: University of California Press, 1970), 33–34.

15. These verbs are found in the same sequence with the word *kadosh,* "holy" in Ps. 65:6.

16. Rashbam.

17. In the old script, the letters *vav* and *kaf* were occasionally confused (R. Weiss, in a written communication).

18. Mish. Tam. 1:3, 5:5.

19. Sot. 13b, Num. R. 18:18.

20. G. B. Gray.

21. So LXX, perhaps reading *shime'uni* for *shime'u na'* (cf. 20:10 LXX; Gen. 23:8).

22. Ibn Ezra.

23. Ibid.

24. Keter Torah, Ehrlich; cf. 4:1–20.

25. Num. R. 18:9.

26. Cf. Ibn Ezra, Rashbam, Hazzekuni. Akk. *elû* also records this meaning as well as "submit," which provides the alternative rendering "we will not submit."

27. Targ. Jon. on 14; Meyuḥas.

28. Cf. Rashbam, Gray, etc. for the style.

29. Targ. Jon. on Exod. 2:14.

30. Targ. Jon.

31. G. B. Gray.

32. Cf. Rashbam.

33. Ibn Ezra.

34. Rashi.

35. Ibid.

36. Ibn Ezra.

37. S. E. Loewenstamm, EB (Hebrew), s.v. "*koraḥ, datan, ve-aviram.*"

38. A similar usage is attested in the Akk. cognate *našû.*

39. *Ḥamor.* LXX reads *ḥamud,* "desirable object." However, the MT is supported by Samuel's defense of his administration (1 Sam. 12:3) and by a similar formula in the El-Amarna letters (280.21–24).

40. *'Attah ve-khol.* LXX reads instead *kaddesh,* "sanctify," but it may only be interpreting the text, albeit correctly, since a theophany requires ritual sanctification on the day before (cf. v. 5; 11:18; and Excursus 27).

41. Cf. R. Gradwohl, "Das 'fremde Feuer' von Nadab und Abihu," ZAW 75 (1963): 288–296.

42. J. C. H. Laughlin, "The Strange Fire of Nadab and Abihu," JBL 95 (1976): 559–565.

43. Heb. *U-mosheh ve-'aharon.* Some versions (LXX, Pesh., Vulg.) read *mosheh* (without the conjunction), implying that Moses and Aaron stood at the Tent of Meeting with the rebels. However, a fulfillment statement is needed to inform us that the chieftains who were commanded to offer incense "before the Lord" (vv. 16, 17) did indeed do so. Also, the presence of Moses and Aaron at the Tent of Meeting is mentioned in the next verse and would be superfluous here. Finally, the order in the Heb., placing part of the subject at the end of the sentence, would be bizarre.

44. Rashi.

45. But LXX reads *kol 'adato,* "all his community," i.e., Korah's fellow schismatics. The correct reading can be determined after noting that there is a consistent distinction in the chapter between *ha-'edah,* "the community" (vv. 3, 9, 23, 26), which refers to all Israel, and "his community" (vv. 4, 6) and "your community" (vv. 11, 16), with a pronominal suffix that refers to Korah's cohorts. If so, then *'edah* in vv. 19, 22, 24 must refer to Israel, and the whole thrust of vv. 19–24 is that Korah succeeded in rallying the entire community against Moses and Aaron. Thus the LXX reading cannot be correct; it is just an

attempt to harmonize the contradiction implied by the text that the *'edah* that had gathered at the Tent of Meeting is suddenly shifted to the rebels' dwellings (vv. 24, 26), on which see v. 24, below, and Excursus 39.

46. Targ. Jon., Ibn Ezra.

47. Num. R. 18:11.

48. *Ha-'ish;* the first vowel should be a *pataḥ,* indicating an interrogative, not a *kamets,* implying the definite article.

49. J. H. Greenstone, *Numbers with Commentary* (Philadelphia: Jewish Publication Society of America, 1939).

50. Cf. Milgrom, *Studies in Levitical Terminology,* pp. 21–33.

51. *He'alu min,* a Nifal with a reflexive meaning: "remove yourselves from" (cf. 2 Sam. 2:27; Jer. 37:5).

52. J. de Vaulx, *Les Nombres* (Paris: J. Gabalda, 1972).

53. The LXX reads only Korah here and in v. 27, another indication that at this point the text was in disarray.

54. Ibn Ezra, Baḥya.

55. Abravanel.

56. Ibn Ezra.

57. *Tissafu,* but reading *tasufu* from *suf* (so LXX) or rendering "swept away" from *safah.*

58. *Be-khol ḥatto'tam,* the *bet* of exchange (Ibn Ezra; cf. Gen. 19:15).

59. Note that *va-ye'alu me-'al . . . mi-saviv* is a conflation of two previous expressions *he'alu mi-saviv* (v. 24) and *me-'al* (v. 26), indicating that v. 27a may have been rewritten (cf. the Comment to v. 24).

60. Cf. 2 Kings 2:24, Shab. 34a, Ehrlich.

61. Tanḥ. Korah 22.

62. Ramban.

63. Ibn Ezra.

64. Rashi.

65. Ibn Ezra; P. D. Hanson, "The Song of Heshbon and David's Nir," HTR 61 (1968): 297–320; a meaning attested for the Piel pattern of *bara'* (see Josh. 17:15, 18; Ezek. 21:24; 23:47).

66. Num. R. 18:4.

67. My student, N. Ben-Dov.

68. Cf. UT 49.II, 15–23.

69. Ibn Ezra.

70. Alternatively, see Ramban's view (v. 33).

71. Ant. 4.50.

72. Cf. 14:11, 30.

73. Cf. Isa. 5:14 for the same idiom with Sheol.

74. Sanh. 110a.

75. Ramban; see also G. Hort, "The Death of Qorah," AusBR 7 (1959): 2–26.

76. Cf. Ibn Ezra.

77. In the putative original version, this verse may have followed verse 24 or 27a since it continues the story of the chieftains. However, the perfect *yatse'ah* (rather than *va-tetse';* cf. Lev. 9:24; 10:2), which should be rendered "had gone forth," supports the present order of the text; i.e., after describing the death of the principals by earthquake, the narrative reverts to the simultaneous death of the 250 chieftains at the Tabernacle. And 26:10 also supports this interpretation, showing that chap. 26 had the MT of chap. 16 before it and, hence, that the Dathan and Abiram story was fused with the Korah and the chieftains story at an early stage.

Chapter 17

1. G. B. Gray; cf. Lev. 10:4; 21:10.

2. Ehrlich.

3. On the analogy of Lev. 10:4.

4. Rashi, Ibn Ezra, Ramban.

5. Targums, LXX.

6. So Targ. Jon., Pesh.

7. The particle *'et,* which begins the verse, is not a problem since it may precede the subject as a sign of the predicate; cf. Gen. 27:42; Deut. 12:22.

8. *Be-nafshotam* (cf. 2 Sam. 23:17; 1 Kings 2:23), the *bet* of exchange. For *nefesh* as the life essence, see 31:50.

9. *Ve'asu 'otam,* literally "and they shall make them," the verb understood as a passive with an impersonal subject.

10. The verb *raka',* "hammer," yields *rakia',* "firmament," the sky-dome hammered thin and stretched over the earth (Gen. 1:6).

11. *Hikrivum,* a pluperfect construed as a passive.

12. Heb. *'ot,* literally "sign," goes together with *zikkaron,* "reminder" (v. 5). Cf. Gen. 9:12, 13, 15; Exod. 12:13, 14, where the sign signals God's favorable intervention (also 14:11), but here it is a stern warning to potential encroachers upon priestly functions (cf. also 15:40).

13. Rashbam, Ramban, Bekhor Shor, Radak.

14. *Yikrav,* literally "qualify" (cf. 16:5 and J. Milgrom, *Studies in Levitical Terminology* [Berkeley: University of California Press, 1970], 33–35), and with the negative particle *lo'* means "encroach" (ibid., pp. 16–33).

15. Mid. Ag.

16. Ibn Ezra, Rashbam, Ramban.

17. *Va-yavo' 'el penei,* literally "came to the front." *'El penei* is equivalent to *lifnei,* the former used after the verbs of motion, the latter after verbs of rest (e.g., 20:10).

18. The LXX, however, adds "and Aaron."

19. *Herommu,* Nifal with reflexive meaning, synonymous with *he'alu* (16:23) and *hibbadelu* (16:21).

20. Cf. David's sacrifice (2 Sam. 24:16, 25).

21. Mekh. Bo' 11.

22. Bekhor Shor.

23. Ibn Ezra.

24. Mid. Ag.

25. *Holekh,* a Hifil. For the meaning "take," cf. Exod. 2:9 (Targums, Ibn Ezra). The word "it" is understood (cf. 12) or read *holikhah.*

26. Cf. the illustration in O. Keel, "Kanaanäische Sühneriten," VT 25 (1975): 421, fig. 5.

27. O. Keel-Leu, *Jahwe-Visionen und Siegelkunst* (Stuttgart: Verlag Katholisches Bibelwerk, 1977).

28. Cf. Rashi, Shab 89a.

29. Targ. Jon.

30. Mekh. Bo' 11; cf. Milgrom, *Studies in Levitical Terminology,* nn. 75, 109.

31. Not in the text but understood.

32. Shadal.

33. N. H. Snaith, *Leviticus and Numbers* (London: Nelson, 1967).

34. G. J. Wenham.

35. According to Herodotus 1.195.

36. The only precise synonym is *shevet,* which, however, just like *matteh* also connotes both tribe and staff; alternating it with *matteh,* "rod," would result in chaos; cf. v. 23 for a similar substitution. Probably the term *beit 'avot* is intended (as in v. 18) since the *nasi'/ro'sh* is the head of a clan *(beit 'avot/mishpaḥah;* see the Comment to 1:4, 16, 44) not a household *(beit 'av).*

37. Rashi, Ibn Ezra, Ramban.

38. Ant. 4.63–66.

39. *'Asher 'ivva'ed,* imperfect tense, implying "where I regularly meet" (Ibn Ezra). *'Ivva'ed* and *ha-'edut* resemble each other in sound (homonyms)—although their roots are different (*y-'-d* and *'-w-d,* respectively)—providing a play on words.

40. This latter reading predicates that the *mem* of *lakhem* is a dittography of the following *shin;* in the ancient Heb. alphabet, *mem* and *shin* resemble each other.

41. Snaith, *Leviticus and Numbers.*

42. A. Dillmann, *Die Bücher Numeri, Deuteronomium, und Josua* (Leipzig: S. Hirzel, 1897).

43. Note that the previous mention of this clause (v. 19) interchanges the terms in chiastic order, "in the Tent of Meeting before the Pact" (my student, E. Adler).

44. H. Bonnet, "Gottesstab," in *Reallexikon der ägyptischen Religionsgeschichte* (Berlin: de Gruyter, 1952), 254–256.

45. Cf. Exod. R. 27:9.

46. M. V. Fox, "The Sign of the Covenant: Circumcision in the Light of the Priestly *'Ot* Etiologies," RB 81 (1974): 557–596.

47. Sefer ha-Mivḥar.

48. Reading *u-tekhal,* an active verb (Piel), as *ve-tekhal* (Kal).

49. Cf. Num. 1:54; 8:21; Exod. 39:32b; 40:16.

50. Pesh. understands it as an emphatic, "behold."

51. The first verb acting as an auxiliary, with the adverbial meaning "entirely, wholly," e.g., *tamnu nikhratu,* "wholly cut off" (Josh 3:16); *safu tammu,* "entirely consumed" (Ps. 73:19).

Chapter 18

1. Cf. Rashi, Ibn Ezra.

2. Rashi, Ibn Ezra.

3. J. Milgrom, *Cult and Conscience* (Leiden: E. J. Brill, 1976), 3–11.

4. Mish. Sanh. 9:6; cf. Tosef. Kelim BK 1:6.

5. *Hakrev.* The Hifil, the causative conjugation of *karav,* "qualify," means "make qualify, render eligible, associate" (see 3:6; 16:5, 9–10).

6. Cf. J. Milgrom, "Priestly Terminology and the Political and Social Structure of Pre-Monarchic Israel," JQR 69 (1978): 65–81.

7. Ehrlich.

8. The verb *sheret,* "assist," is associated with *mishmeret,* "guard duty" (cf. 1:50b, 53b; 3:6b, 7a; 8:26). *Sheret,* which originally may have meant "serve," developed multiple connotations reflecting various kinds of "service": Priests "officiate" (e.g., Exod. 39:26 [the direct object rarely being used]), whereas Levites "guard" the Tabernacle (e.g., 8:26) and "assist" the laity (e.g., 16:9) and priesthood (e.g., 3:6).

9. Sif. Zut. on Num. 18:2, Sifra Tsav, par. 2:12, 3:5, Mish. Tam. 1:1–2, Mish. Mid. 1:1, 6, 9, Sif. Num. 116.

10. *Lamed* before *kol* at the end of a series means "including" (e.g., 3:26; 4:27, 32, 33).

11. For *karav* as "qualify, be associated," cf. v. 2; 16:9–10.

12. *Lakhem mattanah netunim le-YHVH* (cf. 3:9 and the Comment to 8:16).

13. Abravanel.

14. Sforno.

15. *Le-khol devar.* For this usage see 1 Chron. 26:32; 27:1; 2 Chron. 19:11.

16. *U-lemibbet,* literally "inside." *Bayit* and *ḥuts* mean inside and outside, respectively (e.g., Gen. 6:14; Exod. 26:35; 1 Kings 7:9). The prefixed *lamed* has emphatic force (e.g., 2 Sam. 7:19; Jer. 42:8; cf. Jer. 42:1; Keter Torah) or is a repetition of the *lamed* of previous *le-khol.*

17. *Va-'avadtem 'avodat mattanah 'etten 'et-kehunatkhem.* The rendering cited here (1) follows Speiser. However, it fails on three counts: *(a)* It requires taking the previous words *tishmeru* and *va-'avadtem* as a hendiadys, "be careful to perform," even though they are separated from each other by eight words. *(b)* The priesthood has to be construed as a *mattanah,* "dedication," although this term implies subordination. Indeed it is so applied to the subordinated Levites (3:9; 8:16, 19; 18:6) and emoluments (18:8, 11, 12, 19), whereas priests are never "dedicated" *(natan)* but "consecrated" (*kiddesh;* cf. Exod. 29:1). *(c)* Most crucial of all, *'avodah,* "labor," is never assigned to the priests but only to the Levites.

Additional but equally unsatisfactory solutions have been proposed: (2) Following LXX, Sam., Pesh., some commentaries have proposed reading *va-'avadtem 'avodah,* "and you shall perform the labor," but the problem of priestly *'avodah* still remains, and the word *mattanah* is left hanging. (3) A radical solution regards the entire clause as a gloss. Indeed, it is missing in the parallel verse 3:10 (to be sure, LXX inserts it there, but the changed vocabulary betrays the hand of the glossator [Daniel]). Further supporting this conjecture is that after deleting this clause the two similar verses, 3:10 and 18:7, would have the injunction "to guard" logically followed by the penalty to encroachers. Finally, the origin of this clause could be explained as a gloss to anticipate the priests' *mattanah* of "gifts" (rather than "dedication") and it would mean that the priests are rewarded with gifts (vv. 9–20) for incurring mortal dangers in their *'avodah* of guarding the inner sancta, just as the Levites are rewarded with the tithes (vv. 21–24) for their hazardous *'avodah* in transporting the sanctuary. The crux remains unresolved.

18. *Ha-zar ha-karev* (see Excursus 5). Targ. Neof. glosses correctly, "any layman who approaches to serve" (also Sif. Num. 116).

19. Sif. Num. 119; for a slightly different classification, cf. Tosef. Ḥal. 2:7–10, BK 110b, Ḥul. 113b.

20. Sif. Num. 117.

21. Ehrlich.

22. Suk. 38b, Rashi.

23. N. H. Snaith, *Leviticus and Numbers* (London: Nelson, 1967).

24. Sforno.

25. Akk. *mašāḫu* means "to measure," and *mišiḫtu* is "a measured area"; similarly, *mšḥt* in imperial Aram. (DISO).

26. *Ḥok. 'olam* (Num. 18:11, 19; Exod. 29:28; 30:21; Lev. 6:11, 15; 7:34, 10:15; 24:9).

27. One would usually expect the form *me-'ishai* (e.g., Lev. 6:10) or *me-'ishei YHVH* (Lev. 2:3, 10) from *'isheh* (so reads the LXX), which probably means "gifts" (cf. the Comment to 15:25). However, since the purification offering listed here is never called an *'isheh*—an expiatory sacrifice is not a gift—the text is forced to use another term, "the offerings by fire."

28. Sif. Zut.

29. Sefer ha-Mivḥar.

30. Targ. Onk., Ramban.

31. The *bet* may possibly be construed as a *kaf,* i.e., "as" (Ehrlich; cf. v. 26).

32. Cf. Mish. Zev. 5:6, 7.

33. Sif. Num. 117.

34. Mish. Ter. 4:3.

35. Mish. Bik. 1:3; Targ. Jon. only specifies fruit trees.

36. Targ. Neof.; and cf. v. 24.

37. Mish. Bik. 3:2–9.

38. Snaith, *Leviticus and Numbers.*

39. Sif. Num. 117.

40. Tosef. Shab. 15:7, Num. R. 4:3.

41. MK 24b.

42. Cf. Bek. 12b.

43. W. G. Plaut, *The Torah: Numbers* (New York: Union of American Hebrew Congregations, 1981), 1142.

44. The final letter *(kaf)* is not to be read as a pronominal suffix (Rashi on Lev. 27:3) but may be a "pronominal suffix that has become fossilized and absorbed into the nominal stem" (E. A. Speiser, "Leviticus and the Critics," in *Yehezkel Kaufmann Jubilee Volume,* ed. M. Haran [Jerusalem: Magnes Press, 1960], 30–33), whereby "your valuation" becomes the equivalent of "valuation."

45. Laws 1.139.

46. Ibn Ezra.

47. Sif. Num. 118.

48. See also Lev. 10:9, 14, 15. The possibility was noted by M. Brettler, "The Promise of the Land of Israel to the Patriarchs in the Pentateuch," *Shnaton* 5/6 (1978–1979): ix n. 9.

49. Cf. Targ. Jon.

50. R. F. Harper, *Assyrian and Babylonian Letters* (London: Luzac, 1892–1914), 747, v. 6.

51. G. B. Gray.

52. A. Dillmann, *Die Bücher Numeri, Deuteronomium, und Josua* (Leipzig: S. Hirzel, 1897).

53. *Ḥelek* and *naḥalah* are found in poetry, in synonymous parallelism (e.g., Deut. 32:9; 2 Sam. 20:1; Job 20:9; 27:13), and in prose, linked in this order by a *vav* (also Gen. 31:14; Deut. 10:9; 12:12; 14:27; 18:1). Strikingly, the Akk. term *zittu* also means both "share" and "(nonpurchased) hereditary land" (J. N. Postgate, "Land Tenure in the Middle Assyrian Period: A Reconstruction," BSOAS 34 [1971]: 496–520).

54. *Ḥelef* (v. 31). *Ḥlp /t* in Aram., Phoen. means "substitute, compensation."

55. Milgrom, *Cult and Conscience,* pp. 7–9.

56. E.g., Esther 9:1; Ehrlich.

57. Ibn Ezra.

58. The initial *bet* can mean "as" or "or" (e.g., v. 10; 26:53; 34:2; Josh. 13:6; Ezek. 46:16; 47:14), the equivalent of initial *lamed* (21:24).

59. *Ve-neḥshav lakhem terumatkhem.* The customary translation is "your contribution shall be accounted to you (as the new grain)"; cf. v. 30. However, since the verb is masculine, the noun "contribution," which is feminine, cannot be the subject. Hence, the given translation is preferable (cf. Ehrlich).

60. Cf. Rashi. The construction is *ke . . . ken,* "as . . . so . . ." (8:4; 9:14; especially 15:20).

61. *Terumat YHVH,* an objective genitive (Ehrlich).

62. Cf. Lev. 19:30, Sefer ha-Mivḥar, although it is possible that the vocalization is original, signifying the construct of *mikdesh* (a noun formation like *misped*) meaning "the consecrated part" (Lev. 16:33, Ehrlich).

63. "Even in a tomb," Sif. Num. 122.

64. *Ḥelef* (cf. v. 21). Targ. Onk. on *taḥat,* "in place of" (Gen. 4:25), reads *ḥelef* (Radak).

65. Targ. Jon.; cf. Lev. 7:20–21.

66. Milgrom, *Cult and Conscience,* pp. 32, 33 n. 123.

Chapter 19

1. Lev. 21:1–4, 10; 22:4–7; Num. 5:2; 6:6–13; 9:6.

2. The anomaly is noted in Tanḥ. B. Num. 115, PdRK 69, Num. R. 19:4.

3. Although connections have been suggested: that the preceding chapter also contains rules for priests (Ibn Ezra) or that the following chapter gives a concrete case, the death of Miriam (Josephus, Ant. 4.4, 6).

4. Ramban.

5. Sif. Num. 123.

6. A. Brenner, *Colour Terms in the Old Testament* (Sheffield: JSOT, 1982), 62–65.

7. Sif. Num. 123.

8. Deut. 15:19.

9. "Instructions for Temple Officials" ii.18 (ANET, p. 208).

10. Mish. Par. 4:1, Tosef. Par. 3:8, 4:7, Sif. Zut. 19:3; also Philo, Laws 1.268, Josephus, Ant. 4.4, 6.

11. Sif. Num. 123.

12. Mish. Mid. 2:4.

13. Par. Mish. 3:9, Sif. Num. 124.

14. Heb. *pirshah;* cf. Akk. *paršu,* Syr. *perta'*; Jewish Aram. *parta'.*

15. Targ. Jon.

16. ii.12, 18, 19 (ANET, p. 335).

17. Tosef. Neg. 8:2; see RH 23a.

18. Rashi on Lev. 14:4.

19. J. M. Grintz, "Early Terms in the Priestly Torah," *Leshonenu* 39 (1974/1975): 174–178.

20. Targ. Jon., Tosef. Par. 4:10, Sif. Num. 124, Sif. Zut.

21. Ibn Ezra.

22. E.g., Num. 19:21; Lev. 15:5, 6, 7, 8, 10, 16, 17, 18.

23. The first mention of "in water" in this verse is deleted in some manuscripts, LXX, Pesh. (vv. 7, 10, 19).

24. Sif. Num. 124.

25. Mish. Par. 3:11, Tosef. Par. 3:14; cf. Sif. Zut.

26. The LXX and the Targums render "waters of aspersion," where the root *n-d-h,* like Akk. *nadû* and Ugar. *ndy,* would mean "throw, sprinkle"; e.g., "the water he was carrying he threw over me" (W. G. Lambert, *Babylonian Wisdom Literature* [Oxford: Clarendon Press, 1960], 49).

27. With Mish. Par. 2:1; 3:4; 4:1; Sif. Zut.

28. E. Ebeling, "Beiträge zur Kenntnis der Beschwörungsserie Namburbi," RA 48 (1954): 178–181.

29. YD, Laws of Mourning 380.

30. With LXX, Sam., Pesh., requiring only the change of a *yod* to a *vav.*

31. Tosef. Par. 3:14; 10:2; 5:6; 7:4.

32. Sif. Zut.

33. Since there is no passive of the root *n-z-h,* which corresponds to Hifil *hizzah,* the synonym *zorak* is used (my student, D. P. Wright).

34. LXX and Sam. add the conjunctive *vav,* thereby connecting this verse with the preceding passage.

35. LXX.

36. Sif. Num. 126.

37. See Sif. Num. 126, Targums, and the Comment to the end of this verse.

38. Targums, LXX.

39. Sif. Num. 126.

40. D. P. Wright, "Purification from Corpse-Contamination in Numbers XXXI: 19–24," VT 25 (1985): 213–223.

41. 11QTemple 49:8–9.

42. With LXX, Pesh. (see S. C. Reif, "A Note on a Neglected Connotation of *NTN,*" VT 20 [1970]: 114–116; H. J. van Dijk, "A Neglected Connotation of Three Hebrew Words," VT 18 [1968]: 16–30). Also read *ve-natenu* (pl.) to conform to *ve-lakeḥu,* "shall be taken" (also pl.), with LXX, Sam., Pesh.

43. In Sif. Num. 128.

44. My son, A. M. Milgrom.

45. Sefer ha-Mivḥar.

46. My student, D. P. Wright.

47. Ibn Ezra, Ramban.

48. J. Milgrom, "Priestly Terminology and the Political and Social Structure of Pre-Monarchic Israel," JQR 69 (1978): 65–81.

49. Targ. Jon.

Chapter 20

1. G. J. Wenham.

2. Num. R. 19:16.

3. As understood by SOR 9 and Josephus, Ant. 4.78.

4. SOR 9, Josephus, Ant. 4.78, Ibn Ezra, Rashbam.

5. Ramban, Sefer ha-Mivḥar.

6. Or to another city with the same name, Ibn Ezra on v. 14.

7. M. Harel, *The Sinai Journeys* (Hebrew) (Tel Aviv: Am Oved, 1968).

8. Targ. Jon.; scholium to Meg. Ta'an. 2.

9. *Bi-geva',* an infinitive formation like *shelaḥ* (Isa. 58:9; cf. 22:15, Keter Torah).

10. *La-mut,* LXX reads *le-hamit,* "to kill" (us and our beasts). However this would also mean changing *'anaḥnu,* "we," to *'otanu,* "us."

11. Sefer ha-Mivḥar.

12. Ibn Ezra; see W. H. Propp, "The Rod of Aaron and the Sin of Moses," JBL 107 (1988), 19–26.

13. Ibn Ezra, 17:10.

14. Netiv ha-Shalom 14:5, 16:4.

15. E.g., Exod. 17:2; Num. 16:8–9; but see the Comments to 11:10b–15; 14:5–10.

16. F. Kohata, "Die pristerschriftliche Überlieferungsgeschichte von Numeri," *Annual of the Japanese Biblical Institute* 3 (1977): 3–34.

17. Rashbam.

18. My student, D. Levy.

19. Kohata, "Die pristerschriftliche Überlieferungsgeschichte."

20. M. Margaliot, "The Transgression of Moses and Aaron: Num. 20:1–13," JQR 74 (1983): 196–228.

21. Num. R. 19:10.

22. Targ. Neof., Rashi; see Gen. 4:15; 1 Kings 14:7–10; Jer. 29:31–32.

23. My student, D. Levy.

24. E.g., Gen. 14:2, 3, 7, 8, 17; 23:2, 19; 48:7; Josh. 15:10, 25, 49, 60.

25. Mekh. SbY to Exod. 15:24, Sanh. 110a.

26. Actually, Ps. 106 harmonizes the two accounts in Num. and Deut.

27. S. E. Loewenstamm, "The Death of Moses" (Hebrew), *Tarbiz* 27 (1957/1958): 142–145. The Sam. interpolates Deut. 3:26b–28 at this point.

28. The verb is a Nifal reflexive and is so understood by 1QM 17:2, which renders the Nifal of Lev. 10:3 as ***hitkaddesh,*** "sanctified Himself."

29. Moses and Aaron, according to Targ. Jon., Ibn Ezra, Baḥya; the waters, according to Rashi, Rashbam, Ramban, Shadal; Israel, according to Mid. Ag. to Num. 10:13.

30. S. E. Loewenstamm, EB (Hebrew), s.v. ***merivat kadesh.***

31. R. de Vaux, *The Early History of Israel* (Philadelphia: Westminster Press, 1978), 551–563.

32. C. Carmichael, "A New View of the Origin of the Deuteronomic Code," VT 19 (1969): 273–289.

33. P. Buis, "Qadesh: Un lieu maudit?" VT 24 (1974): 268–285.

34. See Num. R. 19:15.

35. The first Assyrian "kings" living in tents (ANET, p. 564b).

36. E.g., Sumerian (ANET, p. 480), El-Amarna (ANET, pp. 484–490), Mari (ANET, pp. 630–632).

37. See E. A. Speiser, *Genesis* (New York: Doubleday, 1964), the Comment to 19:11, p. 140.

38. Tanḥ. Hukat 12; cf. Ramban on v. 19.

39. D. Daube, *The Exodus Pattern in the Bible* (London: Faber and Faber, 1963), 24–25.

40. See Exod. 14:29; 23:20; 33:2.

41. Ramban.

42. E. Weidner, "Assyrische Itinerare," AfO 21 (1966): 42–46.

43. Cf. Targ. Yer.; also on 21:22.

44. Keter Torah.

45. Some manuscripts of Sam. read ***mesulla',*** "rocky road," i.e., through the mountains (so LXX), also implying an alternative, more difficult route.

46. Num. R. 19:15.

47. Ehrlich.

48. So it is understood by Targ. Onk. and Targ. Jon.: "without doing wrong."

49. Targ. Jon. adds: "since the time had not yet arrived for the revenge upon Edom to be administered at their hands" (see 2 Sam. 8:12, 14, reading Edom for Aram).

50. M. Weinfeld, "The Awakening of Israel's National Consciousness in the Seventh Century" (Hebrew), in *Oz LeDavid* (Jerusalem: Kiriat Sefer, 1964), 396–420.

51. Josephus, Ant. 4.82; Eusebius, Onomasticon 176.6, 7.

52. Y. Aharoni, *The Land of the Bible* (Philadelphia: Westminster Press, 1967), 185.

53. Cf. Num. 3:4; 14:37; 15:36; 20:1; 27:3; Gen. 11:32; 23:2; 35:19; 36:33–39; Exod. 2:3.

54. B. Alfrink, "L'expression ***ne'esap 'el 'amayv,***" OTS 5 (1948): 118–131.

55. Keter Torah.

56. Num. R. 19:19.

57. A. Dillmann, *Die Bücher Numeri, Deuteronomium, und Josua* (Leipzig: S. Hirzel, 1897).

58. de Vaux, *Early History of Israel,* p. 399.

59. Alfrink, "L'expression ***ne'esap 'el 'amayv.***"

60. Ehrlich.

61. Num. R. 19:20.

62. Targ. Jon.; cf. Targ. Yer.

63. SER 13:63; 20:112; 25:128; ARN[1] 12, 48–51; ARN[2] 24, 48–51, and supplements 161, 163, as rendered in L. Ginzberg, *The Legends of the Jews,* vol. 3 (Philadelphia: Jewish Publication Society of America), 323, 328–329.

Chapter 21

1. Cf. Gen. 36:21, Exod. 15:14–15; Amos 1:5, 8; Akk. ***wāšib mari,*** "ruler of Mari"; Ugar. ***ytb b'ṯtrt,*** "ruler of Ashtaroth" (M. I. Gruber, "The Many Faces of *Naso' Panim,* (Lift up the Face,'" ZAW 95 [1983]: 257 n. 25), derived from the idiom ***yoshev 'al ha-kisse',*** "he who sits or occupies the throne," i.e., the king or God (1 Kings 22:19; cf. also He who sits "Enthroned on the Cherubim" [1 Sam. 4:4], a reference to the Lord on his heavenly throne; and Akk. ***āšibūt kussi,*** "he who occupies the throne").

2. Perhaps "King of Arad" is a gloss, for the following reasons: (1) the first word, ***ha-kena'ani,*** means "Canaanites" (e.g., 13:29; 14:43), as in v. 3 and should be so rendered. It is a collective noun and cannot be in apposition to an individual, the king of Arad; (2) if ***yoshev*** means "dwelt," the last two words, ***yoshev ha-negev,*** are only appropriate for a people or community. For an individual to dwell in an area the verb would take the preposition ***be*** and not the definite article ***ha.*** The latter usage is only attested for a people who occupy the entirety of the designated area (e.g., Gen. 50:11; Exod. 34:12, 15; Num. 14:14; Josh. 24:18; Judg. 11:21; 2 Sam. 5:6; Jer. 47:2; Ezek. 7:7). Indeed when the glossator of Num. 33:40 inserts these same words into Israel's wilderness itinerary he alters them to ***yoshev ba-negev,*** in accordance with correct grammatical usage; (3) the king is omitted in the rest of the passage, which only mentions the Canaanites being put under ban and delivered into Israel's hands. There is not a word about the king. Without this gloss the text would be rendered: "the Canaanites who dwelt in the Negeb," solving a severe chronological problem (see Excursus 55). Perhaps it is the juxtaposition of the kings of Hormah and Arad with the kings defeated by Joshua (Josh. 12:14) that accounts for the gloss.

3. See Targ. Jon., TJ Yoma 1, 38b, TJ Sot. 1, 17b, Tanḥ. B. Num. 125, Num. R. 19:20.

4. LXX and Sam. add ***be-yado,*** "into its hands," as in v. 2.

5. The Sam. has a different verb, ***hotse'tanu,*** "take us out" (as does the LXX), but also in the singular. Perhaps this is the reason that all the Targums render: "the people spoke against the ***memra'*** of the Lord and murmured against Moses: "Why . . ."

6. Two radicals of the root are doubled as in ***'adamdam*** (Lev. 13:42) and ***sa'se'ah*** (Isa. 27:8). In Ugar. ***qlql*** seems to stand for horse fodder (UT 53.8), i.e., menial food.

7. See also Targ. Jon.

8. Ehrlich.

9. Esarhaddon's campaign to Egypt (ANET, p. 293, col. 2; Strabo, Geography 16.2,30).

10. *Revolt in the Desert* (New York: George H. Doran Co., 1927), 93.

11. Bekhor Shor.

12. See also Mish. RH 3:8, cited in Excursus 52.

13. Gen. R. 31:8.

14. B. Rothenberg, "Un temple égyptien découvert dans la Arabah," BTS 123 (1970): 3, 8–9. The possibility must be entertained that both the Tabernacle (tent shrine) and the copper snake were borrowings from Midianite religion, presumably via the Jethro-Moses channel.

15. F. M. Cross, *Canaanite Myth and Hebrew Epic* (Cambridge: Harvard University Press, 1973).

16. The proposed reconstruction of the original text would accord with the attested redactional technique of grouping a number of stations (see Exod. 15:22a; 16:1; Num. 10:12) under a general designation. In this case, the itinerary 33:42–48a would have been subsumed under the summary phrase: "the wilderness bordering on Moab to the east."

17. The text itself is in doubt judging by the versions, e.g., Akelgai (LXX[A]), Kalgaei (LXX[B]), *'ayin* (Pesh.). Targ. Onk. and Targ. Neof. render "ford of the Hebrews" (reading *ha-'ivrim*), indicating a site on Wadi Zered, the boundary between Edom and Moab (which Israel had to cross).

18. R. de Vaux, *The Early History of Israel* (Philadelphia: Westminster Press, 1978).

19. Z. Kallai, "The Wandering-Traditions from Kadesh-Barnea to Canaan: A Study in Biblical Historiography," JJS 33 (1982): 175–188.

20. M. Ottosson, TDOT, s.v. "gebhul."

21. LXX reads: "set on fire Zahab" *('et zahav saraf/safah);* Targ. Neof. and Targ. Onk. read: "(wonders which the Lord) wrought (with Israel when they stood) by the Reed Sea" *('et yahav ba-suf)*. A more fanciful interpretation is given by Targ. Yer. (cf. Ber. 54a–b), whereby the mountains are fused to give Israel a level passage across the wadis.

22. Enclitic *mem* as in Gen. 14:6; W. F. Albright, *Yahweh and the Gods of Canaan* (Garden City, N.Y.: Doubleday, 1968), 44.

23. G. A. Smith, *The Early Poetry of Israel in its Physical and Social Origins* (London: Oxford University Press, 1927).

24. D. L. Christensen, "Numbers 21:14–15 and the Book of Wars of YHWH," CBQ 36 (1974): 359–360.

25. In this reconstruction, *'et* is to be rendered *'ata* "came," (*'et* is inappropriate in ancient poetry); *'eshed* > *'isher,* "march" (ד = *d* > ר = *r*, as in Sam.), and *'asher* should be deleted as a dittography. For *sufah* as "whirlwind," see Nah. 1:3 (Keter Torah).

26. So rendered by LXX and Pesh.

27. I. Rabinowitz (written communication) shows that *'az* followed by the imperfect is a redactional device that indicates the simultaneity of the events that precede and follow, not their sequentiality.

28. Num. R. 19:26.

29. RH 31a.

30. *'Ali.* LXX reads *'ale,* "at," rendering the clause "sang this song at the well . . ."; however, there is no article on *be'er,* "well." Sam. reads *'olah,* "(the well) ascends"; however, the following clause contains the imperative "sing." Thus the MT is the probable reading.

31. A. Musil, *Arabia Petraea,* vol. 3 (Vienna: A. Hölder, 1908), 259.

32. G. A. Smith, *The Early Poetry of Israel,* p. 64.

33. D. N. Freedman, "The Broken Construct Chain," Bib 53 (1972): 534–536.

34. E.g., Egyptian (ANEP, no. 379); Mesopotamian (ANEP, nos. 442, 447); N. Syrian (ANEP, no. 461).

35. ANEP, no. 463.

36. L. Kopf, "Arabische Etymologien und Parallelen zum Bibelwörterbuch," VT 9 (1959): 255–256.

37. Targums, Num. R. 19:26; also Rashi, Ramban, Bekhor Shor, Baḥya.

38. K. Budde, "The Song of the Well," *New World* 4 (1895): 136–144.

39. J. M. Grintz, "Some Observations on the High-Place in the History of Israel," VT 27 (1977): 111–113.

40. *Ve-nishkefah.* Alternatively, *ha-nishkefah* (LXX; see 23:28) or *ha-nishkaf* (Sam.), masculine, modifying *ro'sh* (as in 23:28). In any event, a modifying participle is needed.

41. TJ Bik. 1:12 (64b), Sif. Deut. 289, Ramban.

42. However, if vv. 12–20 belong to an interpolated itinerary list (see the Comment to v. 11), then v. 21 would originally have followed v. 11, with Israel stationed at Iye-abarim.

43. B. Mazar, "Canaan on the Threshold of the Age of the Patriarchs" (Hebrew), *Eretz-Israel* 3 (1954): 18–32.

44. Num. R. 19:33.

45. Onom. 131.17.

46. Mesha 20–21.

47. A terminus can only be a place and not a people. The accidental omission of Az, *'az,* can be explained as a haplography of *'ad,* "as far as." However, the existence of a place name Az is in doubt (see below). Moreover, *benei 'ammon* may mean (the land of) "Ammon" as well as "Ammonites." Only twice in the entire Bible does *'ammon* appear alone (1 Sam. 11:11; Ps. 83:8), otherwise *benei 'ammon,* even when referring to the land and not the people (Gen. 19:38; Judg. 11:15; 1 Sam. 14:42; etc.). In Akk. inscriptions the land is also called by a compound name, Bit Ammana and Bānammana (= *benei 'ammon*). The LXX also renders the compound literally "sons of Ammon" (even in 1 Sam. 11:11). If one renders "as far as Ammon" no reconstruction is needed.

48. Targ. Onk. apparently read *ha-meshalim,* and Pesh., Vulg., *ba-meshalim,* referring to the compositions rather than their performers as does the introduction to the previous song in v. 14. The latter, however, is appropriate since it is a quotation from a book. Here no written form is indicated; the composition is transmitted orally by its reciters.

49. Here the pausal disjunctive accent *(etnaḥtah)* should be placed under *tibbaneh.*

50. However, H. Olivier (at the Heidelberg conference of the Society of Biblical Literature, 1987) has, on archaeological grounds, identified Ar-Moab with er-Rabba (= Rabbath Moab). Adding further to the ambiguity, Targ. Onk. and Targ. Neof. read *'are,* "cities," which in ancient Heb. would have been written as *'r* and read as *'ar.*

51. "Captive," *ba-shevit,* is read *ba-shevi* in Sam. and one manuscript, the usual form. The parallel in Jer. 48:46 reads *ba-shivyah.*

52. P. D. Hanson, "The Song of Heshbon and David's Nir," HTR 61 (1968): 297–320.

53. Ibid. Alternative readings are *va-ninam,* "their descendants" (LXX); *ve-niram,* "their fields" (Pesh.; see Hos. 10:12); *va-nirem,* "we destroyed them" (Ibn Ezra, from *yarah,* "shoot"); *ve-nimrim,* "Nimrim," a place in Moab (Isa. 15:6; Jer. 48:34; N. H. Tur-Sinai, *The Plain Meaning of Scripture* [Hebrew], vol. 1 [Jerusalem: Kiriat Sefer, 1962]).

54. The LXX renders "women kindled (fire)," reading *ve-nashim nafḥu.* The rendering "We have wrought desolation" derives from the Hifil of *shamam,* "destroy." Also conjectured is the reading *nesi'im,* "chieftains," a parallel to "dominion" (J. van Seters, "The Conquest of Sihon's Kingdom: A Literary Examination," JBL 91 [1972]: 182–197). The crux remains.

55. Other conjectured readings are *mishor,* "tableland" (Josh. 13:19; M. Ottosson, "Once Again: The Conquest of Sihon's Kingdom," JBL 99 [1908]: 117–119), and *sho'ah,* "destruction" (W. Rudolph, *Numeri et Deuteronomium* [Stuttgart: Württembergische Bibelanstalt, 1972]).

56. "They captured its dependencies," *va-yilkedu benoteha.* The LXX reads *va-yilkeduha u-venoteha,* "they captured it and its

dependencies"; "dispossessed," *va-yoresh,* is singular. The versions, however, read it as a plural.

57. Kallai, "The Wandering-Traditions."

58. Num. 32:33; Deut. 1:4; 4:47; 29:6; 31:4; Josh. 2:10; 9:10; Neh. 9:22; Pss. 135:11; 136:20.

59. However, see the Comment to 32:39–42. This is another indication that this account of the conquest of the Bashan (vv. 33–35) is a later version.

60. A. Dillmann, *Die Bücher Numeri, Deuteronomium, und Josua* (Leipzig: S. Hirzel, 1897).

Chapter 22

1. Rather, "Book of Balaam"; BB 14b, Munich MS.

2. R. Johanan in Git. 60a.

3. P. Volz, Review of A. F. von Gall, *Zusammensetzung und Herkunft der Bileam-Perikope in Num. 22–24* (Giessen: J. Ricker, 1900); TLZ 14 (1901):383–385.

4. The kingdom of Og is called Amorite only by Deut. (Deut. 3:8; 4:47; 31:4).

5. Contrast the similar idiom *kats be*, "loathe" (21:5; Gen. 27:46; Lev. 20:23).

6. G. E. Mendenhall, *The Tenth Generation* (Baltimore: Johns Hopkins University Press, 1973).

7. Num. R. 20:4; cf. Josephus, *Ant.* 4.100–102, Sif. Num. 157, Sanh. 105a, Tanḥ. B. Num. 134.

8. Targ. Jon., Meyuḥas.

9. *Yelaḥakhu . . . kileḥokh*. The subject of the first verb is the horde and of the second, the ox. Hence, the first verb is in the Piel (intensive) pattern and the second in the Kal (simple) (cf. Judg. 7:5 with vv. 6 and 7; Ehrlich).

10. The name occurs in the Mesopotamian onomasticon, both in Old Babylonian (Amorite) and New Assyrian; R. Zadok, "Notes on the Biblical and Extra-Biblical Onomasticon" JQR 71 (1980), 69–85.

11. His identification with Bela son of Beor the Edomite (Gen. 36:32) must be rejected (Ibn Ezra).

12. Philo, De Cherubim 22.

13. Targ. Jon.

14. Targ. Jon.

15. Sanh. 105a.

16. *Beʿir*; Sanh. 105a.

17. The name Bilʿam is characteristic of the second millennium. A Bil-amma was known in the fifteenth century. It is identical with the name of the Canaanite town Bileam (1 Chron. 6:55) or Ibleam (Josh. 17:11) in western Manasseh. "The original form of the name may have been *Yabil-ʿammu*, probably meaning 'May the clan lead'" (W. F. Albright, EncJud, s.v. "Balaam.")

18. M. Görg, "Die 'Heimat' Bileams," *Biblische Notizen* 1 (1976):24–28.

19. A. Malamat, "The Arameans," in *Peoples of Old Testament Times*, ed. D. J. Wiseman (Oxford: Clarendon Press, 1973), 134–155.

20. Targ. Jon., Targ. Neof., Pesh., BAP 18.2.

21. Num. R. 20:7, Tanḥ. B. Num. 134.

22. Sam., Pesh., Vulg.

23. A. S. Yehuda, "The Name of Balaam's Homeland," JBL 64 (1945):547–551; W. F. Albright, *Yahweh and the Gods of Canaan* (Garden City, N.Y.: Doubleday, 1968), 15 n. 38.

24. W. Gross, "Bileam," SANT 38 (1974); Görg, "Die 'Heimat' Bileams."

25. Cf. Krt A.104 (ANET, p. 144), Taylor Cylinder 5.42–45.

26. Ehrlich.

27. *'Ukhal nakkeh bo*. If *nakkeh* is first person plural, then read *nukhal* to correspond, yielding: "we can thus defeat them"; or understand *nakkeh* as a Piel infinitive (Ibn Ezra), corresponding to *le-hilaḥem*, "engage in battle" (v. 11). The intensive verb pattern of *nakkeh* occurs once again (Exod. 9:31–32) in the Pual (Keter Torah).

28. Ibn Ezra.

29. Ehrlich.

30. Tanḥ. B. Num. 135, Num. R. 20:8, followed by Rashi, Sforno, Ramban, Abravanel.

31. L. Schmidt, "Die alttestamentliche Bileamüberlieferung," BZ 23 (1979):235–261.

32. Targ. Jon., Philo, 1 Mos. 26b, Samuel ha-Nagid, cited by Ibn Ezra, just as *besorah* can mean "tidings" and "the fee for tidings" (2 Sam. 4:10) and *peduyim* can mean "ransom" and the "ransom price" (3:46) and *peʿulah* can mean "work" and "the wages for work" (Lev. 19:13).

33. See Isa. 3:2; Mic. 3:6,7,11; Jer. 29:8; Ezek. 12:24; 13:19; 21:34.

34. E.g., Gudea A.2.24 and 3.9–11, Rassam Cylinder 3.118–124, and possibly Solomon in the Gibeon sanctuary, 1 Kings 3:5.

35. H. Reviv, "History and Historiography during the Time of the Division of the Kingdoms: Toward an Understanding of the Term *Edah* in 1 Kings 12:20" (Hebrew), *Zion* 50 (1985):59–63.

36. Ibn Ezra.

37. Ehrlich. For *mi* meaning "what," see Gen. 33:8; Judg. 13:17; Mic. 1:5; Ruth 3:16 (Ibn Janaḥ).

38. *Ha-ʿam ha-yotse'*, literally "the people that came out," which perhaps should be rendered "this people that came out." However, LXX, Targums, and Sam. read *ʿam yatsa'*, "a people that came out," as in v. 5.

39. Targ. Jon., BAP 18.5–6, Mid. Lek. Tov.

40. ARN[2] 45, 125; cf. Num. R. 20:10, Tanḥ. B. Num. 136.

41. Ibn Ezra.

42. *Timmanaʿ min*, literally "be withheld, prevented" (Joel 1:13; Job 38:15). But the Nifal pattern can also express a reflexive, that is, "restrain yourself."

43. Ibn Ezra. Also, in Ugar. *kbd* is an ellipsis for a "heavy shekel" (UT 90.6, 7; cf. 9.13; 171.1; 1024.25; my student S. Pfann).

44. My son, A. M. Milgrom.

45. M. Margaliot, "The Connection of the Balaam Narrative with the Pentateuch," *Proceedings of the Sixth World Congress of Jewish Studies*, vol. 1 (Jerusalem: World Union of Jewish Studies, 1977), 279–290.

46. *Ba-zeh*, equivalent of *poh* (v. 8); see also 23:1, 2a; Gen. 38:21; Exod. 24:14.

47. Anabasis 6.4.19.

48. ANET, p. 350; L. Rost, "Fragen um Bileam," in *Beiträge zur alttestamentlichen Theologie*, ed. H. Donner et al. (Göttingen: Vandenhoeck und Ruprecht, 1977), 377–387.

49. J. Pedersen, "The Role Played by Inspired Persons among the Israelites and the Arabs," in *Studies in Old Testament Prophecy*, ed. H. H. Rowley (Edinburgh: Clark, 1950), 133.

50. Ber. 7a.

51. Ehrlich.

52. Mak. 10b, Num. R. 20:18.

53. Shab. 104a, Yoma 38b.

54. M. M. Kalisch, *Bible Studies: The Prophecies of Balaam* (London: Longmans, 1877).

55. Y. Zakovitch, "The Pattern of the Numerical Sequence Three-Four in the Bible" (Hebrew) (Ph.D. diss., Hebrew University, 1977).

56. Rost, "Fragen um Bileam." The use of the two divine names, YHVH and Elohim, also seems to follow a definite scheme: Throughout the story, Elohim is used in the narration and YHVH in Balaam's speech (vv. 8, 13, 18, 19), thereby emphasizing that He is Balaam's Deity. The exceptions are 22:8; 23:5, 16; 24:1, on which see the Comments. In vv. 22–35, only YHVH is used (for the ostensible exception of v. 22, see the Comment), which raises the possibility that the ass story is an interpolation from another hand. For other evidence pointing to the same conclusion, see Excursus 57.

57. Targ. Onk., Rashi, Rashbam, Tosafot.

58. Elohim. One manuscript of the MT, two manuscripts of the LXX, and the Sam. read YHVH, "Lord," the name of the Deity used consistently in the ass episode (vv. 22–35). Since the LXX frequently reads "God" when MT has "Lord," its reading "Lord" here where MT reads "God" argues for its authenticity. The change in the MT is probably due to the influence of the previous pericope, vv. 2–21, where "God" is consistently used in the narrative.

59. *Ki holekh hu'*. A verbal reference to v. 21b, illustrating the technique used by the redactor to lock the ass episode into place here. For other similar examples of this editorial technique, see Josh. 3:17; 4:1–10; Judg. 6:6,7–10; 1 Sam. 17:57; 18:6; 1 Sam. 23:14,15–18 (A. Rofe, *The Book of Balaam* [Hebrew] [Jerusalem: Sinai, 1979]), 56.

60. Num. R. 20:13; cf. Lev. R. 26:7.

61. Num. R. 20:14.

62. R. Largement, "Les oracles de Bile'am et la mantique Suméro-Akkadienne," in *Mémorial du Cinquantenaire* (Paris: Bloud, 1964), 37–50.

63. Ibn Ezra.

64. So rendered by the Targums.

65. See LXX. For *sha'al*, see 1 Kings 20:10; Isa. 40:12; Ezek. 13:19.

66. *Va-tilaḥets*, a Nifal reflexive.

67. Ibn Ezra.

68. Mish. Avot 5:6.

69. *Zeh* (see Num. 14:22; Gen. 31:38).

70. H. L. Ginsberg, *The Israelian Heritage of Judaism* (New York: Jewish Theological Seminary of America, 1982), n. 68.

71. *Hit'allalt*. See Exod. 10:2; 1 Sam. 6:6; elsewhere this word connotes physical abuse (Judg. 19:25; 1 Sam. 31:4; Jer. 38:19).

72. Zohar, Balak; cf. Num. R. 20:14.

73. *Me-'odekha*, literally "all your life" (Gen. 48:15, Pss. 104:33; 146:2, synonymously parallel with "life").

74. So Targ. Onk. and Rashi (see Ps. 139:3; Job 22:2,21).

75. Num. R. 20:14.

76. Zakovitch, "The Pattern of the Numerical Sequence"; L. Rost, "Fragen um Bileam."

77. *Ki yarat ha-derekh le-negdi* (so Targ. Onk.). LXX, Sam., and Vulg. read *darkekha*, "your manner" (for this connotation of *derekh*, see Gen. 6:12; 18:19; 19:31; 31:35). *Yarat* is a hapax, which is alternately rendered "twisted" (Ibn Ezra, Ramban, Abravanel) or "blocked" (Mid. Lek. Tov, Meyuḥas), interpreting *derekh* as "road."

78. *Le-fanai*. Rather, "before me," equivalent to *mi-panai* in the second half of the verse. See Sam., which conflates, *mi-lefanai*. For the *lamed* equivalence to *mem*, see 2 Sam. 24:4 (My student, D. P. Wright); Ps. 36:4 (Ramban). In Ugar., the exchange of the prepositions *lamed* and *mem* is frequently attested (see C. H. Gordon, *Ugaritic Textbook: Grammar*) [Rome: Pontificum institutum biblicum, 1965], 92).

79. Abravanel.

80. *'Ulai* in the sense of *lule'* (Targ. Onk., Targ. Jon., Ibn Janaḥ, Rashi, Ibn Ezra), which frequently begins a conditional clause followed by a main clause beginning with *ki 'attah* (e.g., Gen. 31:42; 43:10), as here.

81. Ehrlich.

82. Meyuḥas.

83. *'Ashuva li*, literally "I will take myself back," a reflexive usage like *lekh lekha*, literally "take yourself forth" (Gen. 12:1).

84. Thus, the possibility exists that the original ending of the ass story had Balaam return home; the editor then lopped it off and replaced it with v. 35 in order to fit the interpolated ass story harmoniously into the main narrative (J. Wellhausen, *Die Composition des Hexateuchs*, 3rd ed. [Berlin: G. Reimer, 1899]). Alternatively, the ass story may also have had the same ending as the narrative, i.e., Balaam's blessing of Israel, in which case v. 35a would be part of the ass story and v. 35b, the editor's repetitive resumption of v. 21b. "So Balaam went on with Balak's dignitaries" (v. 35b) repeats v. 21b. Moreover, "Go with the men. But you must say nothing except what I tell you" (v. 35a) is an almost literal repetition of v. 20a,b. Thus, this entire verse is a repetitive resumption that locks the ass episode into the narrative—unassailable proof that the ass story (vv. 22–34) is an interpolation (see Excursus 57).

85. *Ve-'efes* (*'et*), the equivalent of *'akh*, "but" (v. 20; see the Comment to 23:13). It is usually expressed by the compound *'efes ki* (e.g., 13:28; Deut. 15:4; Judg. 4:9).

86. M. Noth, *Numbers: A Commentary*, trans. J. D. Martin (London: S. C. M. Press, 1968); cf. Gen. 16:13a with vv. 7–12.

87. Saadia.

88. Plutarch, Symposium 5.7.6.

89. Ehrlich.

Chapter 23

1. Shab. 66b.

2. Cited in R. Largement, "Les oracles de Bile'am et la mantique Suméro-Akkadienne," in *Mémorial du Cinquantenaire* (Paris: Bloud, 1964), 46; cf. Virgil, Aeneid 6.38–39.

3. Num. R. 20:8.

4. Targums, Saadia, Ibn Ezra.

5. M. Weinfeld, "Ancient Near Eastern Parallels in Prophetic Literature," VT 27 (1977): 186–187.

6. Anabasis 5.6.29.

7. 1QM 2:3–5.

8. Mish. Ta'an. 4:2.

9. D. Daiches, "Balaam: A Babylonian Bārū," in *Hilprecht Anniversary Volume* (Leipzig: J. C. Hinrichs, 1909), 63.

10. L. Rost, "Zu der Festopfervorschriften von Numeri 28 and 29," TLZ 83(1958):329–334.

11. See Bel and Dragon 11–18.

12. With Targ. Jon. The Nifal of *k-r-h* implies chance or accident, as in 2 Sam. 1:6; 18:9. It is used deliberately here and in vv. 3,15,16 and in the context of a divine manifestation elsewhere only in Exod. 3:18; 5:3, in an address to a foreigner whose encounter with God cannot be counted on. In the Hifil causative, as in Gen. 24:16, it attributes the encounter directly to God. The same root, *kry*, in South Arabian inscriptions denotes oracular appearances of the deity (T. H. Gaster, *Legend, Myth, and Custom in the Old Testament* [New York: Harper and Row, 1969]).

13. So Targums; cf. Saadia, Rashi.

14. Ehrlich.

15. Ibn Ezra.

16. Ramban.

17. E. Gruenhut, *Sefer ha-Likkutim*, 6 vols. (Jerusalem, 1898–1902), Num. 64.

18. J. Wellhausen, *Die Composition des Hexateuchs*, 3rd ed. (Berlin: G. Reimer, 1899); Ehrlich.

19. So Ibn Ezra.

20. Ramban.

21. A. Rofē, *The Book of Balaam* (Hebrew) (Jerusalem: Sinai, 1979).

22. *Va-yisa'* (vv. 18; 24:3,15,20,21,23), i.e., took up on the lips, "uttered," e.g., a curse (1 Kings 8:31), a dirge (Jer. 7:29), a prayer (Isa. 37:4), a song (Ps. 81:3), a name (Exod. 20:7), a rumor (Exod. 23:1). The nominal form *massa'* means "oracle" (Isa. 15:1; 17:1; 19:1), and it occurs in the Deir 'Alla inscription concerning Balaam (see Excursus 60).

23. A. Malamat, "The Arameans," in *Peoples of Old Testament Times*, ed. D. J. Wiseman (Oxford: Clarendon Press, 1973), 134–155.

24. ANET, p. 19.

25. M. Görg, "Die 'Heimat' Bileams," *Biblische Notizen* 1 (1976):24–28.

26. Perhaps Balaam's provenance must be sought elsewhere: e.g., the Hauran Mountains in lower Syria (H. P. Müller, "Die aramäische Inschrift von Deir ʿAlla und die älteren Bileamsprüche," ZAW 94 [1982]: 214–244 or the land of Ammon, according to 22:5, Sam., Pesh. Alternatively, *kedem* can be rendered "of old" since it appears frequently in parallel with *ʿolam* (e.g., Deut. 15:33; Isa. 51:9; my student, H. Chapnick).

27. My student, H. Chapnick.

28. S. Gevirtz, *Patterns in the Early Poetry of Israel* (Chicago: University of Chicago Press, 1963).

29. *Tsurim*. Paired with "heights," it appears only in Ugar. If, however, *harim* "mountains" is read, then the ensuing word pair occurs thirty-one times in the Bible (Gevirtz, *Patterns in the Early Poetry*).

30. H. Chapnick.

31. Targ. Onk.; cf. Rashi.

32. Targ. Jon.; Targ. Yer.; see Philo, 1 Mos. 278. The emendation *la-vetaḥ yashav*, "resting secure," has also been proposed, on the basis of the parallelism of Deut. 33:28; Jer. 49:31 (Gevirtz, *Patterns in the Early Poetry*), and since the verbs *shakhan* and *ḥashav* are found nowhere else in parallel cola.

33. H. Chapnick.

34. See CAD, s.v. *eperu* 1b.

35. Gevirtz, *Patterns in the Early Poetry*.

36. *U-mispar*, reading *mi safar* with the Gk. and manuscripts of Sam., which read *my spr*, *myspr*. In tannaitic Heb., *mi* was frequently attached to the following word (J. N. Epstein, *Introduction to the Text of the Mishnah* [Hebrew], vol. 2 [Jerusalem: Magnes Press, 1948], 1218; but cf. Y. Kutscher, *Studies in Hebrew and Aramaic* [Hebrew] [Jerusalem: Magnes Press, 1977], 137). For the coupling of *manah* and *safar*, see 1 Kings 3:8 and UT 77.45–46 (S. E. Loewenstamm, "Notes on the Origin of Some Biblical Figures of Speech" [Hebrew], in *Studies in the Bible Presented to M. H. Segal*, ed. J. M. Grintz and S. Liver [Jerusalem: Kiriat Sefer, 1964], 183).

37. W. F. Albright, "The Oracles of Balaam," JBL 63 (1944):213 n. 28.

38. Loewenstamm, "Notes on the Origin," p. 186.

39. The exact parallel of dust/dust-cloud, *ʿafar/turbaʿ* is found in Akk.: *epram piki tarbuʾam paniki*, "with the dust of your mouth, with the dust-cloud of your face." Also the Sam. Targum reads *ʿafar*, "dust" (Gen. 18:27), as *rbwʿ* and this root has the same meaning in Arab. The change from projected consonantal *trbʿ* to *ʾt rbʿ* can be accounted for. In the Bar Kokhba letters, the particle *ʾet* is frequently found fused with the following word where the initial *alef* is dropped. This is what some Masorete thought happened to *trbʿ*, and he accordingly divided it into *ʾt rbʿ* (Loewenstamm, "Notes on the Origin," p. 186).

40. E.g., "the dustclouds, *turbû*, of the feet of my armies," H. R. Cohen, *Biblical Hapax Legomena in the Light of Akkadian and Ugaritic* [Missoula, Mont.: Scholars Press, 1978]), 37–39.

41. E.g., Targ. Onk.

42. Assuming that letters *tsadi* and *ayin* can be interchanged.

43. G. B. Gray.

44. Literally, "Constellation," a popular saying; see RH 16b; BM 75b.

45. Shadal.

46. Cf. *har ha-tsofim*, "Mount Scopus"; cf. W. H. Propp, "On Hebrew *śāde(h)*, 'Highland,'" VT 37 (1987):230–236.

47. Sanchuniaton, quoted by Eusebius, Praep. evang. 1.6. Heb. *matsor*, "watch post" (Hab. 2:1), is equivalent to its Akk. cognate *maṣṣertu*, "the watch for astronomical observation" (CAD *maṣṣertu* 3b). Both roots are attested in Habakkuk: "I ... will take up my station at the post [*matsor*; *matsori*, "my post," 1 QpHab] and wait [*ʾatsappeh*] to see ..." (Hab. 2:1).

48. Wellhausen conjectured that since all other occurrences of this verb have God as the subject, they should be revocalized to read as Kal not Nifal as here. However, see the Comment to v. 3, where the MT Nifal is justified.

49. 1 Mos. 282.

50. Meyuḥas, Keter Torah. And see also Gen. 19:35; 27:19; Ezek. 3:22; Isa. 32:9.

51. For this meaning, see Amos 4:6 (Ibn Janaḥ, Ibn Ezra) or read *ʿedi*, "my witness," as in Job 16:19 (LXX, Pesh.).

52. *Beno* (instead of *ben*). The nominative case ending was preserved before a genitive in both Canaanite and biblical poetry (e.g., Pss. 104:11,20; 114:8).

53. Also *ben yonah*, "pigeon" (Lev. 12:6); *bin hakkot*, "one deserving of a flogging" (Deut. 25:2); *ben ḥorim*, "freeman" (Ecclus. 10:17); *ben ḥakhamim*, "wise man" (1 Kings 20:35).

54. A Hitpael that, however, elsewhere means "take comfort/satisfaction" (e.g., Gen. 27:42; Deut. 32:36). The meaning "change one's mind" is attested in the Nifal (e.g., Exod. 13:17; 32:12,14; 1 Sam. 15:19). See S. Morag, "Layers of Antiquity: Some Linguistic Observations on the Oracles of Balaam" (Hebrew), *Tarbiz* 50 (1980/1981): n. 76.

55. R. Caplice, "Namburbi Texts in the British Museum," *Orientalia* 34 (1965):116.

56. J. A. Holstein, "The Case of *ʾîš hāʾĕlōhîm* Reconsidered," HUCA 48 (1977): 69–81.

57. *Yekimennah*. The final syllable is for emphasis (energetic *nun*) and is not to be translated.

58. *Lakaḥti*. Read as a passive *lukaḥti* (LXX, Pesh.), it would be rendered "I was summoned" (see on v. 11; Albright, "The Oracles of Balaam," p. 214 n. 38 or render "I perceived, heard" (Jer. 9:19; Job 4:12; Ehrlich).

59. *U-berekh*, (1) understood as a perfect with a sequential *vav*. Alternatively, (2) "He has blessed" (beforehand; see 22:12), the *vav* taken as conjunctive (Rashi, Ibn Ezra, Rashbam, Sforno) or (3) vocalizing *barekh*, infinitive absolute (see v. 25), render "to bless," as in the previous line, or (4) read as a first person singular, *ʾavarekh*, "I shall bless" (LXX, Targums).

60. Targ. Onk., Targ. Jon., Rashi, Ibn Ezra, Ramban.

61. *Hibbit ... raʾah*, literally "He sees ... views," i.e., God (Rashi), but it is best to think of an impersonal subject (LXX, Targums, Pesh., Ramban).

62. *Melekh*. Read as *malko* (Targ. Onk., Pesh.), referring to the Lord (Exod. 15:18; Deut. 33:5; 1 Sam. 8:7; 12:12; Ps. 68:25).

63. With Targ. Onk.

64. *Motsiʾam*, which perhaps should be read *motsiʾo* (as in 24:8), in keeping with the other third person singular suffixes in this oracle. The variation can be accounted for as a dittography of the initial *mem* in the next word (Ehrlich).

65. G. B. Gray.

66. J. H. Greenstone, *Numbers with Commentary* (Philadelphia: Jewish Publication Society of America, 1939).

67. Tanḥ. Balak 22.

68. Gilgamesh VI. 169–185 (ANET, p. 85). Albright renders "stormed like" from Arab. *wgf*, "run fast," i.e., Israel moves with swiftness and strength.

69. Saadia.

70. Ibn Ezra.

71. B. Mazar et al., *Views of the Biblical World*, vol. 1 (Chicago: Jordan Publications, 1959), 228.

72. *Be-yaʿakov ... be-yisraʾel*, so the Gk., Rashi, Ibn Ezra, Rashbam, Ramban, whereas others, like Targ. Onk., render the preposition *be* as "against." However, the context points to the rendering "in." Moreover, there is no indication in either the prose or the poetry (except in the ass episode) that Balaam ever intended to curse Israel. Finally, augury and divination, the craft of Balaam, are used for prediction, not "against" (see Excursus 59).

73. For this meaning of *loʾ* in a request, see Exod. 8:24; 1 Sam. 14:36; 1 Kings 2:6 (Rofé, *The Book of Balaam*).

Chapter 24

1. *Tov be-ʿeinei*, synonymous with *yashar be- ʿeinei* (23:27); see Deut. 6:18; 12:28; Ps. 25:8; 2 Chron. 14:1; 31:20.

2. I.e., the first two oracles (25:7–10, 18–24). *Ke-faʿam be-faʿam* is used of successive occurrences (Judg. 16:20; 20:30–31; 1 1 Sam. 3:10; 20:25).

3. E. L. Greenstein, "Trans-Semitic Idiomatic Equivalency and the Derivation of Hebrew *Ml'kh*," UF 11 (1979):329–336.

4. Abravanel.

5. Ramban.

6. D. Vetter, *Seherspruch und Segensschilderung* (Stuttgart: Calwer, 1974).

7. My son, A. M. Milgrom.

8. 4QSam[a].

9. Read as *shettammah ʿeino*, where no consonantal change is required (J. Wellhausen, *Die Composition des Hexateuchs*, 3rd ed. [Berlin: G. Reimer, 1899]; cf. LXX; Targ. Onk.). For the *shin* as a relative in old biblical Heb., see Gen. 6:3; 49:10; Judg. 5:7; 6:17; 7:12.

10. Mish. Av. Zar. 5:3, Tosef. Av. Zar. 7[8]:13; cf. Targ. Onk., Saadia, Rashi, Ibn Ezra, Rashbam. See S. Morag, "Layers of Antiquity: Some Linguistic Observations on the Oracles of Balaam" (Hebrew), *Tarbiz* 50 (1980/1981):12–14.

11. Aq., Sym., Theodotian.

12. Num. 22:31, Ned. 31a, Sanh. 105a.

13. W. F. Albright, "The Names Shaddai and Abram," JBL 54(1935):180–187; F. M. Cross, *Canaanite Myth and Hebrew Epic* (Cambridge: Harvard University Press, 1973), 52–66.

14. R. de Vaux, "El et Baal: Le Dieu des pères et Yahweh," *Ugaritica*, vol. 6 (Paris: Geuthner, 1969); W. Wifall, "El Shaddai or El of the Fields," ZAW 92 (1980):24–32.

15. M. M. Kalisch, *Bible Studies: The Prophecies of Balaam* (London: Longman, 1877). Cf. also Ezek. 1:28; 3:23; 43:3.

16. Vetter, *Seherspruch und Segensschilderung*.

17. The Akk. semantic equivalent *igigallu*, "large eye," is used of either man or deity possessing insight (T. H. Gaster, *Myth, Legend, and Custom in the Old Testament*, vol. 1 [New York: Harper and Row, 1969], 306).

18. A verbal form (Gen. 14:3).

19. Targ. Jon., Targ. Yer.

20. E. B. Smick, "A Study of the Structure of the Third Balaam Oracle," in *The Law and the Prophets*, ed. J. M. Skilton (Nutley, N.J.: Presbyterian and Reformed Pub. Co., 1974); but cf. Morag, "Layers of Antiquity," n. 54.

21. See Ps. 45:9; Prov. 7:19; Song 4:14; see Targ. Onk.

22. RH 23a.

23. G. B. Gray.

24. Rashi, see Isa. 44:3; 66:12; Ps. 65:10–11.

25. My son, A. M. Milgrom. Some commentators suggest reading instead of *ve-zarʿo be-mayim*, *u-zeroʿo be-ʿammim*, "their arm shall be upon many peoples" (hinted by LXX, Targ. Onk.), thereby avoiding the repetition of "water." However, this image of physical might would conflict with that of arborescent fertility in the first line. Also, the fact that Qumran did not interpret this verse messianically (as it did v. 17) indicates that their text was probably in agreement with the MT and Sam. against LXX (Smick, *The Third Balaam Oracle*).

26. Targ. Yer., Rashi, Ibn Ezra.

27. W. F. Albright, "The Oracles of Balaam," JBL 63 (1944):218 n. 69.

28. Targ. Yer., Targ. Neof.; also LXX and Sam., which identify the king as Gog.

29. *Motsi'o* (see 23:22), but LXX and Sam. read *nahahu*, "led them" (see 23:7; Exod. 13:17), which may be original.

30. The image as it stands is incongruous since the verb *mahats*, "smash," usually takes as its object the head (Ps. 68:22), the legs (Ps. 68:24), the loins (Deut. 33:11), the temples (v. 17)—implying the use of a club. Equally inappropriate is the reading *behitsav*, "smash (the enemy) with their arrows" (LXX, Targ. Jon., Bekhor Shor). *Lohatsav*, "oppressors" (A. Dillmann, *Die Bücher Numeri, Deuteronomium, und Josua* [Leipzig: S. Hirzel, 1886]) destroys the symmetry of bodily organs in this verse. Preferable, then, is the reading *halatsav*, "loins" (Pesh., Ehrlich; see Deut. 33:11), in parallelism with "bones." See also the Comment to v. 17.

31. The suggestion has also been made to switch cola 9a and 8b so that it is the lion who consumes the enemy and breaks its bones (Vetter, *Seherspruch und Segensschilderung*).

32. GKC, sec. 145, 1; Vetter, *Seherspruch und Segensschilderung*.

33. Ehrlich.

34. G. Coats, "The Way of Obedience," *Semeia* 24 (1982): 53–79, esp. 72.

35. Y. Zakovitch, "The Pattern of the Numerical Sequence Three-Four in the Bible" (Hebrew) (Ph.D. diss., Hebrew University, 1977).

36. *Mal'akhekha* (see 22:5). Vv. 12–13 repeat 22:18 with slight variations.

37. Kalisch, *Bible Studies*; see Excursus 56.

38. Kalisch, *Bible Studies*.

39. L. Schmidt, "Die alttestamentliche Bileamüberlieferung," BZ 23 (1979), 235–261.

40. I. Goldziher, *Abhandlungen zur arabischen Philologie* (Leiden: Brill, 1896).

41. Meyuhas.

42. Targ. Jon.; cf. Sanh. 106a.

43. Philo, 1 Mos. 294–301; Josephus, Ant. 4.126–130, TJ Sanh. 28cd.

44. Kalisch, *Bible Studies*.

45. The many parallels between this fourth oracle and Ps. 110: *ne'um* (24:15; Ps. 110:1), *redeh*, "rule" (24:19; Ps. 110:2), *mahats*, "crush" (24:17; Ps. 110:6) as well as synonyms for "scepter," "heads" (24:17/Ps. 110:2; 24:17/Ps. 110:6) make it likely that the psalmist knew Balaam's oracle (J. de Vaulx, *Les Nombres* [Paris: J. Gabalda, 1972]).

46. With Targ. Onk.

47. Targ. Jon.; see Ber. 7a.

48. Rashi.

49. Perhaps *daʿat* should be vocalized *deʿot* (pl.) in parallel with *'imre*, "speech" (also pl.), as in 1 Sam. 2:3; Job 36:4 (Vetter, *Seherspruch und Segensschilderung*).

50. *'El ʿelyon* of Gen. 14:18–22 is divided into the synonymous parallel lines here and elsewhere (e.g., Pss. 73:11; 77:10–11; 78:17–18; 107:11; Sfire A.11).

51. Rashi, Ibn Ezra.

52. Targ. Onk., Targ. Jon., 1QM 11:6–7, CD 7:19, Rev. 22:16 (Jesus), Test. Patr. Levi 18:3, Test. Patr. Judah 24:1.

53. TJ Taʿan. 68d.

54. C. Roth, "Star and Anchor: Coin Symbolism and the Early Days," *Eretz Israel* 6(1960):13–16.

55. M. Weinfeld, "'They Fought from Heaven': Divine Intervention in War in Israel and in the Ancient Near East," *Eretz Israel* 14(1978):23–30.

56. S. Gevirtz, *Patterns in the Early Poetry of Israel* (Chicago: University of Chicago Press, 1963).

57. A prophetic perfect (without the conversive *vav*).

58. Albright, "The Oracles of Balaam," p. 219 n. 83.

59. Weinfeld, "'They Fought from Heaven.'"

60. Ber. 48b.

61. Weinfeld, "'They Fought from Heaven.'"

62. M. Lichtheim, *Ancient Egyptian Literature*, vol. 2 (Berkeley: University of California Press, 1976), 37.

63. E.g., ANEP, no. 317.

64. *Mahats*. Its Akk. cognate *mahāṣu* is used with a country as its object (e.g., ARM 1.123). In the Bible, its objects are "head" (Hab. 3:13), "loins" (Deut. 33:11), kings (Ps. 110:5), the monster Rahab (Job 26:12); see the Comment to v. 8.

65. *Pa'atei.* Dual in form: "temples" or, if taken figuratively, "chiefs" (LXX; cf. Targ. Onk., Targ. Jer., Pesh.) or "frontiers" ("regions," Sym.), since *pe'ah* means "edge, rim" (e.g., Exod. 25:26; 27:9; Lev. 19:9; 23:22) also in its Ugar. and Akk. cognates (UT 52.68; Krt 105, 193–194; ARM 2.35.7–8; Albright "The Oracles of Balaam," p. 220 n. 86; Gevirtz, *Patterns in the Early Poetry*).

66. *Ve-karkar*, reading *ve-kadkod* on the basis of Sam. and Jer. 48:45. Alternatively, render "the borders of" since Akk. *qaqqaru* means "ground, territory," just as Heb. *kadkod* = Akk. *qaqqadu*, "head" (*kdkd* of Jer. 48:45 may be an error for *krkr*; Gevirtz, *Patterns in the Early Poetry*).

67. A. H. Sayce, "Balaam's Prophecy (Numbers 24:17–24) and the God Sheth," *Hebraica* 4 (1887):1–6; Albright, "The Oracles of Balaam," p. 220 n. 89.

68. Some read *benei sha'on*, "the people of Shaon" (Jer. 48:45; Amos 2:2, parallel to Moab), perhaps an old name for Moab.

69. The order of the MT, abc acb', is characteristic of Ugar. poetry (C. H. Gordon, *Ugaritic Grammar* [Rome: Pontificum institutum biblicum, 1965], 133; Albright, "The Oracles of Balaam," p. 221 n. 94).

70. *Yereshah.* Perhaps should be vocalized *yerushah*, "dispossessed," a passive participle (Albright, "The Oracles of Balaam," p. 221 n. 92).

71. *'Oyevav*, literally "its enemies." It has been suggested to transpose it to the end of v. 19a (Albright "The Oracles of Balaam," p. 221 n. 92). A radical solution is to emend *se'ir* to *sha'ar*, yielding: "the gate (of) its enemies will become a possession" (Gen. 22:17; Ehrlich).

72. Targ. Jon., Saadia, Ibn Ezra, Rashbam.

73. Albright, "The Oracles of Balaam," p. 221 n. 93.

74. K. Seybold, "Das Herrscherbild des Bileamorakels Num. 24, 15–19," TZ 29 (1973):1–19.

75. Kalisch, *Bible Studies*.

76. Either vocalize *'adei 'avod* (infinitive absolute, as in Deut. 7:20), read as *'ad yo'ved* (shifting the *yod*), literally "until it will perish forever," or regard the participle as an abstract noun "destruction" (P. Wernberg-Möller, "Observations on the Hebrew Participle," ZAW 71 [1959]:55) requiring no textual alteration.

77. Aram. and Syr.; see Targum to Judg. 17:4; Jer. 10:9; Ps. 66:10; TJ BB 2:2 (13b).

78. Some add "Kain" (from v. 22) here for the sake of the meter (Albright, "The Oracles of Balaam," p. 222 n. 99). Jer. 49:16 and Obad. 4 borrow from this verse.

79. *Sim*, a passive participle (1 Sam. 9:24; Obad. 4).

80. Some transpose it to the previous verse (after "secure") for the sake of the meter (Albright, "The Oracles of Balaam," p. 222 n. 99).

81. Ibid.

82. Albright ("The Oracles of Balaam," p. 222 n. 103) renders "the while I gaze" taking *'ad* as meaning "while" (1 Sam. 14:19; Job 14:12); *mah* as an untranslatable enclitic (see Sam.); and reading *'ashur*, "I gaze" (23:9; 24:1). However, his reading *toshavekha*, "your sojourners," for *tishbekha* makes little sense. A third possibility is the rendering "Asher" instead of "Asshur" (W. Wifall, "Asshur and Eber, or Asher and Heber," ZAW 82[1970]:110–114). It would refer to the possible conquest and absorption of the Galilean Kenite clan of Heber (Judg. 4:11), which earlier was allied with the Canaanites (Judg. 4:17) by the tribe of Asher (26:45; Gen. 46:17).

83. Albright, "The Oracles of Balaam," p. 222 n. 106.

84. S. Morag, "Layers of Antiquity."

85. Ant. 1.128.

86. Targ. Yer.

87. Y. Aharoni, *Arad Inscriptions* (Jerusalem: Israel Exploration Society, 1981), 12–13.

88. See LXX.

89. Albright, however, would read *mi-yarketei yam*, "from the furthest sea" ("The Oracles of Balaam," p. 223 n. 111).

90. de Vaulx, *Les Nombres*.

91. Wifall, "Asshur and Eber."

92. Gaster, *Myth, Legend, and Custom*, p. 308, following mainly Albright, renders vv. 23–24 so as to substitute "wild beasts" for the ethnic names. This is based on Isa. 13:21–22; 34:14: "Howling beasts (*'iyyim*) come hieing from the Northland/And yowling beasts (*tsiyyim*) from the far reaches of the West/But even as I look, they have passed by/So too shall this one disappear."

93. *Va-yakom va-yelekh.* For the idiom, see Gen. 23:3; 24:10; Judg. 13:11; 19:3,10.

Chapter 25

1. G. J. Wenham.

2. D. T. Olson, *The Death of the Old and the Birth of the New* (Chico, Calif.: Scholars Press, 1985), 160.

3. Sif. Num. 131.

4. Ant. 5.1.

5. Ant. 4.176.

6. *Va-yaḥel* (Hifil of *ḥ-l-l*) with LXX, repointed to *va-yeḥel* or *va-yeḥal* (Nifal reflexive; see Lev. 21:4,9), a root that goes with *zanah*, "whore" (e.g., Lev. 19:29; 21:9).

7. *'El.* A construction attested elsewhere with *zanah* (e.g., Ezek. 16:26,28) to describe Israel's religious and political defections.

8. For biblical *marzeaḥ*, see Jer. 16:5; Amos 6:7.

9. Lev. R. 5:3.

10. PRU 3.

11. Ehrlich. The sexual connotation of this term is attested in an old, bilingual Mesopotamian text: "A girl who did not reach her bloom . . . *eṭlu la ṣum[mudu]* a boy who remained unyoked" (CAD, s.v. *ṣummudu*).

12. Buber, *Moses* (Oxford: Phaidon, 1947), 193.

13. R. de Vaux, *The Early History of Israel* (Philadelphia: Westminster Press, 1978).

14. Rashi.

15. Ehrlich would even go so far as to insist that only the innocent were selected since their execution was dedicated to God, and a sacrificial expiation mandated pure, i.e., innocent, victims.

16. Num. R. 20:23, Tanḥ. Balak 19, Tanḥ. B. 28.

17. Sif. Num. 131; cf. Targ. Jon.

18. The Sam. actually contains a different text for v. 4a: "command that they (i.e., the leaders) slay all the men who have attached themselves to Baal-peor," i.e., Moses' taking of the leaders was to charge them with the responsibility of executing the guilty (equating leaders with "judges" in v. 5). This view is followed by the Targums: "judge and slay him who is guilty of death" (Targ. Onk.); "let them give the judgment to put to death the people who have gone astray after Peor" (Targ. Jon.); "set them for a Sanhedrin before the Lord and let them hang all who are worthy of death" (Targ. Yer.; cf. Targ. Neof.). This interpretation, however, runs into grammatical obstacles: "Them" would have no antecedent and "take" is hardly the proper word for charging the leaders. It would therefore seem that all the leaders fell under the decree (see Excursus 61).

19. Cf. also Sfire 1.C.5 (reconstructed).

20. W. R. Smith, *Lectures on the Religion of the Semites*, 3rd ed. (London: A. and C. Black, 1927).

21. R. Polzin, "'HWQY' and Covenantal Institutions in Early Israel," HTR 62(1969):227–240.

22. Sfire 1.A.40.

23. Mish. Sanh. 6:4.

24. Sanh. 34b.

25. Middle Assyrian laws, par. 53; cf. Hammurabi, par. 153.

26. J. Milgrom, "The Shok Haterumah: A Chapter in Cultic History" (Hebrew), *Tarbiz* 42 (1972/1973):1–11; idem, "The Tenufah" (Hebrew), in *Zer li-gevurot: The Zalman Shazar Jubilee Volume*, ed. B. Z. Lurie (Jerusalem: Kiriat Sefer, 1973), 38–55; idem, *Studies in Cultic Theology and Terminology* (Leiden: E. J. Brill, 1983), 140, 160–161.

27. Cf. also "A Letter from the Time of Josiah" (ANET, p. 568).

28. M. Weinfeld, "Judge and Officer in Ancient Israel and in the Ancient Near East," *Israel Oriental Studies* 8 (1977):65–88.

29. See Ramban.

30. Ibn Ezra.

31. Ramban, Shadal; and see Excursus 61.

32. *Ve-hinneh . . . ba'*. The use of the perfect rather than the imperfect with the sequential *vav* indicates simultaneity of action.

33. Josephus, Ant. 4.150–151.

34. Targ. Jon.; see Sif. Num. 111, Sanh. 82a.

35. Cf. Judg. 21:2; 2 Sam. 15:23; Isa. 30:19; Ezek. 27:30; Mic. 1:10.

36. For his subsequent accomplishments as High Priest, see Num. 31:6; Josh. 22:13, 30–32; 24:33; Judg. 20:28. His zeal set an example for subsequent generations (Ecclus. 45:28; 1 Macc. 2:26; 4 Macc. 18:12).

37. So LXX, Pesh. Others render "tent" (Targums), and in Arab. *al-qubbat* (whence English "alcove") means a "domed tent," as in rabbinic Heb. (Ta'an. 8b BB 25b; cf. Latin *cupa*, *cupula*).

38. J. Morgenstern, "The Ark, the Ephod, and 'Tent of Meeting,'" HUCA 17(1942/1943): 153–265; S. C. Reif, "What Enraged Phineas?: A Study of Numbers 25.8," JBL 90 (1971): 200–206.

39. F. M. Cross, "The Priestly Tabernacle," BA 10 (1947): 45–68.

40. Morgenstern, "The Ark."

41. Ibn Janaḥ.

42. Targ. Jon., Sif. Deut. 165, Ḥul. 134b.

43. LXX, Targ. Onk.

44. Sif. Num. 131, Sanh. 82b, Radak, and Ḥazzekuni (citing 2 Kings).

45. See the Comment to 5:21 and Philo, 1 Mos. 302.

46. Radak.

47. Reif, "What Enraged Phineas?"

48. TJ Sanh. 9 (27b).

49. B. H. Epstein, *Pentateuch and Five Megillot: Torah Temimah* (Hebrew), 5 vols. (Tel Aviv: Am Olam, 1955–1956).

50. Y. Muffs, "Between Justice and Mercy: The Prayer of the Prophets" (Hebrew), in *Torah Nidreshet* (Tel Aviv: Am Oved, 1984), 79.

51. Olson, *The Death of the Old*.

52. *Heshiv 'et ḥamati*. For the idiom, see Jer. 18:20; Ps. 106:23.

53. So the Targums.

54. A. Dillmann, *Die Bücher Numeri, Deuteronomium, und Josua* (Leipzig: S. Hirzel, 1886).

55. Shadal on Exod. 20:5; see the Comment to 5:14.

56. Ramban.

57. Targ. Jon., Targ. Yer., Targ. Neof.

58. Ibn Ezra.

59. Philo, 1 Mos. 304, Ramban, Zohar, Noah 66.

60. See also Jer. 33:20, 25. It is confirmed by the equivalent Akk. terms *riksu u šalāmu* (second millennium) and *adê salīme* (first millennium [M. Weinfeld, "Brit," Bib 56 (1975):123]) as well as in biblical passages where *shalom* and *berit* are almost synonymous (e.g., Josh. 9:15; 1 Kings 5:26). For the full range of the term *shalom*, see at 6:26.

61. Ibn Ezra, Abravanel.

62. For identification of Phinehas with Elijah, see BAP 48.1–2 and later midrashim.

63. E.g., Gen. 9:16; Exod. 31:16; Lev. 24:8; Num. 18:19; 2 Sam. 23:5; Isa. 55:3; 61:8; Jer. 32:40; Ezek. 16:60; 37:26; Ps. 105:10.

64. Zev. 101b, Rashi.

65. See Ecclus. 45:24, Ibn Ezra, Shadal.

66. The names of Eli and Abiathar are conspicuously missing in the line of Phinehas; 1 Chron. 5:30–41.

67. J. Milgrom, *Studies in Levitical Terminology* (Berkeley: University of California Press, 1970), 28–31.

68. Philo, 1 Mos. 303.

69. Josephus, Ant. 4.154.

70. With LXX, Sam.

71. A. Malamat, "*Ummatum* in Old Babylonian Texts and Its Ugaritic and Biblical Counterparts," UF 11(1979):527–536.

72. *Tsaror*, an infinitive absolute used with imperative force. Literally, "be a foe, harass" (Exod. 23:22; Num. 10:9; 33:55; Deut. 2:9). Cf. Akk. *ṣēru*, "foe," and Ugar. *ṣr*, "vex," and *ṣrt*, "hostility."

73. N. K. Gottwald, *The Tribes of Yahweh* (New York: Orbis Books, 1979), 432.

74. *Be-nikhlehem 'asher nikkelu* (so Radak; see Targ. Onk. on Exod. 21:14). Akk. *nakālu* means "be crafty, cunning."

75. Ehrlich.

76. The interchangeability of *nasi'* and *ro'sh* has already been noted (7:2; see 30:2; 32:38; and see Excursus 1).

77. See Keter Torah.

78. 1 Mos. 305–318.

79. D. Jobling, "'The Jordan a Boundary'! A Reading of Numbers 32 and Joshua 22," in *Seminar Papers, Society of Biblical Literature* (Chico, Calif.: Scholars Press, 1980), 183–207 (= *The Sense of Biblical Narrative*, JSOT 39 [Sheffield: Univ. of Sheffield, 1986], 88–123); Olson, *The Death of the Old*.

Chapter 26

1. M. Kochman, in *Numbers* (Hebrew), ed. J. Milgrom et al. (Ramat Gan: Revivim, 1985).

2. M. Weinfeld, in *Numbers* (Hebrew), ed. J. Milgrom et al (Ramat Gan: Revivim, 1985).

3. B. Jacob, *Die Abzählungen in den Gesetzen der Bücher Leviticus und Numeri* (Frankfurt aM: J. Kaufmann, 1909), 92–98, 113.

4. Rashi.

5. Ramban.

6. *Va-yedabber . . . 'otam*. This rendering tries to make sense of a very difficult construction, sincer *dibber 'et* should be followed by a direct object. However, it requires the emendation [*'al*] *'o[do]tam* (12:1; Josh. 14:6, following *dibber*). Some versions read *'ittam*, "(spoke) with them" (Targ. Neof., Pesh.), in which case *'alehem*, "to them," would be expected since a direct quotation follows. LXX deletes *'otam*, which leaves the direct quotation in v. 4 without a subject and verb. Targ. Jon. adds: "spoke [to the officers and said to count] them" (see also Targ. Onk.). Some moderns emend *va-yedabber* to *va-yispor, va-yif kod*, or *va-ya'aver* (see Exod. 30:13; Ehrlich), all synonyms meaning "counted"—which, however, would require deleting *le'mor*, "namely," (with Pesh.), for which there is no textual warrant.

7. *'Al*. In 22:1; 34:15 the more precise preposition *me-'ever*, "opposite," is used (but see 26:63; 31:12; 33:48,50; 35:1; 26:13).

8. Sforno, Shadal, Ehrlich; see Targ. Onk., Targ. Jon.

9. *Va-yiheyu fekudeihem*, alternatively, *u-fekdeihem* (vv. 34, 41,50), indicating that this term and the sum that follows form a single sentence that was (subsequently?) added on to the clan list and that the construction *li-fekudeihem* (vv. 18,22,25,27,37, 43,47), which grammatically belongs with its previous phrase, is probably not original.

10. *Benei*, literally "sons of." Rather, "son of." The plural for a single name occurs in genealogies (see v. 36; Gen. 46:23; 1 Chron. 1:41). See Ramban on Gen. 46:23 and BB 143b.

11. J. Liver, "Korach, Dathan, and Abiram," *Scripta Hierosolymitana* 8(1961):201–214.

12. *Keri (v) 'ei (ha-'edah)*. Rather, "called to" (1:16; 16:2; see Excursus 1).

13. *Hitstsu*, occurs again only in the title to Ps. 60. The Targums render "gathered," which corresponds to the reading in the Sam., *ho'adu* (= *no'adu*?). That this verb is absent from the main account, chap. 16, means that this addition (vv. 8–11) is not a copy but a reworking of the account.

14. Ibn Ezra.

15. Inscription 49.

16. M. Noth, *Numbers: A Commentary*, trans. J. D. Martin (London: S. C. M. Press, 1968).

17. Read *pu'ah* (LXX, Sam., Pesh., and 1 Chron. 7:1).

18. J. Liver, "The Israelite Tribes," in *The World History of the Jewish People*, vol. 3, ed. B. Mazar (Tel Aviv: Jewish History Publications, 1971), 183–211.

19. Note the similar spelling, *'(y)lwn / 'ylwn*.

20. G. B. Gray.

21. J. M. Sasson, "A Genealogical 'Convention' in Biblical Chronography?" ZAW 90 (1978), 171–185.

22. Recently dated at 784/3 B.C.E. by A. F. Rainey, "Toward a Precise Date for the Samaria Ostraca," BASOR 272 (1988): 69–74.

23. Noth, *Numbers: A Commentary*.

24. Kochman, in *Numbers*, ed. J. Milgrom et al.

25. Num. 27:1; 36:1; Josh. 17:1,3; 1 Chron. 2:21,23; 7:14,16,17; Liver, "The Israelite Tribes."

26. A. Lemaire, "Le 'pays de Hépher' et les 'filles de Zelophehad' à la lumière des ostraca de Samarie," Sem 22 (1972):13–20.

27. Lemaire, "Le 'pays de Hépher.'"

28. Ibid.

29. *'Erets*; 1 Kings 4:10; cf. Josh. 17:5; 1 Kings 9:13.

30. Liver, "The Israelite Tribes."

31. Abravanel.

32. Ramban.

33. See the discussion in BB 122a.

34. For decision making (Ezek. 21:20; Mic. 2:5), to prevent disputes (Prov. 16:33; 18:18), to divide spoils (Joel 4:3; Ps. 22:19; Prov. 1:4; 1 Macc. 3:36), to select both persons (Judg. 20:9; 1 Sam. 10:19–20; Nah. 3:10; Neh. 11:1) and the two goats on Yom Kippur (Lev. 16:8), to determine the priestly and Levitical courses (1 Chron. 24:5; 26:13–16), and the sequence of wood offering contributions (Neh. 10:35).

35. E.g., ARM 1.7, Middle Assyrian laws B.1.

36. F. M. Cross, *Canaanite Myth and Hebrew Epic* (Cambridge: Harvard University Press, 1973), 195–215.

37. K. Möhlenbrink, "Die levitischen überlieferungen des Alten Testaments," ZAW 12 (1934): 184–231.

38. J. Liver, *Chapters in the History of the Priests and Levites* (Hebrew) (Jerusalem: Magnes Press, 1968).

39. S. E. Loewenstamm, EB (Hebrew), s.v. *kohat*.

40. W. F. Albright, "The Lachish Cosmetic Burner and Esther 2:12," in *A Light unto My Path*, ed. H. N. Bream et al. (Philadelphia: Temple University Press, 1974), 25–32.

41. See the titles of Pss. 43–49, 84–85, 87–88; 1 Chron. 6:18–23—the singer Heman is a descendant of Korah.

42. Loewenstamm, *kohat*.

43. The rendering here follows Targ. Jon., Targ. Neof., and Pesh., ignoring *'otah* and rendering as though vocalized *yuledah*.

44. Ibn Ezra, Ramban.

Chapter 27

1. *le-mishpeḥot* (pl.), following the LXX which vocalizes *le-mishpaḥat* (sing.). Also render "of a (Manassite) clan."

2. Sif. Num. 133, Sif. Zut. on 27:1, Num. R. 21:10.

3. *Le'mor*, an ellipsis for *va-to'marnah le'mor* (Meyuḥas).

4. *Ki*, synonymous with *ki 'im* (see Gen. 3:5; 24:4; Ps. 115:1; H. L. Ginsberg, *The Israelian Heritage of Judaism* [New York: Jewish Theological Seminary of America, 1982]).

5. Targ. Jon., Sif. Num. 133.

6. So rendered by LXX.

7. Thus "shave" (Isa. 15:2; Jer. 48:37 and in Syr., Aram., South Arab., and by extension (in the Nifal) "be diminished" (36:3; Exod. 5:11; Lev. 27:18) and "be deprived, excluded" (9:7).

8. My student, S. Rattray.

9. Targ. Jon.

10. Num. R. 21:12.

11. *ken*. For this usage, see Exod. 10:29; 2 Kings 7:9; 17:9; Jer. 8:6. It is an adjective from the root *k-w-n*.

12. S. Rattray.

13. Deut. 32:49 is patently from another source.

14. Except for the verbal form *hitnaḥel* (Lev. 25:46).

15. Num. R. 21:12.

16. Ibn Ezra.

17. Sif. Num. 134, BB 109b.

18. *Naḥalah*. The same usage is attested in Mari Akk.: the verb *naḫālu* means "assign (hereditary) property, apportion" (see ARM 8.11.23–31; 13.11–14); the noun *niḫlatu* means "hereditary property, patrimony" (see ARM 1.91.15, 26–27), i.e., "inalienable land whose transfer is only effected through inheritance not purchase" (A. Malamat, "Mari and the Bible," JAOS 82 [1962], 147–150.

19. Ibn Ezra.

20. BB 109b–110a, Sif. Num. 134.

21. *She'ero*. Like Ugar. *šir* and Akk. *šīru*, the basic meaning of *she'er* is "flesh, body" (see Prov. 11:17; Mic. 3:2) and, by extension, "a flesh (blood) relative" (see Lev. 18:6,12,13,17; 25:49).

22. Num. R. 21:13.

23. *Ka'asher*. This usage is attested, if rarely (1 Sam. 28:18; Mic. 3:4). The Sam. reads *'asher* (implying that the MT is a dittography from preceding *'avikha*) meaning "inasmuch as."

24. *Meritem pi* (so Targ. Neof.). The nature of Moses' sin is found in 20:1–3 and explained in Excursus 50.

25. *Hem*, referring to preceding "water," which is plural, *mayim*. Perhaps it betrays an editorial gloss, to correspond with Deut. 32:51.

26. A play on *merivah*, "strife" (20:13; repeated in Deut. 32:51).

27. Num. R. 21:15; see Ibn Ezra.

28. M. Greenberg, *Biblical Prose Prayer* (Berkeley: University of California Press, 1983).

29. Sif. Num. 138.

30. Mid. Song on 1:10.

31. Cf. Josh. 14:11; 1 Sam. 18:13,16; 29:6. So Targums, Sif. Num. 139, Ibn Ezra.

32. Sif. Num. 139.

33. Elsewhere, the abbreviated idiom "go and come" without persons as the object does not mean "lead" but is to be understood either literally (referring to relays of guards, as in 2 Kings 11:9, or warriors, as in 1 Chron. 27:11) or figuratively as "manage, conduct one's affairs" (see Deut. 28:6; 1 Kings 3:7).

34. See M. Weinfeld, *Deuteronomy and the Deuteronomic School* (Oxford: Clarendon Press, 1972), 181 n. 3.

35. Targums.

36. Saadia.

37. D. Daube, *The New Testament and Rabbinic Judaism* (London: University of London and The Athalone Press, 1956), 224–246; idem., "Neglected Nuances of Exposition in Luke-

Acts," *Aufstieg und Niedergang der römischen Welt,* vol. 2, *Principat* 25 (Berlin: de Gruyter, 1985), 232–235.

38. Ḥag. 16b; see Men. 93b and Targ. Jon. on this verse.

39. With LXX.

40. R. Péter, "L'imposition des mains dans l'Ancien Testament," VT 27 (1977), 48–55.

41. Ehrlich.

42. *Ve-tsivvita 'oto.* For this meaning of *tsivvah,* see 1 Sam. 13:14; 25:30; 2 Sam. 6:21; 7:11; Neh. 5:14 (Ramban). But see Deut. 31:14,23 for a different tradition of Joshua's investiture.

43. Targ. Jon.; see Exod. 34:30.

44. Sif. Num. 140.

45. *Yishme'u* (see Gen. 42:22; Deut. 1:43; Isa. 1:19). LXX, Pesh., Targums read "obey him."

46. *Ve-sha'al be* (see Judg. 1:1; 20:18; 1 Sam. 22:15; 21:26 for this usage). LXX reads *ve-sha'alu,* "they (the Israelites) shall seek."

47. *Mishpat* as in "the breastpiece of decision." See Exod. 28:15,29,30; cf. Prov. 16:33; also in Ugar. (*Ugaritica,* vol 5 [Paris: Greuthner, 1968], 564).

48. 11QTemple 58:15–21.

49. Ehrlich.

50. LXX renders "with one accord," which misses the point.

51. G. J. Wenham.

52. See Josh. 21:8 for the same formula (also 1:19; 2:34; 5:4; 8:22; 17:26 for its variations).

Chapter 28

1. See 11QTemple 25:7–8, Mish. Zev. 10:1.

2. Noted by G. B. Gray.

3. M. H. Segal, *Introduction to the Bible* (Hebrew), vol. 1 (Jerusalem: Kiriat Sefer, 1950–1951), 100.

4. *Tishmeru.* Found frequently in Deut., where it is the auxiliary to the infinitive *la'asot,* "to do" (rather than *le-hakriv,* "in presenting," as here).

5. The Hittite "Instructions for Temple Officials" stipulates that "if you do not celebrate the festivals at the time proper for the festivals . . . the gods will seek to take revenge on you in the future" (ANET, pp. 208–209).

6. Even animals follow their "stated times" (Jer. 8:7).

7. Generally the suffix is a subjective genitive referring to the person who makes the offering, but when the suffix refers to God it is an objective genitive, in regard both to "offering" (9:7,13; 31:50; Lev. 23:14) and to "food" (Ezek. 44:7; Lev. 21:6,8,17,21,22).

8. Cf. Bel and Dragon, Num. R. 21:15.

9. Sif. Num. 143.

10. Num. R. 21:19.

11. Sif. Zut. on v. 2; Josephus, Ant. 3.123; idem, *Against Apion* 2.6.

12. Sam. reads *'olat tamid* (as in vv. 10, 15).

13. Just as *'aruḥat tamid* (2 Kings 25:29–30) refers to food regularly served on the king's table, *'anshei tamid* (Ezek. 39:14) means "men in regular employment" (N. H. Snaith, *Leviticus and Numbers* [London: Nelson, 1967]), and *ner tamid* (Exod. 27:20) refers to the regular lighting of the menorah each evening.

14. *'Eḥad.* Sam. reads *ha-'eḥad* (see Exod. 29:39), to correspond to *ha-sheni,* "the other," in the next clause.

15. Mish. Pes. 5:1, Pes. 58a.

16. Sif. Zut. ad loc.

17. So Ehrlich.

18. See Ḥag. 6b, Sif. Zut. on 9:5; 28:6.

19. J. Milgrom, "Concerning Jeremiah's Repudiation of Sacrifice," ZAW 89 (1977):273–275.

20. So Targ. Onk.

21. Targ. Jon.

22. Tosef. Suk. 3:15; Sif. Zut. ad loc.

23. See Ecclus. 50:15, Josephus, Ant. 3.234. *Kodesh,* a very plastic term (M. Haran, "The Priestly Image of the Tabernacle," HUCA 36 [1965]:191–226), can refer to the sacred precincts (see Exod. 28:43; Lev. 10:17) or to the sacred cult objects (3:28; 4:15, 20), in which case it always refers to the collective but never to the altar alone. Besides, the preposition *be,* "in," would not be appropriate for a libation on the altar.

24. Targums.

25. Ramban.

26. BB 97a, Ker. 13b.

27. Saadia.

28. Sif. Num. 144, Yoma 33a.

29. B. A. Levine, orally.

30. This passage is verbless and must be attached to the preceding *tamid,* addressed to the Israelites, v. 3.

31. W. H. Hallo, "New Moons and Sabbaths: A Case Study in the Contrastive Approach," HUCA 48(1977):1–18 (see note 34).

32. 11QTemple 13:17.

33. Marti cited by G. B. Gray.

34. Sif. Num. 144.

35. 4QSerekh Shirot 'Olat ha-Shabbat.

36. *'Al* used also in vv. 15b,24b, whereas the synonym *milvad* is mainly used (28:23,31; 29:6,11,16,19,22,25,28,31,34,38). *'Al* is used with the same meaning in Ugar. sacrificial text, no. 612 (*Ugaritica,* vol. 5 [Paris: Greuthner, 1968], 588), giving rise to the possibility that 28:9–25 is the oldest part of the calendar (L. R. Fisher, "A New Ritual Calendar for Ugarit," HTR 63 [1970]:485–501). See also the Comment to v. 23.

37. Ramban.

38. Hallo, "New Moons and Sabbaths."

39. Moses Cohen the Spaniard, cited by Ibn Ezra.

40. *Yihyeh,* "will be," is absent throughout the sacrificial catalogue and is superfluous here. It is therefore read as *yayin,* "wine" (with Sam. and Pesh.), needed for the beginning of the list. The word *yayin* at the end of 14a (after "lamb") should be deleted (with Sam. and Vulg.).

41. Ramban.

42. See Josephus, Ant. 3.249, Mish. Men. 11:7, Men. 100a.

43. Hallo, "New Moons and Sabbaths."

44. Abravanel.

45. See 11QTemple 18:4–6; 25:5–6,12–15.

46. Mish. Men. 9:6, Men. 90b–91b.

47. E. Kutsch, "*Miqra'*," ZAW 65(1953):247–253; M. Brettler, "*Miqra' Kodesh*" (Unpublished).

48. Ramban on Lev. 21:2; Shadal on Exod. 12:16.

49. RH 24a, 32a; Rashi on Exod. 12:16 (see Siftei Ḥakhamim); J. Morgenstern, "*Miqra' Qodeš* and *Miqra'*," JBL 43 (1924): 314–320; M. Noth, *Numbers: A Commentary,* trans. J. D. Martin (London: S. C. M. Press, 1968); see UText 3.7–8.

50. J. Milgrom, *Studies in Levitical Terminology* (Berkeley: University of California Press, 1970), n. 297.

51. So too all *milvad* statements (28:31; 29:6,11b,16b,19b, 22b,25b,28b,31b,34b,38b) can be regarded as editorial interpolations (I. Knohl, "The Concept of God and Cult in the Priestly Code and Holiness School" [Ph.D. diss., Hebrew University, 1988]). Ugar. texts use *'al* exclusively, proving that the *'al* passages in chaps. 28–29 are older (L. R. Fisher, ed., *Ras Shamra Parallels* [Rome: Pontificum institutum biblicum, 1975]).

52. Mish. Zev. 10:1.

53. Sam.

54. Mish. Men. 4:2–3, Sif. Num. 149.

55. M. Haran, *Temples and Temple-Service in Ancient Israel* (Oxford: Clarendon Press, 1978), 287.

56. Targ. Onk., Mish. Meg. 3:5, Mish. MK 3:6.

57. 11QTemple 19–23.

58. The LXX and Sam. add ***temimim (yihyu lakhem)***, "(see that they are) without blemish" (as in 28:11,19; 29:2,8,13,17, etc.), a word that perhaps was accidentally misplaced in v. 31b and should be moved up to here.

59. Some manuscripts, LXX, Sam.

Chapter 29

1. My student, S. Rattray.
2. Mekh. Bo', 1, Mish. RH 1:1.
3. Bekhor Shor.
4. M. Weinfeld, "Social and Cultic Institutions in the Priestly Source Against Their Ancient Near Eastern Background," in ***Proceedings of the Eighth World Congress of Jewish Studies: Bible Studies and Hebrew Language, 1981*** (Jerusalem: World Union of Jewish Studies), 100.
5. Targ. Jon., Mish. Yoma 8:1.
6. S. Rattray.
7. The form ***kippurim*** is an abstract plural (see Exod. 29:36; 30:16).
8. The Sam. inserts ***ve-niskeihem***, "and their libations," at the end of the verse, as found in the subsequent days of the festival (vv. 18,21,24,27,30,33).
9. *Ve-niskeihem*. Since the libations for the festival burnt offering were already mentioned (v. 18), a few manuscripts, the Pesh., and Vulg. read ***ve-niskah***, "its libation" (of the ***tamid*** burnt offering), as in the prescriptions for the other days (vv. 16, 22,25,28,34; see note 10, below).
10. Many manuscripts, Pesh., and Targ. Jon. read ***ve-niskah***, "its libation," as in the prescriptions for the other festival days (see note 9).
11. Ta'an. 2b; see Mish. Suk. 4:9.
12. Sif. Num. 150.
13. Targ. Jon.
14. Num. R. 21:24.
15. With Targ. Onk., Targ. Jon., Sif. Num. 151.
16. H. L. Ginsberg, ***The Israelian Heritage of Judaism*** (New York: Jewish Theological Seminary of America, 1982).
17. See also Josephus, Ant. 3.252.
18. Keter Torah.
19. Sif. Num. 152, Rashi.

Chapter 30

1. Rashbam, Ramban.
2. Cf. Num. 15:3; 29:35; Lev. 7:13; 27:1–13; Ps. 116:17–19; 11QTemple 53:9–54:5.
3. See Num. 32:28; Josh. 14:1; 21:1; in its only other attestation (1 Kings 8:2 [= 2 Chron. 5:2]), this title is glossed by ***nesi'ei ha-'avot***, "the chieftains of the clans."
4. Ned. 66b, Ramban.
5. For a similar construction, see Exod. 16:32; Lev. 9:6 (Ramban).
6. Sif. Num. 153, Targ. Jon.
7. Sif. Zut. on v. 4.
8. See Rashbam.
9. Num. 6:4a, 5a, 6a; Excursus 11.
10. In the scripture of the Dead Sea sectaries, this phrase reads "vow to Me" (11QTemple 53:14) since, in their text, God speaks in the first person.
11. *Hishava' shevu'ah*. For an example of the similar use of the infinitive absolute instead of the imperfect, see Lev. 25:14.
12. Identical to ***riksa rakāsu*** (Akk.), ***išḫiul išḫija*** (Hittite), and like the Sum. idiom ***inim KA kéš***, the binding is associated here with the word of the mouth (M. Weinfeld, "Brit," Bib 56 [1975]:123).
13. Sif. Num. 153. The Hifil of this root is found only once more in the Bible (Ezek. 39:17); all other instances use the Piel (e.g., Ps. 85:35, a similar context).
14. W. G. Lambert, "Dingir šà. dib. ba. Incantations," JNES 33(1974):280, line 124.
15. CD 16:9–10; cf. Mish. Ned. 2:2, Tosef. Ned. 1:4.
16. Ned. 22a.
17. Mish. Ter. 3:8.
18. Sif. Zut.
19. Ibn Ezra. ***ve*** = ***'o***, "or" (vv. 5,6,7; see vv. 3,7,11,15); 11QTemple 53:17 actually reads ***'o***.
20. Sif. Num. 153.
21. Ned. 47b.
22. So in vv. 6,8,9,12,13,16. For this usage, see, e.g., 1 Kings 5:14.
23. Yev. 87b.
24. See Gen. 23:17,20; Lev. 27:14; Deut. 19:15. Read ***yakumu*** (pl.) for ***yakum*** with LXX, Sam., Targums, and 11QTemple 53:19. The ***vav*** probably fell out by haplography.
25. 32:7,9; Ps. 33:10; and see the Comment to 14:34.
26. R. Jonathan in Sif. Num. 153, Targ. Jon., Ibn Ezra, Rashbam, Bekhor Shor.
27. See Ramban.
28. See Ehrlich and vv. 11–13.
29. Ibn Ezra.
30. Targ. Jon., Sif. Num. 153.
31. *Be-yom shome'o*, transposed after ***ve-heḥerish lah*** (with LXX) for clarity, as in v. 15b.
32. *Ve-hefer*; see ***parāru*** (Akk.) "break, crumble" and the Piel ***perer*** in rabbinic Heb. (e.g., Mish. Pes. 2:1).
33. *Ve-'et*, understood or read as Sam' ***o***.
34. Ehrlich.
35. 11QTemple 54:4–5.
36. See Ibn Ezra on v. 11.
37. Ehrlich.
38. CD 16:10–16.
39. 11QTemple 54:2–3.
40. *Ve-khol*. The 11QTemple 54:2 reads ***'o***, "or."
41. Sif. Num. 156.
42. So Mish. Ned. 10:8; see Tosef. Ned. 6:1; also in the Dead Sea Scrolls, CD 9:6, 1QSa 6:1.
43. Ibn Ezra.
44. Rashbam.
45. Ramban.
46. 11QTemple 54:2.
47. Sif. Num. 155, Targ. Jon., Ramban.

Chapter 31

1. Jer. 50:15,28; 51:11; Ezek. 25:14–17; G. Mendenhall, ***The Tenth Generation*** (Baltimore: Johns Hopkins University Press, 1973), 69–104.
2. Shadal.
3. LXX, Targums, Pesh.
4. And the LXX, Pesh.
5. 1QM 2:7–8.
6. Ehrlich.
7. Abravanel.
8. Z. Ben Hayyim, "Mesorah, Mesoret" (Hebrew), ***Leshonenu*** 21 (1957):283–292.
9. 1QM 3:3,12.
10. Ben Hayyim, "Mesorah, Mesoret."
11. Targ. Yer. on v. 8; Sanh. 106b.
12. With Ehrlich.
13. Mish. Sot. 8:1; and see Lev. R., 20:2, where Phinehas is so named.
14. So Philo, 1 Mos. 306; Josephus, Ant. 4.163.

15. Shadal.
16. Num. R. 22:4.
17. Sif. Num. 157; and see v. 49.
18. Sif. Num. 154, Sot. 43a.
19. Rashi.
20. A. Dillmann, *Die Bücher Numeri, Deuteronomium, und Josua* (Leipzig: S. Hirzel, 1897).
21. Targ. Jon., Num. R. 22:4.
22. Sif. Num. 157.
23. Ehrlich.
24. A. Malamat, "History and the Prophetic Vision in a Mari Letter," *Eretz Israel* 5(1959):67.
25. J. M. Grintz, "Early Terms in the Priestly Torah" (Hebrew), *Leshonenu* 40 (1975/1976): 17–18; idem, "Studies in the Antiquity of the Priestly Code" (Hebrew), in *Proceedings of the Sixth World Congress of Jewish Studies* (Jerusalem: World Union of Jewish Studies, 1977), 69–70.
26. Parallel to *'oholim*, "tents," in Ps. 69:26; cf. Gen. 25:16; Ezek. 25:4; 1 Chron. 6:39.
27. In Num., *pekudim* has an entirely different meaning (1:46; 2:4, 22, 23, etc.), a fact that suggests revocalizing it to *pekidei* (Gen. 41:34; Jer. 29:26; Ehrlich) or that this verse stems from a different source.
28. 1 Sam. 16:14,23; Jer. 32:40; Ezek. 6:9; Ehrlich.
29. R. Ishmael in Sif. Num. 157.
30. Gen. 4:1; 19:8; 1 Kings 1:4.
31. See especially *zikram la iduma*, "has not known a male" (CH 130).
32. Keter Torah.
33. See Judg. 21:12,14; Ehrlich.
34. See Deut. 21:10–14; Judg. 21:11–12.
35. H. M. Wiener, *Essays in Pentateuchal Criticism* (Oberlin: Bibliotheca Sacra Co., 1909), 99 n. 1. See Excursus 67.
36. Targ. Jon., Yev. 60b.
37. Sif. Num. 157.
38. Av. Zar. 75b, Ramban.
39. See Lev. 6:21; 11:33; 15:12; and see the Comment to 19:15.
40. *Tithatta'u*, the Hitpael used actively (Saadia), a rare but attested usage (see 34:10); or read *tehatte'u* as a Piel (the MT having been influenced by *tithatte'u* of the previous verse); or render "cleanse for yourselves," i.e., in your own interest, a use of the Hitpael attested in 33:54 and 34:10 (GKC, sec. 54f.).
41. Sif. Num. 157.
42. Ehrlich.
43. So the rabbis; Mish. Kel. 10:1, Mish. Oho. 5:5, Sif. Num. 126, Sifra Metsora 2:4.
44. 11QTemple 48:14.
45. G. M. Beckman, "Hittite Birth Rituals" (Ph.D. diss., Yale University, 1977), 173.
46. GKC, sec 126n.
47. D. P. Wright, "Purification from Corpse-Contamination in Numbers XXXI: 19–24," VT 25(1985):213–223.
48. Ibid.
49. Ibid. Heb. *he'evir ba-mayim* means "immerse" (Ezek. 47:3,4; Ps. 136:14).
50. B. Baentsch, "Exodus, Leviticus, Numeri," in HKAT, vol. 2 (Göttingen, 1903).
51. 1QM 14:2–3.
52. J. Milgrom, "Studies in the Temple Scroll," JBL 97 (1978):520–521.
53. J. Milgrom, *Cult and Conscience* (Leiden: E. J. Brill, 1976), 55–62.
54. 11QTemple 58:11–15.
55. *Shevi* here is not a noun but a past participle.
56. The full title is *ra'shei beit ha-'avot*, but the word *beit* is dropped when *'avot* is in construct (or in genitival relation) with the preceding and following nouns (see 36:1; and contrast Exod. 6:14; Josh. 22:14).
57. PRU 3.16.276.
58. Rather than assuming that this word entered Heb. via Aram. (B. A. Levine, "On the Study of the Priestly Source: The Linguistic Aspect" [Hebrew], *Eretz Israel* 16 [1982]:131, v. 30), it is more likely that this word "could just as well have entered Canaanite during the Amarna age when Akkadian was the *lingua franca*" (J. C. Greenfield's book review in JBL 87 [1968]: 232–234).
59. The noun *nefesh* is feminine and should precede its adjective. True, it is also attested in the masculine (see Gen. 46:25,27), and the irregular order may have been determined by the parallel phrase *'eḥad 'aḥuz* (see the Comment to v. 30); but the absence of *nefesh* in the latter verse would seem to render it superfluous here. Sam. reads *'aḥat*, correcting the gender but not the order. However, that *nefesh* applies to beasts as well as humans is hardly an anomaly; it is the rule in the priestly literature (e.g., Gen. 1:20; 9:10,12; Lev. 11:10,46).
60. *Terumat YHVH*, an objective genitive.
61. CAD, s.v. *ṣibtu* C.
62. Cf. chap. 1 with chaps. 3–4 and 26:1–56 with 26:57–63.
63. *U-mi-maḥtsit* perhaps should be read *u-mi-meḥtsat* as in v. 43, which takes the objective genitive, i.e. "the half belonging to" (Ehrlich).
64. See Num. 3:6; 7:3; 18:2; 28:26; Exod. 28:1; Lev. 8:6,19; 23:16.
65. *'Ets'adah*. So "*'ets'adah* from his arm" (2 Sam. 1:10), which, perhaps, should be distinguished from *tse'adah* (Isa. 3:20), "anklets," deriving from *tsa'ad*, "step" (Targ. Jon. on Isa. 3:20; Radak).
66. *Tsamid*. So "*tsemidim* on your hands" (Ezek. 16:11; cf. 23:42).
67. *'Agil*. So "*'agilim* on your ears" (Ezek. 16:12).
68. *Kumaz* (Exod. 35:22), perhaps related to Arab. *kumzat*, "bunch, heap," i.e., a cluster of small ornaments (N. A. Snaith, *Leviticus and Numbers* (London: Nelson, 1967). The rabbis understood it is as ornament that covered a woman's genitals (Shab. 64a).
69. A. Schenker, *Versöhnung und Sühne* (Freiburg: Swiss Catholic Bible Society, 1981), 100.
70. Philo, 1 Mos. 317.
71. Ehrlich.
72. J. Milgrom, "A Prolegomenon to Leviticus 17:11," JBL 90 (1971):149–156.
73. G. B. Gray.
74. Ehrlich.
75. Ramban.
76. *Bedek ha-Bayit*, Ket. 106b.
77. Targ. Neof.; see Targ. Jon., Targ. Yer., Philo, 1 Mos. 57.

Chapter 32

1. See Deut. 33:20–21 and contrast v. 6; Ibn Ezra, Ramban.
2. Abravanel.
3. Num. R. 22:8.
4. G. A. Smith, cited by G. B. Gray.
5. Ibn Ezra.
6. This phrase contains three grammatical peculiarities: a Kal passive, followed by an accusative, and a mixed gender. However, the Kal passive, though rare, is attested (e.g., Gen. 37:33; 40:15); an impersonal passive third person singular can take an accusative (e.g. Gen. 4:18; 27:42; Deut. 20:8; 2 Sam. 21:11); and *'erets* can be masculine (26:55; Gen. 13:6; Isa. 9:19; Ibn Ezra), particularly when the verb precedes.
7. Josephus, Ant. 4.167, Ramban.
8. Keter Torah.
9. M. Ottosson, *Gilead: Tradition and History* (Lund: Gleerup, 1969), 53–73.

10. M. Noth, *Numbers: A Commentary*, trans. J. D. Martin (London: S. C. M. Press, 1968).

11. Num. R. 22:7.

12. G. Brin, "The Formulae 'From . . . and Onward/ Upward,'" JBL 99 (1980):161–171.

13. 1QSa 1:10–11.

14. H. L. Ginsberg, *The Israelian Heritage of Judaism* (New York: Jewish Theological Seminary of America, 1982).

15. Sot. 12a, 34b; H. J. Schoeps, "Die griechischen Übersetzer zu Num. 32, 12," Bib 26 (1945): 307–309.

16. Y. Ben-Shem, "Kalev ben Yefunne Ha-kenizzi" (Hebrew), *Beth Mikra* 51 (1972): 498–500.

17. Saadia.

18. *Tarbut*, from the root *r-b-h*, "increase," is related to *tarbit*, "(monetary) interest." Like the other nominal form *marbit* (1 Sam. 2:33), it carries a derogatory connotation (Ehrlich). Alternatively, it may derive from *rav* (root *r-b-b*), "mighty," yielding the rendering "a force" (Meyuḥas).

19. *Li-spot*, ostensibly from the root *s-f-h*, which, however, does not mean "add." Hence, it must derive from the root *y-s-f* (clearly so with the same idiom in the next verse), whose infinitive construct bears this form in one attested case (Isa. 30:1); otherwise, vocalize *la-sefet*. For this usage in the Kal, see Lev. 22:14; Deut. 19:19; Isa. 29:1; 38:5.

20. *Le-hanniḥo* (see Jer. 14:9; Ps. 119:121 for this usage). However, with a place as the object, this verb means "to set down" (e.g., Num. 17:19; 19:9; Deut. 14:28) and always in a favorable sense (e.g., Gen. 2:15; Isa. 14:1; Jer. 27:11; Ezek. 37:14). Perhaps, then, one should read *le-hani'o* (with LXX, Sam.) to correspond with v. 13.

21. Saadia.

22. This leads to the possible inference that originally v. 16 followed on v. 6 and that vv. 7–15, the reference to the scout episode, is a later interpolation. So S. E. Loewenstamm, "The Relation of the Settlement of Gad and Reuben in Num. 32:1–38: Its Background and Its Composition" (Hebrew), *Tarbiz* 42 (1972–1973): 12–26.

23. O. Eissfeldt, "Gabelhurden im Ostjordanland," *Forschungen und Fortschritte* 25 (1949):9–10; G. L. Harding, "The Cairn of Hani'," ADAJ 2 (1953): 8–56; Y. Yadin, "The Earliest Record of Egypt's Military Penetration into Asia," IEJ 5 (1955): 3–10.

24. Yadin, "The Earliest Record," p. 8, fig. 7.

25. Rashi.

26. Loewenstamm, "The Relation of the Settlement."

27. Num. R. 22:9.

28. *Ḥushim*, from *ḥush* (Targums); or, preferably, read *ḥamushim* (Exod. 13:18; Josh. 1:14; 4:12; Judg. 7:11), which, akin to Akk. *ḫumašû*, "warrior's belt," means "armed, girded for battle" (J. M. Sasson, "Reflections on an Unusual Practise Reported in ARM X:4," *Orientalia* 43 [1974]: 404–410).

29. Ramban.

30. Bekhor Shor.

31. *Lifnei benei yisra'el* (Deut. 3:18; Josh. 1:14; 4:12), semantically equivalent to "before the Lord," i.e., His Ark (see the Comment to v. 20).

32. *'Ad 'asher 'im*. This phrase is used only in a future sense (see Gen. 28:15; Isa. 6:11).

33. With LXX, Targ. Onk., Targ. Neof., Saadia, Rashi.

34. Ramban.

35. It can be shown that *ba' 'el* is the biblical equivalent of Aram. *'l'l*, a legal term that expresses the idea of receipt (Y. Muffs, *Studies in the Aramaic Legal Papyri from Elephantine* [Leiden: E. J. Brill, 1969]).

36. For this usage, see Gen. 17:18; 27:7.

37. Ibn Ezra.

38. See Rashi on v. 17.

39. See Num. 5:19,28; Gen. 24:8,41; Josh. 2:17,20; Zech. 5:3.

40. Mish. Shek. 3:2.

41. Ehrlich.

42. See LXX, Philo, 1 Mos. 326, Saadia.

43. J. Milgrom, *Cult and Conscience* (Leiden: E. J. Brill, 1976), 1–12.

44. The verb *matsa'* can mean "strike" (20:14; cf. Deut. 31:17, 21).

45. Targ. Jon., Rashi.

46. *Sham*, literally "there"; perhaps delete with LXX (Origen) and Pesh.

47. Rashi, Abravanel.

48. *Lahem*, literally "for them," equivalent to *'aleihem* (Rashi).

49. *Ra'shei 'avot*. Rather, "the clan heads," short for *ra'shei beit 'avot* (see the Comments to 31:26; 36:1) and equivalent to *nesi'ei*, "chieftains" (see v. 2 and Excursus 1).

50. Mish. Kid. 3:4.

51. Git. 75a, BM 94a, Maimonides, Yad, 'Ishut 6.1–2.

52. Tosafot on Kid. 61b, s.v. *'i lo' katan*; Ehrlich; cf. Ibn Ezra, Ramban, Bekhor Shor.

53. Ramban. However, there is no indication that the conditions imposed upon Gad and Reuben stemmed from the Lord. To the contrary, they were self-imposed (vv. 16–19). Perhaps render *'adoni*, "my lord," i.e., Moses (as in vv. 25,27), which a scribe read as *'adonai*, the Masoretic surrogate pronunciation of the Tetragrammaton. Additional support for this reading is that v. 31b now stands in chiastic relation to v. 25b.

54. *'El*, literally "to," but with the meaning of *'al*. However, if the Tetragrammaton is changed to *'adoni* (see note 53) then *'el* need be neither emended nor reinterpreted; it would refer to Moses' reformulation of the conditions (vv. 25–27).

55. Rashi.

56. Meyuḥas.

57. M. Noth, *Numbers: A Commentary*, (London: SCM Press, 1968).

58. The phrase appears in this chapter for the first time and is probably a later addition (cf. Ramban; and see Excursus 70).

59. Num. 21:24; Deut. 29:6–7; see Deut. 2:36; 3:8; Josh. 12:2–5.

60. *Ha-'arets le-'areha bi-givulot 'arei ha- 'arets saviv*. An educated guess. Obscure.

61. Cf. Rashi.

62. Ramban, Ehrlich.

63. Equivalent to Sebam (see v. 3).

64. *Be-shemot*, reading with the LXX either *bi-shemotan* (fem. suffix), i.e., the original names of the towns (Ramban, Keter Torah), or *bi-shemotam* (masc. suffix), i.e., the new names provided by the Israelites.

65. R. de Vaux, *The Early History of Israel* (Philadelphia: Westminster Press, 1978), 567–569; Y. Aharoni, *The World History of the Jewish People* vol. 3 (Jerusalem: Masada Press, 1971); M. Weinfeld, "The Extent of the Promised Land—the Status of Transjordan," *Das Land Israel in biblischen Zeit*, ed. G. Strecker (Göttingen: Vandenhoeck and Ruprecht, 1983), 59–75. These are opposed by M. H. Segal, "The Settlement of Manasseh East of the Jordan," PEF 50 (1918): 124–131; A. Bergman, "The Israelite Tribe of Half-Manasseh," JPOS 16 (1936): 224–254; A. Lemaire, "Galaad et Makîr: Remarques sur la tribu de Manassé à l'est du Jourdain," VT 31 (1981): 39–61; and see Excursus 70.

66. *Va-yeleku . . . Va-yilkeduha*. The combination of these two verbs is present in Num. only here but common in Judg. (e.g., Judg. 1:3,10–13,17–18).

67. Vocalize *va-yorishu* (pl.) with Sam., Pesh., and Targ. Jon.

68. In Ugar. *ḥeya* is glossed by Akk. *dimtu*, "fortification" (PRU 3.95.6). See also UT 206.2.A, B.2. It also occurs in a proto-Sinaitic inscription (A. F. Rainey, "Notes on Some Proto-Sinaitic Inscriptions," IEJ 25 [1975]: 109).

69. A. Bergman, "The Israelite Tribe of Half-Manasseh," JPOS 16 (1936): 224–254.

70. Mentioned also in Deut. 3:14; Josh. 13:30; Judg. 10:4; 1 Kings 4:13; 1 Chron. 2:23.

71. Ramban.

72. B. Oded, EB (Hebrew), s.v. *kenat*.

73. Tosef. Shevi. 4:11, TJ Shevi. 6:1.

Chapter 33

1. Guide 3.50 (ed. and trans. S. Pines [Chicago: University of Chicago Press, 1963]).

2. Num. R. 23:1.

3. Num. R. 23:3.

4. E.g., Num. 3:3; 4:15; Gen. 36:15,20,31; 1 Chron. 2:1.

5. For other references to Mosaic authorship, see Exod. 17:14; 24:4; 34:27–28; Deut. 31:9,24.

6. A sense conveyed by the participle *mekabberim*.

7. *Va-yashov* is singular; the Sam. reads *va-yashuvu* in keeping with the plural of the other verbs. See Exod. 14:2.

8. J. Simons, *The Geographical and Topographical Texts of the Old Testament* (Leiden: E. J. Brill, 1959).

9. M. Harel, "The Wilderness of Sinai and the Negeb and the Location of Kadesh-Barnea" (Hebrew), in *B. Z. Luria Volume* (Jerusalem: Kiriat Sefer, 1979), 287–297.

10. Targ. Jon.

11. Harel, "The Wilderness of Sinai."

12. B. F. Batto, "The Red Sea: Requiescat in Pace," JBL 102 (1983):27–35.

13. Harel, "The Wilderness of Sinai."

14. M. Noth, "Der Wallfahrtsweg zum Sinai (Nu 33)," PJB 36 (1940): 5–28; G. J. Davies, "The Wilderness Itineraries and the Composition of the Pentateuch," VT 33 (1983): 7.

15. Harel, "The Wilderness of Sinai."

16. Ramban.

17. Harel, "The Wilderness of Sinai."

18. These latter places probably stem from a discrete topographical list unknown to the redactor of this chap. (see the Comments to 21:11,21; and see Excursus 55).

19. Possibly v. 18 has suffered haplography and should read, ". . . Hazeroth and they *encamped* [in the wilderness of Paran and they set out from the wilderness of Paran and they *encamped*] in Ritmah" (see 12:16; F. M. Cross, *Canaanite Myth and Hebrew Epic* [Cambridge: Harvard University Press, 1973]; see Excursus 71).

20. Harel, "The Wilderness of Sinai."

21. Z. Meshel, "On the Problem of Tell el-Kheleifeh, Elath, and Ezion-geber" (Hebrew), *Eretz Israel* 12 (1975): 49–56.

22. B. Mazar, "Ezion-geber and Ebronah" (Hebrew), *Eretz Israel* 12 (1975): 46–48.

23. Y. Aharoni, *The Land of the Bible* (Philadelphia: Westminster Press, 1967), 184–192.

24. H. Ewald, *History of Israel*, trans. R. Martineau (London: Longmans Green, 1902).

25. H. M. Wiener, *Essays in Biblical Criticism* (Oberlin: Bibliotheca Sacra Co., 1909), 127; see A. Dillmann, *Die Bücher Numeri, Deuteronomium, und Josua* (Leipzig: S. Hirzel, 1897).

26. *Be-vo'*, changed from the probable original *ki ba'*, "that [Israel] came" (20:1), in order to allude to the entire story.

27. N. H. Snaith, *Leviticus and Numbers* (London: Nelson, 1967).

28. Ant. 5.4.

29. Eruv. 55b, Yoma 75 b.

30. Abravanel.

31. Ibn Ezra.

32. *Ve-'ibbadetem*. The Piel of the stem *'-b-d* occurs twice in this verse and elsewhere in the Torah only in Deut. 11:4; 12:2.

33. *Masekhotam*, a nominal form, perhaps chosen because it is a near homonym to *maskiyotam*.

34. M. Haran, *Temples and Temple-Service in Ancient Israel* (Oxford: Clarendon Press, 1978), 43–57.

35. Ramban.

36. *Ve-hitnaḥaltem*, a Hitpael with reflexive meaning (Keter Torah).

37. Ramban.

38. My student, E. Adler.

39. Targ. Onk.

40. See J. Milgrom, "Religious Conversion and the Revolt Model for the Formation of Israel," JBL 101 (1982): 169–176.

Chapter 34

1. Ibn Ezra.

2. This rendering is preferred by Ramban, who points to the similar construction, "the king, David" (1 Kings 1:1).

3. Ibn Ezra. Otherwise drop the definite article (so Sam.; see 33:51) or drop *kena'an*, reading "the land" (Ehrlich; see Lev. 19:23).

4. Abravanel; and see the Comments to 33:50–56.

5. See Targums, Ibn Ezra, Rashbam.

6. Rashbam.

7. M. Harel, "The Wilderness of Sinai and the Negeb and the Location of Kadesh-barnea" (Hebrew), in *B. Z. Luria Volume* (Jerusalem: Kiriat Sefer, 1979), 287–297.

8. C. H. J. de Geus, "Kadesh Barnea: Some Geographical and Historical Remarks," OTS 20 (1977): 56–66.

9. Y. Aharoni, EB (Hebrew), s.v. *kadesh*.

10. With Ehrlich.

11. See Saadia.

12. *Teta'u*. The root is *t-'-h*, perhaps a by-form of *t-v-h* (Ezek. 9:4; Ibn Ezra on v. 10). Alternatively, regard the root as *'-v-h* (as in v. 10) or read *teta'ru* from *t-'-r*, "mark"; see Josh. 15:9,11; T. K. Cheyne, *Encyclopaedia Biblica* (London: Macmillan, 1902), 2109.

13. R. de Vaux, "Le pays de Canaan," JAOS 88 (1968): 23–29.

14. Targ. Jon., Mid. Song on 4:8, Mish. Shevi. 6:1, Tosef. Ter. 2:12, C. Albeck, *Six Orders of the Mishnah: Seeds* (Hebrew) (Jerusalem: Mosad Bialik, 1957), 379.

15. Alternatively, with Sam. and LXX, read Arbel.

16. Ibn Ezra.

17. Ehrlich.

18. Tosef. BK 18:8.

19. *Ve-ḥatsi matteh menashe lakeḥu*. This second mention of the verb *lakeḥu*, "received," may indicate that this phrase (as well as v. 15) is an interpolation. The absence of the term "ancestral houses" in this phrase may be attributed to the fact that only a few of the Manassite clans settled in Transjordan (see Excursus 70).

20. Read the verb as a Piel as in v. 29 (and Josh. 13:32; 14:1; 19:51) or keep as is, since the Kal as transitive is attested both in biblical Heb. (e.g., Exod. 34:9; Zech. 2:16) and in Akk. (ARM 8.11.26; 12.5; 13.4,9).

21. Ibn Ezra.

22. Keter Torah.

23. Instead of *benei binyamin*, "Benjamite (tribe)," comparable to the other tribal listings. Perhaps *benei* fell out by haplography. However, the absence of *benei* for Judah (v. 19) has not been satisfactorily resolved.

24. Pharnaces (Herodotus 7.66; 9.41). Hardly the work of the author, it is rather the error of a scribe who lived in the Persian period (A. Dillmann, *Die Bücher Numeri, Deuteronomium, und Josua* [Leipzig: S. Hirzel, 1897]).

Chapter 35

1. 1:47–54 after vv. 1–46; chaps. 3 and 4 after chap. 2; 26:57–62 after vv. 1–56.

2. Where the Aaronides are awarded thirteen towns in Judah, Simeon, and Benjamin; the Kohathites, ten towns in Ephraim, Dan, and western Manasseh; the Gershonites, thirteen towns in Issachar, Asher, Naphtali, and eastern Manasseh; and the Merarites, twelve towns in Reuben, Gad and Zebulun.

3. It contrasts sharply with Ezekiel's utopian scheme whereby the priests and Levites are settled around the Temple (Ezek. 48:8–15). The Levitical towns are again referred to in Lev. 25:32, 34; Josh. 14:4; 1 Chron. 13:2; 2 Chron. 11:14; 31:15,18; Ezra 2:70 (= Neh. 2:7,73); Neh. 11:3,20.

4. Bekhor Shor.

5. Rashi on Lev. 25:33.

6. Perhaps as ***midbar***, "wilderness," is related to ***dibber*** (Song 5:6) and Akk. ***dubburu***, "expel, drive out." However, this etymology has rightly been disputed (J. Barr, "*Migraš* in the Old Testament," JSS 29 [1986]: 15–31).

7. Usually called ***sadeh***, "field"; see Lev. 27:16,17.

8. ***Moshav***; see Ezek. 48:15–17.

9. Josh. 14:4; 21:2; see Mish. Ar. 9:8.

10. See LXX.

11. LXX, Targ. Onk., Pesh.

12. Sefer ha-Mivḥar.

13. M. Greenberg, "Idealism and Practicality in Numbers 35:4–5 and Ezekiel 48," JAOS 88 (1968): 59–63.

14. Targ. Jon., Targ. Neof.

15. LXX, Sam., Pesh., Targ. Jon., Targ. Neof. (margin).

16. Targums.

17. Josh. 21, except for the discrepancy of vv. 16,32.

18. ***Yinḥalu*** is plural, but Sam., Pesh., and Targums read ***yinḥal***, singular.

19. ***Ve-hikritem*** (Targums, Sif. Num. 159, Rashi). The etymology is obscure. The only other occurrences of ***hikrah*** (Gen. 24:12; 27:20) bear a different meaning. Ibn Ezra renders "you shall build," associating the verb with ***kiryah***, "city."

20. The biblical root is the antithesis of ***tsara'***, "stretch" (Lev. 22:23; cf. Lev. 21:18; Isa. 28:20), and thus may mean "confine, crib" (in Arab. ***qula'ṭ*** means "pygmy")—in which case the term may be rendered "confinement/prison cities" (M. Sulzberger, *The Ancient Hebrew Law of Homicide* [Philadelphia: J. H. Greenstone, 1915]).

21. ***Yamut***. Some Sam. manuscripts read ***yumat***, "put to death" (see Saadia).

22. ***'Amdo***, literally "stood." For this judicial usage of ***'amad***, see Num. 27:2; Deut. 19:17; Josh. 20:6; Isa. 50:8.

23. Ramban.

24. My student, D. P. Wright.

25. Sif. Num. 160, Sanh. 76b.

26. Targ. Onk.; see Ezek. 33:9.

27. Sif. Num. 160.

28. A. Dillmann, *Die Bücher Numeri, Deuteronomium, und Josua* (Leipzig: S. Hirzel, 1897).

29. ***'o***, literally "or." Some manuscripts, LXX, Sam. read ***ve'im***, "if." However, the MT is preferable since vv. 18, 19 present similar cases.

30. Sif. Num. 160.

31. Targums, Rashi.

32. Targums; see the Comment to 6:9; and see Ker. 9a (baraita).

33. See Mish. Sanh. 1:6.

34. See Mish. Mak. 2:6.

35. ibid.

36. Mak. 11b, Lev. R. 10:6.

37. As claimed by G. B. Gray.

38. A. Phillips, "Another Look at Murder," JJS 28 (1977): 105–126.

39. See Gen. 36:43; Josh. 22:4,9 for the expression ***'erets 'aḥuzzato***.

40. ***Ve-hayu 'eleh***, literally "And these," i.e., the above criteria (see the Comment to 27:11).

41. Saadia.

42. ***La-nus***. Rather, "from the one who has fled" (Targ. Jon.), reading ***lannus***, a past participle (not an infinitive) as ***shuvei*** (Mic. 2:8), ***nugei*** (Zeph. 3:18) (Rashi). The past participles of intransitive verbs refer to the person who has completed the action, e.g., ***surah*** (Isa. 49:21), ***shurai*** (Ps. 92:12) (Shadal).

43. ***Ba-arets***, literally "on the land" (see v. 28).

44. LXX, Sam., Pesh.

45. ***Bah***, literally "are on it." Some manuscripts, LXX, Pesh., and Targ. Neof. read ***yoshevim bah*** (as in v. 34), which, like this translation, is an interpretation not a translation.

46. ***Be-dam***, i.e., in exchange for—***bet*** of price (e.g., Gen. 9:6; Lev. 17:11; Deut. 21).

47. Sif. Num. 161.

Chapter 36

1. W. G. Plaut, ***The Torah: Numbers*** (New York: Union of American Hebrew Congregations, 1981).

2. D. T. Olson, ***The Death of the Old and the Birth of the New*** (Chico, Calif.: Scholars Press, 1985), 175; and see the Introduction.

3. So Sam., Pesh.

4. Ibn Ezra.

5. ***Tsuvah***. The passive (Pual) pattern of this verb is not rare (see 3:16; Exod. 34:34; Lev. 8:35; 10:13).

6. ***Be-YHVH***. For the ***bet*** of agency in connection with the Lord and following a passive verb, see Deut. 33:29; Isa. 45:17.

7. Cf. the Comment to 27:4.

8. Saadia, Ibn Ezra. For this usage, see Gen. 24:19 (cf. v. 22); Isa. 4:4.

9. Rashi, Ibn Ezra.

10. D. J. Gilner, "The Case of the Daughters of Zelophehad" (Unpublished).

11. Targ. Jon., BB 120a; Sif. Deut. 233.

12. ***Mishpaḥat***. Alternatively, "the clan," i.e., of Hepher. The LXX adopts the same interpretation by omitting the following word, ***matteh***, "tribe," thus yielding "their father's clan," which may be the original reading (see Excursus 77).

13. Ibn Ezra.

14. See Targ. Jon. on v. 6; BB 120a, 121a.

15. P. Ne'eman, "The Inheritance of the Daughters According to the Torah and the Halakha" (Hebrew), ***Beth Mikra*** 47 (1971): 476–489.

16. ***Mi-mishpaḥat matteh 'aviha***. The LXX omits ***matteh***, "tribe," yielding "from her father's clan" (as in v. 6). According to this reading, her land would have to remain in her clan, not just in her tribe (see Excursus 77). The Sam. tries to remove this textual difficulty by reading the plural ***mishpeḥot***, "clans," both here and in v. 6.

17. See Ezra 2:61 and the Comment to 27:7.

18. A. Dillmann, ***Die Bücher Numeri, Deuteronomium, und Josua*** (Leipzig: S. Hirzel, 1897).

19. D. W. Baker, private communication.

EXCURSUSES

EXCURSUS 1

Some Political Institutions of Early Israel (chap. 1)

The government of early, premonarchic Israel (before 1000 B.C.E.) can be described by reference to several technical terms found in the first chapter of Numbers: *ʿedah, nasiʾ, matteh,* and *ʾelef.*

The term *ʿedah* represents either all the Israelites, the adult males, or the chieftains (see v. 2). It constitutes a national political body vested with legislative and judicial powers; when it is made up of only the chieftains it exercises executive powers as well. Thus the *ʿedah* brings to trial and punishes violators of the covenant, be they individuals (e.g., Num. 35:12,24–25), cities, or tribes (e.g., Josh. 22:16; Judg. 21:10). It also crowns kings (1 Kings 12:20) and even reprimands its own leaders (Josh. 9:18–19).

In the immediate postconquest period, there is no trace of a continuous and representative political unit operating on behalf of the entire nation. During the era of the judges (*shofetim*), there is no record of the *ʿedah* selecting the *shofet.* On the contrary, the *shofet* acts on his own initiative and never in consultation with the *ʿedah.* The individual tribe or tribal leader (*nasiʾ*) also takes action without recourse to this body (e.g., Judg. 8; 12:1–6). The last incident in which all Israel is directed by an *ʿedah* is the civil war against Benjamin (Judg. 19–21), a time when there was no national leader. Thus the *ʿedah* was an ad hoc emergency council called together by the tribal chieftains whenever a national transtribal issue arose. Once the monarchy was firmly established in Israel, the *ʿedah* fell into disuse and disappeared. It was replaced by the synonymous *kahal.* Another synonym for *ʿedah* is *moʿed* (see 16:2, a parallel to 1:16), an even more precise term for "council" attested in an eleventh-century account of the Egyptian Wen-Amon (ANET, p. 29) in regard to the assembly called together by the king of Byblos (on the Phoenician coast) and in the even earlier documents from Ugarit (just north of Byblos; UT 137.14, 31).

Interestingly, the nature and history of the biblical *ʿedah* closely corresponds to, and, in fact, has been greatly illuminated by, the premonarchic and early monarchic political systems of the Sumerian city-states, located near the Persian Gulf, in the third millennium B.C.E. Here a council of elders normally handled the affairs of state, but in times of emergency a general assembly of all adult freemen constituted a provisional ad hoc decision-making body in which ultimate sovereignty resided.

Nasiʾ means "chieftain" or clan leader (v. 16). The term, however, may also designate the leader of an entire tribe. Also, to judge by the name lists of the chieftains in the Book of Numbers, those who supervised the census (1:5–16) and brought dedicatory gifts to the Tabernacle (chap. 7) are identical with those who led the tribes in war (2:10,14). That the *nasiʾ* could have national as well as tribal functions is clearly indicated by Numbers 10:3–4. Here the chieftains are expressly defined as clan leaders; yet they also act in an executive capacity on behalf of the *ʿedah.* It is highly probable that in a national crisis the chieftains of each tribe would elect one of their peers to be the tribal representative on a twelve-member, intertribal *ʿedah.* In the Mari archives the title for the family head, *abu bītim,* literally "father of the household," could also designate the tribal chief.

The term *nasi'* occurs over one hundred times in the Bible in a striking distribution. It clusters in the first four books of the Torah and in Joshua and again in Ezekiel and the postexilic books. It is totally absent from Deuteronomy, Judges, Samuel, and all the other prophets. Thus the term is densely concentrated in the wilderness and conquest traditions and does not resurface until the exile, when it is resurrected in the futuristic visions of Ezekiel, not in the original sense of "chieftain" but applied only to the king.

The antiquity of the term *nasi'* is corroborated by its occurrence only among those non-Israelite societies that are nomadic: Ishmaelites (Gen. 17:20; 25:16) and Midianites (Num. 25:14). Moreover, the institution of the *nasi'* persists in Israelite records only in the border tribes of Simeon (1 Chron. 4:38), Reuben (1 Chron. 5:6), and Asher (1 Chron. 7:40), where a sedentary style of life was slow in developing.[1]

Matteh, "tribe," and *'elef,* "clan," are equally old terms. As shown (see vv. 4 and 16), they are found in texts that refer to Israel as a society controlled by clans. Once the monarchy is established these terms disappear and their respective synonyms, *shevet* and *mishpaḥah,* take their place. This means that *matteh* and *'elef* cease to exist as living institutions.

In sum, the terms describing the organization of Israel in this opening chapter of Numbers, *'edah, nasi', matteh,* and *'elef,* support the conclusion that the priestly account of the wilderness sojourn has faithfully preserved a host of institutions that accurately reflect the social and political realities of Israel's premonarchic age.[2]

EXCURSUS 2

The Census and Its Totals (1:1–46)

The purpose of the census is conscription: "They must set out at once for the Land of Israel and those [above] twenty are capable of waging war" (Rashbam on Num. 1:2).

Military censuses are frequently attested under the monarchy (e.g., under David in 2 Sam. 24:9; under Asa in 2 Chron. 14:7; under Jehoshaphat in 2 Chron. 17:13–18; under Amaziah in 2 Chron. 25:5; and under Uzziah in 2 Chron. 26:11–13; see also 2 Kings 15:19–20). Amaziah's census also began at age twenty. In the classical world, military service began at twenty in Sparta, eighteen in Athens, and seventeen in Rome. A head count of the troops took place regularly before a campaign (Josh. 8:10; 1 Sam. 11:8; 13:15; 15:4; 2 Sam. 18:1; 1 Kings 20:15,26–27; 2 Kings 3:6) and at its conclusion, to determine the missing (Num. 31:49; cf. 1 Sam. 14:17).

The census is a hoary institution, essential to any government levy upon persons or property. However, what makes the census of Numbers 1 redolent of antiquity is its use of the same census terminology and procedures found in anterior cultures intimately associated with Israel's origins: Mari, Alalakh, and Ras Shamra (located in northern Syria). At Mari, in particular, the verbal parallels abound. The Akkadian for "muster the troops" is the exact cognate of Hebrew *pakad tsava'* (e.g., ARM 3.19.7; 21.5; cf. Num. 1:3). The men are "inscribed on a tablet by name" (ARM 1.42.5–11,22–25; cf. Num. 1:3,18; 4:32). It has already been noted (in the Comment to vv. 5–15) that most of the chieftains' names never recur in the later literature of the Bible but have analogues with the Near Eastern onomasticons of the second millennium. Again, as explained in Excursus 1, key terms such as *'edah, nasi', matteh,* and *'elef* also reflect the earlier strata of Israel's social and political organization. To

these can be added specific idioms of the chapter, such as *yityalledu* (see the Comment to v. 18) and *mi . . . va-ma'lah* (v. 3), that are expressed differently in the later literature.[1]

The question has been asked: Since all names had to be recorded (v. 2), how could it have been done in fewer than twenty days (cf. Num. 1:1 with 10:11)? By contrast, King David's census, involving approximately the same totals, took twenty days and nine months (2 Sam. 24:8). The answer lies in the use of different procedures. David's census was conducted tribe by tribe, district by district. Moses, on the other hand, made each clan responsible for its own count (vv. 2,18,20,etc.), while he and the tribal chieftains merely supervised. Thus all clans were mustered simultaneously and their respective lists needed only to be collated. In this sense, it resembled a modern election. That this procedure has ancient roots is shown by the practice at Mari, where the mustering of the tribal population was delegated to its chieftains, the *šugagu* (e.g., ARM 3.21.5ff.). Indeed, it is attested of some Judean kings that they continued to base their conscription upon the household, the basic structural unit of the society (e.g., Jehoshaphat, 2 Chron. 17:14; Amaziah, 2 Chron. 25:5). Recently, an ostracon (pottery shard containing writing) was found at Tell 'Ira (near Beersheba), dated from the eighth or beginning of the seventh century B.C.E. It has been rendered: "The census of (the house of) Berechiah: Gibbeah, Mokir, Shelemiah."[2] If this reading proves correct,[3] the ostracon would then exemplify the method used by Moses to conduct the census. The names of all men of military age in each household were written down by the head of the household. The written materials were collected by each clan, then by each tribal chieftain, and, finally, handed over to Moses. This answer is not intended to defend the authenticity of the twenty-day interval. Indeed, a more plausible solution will be presented below. However, it should be clear that the editors of Numbers did not consider this tradition a problem since they knew full well that a census by clan could be a speedy procedure.

The Levites' separate mustering (1:49–50; chaps. 3–4) is illumined by the Mari documents. One of its censuses is divided into three discrete registrations: soldiers, personnel exempt from military service (?), and the aged (ARM 3.19.23ff.). Thus the Levites, who were exempt from the regular militia, could have been expected to be mustered separately.

The Mari evidence leads to a more fundamental question. If the census in Numbers was in reality a conscription why was there a lower age limit (twenty years) but no upper one? Or, why was there not a separate census of the aged, as at Mari? And a specific exemption for the sick, the lame, the blind, and all others physically incapable of bearing arms (as was later granted to those physically and psychically incapacitated; see Deut. 20:5–8)? Indeed, the censuses that follow in Israel are expressly limited to the militarily fit (2 Sam. 24:9; 2 Chron. 14:7, etc.). The answer may perhaps be contained in *The Legend of King Keret* (Krt), found at Ugarit, on the Syrian coast, dated in the centuries immediately preceding the Exodus. The pertinent lines follow:

> Let the multitude be gathered and go forth, let a mighty army be gathered. Let the multitude go forth *together*: your army a considerable force, three hundred myriads, *peasant levies* without number, *regular levies* beyond counting, marching in thousands *like storm clouds,* and in myriads *as autumn rains.* Two marching after two; after three, all of them. Let the solitary man shut up his house, the widow hire herself out. Let the sick man be carried in bed, the blind man *grope his way.* Let the newwed groom go forth. (Krt A.85–101 [See also ANET, p. 143])

Keret is a legendary account of an expedition to capture a bride. Nonetheless, since the instructions of which these lines are a part stem from the god El (just as the Mosaic

conscription issued from divine fiat), the expedition is mandatory; no one is exempt, neither the bachelor, the widow, the sick, the blind, nor even the groom (contrast Deut. 20:7). Striking support is given by early rabbinic law, which applies the exemptions of Deuteronomy 20 to imperialist wars (*reshut*) but not to compulsory, defensive, wars (*ḥovah*), for in the latter not even the bride and groom could be released from military service (Mish. Sot. 8:7, Tosef. Sot. 7:23). Of course, in the rabbinic view, the love-requiting expedition in Ugarit's Keret (and Homer's *Iliad*) could never justify drafting such individuals as the newlywed and the disabled.

This hypothesis that no exemptions were granted in Moses' census is corroborated by the account of the Levite census: Its labor force is indeed given an upper age limit but not its sanctuary guards. The text specifies emphatically: "At the age of fifty they [the Levites] shall retire from the work force and shall serve no more. They may assist their brother Levites at the Tent of Meeting by standing guard, but they shall perform no labor. Thus you shall deal with the Levites in regard to their duties" (8:25–26; the perpetual and crucial guarding of the sanctuary is discussed in Excursus 3). Here then, is clear evidence that in critical wars, there is neither exemption nor retirement from military service. Therefore the absence of an upper age limit and other physical criteria in the military census of Numbers 1 is eloquent testimony to the priority of its goal: the conquest of the promised land.

The account of the earlier census (Exod. 30:12–16) taken during the first year in the wilderness while the Tabernacle was under construction (see the Comment to v. 46) also creates difficulties. Its totals were exactly the same as those of Numbers 1 (cf. Exod. 38:25–28). Rather than make the puzzling assumption that there was a need for two distinct censuses only a few months apart, it is more reasonable to presume that the same census is meant and that Exodus provides its original and authentic setting. Concurrent with the Tabernacle construction, blueprints were drawn up for the deployment of the camp at rest and at march and for the Levites' duties in the transport and guarding of the sancta (see chaps. 3–4). For those projects an accurate census of the people and the Levites would have been required. This also means that the Levites were chosen for their role before the erection of the Tabernacle, possibly as a result of the golden calf apostasy (see Exod. 32:29; Deut. 10:8), and that they were not required to pay the half-shekel ransom (Exod. 30:13). The reason for this tax exemption is probably that the Levites were counted not by man but by God Himself (see the Comment to 3:16). The narrative material was then rearranged so that the accounts of the census and the functions of the Levites (Num. 3–4, 8) would have preceded the account of the march from Sinai (Num. 10). Only the prescription to pay the half-shekel remained in its original place, because it was intended as a general rule for all censuses: *ki tissa'*, "When you take a census" (Exod. 30:12). Thus Numbers 1, according to this hypothesis, would presuppose the payment of the half-shekel by each counted Israelite male (so Rashi and Ramban to 1:2). For the purpose of the half-shekel, see the Comment to 31:48–54.

The totals given for each tribe both in this chapter and in chapter 26 have not been satisfactorily explained. There is, however, a relationship between these numbers and the solar and lunar calendar as well as the synodical periods of the planets, computations well known to the ancient Babylonian astronomers,[4] which suggests the possibility that the tribal figures were made to correspond to celestial movements and thus present Israel as the (literally) "armies of the LORD" (Exod. 12:41; cf. Exod. 7:4), corresponding to the astral bodies, the Lord's celestial armies (Gen. 2:1; Deut. 17:30).

The figure of over 600,000 creates serious difficulties. It presupposes a population of

over two million supporting itself for forty years in the Sinai Peninsula. Apart from the logistical problem, it also clashes with other demographic statistics concerning early Israel. For example, the Song of Deborah (Judg. 5:8), written scarcely a century after the wilderness wanderings, relates that six tribes could only mobilize 40,000 fighting men, whereas the same tribes yielded a total of 273,000 in the census of Numbers 1 and 301,000 in the census of Numbers 26. Furthermore, the totals clash with other figures derived from the same census. For example, 22,273 first-born males (Num. 3:40–43) implies—assuming there were as many females as males in the population—that only one in thirteen females above age twenty were mothers. Alternatively, since the ratio of adult males to first-born males was about 27:1, an average family would have consisted of twenty-seven sons. Presuming an equal number of males and females, the average mother would have had fifty children! It has been proposed that these figures represent the population of Israel during King David's reign.[5] Even then the figures are too large.[6]

A more ingenious proposal is that since the term *'elef,* "thousand," can also mean "clan," it refers in the census to the military force of the clan, and the hundreds digits in the tribal census refer to the number of contingents subject to conscription.[7] According to this system, Israel's fighting force would have totaled 598 contingents numbering 5,550 men. This latter figure is entirely compatible with the size of armies in the ancient Near East. For example the armies cited in the Mari archives number 6,000 and 10,000 men (ARM 1.23.42; 6.33.65).[8] Thus the tribe of Reuben, allegedly totaling 46,500, actually mustered forty-six contingents numbering 500 men (Num. 1:21), allowing for ten or eleven men per unit. By the time of the monarchy, the unit had grown and was standardized at 1,000.[9] The major difficulty with this theory, aside from the minuscule and variable size of the *'elef,* is that in the early texts *'elef* stands for the entire clan and not just the fighting force (e.g., 1 Sam. 23:23; Mic. 5:1; and see the Comment to Num. 1:16). Alternatively, it has been proposed that *'elef* is the designation for any large number and that 600 was the basic military unit. Thus the so-called 600,000 really means a large number (*'elef*) of military units (of 600 each).[10] Arguing against this theory are the tribal totals in this census as well as the credible conscription figures of early Israel, neither of which is divisible by 600 (e.g., Judg. 5:8; 20:15). Finally, since *'elef* revocalized as *'alluf* means "clan leader" (see v. 16), it has been argued that *'elef* in Numbers 1 is actually the term for officer or for a professional, fully armed soldier.[11] However, even granting this emendation, there is no proof that it carries this conjectural meaning.

At present, then, there is no choice but to assume that the number 600,000 was meant to be understood literally. This can be compared with the Chronicler who marshals massive armies for his wars (e.g., 2 Chron. 13:3; 14:8; 17:14–19). Reference to the Keret text quoted above may offer additional illumination. It speaks of thousands and myriads, but once it cites a specific number: three hundred myriads, that is, three million fighting men—five times Israel's forces! Thus the tendency of ancient epics to inflate numbers is well attested.

EXCURSUS 3

The Encampment (chap. 2)

Israel's camp in the wilderness was arranged in the shape of a square and can be represented diagrammatically as follows:

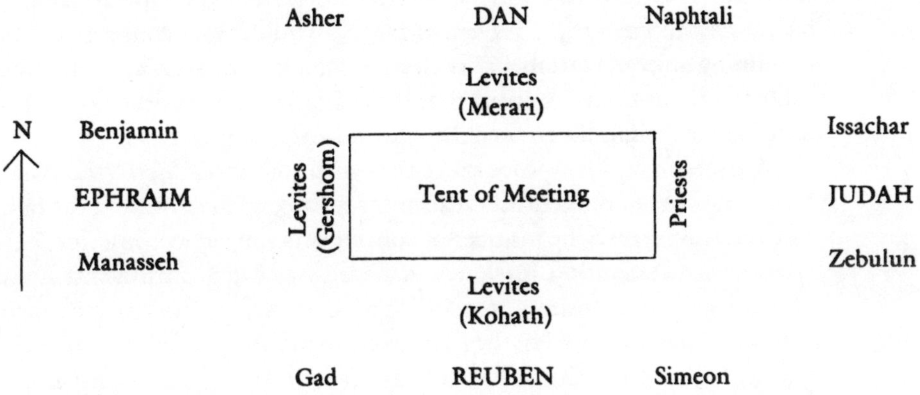

In later Israel the war camp was arranged in the round (cf. 1 Sam. 17:20; 26:5–7). Assyrian reliefs of the first millennium also favor the circular shape.[1] The closest parallel to Israel's wilderness camp is the Egyptian camp of Ramses II (the probable Pharaoh of the Exodus).[2] Pharaoh's camp, like that of Israel, is also square in shape. Strikingly, his tent is in the center. Its walls clearly are thick, a remarkable fact since the camp, formed solely for the purpose of attacking the Hittite stronghold of Kadesh, was only temporary. But it must be remembered that Pharaoh was considered a god and his tent was a sanctuary (as is indicated in an illustration by the figures kneeling before his cartouche) and had to be protected against human and demonic defilement. Israel's monotheistic faith abolished the world of the demons, but the residence of its God still required protection against human agents of defilement—a protection supplied by the Levitical cordon (see Excursus 4). Thus the possibility must be recognized that Israel's camp of the Exodus was modeled upon a contemporary Egyptian pattern.

A few comments on the grouping of the tribes are in order. The Leah tribes comprise the first two divisions located in the east and the south but not in order of birth (contrast Gen. 29:31–30:20; Exod. 1:1–4). This is to enable Judah, Leah's fourth son, to be given the choicest role (cf. Gen. 49:10) as the leader of the eastern unit, whereas the first-born, Reuben, is assigned the leadership of the southern unit. Furthermore, since Levi, Leah's third-born, has not been mustered with his fellow tribes (but is assigned the task of guarding the sanctuary, 1:53), he is replaced by Gad. This is either because Gad is close to Reuben geographically (they adjoin each other in their Transjordanian settlements) or because he is the first-born of Leah's concubine, Zilpah (Gen. 30:9–11). The eastern side of the camp is the choicest because it is there that the Aaronides (and Moses) are encamped at the entrance to the Tabernacle (3:38). This association of the priests with Judah is preserved in the list of Levitical cities, which locates the priests in the tribe of Judah (Josh. 21:13–16).

The southern side is next in importance since the rotation (assuming one is facing east) is always to the right. The Kohathites among the Levites and the Reuben unit of the Israelites occupy this position.

The Rachel tribes are located in the west (vv. 18–24), headed by Ephraim, who must have become the chief of the Rachelites (see Gen. 48:19–20). Last of the order, corresponding to the order of the march (see chap. 10), is the Danite division in the north. Dan had developed a reputation for military prowess (Gen. 49:16–17); by contrast, its subordinate tribes, Asher and Naphtali, were remembered for their pacific nature (Gen. 49:20–21). The Danite division continued to operate in the conquest and settlement of Canaan (Judg. 13:25; 18:12).

The order of the tribes in this chapter is again followed in the account of the gifts of the tribal chiefs to the newly consecrated altar (Num. 7) and in the order of the march (Num. 10:14–28).

It is of interest that the Dead Sea sectarians also envisaged the eschatological war of "the sons of light against the sons of darkness" against the backdrop of Israel's military experience in the wilderness. The formation of the war camp is identical. The standing army of 28,000 infantry and 6,000 cavalry is divided into four camps, each grouped in a square around four camps of the Levites: Aaronides, Kohathites, Gershonites, and Merarites, as in Numbers 3. Much of the same terminology is used.[3]

EXCURSUS 4

The Levites: Guards of the Tabernacle (3:5–43)

To leave the sanctuary or its sancta without protection was unthinkable. Indeed, no sooner did Israel recover the Ark from the Philistines than someone was consecrated to guard it (1 Sam. 7:1). Of the two major Levitical roles, guarding and removal, there can be no doubt which was more important: The labor force was to be activated only when the camp was on the move, but guard duty was a perpetual responsibility. It is significant that when the Levites subsequently were apportioned their share of the Midianite spoils the text twice identifies them as the Tabernacle guards (Num. 31:30,47).

Ancient Israel's neighbors employed not only human but divine guards for the protection of the sanctuary. Thus the ***lamassu*** and ***šēdu*** in Mesopotamia and the gargoyles in Egypt were placed in front of the temples. Israel, however, knew not of the world of demons. Its monotheism allowed for only one power in the universe. Therefore it had but to protect the sanctuary against the only remaining adversary—man.

Guard duty was performed around the clock. The nomadic ***šādin*** in the Arabian desert slept in the sanctuary of which he was the solitary guardian. So, at Shiloh, did young Samuel (1 Sam. 3:2–3), to whom this task was delegated because the priest Eli was nearly blind. According to one tradition, young Joshua was the full-time guard of the wilderness Tent-shrine since he "would not stir out of the Tent" (Exod. 33:11). Priests performed nocturnal guard duty in Mari (ARM 10.50.16–17) and in the Hittite temples ("Instructions for Temple Officials" iii.9,12,30; ANET, p. 209). Akkadian ***naṣāru maṣṣarta*** (the root ***n-ts-r*** also means "guard" in Hebrew, e.g., Isa. 27:3) is the exact semantic cognate of ***shamar mishmeret*** and also is used in reference to the guarding of temples (e.g., Yale Oriental Series 7.89.4). In a Mari letter, the ***āpilum***-diviner "is standing guard over the tent-shrine"

(A.1121:11,27,37–38); Akkadian ***maškanam inaṣṣar*** is the equivalent of biblical ***shamar (mishmeret) mishkan.***[1]

In the Second (Herodian) Temple, the Levitical watch was stationed at twenty-four points: the five Temple gates, the four inner corners, the five gates of the Temple court, the latter's four corners, behind the Temple building, and in five chambers (Mish. Mid. 1; Mish. Tam. 1:1). According to Josephus, more than two hundred gatekeepers closed the Temple gates and these men probably remained at their posts (Apion 2.119). Philo records that Levite guards made the rounds day and night to ensure the purity of the Temple and its visitors (1 Laws 156). These guards were supervised by an officer of the Temple Mount who at night "would make the rounds of every watch preceded by kindled torches" (Mish. Mid. 1:2; cf. Papyrus Oxyrhinchus 5.840). The guard duty was not just ceremonial. During the administration of the Roman governor Coponius (6–9 C.E.), the Temple was defiled, apparently by Samaritans who planted bones there at night (Josephus, Ant. 18.29–30).

When the object of ***mishmeret*** is not the Tabernacle but the Lord, the context always involves proscriptions and taboos, so that the basic meaning of "guarding" is extended to that of being wary of violations, for example, regarding priestly consecration (Lev. 8:35); sexual prohibitions (Lev. 18:30); the defiled priest and his food (Lev. 22:9); God's direction for the march (Num. 9:19,23); priestly taboos concerning the altar and the shrine (Num. 18:7a); and the priestly gifts (Num. 18:18).

Mishmeret in the general sense of "duties" is not found until later biblical sources. *Mishmeret* as a service unit, the sense it assumes in rabbinic literature on the Second Temple, does not occur in the Bible at all.[2] Thus the use of ***mishmeret*** exclusively for guard duty in these pericopes of Numbers attests to their antiquity.

EXCURSUS 5

The Encroacher and the Clergy (chap. 3)

The key word to the understanding of Numbers 3 is ***karev,*** which should be rendered not as "approach" but, in prohibitive contexts, as "encroach" and, in permissive contexts, as "qualify" (Num. 3:6; 18:2; Jer. 30:21; Ezek. 42:13; 44:16). So ***karev*** means "qualify" at Qumran (e.g., 1QS 6:16–19, 7:21, 8:18–20) and in rabbinic Hebrew (e.g., Mish. Eduy. 5:7, 8:7). The Akkadian cognate ***qerēbu*** also attests the prohibitive sense "encroach."[1]

The prohibition against encroaching upon the sanctuary is expressed in the formula ***ha-zar ha-karev yumat,*** "a stranger who encroaches shall be put to death." This formula occurs four times, all in the Book of Numbers (1:51; 3:10,38; 18:7). In the first two instances it is directed to the Levitical cordon outside the sanctuary, and in the latter two, to the priestly cordon within. It decrees that the sacerdotal guards are to put to death any unauthorized encroacher upon the sancta. The uniqueness of this formula is contained in its penalty. Elsewhere crimes against the sanctuary are punishable by God alone, never by man (e.g., improper officiating by priests, in Exod. 28:43; 30:20–21; Lev. 10:6,9; improper handling of the sancta by Levites, in Num. 4:15,19–20—note the Kal form of the verb ***yamut***). Only here is a crime against the sanctuary punishable by human agency (Hofal, ***yumat***). The reason lies in the consequences of the act indicated by the verb ***karev,*** "encroach." Illicit contact with sancta produces divine wrath (***ketsef,*** e.g., Num. 1:53) or plague (***negef,*** e.g., Num. 8:19), which not only is liable to strike down the sinner but to engulf the entire community

as well (e.g., Num. 17:11–15,27–28; 25:9,18–19; 31:16). That is why the establishment of the sacral guards is often coupled with the motive clause "that wrath shall no longer strike the Israelites" (Num. 1:53; 18:5; see 8:19). It is therefore crucial that the intruder be stopped before he carries out his intended encroachment lest he trigger the deadly consequences. The sanctuary guards must cut down the criminal before God cuts down everyone else!

The right to kill with which the sacral cordon is empowered is not to be confused with the legal category of capital punishment whereby death is set as just payment for a particular crime. The action of the guards has nothing to do with justice. The proper category for describing their function goes back to the root purpose of their guarding: ***mishmeret*** as a military category. The encroacher, though he be an Israelite, is the enemy who has it in his power to cause the death of all Israel. Since he is bent on encroachment, words will not dissuade him; in fact, to argue can only augment the danger. He must be struck down in his tracks.

However, what if the guards fail in their responsibility and encroachment takes place? Will the entire community of Israel be exposed to God's unbounded wrath? Despite the foregoing remarks, the answer is ***no;*** only the guards bear the brunt of divine anger. This revolutionary teaching, this unprecedented self-imposed restriction of God's powers, is the innovation of Numbers 18 and is discussed in Excursus 40.[2]

EXCURSUS 6

"ʿAvodah": The Levites' Work Profile (chap. 4)

The second census of the Levites is concerned solely with the work force, that is, the physically qualified males. Thus the census is restricted to those between the ages of thirty and fifty, a fact that, significantly, is mentioned seven times in chapter 4: three times in the introductions (vv. 2,23,30) three times in the sums (vv. 35,39,43), and once in the grand total (v. 47). This last verse is a complexly structured sentence that also clarifies the purpose of the census—***ʿavodah.*** Levitical ***ʿavodah*** never veers from the root meaning of "physical labor." Within this range it can refer to (1) physical labor in general (e.g., v. 33); (2) the job of moving the Tabernacle in particular (e.g., v. 30); and (3) a portion of this job, either (a) to dismantle and reassemble the Tabernacle (e.g., v. 27) or (b) to transport it (e.g., v. 4). The context determines the usage. When ***ʿavodah*** stands in apposition to porterage, ***massa'***, it assumes the more restricted meaning of dismantling and reassembling the Tabernacle. This apposition can take the simple form ***ʿal ʿavodato ve-ʿal massa'o,*** "according to his [literally] packing and porterage" (v. 49), or is expressed as a compound ***la-ʿavod u-le-massa',*** "as to packing and porterage" (v. 24). Finally, there is the more complex passage, containing four consecutive ***ʿavodah*** words: ***la-ʿavod ʿavodat ʿavodah ve-ʿavodat massa'*** (v. 47). Once it is recognized that ***ʿavodah*** and ***massa'*** are in complementary apposition, there is no difficulty in rendering this passage as follows: "to do the packing work and the porterage work."

Why this verbiage? Is it pleonastic inexactness or, the contrary, technical precision? The answer surfaces as soon as it is recognized that this complementary apposition of ***massa'-ʿavodah*** occurs only in Gershonite and Merarite passages or in summaries that include them (vv. 24,27,31,47,49). The fact remains that these two Levitical clans have no porterage (***massa'***) duties at all; the curtains and planks assigned them are carried by oxcart (7:7).

Loading and unloading is the full extent of their removal toil, so that the term *'avodah,* in their case, is reserved exclusively for their labors in making and breaking camp.

On the other hand, *'avodah* for the Kohathites is precisely the opposite of that of their brother clans. Whereas the Tabernacle's curtains and planks are transported on oxcarts, leaving the Gershonites and Merarites no porterage duties, the sacred objects—the specific charge of the Kohathites—must be carried by shoulder (Num. 7:9; cf. 4:15). And whereas the brother clans concentrate upon dismantling and reassembling, the Kohathites must have this work done for them by the priests (4:4–15). Thus it is hardly surprising that Kohathite *'avodah,* rather than being the complement of *massa',* should become its synonym; their labor *is* their porterage (v. 4; cf. v. 15b).

Another boon resulting from this analysis of Levitical *'avodah* is the insight provided by the literary structure of the two censuses, chapters 3 and 4. Since *'avodah* is what is stressed in chapter 4, then the guarding duty of the clans, *mishmeret,* is mentioned only as an afterthought (4:27,28,31,32). In chapter 3, however, the word *mishmeret* outnumbers *'avodah* seven to three. Moreover, a different formulation is found: The framework for each clan reads *mishmeret . . . ve-khol/le-khol 'avodato,* "guarding duties . . . inclusive of their removal labors" (3:25–26,31,36). In chapter 3, then, *'avodah,* the removal labor, is the afterthought.

Perhaps the most remarkable fact concerning *'avodah* is that it describes only the work of the Levites, *never of the priests.* (See the alleged exception of Numbers 18:7.) This is remarkable because in the later postexilic books of the Bible and in rabbinic literature, *'avodah* means "cultic service." These two meanings can never have been used simultaneously because they contradict each other. *'Avodah* as cultic service is the prerogative of the priests alone; the Levite who usurps this function is summarily put to death (see Excursus 5). Thus the conclusion is inescapable that the audience whom the Torah addressed was completely unaware of the meaning of *'avodah* as cultic service, else they would have been bewildered by its use in conjunction with the Levites. This is but another indication that the priestly sources in the Torah predate the exile and were written down before *'avodah* as "cultic service" came into use.[1]

EXCURSUS 7

The Rationale for Biblical Impurity (5:1–4)

Studies in the concept of impurity have generally identified its underlying cause as the fear of the unknown or of demonic possession.[1] Aside from the total inapplicability of this definition to biblical impurity, it has been challenged on its own grounds by Douglas (and others),[2] who points out that from earliest times human beings reacted to the mysteries of nature as much out of awe as of fear.

Douglas's own theory is also not without its flaws. She equates impurity with what we call dirt, which she defines as matter out of place. Applying this definition to Leviticus 11, she declares that the forbidden animals are "out of place" in their media as determined by their means of locomotion. This insight proves helpful but inadequate in explaining why only certain animals were permitted and not others. More valuable is her utilization of the Durkheimian hypothesis that the animal world is a mirror of human society.[3]

The opposite of "dirt out of place" is, of course, order, which in the Bible would

correspond to the sphere of the holy. This accounts for Douglas's definition of the holy as "wholeness and completeness,"[4] and she correctly points to the biblical injunctions that priests and sacrificial animals must be unblemished. That wholeness (Heb. *tamim*) is a significant ingredient of holiness cannot be gainsaid. Indeed, it is precisely for this reason that the Qumran sectaries ban blemished persons from residing in the Temple city (11QTemple 45.12–14).

However, this definition falls short because it fails to take into account the two pairs of antonyms laid down by the priestly legislators: holy-common and impure-pure (Lev. 10:10). A blemished animal or priest is not impure but common (*ḥol*). As for the prohibition against the blemished in the sanctuary, it only applies to priests officiating in the sanctuary and to animals offered on the altar. However, any blemished Israelite—priest and lay person alike—may enter the sacred precincts and offer his sacrifices. If the holy and the impure are lethal antagonists, and they certainly are, then they clash not in the matter of "wholeness" but on an entirely different plane.

It is best to begin again with some comparative data. Meigs, who critiqued Douglas so trenchantly on her "dirt" hypothesis, comes close to the mark in defining impurity as "(1) substances which are perceived as decaying, carriers of such substances and symbols of them; (2) in those contexts in which the substances, their carriers, or symbols are threatening to gain access to the body; (3) where that access is not desired."[5] Meigs's conclusions are founded on her investigations of the Hua of New Guinea. They are congruent with those reached in Culpepper's study of Zoroastrian practices: "All sickness and body excretions were understood to participate in death-impurity"[6] and in Burton's evaluation of Nuer impurity: "The necessity of maintaining the distance between bleeding youth (undergoing initiation) and pregnant women, and between bleeding women (menstruants) and potential life (intercourse) is thus a symbolic statement of the necessity for keeping life-creating processes from potentially life-destructive forces."[7] The common denominator in all of these conclusions is that impurity is associated with the sphere of death. This approach has been taken by some biblical researchers, and their suggestion merits consideration.[8]

A mere glance at the list of impurity bearers in the Torah—the leper, gonorrheic, corpse-contaminated (Num. 5:1–4), parturient (Lev. 12), emitter of semen, menstruant (Lev. 15:16–24)—suffices to reveal that this list is arbitrary and artificial. It does not focus on disease or even on disorders, if by that is meant unnatural disruptions of bodily functions; the inclusion of the parturient, menstruant, and emitter of semen contravenes such a notion. Furthermore, to judge by the high percentage of medical texts in the cuneiform documents of ancient Mesopotamia,[9] there can be no doubt that many diseases were also diagnosed, catalogued, and treated in ancient Israel. Thus, the conclusion is inescapable that the impurities entered into this list have no intrinsic meaning in themselves but were selected because they serve a larger, overarching purpose. It is of no small significance that the dietary laws of the priestly system (Lev. 11), which are contiguous with and inseparable from the bodily impurities in this list (covering Lev. 12–15), are also governed by criteria, such as chewing the cud and having a split hoof, that are equally arbitrary and meaningless in themselves but serve a larger, extrinsic purpose. This purpose can be deduced both from the explicit rationale of holiness (Lev. 11:43–45) and the implications of relevant texts (e.g., Gen. 9:4; Lev. 17:3–5,10–14), to wit: to treat animal life as inviolable except for a few animals that may be eaten—provided they are slaughtered properly and their blood is drained.[10]

I submit that the same rationale or, more precisely, its complement obtains here. The bodily impurities in the above list focus on four phenomena: death, blood, semen, and skin disease. Their common denominator is death. Blood and semen represent the forces of life; their loss, therefore, signifies death. In the case of scaly disease (so-called leprosy) this symbolism is made explicit: Aaron prays for his stricken sister: "Let her not be as one dead" (Num. 12:12). Furthermore, such disease is powerful enough to contaminate someone who is under the same roof, and it is no accident that it shares this feature with the corpse (Num. 19:14). The wasting of the body, the common characteristic of all biblically impure skin diseases, symbolizes the death process as much as does the loss of blood and semen.

Thus biblical impurity and holiness are semantic opposites. And since the quintessence and source of holiness resides with God, it is imperative that Israel control the occurrence of impurity lest it impinge upon the realm of the holy God. The forces pitted against each other in the cosmic struggle are no longer the benevolent and demonic deities who populate the mythologies of Israel's neighbors but the forces of life and death set loose by man himself through his obedience to or defiance of God's commandments. Of all the diachronic changes that occur in the development of Israel's impurity laws, this clearly is the most significant: the total severance of impurity from the demonic and its reinterpretation as a symbolic system reminding Israel of its imperative to cleave to life and reject death. "You shall keep My laws and My rules, by the pursuit of which man ***shall live [ve-ḥai bahem]:*** I am the LORD" (Lev. 18:5).[11]

EXCURSUS 8

The Judicial Ordeal (5:11–31)

Ancient Near Eastern ritual is generally composed of two parts: an act and an incantation. The latter empowers the former. The magic that inheres in incantation formulas guarantees the efficacy of the ritual. (Note how the pagan general Naaman expected the prophet Elisha to cure him of his leprosy in 2 Kings 5:11). The incantation is of even greater efficacy when it takes the form of a warning entreaty and a curse. By accepting the curse (e.g., by responding "amen"; 5:22), the warned person calls upon himself the wrath of the gods. It would therefore seem logical that the water ordeal for the suspected adulteress would have to be accompanied by an adjuration in order to ensure its efficacy. This is confirmed by two examples of water ordeals recorded in Middle Assyrian texts. In one the victim invokes the gods to vindicate him before he undergoes the ordeal. In the other the sequence of the ordeal is as follows: "They will draw [water], drink, swear and be pure."[1] A letter from Mari (ARM 10.9) reads as follows: "The dirt and the jamb of the gate of Mari they took and dissolved in water, and then . . . drank. Thus [spoke] Ea: 'Swear to the gods. . . .'"[2] This striking analogy of the Mari letters to our text is discussed in the Comment to v. 17. For our purpose, however, let the inseverable tandem of water ordeal-oath be noted.

In the ancient Near East the water ordeal provided the punishment as an integral part of the test in which the victim was thrown into the river. If guilty, he sank; if innocent, he floated (Hammurabi, par. 2; ANET, p. 166) or swam a certain distance (in Mari).[3] By contrast, if an ordeal (e.g., "draining the rhyton of the life of the god") only convicted the suspect, then he would be executed by the court together with his family (Hittite "Instruc-

tions for Temple Officials"; ANET, p. 210). Our text stands in close relationship to a river ordeal since it, too, provides that the punishment is built into the ordeal. However, the punishment differs: The guilty woman does not die but becomes sterile (see Excursus 9 for its significance).

Admittedly the text of the case of the suspected wife, verses 12b–14, is verbose and redundant. Its difficulties are further compounded when one compares it with its resumptive summation, verses 29–30. Both formulations of the case seem to consist of two parts, separated by the word "or." In the initial formulation, the "or" occurs in verse 14b, that is, preceding the case in which the husband suspects his wife and she is innocent. However, in the concluding formula, the "or" clause (v. 30) refers to the case where the husband is suspicious, without specifying whether she is innocent or not. One solution suggests that verse 30 refers only to the innocent woman, thus repeating verse 14b (so Bekhor Shor). However, verse 30 provides no textual warrant for this assumption. Perhaps, then, the simpler formulation of the summation, verses 29–30, should be taken at face value, that the suspicious husband is only involved in the second case (v. 30; cf. Sif. Num. 21). This surmise could find support by the water ordeal-oath laws found in the Code of Hammurabi (pars. 131–132; ANET, p. 171), which merit quoting in full (but in reverse order):

132. If a finger has been pointed at a man's wife because of another man, but she has not been caught lying with that other man, she shall leap into the River for the sake of her husband. 131. If a man's wife was accused by her husband, but she was not caught while lying with another man, she shall make an oath by the god and return home.

The two Babylonian laws on the suspected but unapprehended adulteress are distinguished from each other by their cause: In 132, suspicion arises from a third party (perhaps someone has seen her enter the house of another man), resulting in public demand for the ordeal; in 131, it is the husband himself who suspects his wife. This bifurcation in the law of the suspect adulteress may also be present in our text. It is clearest in the summary statement (vv. 29–30), where the second case ("or," v. 30) focuses exclusively upon the suspicious husband as the cause. The opening formulation, verses 12b–14, may lead to a similar interpretation if the initial particle (*vav*) of verse 14 is rendered "or." This arrangement provides the immediate advantage of allocating the two occurrences of ***nitma'ah***, "defiled herself" (vv. 13,14), into discrete cases. Thus verses 12b–13,29 would present the case of a rumor (e.g., "a finger has been pointed," Hammurabi, par. 132) of this woman's infidelity reaching her husband, whereas verses 14,30 would present a second case (equals Hammurabi, par. 131) in which the husband himself is the author of the suspicion.[4]

However, it is more likely that the text must be taken at face value. The husband's suspicions are aroused that his wife has strayed (vv. 12b–14a=29b) and he is suspicious even if she has not strayed (v. 14b=30a); the two cases, in both the introduction and subscript, are set off by the particle *'o*, "or."[5] The subscript (vv. 29b–30a), on the other hand, is abridged, and the husband's suspicions must be assumed to lie behind the first as well as the second case. The Babylonian parallel that speaks of suspicion arising from a third party (Hammurabi, par. 132) is nowhere indicated in the biblical case. In any event, the biblical law did not follow the Babylonian precedent completely. It clearly introduced the following modifications: (1) if the rumor originated in the community it was still only the husband who could press charges (v. 15); (2) the judicial procedures, the oath and ordeal, that occurred separately in Mesopotamian law were combined in Israel and, as indicated

above, with good precedent in the ancient Near East; (3) the ordeal itself took another form, with the punishment of the guilty woman resulting in her sterility, not death (see Excursus 10).

There may be another example of a water ordeal in the Torah. After the apostasy of the golden calf, Moses ground down the idol, mixed its dust with water, and "made the Israelites drink it" (Exod. 32:20). The purpose of this act is not stated but it could well have been as an ordeal to distinguish the guilty from the innocent (so Targ. Jon., Av. Zar. 44a, Liber antiquitatum Biblicarum 12.77.[6] How else would the Levites have known whom to strike down (cf. Ibn Ezra on Exod. 32:26–28)?

There is no other attestation in Scripture that the ordeal was applied or was effective. According to Ramban, this ordeal is the only case in biblical law where a judicial decision depends upon a miracle.

Tannaitic sources attest that the ordeal for the suspected adulteress was suspended by Rabbi Johanan ben Zakkai, who lived at the time of the destruction of the Second Temple (cf. Mish. Eduy. 5:6, Ber. 19a, TJ Sot. 18a). Mishnah Sotah 9:9 ascribes the suspension to the rampant increase of male adulterers; that is, it became ludicrous to put only women to the ordeal. Tosefta Sotah 14:2 gives a more plausible reason: Adultery was practiced in the open, thus removing the very legal grounds for the ordeal—it was no longer a clandestine, unapprehended act. Clearly, the threat of the ordeal was no longer a deterrent.

The precise architectural details concerning the construction and function of installations in the Temple court for the execution of the ordeal further corroborate the presumption that it had continued to be a living practice. To cite but a few of these details: The officiating priest was chosen by lot (Tosef. Sot. 1:2); he prepared the potion by mixing the holy water from the laver with dust taken from the Temple court, from beneath a slab one cubit square, located at the right of the entrance; the slab was affixed with a ring so that it could be easily lifted (Mish. Sot. 2:2); the verses containing the imprecation were inscribed on a golden tablet hung on the Temple wall so that it was visible from the court (Tosef. Sot. 2:1). Such a tablet was one of the many donations of Queen Helena of Adiabene (Mish. Yoma 3:10). Its purpose was to obviate the need to bring in a Torah scroll in order to copy out the appropriate verses (cf. Rashi on Sot. 37a). Despite the evidence of these facilities and of cases of the ordeal, the many restrictions imposed by the rabbis for its administration render it likely that it was a rare occurrence.

EXCURSUS 9

Adultery in the Bible and the Ancient Near East (5:11–31)

Throughout the ancient Near East, adultery was conceived as a crime not just against the husband but also against the gods. Witness these three Genesis narratives: 20:6, 26:10, 39:9b. Not only do all of them specify that adultery is a sin against God but the specification itself is made to or by a non-Israelite. Thus the narrator assumes that Israel shared with its neighbors the conviction that adultery was an affront to the deity. This is confirmed by yet another bit of evidence from the first narrative, Genesis 20:9, that not only the king but also his entire kingdom stands to suffer for the crime, thus making it certain that the wrath of God has been aroused. Furthermore, adultery here is described as "a great sin." It is now known that this is a technical term for adultery throughout the ancient Near East. In Egypt,

four ninth-century marriage documents label adultery as the "great sin."[1] In Babylonia, the adulterer is listed among those who have offended Ninurta by his "weighty sin"; "he who covets his neighbor's wife will [. . .] before his appointed day";[2] and adultery is specified as one of the sins that Marduk punishes.[3] The "great sin" on account of which the king of Ugarit extradites his wife from her native land and puts her to death can only be adultery (PRU 4.129–148). Thus the identification of the "great sin" as adultery in both Israel and its environment together with the explicit claim in Genesis that Israel's neighbors reckoned adultery as a sin against the deity lead to the conclusion that adultery was regarded in the ancient Near East as both a civil and a religious crime, a "great sin" against the gods. Further confirmation of Israel's view is provided in the priestly laws themselves, which include adultery among the sexual offenses for which God banishes the Israelites from their land and sentences them to death (*karet,* Lev. 18:20,25ff.).

Yet, despite the fact that ancient Near Eastern laws regard adultery as a religious sin, they all—except for the Bible—allow the husband to mitigate or even waive the death penalty against the adulterer (e.g., Hammurabi, par. 129; Middle Assyrian laws, pars. 14–16; Hittite laws, pars. 192f.; ANET, pp. 171, 181, 196). Thus the fact that the ancient Near Eastern codes permit monetary compensation for adultery does not render it likely that its theological aspect had any influence upon the legislation. However, this does not hold true for Israel. The death sentence for adultery in the Bible may not be commuted, pointing to the unique element that distinguishes Israel from its neighbors. All biblical sources agree that the prohibition against adultery was incorporated into the national covenant at Sinai to which every Israelite swore allegiance (Exod. 24:1–8; Deut. 5:24–26) and to which subsequent generations were bound (Deut. 29:9–14). Indeed, when both Hosea and Jeremiah score Israel for violating the Sinaitic covenant they specify the sin of adultery (e.g., Hos. 4:2; Jer. 7:9). The testimony of Jeremiah is particularly striking since he expressly pinpoints adultery as the cause of Israel's national doom (Jer. 5:7–9; 7:9–15; 29:23a).

Thus elsewhere in the ancient Near East, although adultery was considered a sin against the gods, it still had no juridical impact, whereas in Israel its inclusion in the Sinaitic covenant guaranteed legal consequences. Unless it was punished with death, God would destroy the malefactors and indeed the entire community that had allowed it to go unpunished.

The background of adultery in the Bible and its environment projects into clear relief the dimensions of the paradox offered by our text. For the adulteress, proved guilty by the ordeal, that is, by God Himself, is not punished with death! True, her punishment is just, "poetically" just. She who opened herself to illicit sex is doomed to be permanently sterile. Yet the gnawing question remains: Having been proved guilty of adultery, why is she not summarily put to death?

The key to the answer lies in the fact that the guilty woman did not go apprehended by man. That this element is the most significant in her case is shown by the fact that it is cited four times in her indictment, each in a different manner: (1) "unbeknown to her husband"; (2) "she keeps secret" (or "it was done clandestinely"); (3) "without being apprehended"; (4) "and there is no witness against her" (v. 13). These clear redundancies, among others, lead one critic to assert that their purpose is "to give weight to what might (and all too correctly!) be seen as a transparent charade . . . to protect the woman as wife in the disadvantaged position determined for her by the mores of ancient Israel's society."[4] This stylistic inflation, however, may have been deliberately written with a judicial purpose in

mind: to emphasize the cardinal principle that the unapprehended criminal is not subject to the jurisdiction of the human court. Since the adulteress has not been apprehended—as the text repeats with staccato emphasis—then the community and, especially, the overwrought husband may not give way to their passions to lynch her. Indeed, even if proved guilty by the ordeal, they may not put her to death. Unapprehended adultery remains punishable only by God, and there is no need for human mediation. The punishment for this sin against man (the husband) and God is inherent in the ordeal.

Supportive evidence may also be adduced from the absence of the technical verb for committing adultery, ***na'af***, which is found in the Decalogue (Exod. 20:13; Deut. 5:17) and the priestly code itself (e.g., Lev. 20:10, four times in this one verse!). Thus, although the legislator expressed the woman's infidelity in four different ways, it may be no accident that he refrained from using the legal term ***na'af***, for he wished to disassociate this woman's fate from the death penalty imposed for adultery. The glaring omission of the term ***na'af*** is then but another indication that jurisdiction in this case lies outside the human court.

A word needs to be said concerning the penalty itself. Whereas man has no choice but to put the apprehended adulteress to death, God metes out a more precise retribution. It is called the measure for measure principle, poetic justice, individually fashioned for each criminal so that the punishment precisely fits the crime. For example, Jacob, who deceived Isaac with a goatskin garment (Gen. 27:16), is himself deceived by a similar garment (Gen. 37:31–35). God's sentence that Israel must wander forty years in the wilderness is retribution for the forty days the spies spent gathering their demoralizing data (Num. 14:33–34; see also Ezek. 4:4–6). So the adulteress who acquiesced to receive forbidden seed is doomed to sterility for the rest of her life. (The rabbis reveal great ingenuity in discovering other instances of measure for measure punishment in her case; cf. Num. R. 9:24 and Tosef. Sot. 3:1–19.) The ordeal clearly presumes the belief in its efficacy, to wit: The guilty woman would be so fearful of its consequences that she would rather confess than subject herself to them. Thus at an attested river ordeal in the city of Mari, one of the litigant's representatives drowns in the "river-god." He then requests that the lives of his three remaining representatives be spared the ordeal and he will renounce his claim.[5]

Finally, that the suspected adulteress is not put to death either by man or God provides the necessary clue to explaining how an ordeal—with its inherent magical and pagan elements—was allowed to enter the legislation of the Torah, or to answer the paradox as it was phrased by Ramban: This is the only case in biblical law where the outcome depends on a miracle. The answer, I submit, is inherent in the ordeal. It provides the priestly legislator with an accepted practice by which he could remove the jurisdiction over and punishment of the unapprehended adulteress from human hands and thereby guarantee that she would not be put to death.[6]

EXCURSUS 10

The Case of the Suspected Adulteress: Redaction and Meaning

(5:11–31)

Modern critics uniformly regard the text of the law of the suspected adulteress (Num. 5:11–31) as a conflation of at least two sources. Two procedures are employed to test the suspect, an oath and an ordeal (vv. 16–24,27–28) with a sacrifice perhaps constituting a third test

(vv. 15,25–26). Moreover, repetitions abound (v. 16b = v. 18a; v. 19a = v. 21a; v. 21b = v. 22a; v. 24a = v. 26b = v. 27a; vv. 12b–14 = vv. 29–30). Notwithstanding this evidence for multiple sources, two recent scholars, M. Fishbane and H. C. Brichto, have shown convincingly that this text is a logical and unified composition.[1] It is submitted that their conception of the text is correct, with the exception of two additions, verses 21 and 31, which, however, provide the key to unlock the redaction and meaning of the text.

The text is cemented together by the sevenfold repetition of the verb ***tame'***, "pollute" (vv. 13,14[2],20,27,29); and it points to the reason for the placement of this case here. The chapter begins with the demand that those who suffer from severe physical impurities should be banished from the camp (5:1–4). This is followed by the law of sacrilege (***ma'al***) against the Lord's sancta (5:5–8)—an act equally offensive to the Deity. The case of the suspected adulteress is also one of sacrilege and pollution but in a moral rather than a ritual sense (see the Comment to v. 13). The implication is clear: This kind of defilement is no less offensive to God and, if not punished, will lead to His abandonment of Israel.

THE SUSPECTED ADULTERESS (5:11–31)

A. *The Case* (vv. 11–14)
  1. introduction (vv. 11–12a)
  2. the wife has strayed (vv. 12b–14a)
  3. the wife is innocent (v. 14b)
    B. *Preparation of the Ritual Ordeal* (vv. 15–18)
      1. ***minḥah*** (v. 15)
      2. water (v. 17)
      3. woman (vv. 18 [16])
        X. *The Oath-Imprecation* (vv. 19–24)
          1. oral adjuration (vv. 19–22)
            [interpolation, v. 21]
          2. written adjuration dissolved and to be imbibed (vv. 23–24)
    B'. *Execution of the Ritual Ordeal* (vv. 25–28)
      1. ***minḥah*** (vv. 25–26a)
      2. water (v. 26b)
      3. woman, effect on (vv. 27–28)
A'. *The Case* (vv. 29–30) (resumptive subscript framed by inverse inclusion)
  1. introduction (v. 29a)
  2. the wife has strayed (v. 29b)
  3. the wife is innocent (v. 30)
      [postscript, v. 31]

The unity of the text is projected into clear relief by its structure. As can be seen by the diagram, it consists of five sections arranged in introverted (chiastic) order. The facts of the case begin and end the text (A, vv. 12–14; A', vv. 29–30). And they contain the following common elements: ***tisteh 'ishah*** (vv. 12,29); ***nitma'ah*** (vv. 12,13,14,29); ***ta'avor 'alav ruaḥ kine'ah*** (vv. 14,30); and ***kinne' 'et 'ishto*** (vv. 14,30). Although the closing statement (A') is only a summary of the case, it nevertheless articulates all its essential elements: the wife's straying and defilement and the husband's suspicions.

The introverted structure of this text is projected in the clearest relief by comparing the preparation and execution sections of the ritual ordeal (B, vv. 15–18; B', vv. 25–28). First, these sections contain common expressions: ***minḥat kena'ot*** (vv. 15,18,25); ***'azkaratah/***

mazkeret/zikkaron (vv. 15,18,26); ***ve-lakaḥ ha-kohen*** (vv. 17,25); ***lifnei YHVH*** (vv. 16,18,25); and ***ve-hikriv 'otah*** (vv. 16,25). Secondly, the structure of the components of each section is identical: ***minḥah***-water-woman. The recognition of this similar substructure clarifies two seeming anomalies. First, the text ostensibly states that the woman was placed at the altar (v. 16) before the preparation of the water (v. 17). However, by using a repetitive resumption (v. 18a), the author thereby indicates that the waters were prepared by the priest prior to the placement of the woman before the altar. The structure indicates the same sequence both in the preparation and in the execution: The woman's role follows that of the water. Secondly, the purpose of verses 27–28 is now seen in proper perspective. These verses are not just an editorial summation of a "prognosis,"[2] but again, in keeping with structural symmetry, they provide a kinetic counterpart to the static picture of verse 18. Both passages find the woman standing before the altar. In verse 18 she holds the ***minḥah*** in her hands; in verses 27–28, the waters are working their effect within her.

Sections B and B′ reveal another inverse symmetry not in language but in procedure, as illustrated in the following diagram.[3]

THE RITUAL ORDEAL

minḥah:	barley flour → (***minus*** holy oil and frankincense)	in woman's hands → during oath	priest's → mediation (***tenufah***)	God (altar)
		↕		
water:	holy water → (***plus*** holy dust and divine curses)	in priest's hands → during oath	priest's → mediation	woman

The ***minḥah*** offering brought by the woman or rather by the husband on her behalf (v. 15) is of the cheapest edible grain, barley (cf. 2 Kings 7:1), and it is deprived of the otherwise two essential elements of the ***minḥah,*** the oil and frankincense (Lev. 2). During the oath it remains in the hands of the woman but, thereafter, it is transferred by the priest in a dedicatory rite to the altar, that is, to the realm of God. The ordeal water undergoes a procedure symmetrically opposite to the ***minḥah.*** It originates in God's realm, the sanctuary laver, from which the priest draws it forth. In contrast to the two elements ***withdrawn*** from the woman's ***minḥah,*** two elements are ***added*** to the water to increase its sanctity and, hence, its efficacy: the dust from the sanctuary floor and the written oath containing the divine name. During the recitation of the adjuration, this water is in the priest's hands while the woman holds the ***minḥah*** in her hands. The priest, then, transfers the woman's ***minḥah*** to the sacred realm of the altar and transfers the sacred water to the profane realm of the woman's body. Thus the introversion is symmetrically balanced: The priest is the medium by which the woman's profane offering is dedicated to the Lord and the divinely empowered water enters her profane body.

The middle section (X, vv. 19–24), the oath, is the pivot of the entire structure and hence its most important section. Its verbal elements tie it to all the other sections. Thus it twice repeats the following elements from A and in chiastic order: ***shakhav 'ish 'otakh, satit, tume'ah*** (vv. 12–13,19–29), and from B it repeats ***mei ha-marim ha-me'ararim*** (vv. 12,18,24).

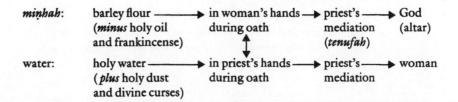

From B′ it borrows ***ha-mayim ha-me'ararim le-marim*** (vv. 24,27), ***ve-tsavetah bitnah ve-naflah yerekhah*** (vv. 21,22,27), ***'alah be-kerev 'ammah*** (vv. 21,27), ***ve-nikketah*** (vv. 19,28), ***ve-nitme'ah*** (vv. 19,20,27,28); and from A′, ***tisteh tahat 'ishah*** and ***nitma'ah*** (vv. 19,20,29). The conditions of the curse are stated in negative form before the positive (vv. 19,20), but in their recapitulation they appear in reverse order (vv. 27,28).

Section X exhibits inner cohesion through the use of introverted or chiastic phraseology. Thus the element of ***shakhav*** in the adjuration begins the negative statement of the oath and ends its positive restatement (vv. 19–20). The oath-imprecation, ***shevu'ah-'alah,*** mentioned twice in verse 21, is also introverted. Moreover, the compound expression for the ordeal water, "spell-inducing ***marim*** water" (vv. 19,24) is not only introverted (in the last verse where it occurs, v. 24) but is also broken into single components, "spell-inducing water" (v. 22) and "***marim*** water" (v. 23). Thus every possible permutation of this compound is accounted for.

Yet it is patently clear that section X is inflated because of the intrusion of verse 21. Not only is the notice that the priest adjures the woman repeated here (vv. 19a,21a) but also the content of the adjuration (vv. 21b,22a). Thus the beginning and end of the oath is not clearly demarcated in the text, the result being that both the Mishnah (Sot. 2:3) and Philo (Laws 3.60) acknowledge differences of opinion concerning its exact wording. Nevertheless, there can be little doubt that originally verse 22 followed verse 20, for then the adjuration reads smoothly and lucidly: ". . . If a man other than your husband has had carnal relations with you, may this water that induces the spell enter your body causing the belly to distend and the thigh to sag. . . ." Furthermore, even if the redundancies of verse 21 could be justified there is no way of harmonizing the jarring and abrasive juxtaposition of verse 22 to verse 21, which implies that first her physical condition will make her a curse and then she will drink the water. However, it is clear that the sagging thigh and distended belly are not the cause but the effect of the water. Hence instead of the sequential verb ***u-va'u,*** "May (this water) enter" (v. 22), one would have expected the infinitive construct ***be-vo',*** "As (this water) enters," the same construction as the previous ***be-tet,*** "As (the Lord) causes" (v. 21). However, ***u-va'u*** follows both logically and grammatically after verse 20, for then the prescribed ordeal is a consequence of the accusation.

Fortunately, the reason for the interpolation of verse 21 is not too difficult to discern. Without it the adjuration contains no mention of the name of God, and the formula gives the impression that the powers of the curse inhere in the water. It was therefore essential to add verse 21 to the adjuration to emphasize that the imprecation derives its force not from the water but from the Lord. It may therefore be conjectured that originally the present formula (minus v. 21) was an ancient Near Eastern incantation for an ordeal employing magical water that did not invoke the name of any deity. It may have been incorporated into the Israelite cult at local high places or shrines and converted into an oath by having the suspected adulteress respond "amen" (v. 22b). The priestly legislator, however, found the formula unacceptable because it ostensibly attributed the effect of the oath to the water itself. But since the formula was already accepted and in widespread use, he would have incurred too much resistance had he attempted to alter its wording. Instead he followed the simple and more acceptable expedient of adding a statement affirming that the efficacy of the oath was due to the God of Israel (v. 21b). And to forestall the protest that no change in the text was necessary since an oath implied the invocation of the Deity, he also added a new thought, that the convicted adulteress would become a curse among her people (v. 21a;

cf. Jer. 29:22). The wording of these two clauses that now comprise the text of the oath in verse 21 was made to fit artistically and coherently with the rest of the oath formula. Thus the Lord will make (*yitten,* v. 21) her a curse in a response to *her* allowing (*va-yitten*) a man other than her husband to have carnal relations with her (v. 20b). Also the effect of the imprecation in verse 21b is given in the reverse order of verse 22a, the thigh preceding the belly, again providing a chiastic balance. Another chiasm was produced within verse 21 with the words *shevu'ah,* "oath," and *'alah,* "imprecation." Finally, the repetition of the instruction to the priest (v. 21a) was added, underscoring the fervent insistence of the legislator that this new element be added to the imprecation. Of course, it is this repetition that fully exposes the interpolation, but it is even more tellingly betrayed, as already indicated, by the discrepancy in the order of events: the effect ostensibly anticipates the cause. We are first informed that she will become a curse (v. 21b) and only afterward that her condition will be caused by the water (v. 22a).

Nonetheless, there can be no doubt that the interpolation of verse 21 took place during the early formation of the text and not during its final stages. This, for the compelling reason that the clause stating that the guilty woman will become an object of derision (v. 21a) is also present in the execution section (v. 27b). Indeed, the presence of the curse in the execution passage (B′) presumes that it was already an element of the adjuration X.

There is a second interpolation in the text that needs to be explained: the postscript of verse 31. That it is a postscript and is not an organic part of the text is clear from the structure of the final section (A′, vv. 30–31). The section is encased by an inverted inclusion *zo't torat . . . ha-torah ha-zo't* (cf. also 6:21). Thus in thought and in form, the law of the suspected adulteress is finished and sealed by this concluding inclusion. What then is the purpose of the postscript of verse 31? First, let us understand its meaning. The first half, "the husband shall be free from punishment," is clearly addressed to the husband; it is to assure him that he has nothing to lose by bringing his wife to the ordeal. His suspicions will either be proved or laid to rest, and in the latter case, a harmonious relationship may be restored. The second half of the verse, "that woman shall suffer her punishment," would seem to be addressed to the suspected adulteress. Understood in this way, this addendum is a pointless redundancy; however, one should not forget that the idiom *nasa' 'avon* implies that she is punished through divine agency (e.g., Lev. 5:1,17; 7:18; 17:16; 19:9; 20:17; Num. 9:13 [with the synonym *ḥet'*]; 14:34; 30:16).[4] Thus this clause is not addressed to the woman but to her husband and community. It reminds them that if the adulteress is convicted by the ordeal, her punishment rests not with them but solely with God.

This, then, is the meaning of the subscript, verse 31. It encourages the suspicious husband to bring his wife to the ordeal by promising him complete exoneration if his suspicions are proved unfounded. It also reminds him and the rest of his community that since the woman's alleged crime was unapprehended by man, she is removed from the jurisdiction of man.

If this subscript is a gloss, as the structure of the text has indicated, it is a correct one. Its author has understood the thrust of this law and its place in biblical jurisprudence, and by inserting it he has made sure that we will understand it too. In sum, the biblical law of the suspected adulteress provides a unique example of how the priestly legislators made use of a pagan ordeal in order to protect a suspected but unproved adulteress from the vengeance of an irate husband or community by mandating that God will decide her case.[5]

EXCURSUS 11

The Nazirite (chap. 6)

The biblical Nazirite, though an ascetic, is definitely not a hermit. He does not lead a monastic existence apart but, to the contrary, is an active participant in all his familial and communal affairs. What sets him apart from his fellows is his meticulous observance of three prohibitions: he may not cut his hair, drink wine, or come in contact with a corpse.

Scripture records two kinds of Nazirite status: lifelong and temporary, both of which result from a vow. In the case of a lifelong Nazirite, the vow is imposed by others, usually by a pregnant mother, whereas the vow of a temporary Nazirite is self-imposed.

The two lifelong Nazirites recorded in the Bible had barren mothers (so too John the Baptist, Luke 1:7). It was therefore not surprising that those women devoted their sons to the Lord as Nazirites both as a thanksgiving offering and a first fruits offering, in the hope that the Lord would bless them with future progeny (such is the purpose of the first fruits; cf. Lev. 19:24–25; 23:10–11; Prov. 3:9–10). And indeed so it happened to Hannah, Samuel's mother (1 Sam. 2:21).

The law of the Nazirite in Numbers 6 does not mention the lifelong Nazirite. Its concern, rather, is with the various sacrificial gifts accruing to the priests and rituals falling under their responsibility in keeping with the theme of the previous passages: the defrauder who takes a false oath (5:6–8); the priest's rights to sacrificial gifts (5:9–10); the ritual of the suspected adulteress (5:11ff.); as well as with the following passage that details the offerings of the tribal chieftains at the sanctuary dedication (chap. 7). Since the lifelong Nazirite incurs no sacrificial obligations—even when he violates his vow—it is of no interest to the priestly legislation presented here.

The two lifelong Nazirites attested in Scripture, Samson and Samuel, were dedicated as such from the moment of conception, "from the womb till the day of his death" (Judg. 13:7; cf. 1 Sam. 1:11,21 [4QSam^a]; Ecclus. 46:13; Mish. Naz. 9:5); so too John the Baptist (Luke 1:15). In this respect the Nazirites resembled the prophets who also felt they were predestined for their role before they were born (cf. Jer. 1:5). And they were akin to the prophets in yet another way: Both felt they served a divine purpose (Amos 2:11).[1]

However, it is more accurate to compare the temporary Nazirite to the priest. Through this institution, the ordinary Israelite was given a status resembling a priest, for he too became "holy to the Lord" (Lev. 21:6; Num. 6:8; cf. Philo, 1 L.A. 249). Actually, in his taboos (as noted in Sif. Naso' 26, Num. R. 10:11, and the Sam.), the Nazirite approximated even more the greater sanctity of the High Priest. (1) He could not contaminate himself with the dead of his immediate family (Lev. 21:11; Num. 6:7; contrast the ordinary priest, Lev. 21:1–4). (2) For him, as for the High Priest, the head was the focus of his sanctity (Exod. 29:7; Num. 6:11b; note the similar motive clauses, Lev. 21:12b; Num. 6:7b; and contrast the dedication of the ordinary priest, Exod. 29:21). (3) He abstained from intoxicants during his term (Num. 6:4), actually a more stringent requirement than that of the High Priest, whose abstinence, like that of his fellow priests, was limited only to the time he was inside the sacred precincts (Lev. 10:9).

An even more illuminating comparison with the temporary Nazirite is the land dedicated to the sanctuary (Lev. 27:16). Naziriteship and the dedication of land to the sanctuary are both votive dedications (Lev. 27:16; Num. 6:2) that are in force for limited periods, the

land reverting to its owner on the Jubilee and the Nazirite reverting to his lay status upon the termination of his vow (Lev. 27:21, by implication; Num. 6:13). In both cases the period of dedication can be terminated earlier: the Nazirite's by contamination (Num. 6:9–12), the land's by redemption (Lev. 27:16–19). In the case of premature desanctification, a penalty is exacted: The Nazirite pays a reparation offering, *'asham,* to the sanctuary, and the owner of the land pays an additional one-fifth of the redemption price to the sanctuary. If the dedication period is completed, no desanctification penalty is incurred. True, the Nazirite offers up an array of sacrifices together with his hair (Num. 6:13–20), but the sacrifices are mainly for thanksgiving, and the hair, which may not be desanctified, must be burned. Similarly, dedicated land (so the text of Lev. 27:22–24 implies) reverts to its original owner on the Jubilee without cost.

Of the three prohibitions incumbent on the temporary Nazirite, two of them are clearly binding for the lifelong Nazirite. Amos pointedly accuses Israel of causing the Nazirite to sin with wine (Amos 2:11–12). Samson's mother is expressly forbidden during her pregnancy to drink wine (Judg. 13:7) or to partake of "anything that comes from the grapevine" (Judg. 13:14; cf. Num. 6:4). By implication, that which her child could not imbibe in the womb was also forbidden to him during his lifetime. To be sure, Samson sponsors a seven-day feast following his wedding (Judg. 14:10–17), but there is no indication that he partook of the wine. Indeed, the writer's comment, "Samson made a feast there, as young men used to do," indicates that Samson was reluctant to play the host—perhaps for the very reason that intoxicants would be imbibed.

What is of interest is the law that the Nazirite could not partake of the grape even in a nonfermented state. Behind this prohibition may lie an ancient ban deriving from nomadic society in which the vine was considered the symbol of the corruption of sedentary life (cf. Noah's drunkenness in the wake of cultivating the vine, Gen. 9:20–21 and the nomadic Rechabites who eschewed both the building of a house and the planting of a vine, Jer. 35:6–11). It is probably not coincidental that the nomadic Nabateans and the pre-Islamic Arabs were also forbidden to use wine and that the Roman high priest, the Flamen Dialis, was prohibited not only from drinking wine but even from touching the vine.[2]

The uncut hair of the Nazirite is truly his distinction (Judg. 16:12; 1 Sam. 1:11). In this respect, he differed from the priest who, though forbidden to shave his hair, was compelled to trim it (Ezek. 44:20). Thus the Nazirite could always be recognized by his appearance and it is no wonder that the term for Nazirite can also refer to his hair (Num. 6:6,7,12,18; Jer. 7:29; note the parallelism in Gen. 49:26; Deut. 33:16). The possibility exists that during Israel's early wars to conquer the land of Canaan, whole armies would vow not to cut their hair until victory was won.[3] This would explain Samson's lifelong dedication to battle the Philistines, the association of Nazirites (and prophets) with the conquest in Amos 2:10–11, and the possible Nazirite vow taken by Deborah's soldiers (cf. Judg. 5:2, "when they grew their hair long in Israel").

Since hair continues to grow throughout life (and apparently for a time after death), it was considered by the ancients to be the seat of man's vitality and life-force, and in ritual it often served as his substitute. A bowl dating from the ninth century B.C.E. found in a Cypriot temple contains an inscription on its outside surface indicating that it contained the hair of the donor. It was placed there, if the reconstructed text is correct, as "a memorial" to Astarte (certain gifts and rites in Israel's sanctuary also served as memorials, e.g., Exod. 28:12,29; 30:16; Num. 10:10; Zech. 6:14), that is, as a permanent reminder to the goddess of the donor's devotion. However, one must be careful not to attribute Samson's

superhuman powers to his Nazirite vow. The story of his magic locks is a prevalent motif in Greek mythology that may have entered into the folklore of the Danites, Samson's tribe, through their contact with their neighbors, the Philistines—former residents of the Greek world.[4]

The offering of hair is also attested in later times in Babylonia (ANET, pp. 339–340), Syria (Lucian, 55, 60), Greece,[5] and Arabia.[6] Lucian's comment merits quotation: "The young men make an offering of their beards, while the young women let their 'sacred locks' grow from birth and when they finally come to the temple, they cut them. When they have placed them in containers, some of silver and many of gold, they nail them up to the temple, and they depart after each inscribes his name. When I was still a youth I, too, performed this ceremony and even now my locks and name are in the sanctuary" (De Dea Syria 60). Absalom was wont to cut his hair ***mikkets yamim la-yamim*** (2 Sam. 14:26). If this phrase is rendered "annually at the yearly feast" (see 1 Sam. 1:21), then the possibility exists that Absalom offered up his shorn hair at the sanctuary. It was customary for pre-Islamic Arabs to deposit their shorn hair at a tomb of a revered saint as a sacrificial act.[7] An analogy persists in the custom of present-day Hasidim who pilgrimage to Meron in the Galilee on Lag ba-Omer in order to cut their children's hair for the first time at the purported tomb of Rabbi Simeon Bar Yoḥai.

The third prohibition, corpse contamination, distinguishes the temporary from the lifelong Nazirite. Samson clearly defiled himself with the dead (Judg. 14:9,19; 15:8,15) and so did Samuel (1 Sam. 15:33). That they were not bound by such a prohibition can be inferred from the instruction of the angel to Samson's mother. She is enjoined to eschew forbidden food (Judg. 13:14), but nothing is said about contracting impurity from the dead, which, according to the priestly code, would have automatically defiled her embryo (cf. Num. 19:22). Here, we must assume that the lifelong Nazirite was subject to the same law as the priest, for whom corpse contamination only suspended his priesthood for a prescribed period of impurity (seven days, as for a layman, inferred from Lev. 22:4) but did not cancel it. The rabbis resolved this discrepancy by presupposing a less observant Samsonite type of Nazirite alongside of a lifelong Nazirite; the latter was required to bring a purification offering, but the former was not (Mish. Naz. 1:2).

How did the priesthood regard the Nazirite institution: with favor, as an opportunity for the layman to achieve holiness, or with disfavor, as an unproductive, wasteful form of life? The priestly texts give no explicit answer; one, nonetheless, is implied. Israel indeed can aspire to holiness: "You shall be holy, for I, the LORD your God, am holy" (Lev. 19:2)—but not in the way of the Nazirite. Rather, Israel achieves holiness by adhering to a series of moral and ritual rules that impinge on the total life of the individual, affecting as much the relationship with his fellow as with his God (vv. 3ff.). Holiness, the priests would aver, is not achieved by imitating the priest. The latter, at least, by virtue of his sanctuary duties is committed to lifelong service to God. He is a two-way channel that conveys, via the altar, the people's petitions and prayers to the Lord and, conversely, that conveys the Lord's ***torah,*** preserved in the sanctuary archives, to the people. The Nazirite, on the other hand, owes no service either to his God or to his people. His priestlike abstentions may satisfy his inner emotional need but they are of benefit to no one else. Only a behavioral transformation, especially as it alleviates the plight of the underprivileged in society, is the true gauge of holiness.

Hence, the possibility must be considered that the institution of the temporary Nazirite is of priestly invention. It effected three major changes. (1) The Nazirite period was

reduced—and entered into on the initiative of the votary and not his parents. (2) The abstinences were severely limited—preventing excessive asceticism. And (3) it could be terminated only by a sacrificial regimen and thus brought under priestly control. By the end of the Second Temple period both priests and rabbis are united in their deprecation of the Nazirite. But the root of their disfavor may be traceable to the holiness laws in Leviticus, which, by their silence regarding the Nazirite, tell us forcefully enough that this is not the preferred way.

The popularity of the Nazirite vow at the close of the Second Temple period can be explained by the relative ease in fulfilling it. By then, the rabbis had reduced the term to thirty days (Mish. Naz. 1:3), unless the votary specified otherwise. More importantly, the cost for the terminal sacrifice could be assumed by others, whereas all other vows had to be fulfilled by the votary himself. Thus Rabbi Simeon ben Shetaḥ split the costs of the sacrifices for the three hundred Nazirites with King Jannai (TJ Ber. 11b), and King Agrippa "arranged for a very considerable number of nazirites to be shorn" (Josephus, Ant. 19.6.1). In like manner the apostle Paul assumed the costs for the sacrifices of four contaminated Nazirites (Acts 21:23–24).

By including women among those who undertook the Nazirite vow, our legislation suggests that the temporary Nazirite was a widespread phenomenon. This is amply attested for the period of the end of the Second Temple (e.g., 1 Macc. 3:49, Josephus, Ant. 19.6.1). We even learn of Nazirite women in the Diaspora (Mish. Naz. 3:6, 5:4), some by name, for example: Queen Helena of Adiabne (Mish. Naz. 3:6), Berenice, sister of King Agrippa II (Josephus, Wars 2.313), and Miriam the Tadmorite (Mish. Naz. 6:11). The great numbers of Nazirites can be inferred from the aforementioned text (TJ Ber. 11b) that records the appearance of hundreds of Nazirites simultaneously before R. Simeon ben Shetaḥ (1st cent. B.C.E.). Some of the early Christians were also Nazirites (Acts 21:23–24).

It is clear that the rabbis frowned upon the Nazirite state both because of its ascetic tendencies, which they opposed (cf. Ned. 9a–10a; Taʿan. 11a), and because it had degenerated through use in wagers. One might say, "I'll be a Nazirite if that man is not so-and-so" (Mish. Naz. 5:5–7). "Simon the Just [High Priest *ca.* 300 B.C.E.] said: In the whole of my life, I ate of the reparation offering of a defiled Nazirite [only once]. This man came to me from the south country, had beauteous eyes and handsome features with his locks heaped into curls. I asked him: Why, my son, did you resolve to destroy such wonderful hair? He answered: In my native town, I was my father's shepherd, and, on going down to draw water from the well, I used to gaze at my reflection [in its waters]. Then my evil inclination assailed me, seeking to compass my ruin and so I said to it, 'Base wretch! Why do you plume yourself on a world that is not your own, for your latter end is with worms and maggots. By the [Temple] service, [I swear] I shall shear these locks to the glory of Heaven!' Then I rose, and kissed him upon his head, and said to him: 'May there be many Nazirites like you in Israel'" (Naz. 4b). This story resembles that of the familiar Narcissus (Ovid, Metamorphosis 30.402ff.) but sharply contrasts with it in its spirituality. But it must be remembered that it is precisely its exceptional nature that caused it to be remembered by the rabbis; the Nazirites of their time could not claim such virtue. "Simon the Just was of the opinion that people make the Nazirite vow in a fit of temper [i.e., impetuously, flippantly]; and since they vow in a fit of temper they will ultimately come to regret it" (Num. R. 10:7).

EXCURSUS 12

The Structure of Numbers 6:1–21

The law of the Nazirite reveals the following introverted structure:

A. Introduction (vv. 1–2)
  B. Prohibitions (vv. 3–8)
    X. Defilement (vv. 9–12)
  B′. Completion (vv. 13–20)
A′. Summary (plus voluntary offerings) (v. 21)

A and A′ introduce and conclude the case of the completed Nazirite term. B and B′ provide the details: prohibitions incumbent on the Nazirite during his term and the desanctification procedure at the end of the term. X, the pivot in this scheme, is the case of the defiled Nazirite; being anomalous, it stands alone. Moreover, being in the pivotal position and, hence, the main point of the scheme, it throws light on the question of why the pericope on the Nazirite was placed here. The concern of the previous chapter is the pollution of the camp and the consequential alienation of the Deity: 5:1–4 prescribes the banishment of the bearers of severe impurity; 5:5–8 mandates reparation to God for the defilement of His name; 5:11–31 deals with the impurity of the suspected adulterers; and here, we have the case of the defiled Nazirite who also must make reparation to the Lord.

The prescriptions are simple and unelaborated. Yet in the few places where the redactor could show his hand and in the connective phrases, a design can be detected. This unit is marked by two inclusions. One frames B′ (vv. 13–14aα,21a), the section dealing with the rites at the successful termination of the Nazirite period. The parallel phrases in the inclusion are here set out. They are not only equivalent but are in chiastic relationship.

ve-zo't torat ha-nazir . . . *nizro* . . . *korbano le-YHVH* (vv. 13–14a)
zo't torat ha-nazir . . . *korbano le-YHVH* . . . *nizro* . . . *torat ha-nazir* (v. 21a)

Another inclusion frames the prohibitions laid upon the Nazirite. Four times the instruction to the Nazirite begins with the phrase ***kol yemei,*** "throughout." In the first and last, the completion of the phrase is identical: ***kol yemei nizro,*** "throughout his term" (vv. 4,8). The middle two phrases are completed with ***neder nizro,*** "his vow as a nazirite" (v. 5), and ***hazziro le-YHVH,*** "he has set apart for the Lord" (v. 6), the latter borrowed from verse 2b, thereby linking sections AB (vv. 1–2,3–8).

The three major sections are linked to each other by common phrases, for example, XB′, ***ro'sh nizro*** (vv. 9,18); BXB′, ***yemei nizro*** (vv. 4,8,12,13); and the root ***k-d-sh,*** "holy" (vv. 5,8,11,20).

Thus, the little freedom that this legal and cultic material allowed to the redactor was utilized by him to create an artistic as well as cohesive unit.

EXCURSUS 13

The Priestly Blessing (6:22–27)

There is only one Hebrew verb meaning bless: ***berekh*** (noun, ***berakhah***). In the Bible (and in contemporary Northwest Semitic inscriptions employing the same root) the range of blessing is as follows: when uttered by the Deity it is a decree (e.g., Gen. 17:16,20); uttered by man it is a prayer. In the latter case, with the Deity as the direct object, it is a prayer of praise (e.g., Pss. 115:18; 134:2); with man as the direct object and the Deity as the expressed or implied subject, the prayer is a request for blessing (e.g., Pss. 115:12–13,15; 118:26; 134:3). Even the ordinary greeting using the passive ***barukh,*** without invoking the Deity by name, implies a request for blessing (1 Sam. 25:33; 26:25; cf. Judg. 5:24). A number of passages contain more than one of the above meanings, for example, Genesis 12:3; 14:19–20, Psalms 115:12–13,15,18, and 134:2–3.

The claim that the blessing (or curse) has inherent powers of fulfillment is not to be found in Scripture except in Genesis 27:34–38. There a vestige of an earlier, pre-Israelite view is still present. The patriarch has the power to confer blessing, and neither its content nor its recipient requires the approval of God ("with the LORD's approval" [Gen. 27:7] is an editorial interpolation). Also presumed is that once the blessing (or curse) is uttered, its force operates independently of its author. Such is the implication of Genesis 27:37. "But *I* have made him master over you: *I* have given him all his brothers for servants, and [literally] *I* have sustained him with grain and wine. What, then, can *I* still do for you, my son?" Thus Isaac, four times, asserts that "I" am the source of blessing, which once uttered cannot be revoked (see also v. 33). Otherwise all utterances, whether blessing or curse, are in effect prayers: Their efficacy depends upon the acquiescence of God. The Bible records another nuance to ***berekh:*** With God as the object it is a euphemism for ***killel,*** "to treat God lightly, disparagingly" (e.g., 1 Kings 21:13; Job 1:5,11; 2:9). Thus to bless God is more than to praise (or curse) Him; it implies that one must demonstrate to Him reverence and loyalty in deeds as well as words.

In the cult, blessing is offered upon entering the sanctuary (Ps. 118:26) but more commonly, upon the conclusion of the service, before departure (Lev. 9:22–23; 2 Sam. 6:18; 1 Kings 8:14,55; 2 Chron. 30:27; Ecclus. 50:20–21). The blessing, as noted above, was the expressed function of the priest (cf. Num. 6:23–27; Deut. 10:8; 21:5; 1 Sam. 2:20; 1 Chron. 23:13; 2 Chron. 30:27; Ecclus. 45:15). However, the historical records show that the king also assumed this prerogative (e.g., David, in 1 Sam. 6:18 [= 1 Chron. 16:2]; Solomon, in 1 Kings 8:14,55 [= 2 Chron. 6:3]; Hezekiah, in 2 Chron. 31:8).

The formula of the Priestly Blessing is probably early. Two Mesopotamian documents reveal a remarkable similarity of language and literary form. A ninth-century boundary stone inscription contains the following terms: "his countenance brightened . . . he turned his attention . . . with his bright gaze, shining countenance . . . he granted his servant." A sixth-century document reads: "turned her countenance toward me; with her shining face she (the goddess Gula) faithfully looked at me and actually caused (him, the god Marduk) to show mercy."[1] The latter passage is particularly striking in indicating, as does the Priestly Blessing, that the turning and bestowing of a shining face results in a bestowal of mercy. Of more direct relevance is the eighth-century Hebrew inscription written in paint on a large jar at Kuntillet 'Ajrud in the upper Sinai containing the words "the Lord bless you and keep

you and be with you." The language of the Priestly Blessing indicates that it was influenced by the formulas of greeting used in Israelite society. Thus the harvesters greet Boaz, (literally) "May the Lord bless you" (Ruth 2:4); Joseph says to Benjamin, "May God be gracious to you (*yaḥnekha*), my boy!" (Gen. 43:29). For further examples, see Jeremiah 31:23, Psalm 128:5, and 134:3.[2]

The antiquity of the Priestly Benediction has been dramatically verified by the discovery of their inscription on two cigarette-sized silver plaques dating back to the seventh or sixth century B.C.E. These amulets were uncovered in a tomb outside ancient Jerusalem on the western slope of the Hinnom valley, just below St. Andrew's church. On the larger plaque, the Priestly Benediction is almost identical with the Masoretic text. On the smaller one, the second and third blessings are combined as follows: *y'r yh[wh] pnyw ['l]yk w[ys]m lk sh[l]wm,* "The Lord make his face to shine upon you and grant you peace." The contraction not only makes sense logically but can also be explained as an error called *homoeoteleuton*, whereby the scribe's eye falls upon the same word (in this case *'lyk*) further down, leading him to omit the intervening words. However, the shortened formula need not be ascribed to a scribal error since the size of the smaller amulet (11.5 x 5.5 mm.) may have mandated an abbreviated version. The antiquity of these amulets is therefore testimony to the antiquity of the Priestly Blessing (see p. 51).

The early prominence of the Priestly Blessing is supported by the host of biblical passages that were clearly influenced by it. For example, Psalm 67:2 cites the blessing formula in summary form. Psalm 4 unmistakably refers to it in *nesah-ʿalenu 'or panekha,* "Lift up the light of your countenance upon us" (v. 7). The songs of ascents (Pss. 120–134), with their emphasis upon the roots *b-r-k, ḥ-n-n, sh-m-r,* and *sh-l-m,* may be an expansion of the Priestly Blessing.[3] Of even greater interest is the stunning tour de force achieved by the prophet Malachi who turns the Priestly Blessing into a blistering attack against the priests themselves.[4] Note the following example: (literally) "will he lift your countenance (*ha-yissa' panekha*) . . . that He may be gracious to us (*vi-ḥannenu*) . . . will He lift His countenance (*ha-yissa' panim*)? Would that you not light (*ta'iru*) My altar in vain (*ḥinnam*)" (Mal. 1:8–10; cf. also 1:6–7,11–14; 2:2–9). The prophet has taken the contents of the Priestly Blessing, negated it, and hurled it like a boomerang back at the priests. "The gift in the Priestly Blessing of a brightened divine countenance which leads to grace/favor (*ya'er Y. panav 'elekha viḥunnekka*) and the raising of the divine countenance (*yissa' Y. panav 'elekha*), which leads to peace or well-being, are punningly countered by the prophet's will that the priests no longer ignite (*ta'iru*) the altar in vain (*ḥinnam*)."[5]

An elaboration on the Priestly Blessing has been found in the writings of the Dead Sea sect of Qumran, as follows: "MAY HE BLESS YOU with all good AND KEEP YOU from all evil, and ILLUMINE your heart with insight into life, AND GRACE YOU with knowledge of things eternal and LIFT UP HIS gracious COUNTENANCE TO YOU for everlasting PEACE" (1QSb 3.3f.; the capitalized words are found in the biblical text); and in a much expanded form for blessing the layman, the High Priest, the priest, the king, and the community prefect (A Formulary of Blessings).

Rabbinic literature records many interpretations of the Priestly Blessing. For example, on the words "and keep you" (v. 24), Rabbi Isaac says: "This means, keep you from the evil inclination, even as Scripture declares, 'For the LORD will be your trust: He will keep your feet from being caught' (Prov. 3:26). Another explanation is that the words mean keep you from the demons, even as Scripture says, 'For He will order His angels to guard you wherever you go' (Ps. 91:11). Yet another explanation is that they mean that God will keep

unto you the covenant made with your fathers as it said, 'the LORD your God will maintain faithfully for you the covenant that He made on oath with your fathers' (Deut. 7:12). Or again, the words may be taken to mean that God will keep (in mind) for you the appointed consummation, as the Scripture says: 'Watchman (Heb. Keeper), what of the night? Watchman, what of the night? The watchman replied, "Morning came, and so did night"' (Isa. 21:11–12). Lastly, the words may be referred to God's keeping of the soul at the hour of death, even as Scripture says, 'The life of my lord will be bound up in the bundle of life' (1 Sam. 25:29); or of His keeping your feet from Hell, as it is said 'He guards and keeps the steps of His faithful' (1 Sam. 2:9)" (Sif. Num. 40).

According to the rabbis (Mish. Sot. 7:6, Mish. Tam. 7:2) the Priestly Blessing was recited as a single unit in the Temple but as three separate blessings outside the Temple, each answered with "amen" (as in the synagogue today). In the Temple, the priests held their hands over their heads, but only up to their shoulders outside the Temple (and in the synagogue today). The Tetragrammaton was pronounced in the Temple but not outside (Philo, 2 Mos. 114). One rabbinic source claims that the use of the Tetragrammaton ceased with Simon the Just (Tosef. Sot. 13:8); however, Rabbi Tarfon, who lived while the Temple service still functioned, claims that it continued to be used (Sif. Zut. to 3:27, Kid. 71a).

EXCURSUS 14

The Chieftains' Gifts and Sacrifices (chap. 7)

Some of the contributions of the chieftains to the Tabernacle clearly nettled the rabbis:

> Three things which the chieftains did improperly the Holy One, blessed be He, accepted. They are as follows: In every other instance an individual may not present incense as a free-will offering; but the princes brought each "one gold ladle of ten shekels, laden with incense" (Num. 7:14). In every other instance an individual may not bring a purification offering except after becoming aware of his wrongdoing; but these brought a he-goat independently of any sin. In every other instance the offering of an individual does not override the Sabbath; but here the offering of the individual did override the Sabbath (Num. R. 13:2; cf. Sif. Num. 51, MK 9a).

There is yet another difficulty. The Tabernacle was completed on the first of Nisan, as explicitly stated in Exodus 40:17, a date supported by Rabbi Akiba (Sif. Num. 68). This conflicts with the main rabbinic position (Sif. Num. 44, SOR 7) that the Tabernacle was erected on the twenty-third of Adar. This would imply that the Tabernacle and the priests were consecrated between the first and seventh of Nisan (cf. Lev. 8:33) and that the offerings of the chieftains took place between the eighth and nineteenth of Nisan—overlapping the Passover!

In reaching for a solution, the first step is to negate the notion that these problems can be dismissed on the grounds that the entire account is fictional and artificial and, hence, bears no correspondence to concrete dates and events.[1] B. A. Levine[2] has demonstrated the antiquity of this account by comparing it with archival records of ancient Near Eastern cult offerings. He finds that this document fits the typology of two-dimensional accounts in which items are listed horizontally according to genre and each genre column is summed up at the bottom of the list (cf. vv. 84–88). Other similarities between Numbers 7 and its ancient Near Eastern counterparts are: (1) The sum for each column is preceded by the

word for "total" (Sum. ŠU.NIGIN, Akk. ***napḫaru,*** Heb. ***kol*** [vv. 85–88]). (2) The standard measurements in weights are inserted parenthetically in the headings (vv. 13,19,25,etc.). (3) In Northwest Semitic inscriptions (Ugar., Aram., Phoen., and also Gk.) the numeral, rather than the word for the numeral, follows each item (for the Bible, see also Num. 28–29; Josh. 12:9–24), for example, bulls, 2; rams, 5; he-goats, 5; yearling rams, 5 (vv. 17,23,29,etc.). Hittite cultic texts also conclude a description of the daily or festival ritual with a summary of the sacrifices offered.[3] Numbers 7, then, follows a two-dimensional scheme with the aforementioned characteristics that obtained in anterior and contemporary but not in later cultures. Thus, the prevalence of this kind of archival notation in the ancient Near East puts the stamp of authority and antiquity upon this chapter.

This conclusion, however, only serves to underscore and aggravate the questions raised above: How could the authors of this document have conceived of a succession of twelve days of offerings by the chieftains of Israel that violates the sacrificial rules for individuals, the Sabbath, and the Passover? I submit that all these questions are resolved with one stroke as soon as it is realized that none of these offerings was actually sacrificed on the day it was brought to the Tabernacle. It was not to accommodate the large total of their animal offerings (Num. 7:87–88) on the altar that separate days were ordained for the chieftains' contributions. Rather, as Ramban has proposed (on Num. 7:2), the purpose may well have been to honor another chieftain and, through him, his tribe on each day. In fact, that the animals are summed up at the end of this Tabernacle document can only mean that they were not sacrificed the very day they were contributed but were transferred (like the silver and gold vessels) to the charge of the sanctuary priests to be offered up in the public cult whenever needed.

Corroboration for this hypothesis stems from similar archival documents in the ancient Near East. There are Hittite texts that list both objects and sacrificial ingredients in inventories of donations to the temple treasury (not in sacrificial rites for the altar). For example, "a mace of bronze, a copper knife, 10 scepters, a ring plated with silver . . . 1 handful of flour, 1 cup of beer."[4] Indeed, the two-dimensional documents that deal with cult offerings, cited above, are not lists of sacrifices offered on a particular occasion but are inventories of gifts to the Temple.

Support for this hypothesis also stems from the biblical text itself. First, it should be noted that all the sacrificial genres appear in the donations: burnt, cereal, well-being, and purification offerings. This means that the chieftains were intent on supplying an initial stock of animals for the public service. One sacrifice, however, is conspicuous by its absence: the ***'asham,*** the reparation offering. Its absence can now be readily explained: It is the ***only*** sacrifice that is exclusively individual and voluntary; it never appears in the fixed order of public worship. Moreover, only the assumption that the sacrificial animals were intended for public offerings explains why all the animals were males (cf. Lev. 9:4; 23:19; Num. 28–29); individual offerings could be females of the herd and flock in the case of the well-being offering (Lev. 3) and had to be females in the case of the purification offering (Lev. 4). Furthermore, the fact that the purification offering is not voluntary but mandatory, brought for acknowledged wrongdoing, and that an individual may not bring an incense offering does not mean that the chieftains were granted a special dispensation (cf. Men. 50b). Rather, the chieftains brought them as a gift to the sanctuary for the public cult and not for themselves.

Lastly, by positing that the sacrificial ingredients were not offered up on the day they were contributed but kept in store by the priests, the four problems that plagued the rabbis

are thereby circumvented: the prohibition against offering individual sacrifices on the Sabbath, the intervention of the Passover, the incense offering that an individual was not permitted to contribute, and the purification offering that could only be brought for one's acknowledged sin.

However, the theory that the chieftains' sacrificial donations were not offered up on the altar on the day of their contribution runs into the difficulty that the choice flour they brought was mixed with oil; since, ostensibly, it would quickly spoil, its sacrifice could not have been delayed. This objection was tested. Since the relative proportions of oil to flour are given (Num. 15:1–10), it became possible for my doctoral student, Susan Rattray, to make up a batch and test its durability. Her sample was made on April 13, 1982. It was sealed in an ordinary plastic container, placed in a cupboard, and never refrigerated. As of the date of this writing, October 15, 1985—three and a half years later—it is perfectly edible, with no trace of spoilage.

One final note. The alleged discrepancy of the overlapping dates (Sabbath and Passover) is obviated on other, philological grounds. The assumption that the chieftains began to bring their gifts on the date the Tabernacle was erected depends on translating the word ***be-yom*** in 7:1 as "on the day [Moses completed]." Its accurate rendering is simply "when" (see the Comment to v. 1). This rendering is necessitated by the context: The consecration of the altar by its anointing (v. 1b) did not take place on one day but over the course of seven. The rendering "when" is also indicated for two other occurrences of this word in this chapter (vv. 10,84). The chieftains did not bring their offerings ***be-yom,*** "on the day," the altar was anointed (v. 10). The altar was anointed for seven days, not one (Exod. 29:36; cf. Abravanel), and the chieftains brought their gifts over twelve days, not one. The same holds for ***be-yom*** of verse 84. It should be noted that this verse opens an inclusion that is closed by verse 88b; but, instead of ***be-yom,*** the text there reads *'aḥarei,* "after."

The rendering of "when" for ***be-yom*** resolves another ancient crux: the chronological discrepancy that results from having Israel's chieftains referred to as the supervisors of the census (Num. 1:2–16) and having them contribute carts to the Levite clans for their removal work after the latter's census and job description (chaps. 3 and 4). The censuses took place immediately after the first day of the second month (Num. 1:1), whereas the Tabernacle was erected on the first day of the first month (Exod. 40:17). How then could the Levites be given the means to perform their labor before their labor was defined? Now, however, that the chieftains' gifts have no fixed date there is no difficulty in the textual sequence that places their gifts to the Levites after their work assignment. The former no longer must be attributed to the day the Tabernacle was erected; it could well have taken place later, after the census.

In sum, a host of alleged contradictions within the sacrificial system and the chronology and sequence of events is resolved by the understanding that the chieftains' gifts of chapter 7 constitute an inventory of their contributions to the Tabernacle store for use in the public cult. They are not individual sacrifices offered up on the altar on the very day they were brought.[5]

EXCURSUS 15

Moses' Audience with God (7:89)

In the Comment to 7:89, it was implied without substantiation that Moses never entered the Holy of Holies in view of the Ark and cherubim. Yet there is the unequivocal affirmation in the early epic traditions that Moses spoke to God "face to face" (Exod. 33:11; Deut. 34:10) and "mouth to mouth" (Num. 12:8) and that he beheld "the likeness of the Lord" (Num. 12:8). Nonetheless, this anthropomorphic language must be discounted as hyperbole. The "face" of the Deity must refer to His Presence rather than His form, since "you cannot see My face, for man may not see Me and live" (Exod. 33:20; cf. Judg. 6:22f.; 13:22), a view that Israel shares with its Canaanite neighbors (e.g., UT 2 Aqht 2.45).

Moreover, scholars agree that these attestations of a direct theophany cannot stem from the priestly tradition, which, to the contrary, takes great pains to deny that Moses ever viewed the divine Presence inside the Holy of Holies. First, just like his fellow Israelites, Moses is only granted a vision of the ***kavod,*** the fire-cloud that envelops God (cf. 9:15–16). His only distinction is that he is permitted to enter the Tent and hear the voice of God as he stands before the ***parokhet***-veil that conceals the Ark from view. The reason for this distinction is clear: He needs to be alone when God communicates with him. Thus, when Moses is in the company of Aaron or his people, the ***kavod*** is beheld in the Tabernacle courtyard (e.g., Exod. 29:42–43; Lev. 9:4,23–24; Num. 14:10; 16:19; 17:8,15; 20:6) to which all of Israel has access (cf. Lev. 8:3–4). However, when Moses meets with God—not for a theophany but for a revelation—he enters the Tent and takes his stand before the ***parokhet***-veil (Exod. 25:22; 30:6,36; Num. 7:89; 17:19). But in the priestly tradition he never passes through the veil to stand before the Ark. Of the medieval exegetes, only Sforno (on Lev. 1:1) holds this view.

What has heretofore allowed for confusion is the ambiguity in the verb ***noʿad,*** "meet," and its noun ***moʿed,*** "meeting." Thus, the Tabernacle is frequently termed the ***'ohel moʿed,*** "The Tent of Meeting," referring to the place where the meeting between God and man takes place. However, nothing in this term implies a face to face meeting. Moreover, the term bears a temporal as well as spatial sense; ***moʿed*** can refer to the ***time*** of a meeting (e.g., 2 Sam. 20:5). And, indeed, in the priestly texts, it is the technical term for the fixed calendrical festivals, ***moʿadei YHVH,*** "the fixed times of the Lord" (e.g., Lev. 23:1,4,37). Thus the Lord meeting (***noʿad***) with Moses in the Tent of Meeting (***moʿed***) refers as much to the fixing of the time (i.e., an appointment) as to the place.

The priestly opposition to having Moses admitted into the Holy of Holies finds its clearest expression in the account of the erection of the Tabernacle (Exod. 40:34–Lev. 1:1). The cloud-encased ***kavod***-fire settles on the Tent and fills it so that Moses is prevented from entering. Thus, he must learn the rules of the sacrificial cult (Lev. 1–5) while standing in the courtyard. Now, as previously noted, whenever God wishes to communicate with Moses and, conversely, when Moses wishes to inquire of God, Moses enters the Tent while God's Presence descends upon the Tent and condenses upon the cherubim-flanked ***kapporet***-throne. Why then does this text (Exod. 40:35) stress the point that Moses was unable to penetrate the cloud? The answer surfaces when this statement is juxtaposed to that of the Sinaitic account—also a priestly text—that Moses did indeed enter the divine cloud, as it rested on Mount Sinai (Exod. 24:18), to receive the Decalogue (Exod. 31:18; 34:18). The encounter made his face radiant with a powerful, perhaps lethal, light (Exod. 34:29–35). For

this reason, the very next time Moses is called to an audience with God—in the newly erected Tabernacle—he can no longer enter the divine cloud. The Torah insists that the Sinaitic theophany was unique in the history of the world: Even Moses was not vouchsafed this experience again.

When henceforth Moses is permitted to enter the Tent, it is to hear the voice of God not to see Him (note the verb ***dibber,*** "speak," in Exod. 25:22; 29:42; Lev. 1:1; Num. 7:89). Moses is barred from the Holy of Holies where the Presence is enthroned on the Ark-throne. He stands in the outer shrine, his view of the Ark blocked by the veil. What holds for Moses holds, therefore, for all other humans. It has already been observed that when the priests dismantle the Tabernacle (ahead of its Levite porters), they shield their eyes from the Ark and then cover it with the upraised ***parokhet***-veil (4:5). And even Aaron, who has no choice but to enter the Holy of Holies in order to purge it of Israel's iniquities and impurities, is expressly warned that unless he blocks his vision by raising up a cloud of incense his entry will prove fatal (Lev. 16:2,13).

Thus, the priestly writers of the Torah de-emphasized the legendary superhuman status that had accrued to the figure of Moses. Not that they denied his greatness or that he was, indeed, the greatest of men. But ever wary of subsequent veneration that might lead to a Moses cult, they took pains to underscore his mortal dimensions.

EXCURSUS 16

Determining the Date of the Chieftains' Contribution (chap. 7)

There are two systems of reckoning the exact dates on which the chieftains offered their gifts. They depend on the date chosen for the consecration of the Tabernacle. Rabbinic tradition, in the main, holds that the seven-day consecration ceremony took place at the end of Adar (Sif. Num. 44, Num. R. 12:5, 13:2, TJ Yoma 1:1) and that on the first day of Nisan (the eighth day, Lev. 9) the first of the chieftains brought his gifts. (Ramban registers the view that the chieftains' gifts were brought between the eighth and nineteenth days.) With this reckoning the problem of the Passover is averted, since the last chieftain offered his gifts on the twelfth day of Nisan. But it does not solve the problem of the Sabbath, for at least one of the twelve days coincided with the Sabbath, when individual sacrifices, particularly the well-being offering, are forbidden (see Excursus 14). The Qumranites (Temple Scroll) and the Karaites (e.g., Sefer ha-Mivḥar on Lev. 8:33; 9:1), supported by Ibn Ezra (on Exod. 40:2; Num. 7:48), hold to the principle of "skipping": The Sabbath was not included among the twelve days. Similarly, they claim that the seven-day march around the walls of Jericho (Josh. 6:3–4,14–15) did not take place on the Sabbath; nor did the fourteen-day dedication of the First Temple between the seventh and twenty-first of Tishrei include the Day of Atonement (1 Kings 8:65–66; 2 Chron. 6:9–10). (However, they make no such claim for the seven-day consecration of the Tabernacle; since the sacrifices were public not private, no violation of the Sabbath occurred.) The possibility of "skipping" the holy day in the enumeration occurred to the rabbis as well, but the view is vigorously rejected (MK 9a). To the contrary, the rabbis claim that Jericho was conquered on the Sabbath (SOR 11, Num. R. 14:1); the fast of Yom Kippur was suspended by the rejoicing for the Temple dedication, and the ***shelamim*** of the chieftain was sacrificed on the Sabbath (MK 9a). However, the controversy is obviated if the explanation offered in Excursus 14 is accepted: that the initiatory gifts eligible for the altar were not sacrificed on the day they were donated.[1]

EXCURSUS 17

The Menorah (8:1–4)

Carol L. Meyers[1] has demonstrated convincingly that the design of the Tabernacle menorah stems from the Mosaic, Late Bronze period. Her main evidence is the following:

1. The six branches plus central axis configuration of the menorah is the form assumed by the stylized tree in the decorative motifs that predominate in the Mesopotamian, Aegean, and Syro-Palestinian regions during the Late Bronze Age.

2. It would have been constructed according to artistic procedures that prevailed in Syro-Palestine while under Egyptian hegemony during the Late Bronze Age. For example, the ring or series of rings found on lampstands from earliest times turns into a series of downward-turned floral capitals, a design first found on Palestinian pottery in the Late Bronze Age.

3. The double bowl (or "cup and saucer") lamp (*gavia'*, Exod. 25:31) appears in Palestine from the end of the Late Bronze Age until it dies out in the sixth century.

4. The thickened lower portion of the stem (*yarekh,* 8:4) is not attested past the Iron Age, when it begins to be replaced by a tripodal metal stand.

5. Acacia wood used in the manufacture of the other Tabernacle sancta (e.g., the Ark, Exod. 25:11; the table of Presence, Exod. 25:24; the incense altar, Exod. 30:3; the pillars supporting the veil, Exod. 26:32—like the menorah plated with gold) was probably the material used for the menorah. Acacia wood is indigenous mainly to the desert areas south of Canaan where Israel was located during its wilderness sojourn.

6. Vegetal motifs (*kaneh,* "reed"; *meshukadim,* "almond-shaped"; *peraḥ,* "lily"; *kaftor,* "apple or pear," Exod. 25:33) are the trademarks of ancient Egyptian art that would have provided the artistic frame of reference for the Hebrew craftsmen.

7. The objection that the Tabernacle menorah was too costly and intricate to have been conceived and executed by a seminomadic people in the wilderness is parried by the following considerations:

a. That Israel could not adjust to wilderness life but pined for the settled life of Egypt is a recurrent motif of the wilderness narratives (e.g., 11:4–5; 14:1–3). Israel, then, was much more at home in Egypt, whose civilization, especially its artistic development, was highly advanced.

b. Israel suffered no shortage of precious metals for the construction of the menorah: It had despoiled the Egyptians (Exod. 3:22; 12:35–36; and especially Ps. 65:37).

c. The Egyptian origin of the production techniques evidenced in the menorah is best explained by the apprenticeship of Israel's artisans (Bezalel and his assistants, Exod. 35:30–36:6) to Egyptian craftsmen. Indeed, Aaron too is said to have fashioned the golden calf (Exod. 32:4). This situation contrasts sharply with the Solomonic period, when a foreign artisan (Hiram, 1 Kings 7:13) had to be imported for the construction of the Temple and its furnishings.

8. Perhaps the most telling evidence of the antiquity of the menorah is its subsequent history. Whereas the Tabernacle menorah corresponds in detail to the lampstands of the Late Bronze Age, its successors in Solomon's Temple and in later exemplars (e.g., Zech. 4:1–3,11–14) are of an entirely different design and construction.

EXCURSUS 18

The Literary Structure of Numbers 8:5–22

The text of Numbers 8:5–22, the purification rites of the Levite work force, reveals the following structure:

A. Introduction (v. 5)
  B. Prescriptive Procedure (vv. 7b–13)
    1. The Levites (v. 7)
      a. lustral water
      b. shaving
      c. laundering
      d. bathing
    2. The Sacrificial Procedure (vv. 8–12)
      a. hand leaning by Israel on Levites
      b. *tenufah* of Levites
      c. hand leaning by Levites on bulls
    3. Levites subordinated to priests (v. 13)

      X. The Rationale (vv. 14–19)
        1. Separate Levites for God (v. 14)
        2. Qualify Levites for sanctuary labor (v. 15)
        3. Replace first-born with Levites (vv. 16–18)
        4. Ransom Israelites from sacrilege of encroachment (v. 19)

  B′. Descriptive Procedure (vv. 20–22a)
    1. The Levites
      a. lustral water (shaving)
      b. laundering (bathing)
    2. The Sacrificial Procedure
      tenufah of Levites (by Aaron, v. 1)
      (presupposes hand leaning)
    3. Levites subordinated to priests
A′. Conclusion (v. 22b)

The introverted structure suggested by this diagram (ABXB′A′) is fully verified when parallel sections are compared. The Introduction and Conclusion (AA′) feature the verb *'asah,* "do"; that is, what Moses was commanded to do he did, together with Aaron and Israel (vv. 7,22). This verb also forms the inclusion for section B′ (vv. 20,22b; see the Comments to those vv.).

BB′ being the prescription and description of the same ritual, as expected, yields a commonality of ideas (B.1,2,3 ‖ B′.1,2,3; see the Comments to these vv.) and phrases. The latter is exemplified by the following: "the whole Israelite community" (vv. 9,20); "water of purification"/"purified themselves" (vv. 7,21); "wash their clothes"/"washed their clothes" (vv. 7,21); "let Aaron perform *tenufah* with the Levites before the LORD"/"Aaron performed *tenufah* with them before the LORD" (vv. 11,21, rendered literally); "make expiation for the Levites"/"made expiation for them" (vv. 12,21); "perform the work of the LORD"/"perform their work in the Tent of Meeting" (vv. 11,22); "place the Levites before Aaron and before his sons"/"the Levites were qualified . . . before Aaron and before his sons" (vv. 13,22, rendered literally).

Two phrases are common to the three major sections, BXB′, and, significantly, they deal with the major theme of the rite. The first states the very purpose of the Levites' purification: "perform the work of the LORD"/"thereafter the Levites shall be qualified for the work of the Tent of Meeting"/"thereafter the Levites were qualified to perform their work of the Tent of Meeting" (vv. 11,15,22), where verses 15 and 22 (XB′) are exact equivalents but for the change in verb tense. The second common phrase refers to the *tenufah,* thereby emphasizing that the Levites must first be ritually dedicated to the Lord before they can qualify for their lethally dangerous role of handling the sancta while transporting the Tabernacle: (literally) "let Aaron perform *tenufah* with the Levites before the LORD"/"perform *tenufah* with them"/"Aaron performed *tenufah* with them before the LORD" (vv. 11,13,15,21). The middle citation is found twice, in verses 13 and 15, where once would have been enough. Perhaps the repetition reflects the redactor's attempt to lock sections B and X together. And the phrase "cleanse them" (vv. 6,15) serves a similar function for sections A and B.

The pivotal section X stands alone since its content, the rationale for the Levitical role in the sanctuary, is unrelated to the vocabulary of the rite and is borrowed from a previous source (3:9,12–13). It also adds a new and essential element to the rationale: the Levites as ransom for the Israelites, as explained in Excursus 19.[1]

EXCURSUS 19

Levitical "Kippur" (8:19)

Kippur as a function of the Levites is clarified by the context of their purification ritual. After they are purified, they undergo two cultic rites: The Israelites lean their hands upon the Levites' heads (8:10), and Aaron dedicates them to the Lord by means of the elevation ceremony (8:11; cf. vv. 13,15,21). These two rites are everywhere else reserved for animal offerings and are never used with humans. The hand leaning on Joshua (27:18) and the blasphemer (Lev. 24:14) serves another purpose. The Levites in the work force are the sole exception to the rule because they are literally sacrifices brought by the Israelites. In the case of the *tenufah* the text is quite explicit: The Levites are "an elevation offering from the Israelites to the Lord" (8:11). The hand leaning ritual is even more instructive. Its meaning is unambiguous: The Levites are the Israelites' sacrifice. The Israelites lean their hands upon the Levites just as worshipers do upon their animals (e.g., Lev. 1:4; 3:2; 4:15,24,29) and, indeed, as the Levites themselves do upon the animal offerings that they bring. Note the parallelism:

> The Levites shall lean their hands upon the heads of the bulls . . . *le-khapper ʿal* the Levites (v. 12).
> Let the Israelites lean their hands upon the Levites . . . *le-khapper ʿal* the Israelites (vv. 10,19).

ʿAl, as the preposition of *kipper* and followed by a human object, always means "on behalf of."[1] Thus, just as the bulls are the *kippur* on behalf of the Levites, so the Levites are the *kippur* on behalf of the Israelites. This equation is important. Elsewhere, where the priest is the subject of *le-khapper,* it means "to perform the *kippur* rite"; here, where the subject of *le-khapper* is both the bulls and the Levites, it can only mean "to be the means of *kippur*" (similarly, see 28:22,30; 29:5). Thus the Levites, unlike the priests, do not perform *kippur*; rather, *kippur* is performed with them.

What is the nature of this Levitical *kippur*? The analogy with sacrifices can be pursued no further because the Levites are patently not offered up on the altar. Only extrasacrificial *kippur* can provide assistance, of which the most helpful cases are the *kippur* payment for the military census (Exod. 30:16; Num. 31:50; cf. 2 Sam. 24:10) and the *kippur* death for homicide (35:33; cf. 2 Sam. 21:1–16) and for idolatry (25:4,11,13; cf. Josh. 22:17–18; Ps. 106:29–30).

All these cases share with Levitical *kippur* a common goal, stated explicitly in each case: to prevent God's wrath (*ketsef*) or plague (*negef*) from spending itself upon the entire community as well as upon the sinners (cf. Exod. 30:12; Num. 25:9,18–19; 31:16; Josh. 22:17; 2 Sam. 21:1,3; Ps. 106:29). These cases of *kippur* are not to be confused with *kippur* performed on the altar by the purification offering. The latter's purpose is to purge the sanctuary of accumulated impurities that make it impossible for God's Presence to manifest itself (see 5:1–4 and Excursus 49). The *kippur* cases adduced here, however, have the immediate goal of preventing the already kindled divine wrath (*ketsef*) from incinerating innocent and guilty alike.

The specific case of *kippur* payment is more informative. First, it should be noted that the notion of monetary payment to prevent divine wrath is present throughout the ancient Near East. In Babylonian exorcistical rites, for example, the patient offers the god Shamash a silver image as his ransom.[2] This motif is also prevalent in the Hittite religion.[3] More importantly, this biblical passage expressly associates the expression "*le-khapper* for your lives" (Exod. 30:15–16) and "*kofer* for your life" (Exod. 30:12). This latter term is a noun whose meaning is undisputed—ransom—as in Exodus 21:30, where it is synonymous with *pidyon,* "redemption."

The notion of ransoming a person or community from divine anger is prevalent throughout the Bible. Wisdom teaching proclaims: "The wicked are the ransom (*kofer*) of the righteous; The traitor comes in place of the upright" (Prov. 21:18; cf. 11:5). The prophets also speak of a human *kofer:* Israel's life is ransomed by the nations (Isa. 43:3). Phinehas's *kippur*-execution performed for Israel (Num. 25:12) cannot be disassociated from his laudation: he "turned back My wrath from the Israelites" (v. 11) nor from the earlier demand for the public impalement of the ringleaders, "so that the LORD's wrath may turn away from Israel" (v. 4). Again, a corresponding wisdom teaching informs us: "The king's wrath is a messenger of death, But a wise man can appease it" (*yekhapperenah,* Prov. 16:14). Perhaps the most illuminating passage is to be found in the sacrificial texts themselves: The blood of an animal slaughtered for food must be poured on the altar to serve as a ransom for the person who has taken its life and who otherwise would be guilty of murder (Lev. 17:11; cf. Lev. 17:4).[4] It is significant that both this passage and that of the military census (Exod. 30:12–16), the one calling for sacrifice and the other for monetary payment, declare that these means have as their purpose "to ransom (*le-khapper*) for your lives" (cf. Lev. 17:11; Exod. 30:15–16). Thus priest, prophet, and sage concur on the prevention or removal of divine wrath through *kofer/kippur* ransom.

It is not accidental that in rabbinic Hebrew the term "ransom" is expressed by *kapparah* (so explicitly, *kufra' kapparah,* BK 40a). In tannaitic literature, this word clearly is present in the living language of the people, for it is used whenever the speaker wishes to take upon himself whatever evil might befall his fellow (e.g., Mish. Sanh. 2:1 [= Tosef. Sanh. 4:1], Tosef. Shevu. 1:4 [= Tosef. Yoma 1:12], Mish. Neg. 2:1). An interesting extension of the concept of ransom is found in the following rabbinic statement: "Students of the Torah who are the *kapparah* for the entire world will not be affected by any of the demons" (Tosef.

BK 7:6). It is not that biblical *kofer* has changed into rabbinic *kapparah,* for *kofer* still survives in rabbinic Hebrew with the connotation of "fine." It is more likely that *kapparah* is a verbal noun derived from *kipper* with the connotation of "ransom."

Therefore, the probability is that all texts that construe *kippur* with *ketsef/negef* have *kofer* in mind: innocent life ransomed by the guilty parties or their representatives. And our text, 8:19, would then imply that the Levites are ransom for Israel, a lightning rod to attract God's wrath upon themselves whenever an Israelite has encroached upon the sancta. This cryptic hint of the fundamental purpose of the Levitical role in the Tabernacle is fully developed in 18:21–23 and is discussed in Excursus 40.[5]

EXCURSUS 20

The Second Passover (9:1–14)

From 9:1–14, it can be inferred that the law of the second Passover applies only to the paschal sacrifice (*pesaḥ*) of the fourteenth day (v. 11) but not to the seven-day Feast of Unleavened Bread (*matsot*), which begins on the fifteenth day (Num. 28:17; Lev. 23:6). That the latter festival was not observed during the second month can also be inferred from the fact that Israel began its march on the twentieth day of the second month—which would have fallen during the festival. The festivals of the *pesaḥ* and the *matsot* are discrete in all the early sources (Exod. 12:1–13,14–20,21–28,40–51; 13:3–10; Lev. 23:5,6–8; Num. 28:16,17–23). They are fused together first in Deuteronomy (Deut. 16:1–7) and in postexilic sources (Ezek. 45:21; Ezra 6:20–22; 2 Chron. 30:2,5,13,15; 35:17).

The reason for the discreteness of the two festivals is clear. The Feast of Unleavened Bread, according to the priestly texts, involves no sacrifice and therefore does not mandate the state of purity regularly required for visits to the sanctuary. The Israelite and resident alien need but cleanse their homes of all leaven and eat *matsot* instead of bread during the seven-day period (e.g., Exod. 12:15–20). Even impure persons, such as the corpse-contaminated individual cited in our passage, could observe this in their homes. But they could not make the pilgrimage to the sanctuary in order to sacrifice "the LORD's offering" (vv. 7,13). The assumption here is that of the Book of Deuteronomy—that after the paschal sacrifice is offered, the worshiper is free to return home to observe the Feast of Unleavened Bread (Deut. 16:7–8; cf. also Exod. 13:6–7). Thus, those whose impurity had invalidated them from offering the paschal sacrifice are still enjoined to remove the leaven from their homes and eat *matsot* for seven days at the same time as their fellow Israelites, whereas their paschal offering is postponed for one month. This inference is corroborated by the halakhah of the rabbis that the second Passover is observed for one day (Tosef. Pes. 3:7) and that leaven may be eaten (Mish. Pes. 9:3).

The severing of the paschal sacrifice from the *matsot* for impure persons points to the probability that the two festivals were originally discrete and that they were combined only in a later age. The consensus of scholarship holds that both originated as first fruit festivals, the paschal sacrifice observed by shepherds and the unleavened bread, by farmers, to assure the fertility of their respective flocks and crops. Thus, the Israelite pastoral nomads combined their observance of the paschal sacrifice (see Exod. 5:1; 10:9) with the Feast of Unleavened Bread after they abandoned their wilderness wandering and settled permanently on the soil of the Holy Land. Indeed, the fact that these two festivals originally were

discrete enabled the rabbis to enjoin the celebration of the Feast of Unleavened Bread, that is, the present-day Passover, even after the cessation of sacrifices with the destruction of the Temple.

Our passage presumes that the paschal sacrifice must be offered at the one authorized sanctuary: the Tabernacle or, once Israel is settled in its land, its legitimate successor. Only this assumption renders plausible the contingency that someone on a journey is not able to offer the sacrifice (vv. 10,13). For if multiplicity of altars were assumed, then the journeyer would simply turn to the closest altar in order to fulfill the requirement of the paschal sacrifice, just as the contemporary Jewish traveler who wishes to fulfill his liturgical obligations plans his itinerary so that he can attend a synagogue. Nor does the factor of distance favor the interpretation that the paschal sacrifice was performed at home as in the case of the first Passover (Exod. 12:1–28), since the text expressly calls the *pesaḥ* a "sacrifice" (vv. 7,13); that is, its blood was dashed on the altar and not on the doorposts of their homes.

There are no recorded instances of the observance of the second Passover in the Bible except the one attributed to King Hezekiah (2 Chron. 30). Since the purification of the Temple lasted until the sixteenth of Nisan (2 Chron. 29:17), one full day past the required time for the paschal sacrifice, the latter was postponed to the fifteenth of the following month. The dependency of this deferred paschal sacrifice on this passage is clear: The two reasons cited for the postponement, impurity (of the priests) and distance (for the people, 2 Chron. 30:3), correspond to the ones explicitly allowed by the paschal law in our passage (see the Comment to v. 10).[1] However, Hezekiah postpones not just the paschal sacrifice but the seven-day Feast of Unleavened Bread as well (2 Chron. 30:21). Because of this and other discrepancies, the rabbis tend to attribute the special case of Hezekiah's deferment of both of the festivals to a calendrical problem: A thirteenth month had to be intercalated and Hezekiah chose a second Nisan (cf. Pes. 56a). Others maintain that the basis for Hezekiah's decree rests in the fact that grain ripens later in the territory of the northern tribes. Thus, since the *omer*-rite with the first grain (barley) has to take place after the paschal sacrifice (Lev. 23:10–11), the northern tribes had no choice but to celebrate it in the second month. Hezekiah, in his attempt to reunite the northern tribes to his kingdom, deliberately postponed the paschal sacrifice to the second month and then invited the northern tribes to celebrate it in Jerusalem (2 Chron. 30:1–2). The calendric difference between Judah and the northern tribes is clearly evident in regard to the Festival of Sukkot: Judah celebrated it in the seventh month (Lev. 23:34; Num. 29:12) and the northern tribes, by edict of their first king Jereboam I, in the eighth month (1 Kings 12:33).[2] It should also be noted that the sectaries of Qumran at the Dead Sea incorporated the second Passover into their calendar.[3]

EXCURSUS 21

Trumpet and Shofar (10:1–10)

The difference between the trumpet and the shofar is clearly indicated by the Septuagint on Psalms 98:6 where the *ḥatsotserah* is called a "metal trumpet" (*salpinx*) and the shofar is called a "horn trumpet" (*keratinēs*), that is, made from the horn of an animal. In Scripture the shofar is used as follows: to muster an army (Judg. 3:27; 6:34); to frighten the enemy (Judg. 7:8,16–22); to proclaim victory (1 Sam. 13:3); to terminate a battle (2 Sam. 18:16;

20:22); to proclaim rebellion (2 Sam. 20:1); to warn of an approaching enemy (Jer. 4:21; Hos. 5:8; Neh. 4:12–14); to install the Ark in David's tent (2 Sam. 6:15); and to proclaim the coronation of kings (2 Sam. 15:10; 2 Kings 9:13; cf. Pss. 47:6; 98:6). When the function of the shofar is compared with that of the trumpet (enumerated in the introductory Comment to this chap.), it is clear that they often overlap. This does not mean, however, as claimed by many critics, that since the trumpet occurs mainly in late sources (the priestly texts in Numbers, according to these critics, are late), the shofar, the original instrument, was replaced by the trumpet in Second Temple times. This theory must be rejected because a number of attestations of the trumpet are clearly preexilic (e.g., 2 Kings 11:14; 12:14; Hosea 5:8). It is more likely that the two instruments were used at the same time and they were distinguished not by their use but by their users: The trumpets were sounded exclusively by the priests. Thus Chronicles deliberately adds to the account in Samuel that a corps of trumpeter priests participated in the celebration when David brought the Ark up to Jerusalem (2 Sam. 6:15; 1 Chron. 15:24,28; see the Introduction). Moreover, it is likely that the nonpriestly sources did not distinguish between the two instruments, calling both of them by the name shofar. This phenomenon is paralleled in another cultic area: The only expiatory sacrifice known in nonpriestly sources (except for 2 Kings 12:17) is the *ʿolah,* whereas the priestly texts also speak of the *ḥatta't* and *'asham.* Thus the masses may not have been aware of the technical name for the wind instrument blown by the priests. This possibility is supported by the account of the battle of Jericho in which the shofar plays a central role. But whereas the people blow the shofar (Josh. 6:9,13b,20), the priests blow the *shoferot hayovelim* (Josh. 6:4,6,8,13a). Thus this nonpriestly source recognizes that the priests resort to a special kind of shofar; only the priestly tradition identifies it with the *ḥatsotserah,* the trumpet. The rabbis escape this textual dilemma by positing that the trumpet was only used during the time of Moses but not by Joshua and later generations (Sif. Num. 75). Certainly by the time of the rabbis of the Gemara, the amoraim, the distinction between the shofar and trumpet was no longer known (Shab. 36a, Sot. 43a; cf. Mish. Kin. 3:6).

EXCURSUS 22

The Ark in War (10:33–36)

This section illustrates vividly the military function of the Ark as both a guide (v. 33) and a palladium, a sign of God's Presence in battle (vv. 35–36). The Ark guides Israel across the Jordan (Josh. 3:4,6) circles Jericho to effect its conquest (Josh. 6:6–7), and accompanies Israel in the battle of Aphek (1 Sam. 4), in the siege of Rabbah of the Ammonites during the time of David (2 Sam. 11:11), and indeed in all the other battles in the wilderness and conquest periods (as we can infer from Num. 14:44). The description of the battle of Aphek is especially illuminating since the Philistines equate the Ark with Israel's God: "When they learned that the Ark of the LORD had come into the camp, the Philistines were frightened; for they said, 'God has come to the camp.' And they cried, '. . . Woe to us! Who can save us from the power of this mighty God?'" (1 Sam. 4:6–8). The Philistines, who brought images or standards of their own gods into battle (cf. 2 Sam. 5:21) as indeed did all the ancient peoples (e.g., Carthaginians: Polybius 7–9.2; Mesopotamians: A. Falkenstein and W. von Soden),[1] clearly viewed the Ark as a representative of Israel's God. Israel's religion, however, was imageless from the outset (cf. the Decalogue, Exod. 20:4; cf. Exod.

20:23) and regarded the Ark not as a representation of the Deity but only as His footstool. This is apparent from the title of Israel's God given in the account of the battle of Aphek, "YHVH of Hosts Enthroned on the Cherubim" (1 Sam. 4:4; cf. 2 Sam. 6:2; 2 Kings 19:15). Thus the cherubim frame the divine chariot-throne, and the Ark, resting beneath the wings of the cherubim (cf. 1 Kings 8:6–7), is His footstool. It is called this elsewhere as well (Pss. 99:5; 132:7; 1 Chron. 28:2). The image of the footstool is particularly apt since the Ark was built in the shape of a chest to serve as a receptacle for the tablets of the Decalogue, the instrument of Israel's covenant with the Lord (Exod. 25:21; Deut. 10:1–5; cf. Deut. 31:26). Throughout the ancient Near East copies of treaties, affixed with sworn oaths to the gods, were deposited "beneath the feet" of the gods, presumably in similar kinds of chests.[2]

The image of God resuming His place on His throne after vanquishing His enemies (originally pagan nature gods) is found in Psalms 29 and 89:16–19 (cf. Pss. 92:8–10; 93) and was probably modeled after Canaanite prototypes that describe the march of the divine warrior god into battle and his enthronement as king of the gods upon his victorious return.[3] A closer analogy is found among the Egyptians where the image of the gods is borne along with a shrine or a special bark, and the shrine has "carrying-poles, overlaid with fine gold, engraved with thy (the god's) name."[4] In Israel, this mythic pattern has been replaced by an epic pattern: The Lord rises from his Ark-cherubim throne to lead Israel to victory throughout its march in the Exodus, the wilderness, and the conquest, ultimately to take up residence in His sanctuary in "Your [the Lord's] own mountain" (Exod. 15:17–18).

The mention of the Ark by itself does not mean that it was taken into battle uncovered or unaccompanied by other sacred objects. In Israel's wilderness battle against the Midianites, we are expressly told that "the sacred utensils and the trumpets" were brought by the priest Phinehas into the war camp (Num. 31:6). Moreover, it is explicitly stated that the Ark was covered in David's war camp (2 Sam. 11:11). Finally, the Ark was probably housed in a tent in the war camp and concealed from view (4:5–6), since the consequences of viewing it or touching it while exposed were regarded as fatal (cf. Num. 4:15,20; 1 Sam. 6:19; 2 Sam. 6:6–7).

Is the Ark the permanent residence of the Lord, or is His association with it temporary, unpredictable, and symbolic? The preponderant view of the texts indicates that the latter is the case: For the Lord to manifest Himself or to speak from the Ark, He arranges to "meet" with Moses or "appears"—His *kavod* is visible—to Israel (e.g., 14:10; 16:19; 17:7; 20:6). Alhough the Tabernacle is perpetually covered by a cloud (Exod. 40:34–38; Num. 9:15–23), God's Presence or *kavod*, indicated by the fire within the cloud (9:15–23), remains inside the cloud *above* the Tabernacle so that it can be visible at night (Exod. 40:38; Num. 9:15). Thus according to these priestly texts, the Lord does not reside in the Tabernacle between the wings of cherubim but only descends upon it from the suspended cloud whenever He wishes to address Moses (e.g., 17:7; 20:6) or appear to Israel (e.g., 14:10; 16:19). And when Moses and Aaron seek an audience on their own initiative, the *kavod* must appear before they can be sure that the Deity has descended onto His throne and will grant them an audience (17:7–8; 20:6–7).

This view seems to be contradicted by sources that speak with assurance that the Lord has taken permanent residence upon the Ark.[5] Thus Hezekiah "spread it [the letter] out before the LORD . . . and said 'O LORD of Hosts Enthroned on the Cherubim'" (2 Kings 19:14–15); and David, in dancing before the Ark, danced "before the LORD" (2 Sam. 6:14,21). These verses, however, are not to be taken literally. Sacrifices are always said to be

offered "before the Lord" without implying that He is physically present in the sanctuary. Indeed, that the cherubim are winged means that the divine seat is in reality a chariot: His dominion is the world and only when He wishes to manifest Himself to Israel does He condense His Presence upon the Ark-cherubim inside the Holy of Holies. From there, hidden from human sight by the ***parokhet***-veil (Exod. 26:33) or the cloud of incense (Lev. 16:2,13), He summons Moses to receive His commands (e.g., Exod. 25:22; Lev. 1:1). Another tradition informs us that even when Moses enters the Tent on his own initiative, for oracular purposes, there is no guarantee that the Lord will answer him or even that He is there. Only the descent of the pillar of cloud at the entrance to the Tent indicates that the Lord is present and is ready for an audience (Exod. 33:8–9).

Moreover, the Ark was not conceived as the permanent residence of the Lord; this is clear from the song of the Ark itself. The song is only a prayer (the imperative "Arise," "Rest" are not written in the usual form ***kum, shuv*** but are lengthened to ***kumah, shuvah*** and thus may be expressing a wish). Moses petitions the Lord to arise from His throne and attack the enemy and then to return to His throne on the Ark-cherubim after the battle is over. There is no assurance that He will do either.

Thus even in the oldest sources, the Ark does not guarantee that the God of Israel is with Israel in all of its endeavors. Because of its special sanctity, its hallowed tradition, and, above all, the belief that the Lord ordained the Ark as the place where He will make His will and Presence manifest, the assurance that the Ark is within the Tabernacle during peace and is visibly present with the army during war suffices to give Israel courage and hope that when she turns to God He will answer.

EXCURSUS 23

The Inverted "Nuns" (10:35–36)

This poetic couplet is bracketed by marks (*simaniyot*, ARN[1] 34) called ***nun menuzzeret***, "isolated ***nun***," or ***nun hafukhah***, "inverted ***nun***." Other shapes and positions for these marks are attested in biblical manuscripts. For example, they can be shaped like a shofar (Sot. 6:1); like a ***kaf***, a mark identical with the ***antisigma***, a critical sign employed by the Alexandrian Greeks to designate misplaced verses; or in the form of a ***diplē***, a sign calling for special interpretation.[1] The rabbis offer two explanations: "[These two verses] are marked at the beginning and at the end to show that this is not their proper place. Rabbi [Judah the Prince] said: [They are marked] to indicate that they form a separate book" (Sif. Num. 84). According to the explanation of Rav Ashi (Shab. 116a), its proper place is the passage on units, ***degalim*** (after 2:17; cf. Baḥya, Baʿal ha-Turim, or, after 10:21, cf. Ḥazzekuni). The Septuagint transposes these verses before verse 34. On the other hand, the claim by Rabbi Judah the Prince that the enclosed two verses form a separate book is supported by the Mishnah: "A biblical scroll that contains eighty-five letters, as in the section that begins: 'when the Ark was to set out,' defiles the hands" (Mish. Yad. 3:5) and is confirmed by similar signs in Greek papyri and grammatical literature.[2]

There is an interesting medieval tradition, attested in an eleventh-century manuscript from Cairo, that these verses are excerpted from a source known as "The Prophecy of Eldad and Medad" (Ginzei Mitsraim) which, according to Lieberman, may underline the para-

phrase of Rabbi Judah the Prince found in an earlier source: "These two verses stem from an independent book that existed but was ***nignaz,*** suppressed" (Mid. Prov.; cf. also Mid. Ḥaserot ve-Yeterot). The attribution of these verses to Eldad and Medad (cf. 11:27) not only represents a rare medieval instance of the denial of Mosaic authorship to a part of the Torah but also indicates that there was continuous awareness in traditional sources that the process of the canonization of Scripture was a highly selective one: Much was "suppressed," that is, rejected.

EXCURSUS 24

The Structure of Chapters 11–12

These two chapters comprise three units of complaints: (1) Israel's at Taberah regarding its forced march (11:1–3; cf. 10:33 and Mid. Ag. and Ramban on 11:1); (2) Israel's at Kibroth-hattaavah regarding meat, intertwined with Moses' regarding his leadership burden (11:4–34); and (3) Miriam's, backed by Aaron, at Hazeroth regarding Moses' leadership monopoly (12:1–15). These complaints are interrelated stylistically and thematically, thereby revealing their structural unity. It can be demonstrated, first, by the common pattern of topical progression (a–f) undergirding the first and last complaints that frame the two chapters as an inclusion.

Complaint 1: Taberah (11:1–3)	***Complaint 3: Hazeroth (12:1–15)***
a. People complain (v. 1a)	a′. Miriam and Aaron complain (vv. 1–2a)
b. God hears, fumes, punishes (v. 1b)	b′. God hears, fumes, punishes (vv. 2b, 4–5, 9–10)
c. people appeal to Moses (v. 2a)	c′. Aaron appeals to Moses (vv. 11–12)
d. Moses intercedes (v. 2bα)	d′. Moses intercedes (v. 13)
e. Appeal answered (v. 2bβ)	e′. Appeal answered (v. 14)
f. March delayed	f′. March delayed (v. 15)

The last component, the nature of the punishment (ff′), requires a word of explanation. Not only are the guilty punished—Miriam (12:9–10) and the outskirts of the camp (or the leaders?, 11:1)—but the entire people suffer the consequence by having their journey delayed: seven days in the case of Miriam, as the text makes explicit (12:15), and an unspecified period at Taberah. The very fact that there is no travel notice between Taberah and Kibroth-hattaavah, as would normally be expected at the end of 11:3, means that for the redactor the two sites are identical. This is confirmed by the list of stations in chapter 33, which lists Kibroth-hattaavah but omits Taberah (33:16). (Deut. 9:22 represents a different tradition.) Also, the brief aside on Moses' uniqueness in chapter 12 comprises an editorial comment (12:3) and a poetic insert (12:6–8).

The middle unit, complaint 2, is itself a conflation of two complaints: Israel's about meat and Moses' about leadership (11:4–35). The two may originally have been discrete but were intertwined (e.g., vv. 11–15) to create the impression that the grumbling of the people triggered an equivalent response from Moses. The result is that instead of interceding for

the people and attempting to stay God's wrath, he actually adds his complaint to theirs. In the long list of instances where Moses acts as Israel's defender before the Lord, this section stands out as the lone exception. Elsewhere Moses' intercessions are of two types: Whenever God announces the punishment beforehand, Moses tries to abort it.[1] However, when God punishes without warning (only, it should be noted, in those incidents where the people defy Him directly), Moses can only try to mitigate the punishment.

There are three ostensible anomalies: (1) God punishes Miriam and Aaron without notifying Moses (the second type) and all Moses can do is to ask for mitigation (chap. 12); yet the sinners have attacked not God but Moses. Here the reason for God's punitive action is patently clear: Miriam and Aaron contest Moses' leadership and God punishes them to vindicate Moses. Indeed, that Moses does not intercede in his own behalf leads the redactor to comment, "Moses was a very humble man" (12:3). (2) In the rebellion of Dathan and Abiram—in distinction to the rebellion of Korah (chap. 16)—Moses does not intercede to avert or mitigate their punishment. To the contrary, Moses not only requests punishment but even specifies its form (16:28–30). Yet here too the punishment serves to vindicate Moses. Moreover, it must spring from Moses' initiative if it is to authenticate his leadership.

(3) However, the Kibroth-hattaavah episode (11:4–34) is truly an exception. Here God's wrath against Israel (v. 10) is not followed by Moses' intercession but by his personal complaint (vv. 11–15), climaxed by his doubts concerning God's powers (vv. 21–22). Indeed, it is Moses' failure to "stand in the breach" (cf. Ezek. 22:30; Ps. 106:23) that explains why the story of the elders is interwoven with the story of the quail: to provide punishment for Moses! As is clear from the Deuteronomic parallels (Deut. 1:12), Moses had requested ***human*** help to ease his leadership burden. But in this pericope, his plea for assistance (vv. 11–13) is inserted into the people's demand for meat (vv. 4–9,13), thus showing that he expected his assistance to come from God. Evidently the fusion of these two stories is an attempt to demonstrate that Moses was punished by the diminution of his spiritual powers (the story of the elders) for failing to intercede on Israel's behalf when it craved meat (the story of the quail) and for failing to believe that God could provide it. The literary structure of the pericope bears out my contention that this purpose underlies the coalescence of the two stories, as follows:

Complaint 2: Kibroth-hattaavah (11:4–34)

A. People's Complaint: Meat (vv. 4–10a,bα)
    Riffraff instigate people (vv.4–6)
    God fumes (v. 10bα)
    B. Moses' Complaint: Assistance (vv. 10bβ–15)
        Moses is upset with God (v. 10bβ)
        Moses indulges in self-pity (vv. 11–15)
            Give me assistance or death (vv. 11–12,14–15)
            I cannot supply meat (v. 13)
        X. God's Answer to Both Complaints (vv. 16–24a)
            God instructs Moses to:
            Choose elders: God will authorize them (vv. 16–17)
            Ready people: *He* will provide meat (vv. 18–20)
            Moses: Where will you get meat (vv. 21–22)
            God: Wait and see (v. 23)
            Moses tells people to get ready (v. 24a)

B′. God Authorizes Elders: Diminishes Moses (vv. 24b–30)
Moses chooses and assembles elders (vv. 24b–30)
God distributes Moses' spirit (v. 25)
Eldad and Medad prophesy (v. 26–27)
Joshua protests (v. 28)
Moses acquiesces (v. 30)
Moses and elders return to camp
A′. God Supplies Meat: Punishes Complainers (vv. 31–34)
Meat brings death (vv. 31–33)
Dead are buried giving name to site (v. 34)

Complaint 2 contains five sections. The actual complaints are expressed in A and B. The middle section, X, comprises God's answer to AB and anticipates the fulfillment B′A′. The fulfillment occurs in introverted order (see the Introduction, p. xxiii). This pattern can only be appreciated when apposite parts are compared.

A and A′ both deal with the people's complaint. They exhibit the same language: *va-yiḥar 'af YHVH . . . ve-'af YHVH ḥarah* (vv. 10,33); *ha'asafsuf–va-ya'asfu . . . 'asaf* (vv. 4,32); *hit'avvu ta'avah ha-ta'avah . . . ha-mit'avvim* (vv. 4,34). The language also highlights contrasts: They sat and wept (v. 4) and only rose (v. 32) to gather quail; they recall the free food spread about on Egyptian soil (v. 5) and now the free quail is spread about in the camp (vv. 31–32); in the desert they have seen no food but manna (v. 6) and now they see only quail (v. 31); their punishment fits the crime: their parched gullets (v. 6) are now stuffed with the quail of death (v. 33).

B and B′ deal with the private complaint of Moses, a complaint filled with self-pity. His plea shows a self-contained, introverted structure, beginning and ending with the identical self-pitying expressions. The specific nature of his complaint—his inability to procure the needed food (v. 13)—comes at the midpoint.[2] Moses begins and ends with an accusation that God has wronged him (root *r-'-'*, vv. 10b, 15). He says that if the Lord really loved him (*matsa' ḥen be-'einei,* vv. 11,15) He would let him die rather than lead this people. The people's complaint for meat (A) is echoed in Moses' complaint (v. 13) because, again in his self-pity, he imagines it is *his* responsibility to supply the meat (vv. 21–22). Moses' collapse deserves not only an answer but a rebuke, and that rebuke is already intimated in God's response (X). God will ordain assistants but only by drawing from Moses' power (v. 17); they may not be his equals but he cannot but be diminished. However, in the fulfillment section (B′) something unanticipated happens. Eldad and Medad receive the gift of prophecy directly from God and not from Moses (v. 26). Moreover, they continue to prophesy. Their gift, then, is permanent and not transient like that of the elders (v. 25). And Joshua astutely recognizes the implication: Moses has rivals. Moses' powers are not merely diminished; he is actually faced with qualified competitors. This unanticipated event, which alarms Joshua (v. 28), is Moses' punishment. It may even have given Miriam and Aaron sufficient grounds for their rebellion against Moses' authority (12:2). Moses, however, greets this verdict with neither resistance nor resignation but with joy. By this response, he demonstrates his humility and greatness. He is rewarded by being elevated to the status of prophet par excellence (12:6–8).

The complaints (AB) and their solution (B′A′) exhibit inner linkage. The two complaints have in common the term *be-kerev* (vv. 4,20,21), referring to each of the dramatis personae of this story. The *'asafsuf* "in the midst of" Israel (v. 4) arouses a lust that

displaces the Lord who hitherto had been in Israel's "midst" (v. 20) and instigates Moses to complain about his role in Israel's "midst" (v. 21).[3] Moreover, the complaints share the word *'akhal*, "eat," which appears seven times (vv. 1,4,13,18[2],19,21). That the redactor may have purposely chosen the number seven for the occurrences of *'akhal* is supported by the absence of the verb in the account of the eating of the quail (A', vv. 31–33), where it might have been expected. The two solutions (B'A') are tied together by the word *ruaḥ*, meaning both spirit and wind: God's *ruaḥ* invests the elders and Eldad and Medad (vv. 25,26,29), and it brings the quail (v. 31).

Section X is pivotal: God reminds the people of their lament (vv. 4,18) and quotes verbatim their demand for meat (vv. 4b, 19a), while indicating that He has seen through the complaint to the rebellion that motivates it (v. 20b). Similarly, God responds to Moses with the promise that He will lighten his administrative load. The answer to the people's complaint is not revealed, even to Moses, since it comprises their punishment. Yet it is subtly intimated by the precise fulfillment of Moses' skeptical challenge: Where will God get animals (meat) for the people to gather and slaughter? (vv. 22,32).

The structure of chapters 11–12 can be represented by the following diagram:

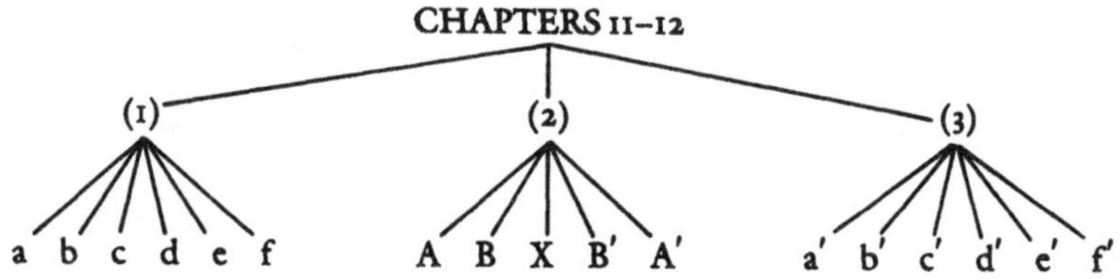

The three complaint units are themselves sequentially and thematically linked: 1 and 2 are bound by the key word *ra'*. The very first verse (11:1) labels the complaint *ra'*, "evil". Indeed, the people's complaint has totally reversed the divine promise of *tov*, "good," emphasized in the previous section (10:29,32), for they now refer to Egypt as *tov* (11:18; cf. 14:3). As noted, Moses himself is so demoralized by the people's complaints that he too attributes *ra'* to God (11:10,11,15). Also, fire *eats* the camp edge (*'asafsuf?*, in 1); the people *eat* the quail gathered at the camp's edge (11:18[2],19,21,32–33, in 2) in answer to their request for food (11:4,13,18, in 2). The alien elements (2) provoke Israel to grumble about the food; the latter, in turn, provoke Moses to grumble about his leadership burden (2). Thus Moses provides a basis for Miriam and Aaron's grumblings about his monopoly of leadership (3). When they also complain about Moses' alien wife, the circle of complaints that was begun by aliens is now closed. Finally, units 2 and 3 are linked by the similar images and vocabulary that picture the fate of those who lust and that was almost experienced by Miriam: her half-eaten *basar* (12:12) is reminiscent of the half-eaten "*basar* still between their teeth, not yet chewed" (11:33).

The figure of Moses unites all the incidents, and his manifestations form a symmetrical pattern. At the beginning and end (complaints 1, 3) he relays appeals to God (11:1; 12:13), that is, he performs his prophetic function. In the interim, incited by the people, he himself complains (complaint 2, 11:11–15). He is rebuked by challenges to his leadership (complaint 2, 11:25–29; complaint 3, 12:2–3). Moses meets these tests, demonstrating his humility (complaint 3, 12:3) and his sincere desire to share his power (complaint 2, 11:29), and

thereupon, God declares him the unique prophetic leader (complaint 3, 12:6–8). Another common motif is the apparent concession God makes to the rebels, which ultimately proves to be a deception.[4] He provides meat that deals death (complaint 1, 11:4; complaint 2, 19–20,31–34); provides Moses with assistants who (temporarily) diminish him (complaint 2, 11:11–12,14–15,24–29); and summons Aaron and Miriam together with Moses before he separates them from Moses in order to punish Miriam (complaint 3, 12:4–5,9–10).

Finally, another unifying element is the inherent topographic code.[5] Israel has departed from impure Egypt and is headed for the Holy Land, Canaan. The wilderness lying in between is ambiguous terrain, and hence the camp must be kept sacred. The areas inside and outside the camp represent discrete domains. For instance, the manna of blessing falls inside, the quail of punishment outside. The edges of the camp burnt by God's wrath (11:1) may be synonymous with the *'asafsuf,* "the gathered ones" (11:4), the alien edge of society. God's grace toward Israel is marked by movement toward Canaan (11:35; 12:16), his punishment, by delays: at least two days for gathering the quail and burying the dead (11:32, 34; it could have lasted a whole month, 11:20–21) and seven days for Miriam (12:15). Corresponding to this horizontal plane is a vertical one: up-down stands for Canaan-Egypt. The manna is heavenly food but the fish/meat and vegetables stem from below. The quail ostensibly fall from the air, but this is a deception for, according to 11:31, it arises from the sea.

The itinerary notices (11:35; 12:16) link the units (the omission of a link between complaints 1 and 2 being deliberate; cf. the Comment to 11:4–35). They are the last stage in the redaction.[6]

EXCURSUS 25

Ecstatic Prophecy in Israel and the Ancient Near East (11:24–30)

In Israel, God frequently communicated with the prophets by possession, as attested by the following expressions: "the hand of the Lord God fell upon me" (Ezek. 8:1), "a spirit lifted me up" (Ezek. 8:3), "a spirit entered into me" (Ezek. 2:2), "the word of the LORD came to me" (Jer. 1:4), "the spirit rested upon them" (Num. 11:25–26), "the spirit of the Lord God is upon me" (Isa. 61:1), "the spirit [of the LORD] enveloped Gideon/Amasai/Zechariah" (Judg. 6:34; 1 Chron. 12:19; 2 Chron. 24:20). These expressions indicate possession but do not necessarily imply ecstasy. The former denotes the *process* by which communication between the human and divine worlds takes place; the latter, as used by anthropologists, refers to a *type of behavior,* specifically the trance.[1]

A survey of the verb *hitnabbe',* "act like a prophet, exhibit the behavior characteristic of a prophet,"[2] a Hitpael denominative from *navi',* "prophet," shows that it sometimes designates ecstatic or trance behavior but not always. Thus, the seventy elders literally "act like prophets" (Num. 11:24–25), as do Eldad and Medad who remain in the camp (Num. 11:26–27). In either case, the precise nature of their behavior is not clear, although it is recognized by the people as prophetic. It was not their speech that marked them as prophets but their behaving in recognizable patterns by which true prophets can be distinguished from pretenders and the mentally disturbed. Clearly their behavior was evaluated positively: Possessing spirit was not demonic but stemmed from the Lord. Joshua did not object to their behavior per se but, on the contrary, he recognized in it a validation of the

divine choice and, hence, a potential threat to Moses. Moses counters Joshua's fears by asserting that the sharing of prophecy is indeed the divine will (Num. 11:28–29).

A second early reference to possession behavior occurs in 1 Samuel 10:1–13. Saul is told that he will encounter a band of prophets exhibiting characteristic prophetic behavior (***mitnabbe'im***). That they play musical instruments suggests that trance may be involved, although it does not incapacitate them since they engage in normal human activities such as walking and playing music. Saul enters the group and exhibits similar behavior (***va-yitnabbe' betokham***). Indeed, it is his behavior that marks him as a prophet and prompts his acquaintances to ask, "Is Saul also among the prophets?"—thus suggesting that prophets at that particular time exhibited stereotypical behavior that was evaluated positively. If their behavior involved ecstasy, it was controlled and not incapacitating.[3]

A negative view of Saul's prophetic behavior is found in 1 Samuel 18:10–11. An evil spirit sent by the Lord possesses him and causes him to "act like a prophet" (***va-yitnabbe'***). His behavior is violent and uncontrolled, leading him to attack David. This negative view may also be reflected in 1 Samuel 19:8–24. Messengers sent by Saul to apprehend David encounter prophets and then they too "act like prophets" (***va-yitnabbe'u***) with the result that they are incapacitated and cannot reach David. Finally Saul himself takes up the pursuit, encounters the prophets, and he too exhibits characteristic prophetic behavior (***va-yitnabbe'***): He tears off his clothes and lies naked and helpless all day and night. This, the narrative concludes, is the real origin of the question "Is Saul among the prophets?" The implied answer is "No, Saul is no prophet; he is insane."[4]

Subsequent usages of ***hitnabbe'*** (e.g., 1 Kings 22:8,10,18; Jer. 23:13; 26:20; 29:24–28; Ezek. 13:17; 37:10; 2 Chron. 20:37) focus on speech as the main characteristic of the prophet's behavior and so merge with the verb ***nibba'***, the Nifal denominative of ***navi'***, "prophet," the normal verb for prophetic speech.

There is a clear attempt in the Bible to distinguish between ecstatics and other prophets by the use of two different nouns derived from the same root: ***navi'*** and ***mitnabbe'***. The latter, a Hitpael formation, carries a pejorative connotation, "to act or play the prophet," and it points, in particular, to the ecstatic frenzy that is its chief characteristic. Thus the ecstatic is equated with a madman (cf. Jer. 29:26; Hos. 9:7), and when the prophet Elisha sends one of his disciples to anoint Jehu king of Israel, the latter is asked: "Is all well? What did that madman come to you for?" (2 Kings 9:11). One could hardly be surprised that the ecstatic was regarded as a lunatic since he was capable of such bizarre behavior as stripping himself of his clothing and lying naked all day and night (1 Sam. 19:24) or mutilating his own body (1 Kings 20:35ff.; 2 Kings 1:8; Zech. 13:4,6; cf. 1 Kings 18:28). Nonetheless, judging from the frequent attestation of prophets overwhelmed by the Lord's spirit or hand (cf. especially Ezek. 2:2; 3:14,24; passim), ecstasy was considered a valid characteristic of the Israelite prophet.

The roots of prophetic ecstasy lie deep in the ancient Near East. Especially at Mari, nearly a millennium before Israel appears as a nation on its own land, prophecy is found to be a living institution practiced by two similar groups: the ***āpilum*** (fem. ***āpiltum***), "respondents," corresponding in the main to the court prophets in the service of Israelite kings (cf. Excursus 26) and the ***muḫḫûm*** (fem. ***muḫḫūtum***), "ecstatics," corresponding to the ***mitnabbe'***, the Israelite ecstatics. The violent nature of the ***muḫḫûm*** is captured by the terminology that is derived from ***meḫû***, "storm, wind." Thus the verb ***namḫu*** (a Nifal formation attested at Mari) is the equivalent of the spirit (wind, storm), which rests on (11:25ff.) or comes upon (24:2) or envelops (2 Chron. 24:20) the Israelite ***mitnabbe'***. The

most vivid description of an ecstatic fit is found in the eleventh-century tale of the Egyptian Wen-Amon, which takes place in the Canaanite milieu of Byblos. It relates that while the king "was making offering to his gods, the god seized one of his youths and made him possessed. And he said to him, 'Bring up [the] god! Bring the messenger who is carrying him! Amon is the one who made him come!' And while the possessed [youth] was having his frenzy on this night . . ." (ANET, p. 26).

The ecstatic trance is usually induced by music: "As the musician played, the hand [= spirit] of the LORD came upon him" (2 Kings 3:15). Musical instruments are associated with ecstatic bands (1 Sam. 10:5). A vestige of the inextricable bond between ecstasy and music is found in the description of the Levite musicians in the Second Temple as prophets and visionaries (1 Chron. 25:1ff.; 2 Chron. 29:30). Dancing and other dervish motions must also have characterized the ecstatic phenomenon but it is only attested for the prophets of the Canaanite god, Baal (1 Kings 18:26).

Ecstatic prophecy in the Bible is ascribed to groups as well as to individuals. With the kings of Israel and Judah in attendance, four hundred prophets emerge from their ecstatic trance pronouncing victory in battle (1 Kings 22:6). Eight hundred and fifty Canaanite prophets of Baal and Asherah "shouted louder, and gashed themselves with knives and spears, according to their practice, until the blood streamed over them. When noon passed, they [literally] prophesied in ecstasy" (1 Kings 18:28–29).

The main function of the ecstatic prophet seems to lie in the military sphere: He arouses fervor for battle, as in the example of 1 Kings 22, when the kings of Israel and Judah are preparing to engage the Arameans in battle. It is also no accident that only after his ecstatic experience is Saul inspired to fight the Ammonites (1 Sam. 11:6). Indeed, one of Deborah's explicit functions as a prophetess (Judg. 4:4) is to arouse Barak (and all Israel) to wage war against the Canaanites (Judg. 5:12).

The ecstatic trance is graphically described by Ezekiel, the ecstatic par excellence among the classic prophets: He sees the vision and falls on his face; the spirit enters him and makes him stand on his feet; and then he prophesies (Ezek. 1:28; 2:2; 3:22–24; cf. Dan. 8:17f.; 10:4ff.). This procedure also describes the Mari ecstatic, a fact that renders plausible the assumption "that the professional was usually sitting, kneeling or crouching until inspiration seized him. . . . (Then) we may imagine him arise and, facing the statue toward the worshippers, become *vox dei.* For the witnesses this must have been an impressive and at times even terrifying experience."[5]

For all the similarities between the Israelite ecstatic and his ancient Near Eastern counterpart, the Bible takes pains to emphasize that the ecstatic phenomenon is not to be equated with divine revelation but is only the psychological preparation for its reception. Above all, the revelation is never self-induced; there is no automatic cause and effect between the trance and the revelation. The latter is always attributed to and dependent on the hand or spirit of the Lord (e.g., 1 Sam. 10:6,10; 18:10; 19:20,23; passim).

Furthermore, although the ecstatic medium is recognized as an authentic vehicle for transmitting the divine message, it is sometimes conceived as an instrument deliberately utilized by God to deceive its audience. Thus the prophets who unanimously predict victory for the kings of Israel and Judah are not liars ("false prophets") but are misled by a "lying spirit," deliberately sent to them by the Lord to deceive their audience (1 Kings 22:19–23).

There is even one case where the ecstatic experience is totally negated as a means of divine communication: "An evil spirit of God (*ruaḥ 'elohim ra'ah*) gripped Saul and he

[literally] became ecstatic (*va-yitnabbe'*) in the house, while David was playing" (1 Sam. 18:10). Here we have all the elements of ecstatic prophesy: induction by music, the descent of the spirit, and the ecstatic result. Yet the spirit is called evil and the effect of the ecstasy is neither prophecy nor inspiration. The Targum to this verse correctly renders *va-yitnabbe'* as *va-'ishtati,* "he [Saul] raved." By the same token most of the other biblical cases of ecstasy also do not lead to a divine message. The contagious ecstatic frenzy of Samuel and his disciples is passed on to Saul's messengers and finally to Saul himself (1 Sam. 19:20–24). But for none of these participants does it yield a divine message. Thus the ecstatic phenomenon is only a symptom of supernatural possession, but its author may be demonic as well as divine; and by no account is it the conveyer of a message.

This limitation upon ecstasy is also affirmed by this chapter and the following one (see Excursus 26), especially by the telling admission concerning the ecstasy of the elders, namely, that it never happened again (v. 25). Thus the ecstatic experience was not for the purpose of transmitting a divine message—no result occurs—but merely as a divine authentication of the election of the elders to leadership. Thereafter, the counsel of the elders stems from their rational judgment and not from their ecstatic experience. True, Moses proclaims: "Would that all the LORD's people were prophets" (v. 29), but this is said in reaction to the spirit of the Lord possessing two individuals (Eldad and Medad) directly, patently bypassing Moses' authority. Thus, by his remark Moses does not come out in favor of ecstasy as a means of prophecy but, in keeping with his humble nature (cf. 12:4), he gives voice to his personal wish that he might share his leadership with all of Israel. In a similar manner, Saul's designation as Israel's *nagid* by Samuel (1 Sam. 10:1) is ratified by God only when Saul experiences ecstatic prophecy (1 Sam. 10:6,10).[6]

Ecstasy, then, is valid because it stems from God and can designate, as in this case, divine election. It can, however, also lead to prophecy that may be false as well as true. It is certainly not a mark of authentic prophecy. Even among authentic prophets, those called by the title *navi',* there is a hierarchy, as reflected in their respective modes of revelation, a matter that is discussed in Excursus 26.

The story of the seventy elders is the prototype for the seventy members of the Sanhedrin (Sif. Num. 92, Sanh. 2b, 17a). Similarly the tradition that charismatic or spiritual gifts were bestowed upon the founders of the first Christian congregation (1 Cor. 12:10,28; Acts 10:44–45) also derives from the story of the seventy elders.[7]

EXCURSUS 26

Prophecy in Israel and the Ancient Near East (11:24–30)

"The *navi'* of today was formerly called a *ro'eh*" (1 Sam. 9:9). In this telling gloss, the biblical writer attests to the original fusion and confusion of the prophet with the clairvoyant (seer). Other offices that must be distinguished from the prophet are the *mitnabbe',* "ecstatic" (Excursus 25), and the *ḥozeh,* "seer." This latter term is first applied to Gad (2 Sam. 24:11, where he is also called a *navi'*). And since there is semantically no distinction between *ḥozeh* and *ro'eh*—both terms imply clairvoyance—the fact that *ḥozeh* is the only term found in reference to a king (*ḥozeh ha-melekh*) implies that it was the official title given to seers attached to the court, the so-called court prophets. This title also seems to have been the common West Semitic designation for clairvoyance since it is attested in the

inscription of King Zakir of Hamath dating to the early eighth century B.C.E.: "I lifted up my hands to Baalsha[mey]n and Baalshameyn answered me [and spoke] to me through *ḥzwn* clairvoyants" (ANET, p. 655, lines 11–12). Similarly, in the eighth-century Deir ʿAlla inscription, biblical Balaam, a true clairvoyant, is referred to as a *ḥozeh* (details in Excursuses 59 and 60).

The clairvoyants mentioned above must, however, be distinguished from diviners who rely upon their magical skill to pry out divine secrets. Divination in all its forms is strictly forbidden in the Bible (e.g., Lev. 19:26,31; cf. especially Deut. 18:10–11). God cannot be coerced by any humanly devised means to reveal His designs. He will communicate His will through dreams and visions but only on His own initiative.

Israel, however, is not the originator of this kind of prophecy. Its antecedents can be traced back fully a millennium to ancient Mari, where charismatic individuals spontaneously appear before the king to deliver a message from the deity. These divinely commissioned messengers are either given the title *muḫḫûm* (fem. *muḫḫūtum*), "ecstatics" (see Excursus 25), or *āpilum* (fem. *āpiltum*), "respondents." The latter appear to be members of a professional group attached to the royal palace or cult and may correspond to the Israelite court prophets, such as Gad and Nathan (e.g., 2 Sam. 7:2; 24:11). As in Mari, Israel also witnesses female prophetesses, including Miriam (Exod. 15:20), Deborah (Judg. 4:4), Huldah (2 Kings 22:14), and Noadiah (Neh. 6:14).

There are noteworthy differences between Israelite prophecy and its Mari antecedents. At Mari the prophet delivers the divine message only to the king never to the people. The message, moreover, is devoid of social or ethical demands. Then, too, the prophet does not have the last word; not only can the king reject the message, its very authenticity can be challenged and the prophet's word submitted to omens for verification. Finally, as noted, no divination is practiced or countenanced in Israel. True, God will reveal Himself in dreams as well as by prophecy (vv. 6–8) and by officially sanctioned and priestly operated Urim and Thummim (27:21; cf. Exod. 28:30) and ephod (1 Sam. 23:9–12); but these latter instruments are equally characterized by the absence of human skill that would imply a coercive effect on the deity. To the contrary, they are the vehicles of the unpredictable and uncontrollable divine communication.[1]

EXCURSUS 27

Sanctification: Preparation for Theophany (11:18)

Israel is commanded in 11:18: (literally) "sanctify yourselves for tomorrow and you shall eat meat." What does "sanctify yourselves" mean? And what has it to do with the following day, "tomorrow"?

Hitkaddesh, "sanctify oneself," is a technical term used by the nonpriestly texts for the process of purification through bathing in order to receive the Presence of the Lord the following day either in the sanctuary or in a theophany.

The *locus classicus* for this phenomenon is the theophany at Sinai. In preparation for this event Moses is commanded: "Go to the people and sanctify them (*ve-kiddashtam*) today and tomorrow. Let them wash their clothes. . . . For on the third day the LORD will come down, in the sight of all the people, on Mount Sinai. . . . Moses came down from the mountain to the people and sanctified (*va-yekaddesh*) the people, and they washed their

clothes. And he said to the people, 'Be ready for the third day: do not go near a woman'" (Exod. 19:10–15). It is clear from this text that the sanctification is accompanied by a laundering and that sexual congress (causing ritual impurity; cf. Lev. 15:18; 1 Sam. 21:5–6) is forbidden. The notion of this sanctification is qualified by the priestly texts, for wherever laundering is commanded so is ritual bathing (Num. 19:19; cf. Lev. 15:5–11,21–22,27). That the term *hitkaddesh* in the epic narratives refers to the ritual bath of purification is attested by the story of David and Bathsheba: "From the roof he saw a woman bathing. . . . She had just purified herself (*mitkaddeshet,* lit. sanctified herself) after her period" (2 Sam. 11:2,4).

The matter of the time element involved in this "sanctification" can be clarified by a few examples. (1) Before crossing the Jordan, "Joshua said to the people, '*Sanctify yourselves,* for *tomorrow* the LORD will perform wonders in your midst'" (Josh. 3:5). Thus, for the waters of the Jordan to rise up miraculously "in a single heap" (Josh. 3:16; cf. Exod. 15:8), that is, for God's Presence to be experienced by Israel, the entire people have to sanctify themselves on the preceding day. (2) Later, during the crisis of Ai, the command is issued: "*Sanctify yourselves* for *tomorrow*. . . . *Tomorrow morning* you shall present yourselves by tribes. Whichever tribe the LORD [literally] marks out with the lot . . ." (Josh. 7:13–14). The casting of lots no less than the miracle of the crossing requires the immediacy of God—on condition that Israel is sufficiently holy to receive Him. Again, their purification takes place on the day preceding the revelation. (3) One of the oldest sources speaks of Jacob's pilgrimage to Bethel in similar terms: "Rid yourselves of the alien gods in your midst, purify yourselves (*ve-hittaharu*), and change your clothes. Come, let us [promptly] go up to Bethel, and I will build an altar there to God . . ." (Gen. 35:2–3). Thus the arrival at the sacred site of Bethel, obviously on the next day (Gen. 35:5–6), must be preceded by bathing and new garments (the equivalent of laundering).

The common denominator in all these examples is that bathing and laundering take place on the day before one is permitted to enter into the Presence of the Lord. Thus it can be assumed that when Korah and his followers are commanded to appear before the Lord the following morning (Num. 16:5,7,16) they must purify themselves by bathing and laundering before nightfall. Conversely, in 1 Samuel 16:5, when the elders of Bethlehem together with Jesse and his sons are commanded by Samuel to sanctify themselves (*hitkaddeshu*) before participating with him in the sacrifice (and Samuel makes sure to sanctify *[va-yekaddesh]* Jesse and his sons so that they, in particular, will show up for the sacrifice), we can be certain that the sacrifice took place only the following morning.

Returning to the theophany at Sinai, we can now understand why the sanctification procedure, bathing and laundering, extended over two days. Because of Israel's momentous confrontation with the divine, especially thorough purifications were indicated, and the theophany took place on the third day.

It is therefore no surprise that the command to gather in the Temple for solemn fasts contains the imperative *kaddesh* (Joel 1:14; 2:15–17). Even the worship of the Canaanite god, Baal, we must assume, prescribed prior purification for the adherents (2 Kings 10:20). The same rules obtained in the war camp. If a soldier "has been rendered unclean by a nocturnal emission, he must leave the camp, and he must not reenter the camp. Toward evening he shall bathe in water, and at sundown he may reenter the camp. . . . Since the LORD your God moves about in your camp . . . let your camp be holy" (Deut. 23:11–15). Thus bathing is a prerequisite for purification. But in this case it is not enough. The war camp is holy, so there must be a time lapse for the residual impurity to wear off totally—the day must end—before the soldier can regain admittance. Of course, sexual congress in the war camp (just

as expressly at Sinai, Exod. 19:15) is strictly forbidden (1 Sam. 21:5–6; 2 Sam. 11:11). Thus it is not surprising that the expression "to prepare for battle" employs the verb ***kiddesh*** (e.g., Jer. 6:4; Joel 4:9; Mic. 3:5).

Finally it should be noted that the priestly texts never use the verb ***kiddesh*** or ***hitkaddesh*** for ritual bathing. This is because they reserve the root ***k-d-sh*** for sacred objects or persons (cf. the Comment to 6:8) and will use that term only when prescribing for Israel a regimen of conduct that will endow all the people with a holy status (e.g., Lev. 11:44; 19:2; 20:26; Num. 15:40). Hence while it eschews the verb "sanctify," it uses the unambiguous verb ***raḥats,*** "wash" (e.g., Num. 19:19; Lev. 14:8–9; 15:5–13; 16:25,28) or, as noted, the verb ***taher,*** "purify" (Num. 8:7; 31:24).

EXCURSUS 28

The Tent of Meeting: Two Traditions (11:16; 12:5)

That there are two traditions concerning the ***'ohel mo'ed,*** "the Tent of Meeting," is clear merely from its two loci: According to the priestly tradition it is located in the very center of the camp (e.g., 2:17; 3:38), and according to the epic tradition it is located outside the camp (e.g., 11:24–27; 12:4–5). Do they refer to the same Tent? Some scholars say yes.[1] There is, however, a rabbinic source that speaks of two Tents, one inside the camp for cultic purposes, the other outside the camp for oracular purposes (Exod. R. 51:2, Tanḥ. Pekudei 5; Tanḥ. B. Exod. 127; Yal. 1.737). Indeed, most moderns follow this rabbinic tradition.[2]

It should be recalled that the priestly Tent also served an oracular function, for it was the focus of God's revelation (see Excursus 15). This can be inferred not only from the meaning of the name of the Tent, that is, "the Tent of Meeting (between God and Moses)" but from the fact that the text frequently takes pains to explain it in that way (Num. 7:89; 17:19; cf. Exod. 25:22,42; 30:6,36). Since the outside Tent, as has been shown, was clearly used for revelation (11:16–30; cf. 12:4–10; Exod. 33:7–11), then both traditions agree that the basic purpose of the Tent was to provide a "meeting" between God and man. However, they definitely differ concerning the mode of revelation. First, whereas the priestly Tent allows only Moses to hear God's voice (and, on occasion, Aaron—but in the courtyard not in the Tent; cf. 16:18–20; 20:6), the outside Tent is available to anyone who seeks an oracle (Exod. 33:7). In the latter instance, Moses or the petitioner stations himself inside while the pillar of cloud descends upon the entrance (e.g., 12:5). This procedure is the prototype for the theophany to Moses and Elijah at Sinai/Horeb when they enter into a scissure and cave, respectively, as the Presence of the Lord passes them by (Exod. 33:22–23; 1 Kings 19:9–14). Moreover, in the priestly Tent, Moses is allowed to enter only the outer room, after the ***kavod***-fire descends from the enveloping cloud onto the Ark-cherubim throne located in the inner room of the Tent (cf. Excursus 22). Thus Moses can hear the voice of the Deity emanating from the inner side of the ***parokhet***-veil; but he cannot behold His Presence (cf. Excursus 15). And, as noted, when God speaks to Aaron or allows Israel to behold His ***kavod,*** the site of the revelation is not inside the Tent at all but in the courtyard of the sacred enclosure. Nonetheless, despite these differences in the mode of revelation, the two Tent traditions concur that the Tent was the medium for revelation.

Another distinction is alleged: The outer Tent did not contain the Ark; in fact, it was empty. However, R. de Vaux has mustered compelling arguments to refute this allegation.[3]

First, the Ark is attested in other narratives as an oracular instrument (Judg. 20:27–28; 1 Sam. 3). Moreover, Joshua was stationed permanently within the Tent (Exod. 33:11; cf. the Comment to 11:28); the only possible reason would be to guard the Ark as Samuel did at Shiloh (1 Sam. 3:3) and Eleazar at Kiriath-jearim (1 Sam. 7:1). Then, too, if the Ark were not in the Tent of Meeting where would it be? It would still require a shelter, a deduction that is confirmed by the tradition that God's Presence was always inside a Tent (2 Sam. 7:6). This must have been a hallowed tradition; otherwise David would not have been prompted to erect a tent for the Ark as soon as he brought it to Jerusalem (2 Sam. 6:17). And as for the objection that the Ark in the epic tradition was in the midst of the camp (Num. 14:44), the term ***bekerev*** may only be a general reference without specifying any particular location (e.g., Deut. 7:14–15; 23:15; and see the translation of Num. 14:44). Thus the probability is strong that the outside Tent also contained the Ark, a factor that would underscore the Tent's oracular function.

Finally, the question needs be asked whether this outside Tent also served a cultic function. Once again, the texts are silent. True, the epic tradition reports that Moses erected altars and officiated on them (Exod. 17:15; 24:3–8; cf. Ps. 99:6). But, significantly, these acts take place before the Sinaitic revelation, that is, before the cultic Tent of Meeting of the priestly tradition was erected. Similarly, the priestly tradition admits that before the consecration of the Aaronide priesthood, Moses himself officiated as a priest (Exod. 29; Lev. 8). However, after Sinai, the epic tradition says nothing concerning sacrifices or any other form of worship. Does this mean that the epic sources knew of a cultic Tent (a view which would be consonant with the rabbinic tradition) but omitted any mention of it sheerly by accident? Or, conversely, did the epic source not have such a tradition? And were references to those sacrifices that continued to be offered up on improvised altars even after Sinai edited out of the text because they conflicted with the priestly Tent tradition? This issue has yet to be resolved.

EXCURSUS 29

The Structure of Chapters 13–14

The overall structure of Numbers 13–14 can be outlined as follows:

A. The Scouts' Expedition (13:1–24)
  1. God decides on reconnaissance (and conquest) (vv. 1–2)
  2. Moses chooses and instructs scouts (vv. 3–20)
  3. Expedition fulfilled: (vv. 21–24)
    [a. All of Canaan] (vv. 21)
    b. The Hebron area (vv. 22–24)
  B. The Scouts' report (13:25–33)
    1. Majority report: objective (vv. 25–29)
    2. Caleb's counterreport (v. 30)
    3. Majority report: subjective (vv. 31–33)
      X. The People's Response (14:1–10a)
        1. Majority response: abandon project (vv. 1–5)
        2. Joshua and Caleb's counterresponse (vv. 6–9)
        3. Majority response: stone opposition (v. 10a)

B′. God's Response (14:10b–38)
    1. Destroy Israel except Moses (vv. 10b–12)
    2. Moses intercedes (vv. 13–19)
    3. God mitigates decree (vv. 20–35)
        [a. Adults die save Caleb (vv. 20–25)]
        [b. Adults die except Joshua and Caleb (vv. 26–35)
        —anticipation of fulfillment (death of spies) (vv. 36–38)]
A′. The People's Expedition (14:39–45)
    1. People decide on conquest (vv. 39–40)
    2. Moses protests (vv. 41–43)
    3. Expedition aborted (vv. 44–45)

Four of the five sections contain three components, as follows: destruction planned, intercession attempted, and destruction fulfilled. Only in the first (A) is there a harmonious progression from God to man to fulfillment. In the other four sections, the first component points to destruction (initiated by scouts, God, or people), the second attempts to avert the destruction, and the third shows that the attempt has failed (except for partial success in B′). The introverted structure of these two chapters becomes apparent upon comparing the parallel sections. A and A′ frame the structure in an inclusion: The people's attempt to retrace the steps of the scouts for the purpose of conquest. They act, however, in defiance of God, and their expedition is aborted. The goal is the same: *ʿalah ha-har,* "go up into the hill country" (13:17; 14:40,44). However, the second expedition meets with frustration, as indicated by the opposite results: "by the LORD's command," "transgress the LORD's command" (13:3; 14:41); "they went up into the Negeb," "the Amalekites . . . came down" (13:22; 14:45); land of fertility, land of destruction (13:23; 14:45).

It is only in BB′ that we find the word *yakhol,* "can [conquer]" (13:30,31; 14:16). The scouts assert that Israel cannot conquer the land; Caleb avers that it can; but if it does not the nations will conclude that it is God who cannot. Therefore, when the scouts say that Israel cannot conquer the land, they really mean that God cannot (cf. also 14:3,4,43). Israel believes its scouts, who see only giants (13:28,32,33). But Israel has been privileged to see God's wonders (14:26) and even His Presence (14:10,14), in contrast to other nations who have only heard (14:13,14,15). Therefore, those whose view is distorted will not view the promised land (14:23).

The middle section, X, is the pivot around which the entire story turns. It follows logically from the preceding, as indicated by the repetition of the following key idioms: Caleb and Joshua confirm that the land indeed is "flowing with milk and honey" (13:27; 14:8) and is "an exceedingly good land" (13:19; 14:7); and as for "the people who inhabit the country" (13:28; 14:9), Israel will devour them and not be devoured (13:32; 14:9). Section X is even more tightly linked to the sections that follow, for it is the people's reaction to the scouts' report that determines the nature and form of their punishment. The murmuring against Moses is exposed as murmuring against God (14:2,27) and is tantamount to rebellion (14:9,11,23,35). Those who would rather die in the desert are destined to do so (14:2,28–29,32). Those who made Moses and Aaron fall in fear of being stoned by the people will fall in death (14:5,29,32). Their children—whom they were certain would be taken captive—are destined to enter the land (14:3,31). In the meantime, only the leaders whom they wished to depose will be saved (14:4,12), whereas those who would rather return to Egypt will now have their wish, only to die on the way (14:4,25). In time, those who feared to die by the sword have their fears realized (14:3,43), those who did not believe

that "God is with us" now discover that He is not (14:9,42–43), and those who would have killed the faithful scouts are killed by the enemy (14:10,45).

Literary criticism has dissected these two chapters into two main sources. Glosses, redundancies, and inconsistencies have been detected (cf. Gray).[1] These trouble spots are debatable but two inconsistencies are irrefutable: (1) The country reconnoitered by the spies is, on the one hand, the entire land of Canaan (13:2,17) from its southern to its northern extremity (13:21), and, on the other hand, it includes only the area around Hebron in the south (13:22–24). (2) Although Caleb appears as both the lone dissenter to the spies' report (13:30) and the lone exemption from the punishment (14:24), he is also joined by Joshua in both these roles (14:6–7,38).

The literary structure of these chapters supports this two-source theory. Section B′, in particular, is ponderous in size (28 verses) and shows signs of duplication and accretion. Thus, verses 36–38 are a redactional interpolation anticipating the long-range result of God's decision. More importantly, there are two passages that describe the mitigation of the divine decree (14:20–25,26–35) and that show not only signs of duplication (e.g., cf. vv. 11 and 25–26; vv. 21 and 28) but contradiction. The first passage (vv. 20–25) posits that, of the adults, only Caleb—and Moses—will survive the trek (14:24); the second (vv. 26–35) includes Joshua (and presumably Aaron; 14:26,30). Section A is also top-heavy (24 verses), due to the inclusion of both the scout list (vv. 4–16) and the two traditions concerning the extent of the territory reconnoitered by the scouts: the Negeb up to Hebron and the entire length of the promised land (e.g., 13:22–24; 21). The two interpolations (13:21; 14:26–38) are attributed by the critics to the priestly source. However, even the main, hypothetically original story contains priestly material. For example, the section 14:1–10 is replete with priestly vocabulary. Thus, one should speak of priestly recensions rather than sources. Diagrammatically, the subdivisions of chapters 13–14 appear as follows:

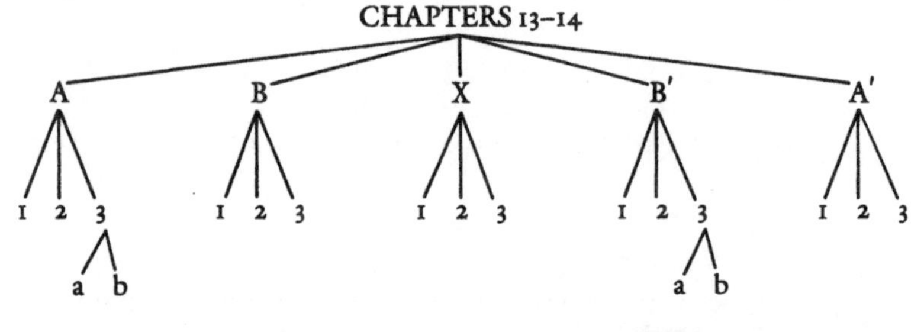

The existence of two separate traditions is confirmed by the Deuteronomic account (Deut. 1:19–46) and its reflex in Joshua (Josh. 14:6–15), which assume that the scouts got only as far as the Hebron area (Deut. 1:24; cf. Num. 32:9) and that Joshua was not among them. This latter point is underscored in Deuteronomy 1:37–38, where another reason is given for Joshua's qualification to enter the land: his appointment as Moses' successor. This can also be deduced from Caleb's remark to Joshua (Josh. 14:7–8), which, by implication, denies that Joshua was a member of the expedition: "Moses . . . sent me [not "us"] . . . and I [not "we"] gave him a forthright report. While my companions who went up with me [not "us"] took the heart out of the people, I [not "we"] was loyal to the LORD my [not "our"] God." Moreover, the Deuteronomic account (as noted in 13:2) attributes the reconnaissance to the initiative of the people (Deut. 1:22) rather than of God (Num. 13:1–3).

As shown by the composite structure, the two traditions have been artfully woven together. However, in one instance in particular, God's response (B′), there is an extra large bulge. The doublet 14:20–25,26–35 throws the structure out of balance. But each contains vital information, and this made it impossible for the redactor to keep one and omit the other. The first includes the promise of Hebron to Caleb (14:25), and the second includes Joshua among the survivors (14:30). Moreover, the two doublets in the structure (A3, B′3) stand in chiastic relationship to each other: The Joshua tradition precedes in the first doublet (A3a), whereas the Caleb tradition precedes in the second (B′3a).[2] Most critics would also claim that the first tradition assumes that only Caleb and his descendants would inherit the land and that the rest of the Israelites, including their children, would die in the desert. However, this is unlikely for it would imply that the only concession Moses won from God (14:20) was for Caleb to enter the land instead of himself (14:12)! Rather, it must be assumed that the first tradition as well as the second posited that the punishment does not include the children (see the Comment to 14:22). This is confirmed by Deuteronomy 1:35, which explains that the term "not one of these men" (cf. Num. 14:22) means "this evil generation."

Despite the dependence of Deuteronomy upon the first tradition (Caleb-Hebron), it is clear that at least in its final form, Deuteronomy had both traditions before it. As shown by the following considerations, the entire text of Numbers 13–14 is reflected in Deuteronomy 1:19–46: (1) The judgment against the adults (Deut. 1:35) implies the exemption of the children. The explicit mention of this in Deuteronomy 1:39 is in the same style and idiom as Numbers 14:31,33 (see chap. 14, Note 50)—the second tradition. (2) Deuteronomy 2:14 is also dependent on 14:33—the second tradition. (3) The expedition consists of one member from each tribe (Deut. 1:23) and is thus based on 13:2, which critics assign to the second tradition. Since the Deuteronomic account gives no indication of having been edited later to harmonize with Numbers 13–14, it must be concluded that the present, composite text of Numbers is old and, more importantly, that *both* traditions preceded the writing of Deuteronomy.

Additional allusions to the composite account of the scouting expedition of Numbers 13–14 can be found in Numbers 26:64–65 and 32:8–13, Psalms 95:10–11 and 106:24–26, and Nehemiah 9:15–17.[3]

EXCURSUS 30

The Scout Typology

In addition to Numbers 13–14, there are other scouting expeditions attributed to Israel during the wilderness and conquest period: at Jazer in Transjordan (Num. 21:32), Jericho (Josh. 2), Ai (Josh. 7:2–3), Bethel (Judg. 1:23), and Dan (Judg. 18). These stories have many elements in common,[1] but, as A. Malamat has observed,[2] the scouting narratives of Israel in the wilderness and the tribe of Dan differ from the others in that their purpose is to gather not only strategic military intelligence but also economic, demographic, and political information. Malamat discusses ten themes common to the two narratives, which can be regrouped as follows:

1. The Danites are an unsettled group, living in temporary encampments (Judg. 18:1,12).

2. Scouts selected from tribal notables are commissioned to gather intelligence in preparation for a military campaign (Judg. 18:2).

3. Regarding the scouts' report—in deliberate contrast to their wilderness forerunners, the Danite scouts bring in a unanimous, favorable report (Judg. 18:7–10).

4. The Danites are momentarily hesitant (Judg. 18:9b)—a faint echo of their ancestors' rebelliousness—but they speedily proceed to the attack.

5. The campaign is conducted in stages, employing the same vocabulary as the wilderness trek: ***va-yiss'u,*** "set out," and ***va-yaḥanu,*** "encamped" (Judg. 18:11–12; cf. Num. 12:16) and giving rise to etiologies concerning the names of the encampments (Judg. 18:12; cf. Num. 11:3,34).

6. An entire ethnic grouping accompanies the soldiers, including women, children, the aged, and their cattle and chattels (Judg. 18:21; cf. Exod. 12:35–38).

7. The Danites bring with them cultic apparatus (Judg. 18:14,17,18,20), which is installed at the final destination (18:30–31), comparable to the Ark and Tabernacle, which accompanied Israel through the wilderness, ultimately to be installed at Shiloh (Josh. 18:1; cf. Judg. 18:31).

8. A Levite priest is engaged for oracular consultation (Judg. 18:19–20; cf. Num. 27:21).

9. The Levite priest of the Danites is identified as Jonathan the son of Gershom the son of Moses; and the priest of the conquest is also of the third generation: Phinehas the son of Eleazar the son of Aaron (Num. 25:7ff.; 31:6; Josh. 22:13).

10. Places conquered and resettled are renamed (Judg. 18:29; cf. Num. 32:41–42).

The striking similarities between the story of the Danite migration and Israel's wilderness journey suggest that the memory of the latter created an archetype, or typology, that imprinted itself on subsequent historical events.

EXCURSUS 31

Caleb (chaps. 13–14)

As indicated in Excursus 29, the scouting expedition of Numbers 13–14 is a conflation of two traditions. The earlier features Caleb as the head of a reconnaissance mission to Hebron and its vicinity. He alone opposes the negative impact of the resident Anakites, in return for which he and his seed are promised the very land he scouted (cf. 13:22,28,30; 14:24). This tradition of an earlier Calebite reconnaissance of the south is supported by Numbers 32:9, by Deuteronomy 1:24, and especially by Joshua 14:7–9, where Caleb informs Joshua (apparently for the first time) that Moses promised him the land that he alone (i.e., without Joshua) reported as conquerable. The subsequent conquest of Hebron is actually attributed to three parties: Caleb (Josh. 14:12–14; 15:13–14), Joshua (Josh. 10:36–37; 11:21), and the tribe of Judah (Judg. 1:10,19–20). However, the tradition that assigns the conquest to Caleb is assuredly more reliable, since it is hardly conceivable that a later period would have attributed the conquest of such an important city—the capital of Judah and the birthplace of King David—to a non-Israelite.

That Caleb was not an Israelite is indicated by his ethnic designation as a Kenizzite (e.g., 32:12). The Kenizzites were originally an Edomite clan (Gen. 36:11,15,42) that later affiliated itself with the tribe of Judah. In this respect they resemble the Kenites who under their leader Hobab also attached themselves to Israel (see the Comment to 10:29) and also

assimilated into the tribe of Judah (1 Sam. 27:10). It can be assumed that the Calebites settled in the Negeb of Judah in the vicinity of Maon and Carmel (on the eastern slopes of the mountain range south of Hebron), since Nabal who lived in this region (1 Sam. 25:2–3) was a Calebite (v. 3b LXX; Targums). It has been suggested that Nabal was a chieftain of the Calebites and that, by marrying his widow Abigail, David laid claim to this position (1 Sam. 25). Thus the magnification of Caleb in the early tradition reflects and legitimates David's coronation in Hebron (the home of the Calebites) as king of Judah.[1] Also the replacement of Nahshon, the leading chieftain of Judah (1:7; 2:3; 7:12,17; 10:14) by Caleb, first among the scouts and later as representative of Judah (34:19), reflects the ascent of David: In the earlier genealogies, he is a descendant of Nahshon (1 Chron. 2:9–17), and, in what is clearly later material, he descends from Caleb (1 Chron. 2:50–51)—all this to legitimate the claim of David to Calebite Hebron.[2] Also, the Negeb of Caleb is listed as a geographic and hence demographic region apart from the territory of Judah (1 Sam. 30:14; cf. 1 Sam. 27:10).

The genealogies of the Book of Chronicles try to attach Caleb to the line of Hezron the son of Perez the son of Judah (1 Chron. 2:1–5) but the linkage is patently artificial since Caleb is not directly attached to the patriarch Judah or his sons (i.e., the principal families of the tribe; cf. also Gen. 46:12; Num. 26:19–22) but to Hezron, the third generation. This can only mean that the main genealogy of Judah had already been established before a place was found for Caleb. The genealogy of 1 Chronicles 4 is important in that it is commonly held that it goes back to the time of King David, which means that the Calebites had affixed themselves to the tribe of Judah before then. Y. Kaufmann believes that the Kenizzites were part of the Judahite stock even in patriarchal times but there is no textual warrant for this hypothesis.[3] The most that can be said with some degree of certainty is that the Calebites are found joined to Israel at Kadesh during the wilderness sojourn and that they are awarded the territory of Hebron as their inheritance.

EXCURSUS 32

Judgment and Mercy: Vertical Retribution and "Salaḥ" (14:18–20)

As noted in the Comment to 14:18, the full form of the formula of God's attributes is found in Exodus 34:6–7: "a God compassionate and gracious, slow to anger, abounding in kindness and faithfulness, extending kindness to the thousandth generation, forgiving iniquity, transgression, and sin; yet He does not remit all punishment [lit. "remit (punishment) he does not remit"] but visits the iniquity of parents upon children and children's children, upon the third and fourth generation."

The formula as it stands divides into two categories: The first speaks of God's mercy, the second (beginning with "yet"), of His justice; that is, punishment is not canceled by mercy but is carried out upon subsequent generations. This formula is basic to the penitential prayers of the Jewish liturgy. Strikingly, however, only the first part of the formula is quoted. Moreover, the quotation stops with ***nakkeh,*** "remit (punishment)," splitting off the rest of the phrase *lo' yenakkeh,* "He does not remit," and thereby totally reversing its actual meaning from "He does not remit all punishment" to "He does remit punishment." Thus it seems that the rabbis have not only quoted selectively but have even done violence to the text by sundering an indissoluble compound idiom in order to force the formula to yield a

meaning of total and unqualified mercy—a meaning it clearly does not have. What has given the rabbis such audacious, indeed scandalous, license?

The first point to remember is that the rabbis are following good biblical precedent. The formula surfaces frequently in biblical petitions and, significantly, always in truncated form. Let these few examples suffice: "But You, being a forgiving God, gracious and compassionate, long-suffering and abounding in faithfulness, did not abandon them. Even though they made themselves a molten calf . . ." (Neh. 9:17–18). What is remarkable about this passage is that it clearly refers to the episode of the golden calf and the original version of the formula; yet the latter is only quoted in part so that God's mercy will appear unqualified! Note also the following: "You are a compassionate and gracious God, slow to anger, abounding in kindness" (Jon. 4:2); "for He is gracious and compassionate, Slow to anger, abounding in kindness" (Joel 2:13); "But You, O LORD, are a God compassionate and merciful, slow to anger, abounding in steadfast love and faithfulness" (Ps. 86:15; cf. Pss. 103:8; 145:8). Thus there is good biblical authority for quoting the formula partially in order to appeal exclusively to God's mercy.

Moreover, one has to recall that the prophetic doctrine of repentance has intervened between the Pentateuchal notion of God's attributes and the later references to God's mercy, cited above. The prophets taught that repentance (*shuv*) not only averts punishment (see Jer. 18:7–11; Joel 2:13–14; Jon. 3:10) but eradicates sin (note the verbs: *maḥah,* "erase," in Isa. 43:25; 44:22; Jer. 18:23; *hilbin,* "whiten," in Isa. 1:18; *rafa',* "heal," in Isa. 6:10; Hos. 14:5; *hishlikh,* "cast [into the sea]," in Mic. 7:19). Therefore, the person who has truly repented need not fear that he will ever face divine retribution for his sin (contrast Exod. 32:34–35; Num. 14:28–35), since his sin no longer exists. It has been expunged from his "book of life" (see Exod. 32:32) such that he starts out life afresh, newborn. Indeed, repentance generates such power that God Himself is overcome by it. If He is determined to punish, He must commission His prophet to stop the people from repenting lest it "save itself" (Isa. 6:10). Thus, if man's repentance can overwhelm God's justice so that only His mercy remains to be activated, is it any wonder that the rabbis, following their prophetic predecessors, felt it only proper and logical to omit God's attribute of retribution when appealing to His mercy.

Finally, as for the "outrage" to biblical grammar by splitting the verbal compound, as noted in the Comment to 14:18, it is attested as early as the Targum: "Pardon those who return to His law but not pardoning those who do not return" (Targ. Onk.; cf. Targ. Jon., Yoma 86a).

Yet the rabbis believed that the entire formula—even its conclusion of vertical retribution—is a plea to God's mercy. Note this example: "R. Judah said: A covenant has been made with the thirteen attributes (Exod. 34:6–7) that they [Israel] will not be turned away empty-handed [when they recite them], as it says, 'Behold I make a covenant' (Exod. 34:10)" (RH 17b). Is there justification for their belief? The meaning of the retribution clause "visiting the iniquity of the parents upon the children" requires closer examination.

There can be no doubt that Israel, along with others in the ancient Near Eastern world, originally held to a strict and literal doctrine of vertical retribution: the deity transferred punishment due to the fathers to their descendants, even though the latter were guiltless. Thus the Hittite king Mursilis exclaims in resignation: "And so it is, the sins of the father have come upon the son; and so my father's sins have come upon me."[1] The historical narratives of the Bible confirm over and over again that this doctrine is part of God's

design. For example, Ahijah the prophet announces that the sins of Jeroboam will be visited upon his son, Abijah (1 Kings 14:10–18). Similarly, the prophet Jehu announces that the sins of Baasha will be visited upon his son Elah (1 Kings 16:1–12). This doctrine undergirds the complaint of the widow of Zarephath to Elijah: "What harm have I done you . . . that you should come here to recall my sin and cause the death of my son?" (1 Kings 17:18). (For other examples, see Lev. 26:39–40; Isa. 14:21; Zech. 8:14; Ps. 109:14; Neh. 9:2.) The stark literalness of this doctrine was well understood by the rabbis: "If it goes ill with the righteous man, his father was wicked" (Ber. 10a).

It is important to note that within the Bible itself, particularly the Deuteronomic corpus, the sharp edge of this doctrine was blunted. Not that the divine right to transfer punishment vertically was denied, but it was qualified: God would visit the fathers' sins upon the children only if the latter themselves proved wicked. This modification (attributable to the Deuteronomist; cf. Deut. 7:9) is particularly impressive in the Decalogue: God visits the sins of the fathers only upon the children "who reject Me" (Exod. 20:5; Deut. 5:9). Conversely, God will show mercy to the thousandth generation "of those who love Me and keep My commandments" (Exod. 20:6; Deut. 5:10). Its influence is felt in other biblical texts, for example, "But the Lord's steadfast love is for all eternity toward those who fear Him, and His beneficence is for the children's children of those who keep His covenant and remember to observe His precepts" (Ps. 103:17–18).

To be sure, even in its ameliorated form this doctrine met opposition within Scripture, especially from the prophetic champions of the opposing doctrine of individual retribution (e.g., Ezek. 18). Nevertheless, the right of God to punish collectively is never explicitly challenged. Indeed, there is one passage in which the two doctrines are juxtaposed: "You show kindness to the thousandth generation, but visit the guilt of the fathers upon their children after them. A great and mighty God whose name is Lord of Hosts, wondrous in purpose and mighty in deed, whose eyes observe all the ways of man, so as to repay every man according to his ways, and with the proper fruit of his deed!" (Jer. 32:18–19). Jeremiah's statement is ostensibly self-contradictory. However, the Deuteronomic modification (Jeremiah's dependency on Deuteronomy is well known) effectively harmonizes the opposing views. For in the same chapter, Jeremiah explains: "The people of Israel and Judah have done nothing but evil in My sight *since their youth*. . . . This city has aroused My anger and My wrath *from the day it was built until this day*" (vv. 30–31). Thus, according to Jeremiah (and Deuteronomy) God punishes the wicked together with their children only if the latter continue in their fathers' ways or, as the rabbis express it, "if they hold the deeds of their fathers in their hands" (Sanh. 27b). For the prophet, then, collective and individual retribution coexist simultaneously in the divine sphere. Both doctrines are legitimate expressions of God's justice. They differ only in their target, the range of humans subject to their jurisdiction. God punishes individually, visiting punishment on the sinner; he in turn passes on the punishment to his progeny if they follow his evil ways.

However, reverting to the Mosaic formula, we note that it is unmitigated by this Deuteronomic qualification: God's punishment will be inflicted on the innocent children. How then can Moses include it in his appeal for mercy? It has been argued that vertical retribution is in reality an aspect of God's mercy: If the sinner will only show contrition, then God, in His mercy, will delay the punishment to a future generation.[2] Certainly, this is the postulate that underlies the death of David's son (2 Sam. 12:13–14) and the postponement of Ahab's punishment. Note the explicit wording in the latter case: "Because he [Ahab] has humbled himself before Me, I will not bring the disaster in his lifetime; I will

bring the disaster upon his house in his son's time" (1 Kings 21:29; cf. 2 Kings 22:19–20 for a similar verdict for Josiah). Perhaps Moses' plea was informed by the same intention—to spare the parents. This supposition finds support in God's response: "Nevertheless . . . none of the men . . . shall see the land" (14:21–23), implying that ordinarily the entire punishment would have been passed on to the children, but Israel's sin being so great or, more probably, because Israel showed no remorse, God insists on punishing them for their sins. (Perhaps it is Israel's explicit show of contrition following the apostasy of the golden calf, Exodus 33:4, that accounts for God's readiness to renew his covenant *with them;* Exod. 34:10).

Further support for this theory can be adduced from the fact that the children of the Exodus generation do indeed bear the sin of their fathers: "while your children roam the wilderness for forty years, *suffering for your faithlessness,* until the last of your carcasses is down in the wilderness" (14:33). Thus it would seem that the innocent children are suffering because their fathers' punishment has been lightened. Indeed, if the sinful generation had been struck down at once as God originally intended (14:12), then, theoretically at least, God might have taken the children straightaway to Canaan. But since God has allowed the parents to die a natural death in the wilderness, the price for this amelioration has to be paid by the children, who must now abide in the wilderness until the last of the parents has died. (Ramban takes a somewhat similar view in his comment on that verse.)

This solution is not without its difficulties, chiefly in the Decalogue, where a quality of mercy has no place in the demand for retribution. First, let it be noted that the doctrine of vertical retribution in the Decalogue is mentioned ahead of God's doctrine of mercy (Exod. 20:5; Deut. 5:9), the exact reverse of what we find in Numbers 14 (and Exod. 34), where it is the last in the attribute chain. This is what we would expect. For when Moses pleads for God's mercy (Exod. 34; Num. 14), he hides the principle of retribution at the end, but when God states the consequences of defection from His worship in the Decalogue, he states the principle of retribution first. Here, then, it cannot mean a transfer of the punishment but its extension to the children: The wrath of God will be so great that it will not burn itself out until a number of generations are consumed. Thus, to judge by the Decalogue, there is no way that the doctrine of retribution can be interpreted as an aspect of God's mercy. To the contrary, it legalizes the divine right not to be bound by the principle of individual retribution that prevails in human justice (Deut. 24:16)—the divine right to punish the innocent along with the guilty. Ibn Ezra was surely correct in observing that the word *salaḥ* cannot be associated with forgiveness in Numbers 14: "Since we have the verse 'they shall not see the land' (14:20) after God said 'I pardoned, as you asked' (v. 20) we know that the expression *selaḥ na',* 'pardon, I pray' (v. 19), [is a prayer that God be] long-suffering [to them but not that they be forgiven]." The question, then, still stands: How could Moses have asked for forgiveness while reminding God of His divine right to punish innocent children as well as guilty fathers?

Another answer can now be put forth. It resides in the meaning of the root *salaḥ,* generally rendered "pardon." Moses requests *salaḥ* (14:19) and receives *salaḥ* (v. 20). Whatever its meaning, the first point to remember is that it is exclusively a divine gift. Only God can be the subject of *salaḥ,* never man! Thus, the inherent parameters of this word set it apart from anthropopathic notions: It does not convey the pardon or forgiveness that man is capable of extending. This point is graphically demonstrated in the series of four intercessions recorded by the prophet Amos: The verb *salaḥ* is synonymous with *ḥadal,* "refrain," and *'avar,* "pass by," and God (on the first two occasions) *niḥam,* "relents"; that

is, He cancels (temporarily) the punishment but not the sin (Amos 7:1–8; 8:1–2). The rabbis share the same view. "It was taught in the school of R. Ishmael (on Mic. 7:18): He puts aside every first [iniquity] and herein lies the attribute of grace. Rabba said: The iniquity itself is not obliterated" (RH 17a). The second point to remember is etymological: In Akkadian the verb ***salāḫu*** means "asperse," and it is the common term in rituals of healing.[3] Thus when God extends man His boon of ***salaḥ,*** He thereby indicates His desire for reconciliation with man in order to continue His relationship with him—in Israelite terms, to maintain His covenant. (For ***salaḥ*** in a covenantal context, see Deut. 29:19; 1 Kings 8:50–51; 2 Kings 24:4; Jer. 5:1,7; Lam. 3:42).

It thus hardly occasions any surprise that Moses' plea for ***salaḥ*** after the apostasy of the golden calf (Exod. 34:9) is met with the following affirmative response by God: "He said, I hereby make a covenant" (v. 10). Since the covenant had been broken, as symbolized by the smashed tablets (Exod. 32:19), it had to be renewed. Its reaffirmation, then, is the most apposite form of divine "pardon" (as recognized by the rabbis in RH 17b).

The matter is entirely the same in the scout episode, indeed, in an even more striking fashion. For Moses bases his plea "according to Your great ***ḥesed***" (14:19), a word that has been rendered as "kindness." But this rendering is a pale reflection of the multivalent richness of this term. Indeed, when God is a subject of ***ḥesed,*** its relation to "kindness" is extremely remote. Rather, it refers to God's fidelity to His commitments, that is, to His covenant. In fact, ***ḥesed*** can actually be a synonym of ***berit,*** "covenant" (e.g., Deut. 7:9,12; 2 Sam. 7:15; 1 Kings 3:6; Pss. 86:5; 89:25,50). Thus, if from the long list of God's attributes, Moses asks Him to operate according to His ***ḥesed,*** he is imploring God to continue to maintain His covenantal relationship with His people (see Rashbam on Exod. 33:18). And when God responds ***"salaḥti"*** (14:20), it can only mean that the covenantal promise of Israel's continuity in its promised land is assured, albeit (***ve-'ulam,*** v. 21) it will only be the next generation that will see its fulfillment.

Thus the problem raised at the outset turns out to be no problem at all. Moses asks for reconciliation not forgiveness, for assurance that Israel will be brought to its land and not that the sin of the Exodus generation will be exonerated. Moses is quite content to invoke the dreaded doctrine of vertical retribution, provided that ***salaḥ*** will also be dispensed, justice will be tempered by mercy, and God will continue as Israel's God and fulfill the promise of His covenant. The text records: "And the LORD said ***salaḥti,*** as you have asked."

EXCURSUS 33

Repentance in the Torah and the Prophets (14:19–20)

In the religion of ancient Israel, as distinct from that of its neighbors, rituals were not inherently efficacious—a point underscored by the sacrificial formula of forgiveness. The required ritual is carried out by the priest, but its desired end, forgiveness, is granted solely by God: "The priest shall make expiation on his behalf for his sin, that he may be forgiven" (Lev. 4:26). Moreover, contrition and confession are indispensable elements of all rituals of forgiveness, whether they are expiatory sacrifices (Lev. 5:5–6) or litanies for fasting (Joel 2:12–14; 1 Sam. 7:5–9).

Indeed, man's involvement, both in conscience and deed, is a ***sine qua non*** for securing divine forgiveness. It is not enough to hope and pray for pardon: Man must humble

himself, acknowledge his wrong, and resolve to depart from sin (e.g., David, in 2 Sam. 12:13ff.; Ahab, in 1 Kings 21:27–29). The Book of Psalms provides ample evidence that penitence and confession must be integral components of all prayers for forgiveness (Pss. 32:5; 38:19; 41:5; Lam. 3:40–42). The many synonyms for contrition testify to its primacy in the human effort to restore the desired relationship with God: seek the Lord (2 Sam. 12:16; 21:1); search for Him (Amos 5:4); humble oneself before Him (Lev. 26:41); and direct the heart to Him (1 Sam. 7:3). If the heart is not involved, the rituals of penitence, such as weeping, fasting, rending clothes, and donning sackcloth and ashes, are unqualifiedly condemned by the prophets (Isa. 1:10ff.; 29:13; Hos. 7:14; Joel 2:12–13).

At the same time, inner contrition must be followed by outward acts; remorse must be translated into deeds. Two substages are involved in this process: first, the negative one of ceasing to do evil (Isa. 33:15; Ps. 15), and then the positive, active step of doing good (Isa. 1:17; Jer. 26:13; Amos 5:14–15). Again the language used to describe man's active role in the process testifies to its centrality: incline the heart to the Lord (Josh. 24:23); make oneself a new heart (Ezek. 18:31); circumcise the heart (Jer. 4:4); wash the heart (Jer. 4:14); and break one's fallow ground (Hos. 10:12). However, all these expressions are subsumed and encapsulated by one verb, which dominates the penitential literature of the Bible, *shuv,* "turn, return." This root combines in itself both requisites of repentance: to turn from evil and to turn to good. The motion of turning implies that sin is not an eradicable stain but a straying from the right path and that by the effort of turning, a power God has given all men, the sinner can redirect his destiny.

It is clear that the term for repentance is not a prophetic innovation but goes back to Israel's ancient traditions: Amos, the first writing prophet, uses it without bothering to explain it (Amos 4:6–11). Moreover, the concept of repentance (though not the term *shuv*) is also assumed in the early narratives about Pharaoh (Exod. 7:3–4; 10:1; 11:10) and the sons of Eli (1 Sam. 2:25). These accounts say that God deliberately blocks their repentance. Finally, the motif of repentance occurs in the tales of the early heroes: David (2 Sam. 12:13–14; 24:10–14), Ahab (1 Kings 21:27–29), and Josiah (2 Kings 22:18–20).

Nonetheless it must be noted that the repentance of these narratives is not the same as that taught by the prophets. First, repentance in the narratives is ineffectual. At best it mitigates retribution (e.g., David) or postpones it (Ahab, Josiah). And on occasion it is of no avail (e.g., to Moses himself; Deut. 3:23–26). Repentance, it is true, is found in the admonitions of the priestly and Deuteronomic texts (Lev. 26:40–42; Deut. 4:29–31; 30:1–10). But in those instances, in contrast to the prophets, it only terminates the punishment; it cannot prevent its onset. The limited scope of repentance in these stories can best be appraised by contrasting it with the success of the people of Nineveh in averting their doom (Jon. 3:1–10).

Secondly, wherever repentance occurs in the early narratives, it is a human virtue. God does not call upon man to repent or upon his prophet to rouse him to repentance. The role of Moses is to intercede for Israel so that God will annul his evil decree (e.g., Exod. 32:11–13,31–34; 34:9; Num. 12:11–13; 14:13–19; Deut. 9:16–29), but not once is he expected to bring his people to repentance so that they might merit divine forgiveness. Other intercessors are also recorded in the early narratives: Abraham (Gen. 18:23–33), Samuel (1 Sam. 7:5–9; 12:25), Elijah (1 Kings 17:17–23), Elisha (2 Kings 4:33; 6:15–20), and Job (Job 42:7–9). These righteous leaders, just like Moses, turn to God to ask for pardon but not to man to urge repentance.

It is against this backdrop that the innovation of the priestly legislation can be

measured. Repentance is operative in sacrificial expiation, as indicated by the terms *hitvaddah,* "confess" (Lev. 5:5; Num. 5:7), and *'asham,* "feel guilt." However, the term *shuv* meaning "repent" never appears in priestly texts. Neither does it appear in the Tetrateuch and early narratives. *Shuv* does occur in four passages in this literature but in the opposite sense of apostasy, turning away from the Lord (Num. 14:43; 32:15; Josh. 22:16,18,23,29; 1 Sam. 15:11). This is as expected, since in the early sources, although Israel is guilty of apostasy, it is never expected to repent.

Shuv as "repent" exhibits the following distribution pattern: twenty-three times in the eighth-century prophets, Amos, Hosea, and Isaiah; fifty times in Jeremiah and Ezekiel; and twenty-eight times in nine postexilic books. Conversely, the use of *'asham,* "feel guilt," which approximates the notion of "repent," is found only in the priestly code (P). Thus it may be concluded that P derived its penitential terminology at a time when *shuv* had not become the standard idiom for repentance. However, under the influence of the prophets, especially Jeremiah and Ezekiel, the root *shuv* overwhelmed all of its competitors. That the priestly doctrine of repentance is preexilic is supported by an additional consideration. Though the power of repentance in P is such that it can reduce a deliberate sin to an unintentional one, P insists that sacrificial expiation (*k-p-r*) is mandatory for the complete annulment of sin. It does not know the prophetic teaching that repentance in itself suffices to nullify sin.

The prophets differ among themselves on the function of repentance, especially in their eschatological prophecies. Isaiah, for example, withdraws the offer of repentance at an early point in his career (cf. Isa. 1:16–20 with 6:9–13). He insists that only the few survivors of God's purge will be allowed to engage in a program of repentance that will qualify them for the new Zion (e.g., Isa. 32:1–8,15–17; 33:5–6). Indeed, he even gives his first-born a name that carries the message: "[Only] A Remnant Will Repent" (Isa. 7:3). In the teaching of Jeremiah, on the other hand, the call to repent is never abandoned. When Jeremiah despairs of men's capability of self-renewal, he postulates that God will provide a "new heart," which will overcome sin and merit eternal forgiveness (Jer. 31:33; Deut. 30:6; Ezek. 36:26–27).[1]

EXCURSUS 34

The "Ger" (15:27–29)

In return for being loyal to his protectors (Gen. 21:23) and bound by their laws (e.g., Lev. 24:22), the *ger,* as indicated by its Arabic cognate *jâr,* was a "protected stranger."[1] Israel regarded itself as a *ger* both in its own land (during the time of the forefathers; Gen. 14:13; 23:4) and in Egypt (Exod. 2:22; Lev. 19:34). Moreover, since the land belonged to God, Israel's status upon it was theologically and legally that of a *ger* (Lev. 25:23). Strangers had attached themselves to Israel during their flight from Egypt (Exod. 12:38,48; Num. 11:14), as did many Canaanites after the conquest (e.g., Josh. 9:3ff.). Therefore, *gerim* could not own landed property and were largely day laborers and artisans (Deut. 24:14–15) or were among the wards of society (Exod. 23:12). Indeed, since the Levites—though Israelites—were also landless, they were dependent on the tribes in whose midst they settled and, hence, they too could be termed *gerim* (e.g., Judg. 17:7; 19:1; Deut. 18:6). Although some

gerim did manage to amass wealth (Lev. 25:37), most were poor and were bracketed with the poor as recipients of welfare (cf. Lev. 19:10; 23:22; 25:6).

Though the *ger* enjoyed equal protection with the Israelite under the law, he was not of the same legal status; he neither enjoyed the same privileges nor was bound by the same obligations. Whereas the civil law held the citizen and the *ger* to be of equal status (e.g., Lev. 24:22; Num. 35:15), the religious law made distinctions according to the following underlying principle: The *ger* is bound by the prohibitive commandments but not by the performative ones. For example, the *ger* is under no requirement to observe the festivals. The paschal sacrifice is explicitly declared a voluntary observance for the *ger:* Whereas an Israelite abstains from the sacrifice on pain of *karet,* the *ger* may observe it provided he is circumcised (Exod. 12:47–48; Num. 9:13–14). In fact, the injunction to dwell in *sukkot* is explicitly directed to the "Israelite citizen" (Lev. 23:42), which, by implication, excludes the *ger.* Similarly, the *ger* may participate in the voluntary sacrificial cult if he follows its prescriptions (Num. 15:14–16; Lev. 22:17ff.).

The injunction that "there shall be one law for you and for the resident stranger" (Num. 15:15; cf. Exod. 12:48–49; Lev. 7:7; 24:22; Num. 9:14; 15:29–30) should not be misconstrued. It applies only to the case given in the context; it is not to be taken as a generalization (cf. Ibn Ezra). Yet, according to the priestly legislation, the *ger* is equally obligated to observe the prohibitive commandments. This conclusion can be derived from the following prohibition incumbent upon the *ger:* "Any person, whether citizen or *ger,* who eats what has died or has been torn by beasts shall wash his clothes, bathe in water, and remain unclean until evening; then he shall be clean. But if he does not wash [his clothes] and bathe his body, he shall bear his punishment" (Lev. 17:15–16). Thus the *ger* and the Israelite are not forbidden to eat carrion but are required to clean themselves of the impurity. The rationale is clear: Failure to eliminate impurity threatens God's land and sanctuary. The welfare of all Israel residing in God's land and under the protection of His sanctuary is jeopardized by the prolongation of impurity. The principle is underscored by chapter 15, which requires the bringing of a communal purification offering to atone not only for individual wrongs of Israelites but for the *gerim* as well (Num. 15:26).

No wonder, then, that the *ger* and the Israelite are equally obligated to refrain from violations that produce impurity. The penalty is *venasa' ʿavono,* "he will bear his punishment," which, in the priestly system, means a purification offering for inadvertent violations (Lev. 4) and *karet* for presumptuous ones (Num. 15:30–31). Moreover, the requirement of a purification offering is imposed for the inadvertent violation of any prohibitive commandment (Lev. 4:2,13,22,27). Perhaps, originally, this sacrifice was limited to those cases where it was explicitly required: the parturient (Lev. 12:6,8), the gonorrheic (Lev. 15:14–15,29–30), the leper (Lev. 14:13,19,30–31), and so on. These cases, it will be noted, deal explicitly with ritually impure persons. However, the heading of Leviticus 4 makes it emphatically clear that this sacrifice is called for upon the inadvertent violation of all prohibitive commandments. Again, the underlying principle is that the violation of all prohibitive commandments creates impurity and consequently pollutes God's sanctuary and land: Sexual offenses and homicide, for example, pollute the land (Lev. 18:27–28; Num. 35:34–35), and Molech worship and corpse contamination pollute the sanctuary (Lev. 20:3; Num. 19:13,20). It therefore makes no difference whether the polluter is Israelite or non-Israelite. Anyone in residence on the Lord's land is capable of polluting it or His sanctuary.

On the other hand, performative commandments are violated by refraining or

neglecting to do them (in rabbinic terms *shev ve-'al ta'aseh,* "sit and do nothing"). These violations are sins not of commission but of omission. They too can lead to dire consequences but only for the Israelite who is obligated by his covenant to observe them. The *ger,* however, is not so obligated. And since they are acts of omission, of nonobservance, they generate no pollution either to the land or to the sanctuary. Thus the *ger,* the resident non-Israelite, does not jeopardize the welfare of his Israelite neighbor by not complying with the performative commandments. As a result, he need not, for example, observe the paschal sacrifice. But if he wishes to, he must be circumcised (Exod. 12:48) and, presumably, must be in a state of ritual purity (Num. 9:6–7,13–14). However, under no circumstances may he possess leaven during the festival (Exod. 12:19; 13:7).

Does this mean that the *ger* is required, as is the Israelite, to observe the minutiae of ritual and ethical prohibitions, such as not wearing garments of mixed seed (Lev. 19:19) or not spreading gossip (Lev. 19:16)? The answer is not clear. Most likely the *ger* is limited in his obligations to refrain only from those violations that engender ritual impurity (Lev. 17:15). True, it would seem from this section, 15:27–29, that the *ger* is required to bring a purification offering for the violation of all commandments, but the meaning of this pericope is unclear (see Excursus 35).

Ostensibly, there is one exception, but it only proves the rule. The exception is the right of the *ger* to slaughter his animals profanely, that is, not as a sacrifice. The priestly tradition equates the *ger* and Israelite in almost all laws of Leviticus 17 that deal with legitimate means of providing meat for the table (vv. 8–9,10,12,13–14,15–16). There are two exceptions: the prohibition of profane slaughter (vv. 3–7) and the requirement to bring the blood of the slain animal to the altar (v. 11). The *ger* is conspicuously absent in the first of these two laws (vv. 3,5). The second law (v. 11) implies this as well by its pronominal suffixes. In verses 10–14, the larger context of which verse 11 is part, the Israelite is addressed in the second person; the *ger* is always in the third person. Thus "to you" and "your lives" (v. 11) can only refer to the Israelites ("to you" but not to others; Sifra 'Aḥarei Mot, parashah 8). These two laws complement each other perfectly. The first states that an Israelite who slaughters the animal for its meat without offering it as a sacrifice is a murderer. The second provides the rationale that the purpose of this sacrifice—indeed, of dousing the animal's blood on the altar—is to atone for killing it. The omission of the *ger* from this law now becomes understandable. The *ger* is permitted nonsacrificial slaughter because (like the non-Israelite in Gen. 9:3–4) he need only drain the blood (the animal being treated like game, vv. 13–14). Conversely, he need not bring his animal as a sacrifice since its slaughter is not sinful for him and requires no sacrificial expiation.

This distinction between the *ger* and the Israelite is also apparent in the corollary prohibition concerning the animal suet: The *ger* may eat it, but the Israelite may not (Lev. 3:17; 7:25). The reason is clear: Suet of sacrificial animals must be offered on the altar (Lev. 7:25), from which may be inferred that suet of game may be eaten. (Note also the contrast: Whereas the prohibition against eating suet falls on sacrificial animals alone, the prohibition of eating blood falls on all animals, including birds; Lev. 7:26.) This leniency toward the *ger* in regard to suet follows logically from his distinction from the Israelites regarding the blood: If the *ger*'s meat need not be offered as a sacrifice, why then his suet?

There is good reason to believe that the status of the *ger* in the priestly laws served as a model for Deuteronomy's subsequent concession of profane slaughter to the Israelite. When it abolished the local altar and declared that the central sanctuary was the only legitimate one, it became impossible to require the Israelite to journey to the central

sanctuary each time he desired meat for his table. Thus the concession was made to the Israelite that he might slaughter his animals profanely, at home, but with the proviso that the blood would not be imbibed (Deut. 12:15–16,20–25).

By suspending the rules of purity governing the eating of sacrificial flesh (Lev. 7:16–21) and by declaring that, henceforth, all animals eligible for food were to be treated as the gazelle and deer (Deut. 12:15,22), Deuteronomy bestowed on them the status of game (cf. Lev. 17:13–14). Moreover, although Deuteronomy takes great pains to reiterate the blood prohibition, it is conspicuously silent regarding the suet. This silence is explicable in the light of the limitation of the suet prohibition to sacrificial animals alone (Lev. 7:25). Thus, in allowing the Israelites to treat all animals as game—in suspending the laws of purity regarding the eating of animals and in conceding, implicitly, the suet of animals as food—Deuteronomy accorded the Israelite the same status as the *ger*. Placed in its historical perspective, the legislation concerning the *ger* served as the model for the Deuteronomic concession to the Israelite concerning the slaughter and eating of animals.

However, Deuteronomy allowed, or rather created, one distinction between the *ger* and Israelite. In the older legislation, the Israelite is forbidden to eat *terefah,* flesh torn by beasts in the field (Exod. 22:30); Deuteronomy forbids him to eat *nevelah,* carrion of animals that died a natural death (Deut. 14:21). The priestly tradition prohibits neither *terefah* nor *nevelah* to the Israelite and the *ger* but only requires a purification ceremony in the event they are eaten (Lev. 17:25–26). Deuteronomy, in forbidding the *nevelah* to the Israelite, has thereby added a prohibition not found in the early sources, presumably so as not to obliterate completely the distinction in this regard between the *ger* and the Israelite; at the same time it imposes the knowledge and the fulfillment of its Torah upon the *ger* (Deut. 31:12).

In sum, the *ger* was expected to observe all the prohibitive commandments, lest their violation lead to the pollution of God's sanctuary and land, which in turn results in God's alienation and Israel's exile. In this regard, both the *ger* and Israelite are subject to the same law, with the exception—explicitly stated—that the *ger* does not have to slaughter his animal at the authorized altar but may slaughter it, like game, in the field. In essence, this concession is only a concomitant of the main distinction between the *ger* and the Israelite: The *ger* must observe the prohibitive commandment not to worship other gods (Lev. 17:8–9), but he is not compelled to observe the performative commandment to worship Israel's God.

It must be remembered that the *ger,* the resident alien of biblical times, is a far remove from the *ger,* the convert of rabbinic times. Conversion as such was unknown in the ancient world. Ethnicity was the only criterion for membership in a group. The outsider could join only by marriage (e.g., Ruth). In fact, it was not those who intermarried but the subsequent generations that succeeded in assimilating and even then not always (e.g., Deut. 23:1–9). Some *gerim,* like the Kenites (Moses' family; Judg. 1:16), were ultimately absorbed into Israel, presumably by marriage. Others, like the Gibeonites, maintained their slave status throughout the biblical period (Josh. 9:27; cf. Ezra 2:58).

The first glimmer of a new status for the *ger* is found in the words of the Second Isaiah at the end of the sixth century B.C.E. In the Babylonian exile, non-Jews had been attracted by the Jewish way of life, particularly by the Sabbath. Isaiah calls upon these would-be proselytes to "make *ʿaliyah*" with the Israelites; and although he cannot promise them that they will be part of the *ʿam,* the peoplehood of Israel—conversion as such was unknown—he assures them that the Temple service will be open to them because "My house will be

called a house of prayer for all peoples" (Isa. 56:7). The way is now open to the next stage of religious conversion, a stage already reached by the year 200 B.C.E. At that time Antiochus III issued a decree fining any foreigner who entered the Israelite court of the Temple (equivalent to "the entrance of the Tent of Meeting") the sum of 3,000 silver drachmas, payable to the priests[2]—a far cry from the biblical *ger* who could enter the Tabernacle court to offer his sacrifices. Clearly, the Jews of the third century B.C.E. were not in violation of the Torah for by then they had reinterpreted the Torah's *ger* to denote the convert.[3]

EXCURSUS 35

The Two Sections on the Purification Offering

(Lev. 4:3–21 and Num. 15:22–31)

Leviticus 4:3–21 and Numbers 15:22–31 seem to be dealing with the same issue: the inadvertent wrong committed by the entire community, which is expiable by sacrifice. However, they are not identical. First, the sacrifices are not the same: Leviticus 4 requires a bull for a purification offering, whereas Numbers 15 requires a bull for a burnt offering and a male goat for a purification offering (and appropriate supplements for the burnt offering). Second, the nature of the sin is not the same: Leviticus 4 deals with the inadvertent violation of a prohibitive commandment (vv. 2,13,22,27), whereas Numbers 15 is concerned with the inadvertent violation of any commandment (vv. 22–23). These differences lead Ibn Ezra (on Num. 15:27) to postulate that these ostensibly similar laws are in reality dealing with two different sins: Leviticus 4 with prohibitive commandments (*lo' ta'aseh*) and Numbers 15 with performative commandments (*'aseh*). And therefore they require different expiatory sacrifices. Thus if the community inadvertently violated the Passover (e.g., they mistakenly celebrated it on the wrong day), they would have brought (1) the purification offering of Leviticus 4 for violating the prohibition against eating leaven during the actual festival (Exod. 12:15) and (2) the required sacrifices of Numbers 15 for neglecting to perform the Passover sacrifice on the proper day (Num. 9:13).

This solution, however, was faulted by Ramban who noted that the Numbers passage cannot be limited to performative sins alone since the verb *'asah,* "do, act," in "if this was done unwittingly" (v. 24), "anyone who acts in error" (v. 29), and "who acts defiantly" (v. 30) predicates an active violation, one that involves actually doing something rather than passively neglecting to do something.

Indeed, as noted by *Sefer ha-Mivḥar,* the language of Numbers 15: *kol hamitsvot* . . . *kol'asher tsivvah,* "any of the commandments . . . anything that the LORD has enjoined" (vv. 22,23), must be understood literally: the word *kol* embraces all the commandments, positive and negative, performative and prohibitive. Abetting this insight is the recognition that not only this section but indeed the entire chapter emphasizes the totality of the commandments. First, it should be noted that verses 22b–23, clearly an editorial interpolation, have been added to underscore the fact that all the commandments are involved. It says in effect that sacrificial expiation is required for the violation not only of prohibitive commandments of Leviticus 4 but of all commandments, including performative ones. Second, as noted, this section contains no heading, thus connecting it with the previous section of *ḥallah* (vv. 17–21). The intent is clear: *ḥallah* and the sacrificial supplements in the preceding section (vv. 1–16) are positive, performative commandments and are there-

fore also subject to the prescribed penalties. Finally, the last unit in this chapter, the *tsitsit* (vv. 37–41), contains the identical emphasis: "all the commandments of the LORD and observe them" (v. 39); "observe all My commandments" (v. 40). Here we find the same usage of *'asah* and *kol mitsvot* as in verses 22,23. The reason for the inclusion of the *tsitsit* ritual in this chapter is now clear: The *tsitsit,* itself a performative commandment, will be a constant reminder to its wearers of the *totality* of the commandments, performative as well as prohibitive, thus preventing or at least lessening the chance of their inadvertent neglect or violation.

In sum, verses 22–31 emphasize that all inadvertencies are subject to sacrificial expiation and the attachment of these verses to other performative commandments that make up this chapter; that is, sacrificial supplements (vv. 1–16), *ḥallah* (vv. 17–21), and *tsitsit* (vv. 37–41) point to a qualification of the position taken in Leviticus 4. Not only prohibitive commandments require sacrificial expiation for their inadvertent violation but also performative ones. Thus one cannot say that Leviticus 4 and Numbers 15 speak of discrete sins, which would therefore warrant discrete sacrificial solutions. Both require sacrificial expiation for inadvertent violation of prohibitive commandments; but Numbers 15 also requires it for the inadvertent violation of performative ones. There is, in other words, an overlap: One must seek another explanation of the relationship between the two.

We would suggest that the purpose of Numbers 15 is to avoid the impression given by Leviticus 4 that only the inadvertent violation of prohibitive commandments is subject to sacrificial expiation. Recently, A. Toeg has gone one step further by proposing that Numbers 15 is actually a reworking of Leviticus 4.[1] Briefly stated, he posits that the Leviticus text was shortened by eliminating the sacrificial procedure and then lengthened in order to emphasize the elements of inadvertency (vv. 25b,26), the stranger (e.g., v. 29), and presumptuousness (vv. 30–31). At the same time, it was subjected to a major change: The purification offering bull became the burnt offering bull to which the purification goat and the former's supplementary meal and wine were added. Thus "a bull of the herd as a purification offering" (Lev. 4:14) was expanded to "one bull of the herd [as a burnt offering of pleasing odor to the LORD, with its proper meal offering and libation, and one he-goat] as a purification offering" (Num. 15:24).

I would add one important bit of evidence in support of Toeg's theory: The sacrificial requirement is governed by the verb *'asah,* "[the community shall] sacrifice" (v. 24). The verb *'asah,* a technical term in the cult, means "sacrifice," that is, perform the entire sacrificial ritual (e.g., Num. 6:11,16,17; 8:12; 9:5; Exod. 10:15; Lev. 4:20; 9:7; 14:19,30; 15:15,30; 16:9,24; 17:9; 23:19). It is therefore a descriptive term that tells exactly how and in what order the sacrificial ritual is to be performed. Now in all rituals calling for the use of both the burnt offering and the purification offering, the latter is invariably offered first.[2] As has already been pointed out in the law of the Nazirite (chap. 6), even though the prescriptive ritual lists the burnt offering ahead of the purification offering (6:10,14), the descriptive ritual puts the latter offering first (6:11,16–17). It is important to realize that the descriptive ritual always uses the verb *'asah* but the prescriptive ritual uses a different verb. Thus in the induction of the Levites, the prescriptive text lists the burnt offering first (8:8), but the descriptive text puts the purification offering first and uses the verb *'asah* (8:12). Indeed, a descriptive ritual can be identified simply by its use of *'asah;* and, conversely, a prescriptive ritual is characterized by the use of some other verb. For example, the sacrificial order for the parturient (Lev. 12:6,8), which ostensibly violates the rule by listing the burnt offering before the purification offering, is in fact only a prescriptive text because it employs the

verbs *hevi'* and *lakaḥ* but not the verb *'asah.* (Lev. 23:18–19 is also not an exception, even though, in this case, *'asah* is used and the burnt offering still precedes the purification offering. In this case, *'asah* refers solely to the purification offering, whereas the burnt offering has its own, different verb.)

Thus Leviticus 4 must be a prescriptive ritual since it does not use the verb *'asah,* whereas Numbers 15 can only be descriptive since it does use the verb *'asah.* However, here we encounter an exception to the rule: Although the verb is *'asah,* the burnt offering is listed first! The solution therefore suggests itself that originally only one sacrifice was listed. And when one compares Numbers 15 with Leviticus 4, it is clear that the sacrifice was the purification offering. Not wanting to detail the complex procedure of Leviticus 4:15–20, the text replaced the verb by *'asah,* thereby telescoping the entire ritual. Thus "the congregation shall offer a bull of the herd for a purification offering" became "the whole community shall sacrifice (*ve-'asu*) one bull of the herd for a purification offering." In other words, the verb *'asah* was correctly applied to one sacrifice. However, when the burnt offering and its accompaniments were added before the purification offering, as noted above, the verb *'asah* remained even though it was not strictly applicable.

This solution, despite its virtues, is subject to two serious objections: (1) It does not explain why the other cases of the purification offering found in Leviticus 4 are missing in Numbers 15. It might be suggested that Numbers 15 has no interest in the cases of the High Priest (Lev. 4:1–12) or of the chieftain (*nasi'*) (Lev. 4:22–26). But why omit the option of offering a ewe by the individual (Lev. 4:32–35)? After all, the ewe—the animal rejected—is attested elsewhere as the individual's purification offering (e.g., by the leper in Lev. 14:10; by the Nazirite in Num. 6:14). In selecting the she-goat as the exclusive offering for the individual (Num. 15:27), the text picked the animal that appears in no other case as a purification offering. (2) In the alleged reworking of the text of Leviticus 4 there is yet another unaccounted-for change. Instead of referring to the community as *kahal* (Lev. 4:14–21), it is consistently called *'edah* (Num. 15:24,25,26). It has already been shown that *'edah* is the old technical term for the Israelite community (see Excursus 1), and it is thereby hardly likely that *kahal* would have been replaced by a more archaic term.

Thus the attempt to find literary dependency between the two purification offering pericopes must be abandoned. There is no alternative but to assume that we are dealing with two independent traditions concerning the purification offering. But what of the term *'asah,* which strongly suggests that only one sacrifice was originally stipulated by Numbers 15:24?

The probability rests with R. Rendtorff,[3] who on other grounds suggests that verse 24 originally stipulated only the burnt offering and that the purification offering was added later. He correctly points to the burnt offering as initially being the sole expiatory sacrifice both for the nation (e.g., Judg. 20:26; 21:2–4; 1 Sam. 7:6; 9:10; 13:12; 2 Sam. 24:25) and for individuals (Jer. 7:21–22; 14:12; especially Job 1:15; 42:7–9). The evidence from this non-cultic literature is confirmed by the priestly code, which continues to permit the use of the burnt offering as the individual's sole expiatory sacrifice (e.g., Lev. 1:4). The rabbis express a similar view: Originally the "open altars (*bamot*) were permitted and only the burnt offering was sacrificed" (Tosef. Zev. 13:1). However, the Torah made this alteration: It added the purification offering to the burnt offering for all fixed, public sacrifices. The precedence of the burnt offering can be detected even here by the fact that all the public sacrifices require male animals; this includes the purification offering, which, however, is limited everywhere else to females (e.g., Lev. 4). That the burnt offering must be a male,

therefore, can only mean that originally it was the only public sacrifice; and when other sacrifices were added to the public cult, they were made to conform to the standard of the burnt offering. (It should be stated parenthetically that other claims made by Rendtorff must be rejected: V. 24a does not refer to an individual whose sin has harmed the community; such a case is predicated only of the High Priest [Lev. 4:3] not of the commoner. And the purification offering described in v. 25b is not a later interpolation: Since the purification offering is not an *'isheh,* it had to be listed separately. See the Comment to that verse.)

Thus, Numbers 15:22–31 represents a tradition of communal expiation different from that of Leviticus 4. In its earlier stage it required only the bull of a burnt offering, but when the purification offering was added, it was made to conform with the male requirement for sacrificial animals used in public, expiatory sacrifices: It thus became a bull and a he-goat. (The combination of a burnt offering bovine and the purification offering he-goat is found in Lev. 9:3 and in the cultic calendar, Lev. 23:18–19 and Num. 28–29.) As for the individual's inadvertency, whereas Leviticus 4 allows either a female goat or sheep, Numbers 15 permits only the female goat. (Even in this common case of the female goat, the language is not the same: e.g., *se'irat 'izzim* in Lev. 4:28; *'ez bat shenatah* in Num. 15:27.) Moreover, the Numbers passage shows important innovations. Foremost among them is the ordinance, found nowhere else, that presumptuous sins are not eligible for sacrificial expiation but are punished by *karet* (vv. 30–31). Other important additions are the inclusion of the resident alien and the special emphasis on the factor of inadvertency. Of equal significance, as noted, is the inclusion of all the commandments—performative as well as prohibitive—under the rule of sacrificial expiation and *karet.*

Finally, once it is accepted that we are dealing with two independent traditions, the possibility must be left open that Numbers 15, like Leviticus 4, speaks only of prohibitive commandments. *'Asah bishgagah,* "do . . . inadvertently" (v. 29), implies an act of commission; that is, a prohibitive commandment has been violated. It is the equivalent of the wording of Leviticus 4:22: "doing (*ve'asah*) inadvertently (*bishgagah*) any of the things which by the commandment . . . ought not to be done." If this be the case, then the commandments referred to in verse 22 cannot refer to the previous performative commandments (vv. 1–20); and the entire pericope (vv. 22–31) may be the displaced conclusion of another legal section. As yet, this problem cannot be resolved.[4]

EXCURSUS 36

The Penalty of "Karet"

Jewish exegesis unanimously holds that *karet* is a divine penalty, but there is disagreement concerning its exact nature. Among the major views of what constitutes *karet* are the following: (1) childlessness and premature death (Rashi on Shab. 25a); (2) death before the age of sixty (MK 28a); (3) death before the age of fifty-two (Rabad); (4) being "cut off" through the extirpation of descendants (Ibn Ezra on Gen. 17:14); (5) the death of the soul at the time of the body's death so that it will not enjoy the spiritual life of the hereafter (Maimonides, Yad, Teshuvah 8.1; cf. Sif. Num. 112 and Ramban on Lev. 20:2). Most moderns, to the contrary, define *karet* either as excommunication or death by man.[1]

The latter theory can be discounted as soon as one classifies the specific instances of the

karet: All fall within the category of religious law not civil law; that is, they are deliberate sins against God not against man. Given the cardinal postulate of the priestly legislation that sins against God are punishable by God—and not by man[2]—it follows that the punishment of *karet* is executed solely by the Deity. The nineteen cases of *karet* in the Torah can be subsumed under the following categories:

A. Sacred time
1. neglecting the paschal sacrifice (Num. 9:13)
2. eating leaven during the Feast of Unleavened Bread (Exod. 12:15,19)
3. working on the Sabbath (Exod. 31:14)
4. working or not fasting on Yom Kippur (Lev. 23:29,30)

B. Sacred substance
5. imbibing blood (Lev. 7:27; 17:10,14)
6. eating suet (Lev. 7:25)
7. duplicating or misusing sanctuary incense (Exod. 30:38)
8. duplicating or misusing sanctuary anointment oil (Exod. 30:33)
9. eating of a sacrifice beyond the permitted period (*piggul*) (Lev. 7:18; 19:8)
10. eating of a sacrifice in the state of impurity (Lev. 7:20–21)
11. encroachment by the Levites upon sancta (Num. 18:3; cf. 4:15,19–20)
12. blaspheming, that is, desecrating God's name (Num. 15:30–31; cf. Lev. 24:15)

C. Purification rituals
13. neglecting circumcision (Gen. 17:14)
14. neglecting purification after contact with the dead (Num. 19:13–20)

D. Illicit worship
15. Molech and other forms of idolatry (Lev. 20:2–5; Ezek. 14:5)
16. consulting the dead (Lev. 20:6)
17. slaughtering animals outside the authorized sanctuary (Lev. 17:4)
18. sacrificing animals outside the authorized sanctuary (Lev. 17:9)

E. Illicit sex
19. effecting forbidden consanguineous and incestuous marriages (Lev. 18:27–29)

Thus the rabbinic view that *karet* is a divine penalty is upheld. As for the exact nature of *karet,* two of the five opinions registered above command attention. The first is that *karet* means extirpation (Ibn Ezra); that is, the offender's line is terminated. In contrast to the death penalty inflicted by man (*yumat*) or God (*yamut*), *karet* need not be directed against the person of the sinner. His life may be aborted but not necessarily. His death need not be immediate as it would be if his execution were the responsibility of a human court. And although the rabbis of the Talmud define *karet* as signifying a premature death (example 2), such cases as are attested in the Torah never use the term *karet* (Nadab and Abihu in Lev. 10; Dathan, Abiram, and Korah in Num. 16; the plagues in Egypt and in the wilderness in Exod. 11; Num. 11–14).

That *karet,* instead, refers to extirpation is supported by the following cases: (1) "May his posterity be cut off (*le-hakhrit*); may their names be blotted out in the next generation" (Ps. 109:13). This verse is significant because of its parallelism: It equates *karet* with extirpation, and it states explicitly that *karet* need not be carried out upon the sinner himself; it will befall his descendants. (2) "That the name of the deceased may not disappear (*yikkaret*) from among his kinsmen" (Ruth 4:10). Boaz the Levir redeems Ruth in order to

perpetuate the line of her deceased husband. (3) "May the LORD (literally) cut off (*yakret*) from him who does this all descendants dwelling in the tents of Jacob" (Mal. 2:12). There is some doubt that *'er ve-'onah* means "descendants," but the context clearly speaks of the extirpation of the line. (4) "[Dathan and Abiram and other families] vanished (*va-yo'vdu*) from the midst of the congregation" (Num. 16:33). Although the root *karet* does not occur, it is replaced by the attested synonym *'avad* (e.g., Lev. 23:30; Deut. 7:24). (5) "The LORD blots out (*u-maḥah*) his name from under heaven" (Deut. 29:19). The context is the clandestine worship of idols. Although the root *karet* does not occur, the Deuteronomic text employs its synonym *maḥah.* Only God can discern the crime (cf. v. 28 and Ibn Ezra), and He punishes it by extirpation. Furthermore, *karet* as extirpation would be consonant with the priestly doctrine that God can hold men collectively accountable: Whereas man may punish only the sinner, God may take out His wrath on the sinner's family and community.

Further illumination is provided by the context of the Malachi passage cited above. The priests are accused of scorning God's name by offering defiled food on the altar and presenting a blind, lame, or sick animal for sacrifice (Mal. 1:6–8). As punishment, the Lord states: "I will strew dung upon your faces, the dung of your festal sacrifices, and you shall be carried out to its heap" (Mal. 2:3). The Hittite "Instructions for Temple Officials" offers a striking parallel: "If . . . the kitchen servant . . . gives the god to eat from an unclean (vessel), to such a man the gods will give dung (and) urine to eat (and) to drink."[3] Furthermore, the *karet* penalty, which the Lord will impose upon the offender and his descendants, is precisely matched in this Hittite text: "Does the god take revenge on him alone? Does he not take revenge on his wife, his children, his descendants, his kin, his slaves, his slave-girls, his cattle (and) sheep together with his crop and will utterly destroy him?"[4] The resemblance between the two documents is so remarkable that the possibility must be entertained that the Hittite text lay before Malachi.[5] In any event, the comparison between the two clarifies the exact meaning of *karet:* extirpation of the entire line of the offender.

The other possible meaning of *karet* is that the punishment is indeed executed upon the sinner but only after his death; that is, he is not permitted to rejoin his ancestors in the afterlife (example 5). This meaning is supported by the idiom that is its opposite in meaning: *ne'esaf 'el,* "be gathered to one's [kin, fathers]" (e.g., Num. 20:24; 27:13; 31:2). Particularly in regard to the patriarchs, the language of the Bible presumes three stages concerning their death: They die, they are gathered to their kin, and they are buried (cf. Gen. 25:8,17; 35:29; 49:33). "It (the term 'gathered') designates something which succeeds death and precedes burial, the kind of thing which may hardly be considered as other than reunion with the ancestors in Sheol."[6] This biblical idiom has its counterpart in the bordering river civilizations of Egypt ("going to one's Ka") and of Mesopotamia ("joining the ghosts of one's ancestors"),[7] all of which is evidence for a belief in the afterlife that permeated the ancient world and for the concomitant fear that a wrathful deity might deprive man of this boon. This interpretation would be in keeping with *karet* as an individual not a collective retribution.

It is difficult to determine which of these two meanings is correct. Since they are not mutually exclusive, it is possible that *karet* implies both: no descendants in this world and no life in the next. Whether *karet* be defined as extirpation or denial of afterlife, or both, it illuminates two cruxes of *karet.* Leviticus 20:2–3 reads that anyone who "gives any of his offspring to Molech shall be put to death; the people of the land shall pelt him with stones. And I will set My face against that man and will cut him off (*ve-hikhratti*) from among his

people." The accepted interpretation, for example, by Abravanel, is that if man does not put the Molech worshiper to death, God will. But the two sentences in the text are not alternatives; they are to be taken conjunctively: Death plus *karet* awaits the criminal. This means that *karet* is not synonymous with death but is another form of punishment, which only the Deity can execute. Thus extirpation or mortality or both fits the context. The same conjunction of judicial death plus *karet* is prescribed for the Sabbath violator (Exod. 31:14). Again, it implies that God and man will punish simultaneously: Man will put him to death, and God will extirpate his line and/or deny him life in the hereafter.

EXCURSUS 37

The Case of the Wood Gatherer (15:32–36)

Moses could not decide the case of the wood gatherer. Was the act in violation of the Sabbath? Assuming that it was, how should the offender be punished? The question of the violation will be dealt with first. Gathering wood on the Sabbath is clearly not mentioned anywhere as an instance of Sabbath desecration. The only explicit Sabbath prohibitions in the Torah regard work and kindling a fire (Exod. 35:2–3). Thus the question before Moses may well have been: Does gathering wood on the Sabbath constitute work?

According to some, however, the answer must have been an unequivocal "yes," in which case there was no need to resort to oracle. The narrative about the gathering of the manna (Exod. 16:22–30) provides a clear analogy. Although there is no explicit formulation of this prohibition, Israel is implicitly warned not to gather manna on the Sabbath: "How long will you men refuse to obey My commandments and My teachings? . . . Let no man leave his place on the seventh day" (vv. 28,29). Moreover, this prohibition can be logically deduced: If the priestly law forbids the gathering of food on the Sabbath even though its consumption is, of course, permitted, how much more so would it forbid the gathering of wood, whose purpose would be for kindling—an explicit sin (Exod. 35:3)? Hence, the law concerning the gathering of wood would have been amply clear to Moses on the analogy of the gathering of manna: It was a willful desecration of the Sabbath. Indeed, there is no doubt that in Jeremiah's time, carrying a burden was a Sabbath violation (Jer. 17:21,27; cf. Neh. 13:15–22), but clearly the origin of this prohibition is older, and it is so intimated by the Torah narratives.

How was this violation of the Sabbath to be punished? For the rabbis, there was no doubt about the verdict: The wood gatherer merited capital punishment. The only question remaining in Moses' mind was the mode of execution. "Our master Moses knew that the wood gatherer [had incurred the penalty of] death, as it is said, 'He who desecrates it shall be put to death' (Exod. 31:14), but he did not know by what mode of execution he should be killed" (Sanh. 78b). Moses then consulted the divine oracle and the response was "death by stoning" (Sif. Num. 112; Sif. Emor 14:5; Targ. Jon. on v. 32; Shab. 96b). This explanation is unconvincing: One could assume that stoning was the accepted mode of execution (Deut. 13:11; 17:5; 21:21; Lev. 20:2,27; 2 Chron. 24:21; Ezek. 16:40; 23:47; 1 Kings 21:13), especially since it is specified by oracle (Lev. 24:14; Josh. 7:25).

The answer suggests itself only upon examination of the Sabbath law itself. The penalty for violating the Sabbath is stated in only one context: the building of the Tabernacle (Exod. 31:14–15; 35:2). Moreover, a double penalty is stipulated: death by man and *karet* by

God (Exod. 31:14). That these penalties are not identical and that they are conjunctive rather than exclusive has been shown in Excursus 36. Indeed, this double penalty is unusual (found elsewhere only with Molech worship; Lev. 20:1ff.). Moreover, it is not the death penalty of *karet* that is striking—sins against God are generally punished by God. Rather, the surprising element is that the violation of the Sabbath calls for death at the hands of man. The reason seems to be that the public violation of the Sabbath and the public worship of idolatry (e.g., the Molech) would demoralize the entire community if not immediately punished.

The novel element of imposing death by man for an offense against God—violating the Sabbath—is projected in clear relief by contrasting the Sabbath penalty with that imposed for the violation of the Day of Atonement. Indeed, the only other day that ranks with the Sabbath in holiness and severity is the Day of Atonement. These two days alone are called a *shabbat shabbaton*, "a sabbath of complete rest" (Lev. 23:3,32). On these days alone is there a total cessation of labor, *kol mela'akhah*, "all work" (Exod. 20:10; Num. 29:7), whereas on all other holidays only *mele'khet 'avodah*, "laborious work," is prohibited (cf. Num. 28:18,25,26; 29:1,12,35).[1] Yet the violation of the Day of Atonement, also a capital crime, is punishable solely by *karet* and not by judicial execution (Lev. 23:29–30).

Thus the prescription of judicial death in addition to *karet* is novel—startling—and demands explanation. That explanation, we submit, is supplied by case law, the precedent of the wood gatherer. The text of this case predicates that Moses indeed did not know the penalty for the violation of the Sabbath. Work was forbidden on the Sabbath, particularly that of gathering, as stipulated by the Ten Commandments (Exod. 20:10) and the case of the manna (Exod. 16:27–29). But in neither instance was a penalty stipulated. To be sure, the penalty is indeed prescribed in the context of the building of the Tabernacle (Exod. 31:14–15; 35:2). But the Sabbath law is not germane to the context; it is an editorial insertion to indicate that the need to build the sanctuary should not overrule the required Sabbath rest.

There is one other example of Moses resorting to an oracle for a legal decision. This is the case of the blasphemer (Lev. 24:10ff.), and it illumines our problem. First, it should be noted that Moses consults the oracle because he does not know the law. Indeed, although the act is proscribed (Exod. 22:27), the penalty is nowhere stated in the Torah. Even the rabbis concede that Moses leaves that answer to God (Sifra Emor 14.5, Sanh. 78b). Similarly, it may have been ignorance of the penalty for Sabbath violation that motivated Moses, once again, to inquire of the oracle. Furthermore, the case of the blasphemer indeed serves as a precedent for the generalized law against blasphemy, as indicated clearly by the context: A citation from a law code dealing with capital punishment and talion is inserted into the narrative of the case (Lev. 24:17–22). Finally, all the ancient traditions agree that it was Moses' exclusive function to consult the oracle for legal decisions: "You represent the people before God: you bring the disputes before God" (Exod. 18:19).

It is therefore proposed that the case of the wood gatherer, which was decided by oracle, provided the precedent for the principle that all work on the Sabbath would be punishable by death and *karet*. Furthermore there is no need to be concerned that the generalization is now found in Exodus and the case in Numbers. The case of the wood gatherer could have happened at any time during the wilderness sojourn. It was placed here in juxtaposition to the *karet* law of 15:30–31 for yet another reason: to inform us that he who "acts defiantly" to "spurn the word of the Lord," "revile the Lord," and "violate His commandments" in respect to the Sabbath shall be not only "cut off from his kin"

(vv. 30–31) but also stoned to death (vv. 35–36). That is to say, whereas brazen violations of God's commandments are punished by *karet,* the brazen violator of the Sabbath is also executed judicially. Of course, the assumption must be made that the wood gatherer acted in open defiance of the prohibition. Had his act been committed inadvertently then he would have been allowed sacrificial expiation (vv. 27–29). Indeed, even the sectaries of Qumran, despite their harsher code of Sabbath observance, also declared: "However, anyone who mistakenly profanes the Sabbath and the festivals shall not be put to death."[2]

EXCURSUS 38

The Tassels "Tsitsit" (15:37–40)

In his commentary on *tsitsit* (Num. 15:37–41), Ibn Ezra writes: "In my opinion one is more obligated to wear the *tsitsit* when not in prayer so that one will remember not to go astray in sin at any time, for in the time of prayer one surely will not sin." Ibn Ezra's comment is a reminder that the *tsitsit* commandment enjoins—and early practice attests—the attaching of the *tsitsit* to the outer garment. They were worn all day long. Indeed, the term *tallit*—the prayer shawl containing the *tsitsit,* which the Jew wraps about himself each morning in prayer—is actually the rabbinic term for outer garment, again alluding to the fact that *tsitsit* were worn throughout the day.

The nature of *tsitsit* is illuminated by the literature and art of the ancient Near East, which shows that the hem was ornate in comparison with the rest of the outer robe. The more important the individual, the more elaborate the embroidery of his hem. Its significance lies not in its artistry but in its symbolism as an extension of its owner's person and authority. Its use is best illustrated by the Akkadian *sissikta batāqu,* "to cut off the hem." For example, an exorcist pronounces an incantation over the detached hem of his patient's garment; a husband who cuts off the hem of his wife's robe thereby divorces her.

A reflex of this practice is found in the Bible in what heretofore was a puzzling dialogue. King Saul has pursued David into the Judean hills. Saul enters a cave and removes his cloak to relieve himself, unaware that David and his men are hiding in the cave. David sneaks up on the unsuspecting Saul and cuts off the hem from his cloak. The text then relates that "afterward David reproached himself for cutting off part of the hem of Saul's cloak. He said to his men, 'The Lord forbid that I should do such a thing.'" When Saul realizes what David has done, he responds: "I know now that you will become king" (1 Sam. 24:6,20). What was the reason for David's remorse and for Saul's response? The answer rests in the meaning of the hem: It was an extension of Saul's person and authority. David felt remorse in taking it because God had not so ordered. Saul, however, regarded it as a sign from God that his authority had been transferred to David: He was now cut off from the throne.

The legal force of the hem in ancient Mesopotamia is evidenced in other ways. In ancient Mari, a professional prophet or dreamer would enclose with his report to the king a lock of his hair and a piece of his hem. They served both as his identification, and more important, as a guarantee that his prediction was true. In effect, these articles gave the king legal control over their owner. Another legal context of the hem is illustrated by clay documents, on which the impression of a hem replaces a signature. Today a nonliterate

might sign with his fingerprints; in ancient Mesopotamia, however, it was the upper class that might use the hem.

E. A. Speiser has made the attractive suggestion that the practice in the synagogue to this day of pressing the edge of the *tallit* to the Torah scroll is a survival of this ancient custom.[1] This act followed by the recital of blessings may well have originated as a dramatic reaffirmation of the participant's commitment to the Torah. He thereby pledges both in words (blessing) and in deed (impressing his "signature" on the scroll) to live by the Torah's commandments.

That *tsitsit* are an extension of the hem is profusely illustrated in ancient Near Eastern art. In one picture, a pendant *tsitsit* is clearly evident, taking the form of a flower head or tassel, thus supporting the rendering "tassel" for *tsitsit.* Our biblical text, moreover, enjoins that *tsitsit* be attached to the corners of the garment. But how can a closed robe or skirt have corners? There are two possibilities. One figure shows that the *tsitsit* are only the extended threads of the embroidered vertical bands, which, instead of being cut off at the hem, are allowed to hang free. These bands terminate at quarter points of the hem, thereby forming four "corners." Another figure illustrates a second possibility. Here the skirts are scalloped and the tassels are suspended where the scallops meet. Our text validates this mode of dress. It prescribes that the *tsitsit* be attached to the *kanaf,* a term that does not mean "corner" but "extremity" or "wing"; and, strikingly, a scalloped hem is the winged extremity of the garment. Thus the significance of the *tsitsit* (as well as of the elaborate hem) lies in this: It was worn by those who counted; it was the identification tag of nobility.

The requirement of the *tekhelet,* the violet cord, gives further support to the notion that *tsitsit* signified nobility. The violet dye was extracted from the gland of the murex snail (*ḥilazon;* Sif. Deut. 354, Shab. 26a, Men. 42b). There are three relevant varieties of the murex snail. The *Murex trunculus* gives a blue-purple or violet color, and the *Thais haemastoma* (also called *Purpura haemastoma*) and *Murex brandaris* give a red-purple color.[2] Both the red-purple dye (Heb. *'argaman;* Akk. *argamannu*) and the blue-purple (Heb. *tekhelet;* Akk. *takiltu*) were used in the manufacture of the inner curtain of the Tabernacle (Exod. 26:1) and of the garments of the High Priest (Exod. 28:6,15,31,33).

The industry based on the dye of the murex snail may have originated in the Greek world rather than in the Phoenician world, as previously supposed. Accumulations of these snail shells have been found in Knossos, Troy, and the Attic coast, dating to the early second millennium B.C.E.[3] On the other hand, similar accumulations of snail shells from the fifteenth century have been found at Ugarit on the Phoenician coast of the Mediterranean.

The *Murex trunculus* can be gathered by hand in the shallow waters off the coast of Lebanon and northern Israel (ancient Phoenicia). Apparently the production of dye from these snails was so important that the city of Haifa in Hellenistic times was called Porphurion (purple). The other two varieties of murex snails used to make the required dye had to be harvested from deeper waters with the use of nets or traps.

The manufacture of the dye is minutely described by Pliny, the Roman historian and naturalist of the first century C.E., in his *Historia Naturalis.* However, his data are insufficient to reproduce the process. Since the mid-nineteenth century, European chemists have attacked the problem but without success.[4] Recently a group from Lebanon has reported success in reproducing the dye.[5] The Center for Maritime Studies of the University of Haifa has been studying the living habits of the snails and simultaneously conducting archaeo-

logical research at several installations where the dye was manufactured: Tell Acre; Tell Mor; Shikhmona; and Tell Keisan, where the dye may have been imported,[6] so we may be very close to solving the mystery of the dye's production.

The method of extracting the dye can be deduced from observing the many ancient shells containing single holes expertly drilled over the locations of the snails' hypobranchial glands. Many others of these ancient shells had been broken at their apex, which also releases the dye.[7]

Though the snails are plentiful, the amount of dye each yields is infinitesimal. In 1909, tests by the Austrian chemist Paul Friedländer[8] demonstrated that 12,000 snails were needed to provide 1.4 grams of pure dye. No wonder that during the reign of Nabonidus, the last king of Babylon (555–539 B.C.E.), purple wool was forty times more expensive than wool dyed with other colors. In 200 B.C.E. one gram of the dye cost $84, or $36,000 per pound. Diocletian paid the equivalent of $8,460 for 328 grams of purple silk from Sidon, or $11,724 per pound. In 300 C.E. the demand raised the price of this Sidonian silk to $98,700 per pound (all figures are in 1984 dollars).[9]

The Bible apparently assumed that even the poorest Israelite could afford at least four violet threads, one for each tassel. Indeed, by using crude instead of pure dye, it is possible to attain ten times the yield.[10] Thus one violet thread would require fewer than fifteen snails. However, only the very rich could afford large quantities of this dye. Indeed, Roman emperors retained for themselves the exclusive privilege of wearing purple mantles, thus giving rise to the color names still used today, "royal blue" and "royal purple." Byzantine emperors were born in purple rooms, that is, "born to the purple," and the title Porphyrogenitus was added to their names. The Bible also affirms that violet cloth was worn by nobility (Ezek. 23:6; Esther 1:6). Thus weaving a violet thread into the *tsitsit* enhances its symbolism as a mark of nobility. Further, since all Jews are required to wear it, it is a sign that Jews are a people of nobility. Their sovereign, however, is not mortal: Jews are princes of God.

Tsitsit have undergone many changes in Jewish practice, and a brief review of their history is indicated. The requirement of the violet cord was suspended in rabbinic times (Mish. Men. 4:1, Num. R. 17:5). The Jewish community following the two Roman wars was so impoverished that many could not afford even the one violet-dyed cord required for each *tsitsit*. Moreover, the dye industry apparently declined and the *tekhelet* became scarce (Men. 42b). To be sure, a cheap counterfeit violet had been developed from the indigo plant but the rabbis disqualified it as *tekhelet* (Sif. Num. 115, BM 61b, Men. 42b–43a). These factors contributed to the suspension of the violet cord requirement, and since then *tsitsit* have been totally white.

Another historical fact revealed by early rabbinic sources is that *tsitsit* were worn by women. In fact, some of the rabbis actually affirmed that *'af ha-nashim be-mashma'*, that is, women are *required* to wear *tsitsit* (Sif. Num. 115, Men. 43a) because they fall into the category of a commandment whose observance is not limited to a fixed time (*she-'ein ha-zeman gerama'*; Tosef. Kid. 1:10).

Finally, because the *tsitsit* marked their wearer as a Jew and because, as a powerless minority within a hostile majority, it might single him out for persecution, it was then ordained that the *tsitsit* should be transferred to an inner garment (*tallit katan*). Nevertheless, among pious Ashkenazi Jews to this day the *tsitsit* are still visible, in fulfillment of the commandment: "and you shall see them" (v. 39).

The purpose of the *tsitsit* is set out by a series of verbs: "look . . . recall . . . observe" (v. 39). These three verbs effectively summarize and define the pedagogic technique of the ritual system of the Torah: sight (i.e., the senses) combined with memory (i.e., the intellect) are translated into action (i.e., good deeds). Thus the experience of rituals and the comprehension of their values lead to loftier ethical behavior. The text also adds a negative purpose: to bridle the passions (v. 39) and thereby, according to the rabbis, prevent heresy and harlotry (Sif. Num. 115).

The final purpose of the *tsitsit* is indicated in verse 40, the conclusion of the pericope: "Thus you shall be reminded to observe all my commandments and to be holy to your God." The ultimate goal of seeing the *tsitsit,* reminding oneself of God's commandments and fulfilling them, is to attain holiness. The nobility to which Israel belongs is not like other power structures characterized by corruption and self-indulgence. Israel is commanded to be "a kingdom of priests and a holy nation" (Exod. 19:6).

But what is there about the *tsitsit* that would remind its wearer of holiness? The earliest rabbinic sources, perhaps dating back to biblical days, taught that the *tsitsit* are *sha'atnez,* a mixture of wool and linen (LXX, Targ. Jon. to Deut. 22:12; cf. Rashi, Ibn Ezra on Deut. 22:12, Men. 39b–40a, 43a, Lev. R. 22:10). In fact white linen cords and dyed woolen cords were found in the Bar Kockba caves, proving that the rabbinic teaching was actually observed. Now the wearing of *sha'atnez* is forbidden to the Israelite (Lev. 19:19; Deut. 22:11), patently because it would resemble some of the priestly garments made from a blend of linen and wool (e.g., Exod. 28:6; 39:29; the colored cloths are wool). In fact, the High Priest's linen turban (Exod. 28:39) is bound by a *petil tekhelet,* a violet woolen cord (Exod. 28:37). Thus *sha'atnez* is forbidden because it is a holy mixture, reserved exclusively for priests and forbidden to nonpriests. That *sha'atnez* is forbidden because it is holy can be derived from the injunction: "You shall not sow your vineyard with a second kind of seed, else the crop—from the seed you have sown—and the yield of the vineyard (literally) will become sanctified (*yikdash*)" (Deut. 22:9); that is, it will belong not to you but to the sanctuary. However, early in the rabbinic period it was taught—perhaps stemming from a biblical practice—that every Israelite should wear *tsitsit* made of *sha'atnez.* (Cf. also Tosafot on Deut. 22:11.) Thus the *tsitsit,* according to the rabbis, are modeled after a priestly garment that is taboo for the rest of Israel!

The *tsitsit,* then, are an exception to the Torah's general injunction against wearing garments of mixed seed. But, in actuality, inhering in this paradox is its ultimate purpose. The resemblance to the High Priest's turban and other priestly clothing can be no accident. It is a conscious attempt to encourage all Israel to aspire to a degree of holiness comparable to that of the priests. Indeed, holiness itself is enjoined upon Israel: "You shall be holy, for I, the LORD your God, am holy" (Lev. 19:2; cf. 11:44; 20:26). True, Israelites not of the seed of Aaron may not serve as priests (cf. 17:5) but they may—indeed, must—strive for a life of holiness by obeying God's commandments. Hence, they are to attach to their garments tassels containing one violet cord, a woolen thread among the threads of linen. Indeed, the use of mixed seed in the prescribed garments reveals a gradation in holiness. The outer garments of the High Priest are *sha'atnez;* the belt of the ordinary priest is *sha'atnez* (Exod. 39:29; cf. Yoma 12b); and the fringes of the Israelite are *sha'atnez* by virtue of one violet woolen thread. The fact that the cord is woolen and violet marks it as a symbol of both priesthood and royalty, thereby epitomizing the divine imperative that Israel become "a kingdom of priests and a holy nation."

It was Aimé Pallière, a French Catholic preparing for the priesthood, who sensed the true significance of the *tsitsit* when he chanced to enter the synagogue on Yom Kippur. He describes his experience in these words:

That which revealed itself to me at that moment was not at all the Jewish religion. It was the Jewish people. The spectacle of that large number of men assembled, their shoulders covered by the tallit, suddenly disclosed to my eyes a far-off past. . . . At first on seeing the prayer-shawls uniformly worn by all the participants in the service, I felt that in a way they were all officiating. . . . It seemed to me that this silent assembly was in expectancy of something to happen . . . a spirit of expectancy and faith in the future which stamps its entire cult with a special seal. In fact, in the synagogue service all Jews are equal, *all are priests* [italics mine], all may participate in the holy functions, even officiate in the name of the entire community, when they have the required training. The dignity which distinguished the Hakham, the doctor, the sage, is not a clerical degree but rather one of learning, and of piety quickened through knowledge. The tallit would have given me the understanding of that peculiarity of Judaism which would have escaped me, had my attention not been captured from the first by this spectacle so new to me, of a multitude of men in white shawls at prayer. It is thus that rites and symbols often constitute a more expressive language than the best of discourses.[11]

To recapitulate: The *tsitsit* are the epitome of the democratic thrust within Judaism, which equalizes not by leveling but by elevating. All of Israel is enjoined to become a nation of priests. In antiquity, the *tsitsit* (and the hem) were the insignia of authority, high breeding, and nobility. By adding the violet woolen cord to the *tsitsit,* the Torah qualified nobility with priesthood: Israel is not to rule man but to serve God. Furthermore, *tsitsit* are not restricted to Israel's leaders, be they kings, rabbis, or scholars. It is the uniform of all Israel.[12]

EXCURSUS 39
Korah's Rebellion: A Study in Redaction (chap. 16)

Numbers 16 is a composite. As such, it is riddled with difficulties. Merely to scan this chapter projects the more obvious ones: In the difficult text of verses 1–2, Korah, Dathan and Abiram, and the chieftains oppose Moses. In verse 3 they oppose Aaron as well as Moses, attacking their exclusive priestly (*kedoshim*) and civil (*titnase'u-nasi'*) power. Moses' response in verses 4–7 predicates that the attack is only against Aaron; he devises an incense test so that God will choose His priest. Moses, however, has been addressing a fourth group of mutineers, the Levites (which implies that *'adato* in v. 5 refers to Levites). Verses 8–11 contain Moses' second response to the Levites: Your sanctuary job is honor enough; in craving the priesthood you defy not Aaron but God. (Again, *'adatekha* means Levites.) In verses 12–15 Dathan and Abiram refuse to answer Moses' summons. (Thus, they were not among the cohorts of Korah who massed against Moses in v. 3.) They murmur not against Aaron's priesthood but against Moses' authority (*tistarer/sar,* v. 13; cf. Exod. 2:14), which they patently crave (v. 15a). The scene in verse 16 shifts back to Korah and his cohorts. The incense test criteria are repeated (vv. 16–17; cf. vv. 6–7), but it is the chieftains and not the Levites who are the antagonists (*'adatekha* in v. 16 means chieftains). Korah then incites the whole community (*'edah*) against Moses and Aaron. The latter

intercede, pleading that only the sinner(s) should suffer. Verses 23–34 find the community at the dwellings of Korah and Dathan and Abiram! Moses, accompanied by the elders, goes there and commands the community to withdraw. Dathan and Abiram have emerged from their tents with their families. Moses prophesies to them that they will be swallowed by the earth. They are—including Korah's people (contra Num. 26:11). In the meantime, the chieftains are incinerated by a divine fire at the Tabernacle (v. 35). The fate of Korah himself is not clear. Undeniably, then, chapter 16 is a composite. Abravanel is surely correct that it contains three rebellions in one; or, more accurately, three rebellions are ***fused*** into one: Dathan and Abiram versus Moses, Korah and the chieftains versus Aaron, Korah and the Levites versus Aaron. In truth, a fourth rebellion should not be overlooked: Korah and the community (***ʿedah***) versus Moses and Aaron, as will be shown below.

Four major problems stand out in this chapter: the discreteness of the Dathan and Abiram rebellion, the ambiguity concerning Korah's death, the incense test doublet (vv. 6–7,16–17), and the abrupt displacement of the community from the Tabernacle to the conspirators' dwellings (vv. 23–34). Each problem requires some elaboration.

The discreteness of the Dathan and Abiram story can best be appreciated by reference to the two following chapters. Although the rebellions of Korah, the chieftains, and the community are mentioned or alluded to in chapter 17 (vv. 5,6, 14,16–21), there is not a word about Dathan and Abiram. Because Dathan and Abiram are neither at the sanctuary nor rebelling against the priesthood, they have no logical place in chapters 17–18, whose theme is the encroachment upon the priesthood and the sanctuary.

It therefore occasions no surprise that Dathan and Abiram have nothing in common with the other rebels in chapter 16. Indeed, the joins between their story and the others bristle with difficulties. Note the following: Dathan and Abiram, in contrast to the other rebels, register no complaint against Aaron. They contend with Moses, yet they are not found with their fellow conspirators when the latter combine against Moses (vv. 3,12). The ***ʿedah*** that assembles at their tents is simultaneously at the Tabernacle (vv. 19,26). Although Moses removes the ***ʿedah*** from this scene before the quake, they are recorded as fleeing from it afterward (vv. 17,34). The transitions between Dathan and Abiram's story and the others are awkwardly abrupt (vv. 12,16,25); moreover, the two stories employ a different terminology: ***suru me-ʿal*** (v. 26) versus ***heʿalu mi-saviv*** (v. 24); ***minḥatam*** (v. 15) and not ***korbanam; ziknei yisraʾel*** and ***yisraʾel*** (vv. 25,34) rather than ***ziknei ha-ʿedah*** and ***ha-ʿedah.*** Thus, all the evidence points to the conclusion that the rebellion of Dathan and Abiram must originally have been an independent story, totally disassociated from Korah and his band. Furthermore, its discreteness is corroborated by the rehearsal of God's wilderness miracles in the Book of Deuteronomy: It reports the fate of Dathan and Abiram but says nothing concerning Korah (Deut. 11:6).

The second major problem of chapter 16 is the ambiguity concerning Korah's death. In linking Korah's dwelling with those of Dathan and Abiram (vv. 24,27), the Masoretic text seems to favor the joint swallowing of Korah and Dathan and Abiram. Moreover, among those specified as engulfed by the quake are ***kol ha-ʾadam ʾasher le-koraḥ,*** "all Korah's people" (v. 32). The objection may be raised that this wording does not state explicitly that Korah himself died in this manner. The objection, however, can be parried when it is realized that this wording may have been modeled after a similar account preserved in Deut. 11:6. The relevant verses are herewith aligned.

Num. 16:32:	*va-tiftaḥ ha-'arets 'et piha va-tivla' 'otam ve-'et bateihem*
Deut. 11:6:	*patsetah ha-'arets 'et piha va-tivla'em ve-et bateihem*
Num. 16:32:	*ve-'et kol ha-rekhush ve-'et kol ha-'adam 'asher le-koraḥ*
Deut. 11:6:	*ve-'et oholeihem ve-'et kol hayekum 'asher be-ragleihem*

The possibility suggests itself immediately that an original *'asher lahem,* a phrase found in the contiguous verses (vv. 30,33), was altered to *'asher le-koraḥ* in order to include Korah in the death of Dathan and Abiram and to exempt his children, who founded the Korahite line (Num. 26:58). Lastly, that this indeed was the reading of the Masoretic text is clear from Numbers 26:10a–11, which states explicitly: "The earth opened its mouth and swallowed them up with Korah. . . . The sons of Korah, however, did not die."

On the other hand, there are sufficient hints in chapter 16 and elsewhere in Scripture that Korah met his death in the sanctuary fire. According to the doublet 16:5–7,16–17 (especially the second passage, which emphasizes the presence of Korah), he was among those who vied against Aaron in the incense test at the Tabernacle. Moreover, if, as postulated above, Korah was not in the original Dathan and Abiram story (v. 32), then he was not swallowed but must have been burned. That Korah perished in the divine fire is also presumed by Numbers 17:5: It states explicitly that "no outsider . . . should presume to offer incense before the LORD and suffer the fate of Korah and his band"; and it glosses "no outsider" with the comment "one not of Aaron's offspring," a pointed reference to Korah and the Levites. Since 17:1–5 is but a continuation of 16:35, which describes the death of the 250 at the Tabernacle fire, the conclusion is ineluctable, at least for the writer of this passage, that Korah shared the fate of the 250. The Samaritan version (26:10) also explicitly reads that Korah died by fire with the 250. Finally, Numbers 27:3 assumes that even if Zelophehad had died with Korah's *'edah* his daughters would have survived, an eventuality that is possible only in the case of fire. In a quake, his entire family, like that of Dathan and Abiram, would have perished.

Thus, the death of Korah remains ambiguous, as both solutions are derivable from the text. The ambiguity is also reflected in the ancient versions and commentaries. Thus, the Samaritan (Num. 26:10) and Josephus (Ant. 4.55–56) opt for death by fire, whereas the Mishnah follows the quake tradition (Sanh. 10:3). Indeed, both traditions are actually recorded in the Talmud (Sanh. 110a).

The third major problem of chapter 16 concerns the doublet of verses 6–7,16–17: In the first, Korah heads the Levites; in the second, he heads the chieftains. The rebellion of the latter is punished by fire (v. 35), but there is nary a word concerning the test to the Levites and its outcome. Yet, that Korah should have led the Levites' uprising makes better sense because he himself is a Levite. Furthermore, what historical reality can lie behind a rebellion of chieftains led by a Levite? But if the chieftains' rebellion was indeed originally dis-associated from Korah, there is no sign of that reality in the Masoretic text, which links Korah's name inextricably with the chieftains. In any event, the chieftains and the Levites represent various traditions of the incense test; and the fact that the Levite story is truncated may point to its being a later insertion.

The fourth major problem concerns verses 23–27, a passage that contains (1) the abrupt displacement of the *'edah* from the Tabernacle to the conspirators' dwellings, (2) the use of *mishkan* for dwellings, a term that can only mean the Tabernacle, and (3) the inclusion of Korah even though he is not an active participant in the debacle to come (vv. 27b–34).

These four problems indicate the location of the last redactional changes—removing them from the text reveals its penultimate stage of organization. The results are presented in the following chapter outlines:

I. PENULTIMATE RECENSION

Introduction: Korah, Dathan and Abiram, chieftains versus Moses and Aaron (vv. 1–4) (earlier version)

A. Dathan and Abiram versus Moses (vv. 12–15)

B. Korah and chieftains versus Aaron (vv. 16–18; *'adatekha* means chieftains)

C. Korah and *'edah* versus Moses and Aaron (vv. 19–22)
1. At the Tabernacle (v. 19)
2. God threatens *'edah* (vv. 20–21)
3. Moses and Aaron intercede (v. 22)

C'. *'Edah* spared at the Tabernacle (vv. 23–24,26a,27a; *mishkan YHVH**)

B'. Korah and the chieftains incinerated at the Tabernacle (v. 35; plus Korah: *va-tetse' 'esh**)

A'. Dathan and Abiram swallowed (vv. 25,26; minus *'edah*; vv. 27b–34; minus Korah, *lahem**)

II. ULTIMATE RECENSION (MT)

Introduction: Korah, Dathan and Abiram, chieftains versus Moses and Aaron (vv. 1–4) [Korah and Levites versus Aaron (vv. 5–7, 8–11; *'adatekha* means Levites)]

A. Dathan and Abiram versus Moses (vv. 12–15)

B. Korah and chieftains versus Aaron (vv. 16–18)

C. Korah and *'edah* versus Moses and Aaron (vv. 19–22)

C'. *'Edah* spared at *dwellings* of Korah and Dathan and Abiram (vv. 23–27a)
1. God orders removal of *'edah* (vv. 23–24)
2. Moses removes *'edah* (vv. 25–27a)

A' + B' (part). Korah and Dathan and Abiram swallowed (vv. 27b–34)

B' (part). Chieftains incinerated (v. 35)

These structural outlines of Numbers 16 lead to certain conclusions: Two stages in the redactional process can now be discerned. Unfortunately, earlier, prepenultimate stages can no longer be separated out; only certain hints remain, such as the unrelatedness of Korah to the rebellions of the chieftains and of Dathan and Abiram. The integrity of the latter story is a certainty, as has been shown. Moreover, its isolation from the narrative (vv. 12–15,25–34*) now allows its literary artistry to be projected in clear relief. The refrain (literally) "we will not go up" forms an inclusion to their address to Moses (vv. 12,14). Moreover, their refusal to "go up" is punished by their being made to "go down" (vv. 30,33). Indeed, for charging that Moses had (literally) "brought us up . . . to have us die in the wilderness" (v. 13), they will "go down alive into Sheol" (vv. 30,33). Thus, the Dathan and Abiram story is an independent literary entity that, perhaps, had already taken the form of an epic prior to its incorporation into our text.

In the penultimate recension, Korah is the leader of the chieftains' rebellion (vv. 16–18; cf. 17:5, 14). However, he is still disassociated from Dathan and Abiram, a fact reflected in the construction of the introductory verse: ***va-yikaḥ koraḥ . . . ve-datan,*** "Korah . . . *and* Dathan took" (v. 1). Also, as indicated above, Korah met his death in the Tabernacle fire while offering incense with the 250 chieftains (vv. 16–18,35) after the rebellious ***'edah,*** instigated by Korah, was removed from the Tabernacle (***mishkan YHVH*;*** vv. 24,27). Verse 35, then, was the original ending of the Tabernacle rebellion account. It would have contained Korah's name.

This penultimate recension reveals a clear introverted structure, ABCC'B'A', that is both logical and aesthetic. The rebellions proceed in an ever-widening scope: They are led respectively by individuals (Dathan and Abiram), 250 chieftains, and finally by the entire community (***'edah***). The rebellions are first against each of the two leaders, Moses and Aaron, and then against them jointly. The outcome of the rebellions is presented in inverse order: The ***'edah*** is spared by the leaders' intercession, but the other mutineers are slain by God; Korah and the chieftains are slain by fire, followed by Dathan and Abiram, who are slain by earthquake. That the penultimate composite reveals a discernible structure leads to the conclusion that a recension of the rebellion materials had been made prior to the Masoretic text.

In the ultimate recension, corresponding to our received text, three changes took place: (1) Korah's death was transferred from the Tabernacle fire to the earthquake that engulfed Dathan and Abiram, for the purpose of associating him with them. The following textual alterations were then mandated: ***Mishkan YHVH**** became ***mishkan koraḥ datan va-'aviram*** (vv. 24,27); ***lahem*** became ***le-koraḥ*** (v. 32), based on Deuteronomy 11:6 (see above), and the ***'edah*** was transposed from the Tabernacle to the ringleaders' dwellings. (2) The Levite passage was inserted (vv. 5–11), becoming the fourth rebellion fomented by Korah. However, the crescendo effect of the structure was thereby broken: A group (Levites; vv. 5–11) now preceded individuals (Dathan and Abiram; vv. 12–15), and a second revolt against Aaron (vv. 5–11) was tacked on, thereby unbalancing the ascending order (Moses, Aaron, Moses and Aaron). The Levite rebellion survives only in its beginnings: Neither the test nor the punishment is accounted for. The reason for this omission is obvious: Both the test and the fate of the Levites are identical with those of the chieftains; hence they could be dispensed with. Neither would these elements have been missed: Korah's ***'edah*** (v. 16) was sufficiently protean a term to stand for the Levites as well. (3) Finally, the verse describing the incineration of the chieftains was transferred to the end of the fused version in order to serve as an introduction to the new account of the salvaging and dedication of the censers (17:1–5) and to the subsequent stories and laws in chapters 17 and 18. In this manner "encroachment upon sancta" becomes the major theme, in keeping with the early chapters of the Book of Numbers. The displacement of verse 35 also broke the chiastic structure, which necessitated the removal of Korah's name from the verse. In sum, new rebellion material was added to the hitherto complete structure in order to attribute all the received traditions about rebellions against Moses to the machinations of Korah.

Subsequent references to Korah's rebellion seem to reflect the Masoretic text and not the penultimate recension. This certainly holds true for Numbers 26:9–11, which groups Korah and Dathan and Abiram in the quake debacle; and by its reference to the incineration as ***ba-'akhol 'esh,*** "when the fire consumed," it reflects the present reading ***ve-'esh yatse'ah,*** literally "a fire had gone forth" (v. 35). It differs from our chapter only by its postscript,

"The sons of Korah, however, did not die" (cf. v. 32), in order to account for the Korahite Levites who played a significant role in the Temple service. Similarly, Numbers 27:3 is also founded on the Masoretic text of chapter 16: *Ha-ʿedah ha-noʿadim ʿal YHVH* reflects the same phrase found in 16:11, a verse that belongs to the Levite passage and inserted, as postulated, by the final redactor. Here, however, the older tradition of Korah's incineration may have been preserved. Finally, Psalms 106:16–18 also reflects our chapter in its received form. Although the Psalm expressly mentions only Dathan and Abiram, Korah is still alluded to in verse 18: "A fire blazed among their party, a flame that consumed the wicked." Furthermore, that the fire follows the earthquake in the sequence reflects the same order of the Masoretic text of Numbers 16. Finally, the reference to "Aaron, the holy one of the LORD" in verse 16 of the Psalm is an allusion to "who is holy" and "he shall be the holy one" (Num. 16:5, 7), which again are from the Levite insert of the final redactor.

Although the second recension distorted the symmetrical introversion of the previous structure, it is not devoid of a redactional art all its own. By the use of the key words ***rav lakhem*** (v. 7) and its semantic opposite ***ha-meʿat*** (v. 9), the Levite insert was locked to the preceding and following pericopes, which contain the same terms. The effect is striking: The former term became an inclusion, a rebuttal by Moses of the mutineers (vv. 3,7), and the latter, a verbal boomerang hurled by Dathan and Abiram against Moses (vv. 9, 13). Equally meritorious is the recension's consistent differentiation between the community, ***ha-ʿedah*** (using the definite article), and Korah's *ʿedah,* qualified by a pronominal suffix (vv. 5,6,11,16; cf. 17:5). However, the rewriting of verses 23–27,32 in order to incorporate Korah into the Dathan and Abiram mutiny and punishment must be adjudged a poor one. Not only has the symmetrical structure been broken, but the breaks have not been adequately patched: The transitions are abrupt, and many inconsistencies still remain, as we have noted.

Can anything be said concerning the dating of these two recensions? Unfortunately, there are no explicit chronological clues. But two different kinds of data point to ***termini ad quem.*** One deals with the historical setting of the various rebellions. First as J. Liver has shown, there can be no doubt that the Dathan and Abiram rebellion reflects the earliest period of Israel's national existence.[1] Dathan and Abiram are Reubenites, and their contention with Moses operates against the background of Reuben the first-born, that is, the erstwhile leader of the tribes, who is subsequently demoted, as reflected in the early patriarchal stories and poems (Gen. 35:22; 49:3–4; cf. 1 Chron. 5:1–2), and who is superseded by Joseph and later by Judah (cf. Gen. 37:18–30 with 42:34–43:15), probably in King David's time. Thus, this rebellion takes place within the context of the wilderness wanderings and the early settlement.

The rebellion of the chieftains poses a more difficult problem. According to our text, they contend with Aaron and not with Moses, and we have no historical record of any struggle for the priesthood outside of Levitical circles. Yet it cannot be gainsaid that in the early sources priestly prerogatives are not limited to the Levites. Indeed, at first the Levites are only a secular tribe, and the patriarchs are the ones who officiate at sacrifices (e.g., Gen. 31:54; 46:1). Although Levites are given preference as priests (Judg. 17), we find judges acting in that capacity (e.g., Gideon in Judg. 6:26; Samuel in 1 Sam. 7:9) and later kings (Saul in 1 Sam. 13:9–10; David in 2 Sam. 6:13,17–18; Ahaz in 2 Kings 16:12–15; Jeroboam in 1 Kings 12:33). Thus, all the old sources agree that lay leaders can be cultic officiants, and since the chieftains (***nesiʾim***) are the leaders par excellence of early Israel, there is sufficient

ground for positing a major clash between the chieftains and the Levites over the rights to the priesthood. Ibn Ezra (on 16:1) may then be correct in associating the rebellion of the chieftains against the Levites with the latter's election as the official clergy (3:11–13) in place of the first-born, the erstwhile priests (3:44–51; 8:16–19). Furthermore, if Josephus's tradition is correct that the contest of the rods (17:16–26) pitted the tribe of Levi against the chieftains of the other tribes (see the Comment to 17:18), we have yet another echo of the rivalry stirred up among the tribes by Levi's election. At any rate, there seems to be no historical basis for the reverse situation: a rebellion of the chieftains led by a Levite. Hence, it may be assumed that Korah's association with the chieftains' rebellion has no historical reality but represents a later attempt to attribute all the early wilderness rebellion traditions to the instigation of Korah.

On the other hand, a Levite rebellion led by Korah makes good historical sense. The Korahites were a powerful Levitical family, to judge by their enumeration among the five direct offspring of Levi (Num. 26:58a). However, as S. E. Loewenstamm has demonstrated, the power of the Korahites could hardly have been felt during the Second Temple period when they served in roles of a lower status, as singers and doorkeepers.[2] From their official genealogy (Exod. 6:16–28; cf. 1 Chron. 6:7), Korah is a first cousin of Moses and Aaron; moreover, he is the first-born of Kohath's second son, hence a legitimate contender for the priesthood. Indeed, the inclusion of Korah the Levite in the genealogy of Exodus 6 is a transparent editorial prolepsis of the forthcoming Korah rebellion. The mention of Korah in the Reubenite genealogy (Num. 26:9–10) and in the inheritance jurisprudence (Num. 27:3) likewise points to the antiquity of the tradition. Liver, then, may be correct in dating the uprising of the Korahite Levites to the beginning of the First Temple period: The Temple hierarchy was still in the process of formation, and the Korahites could have been a major contender for the priesthood. If this be so and since the Levites' rebellion belongs to the last stage of the redaction, then the early monarchy would be a *terminus ad quem* for the final recension of the text.

A second dating criterion stems from a study of the priestly terminology. In particular, the term *ʿedah* is found to be not just preexilic, but also premonarchic, in its historical function. Specifically, *ʿedah* turns out to be an ad hoc emergency body called together by the tribal chieftains whenever a national or transtribal issue arises. The term disappears with the consolidation of the monarchy, a fact that is supported by its absence from any text that can be dated after the ninth century (see Excursus 1).

This redactional analysis of the Korah pericope has wider implications in terms of the new light it sheds on the redactional process of all the wilderness narratives. First and foremost, it should be noted that the contiguous narratives of Kibroth-hattaavah (11:4–34) and the reconnaissance of Canaan (chaps. 13–14) are identical in structure to the penultimate recension of chapter 16, as the following text outlines demonstrate (for the full discussion, see Excursuses 24 and 29).

KIBROTH-HATTAAVAH (11:4–34)

A. People's complaint: meat (vv. 4–10a, bα)
    B. Moses' complaint: assistance (vv. 10bβ–15)
        X. God's answer to both complaints (vv. 16–24a)
    B′. God authorizes elders: diminishes Moses (vv. 24b–30)
A′. God supplies meat: punishes complainers (vv. 31–34)

RECONNAISSANCE OF CANAAN (chaps. 13–14)

A. The scouts' expedition (13:1–24)
   1. God decides on reconnaissance (and conquest) (vv. 1–2)
   2. Moses chooses and instructs scouts (vv. 3–20)
   3. Expedition fulfilled (vv. 21–24)
      [a. All of Canaan (v. 21)]
      b. The Hebron area (vv. 22–24)

B. The scouts' report (13:25–33)
   1. Majority report, objective (vv. 25–29)
   2. Caleb's counterreport (v. 30)
   3. Majority report: subjective (vv. 31–33)

X. The people's response (14:1–10a)
   1. Majority response: abandon project (vv. 1–5)
   2. Joshua and Caleb's counterresponse (vv. 6–9)
   3. Majority response: stone the opposition (v. 10a)

B′. God's response (14:10b–38)
   1. Destroy Israel, save Moses (vv. 10b–12)
   2. Moses intercedes (vv. 13–19)
   3. God mitigates decree (vv. 20–35)
      a. Adults die save Caleb (vv. 20–25)
      b. [Adults die save Joshua and Caleb (vv. 26–35)
         Anticipation of fulfillment (death of spies) (vv. 36–38)]

A′. The people's expedition (14:39–45)
   1. People decide on conquest (vv. 39–40)
   2. Moses protests (vv. 41–42)
   3. Expedition aborted (vv. 41–45)

The structure of chapters 13–14 is given in greater detail than the unit from chapter 11 in order to project the two bulges that distort the balanced symmetry: 13:21 and 14:26–38, indicated by square brackets. Each of the five sections contains three components. All but the first convey the same theme: destruction planned, intercession attempted, and destruction fulfilled. The aforementioned bulges can now be seen as totally anomalous to the structure for they serve only to duplicate the third component of sections A and B′. A detailed breakdown of the chapter 11 unit need not be given here because it exhibits no accretions. Thus, these two units share with the Korah unit a common structure: ABXB′A′. It can hardly be a coincidence.

How do the results of this structural analysis compare with the findings of the documentary hypothesis? Specifically, how do the bulges of chapters 13–14 and the revisions of Korah I by Korah II correspond with the P source, considered by the critics to be the latest of the Pentateuchal sources? First, it should be noted that the last accretions to these stories, 16:5–11 and 13:21 and 14:26–38, do indeed belong to P.[3] Moreover, it can hardly be an accident that 11:4–34 betrays no bulges in its structure: It contains no P! On the other hand, not all of P is accounted for by the bulges. Some P is found within the structure itself: 16:1a,3–4,16–24,26aa,35 in the Korah story and 13:1–16; 14:1a,2,5–7,10 in the reconnaissance story. Thus, if one still wishes to adhere to the documentary theory, two

strands of P would have to be posited: the earlier one (P_1), responsible for the structure; and the later (P_2 or H), which added to and even altered the components of the structure. In chapters 13–14, P_2 or H added some material but not enough to distort the structure, but in chapter 16, P_2 or H disfigured the structure by altering it and adding to it so that it became necessary to dissect the chapter into its rebellion traditions in order to expose the structure. In any event, both P recensions (with the exception of editorial transitions and glosses) must stem from the early monarchy. Moreover, the fact that the P strata are recensions means that, at least in this instance, we can no longer speak of a P source. Finally, the analysis of the redaction of the Korah episode and its structural correspondence with the contiguous narratives offers much promise regarding the solution of the problem of the redaction of the wilderness narrative, in general, and the Book of Numbers, in particular.

Finally it is left for us to consider the place of the Korah episode in the life of Moses and the development of his personality. His enemies and closest associates had charged him with dictatorial ambitions, with the assumption of total power by arrogating all political authority to himself and all religious power (i.e., the High Priesthood) to his brother Aaron. Moses' counterclaim was "that it was the LORD who had sent me to do all these things; that they are not of my own devising" (v. 28). Thus his opponents' murmuring was directed not against Aaron and himself; rather, "it is against the LORD that you and all your company have banded together" (v. 11).

Still, if one compares the Moses of this section with his previous appearances, a profound character change is discernible. Moses had been adjudged the humblest of men because he was impervious to the taunts of his opponents (12:4). This time, however, not only does he ask God to destroy Dathan and Abiram, but he even specifies the means of the destruction. How different is this Moses from the Moses of the plagues, who never initiated either by act or word but as God's obedient servant only fulfilled His command (see Excursus 50). Had Moses confronted the rebels according to his previous pattern he would first have solicited God's decision and having received it would have proclaimed: "Thus says the LORD: Tomorrow at this hour Dathan and Abiram will be swallowed by the earth" (cf. Exod. 9:5).

In truth, signs of Moses' self-inflation had already become visible. His self-pitying utterance at Kibroth-hattaavah: "If You would deal thus with me, kill me rather, I beg You, and let me see no more of my wretchedness" (11:15); his skepticism concerning God's ability to supply Israel with ample meat: "Could enough flocks and herds be slaughtered to suffice them?" (11:22), for which he was rebuked and probably punished (his charisma diminished, 11:25: cf. Excursus 24). Here, however, in prescribing and describing the divine retribution prior to receiving God's consent, his ego reaches new limits. His skepticism concerning God's providence is further exemplified in the scout episode when he prompts the scouts to seek out ***whether*** (rather than ***how***) the land could best be conquered (13:17–20).[4]

It is therefore no accident that the next time Moses is confronted by a new crisis (20:1–13), he loses all restraints and commits the ultimate heresy. Not only does he put himself above his people's woes, not only does he call upon God to affirm his authority through miracle, but in addressing his people he ascribes the miracle to his own powers: In effect, Moses has made himself God (Excursus 50).

At the same time one should not lose sight of the chasm that separates Moses from the dictators of history. With the power at his command, a flick of his finger would have sufficed to have the rebels executed. That he leaves their fate to God suffices in itself to

refute the charge that he had assumed absolute power. To the very end he remains God's faithful servant. This means that all major decisions are referred to God: capital punishment (the Sabbath breaker in 15:32–35), the fate of rebels (the spies in 14:36–38; Dathan and Abiram in 16:28–34; the chieftains in 16:35). He is always ready to intercede for his people, and even when they too rebel, he asks that only the ringleaders be punished (11:2; 14:13–20; 16:20–22). He cannot be accused of seeking personal gain (16:15). Most important of all he is even eager that others achieve his prophetic power (11:26–29).

Thus the physical ordeals of the wilderness and the psychological harassment of his accusers have worn his patience, shaken his equilibrium, and flawed his performance. Still, in the human record, he remains the leader par excellence.[5]

EXCURSUS 40

Sacral Responsibility for Encroachment (chap. 18)

Encroachment is attested in both the secular and the sacred realm. The latter is a major concern of the Korah rebellion (chaps. 16–18) and, indeed, of the early chapters of the Book of Numbers (cf. 1:50–54; 3:5–10,14–39; 4:1–49). Yet the nature of encroachment—precisely how one encroaches upon sacred property—is nowhere stated in the Bible. For that, one has to turn to extrabiblical sources, especially to the Hittite "Instructions for Temple Officials."[1] This text lists types of encroachment by those most likely to commit them: the temple staff (i.46–66; ii.12–58) or the farmers and herdsmen employed in the temple fields (iv.1–75). Encroachment is committed by keeping, eating, using, selling, gifting, delaying, or exchanging the temple's animals, fields, or grain; by expropriating, altering, or wearing the temple's implements or garments; or by changing the time fixed for rites. Women, children and servants, even of the priests, as well as all foreigners, are considered encroachers if they enter the sacred precincts; whereas important Hittite men are granted access provided they are accompanied by guards appointed by the priests (ii.9–12).

In Israel, the issue of encroachment upon the sancta occurs in different literary genres. The narratives record the lethal power of the Ark. God punishes with death Uzzah, for touching the Ark (2 Sam. 6:6–7), and the men of Beth-shemesh, for viewing it (1 Sam. 6:19), both unpremeditated acts. P's earliest traditions on the wilderness period also reflect this belief: The Kohathites will be struck down for accidentally touching covered sancta (Num. 4:15) or viewing uncovered ones (Num. 4:20). However, P's laws introduce a change; they posit inadvertence (***shegagah***) as a mitigating factor in all forms of trespass (***ma'al***) upon the sancta (Lev. 5:14–16). Moreover, P further reduces the contagious power of the sancta: Although it still prohibits nonpriests and disqualified priests from entering the Shrine, it does not penalize them for coming into contact with the sacrificial altar that stands in the open court. This concession can be ascertained from the use of the verbs ***karav/nagash,*** which must be rendered not as "approach" but "encroach"[2] (e.g., Exod. 28:43; 30:20; Lev. 21:23; Num. 1:51; 3:10). Thus only an individual who usurps the priestly monopoly on officiating at the altar is subject to divine sanctions, not one who merely touches the altar, even deliberately. This leads to the corollary deduction that the formula ***kol ha-nogea' be . . . yikdash*** must be rendered "whatever [not whoever] touches . . . is sanctified" (see Excursus 75; cf. Exod. 29:37; 30:29); that is, only objects—not persons—that contact the sancta

absorb their holiness. The specific reason for the reduction of sanctum contagion may lie in P's refusal to grant altar asylum to fugitives from justice (cf. 1 Kings 1:50–53; 2:28–34). P therefore devised in its place the institution of city asylum (Num. 35:9–28).[3]

P's notion of encroachment finds its most significant articulation in its formula *ha-zar ha-karev yumat* (Num. 1:51; 3:10,38; 18:7), which should be rendered "the unauthorized encroacher shall be slain." The context of the formula is invariably the elaboration of the guarding duties of the priestly and Levitical cordons in and around the Tabernacle. Numbers 18 in particular specifies the hierarchy of responsibility in the shared custody of the Tabernacle. The priests are responsible for the encroachment of disqualified priests at the altar and within the Shrine (Num. 18:1,7a; cf. 3:10). Both priests and Levites guard the sancta against possible encroachment by the Levites (Num. 18:3,5a). When, however, the sancta are in transit, the Kohathite Levites who carry them by shoulder (Num. 4:15–20; 7:9) must protect them from Israelite encroachment (Num. 4:18–19). Finally, the Levite cordon stationed outside the Tabernacle guards against possible incursions by Israelites (Num. 18:3,22–23). The gradations of responsibility are in accordance with the physical realities—the actual placement of the sacral guards. The hierarchy of responsibility for encroachment upon the Tabernacle, fully stipulated in chapter 18, is represented by the following scheme:

Verse	*Sacral Class*	*Responsible for*	*Encroachment of*
1b,7a	Priests	Most sacred objects	Disqualified priests
3	Priests and Levites	Most sacred objects (at rest)	Levites
1a	Kohathites	Most sacred objects (in transit)	Israelites
22,23	Levites	The Tabernacle (as a whole)	Israelites

The most significant aspect of this formula is its penalty. Whereas God alone punishes for cultic sin (*yamut* [Kal]), in the case of encroachment upon sancta, death is imposed by man (*yumat* [Hofal]). The graded scale of Tabernacle responsibility clarifies this alleged exception: The wrath of God kindled by the Israelite encroacher does not vent itself on the people but on the negligent Levite guards. The latter, therefore, are empowered to kill the encroacher; as he is their potential murderer, they slay him in self-defense. Indeed, according to P, it is the Levites' mortal risk in guarding the Tabernacle that entitles them to the largesse of the tithes as their reward (Num. 18:21,31). Such ransoming of Israelites by Levites is not an instance of vicarious atonement, whereby the innocent suffer for the sake of the wicked. The formula implies the reverse: Encroaching Israelites are ransomed only by the guilty—that is, negligent—Levite guards. Whereas the doctrine of collective responsibility is the cornerstone of P's theology, a concession is made within the sanctuary to limit its destructiveness to the clergy alone. Thus Numbers 18 is a fitting appendix to the Korahite rebellion of the two preceding chapters. In the wake of the rebellion, God inflicts a plague upon the entire camp (Num. 17:11–15). The people panic; henceforth they will have nothing to do with the Tabernacle (17:28). Chapter 18 is both the remedy and the consolation. Thereafter, the sacral guards will bear the responsibility for lay encroachment. The doctrine of collective responsibility is compromised for Israel's sake so that it may again worship at the sanctuary without fear.[4]

EXCURSUS 41

The "Tenufah" Offering (18:11)

The offerings subject to this ritual are (1) the breast of the well-being offering (*shelamim;* Lev. 7:30; 9:21; 10:14–15; Num. 6:20; 18:18); (2) the right hind thigh and fat of the priestly consecration offering (*millu'im*) and its accompanying bread offering (Exod. 29:22–26; Lev. 8:25–29); (3) the metals for the building of the Tabernacle (Exod. 35:22; 38:24); (4) the reparation offering and the oil for the purification of the healed leper (Lev. 14:12,14); (5) the barley sheaf (Lev. 23:11–14); (6) the two wheat loaves together with two lambs of well-being (Lev. 23:17,20); (7) the meal offering of the suspected adulteress (Num. 5:25); (8) the boiled shoulder of the Nazirite's well-being offering and its accompanying bread offering (Num. 6:20); and (9) the Levites during their ordination (Num. 8:11,15,21).

When the object of the *tenufah* is the Deity, the preposition *lifnei,* "before," is usually used, implying a ritual within the sanctuary (as opposed to the *terumah,* which is always "to the Lord" and never "before the Lord").

The nature of the ritual is nowhere defined. The rabbinic rendering "wave offering" (Mish. Men. 5:6) has been accepted by nearly all translations, dictionaries, and commentaries. The Septuagint exhibits total bewilderment. It renders *tenufah* in the purification ceremonial for the healed leper (Lev. 14) by three words. The Targums, on the other hand, consistently translate *tenufah* and its verbal forms by the root *r-w-m,* "raise, elevate." This rendering is corroborated by most occurrences of *henif* in the Bible (Isa. 10:15; 11:15; 13:2; 19:16), where the rendering "elevate" is clearly superior to "wave." Also, it stands to reason that since the *tenufah* ritual is frequently carried out with many objects simultaneously (Exod. 29:22–24; Lev. 8:25–27), a "waving" motion would topple the entire offering, whereas their "elevation" is physically manageable.

An elevation rite is indeed attested in the Egyptian cult, revealing many characteristics similar to the *tenufah.* (1) The Egyptian formula "elevate . . . before the face of the god" is the exact equivalent of the Hebrew formula (Exod. 29:24). (2) As depicted in the Egyptian relief[1] the offering is an aggregate containing a sampling of all the food placed on the god's table. Correspondingly, all the objects subject to the *tenufah* in a single ritual must undergo the act together, never separately. (3) Like its Egyptian counterpart, the *tenufah* offering is placed on the palms of the hands (so explicitly for the Nazirite; Num. 6:19). A final consideration is that the allegedly parallel waving ceremonial from the ancient Near East turns out to be an exorcistic rite, totally unrelated to the Temple cult. Thus philology, typology, and logic reinforce each other in favor of the rendering of *tenufah* as "elevation offering."

The *tenufah*-elevation is a rite of dedication governed by two postulates. The first is that any offering that still belongs to the owner when it is brought to the sanctuary requires the dedicatory rite of the *tenufah.* Thus nearly all offerings are exempted from the *tenufah* because they are dedicated before they are brought to the sanctuary. The main exception to this rule is the *shelamim,* whose meat belongs to and is eaten by its owner. For the clergy to benefit from the thigh and breast, the owner must first dedicate them to the Lord, that is, subject them to the *tenufah.* The *tenufah* requirement for this offering is supported by the following facts: It is called the offering of the people of Israel (Exod. 29:28) in contrast to the most sacred sacrifices, called an offering to YHVH (Lev. 10:13–14); and the owner is

expressly commanded to bring the dedicatory portions of the *shelamim* "on his hands/ palms" (Exod. 29:24–25; Lev. 7:29–30; Num. 6:19–20). It also explains other anomalies of the ritual. For example, the anointment oil sprinkled on the priests (Exod. 29:7,21; Lev. 8:12,30) does not undergo the *tenufah* because it is inherently holy (Exod. 30:25,32), but the oil for purifying the leper is profane and requires the *tenufah* (Lev. 14:16–17,27–28) in order to sanctify it.

The second postulate is that the most sacred offerings whose composition, procedure, or purpose varies from the norm (Lev. 1–5) require the additional dedication of the *tenufah.* Thus three kinds of grain offering are subject to the *tenufah:* that of the suspected adulteress (Num. 5:25) and of the barley sheaf (Lev. 23:11–14) because they are made of barley and not of wheat, and that of the two wheat loaves (Lev. 23:17–20) because they contain leaven. Moreover, all three lack the usually required frankincense and oil. The reparation offering brought by the healed leper differs from its genre in that its blood, being essential to the ritual, may not be commuted into silver (Lev. 5:15,18,25) and in that it is the first in the sacrificial ritual (Lev. 14:12,24), whereas usually it is last (cf. Num. 6:10–12, Mish. Zev. 10:5). That the aforementioned offerings need reinforced dedication is indicated not only by their abnormal procedure or composition, but more importantly, by their purpose. The barley sheaf and the wheat loaves undergo the *tenufah* ritual "for acceptance in your behalf" (Lev. 23:11), that is, so that the Lord will grant an abundant harvest. The offering of the suspected adulteress is called a "meal offering of remembrance which recalls wrongdoing" (Num. 5:15); that is, God is implored to intercede in this case by guaranteeing that the "water of bitterness" (5:23–26) will reveal the truth. Finally on the eighth day the healed leper is daubed with the blood of the reparation offering and the oil so that he will be qualified to enter the sanctuary to complete his sacrificial rites (cf. Mish. Zev. 10:5).[2]

EXCURSUS 42

The "Terumah" Offering (18:8,11,19)

The sacred gifts called *terumah* are (1) the right hind thighs of the priestly consecration offering, *millu'im,* and well-being offerings, *shelamim* (Exod. 29:27–28; Lev. 7:32,34; 10: 14–15; Num. 6:20); (2) the breast of the well-being offering (Exod. 29:27); (3) the materials for the building of the Tabernacle (Exod. 25:2–3; 35:5,21,24; 36:3,6); (4) the census silver (Exod. 30:13–15); (5) the cakes of the thanksgiving offering, *todah* (Lev. 7:12–14); (6) the first yield of baked bread, *re'shit 'arisah* (Num. 15:19–20); (7) the tithe and its tithe (Num. 18:24–29); (8) the portion of the war spoils assigned to the sanctuary (Num. 31:29,41,52); (9) sacred gifts in general (Num. 5:9; 18:8); and (10) gifts of lesser sanctity in particular (Lev. 22:12,15; Num. 18:11–19). Ezekiel adds to this list the land allotted to the priests and Levites (45:1; 48:8–21) and the sacrificial ingredients levied on the people (45:13,16).

The tannaitic interpretation which regards *terumah* as a ritual in which the offering is subjected to a vertical motion (cf. Mish. Men. 5:6), explains the accepted rendering "heave offering." This rendering, however, is questionable. In the cultic texts of the priestly source, the verb *herim,* used exclusively with the preposition *min* and with the synonyms *hesir* (Lev. 4:8–10,31,35) and *nivdal* (Num. 16:21; 17:10), never means "raise, lift" but only "set apart, dedicate." Consequently, the noun *terumah* can refer only to that which is set apart or dedicated. Hence it must be rendered "dedication, contribution." This rendering is con-

firmed by the Targums (*afreshuta*), by the Septuagint (*aphairema*), and by the Akkadian *tarīmtu* (an exact cognate) and *rīmūtu* (from the root *râmu* III; Assyrian *riāmu*).

The function of the *terumah* is to transfer the object from its owner to the deity. In this respect it is similar to the *tenufah* (see Excursus 41) but with this crucial distinction: The *tenufah* is performed "before the Lord" (*lifnei YHVH*), whereas the *terumah* is never "before" but always "to the Lord" (*le-YHVH*). Thus the *tenufah* and *terumah* constitute two means of dedication to the Lord: the former by a ritual in the sanctuary and the latter by a dedication without ritual outside the sanctuary, effected either by an oral declaration (Judg. 17:3) or by a physical act (Lev. 27:32). This distinction serves to resolve the alleged ambiguities resulting from the same object undergoing both *tenufah* and *terumah* (Exod. 29:22–24,27; 35:24; cf. 38:24). The distinction can be formulated as the following rule: Every *tenufah* (ritual) is preceded by *terumah* (being set apart, designated as an offering).[1]

EXCURSUS 43

First Fruits (18:12–13)

The first issue of all life—called *bikkurim* or *re'shit,* whether from the womb or the soil—was considered intrinsically holy. It had to be transferred to the Deity, the rightful owner, before human beings were permitted to use the crop. Moreover, its transfer to the Deity was considered a prerequisite for the assurance of divine blessing on the remainder of the crop. Both factors, the intrinsic holiness of the first fruits and its pragmatic purpose, are exemplified by the law of the first edible yield of fruit trees: "In the fourth year all its fruit shall be set aside [lit. holy] for jubilation before the LORD; and only in the fifth year may you use its fruit, that its yield to you may be increased" (Lev. 19:24–25). The law of the first fruits of the barley harvest is similar: "You shall bring the first (*re'shit*) *'omer* of your harvest to the priest . . . for acceptance in your behalf" (Lev. 23:10–11). Note also the advice of the wisdom literature: "Honor the LORD with your substance and [literally] with the first fruits (*re'shit*) of all you produce; and your barns will be filled with grain, your vats will burst with new wine" (Prov. 3:9–10). This view is also recorded by the rabbis: "R. Akiba said: The Torah states: bring barley at Passover, since that is the time of ripening barley so that the grain crop may be blessed; and bring the first fruits of wheat at Shavuot since it falls in the time of wheat when the fruits of the tree may be blessed; and bring the water libation at Tabernacles since it falls in the season of the rains in order that you may be blessed with rains" (Tosef. Suk. 3:18).

The gift of the first fruits is due not only from the first ripe crops of the soil but also from certain foods processed from these crops: grain, new wine, new (olive) oil, fruit syrup, leavened food, and bread dough. The priestly legislation preserves the terminological distinction: *Bikkurim* refers to "the first ripe," and *re'shit* to "the first processed." Thus, "all the best of the new oil, wine, and grain, [literally] the first processed (*re'shit*) that they present to the LORD—I give to you. The first ripe (*bikkurim*) of everything in their land, that they bring to the LORD, shall be yours" (Num. 18:12–13; cf. Ezek. 44:30). Grain, wine, and oil as well as fruit syrup, leaven, and dough are clearly processed from plants and are termed *re'shit* in the priestly literature (Lev. 2:12; Num. 18:12; cf. 2 Chron. 31:5; Num. 15:20–21; Ezek. 44:30; also wool in Deut. 18:4). *'Omer re'shit ketsirekhem,* "the first sheaf of your harvest" (Lev. 23:10) is not an exception. *Re'shit* here is not a technical term for first fruits

but simply the adjective "first." Its use emphasizes that the omer is not to be selected from among the many sheaves of the first ripe harvest but must be the very first sheaf (Deut. 16:9; cf. Exod. 23:19; 34:26).

Proof that the *re'shit* refers to processed produce is found in the expression "as with the new grain from the threshing floor" (Num. 18:27), referring to the Israelite's required *re'shit* contribution (Num. 18:12). It is specified that this comes not from the field but from the threshing floor, after the grain is fully separated from the chaff. Indeed this is precisely the way the rabbis understood it when they claimed that the perquisite is removed from the produce only "when its work is completed" (cf. Mish. Ter. 1:10, Maimonides, Zera'im, Ma'aser 3:13), that is, when it is fully processed. The time is specified in the case of the tithe as "grain, after the pile is smoothed off or stacked . . . wine, after it has been skimmed . . . oil, after it has dripped down into the trough" (Mish. Ma'as. 1:6–7; cf. Sif. Num. 121). The use of *re'shit* as first processed fruits seemed to have continued at Qumran. Outside of P, *re'shit* has two other meanings: Either it is equivalent to *bikkurim*, "first ripe (e.g., Deut. 26:2,10; Jer. 2:3), or it means "the best" (e.g., 1 Sam. 2:29b; 15:21; possibly Exod. 23:19; 34:26, but see above).

On the other hand, *bikkurim* consistently refers to the first ripe fruit in all the biblical sources (Exod. 23:16,19; 34:22; Num. 13:20; Neh. 10:37). The term *leḥem bikkurim* (Lev. 23:17,20; 2 Kings 4:42) means bread made from first ripe grain; and *minḥat bikkurim* (Lev. 2:14) refers to the *minḥah* offering made from first ripe barley. The use of *bikkurim* in tannaitic literature is also restricted to first ripe (unprocessed) fruits (e.g., Mish. Bik. 3:1).

The most significant festival involving the first of a crop to ripen was that of the first ripe wheat, which was made to coincide with Shavuot or the Feast of Weeks (Exod. 23:16a; 34:22a; Lev. 23:15–22; Num. 28:26; Deut. 16:9–12). However, it is known from the Temple scroll that the Qumran sectarians also observed two similar festivals for the new wine and the new oil, set apart by fifty-day intervals. Thus in accordance with the Qumran calendar —twelve months of thirty days each, with one added day at the end of every three months—the omer (the first ripe barley) was brought on Sunday (month 1, day 26, the first Sunday after the Passover); Shavuot (the first ripe wheat) was celebrated on Sunday (month 3, day 15); the new wine, on Sunday (month 5, day 3); and the new oil, on Sunday (month 6, day 22). There is a possibility that the practice of multiple *bikkurim* festivals goes back to Nehemiah (Neh. 13:31), for he mentions appointed "times" in connection with the wood offering and the first ripe fruits.[1]

EXCURSUS 44

The Status of "Ḥerem" (18:14)

The term *ḥerem* is generally rendered as "devoted thing." It can be defined as "the status of that which is separated from common use or contact either because it is proscribed as an abomination to God or because it is consecrated to Him."[1] In effect, it is the ultimate in dedication. *Ḥerem* may never be redeemed: *Ḥerem* land belongs permanently to the sanctuary; *ḥerem* animals, if pure, must be sacrificed on the altar and, if impure, become—like land—the permanent property of the sanctuary; and *ḥerem* persons (i.e., certain prisoners of war) must be killed.

Although it is designated within the category of "most sacred" offerings, *ḥerem* proves to be anomalous. It is called "most sacred" in Leviticus 27:28 only to indicate that the object cannot be redeemed. In other respects, however, it is certainly not "most sacred," for both the priests and their families are allowed to partake of this offering (cf. Num. 18:11–19 with 18:9–10).

Ḥerem objects may apply not only to animals but also to lands and human beings. Any animal, whether pure or impure, may become "devoted," in contrast to dedicated impure animals, which may be redeemed. Furthermore, *ḥerem* fields, as distinguished from all other dedicated lands, remain the permanent property of the sanctuary. (Note that despite its holy status, *ḥerem* lands may be farmed by the priests, and the produce used by them.) With respect to humans placed under the *ḥerem*, there is to be no redemption (Lev. 27:29), which means that there is no alternative whatsoever to death. (For an excellent example of this practice, see 1 Sam. 15:3,33, noting the cultic implications of v. 33: "And Samuel cut Agag down before the LORD at Gilgal.")

The taboo of *ḥerem* is found in other narrative sections (Josh. 7:1; 22:20; 1 Kings 20:24; 1 Chron. 2:7), and in addition to Leviticus 27:28 and Numbers 18:14, it is adduced in two other legal documents (Deut. 7:25–26; Ezek. 44:29).

Violation of the *ḥerem* taboo is classified as *maʿal* (Josh. 7:1; 22:20), a legal term denoting a sin against God. More specifically *maʿal* means "trespassing upon the divine realm either by poaching on his sancta or breaking his covenant oath; it is a lethal sin which can destroy both the offender and his community"[2] (see the Comment to Num. 5:6). Although the *ḥerem* taboo was also practiced at Mari, it differed in crucial ways from this case. In the Bible, the *ḥerem* belongs to God, not the king; the death penalty is unquestionably irrevocable; and *ḥerem* property may not be used by the laity or soldiers.

The *ḥerem* injunction of Deuteronomy (Deut. 20:16–17) is unique in the Pentateuchal sources. Exodus 23:20–33 comes closest by demanding the total expulsion of the indigenous population. But expulsion is not extermination. True, *ḥerem* is enjoined once in the Covenant Code: "Whoever sacrifices to a god other than the LORD shall be proscribed" (Exod. 22:19). However, as this injunction is addressed solely to the Israelites (as is the entire Covenant Code; cf. *be-ʿammekha* in Exod. 22:22), it cannot refer to the residents of Canaan. Clearly, as M. Greenberg has pointed out,[3] the hand of the Deuteronomist has been at work. He has taken both the expulsion law of Exodus 23:20–33, directed against the inhabitants of Canaan, and the *ḥerem* law of Exodus 22:19, directed against the individual Israelite, and fused them into a new law that applies *ḥerem* to all idolaters, Israelites (cf. Deut. 13:13–19), and non-Israelites alike, as well as to their sancta (Deut. 7:5,25–26).

The Deuteronomist, however, does not claim that his law is innovative. To the contrary, he says, "as the LORD your God has commanded you" (Deut. 20:17), implying that his *ḥerem* is based on an unambiguous and unimpeachable source. True, as indicated, this source is nowhere in Scripture. Nonetheless, there is evidence that at least once in Israel's history the Deuteronomist's *ḥerem* against the Canaanites was actually invoked. Let us first bear in mind his definition of *ḥerem:* The population is destroyed as well as its cult objects, but its cities and property may be expropriated as spoils (Deut. 6:11). Now it is true that this is precisely the kind of *ḥerem* that Joshua frequently carried out in his conquests. It was imposed on Makkedah, Libnah, Lachish, Eglon, Debir, and other towns both in the south and north (Josh. 10:28–40; 11:10–20). However, the possibility must be reckoned with that the record of the conquest has been made to conform to the Deuteronomic *ḥerem*,

a possibility that is reinforced when we notice that the execution of *ḥerem* continues with the formula, "as the LORD commanded" (e.g., Josh. 10:40; 11:12,15, 20). Then, too, every example of *ḥerem* that stems from an indisputably non-Deuteronomic source actually differs from the Deuteronomic conception: Arad (Num. 21:1–9) and Jericho (Josh. 6:17–19) are subject to total *ḥerem;* Ai and Hazor are burned (Josh. 8:2,28; 11:11–13).

Does this then mean that the Deuteronomist's *ḥerem* is indeed a midrash, "a tendentious revision of history," and that his claim of "as the LORD your God commanded you" is a fiction?[4]

I submit that there is one clear historical precedent for his *ḥerem:* Saul and the Gibeonites. Saul attempted to exterminate the Gibeonites (2 Sam. 21:1). That some Gibeonites succeeded in escaping to Gath (2 Sam. 4:3) underscores the fact that their only haven was outside of Saul's jurisdiction, in non-Israelite territory. Saul confiscated their real property and divided it among his fellow Benjaminite officers (1 Sam. 22:7). Thus Saul's campaign against the Gibeonites follows the precise rules of the Deuteronomic *ḥerem:* the extermination and despoiling of the inhabitants of Canaan. It is clear, when we consider the total picture of Saul's personality and program, that his motives were primarily religious and not economic (although the force of the latter should not be discounted). He stamps out illegitimate divination (1 Sam. 28:3, 9), purifies the cult (1 Sam. 13:32–35), and resorts to prophetic ecstasy (1 Sam. 10:10–12; 19:23–24). Indeed, the text itself labels his persecution of the Gibeonites by the root *k-n-'*, implying religious fanaticism. Thus, it is hardly likely that a God-fearing king would have undertaken the genocide of the Gibeonites unless he felt compelled to do so by divine imperative.

True, Saul is twice portrayed as a rebel against the Lord (1 Sam. 13:13; 15:9ff.). But these texts stem from a Davidide (that is, anti-Saulide) author. The former text probably mirrors Samuel's attempt to contain Saul's desire to officiate at national sacrifices, a royal prerogative attested for later kings (e.g., 1 Kings 8:63–64; 2 Kings 16:15b), and the latter text may in fact be an example of Saul's obedience to God and not his rebelliousness. For it should be remembered that *ḥerem* animals fit for the altar need not be put to the sword but may be sacrificed. Indeed, according to the priestly code they must be sacrificed (Lev. 27:28; Num. 18:14; cf. Ezek. 44:29). The fact that Samuel does not accuse Saul of sparing Agag and actually slaughters Agag as a sacrifice ("before the LORD"; 1 Sam. 15:33), also in keeping with the priestly law of *ḥerem* (Lev. 27:29), is an indication that this is probably what Saul intended to carry out himself. Moreover, that Saul had the "cheap and worthless" animals destroyed on the spot (1 Sam. 15:9) and retained only the best animals accords with the cultic requirement that sacrificial animals must be unblemished (Lev. 22:19). There is, therefore, no reason to doubt Saul's statement that "the troops spared the choicest of the sheep and oxen for sacrificing to the LORD your God" (1 Sam. 15:15). Further evidence that this verse was Saul's true intention is that he spared only "sheep and oxen," a fact confirmed by his antagonist Samuel (1 Sam. 15:14): Saul only took back with him *sacrificial* animals but presumably destroyed animals ineligible for the altar, such as donkeys and camels (1 Sam. 15:3). Thus Saul's assertion that "I have fulfilled the LORD's command" (1 Sam. 15:13) can be fully justified, and it is only the anti-Saulide writer who misrepresents his valid execution of the *ḥerem* as an act of heresy.

In summation, Saul's campaign against the Gibeonites takes on meaning only by assuming that the type of *ḥerem* projected by the Deuteronomist was an old and accepted tradition and that, consequently, his report of the *ḥerem* against most of the captured towns of Canaan is substantially correct.[5]

EXCURSUS 45

The First-Born (18:15–16)

The first-born male of human beings and animals is usually called *bekhor,* less frequently *peter reḥem,* and in the case of human beings, occasionally *rav* (Gen. 25:23) and *re'shit 'oni* (Gen. 49:3). The denominative *bikker* (Piel) is also found (Deut. 21:16).[1] The animal first-born is always that of the mother. For human beings *bekhor* can be either of the mother or of the father or even a metaphor (e.g., Exod. 4:22); *peter reḥem,* "the first issue of the womb," refers exclusively to the first-born of the mother; the remaining terms refer only to the first-born of the father. In most instances, it is the first-born of the father. The first-born of the mother is mentioned for three limited purposes: (1) to stress the child's sanctity (e.g., Exod. 34:19); (2) to emphasize that he is not his father's first-born (e.g., 1 Chron. 2:50); and (3) to underscore the mother's status at the time of his birth (Deut. 25:6; cf. Josephus, Life 76; Luke 2:7).

The genealogical lists point to the importance of the first-born male. He is first in the list, even if the genealogical line is given for all the sons (e.g., 1 Chron. 6:1–14). The family line is continued through the first-born, even if other sons are named (1 Chron. 7:1–4); at times the first-born is the only one named (Gen. 11:12–13). Daughters, even the first-born (*bekhirah*), are listed at the end (1 Sam. 14:49). More significantly, the status of the first-born is indicated by the formula "father/mother/brother/sister of" (Gen. 36:22), indicating that he is the point of reference for the rest of the family.

The hegemony of the first-born is reflected in the early narratives (Gen. 27:1–45; 37:22; cf. 29:32), as in other literature of the ancient Near East.[2] More important, it is concretized in his rights of inheritance: In Israel, the law of Deuteronomy 21:15–17 ordains that the first-born should receive double the portion allotted to each of his brothers (*pi shenayim* means "two portions" of the estate),[3] a division that also obtained in the ancient Near East, in the Middle Assyrian Laws (B.1). But other systems are also attested, for example, one-tenth more, the entire inheritance, the same amount.

The polemical wording of Deuteronomy 21:15–17 indicates that in practice, fathers discriminated in favor of other sons. Indeed, the right of the father to transfer the birthright is evidenced among Israel's neighbors.[4] However, Israel differed in this respect: Although a younger brother might gain the birthright (*bekhorah*), he never acquired the title *bekhor* (cf. 1 Chron. 26:10–11, where he is called *ro'sh,* "chief"; 2 Chron. 11:22, *nagid,* "chief prince"). In Israel the first-born male of the mother held a sacred status (whereas elsewhere his status was likely defined in purely economic terms). Thus the transfer of the birthright—even without the title—is generally recorded as taking place solely by the intervention of God and not by the whim of the father or intrigue of the brothers (e.g., Jacob in Gen. 25:23; Ephraim in Gen. 48:19; David in 1 Chron. 28:4; Solomon in 1 Kings 2:15). In the ancient Near East as well, Ashurbanipal, the youngest son, supports his right to the throne because of divine election.[5]

The laws declaring the sanctity of the first-born consist of a general statement (Exod. 13:1–2; 13:12a; 34:19a; Num. 18:15) and a threefold application: to pure animals, impure animals, and human beings (Exod. 13:12b–13; 34:19b–20; Num. 18:16–18; cf. Exod. 22:28–29; Lev. 27:26–27; Deut. 15:19–23). In the case of the pure animals the law codes differ: In JE (Exod. 13:12–13; 22:28–29; 34:19) the first-born is transferred (*natan, he'evir*) to the Lord,

that is, sanctified either as an *'olah* or as the *shelamim* of the priest; P holds that it is the priest's *shelamim* (Num. 18:17); whereas D maintains it is the owner's (Deut. 15:20). The law codes again differ in the case of the impure animal: JE requires that only the ass be ransomed, but P extends the ransom requirement to all impure animals (D is silent on this case). Here, however, the difference may reflect socioeconomic changes: In JE's time, the ass may have been the only domestically impure animal (cf. Ibn Ezra on Exod. 13:3). The ransom also varies. In JE it is a sheep. However, P's law of Leviticus 27:26–27 stipulates that it is ransomed (*padah*) by its worth as evaluated (*be-'erkekha*) by the priest, but if the owner redeems it (*ga'al*), he adds one-fifth to its value. Since the value of an ass is greater than that of a sheep, the change from JE to P favors the sanctuary.

The verbs used in the laws of the human first-born, "*natan, kiddesh, he'evir* to the LORD," as well as the use of *padah,* "ransom," clearly indicate that the first-born male of the mother is the property of the Deity. This may be a literary reflex of an ancient rule whereby the first-born was expected to care for the burial and worship of his deceased parents. Traces of ancestor worship are found in Mesopotamia: The first-born inherits the family gods at Nuzi and the cultic objects at Nippur; the *kudduru* curses include lack of a son to pour a libation after death. Ancestor worship is also attested in Egypt, among pre-Islamic Arabs, and popularly in Israel (Isa. 8:19; cf. Deut. 26:14). Thus the Bible may be preserving the memory of the first-born bearing a sacred status; and his replacement by the Levites (Num. 3:11–13,40–51; 8:14–18) may reflect the establishment of a professional priestly class. The ransom of the first-born is unspecified in JE, but P sets it at five shekels (Num. 18:16; cf. Lev. 27:6). There is no support for the theory that the first-born was originally offered as a sacrifice.

EXCURSUS 46

The Tithe (18:21–32)

Although the rendering of tithes of property for sacral purposes was common all over the ancient Near East, well-documented, firsthand evidence concerning tithes comes mainly from Mesopotamia (*ešru/eširtû*).[1] These documents date from the Neo-Babylonian period (sixth century B.C.E.), but there is no doubt that the institution as such is much older. In the Syro-Palestine area the tithe (*ma'šārtu;* cf. Heb. *ma'ser*) is found in Ugarit in the fourteenth century B.C.E.[2]

The tithe was not assigned only to temples. As may be learned from 1 Samuel 8:15,17 and from Ugarit,[3] it could also be a royal tax that the king could exact and give to his officials. This ambiguity of the tithe, as a royal due on the one hand and as a sacred donation on the other, is to be explained by the fact that the temples to which the tithe was assigned were royal temples (cf. especially Amos 7:13). As such, the property and treasures in them were at the king's disposal. This can best be exemplified by the two instances of tithe mentioned in older sources of the Pentateuch (JE). In Genesis 14:20 Abraham gives a tithe (after his battle with the four kings of the north) to Melchizedek the king-priest of Shalem (= Jerusalem); and in Genesis 28:22 (cf. Amos 4:4) Jacob vows to pay a tithe at Bethel, the "royal chapel" of the northern kingdom (Amos 7:13). The specific mention of these two "royal temples" in connection with the tithe is not a coincidence. It seems that these two traditions have an etiological slant. The institution of collecting tithes in the

northern royal chapel at Bethel is linked to Jacob, the ancestor hero par excellence of the northern tribes, whereas the institution of the tithe in the royal sanctuary of Jerusalem is traced back to Abraham, whose traditions are mainly attached to the south. As is well known, the kings controlled the treasures of palace and Temple alike (1 Kings 15:18; 2 Kings 12:19; 18:15), which is understandable since they were responsible for the maintenance of the sanctuary and its service not less than for the service of the court (cf. Ezek. 45:17). It stands to reason that the tithe, which originally was a religious tribute, came to be channeled to the court and was therefore supervised by royal authorities. This is actually attested in 2 Chronicles 31:4ff., where Hezekiah is said to organize the collection and the storage of the tribute, including the tithe. Although the description of the event comes from a late and tendentious source, its authenticity is supported by the fact that the Mesopotamian tithe, attested in earlier sources, was organized along similar lines (cf. also the organization of Neh. 10:38; 12:44,47; 13:5,12). The annual tithe of the Carthaginians, which was sent to the Temple of Melqart in Tyre (Diodorus 20.14), is to be understood in a like manner. The Temple of Melqart was the state treasury of Tyre, and so the tribute paid by the Carthaginians had a political aspect in addition to its sacred one.

A further analogy between the sacred tithe and the royal one may be found in the priestly ordinance, according to which the tithes of grain and "flow from the vat" are allocated to the Levites in return for the services that they perform in the Tabernacle (Num. 18:21; cf. v. 27). A similar procedure is attested in Ugaritic grants whereby the king of Ugarit gives the tithe of a whole city to his official for his loyal service;[4] and, like the tithe given to the Levites, it consists of grain and beverage. The same phenomenon is encountered in 1 Samuel 8:15—the king is said to give away to his servants the tithe (grain and wine) taken from the people.

The property that was subject to the tithe in Israel was grain, new wine, and new oil (Deut. 14:23, etc.), as well as cattle and sheep (Lev. 27:32). However, in a general context the tithe appears to embrace all kinds of property. Abraham gives Melchizedek a tenth of everything, which seems to refer to the booty of the war, and Jacob vows that "of all that You give me, I will set aside a tithe for You" (Gen. 28:22). In Mesopotamia, there is evidence of tithes from agricultural produce, cattle and sheep, slaves, donkeys, wool, cloth, wood, metal production, silver, gold, and so on. It seems, therefore, that the specification in the priestly and Deuteronomic codes refers only to the most common objects of tithing in Israel.

Despite the view of most moderns, the tithe in Numbers 18 is not voluntary but mandatory, a conclusion supported by the following evidence: (1) The verb *tikḥu* means "take by force" (cf. the Comment to v. 26), implying that the Levite is not dependent on the whims of the landowner.[5] (2) It would be hard to conceive that the tithes, the only income assigned to the Levites, takes the form of charity—and this in compensation for the ongoing risks involved in laboring for the sanctuary. (The case of Deut. 14:22–29, in which the tithe is indeed a charity, has a totally different sociological motivation: The Levites are unemployed priests and are literally the wards of society.) (3) Since the perquisites for the priestly family of Aaron from the annual produce of the land are mandatory (vv. 12–13), how could the Levitical perquisites from the land, which are supposed to feed a whole tribe (numbering 8,580 males between the ages of thirty and fifty, according to 4:48) be purely voluntary? (4) The history of the Babylonian temple tithe demonstrates that no sooner was a centralized government established than it would have met the need of the sanctuary personnel for a fixed income by imposing an annual sacral tithe.[6]

Underlying all the ancient Near Eastern sources dealing with the tithe is the notion of a tax that is indispensable for the maintenance of the temple and its personnel (except Deut., to be discussed below). As may be learned from the Mesopotamian documents, the tithe was stored in the temple treasuries, and some of the temple representatives were put in charge of these stores. The cattle were marked with a temple mark, and the tithe of grain and dates could be converted into money when desirable. The Babylonian documents also provide evidence on the question of how the tithe was spent by the temple. Most agricultural produce was destined for consumption by the temple personnel, but some was also applied to the maintenance of various enterprises and institutions attached to the temple. Cattle and sheep were used mainly for sacrificial purposes. The tithe was collected by representatives of the temple authorities, who were also responsible for transporting the products to the temple personnel; these collectors themselves were not exempted from the tithe.

A similar picture is obtained when the biblical sources dealing with the tithe are examined in conjunction with the outside sources. Admittedly, as will be shown, one has to take into account the fact that the various sources of the Pentateuch evince different attitudes to the tithe and also that this institution underwent some development during the Second Temple period. However, in general, the nature of the tithe and the way of processing and spending it is quite similar to that known from the outside sources, as presented above. That the tithe was stored in the storehouse of the Temple may be learned from Malachi (3:10), Nehemiah (10:38,39; 12:44; 13:5,12,13), and 2 Chronicles (31:4ff.). The same sources provide information about the custodians of these stores and about the way in which the tithe was distributed among the Temple personnel (e.g., Neh. 13:13). Furthermore, the evidence in Nehemiah 10:38 about Levites as tithe collectors in the provincial cities, which some have regarded as a gloss, is now corroborated by Mesopotamian data, according to which tithe collectors were recruited from the temple administration. Although the Mesopotamian data is from later sources, this does not mean that the whole procedure was a late invention, especially given that the same procedure is attested in outside sources. In fact this is the only realistic way in which the tithe can be conceived. The conversion of tithes of the produce of the land into money, found in Mesopotamian sources, is also mentioned in Leviticus 27:31 and Deuteronomy 14:24–25 (but with the difference that in Deut., one is not bound to pay an additional one-fifth of the tithe for the redemption); and the information that the (Mesopotamian) tithe collectors themselves are bound to pay tithes helps clarify the biblical law that the Levites have to remove the tithes from their income (Num. 18:25ff.).

The law of Deuteronomy (14:22ff.) prescribes the setting aside of a tithe of grain, wine, and oil every year and its consumption at the chosen place (i.e., the central sanctuary). The tithe may be converted into money to be spent on the festive meal in the chosen place. Every third year, however, the tithe has to be left in the local settlement, for the benefit of the Levite, who has no land of his own, the stranger, the fatherless, and the widow (14:28–29). After giving away the tithe to these *personae miserabiles,* the owner has to proclaim a confession in which he declares that he has given it to the indigent and not desecrated it by using it for impure purposes (26:12–14).

This novelty of eating the tithe instead of giving it away to the sanctuary and its ministrants (as was the case before) is to be explained against the background of the cultic reform that stands at the basis of the Deuteronomic law code, especially Deuteronomy

12:19. After the abolition of the provincial sanctuaries and the provincial cultic officials, the Levites, there was no further need for the tithe, which had been destined for the maintenance of these institutions. However, in order to preserve this ancient, sacred institution, the Israelite is commanded to observe the custom of setting aside a tithe from his yield and guarding its holiness by eating it only in the chosen place and by not letting it be defiled. The preservation of another feature of the tithe is also expressed in the allocation of the tithe to the Levite every third year. Called "the year of the tithe" (26:12), this year seems to preserve the old notion of the connection between the Levite and the tithe. It must, however, be admitted that the Levite appears here not as a sacred official but as a destitute person, that is, on the same level as the stranger, orphan, and widow.

The various tithe laws are not in accord on either the matter of what is subject to the tithe or who is its recipient. According to Leviticus 27:30–31, the tithe falls due on all produce and pure animals. Deuteronomy 14:23 ignores the animal tithe and restricts the vegetable tithe to grain, new wine, and olive oil. Numbers 18:21–32 says nothing explicit about either tithe. But from the language of verse 29 it is certain that the animal tithe was ignored ("you shall set aside . . . from . . . its best portion, the part . . . to be consecrated); and it is possible that the crop tithe of verse 30, like Deuteronomy's, was restricted to grain, new wine, and oil ("as the yield of the threshing floor or vat"). However, the discrepancies may be more apparent than real. By any reckoning, grain, new wine, and oil are the major crops of Canaan, and the phrase may simply be a metonym for all the produce of the land. In any event, in the two historical attestations of the tithe in biblical times, the one attributed to King Hezekiah falls due on livestock and "on everything" (2 Chron. 31:5–6), in full agreement with Leviticus 27; and the one attributed to Nehemiah falls due on "the tithes from our ground" (Neh. 10:37), explained as "the contribution of grain, wine and oil" (v. 39), in keeping with Deuteronomy. But here again other vegetable products are not necessarily excluded. Certainly by rabbinic times there was no doubt that all vegetables were subject to the tithe (Mish. Maʿas. 1:1).

On the matter of the tithe recipients, the discrepancies are indisputable. Leviticus assigns them to the sanctuary priests; Numbers, to the Levites; and Deuteronomy, to the Israelite owners. Yet these prescriptions, ostensibly so contradictory, may be related to each other. The produce tithe of Leviticus is redeemable by the owner and thus bears the same status as Deuteronomy's tithe: Every third year it is turned over to the Levites and to other indigents; otherwise it is eaten by its owner. Although Numbers assigns the tithe to the Levites it admits that the tithe has been "set aside for the LORD" in conformance with Leviticus. Thus the change of beneficiary betrays a chronological relationship. (1) Deuteronomy assigns the tithe to its owner but implies that the Levite once had title to it as ordained in Numbers. (2) Numbers, in turn, acknowledges that the tithes originally belonged to the Lord (e.g., sanctuary, priests), a claim only asserted by Leviticus. Thus the Pentateuchal codes affirm that the tithe beneficiary has undergone two changes—from the sanctuary to the Levite to the owner.

At the beginning of the Second Temple period the tithe was considered indispensable for the maintenance of the sanctuary and its personnel. Thus Malachi (3:10) urges the people to bring "the full tithe into the storehouse" that there may be food in the house of God, apparently for the priests. Nehemiah stands on guard so that the people give their tithe to the Levites and do not neglect it (Neh. 10:38; 12:44; 13:10,13). As has already been indicated, the method of organizing the tithe in this period was not different from what is

known about the organization of the tithe in Mesopotamia. Representatives of the Temple were in charge of collecting the tithes from the fields (Neh. 10:38b), and the tithes were stored in the storehouses of the Temple (Mal. 3:10; Neh. 10:39–40; 12:44; 13:5,12,13; cf. 2 Chron. 31:6ff.) under the supervision of priestly officials, who were in charge of their proper distribution (cf. Neh. 13:13). In contrast to the common view, there is no real contradiction between Nehemiah 10:38, which speaks of "the Levites who collect the tithe in all our towns," and passages such as Malachi 3:10 and Nehemiah 12:44 and 13:12, which speak of the people bringing tithes to the storehouses. The latter statements mean that the people made their contribution and not that the people brought the tithes with them in the literal sense of the word. According to the Mesopotamian practice, the temple authorities were responsible for the transportation of the tithe and there is no reason to conclude that the same practice did not prevail in Judah, especially when this is explicitly stated in Nehemiah 10:38. Moreover, this is supported by the rabbinic tradition according to which the tithe was given to the Levites (or rather to the priests, see below) on the threshing floor.[7] On the other hand, it is possible that the petty farmers brought their tithes with them to Jerusalem.

Although the purpose of the tithe and its method of organization in the period under discussion seem quite clear, religious-halakhic factors complicated the issue. From Ezra's time the entire body of Pentateuchal literature was considered to be a unity (the Law of Moses), and the people were expected to comply with the Torah as a whole. This required that the various attitudes toward the tithe as reflected in the different sources (and especially in the priestly code, on the one hand, and the Deuteronomic code, on the other) be combined in a way that reconciled contradictions. Thus for instance, the two types of tithes prevalent at this period, "the first tithe" (*maʿaser riʾshon*) and the "second tithe" (*maʿaser sheni*), are the outcome of the contradiction between Numbers 18:21ff. and Deuteronomy 14:22ff. According to the priestly ordinance, the tithe is to be given to the Levite, whereas according to the Deuteronomic code, it is to be consumed by the owner at the central sanctuary. The rabbis, taking it for granted that both laws are of Mosaic origin and therefore equally binding, interpreted them as two different tributes, one to be given to the Levite, "the first tithe," and the other to be brought to Jerusalem and consumed there, "the second tithe." Theoretically, this was an excellent solution. However, from the practical point of view the implementation of these laws was almost impossible. The excise of 20 percent of the yield was too high; and the destination of the tithe posed an even more serious problem. There were very few Levites in the Second Temple period in contrast to the situation at the monarchical period and so the tithe was automatically shifted to the priests. Because this does not comply with the law, all kinds of explanations had to be provided in order to do away with this legal anomaly. A common explanation was that Ezra punished the Levites for not going up from Babylon to Jerusalem—he allocated the tithe to the priests (Yev. 86b). There were other harmonistic solutions, for example, that the priests are also Levites since they are also descended from the tribe of Levi. But for obvious economic reasons, very few people observed the laws of tithe properly. A conscientious observer of the law could not partake of his yield without first tithing it, and the common people were suspected of not putting aside the sacred portion. This situation caused a lot of problems whose legal aspects are dealt with extensively in a special tractate called Demai.[8]

EXCURSUS 47

The Structure of Chapter 19

This chapter is an ideological and structural unity. As noted by the rabbis (PdRK 58), it contains seven different subjects each mentioned seven times, as follows: (1) the cow and its ashes (vv. 2,5,6,9^2,10,17); (2) burnt items, including skin, flesh, blood, dung, cedar, hyssop, and crimson (vv. 5–6); (3) sprinkling (v. 4); (4) persons who wash (vv. 7 [referring to three priests; vv. 4,6,7],8,10,19,21); (5) contaminated items (by a corpse in a tent: occupants, those who enter, open vessels; and, in an open field: those who touch someone slain, someone who died naturally, a human bone, a grave; vv. 14–16); (6) those that are purified (tent, vessels, persons, one who touched a bone, one who was slain, one who died naturally, a grave; v. 18); (7) priests (vv. 1 [Moses and Aaron], 3,4,6,7^2; that Moses served as a High Priest, see Exod. 29; Lev. 8; PR 14:11).

Besides the septenary principle, this chapter reveals a binary structure, as demonstrated by the following outline:

Panel A	*Panel B*
"This is the ritual law" (v. 2a)	"This is the ritual" (v. 14aα)
Preparation of the ashes	Touching corpse or its derivatives
Renders impure (vv. 2b–10)	Renders impure (vv. 14–16)
Purification procedure (vv. 11–12)	Purification procedure (vv. 17–19)
Penalty for nonpurification (v. 13)	Penalty for nonpurification (v. 20)
	"Law for all time" (v. 21a)
	[Addition (vv. 21b–22)]

Once it is recognized that verses 21b–22 constitute a later addition (the law of one-day impurities resulting from corpse contamination), the two halves of this chapter disclose their structural symmetry. First, they end the same way, with the purification procedure (vv. 11–12, 17–19) followed by the same penalty for neglect (vv. 13,20). The equivalent elements of the latter are cited in parallel columns to allow appreciation of their similarity in phraseology and content:

1. ". . . does not cleanse himself	2. ". . . fails to cleanse himself
defiles the LORD's Tabernacle	that person shall be cut off from
that person shall be cut off from Israel	the congregation for he
Since the water of lustration	has defiled the LORD's sanctuary
was not dashed on him	The water of lustration
he remains unclean" (v. 13).	was not dashed on him
	he is unclean" (v. 20).

The form is abcd||a′c′b′d′. Not only are the middle sections reversed chiastically, but they are also altered slightly by the use of synonyms: Tabernacle/sanctuary and from Israel/from the congregation.

Moreover, the beginning of each panel is also marked by the same phraseology: "This is the ritual law" (v. 2a) and "This is the ritual" (v. 14*a*a); the missing "law," ***ḥukkat,*** has been transferred to the end (v. 21a), thereby framing the entire chapter in an inclusion. In other words, the opening title has been split to provide the same panel with its beginning and its end. Another interlocking element is the term "fire of the purification offering" (v. 17), which has been formed from two phrases of the first panel: "the fire" cleansing (lit. "purification offering"; v. 6b) and "[It is a] purification offering" (v. 9b).

EXCURSUS 48

The Paradox of the Red Cow (chap. 19)

A heathen questioned Rabban Johanan ben Zakkai, saying:

"The things you Jews do appear to be a kind of sorcery. A cow is brought, it is burned, is pounded into ash, and its ash is gathered up. Then when one of you gets defiled by contact with a corpse, two or three drops of the ash mixed with water are sprinkled upon him, and he is told, 'You are cleansed!'"

Rabban Johanan asked the heathen: "Has the spirit of madness ever possessed you?" He replied: "No. Have you ever seen a man whom the spirit of madness has possessed?" The heathen replied: "Yes. And what do you do for such a man? Roots are brought, the smoke of their burning is made to rise about him, and water is sprinkled upon him until the spirit of madness flees."

Rabban Johanan then said: "Do not your ears hear what your mouth is saying? It is the same with a man who is defiled by contact with a corpse—he, too, is possessed by a spirit, the spirit of uncleanness, and Scripture says, 'I will make [false] prophets as well as the unclean spirit vanish from the land'" (Zech. 13:2).

Now when the heathen left, Rabban Johanan's disciples said: "Our master, you put off that heathen with a mere reed of an answer [lit. "you shoved aside that heathen with a reed"], but what answer will you give us?"

Rabban Johanan answered: "By your lives, I swear: The corpse does not have the power by itself to defile, nor does the mixture of ash and water have the power by itself to cleanse. The truth is that the purifying power of the red cow is a decree of the Holy One. The Holy One said: I have set it down as a statute, I have issued it as a decree. You are not permitted to transgress My decree. 'This is the ritual law' (Num. 19:1)" (PdRK 4:7).

The discrepancy between the explanations given by the rabbi to the heathen and to his students reveals the great bewilderment among early Jewish scholars concerning the working and meaning of this ritual. Rabbi Johanan flatly denies that what outwardly looks like an exorcism is indeed so. Yet he is at a loss to find a rationale. His perplexity is aggravated not just by the form of the rite but by its paradoxical effect. Whereas the ashes of the red cow purify those on whom they are sprinkled, they defile those who do the sprinkling (vv. 19,21) and, indeed, anyone who handles them (v. 21) and is involved in preparing them (vv. 6–10). This paradox is neatly captured in the rabbinic apothegm: They purify the defiled and defile the pure (PdRK 4:6).

It is here proposed that the key to unlock the paradox of the red cow is that it is a ***ḥatta't*** sacrifice, as stated unambiguously by the text: "It is a *ḥatta't*" (v. 9). The function of the

ḥatta't sacrifice, as has been demonstrated, is to remove contamination (*ḥitte'* means "decontaminate"). Hence, it should be rendered "purification offering."[1] Since the red cow is labeled a "burnt *ḥatta't* (v. 17), it falls into the category of the *ḥatta't* brought for severe impurities. Its flesh may not be eaten but is burned outside the camp (Lev. 4:6–7,11–12; cf. 6:23; 10:18).[2] Yet the difference in the ritual procedure is glaring: The blood of the red cow is not offered up on the altar in the same manner as is the blood of every *ḥatta't* and, indeed, of every other animal sacrifice. Rather, the whole cow, together with its blood, is incinerated outside the camp (v. 5). Thus it does not appear to be a sacrifice at all.

This discrepancy is a serious one, but it can be resolved. The blood of the red cow is not offered on the altar for the simple reason that it is needed in the ashes as an ongoing *ḥatta't*. It has been shown that the element of the *ḥatta't* that does the decontaminating is the blood. Its placement on the horns of the altars (Lev. 4:4,7,18,25,30,34), in the Shrine (Lev. 4:6,17), or in the adytum (Lev. 16:14) is what purges these sancta of their accumulated impurities (see Excursus 49). True, other traditional purgatives are contained in the ashes—cedar, hyssop, and crimson yarn—but these elements are clearly secondary to the blood, which infuses the ashes with their lustral power.

This single postulate of the red cow as a *ḥatta't* suffices to break the back of the paradox. For the unique characteristic of the *ḥatta't* is that it defiles its handlers. Thus, the one who burns the *ḥatta't* outside the camp "shall wash his clothes and bathe his body in water; after that he may reenter the camp" (Lev. 16:28). Here we have a precise parallel to the defilement incurred by the one who burns the red cow outside the camp and who undergoes a similar purification (v. 8).

It is the very mechanism of the purgation that helps clarify the paradox. In effect, the *ḥatta't* absorbs the impurity it has purged. For that reason, it must be eliminated by incineration. However, this means that anyone involved in the incineration of the *ḥatta't* is infected by it and must undergo purification. Furthermore, since the *ḥatta't* blood now bears the impurity it has absorbed, it contaminates any object it spatters (Lev. 6:20b). Hence the laws of impurity prevail in the cleansing of objects contacted by the *ḥatta't*: earthenware must be broken (cf. Lev. 6:21a with Lev. 11:33,35; 15:12a) and metalware scoured (cf. Lev. 6:21b with Num. 31:22–23).

The residual power of ritual detergents is illustrated by a provision in the Hittite law code (par. 44b): "If anyone has performed a rite of purification on a man, he disposes of the remnants [of the offerings] at the place of burning. If he disposes of them in anyone's field or house, it is sorcery and a case for the court of the king." In the Babylonian exorcism called Shurpu, the patient is rubbed (*kuppuru*) and the impurity, purged by the ritual detergent called *kupiratu*, is then removed to the open country (vii.59–63). The lexical congruence with Hebrew *kipper*, the exclusive term for "purge" used with the *ḥatta't*, needs no additional verification. Thus both ancient Near Eastern rites and vocabulary provide firm precedent for burning or otherwise eliminating the *ḥatta't* because it absorbs the baneful impurity of the object that it has purged. This, then, is the nature of the burnt *ḥatta't*: It transmits impurity from the purified to the purifier; hence, it purifies the defiled and defiles the pure.

The *ḥatta't* postulate commends itself for the additional reason that it accounts for the main details in the preparation of the ashes of the red cow, as follows:

1. *The cow* (v. 2). At first sight, the requirement of a cow clashes with the *ḥatta't* postulate since everywhere else the *ḥatta't* for the individual is either a bull, ewe, or doe.

The discrepancy is chimerical. A bovine is required in order to provide the maximum amount of ashes. However, the bull cannot be chosen since it represents the *ḥatta't* either of the High Priest (Lev. 4:1–12; 16:11) or of the community (Lev. 4:13–21). The red cow, on the other hand, is intended for the exclusive use of the individual Israelite and, according to the priestly code, the individual may bring only a female of the flock for a *ḥatta't* (Lev. 4:22–35; Num. 15:27–29). Thus, since the ashes of the red cow must theoretically supply the purificatory needs of the entire population, the largest female animal is selected—a cow.

2. *red* (v. 2). The association of red with blood is widely attested in primitive cultures.[3] Thus the red hide of the cow symbolically adds to the quantity of blood in the ash mixture (as does the crimson yarn and the [red] cedar; v. 7)[4] and enhances its potency.

3. *without blemish* (v. 2), the basic requirement for sacrificial animals (Lev. 22:17–20).

4. *in his presence* (v. 3) . . . *in his sight* (v. 5). The cow is slaughtered and burned, with Eleazar in attendance. The need for continuous priestly supervision betrays the inherent danger that the ritual may slip back to its pagan moorings, a point that will be developed below. However, incorporating the ritual into the sacrificial regime effectively places it under priestly control.

5. *Eleazar the priest shall take some of its blood with his finger and sprinkle* (*ve-hizzah*) *it seven times toward the front of the Tent of Meeting* (v. 4). Sprinkling the blood toward the Tabernacle proves that the rite is a sacrifice. Instead of sprinkling the blood on the altar—precluded by the need to add the blood to the ashes—the blood is sprinkled toward the altar. The effect is the same: The blood becomes consecrated. In a similar manner the priest sprinkles oil seven times "before the LORD" prior to the purification of the leper (Lev. 14:16); that is, he must consecrate it before he can use it.

An equally cogent parallel is provided by the *ḥatta't* blood on the Day of Atonement. First it is daubed on the horns of the outer altar, and then it is sprinkled on the altar seven times. The purpose of this double manipulation is supplied by the text: *ve-tiharo ve-kiddesho mi-tum'ot benei yisra'el,* "cleanse it [the altar] of [literally] Israel's impurities and consecrate it" (Lev. 16:19). After the altar is cleansed, it needs to be reconsecrated, an act accomplished by the sevenfold aspersion with the *ḥatta't* blood.[5] By the same token, the sevenfold aspersion of the blood of the red cow also consecrates it so that it may always act as a purgative when, in the form of ashes, it is sprinkled upon the impure.

6. *The cow shall be burned in his sight—its hide, flesh, and blood shall be burned, its dung included* (v. 5). The parts of the cow that are burned duplicate those of the *ḥatta't* animal that are burned (Lev. 4:11)—with the notable exception of the blood. Indeed, it is the blood in the ashes that endows them with purificatory powers.

7. *Cedar wood, hyssop, and crimson stuff* (v. 6). These very ingredients, together with blood, are added to the leper's lustral waters (Lev. 14:6,49–50). Thus the mixtures that purify the corpse-contaminated individual and the leper are of the identical composition. Yet their effect upon their manipulators is not the same: The waters for corpse contamination defile; the waters for leprosy do not. The obvious explanation is that the blood used for the leprosy ritual is not a *ḥatta't*. In other words, the first-day ritual for purifying the leper was not incorporated into the *ḥatta't* system, and it retained its pristine, pre-Israelite form.

8. *The priest* who throws the cedar, hyssop, and crimson yarn into the fire (v. 6) is unclean as are the persons who set the cow on fire (vv. 5,8) and collect the ashes (v. 10). However, neither the slaughterer of the cow (v. 3) nor the priest who consecrated its blood (v. 4) is said to have become unclean. The difference is one of time: Only those who come

into contact with the red cow after the consecration of its blood become unclean. This proves that the blood consecration transforms the red cow into a *ḥatta't*, a purification offering, since anyone handling the *ḥatta't* becomes unclean (Lev. 16:28).

9. *It is a ḥatta't* (v. 9). This is the attested formula by which a given sacrifice is declared a *ḥatta't* (cf. Exod. 29:14; Lev. 4:24; 5:9,11,12). However, this formula's use here bears greater significance. It follows upon the sentence that states that the ashes of the red cow are to be "preserved (*le-mishmeret*) by the Israelite community for waters of lustration." "It" (*Ketiv hw'*) is masculine and refers not to the cow but to *'efer,* the ashes. Thus the ashes of the red cow continue to operate as a *ḥatta't*.

In this manner, the *ḥatta't* postulate has unraveled the paradox: The ashes of the red cow are a burnt *ḥatta't*. Hence, they defile their handlers and purify their recipients. Moreover, this postulate has been shown to be the organizing principle in the entire red cow ritual.

One detail, however, remains unexplained by the *ḥatta't* postulate, a detail that occurs not in the preparation of the ashes but in their use. The ashes of the red cow are not sprinkled only on impure objects; they are used primarily on impure persons—constituting a break with the rule that the *ḥatta't* blood is applied solely to objects, indeed, solely to objects within the sanctuary precincts. These sacred objects have been polluted by the physical impurity or the inadvertent wrong of the one who offers the *ḥatta't*. He, the offerer, is cleansed of his physical impurity by his ablutions and cleansed of his wrongdoing by his remorse—but never by the *ḥatta't* blood.[6]

The uniqueness of the aspersion of *ḥatta't* ashes on the body of the corpse-contaminated person is significant because it bears comparison with pre-Israelite precedents. In Mesopotamia, for example, an impure person might be purified by changing or laundering his garments, bathing with pure water, being aspersed with tamarisk and *tullal* plant (the latter remains unidentified) or incensed with censer and torch, and, above all, being wiped with specially prepared detergents. Purification rituals, then, are performed on the body of the afflicted. No wonder then that Rabban Johanan could put off the heathen with his rationale: Exorcisms continued to be performed by aspersing the victim with magical substances, not only in ages gone by but in his time as well.

The question needs to be asked: Why were the ashes retained? Why did not the priestly legislators eliminate this anomaly from the *ḥatta't* purification ritual it prescribed for corpse contamination? The answer surely must be that corpse contamination evoked an obsessive, irrational fear in individuals. In a Mesopotamian Namburbi ritual, the victim is in mortal fear that the evil he saw has infected him with lethal impurity, and he requires an exorcistic incantation in addition to sacrificing, bathing, changing his clothing, and remaining shut up in his house for seven days.[7] That the fear of corpse contamination prevailed into rabbinic times is seen from the report of Josephus that King Herod had to use force to settle Jews in newly constructed Tiberias; to appease them, he even built them homes and gave them tracts of land (Ant. 18.36–38)—all this because he had built Tiberias over a graveyard. Thus it stands to reason that he who had contracted corpse contamination would demand an exorcism, the application of powerful countervailing forces to his body that would drive out the dreaded impurity. Even had the priestly legislators desired to eliminate the use of the ashes (a doubtful supposition), it is hard to believe that the people at large would have let them.

In truth, an exorcism has been preserved in near pristine form in the Bible: the first-day

purification of the healed leper and "leprous" house (Lev. 14:4–8,49–53). As noted above, the same elements that are mixed with the ashes of the red cow are prescribed for the leper's purification: cedar, hyssop, crimson yarn, and, above all, blood. Once again, it is the blood that constitutes the chief detergent because each element must be dipped into the blood (vv. 6,51). Even the decisive verb *ḥitte'*, "purge," is used (vv. 49,52), which indicates that an exorcism is required to remove the impurity from the stricken person or home. Yet the slain bird that has supplied the blood is not called a *ḥatta't*. Nor should we expect it, for the blood is not sprinkled in the direction of the Tabernacle as is the blood of the red cow. The aspersion of the leper, then, must represent the more original rite, and the red cow, transformed into a *ḥatta't*, constitutes a later, Israelite stage.

One additional requirement in the rite of the leper points to its antiquity. It also requires that a live bird be dipped into the blood of the slain bird and then dispatched to the open country (Lev. 14:6–7,51–53). Thus, because it is not enough to exorcise the leper's impurity, it must be sent off to an uninhabited area where it can no longer do harm. There is no comparable requirement in the purification performed with the ashes of the red cow.

This double requirement of removing and dispatching the impurity is also found in the ritual for the Day of Atonement: The impurity of the sanctuary is purged (*kipper;* Lev. 16:16,17,18,20) by the blood of a slain goat and bull. The impurity is then loaded onto the head of a live goat, which is dispatched to an inaccessible place in the wilderness (vv. 21–22). Here, too, the complete ritual, exorcism and elimination, has been preserved for the reason that its locus is the sanctuary. It is not sufficient to purge the impurity of the sanctuary: It must be banished to an inaccessible place whence it can no longer harm the sanctuary. Yet despite the retention of the dispatch ritual, the Israelite transformation has been thoroughgoing: Not only is the blood detergent taken from the *ḥatta't* (vv. 11,15), but the dispatch goat is also called a *ḥatta't* (vv. 5,9), even though it is not sacrificed at all.

The ritual of the red cow partially resembles the rituals of the leper and of the Day of Atonement. Like the latter, the red cow is called a *ḥatta't* and follows, in nearly all respects, the procedure of a *ḥatta't*. And like the former, the blood and the same accompanying ingredients are used to asperse persons. Yet unlike either, there is not a dispatch element—no live animal to carry off the impurity. Thus the Israelite transformation of the presumed original ritual of exorcising and dispatching impurity is more thoroughgoing for corpse contamination than for leprosy or the sanctuary. Except for the use of the ashes, the red cow ritual conforms completely to the Israelite sacrificial system.

The metamorphosis of the red cow ritual is evident in yet another vital area: The power of corpse contamination has been vastly reduced. First, unlike the leper, no ablutions are required of the corpse-contaminated individual on the first day. The reason, I submit, is clear: Whereas the leper is required to bathe before he reenters the camp (Lev. 14:8), the one who is corpse contaminated need not bathe since he has not left his community. True, another, probably older law requires the corpse-contaminated person (and the gonorrheic and the leper) to leave the camp (Num. 5:2). But Numbers 19 implies otherwise: (1) Nowhere does it state that the corpse-contaminated person leaves the camp. (2) The clause "and then he may reenter the camp" found in the prescription for the priest who prepares the ashes (v. 7) and for other impurity bearers who are outside the camp (e.g., Lev. 14:8; 16:26,28) is conspicuously absent from the otherwise detailed purification procedure of Numbers 19. (3) The ashes deposited outside the camp (v. 9) are brought to the one who is corpse contaminated (vv. 17–18a) and not the other way around—implying that he remains

inside the camp. (4) Failure to undergo the water lustration "defiles the LORD's Tabernacle/sanctuary" (vv. 13,20), a consequence that is possible only as long as he remains inside the camp. Thus that the corpse-contaminated individual, unlike the leper, is not required to bathe on the first day and is not banished from the camp during the week of his purification clearly indicates that the priestly legislators eventually downgraded the degree of his impurity.

Further evidence for the diminution of an originally more powerful corpse contamination stems from the fact that the individual brings no sacrifice at the end of his purification. Unlike the parturient, leper, and gonorrheic, who bring a *ḥatta't* on the eighth and final day of their purificatory period (Lev. 12:6–8; 14:10,21–23; 15:14,29), the one who is corpse contaminated completes his purification in seven days and brings no *ḥatta't*. This means that his impurity *ab initio* is not severe enough to pollute the sanctuary as are the other impurities requiring a *ḥatta't*. Only if he delays his purification does his impurity, so to speak, gather force to impinge on the sanctuary, subjecting him to the *karet* penalty if his negligence is deliberate (Num. 15:30–31) or to a *ḥatta't* if he has inadvertently forgotten (Lev. 5:2–3). Lastly, that Numbers 19 reflects a reduction in the potency of corpse contamination is shown by contrasting it with the more conservative view of the priest-prophet Ezekiel: A corpse-contaminated priest must bring a *ḥatta't* at the end of his purificatory period (Ezek. 14:27). This view is still reflected in the priestly text that requires a corpse-contaminated Nazirite—the lay equivalent of a priest—to offer sacrifices on the eighth day of his purification (Num. 6:10–12). In effect, the priestly legislators have reduced the degree of impurity in corpse contamination from the most to the least severe; that is, the impurities requiring a minimum of eight days of purification actually rank as more severe than corpse contamination, which requires seven days of purification and no sacrifice.

In sum, the lustral ashes of the red cow are the only vestige of a pre-Israelite exorcism for corpse contamination. Otherwise, the rite has been totally transformed by the Israelite values inherent in its sacrificial procedures. Above all, the hitherto demonic impurity of corpses has been devitalized, first by denying it the automatic power to contaminate the sanctuary (requiring a *ḥatta't*) upon completion of the purification period and then by denying that the corpse-contaminated individual need leave the camp or city during his purificatory period. Finally, the procedure for preparing the ashes has been restructured to conform to the *ḥatta't* requirements and integrated into Israel's sacrificial system. Because of these changes, the ritual of the red cow, as presently constituted in Numbers 19, is relatively later than the rituals for the severe impurities of Leviticus 12–15, which betray more primitive traces; and that, in the long run, is perhaps what accounts for its insertion in Numbers rather than in Leviticus.

Thus, Rabban Johanan's answer to the heathen reflects the probable origin of the red cow ritual. But neither the rabbi nor his students believed it. For them, and for Judaism, it was inconceivable that any rite was inherently efficacious. In the absence of rational explanation there was, solely and sufficiently, the inscrutable will of God. The break with paganism was complete, but it was not the achievement of their age. More than a half millennium earlier the priestly legislators of this ritual had already severed its pagan roots and remodeled it to accord with their religious beliefs and practice.[8]

EXCURSUS 49

The Effect of the Sinner upon the Sanctuary (chap. 19)

Embodying the priestly theology concerning the effect of sin is the sacrifice called *ḥatta'ṭ,* "purification (or purgation) offering." The question arises at once: Whom or what does it purge? Herein lies the first surprise: It is not the offerer of the sacrifice. It must be remembered that the *ḥatta'ṭ* is brought by an individual in one of two circumstances: He is in a state of severe physical impurity (the parturient, leper, or gonorrheic; Lev. 12–15); or he has committed certain inadvertent sins (e.g., Lev. 4). Clearly, physical impurity is removed by ablution: "He shall wash his clothes, bathe in water" (Lev. 15:8). On the other hand, spiritual impurity caused by inadvertent violation of prohibitive commandments (Lev. 4:22ff.) requires no purificatory rite. The fact that his sin is inadvertent (*bi-shegagah*) and that he feels guilt (*ve-'ashem*) means that he has undergone inner purification.

The contention that the *ḥatta'ṭ* never purifies its offerer is supported by the use of its blood: "Moses took the *ḥatta'ṭ* blood and with his finger put some on each of the horns of the altar, thereby decontaminating (*va-yeḥatte'*) the altar" (Lev. 8:15). The *ḥatta'ṭ* blood, then, is the purging element, the ritual detergent. Its use is confined to the sanctuary, and it is never applied to a person. For example, the rites for the healed leper and the priests' consecration call for both the *ḥatta'ṭ* and the blood daubing, but the latter ritual stems from other sacrificial animals and not the *ḥatta'ṭ* (Exod. 39:20; Lev. 8:22–24; 14:14,25).

Finally, a study of the prepositions used with *kipper* is decisive. In the context of the *ḥatta'ṭ, kipper* means "purge" and nothing else, as indicated by its synonyms *ḥitte'* and *tiher* (e.g., Lev. 14:51–52; Ezek. 43:20,26). When the object is nonhuman, *kipper* takes a preposition, *'al* or *be,* or a direct object. For example, all three usages are attested in the purging of the Holy of Holies—the most sacred area of the sanctuary, containing the holy Ark—on the Day of Atonement (Lev. 16:16–17,20). They must be understood literally, since the *kipper* rite takes place on (*'al*) the *kapporet* and on the floor before it, in (*be*) the adytum; or it can be said that the entire room (*'et*) has been subject to *kipper* (cf. also Exod. 30:10; Lev. 6:23; 16:33). However, when the object of *kipper* is a person, it is never expressed as a direct object but requires the prepositions *'al* or *be-'ad,* both signifying "on behalf of" (e.g., Lev. 16:6,24,30,33; Num. 8:12,21). This means that the purgation rite of *ḥatta'ṭ* is not carried out on the offerer but only on his behalf.

If not the offerer, what then is the object of the *ḥatta'ṭ* purgation? The above considerations lead to but one answer: that which receives the purgative blood—the sanctuary and its sancta. By daubing the altar with the *ḥatta'ṭ* blood or by bringing it inside the sanctuary (e.g., Lev. 16:14–19), the priest purges the most sacred objects and areas of the sanctuary on behalf of the person who caused their contamination by his physical impurity or inadvertent offense.

This conclusion enables us to understand the distinction between the *ḥatta'ṭ* for impurities and inadvertencies. The inadvertent offender is never called "impure" and hence requires no ablutions. In his case the concluding formula reads *ve-kipper hakohen . . . ve-nislaḥ lo,* "the priest shall perform the purgation rite . . . and he may be forgiven" (e.g., Lev. 4:20,26,31,35), whereas for the impure person the formula reads *ve-kipper ha-kohen . . . vetaher(ah),* "the priest shall perform the purgation rite . . . and he [she] shall be clean" (e.g.,

Lev. 12:6,8; 14:9,20). Thus the impure person needs purification and the sinner needs forgiveness.

The inadvertent offender needs forgiveness not because of his act per se—as indicated above, his act is forgiven because of the offender's inadvertence and remorse—but because of the *consequence* of his act. His inadvertence has contaminated the sanctuary and it is his responsibility to purge it with a *ḥatta't*. Confirmation of this thesis is provided by the tannaim: "All the [*ḥatta't* goats] make atonement for the impurity of the Temple and its sancta" (Mish. Shevu. 1:4–5). This rabbinic tradition has preserved the postulate that the *ḥatta't* blood is the ritual detergent employed by the priest to purge the sanctuary of the impurities inflicted upon it by the offerer of the sacrifice.

The *ḥatta't* as the authorized purgative of the sanctuary echoes with a familiar ring for students of ancient Near Eastern cults in which temple purifications play so dominant a role. Impurity was feared because it was considered demonic. It was an unending threat to the gods themselves and especially to their temples, as exemplified by the images of protector gods set before temple entrances (e.g., the *šēdu* and *lamassu* in Mesopotamia and the lion-gargoyles in Egypt) and, above all, by the elaborate cathartic and apotropaic rites to rid buildings of demons and prevent their return. Thus for Israel's neighbors impurity was a physical substance, a miasma that possessed magnetic attraction for the realm of the sacred.

Israel, for its part, thoroughly overhauled this concept of impurity in adapting it to its monotheistic system—although the notion of its dynamic and malefic power, especially in regard to the sancta, was not completely expunged from the priestly texts. Thus, (1) Molech worship is forbidden because it contaminates "My sanctuary" (Lev. 20:3). (2) Whoever is contaminated by a corpse and fails to purify himself "has defiled the LORD's sanctuary" (Num. 19:13,20). (3) Those afflicted with pelvic discharges also need purification, "lest they die through their impurity by defiling My Tabernacle which is among them" (Lev. 15:31). The two latter offenders are banished with the leper, "that they do not defile the camp in whose midst I dwell" (Num. 5:3b). True, the rabbis assumed, in interpreting each of these passages, that impurity came into direct contact with the holy, specifically, that the offender while in an impure state entered the sanctuary or ate of sacred food. However, it is patently clear that these texts are grounded in the axiom, common to all ancient Near Eastern cultures, that impurity is the implacable foe of holiness wherever it exists; it assaults the sacred realm even from afar.

The dynamic, aerial quality of biblical impurity is best attested by its graduated power. Impurity pollutes the sanctuary in three stages:

1. The individual's inadvertent misdemeanor or severe physical impurity pollutes the courtyard altar, which is purged by daubing its horns with the *ḥatta't* blood (Lev. 4:25,30; 9:9ff.).

2. The inadvertent misdemeanor of the High Priest or the entire community pollutes the Shrine, which is purged by the High Priest by placing the *ḥatta't* blood on the inner altar and before the *parokhet*-veil (Lev. 4:5–7,16–18).

3. The wanton, unrepented sin not only pollutes the outer altar and penetrates into the Shrine, but it pierces the veil to the holy Ark and *kapporet,* the very throne of God (cf. Isa. 37:16). Since the wanton sinner is barred from bringing his *ḥatta't* (Num. 15:27–31), the pollution wrought by his offense must await the annual purgation of the sanctuary on the Day of Atonement, which consists of two steps: the purging of the Tent and the purging of

the outer altar (Lev. 16:16–19). Thus the entire sacred area or, more precisely, all that is most sacred, is purged on *Yom ha-kippurim* (Purgation Day) with the *ḥatta't* blood.

Thus the graduated purgations of the sanctuary lead to the conclusion that the severity of the sin/impurity varies in direct relation to the depth of its penetration into the sanctuary. This mathematical relationship between sin and sanctuary is best understood by the accompanying diagram.

DIAGRAM OF SANCTUARY CONTAMINATION

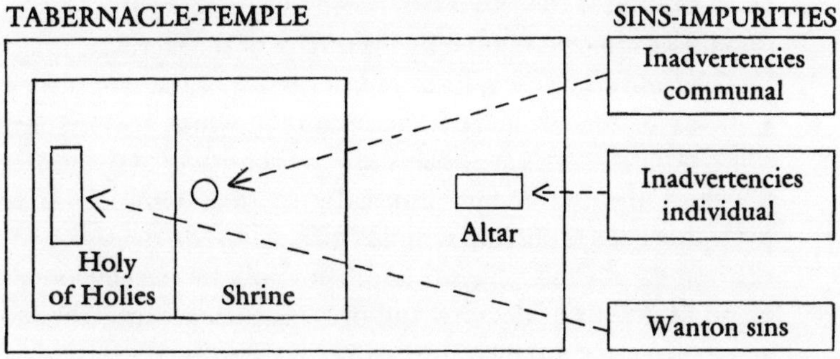

Moreover, this diagram provides graphic illustration of the priestly notion of impurity as a dynamic force, magnetic and malefic to the sphere of the sacred, attacking it not just by direct contact but from a distance. The outer altar is polluted although the wrongdoer is outside the sacred compound; the shrine is polluted although he, a nonpriest, may not even enter it; finally, the adytum is polluted although no man, not even the priest, may enter. Yet despite the fact that Israelites have had no access, the sancta must be purged "of the impurities of the Israelites" (Lev. 16:16).

Significantly, the requirement of two *ḥatta't* goats on Yom Kippur reveals how Israel transformed an ancient exorcism. Demonic impurity was exorcised in three ways: curse, destruction, or banishment. The last was often used; rather than evil being annihilated by curse or fire, it was banished to its place of origin (e.g., netherworld, wilderness) or to some other place where its malefic powers could either work in the interests of the sender (e.g., enemy territory) or do no harm at all (e.g., mountains, wilderness). Thus the scapegoat was sent to the wilderness, which was considered uninhabited except by the satyr demon Azazel. The best-known example of this type of temple purgation is the Babylonian new year festival, when the *urigallu* (high priest) literally wipes the sanctuary walls with the carcass of a ram, which he then throws into the river. Thus the same animal that purges the temple impurities carries them off.

Why then are two goats required in Israel? The text itself provides the answer: The sacrificed goat purges the sanctuary *mi-tume'ot benei yisra'el,* "of Israel's impurities" (Lev. 16:16), whereas the scapegoat carries off *kol 'avonot benei yisra'el,* "all of Israel's transgressions" (Lev. 16:21). The separate functions of the goats are supported by rabbinic tradition: "For impurity that befalls the Temple and its sancta through wantonness, atonement is made by the goat whose blood is sprinkled within the Shrine and by the Day of Atonement. For all other transgressions in the Torah—minor or grave, wanton or inadvertent, conscious or unconscious, of commission or omission—the scapegoat makes atonement" (Mish. Shevu. 1:6). Thus, the slain *ḥatta't* purges the sanctuary, and the live *ḥatta't* purges

the people. The reason for this variance from ancient Near Eastern practice is clear: Israel, the holy people (Lev. 11:44; 19:2; 20:26), needs the same purification as the holy place.

Finally, why the urgency to purge the sanctuary? The answer lies in the postulate that the God of Israel will not dwell in a polluted sanctuary. Although the merciful God will tolerate a modicum of pollution, there is a point of no return. If the pollution continues to accumulate, the end is inexorable: "The cherubs . . . lifted their wings" (Ezek. 11:22). The divine chariot flies heavenward and the sanctuary is left to its doom.

On this point, Israel is in full accord with its neighbors' obsessive compulsion to purify their temples. However, this common ground is split by an unbridgeable chasm. One of Y. Kaufmann's keenest observations is that the ancients feared impurity because it was demonic, even metadivine, capable of attacking the gods.[1] Hence men were summoned, indeed created, for the purpose of purifying temples to aid the benevolent resident gods in their battles with cosmic evil. In Israel, however, there are no traces of demonic impurity. Kaufmann would have us believe that biblical impurity has been completely devitalized. True, the demons have been expunged from the world, but man has taken their place. This is one of the major contributions of the priestly theology: Man is demonized—he falls short of being a demon, but he is capable of the demonic. He alone is the cause of the world's ills. He alone can contaminate the sanctuary and force God out.

If this reconstruction of the priestly theology of the *ḥatta't* is correct, then we have succeeded in uncovering one of the ethical supports upon which the sacrificial system was reared. It constitutes the priestly theodicy. No intellectual circle of ancient Israel evaded the challenge of theodicy; the prophets agonized over it but came up with no solutions. The wisdom literature gave its superficial answer, and its refutation motivated the writing of Job. Thus we should be led to expect a priestly answer, but we search for it in vain. Is it possible that Israel's priests, who had as their prime function to "teach the Israelites" (Lev. 10:11), had nothing to say concerning God's Providence?

Now we know what the priestly theodicy is. It is found not in utterances but in rituals, not in legal statutes but in cultic procedures—specifically, in the rite with the *ḥatta't* blood. The priestly writers claimed that sin may not leave its mark on the face of the sinner, but it is certain to mark the face of the sanctuary, and unless it is quickly expunged God's Presence will depart. In truth, this teaching is not a startling innovation; it is only an extension of the doctrine of collective responsibility, a doctrine that all concur is basic to the priestly theology. It is only natural that they would regard the sanctuary of which they were the stewards as the spiritual barometer by which to measure and explain God's behavior to His people. They knew full well that the prophet was justified in protesting, "Why does the way of the wicked prosper?" (Jer. 12:1), and they provided their answer: Although the sinner may be unscarred by his evil, the sanctuary bears the scars, and, with its destruction, he too will meet his doom.

To summarize: The *ḥatta't* is a vantage point from which to view Israel's cultic ties with its neighbors as well as the gulf that separates them. They hold in common that the impure and the holy are mutually antagonistic and irreconcilable. Thus the sanctuary needs constant purification lest the resident god abandon it as well as his devotees. They differ on one basic issue: The pagan world is suffused with demonic impurity, whereas Israel has eviscerated impurity of its magical power. Only in its nexus with the sancta does it spring to life. However, this malefic impurity does not inhere in nature; it is the creation of man. Man can evict God from His earthly abode—but only to destroy himself.[2]

EXCURSUS 50

Magic, Monotheism, and the Sin of Moses (20:1–13)

Down through the ages, the sin of Moses, as described in Numbers 20:1–13, has been regarded as one of the Gordian knots of the Bible: The punishment is clear; but what is the crime? At least ten explanations given by the medieval Jewish commentators deserve our serious attention.[1] They can be subsumed under three different aspects of the biblical account:

1. Moses' action in striking the rock: (a) that he struck it instead of speaking (Rashi, Rashbam, Arama, Shadal, Malbim); (b) that he chose it although the people wanted another rock (Oraḥ Ḥayyim, Yal., Lek. Tov); (c) that he struck it twice instead of once (Targ. Jon., Ibn Ezra).

2. His character, shown by (a) his blazing temper (Maimonides, Ibn Ezra, Tanḥ. B. 4:210); (b) his cowardice (in fleeing to the sanctuary; v. 6; Albo, Biur); (c) his callousness (in mourning for Miriam while his people died of thirst; Yal., Lek. Tov).

3. His words, (a) which in the form of a question were misconstrued as doubting God (Meir ha-Kohen, Ramban); (b) actually doubting God (Tanḥ. B. 4:121–22; Deut. R. 19:13–14); (c) calling Israel "rebels" (Ibn Ezra); (d) *notsi'*, "shall we draw forth . . ." (Hananel, Ramban).

We shall begin, however, with an eleventh theory—that offered by the consensus of the modern critics. By claiming that the sin of Moses has been lost or deliberately obscured so as not to detract from the glory of Israel's founder, this theory cuts the Gordian knot. An argument from silence is, of course, rarely satisfactory, particularly if the text itself can be made to disclose Moses' sin, as we shall soon discover. As for the notion that Moses' transgression is excised from the narrative, it would have required a severe mutilation of the text to accomplish this purpose. Such a motive, moreover, is not in keeping with what we find elsewhere in the Bible: The biblical editors do not portray infallible heroes and do not hesitate to tarnish them. David's historian, for example, was fiercely loyal to him and his seed, recounting that God would "establish the throne of his kingdom forever" (2 Sam. 7:13,16). Yet he spared no pains to castigate his hero for the sin with Bathsheba (2 Sam. 12:1–14). The Pentateuchal narratives are equally hard on Judah, the ancestor of David, not to speak of Levi, the ancestor of Moses, and Noah, the ancestor of mankind (Gen. 9:21; 34:30; 38; 49:5–7).

Of the ten arguments, we focus first on the popular contention that Moses' irascibility was the source of his sin (2a), a contention that Ramban effectively rebuts: (1) God's condemnation—"You did not trust Me . . . you disobeyed My command" (20:12,24)—cannot refer to anger. (2) Aaron was not guilty of anger. Why was he also punished? (3) Most important of all, our text is not an isolated case of Moses' petulance; for example, Moses was wroth with his army officers (31:14) without provocation. Ramban's apt illustration has Moses venting his spleen only on Israel; we add that it could border on heresy when directed against God (see 11:11–15,21–22). As for his alleged cowardice (2b), we note that Moses was prone to desperation and paralysis for which, however, he never incurred punishment (e.g., Exod. 14:15; 15:25; 17:4; Num. 14:5; 16:4). His alleged callousness (2c) cannot be derived from our texts or from any others.

In dealing with the category of action—striking the rock—we can immediately dis-

count (1b) and (1c) for lack of corroborative evidence. We must, however, address the claim that carries the greatest weight in the tradition: that Moses incurred God's wrath by striking the rock rather than speaking to it (1a). Ramban, again, is most effective in refuting it: (1) When Moses addressed Israel—"Listen, you rebels"—he was also speaking to the rock and therefore fulfilling God's command. (2) How are we to understand that Moses failed to "sanctify" God (Num. 20:12; 27:14; Deut. 32:51) in striking the rock when it is as much a miracle to draw forth water by striking as by speaking? (3) Why would Moses be told at the beginning of this text to "take the rod" (v. 7) if not for the purpose of using it? Indeed, wherever the rod is employed (except for Exod. 17:9), smiting is either specifically mentioned or implied (e.g., Exod. 7:17,20; 8:12; 17:5–6).

Particularly instructive is Exodus 17:5–7, which reports a similar incident. Moses is commanded, "Take along the rod. . . . Strike the rock and water will issue from it." The similarity is more than just in content but, as the quoted passage indicates, also in language. Here we can justifiably ask: If Moses was told once before to obtain water out of the rock by striking it, how could he not but strike again when asked to repeat the miracle, particularly as he was instructed to "take the rod" with him (cf. Exod. 7:15,17)? Furthermore, if the transgression lay in striking, why are we told that God was not sanctified "in the sight of the Israelite people" (20:12a)? The Israelites could not have been aware that a desecration had occurred since they knew nothing about the order to speak to the rock and since their previous experience would have led them to expect Moses to strike it again.

The remarkable parallels in both content and style between Exodus 17 and Numbers 20 have led most critics to posit two variant accounts for the same incident. This possibility was not lost upon one of the medieval Jewish exegetes, Joseph ben Isaac of Orléans, France, known as Bekhor Shor (see Glossary). He postulates the existence of duplicate narratives in our text not just for the rock incident but also for the stories about the manna and the quail. The three episodes are each related twice, once in Exodus and once in Numbers. Evidently, it is the duplication of the quail incident that leads Bekhor Shor to propose his radical solution. For he asks: "If Moses saw that the quail arrived in sufficient quantities the first time, how could he on the second occasion doubt: 'Could enough flocks and herds be slaughtered to suffice them?' (Num. 11:22)."

We can then proceed from this initial clue. Deuteronomy 33:8b reads: "Whom you tested at Massah/Challenged at the waters of Meribah." Since a poetic line consists of parallel clauses, Massah and Meribah must refer to the same incident. The Psalms also interchange the names (e.g., Ps. 95:8–9). Psalms 78:15–31, in particular, which reviews the triad of rock-manna-quail, serves to corroborate Bekhor Shor's thesis. Here, the incident of the quail is mentioned as occurring once. Furthermore, each reference to the rock speaks of it being struck. Lastly, since it is the Numbers version of the quail that is reported here, the psalmist may also have recounted the Numbers version of the rock, and yet he speaks of the rock only as being struck! Perhaps the clearest evidence is that of Deuteronomy 9:22, "Again you provoked the LORD at Taberah, and at Massah, and at Kibroth-hattaavah." The first and third sites are reported in Numbers 11:3,34, whereas Massah is the name given to the rock in Exodus 17:7! It again stands to reason, in the words of the Bekhor Shor, that "the two are one." Finally, attention should be paid to the final verse in the Numbers pericope: "Those are the Waters of Meribah—meaning that the Israelites quarreled with the LORD" (20:13). The wording indicates that the name "Waters of Meribah" has been given previously. And indeed it has, in Exodus 17:7: "The place was named Massah and Meribah, because the Israelites quarreled and because they tried the LORD." Here, then, is

another indication that the two incidents of water from rock are one and the same. Further support for their identity is the mention in this verse of Israel's quarrel with the Lord. However, the quarrel is not with the Lord but with Moses and Aaron (20:2). It is only in the Exodus version that Meribah receives its name because of Israel's "quarrel with the Lord" (Exod. 17:7).

Thus the possibility exists that the two episodes of Moses' drawing water from the rock are but variants of the same tradition. Yet they cannot be equated because of one major difference: In Exodus, Moses is told to strike the rock; in Numbers, he is to speak to it. Ramban suggests two ways of reconciling this difference. First he proposes that *'el*, "to," should be understood as *'al*, "of," citing Jeremiah 27:19 as a precedent, with the result that the verse now reads: "You and your brother Aaron take the rod and assemble the community, and before their very eyes speak *of* the rock so that it will yield its water." Alternatively, Ramban suggests a transposition of *ve-dibbartem* and *'el ha-sela'* with the result that the verse now reads, "You and your brother Aaron take the rod and assemble the community *at* the rock and speak in their presence so that it will yield its water." Thus, according to either rendering, Moses and Aaron are not to speak to the rock but to the assembled Israelites to inform them of the coming miracle, that the Lord will provide water from the rock as soon as Moses strikes it. Indeed some oral explanation is always required in advance of a miracle so that the people will know that it is the work of God and not an accident of nature. Such advance explanation is not only logically expected but is always attested (e.g., the plagues: Exod. 7:16–19,26–29; 8:16–19; 9:1–4,13–19; 10:3–6; 11:4–8; the sea: Exod. 14:13; the wilderness: Exod. 16:6–8; Num. 11:18–20; Sinai: Exod. 19:7,10–11,15–16; Korah: Num. 16:16–17,28–30; 17:16–20).

Ramban's second interpretation is supported by the oft attested usage of *'el* meaning "by, at, in the vicinity of," particularly with reference to natural objects: place (Deut. 16:6; 1 Kings 8:30b), sky (1 Kings 8:30b), water (Jer. 41:12), hill (Josh. 5:3), and particularly by the evidence in this pericope itself. As it stands, verse 8 contains God's command; verses 9–10a describe its execution. Since, as demonstrated, Moses' sin does not lie in the execution of God's command, the two parts—command and execution—should not vary from each other even slightly, either in context or language. But this is not what we find. Verse 10a gives the fulfillment of God's order with the words *'el penei ha-sela'*: "Moses and Aaron assembled the congregation in front of the rock; and he said to them." The fulfillment passage thus clearly states that the gathering is *at* the rock and the speaking is *to the people*. Since these conditions should also obtain in the command, we conclude that *'el ha-sela'* in verse 8 is also the object of the verb *hikhil* and means "at the rock"—the command *ve-dibbartem*, "you shall speak," like *va-yo'mer lahem* (v. 10) is therefore directed to the people and not to the rock.

It may be conjectured that originally Numbers 20:8a read as follows: קח את־המטה והקהל את העדה אתה ואהרן אחיך (ודברתם) אל הסלע[והכית את הסלע] לעיניהם ונתן מימיו/"You and your brother Aaron take the rod and assemble the community before the rock and strike the rock before their very eyes so that it will yield its water." Following the model of the plague narrative where the same vocabulary occurs, it is clear that striking with the rod must take place before those on whom the ensuing miracle must make an impression: ויך את־המים . . . לעיני פרעה ולעיני עבדיו/"He struck the water . . . *in the sight* of Pharaoh and *in the presence* of his servants" (Exod. 7:20; cf. 9:8b). Even more striking is the occurrence of this vocabulary in the Exodus version of the water-rock story: והכית בצור . . . ויעש כן משה לעיני זקני ישראל/ "Strike

the rock. . . . So did Moses ***in the sight*** of the elders of Israel" (Exod. 17:6). We conclude on this basis that the original text of 20:8a very likely contained the command "strike the rock," which, however, accidentally fell out because of the homoeoteleuton. Subsequently ***ve-dibbartem,*** "and speak," was (incorrectly) inserted on the grounds that the fulfillment passage does relate that Moses did speak (20:10b).

A third, more radical approach postulates that the original text called for Moses to strike the rock because an act was needed to bring the Word into fulfillment. This theory posits that the text was altered—to speaking to the rock—in order to bring it into conformity with the alleged later view, reflected in Genesis 1, that God's word was inherently effectual and required no human gesticulation.[2]

In any event, even if we are not disposed to accept the suggested, drastic textual change or either of Ramban's renderings—if we follow the accepted interpretation that Moses and Aaron were ordered to speak to the rock—we cannot gainsay the evidence that the rock was also to be struck with the rod. Thus, their sin lies not in their action but in the only remaining alternative—in Moses' words.

Arguments 3a,b,c are easily dismissed. As to the question in verse 10b implying either unintentional (3a) or deliberate doubt (3b) of God's powers, this is not a first for Moses (e.g., Exod. 4:10–14; 5:22–23; especially Num. 11:11–15,21–22). The answer of the midrash that elsewhere Moses' doubts were uttered in private is unconvincing, for his recurring failure of nerve, another form of doubt and subject to divine censure, occurred at times in full view of the public (e.g., Exod. 14:15; and our own text, v. 6). Finally, since verse 10b is addressed to Israel not to God it is most likely not a question but rather an exclamation of Moses' brittle impatience.

Regarding the use of the word "rebels" as unbecoming (3c), it is apparently not too unbecoming for the Deuteronomist to harp on it (Deut. 1:26,43; 9:7,23–24; 31:27), for Ezekiel to favor it in chastising Israel (e.g., Ezek. 20:8), and for its repeated use by the psalmist (Pss. 78:17; 106:33; 107:11). Indeed, had not God Himself earlier dubbed the Israelites "rebels" (Num. 17:25)? Why should Moses not have availed himself of this divine precedent?

We are left with argument 3d: ***notsi'***. Bekhor Shor has a single terse comment on this word, pointing to the resolution of our enigma: "The sin resulted from saying ***notsi',*** 'shall we draw forth,' and they (Moses and Aaron) should have said ***yotsi',*** 'shall He draw forth,'" meaning God. The Bekhor Shor is not original. This interpretation was proposed earlier by Rabbi Hananel ben Ḥushiel of Kairouwan (ca. 980–1056), and is cited with approval by Ramban (cf. also Ibn Ezra on Ps. 106:33). Rabbi Hananel explains Moses' sin by comparing the circumstances of Massah-Meribah (Exodus 17) with those of Meribah (Num. 20). At the former place, God stood before the seventy elders upon the rock, which for Hananel signifies the cloud of God's glory. But at the latter, there was no visible evidence of God's Presence. Hence, Moses' statement "shall we . . ." clearly implies that what followed was his miracle not God's. In other words, the nature of the sin—far from being obscure or unjustified—is now projected with startling clarity; it was not an ordinary transgression. In defying God, Moses did not merely countermand His order; indeed, his behavior could be interpreted as a denial of God's essence. In the sight of the assembled throngs of Israel, Moses and Aaron missed the opportunity to "sanctify" God (***lo' qiddashtem***) "before the eyes of the children of Israel" (Num. 20:12; 27:24; Deut. 32:51). Instead they showed no trust (***lo' he'emantem;*** Num. 20:12a), acting treacherously (***me'altem;*** Deut. 32:51), rebelling

against God (*meritem pi;* Num. 20:24; 27:14; rendered by Ramban: "you changed My words"), setting themselves up in His place, arrogating to themselves the divine power to draw forth the water miraculously from the rock.

In the face of the magnitude of this sin, all prior incidents of Moses' petulance and doubt pale. Here, in a direct address to his people, Moses ascribes miraculous powers to himself and Aaron. Indeed, by broadcasting one word—*notsi'*, "we shall bring forth"—Moses and Aaron might be interpreted as having put themselves forth as God.

Considering that Moses' generation had hardly been weaned from the bondage of Egypt, his error was neither slight nor pardonable. Israel had to be released from more than chains; it still had to be purged of its pagan background. In being redeemed from Pharaoh, it had yet to be bound to its God.

In his monumental work *The History of the Religion of Israel,* Y. Kaufmann has shown that all polytheistic systems can be reduced to one common denominator: The gods are not ultimately sovereign. Further, "they emerge out of a pre-existent realm and are subject to a transcendent order . . . [which] entails the imposition of natural or supernatural compulsion upon the gods. . . . [Hence] the magical character of the pagan cultus. Magic is an art whose purpose is to move occult powers to act in a desired manner. It utilizes means which are automatically efficient, irrespective of the will of the gods. . . . The power of magic transcends the gods: they themselves employ it, for they too are in need of this almighty instrument which is independent of them and their will. . . . Pagan religion sees the cult as activating the transcendent source of power upon which both the gods and the world depend."[3]

For our purpose it is important to qualify Kaufmann's perception of the magical nature of polytheism by one consideration: Pagan magic may or may not involve a manual act, but it always involves the use of words. In Egypt, as A. H. Gardiner has shown,[4] "the magical rite is always two-fold and comprises (1) an oral rite, consisting of certain words to be recited, and (2) a manual rite, consisting of certain actions to be performed." In the oral rite, the aspect of primary interest to us, the divine force "is treated personally, being commanded, persuaded, cajoled, warned, threatened, or cursed, just like a human being." Gardiner also dwells upon the extensive use of images and amulets in Egyptian magic, noting that "images were not immediately potent of themselves, but had to be charged with magical power in one way or the other. The oral rite is usually recited over them."[5] Thus the oral rite—the use of incantations, charms, curses, and threats—is an indispensable element of Egyptian magic.[6]

Mesopotamian magic reveals the same characteristics: "The act of casting a spell of divine power probably consisted of uttering words extended by conventional movements of the hands," that is, a combination of incantation and gesticulation.[7] "Le rituel d'exorcisme comprenait à la fois des *legomena* [recitation], tous designés par le terme *chiptou* ("incantation") . . . et des *dromena* [performance], c'est-à-dire l'action rituelle," again a combination of incantation and gesticulation, although the oldest material at times contains incantations without ritual.[8] Thus the oral formula is the indispensable ingredient in pagan magic.[9]

The Bible contains a striking confirmation of this twofold nature of pagan magic. The pagan general Naaman is angry that the prophet Elisha did not treat his leprosy as would one of his own magicians: "'I thought,' he said, 'he would surely come out to me, and would stand and invoke the LORD his God by name, and would wave his hand toward the

spot, and cure the affected part'" (2 Kings 5:11). Once again, magic is effected by a combination of incantation (invoking the deity) and gesticulation (waving the hand).

Only when seen against this background can the Mosaic religion as reflected in the Torah be properly understood. In contradistinction to the Egyptian priest or magician who compelled the gods through verbal formulas, Moses performs his miracles in dead silence. In the instance of the plagues, not only does Moses act without speech; but on four different occasions, acceding to Pharaoh's plea to ask for their cessation, he leaves Pharaoh's presence and prays to God alone—so that he not be taken for a heathen magician (Exod. 8:8; 8:25–26; 9:29,33; 10:18; cf. Num. 23:3–7,15–17). Furthermore, Moses always offers his intercessory prayers for Israel in private, again to dissociate him from his pagan counterpart (e.g., Exod. 5:22; 32:11–13,30–31; 33:7–11).

Thus, we see that the Pentateuchal narrators, acutely sensitive to the role of Moses, took extreme care to distinguish him from the Egyptian magician. Moses, the personification of the essential distinction between Israel's new religion and that of its environment, is only the agent of the supreme God, not the initiator of the miraculous but only its executor, a prophet. "These nations that you are about to dispossess do indeed resort to soothsayers and augurs; to you, however, the LORD your God has not assigned the like. The LORD your God will raise up for you a prophet from among your own people . . . him shall you heed" (Deut. 18:14–15).

It is a central element of Moses' prophetic role that he sever Israel from idolatrous seductions. To this end, God helps Moses by showing Israel authenticating "signs" of His power: miracles. But to ensure that Israel understands that they originate in divine will and not as a coincidence of nature, God repeatedly instructs Moses to describe the miracle in advance and to designate the precise moment of its occurrence through a specific manual act. Thus, for example, Moses says to Pharaoh: "'You may have this triumph over me: for what time shall I plead . . .?' 'For tomorrow,' he replied. And [Moses] said: 'As you say—that you may know that there is none like the LORD our God'" (Exod. 8:5–6). Rabbi Samuel ben Hofni (cited by Ibn Ezra) suggests that Pharaoh did not request Moses to stop the plague immediately because he suspected that Moses "the magician" knew by the stars that the plague was destined to cease at once. Therefore, to trick him, he asked that the plague be removed the next day. In any event, Moses makes sure that the time of the miracle is fixed in advance (even allowing Pharaoh to fix it) so that there can be no doubt that God is performing it (see also Exod. 9:5,18; Josh. 11:8). It is precisely here that the danger of mistaken identity can occur. The Israelites, steeped in their experience of Egyptian sorcery, might easily attribute the marvel not to God but to the craft of Moses. Hence, the gulf between Moses and his Egyptian counterpart is made as wide as possible. Moses offers no incantations, recites no formulas, intones no esoteric names; instead, he makes a commonplace gesture—strikes with his rod, pours water, throws up soot (Exod. 4:9; 9:8), puts his hand in his skirt, or raises his arm high (Exod. 4:6–7; 17:11)—all the while remaining silent.

The dialogue between Elisha and Naaman, referred to above, offers a striking analogy. Elisha's act has none of the incantations and gesticulations expected by Naaman, who is told merely to bathe seven times in the Jordan (2 Kings 5:10), an act so ordinary and (from Naaman's point of view) so thoroughly incapable of influencing the divine that he walked away in a frustrated rage (vv. 11–13). This, of course, is the hallmark of Israel's prophet: just the ordinary gesture—and no incantations.

Y. Kaufmann has demonstrated that the priests of the First Temple performed their

ritual in silence.[10] And, with regard to the Torah, this holds true for the prophet (i.e., Moses) as well. The prophet's function, in contrast to that of the priest, is to intercede in prayer for his charges; and if through his agency a miracle comes to pass, he must be silent during its occurrence. In this way, Moses and all his prophetic successors, in their role as vehicles of divine might, differed sharply from their pagan counterparts. The prophets of Israel gestured—albeit with a common gesture—in order to designate the precise moment of the miracle. But they gestured in silence lest the community of observers attribute the miracle to the power of their words rather than to the power of God.

This backdrop of pagan magic should suffice to explain why it cannot be that Moses was commanded to draw forth water from the rock by speaking to it. Had he addressed the rock, he would have committed the quintessential heresy: Those assembled would have taken his words as an incantation and him as a magician who performed the miracle by his own powers rather than by divine agency. Most critics aver that speaking to the rock represents a later tradition that rejected the allegedly cruder rock striking tradition. As we have seen, it is, to the contrary, speaking to the rock in the sight (and hearing) of the Israelites that constitutes Moses' grand heresy: To ascribe this act to the Lord's command is to vitiate all the Pentateuchal passages that impose a uniform silence upon Moses during his initiation of miracles.

The sin of Moses now stands out in its proper perspective. Against the backdrop of the Pentateuchal sensitivity to man's usurping of God's powers, Moses' act is manifestly shocking. Even if we consider the Numbers version authentic, that he was to have spoken to the rock, the heresy lies in what he and Aaron said ("shall *we* . . ."). It is our understanding, however, that the striking of the rock was to have been the same mute performance that characterized his role in other miracles. As final proof that this is the correct reading of the sin of Moses, we submit the testimony of the psalmist: "They [the people] rebelled against Him and he [Moses] spoke rashly" (Ps. 106:33). The text reads literally, "he expressed with his lips," that is, "he blurted out," indicating that his sin may not have been in what he said but in the bare fact that he spoke at all.

Keeping in mind the unrelenting vigilance of the Torah in denying man any share in the manipulation of divine power, we are startled by the contrasts found in the Former Prophets. The Elijah-Elisha narratives, for example, confront us with at least five instances of the prophet performing a supernatural act without the previous consent or command of God; moreover, the prophet takes full credit for the ensuing miracle without even attributing his power to God (1 Kings 17:1; 2 Kings 1:10,12–14; 2:8,9; 4:2–7; 13:21). Other instances can be cited, all of which illustrate the independent power of the prophets. For example, both Moses and Elisha cast wood into water, but whereas the Torah states, "The Lord showed him a piece of wood and he threw it in the water" (Exod. 15:25), the Former Prophets state, "He [Elisha] cut off a stick and threw it in" (2 Kings 6:6). Similarly, according to the Former Prophets, the oath to Caleb is given by Moses (Josh. 14:9), but in the Torah Moses says nothing, for the oath is made by God (Num. 14:21–24,28–30; Deut. 1:34–36). Again, the same miraculous birth announcement stems from Elisha in the Former Prophets (2 Kings 4:16) but from the Lord in the Torah (Gen. 18:10; cf. Gen. 18:14). In the post-Pentateuchal narratives, therefore, there is a blurring of the sharp demarcation between the power of man and God, a nonchalance that contrasts dramatically with the puritan zeal of the Pentateuch.

Finally, the remaining bloc of prophetic narratives, in Chronicles and Daniel, brings us back to the Pentateuchal climate. In Chronicles, as distinct from Kings, the prophet is

shorn of all wonder-working powers: All miracles are performed by God. Even going further than the Pentateuch where the prophet at least was permitted a manual, albeit silent, act the prophet of Chronicles never lifts a finger. He is only a mouthpiece for the Almighty's message. In Daniel as well, we find miracles scrupulously attributed to God and punctuated by homiletic perorations of man's need to trust Him.

How are we to account for the difference in point of view between the folk narratives in the Former Prophets, on the one hand, and the Torah and the Chronicles-Daniel literature, on the other? Surely we cannot say that the Torah was recast by the biblical editors in order to fit the point of view of the later literature, for if so, why did they leave the Former Prophets untouched? We can only conclude that each narrative group, accurately reflecting a different historical period, was entered unrevised into the canon.

What particular circumstances, then, can account for the sensitivity found in the Torah and for the contrasting laxity in the narratives of the Former Prophets? Only one answer is possible. The Torah is religiously militant because it was forged in a period of ideological stress: the monotheistic revolution. This is clearly conveyed by the Pentateuchal narratives: Not only must a pagan Pharaoh be convinced of God's omnipotence, but stiff-necked Israel itself.

The narratives of the Former Prophets, by contrast, are undisturbed by the theological issues that pique the Pentateuchal narrators—exactly what we would expect from our knowledge of that era. It was self-confident and unreflective, marked by a creeping syncretism (e.g., Baal names, household gods, wonder-working prophets, etc.). These borrowings from Canaanite religion, however, were only external—form and not content. Just as the profusion of theophoric names compounded with Baal in the Saul-David era does not indicate wholesale defection from pristine Mosaism—all accounts agree that loyalty to the Lord was uncompromised in that age—so with other syncretistic forms. These too did not meet with the opposition of the prevailing spiritual leadership, priestly and prophetic, because they were not regarded as possible threats to the covenantal faith.

The golden calves of Dan and Bethel serve as an excellent case in point. Even zealots like Elijah and Elisha do not condemn their worship. (Only Hosea, one hundred years later, and he alone of the eighth-century prophets, regards the calves as sinful [Hos. 8:5–6; 10:5–6; 13:2]. But prophesying on the threshold of northern Israel's decline, Hosea is the prescient forerunner of a later age characterized by soul-searching and catharsis, an age that sought an explanation for the destruction of Israel's national life, such as we find in the homiletical historiosophy of the editor of Kings.) Similarly, we note that the existence of pillars (1 Kings 14:15,23), sodomite enclaves (1 Kings 14:24; 15:12), and *gillulim* (1 Kings 15:12), which were built "on every high hill and under every leafy tree," did not incur the wrath of Elijah and Elisha and others of the Former Prophets. In these instances, too, the syncretistic tendencies among the superstition-prone masses were tolerated.

Hence, by the same token, the belief that the prophets were vested with miraculous powers is but another instance of the unconscious osmosis of external pagan notions into Israelite life during this generally unreflective and carefree period. We find support for this historical position in our analysis of Joshua 10:12–14, which quotes from the Book of Jashar to the effect that Joshua commanded the sun and moon to stand still. The editor comments that this miracle, performed "in the presence of the Israelites," is unparalleled since "neither before nor since has there ever been such a day, when the Lord acted on words spoken by man." This, in turn, leads us to the following observations: (1) The Book of Jashar, just as the Elijah-Elisha bloc, has no compunctions in ascribing to man the power to

initiate miracles. Since this book comprises the poetic compositions at least for the period between the conquest and the united kingdom (see 2 Sam. 1:15; 1 Kings 8:13 LXX), it accords with our general conclusion that the monotheistic revolution took place in the preconquest era, and that afterward a more tolerant attitude regarding the wonder-working prophet crept in. (2) The editor was, nevertheless, disturbed by the implication of the poem. Indeed he might well be. It was not only the magnitude of the Gibeon miracle that startled him but especially its inception: Joshua did not request but commanded—the closest we come in the Bible to the polytheistic concept of man controlling the divine. Yet, the editor did not change the material, however much it troubled him. Rather, after dutifully recording the miracle tradition, he allowed himself the luxury of the editorial comment that this event was unique—and never again to be repeated. Thus, our confidence in the authenticity of the biblical narratives receives a new source of support. (3) Finally, we have a clear standard by which to measure the sin of Moses. What was disturbing and unique about the miracle at Gibeon was that man and not God evoked a particular supernatural event, for which the editor found he had to apologize. Moses was guilty in the similar incident of commanding the rock to give forth water. But in attributing the power to himself (and Aaron), he far exceeded Joshua, crossing the border of effrontery and entering the domain of heresy. And for this a commensurate punishment was meted out.

In finally identifying the nature of Moses' sin we have also staked our claim to ancillary conclusions, as follows:

1. With the help of Bekhor Shor, we have lent strength to the hypothesis that duplicate accounts of the wilderness period exist in Exodus and Numbers.

2. The ideal prophet in Israel, as exemplified by Moses, was constrained to speechlessness during the performance of a miracle, a practice that contrasted sharply—deliberately so—with the wonder-workers of other nations.

3. The enforced silence of Moses during the performance of a miracle is matched by his reticence in its initiation. Both of these characteristics clash with the behavior of his successors as related in the prophetic legends; and they cleave the Torah and the early prophets into two independent blocs of narrative material that reflect quite accurately the general theological climate of the periods they describe. In the case of the Torah, this can only mean that the monotheistic revolution was a product of the Mosaic age.

One final observation. If correct, we have uncovered the true pathos in the personal tragedy of Moses. Israel's teacher is condemned for revealing the very failing that he tried to rectify in those charged to his care. He successfully brought his people to a promised land of the spirit, a destination that he himself failed to reach.[11]

EXCURSUS 51

The Encounter with the Canaanites (21:1–3)

This pericope is replete with problems. First, it seems out of place: When Israel should be heading south to skirt Edom (21:4), it is, instead, moving north into the Canaanite-occupied Negeb. If, then, it truly inflicted a crushing defeat on the Canaanites why did it not continue northward to conquer all of Canaan? Second, the victory reported here is refuted by the findings of archaeology: There simply are no Late Bronze remains anywhere

in the Negeb; that is, there were no fortified cities there at the time of Moses and Joshua. In other words, the Israelites who left Egypt could not have been confronted by the forces of the king of Arad; nor could they have destroyed the city of Hormah. Third, the identification of Arad and Hormah is beset with difficulties. Although pinpointing the location of Arad presents no problem—because of the name Tell Arad by which the site is still called today and especially because of the appearance of the name Arad on two ostraca uncovered by the excavation—the excavation also reveals that the site was destroyed during the second phase of the Early Bronze Age (no later than 2700 B.C.E.) and not rebuilt until the Iron Age, no earlier than the time of David and Solomon. Thus, there is no Canaanite city of Arad! The identification of Hormah is just as complicated not only because, as noted, there were no fortified cities in the Negeb during the time of Moses and Joshua but because of conflicting evidence within the Bible itself, which affirms that the city of Hormah was later destroyed by the tribes of Simeon and Judah (Judg. 1:17).

The suggestion—certainly a daring one for its time—was made by Ramban (and earlier by the Karaites; see Sefer ha-Mivḥar and Keter Torah) that the destruction of Hormah in Numbers actually refers to that recorded in Judges. (Of course, this does not imply that Ramban denies the Mosaic authorship of this pericope, as averred by Abravanel; rather, he would say that Moses, through his divinely endowed prophetic gifts, predicted its later destruction.) This suggestion, however, still does not account for an Israelite presence in the Negeb—in the opposite direction from that which they took in circuiting Edom (21:4).

One solution is that Israel initially attempted to skirt Edom by the logical route across Edom's northern border at the Zered River and not by moving southward to the Red Sea. This possibility derives from 14:21, which states that Israel "turned away" from Edom without specifying the direction. When this northern passage was blocked by the Canaanites (21:1–3), Israel was forced to turn southward (21:4).

An alternative solution regards this pericope as originally belonging before 14:45.[1] Thus in the aborted invasion of Canaan from the south, Israel initially conquered Hormah; but when it attempted to penetrate further into the mountains it was soundly defeated by the Amalekites and Canaanites, who then recaptured Hormah (14:45), necessitating its later conquest by the tribes of Simeon and Judah in the time of the Judges (Judg. 1:17). One may argue in support of this solution that the name Hormah is explained here, whereas its origin is taken for granted in 14:45, thereby implying that the events of 21:1–3 are earlier. However, both solutions suffer because of the lack of any evidence of urban settlement in the Negeb during the Mosaic period. All that can be said, then, is that 21:1–3 is related to 14:39–45 in that both correctly reflect an aborted invasion of Canaan from the south. But the topographical names Arad and Hormah continue to present insuperable difficulties.

The third problem, the identification of Arad and Hormah, has elicited the challenging solution of Y. Aharoni.[2] The clue for Arad is to be found in the record of Pharaoh Shishak's campaign in Canaan five years after the death of Solomon. It speaks of two Arads: the fortress of Greater Arad and the Arad of *yrḥm,* possibly the Arad of the Jerahmeelites (1 Sam. 27:10; 30:27). Greater Arad undoubtedly must be Tell Arad; and Arad of the Jerahmeelites may well be the Canaanite Arad that stemmed the Israelite incursion. Now of all the sites in the eastern Negeb only two were occupied and fortified during the Middle Bronze period (with typical Hyksos ramparts): Tell Malḥata and Tell Masos, 12.4 and 16 kilometers (8 and 10 mi.) southwest respectively from Tell Arad. The closer one, Tell

Malḥata, is identified by Aharoni with Canaanite (but not Israelite) Arad, and Tell Masos with Hormah. Their proximity to each other is supported by their juxtaposition in Joshua 12:14. Moreover, since Hormah is probably mentioned in sources of the Egyptian Middle Kingdom (from 1800 B.C.E.), it fits Middle Bronze Tell Masos. And since Tell Masos was clearly the largest fortified settlement in the eastern Negeb before it was destroyed in the eleventh century, it also fits the requirements of Judges 1:17. Regarding the latter's attestation that Hormah was originally called Zephath—though the name Hormah is attested in early Egyptian sources—Aharoni conjectures that since Zephath as derived from the root *ts-f-h* means "watch post," it should be identified with Tell Ira, whose dominant position in the terrain suits this meaning. That is to say, when Tell Ira was fortified during the monarchy, the name of nearby Hormah—in ruins since the days of the judges—was transferred to it, but the meaning of its original name, Zephath, was preserved.

Thus the possibility exists, according to Aharoni, that 21:1–3 faithfully preserves a geographical-historical situation that obtained some 300 years prior to the conquest. This would mean that the wars recorded here against Arad and Hormah are those of Israelite tribes who maintained themselves in the region for several centuries prior to their fusion with the other Israelite tribes that marched across the wilderness from Egypt.

This theory is as tortuous as it is ingenious. Its chief failing is that it does not meet the basic criterion of the verse 21:3—Hormah is not the name of a city but of a region! It is the name given to ***all*** the proscribed Canaanite settlements in the region. The Septuagint may indeed be correct in its rendering "Anathema," which recognizes that, strictly speaking, Hormah is not a specific site. In any event, this Hormah cannot be identified with the city of Zephath/Hormah, conquered much later by the tribes of Simeon and Judah, which lay in the western Negeb.[3]

Thus the pericope may be seen as correctly mirroring an attempt by the Canaanites to stem an Israelite invasion from the south during the days of Moses, and it is these Canaanites who were identified with the later cities of Arad and Hormah. This possibility is enhanced by the likelihood that the term "king of Arad" was later interpolated into the text (see the Comment to verse 1) and that, in fact, Hormah had no connection with the city of that name that flourished during the days of the judges. This being so, the problem of the missing Late Bronze Arad and Hormah disappears. The text merely speaks of an Israelite incursion into Canaanite territory by "the way of Atharim," a route that, unfortunately, cannot be identified. It is possible that the pericope is chronologically correct and reflects an attempt by Israel to skirt Edom at its northern frontier. It is also possible that this event, though of Mosaic provenience, occurred at another time during the wilderness trek and was placed here only because of the redactor's desire to group together Israel's three military victories prior to its invasion of Canaan proper (see 21:21–35).

However, it seems more likely that its placement here fulfilled a larger redactional purpose: to suggest that after the rebuff by Edom (20:14–21) and the death of Aaron (20:22–29), Moses made one desperate attempt to enter the Holy Land directly from the south and thereby defy the divine decree that he must die in the desert (20:12). Thus, Moses duplicated the futile attempt of his own generation to force its way into Canaan in spite of being told that it was doomed to die in the desert (14:22–23,29–35,39–45). Though Moses inflicted a defeat on the Canaanites he was forced to retreat: "to skirt the land of Edom" (21:4). For a discussion of the place of this pericope in the redaction of chapters 20–21, see Excursus 55.

EXCURSUS 52

The Copper Snake (21:4–9)

That a snake provides the therapy for snakebite is an instance of homeopathic, or sympathetic, magic defined as "the belief that the fate of an object or person can be governed by the manipulation of its exact image."[1] One finds biblical examples of such belief in the five golden mice fashioned by the Philistines when these creatures overran their land (1 Sam. 6:5 LXX) and in the bitter water cured by bitter wood and salt (Exod. 15:25; 2 Kings 2:21).

The homeopathic use of snakes is a distinctive feature of ancient Egypt. A serpent-shaped amulet was worn by the living to repel serpents and also by the dead—often mummies—to ward off attacks by serpents and other reptiles in the netherworld. Thus, at the time of Moses, the belief prevailed in Egypt that images of serpents would repel serpents as well as heal wounds caused by them. And it is likely no accident that a copper image of a snake was found at Timna, the copper mining region near Elath on the Red Sea, dating from between 1200 and 900 B.C.E. (see the Comment to 21:9). In other words, we have a copper snake that is similar to the one fashioned by Moses and that originated in the same locale at approximately the same time.

The association of snakes with healing is attested elsewhere in the Near East. The Greek god of healing, Aesculapius, is said to have appeared as a snake. (The serpentine symbol, caduceus, is the insignia of the U.S. Army Medical Corps.) The Phoenician god of healing, Eshmun, is also represented as a snake. "Arabs still regard medicinal waters as inhabited by jinn which are usually of serpentine form."[2] And "Apollonius of Tyana is said to have freed Antioch (in northern Syria) from scorpions by making a bronze image of a scorpion."[3] Rabbinic Judaism also knew of homeopathic magic, which it derived from Scripture. Commenting on Moses' sweetening the bitter water with wood (Exod. 15:25), the rabbis comment:

> See how different are human ways from God's ways. [For] man, the sweet heals the bitter, but this is not so for the Creator (for whom) the bitter heals the bitter. How? He puts a thing that spoils into a thing that is spoiled in order to perform a miracle. So too he (Elisha) went to the spring and threw salt into it. And he said, Thus said the Lord: I heal this water . . . (2 Kings 2:21). Is it not so that when salt is added to good water the water turns bad? How [does the Lord act]? He puts a thing that spoils into a thing that is spoiled in order to perform a miracle (Mekh. Beshallaḥ 1, Mekh. SbY on Exod. 15:25).

The copper snake is also called a *seraph,* which, according to Isaiah (Isa. 14:29; 30:6), was a flying serpent. Again, Egypt is the home for images of winged serpents. For example, the arms on the throne of Tutankhamen consist of two wings of a four-winged snake (uraeus), which rise vertically from the back of the seat. Indeed, the erect cobra, or uraeus, standing on its coil is the symbol of royalty for the pharaoh and the gods throughout Egyptian history. Winged uraei dating from the Canaanite period have been found,[4] proving that the image of the winged serpent was well known in ancient Israel. The *seraphs* of Isaiah's vision (Isa. 6) are best understood in the light of the Egyptian symbol of the winged uraeus:[5] As the uraeus is always standing, so the *seraphs;* as the four wings of the uraeus represent the four corners of the land, so the winged *seraphs* chant, "His presence fills all the earth" (Isa. 6:3); as the Egyptian uraeus belches consuming fire on the pharaoh's

enemies, so the seraphs' repetition of the trisagion ("Holy, holy, holy") shakes the Temple, filling it with smoke (Isa. 6:4); as the winged uraeus can be endowed with hands, legs, and a human face, so the *seraphs* of Isaiah's vision (Isa. 6:2). It is important to note that a *seraph* becomes the agent of healing and purification for Isaiah (Isa. 6:5–7), thereby providing a link between his snake-*seraph* of Isaiah and the therapeutic snake-*seraph* of Moses.

Easily the most significant clue for the identification of the Mosaic copper snake is one of the bronze bowls found in the royal palace of Nineveh, the capital of Assyria. These bowls date to the end of the eighth century and by their inscribed Hebrew names probably indicate that they were booty or tribute delivered to Tiglath-pileser III by King Ahaz (2 Kings 16:8) or to Sennacherib by King Hezekiah (2 Kings 18:14–16). The bowl in question has engraved on its rim a winged snake perched on a standard, precisely as one would imagine it upon recollecting the verse "Moses made a copper serpent (= *saraf,* "seraph") and mounted it on a standard" (v. 9).[6]

A religious reform is attributed to the same King Hezekiah, during which "he also broke into pieces the copper snake that Moses had made, for until that time the Israelites had been offering sacrifices to it; it was called Nehushtan" (2 Kings 18:4). This statement authenticates the antiquity of the story of Moses' copper snake. Could such a story have been written after Hezekiah's time—after the copper snake was declared an idolatrous object? It also allows us to conjecture that like other sacred relics from the Mosaic period, for example, the flask of manna (Exod. 16:34) and Aaron's rod (Num. 17:25), the copper snake was also preserved and treasured. But whereas the above-named relics were kept in the adytum of the Temple, out of people's sight, the copper snake, on top of its standard, was probably erected in the Temple courtyard where it could be seen and worshiped. Undoubtedly, while the *minḥah,* the meal offering, was sacrificed on the altar, the offerer would stare at the snake, hoping to repeat the Mosaic miracle of healing. Thus the sacrifice could in effect have been offered to the snake rather than to Israel's God. Moreover, since the Canaanites regarded the snake as a cultic symbol of renewed life and fertility, it may have become over time a bridge to pagan worship within the Temple itself. Hence, Hezekiah destroyed it. The fear of associating autonomous power with the snake is reflected in the following mishnah: "Could the snake slay or the serpent keep alive? It is, rather, to teach you that whenever the Israelites directed their thoughts on high and kept their hearts in subjection to their Father in heaven, they were healed; otherwise they pined away" (Mish. RH 3:8).

EXCURSUS 53

The Song of the Well (21:17–18)

The fact that the well is directly addressed—"Spring up, O well"—has been taken by scholars to mean that the song is in reality an invocation to the spirit or genie thought to reside in and control its waters. "In Palestine to this day," Robertson Smith notes, "all springs are viewed as seats of spirits and the peasant women, whether Moslem or Christian, ask their permission before drawing water."[1] Support for this animistic belief can be adduced from ancient Near Eastern texts, for example: Amon and the gods dwelling in the well are invoked on behalf of Seti I, the good shepherd who digs the well; waters in the

netherworld hearken to Ramses II when he digs a well;[2] and river gods are called upon as witnesses to the treaty between Ramses II and Hattusilis.[3] Regarding this poem, however, this interpretation is to be totally rejected. Animism, in general, does not figure in the Bible, and this song, in particular, shows no trace of it. Instead it focuses entirely upon the labor of digging the well, and not even the God of Israel is invoked (see the midrash quoted in the Comment to v. 17). The address to the well, then, is nothing but a poetic metaphor.

Philo of Alexandria thought that Israel burst into song when it found its first well on entering cultivated land after leaving the wilderness (Moses 1.46). But the song celebrates the chieftains who dug or, more likely, sponsored its digging (see the Egyptian examples, above, and the Comment to v. 18). Indeed, such a song celebrating the digging of a well with a stick has been found among the Arab Bedouin:[4] "Flow, water, speak abundantly/ Wood, camel, do not scorn it/With sticks we have dug it."

The successful digging of a well in the wilderness is of no small significance. It is a claim to fame—even in Scripture, which praises "Anah who discovered the hot springs in the wilderness" (Gen. 36:24). The importance of wells is underscored by the early stories of Israel, which tell us that the ownership of wells in the parched Negeb was bitterly contested (Gen. 26:18–33; Judg. 1:15).

As researched by Vermes,[5] the Song of the Well has an interesting history, which turns on the meaning that later generations gave to the enigmatic term ***meḥokek***. The Septuagint renders Numbers 21:18 as follows: "Princes dug it, kings of nations delved it, in their kingdom, in their realm." Other biblical occurrences of ***meḥokek*** (Gen. 49:10; Pss. 60:9; 108:9) are rendered in the Septuagint by "ruler, king"—all allusions to royal power. The Targums and the tannaitic midrashim, on the other hand, relate ***meḥokek*** to the teaching of the Torah—the teacher being God, who gave the Torah, or Moses, who is the scribe par excellence, or scribes in general (Targ. Yer. on Gen. 49:10; Deut. 33:21; Targ. Jon. on 21:18; Targ. on Judg. 5:14; Isa. 33:22; Pss. 60:9; 108:9; Sif. Deut. 355). The Qumran writings adopt both interpretations: "royal covenant" (on Gen. 49:10), reflecting the Septuagint tradition, and "interpreter of the Torah" (CD 6:2–11). The latter, an exposition of Numbers 21:18, merits being cited in full:

> But God remembered the covenant He had made with the forefathers and He raised up from Aaron men of understanding, and from Israel men of wisdom, and He commanded them to dig the well: "the well which chieftains dug, which the nobles of the people delved with the ***meḥokek.***" The well is the Torah. They that dug it are penitents of Israel who went out from the land of Judah and dwelt in the land of Damascus. God named all of them "chieftains" because they sought Him, and their fame was not disputed by any mouth. The ***meḥokek*** is the interpreter of the Torah of whom Isaiah said: "He brings forth a tool for His work" (54:16). The "nobles of the people" are those who come to dig the well with their staves [***meḥokekot***] which the lawgiver [***ha-meḥokek***] instituted [***ḥakak***] and in which they must walk during all the time of iniquity. And without them, they shall find nothing until the coming of him who shall teach righteousness (or who is the true teacher) at the end of time.

Thus it is clear that although the Qumranites are fully cognizant of the basic biblical meaning of "staff" for ***meḥokek,*** they have given it a new interpretation, one echoed by later rabbinic tradition: "lawgiver" or "interpreter of the Torah." Vermes may be entirely correct in suggesting that this change of meaning may reflect the changing conditions of authority for the Jewish people from the First to the Second Temple period: Instead of being ruled by kings they were governed by interpreters of the Torah, the predecessors of the rabbis.

Of equal interest is the representation of the well in one of the panels of the Dura

Europos synagogue, which is dated to the mid-third century C.E. and is among the earliest examples of Jewish art.[6] In consonance with Targum Jonathan, the well divides into twelve streams that bring its precious water directly to each of the twelve tribes, each symbolized by an upright figure standing at the entrance of a tent. As has been shown by J. B. Milgrom,[7] the well is placed before the Tabernacle in the center of the camp (Tosef. Suk. 3:11); Moses thrusts a staff into the well, an act that is explained by the following passage from Pseudo-Philo (first century C.E.):

> God commanded many things in Marah. He showed [Moses] the Tree of Life and cut a piece from it, and took it and placed it in Marah and the waters of Marah sweetened, and it went after them in the desert for forty years, going up into the mountains and down the plains.

Thus, not only does this panel picture the well (identified with Marah; Exod. 15:22–25) in the wilderness. On a deeper level Moses' staff is a branch from Israel's tree of life, the Torah; and Israel—even in the Diaspora of Dura—continues to be nourished by its waters. Here the rabbinic interpretation of ***meḥokek*** as relating to Torah is encountered once again but in a novel form—in visual art.

EXCURSUS 54

The Song of Heshbon (21:27–30)

Three theories are current among scholars concerning the origin of the short poem of 21:27–30: (1) as a ninth-century Israelite composition celebrating Omri's conquest of Moab; (2) as a taunt song composed by the Israelites after their conquest of the Amorites challenging them to rebuild Heshbon (the song says, in effect: we dare you Amorites to rebuild your fallen capital as you did when you first conquered it from the Moabites); (3) as the work of an Amorite poet celebrating the victory of his people over Moab.

The first two theories encounter insuperable chronological and textual difficulties. The third theory fits the plain sense of the poem but presupposes that early non-Israelite material could have survived in Israelite circles—and, then, been accepted into the biblical canon. However, this is not the only instance of the Bible citing non-Israelite sources. As shown by Y. Kaufmann,[1] Israel's prophets are not averse to utilizing older, non-Israelite compositions, particularly taunt songs against other nations, which they then rework to convey the Lord's message to the nations (e.g., Isa. 15–16; 21:1–10,23; Jer. 46:1–26; 47:2–7; 48:1–6,20–39,45–46; 49:7–39; Amos. 1:3–2:3).

In fact, the rabbinic sages are unanimous in asserting that this poem is Amorite in origin; moreover, they provide a very compelling explanation of why it was incorporated into the Torah: "In what way does this [poem] concern us? Inasmuch as the Holy One Blessed Be He had commanded 'Do not harass the Moabites' (Deut. 2:9), He therefore said, 'Let Sihon come and take away the land from Moab and then Israel may come and take it away from Sihon'" (Ḥul. 60b). "Had they taken it directly from Moab they would have had in their possession something which they had robbed unjustly. But it was not so. Sihon took it from Moab and Israel took it from Sihon, and so they were free from the charge of robbery" (Num. R. 19:35). This apologetic is also expressed in a biblical tradition

that Sihon controlled all the Moabite territory that would subsequently be conquered by Israel (see the Comment to 21:24), a tradition that was explicitly voiced by Jephthah: "Israel did not seize the land of Moab. . . . Israel took possession of all the land of the Amorites, the inhabitants of that land" (Judg. 11:15,21). The importance of the Song of Heshbon to Israelite historiography is reflected in the fact that it is, in part, cited in Jeremiah 48:45–46 and that the story of the conquest of Moab by the Amorites found its way into a number of prophetic oracles (Isa. 15:2–7; 16:6–11; Jer. 48:1–6,16–24,29–38, 45–46).[2]

Indeed, the different descriptions of Sihon's territory in the Bible also reflect subsequent sensitivity to the justice of Israel's claim to Transjordan. According to Joshua 12:2–3 (also Deut. 2:36; 3:8–12), Sihon's northern boundary was the Sea of Galilee, and, according to Jephthah's claim, it reached the Jabbok (Judg. 11:22), in agreement with the account in Numbers (v. 24). However, it is clear from verse 32 that Sihon's territory did not reach as far as Jazer, which lies close to Heshbon and is far south of the Jabbok (see map 5). Moreover, one can deduce from the Song of Heshbon (vv. 27–30) that Sihon's rule did not extend beyond Heshbon. The possibility strongly exists that the boundaries of Sihon and Og described in Deuteronomy and Joshua reflect the administrative redistricting of Transjordan under Solomon: Og's kingdom and Transjordanian Manasseh correspond to Solomon's seventh and twelfth districts (1 Kings 4:14,19).[3]

One can imagine that subsequent generations of Israelites knew full well—if only by the surviving names, steppes of Moab (21:22), country of Moab (21:20), and Ar of Moab (21:28)—that their ancestors had settled on Moabite land. It was crucial, then, to establish that their fathers had not violated the divine prohibition against possessing Moabite territory. Their descendants accomplished this end by quoting an eyewitness Amorite bard to prove that Israel had actually conquered the Transjordanian territory from its Amorite inhabitants and not from the Moabites.

EXCURSUS 55

The Redaction of Chapters 20–21

The narrative in chapters 20–21 has been the bane of commentators from time immemorial. It is replete with chronological inconsistencies, exegetical cruxes, abrupt transitions, multiple sources, and puzzling insertions. Leaving aside the exegetical problems (discussed in the Commentary), we can group the remaining difficulties into a series of questions, as follows:

1. Why does an incomplete date mark the arrival at Kadesh?

2. Why does Edom's refusal to grant Israel safe passage meet with no resistance (20:14–21), thereby forcing an arduous detour (20:21b; 21:4) in contrast to Israel's aggressive response to a similar refusal by Sihon (21:21–31)?

3. Why is the account of Aaron's death inserted here (20:22–29)?

4. Why, instead of heading south to detour around Edom, does Israel drive due north only to engage the Canaanites who had previously defeated them (14:39–45) and who initially do so again (21:1)? Moreover, why was the encounter with the Canaanites inserted here where it is chronologically out of place (see Excursus 51)?

5. Why has the itinerary formula been broken (21:4a,10b) to allow for the insertion of the incident of the copper snake (21:4–9)?

6. Why has a new itinerary source (21:12–20) containing the explanation of Beer (21:16b) and the Song of the Well (21:17–18) been inserted into the narrative?

7. Why cite an itinerary that takes Israel into the Jordan plain (21:18–20) only to backtrack and recount the conquest of the area (21:21–31)?

8. Why is the conquest of the Bashan telescoped into the same campaign (21:33–35) without mentioning how Israel acquired the intervening territory, that is, the Gilead (cf. 32:39–42)?

It is herewith submitted that the key to all the questions is that the two chapters were redacted to show that despite the continual murmuring of the Israelites, now by a new generation, and the rebellion of their leaders, Moses and Aaron (Excursus 50), God provided His people with all its needs: water, healing, and victory. The questions will be answered seriatim:

1. The station Kadesh may have been improvised and the date of arrival deliberately obscured (see the Comment to 20:1) in order to locate the rebellion of Moses and Aaron at Kadesh and date it in the fortieth year with the contiguous material (see 20:14,22; 33:38). This thereby makes their rebellion the cause for the reverses that followed: the rebuff by Edom, the death of Aaron, and the retreat from Canaan (20:14–21:3).

2. Edom's refusal to allow passage (20:14–21) is a reversal for Israel and a personal blow to Moses who now knows that he cannot enter the land but must die en route. Thus, the reason for avoiding a confrontation with Edom is not that God has forbidden it (the Deuteronomic version; Deut. 2:5) but that Israel buckled before Edom's show of force—a defeat for Israel and Moses.

3. Aaron's death is a premonition that Moses' death is imminent, and delivers the final blow to his hopes of averting the divine decree. It either provokes Moses to attempt an abortive thrust into Canaan (IE_2, below) or ends the unit on the leaders' failures, thereby forming an inclusion with the death of Miriam (see IIA, D3, below).

4. The encounter with the Canaanites (21:1–3) is inserted here either as an inclusion to Israel's Transjordanian victories (21:21–35; see IIA′, D'_3) or as the final blow to Moses' hopes of entering the promised land (IE_3). Moses, that is, panics at the death of Aaron, following as it does on the heels of the rebuff by Edom. He leads a desperate thrust into Canaan only to be blocked at Hormah. Israel thus duplicates the futile attempt of the previous generation to force its way into Canaan (14:39–45), but this time it is Moses who initiates the effort. Although victorious in battle, Israel cannot break through and must retreat (21:4).

5,6,7. The brazen serpent section is inserted into the itinerary (21:4–9), and a new itinerary source is also inserted (21:12–20) to show that even though Israel continues to be contentious (with God!; 21:5), God heals those whom He has afflicted (21:8–9) and provides them with their physical needs (21:16–17) and with victory over their enemies (21:21–35).

8. The successful campaign against Og of the Bashan is included (though no cognizance is taken of the intervening territory) to establish that, by the will of God, all of Transjordan fell into Moses' hands (21:33–35).

After the redactor selected his material (consisting of at least two itinerary lists and several unconnected episodes), he divided it into two parallel panels. The first panel deals

with the failure and punishment of the leaders, the second with the failure, punishment, and ultimate deliverance of the people. Each is subdivided into five parallel sections, with the exception of the middle sections (CD), which follow in reverse order in the second unit (D′C′). Structurally the two resemble the parallel murmuring pericopes 11:1–3 and 12:1–15 (see Excursus 24), which, strikingly, also deal with the failure and punishment, respectively, of both the people and its leaders (Miriam and Aaron).

The short section on the encounter with the Canaanites (21:1–3), falling in the very middle of the two chapters, can be assigned either to the end of the first panel (IE_3) or to the beginning of the second panel (II′A′). This fluidity is possible because it is not clear whether the encounter ranks as a victory or a defeat. True, despite the early loss Israel triumphs in the end, but the next verse (21:4) shows the Israelites in retreat—unable to exploit their victory over the Canaanites and press forward into the promised land. They were, instead, forced to make an arduous detour around Edom. Since both interpretations are possible, two structural outlines are herewith presented; the panels are placed in parallel columns.

GOD PROVIDES DESPITE THE FAILURE OF THE LEADERS AND THE PEOPLE (chaps. 20–21)

First Scheme

I.	*Failure of the Leaders* (32 verses)	I′.	*Failure and Deliverance of the People* (32 verses)
A.	Ominous beginning: Miriam's death (20.1)	A′.	Ominous beginning: arduous detour (21:4)
B.	People murmur for water (20:2–6) and leaders rebel against God (20:9–11a)	B′.	People murmur for water and *they* rebel against God (21:5)
C.	God provides water (20:7–8,11b)	D′.	People punished (21:6)
D.	Leaders punished (20:12–13)	C′.	God heals (21:7–9) and provides water (21:16–18) [insertion of itinerary (21:12–20)]
E.	Three reverses 1. Blocked by Edomites (20:14–21) 2. Mourning for Aaron (20:22–29) 3. Blocked by Canaanites (21:1–3)	E′.	Three victories 1. Sihon (21:21–26,31) [insertion of poem (21:27–30)] 2. Jazer (21:32) 3. Og (21:33–35)

The symmetry of these two panels is readily apparent. First, they are quantitatively equal, each comprising thirty-two verses. Moreover, they exhibit a similar sequence, which is amplified in the second panel. To begin with, the death of Miriam and the forced detour (AA′) are portents of disaster. Rebellions against God follow, initially by Moses and Aaron and then—for the first and only time—by the entire people (BB′). God promptly punishes the rebels (CC′) but nevertheless provides for Israel's needs (DD′).

It should be noted that the sequence of provision-punishment is reversed in the second panel, yielding a chiastic structure within the entire scheme (CDD′C′) that locks the two panels together. That this arrangement is a deliberate, artfully crafted literary technique is demonstrated by its attestations elsewhere in Scripture, for example, Genesis 1.

Day		*Element*		*User*	*Day*
A 1		Light (vv. 3–5)		Luminaries (vv. 14–19)	4 A′
B 2	a.	Sky	b′	Marine life	5 B′
	b.	Terrestial waters (vv. 6–8)	a′	Sky life (vv. 20–23)	
C 3	c.	Dry land	c′	Land animals	6 C′
	d.	Vegetation (vv. 9–13)	d′	Man (vv. 24–31)	

Thus, the scheme of Creation also consists of two parallel panels wherein the elements created during the first three days (ABC) are put to use during the last three days in precisely the same sequence (A′B′C′). However, the sequence of Creation on days two and five, the middle section (BB′), is reversed: Whereas God creates the sky before the terrestrial waters can be defined, He populates the waters before populating the sky. Again, we find here an interlocking device that calls attention to the fact that the two panels are not independent of each other but are knit together into a single scheme.

An itinerary has been inserted into C′ (21:12–20) that belongs chronologically at the end of the chapter. It has been placed here deliberately because it contains a poem (vv. 17–18) that celebrates the fact that Israel's need for water in the wilderness will henceforth be supplied solely by God (see the Comment to v. 16).

The final item in each panel (EE′) matches three reverses with three victories. The Edomites' intransigent refusal to let Israel pass through their land (20:14–21) is followed by a thirty-day delay to mourn Aaron's death (20:22–29) and by a Pyrrhic victory over the Canaanites (21:1–3), which forces Israel into a major detour (cf. 21:4). These three reverses are balanced by three victories (21:21–35).

Another poem (21:27–30) is inserted into the narrative as an eyewitness account, for the purpose of legitimating the seizure of the Transjordan: It was taken from Amorites and not from Moabites (see Excursus 54). Perhaps the need to balance the three reverses with three victories explains why a single verse on the separate campaign against Jazer (21:32) is inserted between the accounts of the major victories over Sihon (21:21–31) and Og (21:33–35).

This first scheme reveals one weak point in the formal analogies: The three reverses (E_3) do not match the three victories (E'_3) in kind; that is, the death of Aaron (E_2) is not a military defeat.

Second Scheme

II.	*Failure of the Leaders* (chap. 20)	II′.	*Failure and Deliverance of the People* (chap. 21)
A.	Miriam's death (v. 1)	A′.	Victory over the Canaanites (vv. 1–3)
B.	People murmur for water (vv. 2–6) and leaders rebel against God (vv. 9–11a)	B′.	People murmur for water and *they* rebel against God (vv. 4–5)
C.	God provides water (vv. 11b,7–8)	C′.	People punished (v. 6)
D.	Leaders punished (vv. 12–29)	D′.	God shows mercy to Israel (vv. 7–35)
	1. No entry (vv. 12–13)		1. He heals (vv. 7–9)
	2. No passage (vv. 14–21)		2. He provides water (vv. 16–18) [insertion of itinerary (vv. 12–20)]
	3. Aaron's death (vv. 22–29)		3. Three victories over the Amorites (vv. 21–35)

The advantage in this scheme is that each panel is framed by an inclusion, the first by a death (AD_3) and the second, by victories ($A'D'_3$). The inclusion technique also reveals why the Canaanite encounter (21:1–3), removed from its original place, was inserted here (A'): to serve the purely redactional function of forming an inclusion with the victories at the end of the unit (D'). On the other hand, this scheme suffers from an imbalance: Three victories separately itemized in the text (21:21–31,32,33–35) are compressed into one subsection (D'_3).

The ambiguity concerning the meaning and place of the Canaanite encounter (21:1–3) within these two chapters has necessitated the presentation of the alternative schemes. However, in every other respect the two schemes are identical, which, we submit, proves that the arrangement of the material in chapters 20–21 is not haphazard but follows a structural scheme that is both aesthetic and logical. It reveals symmetry and purpose and, viewed as a whole and from a distance, satisfactorily resolves all the apparent problems that characterize the text when it is viewed from up close as a series of discrete parts.

EXCURSUS 56

The Unity of the Prose and Poetry in Chapters 22–24

Traditionists and moderns are in agreement that chapters 22–24 (the "Book of Balaam"; BB 14b [Munich MS]) constitute an independent work that was later inserted into the text of the Book of Numbers. Most scholars hold that the narrative and the oracle sections are independent compositions and, indeed, are themselves compilations of different sources. The narrative portion will be examined in Excursus 57. Here the subject is the relationship of the poetry to the prose text.

The conclusion will be stated outright: The poetry was composed for the sake of the prose. Without the narrative, the poetic oracles would make no sense, and all their allusions to personalities, nations, and events would be incomprehensible.

First, let us note that the oracles abound with references to the narrative, indeed to the very prose passages that precede the poetry. The first oracle, 23:7–10, confirms the preceding prose section that (1) King Balak of Moab has summoned Balaam from Aram to curse Israel (23:7; 22:6); (2) the Lord alone determines curse or blessing (23:8; 22:12,24); (3) Balaam views Israel from a height (23:9; 22:41); and (4) finds them numerous (23:10; 22:5, 11). The second oracle (23:18–24) also refers to the narrative since (5) Balak's question is answered immediately (23:18; 23:17) to the effect that (6) the Lord does not alter his decisions although Balak wants Him to (23:19; 22:13; cf. 23:27) and that (7) Israel is blessed (23:20; 22:17) or, alternatively, that Israel will be blessed (23:20; 24:1). (8) Balaam also is taught that he can approach the Lord directly without resort to divination (23:29), and he promptly does so (24:2). The final two oracles (24:3–9,15–19) demonstrate that (9) since Balaam no longer has God's word put into his mouth (23:5,12,16), he composes his own, divinely inspired oracles (24:4,16; 24:2b). (10) His revelation is direct (24:4,16; 24:2); (11) his eyes are open to revelation (24:4,16), a point challenged by the ass episode (22:31); and (12) he sees the entirety of Israel's encampment (24:5–6; 24:20). Thus the poetry is replete with indispensable references to the prose.

Moreover, the oracles keep perfect pace with the thematic progression of the adjoining

narrative text. In both texts, Balaam exhibits a step-by-step development from seer to prophet. In the first oracle (23:7–10), Balaam, brought by Balak from Aram to curse Israel, sees them from a height and realizes, from their strength and numbers, that God has no intention to curse them. In the second oracle (23:18–24), Balaam learns that neither sacrificial ritual nor a select view of Israel's camp can sway God's resolve, that God is with Israel and, hence, no harm can come to them, and that God intends to bless Israel and reveal His plans to them directly. In the third oracle (24:3–9), the theme of blessing approaches a climax. Whereas curse (and blessing) is determined solely by God (23:8), and His word cannot be revoked (23:20), this oracle now teaches that blessing or curse directed to Israel is empowered to redound to its author (24:9). Moreover, now that Balaam knows that the Lord will convey His will to him through prophecy, he renounces divination. Finally, in the fourth oracle (24:15–19), Balaam, who is still possessed by the divine spirit, prophesies that Moab will fall under Israel's domination. The measure for measure principle is invoked: Balak of Moab who hired Balaam to enable him to conquer Israel is now informed by Balaam that Israel will conquer Moab.

Also, Balaam's rise in esteem is inversely matched by the downgrading of Balak. In the first oracle Balak is king of Moab (23:7); in the second, the son of Zippor (23:18), that is, an ordinary mortal; and in the third and fourth oracles, he disappears entirely. Conversely, in the first oracle Balaam is the passive instrument of Balak (23:7); in the second, he gives orders to Balak (23:18); and in the third and fourth, having become the confidant of the Lord, he can ignore Balak altogether (24:4, 16).[1]

Thus the many interlocking details and the parallel development of identical themes in the prose and poetry demonstrate that chapters 22–24 (with the exception of the ass episode—22:21–35; see Excursus 57) form an organic unity. Of course, the possibility must be considered that the poetic oracles and the narrative were originally independent of each other, discrete epics on the same theme, which were fused at a later date by a single editorial hand. However, even were this so, the fusion is so thoroughgoing and skillful that the original seams are no longer visible: The redaction is a new artistic creation.

EXCURSUS 57

Balaam and the Ass (22:22–35)

The opening segment of this episode clearly contradicts its immediate antecedent: God is wroth with Balaam for undertaking a journey (v. 22) that He has just permitted (v.20). There is additional evidence that this episode is not a continuation of the previous narrative: Balak and the Moabites have disappeared from the scene. Balaam's ass traverses cultivated fields and vineyards, hardly the long stretches of desert she would have encountered had she set out from Balaam's home on the Euphrates (see the Comment to 22:24). The protagonists of the story have undergone a radical shift: Heretofore, it was Balak who pitted himself against God; now it is Balaam. Most important of all, Balaam, hitherto the compliant servant of God (Excursus 58), now openly defies Him by consenting to curse Israel without His permission (vv. 22,34). Thus the inconsistencies of this episode point to its discreteness. And its origin can be surmised by its genre—a folk tale, current among many peoples, dealing with the confrontation with a demonic force encountered in the course of a journey. A particularly striking analogy is supplied by an Italian folktale:

> Between Aci Castello and San Filipo, there is an ancient oak, haunted by spirits who prevent anyone from passing. A man who once found himself at the spot around midnight and who wanted at all costs to forge ahead, was knocked so violently against the walls on either side of the road that he died. Another, who likewise reached the place at midnight with his donkey, was forced to turn back. And a laborer who came by one day with a cartload of hay saw the rear-axle of his vehicle buckle and the oxen stop in a fit of terror. He had to take to his heels, leaving everything on the roadside.[1]

The conclusion is inescapable: The ass episode represents a folk theme with a life of its own. Thus, it is a separate composition that was interpolated into the story of Balaam.[2] Various telltale signs bear witness to this fact: the editorial seams, the gross contradiction between verses 20 and 22 at its beginning, and the repetitive resumption in verse 35, repeating verses 20 and 21.

Now that the ass episode is recognized as an interpolation, one can inquire as to its purpose. Why was it inserted here? The goal of the episode is doubtless the humiliation of Balaam, evidenced by the strain of irony that runs through the entire pericope (and recognized by the midrash).[3] Balaam, who desires to subdue Israel with words, cannot even subdue his ass with a stick (Tanḥ. Balak 9). Balaam, who claims prophetic sight (24:4,17), cannot see what his ass sees three times. Balaam, who claims prophetic speech since the Lord puts words into his mouth (22:38; 23:5,12,16), is now matched by his ass (v. 28). Balaam, who boasts that "his knowledge is from the Most High" (24:16), has to admit, "I did not know" (v. 34; Tanḥ. Balak 10). Balaam, who is the wisest of the wise, is bested in a verbal exchange with the most stupid of beasts (v. 30; Gen. R. 93:10; Num. R. 20:14). Balaam, who wishes to slay a whole people with his words, can only kill his ass with a sword (Num. R. 20:14). Balaam, who would slay his ass if only he could find a sword (v. 29), does not see the sword extended by the angel (v. 23). Thus "the ass in this episode plays the role of Balaam—beholding divine visions with eyes unveiled—to Balaam's Balak."[4] In truth, Balaam is depicted on a level lower than his ass: more unseeing in his inability to detect the angel, more stupid in being defeated verbally by his ass, and more beastly in subduing it with his stick whereas it responds with tempered speech.

The lampooning of Balaam, then, serves the purpose of downgrading his reputation. It aims to demonstrate that this heathen seer, who was intent on cursing Israel without God's consent, is in reality a fool, a caricature of a seer, one outwitted even by his dumb beast. This image of Balaam—as wicked—is the one reflected in the later biblical and postbiblical literature. He is depicted as one whose Pharaonic malice toward Israel will be frustrated by Israel's God as He transforms Balaam's curses into blessings (see Excursus 58).

EXCURSUS 58

Balaam: Saint or Sinner? (chaps. 22–24)

If one were to remove the ass episode (22:22–35) from the text, what would remain is a picture of Balaam the saint (see Excursus 57).[1] Over and over again, whether in response to Balak's emissaries or to Balak himself, Balaam harps on a single theme: his unconditional submission to the will of the Lord. He will not allow himself to be hired without the Lord's consent (22:8,13,18). All of Balak's gold and silver will not sway him from pronouncing only that which the Lord has commanded him (22:38; 23:12,26; 24:12–13). Moreover, it is clear from the beginning that Balaam has no intention of cursing Israel:[2] "I could not do

anything, big or little, contrary to the command of the LORD my God" (22:18). He proffers no apologies for his failure to curse Israel and does not offer to try again, but explains as follows: "I can only repeat faithfully what the LORD puts into my mouth" (23:12). Consistently and unflinchingly, Balaam proclaims himself the Lord's obedient servant, who, like Moses, denies that he has ever done anything "of my own accord" (24:13; see 16:28). Indeed, even when he realizes that God wishes him to bless Israel (23:20; 24:1), he does not proceed to do so until he is suffused with God's spirit (24:2; see 24:13). Finally, Balaam is rewarded for his fidelity to God not only by God's promise that "Blessed are they who bless you" (24:9) but by the boon He bestows upon Balaam by granting him a direct revelation without having to resort to divination (24:2).

There was, then, a very old, favorable view of Balaam, as is evident in Micah: "My people, remember what Balak king of Moab plotted against you and how Balaam son of Beor responded to him" (Mic. 6:5). Thus, in eighth-century Judah a tradition existed that pinpointed as the villain of the story not Balaam but Balak. Another passage suggests a similar assessment: "He (Balak) sent for Balaam son of Beor to curse but the Lord your God refused to destroy you" (Josh. 24:9–10 LXX). Again, Balaam emerges as a neutral figure in the confrontation between God and Balak.

Reflexes of this affirmative appraisal of Balaam are occasionally found in the postbiblical literature as well. According to Pseudo-Philo, the night Balaam consulted God (see 22:8), he offered the following prayer: "Wherefore Lord do You tempt the race of men? They therefore cannot sustain it, for You know more than they all that was in the world before You founded it. And now enlighten your servant if it be right that I go with them" (BAP chap. 18, p. 123). And according to the midrash, Balaam gave the following reply to Balak's emissaries: "I cannot undertake to do any evil against Israel with whom is the Lord" (Ag. Ber. 65). The midrash also states that Balaam "was greater in wisdom than Moses" (SER 26:142). Praise of Balaam reaches its summit in the following midrash: "There were three features possessed by the prophecy of Balaam that were absent from that of Moses: (1) Moses did not know who was speaking with him (see Exod. 3:6; Exod. R. 3:1), whereas Balaam knew who was speaking with him (24:4). (2) Moses did not know when the Holy One Blessed Be He would speak with him, whereas Balaam knew (24:16aβ). In illustration of this, Balaam has been compared with a king's cook who knows what fare the king will have on his table and how much is spent by the king on his board. It was in the same way that Balaam knew what the Holy One Blessed Be He would speak to him about. (3) Balaam spoke with Him whenever he pleased, for it says: 'prostrate, but with eyes unveiled' (24:4,16), which signifies that he used to prostrate himself on his face and straightway his eyes were unveiled to anything he inquired about. Moses, however, did not speak with Him whenever he wished (Num. R. 14:20)."[3] Thus, according to this view, Balaam was in some respects even superior to Moses.

Yet the preponderance of the passages on Balaam, biblical and postbiblical alike, are derogatory. The *Grundtext* is in the Balaam section itself, in the episode of the ass (22:22–35): Here Balaam seeks to curse Israel without divine permission (22:22,34; see Excursus 57). Its reflex surfaces first in Deuteronomy with the explicit charge that Balaam set out to curse Israel: "The LORD your God turned the curse into a blessing for you, for the LORD your God loves you" (Deut. 23:6; see Josh. 24:10; Neh. 13:2). Deuteronomy's denigration of Balaam is understandable given its premise that prophets arise only in Israel, whereas their pagan counterparts are abominable magicians (Deut. 18:9–15). And elsewhere Balaam is

censured for another reason: "They [the Midianites] are the very ones who, at the bidding of Balaam, induced the Israelites to trespass against the LORD in the matter of Peor, so that the LORD's community was struck by the plague" (Num. 31:16). Balaam, that is, had advised Balak to demoralize Israel's fighting force by using Midianite women to seduce it into the service of their cult (see the Comment to 24:14). That this tradition is as old as that of Deuteronomy, if not older, is now demonstrable by the eighth-century Deir ʿAlla inscription, which also tells of Balaam advising the establishment of an idolatrous cult (see Excursus 60). Both pejorative traditions are combined in Joshua 13:22, "Together with the others [the Midianites] that they slew, the Israelites put Balaam, the augur, to the sword." That he was an augur points to his condemnation by the law of Deuteronomy 18:10–13, and that he was slain with the Midianites whom he incited against Israel points to Numbers 31:8,16.

The postbiblical texts exaggerate Balaam's vices to such a degree that he becomes an exemplar of villainy. Philo portrays him as more eager even than Balak to curse Israel (1 Mos. 285–286). Josephus also insists that Balaam intended to comply with Balak's wishes (Ant. 4.119–122). The Christian Bible, too, emphasizes Balaam's avarice (2 Pet. 2:15–16; Jude 11) and his counsel of idolatry and debauchery (Rev. 2:14). The tannaitic rabbis claim that "Balaam the Wicked" and all who follow in his ways are cut off from the world to come; that is, they forfeit immortality (Mish. Avot 5:19; see Sanh. 105a–106b, Targums to chaps. 22–24).

Thus the transformation is complete. Later tradition acknowledges almost nothing of Balaam the obedient servant of the Lord, who could not be bribed by all the wealth of Moab. He is, instead, the archetypal enemy of Israel, a Pharaoh or Haman, whose power would threaten to annihilate Israel were it not for the intervention of Israel's God. Yet both traditions, the saint and the sinner, have their roots in Scripture, indeed, in these very chapters of the "Book of Balaam."

EXCURSUS 59

Balaam: Diviner or Sorcerer? (chaps. 22–24)

Magic comprises two categories, sorcery and divination, which differ in their objective: the former attempts to alter the future; the latter, to predict it. The magician who claims to curse or bless is a sorcerer, whereas the one who foretells events but cannot affect them is a diviner.

In Israel, sorcery (*keshafim*) is not only banned (Deut. 18:10) but punished with death (Exod. 22:17). Mesopotamian laws also hold that sorcery (*kishpu*) is a capital crime, but they refer to black magic, for example, hexing an individual and other such antisocial behavior.[1] Sorcery also had a legitimate place in Mesopotamian society, in exorcising demons and countering the effects of black magic (*Shurpu, Maqlu*). In biblical religion, sorcery in any form was, by definition, deemed ineffectual since all events were under the control of the one God. It was also deemed heretical since any attempt to alter the future purported to flout and overrule the will of God. A sorcerer's technique (still not fully understood) is both condemned and ridiculed by Ezekiel: "Woe to those who sew pads on all armjoints and make bonnets for the head of every person, in order to entrap! . . . You have announced the death of persons who will not die and the survival of persons who will not live—lying

to My people, who listen to your lies" (Ezek. 13:18–19). Yet, despite the official ban on sorcery (rather, because such legislation was necessary), we infer that it was widely practiced (see 2 Kings 9:22; Jer. 27:9; Mic. 5:11; Mal. 3:5; 2 Chron. 33:6).

Divination is the science of reading omens, predicated on the assumption that the course of events is predictable: its advance notices are imprinted in natural phenomena or discernible in man-made devices. The following forms of divination are mentioned in Scripture: casting of lots (sortilege; 1 Sam. 14:42–43); interpreting oil or water patterns in a cup (hydromancy or oleomancy; Gen. 44:5,15); inspecting the shape of a sacrificial animal's liver (hepatoscopy; Ezek. 21:6); and consulting (still unidentifiable) ***terafim*** (Judg. 17:5; 18:14; Hos. 3:4; Ezek. 21:26; Zech. 12:2) or the spirits of the dead (necromancy; 1 Sam. 28:9; Isa. 8:19; 19:3; 29:4). In the Bible the king of Israel consults the prophets performing divination before engaging the Arameans at Ramoth-gilead (1 Kings 22:5). Indeed, throughout the ancient Near East divination was widely practiced before battles in order to ascertain the will of the gods. Thus King Hammurabi of Babylon sends his ***bārû***-diviner to "gather omens" before attacking Shabazum.[2] The Hittites divine by stars and birds, and the ancient Greeks consult diviners before military decisions are taken (e.g., Iliad 1.60–120, Anabasis 5.6.29; see the Comment to 23:3).

Divination could be tolerated in Israel since, theoretically, it was not incompatible with monotheism—the diviner could always claim that he was only trying to disclose the immutable will of God. Indeed, according to one source, the prophet originally was called a diviner (1 Sam. 9:9). Thus, the diviner, in contrast to the sorcerer, was never subject to judicial execution. The exception was the necromancer (Lev. 20:27; but not those who consulted him: Lev. 19:31), who laid claim to the sorcerer's power to raise up the dead even against their will (1 Sam. 28:15). Yet certain religious circles condemned divination as an abominable heresy (Deut. 18:10–12; 1 Sam. 15:23)—not that they doubted its efficacy. Rather, God had granted Israel the special boon: He communicated with them directly, either through prophets or dreams (Deut. 12:6–8; 13:2–6). Nonetheless, the official cult did sanction one divinatory medium: the Urim and Thummim, carried on the (High) Priest's ephod (Exod. 28:30–35; 1 Sam. 2:28; 14:3; 23:6,9; 28:6, 30:7).

Into which category of magician does Balaam fall? It has already been noted in the Comment to 23:14 that Balaam required hilltops (and solitude; 23:3) in order to read astronomical signs and other omens—a sure sign of divination. The terminology applied to Balaam confirms this: His craft is called ***naḥash*** (23:23; 24:1) and ***kesem*** (22:7; 23:23). ***Naḥash*** was practiced by Joseph (Gen. 44:5,15), who manifestly sought to read the divine will. ***Kesem*** is the label put on clairvoyance (Zech. 10:2; see Ezek. 13:9; 21:34), necromancy (1 Sam. 28:8), and three other forms of divination (Ezek. 21:26–28). Indeed, in the Deir ʿAlla inscription (Excursus 60), Balaam is expressly called a ***ḥozeh***, a clairvoyant (1.1), indicating that outside of Israel he was also known as a diviner (see Josh. 13:22). Moreover, the list of birds in that inscription (1.7–10) may indicate that Balaam divined by interpreting the omens of birds, and it may be no accident that such is the Balaam tradition preserved in Philo (1 Mos. 282,287).

Yet Balak expects Balaam to curse Israel. This means that Balak regarded him as a sorcerer, one who has the power to determine Israel's destiny. Balak wanted a sorcerer—one who could emasculate Israel with his curses so that the Moabites would prevail over them in battle (see the Comments to 22:6,11). Balaam (rather, Balak's image of Balaam) is paralleled by the practice of pre-Islamic Arabs who would commission a poet (***shāʿir***) reputed to be inspired by the ***jinn*** (spirit) or ***shaiṭān*** to compose a ***hijāʾ***-curse of the enemy.[3]

Indeed, Muhammad himself had a poet curse his opponents before the Battle of Bedr. The curse was conceived in material terms, as an arrow shot from the bow so that "if, when a man was cursed, he was thrown down, it avoided him" (Ibn Hishâm).[4]

Herein lies the major tension in the story. Balak hires Balaam as a sorcerer, but Balaam denies he has such power—his God is the Lord, God of Israel. He can act only as a diviner not as a sorcerer and maintains, again and again, that he can only speak and act as directed by God: "I could not of my own accord do anything good or bad contrary to the LORD's command" (24:13; see 22:8,11,38; 23:3,6,12,26). Balak, just as relentlessly and despite three demonstrations to the contrary, insists that Balaam is a sorcerer and, therefore, responsible not only for his failure to curse Israel but for the fact that he blessed them (23:11,25; 24:10). Balaam does not deny this charge but again insists that he has blessed Israel under the Lord's instructions: "My message was to bless: When He blesses, I cannot reverse it" (23:20; see 24:1,9).

Thus, Balaam never appears as a sorcerer but as a diviner. Indeed, the fact that he is given a northern Mesopotamian provenience corroborates his divining credentials. In Mesopotamian sources there are no instances of a sorcerer who curses the king's enemies. The magician who accompanies the king into battle, as noted above, is the ***bārû***, the diviner. Thus Balaam, if he is a Mesopotamian, should have been expected to divine for Balak not to curse for him. And, in fact, that is precisely how he operates. Twice while Balak is occupied with the sacrificial ritual, Balaam divines that God wants him—indeed, dictates the words to him—to bless Israel (23:3–5,15–16). The third and fourth times, casting divination aside, he rises to the level of prophecy. Needing no dictation from God, but flooded by His spirit, he composes his own utterance (***ne'um***) of blessing (24:1–2).

Balaam's oracles of a blessing are an index of his spiritual growth. The first (23:7–10) expresses praise of Israel's ***present*** status and Balaam's desire to share it. The second (23: 18–24) stresses that God's Presence in Israel obviates the need for divination and endows Israel with leonine power. The third and fourth, Balaam's own compositions, are predictive: Israel will be blessed with prosperity and victory (24:3–9) and, as a result, will crush Balak's nation, Moab, and witness the destruction of other enemies (24:18–23). Thus Israel's blessing moves from the present to the future, from a description of Israel's immediate potential to its eventual fulfillment, reaching its crescendo in the full retribution it will exact from Balak (through his nation) for defying God by attempting to destroy Israel. Balak, in effect, is another Pharaoh whose nation was also punished because he dared to block the divine plan for Israel's salvation. The parallel with Pharaoh is even more apposite since Balak, just as mulishly, tries three times to thwart God's design to bless Israel and thereby brings doom to his own people.

EXCURSUS 60

Balaam and the Deir ʿAlla Inscription

In 1967 a Dutch archaeological expedition, digging at Deir ʿAlla in an ancient delta formed by the juncture of the Jabbok and Jordan rivers, uncovered fragments of an inscription written on wall plaster inside an Iron Age II (900–600 B.C.E.) temple. On both stratigraphic and epigraphic grounds, the inscription has been dated to the eighth century. Its language,

though originally thought to be Aramaic,[1] is clearly a dialect of Hebrew,[2] probably of that very region of Transjordan in which it was found. Judging by the curve of the fragments, the inscription was most likely written on a stele (pillar). And judging by the contents, it may have had something to do with the founding of a temple.

The plaster fragments belong to twelve groups of "combinations," only two of which are large enough to be regarded as continuous texts. The fragmentized state of the inscription allows only a conjectural translation and interpretation. What follows is a tentative translation of combinations 1 and 2.[3] Reconstructions are indicated by square brackets, unclear letters by a superlinear dot, doubtful translations by a parenthetical question mark, and missing text by three dots.

COMBINATION 1

Line

1. [This is] the account of [Balaam, son of Be]or, who was a seėr of the godṡ. The gods came to him in the night, and he saw a vision
2. according to the orȧcle of El. Then they spoke to Ba[laa]m son of Beor: "This he will do . . . in the future(?) . . ."
3. And Balaam rose on the next day . . . and he wept
4. bitterly. And his people came up to ḣim [and said to] hiṁ, "Balaam, son of Beor, why do you fast aṅd weep?" And he
5. said to them: "Siṫ down and I shall relate to you what the ***shadḋa[yin*** are going to do.] Come now and see the work of the gods! The g[o]ds gathered together:
6. the ***shaddayin*** took their places at the assembly and they ṡaid to Sh[eger . . .]: "Sew up, bolt up the heavens with your dense cloud, ordain darkness and not eterṅal light.
7. And place the dark clou[d's se]al [on] your ḃolt, and do not remove it forever! For the swift shall
8. revile the ėagle and the voiċe of the vulture shall sing [. . .], the ẏoung of the ***naḥats***-bird shall claw up the young of the heron, and the swallow shall tear at
9. the pigeon, and the sparrow . . . the staff. At the place where ewes are brought, the hares shall eat branches
10. . . . drink wine and (from) cups. They heard this reproach . . .
11. . . . He will take you to the wise women, mourners, the preparer of myrrh, and the priestess
12. . . . for the prince, a tattered loincloth. The respected man shall respect (others) and the one who gave respect shall be re[spected . . .]
13. . . . The deaf ȯnes shall hear from afar
14. . . . the eyes (?) [of] a ḟool shall see visions. Sheger and Ashtar
15. . . . the panther. The pigling chases the you[ng] of . . .

COMBINATION 2

4. young woman full of love . . .
5. an offspring . . . every moisṫ . . .
6. El will be satisfied. Let him cross ov̇er to the House of Eternity . . .
7. the house where the traveler does not come and bridegroom does not come, the house . . .

8. and the worm from the tomb; from the testicles of men, from the thighs of . . .
9. . . . Will he not take counsel with you? Or will he not take advice from one residing . . .
10. You will cover him with one garment. If you are hostile to him, he will be weak. If . . .
11. I shall pl[ace worms(?)] under your head. You will lie down on your eternal bed to perish . . .
12. . . . in their heart. The offspring sings in his heart . . .
13. . . . kings will see . . . Death will take the newborn child, the suckling . . .
14. . . . the heart of the offspring is hesitant. He comes to . . .
15. . . . to his end . . .
16. . . . a distant vision . . .
17. to make known (lit. "to know") the account he spoke to his people orally (lit. "by tongue") your judgment and your punishment
18. and we shall not drink . . .
35. . . . will drip rain (?) and ton[gue] . . .
36. will drip dew and . . . tongue . . .

The many lacunae and the questionable readings and renderings give some idea why the above translation is largely conjectural. Yet the following is clear. A seer named Balaam the son of Beor has a nocturnal vision in which the gods speak to him (1.1–2)—precisely the circumstances of Numbers 22:8–9,14–20. (Is this why *'elohim*, the plural form of the Deity, is used in the narrative? See chap. 22, note 56). The divine message is obscure but it causes Balaam to weep (1.3–4). His people ask him the meaning of his weeping and fasting, and he tells them that the council of the gods, the *shaddayin*, has decided to inflict a drought on the land (1.4–7). This is followed by a description of desolation that, in certain aspects, is also found in the Bible and the literature of the ancient Near East. The natural world is overturned. Light (*ngh*) is eclipsed by total darkness (*ḥšk*) (1.6–7); compare Amos 5:20: "Surely the day of the LORD shall be/not light, but darkness [*ḥoshekh*],/blackest night without a glimmer [*nogah*]" (see also Ezek. 32:7–8; Joel 2:2,10; Zeph. 1:15). The devastated land is overrun by wild beasts and birds (see Isa. 34:10–15; Zeph. 2:14–15; Sfire I.A. 32–33). Their natures are reversed: The weak birds turn against the strong, and the vulture sings (1.7–9). The land is bereft of joy; the wayfarer and the bridegroom are no longer seen (2.7)—reminding us of Jeremiah 7:34: "I will silence in the towns of Judah and the streets of Jerusalem the sound of mirth and gladness, the voice of bridegroom and bride" (see Jer. 16:9; 25:10), and of Isaiah 33:8: "Highways are desolate,/wayfarers have ceased" (see Isa. 34:10; 60:15). Aristocrats will don loincloths (1.12; see Isa. 3:24), the honored and lowly will exchange roles (1.12; see Isa. 3:5), the deaf will hear from afar (1.13; see Isa. 29:18), and fools will see visions (1.14; see Joel 3:1; Zech. 13:4–6). Death will reign supreme (2.8,11)—snatching the newborn (2.13; see Jer. 9:20; Hos. 9:16) and the youth (2.4,8; see Deut. 32:25; 2 Kings 8:12) and occupying the professional mourners and morticians (1.11; see Jer. 9:16–19; 2 Chron. 16:14; Mark 14:8; 16:1; Ras Shamra 25.460.12).

The names Sheger and Ashtar (1.14) clearly relate to a tandem found in the Bible (Deut. 7:13; 28:4,38,51), where it refers to the offspring of cattle and sheep. Here it stands for two fertility deities: Ashtar, a god well known from the Moabite stone and the Ugaritic texts, and Sheger, a goddess, probably Ashtar's consort, known from the Punic personal name ʿEbhedsheger and from a Ugaritic list of offerings.[4] It is probably they who are responsible for ending the drought with the onset of rain (2.35–36) and, presumably, fertility.

These data most plausibly fit into the following story line: Balaam, having learned in a dream that the gods intend to reverse nature, bringing blight to the land and death to its inhabitants, presumably intercedes with them (in the missing 2.19–34) to revoke their decision. Alternatively, or sequentially, Balaam's intercession may, in the manner of his biblical counterpart, have implored the gods by means of sacrifice (Num. 23:1–2,14,29–30). Perhaps the temple on whose walls this inscription was written was founded to honor the gods (Sheger and Ashtar?) who heeded Balaam's plea/sacrifice.

If this interpretation of the Deir ʿAlla inscription is correct, it has far-reaching implications for the biblical story of Balaam. First, it distinctly shows that the Balaam tradition was very much alive in the eighth century in a non-Israelite, Transjordanian community. Indeed, that it is situated just to the north of the biblical setting of the story may indicate as well that Balaam was not a Mesopotamian from the Euphrates (see the Comments to 22:5; 23:3) but an Aramean (23:7) or an Ammonite (23:5 Sam.), that is, from a nearby region. Moreover, Balaam is not introduced, implying that his name was well known. And furthermore, Balaam is presented as a seer, not as a sorcerer, in keeping with the biblical narrative (see Excursus 59). Equally significant is that Balaam is presented in a positive light, again in agreement with the main biblical story (but not with the ass episode; see Excursus 57). It has also been noted in Excursus 58 that the prophet Micah, also of the eighth century, holds a favorable opinion of Balaam. However, the accusation that Balaam devised the scheme to have the Moabite women seduce Israel into worshipping Baal-peor (Num. 31:16; see Excursus 58) may be traceable to Deir ʿAlla's assertion that Balaam founded a pagan (fertility?) cult. This means that both views of Balaam, positive and negative, are contemporary. In fact, they must be older than the eighth century, since both Micah and Deir ʿAlla refer to the Balaam episode as having occurred long before. Thus we now have extrabiblical confirmation of the antiquity of the Balaam traditions.

EXCURSUS 61

The Apostasy of Baal-Peor (25:1–18)

The major critical problem in the text of the Baal-peor incident is that the solutions to the crisis offered by God and Moses do not agree with each other and that neither one is actually fulfilled. God orders the impalement of all the leaders; Moses orders the "judges" to slay all the idolators, and neither is done. A third solution, the slaying by Phinehas of a sinning couple *in flagrante*, appeases God's wrath.

According to most scholars, three different versions of this incident lie behind the text: The actual impalement of the leaders at God's command, the actual slaying of the guilty at Moses' command, and Phinehas's deed. The editor of the Masoretic text, so runs the theory, truncated the ends of the first two solutions to give the appearance that they were not carried out; Phinehas's solution alone was acceptable to God. From this alleged reconstruction—even if it is correct—we learn nothing, for it does not explain why the partial versions of the first two stories would have been retained. Surely, they must be there for a reason and only by viewing the text as a unity can one hope to disclose what it might be. Moreover, the grounds for maintaining this chapter as a conflation of sources are patently insufficient. There are four criteria by which to separate out literary sources: (1) factual contradictions; (2) expansions or glosses, usually of a tendentious nature; (3)

changed vocabulary, that is, two (or more) different expressions for the same concept or idiom; and (4) variant traditions attested in other biblical texts. The first two criteria are paramount, whereas the latter two are only supportive.

The main source division alleged by the critics, verses 1–5 and verses 6–19, exhibit no inner contradictions. Even the alternation of Moab and Midian can be explained on geopolitical grounds (see the Comments to 22:4,7). There is not a single extraneous bulge. True, the vocabulary used for Phinehas's deed differs from that of the preceding section; however, since his action is spontaneous, a result of his own initiative and is in no way anticipated, it is only to be expected that its language will be novel. Finally, the four literary reflexes of the event do not harbor variant traditions: Psalms 106:28–30 presupposes the Masoretic text of Numbers 25; Hosea 9:10 is noncommittal; Deuteronomy 4:3, which recounts the annihilation of all the wicked of Baal-peor, could have been based on the claim that twenty-four thousand died in the plague (v. 9). Furthermore, Joshua 22:17 does not deny that Phinehas's deed expiated that of Israel; rather, it only avers that the Transjordanian altar is proof that Israel is capable of repeating the sin of Baal-peor.

The only problem lies in verses 1–5. God orders the impalement of the leaders, and just as clearly Moses alters God's decree, appearing to have countermanded God's orders. Perhaps he sought to attain divine forgiveness of the leaders by getting *them* to punish the idolators (see the Targums and Sam. to v. 5). In effect, Moses would be acting as Israel's intercessor, his customary role, seeking to assuage God's anger and avert the natural calamity, which was poised to sweep away guilty and innocent alike. "Once leave has been given to the 'destroyer' to do injury, it no longer discriminates between the innocent and the guilty" (Mekh. Bo' 11; see the Comment to 17:10). Moses, in turn, in ordering the death of the guilty alone is positing an Abrahamic conception of the Deity: "Will you sweep away the innocent along with the guilty?" (Gen. 18:23). This confrontation between the punitive Deity and Moses the intercessor is well documented elsewhere (see 11:2; 12:13; 14:13–19; 16:22; 17:11; 21:7). There is, however, a qualitative difference between Moses' attempt at intercession here and his other intercessions. Whereas the latter are purely didactic in nature, here Moses attempts to alter God's decree. In any event, before either order—God's or Moses'—can be carried out, Phinehas acts. Indeed, the text leaves the impression that Moses and the leaders are so overwhelmed by the rampant plague that they are incapable of any action except to weep and wail at the sanctuary.

The rabbis were uncomfortable with Phinehas's act. Having slain a man impulsively, without either trial or prior warning, he took the law into his own hands, thereby creating a dangerous precedent. No wonder certain sages claim that Moses and the religious leaders would have excommunicated Phinehas were it not for the divine decree declaring that he had acted on God's behalf (TJ Sanh. 27b). However, Phinehas can be defended: He did not act on his own initiative but followed God's command.

First, it should be noted that the text takes special pains to mention the pedigree of the slain—they stem from the leading families of their respective peoples. In other words, Phinehas did indeed attempt to fulfill God's command to impale Israel's leaders. Furthermore, Phinehas's deed in slaying one Israelite leader suffices to ransom (*kipper*) Israel; God requires no additional victims. *Kipper* functions to avert the retribution, to nip it in the bud, to terminate it before it is fully exhausted. Two narratives indeed attest to the fact that *kippur* (ransom) stops a plague in its tracks (Num. 17:11–12; 2 Sam. 24:25).

Phinehas, then, has acted in his capacity as chief of the Tabernacle guards (1 Chron. 9:20; Num. 3:22; see the Comments to vv. 7,13). By his deed, he ransoms (*kipper*; v. 13).

Israel, in keeping with the expiatory function of the sacral guards: (literally) "to ransom [*le-khapper*] the Israelites, so that no ***plague*** [*negef*] may afflict the Israelites for encroaching upon the sanctuary" (Num. 8:19; see 18:22, 23). It follows that the son of and the successor to the chief of the sanctuary guards (3:32), in striking down a leading culprit from both Israel and Midian, thereby stops the plague. The text implies that had they (or other leaders; v. 4a) been slain earlier, many of those who died in the plague could have been saved (v. 4b). Thus, Phinehas's "impassioned action for his God" (v. 13) was actually the ideal—and appropriate—behavior of the sanctuary guard: His prompt action "ransomed" Israel by terminating God's wrath/plague.

Phinehas's role as chief of the sanctuary guards sheds light upon the theological problem presented by God's order: Why should all the leaders, innocent and guilty alike, be impaled? In truth, the same question could be asked of the expiatory function of the guards: Why should the entire Levitical cordon be condemned by God when an Israelite succeeds in encroaching on the sanctuary (18:22–23)? The answer is that the Levitical guards are indeed guilty: It is their negligence that makes encroachment possible (for details, see Excursus 40). Similarly, all of Israel's leaders must share the responsibility for not checking the Israelite apostates at the outset (R. Judah in Num. R. 20:23). However, Phinehas's impassioned act in slaying the perpetrators of this single instance of encroachment suffices to ransom the rest of the people and terminates the plague.

Phinehas's deed implies that the impalement of Israel's leaders, as originally ordered by God, would also have served as ransom. This explanation appears to be confirmed and clarified by two other texts. The first, Exodus 32:26–29, deals with the apostasy of the golden calf where the Levites are called upon to slay the people, even their close relatives, ***indiscriminately***—to assuage the wrath of God. The second text, 2 Samuel 21:1–14, is more illuminating, for it contains the only other mention in the Bible of impalement (*hokia'*). The circumstances, moreover, are strikingly similar. A three-year drought has afflicted the land (v. 1). An oracle pins the blame on Saul's violation of the treaty with the Gibeonites (v. 2). David asks the Gibeonites: "How shall I make expiation [*'akhapper*, i.e., ransom], so that you may bless the LORD's own people?" (v. 3). The Gibeonites demand the impalement of seven sons of Saul "on the mountain [in Gibeon, v. 6 LXX] before the LORD" (v. 9). The passage concludes: "And when all that the king had commanded was done, God responded to the plea of the land thereafter" (v. 14). Thus, impalement before/to the Lord serves an expiatory function, specifically, to assuage the wrath of God, who had blighted the land with drought for the violation of His treaty oath. By the same token, Israel at Shittim had incurred the anger of God in the form of a plague because it had violated the Sinaitic treaty (the Decalogue) forbidding the worship of other gods. The required expiation—the impalement of the leaders—was instead satisfied by Phinehas's impassioned impalement-slaying of two brazen sinners who had brought their idolatrous rite into the sanctuary precincts. Thus, just as the impalement of Saul's sons provided the needed ransom-expiation for ending the drought, so the impalement of Israel's leaders—the original command of God (v. 4) executed through the impalement of Zimri and Cozbi—sufficed to ransom the Israelite community at Baal-peor and thereby bring an end to the pestilence. This indeed must be the meaning of *be-kane'o 'et-kin'ati* (v. 11), literally "in his becoming impassioned with My passion." It is a tacit rebuke of Moses! Only Phinehas obeyed God's orders; only his act was congruent with God's command. And hence he (and not Moses) is entitled to "My pact of friendship" (v. 12).

The historical background for the composition of this text can only be surmised. Many critics (as early as Reggio) have surmised that the struggle over the High Priesthood between the houses of Abiathar and Zadok is reflected here, with victory being awarded to the Zadokites (the line of Phinehas; 1 Chron. 5:30–41). Abiathar and Zadok served jointly as High Priests during the reign of David, but the former was banished from his office by Solomon (1 Kings 2:26–27; cf. 1 Sam. 2:27–36), leaving the office of the High Priest exclusively to the line of Phinehas. However, the text explicitly mentions "a pact of priesthood for all time"—"priesthood" not "High Priesthood." Therefore, it is more likely that the Baal-peor incident was used as justification for the banishment of Abiathar and his entire family from the Jerusalem Temple so that the Zadokites alone remained as its officiating priests. Non-Zadokite priests continued to serve on the staff of the First Temple but not as officiants (Ezek. 40:45–46; 43:19; 44:15–16). Striking confirmation that God's covenant with Phinehas was with all the priests that stemmed from his line is provided by the prophet Malachi, who in Second Temple days speaks of God's covenant with Levi (Mal. 2:4–7; 3:3), that is, with the entire priesthood and not only with the line of Phinehas.

Finally, we must ask, what was the purpose of the licentious cult of Baal-peor and, in particular, of the connubial act of the named couple inside the ***kubbah*** (chamber)? Surely, it was not for sexual gratification. The fact that the act was an integral part of the worship of Baal-peor and that the ***kubbah***, as I understand it, was situated in the sacred precincts means that it was ritual intercourse, deemed essential for the cosmos, for the assurance of divine blessing. But in what way?

The customary interpretation holds that Israel was seduced by the fertility rites of Baal-peor. The sexual union of his human votaries reminds and inspires the Baal (lit. "owner") of the land to impregnate the earth with his rain-seed and thereby assure the fertility of the crops and flocks in the year ahead. "Wherever ample moisture is given to the earth . . . the earth multiplies from within itself whatever seed is placed in it. And this is ascribed to the powerful effects of divine matings."[1]

The problem with this interpretation is that there is absolutely no evidence for it anywhere in the ancient Near East. The only description of sacred prostitution comes from classical sources (Herodotus, Strabo, and Lucian), which completely lack confirmation from primary sources of Mesopotamia, Canaan, and Egypt. To be sure, sacred marriage between a god and goddess or between a goddess and a king is reported in Mesopotamian ritual, but there is no evidence that it was acted out in a sex rite by human participants.[2]

Attempts to find sacred prostitution in the Bible have focused on the ***zonah*** and ***kedeshah***. The former, however, strictly denotes "a harlot" and never refers to a woman who commits a sexual act in a cultic setting. As for the ***kedeshah*** as well as the male ***kadesh*** (see Gen. 38:21–22; Deut. 23:18–19; 1 Kings 15:12; 22:47; 2 Kings 23:7), terms that stem from the word ***kadosh***, "holy"—they probably connote officiants or devotees of an idolatrous cult.[3] The same holds true for the equivalent terms in other Semitic cultures: Ugaritic ***qdšm***[4] and Akkadian ***qadištu***. The latter, in particular, "could marry and have children. She also served as a wet-nurse. She is often designated as a votary of Adad and (in Mari) of Annunitu. There is no evidence of her being a prostitute."[5]

Another interpretation has been suggested: The rites of Baal-peor were not a fertility but a funerary cult.[6] A clue that may point to this interpretation is in Psalms 106:28, one of the later references to this incident: "They attached themselves to Baal Peor, ate sacrifices offered to the dead." Here the dead may not be a derogatory characterization of the pagan

deity but a literal reference to the spirits of the dead who are appeased by these rites. The widespread worship of the ancestral spirits in the ancient Near East is captured by this passage from a Ugaritic epic, which praises the ideal son as follows:

> "So shall there be a son in his house, a scion in the midst of his palace; who sets up the stelae of his ancestral spirits, in the holy place the protectors of his clan."[7]

More significant evidence stems from the ancient Greek festival Anthesteria and the older Mycenaean Festival of the Thirsty (Dead), dedicated to the placation of the spirits of the dead. It was an annual three-day festival of new wine. The first day was called "the opening of the casks [of new wine]" (such a festival name appears in ancient Mari on the Euphrates; ARM 1.52.9–11). The second day was marked by ritual intercourse followed by drinking and revelry, and the third day was given over to the spirits of the dead.[8]

Thus the assumption here is not of idolatry but of necrolatry: Israel engaged in the rites of Baal-peor in a desperate attempt to terminate a deadly (bubonic?) plague caused by the disgruntled spirits of the dead who needed to be appeased by rites similar to the Mycenaean-Greek rites involving ritual feasting and intercourse. The underlying idea is that "the boy or girl who went to death without having experienced sexual intercourse [*la ṣummudu*; see the Comment to v. 3] remained unsatisfied and therefore caused harm to the living. . . . The sequence of sacrifice, food and drink, and ritual intercourse would represent the gamut of those things necessary to put the restless spirits of the age at ease."[9]

The problem with this interpretation is that the god normally associated with plague was Resheph, not Baal (Hab. 3:5; cf. Deut. 32:23–24; Pss. 76:4, 78:48). Baal was the god of fertility and was usually identified with the storm-god Hadad. Thus the contest on Mount Carmel between the Lord and the Baal centers on which deity will break the long drought with abundant rain (1 Kings 18). Moreover, the necrolatry theory has to assume that the plague occurred first and drove the Israelites to Baal-peor, whereas the text implies that the plague was a punitive consequence of their idolatry.

The interpretation adopted in the Commentary (see especially the Comment to v. 2) follows the plain meaning of the text. During their stay at the plains of Moab, many Israelites—including a chieftain—were seduced by Moabite and Midianite women into engaging in sacrificial feasts of the god Baal-peor and into intermarrying with them. Precisely because this was the first such Israelite encounter with the culture of Canaan and because the devastating plague was attributed to divine wrath, Baal-peor came to be etched in the collective memory as a nadir in Israel's history (Deut. 4:3; Hos. 9:10; Ps. 106:28).

EXCURSUS 62

The Apportionment of the Promised Land (26:52–56)

The prescribed method of apportioning the land (vv. 52–56) seems to be based on two mutually exclusive principles: the lot (v. 55) and the need (v. 54). Thus, although the apportionment is decided strictly on the basis of population as determined by the census (vv. 1–51), that decision ostensibly is to be made by lot. Are these two principles reconcilable?

The problem is much discussed by the medieval exegetes. Rashi suggests that God saw to it that the drawn (or cast) lots corresponded to the tribal size; that is, the land was

divided into unequal portions and their distribution determined by lot. Providence then controlled the distribution so that each tribe was assigned the territory it needed. Ramban, on the other hand, maintains there were two discrete distributions: The land was first divided into twelve equal portions, which were distributed by lot. Each tribe then apportioned its assigned territory among its clans according to their size.

Abravanel objects to both of the proposed solutions. Rashi's is contradicted by verse 54; "with larger groups increase the share, with smaller groups reduce the share. Each is to be assigned its share according to its enrollment." This verse states unequivocally that the actual assignment of the land is to be made by Israel and not by God (the lot). Ramban's solution is opposed on two grounds. (1) If the distribution by lot came first it should also have been the first procedure mentioned in the text. But it is second (vv. 55–56). And (2) a reflex of the apportionment of the promised land is found in 33:54: "You shall apportion the land among yourselves by lot, clan by clan: with larger groups increase the share, with smaller groups reduce the share. Wherever the lot falls for anyone, that shall be his. You shall have your portions according to your ancestral tribes." Thus, for Abravanel, only the procedure of the lot seems to be indicated. In addition one can counter Ramban's solution on purely logical grounds: If the tribes divide the land equally then a member of a smaller tribe will more likely receive a larger share than a member of a larger tribe.

Abravanel, then, offers his own solution to parry his objections. There were two divisions: the *location* of each tribe by lot and the *size* of each tribal territory according to population. The location was determined by lot to prevent internecine strife, lest some tribe claim that its territory was not as fertile or not as conquerable as some of the others. The actual extent of each tribal holding would then be determined on an objective basis: The more populous the tribe, as determined by the census, the larger its territory. The rabbis allude to this solution: "The Land of Israel was allocated by [qualitative] assessment" (Sif. Num. 132). The ancient Greeks also followed this procedure. The legislator "must divide the country into twelve sections. The twelve sections should be made equal in the sense that a section should be smaller if the soil is good, bigger if it is poor" (Plato, *Laws* 745).[1]

Subsequent biblical reflexes of the apportionment confirm this solution. Numbers 33:54 indeed stresses that the lot should be used for the location of both tribal and clan holdings (v. 54*aα*,b). However, it also states "with larger groups increase the share, with smaller groups reduce the share" (v. 54a*β*), which implies (here Abravanel errs) that the size of the land parcels each clan receives will not be decided by lot but by the criterion of population. Also, 34:13 asserts that the nine and a half tribes are to receive their share in Cisjordan by lot—again referring only to location. This is followed by 34:16–29, which assigns chieftains as supervisors who will actually draw up the boundaries for each tribe and clan. Finally, Joshua 17:14 explicitly phrases the Josephites' complaint about their land holdings: "Why have you assigned as our portion a single allotment [*goral*] and a single district, seeing that we are a numerous people . . .?"—an allusion to both distribution procedures, by lot and by apportionment. Joshua's answer is to the point: Your territory is large enough; go clear it (Josh. 17:15,18). Again, the implication is manifest: The actual apportionment of the land among the tribes has been equitable since it was based on population.

Abravanel's solution, then, is correct and requires only slight refinement. The key to the literary analysis of this pericope on land apportionment is *'akh* (v. 55), a term that always connotes exclusion, limitation, amendment. Hence, it is the literary marker that divides the section into two procedures of land apportionment: the basic principle of

apportioning the land according to tribal and clan size (vv. 53–54, with Ramban), qualified by the secondary principle that, initially, the location of the tribal and clan territory should be determined by lot (vv. 55–56, with Abravanel). Certainly, simple logic would dictate that the actual location of each tribe and clan could only be decided by lot to prevent suspicions and accusations of inequitable treatment. Indeed, subsequent passages in Scripture confirm that the initial division of Cisjordan was by lot (Num. 34:13; 36:2,3; Josh. 13:6; 14:1–2; especially 18:6–11).

EXCURSUS 63

The Inheritance Rights of Daughters (27:1–8)

Israelite practice contrasts sharply with that of its neighbors regarding a daughter's inheritance rights. It is clear that some other law codes expressly allow a daughter to inherit: Ancient Sumerian law ordains that an unmarried daughter may inherit when there are no sons,[1] and so also do decrees of Gudea (ca. 2150 B.C.E.), ruler of Lagash.[2] Thus, the concession made by the Bible to Zelophehad's daughters was anticipated in Mesopotamia by a millennium. It is also clear from documents of Nuzi[3] and Ugarit[4] (i.e., in places as far apart as the Tigris River and the Mediterranean coast during the middle and second half of the second millennium) that daughters inherited in the absence of sons.[5] Since Mesopotamian women could own property, both real and movable, there was no theoretical bar to a woman inheriting. Indeed, various documents and certain legal passages imply that daughters at times shared in the paternal estate alongside of sons, for example, at Nuzi[6] and in Hammurabi's laws (pars. 171, 175, 176, 178, 180, 181).[7] Documents of ancient Elam (southwest Iran) verify that daughters were equal to sons in matters of inheritance.[8]

A similar situation obtains in Egypt. During the Middle Kingdom (2050–1786), a woman could inherit from her husband if he so provided in his will. In the New Kingdom (1560–1050), the inheritance laws were even more favorable to women: The wife inherited a third of the estate, and the rest was divided equally among the children, male and female alike.[9] Later Ptolemaic law stipulated that a daughter had a legal right to share the inheritance with her brothers if the father died intestate.[10] This may account for Philo's statement that Jewish law (i.e., as practiced in Alexandrian Jewish courts) permitted unmarried daughters with no fixed dowries to share equally in the inheritance with the sons (2 L.A. 125). Hittite law had even fewer restrictions, with wives and daughters inheriting freely.[11]

How then are we to explain the fact that the Bible gives women no inheritance rights except in the case where there are no sons? And in that situation, unmarried daughters inherit for the purpose of transferring the estate to his grandsons! The differences in the law must reflect a difference in the makeup of the respective societies. The Bible, in its earliest stages, presumes a tightly knit clan structure; the foremost goal of its legal system was the preservation of the clan. Biblical law thus rests upon a strict patrilineal-agnatic principle of inheritance that prevents the transfer of land via the daughter to the clan of her husband. By contrast, Israel's neighbors in the great river basins of the Nile and the Tigris and Euphrates were already centralized urban societies even when their earliest laws were promulgated. The clan structure, if it had once existed at all, had disappeared or survived only in marginal seminomadic areas (e.g., Mari). In these societies the agnatic principle could not be rigidly maintained.

It has been alleged that the agnatic principle was not strictly followed in the Bible. But

on closer inspection, these ostensible exceptions prove to be unsubstantiated. Thus, although Job's daughters inherit with his sons (Job 42:15), it should not go unnoticed that this is not really a case of inheritance: "Their father gave them estates together with their brothers" *in his lifetime*. And there is ample additional attestation of the father's right to give parts of his estate as gifts to members of his family while he is alive (see Gen. 25:6; 2 Chron. 21:3; Ecclus. 33:20–24). Indeed, the fact that Deuteronomy has to mandate against violations of the law of primogeniture (Deut. 21:15–17) shows that it was not infrequent that "when he wills his properties to his sons" (v. 16), the father assumes that he has the right to dispose of the properties as he pleases—even to will them to his wives and daughters. Similarly, the money possessed by Micah's widowed mother (Judg. 17:1–4) need not have been an inheritance but property she possessed in her own right. And although the text of Ruth 4:3 is unambiguous in stating that Naomi was permitted to sell the property of her deceased husband, it simply means that after the death of her husband and sons she was declared the guardian of the property until it could be transferred to her descendants, via the levir Boaz, or to the closest relative, that is, the redeemer (Ruth 4:4). Finally, the example of the Jewish colony of Elephantine (near Aswan) in Egypt, which allowed women to inherit, is not germane—that community probably followed Egyptian or Babylonian practice.

The question remains: What happened in postbiblical times, when the clan structure of Israel had completely disintegrated? There would then have been no logical reason for maintaining laws, such as those of inheritance, whose main purpose (to perpetuate the clan) was no longer relevant. But relevant or not, the law had become canon, a divine command that had to be strictly obeyed. Thus, when the rabbis flesh out the law of inheritance to cover cases unanticipated by the biblical law they have no choice but to apply the agnatic principle.

The Torah itself attests that the inheritance law in chapter 27 is not comprehensive. It appends to the Book of Numbers a protest by the clan's leaders against the assignment of Zelophehad's patrimony to his daughters (chap. 36). And the mishnaic formulation of the law (Mish. BB 8:1–2) betrays its numerous and vital lacunae, for example: (1) What if the bequeather leaves behind only grandsons (his sons having predeceased him)? (2) What if one of his two sons predeceases him but leaves behind two sons? (3) In the same case, what if the dead son leaves behind a boy and a girl and the boy dies childless? The rabbis' decree addresses these cases by applying the agnatic rule with impeccable consistency: "Whosoever has precedence in inheritance, his offspring also have precedence" (Mish. BB 8:2). Thus, the bequeather's grandsons inherit him as would his sons (case 1); the surviving son gets half and the two grandsons divide the other half (case 2); the surviving granddaughter inherits the entire estate of her father (case 3). As long as the bequeather leaves descendants, his brothers do not inherit him (despite 27:9). Priority is given to the preservation of the father's line: the plea of Zelophehad's daughters—"Let not our father's name be lost to his clan" (27:4)—is thereby heeded.

A firm precedent for this rabbinic ruling may be found in 2 Samuel 14:5–11, a case of a patent conflict between the surviving son and the brothers of the deceased. The son is guilty of murder, and his uncles, who stand to inherit the estate, press for his execution. King David, however, overrules the hallowed death penalty and spares the life of the son so that the deceased will not be "without name or remnant upon the earth" (2 Sam. 14:7).[12]

What if the bequeather leaves a daughter and a granddaughter (of the dead son)? Rabbinic logic dictates that the granddaughter inherits everything! To which the Sadducees protested: "If my (dead) son's daughter, who represents my son, inherits me, should not

my daughter who represents me inherit me?" (Tosef. Yad. 2:20; BB 115b–116a). Despite the logical and moral weight of this argument, the agnatic principle, ordained by Scripture, is unwaveringly upheld: Inheritance passes through the male line.[13] No wonder that this inequity bothered the rabbis throughout the ages; indeed, they took great pains to compensate the daughter for the deprivation in matters of inheritance. The early tannaitic rabbis went so far as to declare: "If a man died and left sons and daughters and the property was ample, the sons inherit and the daughters receive maintenance; but if the property was small, the daughters receive maintenance and the sons go a-begging" (Mish. Ket. 13:3). However, later tannaim rejected this ruling on the grounds that the sons could protest: "Must I suffer because I am a male?" (Mish. Ket. 13:3). Nonetheless, rabbinic sensitivity to the daughter's plight is reflected in the decree that her support from the father's estate be stipulated in every marriage contract (Mish. Ket. 4:6,11).

Strikingly, the Karaites permitted daughters to inherit equally with sons. They reached this conclusion on the basis of the assumption—clearly, a correct one—that the law of succession deriving from the case of Zelophehad's daughters applied only to the ancestral property in the promised land but not to any other property, either real or movable.[14] It is difficult to determine why the rabbis did not employ the same scriptural exegesis, given their indisputable anguish concerning the disinherited daughter. They were, moreover, well aware that "the wise men of the nations have declared that a son and daughter are equal (in regard to inheritance)" (TJ BB 16a) and that this practice was actually followed in their own country before the Maccabean uprising when Hellenistic law was in force (Meg. Ta'an. 33). That they resisted both the practice of the outside world and the moral urgings of conscience can only mean that they were convinced that inheritance by agnates was an immutable postulate of the Torah.[15]

The hereditary succession according to the rabbis is as follows: (1) sons and their descendants; (2) daughters and their descendants; (3) the father; (4) brothers and their descendants; (5) sisters and their descendants; (6) the father's father; (7) the father's brothers and their descendants; (8) the father's sisters and their descendants; (9) the father's father's father; and so on (Maimonides, *Yad*, Mishpatim Naḥalot 1.1–3). It may seem puzzling that the rabbis give priority to the father when there are no children (BB 115a) even though the father is conspicuously absent from the biblical text. He is omitted in Scripture not because the case where the son predeceases his father is rare (Philo, 1 Mos. 245; and idem, 2 Laws 129–132—hardly a rarity in ancient times!) but for the obvious reason that if the father were alive he would still be in possession of the ancestral property. The rabbis, then, are referring to a different case: property that his son acquired on his own, a matter not discussed in the Bible.[16]

EXCURSUS 64

The Urim and Thummim

The Urim and Thummim are mentioned in Scripture only seven times, as follows:

1. "Inside the breastpiece of decision you shall place the Urim and Thummim, so that they are over Aaron's heart when he comes before the LORD" (Exod. 28:30).

2. "He put the breastpiece on him, and put into the breastpiece the Urim and Thummim" (Lev. 8:8).

3. "But he shall present himself to Eleazar the priest, who shall on his behalf seek the decision of the Urim before the LORD" (Num. 27:21).

4. "And of Levi he said: Let Your Thummin and Urim be with Your faithful" (Deut. 33:8).

5. "And Saul inquired of the LORD, but the LORD did not answer him, either by dreams or by Urim or by prophets" (1 Sam. 28:6).

6,7. "Ordered them not to eat of the most holy things until a priest with Urim and Thummim should appear" (Ezra 2:63; Neh. 7:65).

A few facts can be deduced from these citations. The Urim and Thummim were a form of oracle placed inside a pocket, "the breastpiece of decision," worn by the High Priest on his chest. It was employed exclusively by him; and its use was discontinued in postexilic times (see also Mish. Sot. 9:12, Sot. 48b). But overall, these texts provide little information about the Urim and Thummim. It is hardly any wonder, therefore, that speculation concerning their shape and function has been rife from earliest times. For example, the oldest interpretation, that of the Septuagint, renders the two words as abstract plurals, "revelation" and "truth"—from the words *'or*, "light" and *tam*, "perfection." Another approach suggests that the words are antonyms: "curse" (from the root *'-r-r*) and "perfect, faultless," indicating that which was pleasing to God and that which was not.[1]

In either case, the Urim and Thummim are conceived as two small objects (e.g., pebbles, sticks, arrows) that were cast like dice; depending on the way they turned up, they gave a positive or negative answer. This means that the Urim and Thummim could only give a yes or no answer. An inconclusive answer (no. 5 above) might be obtained, then, only on the assumption that each die was capable of a yes or no (like flipping a coin, heads or tails)—if one came up yes and the other no then the oracle would be considered inconclusive. This theory is supported by the Assyrian fortune-telling practice, psephomancy, which utilized a white and a black stone, called "the desirable die" and "undesirable die," respectively. As with this practice, the Urim and Thummim might also have been two stones that gave a yes or no answer.[2]

To be sure, there is no evidence in the Bible that describes the procedure of using the Urim and Thummim—at least not in the Masoretic text. But the Septuagint has a lengthy expansion of 1 Samuel 14:41 that merits quotation (the Septuagint addition is indicated by brackets): Saul then said to the LORD, the God of Israel ["Why have you not responded to Your servant today? If this iniquity was due to my son Jonathan or to me, O Lord, God of Israel, show Urim, and if You say it was due to Your people Israel] show Thummim."

The reading of the Septuagint is made plausible by the homoeoteleuton involved. The last word of the Masoretic text before the Septuagint's addition and the last word of the Septuagint's addition are the same—Israel. Thus the eye of the scribe may accidentally have skipped from the first "Israel" to the second, causing the long omission. This was a common type of error among ancient scribes and is attested in other scriptural verses as well. Thus, the Septuagint version of this text would corroborate the notion that the Urim and Thummim were two objects that could only give a yes or no answer.

This theory, however attractive, is nonetheless subject to serious objections. For even if the Septuagint represents the correct Hebrew original, (1) the theory does not allow for an inconclusive answer; (2) it does not explain the plural forms of the names Urim and Thummim; and (3) above all, it does not explain how the oracle was able to give more than a mere yes or no reply. That the oracle could indeed do so is shown by the following:

1. "After the death of Joshua, the Israelites inquired of the LORD, 'Which of us shall be

the first to go up against the Canaanites and attack them?' The LORD replied, 'Let Judah go up. I now deliver the land into their hands'" (Judg. 1:1–2).

2. "They proceeded to Bethel and inquired of God; the Israelites asked, 'Who of us shall advance first to fight the Benjaminites?" And the LORD replied, 'Judah first'" (Judg. 20:18).

3. "They inquired of the LORD again, 'Has anyone else [the man (Septuagint)] come here?' And the LORD replied, 'Yes; he is hiding among the baggage'" (1 Sam. 10:22).

4. "Sometime afterward, David inquired of the LORD, 'Shall I go up to one of the towns of Judah' The LORD answered, 'Yes.' David further asked, 'Which one shall I go up to?" And the LORD replied, 'To Hebron.'" (2 Sam. 2:1).

5. "David inquired of the LORD, and He answered, 'Do not go up, but circle around behind them and confront them at the *baca* trees. And when you hear the sound of marching in the tops of the *baca* trees, then go into action, for the LORD will be going in front of you to attack the Philistine forces'" (2 Sam. 5:23–24).

That the Urim and Thummim are being consulted can be deduced by the occurrence, in each of these five instances, of the technical term *sha'al be*, "inquire of (the Lord)." It is also clear that the Urim and Thummim had to be capable of answering more than a mere yes or no: As these citations show, they selected a tribe (1, 2) and a city (4), indicated the hiding place of Saul (3), and detailed a complex military stratagem (5). Thus, the Septuagint's expansion of 1 Samuel 14:41 may not be correct,[3] and, even if it is, the procedure, as indicated, is beset with difficulties and, hence, remains unclear.

Another solution that is worthy of consideration is that the Urim and Thummim comprised the twenty-two letters of the alphabet. "As the basis of the Hebrew language is the triliteral root, it follows that any three letters could provide meaningful words from which the High Priest could extract a message."[4] By the same token, an undecipherable combination would connote God's silence. The names '[*urim*] and *t*[*ummim*] would, then, stand for the first and last letters of the alphabet. They would, in other words, form a merism, denoting all the letters. So with the Greek alphabet: "I am the alpha and omega, the first and the last, the beginning and the end" (Rev. 22:13). And in common parlance we still say "from A to Z" when we wish to signify completeness. Strikingly, the Dead Sea Scrolls have disclosed a new Hebrew word *'wrtwm* (1QH 4:6,23; 18:29), which, according to the context, means "perfect illumination." It is highly probable that it was formed by combining the singulars of *'wr(m)*, "light," and *twm(m)*, "perfect." It would also explain why these words were chosen for the *alef* and *tav*: God created *'or*, "light," first (Gen. 1:3); and *tam*, *tamim* means "complete, finished." These correspond to the rabbinic interpretation of this oracle: "Urim, because it illuminates their (the inquirers') words; Thummim, because it completes (i.e., fulfills) their words" (Yoma 73b, Sif. Zut. to 27:21).

Nonetheless, this theory, like those previously discussed, can, at best, be considered only an attractive speculation. The riddle of the Urim and Thummim still awaits resolution.

EXCURSUS 65

The "Tamid" (chap. 29)

In its outer form, the *tamid* resembles the daily offering of Israel's neighbors, for whom, at least symbolically, it formed the daily diet of the gods. Thus, in Egyptian temples there

were three daily services, but only during the morning and evening were the gods served their meals.[1] In Mesopotamia the parallel is even more striking: "According to an explicit and detailed text of the Seleucid period, the images in the temple of Uruk were served two meals per day. The first and principal meal was brought in the morning when the temple opened, and the other was served at night, apparently immediately before the closing of the doors of the sanctuary. . . . Each repast consisted of two courses, called main and second."[2] Israel's *tamid* also prescribed two offerings daily, a "main course" of a lamb with a meal offering and a libation as "side dishes." However, the menu for the Mesopotamian gods differed sharply from the content of the Israelite *tamid*. "The daily total, throughout the year, for the four meals per day: twenty-one first-class, fat, clean rams which had been fed barley for two years; two large bulls; one milk-fed bullock; eight lambs; thirty *marratu*-birds; thirty . . .-birds; three *cranes* which have been fed . . .-grain; five ducks which have been fed . . .-flour; two ducks of a lower quality than those just mentioned; four *wild* boars; three ostrich eggs; three duck eggs."[3] The contrast is that of Nathan's parable: "The rich man had very large flocks and herds, but the poor man had only one little ewe lamb" (2 Sam. 12:2–3). Indeed, as Abravanel observed, the *tamid* was restricted to the essential staples of the Israelite diet: the flesh of lambs (the most inexpensive meat) and a portion of the three most abundant crops—from which first fruits were prescribed (18:12)—wheat, wine, and (olive) oil.

The biblical sources evidence different traditions concerning the *tamid*. In the First Temple, it was indeed offered twice daily, but the burnt offering was only sacrificed in the morning, and the meal offering, *minḥah*, in the evening (2 Kings 16:5; see 1 Kings 18:29,36). Ezekiel 46:13–15 also prescribes one burnt offering and one meal offering but specifies that both be offered up in the morning. In the postexilic period mention is made of the regular burnt offering and regular meal offering (Neh. 10:34), but their time is unspecified. Here the Torah's twice-daily offering is probably intended, but the meal offering seems to be of equal status with the burnt offering. Although the wine libation is absent in all of the aforementioned references, it is probably incorporated into one of the two offerings (as in 28:19–21; 29:14–15). An earlier association of the meal offering with the evening sacrifice is reflected in the terms "the evening *minḥah*" (Ezra 9:4, 5) and "about the time of the evening *minḥah*" (Dan. 9:21), although undoubtedly the *tamid* as prescribed in the Torah was scrupulously followed. The term persisted in post-Temple times—the afternoon prayer that replaced the second *tamid* offering was also called the *minḥah* (Mish Ber. 4:1, Mish. Pes. 10:1). Some scholars suggest that the text relating to the *tamid* in the Torah also shows signs of having developed from a single daily offering.[4] However, the use of the term "the morning burnt offering" here (28:23) and in the descriptive ritual of Leviticus 9:17 suggests that there was a regular evening offering as well.

The unbroken continuity of the *tamid* in the Temple ritual was reassuring to Israel and its cessation, a traumatic calamity (Dan. 8:11–13; 11:31; 12:11). Legend has it that as long as the *tamid* was uninterrupted the walls of Jerusalem were impregnable (BK 82b). One of the reasons for observing the Fast of the Seventeenth of Tammuz is that on this day the *tamid* ceased (Meg. Taʿan. 4:6). A modern commentator has observed:

> What do moderns consider "primitive" about such rituals? Doubtless, the pre-biblical origins of sacrifice go back to beliefs that the gods desired the food for their consumption. But the Torah itself no longer gives any warrant for the continuation of such beliefs, and Ps. 50:8ff. expressly disavows them. Most likely it is the public nature of the ancient slaughtering process that is repellent to current tastes. We prefer to hide the procedure behind the walls of abattoirs where the animals are killed in a

fashion no less bloody, but without making it necessary for the consumer to witness the life-and-death cycle which goes into his pleasurable nourishment. Moreover, even when we share with others in the eating process, we do not generally experience any of the genuinely worthy emotions which were usually engendered by the sacrifices of old. In the root meaning of the English word, we do not "sacrifice" (i.e., render holy) anything when we eat. This does not mean that our age ought to be ready for any reconsideration of cultic sacrifice. It does suggest that when seen in its own context the biblical order of animal offerings was a genuine form of worship that cannot be quickly dismissed with prejudicial contemporary judgments.[5]

EXCURSUS 66

Oaths, Vows, and Dedications (30:3)

The common denominator of oaths, vows, and dedications is that all are statements that invoke the name of God. Oaths are of two types: assertory and promissory. Assertory oaths are taken to clear oneself of a charge, for example, of misappropriating property (see Exod. 22:7; Lev. 5:20–25). Promissory oaths, the more prevalent type, impose an obligation upon the oath taker, for example, the reputed one made by David that Solomon would reign after him (1 Kings 1:13,17,30). A covenant, by definition, is a promissory oath (e.g., see Gen. 21:22–32; 31:44–53). In this section, the promissory oath, *shevu'at 'issar*, is restricted to an abstention and is exemplified in the case of a married woman who denies to herself (and probably to her husband) a pleasurable (or necessary) act (see the Comments to v. 14 and 29:7). Oaths are generally made in the name of the Deity: *nishba' be-YHVH*, "swear by the Lord." But when the oath entails a promise to God (i.e., God is the recipient of the promissory oath), the term used is *nishba' le-YHVH*, "swear to the Lord" (e.g., 2 Chron. 15:14). In this latter case, the oath approximates the vow, which is also made "to the Lord" (e.g., v. 3). Thus it is possible for the psalmist to say of David: "how he swore to the LORD [*nishba' le-YHVH*], vowed [*nadar*] to the Mighty One of Jacob" (Ps. 132:2).

Vows are promissory by definition, but they differ from promissory oaths in that they are conditional: They are to be fulfilled, for example, if Jacob returns home safely (Gen. 28:20–21), if Israel is victorious over the Canaanites (Num. 21:2), if Jephthah is granted victory over the Ammonites (Judg. 11:30–31), if Hannah is granted a son (1 Sam. 1:11), and if Absalom returns home safely (2 Sam. 15:8). Moreover, all vows in the Bible are dedications to the sanctuary. Thus, in the cases just cited, Israel dedicates the Canaanite spoils as *ḥerem* (see Excursus 44), Jacob promises to build a sanctuary, Jephthah sacrifices his daughter, Hannah dedicates her son to the sanctuary as a Nazirite, and Absalom offers sacrifices at the Hebron sanctuary. Ostensibly, the Nazirite vow resembles the negative promissory oath, since the Nazirite incurs a set of abstentions (see Excursus 11). However, it is the positive aspect of his status that is underscored in his vow. As one who is "consecrated to the Lord" (6:5,8), he belongs to God as with any dedication for the duration of his vow. Moreover, the Nazirite has also vowed a minimum number of sacrifices if he completes his Nazirite period without mishap (see 6:21). Therefore, the text is correct in viewing the Nazirite pledge as a vow and not as an oath. The context of Absalom's vow is also instructive: "Absalom said to the king, 'Let me go to Hebron and fulfill a vow I made to the LORD. For your servant made a vow when I lived in Geshur of Aram: If the LORD ever brings me back to Jerusalem I will worship the LORD [in Hebron'" (LXX)]. (2 Sam. 15:7–8). Thus not only does the term

"vow" automatically denote a dedication to the Lord, but it can be directed, as in Absalom's case, to a specific sanctuary. A singular example where the promissory oath and vow are fused is the case of King David (cited above), of whom the psalmist says: "O LORD, remember in David's favor his extreme self-denial [*ʿunnoto*], how he swore to the LORD [*nishbaʿ le-YHVH*], vowed [*nadar*] to the Mighty One of Jacob" (Ps. 132:2). David denied himself rest (his oath) until he provided a resting place for the Ark (his vow).

Furthermore, the examples cited demonstrate that dedications stemming from a vow need not be animals but can also be persons (Jephthah's daughter, Samuel) and even a sanctuary (for the Ark, Jacob's Bethel). To prevent the tragic case of Jephthah and to discourage the proliferation of Nazirites (see Excursus 9), priestly law provides that vows of persons (except as a Nazirite) must be redeemed by their fixed monetary worth, even allowing for a reduction of the evaluation in cases of indigence (Lev. 27:1–8). That such vows were popular in early Israel is evidenced by King Jehoash's reference to monetary contributions to the Temple of Jerusalem that stem exclusively from "the money equivalent of persons" (2 Kings 12:5). This kind of votive dedication also obtained elsewhere in the ancient Near East. A Ugaritic epic declares: "There [Ke]ret the Noble vo[ws]: As Asherah of Tyre exists, As Elath of Sidon. If Hurriya to my house I take, Bring the lass into my court, Her double I'll give in silver, And her treble in gold."[1] Vowing the monetary equivalent of persons is attested at the end of the Second Temple period as well: "Once the mother of Yurmatia (or Domitia) said, 'I vow my daughter's weight,' and she went up to Jerusalem and weighed her and paid her weight in gold."[2]

Dedications, comprising the third category, are like vows in that they are gifts to the sanctuary. However, they are neither future nor conditional but become effective the moment they are uttered. See, for example, the *ḥerem*-dedication of Jericho (Josh. 6:17–19) and the story of the dedicated silver (Judg. 17:3). The following sacred gifts, according to the wording of the text, were dedicated before they were brought to the sanctuary: first ripe and processed fruits (18:12–13), tithes (Lev. 27:30–33), and most sacred offerings (Lev. 6:18; 7:1–2). Thus the tannaitic dictum "oral dedication is equivalent to transfer [to the sanctuary]" (Mish Kid. 1:6, Tosef. Kid. 1:9) prevails in the Bible as well.

The regular occurrence of vows in the sacrificial laws indicates that a vow was usually fulfilled by a sacrifice (Lev. 7:16; 22:18,21,23; 23:38; Num. 15:3,8; 29:39; Deut. 12:6,11,17,26). The prominent role of vows in the life of the individual is even better evinced by their frequent mention in Psalms (22:26; 50:14; 61:6; 65:2; 66:13; 116:14,18). The popularity of vows is also attested by admonitions in law, wisdom teaching, and prophetic rebuke concerning their potential abuse. A harlot would invite a prospective client to the sacrificial feast she had prepared in fulfillment of her vows (Prov. 7:14), and Deuteronomy finds it necessary to warn: "you shall not bring the fee of a whore or the pay of a dog [i.e., a male prostitute] into the house of the LORD your God in fulfillment of any vow" (Deut. 23:19). Vows were made to the Queen of Heaven (Jer. 44:25) and, presumably, to other gods. The concern in the biblical literature, however, is that impulsive vows may go unfulfilled and thus arouse the divine wrath: "When you make a vow to God, do not delay to fulfill it. For He has no pleasure in fools; what you vow, fulfill. It is better not to vow at all than to vow and not fulfill. Don't let your mouth bring you into disfavor, and don't plead before the messenger [of God] that it was an error; else God may be angered by your talk and destroy your possessions" (Eccles. 5:3–5; see Deut. 24:22–24; Prov. 20:25).

The rabbis evolved an elaborate procedure for annulling vows: They looked for circum-

stances that would have discouraged the individual from making the vow if he or she had been aware of them at the time. Although they took for granted the right to annul vows (Mish. Ned. 2:1,5, etc.), they readily admitted that "the procedure for annulling vows hovers in the air and has nothing to support it" (Mish. Ḥag. 1:8).[3] They were well aware of the example of Jephthah (Judg. 11:30–35) and of others (see Josh. 9:19–20; Judg. 21:7) whose vows and oaths, although made in error, could not be annulled. The absence of annulment in those cases, for which there were rabbinic grounds, is attributed to the ignorance of the vow maker. The rabbis set forth the grounds for the annulment of vows as follows: "Four kinds of vows the sages have declared not to be binding: vows of incitement, vows of exaggeration, vows made in error, and vows of constraint" (Mish. Ned. 3:1). There is a basic distinction between the annulment of a woman's vows by her father or husband and annulment of vows by the rabbis. In the former case, the vows are annulled henceforth; in the latter, the vows are retroactively uprooted so that the sage can say: "The vow or oath is nonexistent" (TJ Ned. 10:8, Ket. 74b, TJ Ket. 7:7). The Karaites also allow for the annulment of mistaken vows (Adderet Eliyahu, Vows, chaps. 7, 16) but their biblical (and only) support (1 Sam. 14:44–45; 25:22,33) is untenable.

EXCURSUS 67

The War Against Midian (chap. 13)

On the surface, the account seems unhistorical. Gray unqualifiedly calls it a midrash "to illustrate certain legal and religious themes"[1] and marshals the following evidence: (1) The Midianites, having been annihilated, should have disappeared from history (but see Judg. 6–8; 1 Kings 11:8; Isa. 60:6). (2) The Israelites incredibly do not lose a single soldier (like the Benjaminites in Judg. 20:1–25). (3) The spoil taken from the Midianites is of astronomical quantities: 32,000 maidens, 675,000 sheep and goats, 72,000 cattle, 61,000 donkeys, and 16,750 shekels of gold seized just by the officers, not to speak of the gold seized by the rank and file. (4) Joshua, though just ordained as Moses' successor, is neither in command of the troops nor even present anywhere in the account; in his stead is the priest Phinehas. Another commentator, de Vaulx, agreeing that it is a midrash, identifies its source as Judges 21:10–12, which also speaks of 12,000 Israelites massacring all the males and married females (of Jabesh-gilead). He concludes that the account does not purport to be a military operation to vanquish a real enemy but a fictitious story of a holy war against the sacrilegious Midianites (v. 16).[2]

Thus, the case against the historicity of this account appears to be strong. Nevertheless, there is too much authentic ancient detail in the narrative to dismiss it cavalierly as spurious. Eissfeldt points to the following:[3] (1) In the Mosaic period, Midian probably enjoyed a protectorate over all of Transjordan (see also Dumbrell).[4] Thus, only the Midianites associated with Moses were decimated, not those linked with the Ishmaelites (Gen. 37:28; Judg. 8:22,24), the Amalekites (Judg. 6:3,33), and Ephah (Gen. 25:4; Isa. 60:6). (2) "Hadad son of Bedad [the Edomite], who defeated the Midianites in the country of Moab" (Gen. 36:35) presumes that Midian had controlled both Edom and Moab but that the Edomites succeeded in regaining their independence. (3) Moses' sojourn in Midian (Exod. 2:15–16; 3:1; 4:19) presumes that Midian was strong enough to provide refuge for Egyptian

fugitives. (4) Moses' request of Hobab the Midianite that he serve as Israel's guide (10:29–32) presumes that the Midianites were at home in the entire wilderness. (5) That there were Midianite chieftains who "dwelt in the land as princes of Sihon" (Josh. 13:21) presumes that the Midianites had accredited ambassadors in Sihon's court (as they had in Moab; see 22:4,7). The argument is considerably strengthened if one renders *yosheve ha-'arets* (Josh. 13:21) as "who ruled the land" (see Exod. 15:15); that is, Midian's hegemony extended over Sihon's kingdom as well. Thus, Moses was forced to fight the Midianites to reach the promised land and, conversely, the Midianites had no choice but to try to block Israel's passage.

Albright (and independently Grintz)[5] adds the important observation that camels are conspicuous in their absence from the inventory of animal booty in Moses' war, whereas they are prominent in the account of Gideon's war against the Midianites (Judg. 6–8). Thus, the Mosaic account must have originated in a historical event that took place before the twelfth/eleventh century B.C.E. Only then, with the development of a camel cavalry, did the Midianites succeed in devastating the settled Israelites (until their own defeat at the hands of Gideon). Albright also points to other ancient elements in the account. The use of handpicked shock-troops is a feature of the premonarchic age (Exod. 17:9; Judg. 6:33–7:2; 1 Sam. 13:2,15). The names of the Midianite chieftains are authentically old and, moreover, reveal the early interrelationship between Midian and Edom (see the Comment to v. 8). Furthermore, the objection concerning Phinehas's role is of no substance since, as shown in verse 6, he was the army's chaplain and not its commander. Finally, it should not be overlooked that Moses permitted the Israelites to marry the Midianite women (v. 18)—something he himself had done (Exod. 2:21; Num. 12:1) and that was permitted by early Israelite law (Deut. 21:10–14). But the practice was strictly prohibited in the days of Ezra and Nehemiah—another sign of the early provenience of this story.[6]

Thus the account of Moses' war against Midian contains a verifiable historical nucleus, even though the quantitative data are not to be taken literally: The amount of spoil is beyond credulity, and one can doubt that the Midianites were annihilated while the Israelites suffered no casualties. Numbers, as already shown (see Excursus 2), most easily fall prey to legendary embellishment. However, the assembled evidence clearly points to the historic reality that Midian was the most powerful and menacing enemy that Israel had to encounter during its migration to Canaan. Indeed, if this account of Israel's victory over the Midianites were not in the Pentateuch it would have to be invented.

EXCURSUS 68

The Literary Structure of Chapter 31

This chapter reveals a chiastic structure, ABB'A'. This introversion is effected by placing at the end of the chapter the account of the ransom of the army by means of the gold booty that the officers dedicated to the sanctuary (A', vv. 48–54). However, this event (rather, the dedication of the booty, vv. 49–50) must have taken place at the field of battle prior to the census (see Exod. 30:12–16) and prior to the purification of the spoils (B, vv. 13–24) and their distribution (B', vv. 25–47). The chapter's structure can be diagrammed as follows:

A. *Battlefront*. The War (vv. 1–12)
Lord's *command* (vv. 1–2)
Moses' *execution* (vv. 3–12)
[B. *Camp*. Moses' Anger and the Purification (vv. 13–24)
Moses' instructions (vv. 13–20,24)
slay nonvirgins (vv. 15–18)
purification (organic spoil)] (vv. 19–20,24)
[Eleazar's instructions (purification of inorganic spoil)] (vv. 21–23)
B′. *Camp*. Distribution of Animate Spoil (vv. 25–47)
Lord's *command* (vv. 25–30)
Moses' *execution* (vv. 31–47)
A′. *Battlefront* (flashback) *and Camp*. The Ransom (vv. 48–54)
dedication of officers' inanimate booty and census (vv. 48–50)
its contribution to the sanctuary (vv. 51–54)

A′, the gold dedication, takes place at the front (a flashback) and thus corresponds to A. The purification instructions (B) and the spoil distribution (B′) take place at the camp. The execution of B, Moses' and Eleazar's instructions, is not recorded and is anomalous in view of A, B′. Moreover, within B, Eleazar's instructions appear as an interpolation (see v. 24). They really represent something new (i.e., not found in chap. 19), thus indicating an editorial hand. Furthermore, A concludes with the notice that the spoil was brought to the camp (v. 12). B′, the distribution of the spoil (vv. 25–47), has the same structure as A (command-execution) and thus seems its logical continuation. Thus B, the instruction regarding the retention and purification of the spoil, may have been a later insertion.

A′ (vv. 48–54) resembles B (vv. 13–24) in that both contain instructions to the army officers (vv. 14,4a), a sign that they were inserted by the same editor. Both also lack the command-execution structure, another sign that they are by the same editor. Finally both B and A′ represent the same kind of material: cultic precautions taken by the army so that God's favor of Israel, magnificently exemplified by the stunning victory over Midian, will not be alienated.

A, the command and execution of the war, must have been a fixed text before the addition of A′. It affords the only explanation of why the A′ data regarding the dedication of the spoil (vv. 48–50) were not inserted where they belong chronologically—in the battle description of A. Moreover, the placement of A′ at the end of the chapter gives it the deliberate literary effect of a chiastic structure.

EXCURSUS 69

The Literary Structure of Chapter 32

The literary cement that binds this chapter into a unified whole is the sevenfold recurrence of five key terms, as follows: (1) *Gad and Reuben*, in this order (vv. 2,6,25,29,31,33,34/37). This may explain why the eighth mention of the tribes contains the reverse order (v. 1) so that the septenary pattern would not be broken; (2) *'aḥuzzah/naḥalah*, "holding/share" (vv. 5,8,19,22,29,32[2]); (3) *'avar*, "cross" the Jordan (vv. 5,7,21,27,29,30,32); (4) *neḥelats, ḥaluts*, "be picked, shock-troops" (vv. 17,20,21,26,29,30,32); (5) *lifnei YHVH*, "before the Lord" (vv. 20,21,22[2],27,29,32). These five terms, in effect, summarize the chapter: If *Gad*

and Reuben cross (the Jordan) as the ***vanguard before the Lord*** (the Ark), they will receive the ***land holdings*** (they desire). Another literary device characterizing the entire chapter is the alternation of positive and negative statements (vv. 12–13,17–18,19a–b,20–23, 29–30).[1]

The unity of this chapter is further revealed by its introverted structure, as follows:

A. *Gad and Reuben Request Land in Transjordan* (vv. 1–6)
  1. They specify nine towns (vv. 1–5)
  2. Moses rejects the request (v. 6)
    [scout episode] [vv. 7–15]

  B. *Their Compromise Proposal is Revised by Moses* (vv. 16–24)
    1. The two tribes' compromise (vv. 16–19)
    2. Moses accepts it, requiring a double condition/oath (vv. 20–24)

    X. *Gad and Reuben Accept Moses' Revisions* (vv. 25–27)

  B′. *Moses' Revised Proposal is Offered the Leaders* (vv. 28–32)
    1. Consequence changes if double condition/oath is rejected (vv. 28–30)
    2. Gad and Reuben repeat their acceptance (vv. 31–32)

A′. *Moses Provisionally Grants Land in Transjordan* (vv. 33–38)
  1. The grant [includes half-Manasseh] (v. 33)
  2. Gad and Reuben rebuild fourteen towns (vv. 34–38)
  [3. Manassite clans Yair and Nobah conquer and rename towns, and Machir settles in its conquered land] [vv. 39–42]

The chapter subdivides into five sections, ABXB′A′. The two bracketed items, Moses' exhortation (vv. 7–15) and the Manassite pericope (vv. 39–42), are interpolations, although the former, containing one of the seven occurrences of *ʿavar*, has been inserted by the chapter's author.

The introverted scheme becomes apparent when parallel sections are compared. AA′ (vv. 1–6,33–38) frame the chapter in an inclusion: Gad and Reuben request that they be given (*yuttan*; v. 5) specified towns (v. 3) and they are given (*va-yitten*; v. 33) these towns and more (vv. 34–38). B is a self-contained section with its own inclusion, chiastically arranged (vv. 16,24). Its structure is further illumined by its mirroring in B′. Furthermore, sections BB′ (vv. 16–24,28–32) form an inner chiasm in subject, content, and style, as follows:

B_1. Gad and Reuben's proposal (vv. 16–19)
  B_2. Moses' revised proposal (vv. 20–24)
  B'_2. Moses' revised proposal (vv. 28–30)
B'_1. Gad and Reuben accept (vv. 31–32)

Units $B_1B'_1$ contain the parallel phrases *ba'ah naḥalatenu me-ʿever* (v. 19), *'ittanu . . . naḥalatenu me-ʿever* (v. 32). Units $B_2B'_2$ both contain the double condition that Moses recites first to Gad and Reuben privately and then before the leaders (vv. 20–24,28–30); and, of course, they show the same vocabulary, especially the key terms in the septenary pattern: *ʿavar, ḥaluts, lifnei YHVH, 'aḥuzzah/naḥalah*. This structure sheds light on the need for Moses to state his proposal twice (vv. 20–24,28–30; $B_2B'_2$) and for Gad and Reuben to accept twice (vv. 16–19,31–32). To be sure, the second time around the proposal is put before the rest of the leadership (v. 28) and the consequences of nonfulfillment are spelled out: Gad and Reuben must settle in Canaan (v. 30). But the repetition of the terms

by Moses and by Gad and Reuben would be superfluous unless it is to answer the requirements of the structure by creating a symmetry of introversion. Here, then, is a clear example where aesthetics alone determines the composition.

The subdivisions of this chapter would appear diagrammatically as follows:

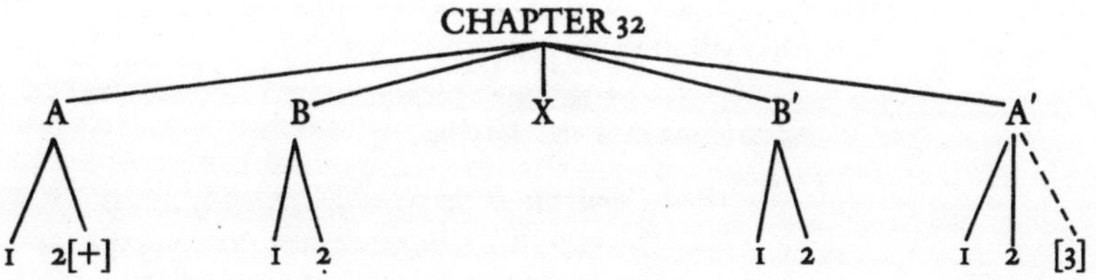

Section X (vv. 25–27) is the true center of the chapter since it expresses Gad and Reuben's full acceptance of the revisions Moses has entered into their proposal. This acceptance is underscored by the twice-repeated ***ka'asher 'adoni metsavveh/dover***, "as my lord commands/orders" (vv. 25,27). Moreover, only here is given the full inventory of those who will remain behind (v. 26). Again, the key septenary terms make their appearance here: ***'avar, ḥaluts***, Gad-Reuben, and ***lifnei YHVH***. Other common terms interlock it with the other sections: Gilead (v. 25; cf. vv. 1,39–40, AA′); ***milḥamah***, "war" (v. 27; cf. vv. 6,20,29, ABB′); ***'avadekha***, "your servants" (vv. 25,27; cf. vv. 5,31, AB′); and ***tappenu, miknenu***, "our dependents, our cattle" (v. 26; cf. v. 16, B). Furthermore, if, as suggested, we read: ***'asher dibber 'adoni ken na'aseh***, "whatever my lord has spoken, that we will do (v. 31, B′), it becomes the chiastically worded ballast to the equivalent phrases in X (vv. 25,27).

The language of the bulge (vv. 7–15) is mainly Deuteronomic, as indicated by the following: (1) Kadesh-barnea (v. 8) is the name of the site that characterizes the Deuteronomic school (Deut. 1:19; 2:14; 9:23; Josh. 10:41; 14:6–7; but see the Comment to 36:4); (2) "going up to the wadi Eshcol" (v. 9; Deut. 1:24); (3) "none except Caleb son of Jephunneh the Kenizzite . . . for they remained loyal to the LORD" (v. 12; Deut. 4:25; 9:18). It thus seems likely that a Deuteronomic editor summarized the full account of the scout expedition (chaps. 13–14) but used his own language. If so, it would be the last editorial hand to rework this chapter, a further indication that the priestly redaction of Numbers that was responsible for chapters 13–14 (see Excursus 29) was earlier (see the Introduction). The Manassite intrusions, which stem from a different hand and not from the author of this chapter, are discussed in Excursus 70.[2]

EXCURSUS 70

The Settlement of Transjordan (chap. 32)

Transjordan can be divided into three discrete geographical regions: (1) Mishor (rendered "Tableland") from the Arnon to wadi Hesban (Josh. 13:9,21; Jer. 48:20), (2) Gilead, and (3) Bashan (Deut. 3:10; 4:43; Josh. 13:9–12; 20:8). The boundary between Gilead and Bashan is not definite, alternating in the sources as either the Jabbok or the Yarmuk (see the Comment to 32:1). If it is the latter, then the three regions correspond to the territory

occupied by the Transjordanian tribes: Reuben in Mishor, Gad in Gilead, and half-Manasseh in Bashan (Deut. 4:43; Josh. 20:8; contrast Josh. 12:2; 13:31). That is, Gad lay to the south of Manasseh, and Reuben lay to the south of Gad, each severed from the other by natural borders. However, this neat congruence of territory and geography is contradicted by our chapter, which places Gadite towns both to the north and south of Reuben. Aroer and Dibon are here assigned to Gad (see the Comment to v. 3); but elsewhere they are assigned to Reuben (Josh. 13:16–17). How can these two irreconcilable positions be explained?

The scholarly consensus, as voiced by R. de Vaux, holds that the contradiction reflects the eventual assimilation of Reuben into the tribe and holdings of Gad. Early in Israelite history, Reuben lost its preeminence, whereas Gad showed increasing strength (see Gen. 49:3–4; Deut. 33:6,20–21); by the time of the kingdom, Reuben had virtually disappeared. Transjordan of Saul's time is described as Gad and Gilead (1 Sam. 13:7); David's census north of the Arnon only mentions Gad (2 Sam. 24:5); Solomon's lower Transjordanian district is called Gad (1 Kings 4:19 LXX) and the Moabite stone (ninth century) refers only to Gad. Reuben does not appear in any of the above references, having been, according to most scholars, absorbed into Gad by the time of the monarchy.

This opinion has been countered by Y. Kaufmann who points to a reference to Transjordan in the time of the Jehu dynasty (end of ninth century) that includes Reuben (2 Kings 10:33).[1] And if one invalidates this reference as a literary stereotype, Kaufmann adduces another text that expressly mentions Reuben as having dwelt on its territory until exiled by Tiglath-pileser III (1 Chron. 5:6,26). His position has been reinforced by B. Oded, who adds the following arguments:[2] (1) Beerah is the *nasi'* of the tribe of Reuben when it is exiled (1 Chron. 5:6). This should be contrasted with Simeon, which, having assimilated into Judah, no longer had a single tribal chieftain but only many clan chieftains (1 Chron. 4:38). (2) Of special significance is the following passage: "He also dwelt to the east as far as the fringe of the wilderness this side of the Euphrates, because their cattle had increased in the land of Gilead. And in the days of Saul they made war on the Hagrites, who fell by their hand; and they occupied their tents throughout all the region east of Gilead" (1 Chron. 5:9–10). Thus, in the time of Saul, the Reubenites had not yet become sedentary, and they pastured their flocks over the entire desert fringe of Transjordan as far north as the Euphrates. Their transhumant existence prevented their consolidation into a centralized political entity, which left them prey to attack by neighboring tribes. It is to this parlous situation that the blessing of Moses adverts: "May Reuben live and not die" (Deut. 33:6). Reuben's pastoral structure is responsible for its weakening in the period of the judges; it did not answer Deborah's summons (Judg. 5:15–16) because it could not. Preferring to live on the eastern, desert fringe, it thus permitted Gad to occupy the southern Mishor, as indicated in this chapter (vv. 3,34) and supported by the Moabite stone. The Levitical cities assigned to Reuben are also located on the desert fringe (1 Chron. 6:63–64), and Heshbon, Reuben's most important town in this chapter (v. 37), is assigned to Gad (Josh. 21:37). The scheme of Levitical cities is of Solomonic origin (see Excursus 75), and Reuben's situation as reflected there accords with prior notices that it did not occupy the Mishor but confined itself to the desert pasturage. Our chapter, which speaks of a Reubenite concentration around Heshbon (see Map 5), must then reflect a later period. It was during the monarchy that Reuben began to penetrate into the Mishor, a movement that was accelerated after Gad was overrun by the Moabites, as attested in the Moabite stone. Thus the chapter stems

from a time between Solomon and the Moabite stone, which Oded pinpoints as the reign of Jeroboam I.

Oded thus reverses the current critical position. Indeed, there is no evidence whatsoever that Reuben assimilated into Gad. The absence of Reuben from early sources such as David's census, Solomon's districts, and the Moabite stone is not due to its disappearance as a tribe entity. Rather, it is due to its preference to remain a pastoral society ranging along the eastern steppe. By degrees, it infiltrated into the Mishor during the period of the divided kingdom and remained settled there until its exile in 733. Four passages, then, show the expansion in Reubenite holdings: Joshua 21:38–39, Numbers 32:37–38, 1 Chronicles 5:8, and Joshua 13:17–23. According to Oded, these can be dated to the periods of Solomon (950–925), Jeroboam I (925–900), Jehu (850–825), and Jeroboam II–Ahaz (750–733), respectively.

Verses 39–42, describing Manassite incursions into upper Transjordan, are a fragment that "probably derives from a fuller narrative, which described how several clans of Manasseh separated from their fellow tribesmen on the *west* of Jordan and acquired settlements in the *east*."[3] That Gad and Reuben rebuilt fourteen towns—having only requested nine—also indicates that these towns were part of another historical document. They therefore did not exactly meet the redactor's desire to create chiastic symmetry. Nevertheless, the longer list may have served his purpose in indicating that Gad and Reuben were rewarded for their fidelity with more than they had requested.

The settlement of Manasseh in Transjordan is obscure. The tradition as recorded in Scripture attributes it to the Mosaic age (Num. 34:14–15; Deut. 3:13–15; 4:43; 29:7; Josh. 1:12; 12:6; 13:29; 14:3; 17:1–16; 18:7). However, the scholarly consensus holds that Manasseh migrated to Transjordan from the west during the period of the judges, the main evidence, first presented by Budde, being Joshua 17:14–18.[4] These verses indicate that the house of Joseph (i.e., Manasseh and Ephraim) received one allotment in Cisjordan and, needing more room, were told by Joshua to clear the forests in the land of the *refa'im*, who (according to Deut. 3:13) lived in upper Transjordan.

This evidence is, however, not without its problems. The clause in Joshua 17:15 dealing with *refa'im* is missing in the Septuagint. Moreover, as M. H. Segal has pointed out, since Joshua charges the Josephites to clear the forests but not to wage war on the *refa'im*, the land must already be in Israel's hands.[5] As for the change in tactics employed by Manasseh, as compared with Gad and Reuben, in obtaining its land—it can be explained by their different situations: Gad and Reuben requested land that had already been conquered by all of Israel, whereas the Manassite clans conducted their own campaigns of conquest. Hence, they did not ask for Moses' permission but for his ratification, which he then granted (v. 40; Deut. 3:13–15).

Nonetheless, it cannot be gainsaid that this Manassite pericope (vv. 39–42) and the phrase "the half-tribe of Manasseh" (v. 33) are interpolations by a later hand (see the Comments to v. 33 and the introductory Comment to vv. 39–42). A similar situation prevails in the story of the suspected heresy of the Transjordanian tribes in the time of Joshua. That account (Josh. 22) mentions Manasseh alongside of Gad and Reuben, except in verses 25, 33 and 34. That account too probably dealt originally with Gad and Reuben; but later, when Manassite clans entered Transjordan, it underwent interpolation to reflect this fact.

In sum, whereas the Gad-Reuben settlement in Transjordan narrows down to the two solutions mentioned above, the paucity and the ambiguity of the information concerning Transjordanian Manasseh do not allow any solution to be anything but a conjecture.[6]

EXCURSUS 71

The Integrity of the Wilderness Itinerary (chap. 33)

The prevailing view in biblical scholarship is that the wilderness itinerary of Numbers 33 is a composite. To cite a recent analysis: verses 5–8 and 43–44 were taken from the Priestly narratives (see Exod. 12:37; 13:20; 14:2; 16:1; 17:1; 19:2; Num. 21:10–11); verses 8–9, from the Jahwist (see Exod. 15:23,27); verses 17–18 from the Elohist (see Num. 11:34–35); and verses 30–33 from the Deuteronomist (see Deut. 10:6–7). Furthermore, a number of verses are editorial glosses (vv. 1–2a,3–4,8–9,38–40). Only verses 12–14, 18–30, 34–35, and 41–42 contain names not found in any of the above-mentioned sources; these were drawn from a discrete document.[1]

However, as early as A. Dillmann,[2] serious objections to this theory have been raised, as follows: (1) Names that are common to both Numbers 33 and the narratives sometimes differ in form and in order (see the Comments to vv. 8,31–33). (2) A few names in the narratives do not appear in Numbers 33 (e.g., 11:3; 21:16,19; and see the Comment to v. 16). And (3) conversely, many names in Numbers 33 do not appear in the narratives (e.g., vv. 18–30). Thus, it is hardly likely that this chapter is a composite of place-names drawn from other Pentateuchal sources. To the contrary, it is more logical to assume that since so many names in Numbers 33 are unattested anywhere else, it represents the master list for the other sources. In other words, the chapter is not a composite text but, in the main, an authentic unified itinerary.

Such, indeed, is the assumption of M. Noth, who has proposed that Numbers 33 represents an ancient pilgrimage route to Mount Sinai, as proof of which he cites Elijah's hurried visit to the "mountain of God" (1 Kings 19).[3] However, it is hazardous, to say the least, to infer the existence of pilgrimages to Sinai in biblical days on the basis of a single prophetic tale, with its emphasis on the miraculous and in the absence of any other corroboration from either biblical or rabbinic sources.

Recently, G. I. Davies has suggested a new approach, based on comparative literary grounds.[4] He notes that the style of the literary chain "they set out from A and encamped at B; they set out from B and encamped in C . . ." (whereby the B name in one link occupies the A position in the next link) is also exemplified in the records of military campaigns in the ancient Near East. Thus a letter of Shamshi-Adad I of Assyria (18th cent. B.C.E.) found in the Mari archive describes the following transport: "from Shubat-Enlil to Tilla, from Tilla to Ashihim, from Ashihim to Iyati, from Iyati to Lakushir, from Lakushir to Sagaratim" (ARM 1.26). Here, just as in Numbers 33, the stations are repeated. The correspondence, however, is not exact since the Mari account is verbless. A more precise parallel is found in the records of the military campaigns of the Assyrian emperors of the ninth century. These utilize the formula "from city A I departed, in city B I spent the night"; and in the next stage, B will occupy the A position. Even more striking is the expansion of this formula as found in the campaign records of Ashurnasirpal II (883–859):

> I spent the night in the city of Shadikanni
> The tribute of Shadikanni—silver, gold, lead, vessels of copper and flocks—I received.
> From the city of Shadikanni I departed.

The expansions in the Ashurnasirpal text deal not only with the receiving of tribute but also with military exploits, river crossings, and the finding of water. What is significant about these expansions is that their content also informs the expansions in Numbers 33: Note the crossing of the sea (v. 8), the problem of water and provisions (vv. 9,14), the battle with the Canaanites (v. 40). Thus, the allegation that these expansions are editorial glosses is refuted. To the contrary, they are integral to the itinerary since, just as in the Assyrian analogue, they record notable events essential to the journey.

In Egyptian itineraries, place-names are not repeated; instead, dates are used to sustain continuity. Even though they display a form that differs from those of the Bible, they record a fact that may be of significance for the biblical itineraries. The annals of Thutmose III (15th cent.) testify that his campaign records "are set down on a roll of leather in the temple of Amon today" (ANET, p. 237). It was, thus, considered vital to preserve the account of the Pharaoh's campaigns in the temple archives, testimony to the glory of the gods who bestowed victory upon Pharaoh: It was incumbent upon the Egyptians to remember and extol them forever. There is, therefore, no a priori reason to doubt the statement that Moses wrote down the itinerary (33:2): By preserving the wilderness stations, Israel would always recall the many benefactions bestowed by the Lord while He brought them to the promised land (see Num. R. 23:1, cited in the introductory Comment to chap. 33).

One can conclude that the list of stations in Numbers 33 is part of a widely attested itinerary genre. In particular, it exhibits the same form and style as the ninth-century campaign records of the Assyrian monarchs: It repeats the names of the campsites and adds pertinent information regarding military exploits, the availability of water and provisions, and the crossing of rivers, but it does not indicate dates or distances covered. Israel's wilderness trek—also a military campaign—was, therefore, written down according to the prevailing ancient Near Eastern style of recording itineraries of military campaigns.

How are the discrepancies between Numbers 33 and the narrative itineraries to be explained? F. M. Cross[5] has observed that there are exactly twelve formulas in the narratives that correspond to the station list of Numbers 33, six which take Israel from Egypt to Rephidim, the stop before Sinai (Exod. 12:37; 13:20; 14:1–2; 15:22; 17:1), and six from Sinai to the plains of Moab (Exod. 19:2; Num. 10:12; 20:1; 20:22; 21:10–11; 22:1). The scheme's symmetry betrays its derivative nature; and Numbers 33 is its likely original source. Cross makes a second plausible suggestion that the narrative itineraries only allude to the stations in the list of Numbers 33. They do not cite them but subsume them under the general designation "wilderness X." Thus, for example, the wilderness of Paran (10:12) covers the stations Rithmah to Ezion-geber (33:19–35).

Although a number of problems still remain, the evidence presented above points to the conclusion that Numbers 33 is an ancient itinerary of the wilderness trek—the master list from which the individual itineraries in the narratives were drawn.

A comparative table of the wilderness itineraries in the Torah follows. Italicized names indicate stations that appear only once. (See also Maps 1 and 2.)

Num. 33	*Exodus, Numbers*	*Deuteronomy*
Rameses	Rameses	
Succoth	Succoth	
Etham	Etham	
Pi-hahiroth	Pi-hahiroth	
Marah	Marah	
Elim	Elim	
Yam Suf		
Sin wilderness	Sin wilderness	
Dophkah		
Alush		
Rephidim	Rephidim/Massah and Meribah	Massah
Sinai wilderness	Sinai wilderness	Horeb
Kibroth-hattaavah	Kibroth-hattaavah/Taberah	Taberah
Hazeroth	Hazeroth	Kibroth-hattaavah
[Paran]	Paran wilderness/Kadesh	Kadesh-barnea
Rithmah		
Rimmon-perez		
Libnah		
Rissah		
Kehelath		
Mount Shepher		
Haradah		
Makheloth		
Tahath		
Terah		
Mithkah		
Hashmonah		
Moseroth		Beeroth-bene-jaakan
Bene-jaakan		Moserah
Hor-haggidgad		Gudgod
Jotbath		Jotbath
Abronah		
Ezion-geber		Ezion-geber and *Elath*
Zin wilderness/Kadesh	Zin wilderness/Kadesh/Me Meribah	
Mount Hor	Mount Hor	
Zalmonah		
Punon		
Oboth	Oboth	
Iye-abarim	Iye-abarim	*Moab wilderness*
	Zered	Zered
	Arnon	Arnon
	Beer	*Kedemoth wilderness*
	Mattanah?	
Dibon-gad	*Nahliel*	
Almon-diblathaim	*Bamoth*	
Hills of Abarim	*the valley/Pisgah*	
	Yahaz	Yahaz
	Edrei	Edrei
Steppes of Moab	Steppes of Moab	the valley/*Beth-peor*

EXCURSUS 72

The Literary Structure of 33:50–56

Introduction: *In the land of Canaan* (vv. 50–51)

A. *The Reward for Obedience* (two apodoses, *ve-horashtem*) (vv. 52–53)
 1. If Israel evicts the inhabitants (v. 52aα)
 2. And destroys their cult objects (v. 52aβb)
 3. Israel will possess and settle the land (v. 53a)
 4. So God has promised (v. 53b)

  X. *The Division of the Land* (v. 54)
   a. by lot for clan location (v. 54aα)
    x. by population for size (v. 54aβ)
   a′. by lot for tribe location (v. 54aγ,b)

A′. *The Punishment for Disobedience* (two apodoses, *ve-hayah*) (vv. 55–56)
 1′. If Israel does *not* evict the inhabitants (v. 55aα)
 2′. They will sting Israel with their cult (v. 55aβ)
 3′. And harass Israel militarily (v. 55b)
 4′. So God, instead, will evict Israel (v. 56)

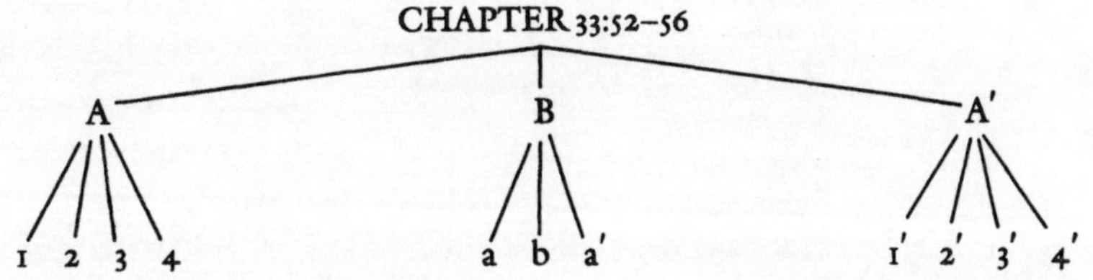

What follows are refinements of an unpublished paper by my student, the late Daniel Levy. Verses 52–56 reveal an introverted structure (AXA′) in which the end (A′) completely reverses the beginning (A). This reversal is carried out in all four statements that comprise A and A′: If Israel does/does not evict the Canaanites (11′), the cult objects Israel fails to destroy will "sting" them (22′), the remaining Canaanites will prevent them from dwelling in the land (33′), and God will, in the end, evict Israel instead of the Canaanites (44′).

The common language underscores the mirror relationship of AA′: 11′ are, but for the negation, precisely the same; 22′ balance each other by the same alliterative sounds *ts* and *sk* (my student, E. Adler; see the Commentary); 33′ also use the same vocabulary (*ha-'arets, yashavh, bah*) with the main verbs reversed: you shall evict (the inhabitants of) the land else they will harass you; and 44′ share the common word *lakhem*, that is, instead of God giving the land "to you," God will do "to you" what He had intended for the Canaanites—evict you from the land. Moreover, the two apodoses that comprise A begin with the same word *ve-horashtem* (vv. 52a,53a) balancing the two apodoses that comprise A′, which also begins with the same word *ve-hayah* (vv. 5aβ,56a).

The pivot of this introversion (X) is itself a miniature introversion (axa′). The same vocabulary is shared by aa′ (*hitnaḥel, goral*), and the two lines also correspond in idea: The lot will determine the location of both the tribe and the clan. The pivot of the minor

introversion (x) stresses that the size of each holding will be determined by population. The language and idea of aa′ are drawn from 26:55; those of × stem from 26:54a. As mentioned in the introductory Comment to 33:50–56, v. 54 (X) had to be repeated because the initial plan to divide Canaan among the twelve tribes (chap. 26) has been compromised by the settlement of Reuben, Gad, and half-Manasseh in Transjordan (chap. 32), necessitating the redivision of the land among the remaining nine and a half tribes.

EXCURSUS 73

The Boundaries of Canaan (chap. 34)

Map 3 shows that the borders of Canaan given in chapter 34 do not correspond with the reality of Israelite settlement in any historical period. The most outstanding discrepancy was established in the time of Moses and detailed in chapter 32—the settlement of two and a half tribes in Transjordan. Throughout the national existence of Israel there were Israelite holdings in Transjordan; yet the promised land as delineated in chapter 34 marks the Jordan River as Israel's easternmost boundary. It was B. Mazar, followed independently by R. de Vaux,[1] who first discovered that these boundaries correspond precisely to those of the province of Canaan of the New Kingdom of Egypt. Beginning in the fifteenth century, Canaan was the official name of Egyptian holdings in Asia. Its northern boundary was fixed in the thirteenth century by the peace treaty between Ramses II and the Hittite empire (ca. 1270), which left the city of Kadesh in Hittite hands and the Damascus region under Egyptian control. Since Egyptian records never mention the Gilead or southern Transjordan—archaeology informs us that they were unsettled until the thirteenth century—it is clear that the Jordan was the eastern border of Egyptian Canaan.

Indeed, all the data in the Book of Numbers confirm that the land of Canaan never extended east of the Jordan (32:29–30; 33:51; 34:2; 35:10; see Josh. 22:9,32), and it is these borders that are alluded to earlier, in 13:17,21, and described in detail in chapter 34 as well as in Joshua 13:2–5 and Ezekiel 47:15–20. (Josh. 13:4–5 adds significant data concerning the northern boundary: Aphek, modern Afqa, 24 kilometers [15 mi.] east of Byblos; Byblos within Canaan; the Amurru kingdom outside Canaan). This view is also held by the rabbis, who declare that the Land of Israel is holy (Mish. Kel. 1:6) but not Transjordan (Sifrei on Deut. 26:2).

The discrepancies between the *promised* land and the *real* land of Israel can be quickly determined by superimposing the map of one on the other. The results, illustrated in Map 3, reveal three kinds of discrepancies: (1) land that was neither apportioned nor annexed—approximating parts of present Lebanon and Syria in the north; (2) land apportioned but not annexed—the coastal strip of Philistia and the one between Acre and Sidon; and (3) land not apportioned but annexed—lower Transjordan. One significant consequence of the latter observation is that upper Transjordan, the Bashan, is within the confines of Canaan. This means that the Manassite clans that settled there did not require special permission to do so. And indeed this is clearly indicated by the evidence of chapter 32. Only Gad and Reuben arouse Moses' ire and must subsequently demonstrate their loyalty to their people, whereas the Manassite passages in this chapter (vv. 33,39–42) as well as in Joshua 22 are later interpolations (see Excursus 70) that are independent of the settlement traditions of Gad and Reuben. Now the reason is clear: The conquest of Bashan—part of

Canaan—would not have raised any objections from Israel's leaders; and, indeed, the text records that Moses gave his consent (32:40). There is yet another map, one that is truly utopian, of the promised land. Its northern borders reach the Euphrates; in the east it extends to the desert (Gen. 15:18; Exod. 23:31, Deut. 1:7; 11:24; Josh. 1:4); and its southern border reaches the Nile Delta (Gen. 15:18; Josh. 13:3). Perhaps it corresponds to the reality of the Davidic-Solomonic empire. Certainly this vast area was under the influence of Israel (see 2 Sam. 8:9–10; 1 Kings 5:1,4). But what is of special interest here is that this is the only map to which the Book of Deuteronomy refers, and it sets the eastern border not as the Jordan but as the wilderness. This means that Deuteronomy acquiesces in the annexation of Transjordan by Israel. To be sure, Deuteronomy acknowledges the patriarchal map, with the Jordan as its eastern boundary (Deut. 2:29; 4:21; 11:31; 12:10; 27:2), but it refrains from stating or implying that the annexation of Transjordan was not sanctioned by God. To the contrary, in distinction to the Book of Numbers, in which Moses attacks Sihon on his own initiative (see the Comments to 21:21–32 and vv. 33–35), Deuteronomy attributes the entire Transjordan campaign to the command of the Lord: "Up! Set out across the wadi Arnon! See, I give into your power Sihon the Amorite, king of Heshbon, and his land. Begin the occupation: engage him in battle" (Deut. 2:24–25).[2]

The contrast between Deuteronomy and (the priestly material in) Numbers could not be sharper. Deuteronomy has accommodated itself to history; Numbers has not. The priestly tradition consistently adheres to the map of Canaan as it existed up to the thirteenth century and does not admit to its slightest alteration in the light of subsequent events. Once again, the priestly texts have proved themselves to be the bearers of Israel's most ancient traditions (see also Excursuses 1, 4, 6).

EXCURSUS 74

The Levitical Town: An Exercise in Realistic Planning (35:1–5)

Those who maintain that the scheme for the Levitical towns is utopian and unrealistic buttress their arguments on the basis of alleged contradictions in the town plan. In particular, they point to the measurements for the pastureland that surrounds the town.

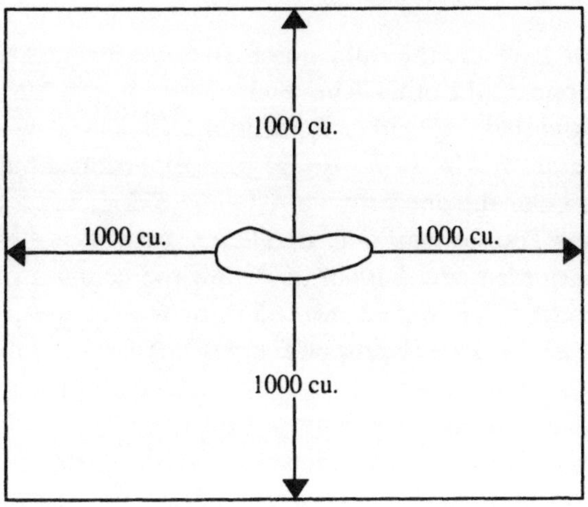

Figure 2

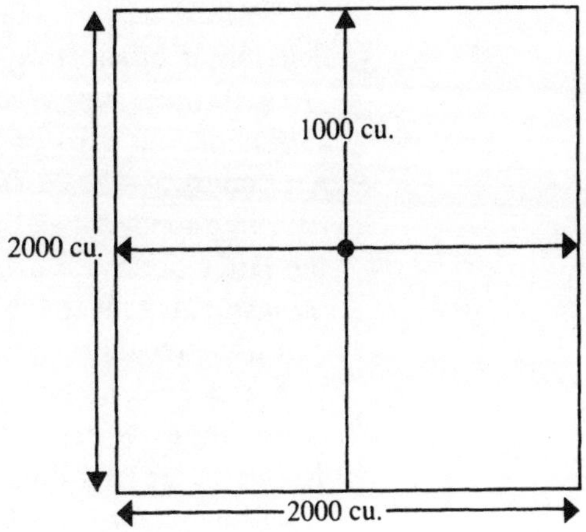

Figure 1

Although it extends 1,000 cubits from the town wall (v. 4), it also extends 2,000 cubits in each direction (v. 5). How can these two ostensibly conflicting data be reconciled?

The breakthrough was provided by Ramban, who realized that the 2,000-cubit measurement refers to the perimeter of the pastureland. His contention is supported by the meaning of *pe'ah* in verse 5, which can only be "side, border," as in all other blueprints, architectural (e.g., Exod. 26:18,20; 27:12,13) and geographical (Josh. 18:12,14,20; Ezek. 48:8,16). Two further terminological refinements clear the way to the solution: (1) ***Mi-kir ha'ir va-ḥutsah*** is to be rendered "from the town wall outward" (see the Comment to v. 4), and (2) ***mi-ḥuts la-'ir*** translates "outside the town" (see the Comment to v. 5). Thus, the measurements for the pastureland form a square of 2,000 cubits per side, whose perimeter is 1,000 cubits in every direction from the town wall.

The only configuration that can contain these two measurements requires that the town be considered as a point, as represented in figure 1.

This postulate, to the best of my knowledge, was first proposed by J. D. Michaelis and J. Clericus and echoed by E. F. K. Rosenmüller.[1] However, their insight remained in the realm of conjecture until recently, when M. Greenberg demonstrated that this postulate was the very one used by the tannaim to calculate the limit of 2,000 cubits that one may walk from his residence on the Sabbath.[2] Regardless of the size or contours of the town, the rabbis measured the 2,000 cubits from the extreme limits of the town in each direction (Eruv. 55a [bar.]; Tosef. Eruv. 4:1–6), as indicated in figure 2.

It can be demonstrated that the tannaim-Greenberg solution not only accounts for all the given data but posits a practical, utilitarian formula for creating a Levitical townsite regardless of its initial size and subsequent growth. From here on, the discussion focuses on figure 3.

A rectangle is circumscribed around the town whose length and width are × and y, respectively. Extend the sides of this rectangle 1,000 cubits in each direction. By enclosing these lines we obtain a new rectangle whose length and width are 2,000 + x and 2,000 + y, respectively. The town, which was a point in figure 2, now provides additional pasturage marked by the shaded area. The total area increase for the pasturage is 1,000x + 1,000y + 1,000x + 1,000y or 2,000(x + y).

It thus becomes evident that the pastureland increases with the growth of the town. For heuristic purposes, let us assume that 2,000 cubits equal a mile (in fact, closer to a half

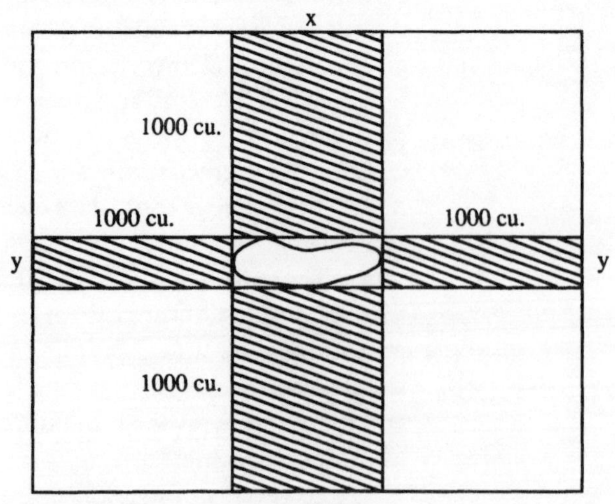

Figure 3

mile). If the town's dimensions are 1 × 2 miles its area would be 2 square miles and the increased pasturage would be 1 (2 + 1) or 3 square miles. If, however, the town extended a mile in length and width so that its dimensions were 2 × 3 miles, its area would be 6 square miles and the additional pasturage would be 1(2 + 3) or 5 square miles. At the same rate of growth, a town 3 × 4 miles would have an area of 12 square miles and an increased pasturage of 1 (3 + 4) or 7 square miles. Thus, the pastureland would grow in strict arithmetic progression (3,5,7,9, . . .) and the town at a faster rate (2,6,12,20, . . .). This is not inappropriate, since every town begins with a fixed pasturage of 2,000 × 2,000 cubits—even before it has a single inhabitant—and a goodly number of its citizens will not be herdsmen but will provide the industrial and commercial services essential to town life.

Additional support stems from elsewhere in the ancient Near East. Mesopotamian cities also provided for an extramural strip, called ***tawwertum/tamertu***, as pasture for livestock.[3] Fourteenth- and thirteenth-century texts from Ugarit (located in Syria, on the Mediterranean coast) testify that fields which were royal property were managed and farmed by nearby villages and that royal pasturelands were leased to nearby pastoral communities. These texts verify the antiquity of the institution, "the village commons."

Thus, the town plan proposed by the legislation of 35:1–8 is based on ancient Near Eastern precedent. But it goes even further. It projects into the future, providing a simple formula guaranteeing that Levitical pastureland will continue to grow, in commensurate fashion, along with the town.[4]

EXCURSUS 75

Asylum Altars and Asylum Cities (35:9–15)

It is a postulate of the early biblical stories that the altar grants asylum to those who grasp it (Exod. 21:13–14; 1 Kings 1:50–51, 2:28–34). It is also attested in the classical world and, therefore, represents a widespread phenomenon. The basic premise is that those who touch the altar absorb its sanctity and are removed from and immune to the jurisdiction of the profane world.

The priestly texts (P) and Deuteronomy (D), however, attribute the power of asylum to certain cities (Num. 35:9–16; Deut. 4:41–43; 19:1–9) rather than to the altar. What, then, is the relationship between the asylum altar and the asylum cities? The common denominator of all the critical theories on the question is that the asylum city was built around a sanctuary, of necessity an important one, whose widely recognized powers of asylum were then extended to the entire city. Although most scholars hold that asylum cities were designated by Israelite rulers to replace the anarchic power of the altar, they are divided on whether the change took place during the reigns of David and Solomon, or of King Josiah; still others maintain that the asylum cities coexisted with the asylum altar from earliest times. Those who hold that the altars and city asylums sprang up simultaneously maintain that the purpose of the city was to provide permanent quarters for the refugee who sought protection at its altar. According to the first theory, cities containing hallowed sanctuaries were expressly chosen to ensure the continuity of asylum once the asylum powers of the sanctuaries were revoked. In both theories the underlying assumption is that asylum cities were sanctuary cities.

P, however, would reject as unlikely, even inconceivable, the premise that asylum cities

contained sanctuaries. Three of the six asylum cities are designated for Transjordan (cf. Deut. 4:43), that is, according to P, outside the promised land (Num. 34:12). In consonance with other ancient traditions, P holds that any territory outside YHVH's land is "impure" (Josh. 22:19; cf. 1 Sam. 26:19; Hos. 9:3; Amos 7:17)—to erect an altar on such land would therefore be tantamount to treason (Josh. 22:16ff.). And when the P strand in Joshua specifies the asylum cities it is very deliberate in its choice of verbs: Those in Cisjordan are "sanctified" (***va-yakdishu***), whereas those in Transjordan are described by the neutral "assigned" (***natnu***; Josh. 20:7–8). The latter, ipso facto, could not be sanctuary cities. Furthermore, it is inconceivable that P would have ordained asylums in cities where murderers could reside in the proximity of, if not within, the sacred precincts, let alone, where ***in extremis*** (e.g., when extradited) they could even grab the horns of the altar. From P's vantage point, this would pose a constant, intolerable threat of pollution to the sanctuary. Finally, P posits a single authorized sanctuary and denies the legitimacy of multiple sanctuaries, thus precluding the very existence of a network of sanctuary asylums.

Having severed the nexus of asylum altar and asylum city, it is no longer possible to say that in P the asylum city is the extension or replacement of the sanctuary. What then is the reason behind P's asylum city? The formula ***kol ha-nogea' yikdash***, "anything [but not anyone] that touches . . . becomes sanctified" (Exod. 29:37; 30:26–29; Lev. 6:11,20), teaches that persons are not subject to the contagion of sancta.[1] The altar, in particular, cannot sanctify persons. Thus, from the beginning P would undoubtedly have looked with alarm at altar asylum, at the attraction of murderers, thieves, assorted criminals—and their pollution—to the sanctuary. P, obsessed with the need to protect the sancta from defilement lest God vent His anger upon the nation, thus adopted a simple if radical expedient. In holding that the above formula does not apply to persons, it could declare that the altar does not give asylum. But the accidental homicide still needed an asylum to escape the revenge of the blood redeemer. P's solution was to establish six asylum cities equitably distributed throughout the land so that one would always be in reach by the homicide before the avenger overtook him.[2]

Thus P's radical reduction of the formula is part and parcel of its establishment of asylum cities. The altar is devitalized of its contagion to persons so that it will not be polluted by criminal elements; the asylum cities that replace it henceforth offer a haven for the accidental homicide. Indeed, P's contention that the altar transmits not holiness but death (Num. 4:15) provides further evidence that P strove to prevent criminals from seeking asylum at the sanctuary: The criminal not only fails to gain immunity by grasping the altar's horns but makes himself liable to death by divine agency. He now has double reason to shy away from the sanctuary.

What historical circumstances account for P's innovation? And what—undoubtedly related—historical events brought an end to the institution of altar asylum? These questions are still debated. Many critics hold that the altar continued to provide asylum until the Deuteronomic reform of Josiah, which "secularized" the asylum by replacing the sanctuaries with asylum cities. However, just as a similar theory for the origin of P's asylum cities was refuted, so it can be shown, albeit on different grounds, that D's asylum cities were not sanctuaries either.

1. There is agreement that D's major innovation is its abolition of the local sanctuaries. Thus, it is not surprising that when D prescribes a sanctuary ritual it invariably states explicitly, emphatically, and repetitively that henceforth it must be observed only at the one chosen sanctuary. However, D's section on asylum cities (19:1–13) contains no reference

whatsoever to centralization. Surely, if the asylum city supplanted the asylum altar some mention of uprooting of the latter through centralization would be expected. Moreover, as Y. Kaufmann has shown,[3] D predicates the establishment of city asylums immediately upon entry into the land (19:1), and the Transjordanian ones even beforehand (4:41); centralization, however, is to be effected only after the conquest is complete and the land is settled and tranquil (12:9). Asylum therefore must be severed from the centralization issue.

2. D uses the term ***makom*** as a holy place both for the central sanctuary that the Lord will choose (*baḥar*; Deut. 12:5,11,14,18,21,26; 14:23,25; 15:20; 16:2,6,7,11,15,16; 17:8,10; 18:6; 26:2; 31:11) and for designating a heathen sanctuary (sing. 12:3,13; pl. 12:2). But it avoids its use in connection with the city asylums and resorts instead to the neutral ***ʿarim***, "cities" (Deut. 4:41–43; 19:1–13).

3. This hypothesis leaves unexplained why Jerusalem was not chosen as an asylum city. Since D does not evidence any objection per se to the concept of altar asylum, it could have continued this institution at the central sanctuary. Moreover, D calls for a high court in Jerusalem for the express purpose of judging difficult capital crimes (17:8).

4. D also had a precedent in the early laws for making Jerusalem the asylum city: "I will assign you a ***makom*** to which he can flee" (Exod. 21:13, JE) to which D could have added, as it did elsewhere, "at the place [*ba-makom*] which the LORD has chosen." That D does not attach its centralizing formula to JE's single asylum can only mean that the tradition of ***multiple*** asylum cities preexisted D. Indeed, D not only assumes their existence but even specifies their names in Transjordan (Deut. 4:41–43).

5. D ordains that "when the LORD your God enlarges your territory, as He swore to your fathers, and gives you all the land that He promised to give your fathers . . . then you shall add three more towns to those three" (Deut. 19:8–9). The unconquered land in this instance cannot be Transjordan since in the Deuteronomic view it had already been conquered and allocated. Moreover D, no less than P, believes that the land sworn to the fathers does not include Transjordan (4:26; 7:1; 8:1; 9:1–5). Indeed, D's chronicle of the conquest of Transjordan avoids any mention of an oath to the fathers (Deut. 2:24–3:15), in contrast to every mention of the conquest of Cisjordan (e.g., Deut. 6:23; 9:5,28; 10:11; 30:20). This being the case, the land yet to be conquered can only be the territory to the north of the tribal settlement, from the sources of the Jordan to the Euphrates (Deut. 1:7) or Lebo-hamath (Num. 34:8; Josh. 13:5). D is saying, in effect, that once the entirety of the promised land has been annexed three additional asylum cities are to be situated there, for an eventual total of nine; three in Transjordan and six in Cisjordan. D, then, cannot have invented the asylum city. It presumes the existence of six cities (three in Cisjordan and three in Transjordan) just as promulgated by P and projects the addition of three more.

These considerations permit of only one conclusion: D no longer knew of the institution of the asylum altar. If the altar had been replaced by the city, it undoubtedly happened long before. D therefore did not invent the city asylum but inherited it from an older source. The only attested altar asylum in the Bible—surely not the first—is David's Tent-shrine in Jerusalem (1 Kings 1:51; 2:28). The existence of asylum in David's Tent-shrine is clear evidence that it was already a hallowed tradition that he did not dare to oppose, for it is inconceivable that he would have invented an institution that held a veto power over his judicial authority.

It is David's son Solomon, a man of very different temperament, who presents himself as the most likely candidate for the role of abolitionist of altar asylum. Solomon was a man determined not to let tradition stand in the way of his administrative goals, a parade

example of which was his redistricting of Israel for tax purposes in defiance of tribal boundaries and authority. Further, two instances of indisputable historicity relate that at the outset of Solomon's reign two of his personal enemies sought asylum at the altar, leading Solomon to recognize that the immunity offered by the altar threatened the throne. It would have been in his personal as well as the national interest to abolish this anarchic institution. And if the Chronicler is correct in attributing the beginning of a judicial system to David (1 Chron. 23:4; 26:29–32)—despite the inflated numbers—then Solomon was already equipped with a system of courts throughout the land capable of handling capital crimes. An even more significant factor pinpoints Solomon as the one who annulled the altar asylum, a factor that would have prevented his father from doing it—Solomon was no longer bound by the Tabernacle tradition. He built the Temple, and though it followed the main architectural plan and cultic appointments of the Tabernacle, it bore the imprint of many an innovation. Above all, it is to be remembered that Solomon installed a new sacrificial altar, one of dimensions and functions that differed from those of its Tabernacle predecessor. Henceforth, the Temple altar did not afford asylum; indeed, it was declared off limits to any nonpriest.

Clearly, altar asylum had ceased by the time of the Second Temple, as can be ascertained from Nehemiah's memoirs. When Shemaiah warns Nehemiah that his life is in danger and that he should lock himself in the Temple, Nehemiah rejects the advice on the grounds that his entry into the Temple would make him subject to the death penalty (Neh. 6:6–7). It must be assumed that the altar no longer afforded asylum, since neither Shemaiah's advice nor Nehemiah's reply mentions that more obvious means of seeking safety.

Furthermore, that the laity was permanently barred from the First Temple may be derived from 2 Kings 21:10: "And the priest Jehoiada took a chest and bored a hole in its lid. He placed it at the right side of the altar as one entered the House of the LORD, and the priestly guards of the threshold deposited there all the money that was brought into the House of the LORD." The logistics are clear. The layman could cross the threshold and enter the Temple court, but he could not personally deposit his contribution in the collection box, which was "at the right side of the altar." But the threshold guards, being priests, had access to the altar and could carry out the task.

In the Second Temple as well, the laity could not come within reach of the altar. Even on the Feast of Tabernacles when many regulations were relaxed and the laity was permitted to circumambulate the altar with its willow branches, only priests (though blemished) were assigned the responsibility of depositing the willows on the altar (Suk. 43b; TJ Suk. 54d).

Finally, the issue of the asylum cities cannot be divorced from the issue of the Levitical cities, for the asylum cities are Levitical cities (Num. 35:6; Josh. 21). And their assignment to the Levites means that they are controlled by the central government. (The complexity of this subject, however, puts it beyond the bounds of this excursus.) It seems probable that the only time at which all of the Levitical cities were in Israelite hands was during the reign of Solomon.[4] Moreover, the clearly archival note of 1 Chronicles 26:29–32 (adduced by Mazar) pointedly demonstrates that the Levites were assigned administrative functions in Transjordan at the end of David's reign. The Chronicler supplies significant, additional information in the High Priestly genealogy (1 Chron. 6:35–38) as the introduction to his list of the Levitical cities. The genealogy cuts off abruptly with Ahimaaz the son of Zadok and concludes with: "These are their dwelling-places according to their settlements within their

borders" (1 Chron. 6:39a; Eng. v. 54a). This verse can only mean that according to the Chronicler the Levitical cities were not just allocated but actually settled during the time of Ahimaaz the son of Zadok—a contemporary of Solomon.[5]

Yet the radical changes in government and worship notwithstanding, it is hard to believe that Solomon could have uprooted a cultic practice as implanted and hallowed as the altar asylum had he not found powerful allies in the priestly hierarchy of Jerusalem under the High Priest Zadok. The latter would have championed the doctrine that sancta do not sanctify persons; hence, the altar cannot provide asylum. It must be conceded that any other monarch might also have found sufficient warrant to institute this change, but the unique cluster of motives, both personal and royal, plus the propitious timing of many other simultaneous cultic changes that attended the building of the Temple favor Solomon over all his successors.

One objection to this dating must be met. It might be argued that the monarchy would rather have abolished the city asylum than create it because an absolute king would not have tolerated the institution of the blood redeemer. He would have stamped it out, thereby eliminating the need for asylum of any kind. However, the account of David's reign is all too rife with blood revenge to allow for the quick death of this visceral institution. One need but note its role in the slaying of Abner (2 Sam. 3:29–30), Saul's sons (2 Sam. 21:1–6), and the son in the Tekoite's fable (2 Sam. 14:7; cf. Middle Assyrian laws B, par. 2). Indeed the Tekoite's story clearly demonstrates that the asylum city was not yet in existence during the reign of David, else her plea for the king's immediate intervention would have been superfluous. Moreover, the slaying of Saul's sons proves that when David did not execute them by his royal order but surrendered them to the Gibeonites, the institution of the blood redeemer was very much alive—even the power of the throne could not overrule it.[6] Finally, since D not only espouses the asylum city but concedes the redeemer's right to act as the state executioner (Deut. 19:12), this can only mean that the state was forced to make concessions to the clan privilege of blood redemption down to the very end of the monarchy.

Thus, P's laws of homicide are not utopian. They reflect a series of concessions to the social reality—precisely what one would expect at the beginning of the monarchy before the central government could effectively usurp tribal and local jurisdiction. In sum, Solomon's innovation lies in the implementation, not the authorship, of the asylum city. It is in his reign that the interests of the crown and the clergy coincided to abolish the asylum of the altar and to replace it with cities of asylum.

Analysis of the biblical sources on the law of asylum leads to the following diachronic scheme:

1. Exodus 21:13–14 is the earliest known stage of altar asylum, and it already curtails its contagious power: It is not available to murderers.

2. Shortly after the Temple was built, most likely during the lifetime of Solomon, the institution of the asylum altar was abolished in every sanctuary (and forbidden in the Temple). It was replaced with six asylum cities in the land, in keeping with the teachings of the Jerusalem priesthood, as incorporated in the Priestly Code.

3. P's system of asylum cities is adopted by D with two minor changes: their number and the date of their inauguration. In fact, D is historically more accurate than P in specifying that the city asylum should be instituted after the completion of the conquest (Deut. 19:1; contrast Num. 35:9–11; Josh. 21). The completion of the conquest is also the time designated by D for the centralization of worship (Deut. 12:9), which the Deuteronomist expressly identifies with the reign of Solomon (1 Kings 3:2).

4. Ezekiel's constitution for the restored Israel does not call for asylum cities. This omission may be due to a textual accident or to the virtual elimination of incidences of blood revenge by the end of First Temple times, which rendered the institution of asylum obsolete.

In sum, the reduction of sancta contagion discernible in the history of the formula ***kol ha-nogea' yikdash*** provides the key to the understanding of how the institution of the asylum altar was replaced by the asylum city. The process had already begun with the exclusion of the murderer from the jurisdiction of the altar. However, it achieves its revolutionary transformation in P, which interprets the formula in such a way that the altar (together with the rest of the sancta) is denied the power to transmit its holiness to persons. P then institutes the asylum cities to compensate for the neutralized altar. And, in turn, D adopts P's innovations with slight quantitative modifications.[7]

EXCURSUS 76

The Postulates of the Laws of Homicide (35:16–28)

The biblical concept of bloodguilt derives from the belief that deeds generate consequences and that punishment inheres in sin. The most vivid examples of this belief appear in connection with unlawful homicide, where innocent blood (***dam naki'***; Jonah 1:14) cries out for vengeance (Gen. 4:10). Rejected by the earth (Isa. 26:21; Ezek. 24:7), it attaches itself to the slayer and his family, literally "dancing around their heads" (2 Sam. 3:28–29) for generations (2 Sam. 21:4–6; 2 Kings 9:26) and even affecting his city (Deut. 21:1–9; Jer. 26:15), nation (Deut. 19:10,13), and land (Num. 35:33–34). The latter two citations illustrate the variant grounds that provide the rationale for the homicide laws in the Deuteronomic and priestly texts. In the former, the people Israel bear the bloodguilt; in the latter, it is the land that is polluted by it. The technical term for bearing bloodguilt, ***damo bo*** or ***damo be-ro'sho***, meant originally "his blood [remains] on him/on his (the murderer's) head" (Josh. 2:19; 1 Kings 2:33; Ezek. 33:5), and the legal formula ***mot yumat damav bo*** (Lev. 20:9–16) means that in the case of lawful execution, the blood of the guilty victim remains on his own person and does not attach itself to his executioner.

This concept of bloodguilt pervades all sources in the Bible, legal, narrative and cultic, and entails the following system of graded punishments for homicide:

1. *Deliberate homicide*. The penalty is death by man (Exod. 21:12) or, failing that, by God (Lev. 20:4–5). A person can cause death directly (Num. 35:16–21) or indirectly, for example, as a watchman (2 Kings 10:24; Ezek. 33:6), a priest (Num. 18:1,3), a homeowner (Deut. 22:8) or through the agency of a subordinate (1 Kings 2:31–35). The ***go'el ha-dam***, the blood redeemer, is charged with the primary responsibility of punishing the murderer—but only after the murderer is convicted by the court (Num. 35:19; Deut. 19:12).

God is the final guarantor that homicide is ultimately punished (Gen. 9:5–6). His personal intervention is expressed by the verbs ***pakad***, "attend to" (Hos. 1:4), ***nakam***, "seek redress of" (2 Kings 9:7), ***darash***, "exact punishment" (Ezek. 33:6), and ***heshiv***, "return," in the idiom ***heshiv damim 'al ro'sh*** (2 Sam. 16:8; 1 Kings 2:33). The sense is that God will turn back to the slayer the blood of the slain; that is, the punishment the murderer thought he had averted. Furthermore, God may postpone punishment to a later generation (2 Sam. 12:13–14; 1 Kings 21:21; see Excursus 32). Man, however, does not have this option (Deut. 24:16; 2 Kings 14:6) unless divinely authorized (2 Kings 9:7,26).

The concept that there is no commutation of the death penalty for deliberate homicide lies at the foundation of biblical criminal law: human life is invaluable. This idea is not found in any other law corpus of the ancient Near East. In the Bible it is also expressed in the law of talion: "life for life" (Exod. 21:23; Lev. 24:17; Deut. 19:21). However, for good reason this law is not inserted into the homicide provisions of Numbers 35: talion for all other injuries was interpreted to mean monetary compensation. Indeed, even *nefesh taḥath nefesh*, "life for life," when it referred to the animal world came to stand for monetary compensation (Lev. 24:18,21). Hence not only was talion omitted in the homicide laws but a special supplement was required (Num. 35:31–34) to emphasize that the life of the murderer should not be ransomed under any circumstances. The incommutability of the death penalty has its origins in the story of man's creation: He is created in God's "image" (Gen. 1:27; 9:6), an idiom that is used for the father-son relationship (Gen. 5:3). By declaring Himself to be man's kinsman, God automatically becomes man's blood redeemer, obligated to execute each and every murderer. Indeed, although one finds in Atraḫasis, the Assyrian story of creation, the notion that man was created literally out of the spirit (*eṭemmu*) and body of a god, it was only Israel who took this divine origin seriously enough to incorporate it into its legal system.

2. *Involuntary homicide*. Since involuntary homicide also results in bloodguilt, the manslayer may be slain with impunity by the *go'el* (Num. 35:26–27; Deut. 19:4–10). However, as the act was unintentional, the natural death of the High Priest is allowed to substitute for the death of the manslayer (Num. 35:25,28; Josh. 20:6). In the interim, he is confined to a city of refuge to protect him from the *go'el* (Num. 35:9–15; Deut. 4:41–43; 19:1–13; Josh. 20:1–9). In this way the punishment is made to fit the crime: The deliberate homicide is deliberately put to death; the involuntary homicide who took life by chance must await the chance of the High Priest's death in order to be released from the asylum city.[1] And in the interim the refuge offered by the city is a form of exile: The homicide, uprooted from his family, home, and livelihood, is thereby punished for his crime, with full expiation available to him only upon the death of the High Priest. Until then he remains under sentence of death, as is demonstrated by the contingency that if he leaves the city of refuge the *go'el* may kill him with impunity. No wonder that, according to the Mishnah, the mother of a High Priest would personally supply food and clothing to the residents of the cities of refuge so that they should not pray for the death of her son (Mish. Mak. 2:6). In any event, there must be accountability for murder. If the slayer is unknown, the community nearest the corpse must disavow complicity and, by means of a ritual, symbolically wash away the blood of the slain (Deut. 21:1–9).

3. *Homicidal beast*. The supreme value of human life in the Bible is best expressed in the law that a homicidal beast is also guilty: Not only must it be killed by stoning but its carcass, laden with bloodguilt, must be reviled (Exod. 21:28–29; see Gen. 9:5).

4. *Unauthorized slaughter of an animal*. The reverence for life that informs all biblical legislation reaches its summit in the priestly law that sanctions the use of an animal for food on the condition that its blood, containing its life, be drained upon the authorized altar (and thereby symbolically restored to God; Lev. 17:11). Or, in the case of game, the blood must be drained and buried (Lev. 17:13–14). All other animal slaughter is theriocide and punishable by death at the hands of God (Lev. 17:4).

5. *Exceptions*. No bloodguilt is incurred by homicide in self-defense (Exod. 22:1), judicial execution (Lev. 20:9–16), and war (1 Kings 2:5–6). There is also some modification of the view that war is justifiable homicide: It disqualified David from building the Temple (1 Chron. 22:8).

Jackson[2] has taken exception to these postulates, as formulated by Greenberg,[3] on the following grounds: (1) Since integration and systemization are late developments in civilization, it is doubtful that there are principles underlying these early laws. (2) The death penalty is imposed for property offenses in the cases of (a) brigandage, (b) kidnapping, and (c) sacrilege. (3) Composition for homicide was allowed before being outlawed as shown by the laws of (a) the goring ox (Exod. 21:29–30), (b) murder (Num. 35:31–32), (c) miscarriage (Exod. 21:22), and (d) killing a slave (Exod. 21:20). (4) Adultery, a capital crime like murder, is also subject to composition (Prov. 6:32–35).

These objections will be parried seriatim: (1) Systemization is also characteristic of the most primitive societies. Consider, for example, the symbolism of the intricately structured food taboos characteristic of primitive African tribes. (2) The alleged property cases subject to the death penalty are chimerical: (a) death for the brigand is nowhere demanded; (b) kidnapping, literally "stealing a life" (Deut. 24:7), is a crime against life, not property; (c) sacrilege is a crime against God (*fas*) not man (*jus*) and, hence, subject to different criteria (see Excursuses 32, 40, 49). (3) The alleged cases of composition for homicide are also chimerical: (a) the goring ox is the murderer and must die (even when it kills a slave; Exod. 21:32; cf. 21:20), whereas its owner, though responsible, is only an accessory;[4] (b) of course, the prohibition to accept ransom for homicide implies that violations occurred but not that they were once legal; (c) a fetus is not a legal person in rabbinic law (Mish. Oho. 7:6; Mekh. Nezikin 8) and probably not in biblical law either (see the Comment to 3:40); (d) the punishment for killing a slave is ***nakom yinnakem***, "he must be avenged," an idiom that elsewhere only means the imposition of death. Since the blood redeemer may not have access to (or may fear to tamper with) someone else's property the text warns that the slave's death must be avenged. (4) Proverbs 6:35 is an illegal cover-up: By bribing the husband to keep quiet it flouts the absolute injunction that the adulterer must be brought to court as a criminal.[5] Furthermore these two capital crimes are not analogous: Adultery, by nature, is surreptitious and can be hushed up; murder, however, will out.[6]

EXCURSUS 77

The Redaction of Chapter 36

Although chapter 36 and 27:1–11 both deal with the same incident, the claim of Zelophehad's daughters to inherit their father, there is philological and chronological evidence that chapter 36 was written later than its sister passage. First, chapter 36 employs vocabulary that differs not only from chapter 27 but from all other priestly material. It uses ***shevet*** in one verse (v. 3) instead of the expected ***matteh***. The former occurs in priestly texts only when a synonym of ***matteh*** is needed (18:2), in the stock phrase "the twelve tribes" (Exod. 28:21; 39:14), or to indicate the aggregate of (the Kohathite) clans (4:18)—but never for "tribe." Another anomalous term is ***davak***, "cleave" (vv. 7,9) a favorite of Deuteronomy (e.g., Deut. 4:4; 10:20; 11:22; 13:5,18; 28:21,60; 30:20) but never found in the priestly texts. The infiltration of these terms would thus seem to reflect the later composition (or recasting) of this chapter.

These philological observations by themselves would not be significant were it not for more explicitly chronological considerations. As noted in the Commentary (to vv. 3,4,7,8; see LXX), the use of the plural "fathers" (rendered "ancestral") implies that the land has been held in the family for at least several generations; hence, the text cannot be contem-

poraneous with Zelophehad's daughters. Finally—and this above all—the fact that this chapter is at the end of the book indicates that it is truly an appendix, an editorial afterthought that could not be inserted in its logical place, sequential with chapter 27 (or even after chapter 32, in which the Transjordanian Manassites receive their land) because the Book of Numbers had been completed and was now closed.

Moreover, this chapter shows signs of inner expansion. The original form of this chapter may have expressed the fear of the daughters' clan that they would marry outside the clan, not outside the tribe. First, it should be recalled that the tribal census was structured according to clan groupings and that it was to these clans (*la-'elleh*; 26:52; and explicitly 33:54) that the land was to be apportioned (see Excursus 55). Second, that the clan—not the tribe—is the societal unit presumed by this chapter is shown by the law of succession that derives from the Zelophehad case. It specifically restricts the heirs of an estate to the deceased's *clan* (27:11)—and not to his tribe. The law of the Levir (Deut. 35:5–9) is extended to the redeemer, that is, to the nearest relative in the *clan*. At the time of marriage to the widow, he also inherits or must redeem her late husband's property (Ruth 3:12–13; 4:1–10; Tob. 6:10–13) in order not to alienate the family property from the *clan*. Finally, it should be noted that the duty of redeeming sold ancestral land falls on the closest relative *within the clan* (Lev. 25:49), but is not incumbent on members of the tribe. Therefore, since all the fundamental laws regarding ancestral land are grounded in the clan structure, it stands to reason that the original scope of this chapter's ruling restricted an heiress's choice of husband to her clan. Moreover, common sense dictates that her property would lie close to her husband's property (rather than at the other end of the tribal domain) so that he might be able to work both lands simultaneously.[1]

It is then no accident that the daughters actually marry their first cousins; so do the daughters of Eleazar (1 Chron. 23:22). It is only to be expected that the law of succession in inheritance (27:11) would be congruent with the heiresses' choice of husbands—for both would aim at keeping the ancestral land within the clan. Indeed, such must have been the law prevailing in every society before the family unit collapsed under the pressures of urbanization and the centralization of government. The oldest law code of ancient Greece, that of Solon, stipulates that if a man dies leaving an unmarried daughter, the nearest relative may claim her hand—clearly, in order to keep the property in the family.

A clue to the original state of the text of chapter 36 may be preserved in the Septuagint, which omits the term *matteh*, "tribe," in verses 6 and 8 and reads *mishpaḥat*, "clan" (sing.), in verse 12. The Septuagint would then point to the ruling that heiresses must marry someone in their clan and that the daughters of Zelophehad indeed did so. This conjectured original law would have been emended later when tribal authority grew stronger and the daughters' choice of husband was broadened to include members of the same tribe. The fear of intertribal marriage leading to the alienation of tribal property would have been a sufficient reason for the revision of this law. That certain clan names are found in more than one tribe (noted in 26:13,23,24,35,44) may be due not to coincidence or to migration but to the marriage of heiresses to men of other tribes and the subsequent passing of their property to their husband's clans, a process this revised law attempted to check.

NOTES TO THE EXCURSUSES

Excursus 1

1. S. E. Loewenstamm, EB (Hebrew), s.v. ***mifkad.***

2. For a fuller discussion, see J. Milgrom, "Priestly Terminology and the Political and Social Structure of Pre-Monarchic Israel," JQR 69 (1978): 65–81.

Excursus 2

1. A. Hurvitz, "The Evidence of Language in Dating the Priestly Code," RB (1974): 24–56.

2. I. Beit-Arieh, "A First Temple Period Census Document," PEQ 115 (1983): 105–109; A. Hurvitz, "How the Israelites Were Mustered: Numbers 1:2 and Its Congeners in the Light of a New Inscription from Tell ʿIra" (Hebrew) (forthcoming).

3. However, see the strictures of Y. Garfinkel, "The Meaning of the Word *MPQD* in the Tel ʿIra Ostracon," ***Palestine Exploration Quarterly*** (1987): 19–23.

4. M. Barnouin, "Les recensements du livre des Nombres et l'astronomie babylonienne," VT 27 (1977): 280–303.

5. A. Dillmann, ***Die Bücher Numerii, Deuteronomium, und Josua*** (Leipzig: S. Hirzel, 1886); W. F. Albright, "The Administrative Divisions of Israel and Judah," JPOS 5 (1925): 20–25.

6. R. de Vaux, ***Ancient Israel*** (New York: McGraw-Hill, 1961), 65–67.

7. W. M. F. Petrie, ***Egypt and Israel*** (London: Society for Promoting Christian Knowledge, 1911), 42–46; G. E. Mendenhall, "The Census Lists of Numbers 1 and 26," JBL 77 (1958): 52–66.

8. J. M. Sasson, "Reflections on an Unusual Practise Reported in ARM X:4," ***Orientalia*** 43 (1974): 404–410.

9. M. Noth, ***Numbers: A Commentary,*** trans. J. D. Martin (London: S. C. M. Press, 1968), 21–22.

10. A. Malamat, EB (Hebrew), s.v. ***gedud;*** S. E. Loewenstamm, EB (Hebrew), s.v. ***mifkad.***

11. J. W. Wenham, "Large Numbers in the Old Testament," TynBul 18 (1967): 19–57.

Excursus 3

1. Y. Yadin, ***The Art of Warfare in Biblical Lands*** (New York: McGraw-Hill, 1963) II, 292–293.

2. Ibid. I, 236–237.

3. Y. Yadin, ***The Scroll of the War of the Sons of Light Against the Sons of Darkness*** (London: Oxford University Press, 1962), 38–64; A. M. Gazov-Ginzberg, "The Structure of the Army of the Sons of Light," RevQ 5 (1965): 163–175.

Excursus 4

1. A. Malamat, "History and Prophetic Vision in a Mari Letter," ***Eretz Israel*** 5 (1959): 67. Cf. A. Lods, "Une tablette inédite de Mari, interessante par l'histoire ancienne de prophétisme semitique," in ***Studies in Old Testament Prophecy,*** ed. H. H. Rowley (Edinburgh: Clark, 1950), 103–110.

2. J. Milgrom, ***Studies in Levitical Terminology*** (Berkeley: University of California Press, 1970), n. 44.

Excursus 5

1. CAD, s.v. ***qerēbu*** 3.

2. For a fuller discussion, see J. Milgrom, ***Studies in Levitical Terminology*** (Berkeley: University of California Press, 1970), 16–32.

Excursus 6

1. For a fuller discussion, see J. Milgrom, "The Levitical ʿAboda," JQR 61 (1970): 132–154.

Excursus 7

1. L. Levy-Bruhl, ***Primitives and the Supernatural*** (New York: Dutton, 1935). W. Kornfeld, "Reine und unreine Tiere im Alten Testament," ***Karios*** 7 (1965): 134–147; K. Elliger, ***Leviticus*** (Tübingen: Mohr, 1966).

2. M. Douglas, ***Purity and Danger*** (London: Routledge and K. Paul, 1966), 1; W. Paschen, "Reine und Unrein," SANT 24 (1970): 62.

3. J. Milgrom, "When Durkheim Meets Leviticus," ***Direction*** 12/2 (1981): 4–6.

4. Douglas, ***Purity and Danger,*** p. 51.

5. A. Meigs, "A Papuan Perspective on Pollution," ***Man*** 13 (1978): 304–318.

6. E. Culpepper, "Zoroastrian Menstrual Taboos," in ***Women and Religion,*** ed. J. Plaskow (Missoula, Mont.: Scholars Press, 1974), 205.

7. J. W. Burton, "Some Nuer Notions of Purity and Danger," ***Anthropos*** 69 (1974): 530.

8. A. Dillmann, ***Exodus und Leviticus,*** 3rd ed. (Leipzig: Hirzel, 1897), 523. G. von Rad, ***Old Testament Theology,*** vol. 1 (New York: Harper, 1962), 272; Kornfeld, "Reine und unreine Tiere"; Paschen, "Rein und Unrein," p. 63; E. Feldman, ***Biblical and Post-Biblical Defilement and Mourning*** (New York: Yeshiva University Press, 1977), 35–37; N. Füglister, "Sühne durch Blut zur Bedeutung von Leviticus 17,11," in ***Studien zum Pentateuch,*** ed. G. Braulik (Vienna: Herder, 1977).

9. A. L. Oppenheim, ***Ancient Mesopotamia*** (Chicago: University of Chicago Press, 1964), 288–305.

10. J. Milgrom, "The Biblical Diet Laws as an Ethical System," Int 17 (1963): 288–301.

11. For greater detail, see J. Milgrom, ***Leviticus,*** Vol. I, Anchor Bible 3A (New York: Doubleday, 1991), chaps 11–15.

Excursus 8

1. M. Fishbane, "Accusations of Adultery: A Study of Law and Scribal Practice in Numbers 5:11–31," HUCA 45 (1974): 25–45.

2. W. L. Moran, "New Evidence from Mari on the History of Prophecy," Bib 50 (1969): 15–59.

3. See G. Dossin, "L'ordalie à Mari," CRAIBL (1958): 387–392.

4. Fishbane, "Accusations of Adultery."

5. T. Frymer-Kensky, "The Strange Case of the Suspected Sotah," VT 34 (1984): 11–26.

6. Guido Kisch, ed., *Pseudo-Philo's Liber antiquitatum Biblicarum* (Notre Dame, Ind.: University of Notre Dame, 1949), 48.

Excursus 9

1. J. J. Rabinowitz, "The 'Great Sin' in Ancient Egyptian Marriage Contracts," JNES 18 (1959): 73.

2. W. G. Lambert, *Babylonian Wisdom Literature* (Oxford: Clarendon Press, 1960), 119, 130f.

3. E. Reiner, *Šurpu* (Graz: Archiv für Orientforschung, 1958), 25.

4. H. C. Brichto, "The Case of the Sota and a Reconsideration of Biblical 'Law,'" HUCA 46 (1975): 55–70.

5. G. Dossin, "L'ordalie à Mari," CRAIBL (1958): 387–392.

6. For a fuller discussion, see J. Milgrom, "The Case of the Suspected Adulteress, Numbers 5:11–31: Redaction and Meaning," in *The Creation of Sacred Literature,* ed. R. F. Friedman (Berkeley: University of California Press, 1981), 69–75.

Excursus 10

1. M. Fishbane, "Accusations of Adultery: A Study of Law and Scribal Practice in Numbers 5:11–31," HUCA 45 (1974): 25–45; H. C. Brichto, "The Case of the Sota and a Reconsideration of Biblical 'Law,'" HUCA 46 (1975): 55–70.

2. Brichto, "The Case of the Sota."

3. My student, S. Feldblum; G. B. Gray, *A Critical and Exegetical Commentary on Numbers* (New York: Scribner's, 1903).

4. W. Zimmerli, "Die Eigenant der prophetischen Rede des Ezekiel," ZAW 66 (1954): 1–26.

5. For a fuller discussion, see J. Milgrom, "The Case of the Suspected Adulteress, Numbers 5:11–31: Redaction and Meaning," in *The Creation of Sacred Literature,* ed. R. F. Friedman (Berkeley: University of California Press, 1981), 69–75; and idem, "On the Suspected Adulteress," VT 35 (1985): 368–369.

Excursus 11

1. See, however, the recent demurrer of Y. Amit, "Life-long Naziriteship: The Evolution of a Motif," *Te'udah* 4 (1986): 23–26 (Hebrew).

2. Cited in Gray.

3. M. Weber, *Ancient Judaism,* trans. H. Gerth and D. Martingale (Glencoe, Ill.: Free Press, 1952), 95.

4. A. Margalit, "Num. 12: The Nature of Moses' Prophecy" (Hebrew), *Beth Mikra* 81 (1980): 132–149.

5. K. Meuli, "Griechische Opferbräuche," in *Phyllobolia für Peter von der Mühll* (Basel: Schwabe, 1946), 185–288.

6. W. R. Smith, *Lectures on the Religion of the Semites,* 3rd ed. (London: A. and C. Black, 1927), 331, 486.

7. I. Goldziher, *Muhammedanische Studien,* vol. 1 (Halle: M. Niemeyer, 1889), 249.

Excursus 13

1. Y. Muffs, *Studies in the Aramaic Legal Papyri from Elephantine* (Leiden: E. J. Brill, 1969), 130–134.

2. U. Cassuto, EB (Hebrew), s.v. "Priestly Benediction."

3. L. J. Liebreich, "The Songs of Ascent and the Priestly Blessing," JBL 74 (1958): 33–36.

4. M. Fishbane, "Forms and Reformulation of the Biblical Priestly Blessing," JAOS 103 (1983): 115–121.

5. Ibid.

Excursus 14

1. J. Wellhausen, *Die Composition des Hexateuchs,* 3rd ed. (Berlin: G. Reimer, 1899), 179; M. Noth, *Numbers: A Commentary,* trans. J. D. Martin (London: S. C. M. Press, 1968).

2. B. A. Levine, "The Descriptive Tabernacle Texts of the Pentateuch," *Journal of the American Oriental Society* 85 (1965), 307–318.

3. A. M. Dinçol and M. Darga, "Die Festen von Karahna," *Anatolica* 3 (1969/1970): 105; M. Weinfeld, "Julius Wellhausen's Understanding of the Law of Ancient Israel and its Fallacies" (Hebrew), *Shnaton* 4 (1980): 62–97.

4. C. W. Carter, *Hittite Cult-Inventories* (Chicago: University of Chicago Library, 1962), 54ff.; M. Weinfeld, "Social and Cultic Institutions in the Priestly Source? Against their Ancient Near Eastern Background," in *Proceedings of the Eighth World Congress of Jewish Studies, Bible Studies,* 1981 (Jerusalem, 1983), 95–129.

5. For a fuller discussion, see J. Milgrom, "The Chieftains' Gift: Numbers, Chapter 7," *Hebrew Annual Review* 9 (1986): 221–226.

Excursus 16

1. For a fuller discussion, see J. Milgrom, "The Chieftains' Gift: Numbers, Chapter 7," *Hebrew Annual Review* 9 (1986): 221–226.

Excursus 17

1. C. L. Meyers, *The Tabernacle Menorah* (Winona Lake, Ind.: Eisenbrauns, 1976).

Excursus 18

1. For a fuller discussion, see J. Milgrom, "The Literary Structure of Numbers 8:5–22 and the Levitic *kippûr,*" in *Perspectives on Language and Text: F. A. Andersen Volume,* ed. E. W. Conrad and E. G. Newing (Winona Lake, Ind.: Eisenbrauns, 1987), 205–209.

Excursus 19

1. J. Milgrom, "*Kipper al/b'ad*" (Hebrew), *Leshonenu* 35 (1970): 16–17.

2. E. Reiner, "La magie babylonienne," in *Le monde du sorcier* (Paris: Editions du Seuil, 1966), 85.

3. M. Vieyra, "La magie hittite," in *Le monde du sorcier,* pp. 110–115.

4. J. Milgrom, "A Prolegomenon to Leviticus 17:11," JBL 90 (1971): 149–156.

5. For a fuller discussion, see J. Milgrom, IDBSup, s.v. "Atonement in the Old Testament."

Excursus 20

1. For details, see J. Milgrom, "Hezekiah's Sacrifices at the Dedication Services of the Purified Temple (2 Chronicles 29:21–

26)," in *Biblical and Related Studies Presented to Samuel Iwry* (Winona Lake, Ind.: Eisenbrauns, 1986), 159–161.

2. S. Talmon, "Divergences in Calendar-reckoning in Ephraim and Judah," VT 8 (1958): 48–74.

3. J. T. Milik, *Ten Years of Discovery in the Wilderness of Judea* (London: S. C. M. Press, 1959), 109.

Excursus 22

1. A. Falkenstein and W. von Soden, *Sumerische und akkadische Hymnen und Gebete* (Zurich: Artemis, 1953), 151–152.

2. R. de Vaux, "Ark of Covenant-Tent of Reunion," in *The Bible and the Ancient Near East* (New York: Doubleday, 1971), 148; M. Görg, "Zur 'Lade des Zeugnisses,'" *Biblische Notizen* 2 (1977): 13–15.

3. F. M. Cross, *Canaanite Myth and Hebrew Epic* (Cambridge: Harvard University Press, 1973), 91–194.

4. J. H. Breasted, *Ancient Records of Egypt: Historical Documents*, vol. 4 (Chicago: University of Chicago Press, 1906), sec. 315.

5. de Vaux, "Ark of Covenant-Tent of Reunion."

Excursus 23

1. S. Lieberman, *Hellenism in Jewish Palestine* (New York: Jewish Theological Seminary of America, 1950), 38–43.

2. Ibid.

Excursus 24

1. D. Jobling, *The Sense of Biblical Narrative*, JSOTSup 7 (Sheffield: Sheffield Academic Press, (1978): 26–62.

2. B. Jones (written communication); G. J. Wenham, *Numbers* (Leicester: Inter-Varsity Press, 1981).

3. J. Milgrom, "The Structure of Numbers: Chapters 11–12 and 13–14. Preliminary Groupings," *Judaic Perspectives on Ancient Israel*, ed. J. Neusner, et al. (Philadelphia: Fortress, 1987), 49–61.

4. Jobling, "The Sense of Biblical Narrative."

5. Ibid.

6. For a fuller discussion, see J. Milgrom, "The Structure of Numbers, Chapters 11–12, 13–14."

Excursus 25

1. R. R. Wilson, "Early Israelite Prophecy," Int 32 (1978): 3–30.

2. Ibid.

3. Ibid.

4. Ibid.

5. W. L. Moran, "New Evidence from Mari on the History of Prophecy," Bib 50 (1969): 15–59.

6. Z. Weisman, "The Personal Spirit as Imparting Authority," ZAW 93 (1981): 225–234.

7. M. Weinfeld, "Ancient Near Eastern Patterns in Prophetic Literature," VT 27 (1977): 178–195.

Excursus 26

1. For a fuller discussion, see S. M. Paul, "Prophets and Prophecy," *EJ*, 1150–1175.

Excursus 28

1. R. de Vaux, "Ark of Covenant-Tent of Reunion," in *The Bible and the Ancient Near East* (New York: Doubleday, 1971), 136–151.

2. E.g., M. Haran, "The Ark in Deuteronomy," IEJ 9 (1959): 30–38, 89–94.

3. de Vaux, "Ark of Covenant-Tent of Reunion."

Excursus 29

1. G. B. Gray.

2. I. Ball (written communication).

3. For a fuller discussion, see J. Milgrom, "The Structure of Numbers, Chapters 11–12, 13–14, and Their Redaction: Preliminary Groupings." *Judaic Perspectives on Ancient Israel*, ed. J. Neusner, et al. (Philadelphia: Fortress, 1987), 49–61.

Excursus 30

1. S. Wagner, "Die Kundschaftergeschichten im Alten Testament," ZAW 76 (1964): 255–269.

2. A. Malamat, "The Danite Migration and the Pan-Israelite Exodus-Conquest: A Biblical Narrative Pattern," Bib 51 (1970): 1–16.

Excursus 31

1. J. D. Levenson, "1 Samuel 25 as Literature and as History," CBQ 40 (1978): 11–28.

2. J. D. Levenson and B. Halpern, "The Political Import of David's Marriages," JBL 99 (1980): 507–518.

3. Y. Kaufmann, *The Babylonian Captivity and Deutero-Isaiah*, trans. C. W. Efroymson (New York: Union of American Hebrew Congregations, 1970), 670–672 (= *The History of Israelite Religion* [Hebrew], vol. 4 [Jerusalem: Mosad Bialik, 1956], 545–546).

Excursus 32

1. ANET, p. 395.

2. Ramban, Bekhor Shor; Y. Muffs, "Between Justice and Mercy: The Prayer of the Prophets" (Hebrew), in *Torah Nidreshet* (Tel Aviv: Am Oved, 1984), 39–87.

3. E.g., E. Reiner, *Šurpu* (Graz: Archiv für Orientforschung, 1958), I.4.13; CAD, s.v. *salāḫu* A1.

Excursus 33

1. For a fuller discussion, see J. Milgrom, IDBSup, s.v. "Repentance."

Excursus 34

1. W. R. Smith, *Lectures on the Religion of the Semites*, 3rd ed. (London: A. and C. Black, 1927), 75–79.

2. Josephus, Ant. 12.145–146.

3. For a fuller discussion, see J. Milgrom, "Religious Conversion and the Revolt Model for the Foundation of Israel," JBL 101 (1982): 169–176.

Excursus 35

1. A. Toeg, "A Halakhic Midrash in Num. 15:22–31" (Hebrew), *Tarbiz* 43 (1973/1974): 1–20.

2. J. Milgrom, *Cult and Conscience* (Leiden: E. J. Brill, 1976), nn. 251, 295.

3. R. Rendtorff, *Studien zum Geschichte des Opfers in alten Israel* (Neukirchen-Vluyn: Neukirchener Verlag des Erziehungsvereins, 1967), 22–23, 81–83.

4. For a fuller discussion, see J. Milgrom, "The Two Pericopes on the Purification Offering," in *The Word of the Lord Shall Go Forth: Essays in Honor of David Noel Freedman*, ed. C. L. Meyers and M. O'Connor (Winona Lake, Ind.: Eisenbrauns, 1983), 251–261.

Excursus 36

1. E.g., G. von Rad, *Old Testament Theology*, vol. 1 (New York: Harper, 1962), 264 n. 182.

2. J. Milgrom, "The Function of the *Ḥaṭṭā't* Sacrifice" (Hebrew), *Tarbiz* 40 (1970): 5–8.

3. ANET, p. 209.

4. Ibid., p. 208.

5. P. Segal, "Further Parallels between the Priestly Literature in the Bible and the Hittite Instructions for Temple Servants" (Hebrew), *Shnaton* 7–8 (1983/1984): 265–273.

6. B. Alfrink, "L'expression *ne'esap 'el 'amayw*," OTS 5 (1948): 128.

7. D. J. Wold, *The Biblical Penalty of Kareth* (Ann Arbor, Mich.: University Microfilms, 1978).

Excursus 37

1. J. Milgrom, *Studies in Levitical Terminology* (Berkeley: University of California Press, 1970), 60ff.

2. CD 12:3–4.

Excursus 38

1. E. A. Speiser, "Palil and Congeners: A Sampling of Apotropaic Symbols," *Assyriological Studies* 16 (1965): 393.

2. A. Dedekind, "La pourpre verte et sa valeur pour l'interpretation des écrits des anciens," *Archives de zoologie experimentale et générale*, 3rd ser., 6 (1898): 467–480; I. I. Ziderman, "The Blue Thread of the Tzitzit: Was the Ancient Dye Prussian Blue or Tyrian Purple?" *Journal of the Society of Dyers and Colourists* 97 and 98 (1981 and 1982): 362–364 and 247; idem, "First Identification of Authentic *Tĕkēlet*," BASOR 265 (1987): 25–36.

3. M. Eilat, EB (Hebrew), s.v. *tekhelet ve-'argaman*. See also D. S. Reese, "Palaikastro Shells and Bronze Age Purple Dye Products in the Mediterranean Basin," ABSAA 82 (1987): 201–206.

4. L. B. Jensen, "Royal Purple of Tyre," JNES 22 (1963): 104–118.

5. J. Doumet, *A Study in Ancient Purple Color*, trans. R. Cook (Beirut: Imprimerie catholique, 1980).

6. E. Linder, E. Spanier, and N. Karmon, *A Report to the National Academy of Science, Israel: Purple Dye Biology, Archaeology and History* (Haifa: University of Haifa, Center for Maritime Studies, 1980).

7. N. Jidejian, *Tyre through the Ages* (Beirut: Dar el-Mashreq, 1969).

8. P. Friedländer, "Über der Farbstoff des antiken Purpurs aus *Murex Brandaris*," *Berichte der deutschen chemischen Gesellschaft* 42 (1909): 765–770.

9. Jensen, "Royal Purple of Tyre."

10. H. Fouquet and H.-J. Beilig, "Biological Precursors and Genesis of Tyrian Purple," *Angewandte Chemie: International Edition in English* 10 (1971): 816–817.

11. A. Pallière, *The Unknown Sanctuary* (New York: Bloch, 1928), 20–22.

12. For a fuller discussion, see J. Milgrom, "The Tassel and the Tallit," The Fourth Annual Rabbi Louis Feinberg Memorial Lecture (University of Cincinnati, 1981), 10 pp.; idem, "Of Hems and Tassels," BARev 9/3 (1983): 61–65; idem, "The Tassels Pericope, Numbers 15:37–41" (Hebrew), *Beth Mikra* 92 (1983): 14–22.

Excursus 39

1. J. Liver, "Korach, Dathan, and Abiram," *Scripta Hierosolymitana* 8 (1961): 201–214.

2. S. E. Loewenstamm, EB (Hebrew), s.v. "Korah, Dathan, and Abiram."

3. Or H (the Holiness source), according to I. Knohl, "The Conception of God and Cult in the Priestly Torah and Holiness School" (Hebrew) (Ph.D. diss., Hebrew University, 1988).

4. Cf. J. S. Ackerman, "Numbers," *The Literary Guide to the Bible*, ed. R. Alter and F. Kermode (Cambridge, MA: Harvard University Press, 1987), 83.

5. For a fuller discussion, see J. Milgrom, "The Rebellion of Korah, Numbers Chapter 16: A Study in Redaction," in *De la Torah au Messie*," ed. J. Doré et al. (Paris: Desclée, 1981), 135–146, 66–75. Idem, "The Korah Rebellion, Numbers 16–18: A Study in Tradition History," *SBL Seminar Papers* (Atlanta: Scholars Press, 1988), 570–573; Knohl, "The Conception," 66–70.

Excursus 40

1. ANET, pp. 207–210.

2. J. Milgrom, *Studies in Levitical Terminology* (Berkeley: University of California Press, 1970), 16–22.

3. J. Milgrom, "Sancta Contagion and Altar/City Asylum," VTSup 32 (1981): 278–310.

4. For a fuller discussion, see Milgrom, *Studies in Levitical Terminology*, pp. 16–59.

Excursus 41

1. See H. H. Nelson, "Certain Reliefs at Karnate and Medinat Habu and the Ritual of Amenophis I," JNES 8 (1949): 201–232, 310–345.

2. For a fuller discussion, see J. Milgrom, "The Alleged Wave Offering in Israel and the Ancient Near East," IEJ 22 (1972): 33–38; idem, "The Tenufah" (Hebrew), in *Zer li-gevurot: The Zalman Shazar Jubilee Volume*, ed. B. Z. Lurie (Jerusalem: Kiriat Sefer, 1973), 38–55 [= *Studies in Cultic Theology and Terminology* (Leiden: E. J. Brill, 1983), 138–158].

Excursus 42

1. For a fuller discussion, see J. Milgrom, *Studies in Cultic Theology and Terminology*, 159–170, 171–172 (reprinted essays). (Leiden: E. J. Brill, 1983).

Excursus 43

1. For a fuller discussion, see J. Milgrom, "The Tenufah" (Hebrew), in *Zer li-gevurot: The Zalman Shazar Jubilee Volume,* ed. B. Z. Lurie (Jerusalem: Kiriat Sefer, 1973), 46 n. 28 [= *Studies in Cultic Theology and Terminology* (Leiden: E. J. Brill, 1983), 148 n. 28]; idem, IDBSup, s.v. "First Fruits; First Processed."

Excursus 44

1. M. Greenberg, EncJud, s.v. "Ḥerem."
2. J. Milgrom, *Cult and Conscience* (Leiden: E. J. Brill, 1976), 21.
3. Greenberg, "Herem."
4. Ibid, p. 349.
5. For a fuller discussion, see J. Milgrom, "Profane Slaughter and a Formulaic Key to the Composition of Deuteronomy," HUCA 47 (1976): 6–9.

Excursus 45

1. Also in Ugarit; cf. Krt B.iii.16 (ANET, p. 146).
2. E. Reiner, *Šurpu* (Graz: Archiv für Orientforschung, 1958), II.35, 89; IV.58; VIII.59; Hymn to Enlil I.32 (ANET, p. 574); Legend of Naran-Sin 1.40.
3. See LXX, Targ. Onk., Targ. Jon., Philo, Laws 2.130, Josephus, Ant. 4.249; BB 122b–123a.
4. Nuzi: E. R. Lacheman, *Family Law Documents* (Cambridge: Harvard University Press, 1962); Egypt: G. Mattha, "Rites and Duties of the Eldest Son," *Bulletin of the Faculty of Arts, Cairo University* 12 (1958): 114; Ugarit: RS 8.145.
5. S. Parapola, *Letters from Assyrian Scholars to the Kings Esarhaddon and Assurbanipal,* vol. 1 (Neukirchen: Kevelaer Butzon and Bercker, 1970), letter 132.

Excursus 46

1. Cf. M. S. Dandamaev, "Chramowaja Desjatina w Pozdnej Babilonii," *Vestnik Drevney Istorii* (1965), 14–34.
2. PRU 3.147.9, 11.
3. Ibid.
4. Ibid., 16.153, 244; cf. 16.132.
5. J. Milgrom, *Studies in Levitical Terminology* (Berkeley: University of California Press, 1970), n. 246; cf. Z. Ben-Barak, "The Verb *lkḥ* as an Indicator of Types of Governance in Israel" (Hebrew), in *B. Ben-Yehuda Volume,* ed. B. Z. Lurie (Tel Aviv: Society for Biblical Research, 1981), 175–183.
6. See J. Milgrom, *Cult and Conscience* (Leiden: Brill, 1976), 55–62.
7. Tosef. Pe'ah 4:3, 6, Ket. 26a, TJ Ket 2:7 (26d); cf. Josephus, Ant. 20.181.
8. For a fuller discussion, see M. Weinfeld, *EJ,* s.v. "Tithe."

Excursus 48

1. J. Milgrom, "Sin-offering or Purification-offering?" VT 21 (1971), 237–239.
2. J. Milgrom, "Two Kinds of *Ḥaṭṭā't,*" VT 26 (1976): 333–337.
3. E. Feldman, *Biblical and Post-Biblical Defilement and Mourning* (New York: Yeshiva University Press, 1977), 153–155.
4. The hyssop provides additional ashes, Tosef. Parah 4:10.
5. T. C. Vriezen, "The Term *Hizza:* Lustration and Consecration," OTS 7 (1950): 201–235.
6. J. Milgrom, "The Function of the *Ḥaṭṭā't* Sacrifice" (Hebrew), *Tarbiz* 40 (1970): 1–8; idem, "Israel's Sanctuary: The Priestly 'Picture of Dorian Gray,'" RB 83 (1976): 390–399.
7. Cf. E. Ebeling, "Beiträge zur Kenntnis der Beschwörungsserie Namburbi," RA 48 (1954): 178–181.
8. For a fuller discussion, see J. Milgrom, "The Paradox of the Red Cow (Num. XIX)," VT 31 (1981): 62–72.

Excursus 49

1. Y. Kaufmann, *The Religion of Israel,* trans. Moshe Greenberg (Chicago: University of Chicago Press, 1960), 21–24.
2. For a fuller discussion, see J. Milgrom, "The Function of the *Ḥaṭṭā't* Sacrifice" (Hebrew), *Tarbiz* 40 (1970): 1–8; idem, "Sin-Offering or Purification-Offering," VT 21 (1971): 237–239; idem, "Israel's Sanctuary: The Priestly 'Picture of Dorian Gray,'" RB 83 (1976): 390–399; idem, IDBSup, s.v. "Sacrifices and Offerings, Old Testament"; idem, IDBSup, s.v. "Atonement in the Old Testament."

Excursus 50

1. For others, see S. D. Fraade, "Moses at Meribah," *Orim* 2 (1986): 43–67; W. H. Propp, "The Rod of Aaron and the Sin of Moses," JBL 107 (1988): 19–26.
2. F. Kohata, "Die priesterschriftliche Überlieferungsgeschichte von Numeri," *Annual of the Japanese Biblical Institute* 3 (1977): 3–34.
3. Y. Kaufmann, "The Biblical Age," in *Great Ages and Ideas of the Jewish People,* ed. L. W. Schwarz (New York: Random House, 1956), 9–10.
4. A. H. Gardiner, *Encyclopaedia of Religion and Ethics* (1923), s.v. "Magic, Egyptian."
5. Ibid.
6. See also ANET, pp. 6–7, 12–14.
7. S. Langdon, *Encyclopaedia of Religion and Ethics* (1923), s.v. "Expiation."
8. E. Reiner, "La magie babylonienne," in *Le monde du sorcier* (Paris: Éditions du Seuil, 1966), 8.
9. For Mesopotamian examples of rituals comprising incantations and manual acts, see ANET, pp. 335–338; for Hittite examples, see ANET, pp. 346–356.
10. Y. Kaufmann, *The History of Israelite Religion* (Hebrew), vol. 2 (Tel Aviv: Dvir, 1947), 476–478.
11. For a fuller discussion, see J. Milgrom, "Magic, Monotheism, and the Sin of Moses," in *The Quest for the Kingdom of God: Essays in Honor of G. E. Mendenhall,* ed. H. B. Huffmon et al. (Winona Lake, Ind.: Eisenbrauns, 1983), 251–261.

Excursus 51

1. H. M. Wiener, *Essays in Pentateuchal Criticism* (Oberlin: Bibliotheca Sacra Co., 1909), 121–129.
2. Y. Aharoni, "Nothing Early and Nothing Late: Rewriting Israel's Conquest," BA 39 (1976): 55–76.
3. N. Na'aman, "The Inheritance of the Sons of Simeon," ZDPV 96 (1980): 136–152.

Excursus 52

1. K. R. Joines, "The Bronze Serpent in the Israelite Cult," JBL 87 (1968): 245–256.
2. W. R. Smith, *Lectures on the Religion of the Semites,* 3rd ed. (London: A. and C. Black, 1927), 168.

3. J. G. Frazer, *The Golden Bough*, vol. 2, 3rd ed. (London: Macmillan and Co., Ltd., 1911–1915), 426–427.

4. A. Reifenberg, *Ancient Hebrew Seals* (London: East and West Library, 1950), figs. 4, 5, 14.

5. K. R. Joines, "Winged Serpents in Isaiah's Inaugural Vision," JBL 86 (1967): 410–415.

6. R. D. Barnett, "Layard's Nimrud Bronzes and Their Inscriptions," *Eretz Israel* 8 (1967): 3, fig. 2.

Excursus 53

1. W. R. Smith, *Lectures on the Religion of the Semites*, 3rd ed. (London: A. and C. Black, 1927), 169 n. 3.

2. J. H. Breasted, *Ancient Records of Egypt: Historical Documents*, vol. 3 (Chicago: University of Chicago Press, 1906), 195, 292.

3. ANET, p. 201; also pp. 205a, 206a.

4. A. Musil, *Arabia Petraea*, vol. 3 (Vienna: A. Hölder, 1908), 259.

5. G. Vermès, *Scripture and Tradition in Judaism* (Leiden: Brill, 1961), 49–55.

6. C. H. Kraeling, *The Synagogue* (New Haven: Yale University Press, 1956), pl. LIX.

7. J. B. Milgrom, "Moses Sweetens the 'Bitter Waters' of the 'Portable Well': An Interpretation of a Panel at Dura-Europos Synagogue," *Journal of Jewish Art* 5 (1978): 45–47.

Excursus 54

1. Y. Kaufmann, *The History of Israelite Religion* (Hebrew), vol. 2 (Jerusalem: Mosad Bialik, 1947): 40–48.

2. M. Dimon (Haran), "Ancient Remnants in Prophetic Literature" (Hebrew), *Yediot* (1947): 7–15.

3. G. Galil, in *Numbers* (Hebrew), by J. Milgrom et al., *Encyclopedia of the Biblical World* (Ramat Gan: Revivim, 1985).

Excursus 56

1. My student, H. Chapnick.

Excursus 57

1. T. H. Gaster, *Myth, Legend, and Custom in the Old Testament*, vol. 1 (New York: Harper and Row, 1969), 310.

2. M. M. Kalisch, *Bible Studies: The Prophecies of Balaam* (London: Longman, 1877); A. Rofē, *The Book of Balaam* (Hebrew) (Jerusalem: Sinai, 1979).

3. See also Y. Zakovitch, "The Pattern of the Numerical Sequence Three-Four in the Bible" (Hebrew) (Ph. D. diss., Hebrew University, 1977).

4. R. Alter, "Biblical Narrative," *Commentary* (May 1976): 61–67.

Excursus 58

1. M. M. Kalisch, *Bible Studies: The Prophecies of Balaam* (London: Longman, 1877).

2. G. W. Coats, "Balaam: Sinner or Saint?" BR 18 (1973): 1–9.

3. A. J. Heschel, *Theology of Ancient Judaism* (Hebrew), vol. 2 (London: Soncino, 1965), 328–332.

Excursus 59

1. Middle Assyrian Laws, par. 47; CH, par. 2.

2. ARM 1.22 (ANET, p. 482).

3. I. Goldziher, *Abhandlungen zur arabischen Philologie* (Leiden: Brill, 1896), 1–121; J. Pedersen, "The Role Played by Inspired Persons among the Israelites and the Arabs," in *Studies in Old Testament Prophecy*, ed. H. H. Rowley (Edinburgh: Clark, 1950), 127–142.

4. Cited by Goldziher, *Abhandlungen*, p. 29 n. 1; see Prov. 26:2.

Excursus 60

1. J. Hoftijzer, *Aramaic Texts from Deir ʿAlla* (Leiden: E. J. Brill, 1976); J. A. Fitzmeyer, review of *Aramaic Texts from Deir ʿAlla*, CBQ 40 (1978), 93–95; A. Caquot and A. Lemaire, "Les textes araméens de Deir ʿAlla," Syria 54 (1977): 189–208; H. P. Müller, "Einige alttestamentliche Problema zur aramäischen Inschrift von Deir ʿAlla," ZDPV 94 (1978):56–67; P. K. McCarter, "The Balaam Texts from Deir ʿAlla: The First Combinations," BASOR 239 (1980): 49–65.

2. M. Dahood, review of *Aramaic Texts from Deir ʿAlla*, Bib 62 (1981): 124–127; J. C. Greenfield, review of *Aramaic Texts from Deir ʿAlla*, JSS 25 (Chico, CA: Scholars Press, 1980): 248–252; J. A. Hackett, *The Balaam Text from Deir ʿAlla* (Chico, Calif.: Scholars Press, 1984), A. Rofē, *The Book of Balaam* (Hebrew) (Jerusalem: Sinai, 1979).

3. See especially Hackett, *The Balaam Text*; and M. Weinfeld, "The Prophecy of Balaam in the Inscription from Deir ʿAlla (Sukkoth)" (Hebrew), *Shnaton* 5–6 (1982):141–147.

4. *Ugaritica*, vol. 5 (Paris: Geuthner, 1968), text 9, verso 8–9.

Excursus 61

1. M. Buber, *Moses* (Oxford: Phaidon, 1947), 192.

2. S. E. Loewenstamm, EB (Hebrew), s.v. *kedeshah*.

3. Ibid.; M. I. Gruber, "The *Kadesh* in the Book of Kings and in Other Sources," (Hebrew) *Tarbiz* 52 (1982/1983):167–176; idem, "Hebrew *qĕdēšāh* and her Canaanite and Akkadian Cognates," UF 18 (1986): 133–148.

4. AHW, s.v. *qdšm*.

5. CAD, s.v. *qadištu* 2e.

6. G. E. Mendenhall, *The Tenth Generation* (Baltimore: Johns Hopkins University Press, 1973).

7. ANET, p. 150

8. L. R. Palmer, *The Interpretation of Mycenaean Greek Texts* (Oxford: Clarendon Press, 1963), 250–255.

9. Mendenhall, *The Tenth Generation*, p. 111.

Excursus 62

1. M. Weinfeld, in *Numbers* (Hebrew), ed. J. Milgrom et al. (Ramat Gan: Revivim, 1985).

Excursus 63

1. UM 55.21–71; M. Civil, "New Sumerian Law Fragments," *Assyriological Studies* 16 (1965): 1–8.

2. Gudea B.vii.44.

3. ANET, p. 220.

4. *Ugaritica*, vol. 5 (Paris: Geuthner, 1968), 9–10.

5. Z. Ben-Barak, "Inheritance by Daughters in the Ancient Near East," JSS (1980): 22–23.
6. J. Paradise, "A Daughter and Her Father's Property at Nuzi," JCS 32 (1980): 189–207.
7. G. R. Driver and J. C. Miles, *The Babylonian Laws*, vol. 1 (Oxford: Clarendon Press, 1956), 335–341.
8. Ben-Barak, "Inheritance by Daughters."
9. J. Vercoutter, "La femme en Égypte ancienne," in *Histoire mondiale de la femme*, ed. P. Grimal (Paris: Nouvelle librairie de France, 1965), 143–146.
10. S. Belkin, *Philo and the Oral Law* (Cambridge: Harvard University Press, 1940), 19–20.
11. J. Danmanville, "Anatole hittite," in *Histoire mondiale de la femme*, ed. P. Grimal (Paris: Nouvelle librairie de France, 1965), 248–255.
12. D. J. Gilner, "The Case of the Daughters of Zelophehad" (Unpublished).
13. P. Ne'eman, "The Inheritance of the Daughters according to the Torah and the Halakha," (Hebrew) *Beth Mikra* 47 (1971): 476–489.
14. M. Zucker, *Rav Saadya Gaon's Translation of the Torah* (Hebrew) (New York: Feldheim, 1959), 485–493.
15. S. Lieberman, in a private communication.
16. S. E. Loewenstamm, EB (Hebrew), s.v. *kohath*.

Excursus 64

1. J. Wellhausen, *Die Composition des Hexateuchs*, 3rd ed. (Berlin: G. Reimer, 1899), 110ff.
2. E. Lipinski, "Urim and Tummim," VT 20 (1970): 495–496.
3. J. Lindblom, "Lot-Casting in the Old Testament," VT 14 (1964): 67–74.
4. E. Robertson, "The Urim and Tummim: What Are They?" VT 14 (1964): 67–74.

Excursus 65

1. S. Sauneron, *The Priests of Ancient Egypt* (New York: Grove Press, 1960).
2. A. L. Oppenheim, *Ancient Mesopotamia* (Chicago: University of Chicago Press, 1964).
3. ANET, p. 344.
4. R. Rendtorff, *Studien zur Geschichte des Opfers in alten Israel* (Neukirchen-Vluyn: Neukirchener Verlag des Erziehungsvereins, 1967), 22–23, 81–83.
5. W. G. Plaut, *The Torah: Numbers* (New York: Union of American Hebrew Congregations, 1981), 1213.

Excursus 66

1. Krt A.200–205 (ANET, p. 145).
2. Mish. Ar. 5:1; see Tosef. Ar. 3:1.
3. See Josephus, Ant. 5.169, Philo 2 L.A. 9.

Excursus 67

1. G. B. Gray, p. 418.
2. J. de Vaulx, *Les Nombres* (Paris: J. Gabalda, 1972).
3. O. Eissfeldt, "Protektorat der Midianiter über ihre Nachbaren in letzten Viertel des 2. Jahrtausends v. chr.," JBL 87 (1968):383–393.
4. W. J. Dumbrell, "Midian: A Land or a League?" VT 25 (1975): 323–337.
5. W. F. Albright, "Midianite Donkey Caravans," in *Translating and Understanding the Old Testament*, ed. H. T. Frank and W. L. Reed (Nashville, Tenn.: Abingdon Press, 1970), 197–205; J. M. Grintz, "Studies in the Antiquity of the Priestly Code" (Hebrew), in *Proceedings of the World Congress of Jewish Studies* (Jerusalem: World Union of Jewish Studies, 1977), 69–70; but cf. P. Wapnish, "Camel Caravans and Camel Pastoralists at Tell Jemmeh," JANES 13(1981):101–121.
6. H. M. Wiener, *Essays in Pentateuchal Criticism* (Oberlin: Bibliotheca Sacra Co., 1909), 99.

Excursus 69

1. M. Ottosson, Gilead, *Tradition and History* (Lund: Gleerup, 1969), 53–73.
2. For the structural relationship between this chapter and its fulfillment (Josh. 22), see D. Jobling, "'The Jordan a Boundary': A Reading of Numbers 32 and Joshua 22," in *Seminar Papers, Society of Biblical Literature* (Chico, Calif.: Scholars Press, 1980), 183–207. [=*The Sense of the Biblical Narrative* II, JSOT Suppl. 39 (Sheffield: Sheffield University Press, 1986), 88–134.]

Excursus 70

1. Y. Kaufmann, *The Book of Joshua* (Hebrew) (Jerusalem: Kiriat Sefer, 1966), 270–282.
2. B. Oded, "The Settlement of Reuben in the Mishor Region" (Hebrew), *Studies in the Jewish People and the Land of Israel* 1 (1970):11–36.
3. G. B. Gray.
4. K. Budde, *Das Buch der Richter* (Freiburg: Mohr, 1897), 12–13.
5. M. H. Segal, "The Settlement of Manasseh East of the Jordan," PEF 50 (1918): 124–131.
6. See also Z. Kallai, "Conquest and Settlement of Trans-Jordan," ZDPV 99 (1983): 110–118; idem., *Historical Geography of the Bible* (Jerusalem: Magnes Press, 1986), 241–259; M. Weinfeld, "The Extent of the Promised Land—the Status of Transjordan," *Das Land in biblischer Zeit,* ed. G. Strecker (Göttingen: Vandenhoeck and Ruprecht, 1983), 60–62.

Excursus 71

1. J. de Vaulx, *Les Nombres* (Paris: J. Gabalda, 1972).
2. A. Dillmann, *Die Bücher Numerii, Deuteronomium, und Josua* (Leipzig: S. Hirzel, 1897).
3. M. Noth, "Der Wallfahrtsweg zum Sinai (Nu33)," PJ 36 (1940): 5–28.
4. G. J. Davies, "The Wilderness Itineraries: A Comparative Study," TynBul 25 (1974): 46–81.
5. F. M. Cross, *Canaanite Myth and Hebrew Epic* (Cambridge: Harvard University Press, 1973).

Excursus 73

1. B. Mazar, "Canaan on the Threshold of the Age of the Patriarchs" (Hebrew), *Eretz Israel* 3(1954): 18–32; R. de Vaux, "Le pays de Canaan," JAOS 88 (1968):23–29.
2. See M. Weinfeld, "The Boundaries of the Promised Land: Two Different Conceptions," (Hebrew) *Cathedra* 47 (1988): 3–16.

Excursus 74

1. J. Clericus, *Pentateuchus Mosis* (Amsterdam: J. Wetstenium and G. Smith, 1735); E. F. K. Rosenmüller, *Scholia in Vetus Testamentum* (Leipzig: J. A. Barthii, 1820–1834).
2. M. Greenberg, "Idealism and Practicality in Numbers 35:4–5 and Ezekiel 48," JAOS 88(1968):59–63.
3. AHw, s.v. *tawwertum/tamertu*.
4. For a fuller discussion, see J. Milgrom, "The Levitic Town: An Exercise in Realistic Planning," JJS 33 (1982): 185–188.

Excursus 75

1. J. Milgrom, "Sancta Contagion and Altar/City Asylum," VTSup 32 (1981): 278–310.
2. See Philo, 1 Laws 159.
3. Y. Kaufmann, *The Book of Joshua* (Hebrew) (Jerusalem: Kiriat Sefer, 1959), 258–270.
4. S. Klein, "The Cities of the Priests and Levites and the Cities of Refuge" (Hebrew), *Kobets* of the Palestine Exploration Society 3 (1934):81–107; W. F. Albright, "The List of Levitical Cities," in *Louis Ginzberg Jubilee Volume* (New York: American Academy for Jewish Research, 1945), 49–73; B. Mazar, "The Cities of the Priests and the Levites," VTSup 7 (1950):193–205; Z. Kallai, "The Cities of Refuge" (Hebrew), *Zion* 45(1980):29–34.
5. S. Japhet, "Conquest and Settlement in Chronicles," JBL 98 (1979): 210–212.
6. S. E. Loewenstamm, EB (Hebrew), s.v. *mishpat*.
7. For a fuller discussion, see J. Milgrom, "Sancta Contagion and Altar/City Asylum."

Excursus 76

1. Ehrlich.
2. B. S. Jackson, "Reflections on Biblical Criminal Law," JJS 24 (1973): 8–38.
3. M. Greenberg, "Some Postulates of Biblical Criminal Law," in *Yehezkel Kaufmann Jubilee Volume*, ed. M. Haran (Jerusalem: Magnes Press, 1960), 5–28.
4. A. Phillips, "Another Look at Murder," JJS 28 (1977): 105–126.
5. Ibid.
6. See M. Greenberg, "More Reflections on Biblical Law," in *Studies in Bible*, ed. S. Japhet, *Scripta Hierosolymitana* 31 (Jerusalem: Magnes Press, 1986), 1–17.

Excursus 77

1. N. K. Gottwald, *The Tribes of Yahweh* (New York: Orbis Books, 1979), 265–267.